Lecture Notes in Computer Science   8479

Commenced Publication in 1973
Founding and Former Series Editors:
Gerhard Goos, Juris Hartmanis, and Jan van Leeuwen

Ioana Boureanu   Philippe Owesarski
Serge Vaudenay (Eds.)

Applied Cryptography and Network Security

12th International Conference, ACNS 2014
Lausanne, Switzerland, June 10-13, 2014
Proceedings

Springer

Volume Editors

Ioana Boureanu
Akamai EMEA
Addlestone, UK
E-mail: icboureanu@gmail.com

Philippe Owesarski
LAAS-CNRS, SARA
Toulouse, France
E-mail: owe@laas.fr

Serge Vaudenay
EPFL, IC LASEC
Lausanne, Switzerland
E-mail: serge.vaudenay@epfl.ch

ISSN 0302-9743   e-ISSN 1611-3349
ISBN 978-3-319-07535-8   e-ISBN 978-3-319-07536-5
DOI 10.1007/978-3-319-07536-5
Springer Cham Heidelberg New York Dordrecht London

Library of Congress Control Number: 2014939351

LNCS Sublibrary: SL 4 – Security and Cryptology

Typesetting: Camera-ready by author, data conversion by Scientific Publishing Services, Chennai, India

Printed on acid-free paper

Springer is part of Springer Science+Business Media (www.springer.com)

Preface

The 12th International Conference on Applied Cryptography and Network Security (ACNS) was held during June 10–13, 2014 in Lausanne, Switzerland. It was hosted by the Ecole Polytechnique Fédérale de Lausanne (EPFL).

The conference received 147 submissions. They went through a doubly-anonymous review process and 33 papers were selected. We were helped by 41 Program Committee members and 156 external reviewers.

We were honored to host Phillip Rogaway and Nadia Heninger as invited speakers.

This volume represents the revised version of the accepted papers along with the abstract of the invited talks.

Following the ACNS tradition, the Program Committee selected a paper to award. To be eligible, the paper had to be co-authored by one full time student who presented the paper at the conference. This year, the Best Student Paper Award was given to Annelie Heuser for her paper

"Detecting Hidden Leakages"

written in collaboration with Amir Moradi and Sylvain Guilley.

The submission and review process was done using the iChair Web-based software system developed by Thomas Baignères and Matthieu Finiasz. They provided us with great help by updating iChair to our needs.

We would like to thank the authors of all submitted papers. Moreover, we are grateful to the members of the Program Committee and the external sub-reviewers for their diligent work, as well as to the staff members of the Security and Cryptography Laboratory (LASEC) of EPFL for their kind help in the organization of the event. We would also like to acknowledge the Steering Committee for supporting us.

Finally, we heartily thank the following bodies, for their kind financial support: the Swiss National Science Foundation, the Hasler Foundation, the Federal Office of Communications, the Center of Risk Analysis and Risk Governance (CRAG) of EPFL, Baidu, and the Distributed Systems Laboratory (LSR) of EPFL, headed by André Schiper. All financial risks were taken by LASEC at EPFL.

April 2014

Ioana Boureanu
Philippe Owesarski
Serge Vaudenay

Organization

Program Committee

Frederik Armknecht	University of Mannheim, Germany
Gildas Avoine	INSA Rennes and UCL, France and Belgium
Marinho P. Barcellos	Federal University of Rio Grande do Sul, Brasil
Alex Biryukov	University of Luxembourg, Luxembourg
Christina Brzuska	Tel-Aviv University, Israel
Anne Canteaut	Inria Paris-Rocquencourt, France
Barbara Carminati	University of Insubria, Italy
Isabelle Chrisment	University of Lorraine, France
Véronique Cortier	CNRS, France
Xuhua Ding	Singapore Management University, Singapore
Jordi Forné	Technical University of Catalonia, Spain
Peter Gutmann	University of Auckland, New Zealand
Cătălin Hrițcu	University of Pennsylvania and Inria Paris-Rocquencourt, USA and France
Marc Joye	Technicolor, France
Steve Kremer	Inria, France
Kaoru Kurosawa	Ibaraki University, Japan
Ralf Küsters	University of Trier, Germany
Xuejia Lai	Shanghai Jiao Tong University, China
Javier Lopez	University of Malaga, Spain
Matteo Maffei	Saarland University, Germany
Wojciech Mazurczyk	Warsaw University of Technology, Poland
Ludovic Mé	Supelec, France
Ilya Mironov	Microsoft Research Silicon Valley, USA
Katerina Mitrokotsa	Chalmers University of Technology, Sweden
Atsuko Miyaji	JAIST, Japan
Svetla Nikova	KU Leuven, Belgium
Miyako Ohkubo	NICT, Japan
Kenny Paterson	Royal Holloway, UK
Goutam Paul	Indian Statistical Institute Kolkata, India
Christophe Petit	UCL, Belgium
Carla Ràfols	Ruhr University Bochum, Germany
Christian Rechberger	DTU, Denmark
Reza Reyhanitabar	EPFL, Switzerland
Mark Ryan	University of Birmingham, UK
Rei Safavi-Naini	University of Calgary, Canada
Jennifer Seberry	University of Wollongong, Australia
Asia Slowinska	Vrije Universiteit Amsterdam, The Netherlands

Gilles Van Assche   STMicroelectronics, Belgium
Michael Waidner   Fraunhofer SIT & TU Darmstadt, Germany
Bogdan Warinschi   University of Bristol, UK
Jianying Zhou   Institute for Infocomm Research, Singapore

External Reviewers

Aysajan Abidin   Gerardo Fernandez
Isaac Agudo   Daniel Fett
Ahmad Ahmadi   Nils Fleischhacker
Martin Albrecht   Jun Furukawa
Cristina Alcaraz   Yuichi Futa
Mohsen Alimomeni   David Galindo
Hoda A. Alkhzaimi   Sébastien Gambs
Elena Andreeva   Wei Gao
Radoniaina Andriatsimandefitra   Pierrick Gaudry
Subhadeep Banik   Asadullah Ghalib
David Bernhard   Benedikt Gierlichs
Rishiraj Bhattacharyya   Zheng Gong
Christophe Bidan   Vincent Grosso
Olivier Blazy   Felix Günther
Céline Blondeau   Siyao Guo
Alexandra Boldyreva   Jens Hermans
Özkan Boztaş   Geshi Huang
Krzysztof Cabaj   Jialin Huang
Eleonora Cagli   Mitsugu Iwamoto
Angelo De Caro   Angela Jäschke
Xavier Carpent   Jérémy Jean
Anrin Chakraborti   Mahavir Jhawar
Kaushik Chakraborty   Han Jinguang
Anupam Chattopadhyay   Saqib A. Kakvi
Jiageng Chen   Aniket Kate
Céline Chevalier   Dmitry Khovratovich
Thibault Cholez   Stefan Kölbl
Sherman S.M. Chow   Junzuo Lai
Oana Ciobotaru   Virginie Lallemand
Cas Cremers   Enrique Larraia
Joan Daemen   Liran Lerman
Gareth T. Davies   Gaëtan Leurent
Antoine Delignat-Lavaud   Wei Li
Patrick Derbez   Kaitai Liang
Xinshu Dong   Benoît Libert
Alexandre Duc   Jia Liu
Xiwen Fang   Joseph K. Liu
Sebastian Faust   Zhe Liu
Florian Feldmann   Yu Long

Atul Luykx
Vadim Lyubashevsky
Xianping Mao
Giorgia Azzurra Marson
Takahiro Matsuda
Matthijs Melissen
Bart Mennink
Marine Minier
Francisco Moyano
Imon Mukherjee
Shishir Nagaraja
Pablo Najera
Gregory Neven
Ana Nieto
David Nuñez
Kazumasa Omote
Cristina Onete
Mihai Ordean
Kim Pecina
Roel Peeters
Léo Paul Perrin
Joshua Phillips
Le Trieu Phong
David Pointcheval
Gordon Proctor
Ivan Pustogarov
Elizabeth Quaglia
Sasa Radomirovic
David Rebollo-Monedero
Manuel Reinert
Christian Reuter
Vincent Rijmen
Ruben Rios
Arnab Roy
Elzbieta Rzeszutko
Kai Samelin
Somitra Sanadhya
Pratik Sarkar
Santanu Sarkar

Alessandra Scafuro
Enrico Scapin
Guido Schmitz
Peter Scholl
Stefaan Seys
Ben Smyth
Chunhua Su
Koutarou Suzuki
Tsuyoshi Takagi
Keisuke Tanaka
Satoru Tanaka
Qiang Tang
Susan Thomson
Tyge Tiessen
Valérie Viet Triem Tong
Tomasz Truderung
Mathieu Turuani
Kerem Varici
Vesselin Velichkov
Srinivas Vivek Venkatesh
Frederik Vercauteren
Lei Wang
Pengwei Wang
Gaven Watson
Hoeteck Wee
Patrick Weiden
Jakob Wenzel
Hong Xu
Jia Xu
Rui Xu
Shota Yamada
Anjia Yang
Masaya Yasuda
Kazuki Yoneyama
Maki Yoshida
Tsz Hon Yuen
Jiangshan Yu
Liang Feng Zhang
Tongjie Zhang

Conference Chairs

Ioana Boureanu   HEIG-VD, Switzerland
Philippe Owezarski   CNRS, France
Serge Vaudenay   EPFL, Switzerland

Invited Talks

How Not to Generate Random Numbers

Nadia Heninger

Department of Computer and Information Science,
University of Pennsylvania

Abstract. Randomness is essential to cryptography: cryptographic security depends on private keys that are unpredictable to an attacker. But how good are the random number generators that are actually used in practice? In this talk, I will discuss several large-scale surveys of cryptographic deployments, including TLS, SSH, Bitcoin, and secure smart cards, and show that random number generation flaws are surprisingly widespread. We will see how many of the most commonly used public key encryption and signature schemes can fail catastrophically if used with faulty random number generators, and trace many of the random number generation flaws we encountered to specific implementations and vulnerable implementation patterns.

The Emergence of Authenticated Encryption

Phillip Rogaway

Dept. of Computer Science,
University of California, Davis, USA

Abstract. Although practical schemes for symmetric encryption (eg, blockcipher modes) are one of the main "exports" of cryptography, for years serious cryptographers mostly ignored this corner of our field. In recent years this has dramatically changed: there has been a quiet revolution in our understanding of *what definitions* general-purpose symmetric encryption schemes should meet and *what algorithms* should be employed to satisfy them. On the definitional side we have come to recognize that semantic security under a chosen-plaintext attack is too weak a notion for a general-purpose scheme. Notions for *authenticated encryption* (AE), which deliver both privacy and authenticity, have emerged as a stronger alternative. On the algorithmic side, security practitioners have increasingly abandoned classical modes like CBC, choosing AE schemes like CCM and GCM in their place.

One reason for this evolution in definitions and schemes is recognition of the fact that a scheme that delivers both privacy and authenticity can be more efficient than the amalgamation of separate privacy and authenticity techniques. Another reason for the change is the realization that an encryption scheme that delivers more is less likely to be misused.

In this talk I'll trace the history of AE, exploring why it emerged, how it evolved, and what some new schemes have come to look like. We'll explore how the basic syntax of AE has changed, and how security notions for AE continue to evolve, including the introduction of misuse-resistance, online, and robust AE. I'll look afresh at generic composition. I'll describe a new AE scheme that I recently co-developed, AEZ. Finally, I'll talk about the CAESAR competition for AE schemes, a contest that has drawn a remarkable 57 round-1 submissions.

AE is rare topic insofar as cryptographic theory and practice have been tightly linked; in particular, practice-oriented provable security has been at the center of this area. The dialectic around AE between theory-oriented and practice-oriented individuals has been unusually strong, with the interaction resulting in better theory and better practice.

Keywords: Authenticated encryption, modes of operation, practice-oriented provable security, symmetric encryption.

Table of Contents

Hashing

Cryptanalysis & Attacks (Symmetric Cryptography)

Network Security

Signatures

System Security

Secure Computation

New Modular Compilers for Authenticated Key Exchange

Yong Li[1,*], Sven Schäge[2,**], Zheng Yang[1,***],
Christoph Bader[1], and Jörg Schwenk[1]

[1] Horst Görtz Institute for IT Security, Ruhr-University Bochum, Germany
{yong.li,christoph.bader,joerg.schwenk}@rub.de
[2] University College London, United Kingdom
s.schage@ucl.ac.uk
[3] Chongqing University of Technology
zheng.yang@rub.de

Abstract. We present two new compilers that generically turn passively secure key exchange protocols (KE) into authenticated key exchange protocols (AKE) where security also holds in the presence of active adversaries. Security is shown in a very strong security model where the adversary is also allowed to i) reveal state information of the protocol participants and ii) launch theoretically and practically important PKI-related attacks that model important classes of unknown-key share attacks. Although the security model is much stronger, our compilers are more efficient than previous results with respect to many important metrics like the additional number of protocol messages and moves, the additional computational resources required by the compiler or the number of additional primitives applied. Moreover, we advertise a mechanism for implicit key confirmation. From a practical point of view, the solution is simple and efficient enough for authenticated key exchange. In contrast to previous results, another interesting aspect that we do not require that key computed by the key exchange protocol is handed over to the compiler what helps to avoid additional and costly modifications of existing KE-based systems.

Keywords: Protocol Compiler, Authenticated Key Exchange, Security Model.

1 Introduction

Authenticated key exchange (AKE) protocols are among the most important building blocks of secure network protocols. They allow a party A to i) authenticate a communication partner B and ii) securely establish a common session

---

* Corresponding author supported by secure eMobility grant number 01ME12025.
** Corresponding author supported by EPSRC grant number EP/G013829/1.
*** Corresponding author supported by CSC china. Part of the work done at Ruhr University Bochum as a doctoral student in 2013.

I. Boureanu, P. Owesarski, and S. Vaudenay (Eds.): ACNS 2014, LNCS 8479, pp. 1–18, 2014.

key with B. In many existing systems both of these tasks are addressed by a single protocol. This can yield very efficient solutions. However, there are several scenarios where these two tasks are actually addressed by separate protocols. For example in typical browser-based applications, the user relies on TLS to exchange a session key k with an authenticated server. The user, on the other hand, often uses a simple username/password combination which is encrypted with k to authenticate himself. In this paper, we consider generic and very efficient constructions that securely combine authentication protocols (AP) and passively secure key exchange protocols (KE) to yield authenticated key exchange.

While combined solutions may be more efficient in general, there are several advantages for the modular design of AKE systems. One is flexibility as one can resort to a rich collection of existing authentication and key exchange protocols that can be combined to yield new AKE systems which are specifically crafted to fit a certain application scenario. The second reason is applicability, as a generic compiler (ideally) does not require any modifications in existing implementations of the input protocols (which are often costly or error-prone in practice). Instead, security can be established by simply 'adding' the implementation of the compiler to the system. Finally, a generic compiler can considerably simplify the security analysis, as only the input protocols have to be analysed to meet their respective security requirements. Security of the entire AKE protocol follows from the security proof of the compiler. This greatly pays off in the setting of key exchange protocols, as here, we usually only require the underlying key exchange protocol to be passively secure (which is a comparably simple security notion) while the output protocol must be secure even under active attacks (where the adversary is granted several additional attack capabilities).

1.1   Contribution

We present two very efficient compilers that construct secure AKE systems from authentication protocols (AP) and passively secure key exchange protocols (KE). To the best of our knowledge, they are the first such compilers that are efficient and truly generic, i.e. they do not require any modifications in the underlying AP and KE protocols. Thus, they are easily applicable to existing systems, what makes them very useful in practice. Previous compilers require costly modifications on the key exchange protocol such that either the messages have to be modified or the secret session key k also has to be output to the compiler. A new session key is computed using e.g. the requested key derivation function (KDF), i.e. the compilers require the session key of the underlying key exchange KE protocol as input. We stress that in some scenarios it is very difficult or impossible (for example because the network application is closed-source) to realize these modifications. Our compilers, in contrast, avoid such problems as they only require the public transcript of the key exchange protocol but not the secret session key from the passively secure KE protocol as input. Our compilers are very efficient but restrict the class of KE protocols to those which do not rely on long-term keys. We have chosen to restrict our attention to this class of key exchange protocols because they i) allow for efficient protocols with very high security guarantees (like forward secrecy) and ii) they can efficiently be recognized. Let us elaborate on this. As a consequence of our restriction long-term keys are only used in the authentication protocol, whereas in the KE protocol, all values are freshly drawn in each new communication session. Our restriction is useful to design protocols with forward secrecy, which states that even after the compromise of long-term keys previously executed sessions remain secure. The same restriction is made on the KE protocols which are used in the recent compiler by Jager, Kohlar, Schäge, and Schwenk (JKSS) [7]. The well-known compiler by Katz and Yung (KY) uses a slightly different approach by directly requiring that the input protocol provides forward secrecy [9]. We present two compilers each of which relies on a different authentication mechanism. Our first compiler is very efficient. It relies on signature schemes and only requires two additional moves in which signatures are exchanged. The second compiler relies on public key encryption systems. Although the first compiler is more efficient, the second compiler accounts for scenarios where the parties do not have (certified) signature keys but only encryption keys. This can often occur in practice. For example, the most efficient (for the client) and most wide-spread key exchange mechanism in TLS is RSA key transport. The latter can be extended to symmetric-based authentication systems in which the communication parties have secure pre-shared keys. All our solutions work in the standard model, i.e. without assuming random oracles.

Technical Contribution. Our efficiency improvements rely on the following techniques. First, we do not use explicit key confirmation to thwart unknown-key share attacks. Instead we use a form of implicit key confirmation where we include the identities of the partners in the messages that are authenticated. At the same time, this helps to also counter strong attacks that an adversary might launch with the help of the extended attack capabilities (state reveals and PKI-based attacks) of our strong security model. In terms of efficiency, this helps us to save the exchange of two MAC values (as compared to the JKSS compiler). As our second efficiency improvement, we formally show that for security we do not have to exchange uniformly random nonces after the key exchange protocol as in the JKSS compiler. In the JKSS compiler these nonces are solely used to make every session's transcript unique. We can prove that instead it is sufficient to use the public ephemeral keys which are exchanged in the key exchange protocol. Technically, we show that if a key exchange protocol that does not rely on long-term keys is passively secure, then with negligible probability there are no collisions among the ephemeral public keys. This is sufficient to show that even in the presence of active attackers each transcript is unique as long as one party is uncorrupted. Finally, our efficient compilers only require the public transcript of the key exchange protocol, denoted here as KE, but not the secret key k_{KE} from KE as input. Our approach helps us to save the additional computation of a new session key for authenticated key exchange (as compared to previous compiler). In other words, our compilers require no cryptographic session key generator other than KE itself.

1.2   The Security Model

Our proofs of our compilers hold in two very strong security models respectively. These models rely on the concept of indistinguishability of session keys which first emerged in the seminal work of Bellare and Rogaway [2] and later extended by [4,15,12] to the public key setting. In contrast to previous works, we explicitly model the strong and practical PKI-based attacks (via a RegCorruptParty query) like the public key substitution attack (PKS) [3,13] or the duplicate-signature key selection (DSKS) attack [13,10]. To model strong and practical PKI-related attacks we use the RegCorruptParty query into our models that allows attackers to register adversarially chosen public keys and identities. Observe that the adversary does not have to know the corresponding secret key. In practice, most certification authorities (CAs) do not require the registrant to deliver proofs of knowledge of the secret key. Using RegCorruptParty query the adversary may easily register a public key which has already been registered by another honest user U. Since the public keys are equal, all the signatures that are produced by U can be re-used by the adversary. Such attacks can have serious security effects [3,13,10]. Our model also formalizes the revelation of state information of sessions (via a RevealState query) and perfect forward secrecy. We believe that the revelation of state information is much more realistic than (just) the revelation of keys. For forward secrecy, it is a very strong form of security which guarantees that past sessions remain secure even if the long-term keys get exposed in later sessions. We use a formal definition of forward secrecy that is adopted from [8].

1.3   Related Work

In 1998, Bellare, Canetti and Krawczyk (BCK) were the first to consider a modular way for the development of AKE [1]. They propose to first design a protocol in the authenticated link model, an idealized model where the links between parties are always authenticated. Then they systematically transform the protocol into a protocol which is also secure in the unauthenticated link model, in which the adversary has control over all the message flows in the network, by applying a so-called authenticator. Basically, for every message A needs to transmit to B there will be some additional communication with B in which B sends a random nonce to A and A responds with an application of an authentication mechanism on this nonce (in a challenge-response like fashion). For example, when instantiated with a signature scheme or with a combination of an encryption system and a message authentication code, the authenticator adds another two messages to every message sent in the original protocol. Altogether, this amounts for a 200% increase in the number of moves of the protocol and the number of messages sent.

   In 2003, Katz and Yung presented a generic compiler for group key agreement [9]. The KY compiler first adds an initial round to a passively secure group key exchange protocol where each party chooses a random nonce and broadcasts it to its communication partner. In the next step, the compiler basically adds to every message of the original protocol a signature which is also computed over all the random values that have been computed in the first phase. When restricted to the two-party case, this compiler is much more efficient in terms of protocol moves, in contrast to the BCK compiler, each message sent does not need to be authenticated interactively. The KY compiler only accounts for a single round that is added to the input protocol. However, the compiler still modifies each message sent in the protocol by basically adding a signature to that message. As before, this approach amounts for a huge decrease in efficiency due to the additional signature generation and verification operations each user has to execute. The KY compiler outputs protocols which guarantee forward secrecy. However, it does require that the input group key protocols already provide forward secrecy. This assumption is similar to our (and the JKSS) assumption on the KE protocol to not rely on long-term keys. Our restriction is, in some sense rougher than that of KY but it allows for a very simple verification by inspection. We stress that we could adapt the KY definition and yield a slightly more general result. We think, however, that in scenarios where a complex, practical protocol is given it might be hard to inspect if the KY compiler is applicable at all. Intuitively, our approach implies forward-secrecy because if all values which are used to generate the session keys are freshly computed in each session of the passively secure key exchange protocol then the keys computed in the different sessions are independent. This intuition is formalized in the security proofs of the subsequent sections. In 2010 Jager et al. presented the first compiler which accounts only for a constant number of additional messages (which is independent of the KE protocol) to be exchanged [6], denoted here as JKSS compiler. In terms of efficiency, this compiler is closest to our results. Basically, the compiler, after executing the KE protocol, makes A and B additionally exchange 1) random nonces, 2) signatures over these nonces and the KE transcript and 3) two MAC values (using a MAC-key K_{mac} generated using the session key from the passively secure KE protocol) which have been computed over all the previous messages. As mentioned above this compiler is less efficient than our solution. At the same time all of the above compilers do neither consider state reveals nor PKI-related attacks in their security analysis.

2   Security Assumptions

Let $[n] = \{1, \ldots, n\} \subset \mathbb{N}$ be the set of integers between 1 and n, and $\kappa \in \mathbb{N}$ be a security parameter. We write $a \xleftarrow{\$} S$ to denote the action of sampling a uniformly random element a from a set S. Let '$||$' denote the operation concatenating two binary strings. To state our results, we will rely on standard security definitions for the collision-resistant cryptographic hash functions, IND-CCA2 secure public key encryption schemes, unforgeable signature schemes, UF-CMA secure one-time message authentication code schemes and a class of passively secure key exchange protocols. Due to space restrictions, we only give generic definitions of passively secure key exchange protocols in this section.

KEY EXCHANGE PROTOCOLS. A two party key-exchange (KE) protocol is a protocol that enables those two parties to compute a shared secret key. In the following, we formally provide a very technical definition of KE which is more detailed than in most other works. This is solely for the purpose of deriving a technical result on general KE protocols without long-term keys. In other words, we require that every secret keys used to generate the session keys must be chosen freshly in each session. For simplicity we first focus on the practically most important class of two-move key exchange protocols. We stress that our definitions and results can easily be generalized to y-move key exchange protocols as sketched below.

A key exchange scheme $\mathsf{KE} = (\mathsf{KE.Setup}, \mathsf{KE.EKGen}, \mathsf{KE.SKGen})$ consists of three algorithms which may be called by a party $\mathsf{ID} \in \mathcal{IDS}$ in each session. Let $\mathcal{M}_{\mathsf{KE}}$ be the message space and $\mathcal{ESK}$ be the space for ephemeral secret key and $\mathcal{EPK}$ be the space for ephemeral public key. Let T be the transcript of all messages exchanged in a KE protocol instance (see Figure 1).

- $pms^{ke} \leftarrow \mathsf{KE.Setup}(1^{\kappa})$: This probabilistic polynomial time algorithm takes as input the security parameter κ and outputs a set of system parameters pms^{ke}. The parameters pms^{ke} might be implicitly used by other algorithms for simplicity.

- $(esk_{\mathsf{ID}}, epk_{\mathsf{ID}}, m_{\mathsf{ID}}) \xleftarrow{\$} \mathsf{KE.EKGen}(pms^{ke}, \mathsf{in})$: The probabilistic polynomial time algorithm takes as input the system parameters pms^{ke} and message $\mathsf{in} \in \mathcal{M}_{\mathsf{KE}}$ and outputs an ephemeral key pair $(esk_{\mathsf{ID}}, epk_{\mathsf{ID}})$, where $esk_{\mathsf{ID}} \in \mathcal{ESK}$ and $epk_{\mathsf{ID}} \in \mathcal{EPK}$, and a message $m_{\mathsf{ID}} \in \mathcal{M}_{\mathsf{KE}}$ that requires to be sent in a protocol move. The execution of this algorithm might be determined by the input message (in) which could be any information including for example identities of session participants, ephemeral public key or just empty string $\emptyset$. If $m_{\mathsf{ID}} = \emptyset$, for simplicity we may write $(esk_{\mathsf{ID}}, epk_{\mathsf{ID}}) \xleftarrow{\$} \mathsf{KE.EKGen}(pms^{ke}, \mathsf{in})$.

- $k \leftarrow \mathsf{KE.SKGen}(esk_{\mathsf{ID}}, T)$: The session key generator is a deterministic polynomial time algorithm which takes as input esk_{ID} of a session participant ID and transcript T of all messages exchanged in this session, and outputs a session key k.

CORRECTNESS. We say a correct key exchange protocol without long-term key if for any protocol instance with session key generated as $k := \mathsf{KE.SKGen}(esk_{\mathsf{ID}}, T)$ it holds that esk_{ID} is generated freshly by $\mathsf{KE.EKGen}$ in corresponding protocol instance. That is, each party computes each session key using only ephemeral secret key which is freshly generated by $\mathsf{KE.EKGen}$ in corresponding protocol instance. We consider key exchange protocols with perfect correctness that is

$$Pr \begin{bmatrix} \mathsf{KE.SKGen}(esk_{\mathsf{ID}_1}, T) = \mathsf{KE.SKGen}(esk_{\mathsf{ID}_2}, T); \\ (esk_{\mathsf{ID}_1}, epk_{\mathsf{ID}_1}, m_{\mathsf{ID}_1}) \xleftarrow{\$} \mathsf{KE.EKGen}(pms^{ke}, \mathsf{in}_1), \\ (esk_{\mathsf{ID}_2}, epk_{\mathsf{ID}_2}, m_{\mathsf{ID}_2}) \xleftarrow{\$} \mathsf{KE.EKGen}(pms^{ke}, \mathsf{in}_2), \\ (m_{\mathsf{ID}_1}, m_{\mathsf{ID}_2}) \in T. \end{bmatrix} = 1.$$

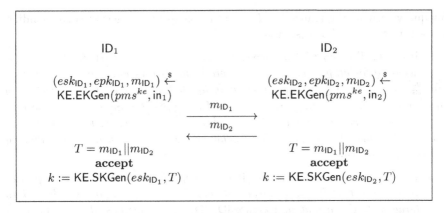

Fig. 1. General Two-move KE Protocol

We observe that in a passively secure key exchange protocol where we do not rely on long-term keys it is necessary that the values epk_{ID_1} and epk_{ID_2} are non-empty and 'meaningful'. This is because both parties have to keep the session key secret from a curious adversary. For example in ephemeral Diffie-Hellman key exchange (EDH) [5], the KE.EKGen is executed without any additional message, i.e. $\mathsf{in}_1 = \mathsf{in}_2 = \emptyset$, and the generated messages such that $m_{\mathsf{ID}_1} = epk_{\mathsf{ID}_1}$ and $m_{\mathsf{ID}_2} = epk_{\mathsf{ID}_2}$. In some KE protocols, the KE algorithms of the initiator ID_1 can be very different from those of the responder ID_2 like for example in encrypted key transport with freshly chosen key material (FEKT), in which case we could instantiate those messages in Figure 1 as: $\mathsf{in}_1 = \emptyset$, $\mathsf{in}_2 = m_{\mathsf{ID}_1} = epk_{\mathsf{ID}_1}$. We stress that the key pairs $(esk_{\mathsf{ID}_1}, epk_{\mathsf{ID}_1})$ and $(esk_{\mathsf{ID}_2}, epk_{\mathsf{ID}_2})$ may have distinct forms depending on specific KE protocol, which are also determined by the forms of messages $(\mathsf{in}_1, \mathsf{in}_2)$ while running KE.EKGen.

In case both parties 'contribute' values which are used to computed the session key, i.e. $k \neq esk_{\mathsf{ID}_2}$ and $k \neq esk_{\mathsf{ID}_1}$, this is very obvious as the contribution of ID_1 has to be transmitted to ID_2 and vice versa. However, if only one party $\mathsf{ID}_c \in \{\mathsf{ID}_1, \mathsf{ID}_2\}$ decides on the session key $esk_{\mathsf{ID}_c} = k$, then k has to securely be transferred to the other party (ID'_c) via some form of encryption of k. In order to guarantee that only the single party ID'_c can decrypt the session key, the encryptor has to encrypt the session key exclusively for ID'_c using an ephemeral public key of ID'_c. As we do not rely on long-term keys, ID'_c has to generate this key freshly and send it to ID_c as $epk_{\mathsf{ID}'_c}$ in the first move of the key exchange protocol, resulting in $\mathsf{ID}'_c = \mathsf{ID}_1$ and $\mathsf{ID}_c = \mathsf{ID}_2$.

In order to model passive attacks we define an $\mathsf{Execute}(\mathsf{ID}_1, \mathsf{ID}_2)$ query. The adversary can use the query to perform passive attacks in which the attacker initiates and eavesdrops on honest executions between parties ID_1 and ID_2. Note that each identity should be uniquely chosen from the identity space $\mathcal{IDS}$. By using this query the adversary can obtain the transcripts that were exchanged during the honest execution of the protocol. For each $\mathsf{Execute}(\mathsf{ID}_1, \mathsf{ID}_2)$ query, an instance of KE protocol is executed between ID_1 and ID_2. After simulation this query returns the transcript T of all messages exchanged in corresponding protocol instance and a session key.

Definition 1. *We say that a correct key-exchange protocol* KE *is* (t, ϵ_{KE}) *passively secure if for all probabilistic polynomial-time (*PPT*) adversary* $\mathcal{A}$ *holds that* $|[\text{EXP}^{ps}_{KE,\mathcal{A}}(\kappa) = 1] - 1/2| \leq \epsilon_{KE}$ *for some negligible function* $\epsilon_{KE}(\kappa)$ *in the security parameter* κ *in the following experiment* $\text{EXP}^{ps}_{KE,\mathcal{A}}(1^\kappa)$*: On input security parameter* 1^κ*, the security experiment is proceeded as a game between a challenger* $\mathcal{C}$ *and an adversary* $\mathcal{A}$ *based on a key exchange protocol* KE*, where the following steps are performed:*

1. *$\mathcal{C}$ generates a set of identities $\{ID_1, \ldots, ID_\ell\}$ for potential protocol participants where $\ell \in \mathbb{N}$. $\mathcal{A}$ is given all identities as input and is allowed to interact with $\mathcal{C}$ via making $\text{Execute}(ID_i, ID_j)$ query at most d times for each party where $d \in \mathbb{N}$ and $i, j \in [\ell]$. As response, $\mathcal{C}$ returns (T, K_0) to $\mathcal{A}$.*
2. *At some point, $\mathcal{A}$ outputs a special symbol $\top$ and sends $\top$ to $\mathcal{C}$. Given $\top$, $\mathcal{C}$ runs a new protocol instance and outputs the transcript T^* and the session key K_0^*. Then, $\mathcal{C}$ samples K_1^* uniformly at random from the key space of the protocol, and tosses a fair coin $b \in \{0, 1\}$. Then $\mathcal{C}$ returns (T^*, K_b^*) to $\mathcal{A}$. After that $\mathcal{A}$ may continually perform $\text{Execute}(ID_i, ID_j)$ queries. Finally, $\mathcal{A}$ may terminate with returning a bit b' as output.*
3. *At the end of the experiment, 1 is returned if $b' = b$; Otherwise 0 is returned.*

In the following, we formally show that for every passively secure key exchange protocol after polynomially calls to KE.EKGen there cannot be any collisions among the ephemeral public keys generated by certain type of KE.EKGen. This lemma will be useful in the security proofs of our compilers to show that a compiler does not have to exchange additional random values after the KE run to guarantee that the transcripts which are authenticated with the authentication mechanism are unique. We can therefore discard the random values which are used in the JKSS compiler. Please note that for a two-move and two-party (ID_1 and ID_2) KE-protocol there exist at most two types of KE.EKGen algorithms which may be determined by input messages in_1 and in_2. We here explicitly classify the algorithm KE.EKGen into two types denoted by $KE.EKGen_{ID_1}$ for party ID_1 and $KE.EKGen_{ID_2}$ for party ID_2. While considering the collisions among ephemeral keys, let *Coll* denote the event that: after a polynomial number q times execution of KE.EKGen algorithm there exist at least two ephemeral public keys epk and epk' generated by the ephemeral key generator KE.EKGen are identical, where the number q is determined by time t. Let probability ϵ_{coll} denote the event *Coll* occurred within time t. We say all ephemeral keys generated by KE.EKGen are (q, t, ϵ_{coll})-distinct if those ephemeral keys are generated by KE.EKGen after q times execution of KE.EKGen algorithm within time t and there exists no collision among those ephemeral keys except for probability ϵ_{coll}. For space reasons we only provide a sketch of the proof.

Lemma 1. *Assume* KE *is a* (t, ϵ_{KE})*-passively secure protocol without long-term key as defined above. Then all ephemeral public keys generated by* KE.EKGen *in the runs of* KE *are* (q, t, ϵ_{coll})*-distinct such that* $\epsilon_{coll} \leq q \cdot \epsilon_{KE}$*.*

Proof. We first consider the case that the ephemeral keys are generated by different types of ephemeral key generators, i.e. $\mathsf{KE.EKGen}_{\mathsf{ID}_1} \neq \mathsf{KE.EKGen}_{\mathsf{ID}_2}$. Obviously, in this case there is no collision between ephemeral keys epk_{ID_1} and epk_{ID_2}, because those keys are assumed to be generated from different key spaces, so we only need to evaluate the collision probability among ephemeral keys generated by the same type of ephemeral key generators, i.e. $\mathsf{KE.EKGen}_{\mathsf{ID}_1} = \mathsf{KE.EKGen}_{\mathsf{ID}_2}$. For this case, we assume that with non-negligible probability ϵ_{coll} there will be a collision among the epk_{ID_1} after q protocol runs, or a collision among the epk_{ID_2} after q protocol runs. According to the protocol specification the epk_{ID_1} values are computed by randomized runs of $\mathsf{KE.EKGen}_{\mathsf{ID}_1}$ while the epk_{ID_2} values have been computed by randomized runs of $\mathsf{KE.EKGen}_{\mathsf{ID}_2}$. In particular, the computation of the epk_{ID_1} and epk_{ID_2} are deterministic in system parameters pms^{ke}, message in_1 (resp. in_2) and the internal random coins ω_{ID_1} used by ID_1 and ω_{ID_2} used by ID_2. The ω_{ID_1} and ω_{ID_2} are drawn uniformly random and in particular independently.

Let $epk^*_{\mathsf{ID}_1}$ and $epk^*_{\mathsf{ID}_2}$ be the ephemeral public keys that are exchanged in the test session and given, together with the challenge key k^*_b and transcript T^*, to the adversary. Let $esk^*_{\mathsf{ID}_1}$ and $esk^*_{\mathsf{ID}_2}$ be the corresponding ephemeral secret keys. These keys have also been computed using $\mathsf{KE.EKGen}_1$ (resp. $\mathsf{KE.EKGen}_2$) with random coin ω_{ID_1} (resp. ω_{ID_2}) and in_1 (resp. in_2). The adversary first guesses whether the collision occurs among the epk_{ID_1} or the epk_{ID_2} with probability $\geq 1/2$. In the first case, the adversary can re-run $\mathsf{KE.EKGen}_{\mathsf{ID}_1}$ $(q-1)$ times with $\omega_{\mathsf{ID}_1,i}$ and $\mathsf{in}_{1,i}$ to output $\{esk_{\mathsf{ID}_1,i}, epk_{\mathsf{ID}_1,i}\}$ for $i \in [1; q-1]$ in time less than t. With the same probability ϵ_{coll} it obtains two values $epk'_{\mathsf{ID}_1}, epk''_{\mathsf{ID}_1}$ among the q values $epk^*_{\mathsf{ID}_1}, epk_{\mathsf{ID}_1,1}, \ldots, epk_{\mathsf{ID}_1,(q-1)}$ with $epk'_{\mathsf{ID}_1} = epk''_{\mathsf{ID}_1}$. Since it holds with probability $\geq 2/q$ that either $epk'_{\mathsf{ID}_1} = epk^*_{\mathsf{ID}_1}$ or $epk''_{\mathsf{ID}_1} = epk^*_{\mathsf{ID}_1}$. In this case the adversary knows one pair $(\omega_{\mathsf{ID}_1,i}, \mathsf{in}_{1,i})$ that maps to $epk^*_{\mathsf{ID}_1}$. Let esk'_{ID_1} be the corresponding ephemeral secret key. We now have to show that esk'_{ID_1} helps us to break the passive security. This simply follows from the determinism of $\mathsf{KE.SKGen}$ and correctness of KE. Since we have perfect correctness the adversary $\mathcal{A}$ can compute the session key k by using the ephemeral secret key esk'_{ID_1} and transcript T^*. Next the adversary can compare whether $k^*_b = k$ and correctly guess the value b. In case there is a collision among the epk_{ID_2} the situation is similar. Hence, due to the security of KE protocol, we have that the probability bound $\frac{\epsilon_{coll}}{q} \leq \epsilon_{\mathsf{KE}}$.

GENERAL KEY EXCHANGE PROTOCOLS. The above definition of KE, the corresponding security definition, and the results of the above lemma can easily be extended to y-move KE protocols. Concretely, besides the $\mathsf{KE.Setup}$ and $\mathsf{KE.SKGen}$ algorithms, each party may run at most $\lceil y/2 \rceil$ different *types* of $\mathsf{KE.EKGen}$ algorithms in each protocol instance depending on the input messages $\mathsf{in}_i : 1 \leq i \leq y$. Namely, each session participant can call at most $\lceil y/2 \rceil$ of times of $\mathsf{KE.EKGen}$ algorithms during protocol execution. We let each invocation of algorithm $\mathsf{KE.EKGen}$ in i-move $(1 \leq i \leq y)$ as $\mathsf{KE.EKGen}_i$ which is used to compute the message for i-move. Consequently, we may have (for instance when y is even) a series of executions: $\{(esk_{\mathsf{ID}_1,1}, epk_{\mathsf{ID}_1,1}, m_{\mathsf{ID}_1,1}) \xleftarrow{\$} \mathsf{KE.EKGen}_1(pms^{ke},$

in$_1$), $(esk_{ID_2,2}, epk_{ID_2,2}, m_{ID_2,2}) \xleftarrow{\$} \text{KE.EKGen}_2(pms^{ke}, \text{in}_2), \ldots, (esk_{ID_1,(y-1)}, epk_{ID_1,(y-1)}, m_{ID_1,(y-1)}) \xleftarrow{\$} \text{KE.EKGen}_{(y-1)}(pms^{ke}, \text{in}_{(y-1)}), (esk_{ID_2,y}, epk_{ID_2,y}, m_{ID_2,y}) \xleftarrow{\$} \text{KE.EKGen}_y(pms^{ke}, \text{in}_y)\}$. We could therefore apply the result of Lemma 1 to y-move KE protocols, namely with overwhelming probability there is for instance no collision among all epk_{ID_b} generated by KE.EKGen_{ID_b} with $b \in \{1,2\}$.

3   Security Model

In this section we present a formal security model for a two-party AKE protocol. We follow the important line of research that was initiated by Bellare and Rogaway [2], and later modified and extended in [4,12]. In these models the adversary is provided with an execution environment, which emulates the real-world capabilities of an active adversary.

Execution Environment. Let $\mathcal{K} \in \{0,1\}^\kappa$ be the key space of session keys, and $\{\mathcal{PK}, \mathcal{SK}\} \in \{0,1\}^\kappa$ be key spaces of long-term public/private keys respectively. Fix a set of honest parties $\{P_1, \ldots, P_\ell\} \in \{0,1\}^\kappa$ for $\ell \in \mathbb{N}$, where each honest party $P_i \in \{P_1, \ldots, P_\ell\}$ is a potential protocol participant and has a pair of long-term public/private key $(pk_i, sk_i) \in (\mathcal{PK}, \mathcal{SK})$ that corresponds to its identity i. In order to formalize several sequential and parallel executions of the protocol, each party P_i is characterized by a polynomial number of oracles $\{\pi_i^s\}$ where $s \in [d]$ is an index for a range such that $d \in \mathbb{N}$. An oracle π_i^s represents a process in which the party P_i executes the s-th protocol instance with access to the long-term key pair (pk_i, sk_i) of party P_i and to all public keys of the other parties. Moreover, we assume each oracle π_i^s maintains a list of independent internal state variables as described in Table 1.

Table 1. Internal States of Oracles

Variable	Decryption
PID_i^s	records the identity $j \in \{1, \ldots, \ell\}$ of intended communication partner P_j
Φ_i^s	denotes $\Phi_i^s \in \{\texttt{accept}, \texttt{reject}\}$
K_i^s	records the session key $\text{K}_i^s \in \mathcal{K}$
STA_i^s	records some secret states used to compute the session key K_i^s
T_i^s	records all messages sent and received in the order of appearance by oracle π_i^s

The internal state of each oracle π_i^s is initialized as $(\text{PID}_i^s, \Phi_i^s, \text{K}_i^s, \text{STA}_i^s, \text{T}_i^s) = (\emptyset, \emptyset, \emptyset, \emptyset, \emptyset)$, where $\emptyset$ denotes the empty string. We assume that the session key is assigned to the variable K_i^s such that $\text{K}_i^s \neq \emptyset$ iff each oracle completes the execution with an internal state $\Phi_i^s = \texttt{accept}$.

Adversary Model. An active adversary $\mathcal{A}$ is able to interact with the execution environment by issuing the following queries:

- Send(π_i^s, m): $\mathcal{A}$ can use this query to send any message m of his own choice to oracle π_i^s. The oracle will respond according to the protocol specification and depending on its internal state. If m consists of a special symbol $\top$ ($m = \top$), then π_i^s will respond with the first protocol message.
- Corrupt(P_i): Oracle π_i^1 responds with the long-term private key sk_i of party P_i. If Corrupt(P_i) is the τ-th query issued by $\mathcal{A}$, then we say that P_i is τ-corrupted. For parties that are not corrupted we define $\tau := \infty$.
- RegCorruptParty(pk_c, P_c): This query allows $\mathcal{A}$ to register a new party P_c ($\ell < c < \mathbb{N}$), with a static public key pk_c on behalf of P_c. If the same party P_c is already registered (either via RegCorruptParty-query or $r \in [\ell]$), a failure symbol $\perp$ is returned to $\mathcal{A}$. Otherwise, P_c is registered, the pair (P_c, pk_c) is distributed to all other parties, and a symbol of success $\triangle$ is returned. This query formalizes a malicious insider setting which can be used to model unknown key share (UKS) attacks and other chosen public key attacks [3,15,14]. We here formalize the arbitrary key registration policy via this query. Parties established by this query are called corrupted or adversary-controlled.
- Reveal(π_i^s): Oracle π_i^s responds to this query with the contents of variable K_i^s to $\mathcal{A}$. This query models the attacks that loss of a session key should not be damaging to other sessions.[1]
- RevealState(π_i^s): Oracle π_i^s responds with the contents of the secret state stored in variable STA_i^s.
- Test(π_i^s): This query may only be asked once throughout the game. Oracle π_i^s handles this query as follows: if the oracle has state $\Phi_i^s \neq \mathtt{accept}$, then it returns some failure symbol $\perp$. Otherwise it flips a fair coin b, samples a random element $k_0 \overset{\$}{\leftarrow} \mathcal{K}$, sets $k_1 = \mathsf{K}_i^s$ to the 'real' session key, and returns k_b.

Security Definitions. We model the partnership of two oracles via the concept of *matching conversations* which was first introduced by Bellare and Rogaway [2] and later refined in [8,11]. Let T_i^s denote the transcript of messages sent and received by oracle π_i^s. We assume that messages in a transcript T_i^s are represented as binary strings. Let $|T_i^s|$ denote the number of the messages in the transcript T_i^s. Assume there are two transcripts T_i^s and T_j^t, where $w := |T_i^s|$ and $n := |T_j^t|$. We say that T_i^s is a prefix of T_j^t if $0 < w \leq n$ and the first w messages in transcripts T_i^s and T_j^t are pairwise equivalent as binary strings.

Definition 2 (Matching Conversations). *We say that π_i^s has a matching conversation to oracle π_j^t, if*

- *π_i^s has sent the last message(s) and T_j^t is a prefix of T_i^s, or*
- *π_j^t has sent the last message(s) and T_i^s is a prefix of T_j^t.*

We say that two oracles π_i^s and π_j^t have matching conversations if π_i^s has a matching conversation to process π_j^t or vice versa.

---

[1] Note that we have $\mathsf{K}_i^s \neq \emptyset$ if and only if $\Phi_i^s = \mathtt{accept}$.

Definition 3 (Correctness). *We say that a two-party* AKE *protocol,* Σ, *is correct if for any two oracles,* π_i^s *and* π_j^t, *that have matching conversations it holds that* $\Phi_i^s = \Phi_j^t = \text{accept},$ $\text{PID}_i^s = j$ *and* $\text{PID}_j^t = i$ *and* $\mathsf{K}_i^s = \mathsf{K}_j^t$.

Definition 4 (Security Game). *We formally consider a security experiment that is played between an adversary* $\mathcal{A}$ *and a challenger* $\mathcal{C}$. *The challenger* $\mathcal{C}$ *implements the collection of oracles* $\{\pi_i^s : i \in [\ell], s \in [d]\}$. *At the beginning of the game, long-term public/private key pairs* (pk_i, sk_i) *for each honest entity* i *are generated by* $\mathcal{C}$. *The adversary receives public keys* $pk_1, \ldots, pk_\ell$ *as input. Now the adversary may start issuing* Send, RevealState, Corrupt, RegCorruptParty *and* Reveal *queries, as well as one* Test *query at some point of the game. Finally, the adversary outputs a bit* b' *and terminates.*

Definition 5 (Freshness). *Let* π_i^s *be an accepting oracle held by a party* P_i *with intended partner* P_j. *Meanwhile, let* π_j^t *be an oracle (if it exists), such that* π_i^s *and* π_j^t *have matching conversations. Then the oracle* π_i^s *is said to be* τ_0-*fresh when the adversary* $\mathcal{A}$ *issues its* τ_0-*th query and none of the following conditions holds:*

- *The party* P_j *has been established by the adversary* $\mathcal{A}$ *via the* RegCorruptParty *query,*
- P_i *is* τ_i-*corrupted with* $\tau_i \leq \tau_0$ *and* P_j *is* τ_j-*corrupted with* $\tau_j \leq \tau_0$,
- $\mathcal{A}$ *has either made a* RevealState(π_i^s) *query or a* RevealState(π_j^t) *query (if* π_j^t *exists),*
- $\mathcal{A}$ *has either made a query* Reveal(π_i^s) *query or a* Reveal(π_j^t) *query (if* π_j^t *exists).*

Definition 6. *We say that a two-party* AKE *protocol* Σ *is* (t, ϵ)-*secure, if for all adversaries* $\mathcal{A}$ *running the* AKE *security game within time* t *while having some negligible probability* $\epsilon = \epsilon(\kappa)$, *it holds that:*

1. *When* $\mathcal{A}$ *terminates, there exists no* τ_0-*fresh oracle* π_i^s *(except with probability* ϵ), *such that*
   - π_i^s *has internal states* $\Omega = \text{accept}$ *and* $\Psi = j$, *and*
   - *there is no unique oracle* π_j^t *such that* π_i^s *and* π_j^t *have matching conversations.*
2. *When* $\mathcal{A}$ *returns* b' *such that*
   - $\mathcal{A}$ *has issued a* Test-*query to oracle* π_i^s, *and*
   - *the oracle* π_i^s *is* τ_0-*fresh throughout the security game,*
   then the probability that b' *equals the bit* b *sampled by the* Test-*query is bounded by*
   $$|\Pr[b = b'] - 1/2| \leq \epsilon.$$

4   Authenticated Key Exchange Compiler from Signature

4.1   Protocol Description

The compiler takes as input the following building blocks: a passively secure key exchange protocol KE and a digital signature scheme (SIG.Gen, SIG.Sign,

SIG.Vfy). Each party A is assumed to possess a pair of long-term keys generated as $(sk_A, pk_A) \overset{\$}{\leftarrow} \text{SIG.Gen}(1^\kappa)$. In the sequel, we will use the superscript 'A' to highlight the message recorded at party A (resp. party B). The compiled protocol between two parties A and B proceeds as follows, which is also informally depicted in Figure 2.

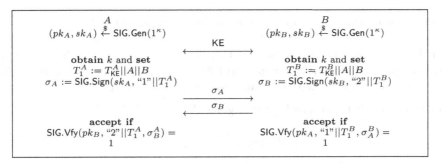

Fig. 2. AKE Protocol from Signature

1. First, A and B run the key exchange protocol KE. They obtain the secure key k from the key exchange phase (as the session key of AKE) and record the transcript as T_{KE}^A and T_{KE}^B, where T_{KE}^D consists of the list of all messages sent and received by party $D \in \{A, B\}$.
2. A sets $T_1^A := T_{KE}^A \parallel A \parallel B$, computes $\sigma_A := \text{SIG.Sign}(sk_A, \text{"1"} \parallel T_1^A)$ and sends σ_A to B. Meanwhile, B sets $T_1^B := T_{KE}^B \parallel A \parallel B$, computes $\sigma_B := \text{SIG.Sign}(sk_B, \text{"2"} \parallel T_1^A)$ and sends σ_B to A.
3. Upon receiving signature on each side, A accepts if and only if $\text{SIG.Vfy}(pk_B, \text{"2"} \parallel T_1^A, \sigma_B^A)=1$. B accepts if and only if $\text{SIG.Vfy}(pk_A, \text{"1"} \parallel T_1^B, \sigma_A^B)=1$.

Session States: In the following we assume that the ephemeral secret vector esk used in each KE protocol instance will be stored in the variable STA.

4.2 Security Analysis

Theorem 1. *Assume that the KE protocol without long-term key is (t, ϵ_{KE})-passively secure (Definition 1), and the signature scheme SIG is deterministic and $(q_{sig}, t, \epsilon_{SIG})$-secure (EUF-CMA), then the above protocol is a (t', ϵ)-secure AKE protocol in the sense of Definition 6 with $t' \approx t$, and $q_{sig} \geq d$, and it holds that*

$$\epsilon \leq 2\ell \cdot \epsilon_{SIG} + d\ell(d\ell + 2) \cdot \epsilon_{KE}.$$

We prove Theorem 1 in two stages. First, we show that the AKE protocol is a secure authentication protocol except for probability ϵ_{auth}, that is, the protocol fulfills security property 1.) of the AKE definition. In the next step, we show that the session key of the AKE protocol is secure except for probability ϵ_{ind} in the sense of the Property 2.) of the AKE definition. Due to space restrictions, we only provide a sketch of the proof.

Lemma 2. *If the* KE *protocol is* $(t, \epsilon_{\mathsf{KE}})$*-passively secure definition 1, and the signature scheme* SIG *is deterministic and* $(q_{sig}, t, \epsilon_{\mathsf{SIG}})$*-secure (EUF-CMA), then the above protocol meets the security Property 1.) of the* AKE *security definition 6 except for probability with*

$$\epsilon_{auth} \leq d\ell \cdot \epsilon_{\mathsf{KE}} + \ell \cdot \epsilon_{\mathsf{SIG}},$$

where all quantities are as the same as stated in the Theorem 1.

Proof. Let $\mathsf{break}_\delta^{(1)}$ be the event that there exists a τ and a τ-fresh oracle $\pi_i^{s^*}$ that has internal state $\varPhi = \mathtt{accept}$ and $\mathsf{PID}_i^s = j$, but there is no unique oracle π_j^t such that π_i^s and π_j^t have matching conversations, in Game δ.

GAME 0. This is the original security game. We have that

$$\Pr[\mathsf{break}_0^{(1)}] = \epsilon_{auth}.$$

GAME 1. In this game, the challenger proceeds exactly like the challenger in Game 0, except that we add an abortion rule. The challenger raises event $\mathsf{abort}_{\mathsf{eph}}$ and aborts, if an ephemeral key epk_i^s is computed by an oracle π_i^s but it has been sampled by another oracle before with the same type of ephemeral key generator. From the result of Lemma 1, we have that

$$\Pr[\mathsf{break}_0^{(1)}] \leq \Pr[\mathsf{break}_1^{(1)}] + d\ell \cdot \epsilon_{\mathsf{KE}}.$$

GAME 2. This game proceeds exactly as before, but the challenger raises event $\mathsf{abort}_{\mathsf{sig}}$ and aborts if the following condition holds:

- there exists a τ-fresh oracle π_i^s that has $\mathsf{PID}_i^s = j$ and $T_1^{i,s} = T_{\mathsf{KE}}^{i,s}||\mathsf{ID}_i||\mathsf{ID}_j$ and $\varPhi_i^s = \mathtt{accept}$,
- π_i^s received a signature σ_j^i that satisfies $\mathsf{SIG.Vfy}(pk_{\mathsf{ID}_j}, \text{``2''} || T_1^{i,s}, \sigma_j^i)=1$, but there exists no oracle π_j^t which has previously output a signature σ_j^i over transcript $T_1^{i,s}$.

Clearly, we have

$$\Pr[\mathsf{break}_1^{(1)}] \leq \Pr[\mathsf{break}_2^{(1)}] + \ell \cdot \epsilon_{\mathsf{SIG}}.$$

Note that the RegCorruptParty query does not affect security, since all registered identities should be distinct to the identities of honest parties. So in Game 2 each accepting oracle π_i^s has a *unique* 'partner' oracle π_j^t sharing the same transcript T_1. With respect to other queries, they will be simulated honestly as in the previous game without any modification since those values are not used for authentication. Thus, if π_i^s accepts, then it must have a matching conversation to π_j^t. So we have $\Pr[\mathsf{break}_2^{(1)}] = 0$. Sum up probabilities from Game 0 to Game 2, we proved Lemma 2.

Lemma 3. *If the KE protocol is (t, ϵ_{KE})-passively secure 1, the signature scheme SIG is deterministic and $(q_{sig}, t, \epsilon_{SIG})$-secure (EUF-CMA), then for any adversary running in time $t' \approx t$, the probability of $\mathcal{A}$ to correctly answer the Test-query is at most $1/2 + \epsilon_{ind}$ with*

$$\epsilon_{ind} \leq \ell \cdot \epsilon_{SIG} + d\ell(d\ell + 1) \cdot \epsilon_{KE},$$

where all quantities are as the same as stated in the Theorem 1.

Proof. Let $\mathsf{break}_\delta^{(2)}$ denote the event that the $\mathcal{A}$ correctly guesses the bit b sampled by the Test-query in Game δ, and $\mathsf{Test}(\pi_i^{s^*})$ is the τ-th query of $\mathcal{A}$, and $\pi_i^{s^*}$ is a τ-fresh oracle that is ∞-revealed throughout the security game. Let $\mathsf{Adv}_\delta := \Pr[\mathsf{break}_\delta^{(2)}] - 1/2$ denote the advantage of $\mathcal{A}$ in Game δ. Consider the following sequence of games.

GAME 0. This is the original security game. Thus we have that

$$\Pr[\mathsf{break}_0^{(2)}] = \epsilon_{ind} + 1/2 = \mathsf{Adv}_0 + 1/2.$$

GAME 1. The challenger $\mathcal{C}$ in this game proceeds as before, which aborts if the test oracle accepts without unique partner oracle. Clearly, we have

$$\mathsf{Adv}_0 \leq \mathsf{Adv}_1 + \epsilon_{auth} \leq \mathsf{Adv}_1 + d\ell \cdot \epsilon_{KE} + \ell \cdot \epsilon_{SIG},$$

where ϵ_{auth} is an upper bound on the probability that there exists an oracle that accepts without unique partner oracle in the sense of Definition 6 (cf. Lemma 2).

GAME 2. This game proceeds exactly as the previous game but the challenger aborts if it fails to guess the test oracle $\pi_i^{s^*}$ and its partner oracle $\pi_j^{t^*}$ such that $\pi_i^{s^*}$ and $\pi_j^{t^*}$ have matching conversations. We have that

$$\mathsf{Adv}_1 \leq (d\ell)^2 \cdot \mathsf{Adv}_2.$$

GAME 3. Finally, we replace the key k^* of the test oracle $\pi_i^{s^*}$ and its partner oracle $\pi_j^{t^*}$ with the same random value $\widetilde{k^*}$. Exploiting the security of key exchange protocol, we obtain that

$$\mathsf{Adv}_2 \leq \mathsf{Adv}_3 + \epsilon_{KE}.$$

In this game, the response to the Test query always consists of a uniformly random key, which is independent to the bit b flipped in the Test query. Thus we have $\mathsf{Adv}_3 = 0$. Lemma 3 is proved by putting together of probabilities from Game 0 to Game 3.

5 Authenticated Key Exchange Compiler from Public Key Encryption

5.1 Protocol Description

The compiler takes the following building blocks as input: a passively secure key exchange protocol KE, a public encryption scheme PKE, a collision resistant hash function CRHF and a one-time message authentication scheme OTMAC. The compiled protocol between two parties A and B proceeds as follows, which is also depicted in Figure 3.

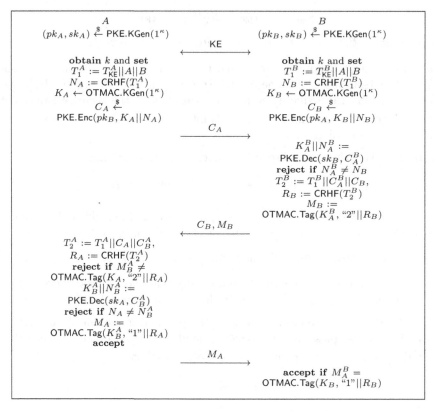

Fig. 3. AKE Compiler from PKE and OTMAC

1. First, A and B run the key exchange protocol KE, then both parties obtain the key k from the key exchange phase (as the session key of AKE protocol) and record the transcripts as T_{KE}^A and T_{KE}^B, where T_{KE}^D consists of the list of all messages sent and received by party $D \in \{A, B\}$.
2. A sets the transcript $T_1^A := T_{KE}^A \| A \| B$ and computes $N_A := \mathsf{CRHF}(T_1^A)$. Then, it runs $K_A \xleftarrow{\$} \mathsf{OTMAC.KGen}(1^\kappa)$ and computes a ciphertext $C_A \xleftarrow{\$} \mathsf{PKE.Enc}(pk_B, K_A \| N_A)$ under B's public key pk_B and transmits C_A to B. Meanwhile, B sets $T_1^B := T_{KE}^B \| A \| B$ and computes $N_B := \mathsf{CRHF}(T_1^B)$. It runs $K_B \xleftarrow{\$} \mathsf{OTMAC.KGen}(1^\kappa)$ and computes $C_B \xleftarrow{\$} \mathsf{PKE.Enc}(pk_A, K_B \| N_B)$ under A's public key pk_A.
3. Upon receiving the ciphertext C_A^B, B sets $T_2^B := T_1^B \| C_A^B \| C_B$ and computes $R_B := \mathsf{CRHF}(T_2^B)$. It decrypts C_A^B (i.e. $K_A^B \| N_A^B := \mathsf{PKE.Dec}(sk_B,$

C_A^B)). Then B checks whether $N_A^B = N_B$. If the check is not passed, then B rejects. Otherwise, it computes $M_B := \mathsf{OTMAC.Tag}(K_A^B, \text{"2"} \,\|\, R_B)$ and transmits (M_B, C_B) to A.

4. Upon receiving messages (M_B^A, C_B^A), A sets $T_2^A := T_1^A \,\|\, C_A \,\|\, C_B^A$ and computes $R_A := \mathsf{CRHF}(T_2^A)$. A rejects if $M_B^A \neq \mathsf{OTMAC.Tag}(K_A, \text{"2"} \,\|\, R_A)$. Then it decrypts the ciphertext C_B^A (i.e. $K_B^A \,\|\, N_B^A := \mathsf{PKE.Dec}(sk_B, C_B^A)$) and checks whether $N_A = N_B^A$. If the check is not passed, then A rejects. Otherwise, A computes $M_A := \mathsf{OTMAC.Tag}(K_B^A, \text{"1"} \,\|\, R_A)$, and sends M_A to B. Finally, A accepts the session.

5. Upon receiving M_A^B, B accepts if and only if $M_A^B = \mathsf{OTMAC.Tag}(K_B, \text{"1"}\|R_B)$.

Session States: We assume the ephemeral secret vector esk used in each KE protocol instance and the random key K_A and K_B used by PKE.Enc will be stored in the variable STA.

5.2   Security Analysis

Theorem 2. *Assume that the KE protocol without long-term key is $(t, \epsilon_{\mathsf{KE}})$-secure (Definition 1), the public key encryption scheme PKE is $(q_{pke}, t, \epsilon_{\mathsf{PKE}})$-secure (IND-CCA2), and the hash function CRHF is $(t, \epsilon_{\mathsf{CRHF}})$-secure and the one-time authentication code scheme OTMAC is deterministic and $(t, \epsilon_{\mathsf{OTMAC}})$-secure. Then the above protocol is a (t', ϵ)-secure AKE protocol in the sense of Definition 6 with $t' \approx t$ and $q_{pke} \geq d$ and holds that*

$$\epsilon \leq 2\epsilon_{\mathsf{CRHF}} + d\ell \cdot (2\ell \cdot \epsilon_{\mathsf{PKE}} + 2\epsilon_{\mathsf{OTMAC}} + 2\epsilon_{\mathsf{KE}}) + (d\ell)^2 \cdot \epsilon_{\mathsf{KE}}.$$

We prove the theorem 2 with two lemmas, similar to the proof of Theorem 1. For space reasons we only provide two lemmas 4 5.

Lemma 4. *Assume that the KE protocol is $(t, \epsilon_{\mathsf{KE}})$-passively secure (Definition 1), the public key encryption scheme PKE is $(q_{pke}, t, \epsilon_{\mathsf{PKE}})$-secure (IND-CCA2), and the hash function CRHF is $(t, \epsilon_{\mathsf{CRHF}})$-secure and the one-time authentication code scheme OTMAC is deterministic and $(t, \epsilon_{\mathsf{OTMAC}})$-secure. Then the above protocol meets the security property 1.) of the AKE security definition 6 except for probability with*

$$\epsilon_{auth} \leq \epsilon_{\mathsf{CRHF}} + d\ell \cdot (\epsilon_{\mathsf{KE}} + \ell \cdot \epsilon_{\mathsf{PKE}} + \epsilon_{\mathsf{OTMAC}}),$$

where all quantities are as the same as stated in the Theorem 2.

Lemma 5. *Assume that the KE protocol is $(t, \epsilon_{\mathsf{KE}})$-passively secure (Definition 1), the public key encryption scheme PKE is $(q_{pke}, t, \epsilon_{\mathsf{PKE}})$-secure (IND-CCA2), and the hash function CRHF is $(t, \epsilon_{\mathsf{CRHF}})$-secure and the one-time authentication code scheme OTMAC is deterministic and $(t, \epsilon_{\mathsf{OTMAC}})$-secure. Then for any adversary running in time t, the probability of A to correctly answer the Test-query is at most $1/2 + \epsilon_{ind}$ with*

$$\epsilon_{ind} \leq \epsilon_{\mathsf{CRHF}} + d\ell \cdot (\epsilon_{\mathsf{KE}} + \ell \cdot \epsilon_{\mathsf{PKE}} + \epsilon_{\mathsf{OTMAC}}) + (d\ell)^2 \cdot \epsilon_{\mathsf{KE}},$$

where all quantities are as the same as stated in the Theorem 2.

Acknowledgements. We would like to thank the anonymous referees for their valuable comments and suggestions.

References

1. Bellare, M., Canetti, R., Krawczyk, H.: A modular approach to the design and analysis of authentication and key exchange protocols (extended abstract). In: STOC, pp. 419–428 (1998)
2. Bellare, M., Rogaway, P.: Entity authentication and key distribution. In: Stinson, D.R. (ed.) CRYPTO 1993. LNCS, vol. 773, pp. 232–249. Springer, Heidelberg (1994)
3. Blake-Wilson, S., Menezes, A.: Unknown key-share attacks on the station-to-station (sts) protocol. In: Imai, H., Zheng, Y. (eds.) PKC 1999. LNCS, vol. 1560, pp. 154–170. Springer, Heidelberg (1999)
4. Canetti, R., Krawczyk, H.: Analysis of key-exchange protocols and their use for building secure channels. In: Pfitzmann, B. (ed.) EUROCRYPT 2001. LNCS, vol. 2045, pp. 453–474. Springer, Heidelberg (2001)
5. Diffie, W., Hellman, M.E.: New directions in cryptography. IEEE Transactions on Information Theory 22(6), 644–654 (1976)
6. Jager, T., Kohlar, F., Schäge, S., Schwenk, J.: Generic compilers for authenticated key exchange. In: Abe, M. (ed.) ASIACRYPT 2010. LNCS, vol. 6477, pp. 232–249. Springer, Heidelberg (2010)
7. Jager, T., Kohlar, F., Schäge, S., Schwenk, J.: Generic compilers for authenticated key exchange (full version). IACR Cryptology ePrint Archive, 2010:621 (2010)
8. Jager, T., Kohlar, F., Schäge, S., Schwenk, J.: On the Security of TLS-DHE in the Standard Model. In: Safavi-Naini, R., Canetti, R. (eds.) CRYPTO 2012. LNCS, vol. 7417, pp. 273–293. Springer, Heidelberg (2012)
9. Katz, J., Yung, M.: Scalable protocols for authenticated group key exchange. J. Cryptology 20(1), 85–113 (2007)
10. Koblitz, N., Menezes, A.: Another look at security definitions. IACR Cryptology ePrint Archive, 2011:343 (2011)
11. Krawczyk, H., Paterson, K.G., Wee, H.: On the security of the tls protocol: A systematic analysis. In: Canetti, R., Garay, J.A. (eds.) CRYPTO 2013, Part I. LNCS, vol. 8042, pp. 429–448. Springer, Heidelberg (2013)
12. LaMacchia, B.A., Lauter, K., Mityagin, A.: Stronger security of authenticated key exchange. In: Susilo, W., Liu, J.K., Mu, Y. (eds.) ProvSec 2007. LNCS, vol. 4784, pp. 1–16. Springer, Heidelberg (2007)
13. Menezes, A., Smart, N.P.: Security of signature schemes in a multi-user setting. Des. Codes Cryptography 33(3), 261–274 (2004)
14. Menezes, A., Ustaoglu, B.: Comparing the pre- and post-specified peer models for key agreement. IJACT 1(3), 236–250 (2009)
15. Okamoto, T.: Authenticated key exchange and key encapsulation in the standard model. In: Kurosawa, K. (ed.) ASIACRYPT 2007. LNCS, vol. 4833, pp. 474–484. Springer, Heidelberg (2007)

Password-Based Authenticated Key Exchange without Centralized Trusted Setup

Kazuki Yoneyama

NTT Secure Platform Laboratories
3-9-11 Midori-cho Musashino-shi Tokyo 180-8585, Japan
yoneyama.kazuki@lab.ntt.co.jp

Abstract. Almost all existing password-based authenticated key exchange (PAKE) schemes achieve concurrent security in the standard model by relying on the common reference string (CRS) model. A drawback of the CRS model is to require a centralized trusted authority in the setup phase; thus, passwords of parties may be revealed if the authority ill-uses trapdoor information of the CRS. There are a few secure PAKE schemes in the plain model, but, these are not achievable in a constant round (i.e., containing a linear number of rounds). In this paper, we discuss how to relax the setup assumption for (constant round) PAKE schemes. We focus on the multi-string (MS) model that allows a number of authorities (including malicious one) to provide some reference strings independently. The MS model is a more relaxed setup assumption than the CRS model because we do not trust any single authority (i.e., just assuming that a majority of authorities honestly generate their reference strings). Though the MS model is slightly restrictive than the plain model, it is very reasonable assumption because it is very easy to implement. We construct a (concurrently secure) three-move PAKE scheme in the MS model (justly without random oracles) based on the Groce-Katz PAKE scheme. The main ingredient of our scheme is the multi-string simulation-extractable non-interactive zero-knowledge proof that provides both the simulation-extractability and the extraction zero-knowledge property even if minority authorities are malicious. This work can be seen as a milestone toward constant round PAKE schemes in the plain model.

Keywords: authenticated key exchange, password, multi-string model, concurrent security.

1 Introduction

Password-based authenticated key exchange (PAKE) is one of most attractive cryptographic primitives because authentication with short PINs or human memorable passwords is getting popular in web-based or cloud services. PAKE provides both the authentication property by passwords and the secrecy of the session key generation (often used to establish a secure channel) simultaneously. We consider the standard two-party setting: two parties share a common short password in advance and can generate a common long session key over an insecure channel like the Internet.

The first PAKE scheme was proposed by Bellovin and Merritt [1]. However, the security of their scheme is not proved formally. To construct a provably secure PAKE

I. Boureanu, P. Owesarski, and S. Vaudenay (Eds.): ACNS 2014, LNCS 8479, pp. 19–36, 2014.
© Springer International Publishing Switzerland 2014

scheme is not so easy because a password has only low entropy. Since a password dictionary is small, an adversary can attempt *off-line dictionary attacks* that the adversary guesses the correct password and *locally* tests guessed passwords with transcripts repeatedly. Also, the adversary can attempt *on-line dictionary attacks* that the adversary guesses the correct password and tries to impersonate some honest party. Though online dictionary attacks cannot be prevented essentially, resistance to off-line dictionary attacks must be guaranteed. Thus, the required security of PAKE is that the advantage of the adversary is bounded by $Q/|\mathcal{D}|$, where Q is the number of impersonations that the adversary attempts and $|\mathcal{D}|$ is the size of a password dictionary $\mathcal{D}$.

First provably secure PAKE schemes [2,3,4] rely on the random oracle (RO) model or the ideal cipher (IC) model. Then, a secure PAKE scheme without ideal primitives (i.e., RO and IC) is proposed by Katz et al. [5] by adopting the *common reference string (CRS) model*. The CRS model assumes that a reference string (e.g., a public-key of a trapdoor function) is honestly created before the beginning of all interactions, and later available to all parties; thus, it is a setup assumption by a trusted third party. Though the CRS model may be practical in some situations where a trusted setup is guaranteed exactly, but it must be very restrictive in general; if an untrustworthy or a corrupted party chooses the reference string, he may be able to learn all parties' passwords by just eavesdropping on the communications. Furthermore, parties cannot detect if CRS is maliciously generated. Almost all existing secure and practical PAKE schemes in the standard model are constructed in the CRS model [5,6,7,8,9,10,11,12,13,14,15,16].

There is another methodology to construct PAKE schemes via secure function evaluation [17,18,19]. These schemes avoid both ideal primitives and the CRS model; that is, these schemes are proved to be secure in the plain model. However, the security is only guaranteed in the case of the non-concurrent (i.e., multiple sessions must be executed sequentially) or bounded concurrent setting. Goyal et al. [20] proposed a PAKE scheme (the GJO scheme) that is secure in the plain model under *concurrent* self-composition. Unfortunately, it is a theoretical scheme because many rounds of communication is necessary (i.e., containing a polynomial number of rounds). Thus, our interest is to construct a concurrently secure and round efficient PAKE scheme without relying on any of ideal primitives and the CRS model.

Our Results.   In this paper, we give a three-move PAKE scheme that is secure without assuming both ideal primitives and a (centralized) trusted setup.

Naturally, the most desirable goal is to construct a practical PAKE scheme in the plain model. However, we have a lot of hurdles to get an efficient construction in the plain model, even for getting constant round. Thus, this paper aims to avoid the drawback of the CRS model as a milestone toward a practical PAKE scheme in the plain model. Our key idea is to adopt the *multi-string (MS) model* [21].

The MS model is a decentralized model of the ordinary CRS model. In the CRS model, a single-authority creates the CRS and parties must trust the authority. For example, in typical PAKE schemes, a public-key is set as the CRS, and then, a password is encrypted with the public-key and the ciphertext is sent in the protocol. If the authority keeps the secret-key corresponding to the public-key, the password can be decrypted. Conversely, in the MS model, there are multiple authorities and each authority creates a random string, respectively. Honest authorities independently generates their reference strings (i.e., each reference string does not depend on other reference strings) while malicious authorities can set their reference strings arbitrarily. It is clearly decentralized because we only assume a majority of authorities generate random strings honestly. The MS model is very realistic because it is possible to be easily implemented in the real world so that authorities just publish their random strings on the Internet, and parties just need to agree on which authorities' strings they want to use. Obviously, the MS model is more relaxed than the CRS model in necessity of a trusted setup.

We introduce a new round-efficient PAKE scheme in the MS model. Our scheme has two attractive points beside existing schemes as follows:

1. *Round-Efficiency.* The drawback of the GJO scheme is in communication complexity; it needs linear number of rounds in the security parameter. Though Groth and Ostrovsky [21] show that any universally composable (UC) multi-party computation protocol can be securely realized in the MS model, such a general construction also needs a large number of rounds. Conversely, our scheme only needs three-moves. The construction is based on the three-move PAKE scheme by Groce and Katz [12] (GK scheme). The GK scheme is (concurrently) secure in the CRS model and most efficient in known PAKE schemes secure in the standard model. To avoid the single CRS (we will mention later), our scheme is not achieved in one-round; but round efficiency of our scheme is comparable with existing schemes. As far as we know, our scheme is first secure round-efficient PAKE scheme without a centralized trusted setup.

2. *Decentralized Setup.* The GK scheme needs a CRS to prove its security. The CRS contains public-keys of semantically secure public-key encryption (CPA-PKE) and chosen ciphertext secure labelled public-key encryption (CCA-lPKE) [22]. Since the simulator needs to know secret keys corresponding to the CRS in order to respond to adversarial messages in the security proof, public-keys have to be the CRS in order that the simulator can generate secret keys. To achieve security in the MS model, we must change the way to use strings in the protocol. Our technique is twofold. One is that public-keys are chosen by parties temporarily in each session, not included in reference strings. Thus, authorities cannot decrypt the ciphertexts; but, the simulator cannot know secret keys in the security proof. To solve this problem, we use the multi-string simulation-extractable non-interactive zero-knowledge (SENIZK) proof [21]. We can simulate responses to adversarial messages without knowing secret keys by relying on simulation-extractability of the SENIZK proof even if minority authorities are malicious. Hence, our scheme does not need a centralized CRS and enjoys the concurrent security as the GK scheme. We will discuss how to avoid the single CRS in detail in Section 3.2.

To show usefulness of our technique, we also show two extended PAKE schemes in the MS model. One is the lattice-based scheme, and the other is the UC scheme. These schemes are obtained by applying our technique to existing PAKE in the CRS model. Thus, while our technique is not generic transformation, it is applicable to a wide class of PAKE schemes such as [7] and its variants.

2 Preliminaries

Throughout this paper we use the following notations. If Set is a set, then by $m \in_R$ Set we denote that m is sampled uniformly from Set. If $\mathcal{ALG}$ is an algorithm, then by $y \leftarrow \mathcal{ALG}(x; r)$ we denote that y is output by $\mathcal{ALG}$ on input x and randomness r (if $\mathcal{ALG}$ is deterministic, r is empty).

2.1 Password-Based Authenticated Key Exchange in Multi-string Model

A PAKE scheme contains two parties (an initiator and a responder, or a client and a server) who will engage in the protocol. We suppose that the total number of parties in the system is at most N. Let passwords for all pairs of parties be uniformly and independently chosen from fixed dictionary $\mathcal{D}$. This uniformity requirement is made for simplicity and can be easily removed by adjusting security of an individual password to be the min-entropy of the distribution, instead of $1/|\mathcal{D}|$. Parties P and P' share a password $pw_{PP'}$. Also, we suppose that the total number of authorities in the system is at most n. Each honest authority publishes reference string ρ without recognizing each other or any other parties.

We denote with Π_P^i the i-th instance of key exchange sessions that party P runs. Parties use reference strings to execute instances. Each party can concurrently execute the protocol multiple times with different instances. We suppose that the total number of instances of a party is at most ℓ. The adversary is given oracle access to these instances and may also control some of the instances itself. We remark that unlike the standard notion of an "oracle", in this model instances maintain state which is updated as the protocol progresses. Also, the adversary can corrupt $n - t_p$ authorities and publish $n - t_p$ reference strings (i.e., there are at least t_p honest reference strings), possibly in a malicious and adaptive manner (i.e., generating corrupted reference strings after seeing honest strings). In particular the state of an instance Π_P^i includes the following variables (initialized as null):

- sid_P^i : the session identifier which is the ordered concatenation of all messages sent and received by Π_P^i;
- pid_P^i : the partner identifier whom Π_P^i believes it is interacting ($\mathsf{pid}_P^i \neq P$);
- acc_P^i : a Boolean variable corresponding to whether Π_P^i accepts or rejects at the end of the execution.

We say that two instances Π_P^i and $\Pi_{P'}^j$ are partnered if the following properties hold: $\mathsf{pid}_P^i = P'$ and $\mathsf{pid}_{P'}^j = P$, and $\mathsf{sid}_P^i = \mathsf{sid}_{P'}^j \neq null$ except possibly for the final message.[1] Partnered parties must accept and conclude with the common session key.

---

[1] The exception of the final message for matching of sid is needed to rule out a trivial attack that an adversary forwards all messages except the final one.

Security Definition. Following [2,12], we show the security definition of PAKE. An adversary is given total control of the external network connecting parties. This adversarial capability is modeled by giving some oracle accesses[2] as follows:

- Execute(P, i, P', j) : This query models passive attacks. The output of this query consists of the messages that were exchanged during the honest execution of the protocol.
- Send(P, i, m) : This query models active attacks. The instance Π_P^i runs according to the protocol specification and updates state. The output of this query consists of the message that the party P would generate on receipt of message m. If the inputted message is empty (say $\perp$), the query means activating the initiator and the output of the query consists of the first move message.
- Reveal(P, i) : This query models leakage of session keys by improper erasure of session keys after use or compromise of a host machine. The output of this query consists of the session key SK of Π_P^i if $\mathsf{acc}_P^i = 1$.
- Test(P, i) : At the beginning a hidden bit b is chosen. If no session key for instance Π_P^i is defined, then return the undefined symbol $\perp$. Otherwise, return the session key for instance Π_P^i if $b = 1$ or a random key from the same domain if $b = 0$. This query is posed just once.

The adversary is considered successful if it guesses b correctly or if it breaks correctness of a session. We say that an instance Π_P^i is fresh unless one of the following is true at the conclusion of the experiment:

- the adversary poses Reveal(P, i),
- the adversary poses Reveal(P', j) if Π_P^i and $\Pi_{P'}^j$ are partnered.

We say that an adversary $\mathcal{A}$ succeeds if either:[3]

- $\mathcal{A}$ poses Test(P, i) for a fresh instance Π_P^i and outputs a bit $b' = b$,
- Π_P^i and $\Pi_{P'}^j$ are partnered, and $\mathsf{acc}_P^i = \mathsf{acc}_{P'}^i = 1$, but session keys are not identical.

The adversary's advantage is formally defined by $\mathsf{Adv}_{\mathcal{A}}(\kappa) = |2 \cdot \Pr[\mathcal{A} \text{ succeeds}] - 1|$, where κ is a security parameter.

Definition 1 (PAKE). *We say a PAKE protocol is t_p-secure if for a dictionary $\mathcal{D}$ and any probabilistic polynomial-time (PPT) adversary $\mathcal{A}$ that makes at most Q_{Send} queries of* Send *to different instances the advantage $\mathsf{Adv}_{\mathcal{A}}(\kappa)$ is only negligibly larger than $Q_{\mathsf{Send}}/|\mathcal{D}|$ for κ, where t_p is the number of honest reference strings.*

---

[2] The model does not contain any explicit corruption oracle access (i.e., to reveal passwords). In the password-only setting, such an oracle is unnecessary because an adversary can internally simulate these oracles by itself. Please see [23, pp.190, footnote 8] for details.

[3] If a PAKE scheme requires mutual authenticity (i.e., an adversary cannot cause an instance to accept without any partnered peer), we add the following condition: $\mathsf{acc}_P^i = 1$ but Π_P^i is not partnered with any other instance.

2.2 Smooth Projective Hash Functions

Smooth projective hash functions play a central role in our scheme. This notion is introduced by Cramer and Shoup [24], and our scheme uses its variant.

Let R be an efficiently computable binary relation. For pairs $(x, w) \in R$ we call x the statement and w the witness. Let X be a set and $L \subset X$ be a NP-language consisting of statements in R. Loosely speaking, hash function H_{hk} that maps X to some set is *projective* if there exists a projection key that defines the action of H_{hk} over the subset L of the domain X. That is, there exists deterministic projection function $F(\cdot)$ that maps key hk into its projection key $hp = F(hk)$. The projection key hp is such that for every $x \in L$ it holds that the value of $H_{hk}(x)$ is uniquely determined by hp and x. In contrast, nothing is guaranteed for $x \notin L$, and it may not be possible to compute $H_{hk}(x)$ from hp and x. A *smooth* projective hash function (SPHF) has the additional property (smoothness) that for $x \notin L$, the projection key hp actually says nothing about the value of $H_{hk}(x)$. More specifically, given x and $hp = F(hk)$, the value $H_{hk}(x)$ is uniformly distributed (or statistically close) to a random element in the range of H_{hk}.

An interesting feature of SPHF is that if L is an NP-language, then for every $x \in L$ it is possible to efficiently compute $H_{hk}(x) = h_{hp}(x, w)$ using projection key $hp = F(hk)$ and witness w of the fact that $x \in L$. Alternatively, given hk itself, it is possible to efficiently compute $H_{hk}(x)$ even without knowing the witness. When L is a hard-on-the-average NP-language, for a random $x \in_R L$, given x and $hp = F(hk)$ the value $H_{hk}(x)$ is computationally indistinguishable from a random value in the range of $H_{hk}(x)$. Thus, even if $x \in L$, the value $H_{hk}(x)$ is pseudorandom, unless the witness is known.

2.3 Multi-string Simulation-Extractable Non-interactive Zero-Knowledge Proof

We borrow the definition of multi-string SENIZK proof from [21].

A multi-string proof system for a relation R consists of PPT algorithms K, P, V, that K means the key generator, P means the prover and V means the verifier respectively. The key generation algorithm can be used to produce common reference string ρ. The prover takes as input (ρ, x, w) where ρ is a set of n different common reference strings and $(x, w) \in R$, and outputs a proof π. The verifier takes as input (ρ, x, π) and outputs 1 if the proof is acceptable and 0 otherwise. We call (K, P, V) a (t_c, t_s, t_z, n)-simulation-extractable NIZK proof system for R if it has the completeness, simulation-extractability and extraction zero-knowledge properties described below. Parameters t_c, t_s and t_z affect these properties in a threshold manner as follows: If t_c out of n reference strings are honestly generated, then the prover holding an NP-witness for the truth of the statement should be able to create a convincing proof (i.e., corresponding to completeness). If t_s out of n reference strings are honestly generated, then it should be infeasible to convince the verifier about a false statement (i.e., corresponding to soundness). If t_z out of n reference strings are honestly generated, then it should be possible to simulate the proof without knowing the witness (i.e., corresponding to zero-knowledge).

Definition 2 (Completeness). *We say* (K, P, V) *is computationally* (t_c, t_s, t_z, n)*-complete if for any non-uniform polynomial time adversary* S*, we have* $\Pr[(\rho, x, w) \leftarrow S^K(1^\kappa);$

$\pi \leftarrow P(\rho, x, w) : V(\rho, x, \pi) = 1$ and $(x, w) \in R] \geq 1 - negl$, where K is an oracle on query i outputting $\rho_i \leftarrow K(1^\kappa)$ and S outputs ρ such that at least t_c of the ρ_i's generated by K are included.

Simulation-extractability is a combining notion of simulation-soundness and proof of knowledge. As simulation-soundness, it guarantees that an adversary cannot prove any false statement even after seeing simulated proofs of arbitrary statements. Also, as proof of knowledge, it guarantees that there are PPT algorithms that can extract a witness from a valid proof. An algorithm SE generates reference string ρ with trapdoor information δ and ξ. An algorithm S uses δ to produce a valid proof from a statement without knowing the corresponding witness. An algorithm E uses ξ to extract the witness from a valid proof.

Definition 3 (Simulation-Extractability). *We say* (K, P, V) *is* (t_c, t_s, t_z, n)-*simulation-extractable if* SE *is a PPT algorithm that outputs* (ρ, δ, ξ) *and for any non-uniform polynomial time adversary* S, *we have* $|\Pr[\rho \leftarrow K(1^\kappa) : S(\rho) = 1] - \Pr[(\rho, \delta, \xi) \leftarrow SE(1^\kappa) : S(\rho) = 1]| \leq negl$, *and if* SE *is a PPT algorithm that outputs* (ρ, δ, ξ), E *is a PPT algorithm that outputs* w *on input* (ρ, ξ, x, π) *and for any non-uniform polynomial time adversary* S, *we have* $|\Pr[(\rho, x, \pi) \leftarrow S^{SE_s, S}(1^\kappa); w \leftarrow E(\rho, \xi, x, \pi) : (\rho, x, \pi) \notin \mathcal{L}$ *and* $(x, w) \notin R$ *and* $V(\rho, x, \pi) = 1] \leq negl$, *where* SE_s *is an oracle on query* i *outputting* (ρ_i, ξ_i) *from* $(\rho_i, \delta_i, \xi_i) \leftarrow SE(1^\kappa)$, S *is an oracle on input* (ρ_j, δ_j, x_j) *outputting* π_j *such that* δ_j *contains* t_z δ_i's *corresponding to* ρ_i's *generated by* SE, $\mathcal{L}$ *is a list of statements and corresponding proofs* (ρ_j, x_j, π_j) *made by* S, *and* ξ *contains* t_s ξ_i's *corresponding to* ρ_i's *generated by* SE.

Extraction zero-knowledge is an extended notion of zero-knowledge according to simulation-extractability. It guarantees that even after seeing many extractions it should still be hard to distinguish real proofs and simulated proofs from one another.

Definition 4 (Extraction Zero-Knowledge). *We say* (K, P, V) *is* (t_c, t_s, t_z, n)-*extraction zero-knowledge if* SE *is a PPT algorithm that outputs* (ρ, δ, ξ), E *is a PPT algorithm that outputs* w *on input* (ρ, ξ, x, π), S *is a PPT algorithm that outputs* π *on input* (ρ, δ, x) *and for any non-uniform polynomial time adversary* S, *we have* $|\Pr[(\rho, x, w) \leftarrow S^{SE_z, E}(1^\kappa); \pi \leftarrow P(\rho, x, w) : S^E(\pi) = 1$ *and* $(x, w) \in R] - \Pr[(\rho, x, w) \leftarrow S^{SE_z, E}(1^\kappa); \pi \leftarrow S(\rho, \delta, x) : S^E(\pi) = 1$ *and* $(x, w) \in R]| \leq negl$, *where* SE_z *is an oracle on query* i *outputting* (ρ_i, δ_i) *from* $(\rho_i, \delta_i, \xi_i) \leftarrow SE(1^\kappa)$, *and* E *is an oracle on input* $(\rho_j, \xi_j, x_j, \pi_j)$ *outputting* w *such that the query contains* t_s ρ_i's *generated by* SE *and* π_j *is not the challenge proof for* S.

3   Three-Move PAKE in Multi-string Model

In this section, we show a PAKE scheme in the MS model based on the Groce-Katz PAKE scheme [12] (GK scheme) in the CRS model. Though our scheme is less efficient both in communication and computational complexity than the GK scheme, the setup assumption is relaxed to a decentralized setup.

3.1   Recalling the GK Scheme

First, we recall the GK scheme that is secure in the CRS model. Fig. 1 shows an overview of the GK scheme.

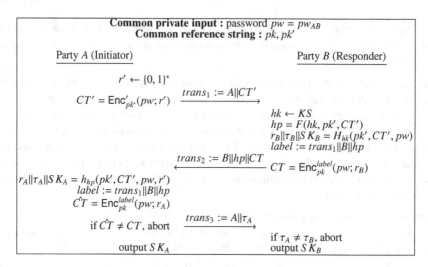

Fig. 1. A high-level overview of the GK scheme

The GK scheme uses a CCA-1PKE $\Sigma = (\mathsf{Gen}, \mathsf{Enc}, \mathsf{Dec})$ where the message space $MS = \mathcal{D}$, PKS is the public-key space and CTS is the ciphertext space, and a CPA-PKE $\Sigma' = (\mathsf{Gen'}, \mathsf{Enc'}, \mathsf{Dec'})$ with an associated SPHF where the message space $MS' = \mathcal{D}$, PKS' is the public-key space and CTS' is the ciphertext space. We define sets X, $\{L_m\}_{m \in \mathcal{D}}$ and language L for Σ' with respect to pk'. Let X be a set $\{(pk', CT', m) | pk' \in PKS'; CT' \in CTS'; m \in \mathcal{D}\}$, L_m be a set $\{(pk', CT', m) | (pk', sk') \leftarrow \mathsf{Gen'}(1^\kappa); \mathsf{Dec'}_{sk'}(CT') = m\}$ and L be a set $\cup_{m \in \mathcal{D}} L_m$.

As described in Section 2.2, the GK scheme uses a family of SPHFs $\mathcal{H} = \{H_{hk}\}$ such that for every hk in the key space KS, $H_{hk} : X \to \{0, 1\}^{3\kappa}$ and $F : KS \times PKS' \times CTS' \to PS$ where PS is the projection key space. Formally, the SPHF that the GK scheme uses is defined by a sampling algorithm that outputs $(KS, \mathcal{H}, PS, F)$ such that:

- There are efficient algorithms that sample a uniform $hk \in KS$, compute H_{hk} for $hk \in KS$ and $x \in X$, and compute $F(hk, pk', CT')$ for all $hk \in KS$, $pk' \in PKS'$ and $CT' \in CTS'$.
- For any $x = (pk', CT', m) \in L$, there is an efficient algorithm that given inputs $hp = F(hk, pk', CT')$ and (pk', CT', m, r') such that $CT' = \mathsf{Enc'}_{pk'}(m; r')$ computes $h_{hp}(x, r') = H_{hk}(x)$.
- For any $x = (pk', CT', m) \in X \setminus L$, distributions $\{hk \leftarrow KS; hp = F(hk, pk', CT') : (hp, H_{hk}(x))\}$ and $\{hk \leftarrow KS; hp = F(hk, pk', CT'); v \leftarrow \{0, 1\}^{3\kappa} : (hp, v)\}$ are statistical indistinguishable in κ.

The GK scheme ensures both correctness and authenticity by relying on the SPHF. First, correctness is guaranteed because of the projection property. Initiator A only knows the projection key hp, but he also knows the randomness r' in generating CT'. Thus, A can derive the correct session key SK with h_{hp} and r'. On the other hand, responder B does not know r', but knows the hash key hk. Thus, B can derive the correct session key SK only with hk. Also, authenticity is guaranteed because of the smoothness property. If a party does not know correct password pw, he cannot determine $r_A = r_B$ and $\tau_A = \tau_B$; hence, the verification of the peer is failed.

3.2 Design Principle

Here, we show our strategy to avoid centralized trusted setup with the MS model.

First, we observe how the CRS model contributes to prove security of the GK scheme. In some step of the security proof, a simulator needs to check if a ciphertext that is generated by the adversary is valid for the correct password. If so, the simulator regards the adversary successful. The simulator can know secret keys sk, sk' for pk, pk' because the CRS is generated by him. Thus, the simulator successfully works in this case with the power of trapdoors of the CRS. In the MS model, the simulator cannot generate all public-keys $(pk_1, \ldots, pk_n)$ because an adversary may publish malicious public-keys as corrupt authorities. Then, the simulator can know trapdoors of only honest authorities. Next, we discuss what is non-trivial to construct PAKE under this setting.

Simple Solutions Do Not Work. A naive idea is that parties encrypt the password with all public-keys and send n ciphertexts. In this case, the simulator can check if a ciphertext that is generated by the adversary is valid for the correct password with a secret key of an honest authority. Obviously, to directly encrypt the password is flawed because the adversary knows secret keys of corrupted authorities and can obtain the password.

Threshold cryptography is widely used in cryptographic protocols involving a multi-authority setting. If we apply it to the PAKE setting, parties transform the password into n shares with a secret sharing scheme like [25], then, encrypt each share with each public-key, and send n ciphertexts. If malicious public-keys are less than the threshold, the password is perfectly protected, and the simulator can reconstruct the password and check the validity of ciphertexts. However, there is a problem that each party cannot know shares of the peer because he does not have any secret key and the share generation algorithm must be probabilistic with local randomness. To compute a common value with the SPHF, parties can input the same encrypted messages to H_{hk} or h_{hp}. Therefore, the approach using threshold cryptography does not work.

Another way is to accumulate all public-keys to a combined public-key. For example, with the ElGamal encryption, the public-keys $(pk_1, \ldots, pk_n)$ are combined as $pk = \prod_1^n pk_i$, and the password is encrypted by pk. In this case, parties can compute a common value with the SPHF. Unfortunately, this approach does not work because a malicious authority can reveal the password. In the MS model, it is not guaranteed that malicious authorities determine their reference strings without seeing other authorities' strings. If a malicious authority observes all other authorities' public-keys before publishing her public-key, she can easily set $pk = \prod_1^n pk_i$ to an arbitrary value that she knows the underlying secret key.

Therefore, these orthodox techniques are not useful in the PAKE setting.

Our Technique. Our main idea is twofold: to use *ad-hoc* public-key and to use a *multi-string SENIZK proof*. Problems we discussed above come from the fact that corrupted authorities can decrypt ciphertexts. Thus, we modify the protocol as each party generates an ad-hoc public-key[4] and encrypts the password with the ad-hoc public-key. Then, the adversary cannot decrypt it. Conversely, the simulator cannot also decrypt the ciphertext that is generated by the adversary because the ad-hoc public-key is also generated by the adversary. We find that what the simulator must do is *not to decrypt the ciphertext but to check if it is valid for the correct password*. Hence, we can solve this problem by using the simulation-extractability of SENIZK. Each party proves that he knows a plaintext and randomness that are used to generate the ciphertext with the public-key. The simulation-extractability ensures that there is a PPT algorithm to extract a witness from a valid proof. The simulator can extract the encrypted plaintext, and check if the plaintext is the correct password.

More formally, the SENIZK proves that ciphertext CT is well-formed in that there exists (pw, r) such that $CT = \mathsf{Enc}_{pk}(pw; r)$. Nobody knows the secret key corresponding to pk. Though the adversary can pose Send query, the simulator can handle such a query with oracle S in the definition of the simulation-extractability. Also, even if arbitrary simulated proofs are provided, the adversary cannot distinguish the simulation environment and the real experiment from the extraction zero-knowledge, and cannot prove any false statement from the simulation-extractability. We use $(0, \frac{n+1}{2}, \frac{n+1}{2}, n)$-SENIZK (i.e., a majority of reference strings are honest). Such a SENIZK is given in [21] for any NP-language. The SENIZK not only allowed us to prove security, but allows us to do so without CCA-lPKE for the responder. A semantically secure labelled public-key encryption (CPA-lPKE) is sufficient.

A remaining problem is how to deal with the SPHF. In the GK scheme, since the SPHF is parameterized by a public-key in the CRS, the public-key is put in the CRS. In our scheme, the SPHF is parameterized by an ad-hoc public-key; thus, we cannot put it in some reference string. This problem is easily resolved. We can simply put the specification of the SPHF in the system-wide parameter without parameterizing by a public-key because the hash key sampling algorithm does not depend on the public-key and other functions are deterministic. The responder can compute projection key hp with an ad-hoc public-key and a ciphertext from the peer. Here, we show an example of the SPHF for the ElGamal encryption: $pk = (g, h)$ is the public-key, r is the randomness to encrypt message m, and $CT = (u = g^r, e = mh^r)$ is the ciphertext. The hash key generation algorithm $HKGen(\mathbb{Z}_p)$ chooses hash key $hk = (a_1, a_2)$ from $\mathbb{Z}_p^2$, and the projection key generation algorithm $HPGen(pk, hk)$ generates projection key hp as $g^{a_1} h^{a_2}$. The hash key-based hash value derivation algorithm $HashHK(CT, m, hk)$ computes the hash value as $u^{a_1}(e/m)^{a_2}$, and the projection key-based hash value derivation algorithm $HashHP(r, hp)$ computes the hash value as hp^r. In this case, the specification of the SPHF without parameterizing by a public-key is set as $(HKGen(\mathbb{Z}_p), HPGen(\cdot, \cdot), HashHK(\cdot, \cdot, \cdot), HashHP(\cdot, \cdot))$. Thus, it can be put in the system-wide parameter without depending on ad-hoc public-keys.

3.3 Our Protocol

A high-level overview of the protocol appears in Fig. 2. Our scheme is formally described as follows:

---

[4] It is unnecessary to keep the secret-key.

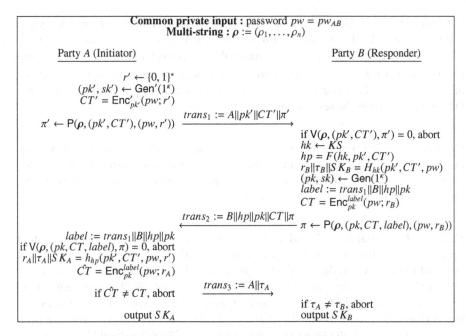

Common private input : password $pw = pw_{AB}$
Multi-string : $\rho := (\rho_1, \ldots, \rho_n)$

Party A (Initiator)   Party B (Responder)

$$r' \leftarrow \{0, 1\}^*$$
$$(pk', sk') \leftarrow \mathsf{Gen}'(1^\kappa)$$
$$CT' = \mathsf{Enc}'_{pk'}(pw; r')$$

$$\pi' \leftarrow \mathsf{P}(\rho, (pk', CT'), (pw, r')) \quad \xrightarrow{\quad trans_1 := A\|pk'\|CT'\|\pi' \quad}$$

if $\mathsf{V}(\rho, (pk', CT'), \pi') = 0$, abort
$hk \leftarrow KS$
$hp = F(hk, pk', CT')$
$r_B\|\tau_B\|S K_B = H_{hk}(pk', CT', pw)$
$(pk, sk) \leftarrow \mathsf{Gen}(1^\kappa)$
$label := trans_1\|B\|hp\|pk$
$CT = \mathsf{Enc}_{pk}^{label}(pw; r_B)$

$$\xleftarrow{\quad trans_2 := B\|hp\|pk\|CT\|\pi \quad} \quad \pi \leftarrow \mathsf{P}(\rho, (pk, CT, label), (pw, r_B))$$

$$label := trans_1\|B\|hp\|pk$$
if $\mathsf{V}(\rho, (pk, CT, label), \pi) = 0$, abort
$$r_A\|\tau_A\|S K_A = h_{hp}(pk', CT', pw, r')$$
$$\hat{CT} = \mathsf{Enc}_{pk}^{label}(pw; r_A)$$

if $\hat{CT} \neq CT$, abort $\xrightarrow{\quad trans_3 := A\|\tau_A \quad}$

if $\tau_A \neq \tau_B$, abort
output $S K_A$ output $S K_B$

Fig. 2. A high-level overview of our basic PAKE scheme

Public Parameters. κ is a security parameter. Let $\Sigma = (\mathsf{Gen}, \mathsf{Enc}, \mathsf{Dec})$ be a CPA-IPKE where the message space $MS = \mathcal{D}$, PKS is the public-key space and CTS is the cipher-text space, and $\Sigma' = (\mathsf{Gen}', \mathsf{Enc}', \mathsf{Dec}')$ be a CPA-PKE with an associated SPHF where the message space $MS' = \mathcal{D}$, PKS' is the public-key space and CTS' is the ciphertext space. We define sets X, $\{L_m\}_{m \in MS}$ and L for Σ'. Let X be a set $\{(pk', CT', m) | pk' \in PKS'; CT' \in CTS'; m \in MS'\}$, L_m be a set $\{(pk', CT', m) | (pk', sk') \leftarrow \mathsf{Gen}'(1^\kappa);$ $\mathsf{Dec}'_{sk'}(CT') = m\}$ and L be a set $\cup_{m \in MS} L_m$. We use a family of SPHFs $\mathcal{H} = \{H_{hk}\}$ such that for every hk in the key space KS, $H_{hk} : X \to \{0, 1\}^{3\kappa}$ and $F : KS \times PKS' \times CTS' \to PS$ where PS is the projection key space. Each authority generates reference string $\rho_i \leftarrow K(1^\kappa)$ for SENIZK. The multi-strings is $\rho := (\rho_1, \ldots, \rho_n)$ where ρ_i is generated by i-th authority.

Protocol Execution. The initiator A generates a randomness $r' \in \{0, 1\}^*$ and a public-key $(pk', sk') \leftarrow \mathsf{Gen}'(1^\kappa)$, and computes the ciphertext $CT' = \mathsf{Enc}'_{pk'}(pw; r')$ with the password pw. Define a language L'_{ZK} as $L'_{ZK} := \{(pk', CT') : \exists pw$ and r' s.t. $CT' = \mathsf{Enc}'_{pk'}(pw; r')\}$. A produces a SENIZK proof π' that $(pk', CT') \in L'_{ZK}$, with the multi-string ρ. A sends $trans_1 := A\|pk'\|CT'\|\pi'$ to the responder B. Upon receiving $A\|pk'\|CT'$ $\|\pi'$, B verifies π' with pk', CT' and ρ. If π' is invalid, B aborts. Otherwise, B generates a hash key $hk \leftarrow KS$ and a public-key $(pk, sk) \leftarrow \mathsf{Gen}(1^\kappa)$, derives the projection key $hp = F(hk, pk', CT')$ and $r_B\|\tau_B\|S K_B = H_{hk}(pk', CT', pw)$, sets $label := trans_1\|B\|hp\|pk$, and computes the ciphertext $CT = \mathsf{Enc}_{pk}^{label}(pw; r_B)$. Define a language L_{ZK} as $L_{ZK} := \{(pk, CT, label) : \exists pw$ and r_B s.t. $CT = \mathsf{Enc}_{pk}^{label}(pw; r_B)\}$. B produces a SENIZK proof π that $(pk, CT, label) \in L_{ZK}$, with ρ. B sends $trans_2 :=$

$B\|hp\|pk\|CT\|\pi$ to A. Upon receiving $B\|hp\|pk\|CT\|\pi$, A sets $label := trans_1\|B\|hp\|pk$, and verifies π with $pk, CT, label$ and ρ. If π is invalid, A aborts. Otherwise, A derives $r_A\|\tau_A\|SK_A = h_{hp}(pk', CT', pw, r')$, computes the ciphertext $\hat{CT} = \text{Enc}_{pk}^{label}(pw; r_A)$, and checks whether $\hat{CT} \neq CT$. If so, A aborts. Otherwise, A sends τ_A to B and outputs the session key SK_A. Upon receiving τ_A, B checks whether $\tau_A \neq \tau_B$. If so, B aborts. Otherwise, B outputs the session key SK_B.

Correctness. When both parties A and B have the common password, the session keys that they compute are the same. This is because the same hash value is obtained when using the hash key hk and when using the projection key hp. This implies that the correctness property holds for the protocol.

Concrete Instantiation. Σ and Σ' can be instantiated by the ElGamal encryption because it can admit a smooth projective hash function. A concrete SENIZK proof in the MS model is introduced in [21]. Specifically, the SENIZK proof is constructed from a CCA-PKE, a zap, and a strong one-time signature. We have efficient CCA-PKE schemes such as the Cramer-Shoup encryption [26]. Zaps are public-coin witness-indistinguishable proofs. While the original SENIZK proof uses a two-move zap [27], we can replace it with an efficient non-interactive zap [28,29] for circuit SAT based on the decisional linear assumption. We can also use an efficient strong one-time signature scheme [30] based on the discrete-log assumption.

3.4 Security

Theorem 1. *Assume that Σ' is a CPA-PKE with an associated SPHF, Σ is a CPA-lPKE, and $(\mathsf{K}, \mathsf{P}, \mathsf{V})$ is $(0, \frac{n+1}{2}, \frac{n+1}{2}, n)$-simulation-extractable and $(0, \frac{n+1}{2}, \frac{n+1}{2}, n)$-extraction zero-knowledge. Then, our scheme in Fig. 2 is $(\frac{n+1}{2})$-secure in the MS model.*

The security proof of our scheme follows the manner of the GK scheme. We proceed to prove the security through a series of hybrid experiment.

Due to space limitation, the proof of Theorem 1 is shown in the full paper. We show a sketch of the proof.

First, we modify the generation of the reference string ρ_i by each honest authority so that ρ_i is generated with trapdoor information by the algorithm SE in the definition of multi-string SENIZK proof. Since honest authorities are majority, this change is indistinguishable from simulation-extractability of SENIZK. Trapdoor information helps to extract the passwords from adversary-generated messages, and the simulator can check the validity of adversary-generated messages in later.

Next, we modify the output of Execute oracle so that all proofs π' and pi are changed to simulated proofs by the algorithm SE in the definition of multi-string SENIZK proof, ciphertexts CT' and CT are changed to encryptions of a fake password, and $H_{hk}(pk', CT', pw)$ is changed to random. Since honest authorities are majority, these changes are indistinguishable from extraction zero-knowledge of SENIZK, CPA security and smoothness of SPHF, respectively. Then, the session key becomes truly random and all transcripts are independent from the real passwords for the output of Execute oracle.

Finally, we modify the output of Send oracle similarly as the case of Execute oracle. We note that the simulator must check the validity of adversary-generated messages by verifying that the correct password is used. However, the simulator does not know the secret key of Σ and Σ' because it is not contained in reference strings. It can be solved by using trapdoor information of reference strings of honest authorities. The simulator can extract a password from the adversary-generated proof. and can check the validity of it. This part is the distinguished point from existing proof scenarios in the CRS model. From extraction zero-knowledge of SENIZK, CPA security and smoothness of SPHF, we can change the output of Send oracle so that the session key becomes truly random and all transcripts are independent from the real passwords.

4   Other Constructions

In this section, we briefly discuss if our technique is applicable to construct other PAKE schemes that have different benefit than our basic scheme in Section 3.3.

4.1   Lattice-Based Three-Move PAKE in Multi-string Model

Katz and Vaikuntanathan [11] propose a lattice-based three-move PAKE scheme (the KV1 scheme) in the CRS model. Because perfect correctness is hard to achieve in lattice-based cryptosystems, the KV1 scheme uses the notion of *approximate* SPHF (i.e., correctness is guaranteed approximately).

We can apply our technique (i.e., generating ad-hoc public-keys and adding the SENIZK proof) to the KV1 scheme. Fig. 3 shows a high-level overview of the lattice-based protocol. We use a family of ϵ-approximate SPHFs $\mathcal{H} = \{H_{hk}\}$ such that for every hk in the key space KS, $H_{hk} : X \to \{0, 1\}^\ell$ and $F : KS \times PKS \times CTS \times LS \to PS$, where KS is the hash key space, PTS is the public-key space, CTS is the ciphertext space, LS is the label space and PS is the projection key space. Let $\mathsf{ECC} : \{0, 1\}^\kappa \to \{0, 1\}^\ell$ be an error-correcting code correcting a 2ϵ-fraction of errors. Let $(\mathsf{Gen}, \mathsf{Enc}, \mathsf{Dec})$ be a CPA-iPKE with an associated ϵ-approximate SPHF. Let $(\mathsf{SigGen}, \mathsf{Sign}, \mathsf{Ver})$ be a one-time signature scheme. The SENIZK proof $(\mathsf{K}, \mathsf{P}, \mathsf{V})$ is for the same language as Section 3.3. Please see [11] for definitions of ϵ-approximate SPHFs and error-correcting codes.

The security proof is similar to the proof in [11]. The main difference is the way to extract the password from the ciphertext that is generated by an adversary. As the proof of Theorem 1, we use the power of simulation-extractability of the SENIZK proof.

For an instantiation, we use the same ingredients as the KV1 scheme except the SENIZK proof. As a building block of the SENIZK proof, while we can use an efficient non-interactive zap [28,29] in the instantiation of our scheme in Section 3.3, it is not suitable for the lattice-based protocol because of the assumption. Thus, we use a two-move zap [27] that is constructed from a general NIZK proof. Therefore, our lattice-based scheme is less efficient than our basic scheme; but, it has an advantage in immunity against quantum attacks.

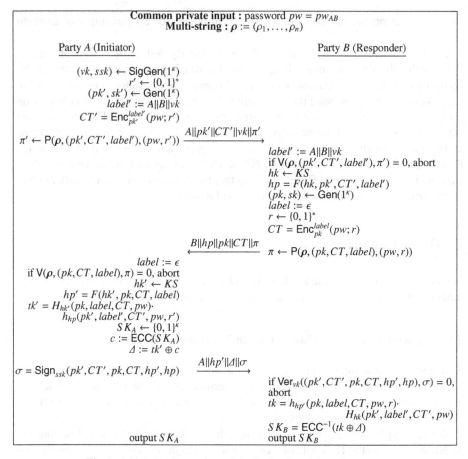

Fig. 3. A high-level overview of the lattice-based PAKE scheme

4.2 Universally Composable Three-Move PAKE in Multi-string Model

Katz and Vaikuntanathan [13] propose a UC one-round PAKE scheme (the KV2 scheme) in the CRS model. The KV2 scheme achieves the UC security by adding a simulation-sound NIZK (SSNIZK) proof that proves that 1) there exists a hash key which is the plaintext of a ciphertext, and 2) a projection key is generated from the hash key.

We also can apply our technique to the KV2 scheme. Fig. 4 shows a high-level overview of the UC protocol. We use the family of SPHFs $\mathcal{H} = \{H_{hk}\}$ that is constructed in [13]. The difference between SPHFs in Section 3.3 and in [13] is that the projection key is generated without inputting the ciphertext in the latter SPHFs (i.e., $hp = F(hk, pk)$).[5] Let (Gen1, Enc1, Dec1) be a CCA-PKE. Let (Gen2, Enc2, Dec2) be a CPA-IPKE with an associated SPHF. The SENIZK proof (K, P, V) is for the same language as Section 3.3. Also, we use a SSNIZK proof (K', P', V') for the following

---

[5] The SPHF based on the ElGamal encryption in [12] indeed satisfies the definition in [13]. Thus, we use the same SPHFs as Section 3.3.

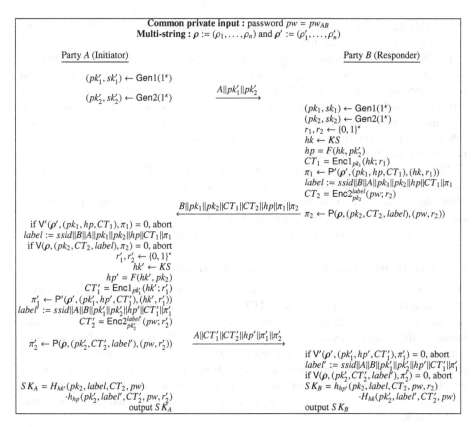

Fig. 4. A high-level overview of the UC PAKE scheme

language: $\{(pk, hp, CT) : \exists hk \in KS \text{ and } r \text{ s.t. } CT = \text{Enc1}_{pk}(hk; r) \text{ and } hp = F(hk, pk)\}$. where the corresponding multi string is $\rho' := (\rho'_1, \ldots, \rho'_n)$. Because SENIZK implies SSNIZK, we can use the SENIZK proof as the SSNIZK proof in the MS model. Please see [31,32,13] for the UC framework and the definition of the simulation-sound NIZK.

The security proof is similar to the proof in [13]. The simulator extracts the password from the ciphertext that is generated by an adversary by simulation-extractability of the SENIZK proof.

The KV2 scheme is one-round protocol, but our UC PAKE scheme needs three-move. We add the first move in order to send initiator's public-keys. The reason we must do that is that the projection key is generated from the hash key and the public-key. In the CRS model, the public-key is put as the CRS, and each party can generate the projection key without interacting with the peer. However, in the MS model, the public-key cannot be put as reference strings because of the discussion in Section 3.2. Hence, we add an additional move to send the public-key.

4.3 Is One-Round PAKE in Multi-string Model Possible?

All our constructions are three-move protocols. Some existing PAKE schemes are one-round such as a scheme in [13] which is secure in the game-based model (i.e., the BPR model [2]). One may wonder why we do not construct a one-round PAKE scheme. Here, we show the reason as follows:

In SPHF-based PAKE, each party must send a projection key without receiving any message from the peer in one-round protocols. However, our methodology requires that public-keys are not put as a CRS but are sent in messages, and the generation of a projection key depends on the public-key of the peer. Therefore, we need an additional message to send the public-key of the initiator. It is the essential reason why our PAKE scheme is not achieved in one-round. All known SPHF-based constructions fall into this problem by adapting our methodology.

The last resort is to use another methodology than the SPHF-based. For example, Canetti et al. [15] proposed a secure PAKE scheme in the CRS model based on an oblivious transfer (OT). Unfortunately, their scheme is not achieved in one-round because it follows the design principle of the GK scheme.

Therefore, a secure one-round PAKE in the MS model is an open problem.

4.4 Semi-Generic Transformation from CRS Model

Our technique is able to be interpreted as a semi-generic transformation from secure PAKE scheme to remove the centralized CRS. Our scheme indeed attaches public-keys to messages, and the SENIZK to prove possession of a password to the GK scheme. However, the technique cannot be applied to any secure PAKE in the black-box manner because it heavily depends on the structure of the underlying scheme. In the GK scheme, a password is encrypted (or committed) by PKE schemes (or a commitment scheme) and the initiator and the responder exchange ciphertexts (or commitments). This structure allows us to prove possession of a password under self-generated public-keys with the SENIZK.

On the other hand, it is applicable to schemes having the same structure like the Gennaro-Lindell framework [7,9], the lattice-based PAKE [11], and the UC PAKE[13] as in 4.1 and 4.2. The common feature of these protocols is that the CRS just contains public-keys to encrypt passwords (and some public information) and the SENIZK property is sufficient to replace NIZKs used in protocols (if any). In this case, we can give the semi-generic transformation from a secure PAKE scheme π is as follows:

1. If π includes NIZKs in the CRS model, the CRS is replaced with the MS for the SENIZK.
2. The initiator I and responder R in π generate public-keys (or commitment CRSs) which are used to encrypt (or commit) the shared password. They exchange their public-keys.
3. When I or R computes a ciphertext or a commitment of the password, the party also generates a proof that public-keys are correctly generated under the password with the SENIZK. Also, if generations of NIZK proofs are contained, these proofs are replaced with the SENIZK.
4. In other parts, I and R execute π.

Though this transformation needs extra two moves for exchanging public-keys, we can optimize the number of moves depending on the structure of the underlying protocol. For example, our constructions in Section 3.3 and 4.1 do not need any extra move, but the construction in Section 4.2 needs an additional move.

5   Concluding Remark

We introduced a first three-move PAKE scheme which is secure without any centralized trusted setup (i.e., in the MS model).

Our idea to construct the PAKE scheme in the MS model is not trivially applicable to a construction in the plain model. The proof in the MS model depends on the fact that there are honest trusted authorities. Thus, we can use the SENIZK proof. Conversely, it is impossible to construct NIZK proofs for non-trivial languages in the plain model [33]. A possible way is to use some (concurrently secure) interactive zero-knowledge proof protocol in the plain model instead of using the SENIZK proof. However, such a protocol needs a large number of rounds.

Therefore, a secure constant round PAKE scheme in the plain model is still hard and an open problem.

References

1. Bellovin, S.M., Merritt, M.: Encrypted Key Exchange: Password-Based Protocols Secure Against Dictionary Attacks. In: IEEE S&P, pp. 72–84 (1992)
2. Bellare, M., Pointcheval, D., Rogaway, P.: Authenticated Key Exchange Secure against Dictionary Attacks. In: Preneel, B. (ed.) EUROCRYPT 2000. LNCS, vol. 1807, pp. 139–155. Springer, Heidelberg (2000)
3. Boyko, V., MacKenzie, P.D., Patel, S.: Provably Secure Password-Authenticated Key Exchange Using Diffie-Hellman. In: Preneel, B. (ed.) EUROCRYPT 2000. LNCS, vol. 1807, pp. 156–171. Springer, Heidelberg (2000)
4. MacKenzie, P.D., Patel, S., Swaminathan, R.: Password-Authenticated Key Exchange Based on RSA. In: Okamoto, T. (ed.) ASIACRYPT 2000. LNCS, vol. 1976, pp. 599–613. Springer, Heidelberg (2000)
5. Katz, J., Ostrovsky, R., Yung, M.: Efficient Password-Authenticated Key Exchange Using Human-Memorable Passwords. In: Pfitzmann, B. (ed.) EUROCRYPT 2001. LNCS, vol. 2045, pp. 475–494. Springer, Heidelberg (2001)
6. Katz, J., Ostrovsky, R., Yung, M.: Forward Secrecy in Password-Only Key Exchange Protocols. In: Cimato, S., Galdi, C., Persiano, G. (eds.) SCN 2002. LNCS, vol. 2576, pp. 29–44. Springer, Heidelberg (2003)
7. Gennaro, R., Lindell, Y.: A Framework for Password-Based Authenticated Key Exchange. In: Biham, E. (ed.) EUROCRYPT 2003. LNCS, vol. 2656, pp. 408–432. Springer, Heidelberg (2003)
8. Jiang, S., Gong, G.: Password Based Key Exchange with Mutual Authentication. In: Handschuh, H., Hasan, M.A. (eds.) SAC 2004. LNCS, vol. 3357, pp. 267–279. Springer, Heidelberg (2004)
9. Gennaro, R.: Faster and Shorter Password-Authenticated Key Exchange. In: Canetti, R. (ed.) TCC 2008. LNCS, vol. 4948, pp. 589–606. Springer, Heidelberg (2008)
10. Katz, J., Ostrovsky, R., Yung, M.: Efficient and secure authenticated key exchange using weak passwords. J. ACM 57(1), 1–39 (2009)
11. Katz, J., Vaikuntanathan, V.: Smooth Projective Hashing and Password-Based Authenticated Key Exchange from Lattices. In: Matsui, M. (ed.) ASIACRYPT 2009. LNCS, vol. 5912, pp. 636–652. Springer, Heidelberg (2009)
12. Groce, A., Katz, J.: A new framework for efficient password-based authenticated key exchange. In: ACM Conference on Computer and Communications Security 2010, pp. 516–525 (2010)

13. Katz, J., Vaikuntanathan, V.: Round-Optimal Password-Based Authenticated Key Exchange. In: Ishai, Y. (ed.) TCC 2011. LNCS, vol. 6597, pp. 293–310. Springer, Heidelberg (2011)
14. Jutla, C.S., Roy, A.: Relatively-Sound NIZKs and Password-Based Key-Exchange. In: Fischlin, M., Buchmann, J., Manulis, M. (eds.) PKC 2012. LNCS, vol. 7293, pp. 485–503. Springer, Heidelberg (2012)
15. Canetti, R., Dachman-Soled, D., Vaikuntanathan, V., Wee, H.: Efficient Password Authenticated Key Exchange via Oblivious Transfer. In: Fischlin, M., Buchmann, J., Manulis, M. (eds.) PKC 2012. LNCS, vol. 7293, pp. 449–466. Springer, Heidelberg (2012)
16. Ben Hamouda, F., Blazy, O., Chevalier, C., Pointcheval, D., Vergnaud, D.: Efficient UC-Secure Authenticated Key-Exchange for Algebraic Languages. In: Kurosawa, K., Hanaoka, G. (eds.) PKC 2013. LNCS, vol. 7778, pp. 272–291. Springer, Heidelberg (2013)
17. Goldreich, O., Lindell, Y.: Session-Key Generation Using Human Passwords Only. In: Kilian, J. (ed.) CRYPTO 2001. LNCS, vol. 2139, pp. 408–432. Springer, Heidelberg (2001)
18. Nguyen, M.H., Vadhan, S.P.: Simpler Session-Key Generation from Short Random Passwords. In: Naor, M. (ed.) TCC 2004. LNCS, vol. 2951, pp. 428–445. Springer, Heidelberg (2004)
19. Barak, B., Canetti, R., Lindell, Y., Pass, R., Rabin, T.: Secure Computation Without Authentication. In: Shoup, V. (ed.) CRYPTO 2005. LNCS, vol. 3621, pp. 361–377. Springer, Heidelberg (2005)
20. Goyal, V., Jain, A., Ostrovsky, R.: Password-Authenticated Session-Key Generation on the Internet in the Plain Model. In: Rabin, T. (ed.) CRYPTO 2010. LNCS, vol. 6223, pp. 277–294. Springer, Heidelberg (2010)
21. Groth, J., Ostrovsky, R.: Cryptography in the Multi-string Model. In: Menezes, A. (ed.) CRYPTO 2007. LNCS, vol. 4622, pp. 323–341. Springer, Heidelberg (2007)
22. Shoup, V. (ed.): Information technology — Security techniques — Encryption algorithms — Part 2: Asymmetric ciphers. International Organization for Standardization, ISO/IEC 18033-2 (2006)
23. Gennaro, R., Lindell, Y.: A Framework for Password-Based Authenticated Key Exchange. ACM Trans. Inf. Syst. Secur. 9(2), 181–234 (2006)
24. Cramer, R., Shoup, V.: Design and Analysis of Practical Public-Key Encryption Schemes Secure against Adaptive Chosen Ciphertext Attack. SIAM Journal on Computing 33, 167–226 (2004)
25. Shamir, A.: How to share a secret. Communications of the ACM 22(11), 612–613 (1979)
26. Cramer, R., Shoup, V.: A Practical Public Key Cryptosystem Provably Secure Against Adaptive Chosen Ciphertext Attack. In: Krawczyk, H. (ed.) CRYPTO 1998. LNCS, vol. 1462, pp. 13–25. Springer, Heidelberg (1998)
27. Dwork, C., Naor, M.: Zaps and Their Applications. In: FOCS 2000, pp. 283–293 (2000)
28. Groth, J., Ostrovsky, R., Sahai, A.: Non-interactive Zaps and New Techniques for NIZK. In: Dwork, C. (ed.) CRYPTO 2006. LNCS, vol. 4117, pp. 97–111. Springer, Heidelberg (2006)
29. Groth, J., Ostrovsky, R., Sahai, A.: New Techniques for Noninteractive Zero-Knowledge. J. ACM 59(3), 11 (2012)
30. Mohassel, P.: One-Time Signatures and Chameleon Hash Functions. In: Biryukov, A., Gong, G., Stinson, D.R. (eds.) SAC 2010. LNCS, vol. 6544, pp. 302–319. Springer, Heidelberg (2011)
31. Canetti, R.: Universally Composable Security: A New Paradigm for Cryptographic Protocols. In: Cryptology ePrint Archive: 2000/067 (2005), http://eprint.iacr.org/2000/067/
32. Canetti, R., Halevi, S., Katz, J., Lindell, Y., MacKenzie, P.D.: Universally Composable Password-Based Key Exchange. In: Cramer, R. (ed.) EUROCRYPT 2005. LNCS, vol. 3494, pp. 404–421. Springer, Heidelberg (2005)
33. Goldreich, O., Oren, Y.: Definitions and Properties of Zero-Knowledge Proof Systems. J. Cryptology 7(1), 1–32 (1994)

A Linear Algebra Attack to Group-Ring-Based Key Exchange Protocols

M. Kreuzer[2], A.D. Myasnikov[1], and A. Ushakov[1,⋆]

[1] Stevens Institute of Technology, Hoboken, NJ, USA
amyasnik,aushakov@stevens.edu
[2] University of Passau, Germany
martin.kreuzer@uni-passau.de

Abstract. In this paper we analyze the Habeeb-Kahrobaei-Koupparis-Shpilrain (HKKS) key exchange protocol which uses semidirect products of groups as a platform. We show that the particular instance of the protocol suggested in their paper can be broken via a simple linear algebra attack.

Keywords: Group-based cryptography, semidirect product, group ring. *Subject Classifications*: 94A60, 68W30

1 Introduction

In this paper we study a key-exchange protocol proposed in [1]. The general protocol uses semidirect products of (semi)groups as a platform. One of its special cases is the standard Diffie-Hellman protocol based on cyclic groups. The authors of [1] conjecture that, when the protocol is used with non-commutative (semi)groups, it acquires several useful features. They suggest the extension of a particular non-commutative semigroup of matrices over a certain finite group ring by a conjugation automorphism as a suitable platform. Our main result is that this particular instance of the protocol can be broken using a linear algebra attack.

Before going into details we would like to mention that the semigroup of matrices over a finite group ring has already been used in a cryptographic context, namely in [3] and in [2]. (The former protocol was analyzed in [5].) For a general introduction to non-commutative cryptography we refer to [4].

2 Description of the HKKS Key Exchange Protocol

Let G and H be groups, let $\text{Aut}(G)$ be the group of automorphisms of G, and let $\rho : H \to \text{Aut}(G)$ be a group homomorphism. The *semidirect product* of G

⋆ The work of the second and third author was partially supported by NSF grant DMS-1318716.

I. Boureanu, P. Owesarski, and S. Vaudenay (Eds.): ACNS 2014, LNCS 8479, pp. 37–43, 2014.

and H with respect to ρ is the set of pairs $\{(g,h) \mid g \in G, \ h \in H\}$ equipped with the binary operation given by

$$(g,h) \cdot (g',h') = (g^{\rho(h')}g', h \circ h').$$

for $g \in G$ and $h \in H$. It is denoted by $G \rtimes_\rho H$. Here $g^{\rho(h')}$ denotes the image of g under the automorphism $\rho(h')$, and $h \circ h'$ denotes a composition of automorphisms with h acting first.

Some specific semidirect products can be constructed as follows. First choose your favorite group G. Then let $H = \text{Aut}(G)$ and $\rho = \text{id}_G$. In which this case the semidirect product $G \rtimes_\rho H$ is called the *holomorph* of G. More generally, the group H can be chosen as a subgroup of $\text{Aut}(G)$. Using this construction, the authors of [1] propose the following key exchange protocol.

Algorithm 1. HKKS Key Exchange Protocol

Initial Setup: Fix the platform group G, an element $g \in G$, and $\varphi \in \text{Aut}(G)$. All this information is made public.

Alice's Private Key: A randomly chosen $m \in \mathbb{N}$.

Bob's Private Key: A randomly chosen $n \in \mathbb{N}$.

Alice's Public Key: Alice computes $(g,\varphi)^m = (\varphi^{m-1}(g)\ldots\varphi^2(g)\varphi(g)g, \varphi^m)$ and publishes the first component $a = \varphi^{m-1}(g)\ldots\varphi^2(g)\varphi(g)g$ of the pair.

Bob's Public Key: Bob computes $(g,\varphi)^n = (\varphi^{n-1}(g)\ldots\varphi^2(g)\varphi(g)g, \varphi^n)$ and publishes the first component $b = \varphi^{n-1}(g)\ldots\varphi^2(g)\varphi(g)g$ of the pair.

Alice's Shared Key: Alice computes the key $K_A = \varphi^m(b)a$ taking the first component of the product $(b,\varphi^n) \cdot (a,\varphi^m) = (\varphi^m(b)a, \varphi^n\varphi^m)$. (She cannot compute the second component since she does not know φ^n.)

Bob's Shared Key: Bob computes the key $K_B = \varphi^n(a)b$ taking the first component of the product $(a,\varphi^m) \cdot (b,\varphi^n) = (\varphi^n(a)b, \varphi^m\varphi^n)$. (He cannot compute the second component since he does not know φ^m.)

Note that $K_A = K_B$ since $(b,\varphi^n) \cdot (a,\varphi^m) = (a,\varphi^m) \cdot (b,\varphi^n) = (g,\varphi)^n$. The general protocol described above can be used with any non-abelian group G and an inner automorphism φ (conjugation by a fixed non-central element of G). Furthermore, since all formulas used in the description of this protocol hold if G is a semigroup and φ is a semigroup automorphism of G, the protocol can be used with semigroups. The private keys m, n can be chosen smaller than the order of (g,ϕ). For a finite group G, this can be bounded by $(\#G) \cdot (\# \text{Aut}(G))$. In an actual implementation, the elements a and b would not necessarily be published, but sent to the other party. Hence our security analysis is based on the assumption that an adversary is able to intercept this transmission without being noticed.

3   Proposed Parameters for the HKKS Key Exchange Protocol

In [1], the authors propose and extensively analyze the following specific instance of their key exchange protocol.

Consider the alternating group A_5, i.e. the group of even permutations on five symbols. It is a simple group containing 60 elements. We denote its elements by $A_5 = \{\sigma_1, \ldots, \sigma_{60}\}$. Let $\mathbb{F}_7 = \mathbb{Z}/7\mathbb{Z}$ be the field with seven elements. Then the group-ring $\mathbb{F}_7[A_5]$ is the set of formal linear combinations

$$A = \sum_{i=1}^{60} a_i \sigma_i,$$

with $a_i \in \mathbb{F}_7$. The addition and multiplication in $\mathbb{F}_7[A_5]$ are defined in the natural way by

$$\left(\sum_{i=1}^{60} a_i \sigma_i \right) + \left(\sum_{i=1}^{60} b_i \sigma_i \right) = \sum_{i=1}^{60} (a_i + b_i)\sigma_i$$

and

$$\left(\sum_{i=1}^{60} a_i \sigma_i \right) \cdot \left(\sum_{i=1}^{60} b_i \sigma_i \right) = \sum_{i=1}^{60} \left(\sum_{\sigma_j \sigma_k = \sigma_i} a_j b_k \right) \sigma_i.$$

By G we denote the monoid of all 3×3 matrices over the ring $\mathbb{F}_7[A_5]$ equipped with multiplication, i.e., we let $G = \mathrm{Mat}_3(\mathbb{F}_7[A_5])$. As usual, by $\mathrm{GL}_3(\mathbb{F}_7[A_5])$ we denote the group of invertible 3×3 matrices over the ring $\mathbb{F}_7[A_5]$.

Furthermore, we choose an inner automorphism of G, i.e., a map $\varphi = \varphi_h : G \to G$ defined by

$$g \mapsto h^{-1}gh,$$

where h is a fixed matrix from $\mathrm{GL}_3(\mathbb{F}_7[A_5])$. Clearly, we have $(\varphi_h)^m = \varphi_{h^m}$ and

$$\varphi^{m-1}(g) \ldots \varphi^2(g)\varphi(g)g = h^{-m+1}gh^{m-1} \ldots h^{-2}gh^2 \cdot h^{-1}gh^1 \cdot g = h^{-m}(hg)^m.$$

Thus we obtain the following specific instance of the HKKS key exchange protocol.

Algorithm 2. HKKS Key Exchange Protocol Using $\mathrm{Mat}_3(\mathbb{F}_7(A_5))$

Initial Setup: Fix matrices $g \in \mathrm{Mat}_3(\mathbb{F}_7[A_5])$ and $h \in \mathrm{GL}_3(\mathbb{F}_7[A_5])$. They are made public.

Alice's Private Key: A randomly chosen $m \in \mathbb{N}$.

Bob's Private Key: A randomly chosen $n \in \mathbb{N}$.

Alice's Public Key: Alice computes $a = h^{-m}(hg)^m$ and makes a public.

Bob's Public Key: Bob computes $b = h^{-n}(hg)^n$ and makes b public.

Shared Key: $K_A = K_B = h^{-n-m}(hg)^{n+m}$.

The security of this protocol is based on the assumption that, given the matrices g, h, $a = h^{-m}(hg)^m$, and $b = h^{-n}(hg)^n$, it is hard to compute the matrix $h^{-n-m}(hg)^{n+m}$. This assumption is similar to the one considered by Stickel in [8] and cryptoanalyzed in [7].

4   Embedding Matrices over Group Rings

In this section we present an embedding of $\mathrm{Mat}_3(\mathbb{F}_7[A_5])$ into $\mathrm{Mat}_{180}(\mathbb{F}_7)$. More generally, fix a finite group $G = \{g_1, \ldots, g_k\}$, where $k = \#G$, and a commutative ring R. We want to construct an embedding of $\mathrm{Mat}_n(R[G])$ into $\mathrm{Mat}_{nk}(R)$.

Let $a, b \in R[G]$ and $c = a \cdot b$. We write

$$a = \sum_{g \in G} a_g \cdot g, \; b = \sum_{g \in G} b_g \cdot g, \; \text{and} \; c = \sum_{g \in G} c_g \cdot g,$$

with $a_g, b_g, c_g \in R$. Next we define a matrix $M_a \in \mathrm{Mat}_k(R)$ and two vectors $\overline{v}_b, \overline{v}_c \in R^k$ as follows:

$$M_a = \begin{pmatrix} a_{g_1 g_1^{-1}} & \cdots & a_{g_1 g_k^{-1}} \\ \cdots & & \\ a_{g_k g_1^{-1}} & \cdots & a_{g_k g_k^{-1}} \end{pmatrix} \; \text{and} \; \overline{v}_b = \begin{pmatrix} b_{g_1} \\ \cdots \\ b_{g_k} \end{pmatrix} \; \text{and} \; \overline{v}_a = \begin{pmatrix} c_{g_1} \\ \cdots \\ c_{g_k} \end{pmatrix}.$$

Then it is easy to see that

$$M_a \cdot \overline{v}_b = \overline{v}_c. \tag{1}$$

In this way, the left multiplication in $R[G]$ by a corresponds to a linear transformation of R^k and can be naturally represented by a matrix in $\mathrm{Mat}_k(R)$.

Proposition 1. *For $a, b \in R[G]$, we have $M_{a \cdot b} = M_a \cdot M_b$. Furthermore, the map $\Phi: R[G] \to \mathrm{Mat}_k(R)$ given by $a \mapsto M_a$ is a ring monomorphism.*

Proof. Since we obviously have $M_{a+b} = M_a + M_b$, it suffices to prove that $M_{a \cdot b} = M_a \cdot M_b$. For $i, j \in \{1, \ldots, n\}$, the entry in position (i, j) of the matrix $M_{a \cdot b}$ is

$$(ab)_{g_i g_j^{-1}} = \sum_{gh = g_i g_j^{-1}} a_g b_h.$$

On the other hand, the entry in position (i, j) of the matrix $M_a \cdot M_b$ is

$$\sum_{m=1}^{k} a_{g_i g_m^{-1}} b_{g_m g_j^{-1}}.$$

Since both elements agree, we have $M_{a \cdot b} = M_a \cdot M_b$. Thus the map $a \mapsto M_a$ is a ring homomorphism. Finally, we note that we can easily reconstruct a from M_a. Consequently, the map $a \mapsto M_a$ is a monomorphism. □

Next, we recall that any matrix $A = (a_{ij}) \in \text{Mat}_n(R[G])$ defines a linear transformation of $(R[G])^n$ in the usual way:

$$\begin{pmatrix} a_{11} & \cdots & a_{1n} \\ \vdots & & \vdots \\ a_{n1} & \cdots & a_{nn} \end{pmatrix} \cdot \begin{pmatrix} b_1 \\ \vdots \\ b_n \end{pmatrix} = \begin{pmatrix} \sum_i a_{1i} b_i \\ \vdots \\ \sum_i a_{ni} b_i \end{pmatrix}.$$

Our goal is now to extend the above embedding of $R[G]$ to vectors and matrices over $R[G]$. For $A = (a_{ij}) \in \text{Mat}_n(R[G])$, we define a block matrix A^* and for a column vector $\bar{b} = (b_1, \ldots, b_n) \in (R[G])^n$, we define a vector $b^* \in R^{kn}$ by

$$A^* = \begin{pmatrix} M_{a_{11}} & \cdots & M_{a_{1n}} \\ \vdots & & \vdots \\ M_{a_{n1}} & \cdots & M_{a_{nn}} \end{pmatrix} \quad \text{and} \quad b^* = \begin{pmatrix} \overline{v}_{b_1} \\ \vdots \\ \overline{v}_{b_n} \end{pmatrix}.$$

Let $\bar{c} = A \cdot \bar{b}$. Then it is straightforward to check that we have

$$c^* = A^* \cdot b^*. \tag{2}$$

Proposition 2. *Let G be a finite group of order k and R a commutative ring. Then the map $\varphi : \text{Mat}_n(R[G]) \to \text{Mat}_{nk}(R)$ given by $A \mapsto A^*$ is a ring monomorphism.*

Proof. For $A, B \in M_n(R[G])$, we obviously have $(A+B)^* = A^* + B^*$. It follows from Proposition 1 that

$$A^* \cdot B^* = (AB)^*.$$

Hence the map φ is a ring homomorphism. Finally, we note that φ is injective because, given A^*, one can reconstruct the matrix A from A^*, since every element a_{ij} is repeated on the main diagonal of $M_{a_{ij}}$. $\qquad\square$

In particular, there exists an embedding of $\text{Mat}_3(\mathbb{F}_7[A_5])$ into $\text{Mat}_{180}(\mathbb{F}_7)$. The following result characterizes the behavior of invertible matrices under this embedding.

Proposition 3. *For a matrix $A \in \text{Mat}_n(R[G])$ we have*

$$A \in \text{GL}_n(R[G]) \iff \varphi(A) \in \text{GL}_{nk}(R).$$

Proof. The implication "$\Rightarrow$" follows from the fact that φ is a ring homomorphism. To prove the implication "$\Leftarrow$", we let $\varphi(A) \in \text{GL}_{nk}(R)$. Let $D(x_1, \ldots, x_n)$ be the determinant polynomial for matrices of size $n \times n$. Using the rule for determinants of block matrices, we know that $\det(\varphi(A)) = \det(D(M_{a_{11}}, \ldots, M_{a_{nn}}))$. The matrix $D(M_{a_{11}}, \ldots, M_{a_{nn}})$ is a polynomial expression in the matrices $M_{a_{ij}}$ which represent the left multiplications by the elements a_{ij}. Since the map Φ in Proposition 1 is a ring homomorphism, we see that the matrix $D(M_{a_{11}}, \ldots, M_{a_{nn}})$ represents the left multiplication by $D(a_{11}, \ldots, a_{nn})$ in $R[G]$. Therefore it is invertible if and only if the element $D(a_{11}, \ldots, a_{nn})$ is an invertible element of $R[G]$. This is equivalent to A being an invertible element of $\text{Mat}_n(R[G])$. $\qquad\square$

5   A Linear Algebra Attack on the HKKS Key Exchange Protocol

In this section we show that the protocol described in Algorithm 2 can be broken using a linear algebra attack. Thus we are breaking an instance of the computational Diffie-Hellman problem in this specific setting. Our attack provides a full session key recovery and makes only use of the public parameters.

Our first observation is that, to impersonate Alice, we do not need to compute her secret key m. It is sufficient to find two matrices $l, r \in G = \mathrm{Mat}_3(\mathbb{F}_7(A_5))$ satisfying the following system of matrix equations:

$$\begin{cases} l \cdot h = h \cdot l, \\ r \cdot (hg) = (hg) \cdot r, \\ a = lr. \end{cases} \tag{3}$$

Indeed, if we know l and r satisfying the equations above, then we can compute the shared key:

$$\begin{aligned} l \cdot b \cdot r &= l \cdot h^{-n}(hg)^n \cdot r \\ &= h^{-n} lr (hg)^n \\ &= h^{-n} h^{-m} (hg)^m (hg)^n = K. \end{aligned}$$

Our second observation is that system (3) has at least one solution with $l \in \mathrm{GL}_3(\mathbb{F}_7[A_5])$, i.e., with an invertible matrix l, namely $l = h^{-m}$ and $r = (hg)^m$.

Therefore, instead of solving system (3), it suffices to solve the system

$$\begin{cases} \ell \cdot h = h \cdot \ell, \\ r \cdot (hg) = (hg) \cdot r, \\ \ell a = r \end{cases} \tag{4}$$

and to recover the matrix l from the equation $\ell \cdot l = 1$.

Our final observation is that, using the embedding of Section 4, the system (4) can be transformed to a system of linear equations over $\mathbb{F}_7$. Indeed, we can write the matrix ℓ in the form

$$\ell = \begin{pmatrix} \sum_{i=1}^{60} l_i^{(1,1)} \sigma_i & \sum_{i=1}^{60} l_i^{(1,2)} \sigma_i & \sum_{i=1}^{60} l_i^{(1,3)} \sigma_i \\ \sum_{i=1}^{60} l_i^{(2,1)} \sigma_i & \sum_{i=1}^{60} l_i^{(2,2)} \sigma_i & \sum_{i=1}^{60} l_i^{(2,3)} \sigma_i \\ \sum_{i=1}^{60} l_i^{(3,1)} \sigma_i & \sum_{i=1}^{60} l_i^{(3,2)} \sigma_i & \sum_{i=1}^{60} l_i^{(3,3)} \sigma_i \end{pmatrix}$$

with unknown coefficients $l_i^{(j,k)} \in \mathbb{F}_7$. Similarly, we can write the matrix r with unknown coefficients $r_i^{(j,k)} \in \mathbb{F}_7$. After performing all matrix multiplications in (4) and applying the embedding of Section 4, we obtain a system of 1620 linear equations in 1080 unknowns $l_i^{(j,k)}, r_i^{(j,k)}$ over the field $\mathbb{F}_7$.

Thus, to break the key exchange protocol, we can proceed as follows.

(1) First we find *any* solution of the described linear system arising from (4) that defines a non-singular matrix ℓ. We know that such a solution exists, since

$\ell = h^{-1}$ and $r = hg$ solve the system. Let us check that randomly chosen solutions of the linear system will lead to a non-singular matrix ℓ with high probability.

In Section 4 we showed that there exists an embedding φ of $M_3(\mathbb{F}_7[A_5])$ into $M_{180}(\mathbb{F}_7)$. By Proposition 3, the matrix ℓ is invertible if and only if $\varphi(\ell)$ is invertible, and this is equivalent to $\det(\varphi(\ell)) \neq 0$. The determinant $\det(\varphi(\ell))$ is a polynomial in the unknowns $l_i^{(j,k)}, r_i^{(j,k)}$ with coefficients from the field $\mathbb{F}_7$. By the Schwartz–Zippel Lemma (see [9,6]), the probability to randomly select a singular solution is at most $1/7$. Hence a sequence of, say 100, trials will produce a non-singular solution of System (4) with very high probability.

(2) After having found ℓ, the determination of l requires merely the solution of another (smaller) linear system corresponding to $l \cdot \ell = I$. Since ℓ is invertible, there is a unique solution for l.

(3) Finally, the computation of the product $l \cdot b \cdot r = K$ reveals the private key.

References

1. Habeeb, M., Kahrobaei, D., Koupparis, C., Shpilrain, V.: Public key exchange using semidirect product of (semi)groups. In: Jacobson, M., Locasto, M., Mohassel, P., Safavi-Naini, R. (eds.) ACNS 2013. LNCS, vol. 7954, pp. 475–486. Springer, Heidelberg (2013)

2. Kahrobaei, D., Koupparis, C., Shpilrain, V.: A CCA secure cryptosystem using matrices over group rings, http://www.sci.ccny.cuny.edu/~shpil/res.html (preprint)

3. Kahrobaei, D., Koupparis, C., Shpilrain, V.: Public key exchange using matrices over group rings. Groups, Complexity, Cryptology 5, 97–115 (2013)

4. Miasnikov, A.G., Shpilrain, V., Ushakov, A.: Non-Commutative Cryptography and Complexity of Group-Theoretic Problems. Mathematical Surveys and Monographs. AMS (2011)

5. Myasnikov, A.D., Ushakov, A.: Quantum algorithm for discrete logarithm problem for matrices over finite group rings, http://eprint.iacr.org/2012/574 (preprint)

6. Schwartz, J.: Fast probabilistic algorithms for verification of polynomial identities. JACM 27, 701–717 (1980)

7. Shpilrain, V.: Cryptanalysis of Stickel's key exchange scheme. In: Hirsch, E.A., Razborov, A.A., Semenov, A., Slissenko, A. (eds.) CSR 2008. LNCS, vol. 5010, pp. 283–288. Springer, Heidelberg (2008)

8. Stickel, E.: A new method for exchanging secret keys. In: Proceedings of the Third International Conference on Information Technology and Applications (ICITA 2005). Contemporary Mathematics, vol. 2, pp. 426–430. IEEE Computer Society (2005)

9. Zippel, R.: Probabilistic algorithms for sparse polynomials. In: Ng, E.W. (ed.) Symbolic and Algebraic Computation. LNCS, vol. 72, pp. 216–226. Springer, Heidelberg (1979)

Improved Constructions of PRFs Secure Against Related-Key Attacks

Kevin Lewi, Hart Montgomery, and Ananth Raghunathan

Stanford University, Stanford, California, United States of America

Abstract. Building cryptographic primitives that are secure against related-key attacks (RKAs) is a well-studied problem by practitioners and theoreticians alike. Practical implementations of block ciphers take into account RKA security to mitigate fault injection attacks. The theoretical study of RKA security was initiated by Bellare and Kohno (Eurocrypt '03). In Crypto 2010, Bellare and Cash introduce a framework for building RKA-secure pseudorandom functions (PRFs) and use this framework to construct RKA-secure PRFs based on the decision linear and DDH assumptions.

We build RKA-secure PRFs by working with the Bellare-Cash framework and the LWE- and DLIN-based PRFs recently constructed by Boneh, Lewi, Montgomery, and Raghunathan (Crypto '13). As a result, we achieve the first RKA-secure PRFs from lattices. In addition, we note that our DLIN-based PRF (based on multilinear maps) is the first RKA-secure PRF for affine classes under the DLIN assumption, and the first RKA-secure PRF against a large class of polynomial functions under a natural generalization of the DLIN assumption. Previously, RKA security for higher-level primitives (such as signatures and IBEs) were studied in Bellare, Paterson, and Thomson (Asiacrypt '12) for affine and polynomial classes, but the question of RKA-secure PRFs for such classes remained open.

Although our RKA-secure LWE-based PRF only applies to a restricted linear class, we show that by weakening the notion of RKA security, we can handle a significantly larger class of affine functions. Finally, the results of Bellare, Cash, and Miller (Asiacrypt '11) show that all of our RKA-secure PRFs can be used as building blocks for a wide variety of public-key primitives.

Keywords: Related-key attacks, pseudorandom functions, learning with errors.

1 Introduction

The usual notions of security for cryptographic primitives do not address the possibility that an attacker could adversarially modify the internal state of hardware devices that implement the primitive. Indeed, fault injection attacks (and other types of side-channel attacks including cold-boot attacks [22], timing attacks [24, 16], and power analysis attacks [27]) have shown that our traditional security definitions are not sufficient for most practical implementations of provably secure cryptographic primitives [12, 13, 33, 6].

To deal with fault injection attacks, cryptographers have developed the notion of related-key attack (RKA) security. RKA security definitions [9] capture the following notion: in addition to allowing the adversary to make input queries on the primitive for a randomly chosen secret key, the adversary is allowed to make input queries on the

I. Boureanu, P. Owesarski, and S. Vaudenay (Eds.): ACNS 2014, LNCS 8479, pp. 44–61, 2014.

primitive for adversarially chosen "related-key deriving" functions $\phi \in \Phi$ of a randomly chosen secret key (where Φ is a function family specified in advance). This notion can be used to show that certain classes of tampering attacks are ineffective against primitives proven secure in the presence of RKAs.

In the past few years, there has been much work in constructing RKA-secure primitives [7, 8, 3, 11, 35, 10]. In addition, RKA security is also of interest to practitioners, particularly in the design of block ciphers [19, 23, 36]. In this work, we will focus our attention on building one of the most basic of the RKA primitives—pseudorandom functions (PRFs). Not only do PRFs find applications in many real-world implementations where side-channel attacks are possible (and hence RKA security becomes relevant) [6], but RKA-secure PRFs are also known to imply RKA security for a wide range of more advanced primitives, including signatures, identity-based encryption, and both public-key and private-key chosen ciphertext secure encryption [8].

1.1 Background and Related Work

Bellare and Cash [7] developed the first RKA-secure PRF for a non-trivial class of functions. Instantiations prior to [7] on RKA-secure PRFs required ideal ciphers, random oracles, or non-standard assumptions [26, 9]. In addition, Bellare and Cash develop a novel framework (which we call the BC framework) for building RKA-secure PRFs, and show how the DDH assumption implies an RKA-secure PRF for the class $\Phi_{\mathsf{lin}} = \{\phi_{\mathbf{a}} : \mathbb{Z}_q^m \to \mathbb{Z}_q^m \mid \phi_{\mathbf{a}}(\mathbf{k}) = \mathbf{k} + \mathbf{a}\}_{\mathbf{a} \in \mathbb{Z}_q^m}$, the class of all linear transformations to the key. Additionally, they construct an RKA-secure PRF under the DLIN assumption [34, 30] for an interesting multiplicative class Φ (where related keys are derived from scalar multiples of components of the key).

Bellare *et al.* [8] explore the possibilities of transferring RKA security from one primitive to another (while preserving the class Φ of related-key deriving functions). In particular, they show that RKA-secure PRFs can be used to construct a wide variety of higher-level RKA-secure primitives. Thus, improvements in building RKA-secure PRFs have wide applicability to RKA-secure public-key cryptographic primitives.

Applebaum *et al.* [3] show how to build RKA-secure symmetric encryption from a variety of hardness assumptions for linear related-key attacks. Wee [35] presents chosen ciphertext RKA-secure public-key encryption scheme constructions from the DBDH and LWE assumptions, also for linear related-key attacks. Finally, Bellare *et al.* [11] show how to build RKA-secure variants from a variety of primitives discussed in [8] for more expressive classes Φ including affine and polynomial function families. However, constructing RKA-secure PRFs for affine or polynomial Φ is notably left open. Concurrently, Bellare *et al.* [10] build RKA-secure signature schemes against related-key deriving functions drawn from such classes of polynomials. Their construction relies on RKA-secure one-way functions which appear to be easier to build under standard assumptions (as opposed to RKA-secure PRFs).

PRFs are extremely well-studied primitives and have been built from a wide variety of assumptions [29, 18, 25, 15, 5, 14]. Currently known RKA-secure PRFs only consider the Naor-Reingold [29] and Lewko-Waters [25] PRFs. We note that PRFs constructed by Boneh *et al.* [14] satisfy an additional "key homomorphism" property which we find useful in constructing RKA-secure PRFs. Our constructions are based on the PRFs considered in this work.

1.2 Our Contributions

Lattice-based RKA-secure PRFs. We present the first lattice-based PRFs secure against related-key attacks. Our construction achieves RKA security under the standard LWE assumption against the class of related-key functions $\Phi_{\mathsf{lin}*} = \{\phi_{\mathbf{a}} : \mathbb{Z}_q^m \to \mathbb{Z}_q^m \mid \phi_{\mathbf{a}}(\mathbf{k}) = \mathbf{k} + \mathbf{a}\}_{\mathbf{a} \in (\frac{q}{p})\mathbb{Z}_q^m}$ over the key space $\mathcal{K} = \mathbb{Z}_q^m$. The class $(\frac{q}{p})\mathbb{Z}_q^m$ here denotes the vectors in $\mathbb{Z}_q^m$ whose entries are all multiples of q/p (where p divides q). This linear RKA class $\Phi_{\mathsf{lin}*}$ is a restricted case of the linear class in [7, Section 6], but our construction offers two advantages: it is the first LWE-based RKA-secure PRF (as opposed to the DDH-based construction in [7]) and its proof does not require a simulator that runs in time exponential in the input length.[1] Ideally we would like to address RKA security for the entire class of linear key shifts, but we only achieve a weaker notion of security. However, these restrictions are quite plausible as they translate to an adversary that can inject faults into the higher order bits of the key.[2]

RKA Security against an Affine Class of Related Keys. Next, we show how the powerful multilinear map abstraction by Garg *et al.* [20] along with the DLIN assumption in this abstraction can be used to construct PRFs with RKA security against a very large and natural class of affine key transformations $\Phi_{\mathsf{aff}} = \{\phi_{\mathbf{C},\mathbf{B}} : \mathbb{Z}_p^{m \times \ell} \to \mathbb{Z}_p^{m \times \ell} \mid \phi_{\mathbf{C},\mathbf{B}}(\mathbf{K}) = \mathbf{CK} + \mathbf{B}\}$ over the key space $\mathcal{K} = \mathbb{Z}_p^{m \times \ell}$. For Φ_{aff}, we require that $\mathbf{C}$ comes from a family of *invertible* matrices and that Φ_{aff} be claw-free—for all $\phi_1, \phi_2 \in \Phi_{\mathsf{aff}}$ and $\mathbf{K} \in \mathcal{K}$, $\phi_1(\mathbf{K}) \neq \phi_2(\mathbf{K})$.

Both restrictions arise from a technical requirement under the BC framework. As noted in [7, 11], some restrictions must be placed on Φ_{aff} in order for PRFs to achieve RKA security against them (for example, Φ_{aff} cannot include constant functions $\phi(\mathbf{K}) = \mathbf{B}$). Hence, our class Φ_{aff} is essentially the most expressive affine class of transformations for which RKA PRF security is still attainable under the Bellare-Cash framework. In fact, there are no known PRFs which are RKA-secure against a class which does not have the claw-free restriction. Bellare *et al.* [11] constructed higher-level primitives RKA-secure against affine classes, but left open the problem of constructing such a PRF (for which we provide an answer).

Unique-input RKA Security against an Affine Class. We note, however, that the assumption that there exists an instantiation of the Garg *et al.* multilinear map abstraction [20] for which DLIN holds is a fairly strong assumption. This raises the following question: Can we achieve a similar result for RKA PRF security against affine transformations from a more standard assumption? We answer this question in the affirmative by considering a slightly weaker notion of RKA security, denoted *unique-input*

---

[1] We note that we require the LWE assumption to hold over superpolynomially-sized modulus q, but this is a well-studied and widely-used assumption [31, 5, 1, 14].

[2] We note that when q and p are powers of 2, $\Phi_{\mathsf{lin}*}$ captures all functions that perform linear shifts on the entries of the key that do not modify the $\log(q/p)$-least significant bits of each entry.

RKA security, where adversary queries are restricted to unique inputs. We build RKA-secure PRFs from the LWE assumption that can handle the class of transformations $\Phi_{\text{ln-aff}} = \{\phi_{\mathbf{C},\mathbf{B}} : \phi_{\mathbf{C},\mathbf{B}}(\mathbf{K}) = \mathbf{C}\mathbf{K} + \mathbf{B}\}$, where $\mathbf{C}$ is a full-rank "low-norm" matrix and $\mathbf{B}$ is an arbitrary matrix in $\mathbb{Z}_q^{m \times m}$ from the LWE assumption. We observe that under this weaker notion of security, our class is significantly more expressive than our first result from lattices because it allows for the addition of arbitrary vectors. However, this requires us to work outside the Bellare-Cash framework. We leave it as an open problem to construct "truly" RKA-secure PRFs from LWE (or other standard assumptions, such as DDH) for an affine class of key transformations.

Unique-input RKA Security against a Class of Polynomials. We further explore the connection between key homomorphism and unique-input RKA security by using the multilinear map abstraction to tackle a polynomial class of related-key functions. More specifically, we consider the class of polynomials $\Phi_{\text{poly}(d)}$ of bounded degree d over matrices $\mathbb{Z}_q^{m \times m}$ and consider a natural exponent assumption over multilinear maps called the Multilinear Diffie-Hellman Exponent (MDHE) assumption. For technical reasons, we require that at least one of the polynomial's non-constant coefficient matrices is full-rank. This natural restriction simply ensures that the output of the polynomial is sufficiently random given a uniformly drawn input of a special form. We note that the MDHE assumption is a natural and fairly plausible generalization of the DLIN assumption.

Finally, we can apply the results of [8] to get Φ-RKA security for signatures, identity-based encryption, and public and private key CCA encryption from our Φ-RKA-secure PRFs.

1.3 Our Techniques

At a high level, we use the Bellare-Cash framework with the (LWE- and DLIN-based) key homomorphic PRFs from Boneh *et al.* [14] to construct RKA-secure PRFs against the classes $\Phi_{\text{lin}*}$ and Φ_{aff}. Below, we give an outline of the framework and note that key homomorphic PRFs are a natural starting point due to the malleability requirement of the framework.

Bellare-Cash Framework. The only known construction of RKA-secure PRFs to date is that of Bellare and Cash [7]. In their framework, Bellare and Cash identify sufficient properties for constructing an RKA-secure PRF. They first consider PRFs $F \colon \mathcal{K} \times \mathcal{X} \to \mathcal{Y}$ that are *key malleable*—PRFs which have an efficient algorithm (denoted a transformer T) that when given an input $(\phi, x) \in \Phi \times \mathcal{X}$ and oracle access to $F(k, \cdot)$ computes $F(\phi(k), x)$. In addition, T must satisfy a *uniformity* property, namely, when $F(k, \cdot)$ is replaced with a random function $f(\cdot)$, the outputs of T on inputs $(\phi_1, x_1), \ldots, (\phi_Q, x_Q)$ for distinct $x_1, \ldots, x_Q$ are uniform and independently distributed. The framework also requires the existence of a *key fingerprint*—an input $w \in \mathcal{X}$ such that for all $k \in \mathcal{K}$ and distinct $\phi_1, \phi_2 \in \Phi$, $F(\phi_1(k), w) \neq F(\phi_2(k), w)$.

For a class Φ with a suitable key malleable PRF, a fingerprint w, and a collision-resistant hash function that satisfies a simple *compatiblity* property H_{com} (see Definition 2.8), under the Bellare-Cash framework, the authors show that the PRF $F_{\text{rka}}(k, x) = F\left(k, H_{\text{com}}(x, F(k, w))\right)$ is Φ-RKA-secure.

Applying the BC Framework to the DLIN-based PRF. Our starting point is the construction of a DLIN-based key homomorphic PRF by Boneh *et al.* [14], who note that key homomorphic PRFs are key malleable. In this work, we generalize this PRF to operate with the key space $\mathcal{K} = \mathbb{Z}_p^{m \times \ell}$ instead of $\mathbb{Z}_p^\ell$. The PRF has public parameters $\mathbf{A}_0, \mathbf{A}_1 \in \mathbb{Z}_q^{\ell \times \ell}$. On input x, the PRF is of the form $(g_\ell)^{\mathbf{W}}$ for $\mathbf{W} = \mathbf{KP}$ where $\mathbf{P} \in \mathbb{Z}_p^{\ell \times \ell}$ is the publicly computable matrix $\mathbf{A}_{x_\ell} \mathbf{A}_{x_{\ell-1}} \cdots \mathbf{A}_{x_1}$ (that only depends on the bits of x) and g_ℓ is the generator of a group with a multilinear map. This additional algebraic structure allows us to consider the class of affine related-key deriving functions of the form $\mathbf{CK} + \mathbf{B}$ for matrices $\mathbf{C} \in \mathbb{Z}_q^{m \times m}$ and $\mathbf{B} \in \mathbb{Z}_q^{m \times \ell}$. The pseudorandomness of the PRF holds by a straightforward hybrid argument, noting that the rows of $\mathbf{K}$ are now identical to independent keys of the original PRF.

Working in the exponent, given access to an oracle that computes $\mathbf{W}$ and an input $\phi_{\mathbf{C}, \mathbf{B}}$, it is easy to construct a transformer that computes $\mathbf{W}' = \mathbf{CW} + \mathbf{BP}$. From some simple algebra, one can verify that this indeed computes the exponent $\mathbf{W}'$ corresponding to $F_{\mathrm{DLIN}}(\phi(\mathbf{K}), x)$. In addition, as long as $\mathbf{C}$ is restricted to the set of full-rank matrices, it follows that the transformer described above outputs uniform matrices if $\mathbf{W}$ corresponds to the outputs of a random function. From this, the rest of the BC framework can be applied and is shown in Section 3.2. We note here that the restriction that Φ is claw-free seems to be inherently required in applying the BC framework (here, we require it in constructing a suitable fingerprint), and we do not overcome this limitation in our construction either.[3]

Applying the BC Framework to the LWE-based PRF. Recollect that Boneh *et al.* construct an "almost" key homomorphic LWE-based PRF F which on input x is of the form $\lfloor \mathbf{Pk} \rfloor_p$, where $\mathbf{P} = \mathbf{A}_{x_\ell} \mathbf{A}_{x_{\ell-1}} \cdots \mathbf{A}_{x_1}$. (Here, $\lfloor x \rfloor_p$ for $x \in \mathbb{Z}_q$ denotes multiplying x by p/q and rounding the result to $\mathbb{Z}_p$.) Unfortunately, the "almost"-ness of the key homomorphism disallows a direct argument of key malleability. Furthermore, a transformer which is "almost" key malleable (in the same sense) is still insufficient for instantiating the BC framework.

This limitation can be overcome by observing that $F(\mathbf{k}_1, x) + F(\mathbf{k}_2, x) = F(\mathbf{k}_1 + \mathbf{k}_2, x)$ if the entries of either $\mathbf{k}_1$ or $\mathbf{k}_2$ are all multiples of q/p. This property is sufficient to show that F is key malleable with respect to the class Φ_{lin^*}, where $\mathbf{k}_2$ is required to be an element of $(\frac{q}{p}) \mathbb{Z}_q^m$. Additionally, this restriction is needed show that any fixed input $w \in \{0, 1\}^\ell$ acts as a key fingerprint for F under the class Φ_{lin^*}. It seems likely that this restriction is in fact necessary for applying the BC framework, leaving this the most expressive class achievable for the LWE-based PRF F.

One natural question to ask is whether the Banerjee *et al.* [5] LWE-based PRF can be used instead of F. We note that their PRF is not key homomorphic and hence the above approach does not apply. However, we leave open the question of achieving unique-input RKA security for their PRF (see Section 6).

Unique-input Adversaries. As was observed by Bellare and Cash, key malleability is intuitively useful in constructing RKA security because it allows us to simulate $F(\phi(k), \cdot)$ without access to the key k but also leads to a simple related-key attack

---

[3] However, in [8], the authors overcome this barrier and achieve RKA security for PRGs, not PRFs, against a class Φ which is not claw-free.

against any class that contains the functions ϕ_{id} (the identity function) and any $\phi' \neq \phi_{\mathsf{id}}$. The difficulty in achieving security lies in the adversary's ability to request multiple related-key deriving functions on the same input x. Given ϕ_{id}, to attack the pseudorandomness, the adversary can run the transformer for ϕ' himself and compare the output of the transformer to the output of the oracle on (ϕ', x). Thus, Bellare and Cash require additional tools.

However, the notion of key malleability suffices to show security against unique-input adversaries, where the adversary's queries are restricted to distinct x's. In extending the RKA-secure LWE-based PRF to a class of affine functions, as discussed earlier in this section, the presence of the rounding does not directly imply key malleability. However, in Section 4, we work through the proof of security of the pseudorandomness of F, along the lines of the proof in [14], to consider its RKA security against the larger class $\Phi_{\mathsf{ln\text{-}aff}}$. We show that the structure of the PRF allows us to simulate, in addition to PRF queries on input x, RKA queries for functions $\phi \in \Phi_{\mathsf{ln\text{-}aff}}$. As in [14], the proof works through several hybrid arguments that modify a challenger from a truly random function to a pseudorandom function that also provides answers to RKA queries $(\phi, x) \in \Phi_{\mathsf{ln\text{-}aff}} \times \{0,1\}^\ell$.

The low-norm restriction on the matrix $\mathbf{C}$ in $\phi_{\mathbf{C},\mathbf{B}} \in \Phi_{\mathsf{ln\text{-}aff}}$ is required to ensure that when using LWE challenges in the hybrids, the noise does not grow larger than what the rounding allows. In the final hybrid, the adversary interacts with uniform and independently chosen outputs corresponding to inputs x_i. As long as the adversary is restricted to unique inputs, this interaction is identical to the game where the adversary receives uniform and independent (consistent) values on queries (ϕ, x). This is sufficient to show RKA security. Whether we can take advantage of the algebraic structure of other pseudorandom functions to directly prove unique-input RKA security is an interesting question.

Unique-input Security against a Class of Polynomials. We have shown how under the DLIN and LWE assumptions we can build RKA-secure PRFs for classes of affine functions, but unfortunately we do know how to extend these results to handle classes of polynomials. However, in Section 5, we show that the PRF F_{DLIN} (defined in Section 3.2) is RKA-secure against unique-input adversaries under the (new) d-MDHE assumption (see Definition 2.5) for a class of degree-d polynomials.

For integers ℓ, d, and a prime p, we consider the class $\Phi_{\mathsf{poly}(d)}$ consisting of all degree-d polynomials over $\mathbb{Z}_p^{\ell \times \ell}$ of the form $P(\mathbf{K}) = \sum_{i=0}^{d} \mathbf{C}_i \cdot \mathbf{K}^i$, where $\mathbf{C}_0, \ldots, \mathbf{C}_d, \mathbf{K} \in \mathbb{Z}_p^{\ell \times \ell}$ and at least one of $\mathbf{C}_1, \ldots, \mathbf{C}_d$ is full rank. To prove the RKA security of F_{DLIN} against unique-input adversaries, we consider a series of hybrid experiments which respond to queries $(\phi_{P(\cdot)}, x) \in \Phi_{\mathsf{poly}(d)} \times \{0,1\}^\ell$, where $P(\mathbf{S}) = \sum_{i=0}^{d} \mathbf{C}_i \cdot \mathbf{S}^i$, by choosing d uniformly random, *independent* secrets $\mathbf{K}_1, \ldots, \mathbf{K}_d$ and computing the weighted sum $\mathbf{C}_0 + \sum_{i=1}^{d} \mathbf{C}_i \cdot \mathbf{K}_i$, as opposed to choosing a single uniformly random secret $\mathbf{S}$ and computing $P(\mathbf{S})$. We show how an adversary which distinguishes between these two cases can be used to break the d-MDHE assumption, and then we use the techniques used to prove the pseudorandomness of F_{DLIN} to complete the argument.

The additional requirement of at least one of $\mathbf{C}_1, \ldots, \mathbf{C}_d$ being full rank is only needed to ensure that a sufficient amount of entropy from the secret key will remain in the output of the PRF. Note that this restriction on $\Phi_{\mathsf{poly}(d)}$ rules out polynomials P for which the output of P on randomly chosen key can be predicted (as an example consider *constant* polynomials $P(\mathbf{K}) = \mathbf{C}$ for some fixed $\mathbf{C} \in \mathbb{Z}_p^{\ell \times \ell}$), for which achieving RKA security is impossible. We believe $\Phi_{\mathsf{poly}(d)}$ captures what is essentially the most expressive class of bounded-degree polynomials for RKA-secure PRFs.

Organization. In Section 2 we introduce preliminary notation and definitions. In Section 3 we construct RKA-secure LWE- and DLIN-based PRFs using the BC framework. Then, in Section 4, we give an LWE-based RKA-secure PRF against unique-input adversaries for an affine class of transformations. In Section 5, we show how the DLIN-based PRF is secure against unique-input adversaries where the related-key attacks come from a class of bounded-degree polynomials. We conclude in Section 6. In the full version, we give additional preliminaries, missing proofs, and more details.

2 Preliminaries

2.1 Notation

Rounding. We define $\lfloor \cdot \rfloor$ to round a real number to the largest integer which does not exceed it. For integers q and p where $q \geq p \geq 2$, we define the function $\lfloor \cdot \rceil_p : \mathbb{Z}_q \to \mathbb{Z}_p$ as $\lfloor x \rceil_p = i$ where $i \cdot \lfloor q/p \rfloor$ is the largest multiple of $\lfloor q/p \rfloor$ which does not exceed x. For a vector $\mathbf{v} \in \mathbb{Z}_q^m$, we define $\lfloor \mathbf{v} \rceil_p$ as the vector in $\mathbb{Z}_p^m$ obtained by rounding each coordinate of the vector individually.

When $p \mid q$, we let $(\frac{q}{p})\mathbb{Z}_q$ denote the subgroup of $\mathbb{Z}_q$ comprising the set $\{(q/p) \cdot x \mid x \in \mathbb{Z}_q\}$. The following lemma follows from some elementary arithmetic.

Lemma 2.1. *For any $u \in (\frac{q}{p})\mathbb{Z}_q$ and $x \in \mathbb{Z}_q$ such that $u \equiv x(q/p) \mod q$ and any $y \in \mathbb{Z}_q$,*

$$\lfloor y + u \rceil_p = \lfloor y \rceil_p + \lfloor u \rceil_p = \lfloor y \rceil_p + x \pmod{p}.$$

Groups. For a matrix $\mathbf{M}$, we let the component-wise exponentiation $g^{\mathbf{M}}$ denote a matrix with entries $g^{\mathbf{M}_{i,j}}$. We let $(g^{\mathbf{A}})^{\mathbf{B}}$ denote the matrix with entries $g^{(\mathbf{AB})_{i,j}}$. We let $\mathbf{Rk}_i(\mathbb{Z}_p^{a \times b})$ denote the set of all $a \times b$ matrices over $\mathbb{Z}_p$ of rank i.

Pseudorandom Functions. Informally, a PRF [21] is an efficiently computable function $F : \mathcal{K} \times \mathcal{X} \to \mathcal{Y}$ such that no efficient adversary can distinguish the function from a truly random function given only black-box access. In this paper, we allow the PRF to additionally take public parameters pp. The advantage $\mathbf{Adv}_F^{\mathsf{prf}}(\cdot)$ against the PRF is defined in a standard manner and deferred to the full version due to space constraints.

2.2 RKA-secure PRFs

For a class of related-key deriving functions $\Phi = \{\phi : \mathcal{K} \to \mathcal{K}\}$, the notion of Φ-RKA security for a PRF $F : \mathcal{K} \times \mathcal{X} \to \mathcal{Y}$ is defined using an experiments between a challenger and an adversary $\mathcal{A}$. For $b \in \{0, 1\}$ define the following experiment $\mathsf{Expt}_b^{\mathsf{prf\text{-}rka}}$:

1. Given security parameter λ, the challenger samples and publishes public parameters pp to the adversary. Next, the challenger chooses a random key $k \in \mathcal{K}$ and if $b = 0$, sets $f(\cdot) \stackrel{\text{def}}{=} F(k, \cdot)$. Otherwise, if $b = 1$, the challenger chooses a random keyed function $f : \mathcal{K} \times \mathcal{X} \to \mathcal{Y}$.
2. The adversary (adaptively) sends input queries $(\phi_1, x_1), \ldots, (\phi_Q, x_Q)$ in $\Phi \times \mathcal{X}$ and receives back $f(\phi_1(k), x_1), \ldots, f(\phi_Q(k), x_Q)$.
3. The adversary outputs a bit $b' \in \{0, 1\}$, and the experiment also outputs b'.

Definition 2.2 (RKA-secure PRF for Φ). *A PRF $F : \mathcal{K} \times \mathcal{X} \to \mathcal{Y}$ is RKA-secure with respect to class Φ if for all efficient adversaries $\mathcal{A}$ the quantity*

$$\mathbf{Adv}_{\Phi, F}^{\text{prf-rka}}(\mathcal{A}) \stackrel{\text{def}}{=} \left| \Pr\left[\text{Expt}_0^{\text{prf-rka}} = 1 \right] - \Pr\left[\text{Expt}_1^{\text{prf-rka}} = 1 \right] \right|$$

is negligible.

Unique-input RKA Security (cf. [7]). We say that an adversary is *unique-input* in the above security game if the input queries $(\phi_1, x_1), \ldots, (\phi_Q, x_Q) \in \Phi \times \mathcal{X}$ are such that $x_1, \ldots, x_Q$ are distinct. A PRF is *unique-input* RKA-secure if it is RKA secure against unique-input adversaries.

2.3 Security Assumptions

Learning with Errors (LWE) Assumption. The LWE problem was introduced by Regev [32] who showed that solving the LWE problem on average is as hard as (quantumly) solving several standard lattice problems in the worst case.

Definition 2.3 (Learning With Errors). *For integers $q > 2$ and a noise distribution χ over $\mathbb{Z}_q$, the learning with errors problem (LWE) over n-dimensional vectors is to distinguish between the distributions $\{\mathbf{A}, \mathbf{A}^{\mathsf{T}} \mathbf{s} + \chi\}$ and $\{\mathbf{A}, \mathbf{u}\}$, where $m = \text{poly}(n)$, $\mathbf{A} \leftarrow \mathbb{Z}_q^{n \times m}, \mathbf{s} \leftarrow \mathbb{Z}_q^n, \chi \leftarrow \chi^m$, and $\mathbf{u} \leftarrow \mathbb{Z}_q^m$.*

Regev [32] shows that for a certain noise distribution $\chi = \overline{\Psi}_{\alpha}$,[4] for n polynomial in λ and $q > 2\sqrt{n}/\alpha$, the LWE problem is as hard as the worst-case SIVP and GapSVP under a quantum reduction (see also [31, 17] for classical reductions). These results have been extended to show that $\mathbf{s}$ can be sampled from a low-norm distribution (in particular, from the noise distribution χ) and the resulting problem is as hard as the basic LWE problem [2]. Similarly, the noise distribution χ can be a simple low-norm distribution [28]. Boneh *et al.* [14] show that the variant of LWE where the entries of $\mathbf{A}$ are binary and $m > n \log q$ is equivalent (modulo a $\log q$-factor loss in dimension) to LWE over n-dimensional vectors. In this work, we let $B \in \mathbb{R}$ be an error bound such that for $\chi \leftarrow \overline{\Psi}_{\alpha}$, $|\chi| \le B$ with overwhelming probability.

---

[4] For an $\alpha \in (0, 1)$ and a prime q, let $\overline{\Psi}_{\alpha}$ denote the distribution over $\mathbb{Z}_q$ of the random variable $\lceil qX \rfloor \pmod{q}$ where X is a normal random variable with mean 0 and standard deviation $\alpha/\sqrt{2\pi}$.

Low-norm Matrix LWE. We work with the right-multiplied matrix form of (low-norm) LWE, namely, that for a uniformly drawn $\mathbf{A} \leftarrow \{0,1\}^{m \times 2m}$, $\mathbf{U} \leftarrow \mathbb{Z}_q^{m \times 2m}$, $\mathbf{S} \leftarrow \mathbb{Z}_q^{m \times m}$, and $\mathbf{X} \leftarrow \chi^{m \times 2m}$, the problem is to distinguish between the distributions $\{\mathbf{A}, \mathbf{SA} + \mathbf{X}\}$ and $\{\mathbf{A}, \mathbf{U}\}$.

To compare it to the low-norm LWE variant in [14], we note that $\{\mathbf{A}, \mathbf{SA} + \mathbf{X}\}$ and $\{\mathbf{A}, \mathbf{A}^\mathsf{T}\mathbf{S} + \mathbf{X}^\mathsf{T}\}$ are distributed identically, and a standard hybrid argument shows that any adversary which can distinguish $\{\mathbf{A}, \mathbf{A}^\mathsf{T}\mathbf{S} + \mathbf{X}^\mathsf{T}\}$ from $\{\mathbf{A}, \mathbf{U}\}$ can be used to distinguish $\{\mathbf{A}, \mathbf{A}^\mathsf{T}\mathbf{s} + \chi\}$ from $\{\mathbf{A}, \mathbf{u}\}$ with only a $(1/m)$-factor loss in advantage.

The DLIN Assumption in Multilinear Groups. In Section 3.2, we rely on the decisional linear (DLIN) assumption (as stated in Boneh *et al.* [14]) for the Garg *et al.* abstraction of graded multilinear maps [20]. Consider a sequence of groups $\vec{\mathbb{G}} = (\mathbb{G}_1, \ldots, \mathbb{G}_\ell)$ with a set of bilinear maps $\hat{e}_i$ for $i \in [1, \ell - 1]$, and a generator g of $\mathbb{G}_1$.

Definition 2.4 (Decisional Linear). *The κ-decisional linear (κ-DLIN) assumption in the presence of a graded ℓ-linear map states that for any integers $a, b \geq \kappa$, and for any $\ell \leq j < \kappa$ the distributions*

$$\left\{g, g^\mathbf{X}\right\}_{\mathbf{X} \leftarrow \mathbf{Rk}_j\left(\mathbb{Z}_p^{a \times b}\right)} \quad and \quad \left\{g, g^\mathbf{Y}\right\}_{\mathbf{Y} \leftarrow \mathbf{Rk}_\kappa\left(\mathbb{Z}_p^{a \times b}\right)}$$

are computationally indistinguishable, in the presence of $\vec{\mathbb{G}}$ and $\{\hat{e}_i\}_{i \in [1, \ell-1]}$.

The Multilinear Diffie-Hellman Exponent Assumption. In Section 5, we will use the Multilinear Diffie-Hellman Exponent (MDHE) assumption, defined as follows. Consider a sequence of groups $\vec{\mathbb{G}} = (\mathbb{G}_1, \ldots, \mathbb{G}_\ell)$ with a set of bilinear maps $\hat{e}_i$ for $i \in [1, \ell - 1]$, and a generator g of $\mathbb{G}_1$.

Definition 2.5 (Multilinear Diffie-Hellman Exponent). *The d-Multilinear Diffie-Hellman Exponent (d-MDHE) assumption in the presence of a graded ℓ-linear map (as abstracted by [20]) states that, in the presence of $\vec{\mathbb{G}}$ and $\{\hat{e}_i\}_{i \in [1, \ell-1]}$, for any integer $j \geq \ell$, the distribution*

$$\left\{g^\mathbf{A}, \left\langle g^{\mathbf{S}^i \cdot \mathbf{A}}\right\rangle_{i \in [d]}, g^\mathbf{B}, \left\langle g^{\mathbf{S}^i \cdot \mathbf{B}}\right\rangle_{i \in [d]}\right\}_{\mathbf{A}, \mathbf{B} \leftarrow \mathbf{Rk}_j\left(\mathbb{Z}_p^{j \times j}\right), \mathbf{S} \leftarrow \mathbb{Z}_p^{j \times j}}$$

is computationally indistinguishable from the distribution

$$\left\{g^\mathbf{A}, \left\langle g^{\mathbf{U}_i}\right\rangle_{i \in [d]}, g^\mathbf{B}, \left\langle g^{\mathbf{V}_i}\right\rangle_{i \in [d]}\right\}_{\mathbf{A}, \mathbf{B} \leftarrow \mathbf{Rk}_j\left(\mathbb{Z}_p^{j \times j}\right), \forall i \in [d], \mathbf{U}_i, \mathbf{V}_i \leftarrow \mathbb{Z}_p^{j \times j}}.$$

We note that the 1-MDHE assumption is essentially equivalent to the 2ℓ-DLIN assumption (where $j = \ell$ and $\kappa = 2\ell$ as in [14]), and hence the d-MDHE assumption can be seen as a generalization of DLIN assumption to the dth exponent of the secret.

2.4 The Bellare-Cash Framework

Bellare and Cash [7] give a general framework (denoted the BC framework) for constructing RKA-secure PRFs for a class Φ using a key malleable PRF, a key fingerprint, and a collision-resistant hash function. We review their definitions and main theorem here.

Definition 2.6 (Key Malleable PRF). *A PRF $F : \mathcal{K} \times \mathcal{X} \to \mathcal{Y}$ is* key malleable *if there exists an efficient algorithm* T, *which on input $\phi \in \Phi$ and $x \in \mathcal{X}$ and with oracle access to $F(k, \cdot)$, which satisfies $\mathsf{T}^{F(k,\cdot)}(\phi, x) = F(\phi(k), x)$, for all $k \in \mathcal{K}$. Also, we require that for any distinct $x_1, \ldots, x_Q \in \mathcal{X}$, if $f : \mathcal{X} \to \mathcal{Y}$ is a truly random function, then $\mathsf{T}^{f(\cdot)}(\phi, x_1), \ldots, \mathsf{T}^{f(\cdot)}(\phi, x_Q)$ are distributed independently and uniformly in $\mathcal{Y}$.*

Definition 2.7 (Key Fingerprint). *An element $w \in \mathcal{X}$ is a* key fingerprint *if for all $k \in \mathcal{K}$ and distinct $\phi_1, \phi_2 \in \Phi$, $F(\phi_1(k), w) \neq F(\phi_2(k), w)$.*

Definition 2.8 (Compatible Hash Function). *For a fingerprint w, a hash function $H_{\mathsf{com}} : \mathcal{X} \times \mathcal{Y} \to \mathcal{R}$ is* compatible *if the set of oracle queries made by $\mathsf{T}^{F(k,\cdot)}(\phi, w)$ over all $\phi \in \Phi$ is disjoint from the set of oracle queries made by $\mathsf{T}^{F(k,\cdot)}(\phi, z)$ over all $z \in \mathcal{R}$ and $\phi \in \Phi$.*

Theorem 2.9 (c.f. [7, Theorem 3.1], paraphrased). *For a fixed class Φ of related-key deriving functions, let $F : \mathcal{K} \times \mathcal{X} \to \mathcal{Y}$ be a key malleable PRF for Φ, $w \in \mathcal{X}$ a key fingerprint for F and Φ, and $H_{\mathsf{com}} : \mathcal{X} \times \mathcal{Y} \to \mathcal{X}$ a compatible hash function. Define $F_{\mathsf{rka}} : \mathcal{K} \times \mathcal{X} \to \mathcal{Y}$ as*

$$F_{\mathsf{rka}}(k, x) = F(k, H_{\mathsf{com}}(x, F(k, w))).$$

For any probabilistic polynomial-time (PPT) adversary $\mathcal{A}$ against the RKA PRF F_{rka} for the class Φ, there exist PPT adversaries $\mathcal{B}$ against the PRF security of F_{LWE} and $\mathcal{C}$ against the collision-resistance of the hash function H_{com} such that

$$\mathbf{Adv}_{\Phi, F_{\mathsf{rka}}}^{\mathsf{prf\text{-}rka}}(\mathcal{A}) \leq \mathbf{Adv}_F^{\mathsf{prf}}(\mathcal{B}) + \mathbf{Adv}_{H_{\mathsf{com}}}^{\mathsf{cr}}(\mathcal{C}).$$

3   New RKA-secure PRFs Using the BC Framework

In this section, we use the BC framework [7] to construct new RKA-secure PRFs. We introduce two classes of related-key functions, a linear (Φ_{lin^*}) and an affine (Φ_{aff}) class, and show that the key homomorphic PRFs from Boneh *et al.* [14] can be used to instantiate the BC framework. The main technical challenge requires using the key homomorphism property to construct appropriate *transformers* required in the BC framework.

3.1   RKA-secure PRFs for a Restricted Linear Class Φ_{lin^*}

Boneh, Lewi, Montgomery, and Raghunathan [14] constructed the following PRF that is *almost* key homomorphic and showed its pseudorandomness under the LWE assumption.

The PRF F_{LWE}. For parameters m, p, and $q \in \mathbb{N}$ such that $p \mid q$, the public parameters of the PRF are binary matrices $\mathbf{A}_0, \mathbf{A}_1 \in \mathbb{Z}_p^{m \times m}$. The PRF key is a vector $\mathbf{k} \in \mathbb{Z}_q^m$. The PRF $F_{\mathrm{LWE}} : \mathbb{Z}_q^m \to \mathbb{Z}_p^m$ is defined as follows:

$$F_{\mathrm{LWE}}(\mathbf{k}, x) = \left\lfloor \prod_{i=1}^{\ell} \mathbf{A}_{x_i} \cdot \mathbf{k} \right\rfloor_p. \tag{3.1}$$

Theorem 3.1 (cf. [14], paraphrased). *The function F_{LWE} is pseudorandom under the LWE assumption for suitable choices of the parameters.*

The Class $\Phi_{\mathsf{lin}*}$. Recall the definition of $(\frac{q}{p})\mathbb{Z}_q$. We consider a class of linear RKA functions defined as follows:

$$\Phi_{\mathsf{lin}*} = \{\phi_{\mathbf{a}} : \mathbb{Z}_q^m \to \mathbb{Z}_q^m \mid \phi_{\mathbf{a}}(\mathbf{k}) = \mathbf{k} + \mathbf{a}\}_{\mathbf{a} \in (\frac{q}{p})\mathbb{Z}_q^m}. \qquad (3.2)$$

In other words, $\Phi_{\mathsf{lin}*}$ is identical to the class $\Phi_{\mathsf{lin}} = \{\phi_{\mathbf{a}} : \mathbb{Z}_q^m \to \mathbb{Z}_q^m \mid \phi_{\mathbf{a}}(\mathbf{k}) = \mathbf{k} + \mathbf{a}\}_{\mathbf{a} \in \mathbb{Z}_q^m}$ of all possible linear transformations of the key (the class for which an RKA-secure PRF is given in [7] under the DDH assumption), except that in $\Phi_{\mathsf{lin}*}$ we have the added restriction that the transformation must be an element of $(\frac{q}{p})\mathbb{Z}_q^m$.

We use the homomorphic property of the PRF to construct a transformer, that we denote $\mathsf{T}_{\mathsf{lin}}^{f(\cdot)}$, in a straightforward manner: $\mathsf{T}_{\mathsf{lin}}^{f(\cdot)}(\phi_{\mathbf{a}}, x) := f(x) + F_{\mathrm{LWE}}(\mathbf{a}, x)$. To use the BC framework, it is necessary to show that for the class of RKA functions $\Phi_{\mathsf{lin}*}$, the PRF and the transformer satisfy the malleability and uniformity properties.

Lemma 3.2 (Malleability). *For all $\mathbf{k} \in \mathbb{Z}_q^m$, $\phi \in \Phi_{\mathsf{lin}*}$, and $x \in \{0,1\}^\ell$, it holds that*

$$\mathsf{T}_{\mathsf{lin}}^{F_{\mathrm{LWE}}(\mathbf{k}, \cdot)}(\phi, x) = F_{\mathrm{LWE}}(\phi(\mathbf{k}), x). \qquad (3.3)$$

Proof. Fix a key $\mathbf{k} \in \mathbb{Z}_q^m$ and $x \in \{0,1\}^\ell$. Let $\phi_{\mathbf{a}}$ denote a function in $\Phi_{\mathsf{lin}*}$ corresponding to $\mathbf{a} \in (\frac{q}{p})\mathbb{Z}_q^m$. Define the product of matrices $\mathbf{P} = \prod_{i=1}^{\ell} \mathbf{A}_{x_i}$. From the definition of the transformer $\mathsf{T}_{\mathsf{lin}}^{F_{\mathrm{LWE}}(\mathbf{k}, \cdot)}$ the left side of equation (3.3) equals $\lfloor \mathbf{Pk} \rfloor_p + \lfloor \mathbf{Pa} \rfloor_p$. The right side of the equation is $\lfloor \mathbf{P(k+a)} \rfloor_p = \lfloor \mathbf{Pk} + \mathbf{Pa} \rfloor_p$. As $\mathbf{a} \in (\frac{q}{p})\mathbb{Z}_q^m$, it holds that $\mathbf{Pa} \in (\frac{q}{p})\mathbb{Z}_q^m$. Applying Lemma 2.1 on each coordinate, it holds that $\lfloor \mathbf{Pk} + \mathbf{Pa} \rfloor_p = \lfloor \mathbf{Pk} \rfloor_p + \lfloor \mathbf{Pa} \rfloor_p$, as required. ∎

The following lemma follows straightforwardly from the definition of $\mathsf{T}_{\mathsf{lin}}^{f(\cdot)}$.

Lemma 3.3 (Uniformity). *If $f : \{0,1\}^\ell \to \mathbb{Z}_p^m$ is a random function and $x_1, \ldots, x_Q \in \{0,1\}^\ell$ are distinct, for any functions $\phi_1, \ldots, \phi_Q \in \Phi_{\mathsf{lin}*}$, the values $\mathsf{T}_{\mathsf{lin}}^{f(\cdot)}(\phi_i, x_i)$ are independently and uniformly distributed in $\mathbb{Z}_p^m$.*

Next, we show that any $w \in \{0,1\}^\ell$ is a key fingerprint for $\Phi_{\mathsf{lin}*}$.

Lemma 3.4 (Fingerprint). *For any $w \in \{0,1\}^\ell$, $\mathbf{k} \in \mathbb{Z}_q^m$, for any distinct $\phi_1, \phi_2 \in \Phi_{\mathsf{lin}*}$, it holds that $F_{\mathrm{LWE}}(\phi_1(\mathbf{k}), w) \neq F_{\mathrm{LWE}}(\phi_2(\mathbf{k}), w)$.*

Proof. For $i \in \{1, 2\}$, let $\phi_i = \phi_{\mathbf{a}_i}$ for vectors $\mathbf{a}_i \in (\frac{q}{p})\mathbb{Z}_q^m$. Let $\mathbf{P} = \prod_{i=1}^{\ell} \mathbf{A}_{w_i}$, the product of full-rank matrices. As ϕ_1 and ϕ_2 are *distinct* and $\mathbf{P}$ is full-rank over $\mathbb{Z}_q$, it holds that $\mathbf{P}(\mathbf{a}_1 - \mathbf{a}_2) = \mathbf{u}$ for some *non-zero* $\mathbf{u}$. Moreover, as $\mathbf{a}_1$ and $\mathbf{a}_2$ are in $(\frac{q}{p})\mathbb{Z}_q^m$, the difference $(\mathbf{a}_1 - \mathbf{a}_2)$ and therefore $\mathbf{u}$ are in $(\frac{q}{p})\mathbb{Z}_q^m$. Now, note that $F_{\mathrm{LWE}}(\phi_1(\mathbf{k}), w) = \lfloor \mathbf{P} \cdot \mathbf{k} + \mathbf{P} \cdot \mathbf{a}_1 \rfloor_p = \lfloor \mathbf{P} \cdot \mathbf{k} + \mathbf{P} \cdot \mathbf{a}_2 + \mathbf{u} \rfloor_p$. Applying Lemma 2.1, this in turn equals $\lfloor \mathbf{P} \cdot \mathbf{k} + \mathbf{P} \cdot \mathbf{a}_2 \rfloor_p + \lfloor \mathbf{u} \rfloor_p = F_{\mathrm{LWE}}(\phi_2(\mathbf{k}), w) + \lfloor \mathbf{u} \rfloor_p$. As $\mathbf{u} \in (\frac{q}{p})\mathbb{Z}_q^m$ and is non-zero, $\lfloor \mathbf{u} \rfloor_p$ is also non-zero in $\mathbb{Z}_p^m$ concluding the proof of the lemma. ∎

Consider a collision-resistant hash function $H\colon \{0,1\}^\ell \times \mathbb{Z}_q^m \to \{0,1\}^{\ell-1}$ and the fingerprint $w = 0^\ell$. We define $H_{\mathrm{com}}^{(\Phi_{\mathrm{lin}^*})}\colon \{0,1\}^\ell \times \mathbb{Z}_q^m \to \{0,1\}^\ell$ as $H_{\mathrm{com}}^{(\Phi_{\mathrm{lin}^*})}(x,y) = 1\|H(x,y)$ and note that it is a compatible hash function. Applying Lemmas 3.2–3.4 and Theorem 3.1 to the BC framework, Theorem 2.9 implies the following result.

Theorem 3.5. *Under the LWE assumption and the collision-resistance of the hash function H, the function $F_{\mathrm{rka\text{-}lin}}\colon \mathbb{Z}_q^m \times \{0,1\}^\ell \to \mathbb{Z}_p^m$ defined as:*

$$F_{\mathrm{rka\text{-}lin}}(\mathbf{k},x) = F_{\mathrm{LWE}}\left(\mathbf{k}, H_{\mathrm{com}}^{(\Phi_{\mathrm{lin}^*})}\left(x, F_{\mathrm{LWE}}\left(\mathbf{k},0^\ell\right)\right)\right)$$

is an RKA-secure PRF with respect to Φ_{lin^*}.

3.2 RKA-secure PRFs for an Affine Class Φ_{aff}

In addition to the LWE-based almost key homomorphic PRF, Boneh *et al.* [14] also constructed a "fully" homomorphic PRF under the DLIN assumption over groups equipped with a multilinear map.

The PRF F_{DLIN}. For parameters m and $\ell \in \mathbb{N}$, let $\vec{\mathbb{G}} = (\mathbb{G}_1, \ldots, \mathbb{G}_\ell)$ be a sequence of groups equipped with a graded ℓ-multilinear map $\{\hat{e}_i\}_{i\in[\ell-1]}$. The public parameters comprise $pp = (g^{\mathbf{A}_0}, g^{\mathbf{A}_1})$, where $\mathbf{A}_0, \mathbf{A}_1 \leftarrow \mathbf{Rk}_\ell(\mathbb{Z}_p^{\ell \times \ell})$. The PRF key $\mathbf{K}$ is a matrix in $\mathbb{Z}_p^{m \times \ell}$. Define $F_{\mathrm{DLIN}}\colon \mathbb{Z}_p^{m \times \ell} \times \{0,1\}^\ell \to (\mathbb{G}_\ell)^{m \times \ell}$ as follows:

$$F_{\mathrm{DLIN}}(\mathbf{K},x) = (g_\ell)^{\mathbf{W}}, \text{ where } \mathbf{W} = \mathbf{K} \cdot \left(\prod_{i=1}^\ell \mathbf{A}_{x_i}\right). \tag{3.4}$$

Theorem 3.6 (cf. [14], paraphrased). *The function F_{DLIN} is pseudorandom under the DLIN assumption for suitable choices of parameters.*

As noted by Boneh *et al.*, the PRF can be evaluated at a point $x = x_1 \ldots x_\ell \in \{0,1\}^\ell$ given the the public parameters pp and secret key $\mathbf{k} \in \mathbb{Z}_p^\ell$ using the graded bilinear maps $\hat{e}_i : \mathbb{G}_1 \times \mathbb{G}_i \to \mathbb{G}_{i+1}$. The matrix multiplication is carried out one step at a time by nesting these bilinear maps as follows:

$$F_{\mathrm{DLIN}}(\mathbf{K},x) = \hat{e}_{\ell-1}\left(g^{\mathbf{KA}_{x_1}}, \hat{e}_{\ell-2}\left(g^{\mathbf{A}_{x_2}}, \ldots \hat{e}_2\left(g^{\mathbf{A}_{x_{\ell-2}}}, \hat{e}_1\left(g^{\mathbf{A}_{x_{\ell-1}}}, g^{\mathbf{A}_{x_\ell}}\right)\right)\right)\right),$$

where $g^{\mathbf{KA}_{x_1}}$ is computed "in the exponent" given $\mathbf{K}$ and $g^{\mathbf{A}_{x_1}}$. A pairing $\hat{e}\left(g^{\mathbf{A}_0}, g^{\mathbf{A}_1}\right)$ of matrices given in the exponent is done by computing the component-wise dot products of rows of $\mathbf{A}_0$ with columns of $\mathbf{A}_1$ using the bilinear map $\hat{e}$.

Observe that this PRF is identical to the DLIN-based PRF in [14] except that the key $\mathbf{K}$ is now a matrix. This is required to define a meaningful affine class over the key space. The pseudorandomness extends to the case where $\mathbf{K}$ is a matrix by considering the rows of $\mathbf{K}$, $\mathbf{k}_1^\mathsf{T}, \ldots, \mathbf{k}_m^\mathsf{T}$ to be m independent keys of the original DLIN-based PRF. The key homomorphism also extends in a straightforward manner.

The Affine Class Φ_{aff}. With the above DLIN-based PRF, we can consider the following affine class of related-key deriving functions. We define

$$\Phi_{\mathrm{aff}} = \{\phi_{\mathbf{C},\mathbf{B}} : \mathbb{Z}_p^{m \times \ell} \to \mathbb{Z}_p^{m \times \ell} \mid \phi_{\mathbf{C},\mathbf{B}}(\mathbf{K}) = \mathbf{CK} + \mathbf{B}\}, \tag{3.5}$$

for matrices $\mathbf{C} \in \mathbb{Z}_p^{m \times m}$ and $\mathbf{B} \in \mathbb{Z}_p^{m \times \ell}$ constrained as follows: (a) the class Φ_{aff} is *claw-free*, and (b) $\mathbf{C}$ is a *full-rank* matrix.

As in Section 3.1, the key homomorphism of F_{DLIN} allows us to construct a transformer, denoted $\mathsf{T}_{\text{aff}}^{f(\cdot)}$, in the following manner: $\mathsf{T}_{\text{aff}}^{f(\cdot)}(\phi_{\mathbf{C},\mathbf{B}}, x)$ sets $f(x) = (g_\ell)^{\mathbf{F}}$ and computes $(g_\ell)^{\mathbf{CF}} \cdot F_{\text{DLIN}}(\mathbf{B}, x)$. In other words, we left-multiply (in the exponent) the output of $f(\cdot)$ with entries from $\mathbf{C}$ and then use the homomorphism of F_{DLIN} to incorporate $\mathbf{B}$. We use the BC framework and show that for the class of related-key functions Φ_{aff}, the PRF and the transformer satisfy the malleability and uniformity properties.

Lemma 3.7 (Malleability). *For all* $\mathbf{K} \in \mathbb{Z}_p^{m \times \ell}$, $\phi \in \Phi_{\text{aff}}$, *and* $x \in \{0,1\}^\ell$, *it holds that*

$$\mathsf{T}_{\text{aff}}^{f(\cdot)}(\phi, x) = F_{\text{DLIN}}(\phi(\mathbf{k}), x). \tag{3.6}$$

Proof. The proof follows from elementary algebra in the exponent. Let $\phi = \phi_{\mathbf{C},\mathbf{B}}$ for arbitrary $\mathbf{C}$ and $\mathbf{B}$. For a key $\mathbf{K}$ and input x, let $\mathbf{W}$ be the matrix in equation (3.4). By definition, $\mathsf{T}_{\text{aff}}^{f(\cdot)}(\phi, x) = (g_\ell)^{\mathbf{C} \cdot \mathbf{W}} \cdot F_{\text{DLIN}}(\mathbf{B}, x) = F_{\text{DLIN}}(\mathbf{CK} + \mathbf{B}, x)$ as required. The last equality follows from the key homomorphism of F_{DLIN}. ∎

The following lemma follows straightforwardly from the definition of $\mathsf{T}_{\text{aff}}^{f(\cdot)}$.

Lemma 3.8 (Uniformity). *If* $f : \{0,1\}^\ell \to (\mathbb{G}_\ell)^{m \times \ell}$ *is a random function and* $x_1, \ldots,$ $x_Q \in \{0,1\}^\ell$ *are distinct, for any functions* $\phi_1, \ldots, \phi_Q \in \Phi_{\text{aff}}$, *the values* $\mathsf{T}_{\text{aff}}^{f(\cdot)}(\phi_i, x_i)$ *are independently and uniformly distributed in* $(\mathbb{G}_\ell)^{m \times \ell}$.

Next, we show that any $w \in \{0,1\}^\ell$ is a key fingerprint for Φ_{lin^*}.

Lemma 3.9 (Fingerprint). *For any* $w \in \{0,1\}^\ell$, *for any* $\mathbf{K} \in \mathbb{Z}_q^{m \times \ell}$, *and for any two distinct* $\phi_1, \phi_2 \in \Phi_{\text{aff}}$, *it holds that* $F_{\text{DLIN}}(\phi_1(\mathbf{K}), w) \neq F_{\text{DLIN}}(\phi_2(\mathbf{K}), w)$.

Proof. We use the fact that the family Φ_{aff} is claw-free. For any key $\mathbf{K}$, this implies that $\phi_1(\mathbf{K}) \neq \phi_2(\mathbf{K})$. For $i \in \{1, 2\}$, let $\mathbf{W}_i$ denote the matrix $\phi_i(\mathbf{K}) \cdot \left(\prod_{i=1}^\ell \mathbf{A}_{w_i} \right)$. The product of full-rank matrices $\mathbf{A}_{w_i}$ is full-rank and as $\phi_1(\mathbf{K}) \neq \phi_2(\mathbf{K})$, it follows that $\mathbf{W}_1 \neq \mathbf{W}_2$. As F_{DLIN} is defined as $(g_\ell)^{\mathbf{W}}$ for generator g_ℓ, it holds that if $\mathbf{W}_1 \neq \mathbf{W}_2$, then $(g_\ell)^{\mathbf{W}_1} \neq (g_\ell)^{\mathbf{W}_2}$ concluding the proof of the lemma. ∎

Consider a collision-resistant hash function $H: \{0,1\}^\ell \times (\mathbb{G}_\ell)^{m \times \ell} \to \{0,1\}^{\ell-1}$ and the fingerprint $w = 0^\ell$. We define $H_{\text{com}}^{(\Phi_{\text{aff}})}: \{0,1\}^\ell \times (\mathbb{G}_\ell)^{m \times \ell} \to \{0,1\}^\ell$ as $H_{\text{com}}^{(\Phi_{\text{aff}})}(x, y) = 1 \| H(x, y)$ and note that it is a compatible hash function. Applying Lemmas 3.7–3.9 and Theorem 3.6 to the BC framework, Theorem 2.9 implies the following result.

Theorem 3.10. *Under the DLIN assumption and the collision-resistance of the hash function* H, *the function* $F_{\text{rka-aff}}: \mathbb{Z}_p^{m \times \ell} \times \{0,1\}^\ell \to (\mathbb{G}_\ell)^{m \times \ell}$ *defined as:*

$$F_{\text{rka-aff}}(\mathbf{K}, x) = F_{\text{DLIN}}\left(\mathbf{K}, H_{\text{com}}^{(\Phi_{\text{aff}})}\left(x, F_{\text{DLIN}}\left(\mathbf{K}, 0^\ell \right) \right) \right)$$

is an RKA-secure PRF with respect to Φ_{aff}.

4 Unique-Input RKA-secure PRFs for an Affine Class

In this section, we construct RKA-secure PRFs from the LWE assumption for a slightly more restricted notion of RKA security, denoted unique-input RKA security. As explained in Section 1.3, we work directly with the pseudorandomness proof of F_{LWE} to show unique-input RKA security against a larger class of affine related-key functions rather than the restricted linear class $\Phi_{\text{lin}*}$ from Section 3.1. To do this, we use the algebraic structure that suits the key homomorphism of F_{LWE} to overcome the restrictions of $\Phi_{\text{lin}*}$ required in order to apply the Bellare-Cash framework. We prove unique-input RKA security for the affine class $\Phi_{\text{ln-aff}} = \{\phi_{\mathbf{C},\mathbf{B}} : \phi_{\mathbf{C},\mathbf{B}}(\mathbf{K}) = \mathbf{CK} + \mathbf{B}\}$, where $\mathbf{C}$ is a full rank matrix in $[-c, c]^{m \times m}$ for a small constant c, and $\mathbf{B}$ is an arbitrary matrix in $\mathbb{Z}_q^{m \times m}$.

We consider the PRF F_{LWE} where the key $\mathbf{k}$, originally a vector, is replaced by a matrix $\mathbf{K}$ in order to obtain the algebraic structure required for $\Phi_{\text{ln-aff}}$. Recollect the definition of F_{LWE} from Equation (3.1). For parameters $m, p, q \in \mathbb{N}$ such that $p \mid q$, the public parameters of the PRF are binary matrices $\mathbf{A}_0, \mathbf{A}_1 \in \mathbb{Z}_p^{m \times m}$. The key is now a *matrix* $\mathbf{K} \in \mathbb{Z}_q^{m \times m}$, and the PRF $F_{\text{LWE}} : \mathbb{Z}_q^{m \times m} \times \{0,1\}^\ell \to \mathbb{Z}_p^{m \times m}$ is defined as follows:

$$F_{\text{LWE}}(\mathbf{K}, x) = \left\lfloor \mathbf{K} \cdot \prod_{i=1}^{\ell} \mathbf{A}_{x_i} \right\rceil_p . \tag{4.1}$$

Recollect the bound B for samples drawn from the LWE error distribution $\overline{\Psi}_\alpha$. In the rest of the section, we set the parameters of the system $q, p, m, c, B, \lambda, \ell > 0$ such that the quantity $(2m)^\ell cBp/q$ is negligible in the security parameter λ. This is along the lines of the parameters chosen in [14]. We state the following theorem for this choice of parameters:

Theorem 4.1. *Under the LWE assumption, the PRF F_{LWE} defined in Equation (4.1) is RKA-secure against unique-input adversaries for the class $\Phi_{\text{ln-aff}}$.*

Proof of Theorem 4.1. In what follows, for a bit string x on ℓ bits, we use $x|_j$ to denote the bit string comprising bits j through ℓ of x. Let $x|_{\ell+1}$ denote the empty string ε^*. Let $\mathcal{A}$ be a probabilistic polynomial time unique-input RKA adversary. We consider the following experiments interacting with $\mathcal{A}$.

Experiment $\mathbf{G}_j$ for $j \in [1, \ell + 1]$.

1. The challenger samples as public parameters full-rank matrices $\mathbf{A}_0, \mathbf{A}_1 \in \{0,1\}^{m \times m} \subset \mathbb{Z}_q^{m \times m}$ which are sent to the adversary.

2. The challenger creates a lookup table L of pairs $(w, \mathbf{Z}) \in \{0,1\}^{\ell-j+1} \times \mathbb{Z}_q^{m \times m}$, and initializes L to contain only the pair $(\varepsilon^*, \mathbf{R})$ for some randomly chosen $\mathbf{R} \in \mathbb{Z}_q^{m \times m}$.

3. For $k \in [Q]$, the adversary (adaptively) sends input queries $\left(\phi_{\mathbf{C},\mathbf{B}}^{(k)}, x^{(k)} \right) \in \Phi_{\text{ln-aff}} \times \{0,1\}^\ell$ to the challenger. For each input query, the challenger checks to see if there is a pair $\left(x^{(k)}|_j, \mathbf{Z} \right)$ in L for some $\mathbf{Z} \in \mathbb{Z}_q^{m \times m}$. If there is no such pair, then the challenger chooses a random $\mathbf{Y} \in \mathbb{Z}_q^{m \times m}$, adds the pair $\left(x^{(k)}|_j, \mathbf{Y} \right)$ to L, and sets

$\mathbf{Z} = \mathbf{Y}$. The challenger returns $\mathbf{N} = \left\lfloor \mathbf{CZ} \prod_{i=1}^{j-1} \mathbf{A}_{x_i^{(k)}} + \mathbf{B} \prod_{i=1}^{\ell} \mathbf{A}_{x_i^{(k)}} \right\rfloor_p$ to the adversary.

4. The adversary outputs a bit $b' \in \{0, 1\}$, which the experiment also outputs.

Experiment H_j for $j \in [1, \ell + 1]$.

1. The challenger samples as public parameters full-rank matrices $\mathbf{A}_0, \mathbf{A}_1 \in \{0, 1\}^{m \times m} \subset \mathbb{Z}_q^{m \times m}$ which are sent to the adversary.
2. The challenger creates a lookup table L of triples $(w, \mathbf{Y}, \mathbf{Z}) \in \{0, 1\}^{\ell - j + 1} \times \mathbb{Z}_q^{m \times m} \times \mathbb{Z}_q^{m \times m}$, and initializes L to contain only the triple $(\varepsilon^*, \mathbf{R}, \boldsymbol{\Delta})$ for some randomly chosen $\mathbf{R} \in \mathbb{Z}_q^{m \times m}$ and $\boldsymbol{\Delta} \leftarrow \overline{\varPsi}_\alpha^{m \times m}$.
3. For $k \in [Q]$, the adversary (adaptively) sends input queries $\left(\phi_{\mathbf{C}, \mathbf{B}}^{(k)}, x^{(k)} \right) \in \varPhi_{\mathsf{ln\text{-}aff}} \times \{0, 1\}^\ell$ to the challenger. For each input query, the challenger checks to see if there is a triple $(x^{(k)}|_{j-1}, \mathbf{Z}, \boldsymbol{\Delta})$ in L for some $\mathbf{Z} \in \mathbb{Z}_q^m$ and $\boldsymbol{\Delta} \leftarrow \overline{\varPsi}_\alpha^{m \times m}$. If there is no such triple, then the challenger chooses a random $\mathbf{Y} \in \mathbb{Z}_q^{m \times m}$ and random $\mathbf{V}_0, \mathbf{V}_1 \leftarrow \overline{\varPsi}_\alpha^{m \times m}$, adds the triples $\left(0 \parallel \left(x^{(k)}|_j \right), \mathbf{Y}, \mathbf{V}_0 \right)$ and $\left(1 \parallel \left(x^{(k)}|_j \right), \mathbf{Y}, \mathbf{V}_1 \right)$ to L, and sets $\mathbf{Z} = \mathbf{Y}$ and $\boldsymbol{\Delta} = \mathbf{V}_{x_{j-1}^{(k)}}$ (i.e., $\mathbf{V}_0$ or $\mathbf{V}_1$ depending on the $j - 1^{\text{th}}$ bit of $x^{(k)}$). The challenger returns to the adversary the value:

$$\mathbf{N} = \left\lfloor \mathbf{C} \left(\mathbf{Z} \mathbf{A}_{x_{j-1}^{(k)}} + \boldsymbol{\Delta} \right) \cdot \prod_{i=1}^{j-2} \mathbf{A}_{x_i^{(k)}} + \mathbf{B} \cdot \prod_{i=1}^{\ell} \mathbf{A}_{x_i^{(k)}} \right\rfloor_p.$$

4. The adversary outputs a bit $b' \in \{0, 1\}$, which the experiment also outputs.

Observe that $\mathsf{G}_{\ell+1}$ responds to the adversary's queries identically as in $\mathsf{Expt}_0^{\mathsf{prf\text{-}rka}}$. Hence, $\Pr\left[\mathsf{Expt}_0^{\mathsf{prf\text{-}rka}} = 1 \right] = \Pr[\mathsf{G}_{\ell+1} = 1]$.

Lemma 4.2. *For all $j \in [2, \ell+1]$, it holds that $|\Pr[\mathsf{G}_j = 1] - \Pr[\mathsf{H}_j = 1]|$ is negligible.*

Proof. In Experiment H_j, let $\mathbf{M}_k = \mathbf{CZA}_{x_{j-1}^{(k)}} \cdot \prod_{i=1}^{j-2} \mathbf{A}_{x_i^{(k)}}$ and $\mathbf{W}_k = \mathbf{C}\boldsymbol{\Delta} \cdot \prod_{i=1}^{j-2} \mathbf{A}_{x_i^{(k)}}$. Since the entries of $\mathbf{C}$ lie within $[-c, c]$, the entries of $\boldsymbol{\Delta}$ lie within $[-B, B]$, and the entries of each of the $j - 2$ matrices $\mathbf{A}_{x_i^{(k)}}$ lie within $\{0, 1\}$, the entries of $\mathbf{W}_k$ must lie within $[-cBm^{j-2}, cBm^{j-2}]$.[5] Since $\mathbf{A}_0$ and $\mathbf{A}_1$ are full rank, the product of these matrices is also full rank. Since $\mathbf{Z}$ is drawn uniformly at random from $\mathbb{Z}_q^{m \times m}$, the matrix $\mathbf{M}_k$ is distributed uniformly in $\mathbb{Z}_q^{m \times m}$. Thus, the probability that $\lfloor \mathbf{M}_k + \mathbf{W}_k \rfloor_p \neq \lfloor \mathbf{M}_k \rfloor_p$ is at most $m^2(cBm^{j-2})p/q$. By taking a union bound over all $x \in \{0, 1\}^\ell$, we have that the probability that there exists some input $x \in \{0, 1\}^\ell$ for which $\lfloor \mathbf{M}_k + \mathbf{W}_k \rfloor_p \neq \lfloor \mathbf{M}_k \rfloor_p$ is at most $(2m)^\ell cBp/q$. Conditioned on the above event not occurring, it holds that for all x, $\lfloor \mathbf{M}_k + \mathbf{W}_k \rfloor_p = \lfloor \mathbf{M}_k \rfloor_p$ which implies that G_j and H_j respond identically to adversary queries. Therefore $|\Pr[\mathsf{G}_j = 1] - \Pr[\mathsf{H}_j = 1]|$ is bounded by the probability of the above "bad" event, which is negligible for a suitable choice of parameters. ∎

---

[5] The fact that entries of $\boldsymbol{\Delta}$ lie within $[-B, B]$ holds only with overwhelming probability, but we will ignore this detail for ease of presentation, as it does not affect the final theorem.

We now state Lemmas 4.3 and 4.4, the proofs of which are deferred to the full version. Applying Lemmas 4.2–4.4 with suitable parameters yields Theorem 4.1.

Lemma 4.3. *Under the LWE assumption, for all* $j \in [2, \ell+1]$, *it holds that the quantity* $|\Pr[G_{j-1} = 1] - \Pr[H_j = 1]|$ *is negligible.*

Lemma 4.4. $\Pr[G_1 = 1] = \Pr\left[\mathsf{Expt}_1^{\mathsf{prf\text{-}rka}} = 1\right].$

5   Unique-Input RKA-secure PRFs for a Class of Polynomials

In this section, under the d-MDHE assumption, we show that F_{DLIN} is RKA-secure against unique-input adversaries with respect to the following class of bounded-degree polynomials. For positive integers ℓ, d and prime p we define

$$\Phi_{\mathsf{poly}(d)} = \left\{ \phi_{P(\cdot)} : \mathbb{Z}_p^{\ell \times \ell} \to \mathbb{Z}_p^{\ell \times \ell} \mid \phi_{P(\cdot)}(\mathbf{K}) = P(\mathbf{K}) \right\},$$

for polynomials P over $\mathbb{Z}_p^{\ell \times \ell}$ of degree at most d which have at least one coefficient matrix (excluding the constant coefficient matrix) which is full rank. In other words, if $P(\mathbf{K}) = \sum_{i=0}^{d} \mathbf{C}_i \cdot \mathbf{K}^i$ for matrices $\mathbf{C}_i \in \mathbb{Z}_p^{\ell \times \ell}$, then there exists a $j > 0$ such that $\mathbf{C}_j \in \mathrm{Rk}_\ell \left(\mathbb{Z}_p^{\ell \times \ell} \right)$. The proof of the following theorem is given in the full version.

Theorem 5.1. *Under the d-MDHE assumption, the PRF* F_{DLIN} *is RKA-secure against unique-input adversaries for the class* $\Phi_{\mathsf{poly}(d)}$.

6   Conclusions

We construct the first lattice-based PRFs secure against related-key attacks. We achieve RKA security under the standard (super-polynomial) LWE assumption for a restricted linear class of related-key functions and this result is comparable to the DDH-based RKA-secure PRF construction by Bellare and Cash [7]. Under the powerful multilinear map abstraction [20], we construct RKA-secure PRFs against a large and natural class of affine related-key deriving functions with minimal restrictions. We believe this to be the most expressive affine class of transformations attainable under the Bellare-Cash framework. We also achieve the weaker notion of unique-input RKA security for an affine class of related-key deriving functions by considering the LWE-based key homomorphic PRF by Boneh et al. [14]. We show that by working with the proof of pseudorandomness and utilizing the algebraic structure of the PRF, we can overcome restrictions on the related-key class that are necessary to apply the Bellare-Cash framework. Finally, we show how, under the d-MDHE assumption in the presence of multilinear maps, we can achieve RKA security against unique-input adversaries for the class of degree-d polynomials. Our work on constructing new RKA-secure PRFs leads to several interesting open problems:

◇ Can we construct LWE-based PRFs under the Bellare-Cash framework for a class less restrictive than Φ_{lin^*}? The only known LWE-based PRFs [5, 14] both require rounding and have "error terms" in proofs that have to be carefully dealt with. This will require a more careful application of the Bellare-Cash framework.

◇ Can we construct unique-input RKA-secure PRFs from other LWE-based PRFs by Banerjee *et al.* [5] and (more recently) Banerjee and Peikert [4]?

◇ Can we construct RKA-secure PRFs against unique-input adversaries for classes of polynomials from more standard assumptions such as LWE or DLIN?

References

[1] Agrawal, S., Boyen, X., Vaikuntanathan, V., Voulgaris, P., Wee, H.: Functional encryption for threshold functions (or fuzzy IBE) from lattices. In: Fischlin, M., Buchmann, J., Manulis, M. (eds.) PKC 2012. LNCS, vol. 7293, pp. 280–297. Springer, Heidelberg (2012)

[2] Applebaum, B., Cash, D., Peikert, C., Sahai, A.: Fast cryptographic primitives and circular-secure encryption based on hard learning problems. In: Halevi, S. (ed.) CRYPTO 2009. LNCS, vol. 5677, pp. 595–618. Springer, Heidelberg (2009)

[3] Applebaum, B., Harnik, D., Ishai, Y.: Semantic security under related-key attacks and applications. In: ICS (2011)

[4] Banerjee, A., Peikert, C.: New and improved key-homomorphic pseudorandom functions. Cryptology ePrint Archive, Report 2014/074 (2014), http://eprint.iacr.org/

[5] Banerjee, A., Peikert, C., Rosen, A.: Pseudorandom functions and lattices. In: Pointcheval, D., Johansson, T. (eds.) EUROCRYPT 2012. LNCS, vol. 7237, pp. 719–737. Springer, Heidelberg (2012)

[6] Barenghi, A., Breveglieri, L., Koren, I., Naccache, D.: Fault injection attacks on cryptographic devices: Theory, practice, and countermeasures. Proceedings of the IEEE 100(11) (2012)

[7] Bellare, M., Cash, D.: Pseudorandom functions and permutations provably secure against related-key attacks. In: Rabin, T. (ed.) CRYPTO 2010. LNCS, vol. 6223, pp. 666–684. Springer, Heidelberg (2010)

[8] Bellare, M., Cash, D., Miller, R.: Cryptography secure against related-key attacks and tampering. In: Lee, D.H., Wang, X. (eds.) ASIACRYPT 2011. LNCS, vol. 7073, pp. 486–503. Springer, Heidelberg (2011)

[9] Bellare, M., Kohno, T.: A theoretical treatment of related-key attacks: RKA-PRPs, RKA-PRFs, and applications. In: Biham, E. (ed.) EUROCRYPT 2003. LNCS, vol. 2656, pp. 491–506. Springer, Heidelberg (2003)

[10] Bellare, M., Meiklejohn, S., Thomson, S.: Key-versatile signatures and applications: RKA, KDM and joint enc/sig. In: Nguyen, P.Q., Oswald, E. (eds.) EUROCRYPT 2014. LNCS, vol. 8441, pp. 496–513. Springer, Heidelberg (2014)

[11] Bellare, M., Paterson, K.G., Thomson, S.: RKA security beyond the linear barrier: IBE, encryption and signatures. In: Wang, X., Sako, K. (eds.) ASIACRYPT 2012. LNCS, vol. 7658, pp. 331–348. Springer, Heidelberg (2012)

[12] Biham, E., Shamir, A.: Differential fault analysis of secret key cryptosystems. In: Kaliski Jr., B.S. (ed.) CRYPTO 1997. LNCS, vol. 1294, pp. 513–525. Springer, Heidelberg (1997)

[13] Boneh, D., DeMillo, R.A., Lipton, R.J.: On the importance of eliminating errors in cryptographic computations. J. Cryptology 14(2) (2001)

[14] Boneh, D., Lewi, K., Montgomery, H., Raghunathan, A.: Key homomorphic pRFs and their applications. In: Canetti, R., Garay, J.A. (eds.) CRYPTO 2013, Part I. LNCS, vol. 8042, pp. 410–428. Springer, Heidelberg (2013)

[15] Boneh, D., Montgomery, H.W., Raghunathan, A.: Algebraic pseudorandom functions with improved efficiency from the augmented cascade. In: ACM CCS (2010)

[16] Bonneau, J., Mironov, I.: Cache-collision timing attacks against AES. In: Goubin, L., Matsui, M. (eds.) CHES 2006. LNCS, vol. 4249, pp. 201–215. Springer, Heidelberg (2006)

[17] Brakerski, Z., Langlois, A., Peikert, C., Regev, O., Stehlé, D.: Classical hardness of learning with errors. In: STOC (2013)

[18] Dodis, Y., Yampolskiy, A.: A verifiable random function with short proofs and keys. In: Vaudenay, S. (ed.) PKC 2005. LNCS, vol. 3386, pp. 416–431. Springer, Heidelberg (2005)

[19] Ferguson, N., Kelsey, J., Lucks, S., Schneier, B., Stay, M., Wagner, D., Whiting, D.L.: Improved cryptanalysis of rijndael. In: Schneier, B. (ed.) FSE 2000. LNCS, vol. 1978, pp. 213–230. Springer, Heidelberg (2001)

[20] Garg, S., Gentry, C., Halevi, S., Sahai, A., Waters, B.: Attribute-based encryption for circuits from multilinear maps. In: Canetti, R., Garay, J.A. (eds.) CRYPTO 2013, Part II. LNCS, vol. 8043, pp. 479–499. Springer, Heidelberg (2013)

[21] Goldreich, O., Goldwasser, S., Micali, S.: How to construct random functions. J. ACM 34(4) (1986)

[22] Alex Halderman, J., Schoen, S.D., Heninger, N., Clarkson, W., Paul, W., Calandrino, J.A., Feldman, A.J., Appelbaum, J., Felten, E.W.: Lest we remember: cold-boot attacks on encryption keys. Commun. ACM 52(5) (2009)

[23] Jakimoski, G., Desmedt, Y.: Related-key differential cryptanalysis of 192-bit key aes variants. In: Matsui, M., Zuccherato, R.J. (eds.) SAC 2003. LNCS, vol. 3006, pp. 208–221. Springer, Heidelberg (2004)

[24] Kocher, P.C.: Timing attacks on implementations of diffie-hellman, RSA, DSS, and other systems. In: Koblitz, N. (ed.) CRYPTO 1996. LNCS, vol. 1109, pp. 104–113. Springer, Heidelberg (1996)

[25] Lewko, A.B., Waters, B.: Efficient pseudorandom functions from the decisional linear assumption and weaker variants. In: CCS (2009)

[26] Lucks, S.: Ciphers secure against related-key attacks. In: Roy, B., Meier, W. (eds.) FSE 2004. LNCS, vol. 3017, pp. 359–370. Springer, Heidelberg (2004)

[27] Messerges, T.S., Dabbish, E.A., Sloan, R.H.: Examining smart-card security under the threat of power analysis attacks. IEEE Trans. Computers 51(5) (2002)

[28] Micciancio, D., Peikert, C.: Hardness of SIS and LWE with small parameters. In: Canetti, R., Garay, J.A. (eds.) CRYPTO 2013, Part I. LNCS, vol. 8042, pp. 21–39. Springer, Heidelberg (2013)

[29] Naor, M., Reingold, O.: Number-theoretic constructions of efficient pseudo-random functions. In: FOCS (1997)

[30] Naor, M., Segev, G.: Public-key cryptosystems resilient to key leakage. SIAM J. Comput. 41(4) (2012)

[31] Peikert, C.: Public-key cryptosystems from the worst-case shortest vector problem: extended abstract. In: STOC. ACM (2009)

[32] Regev, O.: On lattices, learning with errors, random linear codes, and cryptography. In: STOC (2005)

[33] Ristenpart, T., Tromer, E., Shacham, H., Savage, S.: Hey, you, get off of my cloud: exploring information leakage in third-party compute clouds. In: CCS (2009)

[34] Shacham, H.: A cramer-shoup encryption scheme from the linear assumption and from progressively weaker linear variants. IACR Cryptology ePrint Archive (2007)

[35] Wee, H.: Public key encryption against related key attacks. In: Fischlin, M., Buchmann, J., Manulis, M. (eds.) PKC 2012. LNCS, vol. 7293, pp. 262–279. Springer, Heidelberg (2012)

[36] Zhang, W., Zhang, L., Wu, W., Feng, D.: Related-key differential-linear attacks on reduced AES-192. In: Srinathan, K., Rangan, C.P., Yung, M. (eds.) INDOCRYPT 2007. LNCS, vol. 4859, pp. 73–85. Springer, Heidelberg (2007)

Verifiable Multi-server Private Information Retrieval

Liang Feng Zhang and Reihaneh Safavi-Naini

Institute for Security, Privacy and Information Assurance
Department of Computer Science
University of Calgary

Abstract. Private information retrieval (PIR) allows a client to retrieve any block x_i from a database $x = x_1 \cdots x_n$ (stored on a server) such that i remains hidden from the server. PIR schemes with unconditional privacy and sublinear (in n) communication complexity can be constructed assuming multiple honest-but-curious servers. This assumption however cannot be guaranteed in many real life scenarios such as using cloud servers. There are also extra properties such as efficient update of the database. In this paper, we consider a verifiable multi-server PIR (VPIR) model where the servers may be malicious and provide fraudulent answers. We construct an unconditionally t-private and computationally secure k-server VPIR scheme with communication complexity comparable to the best t-private k-server PIR scheme in the honest-but-curious server model. Our scheme supports efficient update of the database, identification of the cheating servers, tolerance of slightly corrupted answers, and multiple database outsourcing.

1 Introduction

Private information retrieval (PIR) allows a client to retrieve any block x_i from a database $x = x_1 \cdots x_n$ (stored on a server) such that i remains hidden from the server. The main efficiency measure of a PIR scheme is its communication complexity and defined to be the total number of bits communicated for retrieving a single bit of x. In a trivial PIR scheme, the client simply downloads x. Although perfectly private, this solution has a prohibitive communication complexity $\geq n$. Chor et al. [5] showed that the trivial solution is optimal in terms of communication complexity if there is only one server and perfect privacy is required. Non-trivial PIR schemes with communication complexity $< n$ have been constructed in information-theoretic (multi-server) setting [5,2,17] and computational (single-server) setting [13]. The former setting still provides privacy even if the server spends unrestricted computational resources to recover i once x_i has been collected. Let $1 \leq t < k$. A k-server PIR scheme is said to be t-private if no collusion of up to t servers can learn any information about i. The most efficient t-private PIR scheme [17] with $t > 1$ has communication complexity $O(n^{1/\lfloor (2k-1)/t \rfloor})$ in the honest-but-curious server model.

The PIR servers' computation complexity can be measured by the total number of database blocks read by the servers and is lower bounded by n in any

I. Boureanu, P. Owesarski, and S. Vaudenay (Eds.): ACNS 2014, LNCS 8479, pp. 62–79, 2014.
© Springer International Publishing Switzerland 2014

PIR schemes [3,1]. Advances in cloud computing makes it possible [14,6,12] to implement multi-server PIR using cloud servers such that the high computation complexity can be offloaded to the powerful clouds. However, the outsourcing requires a stronger adversary model as the clouds may provide incorrect answers due to malicious behaviors or accidental failures. In this paper, we strengthen the honest-but-curious server model of the existing multi-server PIR schemes [5,2,17] to provide security against malicious servers. We require that the client should be able to identify the malicious servers. This is very important as an unidentified malicious server can result in system failure without concern about its reputation. In practice, very few databases stay unchanged over time. Thus, we also would like our PIR scheme to have extra properties such as efficiently updating the outsourced database and catering for multiple databases. In a trivial malicious server PIR scheme the database owner may sign each block x_i of the database using any signature scheme and then send the "extended database" of (block, signature) to the clouds; the client can use any PIR scheme to retrieve x_i along with its signature from the "extended database" and then verify. However, this solution becomes insecure after the first database update as the server can always use old (block, signature) pairs without being detected. To improve this trivial solution, the database owner may consider $x_1, \ldots, x_n$ as leaves of a Merkle tree and publish the root of this tree for verification. To access one block, in this case one leaf of the tree, the client runs a multi-server PIR scheme once for each layer of the tree, obtains the required block and the siblings of all nodes on the path from the leaf to the root and verifies the result against the root of the tree. This solution provides basic update but with higher cost; and more importantly, it does not allow identification of cheating clouds; it treats each database individually with no saving when multiple databases are outsourced.

1.1 Our Contributions

In this paper, we consider verifiable multi-server PIR schemes that support efficient update, cheater identification and multiple database delegations.

VPIR Model. We introduce a verifiable multi-sever PIR (VPIR) model (see Figure 1) that consists of a database owner $\mathcal{D}$, a client $\mathcal{C}$ and k clouds $\mathcal{S}_1, \ldots, \mathcal{S}_k$. Let λ be a security parameter. $\mathcal{D}$ has a database $x = x_1 \cdots x_n \in \mathbb{F}_p^n$, where n is a polynomial of λ and p is a λ-bit prime. The client $\mathcal{C}$ has an index $i \in [n]$ and wants to learn x_i from the clouds, without revealing i. In a VPIR scheme $\Gamma = (\mathsf{KeyGen}, \mathsf{Setup}, \mathsf{Query}, \mathsf{Answer}, \mathsf{Challenge}, \mathsf{Respond}, \mathsf{Verify}, \mathsf{Update})$, $\mathcal{D}$ is responsible to set up the system and update x. To set up the system, $\mathcal{D}$ runs a key generation algorithm $(pk, sk) \leftarrow \mathsf{KeyGen}(1^\lambda, n)$ and a setup algorithm $vk_x \leftarrow \mathsf{Setup}(pk, sk, x)$. It publishes (pk, vk_x) and gives x to every cloud. To update the database from x to x', $\mathcal{D}$ runs an update algorithm $vk_{x'} \leftarrow \mathsf{Update}(pk, sk, vk_x, x')$, publishes $vk_{x'}$ and then instructs each cloud to change x to x'. To retrieve x_i, the client runs a query algorithm $(Q_1, \ldots, Q_k, \mathsf{aux}) \leftarrow \mathsf{Query}(pk, i)$ and sends a query Q_j to $\mathcal{S}_j$ for every $j \in [k]$. The cloud $\mathcal{S}_j$ runs an answer algorithm $A_j \leftarrow \mathsf{Answer}(pk, x, Q_j)$ and replies with A_j. To verify A_j, the client runs a challenge algorithm $(I_1, \ldots, I_k) \leftarrow \mathsf{Challenge}(pk)$ to produce a challenge I_j for every cloud S_j and the cloud S_j must respond with a proof $\sigma_j \leftarrow \mathsf{Respond}(pk, x, Q_j, I_j)$ vouching for the correctness of A_j. At last, if the k answers $A_1, \ldots, A_k$ are all correct, then the client can run an extract algorithm $\mathsf{Extract}(pk, vk_x, \{(A_j, I_j, \sigma_j) : j \in [k]\}, \mathsf{aux})$ to compute x_i. The running time of all algorithms must be polynomial in λ.

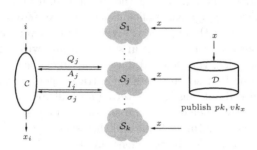

Fig. 1. Verifiable multi-server PIR

We define privacy (information theoretic) and verifiability (computational) of the system in line with the privacy in PIR and the security in VC. The definition is justified because the privacy attacker has unlimited time to break the system, while verifiability of the clouds' answers should be provided without delay. The clouds' answers are verified individually and so the cheating clouds can be identified. The public key pk can be used for outsourcing multiple databases. In fact it can be computed and published once by a third party and used by many database owners. The algorithm Update only requires the difference between x' and x and the algorithm $\mathsf{Extract}$ only requires a small portion of pk. Throughout the paper, the *size* $|w|$ of any string w is defined to be the number of λ-bit blocks it contains.

VPIR Constructions. We propose a basic construction Γ_0 and a main construction Γ_1 of VPIR schemes. The basic construction is obtained by adding verifiability [15] to the best t-private PIR scheme [17]. As a main drawback, the communication complexity of Γ_0 squares that of the underlying PIR scheme [17]. The main construction reduces this cost to be comparable to [17]. Let $t < k$ and $d = \lfloor (2k-1)/t \rfloor$. Let $m > 0$ be such that $\binom{m}{d} \geq n$. The main construction Γ_1 has the following properties.

PRIVACY. The scheme Γ_1 achieves unconditional t-privacy in the sense that any collusion of up to t clouds learns no information about the client's index i, even if they have unlimited computing power.

SECURITY. No cloud S_j can deceive the client into accepting an incorrect answer $\bar{A}_j$ with a forged proof $\bar{\sigma}_j$, except with negligible probability. In particular, the client can identify any cheating cloud by verifying that cloud's answer. The security is based on the $(m + d - 1)$-SBDH assumption (see Definition 2).

COMMUNICATION. Each block of our database x has λ bits and so the communication complexity of our VPIR schemes is the number of λ-bit blocks communicated by the client. To retrieve a block x_i, the client sends a query Q_j of size $O(m)$ to each cloud $\mathcal{S}_j$ and receives an answer A_j of size $O(m)$. It also sends $\mathcal{S}_j$ a challenge I_j of size $O(\log m)$ and receives a proof σ_j of size $O(\lambda m)$. Thus, the communication complexity of Γ_1 is $O(\lambda m) = O(\lambda n^{1/\lfloor (2k-1)/t \rfloor})$.

COMPUTATION. (1) <u>Client</u>: The computation of $Q_1, \ldots, Q_k$ consists of evaluating m univariate polynomials of degree $\leq t$ over $\mathbb{F}_p$. The verification of each answer A_j consists of checking λ equations, where each equation requires $\leq 2m$ bilinear paring computations. The extraction of x_i from $A_1, \ldots, A_k$ consists of interpolating and evaluating a univariate polynomial of degree $\leq 2k - 1$. The client's computation is dominated by $O(m)$ pairing computations. (2) <u>Cloud</u>: The computation of A_j consists of evaluating a polynomial $P_x(z, y)$ (see equation (2)) at $O(m)$ points. The computation of σ_j consists of decomposing P_x (see Lemma 1) and computing $O(m)$ bilinear group elements and $O(m)$ field elements. We show that the response time of each cloud in Γ_1 can be significantly reduced by distributing the PIR server computation to its numerous computing units.

STORAGE. <u>Cloud</u>: In Γ_1, each cloud stores a copy of x. <u>Client</u>: The client uses (vk_x, aux) and $O(m)$ elements of pk for verification and reconstruction. For each retrieval, the client also temporarily stores k triples $\{(A_j, I_j, \sigma_j) : j \in [k]\}$ of total size $O(\lambda m)$.

UPDATE. To change one block of x, say x_i to x_i', $\mathcal{D}$ needs to compute $vk_{x'}$ for $x' = x_1 \cdots x_{i-1} x_i' x_{i+1} \cdots x_n$ using $d + 1$ multiplications in a bilinear group of order p, and then instructs each cloud to change x_i to x_i'. Note that d is a constant. Hence, the update complexity is $O(1)$. The update is verifiable in the sense that any cloud that does not change x accordingly will be detected as cheating in the future executions of Γ_1.

ADDITIONAL PROPERTIES. The construction Γ_1 also provides two additional properties. <u>Error Tolerance</u>: Each cloud's answer in Γ_1 is a codeword under a Reed-Solomon code. We show how to modify Γ_1 such that slight corruptions of each cloud's answer can be tolerated. <u>Multiple Database Delegation</u>: The system public key pk has size $(2d + 2 + o(1))n$ and can be used by any database owner to delegate their database. For each database x, a short (one group element) public verification key vk_x will be published. Updating the database x is done by updating this short key.

1.2   Related Work

PIR with Malicious Servers. Constructing PIR schemes that are secure in a malicious server model is well-motivated and has been put forth by Beimel [1]. The GMW compiler [10] allows one to compile any PIR scheme in the honest-but-curious server model into a PIR scheme in the malicious server model. However, its communication complexity is higher than the trivial PIR scheme and thus much higher than Γ_1. The robust multi-server PIR schemes that tolerate a limited number of malicious servers have been studied in [4,9,7]. The communication complexities of all these schemes are much higher than Γ_1. Furthermore, if all the answering servers in these schemes collude with each other, then the client may be deceived into computing an incorrect value of x_i. In contrast, the client in Γ_1 will reject and not be deceived. More importantly, the PIR schemes of [4,9,7] do not support update, while the database owner in Γ_1 can efficiently and verifiably update its outsourced database x.

Outsourced PIR. The practicality of outsourcing PIR has been demonstrated by [14,6,12]. Mayberry et al. [14] presented a MapReduce-based outsourced single-server PIR scheme called "PIRMAP" which is more than one order of magnitude faster than the trivial PIR scheme. Devet [6] developed parallelization techniques that significantly reduce each cloud's response time by distributing the delegated PIR server computation among its numerous computing units. Huang et al. [12] combined certain multi-server PIR with oblivious RAM to obtain outsourced PIR schemes where the access patterns of the database owner and all clients are hidden from the clouds. None of the schemes [14,6,12] consider malicious clouds.

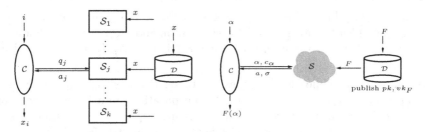

Fig. 2. Private information retrieval and public verifiable computation

1.3   Building Blocks and Our Techniques

Woodruff-Yekhanin PIR Scheme. Let $t, k > 0$ be integers such that $1 \leq t < k$. A t-private k-server PIR scheme (see Figure 2) involves a database owner $\mathcal{D}$, a client $\mathcal{C}$ and k servers $\mathcal{S}_1, \ldots, \mathcal{S}_k$, where $\mathcal{D}$ has a database $x = x_1 \cdots x_n \in \mathbb{F}_p^n$ and $\mathcal{C}$ wants to learn x_i. The $\mathcal{D}$ does not directly communicate with the client but gives x to each server. To privately retrieve x_i, the client computes a query q_j to each server $\mathcal{S}_j$ and receives an answer a_j in return. The queries are computed such that any t of them give no information about i; the k answers allow the client to recover x_i. Let $d = \lfloor (2k-1)/t \rfloor$ and $m = O(n^{1/d})$ be such that $\binom{m}{d} \geq n$. Let $\mathsf{IndEnc} : [n] \to \mathbb{F}_p^m$ be a 1-to-1 index encoding that maps any index $i \in [n]$ to a 0-1 vector of Hamming weight d. Let

$$F_x(\boldsymbol{z}) = \mathsf{PolyEnc}_0(x) \triangleq \sum_{j=1}^{n} x_j \prod_{\ell: \mathsf{IndEnc}(j)_\ell = 1} z_\ell \tag{1}$$

be a polynomial encoding of x of total degree $\leq d$ in $\boldsymbol{z} = (z_1, \ldots, z_m)$ such that $F_x(\mathsf{IndEnc}(i)) = x_i$ for every $i \in [n]$. Woodruff and Yekhanin [17] constructed a PIR scheme Π_{wy} where the client simply computes $F_x(\boldsymbol{z})$ at its private input $\mathsf{IndEnc}(i)$ with the servers. The client computes k queries $q_1, \ldots, q_k$ as k shares of

IndEnc(i) under Shamir's t-private threshold secret sharing scheme; each server S_j answers with $a_j = (F_x(q_j), \frac{\partial F_x}{\partial z_1}|_{q_j}, \ldots, \frac{\partial F_x}{\partial z_m}|_{q_j})$; from $a_1, \ldots, a_k$ the client can interpolate a univariate polynomial of degree $< 2k$ whose evaluation at 0 gives x_i. In Π_{wy} the client sends m field elements (i.e., $q_j \in \mathbb{F}_p^m$) to each server and receives $m+1$ field elements (i.e., a_j). Its communication complexity is $k(2m+1)$.

Papamanthou et al. PVC Schemes. Papamanthou et al. [15] introduced a publicly verifiable computation (PVC) model (see Figure 2) that involves a function owner $\mathcal{D}$, a cloud $\mathcal{S}$ and a client $\mathcal{C}$, where $\mathcal{D}$ has a function $F \in \mathcal{F}$ and $\mathcal{C}$ wants to learn $F(\alpha)$. The function owner computes (pk, vk_F), makes them public and then gives F to the cloud; the client gives α and a challenge c_α to the cloud; the cloud computes $a = F(\alpha)$ and a proof σ using (pk, F); at last, the client can verify a using (pk, vk_F, σ). Let $\mathcal{F} \subseteq \mathbb{F}_p[z]$ be the set of polynomials of total degree $\leq d$ in $z = (z_1, \ldots, z_m)$. Papamanthou et al. [15] constructed a scheme Π_0 (Section B.1, eprint version of [15]) which allows the client to verify the result $F(\alpha)$ from $\mathcal{S}$ for any $(F, \alpha) \in \mathcal{F} \times \mathbb{F}_p^m$ and a scheme Π_1 (Corollary 1, eprint version of [15]) that allows the client to verify the result $\frac{\partial F}{\partial z_\ell}\big|_\alpha$ from $\mathcal{S}$ for any $((F, \ell), \alpha) \in (\mathcal{F} \times [m]) \times \mathbb{F}_p^m$. In both schemes, the client sends a challenge c_α of size $m - 1$ to the cloud and receives a proof of size $O(m)$.

Our Constructions. Our basic VPIR construction Γ_0 is a composition of Π_{wy}, Π_0 and Π_1. In Γ_0, each cloud $\mathcal{S}_j$ performs the computation of the jth server in Π_{wy}. The computation of a_j by $\mathcal{S}_j$ involves one evaluation and m differentiations of the polynomial $F_x(z)$ at q_j. We simply enforce the integrity of these computations using Π_0 and Π_1, respectively.

In Γ_0, the client sends a challenge of size $m - 1$ to $\mathcal{S}_j$ and receives a proof of size $O(m)$ from $\mathcal{S}_j$ for every component of a_j. Thus, the communication complexity of Γ_0 is $k(m+1) \cdot O(m) = O(m^2)$ and squares that of Π_{wy}. Our main construction Γ_1 reduces it to $O(\lambda m)$ by limiting the proof size of each cloud. To do so, a natural idea is using *probabilistic verification*: for every $j \in [k]$, the client verifies only λ random components of a_j. If the cloud $\mathcal{S}_j$ has tampered with a constant fraction (say δ) of a_j, then $\mathcal{S}_j$ will be detected with overwhelming probability $1 - (1 - \delta)^\lambda$. However, a clever $\mathcal{S}_j$ may tamper with only one component of a_j and deceive the client with non-negligible probability $(1 - \frac{1}{m+1})^\lambda$. To thwart this attack, we encode a_j using an error-correcting code $C : \mathbb{F}_p^{m+1} \to \mathbb{F}_p^M$ such that $\mathcal{S}_j$ must change a constant fraction of $A_j = C(a_j)$ in order to change a_j, where $M = O(m + 1)$. Otherwise, the client can decode a_j from A_j. We take C to be the Reed-Solomon code that encodes any message $w = w_0 \cdots w_m \in \mathbb{F}_p^{m+1}$ as $C(w) = (f_w(\gamma_1), \ldots, f_w(\gamma_M))$, where $f_w(y) = w_0 + w_1 y + \cdots + w_m y^m$ and $\gamma_1, \ldots, \gamma_M \in \mathbb{F}_p$ are distinct. Let

$$P_x(z, y) = \mathsf{PolyEnc}_1(x) \triangleq F_x(z) + \sum_{\ell=1}^m \frac{\partial F_x(z)}{\partial z_\ell} y^\ell, \tag{2}$$

where $F_x(z) = \mathsf{PolyEnc}_0(x)$. Then $A_j = C(a_j) = (P_x(q_j, \gamma_1), \ldots, P_x(q_j, \gamma_M))$. The client in Γ_1 learns A_j from $\mathcal{S}_j$ and then randomly verifies λ components of A_j. If $\mathcal{S}_j$ tampers with a constant fraction of A_j, then it will be detected; otherwise, the client can recover a_j. The client can use Π_0 to verifiably compute the $(m+1)$-variate polynomial P_x of total degree $\leq m+d-1$. But that requires a public key of size $\binom{2m+d}{m+d-1} = \exp(O(n))$. We develop a new PVC scheme Π_2 for P_x which requires a public key of size $(2d+2+o(1))n$. In Π_2, the client sends a challenge of size m to the cloud and receives a proof of size $O(m)$. Thus, the λ proofs required by our client have total size $O(\lambda m)$. Our client must send the M challenges for computing A_j, and then ask for the λ proofs only after A_j has been received; otherwise the cloud will know which λ components of A_j will be verified and then break the security by changing other components. However, we observe that these challenges can be chosen such that they are equal to each other without compromising the security. That is, the client can send one *common challenge* of size $O(m)$ for the M computations. Enforcing the integrity of computing P_x using Π_2 with probabilistic verification and common challenge gives us a VPIR scheme of communication complexity $O(\lambda m)$.

2   Preliminaries

2.1   Our Model

We denote any negligible function in λ by $\mathsf{neg}(\lambda)$ and any polynomial function in λ by $\mathsf{poly}(\lambda)$. Our VPIR model (see Figure 1) involves a database owner $\mathcal{D}$, a client $\mathcal{C}$ and k clouds $\mathcal{S}_1, \ldots, \mathcal{S}_k$, where $\mathcal{D}$ has a database $x = x_1 \cdots x_n \in \mathbb{F}_p^n$ and the client $\mathcal{C}$ wants to privately retrieve x_i.

Definition 1. *A k-server VPIR scheme is a tuple $\Gamma =$ (KeyGen, Setup, Query, Answer, Challenge, Respond, Extract, Update) of eight algorithms, where*

- *$(pk, sk) \leftarrow$ KeyGen$(1^\lambda, n)$ is a key generation algorithm which takes as input (λ, n) and outputs a public key pk and a secret key sk;*
- *$vk_x \leftarrow$ Setup(pk, sk, x) is a setup algorithm which takes as input (pk, sk) and any database $x \in \mathbb{F}_p^n$ and outputs a public verification key vk_x;*
- *$(Q_1, \ldots, Q_k, \mathsf{aux}) \leftarrow$ Query(pk, i) is a query algorithm which takes as input pk and any index $i \in [n]$ and outputs k queries $Q_1, \ldots, Q_k$ along with some auxiliary information aux;*
- *$A_j \leftarrow$ Answer(pk, x, Q_j) is an answer algorithm which computes an answer A_j from (pk, x, Q_j);*
- *$(I_1, \ldots, I_k) \leftarrow$ Challenge(pk) is a challenge algorithm that generates k challenges $I_1, \ldots, I_k$ for the clouds;*
- *$\sigma_j \leftarrow$ Respond(pk, x, Q_j, I_j) is a respond algorithm which takes as input (pk, x, Q_j, I_j) and outputs a proof σ_j vouching for the correctness of A_j;*
- *$\{x_i, \bot\} \leftarrow$ Extract$(pk, vk_x, \{(A_j, I_j, \sigma_j) : j \in [k]\}, \mathsf{aux})$ is an extract algorithm that reconstructs x_i or outputs $\bot$ (to indicate failure);*
- *$vk_{x'} \leftarrow$ Update(pk, sk, vk_x, x') is an update algorithm which generates a new public verification key $vk_{x'}$ from (pk, sk, vk_x) and the new database x'.*

The database owner $\mathcal{D}$ is responsible to set up the system and update x. To set up the system, $\mathcal{D}$ runs KeyGen and Setup to compute (pk, sk) and vk_x, publishes (pk, vk_x) and gives x to every cloud. To update the database from x to x', $\mathcal{D}$

runs Update to compute $vk_{x'}$, publishes $vk_{x'}$ and then instructs each cloud to change x to x'. To retrieve x_i, $\mathcal{C}$ runs Query to compute $(Q_1, \ldots, Q_k, \mathsf{aux})$ and sends a query Q_j to the cloud $\mathcal{S}_j$ for every $j \in [k]$. The cloud $\mathcal{S}_j$ runs Compute, computes and replies with A_j. To verify these answers, the client runs Challenge to generate k challenges $(I_1, \ldots, I_k)$. Each cloud $\mathcal{S}_j$ generates a proof σ_j using Respond. At last, the client can run Extract to verify the k answers $A_1, \ldots, A_k$ and then compute x_i if all answers are correct.

Correctness. The scheme Γ is said to be correct if the extract algorithm always outputs the correct value of x_i when all k clouds are honest. Formally, let $(pk, sk) \leftarrow \mathsf{KeyGen}(1^\lambda, n)$. Let $x^{(0)} \in \mathbb{F}_p^n$ and $vk_{x^{(0)}} = \mathsf{Setup}(pk, sk, x^{(0)})$. For $u = 1, \ldots, U(= \mathsf{poly}(\lambda))$, let $vk_{x^{(u)}} \leftarrow \mathsf{Update}(pk, sk, vk_{x^{(u-1)}}, x^{(u)})$. Π is *correct* if for any $u \in \{0, 1, \ldots, U\}$, any $i \in [n]$, any $(Q_1, Q_2, \ldots, Q_k, \mathsf{aux}) \leftarrow \mathsf{Query}(pk, i)$ and any $(I_1, \ldots, I_k) \leftarrow \mathsf{Challenge}(pk)$, it holds that $\mathsf{Extract}(pk, vk_{x^{(u)}}, \{(A_j, I_j, \sigma_j) : j \in [k]\}), \mathsf{aux}) = x_i^{(u)}$, where $A_j = \mathsf{Answer}(pk, x^{(u)}, Q_j)$ and $\sigma_j = \mathsf{Respond}(pk, x^{(u)}, Q_j, I_j)$ for every $j \in [k]$.

t-**Privacy.** The scheme Γ is said to be (unconditionally) t-private if no collusion of up to t servers can learn any information about i. Formally, Γ is (unconditionally) t-private if for any k, n, any $i_1, i_2 \in [n]$ and any set $T \subseteq [k]$ of size $|T| \le t$, the distributions of $\mathsf{Query}_T(pk, i_1)$ and $\mathsf{Query}_T(pk, i_2)$ are identical, where Query_T denotes concatenation of j-th outputs of Query for $j \in T$.

Security. The scheme Γ is said to be secure if no probabilistic polynomial time (PPT) adversary can deceive the client into reconstructing an incorrect value of x_i. Formally, Γ is secure if no PPT adversary $\mathcal{A}$ can win with non-negligible probability in the following security game:

---

1. The challenger picks $(pk, sk) \leftarrow \mathsf{KeyGen}(1^\lambda, n)$ and then gives pk to $\mathcal{A}$.
2. $\mathcal{A}$ picks a database $x^{(0)} \in \mathbb{F}_p^n$ and makes a query $\mathsf{Setup}(pk, sk, x^{(0)})$ to the challenger. The challenger returns $vk_{x^{(0)}}$. For $u = 1, \ldots, U(= \mathsf{poly}(\lambda))$, $\mathcal{A}$ makes a query $\mathsf{Update}(pk, sk, vk_{x^{(u-1)}}, x^{(u)})$. The challenger returns $vk_{x^{(u)}}$ every time.
3. $\mathcal{A}$ picks $u \in \{0, 1, \ldots, U\}$, $i \in [n]$ and then gives (u, i) to the challenger. The challenger gives k queries $(Q_1, \ldots, Q_k)$ to $\mathcal{A}$ and stores a string aux. $\mathcal{A}$ returns k answers $(\bar{A}_1, \bar{A}_2, \ldots, \bar{A}_k)$. The challenger then gives k challenges $(I_1, \ldots, I_k)$ to $\mathcal{A}$ and receives k proofs $(\bar{\sigma}_1, \bar{\sigma}_2, \ldots, \bar{\sigma}_k)$ in return.
4. $\mathcal{A}$ wins if $\mathsf{Extract}(pk, vk_{x^{(u)}}, \{(\bar{A}_j, I_j, \bar{\sigma}_j) : j \in [k]\}, \mathsf{aux}) \notin \{x_i^{(u)}, \bot\}$.

In our security game, $\mathcal{A}$ cannot deceive the client into computing an incorrect value of $x_i^{(u)}$ even if it can freely choose and update the database x. Thus, a VPIR scheme secure under our definition above not only allows the client to verifiably retrieve any block from the database, but also allows $\mathcal{D}$ to verifiably update its outsourced database without compromising the security. The query, answer and communication complexities of Γ are defined to be $\mathcal{QC}_\Gamma = \max\{|Q_j| + |I_j|\}$, $\mathcal{AC}_\Gamma = \max\{|A_j| + |\sigma_j|\}$ and $\mathcal{CC}_\Gamma = \sum_{j=1}^k (|Q_j| + |I_j| + |A_j| + |\sigma_j|)$, respectively.

2.2 Woodruff-Yekhanin PIR Scheme

Let $1 \leq t < k$ and $d = \lfloor (2k-1)/t \rfloor$. Let $m = O(n^{1/d})$ be such that $\binom{m}{d} \geq n$. Let $\beta_1, \ldots, \beta_k \in \mathbb{F}_p^*$ be distinct. Let $\mathsf{IndEnc} : [n] \rightarrow \mathbb{F}_p^m$ be the 1-to-1 index encoding that maps any index $i \in [n]$ as a 0-1 vector of Hamming weight d. Let $F_x(z)$ be the polynomial encoding of any database $x \in \mathbb{F}_p^n$ (see (1)) such that $F_x(\mathsf{IndEnc}(i)) = x_i$ for every $i \in [n]$. Woodruff and Yekhanin's t-private k-server PIR scheme is a triple $\Pi_{\mathrm{wy}} = (\mathsf{Query}, \mathsf{Answer}, \mathsf{Extract})$ of algorithms, where

- $(q_1, \ldots, q_k, \mathsf{aux}) \leftarrow \mathsf{Query}(i)$ is a query algorithm that picks $v_1, \ldots, v_t \leftarrow \mathbb{F}_p^m$; computes a query $q_j = \mathsf{IndEnc}(i) + \beta_j v_1 + \cdots + \beta_j^t v_t$ for every $j \in [k]$ and an auxiliary information $\mathsf{aux} = \{v_1, \ldots, v_t\}$.
- $a_j \leftarrow \mathsf{Answer}(x, q_j)$ is an answer algorithm that computes $a_{j,0} = F_x(q_j)$ and $a_{j,\ell} = \frac{\partial F_x}{\partial z_\ell}\big|_{q_j}$ for every $\ell \in [m]$ and outputs $a_j = (a_{j,0}, a_{j,1}, \ldots, a_{j,m})$.
- $\mathsf{Extract}(a_1, \ldots, a_k, \mathsf{aux})$ is an extract algorithm that interpolates a polynomial $f(y) = F_x(\mathsf{IndEnc}(i) + yv_1 + \cdots + y^t v_t)$ and outputs $f(0) = x_i$.

The algorithm Query will be run by the client to generate k queries and aux; the algorithm Answer will be run by each server to compute an answer; the algorithm $\mathsf{Extract}$ will be run by the client to recover x_i. In Π_{wy}, the k queries $q_1, \ldots, q_k$ are k shares of $\mathsf{IndEnc}(i)$ under Shamir's t-private threshold secret sharing scheme. Thus, no t or less servers can learn any information about i and thus the t-privacy follows. The communication complexity of Π_{wy} is $k(2m+1) = O(m)$.

2.3 Papamanthou et al. PVC Schemes

Papamanthou et al.'s PVC scheme [15] (see Figure 2) is a tuple $\Pi = (\mathsf{KeyGen}, \mathsf{Setup}, \mathsf{Challenge}, \mathsf{Compute}, \mathsf{Verify}, \mathsf{Update})$ of six algorithms, where

- $(pk, sk) \leftarrow \mathsf{KeyGen}(1^\lambda, \mathcal{F})$ is a key generation algorithm that takes as input λ and a function family $\mathcal{F}$ and outputs a public key pk and a secret key sk;
- $vk_F \leftarrow \mathsf{Setup}(pk, sk, F)$ is a setup algorithm that computes a public verification key vk_F for any $F \in \mathcal{F}$ with the knowledge of (pk, sk);
- $c_\alpha \leftarrow \mathsf{Challenge}(pk, \alpha)$ is a challenge algorithm that produces a challenge c_α for any α in the domain of F;
- $(a, \sigma) \leftarrow \mathsf{Compute}(pk, F, \alpha, c_\alpha)$ computes $a = F(\alpha)$ along with a proof σ;
- $\{F(\alpha), \bot\} \leftarrow \Pi.\mathsf{Verify}(pk, vk_F, \alpha, c_\alpha, a, \sigma)$ is a verification algorithm that checks if a is indeed equal to $F(\alpha)$;
- $vk_{F'} \leftarrow \mathsf{Update}(pk, sk, vk_F, F')$ is an update algorithm that computes a public verification key $vk_{F'}$ based on (pk, sk, vk_F) and the changes of the new function F' with respect to F.

In a PVC scheme, $\mathcal{D}$ is responsible to set up the system and update F. To set up the system, $\mathcal{D}$ runs the first two algorithms to compute (pk, sk) and vk_F. It publishes (pk, vk_F) and gives F to the cloud. To update the function from F to F', $\mathcal{D}$ runs Update to compute $vk_{F'}$, publishes $vk_{F'}$ and instructs the cloud $\mathcal{S}$ to change F to F'. To compute $F(\alpha)$, the client $\mathcal{C}$ runs $\mathsf{Challenge}$ and picks a challenge c_α to the cloud. The cloud runs Compute and replies with (a, σ). At last, the client runs Verify to check if a is indeed equal to $F(\alpha)$. The query, answer and communication complexities of Π are defined to be $|\alpha| + |c_\alpha|$, $|a| + |\sigma|$ and $|\alpha| + |c_\alpha| + |a| + |\sigma|$, respectively. Let $\mathbb{F} = \{z_1^{e_1} \cdots z_m^{e_m} : e_1 + \cdots + e_m \leq d\}$ and $\mathcal{F} = \text{span}(\mathbb{F}) \subseteq \mathbb{F}_p[z]$. Papamanthou et al. [15] constructed a PVC scheme Π_0 and a PVC scheme Π_1 for computing the evaluations and differentiations of any $F \in \mathcal{F}$. In both schemes, the client sends a challenge of size $m - 1$ to the cloud and receives a proof of size $O(m)$ in return. We also observe that the Verify in both schemes uses at most $m + d - 2$ out of the $\binom{m+d}{d}$ components of pk.

2.4   Bilinear Maps and Assumptions

Let $\mathcal{G}$ be a generator which takes λ as input and outputs a bilinear map instance $(p, \mathbb{G}, \mathbb{G}_T, e, g)$, where $\mathbb{G} = \langle g \rangle$ and $\mathbb{G}_T$ are cyclic groups of prime order p; and $e : \mathbb{G} \times \mathbb{G} \to \mathbb{G}_T$ is a non-degenerate bilinear map such that $e(g^a, g^b) = e(g, g)^{ab}$ for any $a, b \in \mathbb{F}_p$ and $e(g, g)$ is a generator of $\mathbb{G}_T$.

Definition 2. (*d-SBDH*) *Let* $\Lambda = (p, \mathbb{G}, \mathbb{G}_T, e, g) \leftarrow \mathcal{G}(1^\lambda)$. *Let* $d = \text{poly}(\lambda)$. *We say that the bilinear d-strong Diffie-Hellman assumption holds if for any PPT algorithm* $\mathcal{A}$, $\Pr[s \leftarrow \mathbb{F}_p^* : \mathcal{A}(\Lambda, g, g^s, \ldots, g^{s^d}) = (\theta, e(g, g)^{1/(s+\theta)})] < \text{neg}(\lambda)$, *where* $\theta \in \mathbb{F}_p^* \setminus \{-s\}$.

3   Our Constructions

In this section we first present our basic construction Γ_0 as a composition of Π_{wy}, Π_0 and Π_1. We then improve Γ_0 to our main construction Γ_1 whose communication complexity is comparable to the PIR of [17].

3.1   Basic Construction

In Π_{wy} the PIR servers' computations consist of evaluating and differentiating the polynomial $F_x(z) = \text{PolyEnc}_0(x)$ at k points $q_1, \ldots, q_k$ which are k shares of $\text{IndEnc}(i)$ under Shamir's t-private threshold secret sharing scheme. In Γ_0 (see **Fig. 3**), the k clouds $\mathcal{S}_1, \ldots, \mathcal{S}_k$ perform these computations on behalf of the PIR servers. For every $j \in [k]$, the client runs Π_0 with $\mathcal{S}_j$ to compute $a_{j,0}$ and runs Π_1 with $\mathcal{S}_j$ to compute $a_{j,\ell}$ for every $\ell \in [m]$.

Correctness, Privacy and Security. The correctness of Γ_0 follows from that of Π_{wy}, Π_0 and Π_1. The only information about i that the clouds can learn is from the k points $q_1, \ldots, q_k$ which are k shares of $\text{IndEnc}(i)$ under Shamir's t-private threshold secret sharing scheme. Thus, no collusion of up to t clouds can learn any information about $\text{IndEnc}(i)$, i.e., Γ_0 achieves unconditional t-privacy. In Γ_0, the client runs $k(m+1)$ independent Π_0 and Π_1 instances with the clouds. If any cloud can break one of the instances, then we can simulate that cloud to break the d-SBDH assumption as in the security proofs of Π_0 and Π_1 (see [15] for the proofs). Hence, Γ_0 is secure under the d-SBDH assumption.

Theorem 1. Γ_0 *is an unconditionally t-private and computationally secure VPIR scheme. Its security is based on the d-SBDH assumption.*

KeyGen($1^\lambda, n$): Output $(pk, sk) \leftarrow \Pi_0.\text{KeyGen}(1^\lambda, \text{span}(\mathbb{F}))$, where $sk = \tau \in \mathbb{F}_p^m$.

Setup(pk, sk, x): Output $vk_x \leftarrow \Pi_0.\text{Setup}(pk, sk, F_x)$.

Query(pk, i): Compute $(q_1, \ldots, q_k, \text{aux}') \leftarrow \Pi_{\text{wy}}.\text{Query}(i)$. For every $j \in [k]$ and $\ell \in \{0, 1, \ldots, m\}$, compute $c_{j,\ell} \leftarrow \Pi.\text{Challenge}(pk, q_j)$, where $\Pi = \Pi_0$ if $\ell = 0$ and $\Pi = \Pi_1$ otherwise. Output $Q_j = (q_j, c_{j,0}, c_{j,1}, \ldots, c_{j,m})$ for all $j \in [k]$ and aux $= (\text{aux}', \{c_{j,\ell} : j \in [k], 0 \le \ell \le m\})$.

Answer(pk, x, Q_j): Compute $(a_{j,\ell}, \sigma_{j,\ell}) \leftarrow \Pi.\text{Compute}(pk, F_x, q_j, c_{j,\ell})$, where $\Pi = \Pi_0$ if $\ell = 0$ and $\Pi = \Pi_1$ if $\ell \in [m]$. Output $A_j(= a_j) = (a_{j,0}, a_{j,1}, \ldots, a_{j,m})$.

Challenge(pk): For every $j \in [k]$, set $I_j = \{0, 1, \ldots, m\}$. Output $(I_1, \ldots, I_k)$.

Respond(pk, x, Q_j, I_j): Output $\sigma_j = \{\sigma_{j,\ell} : \ell \in I_j\}$.

Extract($pk, vk_x, \{(A_j, I_j, \sigma_j) : j \in [k]\}, \text{aux}$): Compute $b_{j,\ell} = \Pi.\text{Verify}(pk, vk_x, q_j, c_{j,\ell}, a_{j,\ell}, \sigma_{j,\ell})$, for every $j \in [k]$ and $\ell \in I_j$. where $\Pi = \Pi_0$ if $\ell = 0$ and $\Pi = \Pi_1$ otherwise. If all $b_{j,\ell}$'s are 1, output $x_i = \Pi_{\text{wy}}.\text{Extract}(A_1, \ldots, A_k, \text{aux}')$. Otherwise, output $\perp$.

Update(pk, sk, vk_x, x'): Output $vk_{x'} \leftarrow \Pi_0.\text{Update}(pk, sk, vk_x, \text{PolyEnc}_0(x'))$.

Fig. 3. The scheme Γ_0

Complexity. The database owner $\mathcal{D}$ runs $\Pi_0.\text{KeyGen}$ and $\Pi_0.\text{Setup}$ to set up the system. Both algorithms are executed once and take time $O(n)$. $\mathcal{D}$ may also run $\Pi_0.\text{Update}$ to update x. To change one component of x, $\mathcal{D}$ needs to multiply vk_x with one element from $\{g^{h(\tau)} : h(z) \in \mathbb{F}\}$ (see [15]). Therefore, the update complexity is $O(1)$. The client $\mathcal{C}$ computes and sends Q_j and I_j to the cloud $\mathcal{S}_j$ for every $j \in [k]$. It receives A_j and σ_j. Therefore, $\mathcal{QC}_{\Gamma_0} = \max\{|Q_j| + |I_j|\} = O(m^2)$, $\mathcal{AC}_{\Gamma_0} = \max\{|A_j| + |\sigma_j|\} = O(m^2)$ and $\mathcal{CC}_{\Gamma_0} = O(m^2)$. For verification, the client uses aux ($|\text{aux}| = O(m^2)$) and $m + d - 2 = O(m)$ components of pk. Each cloud stores x, runs $\Pi_0.\text{Compute}$ once and $\Pi_1.\text{Compute}$ m times.

Variant. In Γ_0, the client communicates four messages Q_j, A_j, I_j and σ_j with every cloud $\mathcal{S}_j$ in two rounds. Note that I_j is always equal to $\{0, 1, \ldots, m\}$. We can merge the four messages and obtain a two-message version of Γ_0: the client simply sends Q_j to each cloud $\mathcal{S}_j$ and $\mathcal{S}_j$ replies with (A_j, σ_j). Thus, our basic construction can be made into one round.

3.2   Main Construction

In this section, we reach Γ_1 using a series of modifications to Γ_0. For every $j \in [k]$, the client in Γ_0 sends a query $Q_j = (q_j, c_{j,0}, c_{j,1}, \ldots, c_{j,m})$ and a challenge $I_j = \{0, 1, \ldots, m\}$ to $\mathcal{S}_j$, where $q_j \in \mathbb{F}_p^m$, $c_{j,0}, c_{j,1}, \ldots, c_{j,m} \in (\mathbb{F}_p^*)^{m-1}$. Clearly, $|Q_j| + |I_j|$ contributes $O(m^2)$ to $\mathcal{CC}_{\Gamma_0}$. If we use a common challenge $c_{j,0} = c_{j,1} = \cdots = c_{j,m} = c_j \in (\mathbb{F}_p^*)^{m-1}$ in Γ_0, then $|Q_j| + |I_j|$ would be reduced to $O(m)$ for every $j \in [k]$ and thus $\sum_{j=1}^{k}(|Q_j| + |I_j|)$ will be reduced to $O(m)$. We shall see that this modification will not compromise the security of Γ_0. We denote by Γ_0' this modified version of Γ_0.

In Γ_0', each cloud $\mathcal{S}_j$ answers with $a_j = (a_{j,0}, a_{j,1}, \ldots, a_{j,m})$ and responds with $\sigma_j = (\sigma_{j,0}, \sigma_{j,1}, \ldots, \sigma_{j,m})$, which contributes $|a_j| + |\sigma_j| = O(m) + O(m^2) = O(m^2)$ to $\mathcal{CC}_{\Gamma_0'}$. If we can modify Γ_0' such that only $O(\lambda)$ components of σ_j are needed to verify a_j, then we would reduce $\mathcal{CC}_{\Gamma_0'}$ to $O(\lambda m)$. A natural idea is performing probabilistic verification: instead of requesting the σ_j from $\mathcal{S}_j$, the client requests λ random components of σ_j, say $\{\sigma_{j,\ell} : \ell \in I_j\}$, where $I_j \subseteq \{0, 1, \dots, m\}$ is a random λ-subset; the client accepts a_j only if $(a_{j,\ell}, \sigma_{j,\ell})$ verifies for every $\ell \in I_j$. More precisely, $\Gamma_0'.\mathsf{Challenge}$ will simply output k independent random λ-subsets $I_1, \dots, I_k \subseteq \{0, 1, \dots, m\}$. We denote by Γ_0'' this modified version of Γ_0'. Note that the modification should not compromise the security of Γ_0''. If a constant fraction (say δ) of the elements of a_j have been tampered with by $\mathcal{S}_j$, then except with negligible probability $(1 - \delta)^\lambda$ at least one element of $\{a_{j,\ell} : \ell \in I_j\}$ happens to be tampered with and therefore $\mathcal{S}_j$ will be detected. However, a clever $\mathcal{S}_j$ may tamper with only one element of a_j. This will allow $\mathcal{S}_j$ to deceive the client $\mathcal{C}$ into accepting a_j with non-negligible probability $(1 - \frac{1}{m+1})^\lambda$. Then k such malicious clouds would be able to deceive the client into accepting their answers $a_1, \dots, a_k$ with non-negligible probability as $\lambda = o(m)$ and $k = O(1)$. Whenever this occurs, the client will compute a wrong value of x_i from those answers, i.e., the security of Γ_0'' is compromised.

In order to thwart this attack, we ask the cloud $\mathcal{S}_j$ to return an encoding A_j of a_j under an error-correcting code $C : \mathbb{F}_p^{m+1} \to \mathbb{F}_p^M$, such that $\mathcal{S}_j$ must change a constant fraction of A_j in order to change even one component of a_j. Furthermore, the client turns to verify A_j. Let C be an $[M, m+1, d']_p$ linear code with constant expansion $\rho = M/(m+1)$ and error rate $\delta = (d'-1)/(2M)$, then Γ_0'' can be further modified as below: the cloud $\mathcal{S}_j$ answers with $A_j = (A_{j,1}, \dots, A_{j,M}) = C(a_j)$ instead of a_j; the client gives a random λ-subset $I_j \subseteq [M]$ to $\mathcal{S}_j$ and $\mathcal{S}_j$ returns the proofs for $\{A_{j,\ell} : \ell \in I_j\}$; the client then verifies $A_{j,\ell}$ for every $\ell \in I_j$; it accepts and decodes A_j to a_j only if all the verifications are successful. Let Γ_0''' be this modified version of Γ_0''. If such an idea of modifying Γ_0'' can be realized, then each cloud $\mathcal{S}_j$ can deceive the client into accepting $\bar{a}_j \neq a_j$ only if it tampers with $> \delta M$ components of A_j but $\{A_{j,\ell} : \ell \in I_j\}$ are not tampered with. Clearly, this event occurs with probability $\leq (1-\delta)^\lambda$, which is negligible. On the other hand, if $\mathcal{S}_j$ only tampers with $< \delta$ fraction of A_j, then the client can correctly decode a_j from A_j.

A remaining problem is how to choose C such that the idea can be realized, i.e., enable the verifiable computation of A_j. We take C to be an $[M, m+1, M-m]_p$ Reed-Solomon code with constant expansion $\rho = M/(m+1)$ and error rate $\delta = \frac{1}{2} - \frac{1}{2\rho}$. Under this choice each cloud $\mathcal{S}_j$ answers with $A_j = C(a_j) = (f_{a_j}(\gamma_1), f_{a_j}(\gamma_2), \dots, f_{a_j}(\gamma_M))$, where $f_{a_j}(y) = a_{j,0} + a_{j,1}y + \dots + a_{j,m}y^m$ and $\gamma_1, \dots, \gamma_M \in \mathbb{F}_p$ are distinct. Recall that $a_{j,0} = F_x(q_j)$ and $a_{j,\ell} = \frac{\partial F_x}{\partial z_\ell}\big|_{q_j}$ for every $\ell \in [m]$. Let $P_x(z, y) = \mathsf{PolyEnc}_1(x)$. Then $f_{a_j}(\gamma_\ell) = P_x(q_j, \gamma_\ell)$ for every $\ell \in [M]$, where $(q_j, \gamma_\ell) \in \mathbb{F}_p^{m+1}$. Thus, computing A_j is equivalent to evaluating P_x at M points $(q_j, \gamma_1), \dots, (q_j, \gamma_M)$. The PVC scheme Π_0 can compute m-variate polynomials of total degree $\leq m + d - 1$ which in particular include P_x. However, that requires a public key of size $\binom{2m+d}{m+d-1}$ which is exponential in $n \leq \binom{m}{d}$ as $m = \omega(1)$ and $d = O(1)$. Below we construct a new PVC scheme Π_2 for evaluating P_x. Enforcing the integrity of computing P_x using Π_2 with the common challenge and the probabilistic verification techniques gives us Γ_1.

Let $\mathbb{P}_0$ be the set of all monomials $z_1^{e_1} \cdots z_m^{e_m}$ with $e_1, \ldots, e_m \in \{0,1\}$ and $e_1 + \cdots + e_m = d$. Let $\mathbb{P}_1$ be the set of all monomials $y^u \cdot z_1^{e_1} \cdots z_m^{e_m}$ with $u \in [m], e_1, \ldots, e_m \in \{0,1\}$ and $e_1 + \cdots + e_m = d - 1$. Then

$$P_x \in \mathcal{P} = \mathrm{span}(\mathbb{P}_0 \cup \mathbb{P}_1).$$

For every $i \in [m-1]$, let $\mathbb{B}_i$ be the set of monomials $z_i^{e_i} \cdots z_m^{e_m}$ with $e_{i+2}, \ldots, e_m \in \{0,1\}$ and $e_i + \cdots + e_m \le d - 1$; let $\mathbb{D}_i$ be the set of monomials $y^u z_i^{e_i} \cdots z_m^{e_m}$ with $u \in [m], e_{i+2}, \ldots, e_m \in \{0,1\}$ and $e_i + \cdots + e_m \le d - 2$. Let $\mathbb{B}_m = \{y^u z_m^v : 0 \le u + v \le d - 1\}$ and $\mathbb{D}_m = \{y^u z_m^v : 0 \le v \le d-2, u+v \le m+d-2\}$. We have the following technical lemma.

Lemma 1. *Let $P(z, y) \in \mathcal{P}$, $\alpha = (\alpha_1, \ldots, \alpha_{m+1}) \in \mathbb{F}_p^{m+1}$ and $r = (r_1, \ldots, r_m) \in (\mathbb{F}_p^*)^m$. Then there exist $\Phi_1(z, y) \in \mathrm{span}(\mathbb{B}_1 \cup \mathbb{D}_1), \ldots, \Phi_m(z, y) \in \mathrm{span}(\mathbb{B}_m \cup \mathbb{D}_m)$ and $\phi_0, \ldots, \phi_{m+d-2} \in \mathbb{F}_p$ such that $P(z, y) - P(\alpha) = \sum_{i=1}^{m}(r_i(z_i - \alpha_i) + z_{i+1} - \alpha_{i+1})\Phi_i + (y - \alpha_{m+1})\sum_{j=0}^{m+d-2} \phi_j y^j$. Furthermore, $\sum_{i=1}^{m} |\mathbb{B}_i| \le (1 + O(m^{-1}))\binom{m}{d}$ and $\sum_{i=1}^{m} |\mathbb{D}_i| \le (d + O(m^{-2}))\binom{m}{d}$.*

We defer the proof of Lemma 1 to the full version. Let $\mathbb{P} = \mathbb{P}_0 \cup \mathbb{P}_1 \cup \cup_{i=1}^{m}(\mathbb{B}_i \cup \mathbb{D}_i)$. Below is the scheme Π_2 for verifiably evaluating the polynomials in $\mathcal{P}$.

KeyGen$(1^\lambda, \mathcal{P})$: Pick $\Lambda = (p, \mathbb{G}, \mathbb{G}_T, e, g) \leftarrow \mathcal{G}(1^\lambda)$ and $\tau = (\tau_1, \tau_2, \ldots, \tau_{m+1}) \leftarrow \mathbb{F}_p^{m+1}$. Output $sk = \tau$ and $pk = (\Lambda, \mathbb{M})$, where $\mathbb{M} = \{g^{h(\tau)} : h(z, y) \in \mathbb{P}\}$.

Setup(pk, sk, P): Compute and output $vk_P = g^{P(\tau)}$.

Challenge(pk): Pick $r = (r_1, \ldots, r_m) \leftarrow (\mathbb{F}_p^*)^m$ and output $c = r$.

Compute(pk, P, α, c): Compute $\Phi_1(z, y), \ldots, \Phi_m(z, y)$ and $\phi_0, \ldots, \phi_{m+d-2}$ such that the decomposition of $P(z, y) - P(\alpha)$ in Lemma 1 holds. Compute $w_i = g^{\Phi_i(\tau)}$ for every $i \in [m]$. Output $a = P(\alpha)$ and $\sigma = (w_1, \ldots, w_m, \phi_0, \ldots, \phi_{m+d-2})$.

Verify$(pk, vk_P, \alpha, c, a, \sigma)$: If $e(vk_P \cdot g^{-a}, g) = \prod_{i=1}^{m} e\left(g^{r_i(\tau_i - \alpha_i) + \tau_{i+1} - \alpha_{i+1}}, w_i\right) \cdot \prod_{j=0}^{m+d-2} e\left(g^{\tau_{m+1} - \alpha_{m+1}}, g^{\phi_j \tau_{m+1}^j}\right)$, output 1; otherwise, output 0.

Update(pk, sk, vk_P, P'): Compute $P'(z, y) - P(z, y)$, say it is equal to $\eta h(z, y)$ for $\eta \in \mathbb{F}_p$ and $h(z, y) \in \mathbb{P}$. Output $vk_{P'} = vk_P \cdot (g^{h(\tau)})^\eta$.

Lemma 1 shows that $\Phi_1, \ldots, \Phi_m, z_1, \ldots, z_m, y, y^2, \ldots, y^{m+d-2}$ and $P(z, y)$ all belong to $\mathrm{span}(\mathbb{P})$. Thus the cloud can use pk to compute σ. On the other hand, the $2m + d - 2$ components $pk' = (g^{\tau_1}, \ldots, g^{\tau_m}, g^{\tau_{m+1}}, \ldots, g^{\tau_{m+1}^{m+d-2}})$ of pk suffice for executing Π_2.Verify. It is a trivial generalization of the security proof in [15] to show Π_2 is secure under the $(m + d - 1)$-SBDH assumption.

Theorem 2. *Π_2 is a secure PVC scheme for evaluating the polynomials in $\mathcal{P}$ with $CC_{\Pi_2} = O(m)$. Its security is based on the $(m + d - 1)$-SBDH assumption.*

Due to Lemma 1, we have $|\mathbb{P}| \le (2d + 2 + o(1))n$. Thus, Π_2 only requires a public key of size $(2d + 2 + o(1))n$.

The Main Construction (Γ_1). Recall that the polynomial encoding P_x belongs to $\mathcal{P} = \mathrm{span}(\mathbb{P}_0 \cup \mathbb{P}_1)$. Our main construction Γ_1 is described as below.

KeyGen($1^\lambda, n$): Output $(pk, sk) \leftarrow \Pi_2.\text{KeyGen}(1^\lambda, \mathcal{P})$, where $sk = \tau \in (\mathbb{F}_p^*)^m$.

Setup(pk, sk, x): Output $vk_x \leftarrow \Pi_2.\text{Setup}(pk, sk, P_x)$.

Query(pk, i): Compute $(q_1, \ldots, q_k, \text{aux}') \leftarrow \Pi_{\text{wy}}.\text{Query}(i)$. For every $j \in [k]$, compute $c_j \leftarrow \Pi_2.\text{Challenge}(pk)$. Output $Q_j = (q_j, c_j)$ for every $j \in [k]$ and $\text{aux} = (\text{aux}', c_1, \ldots, c_k)$.

Answer(pk, x, Q_j): For every $\ell \in [M]$, compute $(A_{j,\ell}, \sigma_{j,\ell}) \leftarrow \Pi_2.\text{Compute}(pk, P_x, Q_{j,\ell}, c_j)$, where $Q_{j,\ell} = (q_j, \gamma_\ell)$. Output $A_j = (A_{j,1}, A_{j,2}, \ldots, A_{j,M})$.

Challenge(pk): Output k independent random λ-subsets $I_1, \ldots, I_k \subseteq [M]$.

Respond(pk, x, Q_j, I_j): Output $\sigma_j = \{\sigma_{j,\ell} : \ell \in I_j\}$.

Extract($pk, vk_x, \{(A_j, I_j, \sigma_j) : j \in [k]\}, \text{aux}$): Compute $b_{j,\ell} = \Pi_2.\text{Verify}(pk, vk_x, Q_{j,\ell}, c_j, A_{j,\ell}, \sigma_{j,\ell})$ for every $j \in [k]$ and $\ell \in I_j$. If all $b_{j,\ell}$'s are 1, then decode A_j to $a_j = (a_{j,0}, a_{j,1}, \ldots, a_{j,m})$ for every $j \in [k]$, where $a_{j,0} = F_x(q_j)$ and $a_{j,\ell} = \frac{\partial F_x}{\partial z_\ell}\big|_{q_j}$ for every $\ell \in [m]$; and output $x_i \leftarrow \Pi_{\text{wy}}.\text{Extract}(a_1, \ldots, a_k, \text{aux}')$. Otherwise, output $\bot$.

Update(pk, sk, vk_x, x'): Suppose that x' is not different from x except that $x_i' \neq x_i$. Suppose that the components of $\text{IndEnc}(i)$ are all 0 except those labeled by $i_1, \ldots, i_d \in [m]$. Then $F_{x'}(\mathbf{z}) = F_x(\mathbf{z}) + (x_i' - x_i)\pi$, where $\pi = \prod_{j=1}^d z_{i_j}$. It follows that $P_{x'}(\mathbf{z}, y) = P_x(\mathbf{z}, y) + (x_i' - x_i)\pi(1 + \sum_{j=1}^d z_{i_j}^{-1} y^{i_j})$. The algorithm outputs $vk_{x'} = g^{P_{x'}(\tau)} = vk_x \cdot g^\Delta$, where $\Delta = (x_i' - x_i) \cdot \tau_{i_1} \cdots \tau_{i_d}(1 + \sum_{j=1}^d \tau_{i_j}^{-1} \tau_{m+1}^{i_j})$.

Fig. 4. The scheme Γ_1

Correctness, Privacy and Security. The correctness of Γ_1 follows from that of Π_{wy} and Π_2. The unconditional t-privacy of Γ_1 follows from a similar argument as in Γ_0. In Γ_1, any malicious cloud $\mathcal{S}_j$ that tries to deceive the client into computing an incorrect result must change at least $\delta = 1/2 - 1/(2\rho)$ fraction of its answer A_j. The client in Γ_1 verifies λ random components of A_j. Therefore, $\mathcal{S}_j$ will be detected with overwhelming probability $\geq 1 - (1 - \delta)^\lambda$.

Theorem 3. *Γ_1 is an unconditionally t-private and computationally secure VPIR scheme. Its security is based on the the $(m + d - 1)$-SBDH assumption.*

Proof. Suppose there is an adversary $\mathcal{A}$ that breaks the security of Γ_1 with non-negligible probability ϵ. We construct a simulator that simulates $\mathcal{A}$ and breaks the $(m+d-1)$-SBDH assumption. The SBDH challenger picks a random bilinear map instance $\Lambda = (p, \mathbb{G}, \mathbb{G}_T, e, g) \leftarrow \mathcal{G}(1^\lambda)$ and a random field element $s \leftarrow \mathbb{F}_p^*$. Given Λ and $(g, g^s, \ldots, g^{s^{m+d-1}})$, the simulator proceeds as below:

1. The simulator needs to mimic $\Gamma_1.\text{KeyGen}$ and gives a public key pk to $\mathcal{A}$. To do so, the simulator implicitly sets $\tau_\ell = \mu_\ell s + \nu_\ell$ for every $\ell \in [m+1]$, where μ_ℓ and ν_ℓ are uniformly chosen from $\mathbb{F}_p$; Clearly, the simulator does not know the secret key $\tau = (\tau_1, \ldots, \tau_{m+1}) \in \mathbb{F}_p^{m+1}$ but can compute the public key $\mathbb{M} = \{g^{h(\tau)} : h(\mathbf{z}, y) \in \mathbb{P}\}$. In fact, each monomial $h(\mathbf{z}, y) \in \mathbb{P}$ has total degree $\leq m + d - 1$. Thus, $h(\tau)$ is a polynomial of degree $\leq m + d - 1$ in s whose coefficients are known to the simulator. Thus, the simulator can compute $g^{h(\tau)}$ as it knows $g, g^s, \ldots, g^{s^{m+d-1}}$; At the end, the simulator picks k random field elements $\theta_1, \ldots, \theta_k \leftarrow \mathbb{F}_p$ and gives $pk = (\Lambda, \mathbb{M})$ to $\mathcal{A}$.

2. Given pk, $\mathcal{A}$ picks $x^{(0)} \in \mathbb{F}_p^n$ and makes a query $\Gamma_1.\mathsf{Setup}(pk, sk, x^{(0)})$ to the simulator. The simulator replies with $vk_{x^{(0)}} = g^{P_0(\tau)}$, where $P_0(\boldsymbol{z}, y) = \mathsf{PolyEnc}_1(x^{(0)})$. For every $u = 1, 2, \ldots, U(= \mathsf{poly}(\lambda))$, $\mathcal{A}$ makes a query $\Gamma_1.\mathsf{Update}(pk, sk, vk_{x^{(u-1)}}, x^{(u)})$ to the simulator. The simulator replies with $vk_{x^{(u)}} = g^{P_u(\tau)}$, where $P_u(\boldsymbol{z}, y) = \mathsf{PolyEnc}_1(x^{(u)})$ and $g^{P_u(\tau)}$ can be computed by the simulator although it does not know $sk = \tau$.

3. The adversary $\mathcal{A}$ picks $u \in \{1, \ldots, U\}$, $i \in [n]$ and gives (u, i) to the simulator. The simulator runs $\Pi_{\mathrm{wy}}.\mathsf{Query}(i)$ and picks k points $q_1, \ldots, q_k \in \mathbb{F}_p^m$ along with a string aux'. Furthermore, the simulator needs to choose a challenge $c_j \in (\mathbb{F}_p^*)^m$, define $Q_j = (q_j, c_j)$ for every $j \in [k]$ and $\mathsf{aux} = (\mathsf{aux}', c_1, \ldots, c_k)$. Note that the adversary may control some of the clouds. For every $j \in [k]$, the challenge c_j must be chosen in a way such that the cloud $\mathcal{S}_j$ can be successfully simulated in order to break the SBDH instance if it is corrupted by $\mathcal{A}$ and provides incorrect answers. Therefore, the simulator will not pick the challenge c_j using the $\Pi_2.\mathsf{Challenge}$ as the client in Γ_1 has done. Instead, for every $j \in [k]$, it will guess an index $\ell_j \in [M]$ such that the cloud $\mathcal{S}_j$ will provide an incorrect answer A_{j,ℓ_j}. For notational convenience, for every $j \in [k]$, we denote $Q_{j,\ell} = (q_j, \gamma_{\ell_j}) = (\alpha_{j,1}, \ldots, \alpha_{j,m+1})$. The simulator will carefully compute $c_j = (r_{j,1}, \ldots, r_{j,m}) \in (\mathbb{F}_p^*)^m$ such that

$$r_{j,\ell}(\tau_\ell - \alpha_{j,\ell}) + \tau_{\ell+1} - \alpha_{j,\ell+1} = s_{j,\ell}(s + \theta_j) \tag{3}$$

for every $\ell \in [m]$. Note that the simulator had set $\tau_\ell = \mu_\ell s + \nu_\ell$ for every $\ell \in [m+1]$. It is easy to verify that (3) will hold for any $s \in \mathbb{F}_p$ when

$$r_{j,\ell} = -\frac{\theta_j \mu_{\ell+1} + \alpha_{j,\ell+1} - \nu_{\ell+1}}{\theta_j \mu_\ell + \alpha_{j,\ell} - \nu_\ell} \text{ and } s_{j,\ell} = \frac{\alpha_{j,\ell}\mu_{\ell+1} - \mu_{\ell+1}\alpha_{j,\ell+1} + \mu_\ell \nu_{\ell+1} - \mu_{\ell+1}\nu_\ell}{\theta_j \mu_\ell + \alpha_{j,\ell} - \nu_\ell}$$

for every $\ell \in [m]$. The simulator defines $Q_j = (q_j, c_j)$ for every $j \in [k]$, $\mathsf{aux} = (\mathsf{aux}', c_1, \ldots, c_k)$ and then gives $(Q_1, \ldots, Q_k)$ to $\mathcal{A}$. Note that c_j is uniform over $(\mathbb{F}_p^*)^m$ due to the choices of $\{\mu_\ell, \nu_\ell : \ell \in [m+1]\}$.

4. $\mathcal{A}$ answers with $(\bar{A}_1, \ldots, \bar{A}_k)$, where $\bar{A}_j = (\bar{A}_{j,1}, \ldots, \bar{A}_{j,M})$ for every $j \in [k]$.

5. For every $j \in [k]$, the simulator picks a random $(\lambda - 1)$-subset $I_j' \subseteq [M]$ such that $\ell_j \notin I_j'$ and then set $I_j = I_j' \cup \{\ell_j\}$. It then gives $(I_1, \ldots, I_k)$ to $\mathcal{A}$. Clearly, the distribution of $(I_1, \ldots, I_k)$ is identical to the distribution of those sets generated by $\Gamma_1.\mathsf{Challenge}$. Therefore, $\mathcal{A}$ cannot distinguish between the simulation and the real execution of Γ_1.

6. $\mathcal{A}$ responds with $(\bar{\sigma}_1, \ldots, \bar{\sigma}_k)$, where $\bar{\sigma}_j = \{\bar{\sigma}_{j,\ell} : \ell \in I_j\}$ for every $j \in [k]$.

To deceive the client into computing an incorrect value of x_i, at least one of the k answers $\bar{A}_1, \ldots, \bar{A}_k$, say $\bar{A}_j$, should have Hamming distance $> M\delta$ with the correct answer $A_j = (A_{j,1}, \ldots, A_{j,M})$, where $A_{j,\ell} = \Pi_2.\mathsf{Compute}(pk, P_u, Q_{j,\ell}, c_j)$ for every $\ell \in [M]$. Otherwise, the client would be able to correct the errors and then compute the correct value of x_i using $\Pi_{\mathrm{wy}}.\mathsf{Extract}$. Furthermore, the forged answers $\bar{A}_1, \ldots, \bar{A}_k$ should not be rejected. Equivalently, all of the forged pairs $\{(\bar{A}_{j,\ell}, \bar{\sigma}_{j,\ell}) : j \in [k], \ell \in I_j\}$ should pass the client's verification, i.e.,

$$\Pi_2.\mathsf{Verify}(pk, vk_{x^{(u)}}, Q_{j,\ell}, c_j, \bar{A}_{j,\ell}, \bar{\sigma}_{j,\ell}) = 1 \tag{4}$$

for every $j \in [k]$ and $\ell \in I_j$ because otherwise the client will reject. Let $\mathbf{E}$ be the event that (1) at least one of the forged answers $\bar{A}_1, \ldots, \bar{A}_k$ has Hamming distance $> M\delta$; and (2) the forged answers $\bar{A}_1, \ldots, \bar{A}_k$ are not rejected, i.e., (4) holds for every $j \in [k]$ and $\ell \in I_j$. Due to our assumption, $\Pr[\mathbf{E}] \geq \epsilon$. For notational convenience, we suppose that the Hamming distance between $\bar{A}_{j^*}$ and A_{j^*} is $> M\delta$, where $j^* \in [k]$. Let $L = \{\ell \in [M] : \bar{A}_{j^*,\ell} \neq A_{j^*,\ell}\} \subseteq [M]$ be the set of indices where $\bar{A}_{j^*}$ and A_{j^*} do not agree with each other. Then $|L| > M\delta$. Let $\mathbf{G}$ be the event that $I_{j^*} \cap L = \emptyset$ and let $\neg\mathbf{G}$ be the event that $I_{j^*} \cap L \neq \emptyset$. Since the indices in I_{j^*} are chosen uniformly and independently, $\Pr[\mathbf{G}] = (1 - |L|/M)^\lambda \leq (1 - \delta)^\lambda$, which is negligible. It follows that $\Pr[\mathbf{E}] = \Pr[\mathbf{E}|\mathbf{G}]\Pr[\mathbf{G}] + \Pr[\mathbf{E}|\neg\mathbf{G}]\Pr[\neg\mathbf{G}] \leq (1-\delta)^\lambda + \Pr[\mathbf{E}|\neg\mathbf{G}]\Pr[\neg\mathbf{G}]$. Recall that $\Pr[\mathbf{E}] \geq \epsilon$. We have $\Pr[(\neg\mathbf{G})\wedge\mathbf{E}] = \Pr[\mathbf{E}|\neg\mathbf{G}]\Pr[\neg\mathbf{G}] \geq \epsilon - (1-\delta)^\lambda \triangleq \epsilon_1$, which is non-negligible. In other words, the event $(\neg\mathbf{G})\wedge\mathbf{E}$ that $I_{j^*} \cap L \neq \emptyset$ and the forged answers $\bar{A}_1, \ldots, \bar{A}_k$ are accepted must occur with probability $\geq \epsilon_1$. Recall that the indices $\ell_1, \ldots, \ell_k \in [M]$ have been uniformly chosen by the simulator at step 3 of the simulation. Let $\mathbf{F}$ be the event that $\ell_{j^*} \in L$. Note that ℓ_{j^*} is not different from the other indices in I_{j^*} since c_{j^*} is uniform over $(\mathbb{F}_p^*)^m$ and thus gives no information on ℓ_{j^*}. Thus, we have that $\Pr[\mathbf{F}|\neg\mathbf{G} \wedge \mathbf{E}] \geq 1/|I_{j^*}| \geq 1/\lambda$. When $\mathbf{F}$ and $(\neg\mathbf{G}) \wedge \mathbf{E}$ occur simultaneously, $\mathcal{A}$ can be simulated by a simulator in the security game of the Π_2 instance for computing $\bar{A}_{j^*,\ell_{j^*}}$. Using that simulator, the simulator in the security game of Γ_1 can eventually break the $(m+d-1)$-SBDH instance. Note that $\Pr[\mathbf{F}\wedge(\neg\mathbf{G})\wedge\mathbf{E}] = \Pr[\mathbf{F}|\neg\mathbf{G}\wedge\mathbf{E}]\Pr[(\neg\mathbf{G})\wedge\mathbf{E}] \geq \epsilon_1/\lambda$, which is non-negligible. Recall the security proof for Π_2. By simulating an adversary that breaks the security of Π_2 with probability ϵ_1/λ, one can break a random $(m+d-1)$-SBDH instance with probability $\geq \lambda^{-1}\epsilon_1(1-(m+d-1)/p)$, which is non-negligible. Therefore, the simulator in the security game of Γ_1 can eventually break the random $(m+d-1)$-SBDH instance with non-negligible probability. Therefore, Γ_1 must be secure under the $(m+d-1)$-SBDH assumption. $\square$

Complexity. The database owner $\mathcal{D}$ runs Π_2.KeyGen and Π_2.Setup once. The running time of Π_2.KeyGen is dominated by the computation of $\mathbb{M} = \{g^{h(\tau)} : h(z,y) \in \mathbb{P}\}$ in Π_2 that requires $(2d + 2 + o(1))n = O(n)$ exponentiations. The algorithm Π_2.Setup computes one exponentiation $g^{P_x(\tau)}$. $\mathcal{D}$ also runs Π_0.Update to update x. To change one component of x, $\mathcal{D}$ needs to multiply vk_x with $d+1$ elements from $\mathbb{M}$, i.e., the update complexity is $d+1 = O(1)$. The client $\mathcal{C}$ computes and sends Q_j, I_j to $\mathcal{S}_j$ and receives A_j, σ_j from $\mathcal{S}_j$ for every $j \in [k]$. We have that $\mathcal{QC}_{\Gamma_0} = \max\{|Q_j|+|I_j|\} = O(m)$, $\mathcal{AC}_{\Gamma_0} = \max\{|A_j|+|\sigma_j|\} = O(\lambda m)$ and $\mathcal{CC}_{\Gamma_0} = \sum_{j=1}^k(|Q_j| + |I_j| + |A_j| + |\sigma_j|) = O(\lambda m)$. For each verification, the client uses aux and $2m + d - 2$ elements pk' of pk, where $|\text{aux}| = O(m)$. Each cloud stores x and runs Π_2.Compute M times.

Response Time. A computationally powerful cloud may employ hundreds of thousands of computing units. For example, the Amazon Elastic Compute Cloud (EC2) was employing more than 158000 computing units until May 2013. Mayberry et al. [14] and Devet [6] suggested to outsource the PIR servers' computation to the clouds. Each cloud can distribute the PIR server computation to its computing units and then combine the results of these units. This parallelization technique can effectively reduce the response time of each cloud. It is trivial to see the computation of each cloud in Γ_1 only involves polynomial decompositions, polynomial valuations and exponentiations. All of them can be distributed to multiple computing units. Thus, each cloud can significantly reduce the response time using the parallelization techniques.

Error Tolerance. In Γ_1, the client verifies A_j by checking a random λ-subset of the components of A_j for every $j \in [k]$. If any one of the λk verifications is unsuccessful, then the client rejects; otherwise, it decodes every A_j to a_j and then reconstructs x_i from $a_1, \ldots, a_k$. Note that if a very small constant fraction of a_j has been corrupted, the client will reject with overwhelming probability. For example, the answer A_j will be rejected with overwhelming probability even if $2\delta/3$ fraction of A_j have been corrupted, where $\delta = \frac{1}{2} - \frac{1}{2\rho}$ and $\rho = M/(m+1)$. Recall that $A_j = C(a_j)$ is a Reed-Solomon encoding that can tolerate δ fraction of corruptions. We say that A_j is slightly corrupted if a constant $\delta' \leq 2\delta/3$ fraction of A_j have been corrupted. The client's verification is so severe that a slightly corrupted A_j will be rejected as well while the corruptions can be efficiently corrected. As a result, the client must execute the scheme Γ_1 again to retrieve x_i, which incurs efficiency loss. In particular, if the corruptions were introduced by the infrastructure failures, then rerunning Γ_1 is unlikely to be useful. In this case we can extend (modify) Γ_1 such that the client will not reject A_j except the event $\mathbf{E} : |\{\ell \in I_j : b_{j,\ell} = 0\}| \geq 3\delta|I_j|/4$ occurs. Suppose δ' fraction of $\{A_{j,\ell} : \ell \in I_j\}$ have been corrupted. If $\delta' \leq 2\delta/3$, then the client will not reject and efficiently reconstruct a_j except with probability $\exp(-O(\lambda))$ as $\mathbf{E}$ occurs with probability $\exp(-O(\lambda))$; if $\delta' > \delta$, then $\mathbf{E}$ will occur with probability $1 - \exp(-O(\lambda))$ and thus the client will reject A_j with overwhelming probability.

Multiple Database Delegation. It is an interesting observation that none of the algorithms in Γ_1 actually takes sk as input. As a result, a trusted third party rather than each database owner can run the algorithm KeyGen and then publish pk such that any database owners, clouds and clients can freely use Γ_1. Therefore, Γ_1 actually allows multiple database delegation.

Variant. In Γ_1 the client must communicate with each cloud $\mathcal{S}_j$ in two rounds. In the first round, it sends a query $Q_j = (q_j, c_j)$ and receives an answer A_j; in the second round, it sends a challenge I_j and receives a response σ_j. This two-round communication is essential as sending I_j along with Q_j in the first round would reveal which components of A_j will be verified, and thus enable a cheating cloud to break the security of Γ_1. To get a one-round scheme, the client can consider the M proofs for the M components of A_j as a database and use a single-server PIR [11] with constant communication rate in the honest-but-curious server model to privately retrieve the λ proofs it requires.

4   Conclusions

In this paper, we formally defined verifiable multi-server PIR schemes and constructed an unconditionally t-private and computationally secure VPIR scheme based on the best t-private PIR scheme of Woodruff et al. [17] in the honest-but-curious server model and a new PVC scheme for multivariate polynomial evaluation. Our scheme has communication complexity $O(\lambda n^{1/\lfloor (2k-1)/t \rfloor})$ which is comparable to [17]. Constructing VPIR schemes in the single server setting seems difficult because the known VC with input privacy rely on FHE.

Acknowledgement. This research is in part supported by Alberta Innovates Technology Futures.

References

1. Beimel, A.: Private Information Retrieval: A Primer (2008) (manuscript)
2. Beimel, A., Ishai, Y., Kushilevitz, E.: General Constructions for Information-Theoretic Private Information Retrieval. J. Comput. Syst. Sci. 71(2), 213–247 (2005)
3. Beimel, A., Ishai, Y., Malkin, T.: Reducing the Servers' Computation in Private Information Retrieval: PIR with Preprocessing. J. Cryptol. 17(2), 125–151 (2004)
4. Beimel, A., Stahl, Y.: Robust Information-Theoretic Private Information Retrieval. J. Cryptol. 20(3), 295–321 (2007)
5. Chor, B., Goldreich, O., Kushilevitz, E., Sudan, M.: Private Information Retrieval. In: FOCS, pp. 41–50 (1995)
6. Devet, C.: Evaluating Private Information Retrieval on the Cloud. Technical Report (2013), http://cacr.uwaterloo.ca/techreports/2013/cacr2013-05.pdf
7. Devet, C., Goldberg, I., Heninger, N.: Optimally Robust Private Information Retrieval. In: USENIX Security Symposium (2012)
8. Gennaro, R., Gentry, C., Parno, B.: Non-Interactive Verifiable Computing: Outsourcing Computation to Untrusted Workers. In: Rabin, T. (ed.) CRYPTO 2010. LNCS, vol. 6223, pp. 465–482. Springer, Heidelberg (2010)
9. Goldberg, I.: Improving the Robustness of Private Information Retrieval. In: IEEE Symposium on Security and Privacy, pp. 131–148 (2007)
10. Goldreich, O., Micali, S., Widgerson, A.: How to Play any Mental Game-A Completeness Theorem for Protocols with Honest Majority. In: STOC, pp. 218–229. ACM (1987)
11. Groth, J., Kiayias, A., Lipmaa, H.: Multi-query Computationally-Private Information Retrieval with Constant Communication Rate. In: Nguyen, P.Q., Pointcheval, D. (eds.) PKC 2010. LNCS, vol. 6056, pp. 107–123. Springer, Heidelberg (2010)
12. Huang, Y., Goldberg, I.: Outsourced Private Information Retrieval. In: Workshop on Privacy in the Electronic Society, pp. 119–130. ACM (2013)
13. Kushilevitz, E., Ostrovsky, R.: Replication Is Not Needed: Single Database, Computationally-Private Information Retrieval. In: FOCS, pp. 364–373 (1997)
14. Mayberry, T., Blass, E., Chan, A.: PIRMAP: Efficient Private Information Retrieval for MapReduce. In: Sadeghi, A.-R. (ed.) FC 2013. LNCS, vol. 7859, pp. 371–385. Springer, Heidelberg (2013)
15. Papamanthou, C., Shi, E., Tamassia, R.: Signatures of Correct Computation. In: Sahai, A. (ed.) TCC 2013. LNCS, vol. 7785, pp. 222–242. Springer, Heidelberg (2013), http://eprint.iacr.org/2011/587.pdf
16. Sion, R., Carbunar, B.: On the Computational Practicality of Private Information Retrieval. In: NDSS 2007 (2007)
17. Woodruff, D.P., Yekhanin, S.: A Geometric Approach to Information-Theoretic Private Information Retrieval. SIAM J. Comp. 37(4), 1046–1056 (2007)

Certified Bitcoins

Giuseppe Ateniese[1,2], Antonio Faonio[1],
Bernardo Magri[1], and Breno de Medeiros[3]

[1] Sapienza - University of Rome, Italy
{ateniese,faonio,magri}@di.uniroma1.it
[2] Johns Hopkins University, USA
ateniese@cs.jhu.edu
[3] Google, Inc.
breno@google.com

Abstract. Bitcoin is a peer-to-peer (p2p) electronic cash system that uses a distributed timestamp service to record transactions in a public ledger (called the Blockchain). A critical component of Bitcoin's success is the decentralized nature of its architecture, which does not require or even support the establishment of trusted authorities. Yet the absence of certification creates obstacles to its wider acceptance in e-commerce and official uses. We propose a certification system for Bitcoin that offers: *a*) an opt-in guarantee to send and receive bitcoins only to/ from certified users; *b*) control of creation of bitcoins addresses (certified users) by trusted authorities. Our proposal may encourage the adoption of Bitcoin in different scenarios that require an officially recognized currency, such as tax payments—often an integral part of e-commerce transactions.

1 Introduction

Bitcoin is a peer-to-peer (p2p) electronic cash system, first described in [11]. The Bitcoin p2p network implements a distributed timestamp service that records transactions in a public ledger (called the Blockchain). The timestamp operation is computationally expensive, requiring proof-of-work to verify a transaction and insert it into the Blockchain. In compensation for this effort, the Bitcoin protocol enables the nodes to *mint* coins, i.e., to add into the ledger transactions for self-credit. This distributed minting operation is the source of new currency, dispensing with the need of a central issuer.

Large numbers of users currently transact in Bitcoin, engaging in significantly-sized transactions [13]. The decentralized nature of Bitcoin, wherein confidence on the integrity of the public ledger arises by the cooperative nature of interactions between the participants, is a critical component of its success: Bitcoin removes the necessity for all involved to agree to trust any single entity. However, the converse is also true: Bitcoin does not offer a built-in mechanism to incorporate trustworthiness from real-world entities into the system.

Anonymity In the Bitcoin Protocol. In the Bitcoin Blockchain, users are identified only by addresses, which are pseudonymous public key fingerprints. It is

I. Boureanu, P. Owesarski, and S. Vaudenay (Eds.): ACNS 2014, LNCS 8479, pp. 80–96, 2014.

possible for the user controlling a Bitcoin address to remain unidentified—until information is voluntarily revealed during a purchase or in other circumstances. For this reason Bitcoin has been at times chosen as a payment medium for illegal business. Some governments[1] are also concerned that Bitcoins could be used to skirt capital control laws. On the other hand, legitimate users desirous of privacy should be mindful of the fact that it is possible to link entities that share cash streams—see Ober et al. [13] and Meiklejohn et al. [8] for how an analysis of the Blockchain may reveal that the same real-world entity is behind multiple Bitcoin addresses. Thus, such users should completely segregate their Bitcoin addresses among their different personas.

Our Contribution: Certifiable Bitcoin Addresses. This paper describes an extension of the Bitcoin protocol that preserves its decentralized nature, while also enabling payers to **optionally** specify the involvement of a trusted authority that attests to the identity of the payee, by requiring payees to use *certified* Bitcoin addresses. Conversely, we also enable payees to require that a payer uses a certified Bitcoin address. More specifically, we introduce the concept of Bitcoin addresses that need to be generated with the support of a trusted authority. Those addresses are still anonymous within the Bitcoin system, but the authority can validate the legitimacy of the entity to whom it releases a certified address[2], and other members of the Bitcoin network can attest to the involvement of the trusted authority in issuing the address. These certified addresses are allowed to **co-exist** with the standard auto-generated Bitcoin addresses.

Certified Bitcoin addresses are *blinded*: While the trusted authority can mint coins on behalf of a particular user, it cannot spend any of them. Certified addresses mitigate existing reservations against the adoption of Bitcoin as a currency in commercial uses and against acceptance of the Bitcoin payment protocol as a fully valid alternative to credit card systems.

Identity Theft Mitigation. Our proposal also enhances security against identity theft in Bitcoin. Indeed, consider the case where a man-in-the-middle (MITM) attacker changes the payee's bitcoin address for the attacker's address. For instance, the attacker could deface the payee's website to receive payments intended for the payee. This attack is quite devastating since, in the Bitcoin protocol, once the payment is accepted and registered in the ledger, it is impossible to revert it (unlike credit card payments). With our proposed solution, the payer can first check that the address is certified thus ensuring that the actual identity of the attacker could be recovered by the trusted authority in case of dispute.

1.1 Outline

We briefly recall Bitcoin's transaction mechanism. A Bitcoin transaction is a cryptographically signed statement that transfers an amount of bitcoins from the

---

[1] China [18] has recently declared Bitcoin illegal.

[2] Note that users may be allowed to use simply, e.g., an email address to request Bitcoin addresses. In this case, an email address, rather than an actual identity, is bound to a Bitcoin address.

sender's to the receiver's address. The sender proves ownership of the bitcoins by "redeeming" a transaction already in the ledger that moves at least the same amount of bitcoins to their address. For more details please refer to Section 3.

The standard approach to add certified addresses to the Bitcoin system would be to use PKI-rooted certificates. A trusted authority would sign each newly released certified address by generating an address certificate. This mechanism can be adapted into Bitcoin's infrastructure by using the Bitcoin scripting language. For a certified address one needs to include a certificate from the central authority to each transaction: A new transaction redeems the earlier one only if a) it is verifiable using the sender' address, as with all transactions; and b) the attached certificate is valid. However, there are some disadvantages to incorporating a traditional PKI approach in Bitcoin, to wit:

1. A noticeable modification on the software is needed. We need a signature verification operation that takes as input the certified public key (the message), the certificate (the CA's signature on the message) and the public key of the CA in order to verify the certificate. However the operation OP_CHECKSIG, which in the Bitcoin scripting language provides signature verification, takes only two inputs – a public key and a signature – and assumes as message the transaction's data. The semantic of OP_CHECKSIG would need to be significantly modified or a new operation would have to be added to the scripting language. Any modification of this type would require all the nodes in the system to upgrade their software.
2. In Bitcoin, transaction fees are accounted per bytes: the bigger the size of a transaction, the higher the fees to pay. PKI's addition of certificate chains to (potentially) each address in each transaction would significantly increase transaction costs.
3. The Bitcoin *wallet* software must download the entire ledger. Even an increase of a few gigabytes creates scalability issues, particularly for smartphones or devices with limited bandwidth and data capability. The average size for a block is 156KB and the average number of transactions for each block is 315, which means that the average size of a transaction is approximately 507 Bytes. Considering that the size of a signature in the Bitcoin system's encoding is 71 Bytes, the transaction size will increase by at least 14% [3]. Currently, the size of the ledger is approximately 12GB. In the worst case scenario, where every transaction is being certified, the ledger would be about 1.67 GB bigger.

It would be preferable to add certified addresses in the Bitcoin system *without increasing the size of the transactions* (and, ultimately, the size of the ledger). We achieve this by leveraging the storage and bandwidth cost benefits provided by self-certified public keys. In particular, we adapt techniques developed for self-certified PKI to work within the Bitcoin system. Compared with a standard PKI approach, our solution does not have the drawbacks (2) and (3) outlined above. Moreover, even though we still need to update the software of every

---

[3] By taking the average over all transactions made in 2013.

node in the network, the modification to accommodate self-signed certificates is easier to accomplish. It can be achieved without changes to the the Bitcoin scripting language, or (in alternative implementation) with minimal changes. Indeed, our solution is perfectly compatible with the current ledger and both systems (standard and certified Bitcoin) can run contemporarily on the same ledger.

1.2 Previous Work

Previous Work on Bitcoin. As pointed out earlier, the Blockchain allows to link entities that share cash streams; and the misconception that pseudonymity provides anonymity has been partially unmasked by a series of recent works on the Bitcoin transaction's graph, see for example [16,13,1]. Previous research has thus focused on *strengthening* the privacy guarantees afforded by Bitcoin. In [4] Barber et al. provide a protocol that features *secure* mixing of money, ensuring money is transferred to fresh, and thus unlinkable, addresses through an untrusted third party. A more radical solution to anonymity is given in the paper of Miers et al. [9], where the authors propose an innovative and Bitcoin-compatible system where full anonymity is achieved via zero-knowledge techniques. In this paper, we focus instead on enhancing trust, via certified bitcoins. Without additional measures, this approach would lower the degree of anonymity in the system; but we point out that our solution is compatible with the approaches proposed in [4,9], allowing for both anonymity and certification within the system.

Other works have focused on improving the scalability of Bitcoin, particularly in what regards the bandwidth required to validate the Blockchain. In [4], the authors proposed a secure filtering service that is backward compatible with the current system. The filtering service sends only relevant transactions to nodes allowing for significant space savings. The service does not increase the degree of linkability, and thus has no impact on the privacy of Bitcoin usage, but the need of a fully-trusted third party can be a deterrent in the Bitcoin's context. Indeed, the filtering service could maliciously hide from the user important transactions—the user needs to fully trust the service provider for the filtering service. In contrast, the trusted authority in our certification scheme is only *functionally trusted*, and a pure enhancement to the Bitcoin's ecosystem. As we shall see in Section 3, the trusted party cannot recover the user secret key. In addition, any abuse from the certification authority are detectable via inspection of the Blockchain.

Another line of research has been recently proposed by Andrychowicz et al. [2] where a general protocol for secure multiparty computation using Bitcoin's transactions is proposed. The system guarantees a form of fairness: if a party interrupts the protocol, the outcome is still "tolerable" to the other honest parties.

Previous Work on Self-Certified Public Key. Our proposal can be seen as a weak version of what is referred to as Self-certified (SC) PKI. SC-PKI contemplates public keys that do not need to be accompanied by a certificate in order to be authenticated by other users. To the best of our knowledge, the first schemes to rely on only functionally trusted authorities were described by M. Girault in [7]—where the concept of SC-PKI is itself introduced. That work establishes two SC-PKI constructions, one based on RSA and one based on Elgamal-type public keys. It has been later shown that RSA constructions suffer from a drawback, namely it is possible for the trusted party to safely generate its keys to include trapdoor information that facilitates the recovery of other parties' secrets [17]. This attack applies to every RSA-based construction that results in users reconstructing discrete-log type public keys. Therefore, we concentrate on the case where the trusted party's public keys are themselves of discrete-log type.

We note that Girault's SC-PKI schemes are not ideally suited to the desired Bitcoin application. The key generation protocol for the Girault's scheme takes as common inputs the group's parameters $(\mathbb{G}, g)$, the user's identity I and returns as the user's public key the tuple (r, r^s) where $r \in \mathbb{G}$ and the user's secret key is $s \in \mathbb{Z}_q$.

By necessity, the discrete logarithm of r to base g should not be learned by the user, for this would leak the trusted authority's private key. As a result, two public key pairs $(r_A, r_A^{s_A})$ and $(r_B, r_B^{s_B})$ of users A and B are computed with respect to different bases r_A and r_B, respectively. However, this type of public key (i.e., an element in $\mathbb{G}^2$) does not match the Bitcoin specification.

Another self-certified public key scheme based on Elgamal signatures and provably secure in the Random Oracle Model (ROM) was described by Petersen and Horster [14]. The security analysis relies on Pointcheval and Stern's splitting-lemma security arguments [15], and thus achieves only a *loose* reduction to the Discrete Logarithm Problem (DLP).

However, in the Bitcoin setting, a *tight* proof in the Generic Group Model (GGM) is more desirable than a loose proof in the Random Oracle Model. Indeed, the Bitcoin protocol already relies on the security of the ECDSA standard—which is only shown secure via a GGM (tight) reduction to the Elliptic Curve Discrete Logarithm Problem (ECDLP). Our Certified Addresses construction is thus a better fit for Bitcoin in that it is similarly provably secure in the GGM by a tight reduction to the ECDLP—allowing for the entire security analysis to occur within the same well-defined model.

Ateniese and de Medeiros [3] describe a new self-certified scheme based on the Nyberg-Rueppel signature [12] scheme and its variants. The certification scheme in Section 3 can be seen as a novel self-certified scheme where the certification results from the trusted party applying the modified Nyberg-Rueppel signature [3] to the message $m = 0$.

Description of contents. On Section 2 we begin by giving a description of Bitcoin and its transaction mechanism and then we introduce a few standard cryptographic concepts and terminology that will be used in later sections. On Section 3 we present our contribution with a brief description of an implementation. On Section 4 we provide the security analysis of our proposal. Lastly, on Section 5 we give a brief conclusion of the paper.

2   Background

In this section, we provide an overview of the Bitcoin system and its transaction mechanism. We also introduce a few standard cryptographic concepts and terminology that will be used in later sections.

2.1   Bitcoin Signature Scheme

Bitcoin employs the Elliptic Curve Digital Signing Algorithm (ECDSA) [19] for all of its signatures. ECDSA is a widely used and trusted standard, and it has been extensively analyzed. While a security proof for ECDSA in the *Standard Model* is not known, it has been proved secure against existential forgery by adaptive chosen-message attack in the *GGM* [5].

2.2   Bitcoin Transactions

In order to generate a new Bitcoin address (the core identifier in the Bitcoin protocol), a user first produces a pair of private and public keys for ECDSA: (sk, pk). The Bitcoin address relative to (sk, pk) is the hash of the public key, namely $H(pk)$, where H is a hash function based on SHA-256 and RIPEMD-160. Some extra bytes are appended as a checksum.

The simplest case is a *standard* transaction, say with label T_n, between a sender's address S, with public key pk_S, and one recipient address R. The *payload* of this transaction, which we denote by $[T_n]$ contains: an input index p (which refers to the earlier transaction T_p, already committed to the public ledger), the amount v_n of bitcoins to be transferred, the sender's public key pk_S, and the receiver's address R. In addition to its payload, the transaction includes the sender's signature τ on the transaction payload. More precisely, in addition to the payload, the transaction includes a small, standard program in the *Bitcoin Scripting Language* that when executed validates the sender's signature on the payload, by applying the following simple rules: The signature on T_n is *valid* if and only if $H(pk_S) = S$ and the application of the ECDSA verification algorithm with public key pk_S, message $[T_n]$, and signature τ succeeds. That alone is insufficient for T_n to be accepted: In addition, the value v_n being transferred should not exceed the value v_p in the output of the earlier transaction T_p. If this latter condition holds, then T_n can be accepted to *redeem* transaction T_p, provided that the transaction T_p has not been redeemed earlier (otherwise this is an attempt to double-spend the same set of bitcoins, and the transaction should be rejected).

More advance standard transactions with several inputs and several recipient address can be defined. Since such transactions are not necessary for the understanding of this paper we skip their description and refer to [2]. Bitcoin allows the users to also create non-standard (also called *strange*) transactions. Strange transactions have a *validity policy*, specifically, a strange transaction T_p contains in its output a piece of code in the Bitcoin Scripting Language which implements a redemption *policy*. Subsequent strange transaction T_n that purports to redeem

T_p should thus supply any necessary inputs for the evaluation of T_p's policy code, and the transaction T_n successfully redeems T_p if the evaluation of T_p's policy with inputs provided by T_n outputs true (and again under the restriction that no earlier transaction had redeemed T_p).

3   Certified Bitcoin Address

3.1   Description of the Scheme

In this section we describe our main contribution. First we introduce some mathematical concepts and notation. The additive group of integer residues modulo q is denoted by $\mathbb{Z}_q$. The Certification Authority (CA), denoted by T, has the following public parameters: the description[4] $\mathbb{G}$ of a finite group of size q, a generator g of $\mathbb{G}$, and an additional element y_T of $\mathbb{G}$. The private parameter of the CA is the value $x_T \in \mathbb{Z}_q$ such that $y_T = g^{x_T}$. We also fix a function ρ from $\mathbb{G}$ to $\mathbb{Z}_q$. This function could be fairly simple, e.g., it interprets the binary encoding of an element of $\mathbb{G}$ as the encoding of a positive integer.

(**Certified Address**). A user U can request a certified address to the certification authority T by jointly executing the protocol Certified Key Generation in Table 1. Notice that U samples k uniformly at random in $\mathbb{Z}_q$ (and so does T for k'). At this point, U computes the secret key x and verifies that

$$g^x = c \cdot y_T^{\rho(c)}.$$

The certified address A is the value $H(c)$.

(**Signature Verification**). Given a self-certified public key $c \in \mathbb{G}$, the signature verification process works by first extracting the embedded public key y and then using the standard verification. The only operation that needs to be added is the extracting procedure (step 2 on the right of Table 1).

(**Certified Transaction**). Let S be an address and R a certified address. Before sending bitcoins to the address R, the payer S checks whether there already exists a transaction redeemed by R in the ledger. Notice that R can ensure that such a transaction exists by sending some bitcoins to itself (i.e. a self-transaction). We call the first redeemed transaction of a certified address the *address certification transaction*.

The correctness of the public key derivation follows:

$$g^x = g^{k+k'+\rho(c)x_T} = g^{k+k'} \cdot g^{\rho(c)x_T} = c \cdot y_T^{\rho(c)} \tag{1}$$

For a comprehensive list of the possible interactions between standard and certified addresses we refer to Figure 1.

---

[4] By description here we mean a (binary) encoding of $\mathbb{G}$ and its operations that can be programmed into a computer.

Table 1. Comparison between Bitcoin and Certified Bitcoin. In both systems, the value A represents the Bitcoin address. The certified key generation is blinded while the transaction verification needs only a single extra step (step 2 on the right). All operations on the exponents are taken modulo q.

Standard Bitcoin	Certified Bitcoin
Common inputs: $\mathbb{G}, g$	**Common inputs:** $\mathbb{G}, g, y_{\mathsf{T}}$
Standard Key Generation:	Certified Key Generation:
User 1. $x \leftarrow \mathbb{Z}_q$ 2. $y := g^x$ 3. $A := H(y)$	User / CA 1. $k \leftarrow \mathbb{Z}_q$ 2. $h := g^k$ $\xrightarrow{h}$ 3. $k' \leftarrow \mathbb{Z}_q$ 4. $c := h \cdot g^{k'}$ 5. $e := \rho(c)$ $\xleftarrow{c, \bar{x}}$ 6. $\bar{x} := k' + e \cdot x_{\mathsf{T}}$ 7. $x := \bar{x} + k$ 8. $A := H(c)$.
Standard Verification:	Certified Verification:
1. **Check** $A = H(y)$; 2. **Check** $\mathsf{Vrf}_y^{ECDSA}([T], \tau)$	1. **Check** $A = H(c)$; 2. **Set** $y := c \cdot y_{\mathsf{T}}^{\rho(c)}$ 3. **Check** $\mathsf{Vrf}_y^{ECDSA}([T], \tau)$

3.2 Implementation Designs

Because of how Bitcoin handles transactions internally, it is not possible to check that an address is certified by just looking at the transaction script. A standard transaction script is shown below:

```
scriptPubKey: OP_DUP OP_HASH160 <pubKeyHash> OP_EQUALVERIFY OP_CHECKSIG
scriptSig:    <sig> <pubKey>
```

where `scriptPubKey` is the input script and `scriptSig` is the output script. To verify a transaction, the following actions are performed: (1) after stacking up the signature of the transaction and the redeemer's public key, (2) the latter is hashed by the `OP_HASH160` operation and (3) the hashed valued is compared with the `<pubKeyHash>` value. The problem is that such a value is a hash of the public key and *not* a bitcoin address. The operation `OP_CHECKSIG` is able to

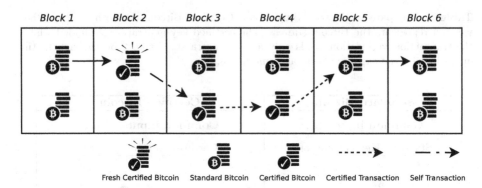

Fig. 1. Certified Bitcoin transactions: The figure shows all possible types of transactions in a ledger with both standard and certified bitcoins. In the second block, a bitcoin is sent to a newly created and supposedly-certified address. This first self transaction in the third block designate that address as indeed certified. In the 5th block, bitcoins are sent from a certified address to a standard address. The last transaction is between standard bitcoin addresses.

distinguish whether the address is certified (by applying the certified signature verification algorithm), but it has no way to report the type of address to the Bitcoin client.

There are a few ways to implement our proposal into the Bitcoin client. We briefly describe three viable options next.

New operation OP_EXTCERTKEY. For this implementation, we extend the scripting language with a new operation OP_EXTCERTKEY that takes a self-certified public key c as input and then extracts the public key y from it, pushing the extracted key y into the stack, and then re-using the standard signature operation OP_CHECKSIG to verify the signature against the extracted key (now in the stack). The size of the transaction would increase by the size of the new operation code (1 byte):

```
scriptPubKey: OP_DUP OP_HASH160 <pubKeyHash> OP_EQUALVERIFY OP_EXTCERTKEY
              OP_CHECKSIG
```

New operation OP_CHECKCERTSIG. Instead, we could extend the scripting language with a new operation OP_CHECKCERTSIG that will exclusively handle certified transactions by first extracting the public key y from the self-certified public key c to later perform the standard signature verification. The transaction script for a *certified* transaction replaces the standard operation OP_CHECKSIG with this new operation:

```
scriptPubKey: OP_DUP OP_HASH160 <pubKeyHash> OP_EQUALVERIFY
              OP_CHECKCERTSIG
```

Modify the operation OP_CHECKSIG. Another way is to just modify the client to interpret each transaction as possibly a certified transaction. In this case, the client would first execute the script normally, but if it failed, it would re-attempt the execution using the certified transaction algorithm (i.e., performing an operation such as OP_CHECKCERTSIG instead of OP_CHECKSIG). The client would then report one of (a) successful standard transaction; (b) successful certified transaction; or (c) verification failure accordingly. The Bitcoin scripting language is unmodified in this approach.

3.3   Security Requirements and Goals

A standard Bitcoin address is self-generated, while a certified address is jointly computed with the involvement of the CA. Thus, it is natural to require that Bitcoin transactions be hard to forge even by a malicious CA. Another security requirement is that certificates must be *unforgeable*—if the adversary does not know the CA's secret key, it cannot generate a certificate and a transaction (signature) through that certificate. Certified Bitcoin addresses share some ideas with both Self-Certified Public Keys [7] and Blind Signatures [6]. The security of our construction holds in the GGM which is the same on which the security of standard Bitcoin relies on. This allows us to provide a security analysis of the protocol within a single and well-defined model.

Crucial to our security formulation is the stipulation that an address be recognized as certified only after it issues a signature (i.e., there is a certified transaction in the public ledger which redeems from it). Indeed, in the absence of the burden of demonstrating knowledge of the secret key, it is trivial for an adversary to "pretend" to have a certificate, since the output c of an (honest-party) execution of the certification protocol is simply an uniformly distributed element in $\mathbb{G}$.

While, by unforgeability of ECDSA, the adversary can not redeem bitcoins from the related address, they may still pretend that the address has been certified. This attack makes no sense in the context of standard Bitcoin addresses: A rational adversary willing to maximize their gain would prefer to exhibit an address for which the secret key is known (to be able to spend any received coins). In our context, on the other hand, if a malicious user falsely claims that an address is certified, it may induce other users to complete unpremeditated transactions.

4   Security of the Certified Bitcoin Addresses

In this section we provide a formal security experiment that captures the informal requirements given in Section 3. Then we show that no PPT generic adversary can win the experiment, providing a formal proof of security to our construction.

We recall that the GGM captures algorithms that access group operations (and indeed the group encoding) through black box function calls. The proofs are inspired by the techniques described in Naccache et al. [10].

In the GGM, the group encoding $\sigma(\cdot) : \mathbb{Z}_q \to \mathbb{G}$ represents an *encoding oracle* that implements a homomorphism from $\mathbb{Z}_q$ onto $\mathbb{G}$.

As before, we employ a function $\rho(\cdot)$ from $\mathbb{G}$ to $\mathbb{Z}_q$, and via notation overload also see $\rho(\cdot)$ as a function from $\mathbb{G}$ to $\mathbb{Z}_q$. To recall, since $\sigma(\cdot)$ encodes elements of $\mathbb{G}$ into binary strings, these strings may thus be interpreted as the binary expansion of an non-negative integer, and that integer can further be *reduced* by computation of its positive remainder modulo q.

In this setting, one describes the public key $y = g^x$ as $\{\sigma(1), \sigma(x)\}$. This notation just means that the homomorphism $\sigma(\cdot)$ maps 1 to g and therefore maps x to y. $\sigma(\cdot)$ is an exponential notation, so x is unrecoverable from $\sigma(x)$.

The group operation oracle $\cdot \oplus \cdot$ takes two encoded group elements $\sigma(v_1)$, $\sigma(v_2)$, and returns the encoded product $\sigma(v_1 + v_2)$. (Since this is exponential notation, the product translate as a sum in the exponents.) Similarly, given $\sigma(v)$ and an integer u, one can implement the square-and-multiply algorithm for exponentiation, using multiple calls to the group operation oracle, to obtain $\sigma(uv)$. One also needs a group inversion oracle $\ominus\sigma(v) \to \sigma(-v)$.

4.1   Unforgeability Formalizations and Proofs

We now provide a rigorous definition of security for the construction in 3.1 by defining the *Signature Unforgeability Experiment*. This is an adversarial game wherein an attacker may obtain one or more certified addresses by executing the protocol with the CA and/or compromise the CA. To succeed in the experiment, the attacker needs to produce a valid message-signature tuple for a fresh certified public key (i.e., one requested by an honest party to the potentially malicious CA).

Notation: k denotes a security parameter, and $\mathsf{poly}(k)$ a value allowed to grow as a polynomial function of k. $\mathcal{A}$ stands for the attacker or adversary. $\mathsf{CKG}_{P,\mathsf{T}}$ represents the Certified Key Generation protocol described in 3.1, where P is some party. In the adversarial game, the adversary has oracle access $\mathcal{O}_\mathsf{T}$ to the trusted party and can execute the protocol $\mathsf{CKG}_{\mathcal{A},\mathcal{O}_\mathsf{T}}$, obtaining new certified keys at will. It may also compromise the trusted party directly, in which case it can execute the protocol $\mathsf{CKG}_{\mathcal{A},\mathsf{T}}$ entirely as a procedure.

The adversary may also request that new (honest) parties P be instantiated and obtain oracle access $\mathcal{O}_P$ with which to execute $\mathsf{CKG}_{\mathcal{O}_P,\mathcal{O}_\mathsf{T}}$ to produce a certified address c for P. Alternatively, if $\mathcal{A}$ has compromised T, it can execute $\mathsf{CKG}_{\mathcal{O}_P,\mathsf{T}}$, which additionally gives it T's view of P's certificate key generation. Finally the adversary can use oracle access $\mathcal{O}_P$ to request signatures $\mathsf{Sign}_{\mathcal{O}_P}^{\mathsf{ECDSA}}(\cdot)$ on arbitrarily chosen messages. The security experiment is described in Fig. 2.

Informally, we say that an adversary wins an experiment if only if the output of the experiment is 1. The security claim is that, under the GGM, there is no efficient adversary that wins the *Signature Unforgeability Experiment*.

Before stating our first security result, we informally recall the hypothesis of the *Security Theorem* of the ECDSA signature scheme in the GGM (Thrm. 2 in D. Brown [5]). The theorem holds under the assumptions that the private keys and ephemeral keys are uniformly random, the hash function is collision resistance and satisfies two other properties called (1) *zero-resistance*, i.e., an

$\mathsf{Exp}_{\mathcal{A}}^{sig-unf}(k):$

1. $(\mathbb{G}, g, x_\mathsf{T}, y_\mathsf{T}) \leftarrow \mathsf{Gen}(1^k)$ where $|\mathbb{G}| = \mathsf{poly}(k)$, and set $L \leftarrow \emptyset$, $S \leftarrow \emptyset$;
2. $\mathcal{A}$ with input $\mathbb{G}, g, y_\mathsf{T}$ has oracle access to $\mathsf{T} = \mathsf{T}(x_\mathsf{T})$ with which can play the protocol $\mathsf{CKG}_{\cdot,\mathcal{O}_\mathsf{T}}$
   Let $(c, \bar{x})$ be the output of T after any execution of $\mathsf{CKG}_{\mathcal{A},\mathcal{O}_\mathsf{T}}$
   L maintains all certificates whose secrets were produced by $\mathcal{A}$:
   Update $L \leftarrow L \cup \{c\}$;
3. Optionally $\mathcal{A}$ can extract the secret key x_T of the trusted party by compromising it;
4. $\mathcal{A}$ may request that arbitrary honest parties P be instantiated. Specifically, an oracle machine $\mathcal{O}_P$ is instantiated and set in pause state;
5. Through oracle access $\mathcal{O}_P$, $\mathcal{A}$ may request that $\mathsf{CKG}_{\mathcal{O}_P,\mathcal{O}_\mathsf{T}}$ be executed to output a certified address $c = c_P$ for P ($\mathcal{A}$ has bystander view of an honest party enrollment);
6. If $\mathcal{A}$ has compromised T, it may request that $\mathsf{CKG}_{\mathcal{O}_P,\mathsf{T}}$ be executed, giving $\mathcal{A}$ the trusted party view of an honest party enrollment;
7. $\mathcal{A}$ may request that honest party P sign arbitrary messages m of $\mathcal{A}$'s choice, executing $\tau \leftarrow \mathsf{Sign}_{\mathcal{O}_P}^{\mathsf{ECDSA}}(m) = \mathsf{SignECDSA}_{c_P \cdot y_\mathsf{T}^{\rho(c_P)}}(m)$
   Let (c_P, m, τ) be the output after any such execution
   S maintains the set of signatures directly given to A:
   Update $S \leftarrow S \cup \{(c_P, m, \tau)\}$;
8. Eventually $\mathcal{A}$ outputs a triple $s = (c, m, \tau)$; if

$$\mathsf{Vrf}_y^{\mathsf{ECDSA}}(m, \tau) = 1 \text{ and } c' \notin L, \text{ and } s \notin S$$

holds where $y = c \cdot y_\mathsf{T}^{\rho(c)}$, then output 1 else 0.

Fig. 2. The $\mathsf{Exp}^{sig-unf}$ experiment

adversary cannot find a message that the hash function maps to 0^k), and (2) *uniformity*, roughly, the distribution of the output value of the hash function on input a uniformly and random message is statistically close to the uniform distribution (see [5] for more details). These two properties are generally believed to hold true in practice for cryptographic hash functions in current usage, in particular the ones employed in the Bitcoin protocol.

Theorem 1. *If the Bitcoin's hash function is collision resistant, zero resistant and uniform, and the ephemeral keys are uniformly random, then there is no efficient, generic adversary that achieves a non-negligible probability of success in* $\mathsf{Exp}^{sig-unf}$.

We prove the theorem by transforming the above experiment into related ones by reasoning about the adversary view (hybrid argument).

First, we note that we can assume that $\mathcal{A}$ always compromises T right after receiving the public parameters. Indeed, the adversarial goal in the experiment is the same whether T is compromised or not, and $\mathcal{A}$'s view of the experiment is strictly enlarged by directly playing the role of T throughout.

Now we look into more detail on the protocol algorithm CKG within the GGM. Whenever a party chooses some random value r and needs to compute $g^r \in \mathbb{G}$, it actually needs to consult the encoding oracle for $\sigma(r)$. The encoding oracle in a GGM simulation maintains a list of previously asked for inputs i_j it has been given and the values it has returned for them: $\{i_1, \sigma_1 = \sigma(i_1), \ldots, i_n, \sigma_n = \sigma(i_n)\}$. If the new input r matches an earlier i_ℓ, it will return the corresponding σ_ℓ. Otherwise, it generates a completely new random binary string z, newly defines $\sigma(r) := z$ and appends to its list $\{i_1, \sigma_1, \ldots, i_n, \sigma_n, i_{n+1} = r, \sigma_{n+1} = \sigma(r) = z\}$, returning z to the caller.

We now modify the experiment simulation to $\overline{\mathsf{Exp}}_{\mathcal{A}}^{sig-unf}$. The only difference between $\overline{\mathsf{Exp}}_{\mathcal{A}}^{sig-unf}$ and $\mathsf{Exp}_{\mathcal{A}}^{sig-unf}$ is as follows: When an honest party P engages with $\mathcal{A}$ (impersonating T) to obtain a certificate, and $\mathcal{A}$ generates k' and attempts to compute $c = hg^{k'} = \sigma(k + k')$, where k is the randomness computed by P; then if the GGM oracle already has some $i_\ell = k + k'$ in its list of previously encoded group elements, the experiment $\overline{\mathsf{Exp}}_{\mathcal{A}}^{sig-unf}$ terminates early, with $\mathcal{A}$ victorious. Let us call Coll this event. Otherwise, it continues identically as $\mathsf{Exp}_{\mathcal{A}}^{sig-unf}$, i.e., the GGM oracle computes an entirely new random string $c = \sigma(k + k')$ and returns it to $\mathcal{A}$.

We claim that $\mathcal{A}$'s additional probability of success in $\overline{\mathsf{Exp}}_{\mathcal{A}}^{sig-unf}$ versus $\mathsf{Exp}_{\mathcal{A}}^{sig-unf}$ is negligible. For if the adversary were able to compute k' such that $k' = i_\ell - k$ for a previously seen i_ℓ, it would also be able to extract the discrete logarithm $k = i_\ell - k'$ from $h = g^k$, given only h. The claim then obviously follows by the standard security assumption of hardness of the Discrete Logarithm Problem in elliptic curves (ECDLP).

Within $\overline{\mathsf{Exp}}_{\mathcal{A}}^{sig-unf}$ it holds that even when honest party P interacts with a malicious trusted party, the protocol execution guarantees that c, and thus the random contribution $\bar{x} = k' + \rho(c) \cdot x_{\mathsf{T}}$ of T to P's private key $x = \bar{x} + k$ is uniformly and randomly distributed.

Specifically, let u be the number of instantiated honest parties P (i.e., u is the number of execution of the CKG protocol between an honest party and the trusted party) and let ϵ bound the probability that a PPT generic algorithm solves the DLP in $\mathbb{G}$, we have that:

$$\Pr\left[\mathsf{Exp}_{\mathcal{A}}^{sig-unf}(k) = 1\right] \leq \Pr\left[\overline{\mathsf{Exp}}_{\mathcal{A}}^{sig-unf}(k) = 1\right] \leq$$

$$\leq \Pr\left[\overline{\mathsf{Exp}}_{\mathcal{A}}^{sig-unf}(k) = 1 \,|\, \neg\mathsf{Coll}\right] + \Pr\left[\mathsf{Coll}\right] \leq$$

$$\leq \Pr\left[\overline{\mathsf{Exp}}_{\mathcal{A}}^{sig-unf}(k) = 1 \,|\, \neg\mathsf{Coll}\right] + u \cdot \epsilon$$

If $\neg\mathsf{Coll}$ holds the experiment guarantees that the honest parties private keys are uniformly and randomly generated. Notice that the experiment $\overline{\mathsf{Exp}}_{\mathcal{A}}^{sig-unf}$ under the condition $\neg\mathsf{Coll}$ is equivalent to u independent and parallel executions of the existential forgery experiment under the chosen-message attack of the ECDSA. We now can directly invoke the security of ECDSA in GGM. In fact, the private keys are uniformly and random, and by hypothesis, the hash function is collision resistance, zero-resistance and uniform and the ephemeral keys are uniformly and random.

Specifically, let ϵ_{crh} be the probability under collision resistance attack for the underlying hash function, then:

$$\Pr\left[\mathsf{Exp}_{\mathcal{A}}^{sig-unf}(k) = 1\right] \leq u \cdot (\epsilon_{crs} + \mathsf{poly}(k) \cdot \epsilon)$$

where the $\mathsf{poly}(k)$ depends on the running time of the adversary.   □

In the above we did *not* prove that the generation of certificates itself was unforgeable—indeed, by disclosing T's private key to $\mathcal{A}$ we made it trivial for $\mathcal{A}$ to generate new certificates. Merely proving that a malicious T cannot bias the selection of private keys by honest parties was sufficient given that the Bitcoin construction requires issuing a signature to complete certificate validation. We now consider the issue of unforgeability of certificates separately.

The property is not strictly necessary to the security of the certified Bitcoin address construction, since without a previously seen signature issued by a Bitcoin address, it cannot be considered certified. However, it provides evidence that our Certified Key Generation mechanism can be used in any cryptographic application, provided that the certificate be accompanied by a proof of knowledge of the certificate's associated private key.

We omit a formal definition of security requirements of self-certified public schemes here for conciseness reasons, and instead refer the reader to [7]. More specifically, we provide an adversarial-game formulation of security for the following claim: When the trusted party is honest, adversaries cannot on their own generate certificates on public keys for which they know the private key.

$\mathsf{Exp}_{\mathcal{A}}^{cert-unf}(k)$:

1. $(\mathbb{G}, g, x_\mathsf{T}, y_\mathsf{T}) \leftarrow \mathsf{Gen}(1^k)$ where $|\mathbb{G}| = \mathsf{poly}(k)$, and set $L \leftarrow \emptyset$;
2. $\mathcal{A}$ with input $\mathbb{G}, g, y_\mathsf{T}$ has oracle access to $\mathsf{T} = \mathsf{T}(x_\mathsf{T})$ with which can play the protocol $\mathsf{CKG}_{\cdot, \mathcal{O}_\mathsf{T}}$
   Let $(c, \bar{x})$ be the output of T after any execution of $\mathsf{CKG}_{\mathcal{A}, \mathcal{O}_\mathsf{T}}$
   L maintains all certificates whose secrets were produced by $\mathcal{A}$:
   Update $L \leftarrow L \cup \{c\}$;
3. Eventually $\mathcal{A}$ outputs x, c; if

$$y = g^x = c \cdot y_\mathsf{T}^{\rho(c)}, \text{ where } c \notin L$$

holds then output 1 else 0.

The security claim is that, under the GGM, there is no efficient adversary $\mathcal{A}$ that wins the *Certificate Unforgeability Experiment* $\mathsf{Exp}^{cert-unf}$.

Theorem 2. *There is no efficient, generic adversary that achieves a non-negligible probability of success in* $\mathsf{Exp}^{cert-unf}$.

As a generic algorithm, $\mathcal{A}$ works as follows: It maintains a list of linear polynomials $\{F_i\}$, where $F_i = \alpha_i + \beta_i X$, and the coefficients lie in $\mathbb{Z}_q$. The list is initiated as $\{F_1 = 1, F_2 = X\}$. The algorithm also maintains a list $\{\sigma_i\}$ of encodings, initiated as $\{\sigma_1 = \sigma(1), \sigma_2 = \sigma(x_\mathsf{T})\}$. At the k-th time the algorithm queries the oracle, it provides the indices i, j and a bit b, and the oracle responds with either $\sigma_k = \sigma_i \oplus \sigma_j$ or $\sigma_i \oplus (\ominus \sigma_j)$, according to the case $b = 0$ or $b = 1$, respectively. The algorithm adds σ_k and $F_k = F_i \pm F_j \mod q$ to each of the respective lists, with the $+$ sign being chosen if $b = 0$. (So it is the same sign as in the definition of σ_k in terms of σ_i and σ_j.) Without loss of generality, we may assume that the F_i are distinct linear polynomials with coefficients in $\mathbb{Z}_q$. If, during the execution of the protocol, it happens that $F_i(x) = F_j(x) \mod q$, with $i \neq j$, it follows that $F = F_i - F_j$ is a non-zero polynomial, with $F(x_\mathsf{T}) = 0 \mod q$. This can allow $\mathcal{A}$ to solve it for x_T, thus extracting the trusted party's secret. If the discrete logarithm is hard in $\mathbb{G}$ this can only happen with negligible probability, and we can rule out the occurrence of such execution sequences from the game simulation (called *unsafe* sequences in GGM terminology).

Consider now an algorithm that produces a tuple (c, x), after u queries to the group operation oracle. Note that in this case, the verification equation implies that $c = \sigma(x - \rho(c) \cdot x_\mathsf{T})$. Let $e = \rho(c)$ and $P = x - e \cdot X$. If P is not in the list of oracle queries performed by the algorithm, augment the list by adding $F_{u+1} = P$ at the end, and increment the number of queries $u \leftarrow u + 1$.

Let F_j be the unique appearance of the polynomial P in the list, without loss of generality. Remind that, from the hardness of DL problem in $\mathbb{G}$, there does not exist a index i such that $F_i(x_\mathsf{T}) \equiv F_j(x_\mathsf{T}) \mod q$. This implies that the group operation oracle may return a random value for σ_j, because F_j represents a query for a new encoding when the encoding oracle is called at step j. The probability that σ_j equals c is therefore, no more than $1/|\mathbb{G}|$, as (almost) all values are now equally likely. In other words, the probability that the adversary will arrive at such an execution sequence is $1/|\mathbb{G}|$ for each oracle query, and thus overall negligible if given only a polynomial number of queries.   □

Implication of Certificate Unforgeability to Identity Theft Mitigation. Let us briefly consider the implications of certificate unforgeability for our construction, where the certification authority is functionally trustworthy, and indeed collects proofs of (real-world) identity from the entities it certifies. Now, recall the attack scenario where a man-in-the-middle (MITM) attacker changes the payee's Bitcoin address for the attacker's address. Since (by the result above) an attacker cannot forge certificates, the payee has a recourse to report the fraud and bind it to the identity of the malicious party, with cooperation of the CA. To provide a full proof of security of this fact we would have to provide (verbose, but intuitively straightforward) formalizations of CA functional trust and of identity theft in the context of our Bitcoin construction—for reasons of brevity we refrain from expanding on it here.

5   Conclusion

The decentralized nature of Bitcoin is a critical component of its success. In this paper we describe an optional Bitcoin address certification mechanism that incorporates trustworthiness from real-world entities into the system, to mitigate against existing reservations to the adoption of Bitcoin as a legitimate currency. We describe how to implement the scheme with the current Bitcoin ledger, allowing certified and non-certified addresses to be used concurrently. In addition, we provide a proof of security within an adversarial-game security model, under the Generic Group Model of computation.

Acknowledgments. This research was supported in part by the PRIN project TENACE.

References

1. Androulaki, E., Karame, G.O., Roeschlin, M., Scherer, T., Capkun, S.: Evaluating user privacy in bitcoin. In: Sadeghi, A.-R. (ed.) FC 2013. LNCS, vol. 7859, pp. 34–51. Springer, Heidelberg (2013)
2. Andrychowicz, M., Dziembowski, S., Malinowski, D., Mazurek, L.: Secure multiparty computations on bitcoin. Cryptology ePrint Archive, Report 2013/784 (2013), http://eprint.iacr.org/
3. Ateniese, G., de Medeiros, B.: A provably secure nyberg-rueppel signature variant with applications. Cryptology ePrint Archive, Report 2004/093 (2004), http://eprint.iacr.org/
4. Barber, S., Boyen, X., Shi, E., Uzun, E.: Bitter to better how to make bitcoin a better currency. In: Keromytis, A.D. (ed.) FC 2012. LNCS, vol. 7397, pp. 399–414. Springer, Heidelberg (2012)
5. Brown, D.R.L.: The exact security of ecdsa. Technical report, Advances in Elliptic Curve Cryptography (2000)
6. Chaum, D.: Blind signatures for untraceable payments. In: Chaum, D., Rivest, R.L., Sherman, A.T. (eds.) CRYPTO, pp. 199–203. Plenum Press, New York (1982)
7. Girault, M.: Self-certified public keys. In: Davies, D.W. (ed.) EUROCRYPT 1991. LNCS, vol. 547, pp. 490–497. Springer, Heidelberg (1991)
8. Meiklejohn, S., Pomarole, M., Jordan, G., Levchenko, K., McCoy, D., Voelker, G.M., Savage, S.: A fistful of bitcoins: Characterizing payments among men with no names. In: Proceedings of the 2013 Conference on Internet Measurement Conference, IMC 2013, pp. 127–140. ACM, New York (2013)
9. Miers, I., Garman, C., Green, M., Rubin, A.D.: Zerocoin: Anonymous distributed e-cash from bitcoin. In: Proceedings of the 2013 IEEE Symposium on Security and Privacy, SP 2013, pp. 397–411. IEEE Computer Society, Washington, DC (2013)
10. Naccache, D., Pointcheval, D., Stern, J.: Twin signatures: an alternative to the hash-and-sign paradigm. In: Proceedings of the 8th ACM Conference on Computer and Communications Security (ACM CCS), pp. 20–27 (2001)
11. Nakamoto, S.: Bitcoin: A peer-to-peer electronic cash system. Consulted 1, 2012 (2008)
12. Nyberg, K., Rueppel, R.: A new signature scheme based on the DSA giving message recovery. In: Proceedings of the First ACM Conference on Computer and Communications Security (ACM CCS 1993), pp. 58–61. ACM Press (1993)
13. Ober, M., Katzenbeisser, S., Hamacher, K.: Structure and anonymity of the bitcoin transaction graph. Future Internet 5(2), 237–250 (2013)

14. Petersen, H., Horster, P.: Self-certified keys – concepts and applications. In: Proceedings of the Third Conference on Communications and Multimedia Security. Chapman & Hall (1997)
15. Pointcheval, D., Stern, J.: Security proofs for signature schemes. In: Maurer, U.M. (ed.) EUROCRYPT 1996. LNCS, vol. 1070, pp. 387–398. Springer, Heidelberg (1996)
16. Ron, D., Shamir, A.: Quantitative analysis of the full bitcoin transaction graph. In: Sadeghi, A.-R. (ed.) FC 2013. LNCS, vol. 7859, pp. 6–24. Springer, Heidelberg (2013)
17. Saeednia, S.: A note on girault's self-certified model. Information Processing Letters 86(6), 323–327 (2003)
18. Wired.com. Bitcoin bubble bursts as china cracks down on digital currency (December 2013),
http://www.wired.com/wiredenterprise/2013/12/china_crackdown/
19. X9.62-2005, Public Key Cryptography for the Financial Services Industry: The Elliptic Curve Digital Signature Standard (ECDSA) (November 2005)

Leakage Resilient Proofs of Ownership in Cloud Storage, Revisited*

Jia Xu and Jianying Zhou

Infocomm Security Department, Institute for Infocomm Research, Singapore
{xuj,jyzhou}@i2r.a-star.edu.sg

Abstract. Client-side deduplication is a very effective mechanism to reduce both storage and communication cost in cloud storage service. Halevi *et al.* (CCS '11) discovered security vulnerability in existing implementation of client-side deduplication and proposed a cryptographic primitive called "proofs of ownership" (PoW) as a countermeasure. In a proof of ownership scheme, any owner of the same file can prove to the cloud storage server that he/she owns that file in an efficient and secure manner, even if a bounded amount of any efficiently extractable information of that file has been leaked. We revisit Halevi *et al.*'s formulation of PoW and significantly improve the understanding and construction of PoW. Our contribution is twofold: Firstly, we propose a generic and conceptually simple approach to construct *Privacy-Preserving* Proofs of Ownership scheme, by leveraging on well-known primitives (i.e. Randomness Extractor and Proofs of Retrievability) and technique (i.e. sample-then-extract). Our approach can be roughly described as Privacy-Preserving PoW = Randomness Extractor + Proofs of Retrievability. Secondly, in order to provide a better instantiation of Privacy-Preserving-PoW, we propose a novel design of randomness extractor with large output size, which improves the state of art by reducing both the random seed length and entropy loss (i.e. the difference between the entropy of input and output) simultaneously.

Keywords: Cloud Storage, Client-side Deduplication, Proofs of Ownership, Leakage Resilience, Privacy-Preserving, Proofs of Retrievability, Randomness Extractor, Sample-then-Extract.

1 Introduction

Cloud storage service (e.g. Dropbox, Skydrive, Google Drive, iCloud, Amazon S3) is becoming more and more popular in recent years [2]. The volume of personal or business data stored in cloud storage keeps increasing [3,4,5]. In face to the challenge of rapidly growing volume of data in cloud, deduplication technique is highly demanded to save disk space by removing duplicated copies of the same file (Single Instance Storage). SNIA white paper [6] reported that the deduplication technique can save up to 90% storage, dependent on applications.

---

* This work is supported by Singapore A*STAR project SecDC-112172014. The full version of this work is available at Cryptology ePrint Archive, Report 2013/514 [1].

I. Boureanu, P. Owesarski, and S. Vaudenay (Eds.): ACNS 2014, LNCS 8479, pp. 97–115, 2014.
© Springer International Publishing Switzerland 2014

Traditional deduplication technique (i.e. server side deduplication [7,8,9,10]) in centralized storage system removes duplicated copies residing in the same server. Unlike server-side deduplication, client-side deduplication in cloud storage system will identify duplicated copies such that one copy resides in the cloud storage server and the other resides remotely in the cloud client, and saves the uploading bandwidth (time, respectively) for the duplicated file. In both server and client side deduplication, all owners of the deduplicated file will be provided a soft link to the unique copy of that file stored in the centralized storage or cloud storage respectively. In contrast to server-side deduplication which saves only storage on server side, client-side deduplication saves not only server storage but also network bandwidth and transmission time, and benefits both cloud server and client.

However, how to implement client-side deduplication *securely* in an untrusted environment, is far more challenging than it first appears [11,12]. Arguably, the root cause of the difference between security requirements of server-side and client-side deduplication, is that server-side deduplication is executed in the trusted server, while client-side deduplication is distributively executed between the trusted[1] cloud server and potentially untrusted cloud client. Here the cloud user is considered as potentially untrusted, since anyone from the untrusted Internet could become a cloud user and the cloud server is unable to distinguish honest users from malicious users (i.e adversaries) in general.

Server side deduplication may simply apply a collision resistant hash function (say SHA256) to identity duplicated files in the storage server, and remove the extra copies to achieve "single instance storage". An existing implementation of client-side deduplication (called as "hash-as-a-proof" method) is as below: Cloud storage server keeps a lookup table, which records hash value of each file in its storage. Cloud user Alice, who tries to upload file F to the cloud storage, will firstly send hash value $\mathsf{hash}(F)$ to the cloud server. If $\mathsf{hash}(F)$ is not found in the lookup table, then Alice should upload file F to the cloud storage and cloud server will update the lookup table by adding entry $\mathsf{hash}(F)$. Otherwise, cloud server has a copy of F already, which could be uploaded by other users. Consequently Alice's uploading process will be saved, and Alice is allowed to download F from cloud server on demand. In the above method, the knowledge of hash value $\mathsf{hash}(F)$ is treated as a "proof" that Alice owns file F. Previously, Dropbox[2] applied the above "hash-as-a-proof" method on block-level cross-users deduplication [12][13].

Halevi *et al.* [12] targets the critical security vulnerability in the above "hash-as-a-proof" method, where the leakage of a short hash value $\mathsf{hash}(F)$ would lead (or amplify) to leakage of entire file F to outside adversary. Their work proposes a cryptographic primitive called "proofs of ownership" (PoW) to address

---

[1] The cloud server is trusted in data integrity and availability in this work.

[2] In Feb 2012, we noticed that Dropbox disabled the deduplication across different users, probably due to recent vulnerabilities discovered in their original cross-user client-side deduplication method. This also indicates the importance and urgency in the study of security in client-side deduplication.

such leakage amplification vulnerability. The distinguishable feature of Halevi *et al.* [12] from all of previous study in security of deduplication (e.g. convergent encryption [7,8,14]), is that Halevi *et al.* [12] adopts a *bounded leakage model* to characterize the untrusted environment in which the client-side deduplication runs. Their formulation requires that, after a setup between one owner of file F and the cloud storage server, any owner of F can efficiently *prove* (in the sense of "interactive proof system" [15]) to the cloud storage server that he/she indeed owns file F without really transmitting F, even if a bounded amount of any efficiently extractable information of F has been leaked via some owner (considered as the accomplice or colluder) of F intentionally or unintentionally.

In this work, we revisit Halevi *et al.* [12]'s formulation, and extend it in two aspects: (1) We shift a significant amount of workload (precisely, the setup procedure) from cloud server to a cloud user, which reflects our understanding of real world setting—the average computation power allocated to each online user by cloud server is typically smaller than the computation power of an average cloud user. (2) We protect data privacy against verifier (e.g. the cloud storage server), during the interactive proof protocol. Halevi *et al.* [12]'s formulation does not address privacy protection of user data against the cloud storage server. Prudent users may have reasons to not trust the cloud server. For example, the cloud server may be hacked (e.g.[16]), making it a single point of failure of user data privacy. In addition, the cloud server may make careless technical mistakes [17,18], which may expose user data to unauthorized persons. In this work, we will trust cloud storage server in data availability and integrity (which is the research topic of proofs of storage [19,20]), but not trust it in data privacy.

1.1 Overview of Our Result

Under the framework of Halevi *et al.* [12], in a secure PoW scheme, if the input file F has k bits min-entropy to the view of adversary at the very beginning and at most T ($< k - \lambda$) bits of message about F is leaked at adversary's (adaptive) choice, then the adversary should not be able to convince the cloud storage server that he/she owns file F with significant probability.

1.1.1 Generic Construction of Privacy-Preserving-PoW.

Intuitively, our generic construction of Privacy-Preserving-PoW is as below: At first, apply a *proper*[3] randomness extractor over file F to output $T + 2\lambda$ ($< k$) bits almost-uniform random number Y_F. Next, apply a *proper* proofs of retrievability (POR [19]) scheme over Y_F. Since the output Y_F of the randomness extractor is statistically close to true uniform randomness, any adversary that learns at most T bits arbitrary information of F, cannot output the $T + 2\lambda$ bits long value Y_F entirely with significant probability, and thus cannot succeed in the verification of POR scheme. The difference $(k - T)$ is like the *entropy loss* in randomness extractor, thus the smaller the difference $(k - T)$ is , the better the PoW scheme is in aspect of leakage resilience.

---

[3] See Theorem 1 and Theorem 2 for the explanation of "proper" randomness extractor and "proper" POR.

Our result can be combined with convergent encryption or Message-Locked Encryption [7,8,21,10,22], in order to construct strong leakage-resilient client-side deduplication scheme for encrypted data in cloud storage and thus protect data privacy against both outside adversary and curious cloud server.

We remark that formulating and constructing privacy-preserving PoW scheme are very challenging. Previous work by Ng *et al.* [23] made the first attempt towards this goal, but gave an unsatisfactory solution: As pointed out by Xu *et al.* [21], Ng *et al.* [23] formulates the privacy property *locally* for each block and their scheme suffers from "divide and conquer" attack: If an input file with N blocks has 1 bit min-entropy in each block *independently*, then this file could be recovered by an outside adversary via brute force search in time $\mathcal{O}(N)$ instead of $\mathcal{O}(2^N)$.

1.1.2   Improved Randomness Extractor. Unfortunately, the state of art [24,25] (with restriction of small seed size and practical computation cost) of randomness extractor only gives us a PoW with $k-T = \Omega(|F|)$ and requires relatively large random seed. We propose a new randomness extractor with shorter random seed and results in a PoW with $k - T = \mathcal{O}(|F|^{1-c})$ for any constant $c \in (0,1)$.

Table 1. Compare our PoW scheme with existing works. Unsatisfactory items are highlighted in italic font and red color.

Scheme	Distribution of input	Seed Size	Computation complexity	Privacy-Preserving	Security Model
PoW1 [12]	Any	$\mathcal{O}(\lambda)$	*Expensive [12]*	*No (Leaking whole file F)*	Stand. Model
PoW2 [12]	Any	$\geq 6T$ †	*Prohibitively expensive [12]*	*No*	Stand. Model
PoW3 [12]	*Generalized block-fixing distribution*	$\mathcal{O}(\lambda)$	Practical	*Unclear*	*Rand. Oracle; Unjustified Assump.‡*
This work	Any	$\mathcal{O}(\lambda)$	Practical	Yes	Stand. Model

†T may take value 64MB.

‡ Theorem 3 in [12] relies on an unproven assumption that the code generated by the third construction PoW3 is "good" and authors of [12] admits that it is very hard to analyze this unproven assumption. See text surrounding Theorem 3 in [12].

Table 2. Compare randomness extractors with output size $\ell\rho$, where ℓ could take value as large as $2^{21} \approx 2$ millions. The input is file F. Unsatisfactory items are highlighted in italic font and red color.

Scheme	Distribution of input	Randomness complexity	Computation complexity	Entropy Loss	Security Model
HMAC(s_1,F)‖⋯‖HMAC(s_ℓ,F)	Any	$\ell\lambda$	$\ell|F|$	small	Random Oracle
Inner Product Universal Hash [26]	Any	$2|F|$	$\Omega(|F|\log(\ell\rho))$	$2\log(1/\epsilon)$	Stand. Model
[24]	Any	$\mathcal{O}(\ell\lambda)$	$2|F|\log\ell$	$\Omega(|F|)$	Stand. Model
This work	Any	$\mathcal{O}(\lambda)$	$2|F|\log\ell$	$\mathcal{O}(|F|^{1-c})$ †	Stand. Model

†$c \in (0,1)$

1.2   Contributions

Our main contributions can be summarized as below:

1. We propose a generic and conceptually simple paradigm to construct proof of ownership scheme: PoW=Randomness Extractor + Proofs of retrievability. To the best of our knowledge, this is the first work that bridges the proof of ownership and randomness extractor. Our result improves previous works on PoW in the following aspects: (1) Complete proof of security in standard model for *any* distribution of input file, while still being practical. (2) The first generic framework to construct PoW and benefited from the future advance in randomness extractor or proofs of retrievability. (3) Privacy-Preserving against verifier (e.g. cloud storage server). A detailed comparison between our work and existing PoW schemes is given in Table 1 (on page 100).

2. We propose a novel construction of randomness extractor with large output size, which improves existing work [24] by reducing both the seed length and entropy loss (i.e. the difference between entropy of input and output) *simultaneously*. This new randomness extractor may have independent interest. A detailed comparison between our work and existing randomness extractors is given in Table 2 (on page 100).

1.3   Organizations

We introduce preliminaries and background in Section 2 and formulation in Section 3. We present our overall solution in a modular approach in Section 4 and Section 5: At first in Section 4, we propose the construction of Privacy-Preserving-PoW and analyze its security, by treating an important component (i.e randomness extractor) as black-box. Next, Section 5 constructs the required randomness extractor with rigorous analysis and completes the description of the proposed solution. Section 6 concludes this paper. Due to space constraint, experiment result and most detailed proofs will be available only in full paper [1].

2   Preliminaries and Background

2.1   Notations and Definitions

Key notations in this paper are defined in Table 3 (on page 102).

Definition 1 (Statistical Difference). *The* statistical difference *between two random variables* $\mathbf{X}$ *and* $\mathbf{Y}$ *on the same space* $\mathcal{U}$ *is defined as*

$$\mathsf{SD}(\mathbf{X}, \mathbf{Y}) = \frac{1}{2} \sum_{a \in \mathcal{U}} \left| \Pr[\mathbf{X} = a] - \Pr[\mathbf{Y} = a] \right| \tag{1}$$

Some useful background information about statistical difference is provided in full paper [1].

2.2   Proofs of Retrievability

We adopt the formulation of proofs of retrievability from existing works [27,28] and make some syntactical modifications according to our needs to construct proofs of ownership scheme.

Table 3. Key Notations

Notation	Semantics
λ	The security parameter.
PPT	Probabilistic polynomial time (w.r.t. security parameter λ, if not explicitly stated otherwise).
$[n]$	The set of integers $1, 2, 3, 4, \ldots, n$.
$h(\cdot)$	Full domain collision resistant hash function (e.g. SHA256).
$F[i]$	The projection of bit-string F onto i-th coordinate (i.e. the i-th bit of F, $1 \le i \le |F|$).
$F[\{i_1, \ldots, i_n\}]$	The projection of bit-string F onto the subset of coordinates (i.e $F[i_1]\|F[i_2]\| \ldots \|F[i_n]$, where $1 \le i_1 < i_2 < \ldots < i_n \le |F|$).
$\mathbf{H}_\infty(X)$	min-entropy of random variable X.
$\mathsf{SD}(X, Y)$	Statistical difference between random variables X and Y.
$X \approx_\epsilon Y$	$\mathsf{SD}(X,Y) \le \epsilon$; X is ϵ-close to Y.
$B|_{A=a}$	The conditional distribution of B given that $A = a$ for jointly distributed random variables (A, B).
$x \sim \mathcal{D}$	Sample x according to distribution $\mathcal{D}$.
$U_{|n|}$	Independent uniform random variable over $\{0, 1\}^n$.
$U_{|n|,1},$ $U_{|n|,2,\cdots}$	Independently and identically distributed uniform random variables over $\{0, 1\}^n$.

Definition 2 (Proofs of Retrievability). *A proofs of retrievability (POR) scheme consists of PPT algorithms* KeyGen, Tag, GenChal, GenProof *and* Verify, *which are described as below*

- KeyGen$(1^\lambda) \to (pk, sk)$. *The key generation algorithm takes a security parameter λ as input and outputs a pair of public-private key (pk, sk).*
- Tag$(sk, \{F_i\}_{i=1}^n) \to \{\sigma_i\}_{i=1}^n$. *The tag generation algorithm computes an authentication tag σ_i for each file block F_i.*
- GenChal$(pk, n, c) \to (C, \Psi_F, \Psi_\sigma)$. *The challenger generation algorithm takes as input the public key pk, erasure encoded file size n (in term of blocks), and the sample size c, and outputs a sample $C \subset [n]$ with $|C| = c$ and meta-data (Ψ_F, Ψ_σ).*
- GenProof$(pk, \{(F_i, \sigma_i)\}_{i=1}^n, C, \Psi_F, \Psi_\sigma) \to (\bar{F}, \bar{\sigma})$, *where $\bar{F} :=$ GenProof$_{\mathsf{data}}(pk, \{F_i\}_{i=1}^n, C, \Psi_F)$ and $\bar{\sigma} :=$ GenProof$_{\mathsf{tag}}(pk, \{\sigma_i\}_{i=1}^n, C, \Psi_\sigma)$. The algorithm* GenProof$_{\mathsf{data}}$ *takes as input the public key pk, file blocks F_i's, a sample set $C \subset [n]$, and meta-data Ψ_F, and outputs an aggregated file block denoted as $\bar{F}$. The algorithm* GenProof$_{\mathsf{tag}}$ *takes as input the public key pk, authentication tags σ_i's, a sample set $C \subset [n]$, and meta-data Ψ_σ, and outputs an aggregated authentication tag denoted as $\bar{\sigma}$.*
- Verify$(K, \bar{F}, \bar{\sigma}, \Psi_F, \Psi_\sigma, C) \to$ Accept *or* Reject. *If K is private key sk, then the POR scheme supports private key verifiability; if K is public key pk, then the POR scheme supports public key verifiability.*

We remark that the above formulation is syntactically different from original [27,28] in the sense that we explicitly decompose the algorithm GenProof into two sub-routines: GenProof$_{\mathsf{data}}$ and GenProof$_{\mathsf{tag}}$, where GenProof$_{\mathsf{data}}$ processes selected data blocks F_i ($i \in C$) and GenProof$_{\mathsf{tag}}$ processes corresponding authentication tags σ_i's. Many existing works (e.g. [27,28] and Merkle Hash Tree based POR) support such decomposition, but a few works (e.g. [19]) do not.

For some POR schemes [27,28], meta-data Ψ_F and Ψ_σ are two seeds from which a list of coefficients $\{\alpha_i\}_{i \in C}$, $\{\beta_i\}_{i \in C}$ can be generated, and the aggregated values are $\bar{F} = \sum_{i \in C} \alpha_i F_i$ and $\bar{\sigma} = \sum_{i \in C} \beta_i \sigma_i$.

Definition 3 (Soundness of POR [19,27,28]). *Let $\epsilon \in (0, 1)$. A POR scheme is ϵ-sound, if there exists a PPT extractor algorithm, such that for any prover* *which can convince the verifier to accept with probability $\geq \epsilon$, then the extractor can output the original file with overwhelming high probability (1 - negl) by executing POR proof protocol with the prover.*

Readers may find more details about POR in [19,27,30,28].

2.3 Randomness Extractor

Definition 4 (Strong Extractor). *We say* $\mathsf{Ext} : \{0,1\}^{\ell_{in}} \times \{0,1\}^{\ell_s} \to \{0,1\}^{\ell_{out}}$ *is a strong* (k, ϵ)-*extractor, if for any distribution X over $\{0,1\}^{\ell_{in}}$ with at least k bits min-entropy, the following inequality holds*

$$\mathsf{SD}\Big((\mathsf{Ext}(X;s),s),\ (U_{\ell_{out}},s)\Big) \leq \epsilon \qquad (2)$$

where the seed s is uniformly randomly chosen from $\{0,1\}^{\ell_s}$ and $U_{\ell_{out}}$ is a uniform random variable over $\{0,1\}^{\ell_{out}}$.

It is well known that the output size ℓ_{out} of any randomness extractor can not exceed the min-entropy k of the input (i.e. $\ell_{out} < k$), and the difference $(k - \ell_{out})$ is called the "entropy loss" of the randomness extractor.

3 Formulation: Proofs of Ownership, Revisited

Halevi *et al.* [12] proposed the formulation of proofs of ownership. In this section, we revisit and revise their formulation and propose our definition for privacy-preserving proofs of ownership.

Definition 5 (Proofs of Ownership [12]). *A proof of ownership scheme (*PoW*) consists of a probabilistic algorithm* S *and a pair of probabilistic interactive algorithm* $\langle \mathsf{P}, \mathsf{V} \rangle$*, which are described as below:*

- *$\mathsf{S}(F, 1^\lambda) \to \psi$: The randomized summary function* S *takes a file F and the security parameter λ as input, and outputs a short summary value ψ, where the bit-length of ψ is short and independent on file size $|F|$.*
- *$\langle \mathsf{P}(F), \mathsf{V}(\psi) \rangle \to$ Accept *or* Reject*: The prover algorithm* P *which takes as input a file F, interacts with the verifier algorithm* V *which takes as input a short summary value ψ, and outputs either* Accept *or* Reject*.*

We are only interested in efficient PoW *scheme, such that* V *is polynomial time algorithm w.r.t. security parameter λ and both* S *and* P *are polynomial algorithms in $|F|$ and λ.*

Definition 6 (Completeness of PoW [12]). *A PoW scheme* $(\mathsf{S}, \langle \mathsf{P}, \mathsf{V} \rangle)$ *is complete, if for all positive integer λ and for any file $F \in \{0,1\}^{poly(\lambda)}$, it holds that*

$$\langle \mathsf{P}(F), \mathsf{V}(\mathsf{S}(F, 1^\lambda)) \rangle \text{ always outputs Accept.}$$

3.1 Two Players Setting and Three Players Setting of PoW

In the original framework [12], PoW runs by two players: verifier and prover. In this paper, we will redefine this system model by introducing a third player, called summarizer, who is responsible to preprocess the data file F during the setup. The PoW scheme in three players setting executes in this way: Summarizer (e.g. data owner of F) runs summary function to obtain $\psi := \mathsf{S}(F, 1^\lambda)$ and sends ψ to verifier (e.g. the cloud storage server). Then prover (e.g. some cloud user claiming to own file F), who runs algorithm $\mathsf{P}(F)$, interacts with the verifier, who runs algorithm $\mathsf{V}(\psi)$. A dishonest prover (e.g. dishonest cloud user) may replace the prover algorithm P with any other PPT program of his/her choice.

Definition 7 (Two/Three Players setting of PoW). *For any PoW scheme $(\mathsf{S}, \langle \mathsf{P}, \mathsf{V} \rangle)$, the two players setting and three players setting are described as below:*

- *in a **two players setting**, the summary algorithm S and verifier algorithm V are executed by the first player—verifier (e.g. cloud storage server), and the prover algorithm P is executed by the second player—prover (e.g. cloud user);*

- *in a **three players setting**, the summary algorithm S is executed by the first player—summarizer (e.g. cloud user owning file F), the verifier algorithm V is executed by the second player—verifier (e.g. cloud storage server), and the prover algorithm P is executed by the third player—prover (e.g. another cloud user claiming to own F).*

Our three players setting will further relieve the computation burden of the cloud storage server, and might make our scheme easier to be adopted by cloud storage servers in real applications—This is exactly our initial motivation to introduce the new three players setting of PoW. We believe that, the average computation resource that a cloud storage server allocates to each online user, is typically less than the computation resource of an average cloud user. Additionally, the fact that many cloud storage servers (e.g. Dropbox, Skydrive, and Google Drive) provide free service to public users, further justifies our attempt to shift some computation burden from cloud server to cloud user.

The change from two players setting to three players setting also leads to the change of trust model and thus impact the security formulation. In the original two players setting of PoW [12], preserving privacy of input file F during the interactive proof $\langle \mathsf{P}, \mathsf{V} \rangle$ (like in zero-knowledge proof) is meaningless, since the verifier, who runs V, also runs the summary function $\mathsf{S}(F, 1^\lambda)$ and has direct access to file F. Therefore, the verifier has to be trusted in data confidentiality of input file F in this two players setting. In contrast, in our three players setting, preserving privacy of F during the interactive proof $\langle \mathsf{P}, \mathsf{V} \rangle$ (like in zero-knowledge proof) is an interesting problem, if the verifier (e.g. cloud storage server) is not trusted in data confidentiality.

3.2 Soundness of PoW

Intuitively, PoW aims to prevent leakage amplification in client-side deduplication: If an outside adversary *somehow* obtain a bounded amount ($\leq T$ bits) of messages about the target user file F via out-of-band leakage, then the adversary cannot obtain the whole file F by participating in the client-side deduplication with the cloud storage server.

The security game $\mathsf{G}_{\mathcal{A}}^{\mathsf{PoW}}(k, T)$ between a PPT adversary $\mathcal{A}$ and a challenger w.r.t. PoW scheme $(\mathsf{S}, \langle \mathsf{P}, \mathsf{V} \rangle)$ is defined as below. Here k is the lower bound of min-entropy of the distribution of the challenged file F at the beginning of the game, and the adversary is allowed to learn at most T bits message related to file F (possibly including random coins chosen when processing F) from the challenger via the leakage query.

Setup. The description of $(S, \langle P, V \rangle)$ is made public. Let $\mathcal{D}$ be a distribution over $\{0,1\}^M$ with min-entropy $\geq k$, where $\mathcal{D}$ is chosen by the adversary $\mathcal{A}$ and M is any public positive integer constant. The challenger samples file F according to distribution $\mathcal{D}$ and runs the summary algorithm to obtain $\psi := S(F, 1^\lambda)$.

Learning. The adversary $\mathcal{A}$ can adaptively make polynomially many queries to the challenger, where each query is in one of the following types and concurrent queries of different types are not allowed[4]. Furthermore, the total amount of messages output by all leakage queries should not be greater than the threshold T, i.e. $\mathcal{Y}_I + \mathcal{Y}_{II} \leq T$, where $\mathcal{Y}_I$ and $\mathcal{Y}_{II}$ will be defined below.

- PROVE-QUERY: The challenger, running the verifier algorithm V with input ψ, interacts with the adversary $\mathcal{A}$ which replaces the prover algorithm P, to obtain $b := \langle \mathcal{A}, V(\psi) \rangle$. The adversary $\mathcal{A}$ is given the value of b.
- LEAK-QUERY-I($\mathcal{P}$): This query consists of a description of a PPT algorithm $\mathcal{P}$ (a variant version of prover algorithm). The challenger responses this query by computing the output y of $\mathcal{P}(F)$ after interacting with $V(\psi)$ (i.e. $y := \mathcal{P}(F)^{V(\psi)}$) and sending y to the adversary $\mathcal{A}$. Denote with $\mathcal{Y}_I$ the sum of bit-lengths of all responses y's for this type of queries.
- LEAK-QUERY-II($\mathcal{L}$): This query consists of a description of a PPT algorithm $\mathcal{L}$. Let transcript$_S$ denote the transcript of all steps of operations in the execution of algorithm "$\psi := S(F, 1^\lambda)$" in the above **Setup** phase. The challenger responses this query by computing the output $y := \mathcal{L}(\text{transcript}_S)$ and sending y to the adversary $\mathcal{A}$. Denote with $\mathcal{Y}_{II}$ the sum of bit-lengths of all responses y's for this type of queries.

Challenge. The adversary $\mathcal{A}$ which replaces the prover algorithm P, interacts with the challenger, which runs the verifier algorithm V with input ψ, to obtain $b := \langle \mathcal{A}, V(\psi) \rangle$. The adversary $\mathcal{A}$ wins the game, if $b = \texttt{Accept}$.

Definition 8 (Soundness of PoW (Refining [12])). *A PoW scheme is (k, T, ϵ)-sound in three players setting, if for any PPT adversary $\mathcal{A}$, $\mathcal{A}$ wins the security game $G_{\mathcal{A}}^{\mathsf{PoW}}(k, T)$ with probability not greater than $\epsilon + negl(\lambda)$.*

$$\Pr[\mathcal{A} \text{ wins the security game } G_{\mathcal{A}}^{\mathsf{PoW}}(k, T)] \leq \epsilon + negl(\lambda). \qquad (3)$$

The (k, T, ϵ)-soundness definition in two players setting is the same as the above, except that the adversary $\mathcal{A}$ is not allowed to make LEAK-QUERY-II in the security game $G_{\mathcal{A}}^{\mathsf{PoW}}(k, T)$ (i.e. $\mathcal{Y}_{II} = 0$).

---

[4] Concurrent PROVE-QUERY and LEAK-QUERY would allow the adversary to replay messages back and forth between these two queries, and eliminate the possibility of any secure and efficient solution to PoW. Therefore, the framework of Halevi *et al.* [12] do not allow concurrent queries of different types in the security formulation. We clarify that, concurrent queries of the same type can be supported. Thus, in the real application, the cloud storage server (verifier) can safely interact with multiple cloud users (prover) w.r.t. the same file concurrently.

We remark that (1) the (k, T, ϵ)-soundness definition in two players setting is essentially the same as the original formulation [12], and (2) soundness in three players setting implies soundness in two players setting, but not vice versa.

3.3 Privacy-Preserving PoW

Intuitively, we say a PoW scheme is privacy-preserving against the verifier, if everything about file F that the verifier can learn after participating the PoW scheme w.r.t. F, can be computed from the short summary value of F and some almost-perfect uniform random number.

Definition 9 (Privacy-Preserving). *A PoW scheme* $(\mathsf{S}, \langle \mathsf{P}, \mathsf{V} \rangle)$ *is* (k, T, ϵ)-*privacy-preserving against the verifier (in the three players setting), if for any distribution $\mathcal{D}$ over $\{0,1\}^M$ with at least k bits min-entropy, for every PPT interactive algorithm V^*, there exists a PPT algorithm Sim and a random variable Z over domain $\{0,1\}^{T+\lambda+\Omega(\lambda)}$, such that*

- $\mathsf{SD}(Z, U_{|Z|}) \leq \epsilon$, *where $U_{|Z|}$ is the uniform random variable over $\{0,1\}^{|Z|}$;*
- *for any function $f : \{0,1\}^M \rightarrow \{0,1\}$, and any (leakage) function $\mathcal{L} : \{0,1\}^M \rightarrow \{0,1\}^{\leq T}$, the following two probabilities (taken over file $F \sim \mathcal{D}$ and the random coins of related algorithms) are equal*

$$\Pr\Big[\mathsf{V}^*\big(\psi\|\mathcal{L}(F)\big)^{\mathsf{P}(F)} = f(F)\Big] = \Pr\Big[\mathsf{Sim}\big(\psi\|\mathcal{L}(F), Z\big) = f(F)\Big],$$

where $\psi := \mathsf{S}(F, 1^\lambda)$ and $\mathsf{V}^*(\mathsf{S}(F, 1^\lambda)\|\mathcal{L}(F))^{\mathsf{P}(F)}$ denotes the output of (dishonest) verifier V^* taking the summary value $\mathsf{S}(F, 1^\lambda)$ and leakage information $\mathcal{L}(F)$ as input and having interaction with interactive prover algorithm $\mathsf{P}(F)$.

As we discussed before, preserving privacy against the verifier for any PoW scheme in the two players setting, is impossible.

3.4 Clarification on Leakage of User ID and Password

We admit that, as the same as Halevi *et al.* [12], this work will consider leakage of user account (i.e. id and password) as out of scope. We assume the user account is associated to user's real identity (e.g. mobile phone number) and sibyl account is hard to create. Thus, leakage of user file stored in cloud storage by disclosure of user account could be traced back to the source and the corresponding account could be disabled without affecting honest users.

4 Generic Construction of Proofs of Ownership

4.1 Some Unsatisfactory Approaches

At first, putting privacy-preserving property aside, we review some straightforward approaches and existing works for PoW as below.

4.1.1 Compute fresh MACs online on Both Sides.
To prove his/her ownership of a file F, the prover can compute a MAC (i.e. Message Authentication Code) value over F with a random nonce as key, where the random nonce is chosen by the verifier. To verify the correctness of this MAC value, the verifier need to re-compute the MAC value of F under the same key. This approach is secure, but rejected for two reasons: (1) in some applications of PoW, the verifier

does not have access to the file F; (2) the stringent requirement on efficiency (including disk IO efficiency) given by Halevi *et al.* [12] does not allow verifier to access entire file F during the interactive proof.

4.1.2   Pre-compute MACs offline. In the summary phase, t number of keys $s_1, \ldots, s_t$ are randomly chosen and t number of MAC values $\mathsf{MAC}_{s_i}(F)$'s are computed correspondingly. The summary value of file F is $\{(i, s_i, \mathsf{MAC}_{s_i}(F)) : i \in [t]\}$. In the i-th proof session, the verifier sends the MAC key s_i to the prover and expects $\mathsf{MAC}_{s_i}(F)$ as response.

This approach is not secure in the setting of PoW [12], since a single malicious adversary could consume up all of t pre-computed MACs easily by impersonating or colluding with t distinct cloud users.

4.1.3   Proofs of Retrievability. Some instance of POR (e.g. [27,32,30]) can serve as PoW. The first construction (i.e. PoW1 as in Table 1) of Halevi *et al.* [12] is just the Merkle Hash Tree based POR scheme (MHT-POR), which combines error erasure code and Merkle Hash Tree proof method[5]. The drawback of this approach is that, the relatively expensive error erasure code[6] is applied over the whole input file, while in our approach, error erasure code is applied over the output of the randomness extractor, which is much shorter than the whole input file.

We notice that recent work by Zheng and Xu [33] attempts to equip proofs of storage (POR or PDP) with deduplication capability. However, their work is not in the leakage setting of Halevi *et al.* [12].

4.1.4   Pairwise-Independent Hash with Large Output Size. The second construction of PoW in Halevi *et al.* [12] is based on pairwise independent hash family (a.k.a 2-independent or 2-universal hash family). A large input file is hashed into a constant size (say about $3T = 3 \times 64\mathrm{MB}$) hash value and then apply the merkle hash tree proof method over the hash value. This construction is secure, but very in-efficient in both computation and randomness complexity. Furthermore, large random seed also implies large communication cost required to share this seed among all owners of the same file. It is worth pointing out that Halevi *et al.* [12] overlooked the disadvantage in large randomness complexity (i.e. at least twice of hash output size, say about $2 \times 3T = 6 \times 64\mathrm{MB}$), although they admitted that this construction is *prohibitively* expensive in computation for practical data size.

A quick thought to reduce the seed length is to apply pseudorandomness generated from a short true random seed. However, in the leakage setting of PoW, any short seed could be leaked to the adversary by some colluded owner of target file. Consequently, the standard computational indistinguishability argument of pseudorandom number generator (or pseudorandom functions) is not applicable.

---

[5] Merkle Hash Tree proof method proves the correctness of a leaf value by presenting as a proof all sibling values along the path from the questioned leaf to the root of Merkle Hash Tree, and verification requires only the root value.

[6] In typical usage of error erasure code, block length is some small constant (say 223 bytes for (255, 223)-reed-solomon code). However, in the usage of POR, the block length has to be as large as the input file, which makes the coding much slower than typical case.

It is unclear whether this pseudorandomness approach works or not without new sophisticated proof (or disproof). Similar issue is discussed in the study of proofs of retrievability by Dodis *et al.* [30], which adopts sampling technique with public coin as seed to replace pseudorandomness.

4.1.5 PoW with respect to Particular Distribution. The third construction of PoW in Halevi *et al.* [12] is the most efficient one among all of three constructions proposed by Halevi *et al.* [12]. In the third construction, the size of random seed is dramatically reduced by treating hash function SHA256 as a random oracle. However, their proof (in random oracle model) of this construction is incomplete: firstly, the distribution of input file is restricted as "generalized bit/block-fixing distribution" [7]; secondly, their proof assumes their algorithm will generate a "good linear code" and the authors admit that it is "very hard to analyze" this unproven assumption (See texts around Theorem 3 in [12]).

We emphasize that, information leakage of file F may have different forms. For example, some plain bits $F[i]$'s are leaked, or some aggregated information of file F (e.g. a hash value) is leaked. In the latter case, file F is hardly considered as fitting in (generalized) fixed-bit/block distribution.

Gabizon *et al.* [35] proposed a randomness extractor for input under bit-fixing distribution. Such extractor can be combined with our generic construction to obtain a secure PoW scheme for bit-fixing input file and with complete security proof in standard model.

Other works on deduplication/PoW include Pietro and Sorniotti [36], which treats a projection $(F[i_1], \ldots, F[i_\lambda])$ of file F onto λ randomly chosen bit-positions $(i_1, \ldots, i_\lambda)$ as the "proof" of ownership of file F. Similar to the "hash-as-a-proof" method, this work is extremely efficient but insecure in the bounded leakage setting [12]. Readers may find more related works in Xu *et al.* [21].

4.2 Our Approach: PoW = Randomness Extractor + POR

Intuitively, our generic construction extracts $(T + 2\lambda)$ bits message Y from the input file F and then apply a proofs of retrievability scheme over Y. It is worth noting that in our usage of proofs of retrievability scheme, algorithm POR.GenProof$_{data}$ runs by prover and algorithm POR.GenProof$_{tag}$ runs by verifier[8], while in the literature [19,27,28], both of these two algorithms run by prover. It is easy to see that, such modification will preserve the soundness of POR scheme.

The detailed construction is given in Figure 1 (on page 110). Before presenting a formal statement in Theorem 2 for the PoW scheme in Figure 1 which

---

[7] A M bits long file F with k bit entropy under "generalized bit-fixing distribution" is generated in this way: (1) Independently choosing k uniform random bits; (2) deriving all other $(M - k)$ bits from these k random bits (Halevi *et al.* [12] applies linear transformation); (3) the file F is a random permutation of these k random bits and $(M - k)$ derived bits. If in the above step (2), all $(M - k)$ bits are constant, then the resulting distribution is called "bit-fixing distribution" with entropy k.

[8] All tag values are stored with the verifier instead of the provers, in order to prevent any potential leakage of partial information of Y from its tag values to the (dishonest) provers.

constructed from a generic randomness extractor algorithm and a generic POR scheme, we will prove a stronger result in Theorem 1 for the special case that the POR scheme is instantiated with MHT-POR[9] scheme in the construction of PoW. The reason that MHT-POR can achieve a stronger result is that, the security of MHT-POR relies on the cryptographic one-way function without trapdoor (precisely the collision resistance hash function). In contrast, most other POR schemes rely on cryptographic trapdoor one-way function (e.g. factorization), and such *short* trapdoor (or private key) might be leaked via some colluded file owner in our stringent security model in three player setting. Once the short trapdoor is leaked to the adversary, the POR scheme can be easily broken.

Theorem 1. *Suppose* Extractor : $\{0,1\}^M \times \{0,1\}^{\ell_s} \rightarrow \{0,1\}^{T+2\lambda}$ *is a strong* (k,ϵ)*-extractor, and the POR scheme is the Merkle Hash Tree based scheme* MHT-POR *(as described in Sec 2.2.1 in the full paper [1]), which is ϵ-sound. Then the PoW scheme constructed in Figure 1 is (k,T,ϵ)-sound and (k,T,ϵ)-privacy-preserving in the three players setting.* *(Proof is in full paper [1])*

Most POR schemes [27,28] require a short private key (e.g. the factorization of a RSA modulus, the secret key of some pseudorandom function) to work and thus cannot resist Type-II leak query LEAK-QUERY-II, from which the adversary could learn the short private key and break the POR scheme. Therefore, for such POR schemes with private key, we have to disable Type-II leak query by switching to the two players setting as below.

Theorem 2. *Suppose* Extractor : $\{0,1\}^M \times \{0,1\}^{\ell_s} \rightarrow \{0,1\}^{T+2\lambda}$ *is a strong* (k,ϵ)*-extractor and* POR *is an ϵ-sound POR scheme. Then the PoW scheme constructed in Figure 1 is (k,T,ϵ)-sound in the two players setting.*

We compare two instantiations of our generic approaches in Table 4 (on page 109).

Table 4. Two instantiations of PoW=RE+POR

Choice of POR	Setting	Summary Value Size (bits)	Communication cost (bits)
MHT-POR	2P,3P	λ	$\lambda \cdot \log_{1-\alpha} \epsilon \cdot \log(T/\alpha)$
Brent-Waters-POR [27]	2P	$T/(\alpha s)$ †	$(s+3)\lambda + 440$

† : s is a system parameter of POR [27] and can take any positive integer value.

5   Randomness Extractor with Large Output Size

In this section, we propose in Figure 2 (on page 111) a novel randomness extractor with large output size using the well-known "sample-then-extract" approach: Repeatedly sample a subset of bits from a weak random source and then apply an existing extractor with small output size over the sample.

Intuitively, the sampling lemma [24,25] states that "if one samples a random subset of bits from a weak random source, the min-entropy rate (i.e. ratio of min-entropy to bit-length) of the source is nearly preserved". Precisely if $X \in \{0,1\}^n$

---

[9] Detailed description of Merkle Hash Tree based POR (MHT-POR) is given in Sec 2.2.1 of the full paper [1]

$S(F, 1^\lambda)$ Summary function.

Input: An M-bit file $F \in \{0,1\}^M$ and security parameter λ in unary form.

Extract: Choose random seed s from domain $\{0,1\}^{\ell_s}$ and compute $Y :=$ Extractor$(F; s)$.

Expand: Apply Erasure-Correcting-Code on Y to obtain $\hat{Y} = (\hat{Y}_1, \hat{Y}_2, \ldots, \hat{Y}_n)$ such that Y can be completely recovered from any αn blocks among $\{\hat{Y}_1, \hat{Y}_2, \ldots, \hat{Y}_n\}$, where constant $\alpha \in (0,1)$ is some system parameter. Generate POR-key pair $(pk, sk) :=$ POR.KeyGen(1^λ), and authentication tags $\{\sigma_i\}_{i=1}^n :=$ POR.Tag$(sk, \{\hat{Y}_i\}_{i=1}^n)$. Let $\pi_F = (pk, sk, \{\sigma_i\}_{i=1}^n)$.
Note: As mentioned in [12], in the construction of PoW, the decoding algorithm of the above Erasure-Correcting-Code is not required to be practical, since the decoding algorithm will not be invoked in the legitimate application of PoW.

Output: The summary value of file F is $\psi = (s, \alpha, \pi_F)$. Output ψ.

$\langle P(F), V(\psi) \rangle$ Interactive proof system between verifier (cloud storage server) and prover (cloud storage client).

Input: The prover has file F as input and the verifier has a summary value $\psi = (s, \alpha, \pi_F)$ as input, where $\pi_F = (pk, sk, \{\sigma_i\}_{i=1}^n)$.

V1: Verifier finds $c = \lceil \log_{1-\alpha} \epsilon \rceil$ (i.e. c is the smallest integer such that $(1 - \alpha)^c \leq \epsilon$) and computes $(C, \Psi_F, \Psi_\sigma) :=$ POR.GenChal(pk, n, c). Verifier sends $(C, s, \alpha, pk, \Psi_F)$ to the prover.

P1: Prover runs the extractor algorithm to obtain $Y :=$ Extractor$(F; s)$, and re-generate the erasure code $\hat{Y}$ from Y using the same Erasure-Correcting-Code with the same parameter α. Prover divides $\hat{Y}$ into n blocks $\hat{Y}_1, \ldots, \hat{Y}_n$ and computes $\bar{F} :=$ POR.GenProof$_{data}(pk, \{\hat{Y}_i\}_{i=1}^n, C, \Psi_F)$. Prover sends $\bar{F}$ to verifier.

V2: Verifier computes $\bar{\sigma} :=$ POR.GenProof$_{tag}(pk, \{\sigma_i\}_{i=1}^n, C, \Psi_\sigma)$ and $b :=$ POR.Verify$(K, \bar{F}, \bar{\sigma}, \Psi_F, \Psi_\sigma) \in \{\texttt{Accept}, \texttt{Reject}\}$, where K is pk if the POR scheme supports public key verification; otherwise K is sk.

Output: Output $b \in \{\texttt{Accept}, \texttt{Reject}\}$.
Note: The subset C requires $|C| \log n$ bits communication cost. We can reduce this communication cost by using Goldreich [29]'s (δ, γ)-hitter sampler[a] to represent C compactly with only $\log n + 3 \log(1/\gamma)$ bits of public random coins.

---

[a] Goldreich [29]'s (δ, γ)-hitter guarantees that, for any subset $W \subset [1, n]$ with size $|W| \geq (1 - \delta)n$, $\Pr[C \cap W \neq \emptyset] \geq 1 - \gamma$. Readers may refer to [29,30] for more details.

Fig. 1. PoW = RE + POR: A Generic Construction of PoW using Randomness Extractor Extractor$(\cdot \; ; \; \cdot)$ and POR scheme (KeyGen, Tag, GenChal, GenProof$_{data}$, GenProof$_{tag}$, Verify). The completeness of the constructed PoW scheme is straightforward.

has δn min-entropy and $X[S] \in \{0,1\}^t$ is the projection of X onto a random set $S \subset [n]$ of t positions, then with high probability, $X[S]$ is statistically close to a random variable with $\delta' t$ min-entropy. We consider the difference $(\delta t - \delta' t)$ as the entropy loss in sampling t bits. Nisan and Zuckerman(Lemma 11 in [24]) gave a sampling algorithm where $\delta' = c\delta/\log(1/\delta)$ for some small positive constant c. Vadhan (Lemma 6.2 in [25]) improved their result and allows $\delta' = (\delta - 3\tau)$ for sufficiently small positive constant τ.

We brief the existing approach [24,38] as below: (1) Independently and randomly choose l number of seeds, in order to get l samples $X_1, \ldots, X_l$ from the input weak source F, which has min-entropy rate δ. (2) Show that $(X_1, \ldots, X_l)$ is a δ'-block-wise source with δ' close to δ, i.e. for each $i \in [l]$, conditional on $(X_1, \ldots, X_i)$, the random variable X_{i+1} has min-entropy rate at least δ'. (3) Apply existing randomness extractor on the *structured* weak random source $(X_1, \ldots, X_l)$ to generate almost-uniform random output $(y_1, \ldots, y_l)$.

Roughly speaking, in the analysis of the above approach in [24,38], to extract each block y_i, the remaining min-entropy of the input F reduces by $|X_i|$ bits—the bit-length of X_i. Unlike previous works [24,25,38], we do not generate block-wise source as intermediate product, and manage to show that the remaining min-entropy of the input F, after extracting each block y_i, reduces by $|y_i|$ bits—the bit-length of y_i which is much smaller than $|X_i|$. Readers may find definition and calculation of remaining (or conditional) min-entropy $\tilde{\mathbf{H}}_\infty(A|B)$ of variable A given variable B in the full paper [1]. In this jargon, we manage to switch the conditional variable B from X_i (as previous works) to y_i in the analysis of our new design.

Extractor$(F; s, s')$ This extractor algorithm will serve as a subroutine to construct PoW scheme.

    Input: An M-bit file $F \in \{0,1\}^M$; $s \in \{0,1\}^{r_0}$ and $s' \in \{0,1\}^{r_1}$ are true random seeds, where $r_0 + r_1 = \rho$.

    Sample-then-Extract-Loop:

        Let $s_1 := s$ and $s'_1 := s'$. Let $h_F := \mathsf{SHA256}(F)$ with $|h_F| \le \rho$.

        For each i from 1 to ℓ:

    Sample: Independently and randomly sample t *distinct* indices from the set $[M]$, using random seed s_i, to obtain $S_i := \mathsf{Samp}([M], t;\ s_i) \subset [M]$.

    Extract: Compute $y_i := \mathsf{Ext}(h_F \| F[S_i];\ s'_i) \in \{0,1\}^\rho$. Let s_{i+1} be the prefix of bit-length r_0 of bit-string y_i, and s'_{i+1} be the suffix of bit-length r_1 of bit-string y_i.

        Note: The hash value h_F is added into the input of Ext, in order to ensure that any change in file F will lead to significant change in the output of randomness extractor.

    Output: Let $Y := y_1 \| y_2 \| \ldots \| y_\ell \in \{0,1\}^{\rho\ell}$. The output is Y.

Fig. 2. A Novel Randomness Extractor with Large Output Size and Short Seed. Ext is some existing strong randomness extractor and Samp is some existing sampling algorithm.

Theorem 3. *Let* $t = M^c$ *and* $\tau = M^{-c}$ *for constant* $c \in (0,1)$. *Let* Ext : $\{0,1\}^{t+256} \times \{0,1\}^{r_1} \to \{0,1\}^\rho$ *be a strong* (k_0, ϵ_0)-*extractor. Let* Samp *be an* (μ, θ, γ)-*averaging sampler [25,38]. Then the algorithm* Extractor : $\{0,1\}^M \times$

$\{0,1\}^\rho \to \{0,1\}^{\rho\ell}$ *constructed in Figure 2 is a* (k_1, ϵ_1)-*extractor, where* $\rho = \lambda + \log(M/t) + \log(1/\gamma) \cdot poly(1/\theta)$, $\rho \cdot \ell = k_1 - (k_0 + 3)M^{1-c}$, *and* $\epsilon_1 = 5\ell(\epsilon_0 + \gamma + 2^{-\lambda} + 2^{-\Omega(\tau M)})$.

We make the following remarks: (1) Our algorithm in Figure 2 requires about $1/\ell$ fraction of the amount of random bits required by [24], since [24] requires that all of sampling seeds $s_1, s_2, \ldots, s_\ell$ should be independent randomness. (2) The choice of value $t = M^c$ ensure that there will be sufficient remaining min-entropy in the last sample (worst case), and this value of sample size t would be much larger than required for the first few samples (good cases). One may use different sample size t_i for the i-th sample $(t_1 < t_2 < t_3 \ldots < t_\ell = M^c)$, in order to reduce the IO reading. (3) Alternatively, we may choose hitter-sampler [29] as in [24] instead of averaging sampler, in order to reduce the seed length ρ (only $\mathcal{O}(\lambda + \log M)$ bits) at the cost of larger value of t. (4) In practice, one may use Tabulation Hashing [39] or CBC-MAC or HMAC as the underlying extractor algorithm Ext (possibly in the companion with hitter sampler which allows small ρ), as analyzed by Dodis *et al.* [40].

To prove Theorem 3, we introduce Lemma 4 and Lemma 5.

Lemma 4 (Amplification). *Suppose the algorithm* $\overline{\mathsf{Ext}} : \{0,1\}^M \times \{0,1\}^\rho \to \{0,1\}^\rho$ *defined as*

$$\overline{\mathsf{Ext}}(X; (s, s')) \stackrel{\text{def}}{=} \mathsf{Ext}\Big(\mathtt{SHA256}(X) \parallel X[\mathsf{Samp}(s)]; s'\Big) \qquad (4)$$

is a strong (k_2, ϵ_2)-*extractor. Then* Extractor : $\{0,1\}^M \times \{0,1\}^\rho \to \{0,1\}^{\rho\ell}$ *constructed in Figure 2 is a* (k_1, ϵ_1)-*extractor, where* $k_1 \geq k_2 + \rho(\ell - 1) + \lambda$ *and* $\epsilon_1 = 5\ell(\epsilon_2 + 2^{-\lambda})$.

Our proof for Lemma 4 in full paper [1] is an analog of *hybrid proof technique* for (computational) indistinguishability [41].

Lemma 5 (Theorem 6.3 [25], sample-then-extract). *Let* $1 \geq \overline{\delta} \geq 3\tau > 0$. *Suppose that* Samp : $\{0,1\}^{r_0} \to [M]^t$ *is an* (μ, θ, γ) *averaging sampler with distinct samples for* $\mu = (\overline{\delta} - 2\tau)/\log(1/\tau)$ *and* $\theta = \tau/\log(1/\tau)$ *and that* Ext : $\{0,1\}^{t+256} \times \{0,1\}^{r_1} \to \{0,1\}^\rho$ *is a strong* $(k_0 = (\overline{\delta} - 3\tau)t, \epsilon_0)$-*extractor. Let* $\rho = r_0 + r_1$ *and define* $\overline{\mathsf{Ext}} : \{0,1\}^M \times \{0,1\}^\rho \to \{0,1\}^\rho$ *by*

$$\overline{\mathsf{Ext}}(X; (s, s')) \stackrel{\text{def}}{=} \mathsf{Ext}\Big(\mathtt{SHA256}(X) \parallel X[\mathsf{Samp}(s)]; s'\Big) \qquad (5)$$

Then $\overline{\mathsf{Ext}}$ *is a strong* (k_2, ϵ_2)-*extractor with* $k_2 = \overline{\delta}M$ *and* $\epsilon_2 = \epsilon_0 + \gamma + 2^{-\Omega(\tau M)}$. *Note: As mentioned in [25],* τ *could be arbitrarily small and approaches 0. In this paper, we set* $\tau = M^{-c}$ *for some constant* $c \in (0, 1)$.

Computational Complexity. Recall that, in order to reduce computation cost, we could choose different sample size t_j for iteration j, where $t_1 < t_2 < \ldots < t_\ell = t = M^c$. The computational complexity of our proposed randomness extractor can be measured by the total number of bits read (or sampled) from the file (double counting repeated bits), i.e. the sum of t_j for $j \in [\ell]$. We will give an upper bound on the sum of t_j.

Lemma 6 (Complexity). *Suppose $M^{1-c} \geq 2$. The total number of bits (i.e. $\sum_{j=1}^{\ell} t_j$) of input file F accessed by the randomness extractor in Figure 2 is in $\mathcal{O}(M \log \ell)$.*

Note: (1) If the underlying extractor Ext *is Tabulation Hashing, then the constant behind the big-O notation is very small—around 2.   (2) Multiple access to the same bit will be counted with its frequency.   (3)   The proof of this lemma is in full paper [1].*

We remark that the extractor algorithm in Figure 2 can be modified into m concurrent threads/processes, while increasing the seed size by m times.

6   Conclusion and Open Problems

We were the first one to bridge construction of PoW with randomness extractor and proofs of retrievability. We also proposed a novel randomness extractor with large output size, which improves existing works in both seed length and entropy loss (i.e. the difference between entropy of input and output). Our proofs of ownership scheme can be applied in client-side deduplication of encrypted (unencrypted, too) data in cloud storage service, and the new randomness extractor may have independent interest.

Whether "partition-then-extract" approach works for *any* distribution of input file and how to apply pseudo-entropy extractor (e.g Yao-Entropy extractor) to construct proofs of ownership scheme, remain two open problems.

References

1. Xu, J., Zhou, J.: Leakage Resilient Proofs of Ownership in Cloud Storage, Revisited. Cryptology ePrint Archive, Report 2013/514 (2013),
   http://eprint.iacr.org/2013/514
2. iHS iSuppli: Cloud Storage Services Now Have Over 375M Users, Could Reach 500M By Year-End, http://goo.gl/BO6zWy
3. Blog, A.: Amazon S3 goes exponential, now stores 2 trillion objects,
   http://goo.gl/NUIEny,
   http://gigaom.com/2013/04/18/
   amazon-s3-goes-exponential-now-stores-2-trillion-objects/
4. Blog, W.A.S.T.: Windows Azure Storage – 4 Trillion Objects and Counting,
   http://blogs.msdn.com/b/windowsazurestorage/archive/2012/07/20/
   windows-azure-storage-4-trillion-objects-and-counting.aspx
5. Blog, D.: Over 175 million people using Dropbox and more than a billion files synced each day, https://blog.dropbox.com/2013/07/dbx/
6. SNIA: Understanding Data De-duplication Ratios. white paper,
   http://www.snia.org/sites/default/files/
   Understanding_Data_Deduplication_Ratios-20080718.pdf
7. Douceur, J., Adya, A., Bolosky, W., Simon, D., Theimer, M.: Reclaiming space from duplicate files in a serverless distributed file system. In: ICDCS 2002: International Conference on Distributed Computing Systems (2002)
8. Douceur, J., Bolosky, W., Theimer, M.: US Patent 7266689: Encryption systems and methods for identifying and coalescing identical objects encrypted with different keys (2007)

9. Storer, M., Greenan, K., Long, D., Miller, E.: Secure Data Deduplication. In: StorageSS 2008: ACM International Workshop on Storage Security and Survivability, pp. 1–10 (2008)
10. Bellare, M., Keelveedhi, S., Ristenpart, T.: Message-Locked Encryption and Secure Deduplication. In: Johansson, T., Nguyen, P.Q. (eds.) EUROCRYPT 2013. LNCS, vol. 7881, pp. 296–312. Springer, Heidelberg (2013), http://eprint.iacr.org/2012/631
11. Harnik, D., Pinkas, B., Shulman-Peleg, A.: Side Channels in Cloud Services: Deduplication in Cloud Storage. IEEE Security and Privacy Magazine, Special Issue of Cloud Security 8(6) (2010)
12. Halevi, S., Harnik, D., Pinkas, B., Shulman-Peleg, A.: Proofs of ownership in remote storage systems. In: CCS 2011: ACM Conference on Computer and Communications Security, pp. 491–500 (2011), http://eprint.iacr.org/2011/207
13. Dropship: Dropbox api utilities (April 2011), https://github.com/driverdan/dropship
14. Storer, M., Greenan, K., Long, D., Miller, E.: Secure data deduplication. In: Proceedings of the 4th ACM International Workshop on Storage Security and Survivability, StorageSS 2008, pp. 1–10 (2008)
15. Goldwasser, S., Micali, S., Rackoff, C.: The knowledge complexity of interactive proof systems. SIAM Journal on Computing 18(1), 186–208 (1989)
16. Wikipedia: PlayStation Network outage, http://en.wikipedia.org/wiki/PlayStation_Network_outage
17. wired.com: Dropbox Left User Accounts Unlocked for 4 Hours Sunday, http://www.wired.com/threatlevel/2011/06/dropbox/, http://blog.dropbox.com/?p=821
18. Twitter: Tweetdeck, http://money.cnn.com/2012/03/30/technology/tweetdeck-bug-twitter/
19. Juels, A., Kaliski, Jr., B.: Pors: proofs of retrievability for large files. In: CCS 2007: ACM Conference on Computer and Communications Security, pp. 584–597 (2007)
20. Ateniese, G., Burns, R., Curtmola, R., Herring, J., Kissner, L., Peterson, Z., Song, D.: Provable data possession at untrusted stores. In: CCS 2007: ACM Conference on Computer and Communications Security, pp. 598–609 (2007)
21. Xu, J., Chang, E.C., Zhou, J.: Weak Leakage-Resilient Client side Deduplication of Encrypted Data in Cloud Storage. In: ASIACCS 2013: Proceedings of the 8th ACM Symposium on Information, Computer and Communications Security (Full Paper), pp. 195–206 (2013), http://eprint.iacr.org/2011/538
22. Bellare, M., Keelveedhi, S., Ristenpart, T.: DupLESS: Server-Aided Encryption for Deduplicated Storage (will appear in Usenix Security Symposium 2013). Cryptology ePrint Archive, Report 2013/429 (2013), http://eprint.iacr.org/2013/429
23. Ng, W.K., Wen, Y., Zhu, H.: Private data deduplication protocols in cloud storage. In: SAC 2012: Proceedings of the 27th Annual ACM Symposium on Applied Computing, pp. 441–446 (2012)
24. Nisan, N., Zuckerman, D.: Randomness is linear in space. Journal of Computer and System Sciences 52(Special issue on STOC 1993) , 43–52 (1996)
25. Vadhan, S.: Constructing Locally Computable Extractors and Cryptosystems in the Bounded-Storage Model. J. Cryptol. 17(1), 43–77 (2004)
26. Stinson, D.R.: Universal hash families and the leftover hash lemma, and applications to cryptography and computing. Journal of Combinatorial Mathematics and Combinatorial Computing 42, 3–31 (2002)
27. Shacham, H., Waters, B.: Compact Proofs of Retrievability. In: Pieprzyk, J. (ed.) ASIACRYPT 2008. LNCS, vol. 5350, pp. 90–107. Springer, Heidelberg (2008)

28. Xu, J., Chang, E.C.: Towards efficient proof of retrievability. In: ASIACCS 2012: Proceedings of the 7th ACM Symposium on Information, Computer and Communications Security (Full Paper) (2012), http://eprint.iacr.org/2011/362

29. Goldreich, O.: A Sample of Samplers - A Computational Perspective on Sampling (survey). Electronic Colloquium on Computational Complexity (ECCC) 4(20) (1997)

30. Dodis, Y., Vadhan, S., Wichs, D.: Proofs of Retrievability via Hardness Amplification. In: Reingold, O. (ed.) TCC 2009. LNCS, vol. 5444, pp. 109–127. Springer, Heidelberg (2009)

31. Xu, J., Chang, E.C., Zhou, J.: Leakage-Resilient Client-side Deduplication of Encrypted Data in Cloud Storage. Cryptology ePrint Archive, Report 2011/538 (2011), http://eprint.iacr.org/2011/538

32. Chang, E.C., Xu, J.: Remote Integrity Check with Dishonest Storage Server. In: Jajodia, S., Lopez, J. (eds.) ESORICS 2008. LNCS, vol. 5283, pp. 223–237. Springer, Heidelberg (2008), http://eprint.iacr.org/2008/346

33. Zheng, Q., Xu, S.: Secure and efficient proof of storage with deduplication. In: CODASPY 2012: ACM conference on Data and Application Security and Privacy, pp. 1–12 (2012)

34. Barak, B., Dodis, Y., Krawczyk, H., Pereira, O., Pietrzak, K., Standaert, F.-X., Yu, Y.: Leftover Hash Lemma, Revisited. In: Rogaway, P. (ed.) CRYPTO 2011. LNCS, vol. 6841, pp. 1–20. Springer, Heidelberg (2011)

35. Gabizon, A., Raz, R., Shaltiel, R.: Deterministic Extractors for Bit-Fixing Sources by Obtaining an Independent Seed. SIAM Journal on Computing 36(4), 1072–1094 (2006)

36. Pietro, R.D., Sorniotti, A.: Boosting Efficiency and Security in Proof of Ownership for Deduplication. In: ASIACCS 2012: ACM Symposium on Information, Computer and Communications Security (Full Paper) (2012)

37. Ateniese, G., Burns, R., Curtmola, R., Herring, J., Khan, O., Kissner, L., Peterson, Z., Song, D.: Remote data checking using provable data possession. ACM Transactions on Information and System Security 14, 12:1–12:34 (2011)

38. Vadhan, S.: Pseudorandomness. Foundations and Trends in Theoretical Computer Science 7(1-3), 1–336 (2012)

39. Patrascu, M., Thorup, M.: The power of simple tabulation hashing. In: STOC 2011: ACM Symposium on Theory of Computing, pp. 1–10 (2011)

40. Dodis, Y., Gennaro, R., Håstad, J., Krawczyk, H., Rabin, T.: Randomness Extraction and Key Derivation Using the CBC, Cascade and HMAC Modes. In: Franklin, M. (ed.) CRYPTO 2004. LNCS, vol. 3152, pp. 494–510. Springer, Heidelberg (2004)

41. Goldreich, O.: Foundations of Cryptography. Basic Applications, vol. 2. Cambridge University Press (2004)

Private Message Transmission
Using Disjoint Paths

Hadi Ahmadi* and Reihaneh Safavi-Naini

Department of Computer Science, University of Calgary, Canada**
{hahmadi,rei}@ucalgary.ca

Abstract. We consider private message transmission (PMT) between two communicants, Alice and Bob, in the presence of an eavesdropper, Eve. Alice and Bob have no shared keys and Eve is computationally unbounded. There is a total of n communicating paths, but not all may be simultaneously accessible to the parties. We let t_a, t_b, and t_e denote the number of paths that are accessible to Alice, Bob and Eve respectively. We allow the parties to change their accessed paths at certain points in time during the PMT protocol. We study perfect (P)-PMT protocol families that guarantee absolute privacy and reliability of message transmission. For the sake of transmission rate improvement, we also investigate asymptotically-perfect (AP)-PMT protocol families that provide negligible error and leakage and behave the same as P-PMT families when message length tends to infinity.

We derive the necessary and sufficient conditions under which P-PMT and AP-PMT are possible and introduce explicit PMT schemes. Our results show AP-PMT protocols attain much higher information rates than P-PMT ones. Interestingly, AP-PMT may be possible even in poor conditions where $t_a = t_b = 1$ and $t_e = n - 1$. We study applications of our results to private communication over the real-life scenarios of multiple-frequency links and multiple-route networks. We show practical examples of such scenarios that can be abstracted by the multipath setting: Our results prove the possibility of keyless information-theoretic private message transmission at rates 17% and 20% for the two example scenarios, respectively. We discuss open question and future work.

1 Introduction

With the rapid growth of online communication, an increasing number of daily activities are moved to the online world and fall under prying eyes resulting in increasing loss of privacy. Personal data can be under surveillance by various entities. Hackers easily tap into WiFi connections to steal online communication data [9]. There are reported news on security agencies watching civilian communications through routers in the Internet [8]. Given massive computational resources accessible to the adversaries, naïve usage of traditional cryptographic

---

* The author has moved to Nulli Identity Solution Inc., Canada (hahmadi@nulli.com).
** This work is in part supported by Alberta Innovates Technology Futures.

I. Boureanu, P. Owesarski, and S. Vaudenay (Eds.): ACNS 2014, LNCS 8479, pp. 116–133, 2014.

systems for protecting communication in many cases creates a false sense of security rather than real protection [7]. Development of quantum algorithms such as Shor's algorithm [13] will also render all today's widely used crypto algorithms insecure. The widely known one-time-pad alternative with information-theoretic security requires prior sharing of long keys, which is impractical.

In this paper, we investigate using multiple paths of communication as an alternative resource for providing privacy against a computationally-unbounded eavesdropper. A path may have different realizations such as a network route, a frequency channel in wireless communication, or a fiber strand in fiber-optics. Using path redundancy for security has been considered in the context of secure message transmission (SMT) [5]. The focus of SMT research however has been security against Byzantine active adversaries, an objective which is impossible in many cases of interest where the majority of paths are corrupted. Note that studying active adversaries is not necessary for networks under surveillance.

1.1   Our Work: PMT in the Multipath Setting

We consider message transmission over the following abstract communication system with three parties: a message sender *Alice*, a message receiver *Bob*, and an eavesdropper *Eve*. Alice wants to send a message to Bob, without leaking information to computationally-unbounded Eve. There is no shared key between Alice and Bob. The system provides n disjoint paths, but not all paths can be accessed simultaneously: Alice, Bob, and Eve can have access to up to t_a, t_b, and t_e paths at a time, respectively. We assume time is divided into intervals of equal length λ, and the parties can change their accessed paths at the beginning of each time interval. The value of λ is determined by the technological limitations of the parties, esp. Eve, in switching between paths.

We refer to this problem as private message transmission (PMT) in the $(n, t_a, t_b, t_e, \lambda)$-multipath setting. We provide formal definitions of PMT protocols in this setting. Foremost, we are interested in necessary and sufficient connectivity conditions, under which PMT is possible. But we do not stop here. We study how to attain the so-called *secrecy capacity*, i.e., highest possible rate (message bits divided by communicated bits). The study of secrecy capacity and optimal constructions is essential due to bandwidth limitations and communication cost in most practical scenarios.

P-PMT and AP-PMT. The security of PMT protocols is measured by reliability (δ) and secrecy (ϵ) parameters. The former shows the probability of "incorrect" transmission and the latter represents information leakage. Ideally, a PMT protocol is expected to provide perfect security $\delta = \epsilon = 0$. Relaxing the security requirements to a desired extent may however let PMT at higher rates. We consider designing of two types of PMT protocol families, namely *perfect (P)-PMT* families with perfectly-secure protocols and *asymptotically-perfect (AP)-PMT* families that allow positive yet decreasing δ and ϵ, with respect to message length. The latter family is particularly interesting because it may provide security for a much wider connectivity range. We define *P-secrecy capacity C_0* and

AP-secrecy capacity $C_{\sim 0}$ as the highest achievable rates by P-PMT and AP-PMT families. We start our investigation in full-access case (when $t_a = t_b = n$), and then extend the study to the general case.

PMT Results. Our precise results on P-PMT and AP-PMT protocols are rather complex (see Section 5). For the sake of a quick overview, we provide in Table 1 an approximation of these results for sufficiently large λ. Section 6 gives details about why assuming large λ is plausible.

Table 1. PMT conditions and capacities in the $(n, t_a, t_b, t_e, \lambda)$-multipath setting

		Full Access		Partial Access	
		One-way	Two-way	One-way	Two-way
Condition	**P-PMT**	$t_e < n$		$t_e < t_{ab}$	
	AP-PMT			$t_e < t_b$	$t_e < n$
Capacity	**C_0**	$\approx 1 - \frac{t_e}{n}$		$\approx [1 - \frac{t_e}{t_{ab}}]_+$	
	$C_{\sim 0}$			$\approx 1 - \frac{t_e}{n}$	$\approx 1 - \frac{t_e}{n}$

In the full-access case, P-PMT and AP-PMT behave the same in rate and connectivity condition. This result is not surprising: When $t_e = n$, Eve can collect all data communicated over the paths to retrieve the message. Conversely when $t_e < n$, message is divided into n shares and sent such that $n - t_e$ shares remain private, implying the secrecy rate of $1 - \frac{t_e}{n}$. We show that relaxing security to asymptotically-prefect does not change the results. Surprisingly however, in the case of partial-access, AP-PMT shows a huge advantage. P-PMT protocols cannot exceed rate $[1 - \frac{t_e}{t_{ab}}]_+$, with $t_{ab} = \min\{t_a, t_b\}$, whereas it is possible to get rates close to $1 - \frac{t_e}{n}$ through AP-PMT. To appreciate this advantage more, consider cases where Alice and Bob possess poor connectivity, but Eve has access to almost all paths (i.e., $t_a, t_b \ll t_e \approx n$): While P-PMT is clearly impossible, one may take the benefit of positive-rate AP-PMT protocols.

We introduce one-round and two-round AP-PMT schemes to prove our AP-secrecy rates. The schemes consist of two primitive blocks, namely a (low-rate) *key establishment block* followed by a (high-rate) *coordinated (keyed) PMT block*. The former allows the parties to share a secret key and the latter allows them to use the secret key for high rate message transmission.

Practical Consideration. To show the practical relevance of our results, we elaborate on two example scenarios of communication over multiple-frequency links and multiple-route networks and show private communication is achieved at rates 17% and 20%, respectively. *This provides a novel attempt to build optimal-rate communication with information-theoretic privacy in these scenarios.*

Secrecy Rates and Multipath Setting Parameters. Although it may not be clearly from Table 1, precise secrecy rates of P-PMT and AP-PMT (see Section 5) depend on all multipath setting parameters $(n, t_a, t_b, t_e, \lambda)$. Here are a few words on how the rates are affected generally by these parameters. First, all secrecy rates are functions of path ratios $\frac{t_a}{n}$, $\frac{t_b}{n}$, and $\frac{t_e}{n}$: As long as these three values are not changed increasing/decreasing the total number n of paths does not affect the derived rates. Next (and intuitively), the rates are improved by allowing Alice and Bob higher connectivity (increasing $\frac{t_a}{n}$ and $\frac{t_b}{n}$) and are decreased when Eve obtains higher connectivity ($\frac{t_e}{n}$ is increased). Finally, having longer time intervals (larger λ) results in better rates: The reason is larger λ implies that Alice and Bob can send more information before Eve switches her accessed paths.

1.2   Related Work and Discussion

Secure Message Transmission. In secure message transmission (SMT) [5], Alice and Bob are connected by n paths, out of which $t \leq n$ can be corrupted by the active adversary, Eve. The objective is to guarantee privacy and reliability of a transmitted message. Our study of PMT deviates in a few directions from SMT. Firstly, we focus on passive attacks and study capacity-achieving constructions. Note that a great portion of threats to online communication are passive and using immediate SMT results is an over-design with sub-optimal solutions.

Secondly, SMT assumes Alice and Bob can use all n paths. In dense networks or wide-band frequency channels however, there are more communication paths than parties can possibly afford access. We address this by allowing partial access for Alice and Bob. Last but not least, there is no concept of time interval in SMT, i.e., Alice and Bob can communicate arbitrarily many bits (in a round) without Eve switching her corrupted paths. In a real-life scenario however, Eve may switch paths if enough time is provided. We capture this by adding a time-interval length parameter λ to our abstract model. A SMT protocol that transmits more than λ bits in one round without accounting for Eve's movements is not necessarily functional in our new model. Note that the last two differences cause our study to be more general than SMT.

Frequency Hopping. Frequency-hopping spread spectrum (FHSS) is a communication technique which transmits data as a sequence of blocks sent over pseudo-random frequency channels. The technology has appeared in early WiFi and Bluetooth applications to enhance resistance against interference and narrow-band noise, and more recently, to countermeasure jamming-based denial of service (DoS) attacks [15]. FHSS originally requires share keys between the communicants. Strasser et al. [14] introduced keyless or uncoordinated frequency hopping (UFH) for jamming-resistant key establishment. Although UFH provides "jamming resistance" security without share keys, its security relies on higher-layer cryptography, which implies two drawbacks: (i) the need for a public-key infrastructure and (ii) only computational security guarantees. Looking at a different objective, our PMT results show the possibility of private communication over multiple-frequency channels. In contrast to UFH, the PMT guarantees (i) do not rely on higher-layer cryptography, and (ii) provide security against computationally-unlimited adversaries.

Notation. For real value x, we denoted $[x]_+ = \max\{0, x\}$. For two random variables $X \in \mathcal{X}$ and $Y \in \mathcal{Y}$, we denote their statical distance by $SD(X, Y) = 0.5 \sum_{x \in \mathcal{X}} |\Pr(X = x) - \Pr(Y = x)|$. Throughout, we use $(n, t_a, t_b, t_e, \lambda)$ as multipath setting parameters, and let $t_{ab} = \min(t_a, t_b)$ and $\Delta = 2^{\frac{\lambda}{2} - 2} - 0.25)^{-1}$. We consider Δ to be negligible for our numerical analysis by assuming large λ.

2   Preliminaries: Ramp and Quasi-ramp Secret Sharing

A secret sharing scheme (SSS) distributes a secret S among a set of m players such that every "qualified" subsets can reconstruct S, while no information is leaked to an "unqualified" subset. The scheme is defined by a pair (**Share**, **Rec**) of functions: **Share** maps secret S to shares $\underline{X} = (X_1, X_2, \ldots, X_m)$ and **Rec** maps shares $\underline{X'} = (X'_1, \ldots, X'_m)$ to a secret reconstruction $\hat{S}$. A (k, m)-threshold SSS [12] distributes the secret via m shares such that any $\geq k$ shares are qualified and any $\leq k - 1$ shares are unqualified. A (k, r, m)-ramp SSS extends the above (to $r \neq 1$) such that any $\geq k$ shares are qualified and $\leq k - r$ shares are unqualified, and information leakage increases by the number of shares.

Polynomial-based ramp SSS. The simplest (k, r, m)-ramp SSS is Shamir's polynomial-based construction [12] denoted by (**Share**$_{pol}$, **Rec**$_{pol}$) and described below. Define integer $p \geq m + r$ and let $S = (S_0, \ldots, S_{r-1}) \in \mathbb{F}_p^r$ be the secret.

- **Share**$_{pol}(S)$ chooses a random polynomial $f(x)$ of degree $\leq k - 1$ over $\mathbb{F}_p[x]$, such that $f(0) = S_0, f(1) = S_1, \ldots, f(r - 1) = S_{r-1}$; it returns m shares $X_1 = f(r), \ldots, X_m = f(r + m - 1)$.
- **Rec**$_{pol}(\underline{X'})$ chooses the first k present shares: If this is not possible, returns $\perp$; otherwise obtains $f(x)$ through interpolation and returns $S = (f(0), f(1), \ldots, f(r - 1))$.

Algebraic-geometric Quasi-ramp SSS. The polynomial-based ramp SSS requires $m + r \leq p$ since there is only p points on the polynomial. Algebraic-geometric constructions relax this requirement by using curves of high genus. Garcia and Stichtenoth [6, Theorem 3.1] show an explicit family of curves with arbitrary genus g and $(\sqrt{p} - 1)g$ many points over $\mathbb{F}_p$ (when p is a square). Chen and Cramer [3] use these curves to construct an algebraic geometric (k, r, g, m)-quasi-ramp SSS for any $m < (\sqrt{p} - 1)g$ shares. A Quasi-ramp SSS allows $\geq k + 2g$ shares to be qualified and any $\leq k - 1$ shares to be unqualified.

(k, r, g, m)-*quasi-ramp SSS* (**Share**$_{alg}$, **Rec**$_{alg}$). Let $\mathcal{C}$ be a Garcia-Stichtenoth curve with genus g over $\mathbb{F}_p$, where p is a square and $(\sqrt{p} - 1)g \geq m + r$. Define Q, $P_0, P_1, \ldots, P_{m+r-1}$ as any $m + r + 1$ distinct rational points on $\mathcal{C}$, $D = (k + 2g).(Q)$ as a rational divisor of $\mathcal{C}$, and $\mathcal{L}(D)$ as the Riemann-Roch space associated with D. Let $S \in \mathbb{F}_p^r$ be the secret.[1]

---

[1] Refer to [3] for the definitions of rational divisor and Riemann-Roch space.

- **Share**$_{alg}(S)$ chooses a random function $f(.) \in \mathcal{L}(D)$ such that $f(P_0) = S_0, f(P_1) = S_1, \ldots, f(P_{r-1}) = S_{r-1}$ and returns shares $X_1 = f(P_r), \ldots, X_m = f(P_{m+r-1})$ over $\mathbb{F}_p$.
- **Rec**$_{alg}(X'_1, \ldots, X'_m)$ chooses the first $k + 2g$ present shares: If not possible, returns $\perp$); otherwise, obtains $f(.)$ through linear interpolation and returns $S = (f(0), f(1), \ldots, f(r-1))$.

The above SSS allows for more shares at the price of increasing the gap between the number of qualified and unqualified players. If field size p is large enough, one can generate $\sqrt{p} - 1$ additional shares by allowing only 2 players gap in SSS. We use this interesting property in our PMT constructions which let $p = 2^\lambda$, for time-interval length λ.

3 Problem Description

3.1 Multipath Setting Abstraction

A *multipath setting* refers to an abstract communication system which consists of n disjoint communication paths, out of which at most t_a, t_b, and t_e can be simultaneously accessed by Alice, Bob, and Eve, respectively. More precisely, time is divided into equal-length intervals each of which corresponds to λ bits of communication over at least one path. In the beginning of a time intervals, the parties choose their access paths and will hold on to their choice till the end of that interval, i.e., until λ bits are communicated over a path. This abstraction of time intervals in bits is obtained by multiplying the bit-transmission speed by path switching time. The value of λ depends on how fast the communicants and (more importantly) Eve can release old paths and capture new paths without possibly missing the live communication. This relates to the actual communication scenario, the communication capability of devices, and the transmission speed. We shed more light on this in Section 6: The practical scenarios considered there suggest typical values of $\lambda > 100$. To summarize, a multipath setting is defined by five public parameters $(n, t_a, t_b, t_e, \lambda)$ and we denote $t_{ab} = \min(t_a, t_b)$ throughout. When $t_{ab} = n$, we refer to the setting as the (n, t_e, λ)-full-access setting. Figure 1 illustrates full-access versus partial-access settings.

(a) Full-access: $t_a = t_b = n$.   (b) Partial-access: $t_a, t_b \leq n$.

Fig. 1. Full-access vs. partial-access multipath settings

3.2   PMT protocol and Secrecy Capacity: Definition

To deliver message S from Alice to Bob, a PMT protocol makes them communicate sequences of data so that Bob can obtain an estimate $\hat{S}$. The protocol leaves Eve with some view $View_E(S)$ of the communication. The randomness in $View_E(.)$ comes from the PMT protocol and the adversary.

Definition 1 (PMT Protocol). *A protocol Π over a multipath setting is a (k, c, δ, ϵ)-PMT protocol if it transmits any k-bit message using c bits of communication such that*

$$Reliability: \quad \forall s \in \{0,1\}^k: \quad \Pr(\hat{S} \neq s) \leq \delta, \tag{1}$$

$$Secrecy: \quad \forall s_1, s_2 \in \{0,1\}^k: \quad SD\left(View_E(s_1), View_E(s_2)\right) \leq \epsilon. \tag{2}$$

Π is called perfect (P)-PMT if $\delta = \epsilon = 0$. The secrecy rate of Π equals $R = \frac{k}{c}$.

In practice, the message length may be unknown beforehand and one needs a family of PMT protocols for arbitrarily long messages. PMT families are desired to have a guaranteed rate for any message length. We refer to this guaranteed rate as the *secrecy rate* of the family.

Definition 2 ((δ, ϵ)-PMT and P-PMT Families). *A (δ, ϵ)-PMT family $\mathcal{F}$ for a multipath setting $\mathscr{S}$ is a sequence $(\Pi_i)_{i \in \mathbb{N}}$, where for each i, Π_i is a $(k_i, c_i, \delta, \epsilon)$-PMT protocol over $\mathscr{S}$ and $k_{i+1} > k_i$. The (δ, ϵ)-secrecy rate of $\mathcal{F}$ equals $R_{\mathcal{F}:\delta, \epsilon} = \inf\{\frac{k_i}{c_i} : i \in \mathbb{N}\}$.[2] When $\delta = \epsilon = 0$, $\mathcal{F}$ is called a perfect (P)-PMT family and the P-secrecy rate is denoted by $R_{\mathcal{F}:0}$.*

Designing P-PMT families is crucial for highly-sensitive data transmission. There are however scenarios which desire non-zero yet negligible δ and ϵ. We define asymptotically-perfect (AP)-PMT families with (δ, ϵ)-PMT protocols, such that the values δ and ϵ tend to zero for longer messages.

Definition 3 (AP-PMT Family). *An AP-PMT family $\mathcal{F}$ for a multipath setting $\mathscr{S}$ is a sequence $(\Pi_i)_{i \in \mathbb{N}}$ where for each i, Π_i is a $(k_i, c_i, \delta_i, \epsilon_i)$-PMT protocol over $\mathscr{S}$, and it holds $k_{i+1} > k_i$, $\delta_{i+1} \leq \delta_i$, $\epsilon_{i+1} \leq \epsilon_i$, and $\lim_{i \to \infty} \delta_i = \lim_{i \to \infty} \epsilon_i = 0$. The AP-secrecy rate of $\mathcal{F}$ is defined as $R_{\mathcal{F}:\sim 0} = \inf\{\frac{k_i}{c_i} : i \in \mathbb{N}\}$.*

We accordingly define the secrecy capacity of a multipath setting as the highest secrecy rate that can be guaranteed for all message lengths. We are particularly interested in two types of capacities.

Definition 4 (Secrecy Capacity). *The P- (resp. AP-) secrecy capacity C_0 (resp. $C_{\sim 0}$) of a setting $\mathscr{S}$ equals the largest P-secrecy (resp. AP-secrecy) rate achievable by all possible P- (resp. AP-) PMT families over $\mathscr{S}$.*

---

[2] The infimum exists as the sequence is bounded from below by zero.

3.3 Relation among P-secrecy and AP-secrecy Capacities

Definition 1 implies that any $(k, c, \delta_1, \epsilon_1)$-PMT protocol is also $(k, c, \delta_2, \epsilon_2)$-PMT for $\delta_2 \geq \delta_1$ and $\epsilon_2 \geq \epsilon_1$. Since families simply consist of protocols, any (δ_1, ϵ_1)-PMT family is also a (δ_2, ϵ_2)-PMT family. This shows $C_0 \leq C_{\sim 0}$. It is important to know whether the above can be replaced by a strict inequality: It is fairly reasonable to tolerate negligible deviation from perfect security to improve rate or to make PMT possible. Below, we study P-PMT and AP-PMT protocols starting from the full-access case (when $t_a = t_b = n$) and extend it to the general multipath setting. Our study leads us the following ultimate conclusion:

For a wide range of settings, it holds $C_{\sim 0} > C_0$.

4 PMT in the Full-access Scenario

In the (n, t_e, λ)-full-access setting (i.e., $t_a = t_b = n$) with infinite interval length $\lambda = \infty$, the PMT problem relates to the SMT work [5] (for passive adversary): The optimal solution, denoted by $\mathcal{F}_0^{pol}$, simply uses a polynomial-based (n, r, n)-ramp secret sharing scheme (SSS), $(\mathbf{Share}_{pol}, \mathbf{Rec}_{pol})$, where $r = n - t_e$. Let $S \in \mathbb{F}_{2^u}^r$ be the secret message, for some integer $u > \log(2n - t_e)$.

- Alice calculates shares $\underline{X} = (X_1, X_2, \ldots, X_n) = \mathbf{Share}_{pol}(S)$ and sends $X_i \in \mathbb{F}_{2^u}$ over path i.
- Having received X_i's, Bob obtains the message as $S = \mathbf{Rec}_{pol}(\underline{X})$.

The perfect reliability and secrecy follow trivially from the properties of (n, r, n)-ramp SSS: n shares are qualified and $n - r = t_e$ shares are unqualified.

Proposition 1. *The scheme $\mathcal{F}_0^{pol}$ gives a family of $(u.r, u.n, 0, 0)$-P-PMT protocols with rate $R_{\mathcal{F}_0^{pol}} = 1 - \frac{t_e}{n}$ over the (n, t_e, λ)-full-access setting with $\lambda = \infty$.*

4.1 P-PMT for Finite λ

When λ is finite, the scheme $\mathcal{F}_0^{pol}$ (without any modification) does not provide us with a P-PMT family since it cannot give P-PMT protocols for message lengths $u.r$ such that $u > \lambda$. There is of course an easy fix to this. One can stay with a constant field size 2^λ and instead repeat $\mathcal{F}_0^{pol}$ for sufficiently many times to send arbitrarily long messages; hence, a PMT family.

Proposition 2. *Repeating $\mathcal{F}_0^{pol}$ for arbitrary times results in a P-PMT family with rate $R_{\mathcal{F}_0^{pol}} = 1 - \frac{t_e}{n}$ in any (n, t_e, λ)-full-access setting with $2n - t_e \leq 2^\lambda$.*

The situation is unfortunate when $2n - t_e > 2^\lambda$: $\mathcal{F}_0^{pol}$ cannot provide any PMT protocol since the polynomial-based SSS cannot generate more points than the field size 2^λ. To resolve this, we propose a P-PMT scheme, $\mathcal{F}_0^{alg}$, that is similar to $\mathcal{F}_0^{Pol}$ but uses the algebraic-geometric SSS of Section 2 with arbitrarily many shares over $\mathbb{F}_{2^\lambda}$ and transmits message in q time-intervals. In precise, the scheme uses a $(qn-2g, r, g, qn)$-quasi-ramp SSS $(\mathbf{Share}_{alg}, \mathbf{Rec}_{alg})$ for the secret message $S = (S_1, \ldots, S_r) \in \mathbb{F}_{2^\lambda}^r$: To generate $qn + r \le (\sqrt{2^\lambda} - 1)g$ points, we choose $g = \lceil \frac{q(2n-t_e)}{2^{\lambda/2}-1} \rceil$ and $r = q(n-t_e)-2g$. The reliability and secrecy properties of $\mathcal{F}_0^{alg}$ follow from the quasi-ramp SSS: $qn-2g+2g = qn$ shares are qualified and $qn - 2g - r = qt_e$ shares are unqualified. The rate equals $R_{\mathcal{F}_0^{alg}} = \frac{r\lambda}{qn\lambda} = 1 - \frac{t_e}{n}$, where (inequality (a) follows by choosing $q \ge \frac{2^{\lambda/2}-1}{t_e} - \Delta$)

$$\Delta = \frac{2\lceil \frac{2qn}{2^{\lambda/2}-1} - \frac{qt_e}{2^{\lambda/2}-1} \rceil}{qn} \overset{(a)}{\le} \frac{4qn}{(2^{\lambda/2} - 1)qn} = (2^{\frac{\lambda}{2}-2} - 0.25)^{-1}. \tag{3}$$

Proposition 3. *The scheme $\mathcal{F}_0^{alg}$ gives a P-PMT family over any (n, t_e, λ)-full-access setting. The P-secrecy rate of the family is $R_{\mathcal{F}_0^{alg}:0} = [1 - \frac{t_e}{n} - \Delta]_+$ where $\Delta \le (2^{\frac{\lambda}{2}-2} - 0.25)^{-1}$.*

Implication to P-secrecy Capacity The existing work on SMT (cf. [11]) suggests the upper-bound $1 - \frac{t_e}{n}$ on achievable P-PMT secrecy rates. This combined with the above results leads us to the following approximation of the P-secrecy capacity for the full-access case:

$$[1 - \frac{t_e}{n} - \Delta]_+ \le C_0^{\mathbf{FA}} \le 1 - \frac{t_e}{n}. \tag{4}$$

It remains an interesting theoretical question to close the gap between the two bounds. For practical scenarios ($\lambda > 100$), the gap Δ is reasonably small.

4.2 AP-PMT in the full-access Case

We are interested in finding whether PMT rates can be improved if reliability or secrecy requirements are relaxed to asymptotically perfect. We already have the trivial lower-bound $C_{\sim 0}^{\mathbf{FA}} \ge C_0^{\mathbf{FA}}$. To derive an upper-bound, we obtain a bound on (δ, ϵ)-secrecy rates and then study its behavior when δ and ϵ approach zero. The bound is obtained by relating to (δ, ϵ)-*secret-key rates for secret-key establishment protocols*. The proof is rather technical and is removed due to lack of space. We refer to the full version [2, Section 4.3] for the proof.

Theorem 1. *There is no (possibly multiple-round) (k, c, δ, ϵ)-PMT protocol in the (n, t_e, λ)-full-access setting with $\frac{k}{c} > \frac{1-t_e/n}{1-1.25\epsilon'-\epsilon' \log \epsilon'}$, where $\epsilon' = \epsilon + \delta$. This implies the AP-secrecy capacity of (using the lower-bound (4))*

$$[1 - \frac{t_e}{n} - \Delta]_+ \le C_{\sim 0}^{\mathbf{FA}} \le 1 - \frac{t_e}{n}. \tag{5}$$

The bounds (4) and (5) show that P-secrecy and AP-secrecy capacities fall in the same range and will equal $1 - \frac{t_e}{t_{ab}}$ assuming $\Delta \to 0$: We can conclude *relaxing security requirements from perfect to asymptotically-perfect does NOT help improve the secrecy rate in the "full-access" case.*

5   PMT in the General Multipath Setting

Unlike full-access, relaxing security to asymptotically perfect benefits PMT in the general setting. We study P-PMT and AP-PMT rates separately.

5.1   P-PMT: Capacity and Construction

We derive lower and upper bounds on the P-secrecy capacity in the general (two-way) multipath communication setting that prove $C_0 \approx [1 - \frac{t_e}{t_{ab}}]_+$ and imply P-PMT impossibility when $t_e \geq t_{ab}$.

Lower-bound via one-round P-PMT. The lower-bound on C_0 is attained by using one-round PMT schemes, $\mathcal{F}_0^{pol}$ or $\mathcal{F}_0^{alg}$, over a fixed (hard-coded) set of t_{ab} paths. The constructions promise the rate $1 - \frac{t_e}{t_{ab}} - \Delta$ when $t_e \leq t_{ab}$ (see (4)).

Upper-bound on P-PMT achievable rates. Any (possibly multiple-round) P-PMT protocol in the multipath setting needs to provide "perfect" secrecy, even in the "worst" case when Eve always captures t_e of the $\leq t_{ab}$ communication paths between Alice and Bob. This suggests the maximum rate $1 - t_e/t_{ab}$ stated in the following Lemma. For the proof, we refer to the full version [2, Appendix D].

Lemma 1. *There is no (possibly multiple-round) $(k, c, 0, 0)$-PMT protocol over the $(n, t_a, t_b, t_e, \lambda)$-multipath setting with rate $R = \frac{k}{c} > [1 - \frac{t_e}{t_{ab}}]_+$.*

Theorem 2 concludes the results on P-secrecy capacity.

Theorem 2. *The P-secrecy capacity of any $(n, t_a, t_b, t_e, \lambda)$ multipath setting satisfies $[1 - \frac{t_e}{t_{ab}} - \Delta]_+ \leq C_0 \leq [1 - \frac{t_e}{t_{ab}}]_+$ and the lower-bound is achieved by an explicit one-round PMT protocol.*

5.2   AP-PMT: Capacity and Constructions

Achievable AP-secrecy rates in the general setting cannot be upper-bounded by some similar approach to the full-access case (as in Section 4.2). This leaves us with the trivial upper-bound

$$C_{\sim 0} \leq U_{\sim 0} \stackrel{\Delta}{=} 1 - \frac{t_e}{n}. \tag{6}$$

At a first look, the upper-bound seems far from tight. It seems impossible to reach secrecy rates up to $1 - \frac{t_e}{n}$, regardless of connectivity parameters t_a and t_b. We prove however that for sufficiently large λ, there are AP-PMT families which can get close to this rate. For one-way multipath setting, the required connectivity condition is $t_b > t_e$; for two-way setting however, AP-PMT is always possible only if $t_e < n$ and $t_a, t_b > 0$.

AP-PMT Approach. We introduce three different AP-PMT schemes for different connectivity ranges. All schemes consist of two primitive blocks: (i) *low-rate key establishment block* and (ii) *high-rate coordinated PMT block*. The key-establishment block lets Alice and Bob share a long secret-key W in q_1 intervals. The coordinated PMT block allows Alice to send her message to Bob in q_2 intervals over the secret paths chosen based on W: Since Eve is unaware of W, the coordinated PMT rate equals (almost) $1 - \frac{t_e}{n}$. The overall rate however takes into account the overhead communication for block (i). Both blocks take use of the algebraic-geometric SSS of Section 2.

One-round AP-PMT for $t_e \leq t_{ab}$. We introduce a one-round AP-PMT scheme $\mathcal{F}_1$ with an AP-secrecy rate close to $1 - \frac{t_e}{n}$. The scheme has perfect reliability, but allows for negligible leakage. It composes a key-transport block and a coordinated PMT block as follows. Given the $(n, t_a, t_b, t_e, \lambda)$ multipath setting, define $w = \lceil \log \binom{n}{t_{ab}} \rceil$. For arbitrarily small $\psi > 0$, and sufficiently large $q_1 \in \mathbb{N}$ (to be determined), define [3]

$$g_1 = \lceil \frac{q_1(2t_{ab} - t_e)}{2^{\lambda/2} - 1} \rceil, \quad r_1 = q_1(t_{ab} - t_e) - 2g_1 \qquad (7)$$

$$q_2 = \frac{r_1 \lambda}{w}, \quad t'_{e,2} = (1 + \psi)\frac{t_{ab}t_e}{n}, \quad g_2 = \lceil \frac{q_2(2t_{ab} - t'_{e,2})}{2^{\lambda/2} - 1} \rceil, \quad r_2 = q_2(t_{ab} - t'_{e,2}) - 2g_2. \quad (8)$$

Let $(\mathbf{Share}_{alg,1}, \mathbf{Rec}_{alg,1})$ be a $(q_1 t_{ab} - 2g_1, r_1, g_1, q_1 t_{ab})$-quasi-ramp SSS over $\mathbb{F}_{2^\lambda}$ used for key transport, and $(\mathbf{Share}_{alg,2}, \mathbf{Rec}_{alg,2})$ be a $(q_2 t_{ab} - 2g_2, r_2, g_2, q_2 t_{ab})$-quasi-ramp SSS over $\mathbb{F}_{2^\lambda}$ used for coordinated PMT. Let $\mathcal{T}_0$ be a set of fixed (public) t_{ab} paths and $S \in \mathbb{F}_{2^\lambda}^{r_2}$ be the message to be transmitted.

One-round $(0, \epsilon)$-PMT scheme $\mathcal{F}_1$.

(i) *Key transport (q_1 intervals).* Alice generates randomly $W = (W_1, \ldots, W_{q_2}) \in \{0, 1\}^{q_2 w}$. She obtains shares $\underline{X} = (X_{i,j})_{1 \leq i \leq q_1, 1 \leq j \leq t_{ab}} = \mathbf{Share}_{alg,1}(W)$ and sends $(X_{i,j})_{1 \leq j \leq t_{ab}}$ over the t_{ab} paths of $\mathcal{T}_0$ in interval $1 \leq i \leq q_1$. Having received shares, Bob reconstructs $W = \mathbf{Rec}_{alg,1}(\underline{X})$.

(ii) *Coordinated PMT (q_2 intervals).* Alice and Bob calculate path sets $\mathcal{T}_i$ of size t_{ab}, for $1 \leq i \leq q_2$, using key $W_i \in \{0, 1\}^w$. Alice calculates message shares $\underline{Y} = (Y_{i,j})_{1 \leq i \leq q_2, 1 \leq j \leq t_{ab}} = \mathbf{Share}_{alg,2}(S)$ and sends the part $(Y_{i,j})_{1 \leq j \leq t_{ab}}$ over $\mathcal{T}_i$ in interval $q_1 + i$. Having received all shares, Bob reconstructs $S = \mathbf{Rec}_{alg,2}(\underline{Y})$.

Theorem 3. *For any small $\psi, \epsilon > 0$, the scheme $\mathcal{F}_1$ gives $(0, \epsilon)$-PMT and AP-PMT families over an $(n, t_a, t_b, t_e, \lambda)$ multipath setting with $t_e < t_{ab} \leq n$. The AP-secrecy rate of the scheme equals*

$$R_{\mathcal{F}_1:\sim 0} = \frac{1 - \frac{t_e}{n} - \Delta}{1 + \xi_1}, \quad where \quad \xi_1 = \frac{\log(\frac{en}{t_{ab}})}{\lambda(1 - \frac{t_e}{t_{ab}} - \Delta)} \quad and \quad \Delta = (2^{\frac{\lambda}{2} - 2} - 0.25)^{-1}.$$

---

[3] Here, we assume that q_1 is chosen such that w divides $r_1 \lambda$.

Proof. See Appendix A.

Remark 1. It is crucial to use the algebraic-geometric (rather than polynomial) SSS. Expecting arbitrarily small $\epsilon > 0$ requires sufficiently many $(q_2 t_{ab})$ shares over field of constant size 2^λ.

The rate $R_{\mathcal{F}_1 : \sim 0}$ shows rate improvement of AP-PMT compared to P-PMT. The rate is however lower than upper-bound (6) mainly due to the key-transport block communication overhead ξ_1.

One-round AP-PMT for $t_e \geq t_{ab}$. The scheme $\mathcal{F}_1$ cannot achieve any positive secrecy rate when $t_e \geq t_{ab}$. We observe the following two restricting properties of $\mathcal{F}_1$: (i) it provides perfect reliability, and (ii) it is non-interactive. In this section, we focus on relaxing perfect reliability and introduce a PMT scheme $\mathcal{F}_2$ that only modifies the key-transport block in $\mathcal{F}_1$: It fixes a larger set $\mathcal{T}_0$ of $\max(t_a, t_b) \leq n' \leq n$ (instead of t_{ab}) paths and requires Alice and Bob to communicate over random subsets of $\mathcal{T}_0$. This sacrifices the reliability, but allows for pushing the multipath connectivity condition to $t_e < t_b$ instead of $t_e < t_{ab}$ (for scheme $\mathcal{F}_1$).

$\mathcal{F}_2$ uses same parameters (8) for coordinated PMT, but updates parameters for key transport: It uses the algebraic-geometric $(q_1 t'_{b,1} - 2g_1, r_1, g_1, q_1 t_a)$-quasi-ramp SSS ($\mathbf{Share}_{alg,1}, \mathbf{Rec}_{alg,1}$), where

$$t'_{b,1} = (1 - \psi) \frac{t_a t_b}{n'}, \quad t'_{e,1} = (1 + \psi) \frac{t_a t_e}{n'},$$

$$g_1 = \lceil \frac{q_1(t_a + t'_b - t'_{e,2})}{2^{\lambda/2} - 1} \rceil, \quad r_1 = q_1(t'_{b,1} - t'_{e,1}) - 2g_1. \tag{9}$$

One-round (δ, ϵ)-PMT scheme $\mathcal{F}_2$.

(i) *Key transport (q_1 intervals).* Alice generates random $W = (W_1, \ldots, W_{q_2}) \in \{0,1\}^w$ and shares $\underline{X} = (X_{i,j})_{1 \leq i \leq q_1, 1 \leq j \leq t_a} = \mathbf{Share}_{alg,1}(W)$. In each round $1 \leq i \leq q_1$, she sends the part $(X_{i,j})_{1 \leq j \leq t_a}$ over t_a (random) paths from $\mathcal{T}_0$, and Bob listens over t_b (random) paths from $\mathcal{T}_0$. If Bob's observation $\underline{X}'$ includes less than $q_1 t'_{b,1}$ shares, he aborts and chooses $\hat{S} \in_R \mathbb{F}_{2^\lambda}^{r_2}$; otherwise, he reconstructs $W = \mathbf{Rec}_{alg,1}(\underline{X}')$.

(ii) *Coordinated PMT (q_2 intervals).* This is the same as $\mathcal{F}_1$.

Theorem 4. *For any small $\psi, \delta, \epsilon > 0$, the scheme $\mathcal{F}_2$ gives (δ, ϵ)-PMT and AP-PMT families over any $(n, t_a, t_b, t_e, \lambda)$ multipath setting with $t_e < t_b$. The AP-secrecy rate of this scheme reaches*

$$R_{\mathcal{F}_2 : \sim 0} = \frac{1 - \frac{t_e}{n} - \Delta}{1 + \xi_2}, \quad where$$

$$\xi_2 = \frac{\log(\frac{en}{t_{ab}})}{\lambda \left(\frac{t_b - t_e}{n'} - \Delta \right)}, \quad n' = \max(t_a, t_b), \quad and \quad \Delta = (2^{\frac{\lambda}{2} - 2} - 0.25)^{-1}.$$

Proving Theorem 4 is similar to Theorems 3. We refer the reader to the full version [2, Appendix F] for the proof.

Remark 2. When $t_b = n$ Scheme $\mathcal{F}_2$ can be simplified to achieve a higher rate: Only Stage (i), key-transport, suffices to serve message transmission at rate $\frac{t_b - t_e}{t_b} - \Delta = 1 - \frac{t_e}{n} - \Delta$, for $n' = n$.

Impossibility of One-way PMT for $t_e \geq t_b$. It is impossible to obtain AP-PMT in one-round when $t_e \geq t_b$. The reason any protocol that lets Bob recover the message will let Eve too. For the proof, refer to [2, Appendix G]

Proposition 4. *When $t_e \geq t_b$, there is no one-round (k, c, δ, ϵ)-PMT protocol of rate $R = \frac{k}{c} > \frac{2\epsilon}{1-\delta-\alpha}$ to transmit $k \geq 3/\alpha$ bits of messages, implying the AP-secrecy capacity of $\mathcal{C}_{\sim 0} = 0$.*

Implication to one-way AP-secrecy capacity. Putting things together, we reach the following on AP-secrecy capacity of one-way communication.

Corollary 1. *For any one-way $(n, t_a, t_b, t_e, \lambda)$-multipath setting, it holds that $\overrightarrow{L}_{\sim 0} \leq \overrightarrow{C}_{\sim 0} \leq \overrightarrow{U}_{\sim 0}$, where*

$$\overrightarrow{L}_{\sim 0} = \begin{cases} [\frac{1 - \frac{t_e}{n} - \Delta}{1 + \min(\xi_1, \xi_2)}]+, & \text{if } t_e < t_{ab} \\ [\frac{1 - \frac{t_e}{n} - \Delta}{1 + \xi_2}]+, & \text{if } t_{ab} \leq t_e < t_b \\ 0, & \text{if } t_e \geq t_b \end{cases}, \quad \overrightarrow{U}_{\sim 0} = \begin{cases} 1 - \frac{t_e}{n}, & \text{if } t_e < t_b \\ 0, & \text{if } t_e \geq t_b \end{cases} \tag{10}$$

AP-PMT: Always Positive Rates via Two-way Communication. We introduce a two-round AP-PMT scheme $\mathcal{F}_3$ that achieves positive rates even when $t_e \geq t_b$. The idea is using an *interactive key-agreement* block, instead of key transport. Bob sends random elements over random paths and Alice publicly responds (over a fixed path) which elements she has received. Having shared common elements, Alice and Bob apply privacy amplification to convert them into a secret-key. We use the algebraic-geometric SSS for privacy amplification.

Scheme $\mathcal{F}_3$ uses same parameters as $\mathcal{F}_1$ for coordinated PMT (8), but updates paraments for key agreement: It uses the $(q_1 t'_{a,1} - 2g_1, r_1, g_1, q_1 t'_{a,1})$-quasi-ramp SSS (**Share**$_{alg,1}$, **Rec**$_{alg,1}$), where

$$t'_{a,1} = (1 - \psi)\frac{t_a t_b}{n}, \quad t'_{e,1} = (1 + \psi)\frac{t'_{a,1} t_e}{n}, \tag{11}$$

$$g_1 = \lceil \frac{q_1(2t'_{a,1} - t'_{e,1})}{2^{\lambda/2} - 1} \rceil, \quad r_1 = q_1(t'_{a,1} - t'_{e,1}) - 2g_1. \tag{12}$$

Two-round (δ, ϵ)-PMT scheme $\mathcal{F}_3$.

(i) *Interactive key agreement (q_1 intervals).* Bob generates $\underline{X} = (X_{i,j})_{1 \leq i \leq q_1, 1 \leq j \leq t_b}$ randomly from $(\mathbb{F}_2^\lambda)^{q_1 t_b}$. In each interval $1 \leq i \leq q_1$, he sends $(X_{i,j})_{1 \leq j \leq t_b}$ over t_b random paths and Alice listens over t_a random paths. If Alice's observation includes $< q_1 t'_{a,1}$ elements from $\underline{X}$, she aborts and Bob outputs $\hat{S} \in_R \mathbb{F}_{2^\lambda}^{r_2}$; otherwise, let $X_A \subseteq \underline{X}$ be the first $q_1 t'_{a,1}$ elements observed by Alice over path sets $(\mathcal{P}_i)_{1 \leq i \leq q_1}$. Alice sends $(\mathcal{P}_i)_{1 \leq i \leq q_1}$ information over a fixed (public) path to Bob. Alice and Bob use X_A as shares to calculate $W = (W_1, \ldots, W_{q_2}) = \mathbf{Rec}_{alg,1}(X_A)$.

(ii) *Coordinated PMT (q_2 intervals).* This is the same as $\mathcal{F}_1$.

Theorem 5. *For any $\psi, \delta, \epsilon > 0$, the scheme $\mathcal{F}_3$ gives (δ, ϵ)-PMT and AP-PMT families over any $(n, t_a, t_b, t_e, \lambda)$ multipath setting with $t_a, t_b > 0$ and $t_e < n$. The AP-secrecy rate of $\mathcal{F}_3$ equals:*

$$R_{\mathcal{F}_3: \sim 0} = \frac{1 - \frac{t_e}{n} - \Delta}{1 + \xi_3},$$

where $\quad \xi_3 = \dfrac{\left(\frac{n}{t_a} + \frac{\log(en^2/(t_a t_b))}{\lambda} \right) \log \frac{en}{t_{ab}}}{\lambda \left(1 - \frac{t_e}{n} - \Delta \right)} \quad$ *and* $\quad \Delta = (2^{\frac{\lambda}{2} - 2} - 0.25)^{-1}.$

The proof is similar to those for Theorems 3 and 4. We refer the reader to the full version [2, Appendix H].

Implication to two-way AP-secrecy capacity. The capacity is trivially upper-bounded by $1 - \frac{t_e}{n}$, unless when $t_a = 0$ or $t_b = 0$. Combining the lower bounds from $\mathcal{F}_1$, $\mathcal{F}_2$, and $\mathcal{F}_3$, we have:

Corollary 2. *For any $(n, t_a, t_b, t_e, \lambda)$-multipath setting, it holds $L_{\sim 0} \le C_{\sim 0} \le U_{\sim 0}$, where*

$$L_{\sim 0} = \begin{cases} [\frac{1 - \frac{t_e}{n} - \Delta}{1 + \min(\xi_1, \xi_2, \xi_3)}]_+, & \text{if } t_e < t_{ab} \\ [\frac{1 - \frac{t_e}{n} - \Delta}{1 + \min(\xi_2, \xi_3)}]_+, & \text{if } 0 < t_{ab} \le t_e < t_b \\ [\frac{1 - \frac{t_e}{n} - \Delta}{1 + \xi_3}]_+, & \text{if } 0 < t_b < t_e \wedge t_a > 0 \\ 0, & \text{else} \end{cases} , U_{\sim 0} = \begin{cases} 1 - \frac{t_e}{n}, & \text{if } t_a, t_b > 0 \\ 0, & \text{else} \end{cases} \quad (13)$$

5.3 Comparison of P-secrecy and AP-secrecy Rates

We have proved that in partial-access multipath communication, Alice and Bob can achieve higher secrecy rates if they choose AP-PMT protocols over P-PMT ones. To give more sense about how much rate improvement is attained by AP-PMT protocols, we compare the P-secrecy and AP-secrecy capacities for typical multipath parameters that match practical scenarios. Figure 2(a) graphs the lower and upper bounds on $C_{\sim 0}$ as well as C_0 for different values of $\beta = \frac{t_e}{n}$, assuming $\lambda = 100$ and $t_a = t_b = 0.2n$. For this value of λ, we approximate $\Delta \approx 0$ and thus $C_0 \approx 1 - \frac{t_e}{t_{ab}} = 1 - 5\beta$ (see Theorem 2). The capacity C_0 and the bounds $L_{\sim 0}$ and $U_{\sim 0}$ are shown by solid, dotted, and dashed lines, respectively. The graph clearly illustrates the benefit of using AP-PMT: While the lower-bound $L_{\sim 0}$ remains positive throughout, C_0 drops fast and equals 0 for $\beta \ge 0.2$. For $\beta \le 0.15$, the lower bound $L_{\sim 0}$ is achieved by one-round AP-PMT and is quite close to the upper bound. Outside of this range, the lower-bound corresponds to our two-round scheme $\mathcal{F}_3$. This is not surprising since one-way AP-PMT is impossible when $\beta \ge 0.2$ (implying $t_e \ge t_b$).

Figure 2(b) graphs the same three quantities (C_0, $L_{\sim 0}$, and $U_{\sim 0}$) with respect to $\alpha = \frac{t_{ab}}{n}$, assuming $\lambda = 100$, $t_a = t_b$, and $t_e = 0.2n$. The gap between

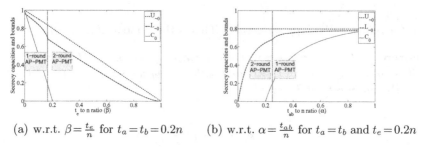

(a) w.r.t. $\beta = \frac{t_e}{n}$ for $t_a = t_b = 0.2n$ (b) w.r.t. $\alpha = \frac{t_{ab}}{n}$ for $t_a = t_b$ and $t_e = 0.2n$

Fig. 2. Comparing the secrecy capacities and bounds

the bounds on $C_{\sim 0}$ bridges as we increase α. What causes more gap for small $\alpha < 0.25$ is small is the two-round AP-PMT communication overhead ξ_3. Finding a better approximation of the AP-secrecy capacity, especially in the low connectivity regime where $t_a, t_b < t_e$ is recommended as future work.

6   Practical Consideration

We discuss two practical applications of our PMT results in the multipath setting model, i.e., sending secret data over (i) multiple-frequency links and (ii) multiple-route networks. Both scenarios include a set of paths that connect communicants and can be tapped into by present eavesdroppers.

6.1   PMT Using Multiple-frequency Links

Multiple-frequency communication environments, such as wireless and fiber-optics, realize our multipath setting. Our PMT results show the possibility of secure communication, provided that the wiretapper does not have simultaneous access to all frequencies (i.e., $t_e < n$ in our setting). The challenge is to design a multiple-frequency system that enforces this property. Existing frequency-hopping solutions do not satisfy this requirement. Bluetooth for example transmits data at speed of 1Mbps over 79 adjacent 1-MHz frequency channels and by the current technology, one can easily capture all the 80-MHz frequency range and store hours of communication in a 1 Terabyte disk.

It is yet possible to design systems that serve our purpose as it is practically infeasible for a single transceiver (and ADC) to deal with wider than 100 MHz ranges [10]. All we need is to use a system whose frequency channels are far apart. Consider for instance a system design that uses $n = 70$ 20-MHz frequency-channels distributed evenly (with 80-MHz distances) over the 57–64 GHz (unlicensed Gigabit WiFi) frequency range. Data transmitted at 100 Mbps speed. Since there is only one frequency channel in each 100-MHz slot, the eavesdropper would require 70 transceiver blocks to access all 70 channels simultaneously. This is not practical in certain scenarios due to expense concern or space restriction (e.g., stealth attack on indoor communication).

Let us assume legitimate devices use only $t_a = t_b = 4$ transceivers, while the wiretapper's device can embed $t_e = 35$ such blocks. The wiretapper may switch between frequencies to learn more information. Fastest frequency synthesizers have switching time around $1\mu s$ [1]. Although one may allow longer switching time for legitimate parties, the $1\mu s$ time determines λ in our design. At the speed of 100 Mpbs, this gives $\lambda = \lfloor 10^{-6} \times 100 \times 2^{20} \rfloor = 104$ bits, implying a $(70, 4, 4, 35, 104)$-multipath setting for which the two-round AP-PMT scheme $\mathcal{F}_3$ sends private data at rate 17%. *This solution does not require pre-shared keys and provides information-theoretic security.*

6.2 PMT Using Multiple-route Networks

Multipath routing has been shown [16] to benefit reliable transmission over large networks such as mobile ad hoc networks (MANETs) and the Internet. We study whether the resource can be used to enhance privacy of communication when middle routers can be tapped into. We focus on MANETs. Studies have shown the average number of node-disjoint paths in a moderately-dense (around 500-node) MANET is over 10. Consider the following scenario: There are $n = 10$ paths between the source and destination nodes. The source can send over only $t_a = 2$ paths while the destination receives data through all $t_b = 10$ paths. The adversary's resources allow for compromising at most $t_e = 8$ paths at a time, and at least 1 millisecond is needed to redirect resources to tap into new nodes (and paths); this is quite plausible, noting the technical challenges of tapping into communicating devices. The source transmits data at the speed of 512 Kbps, implying $\lambda = \lfloor 10^{-3} \times 512 \times 2^{10} \rfloor = 524$. This leads to the $(10, 2, 8, 10, 524)$-multipath setting for which the simplified version of scheme $\mathcal{F}_2$ (Block (i) only – see Remark 2) guarantees private transmission at rate 20%.

7 Conclusion and Future Work

We have derived connectivity conditions for the possibility of P-PMT and AP-PMT in the multipath setting. We also derived lower and upper bounds on the secrecy capacities. Although in the full-access case, P-PMT and AP-PMT behave the same, in general, AP-PMT protocols attain strictly higher rates. The maximum rate for P-PMT is $[1 - \frac{t_e}{t_{ab}}]_+$, whereas AP-PMT protocols can achieves rates close to the upper-bound $1 - \frac{t_e}{n}$. The is yet a gap between the proved achievable rates and this upper-bound. *Bridging the gap is an interesting question which we leave for future work.*

Any practical communication system with path diversity can be a case to test the feasibility our PMT results. We considered the real-life scenarios of communication over multiple-frequency links and multiple-route networks. In both cases, we elaborated on how to derive multipath setting parameters and used our results to provide private communication at rates 17% and 20%, respectively. Showing the possibility of keyless communication with information-theoretic privacy is interesting. *A followup work can be the design of concrete protocols considering all practical and technical concerns that may have been missing in this work.*

References

1. Winradio ms-8323 multichannel telemetry receiver, http://www.winradio.com/home/ms8323.htm
2. Ahmadi, H., Safavi-Naini, R.: Multipath private communication: An information theoretic approach. CoRR, abs/1401.3659 (2014)
3. Chen, H., Cramer, R.: Algebraic geometric secret sharing schemes and secure multiparty computations over small fields. In: Dwork, C. (ed.) CRYPTO 2006. LNCS, vol. 4117, pp. 521–536. Springer, Heidelberg (2006)
4. Chernoff, H.: A measure of asymptotic efficiency for tests of a hypothesis based on the sum of observations. Annals of Mathematical Statistics 23(4), 493–507 (1952)
5. Dolev, D., Dwork, C., Waarts, O., Yung, M.: Perfectly secure message transmission. Journal of the ACM (JACM) 40(1), 17–47 (1993)
6. Garcia, A., Stichtenoth, H.: On the asymptotic behaviour of some towers of function fields over finite fields. Journal of Number Theory 61(2), 248–273 (1996)
7. Leyden, J.: Worried openssl uses nsa-tainted crypto? this bug has got your back (2013), http://www.theregister.co.uk/2013/12/20/openssl_crypto_bug_beneficial_sorta/
8. Lichtblau, E., Risen, J.: Spy agency mined vast data trove, officials report. New York Times (2005)
9. Linder, F.: Cisco ios attack and defense the state of the art. Presented at the 25th Chaos Communication Congress (2008)
10. Löhning, M., Fettweis, G.: The effects of aperture jitter and clock jitter in wideband adcs. Computer Standards & Interfaces 29(1), 11–18 (2007)
11. Patra, A., Choudhury, A., Pandu Rangan, C., Srinathan, K.: Unconditionally reliable and secure message transmission in undirected synchronous networks: Possibility, feasibility and optimality. International Journal of Applied Cryptography 2(2), 159–197 (2010)
12. Shamir, A.: How to share a secret. Communications of the ACM 22(11), 612–613 (1979)
13. Shor, P.W.: Polynomial-time algorithms for prime factorization and discrete logarithms on a quantum computer. SIAM Journal on Computing 26(5), 1484–1509 (1997)
14. Strasser, M., Capkun, S., Popper, C., Cagalj, M.: Jamming-resistant key establishment using uncoordinated frequency hopping. In: IEEE Symposium on Security and Privacy (SP), pp. 64–78 (2008)
15. Wood, A.D., Stankovic, J.A.: Denial of service in sensor networks. Computer 35(10), 54–62 (2002)
16. Ye, Z., Krishnamurthy, S.V., Tripathi, S.K.: A framework for reliable routing in mobile ad hoc networks. In: INFOCOM 2003. Twenty-Second Annual Joint Conference of the IEEE Computer and Communications. IEEE Societies, vol. 1, pp. 270–280. IEEE (2003)

A   Proof of Theorem 3

Given $\psi, \epsilon > 0$, the PMT family from choices of q_1 such that

$$q_1 \geq \frac{2^{\lambda/2} - 1}{t_e} \quad \text{and} \quad q_2 \geq \max\left(\frac{(2+\psi)n}{\psi^2 t_e}\ln\frac{1}{\epsilon}\,,\,\frac{2^{\lambda/2} - 1}{t'_{e,2}}\right).$$

Secrecy Rate. The two blocks communicate $c_1 = q_1 t_{ab}\lambda$ and $c_1 = q_1 t_{ab}\lambda$ bits, respectively. Recalling (7), $t_{ab} = \min(t_a, t_b)$, and $\Delta = (2^{\frac{\lambda}{2}-2} - 0.25)^{-1}$, we calculate

$$R_{\mathcal{F}_1} = \frac{r_2\lambda}{(q_1 + q_2)t_{ab}\lambda} = \frac{q_2\left(1 - \frac{t'_{e,2}}{t_{ab}} - \frac{2g_2}{q_2 t_{ab}}\right)}{q_2 + q_1} = \frac{q_2\left(1 - \frac{t'_{e,2}}{t_{ab}} - \frac{2g_2}{q_2 t_{ab}}\right)}{q_2 + \frac{r_1}{t_{ab} - t_e - \frac{2g_1}{q_1}}}$$

$$= \frac{q_2\left(1 - \frac{t'_{e,2}}{t_{ab}} - \frac{2g_2}{q_2 t_{ab}}\right)}{q_2 + \frac{q_2 w}{\lambda t_{ab}\left(1 - \frac{t_e}{t_{ab}} - \frac{2g_1}{q_1 t_{ab}}\right)}} \overset{(a)}{\geq} \frac{1 - \frac{t'_{e,2}}{t_{ab}} - \Delta}{1 + \frac{\log\left(\frac{n}{t_{ab}}\right)}{\lambda t_{ab}\left(1 - \frac{t_e}{t_{ab}} - \Delta\right)}} \overset{(b)}{\geq} \frac{1 - \frac{t'_{e,2}}{t_{ab}} - \Delta}{1 + \frac{\log(en/t_{ab})}{\lambda\left(1 - \frac{t_e}{t_{ab}} - \Delta\right)}}.$$

Inequality (a) follows by using a similar argument as in (3), noting the choices of g_1 and g_2 (7) as well as $q_1 \geq \frac{2^{\lambda/2}-1}{t_e}$ and $q_2 \geq \frac{2^{\lambda/2}-1}{t'_{e,2}}$. Inequality (b) holds due to Stirling's inequality $\binom{n}{t_{ab}} < (ne/t_{ab})^{t_{ab}}$. The fact that $\psi > 0$ can be arbitrarily small implies that $\lim_{\psi \to 0} \frac{t'_{e,2}}{t_{ab}} = \frac{t_e}{n}$; hence, the rate.

0-reliability. This is trivial: Both key-transport and coordinated-PMT use common paths.

ϵ-secrecy. Leakage occurs only if Eve observes more than $q_2 t'_{e,2}$ of the $q_2 t_{ab}$ secret paths during coordinated PMT (otherwise SSS guarantees no information leakage to Eve). Let $T'_i \leq \min(t_{ab}, t_e) = t_e$ be the number paths that Eve observes in interval $q_1 + i$. For every $s_1, s_2 \in \{0, 1\}^k$, we have

$$SD(View_E(s_1), View_E(s_2)) \leq \Pr(\sum_{i=1}^{q_2} T'_i > q_2 t'_{e,2}) \times 1 = \Pr(\sum_{i=1}^{q_2} T'_i > q_2 t'_{e,2}).$$

We upper-bound the right hand side. T'_i's are independent with hyper-geometric distribution

$$\forall 0 \leq j \leq t_e: \quad \Pr(T'_i = j) = \frac{\binom{t_{ab}}{j}\binom{n-t_{ab}}{t_e-j}}{\binom{n}{t_e}},$$

with an expected value of $\frac{t_{ab}t_e}{n}$. We apply the Chernoff bound [4] to the sum of normalized variables $\frac{T'_i}{t_{ab}}$, with mean $\mu = t_e/n$, to obtain (the last inequality is due to the choice of q_2):

$$\Pr\left(\sum_{i=1}^{q_2} T'_i > q_2 t'_{e,2}\right) = \Pr\left(\sum_{i=1}^{q_2} \frac{T'_i}{t_{ab}} > (1+\psi)q_2\mu\right) < e^{-\frac{\psi^2}{2+\psi}q_2\mu} \leq e^{-\ln(1/\epsilon)} = \epsilon.$$

Partial Key Exposure Attacks
on Takagi's Variant of RSA

Zhangjie Huang[1,2,3], Lei Hu[1,2], Jun Xu[1,2],
Liqiang Peng[1,2], and Yonghong Xie[1,2]

[1] State Key Laboratory of Information Security, Institute of Information Engineering,
Chinese Academy of Sciences, Beijing 100093, China
[2] Data Assurance and Communication Security Research Center,
Chinese Academy of Sciences, Beijing 100093, China
[3] University of Chinese Academy of Sciences, Beijing 100049, China
{zhjhuang,hu,xjun,lqpeng,yhxie}@is.ac.cn

Abstract. We present several attacks on a variant of RSA due to Takagi
when different parts of the private exponent are known to an attacker.
We consider three cases when the exposed bits are the most significant
bits, the least significant bits and the middle bits of the private exponent
respectively. Our approaches are based on Coppersmith's method for
finding small roots of modular polynomial equations. Our results extend
the results of partial key exposure attacks on RSA of Ernst, Jochemsz,
May and Weger (EUROCRYPT 2005) for moduli from $N = pq$ to $N = p^r q$ $(r \geq 2)$.

Keywords: RSA, partial key exposure, Coppersmith's method, lattice
reduction, LLL algorithm.

1 Introduction

In his seminal work [5] in 1996, Coppersmith described a method for finding small
roots of univariate modular polynomial equations in polynomial time based on
lattice basis reduction. Coppersmith showed that for a monic univariate polynomial $f(x)$ of degree d, one can find any root x_0 of $f(x) \equiv 0 \pmod{N}$ in
polynomial time if $|x_0| < N^{1/d}$. The essence of Coppersmith's method is to
find integral linear combinations of polynomials which share a common root
modulo some integer such that the result has small coefficients. Thus one may
obtain a polynomial with the desired root over the integers and one can then
find the desired root using standard root-finding algorithms. This method was
then reformulated by Howgrave-Graham [11] in a simpler way which has been
widely adopted by researchers for cryptanalysis. In general, the reformulation
by Howgrave-Graham is used when we say Coppersmith's method.

Coppersmith's method can be extended to handle multivariate modular polynomial equations with some heuristic assumptions. In the multivariate cases, we
obtain some multivariate integer polynomials and find the final roots by computing the resultants or using Gröbner basis algorithms. At present, there have

I. Boureanu, P. Owesarski, and S. Vaudenay (Eds.): ACNS 2014, LNCS 8479, pp. 134–150, 2014.

been many variants of Coppersmith's method. In 2006, Jochemsz and May [13] described a general strategy for finding small roots of modular or integer multivariate polynomial equations. Their strategy makes it easier to construct lattices and to analyse the bounds for the small roots. More recently, Herrmann and May [9] introduced the technique of unravelled linearization and Aono [1] introduced the Minkowski sum based lattice construction. All these variants make Coppersmith's method a powerful tool in the field of cryptanalysis.

Since the invention of Coppersmith's method, much effort has been made to evaluate the security of RSA and its variants. It was used to break RSA when the private exponent $d < N^{0.292}$ [3] and to attack CRT-RSA when the private exponent is small [14]. It was also used to prove the equivalence between knowing the private exponent d and factoring the modulus N [6,15]. The book [10] is a good survey of these kinds of applications.

In order to gain a faster decryption, Takagi [18] proposed a RSA-type cryptosystem with moduli $N = p^r q$. The polynomial-time equivalence between factoring the modulus and recovering the private exponent for Takagi's scheme was proved in [15]. Later in [12], Itoh, Kunihiro and Kurosawa extended the method of lattice construction in [15] and gave a polynomial-time attack when the private exponent $d < N^{\frac{7-2\sqrt{7}}{3(r+1)}}$ (and improved to $d < N^{\frac{2-\sqrt{2}}{r+1}}$ by using "Geometrically Progressive Matrices"). Both in [15] and [12], the authors constructed lattices in a clever way by taking advantage of the foreknowledge that $y^r z = N$ where variables y, z denote p, q respectively. They substituted N for every occurrence of $y^r z$ while constructing lattices. This kind of foreknowledge was not used in Jochemsz and May's strategy [13]. This trick of substituting was first used in [3] and then also adopted in [7].

In this paper, we consider the partial key exposure attacks on Takagi's variant of RSA. The partial key exposure attacks were first considered by Boneh, Durfee and Frankel in [4]. The work was then followed by Blömer and May in [2] and Ernst *et al.* in [8]. The first attack we present in this paper is for the case when some of the most significant bits (MSBs) of the private exponent are known. Our attack extends the method of constructing lattices in [12]. Our second attack on knowing some of the least significant bits (LSBs) of the private exponent can be achieved in an analogous way as it was done in [12]. We also consider how to attack the case when the known bits lie in the middle of the private exponent. All our attacks are based on Coppersmith's method. We summarize our results in the following theorems and prove them in Section 3.

Our attack results on known MSBs and on known bits in the middle of the private exponent are asymptotically the same, *i.e.*, the two attacks need the same amount of known bits. We state the results of these two attacks in Theorem 1:

Theorem 1 (Known MSBs/Known Bits in the Middle). *For any $\epsilon > 0$ there exists N_0 such that if $N > N_0$ for $N = p^r q$ where p and q are primes with the same bit-length, the following holds: Let $e = N^\alpha$ and $d = N^\beta$ be integers satisfying $ed \equiv 1 \pmod{(p-1)(q-1)}$ and $\gcd(e,p) = 1$. Given about $(1 - \frac{\delta}{\beta})$-fraction of the MSBs or continuous bits in the middle of d, the modulus N can be factored in polynomial time if*

$$\delta \le \frac{7}{4(r+1)} - \frac{1}{4}\sqrt{\frac{24(\alpha+\beta)}{r+1} - \frac{39}{(r+1)^2}} - \epsilon.$$

We show our result of Theorem 1 in Fig. 1 with $r = 2$. The figure shows the relation between the fraction of bits required for an attack and the size of d when we set e as full-size, *i.e.*, $\alpha = 2/(r+1)$. The left rectangle in the figure represents the result of the small key attack from [12].

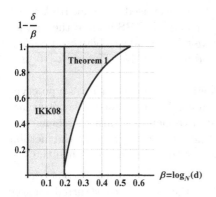

Fig. 1. Known MSBs/Known bits in the middle attack: The relation between the fraction of bits required and the size of d when $r = 2$ and $\alpha = 2/(r + 1)$

Fig. 2. Known LSBs attack: The relation between the fraction of bits required and the size of d when $r = 2$ and $\alpha = 2/(r+1)$

We note that when $r = 1$ and $\alpha = 1$, our result on known MSBs is a little bit weaker than one of the results in [8] (Section 4.1.1 therein):

$$\delta < \frac{5}{6} - \frac{1}{3}\sqrt{1 + 6\beta}.$$

In this case, the way of constructing lattices in [8] is better than ours because our method is not able to make the best of the information we get. We treat an equation which is actually over the integers as a modular equation (see Section 3.1). On the other hand, our result is a general result when $r \ge 1$ in $N = p^r q$. The case of known MSBs can be viewed as a special case of known bits in the middle.

Theorem 2 (Known LSBs). *For any $\epsilon > 0$ there exists N_0 such that if $N > N_0$ for $N = p^r q$ where p and q are primes with the same bit-length, the following holds: Let $e = N^\alpha$ and $d = N^\beta$ be integers satisfying $ed \equiv 1 \pmod{(p-1)(q-1)}$ and $\gcd(e,p) = 1$. Given about $(1 - \frac{\delta}{\beta})$-fraction of the LSBs of d, the modulus N can be factored in polynomial time if*

$$\delta \le \frac{5}{3(r+1)} - \frac{2}{3}\sqrt{\frac{3(\alpha+\beta)}{r+1} - \frac{5}{(r+1)^2}} - \epsilon.$$

Fig. 2 illustrates our result when the least significant bits of d are known. We set $r = 2$ and $\alpha = 2/(r+1)$ in Fig. 2. The figure shows the relation between the fraction of bits required for an attack and the size of d. The left rectangle in the figure represents the result of the small key attack from [12]. Our result when $r = 1$ is the same with the result in [8]. Our result may be seen as an extension of the result in [8] for moduli $N = p^r q$ when $r \geq 2$.

Our results stated above are general results for exponents (e, d) with arbitrary sizes. From the bounds for δ in these two theorems, the relations between the fraction of bits required and the size of e when d is full-size are also clear, we omit the corresponding figures here. One may notice that the size of e (represented as α) and the size of d (represented as β) have the same impact on the attacks. Intuitively, the quality of our attacks depends on the information we know, including the public exponent e and the known bits of d (and others). There is a trade-off between the size of e and the size of known bits of d. We can mount the attacks in the cases when e is smaller and d is larger (which means that we know more bits of d) and vice versa, as long as we know approximately the same number of bits. From this point of view, our results are reasonable intuitively.

The rest of this paper is organized as follows. Section 2 gives some preliminaries on lattices and also a brief description of Takagi's variant of RSA. We derive our problems from Takagi's variant of RSA in Section 3 and give our approaches to the problems. The justification of our approaches is also examined through some experiments in Section 4. Finally, we give our conclusion in Section 5.

2   Preliminaries

Coppersmith's method uses lattice basis reduction to find the polynomials with small coefficients. Hence we briefly introduce a few necessary definitions and facts about lattices. It is common to use the LLL algorithm along with Howgrave-Graham's lemma to estimate the bounds for the small roots. This was stated in Howgrave-Graham's reformulation [11] of Coppersmith's method. Finally we introduce Takagi's variant of RSA.

2.1   Lattices and Howgrave-Graham's Lemma

Let $b_1, \ldots, b_\omega \in \mathbb{Z}^n$ be linearly independent (row) vectors. A lattice L generated by $b_1, \ldots, b_\omega$ is the set of all integral linear combinations of these vectors:

$$L = \mathcal{L}(b_1, \ldots, b_\omega) = \left\{ v \in \mathbb{Z}^n \mid v = \sum_{i=1}^{\omega} a_i b_i, \ a_i \in \mathbb{Z} \right\}.$$

We call n the dimension of L and ω its rank. We often denote the basis $b_1, \ldots, b_\omega$ as a matrix, called the basis matrix of L:

$$B = \begin{pmatrix} b_1 \\ b_2 \\ \vdots \\ b_\omega \end{pmatrix} \in \mathbb{Z}^{\omega \times n}.$$

Then the determinant of L can be computed as $\det(L) = \sqrt{\det(BB^T)}$.

The most famous algorithm for lattice basis reduction is the LLL algorithm [16]. It allows one to find a short vector in a lattice in polynomial time. The proof of the following fact can be found in [17].

Fact 1 (LLL). *Let L be a lattice spanned by the rows of $B = (b_1^T, \ldots, b_\omega^T)^T$. The LLL algorithm outputs a reduced basis $v_1, \ldots, v_\omega$ satisfying*

$$\|v_i\| \leq 2^{\frac{\omega(\omega-1)}{4(\omega-i+1)}} \det(L)^{\frac{1}{\omega-i+1}}, \ 1 \leq i \leq \omega$$

in polynomial time in ω and in the bit size of the entries of the basis matrix B.

When using Coppersmith's method to find the small roots of a modular polynomial equation, the following lemma due to Howgrave-Graham is useful. It states that under which condition a modular equation holds over the integers. The norm of a polynomial $f(x_1, \ldots, x_n) = \sum a_{i_1, \ldots, i_n} x_1^{i_1} \ldots x_n^{i_n}$ is defined as $\|f(x_1, \ldots, x_n)\| = \sqrt{\sum |a_{i_1, \ldots, i_n}|^2}$.

Lemma 1 (Howgrave-Graham [11]). *Let $g(x_1, \ldots, x_n) \in \mathbb{Z}[x_1, \ldots, x_n]$ be a polynomial that consists of at most ω monomials. Suppose that*

1. $g(x_1^{(0)}, \ldots, x_n^{(0)}) \equiv 0 \pmod{N}$ *for $|x_1^{(0)}| \leq X_1, \ldots, |x_n^{(0)}| \leq X_n$, and*
2. $\|g(X_1 x_1, \ldots, X_n x_n)\| < \frac{N}{\sqrt{\omega}}$,

then $g(x_1^{(0)}, \ldots, x_n^{(0)}) = 0$ holds over the integers.

Combining the Howgrave-Graham's lemma with the LLL algorithm, we deduce that if

$$2^{\frac{\omega(\omega-1)}{4(\omega-i+1)}} \det(L)^{\frac{1}{\omega-i+1}} < \frac{N}{\sqrt{\omega}},$$

then the polynomials corresponding to the shortest i reduced basis vectors satisfy Howgrave-Graham's bound. The condition implies

$$\det(L) < 2^{-\frac{\omega(\omega-1)}{4}} \left(\frac{1}{\sqrt{\omega}}\right)^{\omega-i+1} N^{\omega-i+1}.$$

As in previous works, we ignore the terms that do not depend on N and simply check the condition $\det(L) < N^{\omega-i+1}$. In practice, this is convenient when N is large enough. After obtaining enough equations over the integers, one can extract the common roots by computing the resultants of these polynomials under the following heuristic assumption:

Assumption 1. *The resultant computations for the polynomials corresponding to the first few LLL-reduced basis vectors produce non-zero polynomials.*

The above assumption may sometimes fail especially for the cases dealing with four or more variables. If this assumption fails, we may obtain the roots in other ways (See the note in Section 4.).

2.2 Takagi's RSA-Type Cryptosystem

In 1998, Takagi [18] proposed a cryptosystem with moduli $N = p^r q$ based on RSA aiming at a faster decryption process and keeping its security at the same time. We give a brief description of Takagi's cryptosystem here.

Generate two primes p and q with the same bit-length and let $N = p^r q$ for some small integer $r \geq 2$. Let e and d be integers satisfying $ed \equiv 1 \pmod{(p-1)(q-1)}$ and $\gcd(e, p) = 1$. Then set (N, e) as the public key and (p, q, d) as the private key. The encryption of a message $M \in \mathbb{Z}_N^*$ is like in the RSA cryptosystem: $C = M^e \bmod N$. The decryption process is as follows. Firstly, compute $M_p = C^d \bmod p$ and $M_q = C^d \bmod q$. It is clear that $M \equiv M_q \pmod{q}$. Then compute an integer M_{p^r} satisfying $M \equiv M_{p^r} \pmod{p^r}$ from M_p and C using Hensel lifting. At last M is obtained from M_q and M_{p^r} using the Chinese Remainder Theorem. We refer to the original article [18] for more details especially for the Hensel lifting computation.

3   Description of Attacks and Proof of Theorems

In this section, we give our attack methods to the problems when one of the three different parts of the private exponent d in Takagi's variant of RSA is known. Here the three different parts are the most significant bits, the least significant bits and the continuous bits lying in the middle of d. We first describe how to construct lattices from the problems and then prove the results stated in Section 1. The first two types of exposure bits are already considered in [8] and we treat them in an analogous way in this paper. We consider a new type of known bits, *i.e.*, bits in the middle of d. Our methods extend the way of constructing lattices in [12].

3.1   Attack with Known MSBs

Deriving the problem. In Takagi's variant of RSA, we have

$$N = p^r q \text{ and } ed \equiv 1 \bmod (p-1)(q-1),$$

where p and q are two primes with the same bit-length. There exists an integer k such that

$$ed = 1 + k(p-1)(q-1). \tag{1}$$

We assume the exponents $e = N^\alpha$ and $d = N^\beta$. Since the bit-lengths of p and q are the same, then it holds that $p < 2N^{1/(r+1)}$ and $q < 2N^{1/(r+1)}$. Since $e < (p-1)(q-1)$ and $d < (p-1)(q-1)$, we have $0 < \alpha, \beta < 2/(r+1)$. According to (1), we have

$$k = \frac{ed - 1}{(p-1)(q-1)} < \frac{2ed}{pq} < 2N^{\alpha + \beta - \frac{2}{r+1}}.$$

If we know some of the most significant bits of the private exponent d, that is we know $\tilde{d}$ such that $d = \tilde{d} + d_0$, where d_0 is the unknown part of d satisfies $|d_0| = |d - \tilde{d}| < N^\delta$ for $\delta < \beta$. Then we can rewrite (1) as

$$e(\tilde{d} + d_0) = 1 + k(p-1)(q-1),$$

and we know that the polynomial

$$f_{\mathrm{msb}}(w, x, y, z) = x(y-1)(z-1) + ew + 1$$

has a root $(-d_0, k, p, q)$ modulo $N_0 = e\tilde{d}$ ($\approx N^{\alpha+\beta}$). Note that we view an integer equation as a modular equation here. Define

$$W = N^\delta, \; X = 2N^{\alpha+\beta-2/(r+1)} \text{ and } Y = Z = 2N^{1/(r+1)}.$$

We are trying to find a "small" root $(w_0, x_0, y_0, z_0) = (-d_0, k, p, q)$ of

$$f_{\mathrm{msb}}(w, x, y, z) \equiv 0 \pmod{N_0}$$

with the bounds $|w_0| < W$, $|x_0| < X$, $|y_0| < Y$ and $|z_0| < Z$.

Constructing the Lattice Basis. The first step of our attack is to collect some polynomials which share a common root (w_0, x_0, y_0, z_0) modulo N_0^m for some fixed positive integer m which is polynomial in $\frac{1}{\epsilon}$. We define these polynomials as (the form)

$$g_{i_1,i_2,i_3,i_4,i_5}(w, x, y, z) = w^{i_1} x^{i_2} y^{i_3} z^{i_4} f_{\mathrm{msb}}(w, x, y, z)^{i_5} N_0^{m-i_5}, \text{ for } 0 \le i_5 \le m,$$

where the indices $(i_1, i_2, i_3, i_4, i_5)$ will be determined later. We then construct a lattice basis with the coefficient vectors of $g_{i_1,i_2,i_3,i_4,i_5}(wW, xX, yY, zZ)$ as its basis vectors. The principle of the choice for $(i_1, i_2, i_3, i_4, i_5)$ is that we collect an (ordered) list of polynomials $G = \{ g_{i_1,i_2,i_3,i_4,i_5} \}$ such that every polynomial in the list introduces exactly one monomial that does not appear in the previous polynomials. This will make the basis triangular which allows for an easy determinant calculation.

Since our choice for the polynomials is based on the polynomials Itoh, Kunihiro and Kurosawa chose in [12], we briefly introduce the construction of basis in [12]. In [12], they considered the problem of finding the small root (k, p, q) of the modular polynomial

$$\bar{f}(x, y, z) = x(y-1)(z-1) + 1 \bmod e, \tag{2}$$

where e, k, p and q are the same meanings as in (1). They constructed a basis which was triangular by taking advantage of the relation that $y^r z = N$ since $N = p^r q$ is public. Every occurrence of $y^r z$ in the polynomials was replaced

---

Algorithm 1. The way of collecting polynomials in [12] for integers n and s

---

$G_n \leftarrow \emptyset$
for $u = 0, \ldots, n$ **do**
  for $i = 0, \ldots, u - 1$ **do**
    append $\bar{g}_{u-i,0,0,i}$, $\bar{g}_{u-i,1,0,i}$ to G_n
    append $\bar{g}_{u-i,r-1,1,i}$, $\bar{g}_{u-i,r-2,1,i}, \ldots, \bar{g}_{u-i,1,1,i}$ to G_n
  for $j = 0, \ldots, s$ **do**
    append $\bar{g}_{0,j,0,u}$ to G_n
  for $k = 1, \ldots, s$ **do**
    append $\bar{g}_{0,r-1,k,u}$, $\bar{g}_{0,r-2,k,u}, \ldots, \bar{g}_{0,0,k,u}$ to G_n
return G_n

---

by N and thus changed the monomials in the polynomials. All our settings are the same with theirs except that we consider the polynomial

$$f_{\mathrm{msb}}(w, x, y, z) = \bar{f}(x, y, z) + ew \bmod N_0 \tag{3}$$

instead of $\bar{f}(x, y, z)$.

For a fixed positive integer n and some integer s, they defined the list of polynomials, which we denote as G_n here, according to Algorithm 1. In Algorithm 1, $\bar{g}_{j_1,j_2,j_3,j_4} = x^{j_1} y^{j_2} z^{j_3} \bar{f}^{j_4} e^{n-j_4}$, which means that all polynomials in G_n satisfy $\bar{g}_{j_1,j_2,j_3,j_4}(k, p, q) = 0 \bmod e^n$. Obviously, with the same s, $G_n \subset G_{n+1}$ for any $n \geq 0$.

Now we come to our construction. The idea behind our choice for the polynomials is as follows. First we will show that how to order the monomials can we obtain a basis which is triangular. For any positive integer a, we have the binomial expansion

$$f_{\mathrm{msb}}^a = (\bar{f} + ew)^a = \underbrace{(ew)^a}_{w^a} + \underbrace{\binom{a}{1}(ew)^{a-1}\bar{f}}_{w^{a-1}} + \underbrace{\binom{a}{2}(ew)^{a-2}\bar{f}^2}_{w^{a-2}} + \cdots + \underbrace{\bar{f}^a}_{w^0} . \tag{4}$$

We partition the set of monomials in f_{msb}^a into $a+1$ subsets naturally in terms of the exponent of w in the monomials in (4). Therefore, we order all the monomials in f_{msb}^a in the lattice basis by this sequence: the monomials in the term w^a, then the monomials in the term $w^{a-1}f$, and so on.

For $0 \leq b \leq a$, we know from [12] that we can construct a triangular basis from the polynomials in G_b (as in Algorithm 1 when $n = b$) for the monomials in $\bar{f}^b$. Obviously we can construct a triangular basis from the polynomials in $w^{a-b}G_b$ for the monomials in $w^{a-b}\bar{f}^b$. As an abuse of notation, we denote $w^{a-b}G_b$ as the set of polynomials in G_b each multiplied by the term w^{a-b}. We use similar notations hereafter. We then concatenate all the triangular basis for $0 \leq b \leq a$ and end up with a triangular basis for the monomials in f_{msb}^a.

We summarize this process in Algorithm 2. In Algorithm 2, we fix integers m and s and define the list of polynomials G we chose for our problem as follows:

$$G = \bigcup_{i=0}^{m} w^{m-i} G_i = w^m G_0 \bigcup w^{m-1} G_1 \bigcup w^{m-2} G_2 \bigcup \cdots \bigcup w^0 G_m. \tag{5}$$

Algorithm 2. Collecting the polynomials and the corresponding monomials

---

$G \leftarrow \emptyset$, $H \leftarrow \emptyset$
for $v = m, \ldots, 0$ **do**
    for $u = 0, \ldots, m - v$ **do**
        for $i = 0, \ldots, u - 1$ **do**
            append $g_{v,u-i,0,0,i}$, $g_{v,u-i,1,0,i}$ to G
            append $w^v x^u z^i$, $w^v x^u y^{i+1}$ to H
            append $g_{v,u-i,r-1,1,i}$, $g_{v,u-i,r-2,1,i}, \ldots, g_{v,u-i,1,1,i}$ to G
            append $w^v x^u y^{r-1} z^{i+1}$, $w^v x^u y^{r-2} z^{i+1}, \ldots, w^v x^u y z^{i+1}$ to H
        for $j = 0, \ldots, s$ **do**
            append $g_{v,0,j,0,u}$ to G
            if $j = 0$ **then**
                append $w^v x^u z^u$ to H
            else
                append $w^v x^u y^{u+j}$ to H
        for $k = 1, \ldots, s$ **do**
            append $g_{v,0,r-1,k,u}$, $g_{v,0,r-2,k,u}, \ldots, g_{v,0,0,k,u}$ to G
            append $w^v x^u y^{r-1} z^{u+k}$, $w^v x^u y^{r-2} z^{u+k}, \ldots, w^v x^u z^{u+k}$ to H
return G, H

We also denote the list of corresponding monomials introduced by the polynomials in G as H.

Remark 1. We must stress that the G_i in (5) is not totally the same as the ones that Algorithm 1 output. We write (5) for ease of presentation. They differ in two places and the purpose of these two replacements is to make sure that the polynomials we chose in G satisfy $g_{i_1,i_2,i_3,i_4,i_5}(w_0, x_0, y_0, z_0) \equiv 0 \bmod N_0^m$.

1. The factor e is replaced by N_0. This replacement does not influence the structure of polynomials, *i.e.*, the monomials they contain;
2. $\bar{f}$ is replaced by f_{msb}. We will show that this replacement does not affect the property of triangular of the final basis. For some $0 \le i \le m$, we consider the polynomials in $w^{m-i} G_i$. We know from Algorithm 1 that each polynomial $\bar{g}$ in G_i is in the form of $\bar{g} = x^{j_1} y^{j_2} z^{j_3} \bar{f}^{j_4} e^{i-j_4}$ with $j_4 \le i$. After the replacements of e to N_0 and $\bar{f}$ to f_{msb}, the corresponding polynomial in $w^{m-i} G_i$ becomes $w^{m-i} x^{j_1} y^{j_2} z^{j_3} f_{\mathrm{msb}}^{j_4} N_0^{i-j_4}$. Rewrite this as

$$w^{m-i} x^{j_1} y^{j_2} z^{j_3} f_{\mathrm{msb}}^{j_4} N_0^{i-j_4}$$
$$= w^{m-i} x^{j_1} y^{j_2} z^{j_3} (\bar{f} + ew)^{j_4} N_0^{i-j_4}$$
$$= N_0^{i-j_4} x^{j_1} y^{j_2} z^{j_3} \sum_{j=0}^{j_4} \binom{j_4}{j} e^j w^{m-i+j} \bar{f}^{j_4-j}$$
$$= N_0^{i-j_4} x^{j_1} y^{j_2} z^{j_3} w^{m-i} \bar{f}^{j_4} + \underbrace{N_0^{i-j_4} x^{j_1} y^{j_2} z^{j_3} \sum_{j=1}^{j_4} \binom{j_4}{j} e^j w^{m-i+j} \bar{f}^{j_4-j}}.$$

Look at the degrees of w in the last summation, it is $m - i + j$, which is in the interval $[m - i + 1, m]$. The monomials in the summation part are in the polynomials in $\bigcup_{j=1}^{i} w^{m-i+j} G_i$. As stated before, we present the monomials in the basis according to the powers of w in it. Therefore, the monomials in the summation part already appear in the basis. The new monomials introduced are only those in the term $N_0^{i-j_4} x^{j_1} y^{j_2} z^{j_3} w^{m-i} \bar{f}^{j_4}$. The corresponding polynomials for these new monomials are in $w^{m-i} G_i$. Algorithm 1 guarantees that the final basis is triangular.

Calculating the Bound. A list of polynomials $G = \{ g_{i_1,i_2,i_3,i_4,i_5} \}$ is defined above. Denote the basis with the coefficient vectors of $g_{i_1,i_2,i_3,i_4,i_5} (wW, xX, yY, zZ)$ as its basis vectors as M and the lattice generated by M as L. Let $M^{(v,u)}$ be the submatrix whose rows are corresponding to the polynomials for some $v \in [0, m]$, $u \in [0, m - v]$ and columns are corresponding to the monomials in the form of $w^v x^u y^a z^b$ for some integers a and b. We show the structure of M in Table 1 when $m = 2$. All the entries above the main diagonal are zeroes and the entries marked as asterisks are those whose values do not contribute to the determinant.

Table 1. Structure of matrix M with $m = 2$

			w^2	w^1		w^0		
			x^0	x^0	x^1	x^0	x^1	x^2
$v = 2$	$u = 0$		$M^{(2,0)}$					
$v = 1$	$u = 0$		$*$	$M^{(1,0)}$				
	$u = 1$		$*$	$*$	$M^{(1,1)}$			
$v = 0$	$u = 0$		$*$	$*$	$*$	$M^{(0,0)}$		
	$u = 1$		$*$	$*$	$*$	$*$	$M^{(0,1)}$	
	$u = 2$		$*$	$*$	$*$	$*$	$*$	$M^{(0,2)}$

Let $s = \tau m$ for $\tau > 0$ which will be optimized later. In Appendix A, an asymptotic bound concerning the upper bounds for the sizes of the roots, W, X, Y and Z is given:

$$W^{(r+1)(1+4\tau)} X^{2(r+1)(1+2\tau)} Y^{1+4\tau+6\tau^2} Z^{r(1+4\tau+6\tau^2)} < N_0^{(r+1)(1+4\tau)}.$$

Substituting the values for N_0, W, X, Y and Z, we obtain the inequality on τ:

$$\frac{6}{r+1} \tau^2 + 4 \left(\delta - \frac{1}{r+1} \right) \tau + \left(\alpha + \beta + \delta - \frac{3}{r+1} \right) < 0.$$

Let τ be the optimal value $\frac{1}{3}(1 - \delta(r+1))$. Then we obtain the inequality on δ:

$$2\delta^2 - \frac{7}{r+1} \delta + \frac{11}{(r+1)^2} - \frac{3(\alpha + \beta)}{r+1} > 0.$$

This implies that

$$\delta < \frac{7}{4(r+1)} - \frac{1}{4}\sqrt{\frac{24(\alpha+\beta)}{r+1} - \frac{39}{(r+1)^2}}.$$

The dimension of our lattice is $O(m^4)$ which is polynomial in $\frac{1}{\epsilon}$. The bit-sizes of the entries are clearly polynomial in $\log(N)$. Hence, the running time of our method is polynomial in $(\log(N), \frac{1}{\epsilon})$. The result for knowing the MSBs in Theorem 1 is obtained.

3.2   Attack with Known LSBs

In this section, we consider the case when we know some of the least significant bits of the private exponent d.

Following the notations in Section 3.1, we let $e = N^\alpha$ and $d = N^\beta$. Assume d is in the form of $d = d_1 R + \hat{d}$, where $\hat{d}$ denotes the known LSBs and R is some known integer. Let R be $N^{\beta-\delta}$. We deduce that $|d_1| = |\frac{d-\hat{d}}{R}| < |\frac{d}{R}| = N^\delta$. Then we can rewrite (1) as

$$e(d_1 R + \hat{d}) = 1 + k(p-1)(q-1).$$

Define

$$f_{\text{lsb}}(x, y, z) = x(y-1)(z-1) + (1 - e\hat{d}).$$

Then $(x_0, y_0, z_0) = (k, p, q)$ is a root of $f_{\text{lsb}}(x, y, z) \equiv 0 \pmod{N_1}$ where $N_1 = eR (= N^{\alpha+\beta-\delta})$. Define

$$X = 2N^{\alpha+\beta-2/(r+1)} \text{ and } Y = Z = 2N^{1/(r+1)},$$

then $|x_0| < X$, $|y_0| < Y$ and $|z_0| < Z$.

$f_{\text{lsb}}(x, y, z)$ contains the same monomials with the polynomial $\bar{f}$ (See Section 3.1.) considered in [12]. We can construct the lattice in an analogous way with the authors did in [12]. We can also view this problem as a special case of the problem we considered in Section 3.1. We collect polynomials as in Algorithm 2 except that we fix $v = 0$. We then construct a lattice using these polynomials. All the computations are similar to those in Appendix A except that we fix $v = 0$. We leave the calculations for the following condition in Appendix B:

$$X^{(r+1)(2+3\tau)}Y^{1+3\tau+3\tau^2}Z^{r(1+3\tau+3\tau^2)} < N_1^{(r+1)(1+3\tau)}.$$

τ is the same as in previous section. Substituting the values for N_1, X, Y and Z into the condition, we obtain

$$\delta < \frac{5}{3(r+1)} - \frac{2}{3}\sqrt{\frac{3(\alpha+\beta)}{r+1} - \frac{5}{(r+1)^2}},$$

when $\tau = \frac{1}{2}(1 - \delta(r+1))$. The running time of our method is polynomial in $(\log(N), \frac{1}{\epsilon})$ as in the previous section. This completes the proof of Theorem 2.

3.3   Attack with Known Bits in the Middle

When the known bits are in the middle of d, we can write d as $d = d_{2,1} + \bar{d}R_1 + d_{2,2}R_2$, where $\bar{d}$ represents the known bits lying in the middle of d, and $d_{2,1}$, $d_{2,2}$ represents the unknown least significant bits and most significant bits respectively. Moreover, R_1 and R_2 are two known integers. Let us assume that $d_{2,1}$ and $d_{2,2}$ are bounded by N^{δ_1} and N^{δ_2} respectively, then R_2 is about $N^{\beta-\delta_2}$. From (1) we have

$$e(d_{2,1} + \bar{d}R_1 + d_{2,2}R_2) = 1 + k(p-1)(q-1).$$

Rearranging it, we get

$$k(p-1)(q-1) - ed_{2,1} - e\bar{d}R_1 + 1 = eR_2d_{2,2}.$$

Therefore we formulate our problem as finding a small root of the polynomial

$$f_{\mathrm{mid}}(w, x, y, z) = x(y-1)(z-1) - ew + (1 - e\bar{d}R_1)$$

modulo $N_2 = eR_2$ ($\approx N^{\alpha+\beta-\delta_2}$). The root is $(w_0, x_0, y_0, z_0) = (d_{2,1}, k, p, q)$ with $|w_0| < W$, $|x_0| < X$, $|y_0| < Y$ and $|z_0| < Z$ where

$$W = N^{\delta_1}, \ X = 2N^{\alpha+\beta-2/(r+1)} \ \text{and} \ Y = Z = 2N^{1/(r+1)}.$$

The polynomial $f_{\mathrm{mid}}(w, x, y, z) = x(y-1)(z-1) - ew + (1 - e\bar{d}R_1)$ has the same monomials with f_{msb} we considered in Section 3.1. We can construct our lattice in an analogous manner as in Section 3.1 and apply the bound directly. Plugging the values for N_2, W, X, Y and Z into the bound

$$W^{(r+1)(1+4\tau)}X^{2(r+1)(1+2\tau)}Y^{1+4\tau+6\tau^2}Z^{r(1+4\tau+6\tau^2)} < N_2^{(r+1)(1+4\tau)}$$

and doing some routine calculations, we obtain that

$$\delta < \frac{7}{4(r+1)} - \frac{1}{4}\sqrt{\frac{24(\alpha+\beta)}{r+1} - \frac{39}{(r+1)^2}},$$

when $\tau = \frac{1}{3}(1 - \delta(r+1))$. Here we denote $\delta_1 + \delta_2$ as δ. The running time of our method is polynomial in $(\log(N), \frac{1}{\epsilon})$ as in Section 3.1. This completes the proof of Theorem 1.

Table 2. Some results of the experiments with $r = 2$ and $\alpha = 2/3$

	N (bits)	β	δ	m	s	dim(L)	$\log_2(\det(L))$	time (LLL)
MSBs	600	0.10	0.03	6	1	280	7.69×10^5	16.2 hr
	1000	0.05	0.04	6	1	280	1.19×10^6	2.8 hr
LSBs	2000	0.20	0.05	8	2	171	2.28×10^6	54.7 hr
	1000	0.15	0.10	9	2	205	1.32×10^6	33.3 hr
MBs	1000	0.10	0.03	6	1	280	1.26×10^6	36.6 hr
	1000	0.08	0.04	6	1	280	1.21×10^6	14.0 hr

4   Experiments

Our methods are heuristic due to Assumption 1 as stated before. In order to show the correctness of our methods, we ran several experiments on a desktop running Ubuntu with 2.83GHz Intel Core2 CPU and 4GB RAM. As examples, we only ran our experiments with full-size e. Thinking of that the dimensions of our lattices are large even with small parameters (r, m, s), we chose our parameters which are relatively small.

We chose the parameters with the exact expressions, like (6) and (7) in Appendix A, for the dimensions and determinants of lattices. For a specific value of β (representing size of d), we chose a value of δ (representing size of the unknown bits) in the range of our results. Then we chose m and s subject to the condition

$$\det(L) < N_i^{m(\dim(L)-1)}$$

such that the dimension of the lattice is relatively small. We list some parameter settings and the results of the experiments in Table 2. In all our experiments, we could obtain the final roots and thus factored the moduli N.

We found that Assumption 1 may fail on a few occasions. In these cases, two ways may be used to find the final roots.

1. For example, assume we have three polynomials $f_1(x, y, z)$, $f_2(x, y, z)$ and $f_3(x, y, z)$ with a common root (x_0, y_0, z_0). We take $f_{12}(y, z) = \mathrm{Res}_x(f_1, f_2)$, $f_{13}(y, z) = \mathrm{Res}_x(f_1, f_3)$ and then $f_{23}(z) = \mathrm{Res}_y(f_{12}, f_{13})$. If unfortunately $f_{23}(z) \equiv 0$, which means that f_{12} and f_{13} have a nontrivial factor, then we can first take $f'_{12} = \frac{f_{12}}{\gcd(f_{12}, f_{13})}$ and $f'_{13} = \frac{f_{13}}{\gcd(f_{12}, f_{13})}$. Finally, we take $f'_{23}(z) = \mathrm{Res}_y(f'_{12}, f'_{13})$. It ends up with $f'_{23}(z_0) = 0$ but $f'_{23}(z) \not\equiv 0$. Use any standard root-finding algorithm to recover z_0 and then recover y_0 from $f'_{12}(y, z_0) = 0$ and x_0 from $f_1(x, y_0, z_0) = 0$.
2. Another way is to use the technique of Gröbner basis. We found that for sufficiently large N, there were more polynomials which are corresponding to the LLL-reduced basis vectors that share the desired root. This may benefit us when computing the Gröbner basis by adding all these polynomials in the basis.

Unfortunately, both the resultant computations and the Gröbner basis computations consume too much memory and time in our experiments. For some experiments, we just checked that the polynomials we obtained contain the roots indeed but rather than really did the computations.

5   Conclusion

In this paper, we considered partial key exposure attacks on Takagi's variant of RSA with moduli $N = p^r q$ $(r \geq 2)$. We presented three attacks when different parts of the private exponent are exposed to an attacker. Our results showed that when a certain number of bits of the private exponent are exposed, then the modulus N can be factored in polynomial time. We examined the validity of our methods through some experiments.

Acknowledgements. The authors would like to thank anonymous reviewers for their helpful comments and suggestions. The work of this paper was supported by the National Key Basic Research Program of China (2013CB834203), the National Natural Science Foundation of China (Grant 61070172), and the Strategic Priority Research Program of Chinese Academy of Sciences under Grant XDA06010702.

References

1. Aono, Y.: Minkowski sum based lattice construction for multivariate simultaneous Coppersmith's technique and applications to RSA. In: Boyd, C., Simpson, L. (eds.) ACISP. LNCS, vol. 7959, pp. 88–103. Springer, Heidelberg (2013)

2. Blömer, J., May, A.: New partial key exposure attacks on RSA. In: Boneh, D. (ed.) CRYPTO 2003. LNCS, vol. 2729, pp. 27–43. Springer, Heidelberg (2003)

3. Boneh, D., Durfee, G.: Cryptanalysis of RSA with private key d less than $N^{0.292}$. In: Stern, J. (ed.) EUROCRYPT 1999. LNCS, vol. 1592, pp. 1–11. Springer, Heidelberg (1999)

4. Boneh, D., Durfee, G., Frankel, Y.: An attack on RSA given a small fraction of the private key bits. In: Ohta, K., Pei, D. (eds.) ASIACRYPT 1998. LNCS, vol. 1514, pp. 25–34. Springer, Heidelberg (1998)

5. Coppersmith, D.: Finding a small root of a univariate modular equation. In: Maurer, U.M. (ed.) EUROCRYPT 1996. LNCS, vol. 1070, pp. 155–165. Springer, Heidelberg (1996)

6. Coron, J.S., May, A.: Deterministic polynomial-time equivalence of computing the RSA secret key and factoring. J. Cryptol. 20(1), 39–50 (2007)

7. Durfee, G., Nguyên, P.Q.: Cryptanalysis of the RSA schemes with short secret exponent from Asiacrypt '99. In: Okamoto, T. (ed.) ASIACRYPT 2000. LNCS, vol. 1976, pp. 14–29. Springer, Heidelberg (2000)

8. Ernst, M., Jochemsz, E., May, A., de Weger, B.: Partial key exposure attacks on RSA up to full size exponents. In: Cramer, R. (ed.) EUROCRYPT 2005. LNCS, vol. 3494, pp. 371–386. Springer, Heidelberg (2005)

9. Herrmann, M., May, A.: Maximizing small root bounds by linearization and applications to small secret exponent RSA. In: Nguyen, P.Q., Pointcheval, D. (eds.) PKC 2010. LNCS, vol. 6056, pp. 53–69. Springer, Heidelberg (2010)

10. Hinek, M.J.: Cryptanalysis of RSA and Its Variants, 1st edn. Chapman & Hall/CRC (2009)

11. Howgrave-Graham, N.: Finding small roots of univariate modular equations revisited. In: Darnell, M.J. (ed.) Cryptography and Coding 1997. LNCS, vol. 1355, pp. 131–142. Springer, Heidelberg (1997)

12. Itoh, K., Kunihiro, N., Kurosawa, K.: Small secret key attack on a variant of RSA (due to Takagi). In: Malkin, T. (ed.) CT-RSA 2008. LNCS, vol. 4964, pp. 387–406. Springer, Heidelberg (2008)

13. Jochemsz, E., May, A.: A strategy for finding roots of multivariate polynomials with new applications in attacking RSA variants. In: Lai, X., Chen, K. (eds.) ASIACRYPT 2006. LNCS, vol. 4284, pp. 267–282. Springer, Heidelberg (2006)

14. Jochemsz, E., May, A.: A polynomial time attack on RSA with private CRT-exponents smaller than $N^{0.073}$. In: Menezes, A. (ed.) CRYPTO 2007. LNCS, vol. 4622, pp. 395–411. Springer, Heidelberg (2007)

15. Kunihiro, N., Kurosawa, K.: Deterministic polynomial time equivalence between factoring and key-recovery attack on Takagi's RSA. In: Okamoto, T., Wang, X. (eds.) PKC 2007. LNCS, vol. 4450, pp. 412–425. Springer, Heidelberg (2007)
16. Lenstra, A., Lenstra Jr., H.W., Lovász, L.: Factoring polynomials with rational coefficients. Mathematische Annalen 261(4), 515–534 (1982)
17. May, A.: New RSA vulnerabilities using lattice reduction methods. Ph.D. thesis, University of Paderborn (2003)
18. Takagi, T.: Fast RSA-type cryptosystem modulo $p^k q$. In: Krawczyk, H. (ed.) CRYPTO 1998. LNCS, vol. 1462, pp. 318–326. Springer, Heidelberg (1998)

A   The Asymptotic Bound in Section 3.1

Let $\omega_{v,u}$ be the dimension of $M^{(v,u)}$ as in Table 1. It is easy to see that

$$\omega_{v,u} = u(r+1) + (s+1) + sr = (r+1)(u+s) + 1.$$

$M^{(v,u)}$ is lower triangular and the elements on its diagonal are bounds (multiplied by some powers of N_0) for the monomials. Therefore, the determinant of $M^{(v,u)}$ is

$$\det\left(M^{(v,u)}\right) = N_0^{t_n} W^{t_w} X^{t_x} Y^{t_y} Z^{t_z},$$

where t_n, t_w, t_x, t_y and t_z are given as follows:

$$t_n = \sum_{i=0}^{u-1}(m-i)(r+1) + (m-u)(1+s+rs)$$

$$= m((r+1)(u+s)+1) - \frac{1}{2}u((r+1)(u+2s) - r + 1),$$

$$t_w = v\omega_{v,u} = v((r+1)(u+s)+1),$$

$$t_x = u\omega_{v,u} = u((r+1)(u+s)+1),$$

$$t_y = \sum_{i=0}^{u-1}\left(i+1+\frac{1}{2}r(r-1)\right) + \sum_{j=1}^{s}(u+j) + \sum_{k=1}^{s}\frac{1}{2}r(r-1)$$

$$= \frac{1}{2}(u+s)(u+s+r(r-1)+1),$$

$$t_z = \sum_{i=0}^{u-1}(i+(i+1)(r-1)) + u + \sum_{k=1}^{s}(u+k)r = \frac{1}{2}r(u+s)(u+s+1).$$

Then we can compute the dimension of the lattice L:

$$\dim(L) = \sum_{v=0}^{m}\sum_{u=0}^{m-v}\omega_{v,u} = \frac{1}{6}(r+1)(1+3\tau)m^3 + o(m^3), \tag{6}$$

and the determinant of L:

$$\det(L) = \prod_{v=0}^{m}\prod_{u=0}^{m-v}\det\left(M^{(v,u)}\right) = N_0^{s_n} W^{s_w} X^{s_x} Y^{s_y} Z^{s_z}, \tag{7}$$

where

$$s_n = \sum_{v=0}^{m} \sum_{u=0}^{m-v} t_n = \frac{1}{24}(r+1)(3+8\tau)m^4 + o(m^4),$$

$$s_w = \sum_{v=0}^{m} \sum_{u=0}^{m-v} t_w = \frac{1}{24}(r+1)(1+4\tau)m^4 + o(m^4),$$

$$s_x = \sum_{v=0}^{m} \sum_{u=0}^{m-v} t_x = \frac{1}{12}(r+1)(1+2\tau)m^4 + o(m^4),$$

$$s_y = \sum_{v=0}^{m} \sum_{u=0}^{m-v} t_y = \frac{1}{24}(1+4\tau+6\tau^2)m^4 + o(m^4),$$

$$s_z = \sum_{v=0}^{m} \sum_{u=0}^{m-v} t_z = \frac{1}{24}r(1+4\tau+6\tau^2)m^4 + o(m^4).$$

We then apply LLL-reduction algorithm to the lattice L. In order to obtain the root (w_0, x_0, y_0, z_0) by computing the resultants, we need four polynomials which all have (w_0, x_0, y_0, z_0) as a root. Since we already have two such polynomials, which are $f_1 = y^r z - N$ and $f_2 = x(y-1)(z-1) + ew + 1 - e\tilde{d}$, we need another two such polynomials. If the polynomials corresponding to the shortest two vectors in the LLL-reduced basis satisfy Howgrave-Graham's condition

$$\det(L) < N_0^{m(\dim(L)-1)},$$

we get another two such polynomials f_3 and f_4 according to Lemma 1. Then the root (w_0, x_0, y_0, z_0) can be obtained from these four polynomials by using the resultant technique under Assumption 1.

Ignore the terms that do not depend on N_0 and the low order terms $o(m^4)$, we obtain that

$$W^{(r+1)(1+4\tau)} X^{2(r+1)(1+2\tau)} Y^{1+4\tau+6\tau^2} Z^{r(1+4\tau+6\tau^2)} < N_0^{(r+1)(1+4\tau)}.$$

B   The Asymptotic Bound in Section 3.2

We reuse some notations in Appendix A. The dimension of the lattice we construct for the problem in Section 3.2 is

$$\dim(L) = \sum_{u=0}^{m} \omega_{v,u} = \frac{1}{2}(r+1)(1+2\tau)m^2 + o(m^2).$$

The determinant is $\det(L) = N_1^{s_n} X^{s_x} Y^{s_y} Z^{s_z}$ where

$$s_n = \sum_{u=0}^{m} t_n = \frac{1}{6}(r+1)(2+3\tau)m^3 + o(m^3),$$

$$s_x = \sum_{u=0}^{m} t_x = \frac{1}{6}(r+1)(2+3\tau)m^3 + o(m^3),$$

$$s_y = \sum_{u=0}^{m} t_y = \frac{1}{6}(1+3\tau+3\tau^2)m^3 + o(m^3),$$

$$s_z = \sum_{u=0}^{m} t_z = \frac{1}{6}r(1+3\tau+3\tau^2)m^3 + o(m^3).$$

From $\det(L) < N_1^{m(\dim(L)-1)}$, we derive that

$$X^{(r+1)(2+3\tau)}Y^{1+3\tau+3\tau^2}Z^{r(1+3\tau+3\tau^2)} < N_1^{(r+1)(1+3\tau)}.$$

New Partial Key Exposure Attacks
on CRT-RSA with Large Public Exponents

Yao Lu[1,2,*], Rui Zhang[1,*], and Dongdai Lin[1]

[1] State Key Laboratory of Information Security (SKLOIS)
Institute of Information Engineering (IIE)
Chinese Academy of Sciences (CAS)
[2] University of Chinese Academy of Sciences (UCAS)
lywhhit@gmail.com, {r-zhang,ddlin}@iie.ac.cn

Abstract. In Crypto'03, Blömer and May provided several partial key exposure attacks on CRT-RSA. In their attacks, they suppose that an attacker can either succeed to obtain the most significant bits (MSBs) or the least significant bits (LSBs) of $d_p = d \bmod (p-1)$ in consecutive order. For the case of known LSBs of d_p, their algorithm is polynomial-time only for small public exponents e (i.e. $e = \mathrm{poly}(\log N)$). However, in some practical applications, we prefer to use large e (Like $e \approx d_p$, to let the public and private operations with the same computational effort). In this paper, we propose some lattice-based attacks for this extended setting. For known LSBs case, we introduce two approaches that work up to $e < N^{\frac{3}{8}}$. Similar results (though not as strong) are obtained for MSBs case. We also provide detailed experimental results to justify our claims.

Keywords: lattices, RSA, Coppersmith's method.

1 Introduction

Let $N = pq$ be an RSA modulus where p, q are of the same bitsize. The public exponent e and private exponent d satisfy $ed - 1 \equiv 0 \bmod (p-1)(q-1)$. Since the decryption/signing in RSA require taking heavy exponential multiplication modulus of N, low efficiency became a bottleneck of using RSA cryptosystem.

Perhaps the most straightforward solution to speed up RSA decryption/signing process is to choose small d. However, in 1991, Wiener [24] showed that if $d < N^{0.25}$ then the factorization of N can be found in polynomial-time. Later, Boneh and Durfee [2] improved Wiener's bound to $d < N^{0.292}$, in their attack, the proof of the final bound is complicated. Recently, a simple and elementary proof is given to achieve Boneh-Durfee's bound [9,14].

Another sophisticated approach, proposed by Quisquater and Couvreur [18], is to use the Chinese Remainder Theorem (CRT) for decryption/signing. In this case, the public exponent e and private CRT-exponents d_p and d_q satisfy

$$ed_p \equiv 1 \mod (p-1)$$
$$ed_q \equiv 1 \mod (q-1)$$

---

* Corresponding author.

I. Boureanu, P. Owesarski, and S. Vaudenay (Eds.): ACNS 2014, LNCS 8479, pp. 151–162, 2014.
© Springer International Publishing Switzerland 2014

In [24], Wiener stated that decryption/signing time can be further reduced if we use small private CRT-exponents. However, there are several attacks that can break CRT-RSA if the CRT-exponents are sufficiently small. In Crypto'02, May [16] described two attacks when the smaller prime factor is less than $N^{0.382}$. Later, in PKC'06, Bleichenbacher and May [1] improved May's bound to $N^{0.468}$. These two attacks focus on the special case where p and q are unbalanced. In Crypto'07, Jochemsz and May [12] presented an attack on the case of p and q are balanced and e is full size (i.e. $e \approx N$), they showed that CRT-RSA can be broken when d_p and d_q are smaller than $N^{0.073}$.

Partial Key Exposure Attacks on RSA. Even if we choose to use large private exponents, in implementations, it may leaks some bits of the private key, we can still recover the entire private key from this knowledge. This is known as partial key exposure attack. Actually small private key attacks can be seen as partial key exposure attacks where MSBs of the private exponent are known to be equal to zero. In Asiacrypt'98, Boneh, Durfee and Frankel [3] presented several attacks on RSA where the attacker gains knowledge of MSBs or LSBs of d. In their attacks, the public exponent e must be relatively small. In Crypto'03, Blömer and May [11] described several attacks for larger values of public exponent e. Further in Eurocrypt'05, Ernst et al. [5] extended these attacks to work up to full size e. As a follow-up work of [5], recently, Joye and Lepoint [13] provided several attacks on the practical setting of a private exponent d larger than the modulus N.

Partial Key Exposure Attacks on CRT-RSA. In Crypto'03, Blömer and May [11] provided some partial key exposure attacks on CRT-RSA. Suppose $d_p \approx p$, they showed that for small public exponents e (i.e. $e = \text{poly}(\log N)$), known half of the LSBs of d_p are sufficient to factorize N.

Later in PKC'04, May [17] generalized Blömer-May's results [11] to the multi-power RSA [20] (Takagi's scheme: Modulus $N = p^r q$ $(r \geq 2)$). Using Boneh, Durfee and Howgrave-Graham's result [4], May presented polynomial-time attacks that need only a fraction of $\frac{1}{r+1}$ of the MSBs or LSBs of $d_p(d_p \approx p)$ to factor N when the public exponent e is small.

In ACNS'09, Sarkar and Maitra [19] provided another partial key exposure attack on CRT-RSA. In their attack, they assume that certain amounts of MSBs of d_p and d_q are exposed. Actually their attack can be regard as an extension of Jochemsz-May's attack [12].

1.1 Our Contribution

In this paper, we present two extended polynomial-time attacks that even works for all $e < N^{\frac{3}{8}}$ when certain amounts of LSBs of d_p are exposed. Moreover, in our attacks, the upper bound of e can be further improved if one uses a small secret CRT-exponent d_p. As an immediate application, we can utilize our approach to analyze Tunable Balancing of RSA which was introduced by Galbraith et al. [6] in ACISP'05. Moreover, for known MSBs of d_p, we can extend the results of [11] to any small secret exponents d_p. We also point out that there are close relations between our technique and the algorithm of Blömer and May [11].

Additionally, our technique can be easily extended to improve May's attack [17] on Takagi's scheme. However, Takagi's scheme requires the public exponent e extremely small to make the decryption efficient (In the Hensel lifting Step in Decryption, $r - 1$ modular exponentiations with exponent e need to be done). Therefore, we do not discuss these extensions in this paper.

Experimental Results. For all these attacks, we carry out experiments to verify the effectiveness of our algorithms, which are depicted in Sec. 5 in detail. These experimental results demonstrate that our attacks are effective.

2 Preliminaries

2.1 Lattices

Our attacks are based on the techniques that rely on lattice basis reduction. In this section, we review some basic background information about lattices and lattice basis reduction.

A lattice is a discrete additive subgroup of $\mathbb{R}^n$. For our purpose, given $m \leq n$ linearly independent vectors $b_1, \ldots, b_m \in \mathbb{R}^n$, the set

$$\mathcal{L} = \mathcal{L}(b_1, \ldots, b_m) = \{\sum_{i=1}^{m} \alpha_i b_i | \alpha_i \in \mathbb{Z}\}$$

is a lattice. The b_i are called the basis vectors of $\mathcal{L}$ and $\mathcal{B} = \{b_i, \ldots, b_m\}$ is called a lattice basis for $\mathcal{L}$. The determinant of a lattice is defined as $\det(\mathcal{L}) = \det(BB^t)^{\frac{1}{2}}$. When the lattice is full-rank ($m = n$), the formula simplifies to $\det(\mathcal{L}) = |\det B|$.

An important class of reduced basis, are LLL-algorithm, named after Lenstra, Lenstra and Lovász [15]. The following lemma gives bounds on LLL-reduced basis vectors.

Lemma 1 (LLL [15]). *Let $\mathcal{L}$ be a lattice of dimension w. Within polynomial-time, LLL-algorithm outputs a set of reduced basis vectors v_i, $1 \leqslant i \leqslant w$ that satisfies*

$$||v_1|| \leqslant ||v_2|| \leqslant \cdots \leqslant ||v_i|| \leqslant 2^{\frac{w(w-1)}{4(w+1-i)}} \det(\mathcal{L})^{\frac{1}{w+1-i}}$$

We also state a useful lemma from Howgrave-Graham [10]. Let $g(x_1, \cdots, x_k) = \sum_{i_1, \cdots, i_k} a_{i_1, \cdots, i_k} x_1^{i_1} \cdots x_k^{i_k}$. We define the norm of g by the Euclidean norm of its coefficient vector: $||g||^2 = \sum_{i_1, \cdots, i_k} a_{i_1, \cdots, i_k}^2$.

Lemma 2 (Howgrave-Graham [10]). *Let $g(x_1, \cdots, x_k) \in \mathbb{Z}[x_1, \cdots, x_k]$ be an integer polynomial that consists of at most w monomials. Suppose that*

1. $g(y_1, \cdots, y_k) = 0 \bmod p^m$ for $| y_1 | \leqslant X_1, \cdots, | y_k | \leqslant X_k$ and
2. $||g(x_1 X_1, \cdots, x_k X_k)|| < \frac{p^m}{\sqrt{w}}$

Then $g(y_1, \cdots, y_k) = 0$ holds over integers.

Our attacks rely on a well-known assumption which was widely used in the literature [5,2,8].

Assumption 1. *The lattice-based construction yields algebraically independent polynomials. The common roots of these polynomials can be efficiently computed using the* Gröbner *basis technique.*

2.2   Blömer-May's Partial Key Exposure Attacks on CRT-RSA

In [11], Blömer and May proposed two partial key exposure attacks on CRT-RSA. Following we list their results.

Theorem 1 (LSBs). *Let (N, e) be an RSA public key with $N = pq$ and secret key d. Let $d_p = d \mod (p-1)$. Given d_0, M with $d_0 = d_p \mod M$ and*

$$M > N^{\frac{1}{4}}$$

Then the factorization of N can be found in time $e \cdot poly(\log N)$.

Theorem 2 (MSBs). *Let (N, e) be an RSA public key with $N = pq$ and secret key d and $e = N^\alpha$ for some $\alpha \in [0, \frac{1}{4}]$. Furthermore, let $d_p = d \mod (p-1)$. Given $\tilde{d}$ with*

$$|d_p - \tilde{d}| \leq N^{\frac{1}{4} - \alpha}$$

Then N can be factored in polynomial-time.

2.3   Finding Small Root of Bivariate Linear Equations

In Asiacrypt'08, Herrmann and May [8] gave an upper bound on the solutions of a bivariate linear equations modulo an unknown divisor of a known composite, which can also be extended to multivariate linear equations. Recently in ACISP'13 [21], Takayasu and Kunihiro improved Herrman-May's results by taking into account the sizes of the root bound. In this paper we used their approach to find small root of our attack polynomial.

Theorem 3 (Herrmann-May-Takayasu-Kunihiro). *Let N be a sufficiently large composite integer (of unknown factorization) with a divisor $p \geq N^\beta$. Let $f(x_1, x_2) \in \mathbb{Z}[x_1, x_2]$ be a linear polynomial in two variables. Under Assumption 1, we can find all the solutions (y_1, y_2) of the equation $f(x_1, x_2) = 0 \mod p$ with $|y_1| \leq N^\gamma$ and $|y_2| \leq N^\delta$ (Suppose $\delta > \gamma$) if*

$$\begin{cases} \gamma + \delta \leq 3\beta - 2 + 2(1-\beta)^{\frac{3}{2}} & \text{if } \delta < \beta(1 - \sqrt{1-\beta}) \\ \delta(3\beta - \gamma - 2\sqrt{\delta - \gamma}) < \beta^3 & \text{if } \beta^2 > \delta > \beta(1 - \sqrt{1-\beta}) \end{cases}$$

The time and space complexities of the algorithm are polynomial in $\log N$.

3   Key Recovery from Known LSBs

In this section, we assume that the attacker succeeded in getting the least significant bits of d_p

$$d_p = d_1 M + d_0$$

where d_0 is known to the attacker, together with its higher bound M, but d_1 is unknown. (In a special case of known LSBs, M is a power of two.)

3.1   The Description of Our Attacks

In Crypto'03, Blömer and May [11] showed that if half of the lower bits of d_p ($d_p \approx p$) are known, one can factorize N in time $e \cdot \mathrm{poly}(\log N)$. Obviously their attack is of exponential time when the public exponent e is large. However, in some practical applications we need large e (Like $e \approx \sqrt{d_p}$) to satisfy our specific requirements, e.g., Galbraith et al.'s scheme [6] in ACISP'05. In such a situation, the attack of [11] will not work.

We propose two polynomial-time attacks for the case of large e. Our attacks are based on Coppersmith's method for finding small roots of modular equations. The fist step of our attacks is to derive, from an CRT-RSA equation, a multivariate polynomial in some of the unknowns of CRT-RSA parameters, like p, d_p.

Since $d_p = d_1 M + d_0$ and $ed - 1 = k_p(p - 1)$, we can rewrite CRT-RSA equation as

$$eM d_1 + e d_0 - 1 - k_p(p - 1) = 0$$

Suppose that $d_1 \approx N^{\delta_1}$, $d_p \approx N^{\delta}$ and $e \approx N^{\alpha}$, we have

$$k_p = \frac{ed_p - 1}{p - 1} \approx \frac{N^{\delta+\alpha}}{N^{\frac{1}{2}}} \approx N^{\delta+\alpha-\frac{1}{2}}$$

For the first attack, we consider a bivariate modular polynomial

$$f_{LSB1}(x, y) = eMx + y + ed_0 - 1$$

with the root $(x_0, y_0) = (d_1, k_p)$ modulo p. Let $X = N^{\delta_1}, Y = N^{\delta+\alpha-\frac{1}{2}}$, then $|x_0| < X, |y_0| < Y$.

For the second attack, we use a different bivariate polynomial that modulo eM. Specifically, we focus on the polynomial

$$f_{LSB2}(x, y) = x(y - 1) + 1 - ed_0$$

with the root $(x_0, y_0) = (k_p, p)$ modulo eM. Using $X = N^{\delta+\alpha-\frac{1}{2}}, Y = N^{\frac{1}{2}}$, then $|x_0| < X, |y_0| < Y$.

Next we give the details on how to find the small root of f_{LSB1} and f_{LSB2}.

3.2   Attack I: An Approach Modulo p

Theorem 4 (Attack I). *Let $N = pq$, where p, q are primes of the same bit-size. Let the public exponent e ($e \approx N^{\alpha}$) and private CRT-exponent d_p ($d_p \approx N^{\delta}$) satisfy $ed_p \equiv 1 \bmod (p-1)$. Suppose that $d_p = d_1 M + d_0$ where $d_1 \approx N^{\delta_1}$. Given d_0, M, and assume that the following conditions are satisfied*

$$\begin{cases} 2 - \delta - \alpha - 2\sqrt{\delta_1 - \delta - \alpha + 0.5} < \frac{0.125}{\delta_1} & \text{if } 0.5 > \delta_1 > 0.146 > \delta + \alpha - 0.5 \\ 1.5 - \delta_1 - 2\sqrt{\delta + \alpha - \delta_1 - 0.5} < \frac{0.125}{\delta + \alpha - 0.5} & \text{if } 0.5 > \delta + \alpha - 0.5 > 0.146 > \delta_1 \\ \delta_1 + \delta + \alpha - 0.707 < 0 & \text{if } 0.146 > \max\{\delta + \alpha - 0.5, \delta_1\} \end{cases}$$

Then N can be factored in polynomial-time.

Proof. According to the analysis of Sec. 3.1, we try to find the small root $(x_0, y_0) = (d_1, k_p)$ of the polynomial

$$f_{LSB1}(x, y) = eMx + y + ed_0 - 1$$

Applying Theorem 3 and setting $\beta = \frac{1}{2}$, then

$$\beta(1 - \sqrt{1 - \beta}) = \frac{2 - \sqrt{2}}{4} \approx 0.146$$

For the case of $0.146 > \max\{\delta + \alpha - 0.5, \delta_1\}$, we can get $\delta_1 + \delta + \alpha - 0.707 < 0$. For the case of $0.146 < \max\{\delta + \alpha - 0.5, \delta_1\}$, we consider two subcases: $\delta + \alpha - 0.5 > \delta_1$ and $\delta + \alpha - 0.5 < \delta_1$. After some calculations, we obtain the claimed result.   □

3.3   Attack II: An Approach Modulo eM

Theorem 5 (Attack II). *Using the notations of Theorem 4, provided that*

$$\delta + \frac{5}{2}\delta_1 - 3\delta_1^2 + \alpha - \frac{7}{8} < 0$$

Then N can be factored in polynomial-time.

Proof. According to the analysis of Section 3.1, we try to find the small root $(x_0, y_0) = (k_p, p)$ of the polynomial

$$f_{LSB2}(x, y) = x(y - 1) + 1 - ed_0$$

Note that the desired small solution contains the prime factor p, but p is already determined by modulus N. Based on this observation, we apply the technique of Bleichenbacher and May [1]. Define two integers m and t. Then we introduce a new variable z for the prime factor q, and multiply the polynomial $f_{LSB2}(x, y)$ by a power z^s for some s that has to be optimized. Let us look at the following collection of trivariate polynomials that all have the root (x_0, y_0) modulo $(eM)^m$.

$$g_{i,j}(x, y, z) = (eM)^{m-i}x^j z^s f_{LSB2}^i(x, y) \quad \text{for } i = 0, \ldots, m; \ j = 0, \ldots, m - i$$

$$h_{i,j}(x,y,z) = (eM)^{m-i}y^j z^s f^i_{LSB2}(x,y) \quad \text{for} \quad i = 0,\ldots,m; \ j = 1,\ldots,t.$$

For $g_{i,j}(x,y,z), h_{i,j}(x,y,z)$, we replace every occurrence of the monomial yz by N because $N = pq$. Therefore, compared to the unchanged collection, every monomial $x^i y^j z^s (j \geq s)$ with coefficient $a_{i,j}$ is transformation into a monomial $x^i y^{j-s}$ with coefficient $a_{i,j} N^s$. And every monomial $x^i y^j z^s (j < s)$ with coefficient $a_{i,j}$ is transformation into a monomial $x^i z^{s-j}$ with coefficient $a_{i,j} N^j$.

To keep the lattice determinant as small as possible, we try to eliminate the factor of N^j in the coefficient of diagonal entry. Since $\text{GCD}(eM, N) = 1$, we only need multiplying the corresponding polynomial with the inverse of N^j modulo $(eM)^m$ [1].

We have to find two short vectors in lattice $\mathcal{L}$. Suppose that these two vectors are the coefficient vectors of two trivariate polynomial $f_1(xX, yY, zZ)$ and $f_2(xX, yY, zZ)$. There two polynomials have the root (k_p, p, q) over the integers. Then we can eliminate the variable z from these polynomials by setting $z = \frac{N}{y}$. Finally, we can extract the desired root (k_p, p) from the new two polynomials if these polynomials are algebraically independent. Therefore, our attack relies on Assumption 1.

Now we give the details of the condition which we can find two sufficiently short vectors in the lattice $\mathcal{L}$. Let $t = \tau m, s = \sigma m$, the determinate of the lattice $\mathcal{L}$ is

$$\det(\mathcal{L}) = (eM)^{s_{eM}} X^{s_X} Y^{s_Y} Z^{s_Z}$$

where

$$s_{eM} = \sum_{i=0}^{m}\sum_{j=0}^{m-i}(m-i) + \sum_{i=0}^{m}\sum_{j=1}^{t}(m-i) = (2+3\tau)\cdot\frac{1}{6}m^3 + o(m^3)$$

$$s_X = \sum_{i=0}^{m}\sum_{j=0}^{m-i}(i+j) + \sum_{i=0}^{m}\sum_{j=1}^{t}i = (2+3\tau)\cdot\frac{1}{6}m^3 + o(m^3)$$

$$s_Y = \sum_{i=s}^{m}\sum_{j=0}^{m-i}(i-s) + \sum_{i=0}^{m}\sum_{j=\max\{1,s-i\}}^{t}(j+i-s)$$
$$= (1+3(\tau-\sigma)(1+\tau-\sigma))\cdot\frac{1}{6}m^3 + o(m^3)$$

$$s_Z = \sum_{i=0}^{s}\sum_{j=0}^{m-i}(s-i) + \sum_{i=0}^{s}\sum_{j=1}^{s-i}(s-i-j) = 3\tau^2\cdot\frac{1}{6}m^3 + o(m^3)$$

And X, Y, Z are the upper bounds of k_p, p, q. An easy calculation shows the dimension of the lattice is

$$n = \dim(\mathcal{L}) = \frac{1}{6}(3+6\tau)m^2 + o(m^2)$$

---

[1] In Sec. 4 of [1], the authors eliminated the factor N^j by multiplying the inverse of N^j modulo e, in fact it should be e^m to satisfy the first condition of Lemma 2.

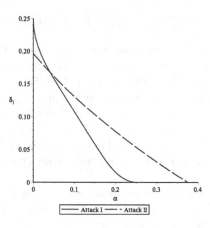

Fig. 1. The Case of Known LSBs of d_p ($d_p \approx p$)

To get two polynomials which sharing the root (k_p, p, q), we get the condition $\det(\mathcal{L}) \leq (eM)^{m \dim(\mathcal{L})}$. Substituting the values of the $\dim(\mathcal{L})$ and neglecting low-order term, we obtain the new condition

$$(2 + 3\tau)(\alpha + \delta - \frac{1}{2}) + \frac{1}{2}(1 + 3(\tau - \sigma)(1 + \tau - \sigma)) + \frac{3}{2}\tau^2 - (1 + 3\tau)(\alpha + \delta - \delta_1) < 0$$

The optimized values of parameters τ and σ were given by

$$\sigma = \frac{1}{2} + \delta_1 \qquad \tau = \frac{1}{2} - 2\delta_1$$

Plugging in this values, we finally end up with the condition

$$\delta + \frac{5}{2}\delta_1 - 3\delta_1^2 + \alpha - \frac{7}{8} < 0$$

$\square$

3.4   Comparison of the Attacks

We give the comparison of our attacks when the private exponent is full sized i.e. $d_p \approx p$. Fig. 1 illustrates our results on known LSBs of d_p when $\delta = \frac{1}{2}$. The maximal size of unknown d_1 ($d_1 \approx N^{\delta_1}$) for an attack is plotted as a function of the size of e ($e \approx N^\alpha$). Notice that the bounds for Attack I and Attack II match when $\alpha \approx 0.04$, thus Attack II is stronger than Attack I for $\alpha > 0.04$. Besides our attacks works up to $\alpha = \frac{3}{8} = 0.375$.

4   Key Recovery from Known MSBs

In this section we consider the case when some MSBs of d_p are known.

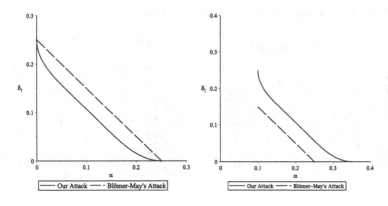

Fig. 2. Known MSBs: $\delta = 0.5$ **Fig. 3.** Known MSBs: $\delta = 0.4$

Theorem 6 (Known MSBs). *Let $N = pq$, where p, q are primes of the same bit-size. Let the public exponent e ($e \approx N^\alpha$) and the private CRT-exponent d_p ($d_p \approx N^\delta$) satisfying $ed_p \equiv 1 \bmod (p-1)$. Given $\tilde{d}$ where $|d_p - \tilde{d}| < N^{\delta_1}$, and assume that the following conditions are satisfied*

$$
\begin{cases}
2 - \delta - \alpha - 2\sqrt{\delta_1 - \delta - \alpha + 0.5} < \frac{0.125}{\delta_1} & \text{if } 0.5 > \delta_1 > 0.146 > \delta + \alpha - 0.5 \\
1.5 - \delta_1 - 2\sqrt{\delta + \alpha - \delta_1 - 0.5} < \frac{0.125}{\delta + \alpha - 0.5} & \text{if } 0.5 > \delta + \alpha - 0.5 > 0.146 > \delta_1 \\
\delta_1 + \delta + \alpha - 0.707 < 0 & \text{if } 0.146 > \max\{\delta + \alpha - 0.5, \delta_1\}
\end{cases}
$$

Then N can be factored in polynomial-time.

Proof. We have that $ed_p - 1 = k_p(p-1)$ for some $k \in \mathbb{N}$. We can rewrite our equation as

$$e(d_p - \tilde{d}) + k_p + e\tilde{d} - 1 \equiv 0 \bmod p$$

Now we try to find the small root $(y_1, y_2) = (d_p - \tilde{d}, k_p)$ of the polynomial

$$f_{MSB}(x_1, x_2) = ex_1 + x_2 + e\tilde{d} - 1$$

Since $d_p - \tilde{d} \approx N^{\delta_1}$, $d_p \approx N^\delta$ and $e \approx N^\alpha$, we have

$$k_p = \frac{ed_p - 1}{p - 1} \approx \frac{N^{\delta+\alpha}}{N^{0.5}} \approx N^{\delta+\alpha-0.5}$$

Applying Theorem 3 and setting $\beta = 0.5$, we obtain the claimed result.   □

4.1   Comparison with Blömer-May's [11] Results

Fig. 2 and Fig. 3 compare the results on known MSBs of d_p. We focus on two cases: $\delta = 0.5$ and $\delta = 0.4$. In Fig. 2, note that Blömer-May's [11] result is better than ours. However, for the case $\delta = 0.4$, our result is better (Fig. 3). Actually our result is better than Theorem 2 if $\delta < 0.457$.

Table 1. Experimental Results for Partial Key Exposure Attacks (LSBs)

(a) LSBs Case: Attack I

e	d	d_1	(m,t)	dim($\mathcal{L}$)	time(sec)
30	512	150	$(10,3)$	66	172.241
60	512	110	$(10,3)$	66	191.304
100	512	60	$(10,3)$	66	250.397
150	512	20	$(10,3)$	66	272.378
85	512	85	$(13,4)$	105	4012.299

(b) LSBs Case: Attack II

e	d	d_1	(m,t,u)	dim($\mathcal{L}$)	time(sec)
30	512	130	$(7,4,2)$	68	95.176
60	512	100	$(7,4,2)$	68	152.295
80	512	100	$(10,6,3)$	132	5642.342
100	512	70	$(7,4,3)$	68	391.281
150	512	35	$(7,4,3)$	68	605.471
200	512	10	$(8,4,4)$	81	3096.707

In fact, we can apply the linearization method on the equation of Theorem 6:

$$\underbrace{e(d_p - \tilde{d}) + k_p}_{x} + e\tilde{d} - 1 \equiv 0 \mod p$$

This can be stated as finding the root of the linear monic polynomial $f(x) = x + e\tilde{d} - 1 \mod p$ where $p = N^{\frac{1}{2}}$. Using Herrmann-May's method [8], we can get the same bound as [11]. In [8], Herrmann and May observed that their algorithm gives much better bounds for a smaller number of unknown variables (From two to one). That is the reason why [11]'s result is better than ours when $\delta = 0.5$. However, as the size of $e(d_p - \tilde{d})$ and k_p increasingly unbalanced, this linearization method can not exploit the relation between the coefficients of the polynomial f_{MSB}. Therefore, our method is more appropriate for this scenario (δ is small). Actually, in [22,7], the authors used the similar technique to improve the bound for solving the Multi-Prime Φ-Hiding Problem.

5   Experimental Results

To verify the effectiveness of our lattice-based approaches, we carry out some experiments[2]. We have implemented our attacks using Magma [23] on a laptop with Intel© Core™ i5-2430M CPU 2.40 GHz, 2 GB RAM. For all the listed-up parameters, we can recover the factorization of N.

In Table 1[3] we illustrate partial known LSBs attacks for 1024-bit RSA modulus N with 512-bit primes p, q. From the data of the table, it is clear that for large e, Attack II works better than Attack I for recovering the whole key, which was already shown in Sec. 3.4.

---

[2] Since the attack of Sec. 4 is similar to the attack of Sec. 3.2, we omit experiments for the MSBs case here.

[3] In Table 1(a), we did not exploit Takayasu-Kunihiro's technique [21] that consider the sizes of the root bound. Because we believe that it is enough to show the efficiency comparison of our two attacks.

Acknowledgments. We would like to thank the anonymous reviewers for helpful comments. This work is supported by the National 973 Program of China under Grant No. 2011CB302400, the National Natural Science Foundation of China under Grant No. 61303257, No. 61100225 and No. 61379139. IIEs Research Project on Cryptography under Grant No. Y3Z001C102, One Hundred Talents Project of the Chinese Academy of Sciences, the Strategic Priority Research Program of the Chinese Academy of Sciences under Grant No. XDA06010701.

References

1. Bleichenbacher, D., May, A.: New attacks on RSA with small secret CRT-exponents. In: Yung, M., Dodis, Y., Kiayias, A., Malkin, T. (eds.) PKC 2006. LNCS, vol. 3958, pp. 1–13. Springer, Heidelberg (2006)

2. Boneh, D., Durfee, G.: Cryptanalysis of RSA with private key d less than $N^{0.292}$. IEEE Transactions on Information Theory 46(4), 1339–1349 (2000)

3. Boneh, D., Durfee, G., Frankel, Y.: Exposing an RSA private key given a small fraction of its bits. In: Full Version of the work from Asiacrypt, vol. 98 (1998)

4. Boneh, D., Durfee, G., Howgrave-Graham, N.: Factoring $n = p^r q$ for large r. In: Advances in Cryptology–CRYPTO 1999, p. 787. Springer (1999)

5. Ernst, M., Jochemsz, E., May, A., de Weger, B.: Partial key exposure attacks on RSA up to full size exponents. In: Cramer, R. (ed.) EUROCRYPT 2005. LNCS, vol. 3494, pp. 371–386. Springer, Heidelberg (2005)

6. Galbraith, S.D., Heneghan, C., McKee, J.F.: Tunable balancing of RSA. In: Boyd, C., González Nieto, J.M. (eds.) ACISP 2005. LNCS, vol. 3574, pp. 280–292. Springer, Heidelberg (2005)

7. Herrmann, M.: Improved cryptanalysis of the multi-prime ϕ - hiding assumption. In: Nitaj, A., Pointcheval, D. (eds.) AFRICACRYPT 2011. LNCS, vol. 6737, pp. 92–99. Springer, Heidelberg (2011)

8. Herrmann, M., May, A.: Solving linear equations modulo divisors: On factoring given any bits. In: Pieprzyk, J. (ed.) ASIACRYPT 2008. LNCS, vol. 5350, pp. 406–424. Springer, Heidelberg (2008)

9. Herrmann, M., May, A.: Maximizing small root bounds by linearization and applications to small secret exponent RSA. In: Nguyen, P.Q., Pointcheval, D. (eds.) PKC 2010. LNCS, vol. 6056, pp. 53–69. Springer, Heidelberg (2010)

10. Howgrave-Graham, N.: Finding small roots of univariate modular equations revisited. In: Möhring, R.H. (ed.) WG 1997. LNCS, vol. 1335, pp. 131–142. Springer, Heidelberg (1997)

11. Blömer, J., May, A.: New partial key exposure attacks on RSA. In: Boneh, D. (ed.) CRYPTO 2003. LNCS, vol. 2729, pp. 27–43. Springer, Heidelberg (2003)

12. Jochemsz, E., May, A.: A polynomial time attack on RSA with private CRT-exponents smaller than $N^{0.073}$. In: Menezes, A. (ed.) CRYPTO 2007. LNCS, vol. 4622, pp. 395–411. Springer, Heidelberg (2007)

13. Joye, M., Lepoint, T.: Partial key exposure on RSA with private exponents larger than n. In: Ryan, M.D., Smyth, B., Wang, G. (eds.) ISPEC 2012. LNCS, vol. 7232, pp. 369–380. Springer, Heidelberg (2012)

14. Kunihiro, N., Shinohara, N., Izu, T.: A unified framework for small secret exponent attack on RSA. In: Miri, A., Vaudenay, S. (eds.) SAC 2011. LNCS, vol. 7118, pp. 260–277. Springer, Heidelberg (2012)

15. Lenstra, A.K., Lenstra, H.W., Lovász, L.: Factoring polynomials with rational coefficients. Mathematische Annalen 261(4), 515–534 (1982)
16. May, A.: Cryptanalysis of unbalanced RSA with small CRT-exponent. In: Yung, M. (ed.) CRYPTO 2002. LNCS, vol. 2442, pp. 242–256. Springer, Heidelberg (2002)
17. May, A.: Secret exponent attacks on RSA-type schemes with moduli $N = p^r q$. In: Bao, F., Deng, R., Zhou, J. (eds.) PKC 2004. LNCS, vol. 2947, pp. 218–230. Springer, Heidelberg (2004)
18. Quisquater, J.-J.: Chantal Couvreur. Fast decipherment algorithm for RSA public-key cryptosystem. Electronics Letters 18(21), 905–907 (1982)
19. Sarkar, S., Maitra, S.: Partial key exposure attack on CRT-RSA. In: Abdalla, M., Pointcheval, D., Fouque, P.-A., Vergnaud, D. (eds.) ACNS 2009. LNCS, vol. 5536, pp. 473–484. Springer, Heidelberg (2009)
20. Takagi, T.: Fast RSA-type cryptosystem modulo $p^k q$. In: Krawczyk, H. (ed.) CRYPTO 1998. LNCS, vol. 1462, pp. 318–326. Springer, Heidelberg (1998)
21. Takayasu, A., Kunihiro, N.: Better lattice constructions for solving multivariate linear equations modulo unknown divisors. In: Boyd, C., Simpson, L. (eds.) ACISP 2013. LNCS, vol. 7959, pp. 118–135. Springer, Heidelberg (2013)
22. Tosu, K., Kunihiro, N.: Optimal bounds for multi-prime ϕ-hiding assumption. In: Susilo, W., Mu, Y., Seberry, J. (eds.) ACISP 2012. LNCS, vol. 7372, pp. 1–14. Springer, Heidelberg (2012)
23. Cannon, J., Bosma, W., Playoust, C.: The Magma algebra system. I. The user language. J. Symbolic Comput. 24(3-4), 235–265 (1997); Computational algebra and number theory, London (1993)
24. Wiener, M.J.: Cryptanalysis of short RSA secret exponents. IEEE Transactions on Information Theory 36(3), 553–558 (1990)

Bit-Flip Faults on Elliptic Curve Base Fields, Revisited

Taechan Kim[1,*] and Mehdi Tibouchi[2]

[1] Seoul National University
[2] NTT Secure Platform Laboratories

Abstract. As part of their investigation of fault attacks on elliptic curve cryptosystems, Ciet and Joye showed, back in 2003, that perturbing the value representing the cardinality of the base field in a physical implementation of ECC could result in a partial key recovery. They had to assume, however, that the perturbed computation would "succeed" in some sense, and that is rather unlikely to happen in practice.

In this paper, we extend their analysis and show that, in a somewhat stronger fault model, full key recovery is possible with a single fault. For example, our fault attack typically reduces 256-bit ECDLP to solving discrete logarithm problems in a few random elliptic curves over fields of less than 60 bits, which typically takes a matter of seconds. More generally, the asymptotic complexity of ECDLP becomes heuristically subexponential under our fault attack.

Our attack also extends to a very efficient full key recovery attack on ECDSA with two faulty signatures.

Keywords: Elliptic Curve Cryptography, Fault Analysis, ECDSA.

1   Introduction

Elliptic Curve Cryptography. Elliptic curves, whose use in public-key cryptography was first suggested by Koblitz and Miller in the mid-1980s [29,31], offer numerous advantages over more traditional settings like RSA and finite field discrete logarithms, particularly higher efficiency and a much smaller key size that scales gracefully with security requirements. This makes them especially well-suited for implementations of cryptography, in both hardware and software, on resource-constrained and embedded devices.

Despite some initial reluctance from practitioners, elliptic curve cryptography (ECC) has become widely accepted in the cryptographic community and has made major inroads in the industry starting from the early 2000s, with the standardization of multiple elliptic curve-based cryptographic primitives [24,3] (ECDSA [18] in particular has been widely adopted), agencies weighing in favor of their use [32], and new embedded applications such as secure e-passports mandating them [25].

---

[*] This work was carried out during the first author's visit to NTT Secure Platform Laboratories.

I. Boureanu, P. Owesarski, and S. Vaudenay (Eds.): ACNS 2014, LNCS 8479, pp. 163–180, 2014.
© Springer International Publishing Switzerland 2014

ECC implementations are now a staple of the modern cryptographic landscape, and it is thus of prime importance to study their security not only from a purely algorithmic point of view, but also against physical attacks. A number of works in recent years have been devoted to attacking ECC implementations with, and protecting them against, both side-channel analysis, fault analysis, and even combined attacks with both passive and active phases. See [14,2,15] for surveys of recent results.

Fault Attacks on Elliptic Curves. In this paper, we are particularly interested in *active* physical attacks against the elliptic curve discrete logarithm problem (ECDLP). Much like the so-called Bellcore attack of Boneh, DeMillo and Lipton [9] allows an attacker to recover an RSA secret key by perturbing the computation of an RSA signature in a signing device, fault attacks on ECDLP seek to recover a secret exponent k by perturbing the computation of the scalar multiplication of an elliptic curve point P by k.

The most common type of fault attack on ECDLP consists of "weak curve attacks", the first of which was introduced by Biehl, Meyer and Müller in 2000 [8]. Their key observation was that at least one of the elliptic curve parameters does not intervene in the expression of the addition and doubling formulas on that elliptic curve; for example, in commonly used coordinate systems, the addition and doubling formulas on the short Weierstrass curve $E\colon y^2 = x^3 + ax + b$ do not involve the parameter b at all. As a result, if one perturbs the computation of a scalar multiplication kP by modifying the coordinates of P into those of a different point $\widetilde{P}$ not on the curve E, the computation carried out by the device is still an elliptic curve scalar multiplication $k\widetilde{P}$, but on a different curve:

$$\widetilde{E}\colon y^2 = x^3 + ax + \tilde{b} \quad \text{where} \quad \tilde{b} = y_{\widetilde{P}}^2 - x_{\widetilde{P}}^3 - ax_{\widetilde{P}}.$$

If the discrete logarithm problem happens to be easy on $\widetilde{E}$ (this happens for example when the group order of $\widetilde{E}$ is a smooth number, or when $\widetilde{P}$ is a point of small order on $\widetilde{E}$), information about k can be deduced from the result $k\widetilde{P}$ of the faulty scalar multiplication.

This type of attack was later called *invalid point attack* because it relies on obtaining, through fault injection, an input point to the scalar multiplication algorithm that lies outside of the elliptic curve. One notable variant is the twist attack of Fouque et al. [19], which assumes that the input point is in compressed form, and which perturbs it (with probability $1/2$) into a point on the twisted curve of E, which is often weaker.

Ciet and Joye [11] extended the work of Biehl et al. in several directions, and showed in particular that faults injected not only on the base point but also on the curve parameters, or the representation of the base field, could cause the scalar multiplication to be performed on a weak curve, and hence allow the recovery of some information on the discrete logarithm.

We consider in particular their attack on the base field. In the prime field case, it can be roughly described as follows: suppose that the elliptic curve E is defined over the field $\mathbb{F}_p$, and that a fault is injected on p, yielding a faulty modulus p'. With high probability, p' is then a composite number $p' = \prod_{i=1}^{r} q_i^{e_i}$. Hence, the faulty computation of kP, *assuming that it proceeds without error*, should really be a scalar multiplication by k on an elliptic curve over the ring $\mathbb{Z}/q_1^{e_1}\mathbb{Z} \times \cdots \times \mathbb{Z}/q_r^{e_r}\mathbb{Z}$, which decomposes as a product $\widetilde{E}_1(\mathbb{Z}/q_1^{e_1}\mathbb{Z}) \times \cdots \widetilde{E}_r(\mathbb{Z}/q_r^{e_r}\mathbb{Z})$. Each of the curves $\widetilde{E}_i$ is defined over a much smaller base than the original curve E, and is therefore weaker, making the discrete logarithm problem potentially tractable.

If one tries to implement that attack, however, one finds that it fails almost all the time, mainly because some of the prime factors q_i of p' are likely to be very small; the reduced curve modulo those primes may either not be an elliptic curve at all (due to having zero discriminant: this happens if one of the q_i's is 2 or 3, for example), or have such a small order that the scalar multiplication will meet the point at infinity modulo that prime with high probability, causing a division by zero or an otherwise erroneous computation.

Our Contributions. Motivated in part by recent work on modulus fault attacks against RSA signatures [10], we revisit Ciet and Joye's attack on the base field representation in such a way as to make it actually work with as few as a single faulty scalar multiplication.

Most of our analysis is in a stronger fault model than random fault model considered by Ciet and Joye: namely, we assume that the adversary can *choose* the fault they inject on the modulus from a certain set. This can be achieved in various ways in practice, such as instruction skipping in software or triggering reset wires in hardware to zero out some chosen bitstring in the modulus, or by using the chosen bit-flip model considered in the original paper of Biehl et al.. Bit flips are often considered tricky to achieve against real devices, but Agoyan et al. [1] have demonstrated that they can be performed in a reproducible way using laser shots on SRAM memory cells.

We show that if one can flip a chosen bit of the modulus p (or otherwise inject a fault chosen from a similarly-sized set), we can ensure that the resulting faulty modulus p' has much smaller prime factors (less than 60 bits each when p is a 256-bit prime, say). This makes it possible to recover almost all the bits of k (all but a couple dozen) from a *single* faulty computation of the scalar multiplication kP in a division-free coordinate system (projective, Jacobian, etc.). The few remaining bits can be quickly found using Pollard's lambda algorithm if, in addition, the result of the non-faulty computation is known. The attack also extends to the more common case when the result is converted back to affine coordinates at the end, unless the device implements a normally useless test to avoid it.

We provide an extensive theoretical analysis of this attack showing, more generally, that a chosen bit-flip on an n-bit elliptic curve modulus allows the recovery of $n - O(\log^2 n)$ bits of the n-bit exponent k from a faulty computation of kP in heuristic (slightly) subexponential time $2^{O(n \log \log n / \log n)}$. And again, all

n bits can be recovered if the correct value of kP is also known, making ECDLP subexponential under this fault model. Note that our fault is chosen from a set of polynomial size: this is in contrast with Biehl et al.'s subexponential complexity result for their invalid point attack (later established more rigorously under reasonable heuristics by Wang and Zhan [35]) which requires superpolynomially many faults, and is therefore of little practical significance.

Furthermore, our attack extends to random faults as well, but several faults are necessary for the recovery of the whole discrete log to become practical: for 256-bit elliptic curves, three or four faults are typically enough.

In addition, we propose a very efficient full key recovery attack on ECDSA with only two faulty signatures based on our attack: each faulty signature reveals most of the bits of the corresponding nonce, so that the ECDSA secret key can easily be found using lattice reduction techniques with just two faults. Moreover, for deterministic implementations of ECDSA, having one correct and one faulty signature on the same message is also enough.

All variants of our attacks have been validated using simulations. In our implementation, the search for the optimal bit flip on a 256-bit modulus takes a few CPU hours (and is easily parallelized) on a standard PC, while the attacks themselves, both on ECDLP and ECDSA, take seconds to minutes to complete.

2   Background on ECDLP and ECDSA

Elliptic Curves. An elliptic curve over a finite prime field $\mathbb{F}_p$, $p > 3$, can be described as the set of points (x, y) on the affine plane curve

$$E\colon y^2 = x^3 + ax + b \tag{1}$$

for some coefficients $a, b \in \mathbb{F}_p$ with $4a^3 + 27b^2 \neq 0$, together with the point at infinity on the projective closure of the affine curve. This set $E(\mathbb{F}_p)$ is endowed with a natural abelian group law which can be defined by a chord-and-tangent process.

The formulas giving the affine coordinates of the sum of two curve points involve divisions, so efficient implementations of elliptic curve arithmetic rely on redundant coordinate systems for which division-free formulas exist. In this paper, we consider in particular Jacobian coordinates $(X : Y : Z)$ for the Weierstrass form (1), given by $(x, y) = (X/Z^2, Y/Z^3)$ as they seem to be the most commonly used in practice (in particular, they are the coordinate system described in the IEEE P1363 standard [23, A.10], and the one recommended over prime fields in [22]). However, our results generalize directly to any other coordinate system with division-free formulas for addition and doubling which are independent of at least one curve parameter (like the formulas for Jacobian coordinates below, which are independent of the parameter b of the Weierstrass equation). This also includes projective coordinates in Weierstrass form, as well as projective coordinates on Hessian and generalized Hessian curves [16], Huff and twisted Huff curves [26], etc., but not Edwards curves [7], for which addition formulas depend on all curve parameters.

Formulas for addition and doubling in Jacobian coordinates are provided in the full version of this paper [28] (as well as many other standard references); they are indeed division-free and do not depend on the parameter b of the curve equation. Such formulas are sufficient to compute scalar multiplications $P \mapsto kP$ in $E(\mathbb{F}_p)$. While this can be done in several ways, we will assume in this paper that the double-and-add algorithm (in either its left-to-right or its right-to-left variant) used for those computations. Nevertheless, we note that our results apply with little to no change to most other scalar multiplication algorithms, including the generalized Montgomery ladder [27], and even to higher radix algorithms (k-ary double-and-add, sliding window, etc.) as long as faults are injected before the corresponding precomputations so that precomputed points lie on the faulty curve as well.

ECDLP. Consider again an elliptic curve E over $\mathbb{F}_p$, and a point $P \in E(\mathbb{F}_p)$ of order N in the group (usually a generator of either $E(\mathbb{F}_p)$ itself or a subgroup of small index). The elliptic curve discrete logarithm problem (ECDLP) in (the subgroup generated by P in) E is the computational problem of finding $k \in \{0, \ldots, N-1\}$ given P and the scalar multiple kP. For almost all isomorphism classes of elliptic curves, this problem is considered hard, and the best known attack has a complexity of $O(\sqrt{N})$.

ECDSA. The elliptic curve digital signature algorithm (ECDSA) is a digital signature scheme based on elliptic curves and standardized as part of the Digital Signature Standard [18]. ECDSA system parameters consist of an elliptic curve E over a finite field (for example a prime field $\mathbb{F}_p$), a generator $P \in E(\mathbb{F}_p)$ of a large subgroup of the curve, of order N, and a hash function $H \colon \{0,1\}^* \to \mathbb{Z}/N\mathbb{Z}$. The secret key is then a random integer $\mathsf{d} \in \{0, \ldots, N-1\}$, and the public verification key is the curve point $\mathsf{d}P$. A message m is then signed as follows: choose a uniformly random $k \in \{1, \ldots, N-1\}$, compute the scalar multiple $kP = (x,y) \in E(\mathbb{F}_p)$, and return the signature as the pair $(r,s) \in (\mathbb{Z}/N\mathbb{Z})^2$ given by $r = x \bmod N$ and $s = k^{-1} \cdot \big(H(m) + r \cdot \mathsf{d}\big) \bmod N$.

3   Our Attack

3.1   Attack Model

We consider a cryptographic device computing the scalar multiplication of a known point $P = (x_P, y_P)$ by an unknown scalar k on a public elliptic curve $E \colon y^2 = x^3 + ax + b$ over the finite prime field $\mathbb{F}_p$, and we try to recover k using fault analysis. To fix ideas, we assume that the scalar multiplication is carried out in Jacobian coordinates using the double-and-add algorithm (although, as mentioned earlier, the approach extends to most curve shapes and coordinate systems admitting division-free addition and doubling formulas, and to essentially any scalar multiplication algorithm with minor changes).

Our fault model is to consider that a permanent fault is injected on the representation of the base field $\mathbb{F}_p$ at the beginning of the computation, so that all arithmetic operations are carried out modulo a different integer p' instead, which is typically composite: $p' = \prod_{i=1}^{r} q_i^{e_i}$. This type of fault is typically achieved using laser beams on RAM cells after the value of p is loaded into memory. Note that the model is only realistic if the device uses a generic implementation of base field operations. Devices using curves with random base fields, such as Brainpool [30] and the French government ANSSI curve [4], do satisfy that property, but in some cases implementations of NIST curves [18] (which have special base fields) do not, and those based on Curve25519 [5] and other "SafeCurves" [6] normally do not either.

As noted in the introduction, the computation of the scalar multiplication by k using the faulty modulus p' essentially amounts to a scalar multiplication by k in the product group $\widetilde{E}_1(\mathbb{Z}/q_1^{e_1}\mathbb{Z}) \times \cdots \times \widetilde{E}_r(\mathbb{Z}/q_r^{e_r}\mathbb{Z})$, where $\widetilde{E}_i$ is the curve over $\mathbb{Z}/q_i^{e_i}\mathbb{Z}$ defined by:

$$\widetilde{E}_i \colon y^2 = x^3 + ax + b_i \qquad \text{where} \qquad b_i = \left(y_P^2 - x_P^3 - ax_P\right) \bmod q_i^{e_i}.$$

More precisely, consider a prime factor q_i of p' of multiplicity 1 ($e_i = 1$) such that the curve $\widetilde{E}_i$ is indeed an elliptic curve over $\mathbb{F}_{q_i}$ (i.e. q_i is prime to $2 \cdot 3 \cdot (4a^3 + 27b_i^2)$, which happens with high probability unless q_i is very small), and let $P_i \in \widetilde{E}_i(\mathbb{F}_{q_i})$ be the point $\left(x_P \bmod q_i, y_P \bmod q_i\right)$. Then, the double-and-add algorithm carried out in Jacobian coordinates modulo q_i correctly computes the Jacobian coordinates of the scalar multiple $kP_i \in \widetilde{E}_i(\mathbb{F}_{q_i})$, *unless* the validity condition for the addition law[1] described in Section 2 (saying that the points being added are different, not inverses of each other and not at infinity) fails at some point in the computation, in which case it is easy to check that the computation returns either the point at infinity on $\widetilde{E}_i$ or the erroneous value $(0 : 0 : 0)$. The same holds modulo primary factors $q_i^{e_i}$ of p of higher multiplicity, except that zeros are replaced by non-invertible elements of $\mathbb{Z}/q_i^{e_i}\mathbb{Z}$.

As a result, it follows from the Chinese Remainder Theorem that when the whole computation is carried out modulo p', the algorithm returns a value $(X' : Y' : Z')$ which, when reduced modulo $q_i^{e_i}$, gives the correct scalar multiple $kP_i \in \widetilde{E}_i(\mathbb{Z}/q_i^{e_i}\mathbb{Z})$ whenever $\widetilde{E}_i$ is indeed an elliptic curve and q_i does not divide Z'. If, moreover, the order N_i of P_i in the group $\widetilde{E}_i(\mathbb{Z}/q_i^{e_i}\mathbb{Z})$ is not too large (hopefully much smaller than 2^n), we can hope to recover $k \bmod N_i$ in time $O(\sqrt{N_i})$ using a generic algorithm for the discrete logarithm such as

---

[1] Note that a typical implementation of scalar multiplication on the curve can omit checking whether the validity condition holds, as it is never satisfied under normal conditions, but even if the check is carried out, it is immaterial for our purposes. Indeed, the check would be done using equality modulo p', and hence would not detect equality modulo a single prime factor of p'.

Pollard's rho.[2] And ultimately, putting all those results together, we should obtain $k \bmod \nu$ where ν is the LCM of the N_i's corresponding to those primary factors for which the computation could be carried out.

There are almost always primary factors for which the computation fails, and even for those where it succeeds, the corresponding N_i's may not be relatively prime, so one cannot hope to recover all of k using a single faulty computation. But as we will see, we can actually come quite close! Our analysis of the attack will proceed as follows:

- In Section 3.2, we assume that the faulty modulus p' is obtained from p by flipping a single chosen bit, and we show that if that bit is selected correctly, we can make p' smooth enough that the discrete logarithm becomes easy in all reduced curves $\widetilde{E}_i$.
- In Section 3.3, we then show that the output of a single faulty double-and-add computation in Jacobian coordinates is then enough to recover $n - O(\log^2 n)$ bits of k (out of n), which is quite close to optimal.
- In Section 3.4, we discuss how the few remaining unknown bits of k can be recovered easily if the correct value of $kP \in E(\mathbb{F}_p)$ is known.[3]
- In Section 3.5, we show that recovering k is still possible if the result of the scalar multiplication is converted back from Jacobian to affine coordinates before being output, under plausible assumptions on the Jacobian-to-affine conversion algorithm. Furthermore, we show that the affine x-coordinate alone is enough to carry out the attack.
- In Section 3.6, we discuss how this fault attack on scalar multiplication easily extends to a full key recovery attack on ECDSA signatures given only two faulty signatures.
- Finally, while all the previous results are obtained assuming chosen bit flip faults, we briefly discuss in Section 3.7 how they extend to the case of random faults when a higher number of faulty results is available.

3.2 Choice of the Faulty Modulus

In Ciet and Joye's fault attack [11], of which the present paper is a variant, faults injected on the modulus were considered random. As a result, for a 256-bit elliptic curve, say, the faulty modulus p' would typically have a prime factor of

---

[2] In practice, N_i is often composite, so it is preferable to first factor this order and then use the Pohlig–Hellman algorithm. Moreover, when $e_i > 1$, we can recover $k \bmod N_i$ even faster by first carrying out the discrete logarithm computation in the reduced curve modulo q_i, and then lifting to q_i^2, q_i^3 and so on until $q_i^{e_i}$. However, factors of p' with multiplicity higher than 1 are usually very small if they exist at all, so it is rarely useful to treat them separately in practice.

[3] Whether the correct value of kP is available to an attacker depends on the protocol implemented by the device. This is typically the case when k is the secret key itself, as in static Diffie–Hellman key exchange, BLS signatures and many other protocols. In other settings like ECDSA, k is randomly chosen anew in each execution of the protocol, but as we show below, we can then break the corresponding schemes using several faults.

size $256\lambda = 256 \cdot 0.642\ldots \approx 164$ bits (where λ is the Golomb–Dickman constant), making the discrete logarithm problem on the corresponding reduced curve likely intractable. As a result, Ciet and Joye's attack can usually only recover a small fraction of the bits of k using a single fault.

By contrast, our analysis is based on the assumption that the attacker can *choose* the fault to some extent: more precisely, we assume that the attack gets to flip a single chosen bit of p. This is a rather powerful fault model, but this type of faults has been shown by Agoyan et al. [1] to be consistently achievable in practice using laser shots on SRAM cells.

In such a setting, we claim that we can ensure that the faulty modulus p' has only relatively small prime factors, making the discrete logarithm probably easy in all reduced curves.

Indeed, there are n integers obtained from p by flipping a single bit, and with respect to the distribution of the sizes of their prime factors, it is reasonable to make the heuristic assumption (as is usually done in the complexity analysis of e.g. factoring algorithms) that they behave like independent random numbers of the same size; our experiments seem to confirm that this assumption holds. Now, recall that for any constant $s > 1$, the asymptotic probability that a random integer x is $x^{1/s}$-smooth (i.e. has all of its prime factors smaller than $x^{1/s}$) is given by Dickman's function $\rho(s)$ [13], which satisfies $\log \rho(s) \sim -s \log s$ (see e.g. [21]).

As a result, the probability that all of the integers obtained from p by flipping a single bit have a prime factor of at least n/s bit is given by $(1 - \rho(s))^n \approx \exp(-n\rho(s))$, which is bounded by $1/e$ as soon as $n\rho(s) \geq 1$, or equivalently, $\log n \geq -\log \rho(s) \sim s \log s$. Therefore, with good probability, at least one of the integers obtained from p by flipping a single bit is $2^{n/s}$-smooth with $s \approx \log n / \log \log n$.

We have seen that our fault model essentially reduces the discrete logarithm problem in $E(\mathbb{F}_p)$ to ECDLP instances in elliptic curves $\widetilde{E}_i$ over base fields $\mathbb{F}_{q_i}$ corresponding to the prime factors[4] q_i of the faulty modulus p'. Since we can choose p' to be $2^{n \log \log n / \log n}$-smooth with good probability by flipping a bit, we obtain that, in this setting, the heuristic complexity of ECDLP-using-a-single-fault is bounded by $O(2^{n \log \log n / 2 \log n})$ which is subexponential in n.

More practically, if we consider 256-bit elliptic curves, say, we find that $(1 - \rho(s))^{256}$ is $0.466\ldots < 1/2$ for $s = 4.2$, and $256/4.2 = 60.9\ldots$. Therefore, this fault attack will typically reduce 256-bit ECDLP to discrete logarithm problems in a few random curves over base fields of less than 61 bits, which are quite easy to solve in practice. Note also that effectively finding the correct bit to flip amounts to factoring 256 numbers of 256 bits each, which can be done in matter of minutes on a standard desktop computer.

The next few sections are devoted to making precise, using properly justified heuristics, in what sense the fault does indeed "reduce" the larger ECDLP instance to the smaller ones.

---

[4] Due to the lifting technique mentioned in a previous note, this is correct even if p' has repeated prime factors, but we reiterate that such factors of higher multiplicity are irrelevant in practice: a prime factor q of p' is repeated with probability $\approx 1/q$, which is small enough to ignore if q is larger than a dozen bits or so.

3.3   Result in Jacobian Coordinates: Recovering Most of the Scalar

In this section, we argue that an attacker who obtains the result of a single faulty scalar multiplication by k as a point in Jacobian coordinates (i.e. that is not converted back to affine coordinates) can recover almost all the bits of k. This is done in three steps. We first show that the computation has a high probability to succeed modulo all the prime factors q_i of p' such that $q_i \gg n \log n$. We call those prime factors "good moduli", and the other ones "bad moduli". We then prove that the bad moduli account for only a small part of the bits of p', in the sense that the bit length of the $O(n \log n)$-smooth part of p' is bounded as $O(\log n)$ with high probability. And finally, we show that, under reasonable heuristics, the bit size of the LCM ν of the orders $N_i = \operatorname{ord}(P_i)$ is not much smaller than n (it is of length $n - O(\log^2 n)$ bits). As a result, since we finally obtain $k \bmod \nu$, our attack recovers $n - O(\log^2 n)$ bits of information out of n on the scalar k using just a single fault.

The Computation Succeeds for Good Moduli. First, we observe that the erroneous computation is unlikely to happen on the large modulus. For a given q_i, we show that the probability that the computation kP on $\widetilde{E}_i(\mathbb{F}_{q_i})$ meets the point at infinity is $O(\frac{n \log q_i}{q_i})$, where n denotes the bit length of k. Our analysis is based on the following reasonable heuristic assumptions:

1. the curve $\widetilde{E}_i$ behaves like a random elliptic curve over $\mathbb{F}_{q_i}$;
2. the point P behaves like a random point in $\widetilde{E}_i(\mathbb{F}_q)$; and
3. the scalar k is a random n-bit integer.

Note that the probability mentioned above is very small for a prime $q_i \gg n \log n$. It is also consistent with the intuition that the point at infinity is much more likely to be encountered as part of the scalar multiplication on a small elliptic curve group than on a large one (and the Hasse–Weil bound implies that the group size is essentially given by the size of the base field).

Assume that the scalar multiplication by k is carried out in the double-and-add approach. The computation fails if a multiple of the order of the point appears somewhere during the scalar multiplication. Under the heuristic assumption that each constant appearing in the scalar multiplication behaves like a random integer of the corresponding bit length, we prove in the full version of this paper [28] that the probabilty of encountering the point at infinity is bounded by $2n/\operatorname{ord}(P)$ for the n-bit scalar multiple k.

Thus for a given curve E defined over $\mathbb{F}_q$, the probability that a random point P would meet the point at infinity becomes $\sum_d \Pr[\operatorname{ord}(P) = d] \cdot (2n/d)$, where d runs over the divisors of the order of the elliptic curve. This leads us to consider the function $\sum_d \frac{\Pr[\operatorname{ord}(P)=d]}{d} = \frac{1}{|E|} \sum_{P \in E} \frac{1}{\operatorname{ord}(P)}$. In the full version of this paper [28], we show that the expected value of $\sum_{P \in E} \frac{1}{\operatorname{ord}(P)}$ asymptotically becomes $O(\log q)$. Consequently, we obtain that the probability $O(\frac{n \log q}{q})$, which is small for $q \gg n \log n$. For example, this explains that for 256-bit elliptic curve the result of the faulty computation gives a correct value on the corresponding curves for large moduli q_i such that $q_i \gg 256 \cdot 8 = 2048$.

Bad Moduli Account for a Small Number of Bits. From the previous subsection, we expect that the computation modulo large factors of p' succeeds with high probability. However, the computation usually fails to give a useful result on "bad moduli" $q_i = O(n \log n)$. Fortunately, in this section we show that the size of the product of these bad moduli is not so large.

For integers B and x, we write $S_B(x)$ for the B-smooth part of x, i.e. the product of all prime factors of x (with multiplicities) which are $\leq B$. Moreover, if u is a B-smooth integer, we define $P_B(u)$ as the asymptotic probability that a random integer x satisfies $S_B(x) = u$. This probability is well-defined, and given by $P_B(\ell^a) = \frac{1}{\ell^a} - \frac{1}{\ell^{a+1}}$ on powers of primes $\ell^a \leq B$, from which the value of $P_B(u)$ for all B-smooth integers u easily follows. Now consider the probability that $S_B(p') \leq B^\alpha$, i.e. $\sum_{u \leq B^\alpha} P_B(u)$. In the full version of this paper [28], we prove:

Theorem 1. *Let $S(x, y)$ be the set of y-smooth integers up to x. For any positive real number $\alpha > 0$, we have*

$$\sum_{u \in S(B^\alpha, B)} P_B(u) \sim \frac{1}{e^\gamma} \cdot \int_0^\alpha \rho(s) ds$$

as $B \to \infty$. Here, ρ is Dickman's function and γ is the Euler-Mascheroni constant.

Consider the right-hand side of the asymptotics of Theorem 1. By definition of Dickman's function, $\rho(s) = \frac{1}{s} \int_{s-1}^s \rho(t) dt$ for all $s > 1$ and $\rho(s) = 1$ for $0 \leq s \leq 1$. It follows that $\rho(s) = 1 - \log s$ for $1 \leq s \leq 2$, and a simple calculation then gives:

$$\frac{1}{e^\gamma} \int_0^2 \rho(s) ds = \frac{3 - 2 \log 2}{e^\gamma} = 0.90603 \cdots .$$

It means that for random n-bit integer p', the inequality $S_B(p') \leq B^2$ holds with about 91% probability. More generally, for $B = O(n \log n)$, the bit length of $S_B(p')$ is $O(\log n)$ with high probability. And in the case of a 256-bit random integer p', we can expect that the product of primes less than $B \approx 256 \cdot 8 = 2048$ is less than $2 \log 2048 = 15.2 \ldots$ bits with high probability.

Size of the LCM of the Good Orders. For each of the good moduli q_i, the faulty computation reveals the point $k\widetilde{P}_i \in \widetilde{E}_i(\mathbb{F}_{q_i})$, and since the discrete logarithm problem on each of these small curves is tractable, we can solve it to obtain $k \bmod N_i$ where $N_i = \text{ord}_{\widetilde{E}_i}(P)$. Then, the total recoverable bit length of k is determined by the size of $\nu := \text{lcm}\{N_i\}$, where the lcm is taken over the set I of indices of the good moduli q_i. Thus, to show that most bits of k can be recovered, we would like to justify that the size of ν is close to n.

This is done in two steps. First, we argue that for each i, the order N_i of $\widetilde{P}_i$ in $\widetilde{E}_i(\mathbb{F}_{q_i})$ is close to the order of the group itself. This can be done under the heuristic assumption that $\widetilde{P}_i$ is a random point on the corresponding curve, and that the curve itself is random in an appropriate sense. Indeed, we can explicitly compute the expected order of a random element in a finite abelian group with at most two invariant factors (it is close to the exponent of the group), and the order of the smaller invariant factor of a random elliptic curve is typically small (precise estimates can be found in [20]). Overall, we prove in the full version of this paper [28] that N_i, the order of P on $\tilde{E}_i$, is only a constant number of bits shorter than $|\tilde{E}_i(\mathbb{F}_{q_i})|$ on average.

As a result, of the LCM ν of the N_i's will be within a constant factor of the LCM of the curve orders $N_i' = |\tilde{E}_i(\mathbb{F}_{q_i})|$. The second step is then to justify that this latter LCM is close to the product of the N_i's, or equivalently of the q_i's, which we know is of size $n - O(\log n)$ bits. To do so, we argue, using the results of Gekeler [20] again, that the distribution of the sizes of the prime factors of the order a random elliptic curve is essentially the same as that of a random integer of the same size. Thus, the LCM of the N_i's should behave like the LCM of $|I|$ random integers of the same sizes. And a recent theorem of Fernández and Fernández [17] provides a bound on the difference between the size of the product and the size of the LCM: it ensures that $\log \prod_{i \in I} N_i - \log \nu = O(|I|^2) = O(\log^2 n)$.

All in all, under reasonable heuristic assumptions, the total recoverable bit length of k is at least $n - O(\log^2 n)$. A more detailed discussion of these heuristic arguments, and full proofs under the appropriate assumptions, are provided in the full version of this paper [28].

3.4 Result in Jacobian Coordinates: Recovering the Whole Scalar

Let $(X_Q : Y_Q : Z_Q)$ be a point in the Jacobian coordinate of the result of the faulty computation with modulus p'. If the scalar multiplication on the modulus q_i contains the point at infinity somewhere, then the Z-coordinate of the result should be zero. Thus, in practice, we detect which modulus is a good modulus by checking the value of the GCD of Z_Q and p'; the good modulus q_i never be a factor of $d := \gcd(Z_Q, p')$.

With the proper choice of the faulty modulus, we have seen how to recover a large part of the exponent, namely $k \pmod{\nu}$ where ν is a known integer of expected bit size $n - O(\log^2 n)$. Assume that we also obtain the value of the *correct* computation kP. From $k = \nu x + (k \bmod \nu)$ for some x in a small interval of length $O(\log^2 n)$, we can recover x by applying Pollard's lambda algorithm to the pair of known points νP and $x \cdot (\nu P) = kP - (k \bmod \nu)P$. This only requires $O(\sqrt{\log^2 n}) = O(\log n)$ arithmetic operations on the elliptic curve $E(\mathbb{F}_p)$, and is therefore quite fast (and in any case, polynomial time).

3.5 Result in Affine Coordinates

In practice, at the end of the computation, the final result is usually converted back to affine coordinates before being output. So, the final point $(X_Q : Y_Q : Z_Q)$ in the Jacobian coordinate should be converted into the affine coordinate $(X_Q/Z_Q^2, Y_Q/Z_Q^3)$. This step requires the inversion of Z_Q in $\mathbb{F}_p$. To invert the element Z_Q modulo p, it is widely used the extended Euclidean algorithm (EEA):

Find integers α and β satisfying $\alpha Z_Q + \beta p = 1$, then compute $(\alpha^2 X_Q \bmod p, \alpha^3 Y_Q \bmod p)$ from the point $(X_Q : Y_Q : Z_Q)$.

In our fault model the inverse of Z_Q does not exist with respect to the faulty modulus p', because Z_Q and p' are not relatively prime in general. However, if we assume that the procedure of conversion from the Jacobian to the affine coordinates is done by the EEA without checking that $\gcd(Z_Q, p') = 1$ (this is a reasonable assumption in the sense that this check is never necessary for field arithmetic: a field element is invertible as soon as it is non-zero, and this is normally verified separately), we obtain the faulty affine coordinates $(\tilde{x}, \tilde{y}) = (\tilde{\alpha}^2 X_Q \bmod p', \tilde{\alpha}^3 Y_Q \bmod p')$, where $Q = (X_Q : Y_Q : Z_Q)$ is the result of computing kP modulo p' and $\tilde{\alpha} Z_Q + \tilde{\beta} p' = \gcd(Z_Q, p')$ in the EEA.

To obtain the value of $kP_i \in \tilde{E}_i$, we need to compute the correct affine coordinates:

$$(x_i, y_i) = (X_Q/Z_Q^2 \bmod q_i, Y_Q/Z_Q^3 \bmod q_i)$$

from the given result $(\tilde{x}, \tilde{y})$. Note that $\frac{Z_Q}{d}$ and $\frac{p'}{d}$ are relatively prime for $d := \gcd(Z_Q, p')$, and we have $\tilde{\alpha} \cdot \frac{Z_Q}{d} + \tilde{\beta} \cdot \frac{p'}{d} = 1$. This induces that $Z_Q^{-1} = \frac{\tilde{\alpha}}{d} \bmod q_j$ for prime factors q_j of $\frac{p'}{d}$, so we deduce that

$$\tilde{x}/d^2 = X_Q/Z_Q^2 \bmod q_j \quad \text{and} \quad \tilde{y}/d^3 = Y_Q/Z_Q^3 \bmod q_j.$$

It remains to recover d from $\tilde{x}$ and $\tilde{y}$. Note that d is the product of the prime factors q_i on which $Z_Q \bmod q_i = 0$.

If the computation of kP involves the point at infinity somewhere for $P \in E_i(\mathbb{F}_{q_i})$, then the final result is of form $(0 : 0 : 0)$. Thus $\gcd(Z_Q, p')$ divides $\gcd(X_Q, p')$.

Conversely, assume that $Z_Q \neq 0 \bmod q_i$. The point $(X_Q/Z_Q^2, Y_Q/Z_Q^3) \bmod q_i$ behaves as a random point on $E_i : y^2 = x^3 + ax + b_i$. The curve E_i has a point of form $(0, y)$ if and only if b_i is a quadratic residue modulo q_i and in this case we have $(0, y) = (0, \pm b_i^{1/2})$. So, the probability that a randomly chosen point has its x-coordinate zero is $\frac{2}{|E_i|} \approx \frac{2}{q_i}$ if it exists. Thus $X_Q \neq 0 \bmod q_i$ with the probability $1 - \frac{1}{2} \cdot \frac{2}{q_i} = 1 - \frac{1}{q_i}$. Thus $\gcd(X_Q, p')$ divides $\gcd(Z_Q, p')$ with probability $\prod_{i=1}^{7}(1 - 1/q_i)$. We deduce that $d = \gcd(Z_Q, p') = \gcd(X_Q, p')$ with high probability.

Finally, we have $\gcd(\tilde{x}, p') = \gcd(\tilde{\alpha}^2 X_Q, p') = \gcd(X_Q, p') = d$, since $\tilde{\alpha}$ is relatively prime to p'/d, and we are able to recover the correct affine coordinates from $(\tilde{x}, \tilde{y})$. The recovery of the exponent can be carried out as before.

Remark 1. Assume that we only have the affine x-coordinate of the faulty computation. In this case, we have two choices of possible point $(x_i \bmod q_i, y_i \bmod q_i)$ for each i. Therefore, if there are w good moduli, we have 2^w possibilities for $k \bmod \nu$. If the exact value of kP is known, we can thus recover k by running Pollard's lambda algorithm 2^w times as before using all of the possible candidates for $k \bmod \nu$. This exhaustive search is quite fast, and in any case polynomial time.

3.6   Attack on ECDSA

Consider two faulty signatures of form

$$(r_1, s_1) := (x_1, k_1^{-1}(h_1 + r_1 \cdot \mathbf{d}) \bmod N) \quad \text{for } h_1 = H(m_1)$$

and

$$(r_2, s_2) := (x_2, k_2^{-1}(h_2 + r_2 \cdot \mathbf{d}) \bmod N) \quad \text{for } h_2 = H(m_2).$$

As before, we know that $k_1 = \nu \mathbf{x}_1 + \eta_1$ and $k_2 = \nu \mathbf{x}_2 + \eta_2$ for the small unknowns $0 < \mathbf{x}_1, \mathbf{x}_2 < 2^{O(\log^2 n)}$. To find $\mathbf{x}_1$ and $\mathbf{x}_2$, we consider the equations obtained by multiplying k_1 and k_2 for each s_1 and s_2:

$$\begin{cases} s_1 \cdot (\nu \mathbf{x}_1 + \eta_1) = h_1 + r_1 \cdot \mathbf{d} \bmod N \\ s_2 \cdot (\nu \mathbf{x}_2 + \eta_2) = h_2 + r_2 \cdot \mathbf{d} \bmod N. \end{cases}$$

Eliminating $\mathbf{d}$, we obtain the equation

$$r_2 s_1 (\nu \mathbf{x}_1 + \eta_1) - r_1 s_2 (\nu \mathbf{x}_2 + \eta_2) = r_2 h_1 - r_1 h_2 \bmod N.$$

Hence the problem reduces to solving the bivariate modular equation $\alpha \mathbf{x}_1 + \beta \mathbf{x}_2 = \gamma \bmod N$ for small $\mathbf{x}_1, \mathbf{x}_2$ and known N which can be solved efficiently with the LLL algorithm when $|\mathbf{x}_1|, |\mathbf{x}_2| \lesssim N^{1/2}$ (since it is an instance of the $(1, 2)$-ME problem in the terminology of Takayasu and Kunihiro [34]; see also [12]), and that bound is of course satisfied in our setting.

3.7   Extending the Attacks to Random Faults

Suppose that we are unable to obtain faults on a specific bit of p, but can instead carry out several faulty executions of the scalar multiplication with the same scalar k in which a different random fault is injected in p every time. Ciet and Joye have shown that, in such a setting, we can assume that each of the faulty moduli p'_j is known, as it can be recovered from the resulting point [11].

Our attack naturally extends to such a setting as follows: while some "good moduli" among the largest factors of the p'_j's may be too large for the corresponding discrete logarithm instances to be tractable, we can use all the results from the available good moduli starting from the easiest Pohlig–Hellman instances, and stop as soon as enough bits have been recovered in the LCM so that all of k is known. Experimentally, we find that for a 256-bit modulus, 3 to 4 random faults are enough to recover all of k in a few minutes. The precise analysis of this multiple random fault variant is left as future work. Note that this attack is similar to the one originally proposed by Ciet and Joye, but does account for "bad moduli" and can therefore be carried out in practice.

Similarly, it is even easier to adapt the ECDSA attack to random faults: if each random fault reveals a bit more than one fourth of the nonce on average, say, the LLL attack above generalizes directly to a full key recovery attack using 4 faulty signatures.

4   Simulation Results

We have implemented the attacks described in the previous section in the Sage computer algebra system [33], and carried out simulations on a mid-range workstation with 16 Xeon E5 CPU cores at 2.9 GHz. All our code was run on a single core of that machine, except the search for optimal bit flips, which was parallelized.

We experimented with several standardized elliptic curve parameters: the 224-bit and 256-bit prime field NIST curves [18], the Brainpool curves of the same sizes [30], and the 256-bit curve recommended by the French government [4]. Indeed, the base fields of NIST curves have a special form, which we thought could yield to a somewhat special behavior with respect to our attacks.

4.1   Search for Optimal Bit Flips

Given an elliptic curve $E/\mathbb{F}_p$ and a corresponding base point $P \in E(\mathbb{F}_p)$, we search for "good" bit faults by trying, for each bit of p, to flip that bit, which yields a certain faulty modulus p'. We then compute the prime factorization $\prod q_i^{e_i}$ of p', and the order N_i of each of the reduced points P_i on the reduced curves $E_i(\mathbb{Z}/q_i^{e_i}\mathbb{Z})$ (for those of them that are actually elliptic curves).

A faulty p' is good if it is quite smooth (i.e. if the bit size of the largest q_i is relatively small), or more precisely if the N_i's themselves are smooth, as the complexity of recovering the discrete logarithm using the Pohlig-Hellman is essentially given by the size of the LCM ν of the N_i's.

It turns out that while the smoothest possible p' is sometimes optimal in the latter respect (this is the case for example for the French government curve FRP256v1, for which flipping bit 184 of the modulus gives both the smoothest p', with a largest prime factor of 59 bits, and the smoothest ν, with a largest prime factor of 35 bits), it is not always the case. For example, although the smoothest possible p' for NIST curve P–256 is obtained by flipping bit 64 (2^{51}-smooth), it is much better to flip bit 5 of NIST curve P256: the corresponding p' is only 2^{113}-smooth, but ν is then 2^{23}-smooth (vs. 2^{34}-smooth for bit 64), providing significantly faster discrete logarithm recovery.

To find the optimal bit flip, we can thus rank each bit position i of p according to the size of the largest prime factor of ν associated with the faulty modulus $p' = p \oplus 2^i$, and keep the best choice. Sometimes, the second or third best choice can be preferred if the size of the largest prime factor of ν is close, but ν itself is larger, as this makes the Pollard lambda step of the attack faster.

By far the most costly part of the attack is the factorization of the faulty moduli p'. Factoring integers of 256 bits or less is not hard on modern computers but can still take a substantial amount of time in unfavorable cases: using the basic `factor` algorithm in Sage (which uses PARI's implementation of ECM and MPQS), we found that the whole search took around 2.5 CPU hours for a 256-bit curve on a single core. Clearly, the search can easily be parallelized by running the computations for different bits i separately. We do it using the `@parallel`

Table 1. Results of the search for optimal bit flips on five standard curve parameters. For each curve, we provide the bit flip yielding the smoothest p', the smoothest ν, and the one we consider optimal for our purposes (ranked 1 to 3 in order of smoothness for ν). The top-left cell "128 $(46, 44, 134)$" means that flipping bit 128 of the modulus for the curve P–224 yields a 2^{46}-smooth p', and a 2^{44}-smooth ν which is 134-bit long in total. Computation time is on the wall clock, on our 16-core machine.

Bit flips	NIST		Brainpool		French gov.
	P–224	P–256	P224t1	P256t1	FRP256v1
Smoothest p'	128 $(46, 44, 134)$	64 $(51, 34, 227)$	58 $(51, 26, 213)$	24 $(60, 48, 228)$	184 $(59, 35, 218)$
Smoothest ν	82 $(60, 29, 219)$	5 $(113, 23, 232)$	10 $(71, 23, 193)$	16 $(88, 35, 239)$	184 $(59, 35, 218)$
Recommended	82 $(60, 29, 219)$	5 $(113, 23, 232)$	58 $(51, 26, 213)$	16 $(88, 35, 239)$	39 $(86, 36, 236)$
Time (s)	116	822	109	887	854

decorator in Sage, which speeds up the computation by a factor of around 11 on our 16-core machine. Detailed results are provided in Table 1.

4.2 ECDLP Attack

As described earlier, given the result of a faulty scalar multiplication kP carried out with our chosen faulty modulus p', we recover the exponent k modulo the order N_i of P on each of the reduced curves using the Pohlig–Hellman algorithm, and combine those result with the Chinese Remainder Theorem to get k modulo ν. Note that for a given exponent k, the number of bits recovered at this step may be lower than the theoretical maximum computed previously, in case the point at infinity on one of the reduced curves is reached at some stage during the scalar multiplication.

If in addition the result of the correct multiplication kP on the curve E is available, we use Pollard's lambda algorithm to find the remaining bits of k.

Our implementation uses Sage's generic group algorithms for both Pohlig–Hellman and Pollard lambda, which is certainly suboptimal, having both high overhead from the unoptimized Python code and naive underlying elliptic curve arithmetic. Nevertheless, the timings that we obtain and report in Table 2 confirm that the attack is very practical.

4.3 ECDSA Attack

In the ECDSA attack, we are given two faulty ECDSA signatures generated with our chosen faulty modulus. We first use our ECDLP attack to recover more than half of the bits of the nonce used in each signature (we can stop when those bits are obtained: we don't have to go through all possible reduced points). We actually recover a set of candidate nonce values to exhaustively search over, due to the sign indeterminacy discussed in the previous section. We then iterate over this exhaustive search space trying to recover the remainder of the nonces, and hence the full ECDSA secret key, using LLL lattice reduction.

Table 2. Ranges for the number of bits recovered and the recovery time in the main (Pohlig–Hellman) and final (Pollard lambda) steps of the ECDLP attack. Each recovery has been carried out on 5 random exponents for each curve, using the optimal bit flip computed before. Timings are given on a single CPU core of our machine.

	NIST		Brainpool		French gov.
Measured attacks	P–224	P–256	P224t1	P256t1	FRP256v1
Main recovered bit size	205–205	232–232	213–213	239–239	228–236
Main recovery time (s)	6.6–7.8	1.5–1.7	2.4–3.1	52–59	27–34
Remaining recovered bit size	20–20	25–25	11–11	18–18	21–29
Remaining recovery time (s)	0.29–2.4	1.0–7.1	0.08–0.10	0.15–0.59	0.54–8.1

Table 3. Timings for the initial as well as LLL stage of the ECDSA attack. Timings are given on a single CPU core of our machine.

	NIST		Brainpool		French gov.
Measured attacks	P–224	P–256	P224t1	P256t1	FRP256v1
Recovered nonce size	153–153	178–178	134–134	182–182	177–177
Number of nonce pairs to search over	64–64	4–4	64–64	16–64	32–64
Nonce recovery time (s)	12–13	2.7–3.2	3.5–4.3	56–68	48–57
LLL recovery time (μs)	2–11	1–2	10–37	4–12	9–27

The attack is very fast, as shown in Table 3. In particular, the LLL step takes negligible time, even though it requires carrying out the exhaustive search discussed in Remark 1.

5   Conclusion

We have proposed and thoroughly analyzed an extension of the Ciet–Joye fault attack on base fields of elliptic curves, and found that it works very well in practice provided that precise enough faults can be obtained on the modulus. It also extends to a very efficient fault attack on ECDSA, using only two faulty signatures.

The original countermeasure suggested by Ciet and Joye (namely, consistency checking of the modulus using a CRC or other cheap redundancy check) does thwart this attack, but our results underscore the importance of using it in actual implementations. Alternatively, using ECC implementations with dedicated arithmetic for a specific base field, as is sometimes done for NIST curves and almost always for rigid curve parameters such as Curve25519 [5] and other "SafeCurves" [6] (but not curves with random base fields like the Brainpool curves [30]), provides intrinsic protection against the attacks from this paper.

Note on the other hand that verifying the signature after generation (a common fault countermeasure especially in the RSA setting) does not help against our attack at all.

We have only considered prime fields, but essentially the same attack carries over in e.g. the binary field setting. It is probably less relevant to practitioners, however, since implementations of binary elliptic curves often use dedicated base field arithmetic as well.

References

1. Agoyan, M., Dutertre, J.-M., Mirbaha, A.-P., Naccache, D., Ribotta, A.-L., Tria, A.: How to flip a bit? In: IOLTS 2010, pp. 235–239. IEEE (2010)
2. Alkhoraidly, A., Domínguez-Oviedo, A., Hasan, M.A.: Fault attacks on elliptic curve cryptosystems. In: Joye, M., Tunstall, M. (eds.) Fault Analysis in Cryptography. Information Security and Cryptography, pp. 137–155. Springer (2012)
3. ANSI X9.63:2001. Public Key Cryptography for the Financial Services Industry, Key Agreement and Key Transport Using Elliptic Curve Cryptography. ANSI, Washington DC, USA (2001)
4. ANSSI. Publication d'un paramétrage de courbe elliptique visant des applications de passeport électronique et de l'administration électronique française (November 2011),
   http://www.ssi.gouv.fr/fr/anssi/publications/
   publications-scientifiques/autres-publications/publication-d-un-
   parametrage-de-courbe-elliptique-visant-des-applications-de.html
5. Bernstein, D.J.: Curve25519: New Diffie-Hellman speed records. In: Yung, M., Dodis, Y., Kiayias, A., Malkin, T. (eds.) PKC 2006. LNCS, vol. 3958, pp. 207–228. Springer, Heidelberg (2006)
6. Bernstein, D.J., Lange, T.: SafeCurves: choosing safe curves for elliptic-curve cryptography (2013), http://safecurves.cr.yp.to (accessed December 1, 2013)
7. Bernstein, D.J., Lange, T.: Faster addition and doubling on elliptic curves. In: Kurosawa, K. (ed.) ASIACRYPT 2007. LNCS, vol. 4833, pp. 29–50. Springer, Heidelberg (2007)
8. Biehl, I., Meyer, B., Müller, V.: Differential fault attacks on elliptic curve cryptosystems. In: Bellare, M. (ed.) CRYPTO 2000. LNCS, vol. 1880, pp. 131–146. Springer, Heidelberg (2000)
9. Boneh, D., DeMillo, R.A., Lipton, R.J.: On the importance of eliminating errors in cryptographic computations. J. Cryptology 14(2), 101–119 (2001)
10. Brier, É., Naccache, D., Nguyen, P.Q., Tibouchi, M.: Modulus fault attacks against RSA-CRT signatures. In: Preneel, B., Takagi, T. (eds.) CHES 2011. LNCS, vol. 6917, pp. 192–206. Springer, Heidelberg (2011)
11. Ciet, M., Joye, M.: Elliptic curve cryptosystems in the presence of permanent and transient faults. Des. Codes Cryptography 36(1), 33–43 (2005)
12. Coron, J.-S., Naccache, D., Tibouchi, M.: Fault attacks against EMV signatures. In: Pieprzyk, J. (ed.) CT-RSA 2010. LNCS, vol. 5985, pp. 208–220. Springer, Heidelberg (2010)
13. Dickman, K.: On the frequency of numbers containing prime factors of a certain relative magnitude. Arkiv för Matematik, Astronomi och Fysik 22A(10), 1–14 (1930)
14. Fan, J., Guo, X., Mulder, E.D., Schaumont, P., Preneel, B., Verbauwhede, I.: State-of-the-art of secure ECC implementations: a survey on known side-channel attacks and countermeasures. In: HOST 2010, pp. 76–87 (2010)

15. Fan, J., Verbauwhede, I.: An updated survey on secure ECC implementations: Attacks, countermeasures and cost. In: Naccache, D. (ed.) Quisquater Festschrift. LNCS, vol. 6805, pp. 265–282. Springer, Heidelberg (2012)
16. Farashahi, R.R., Joye, M.: Efficient arithmetic on Hessian curves. In: Nguyen, P.Q., Pointcheval, D. (eds.) PKC 2010. LNCS, vol. 6056, pp. 243–260. Springer, Heidelberg (2010)
17. Fernández, J.L., Fernández, P.: On the probability distribution of the gcd and lcm of r-tuples of integers. arXiv (2013), http://arxiv.org/abs/1305.0536
18. FIPS PUB 186-3. Digital Signature Standard (DSS). NIST, USA (2009)
19. Fouque, P.-A., Lercier, R., Réal, D., Valette, F.: Fault attack on elliptic curve Montgomery ladder implementation. In: Breveglieri, L., Gueron, S., Koren, I., Naccache, D., Seifert, J.-P. (eds.) FDTC, pp. 92–98 (2008)
20. Gekeler, E.-U.: The distribution of group structures on elliptic curves over finite prime fields. Documenta Mathematica 11, 119–142 (2006)
21. Granville, A.: Smooth numbers: computational number theory and beyond. Algorithmic Number Theory, MSRI Publications 44, 267–323 (2008)
22. Hankerson, D., Menezes, A., Vanstone, S.: Guide to Elliptic Curve Cryptography. Springer (2004)
23. IEEE Std 1363-2000. Standard Specifications for Public-Key Cryptography. IEEE (2000)
24. ISO/IEC 18033-2:2006. Information technology – Security techniques – Encryption algorithms – Part 2: Asymmetric ciphers. ISO, Geneva, Switzerland (2006)
25. ISO/IEC JTC1 SC17 WG3/TF5. Supplemental Access Control for Machine Readable Travel Documents, version 1.01. ICAO (2010), http://mrtd.icao.int/.
26. Joye, M., Tibouchi, M., Vergnaud, D.: Huff's model for elliptic curves. In: Hanrot, G., Morain, F., Thomé, E. (eds.) ANTS-IX. LNCS, vol. 6197, pp. 234–250. Springer, Heidelberg (2010)
27. Joye, M., Yen, S.-M.: The Montgomery powering ladder. In: Kaliski Jr., B.S., Koç, Ç.K., Paar, C. (eds.) CHES 2002. LNCS, vol. 2523, pp. 291–302. Springer, Heidelberg (2003)
28. Kim, T., Tibouchi, M.: Bit-flip faults on elliptic curve base fields, revisited. Cryptology ePrint Archive (2014), Full version of this paper, http://eprint.iacr.org/
29. Koblitz, N.: Elliptic curve cryptosystems. Math. Comp. 48, 203–209 (1987)
30. Lochter, M., Merkle, J.: Elliptic Curve Cryptography (ECC) Brainpool Standard Curves and Curve Generation. RFC 5639 (Informational) (March 2010)
31. Miller, V.S.: Use of elliptic curves in cryptography. In: Williams, H.C. (ed.) CRYPTO 1985. LNCS, vol. 218, pp. 417–426. Springer, Heidelberg (1986)
32. National Security Agency. The case for elliptic curve cryptography (2005), http://www.nsa.gov/business/programs/elliptic_curve.shtml
33. Stein, W., et al.: Sage Mathematics Software (Version 5.11). The Sage Development Team (2013), http://www.sagemath.org
34. Takayasu, A., Kunihiro, N.: Better lattice constructions for solving multivariate linear equations modulo unknown divisors. In: Boyd, C., Simpson, L. (eds.) ACISP. LNCS, vol. 7959, pp. 118–135. Springer, Heidelberg (2013)
35. Wang, M., Zhan, T.: Analysis of the fault attack ECDLP over prime field. Journal of Applied Mathematics, 1–11 (2011)

All-but-One Dual Projective Hashing and Its Applications

Zongyang Zhang[1,4], Yu Chen[2,*], Sherman S.M. Chow[3], Goichiro Hanaoka[1],
Zhenfu Cao[4], and Yunlei Zhao[5]

[1] National Institute of Advanced Industrial Science and Technology (AIST), Japan
[2] State Key Laboratory of Information Security (SKLOIS),
Institute of Information Engineering, Chinese Academy of Sciences, China
[3] Department of Information Engineering, The Chinese University of Hong Kong
[4] Department of Computer Science and Engineering, Shanghai Jiao Tong University
[5] Software School, Fudan University, China
zongyang.zhang@aist.go.jp, chenyu@iie.ac.cn, sherman@ie.cuhk.edu.hk,
hanaoka-goichiro@aist.go.jp, zfcao@sjtu.edu.cn, ylzhao@fudan.edu.cn

Abstract. Recently, Wee (EUROCRYPT'12) introduced the notion of
dual projective hashing as an extension of the Cramer-Shoup projective
hashing, with a simple construction of lossy trapdoor functions, and a
simple construction of deterministic encryption schemes which is chosen-
plaintext-attack secure with respect to hard-to-invert auxiliary input. In
this work, we further extend it to the all-but-one setting by introducing
the notion of all-but-one dual projective hashing.

- We provide a simple construction of all-but-one lossy trapdoor functions. Our construction encompasses many known constructions of
all-but-one lossy trapdoor functions, as presented by Peikert and
Waters (STOC'08), and Freeman et al. (JoC'13). Particularly, we
present a new construction of all-but-one lossy trapdoor functions
based on the DLIN assumption, which can be viewed as an extension
of Freeman et al.'s DDH-based construction to the DLIN setting, and
therefore solves an open problem left by Freeman et al.
- We also provide a general construction of chosen-ciphertext-attack
(CCA) secure deterministic encryption schemes in the standard model,
under an additional assumption about the projective map. This extends the general approach of designing CCA secure deterministic
encryption schemes by Boldyreva, Fehr and O'Neill (CRYPTO'08).
In addition, we present a new construction of CCA secure deterministic encryption schemes based on the DLIN assumption.

Keywords: Smooth projective hashing, ABO lossy trapdoor function,
deterministic encryption, CCA security.

1 Introduction

In 1998, Cramer and Shoup [9] presented the first efficient public key encryption
scheme which is chosen-ciphertext-attack (CCA) secure in the standard model,

---

* Corresponding author.

I. Boureanu, P. Owesarski, and S. Vaudenay (Eds.): ACNS 2014, LNCS 8479, pp. 181–198, 2014.

under the decisional Diffie-Hellman assumption. Towards a general paradigm of constructing CCA secure public key encryption schemes, they [10] abstracted the above work to hash proof system (HPS). At the heart of HPS lies a primitive dubbed "smooth projective hashing". Thereafter, the smooth projective hashing and its variants have found numerous applications beyond CCA security, including password-based authenticated key exchange [15,19], extractable commitment [1], lossy encryption [5], leakage-resilient public key encryption [21], privacy-preserving interactive protocols [6], oblivious transfer [17], etc.

Informally, a smooth projective hashing is a family of keyed hash functions $\{H_k\}$ whose input u is from some hard language (consisting of YES instances and NO instances). There are two ways to compute the function. First, knowing the hashing key k, one can compute the hash function on every instances in its domain. Second, knowing a projective key $\alpha(k)$ where α is a projective map, one can compute the hash function for each YES instance as long as it additionally knows the associated "witness". This means that the hash value $H_k(u)$ is completely determined by $\alpha(k)$ and u, and this is therefore called the *projective* property. The other property, *smoothness*, means that the projective key $\alpha(k)$ gives (almost) no information about the value of the hash function on NO instance, i.e., the value of the hash function is completely undetermined.

Regarding evaluation on NO instances, instead of smoothness, Wee [25] considered *invertibility* that, for any NO instance u, one can compute the hashing key k given the projective key $\alpha(k)$ and the hash value $H_k(u)$ together with an inversion trapdoor of u. This alternative introduced the notion of dual projective hashing (DPH), where "dual" means that roles of u and k are exchanged. This is why it is more convenient to write the function as $\Lambda_u(k) := H_k(u)$. Moreover, in typical applications of smooth projective hashing, YES instances are used for functionality/correctness and NO instances are used to establish security. In contrast, in applications of dual projective hashing, YES instances are used to establish security, and NO instances are used for functionality/correctness.

Wee [25] showed a simple construction of lossy trapdoor functions via dual projective hashing and presented instantiations of dual projective hashing from Diffie-Hellman assumptions like Decisional Diffie-Hellman (DDH) and and Decisional Linear (DLIN), number-theoretic assumptions like Quadratic Residuosity (QR) and Decisional Composite Residuosity (DCR), and lattice-based assumptions like Learning-with-Error (LWE). It unifies (with slight changes) almost all known constructions of lossy trapdoor functions in [22,13]. When considering chosen-ciphertext security for encryption, many constructions based on lossy-trapdoor function rely on a more generalized all-but-one (ABO) lossy trapdoor functions [22]. It is natural to ask whether we can find an abstraction framework to unify existing ABO lossy trapdoor functions.

Dual projective hashing also leads to a simple construction of deterministic encryption scheme (with respect to hard-to-invert auxiliary input) [25]. Since it only achieves chosen-plaintext security, it is natural to ask whether we can achieve CCA security using dual projective hashing, or if we can get another general framework for CCA secure deterministic encryption schemes.

1.1   Overview of Our Results

We introduce the notion of ABO dual projective hashing. We consider a family of projective hash functions $\{H_k\}$ indexed by a hashing key k and whose inputs are (tag, u). Here, we do not consider YES or NO instances. For any initial parameter $tag^* \in \text{TAG}$, and any u generated by some efficient algorithm together with tag^*, if $tag = tag^*$, we require *projective* property that the hash value $H_k(tag, u)$ is completely determined by u and $\alpha(k)$; otherwise we require *invertibility* that there is some inversion trapdoor allowing us to efficiently recover k given $(\alpha(k), H_k(tag, u))$ along with u. In addition, we require the *hidden projective tag* property that a randomly chosen input u under any $tag \in \text{TAG}$ is computationally indistinguishable from a randomly chosen input u' under another different tag $tag' \in \text{TAG}$. When $\text{TAG} = \{0, 1\}$, an ABO dual projective hashing degrades to a dual projective hashing (refer to Section 3.1 for details). We proceed to answer the above two problems using ABO dual projective hashing. Our applications treat u as an index and (tag, k) as an input to some hash function. It is thus more convenient to denote an ABO dual projective hashing by $\Lambda_u(tag, k)$. For clarity, we replace k with x and use $\Lambda_u(tag, x)$ instead.

ABO Lossy Trapdoor Functions. A collection of ABO lossy trapdoor functions is associated with a set, whose members are called branches. The generator of the collection takes an additional parameter $b^* \in B$, and outputs a description of a function $f(\cdot, \cdot)$ together with a trapdoor τ. The function f has the property that for any branch $b \neq b^*$ the function $f(b, \cdot)$ is injective and can be inverted using τ, while $f(b^*, \cdot)$ is lossy, which means each function statistically loses a significant amount of information about its input. Moreover, the hidden lossy branch property requires that a description of a random function f_1 generated with a parameter b_1 should be indistinguishable from a description of a random function f_2 generated with a distinct parameter b_2.

Starting from ABO dual projective hashing, we can build a collection of ABO lossy trapdoor functions as $F_{u,tag} : x \mapsto \alpha(x) \| \Lambda_u(tag, x)$. The parameter u is generated by a key generation algorithm whose inputs are the projective tag tag^* together with some trapdoor information. For the injective branch $tag \neq tag^*$, invertibility guarantees that, x can be efficiently recovered from the output of the hash function. For the lossy branch tag^*, the projective property guarantees that the output is fully determined by $\alpha(x)$ (and u), and therefore preserves at most $\log |\alpha(x)|$ bits information of x. The hidden lossy branch property is implied by the hidden projective tag property of ABO dual projective hashing.

Deterministic Encryption. Deterministic public key encryption, first introduced by Bellare, Boldyreva and O'Neill [2], is proposed as an alternative in scenarios where traditional randomized encryptions exhibit inherent drawbacks, such as failure in supporting efficient search on encrypted data by simple equality test. The only known general construction of CCA secure deterministic encryption schemes was presented by Boldyreva, Fehr and O'Neill [7]. We give a new one follow their approach. The differences are, they used (ABO) lossy trapdoor functions in place of (ABO) dual projective hashing and the lossy mode acts as an universal hash function (called universal hash mode). With a family of universal hash function $\mathcal{H}$ which is universal one-way, a dual projective hashing Λ, and an ABO dual projective hashing Λ', our construction is roughly as follows.

- The key generator chooses a random NO instance u of Λ together with a trapdoor τ, and generates a random instance u' of Λ' together with trapdoor τ' under a default projective tag. The public key is $pk = (u, u', H)$ where h is a hash function chosen at random from $\mathcal{H}$. The secret key is (τ, τ', pk).
- The encryption algorithm encrypts a message m as follows: $H(m)||\alpha(m)|| \Lambda_u(m)||\alpha'(m)||\Lambda'_u(H(m), m)$. Note that Λ'_u uses $H(m)$ as tag.
- The decryption algorithm attempts to decrypt a ciphertext $c = h||c_1||c_2||c_3||c_4$ as follows: It computes m' from c_1, c_2 using the trapdoor τ. Since Λ is invertible on NO instance u, this can be done efficiently. It outputs m' if the ciphertext is well-formed, that means it can be reconstructed from m'.

We show that if both $\alpha(\cdot)$ and $\alpha'(\cdot)$ are strong average-case extractors (where the seed is provided by the public parameter) for high min-entropy sources, then we obtain a CCA secure deterministic encryption scheme for high min-entropy message distributions. With these requirements on α and α', dual and ABO dual projective hashing imply lossy and ABO lossy trapdoor functions with universal hash mode, respectively, so our construction in general follows from their framework. The additional requirements on $\alpha(\cdot)$ and $\alpha'(\cdot)$ are sometimes satisfied under the cost of efficiency (i.e., the sizes of the keys and hash value). We further present an extended general construction with improved efficiency, which eliminates the extra requirement on the (ABO) dual projective hashing, similar to existing technique [7]. In particular, we use an invertible, pairwise-independent hash functions, and then show this extension suffices to provide CCA security by applying a generalized crooked leftover hash lemma [7].

Instantiations. We present instantiations of ABO dual projective hashing from three major classes of cryptographic assumptions, consisting of Diffie-Hellman assumptions like DDH and DLIN, number-theoretic assumptions like DCR, and lattice-based assumptions like LWE. Following similar technique of [25], we rely on hashing keys to be vectors and/or matrices over $\{0, 1\}^*$ (except one of the DCR-based constructions) in order to achieve the invertibility.

Our results also give a unified treatment of all known constructions of ABO lossy trapdoor functions [22,13], since they can be obtained (with slight changes) by applying our generic transformations from ABO dual projective hash to ABO lossy trapdoor functions on these instantiations. In addition, we present a new construction of ABO lossy trapdoor function based on the DLIN assumption, which can be viewed as an extension of Freeman et al.'s [13] DDH-based scheme to the DLIN setting, and therefore solves an open problem left by them[1].

We then discuss instantiations of CCA secure deterministic encryption. Due to the invertibility requirement, hashing keys k are vectors and/or matrices over

---

[1] As explained later, DLIN-based ABO lossy trapdoor functions can be constructed from DLIN-based lossy trapdoor functions by the parallel execution technique [22].

$\{0,1\}^*$. Regarding the general construction, in order to instantiate $\alpha(\cdot)$ and $\alpha'(\cdot)$ as average-case extractors, we resort to random linear functions where the input k are vectors and/or matrices over $\{0,1\}^*$ [21,25]. For the above reasons, our DCR-based construction and the LWE-based construction are less efficient compared with those of Boldyreva, Fehr and O'Neill [7][2]. However, our DDH-based construction achieves almost the same efficiency as theirs. In addition, we present a new construction of CCA secure deterministic encryption based on the DLIN assumption. Regarding the extended general construction, our DCR-based and LWE-based instantiations are as efficient as those in [7].

1.2 Related Work

ABO Lossy Trapdoor Functions. Peikert and Waters [22] presented general constructions of ABO lossy trapdoor functions from lossy trapdoor function using the "parallel execution" technique. As the sizes of the public key and hash value are linear to the length of the branch, this approach yields inefficient constructions. They also presented direct matrix-based constructions based on DDH and LWE assumptions. Freeman et. al. [13] then proposed new and improved instantiations of ABO lossy trapdoor functions based on DDH and DCR assumptions. Recently, Joye and Libert [18] gave a new construction of ABO lossy trapdoor function based on both the k-Quadratic Residuosity and the DDH assumptions, which achieves much shorter outputs and keys than previous DDH-based ones.

Deterministic Encryptions. Bellare et al. [2] first introduced deterministic public key encryption, formalized several notions of security, and gave a construction in the random oracle model. Later, Bellare et al. [4] and Boldyreva, Fehr and O'Neill [7] refined and extended the security notions, and presented constructions in the standard model. Especially, the latter gave general constructions of CPA/CCA secure deterministic encryption schemes, as well as efficient instantiations under number-theoretic assumptions. After that, there are several follow-up works, focusing on hard-to-invert auxiliary inputs [8,25], incrementatlity [20] (i.e., small changes in the plaintext translate into small changes in the corresponding ciphertext), multi-shot adversaries [3] (i.e., adversaries that interactively challenge the scheme with plaintext distributions depending on previous ciphertexts), bounded multi-message security [14] (i.e., the number of messages are bounded before the setup of the system but messages may be arbitrarily correlated), and impossibility for unbounded multi-message security [26].

There are two main limitations in the above work. One is *plaintext unpredictability*, which means security can be satisfied when plaintext are distributed over a large set. This limitation is inherent and essential for deterministic encryption. The other limitation is *key-independent plaintext distributions*, which means plaintext distributions are independent on the public key. It was considered to be inherent, until Raghunathan, Segev and Vadhan [23] showed that this

---

[2] The DDH-based construction in [7] follows the general framework, while the DCR-based and the LWE-based constructions follow the extended general framework.

limitation can be removed, with meaningful security guarantee, by relying on a randomness extraction from seed-dependent distributions. They also presented CCA secure schemes based on lossy trapdoor functions.

2 Preliminaries

Notation. If A is a deterministic algorithm, then $y := A(x)$ denotes the assignment to y of the output of A on input x. If A is a probabilistic algorithm, then $y \leftarrow_\$ A(x)$ denotes the assignment to y of the output of A on input x with a set of uniformly random coins. We write $y := A(x; r)$ to denote the assignment to y of the output of A on input x and random coins r. A function $\mu(\cdot)$, where $\mu : \mathbb{N} \to [0, 1]$ is called *negligible* if for every positive polynomial $p(\cdot)$, for all sufficiently large $\kappa \in \mathbb{N}$, $\mu(\kappa) < 1/p(\kappa)$. We use $\mathsf{negl}(\cdot)$ to denote an unspecified negligible function.

Let $\{0, 1\}^n$ be the set of n-bit strings. For a string $x \in \{0, 1\}^*$, $|x|$ denotes the length of x. For a random variable X, we use notation $x \leftarrow X$ to denote that a value x is sampled according to X. For a finite set $\mathcal{X}$, we write $x \leftarrow_\$ \mathcal{X}$ to denote the assignment to x of a uniformly randomly chosen element of $\mathcal{X}$. We use $|\mathcal{X}|$ to denote the cardinality of the set $\mathcal{X}$.

The *min-entropy* of a random variable X, denoted as $\mathrm{H}_\infty(X)$, is $\mathrm{H}_\infty(X) := -\log(\max_x \Pr[X = x])$. A k-*source* is a random variable X with $\mathrm{H}_\infty(X) \geq k$. A family of hash functions is a pair $\mathcal{H} := (\mathcal{K}, H)$ where the key generation algorithm $\mathcal{K}(1^\kappa)$ returns a key K, and the deterministic hash function H takes K and an input x to return a hash value y. Let $\ell := \ell(\kappa)$ be a polynomial-time computable function. For simplicity, $\{0, 1\}^\ell$ and $\mathcal{R}$ denote the domain and image of $H(K, \cdot)$, respectively. We call $\mathcal{H}$ an ℓ-*bit hash function*. We say that an ℓ-bit hash function $\mathcal{H}$ with image $\mathcal{R}$ is *universal* if for all $x_1 \neq x_2 \in \{0, 1\}^\ell$, $\Pr[H(K, x_1) = H(K, x_2) : K \leftarrow_\$ \mathcal{K}(1^\kappa)] \leq 1/|\mathcal{R}|$. If we have an upper bound of $\epsilon < 1$ on the collision probability, we say that $\mathcal{H}$ is ϵ-*almost universal*. We say that $\mathcal{H}$ is *pairwise-independent* if for all $x_1 \neq x_2 \in \{0, 1\}^\ell$ and $y_1, y_2 \in \mathcal{R}$, $\Pr[H(K, x_1) = y_1 \wedge H(K, x_2) = y_2 : K \leftarrow_\$ \mathcal{K}(1^\kappa)] \leq 1/|\mathcal{R}|^2$.

We say that $\mathcal{H}$ is *universal one-way* (UOW) if for every PPT adversary $A := (A_1, A_2)$, the *UOW-advantage* $\mathsf{Adv}_{\mathcal{H}, A}^{\mathrm{uow}}(\kappa) := \Pr[H(K, x_1) = H(K, x_2) : (x_1, st) \leftarrow A_1(1^\kappa), K \leftarrow_\$ \mathcal{K}(1^\kappa), x_2 \leftarrow A_2(K, st)]$ of A is negligible in κ. We say that $\mathcal{H}$ is *collision-resistant (CR)* if for every PPT adversary A, the advantage $\mathsf{Adv}_{\mathcal{H}, A}^{\mathrm{cr}}(\kappa) := \Pr[H(K, x_1) = H(K, x_2) \wedge x_1 \neq x_2 :, K \leftarrow_\$ \mathcal{K}(1^\kappa), x_1, x_2 \leftarrow A_2(K)]$ of A is negligible in κ. UOW is implied by CR.

Definition 1 (Dual Projective Hashing). *A dual projective hashing* $\mathbf{P}$ *consists of the following polynomial-time algorithms:* Setup, Pub, Priv, Tdinv.

- Setup(1^κ): *takes as input a security parameter* κ *expressed in the unary representation, and generates parameterized instances of the form* para := $(hp, msk, \mathcal{X}, \mathcal{Y}, \mathcal{P}, \mathcal{U} = \Pi_Y \bigcup \Pi_N, \mathcal{W}, \Gamma, \mathbf{H}, \alpha)$, *where* hp *contains global public parameters[3], msk is a master trapdoor related to hp (e.g., the randomness*

---

[3] Throughout the paper, we assume that all algorithms get hp as an input, and sometimes omit hp from the input for brevity.

used to generate hp), Π_Y and Π_N are disjoint sets and correspond to YES and NO instances, respectively, $\mathbf{H} := \{\Lambda_u : \mathcal{X} \rightarrow \mathcal{Y}\}_{u \in \mathcal{U}}$ *is a family of hash functions indexed by* $u \in \mathcal{U}$, *and* $\alpha : \mathcal{X} \rightarrow \mathcal{P}$ *is a projective map (that we will explain later). In addition, we require that there exists a pair of efficient sampling algorithms* SampYes *and* SampNo.

- YES *instance sampling algorithm:* SampYes(hp) *outputs a random pair of values* (u, w) *where* u *is uniformly distributed over* Π_Y *and* w *is the corresponding witness in* $\mathcal{W}$;
- NO *instance sampling algorithm:* SampNo(hp) *outputs a random pairs of values* (u, τ) *where* u *is uniformly distributed over* Π_N *and* τ *is the corresponding trapdoor in* Γ. *Note that for some instantiations,* SampNo(hp) *requires as input the master trapdoor* msk *in order to compute the inversion trapdoor* τ.

- Priv(u, x): *is a deterministic private evaluation algorithm. It takes as input a public parameter* $u \in \mathcal{U}$ *and an input* $x \in \mathcal{X}$, *outputs* $y \in \mathcal{Y}$.
- Pub$(u, \alpha(x), w)$: *is a deterministic public evaluation algorithm. It takes as input a public parameter* $u \in \Pi_Y$, *a projective value* $\alpha(x) \in \mathcal{P}$, *and a witness* w *for* u, *outputs* $y \in \mathcal{Y}$.
- Tdinv$(\tau, \alpha(x), \Lambda_u(x))$: *takes as input a trapdoor information* $\tau \in \Gamma$, *a projective value* $\alpha(x) \in \mathcal{P}$ *for any* $x \in \mathcal{X}$, *and a hash value* $\Lambda_u(x) \in \mathcal{Y}$, *outputs* $x' \in \mathcal{X}$.

Correctness. We require that for all $\kappa \in \mathbb{N}$, all para generated by Setup(1^κ), all $u \in \Pi_Y \bigcup \Pi_N$ and all $x \in \mathcal{X}$, Priv$(u, x) = \Lambda_u(x)$.

Projectiveness. $\mathbf{P}$ *is almost projective if for all* $\kappa \in \mathbb{N}$, all para generated by Setup(1^κ), all $x \in \mathcal{X}$, $\Pr[\mathsf{Pub}(u, \alpha(x), w) = \Lambda_u(x) : (u, w) \leftarrow_\$ \mathsf{SampYes}(hp)] \geq 1 - \mathsf{negl}(\kappa)$. *If this holds with probability 1, we say that* $\mathbf{P}$ *is perfectly projective.*

Invertibility. $\mathbf{P}$ *is almost invertible if for all* $\kappa \in \mathbb{N}$, all para generated by Setup(1^κ), all $x \in \mathcal{X}$, $\Pr[\mathsf{Tdinv}(\tau, \alpha(x), \Lambda_u(x)) = x : (u, \tau) \leftarrow_\$ \mathsf{SampNo}(hp)] \geq 1 - \mathsf{negl}(\kappa)$. *If this holds with probability 1, we say that* $\mathbf{P}$ *is perfectly invertible.*

Subset Membership Assumption. This assumption states that the uniform distributions over Π_Y and Π_N are computationally indistinguishable, even given hp. This is formally captured by the advantage function $\mathsf{Adv}^{\mathrm{sm}}_{\mathrm{DPH},A}(\kappa)$:

$$\mathsf{Adv}^{\mathrm{sm}}_{\mathrm{DPH},A}(\kappa) := \Pr[A(hp, u) = 1 : u \leftarrow_\$ \Pi_Y] - \Pr[A(hp, u) = 1 : u \leftarrow_\$ \Pi_N]$$

where hp is generated by Setup(1^κ). The subset membership assumption states that for all PPT adversary A, $\mathsf{Adv}^{\mathrm{sm}}_{\mathrm{DPH},A}(\kappa)$ is a negligible function in κ.

3   ABO Dual Projective Hashing

Definition 2 (ABO Dual Projective Hashing). *An all-but-one dual projective hashing* $\mathbf{P}$ *consists of the following polynomial-time algorithms:* Setup, Keygen, Pub, Priv, Tdinv.

- Setup(1^κ): *takes as input a security parameter κ expressed in the unary representation, and generates parameterized instances of the form* **para** $:=$ $(hp, msk, \mathrm{TAG}, \mathcal{X}, \mathcal{Y}, \mathcal{P}, \mathcal{U}, \mathcal{W}, \Gamma, \mathbf{H}, \alpha)$, *where hp contains global public parameters, msk is a master trapdoor related to hp (e.g., the randomness used to generate hp), $\mathbf{H} := \{\Lambda_u : \mathrm{TAG} \times \mathcal{X} \to \mathcal{Y}\}_{u \in \mathcal{U}}$ is a family of hash functions indexed by $u \in \mathcal{U}$, and $\alpha : \mathcal{X} \to \mathcal{P}$ is a projective map.*
- Keygen(msk, tag^*): *takes as input a master trapdoor msk and a tag $tag^* \in$ TAG, and outputs (u, w, τ) consisting of a public parameter $u \in \mathcal{U}$, a witness $w \in \mathcal{W}$, and an inversion trapdoor $\tau \in \Gamma$. If no tag input is specified, it is assumed to be a fixed "default" tag.*
- Priv(u, tag, x): *is the deterministic private evaluation algorithm. It takes as input a public parameter $u \in \mathcal{U}$, a tag $tag \in \mathrm{TAG}$ and an input $x \in \mathcal{X}$, and outputs $y \in \mathcal{Y}$.*
- Pub$(u, tag, \alpha(x), w)$: *is the deterministic public evaluation algorithm. It takes as input a public parameter $u \in \mathcal{U}$, a tag $tag \in \mathrm{TAG}$, a projective value $\alpha(x) \in \mathcal{P}$ and a witness w, and outputs $y \in \mathcal{Y}$ if $tag = tag^*$.*
- Tdinv$(\tau, tag, \alpha(x), \Lambda_u(tag, x))$: *takes as input a trapdoor information $\tau \in \Gamma$, a tag $tag \in \mathrm{TAG}$, a projective value $\alpha(x) \in \mathcal{P}$ for any $x \in \mathcal{X}$, and a hash value $\Lambda_u(tag, x)$ for some tag $tag \in \mathrm{TAG}$, and outputs $x' \in \mathcal{X}$ if $tag \neq tag^*$.*

Correctness. We require that for all $\kappa \in \mathbb{N}$, all **para** generated by Setup(1^κ), all $tag^* \in \mathrm{TAG}$, all (u, w, τ) generated by Keygen(msk, tag^*), and all $x \in \mathcal{X}$, Priv$(u, tag, x) = \Lambda_u(tag, x)$.

Projectiveness. We say $\mathbf{P}$ is *almost projective* if for all $\kappa \in \mathbb{N}$, all **para** generated by Setup(1^κ), all $tag^* \in \mathrm{TAG}$, all $x \in \mathcal{X}$, $\Pr[\mathsf{Pub}(u, tag^*, \alpha(x), w) = \Lambda_u(tag^*, x) : (u, w, \tau) \leftarrow_\$ \mathsf{Keygen}(msk, tag^*)] \geq 1 - \mathsf{negl}(\kappa)$. If the projective property holds with probability 1 then we say that $\mathbf{P}$ is *perfectly projective.*

Invertibility. We say $\mathbf{P}$ is *almost invertible* if for all $\kappa \in \mathbb{N}$, all **para** $\leftarrow$ Setup(1^κ), all $tag^*, tag \in \mathrm{TAG}$ where $tag^* \neq tag$, all $x \in \mathcal{X}$, $\Pr[\mathsf{Tdinv}(\tau, tag, \alpha(x), \Lambda_u(tag, x)) = x : (u, w, \tau) \leftarrow_\$ \mathsf{Keygen}(msk, tag^*)] \geq 1 - \mathsf{negl}(\kappa)$. If the invertibility holds with probability 1 then we say that $\mathbf{P}$ is *perfectly invertible.*

Hidden Projective Tag. For every **para** generated by Setup(1^κ) and for any PPT algorithm $A := (A_1, A_2)$, the advantage $\mathsf{Adv}_{\mathbf{P},A}^{\mathrm{hpt}}(\kappa)$ of A is negligible in the security parameter κ:

$$\mathsf{Adv}_{\mathbf{P},A}^{\mathrm{hpt}}(\kappa) := 2\Pr\left[b = b' : \begin{array}{l}((tag_0, tag_1), st) \leftarrow A_1(hp), b \leftarrow_\$ \{0,1\} \\ (u, w, \tau) \leftarrow_\$ \mathsf{Keygen}(msk, tag_b), b' \leftarrow A_2(hp, u, st)\end{array}\right] - 1.$$

Dual projective hashing (DPH) and ABO dual projective hashing are equivalent for appropriate choices of parameters. We show their relationship in Section 3.1.

3.1   Relationship between DPH and ABO DPH

From ABO DPH to DPH. Starting from an ABO dual projective hashing $\mathbf{P} := (\mathsf{Setup}, \mathsf{Keygen}, \mathsf{Pub}, \mathsf{Priv}, \mathsf{Tdinv})$ with tag set $\mathrm{TAG} = \{0, 1\}$, we may derive a dual projective hashing as follows.

- Setup$'(1^\kappa)$: runs $(hp, msk, \{0,1\}, \mathcal{X}, \mathcal{Y}, \mathcal{P}, \mathcal{U}, \mathcal{W}, \Gamma, \mathbf{H}, \alpha) \leftarrow_\$ \mathsf{Setup}(1^\kappa)$, then
  run $(u_0, w_0, \tau_0) \leftarrow_\$ \mathsf{Keygen}(msk, 0)$, and $(u_1, w_1, \tau_1) \leftarrow_\$ \mathsf{Keygen}(msk, 1)$. De-
  note by Π_Y and Π_N the set of possible value of u_0 and u_1, respectively. The
  family of functions $\mathbf{H}' := \{\Lambda'_u : \mathcal{X} \to \mathcal{Y}\}_{u \in \mathcal{U}'}$ is defined as $\Lambda'_u(x) := \Lambda_u(0, x)$.
  Return $(hp, msk, \mathcal{X}, \mathcal{Y}, \mathcal{P}, \mathcal{W}, \mathcal{U}' := \Pi_Y \bigcup \Pi_N, \Gamma, \mathbf{H}', \alpha)$.
  - SampYes(hp): runs $(u, w, \tau) \leftarrow_\$ \mathsf{Keygen}(msk, 0)$ and outputs (u, w).
  - SampNo(hp): runs $(u, w, \tau) \leftarrow_\$ \mathsf{Keygen}(msk, 1)$ and outputs (u, τ).
- Priv$'(u, x)$: outputs $\mathsf{Priv}(u, 0, x)$.
- Pub$'(u, \alpha(x), w)$: outputs $\mathsf{Pub}(u, 0, \alpha(x), w)$.
- Tdinv$'(\tau, \alpha(x), y)$: outputs $x \leftarrow \mathsf{Tdinv}(\tau, 0, \alpha(x), y)$.

From DPH to ABO DPH. We give a general construction of ABO dual projective hashing from a dual projective hashing by "parallel execution" which has
been used in previous works [12,24,22]. Starting from a dual projective hashing
$\mathbf{P} := (\mathsf{Setup}, \mathsf{Pub}, \mathsf{Priv}, \mathsf{Tdinv})$, we can derive an ABO dual projective hashing
for tag set $\{0,1\}^\ell$ as follows.

- Setup$'(1^\kappa)$: runs $(hp, msk, \mathcal{X}, \mathcal{Y}, \mathcal{P}, \mathcal{U} = \Pi_Y \bigcup \Pi_N, \mathcal{W}, \Gamma, \mathbf{H}, \alpha) \leftarrow_\$ \mathsf{Setup}(1^\kappa)$.
  Sets TAG $:= \{0,1\}^\ell$. Sets $\mathcal{Y}' := \mathcal{Y}^\ell, \mathcal{U}' := \mathcal{U}^{2\ell}, \mathcal{W}' := \mathcal{W}^\ell, \Gamma' := \Gamma^\ell$.
  The family of functions $\mathbf{H}' := \{\Lambda'_{u'} : \text{TAG} \times \mathcal{X} \to \mathcal{Y}'\}_{u' \in \mathcal{U}'}$ is defined
  as $\Lambda'_{u'}(tag, x) := (\Lambda_{u_{i,tag_i}}(x))_{i \in [\ell]}$ where u' equals $(u_{i,0}, u_{i,1})_{i \in [\ell]}$. Returns
  $(hp, msk, \text{TAG}, \mathcal{X}, \mathcal{Y}', \mathcal{P}, \mathcal{U}', \mathcal{W}', \Gamma', \mathbf{H}', \alpha)$.
- Keygen$'(msk, tag^*)$: for $i = 1$ to ℓ, runs $(u_{i,tag_i^*}, w_i) \leftarrow_\$ \mathsf{SampYes}(hp)$ and
  $(u_{i,1-tag_i^*}, \tau_i) \leftarrow_\$ \mathsf{SampNo}(hp)$. Sets $u' := (u_{i,0}, u_{i,1})_{i \in [\ell]}$, $w' := (w_i)_{i \in [\ell]}$, and
  $\tau' := (\tau_i)_{i \in [\ell]}$. Outputs (u', w', τ').
- Priv$'(u', tag, x)$: parses u' as $(u_{i,0}, u_{i,1})_{i \in [\ell]}$, and outputs $(\mathsf{Priv}(u_{i,tag_i}, x))_{i \in [\ell]}$.
- Pub$'(u', tag, \alpha(x), w')$: if $tag \neq tag^*$, outputs $\bot$. Otherwise parses u' as
  $(u_{i,0}, u_{i,1})_{i \in [\ell]}$ and w' as $(w_i)_{i \in [\ell]}$, and outputs $(\mathsf{Pub}(u_{i,tag_i}, \alpha(x), w_i))_{i \in [\ell]}$.
- Tdinv$'(\tau', tag, \alpha(x), (y_1, \ldots, y_\ell))$: computes $x_i \leftarrow \mathsf{Tdinv}(\tau_i, \alpha(x), y_i)$ for all i
  such that $tag_i \neq tag_i^*$. Denote the common value by x if all these values
  agree and if not outputs $\bot$. Checks $y_i = \mathsf{Priv}(u_{i,tag_i}, x)$ for all i such that
  $tag_i = tag_i^*$. If all the checks pass, then outputs x; otherwise outputs $\bot$.

4   All-but-One Lossy Trapdoor Functions from ABO DPH

We construct a family of ABO lossy trapdoor functions in Fig. 1.

Theorem 1. *Suppose that* $\mathbf{P} := (\mathsf{Setup}, \mathsf{Keygen}, \mathsf{Pub}, \mathsf{Priv}, \mathsf{Tdinv})$ *is an ABO
dual projective hashing, then the construction in Fig. 1 yields a collection of
$(m, m - \log|\mathrm{Img}\alpha|)$-ABO lossy trapdoor functions, where $m := \log|\mathcal{X}|$.*

Proof. The correctness for injective functions follows from the invertibility property. The lossiness for the lossy branch follows from the projective property. Re-
call that if $tag = tag^*$, then for all $x \in \mathcal{X}$, $\Lambda_u(tag, x)$ is determined by $\alpha(x)$ and
u. This means that the size of image set $\mathrm{Img} f_{u,tag}$ is at most $|\mathrm{Img}\alpha|$. Thus, the
function is $(m, m - \log|\mathrm{Img}\alpha|)$-lossy. The hidden lossy branch property directly
follows from the hidden projective tag property of $\mathbf{P}$.

All-but-One Lossy Trapdoor Function

1. *Sampling a branch:* $B(1^\kappa)$ outputs a value $tag^* \in$ TAG.
2. *Sampling a function:* $S_{\text{abo}}(1^\kappa, tag^*)$ first runs $(u, w, \tau) \leftarrow_\$ \text{Keygen}(msk, tag^*)$, and outputs $(hp||u, \tau)$.
3. *Evaluation:* $F_{\text{abo}}(hp||u, tag, x)$ returns $\alpha(x)||\Lambda_u(tag, x)$. Note $\Lambda_u(tag, x)$ can be computed using $\text{Priv}(u, tag, x)$.
4. *Inversion of injective functions:* Returns $\text{Tdinv}(\tau, tag, \alpha(x), \Lambda_u(tag, x))$ if $tag \neq tag^*$.

Note: $(hp, msk, \text{TAG}, \mathcal{X}, \mathcal{Y}, \mathcal{P}, \mathcal{U}, \mathcal{W}, \Gamma, \mathbf{H}, \alpha) \leftarrow_\$ \text{Setup}(1^\kappa)$.

Fig. 1. ABO lossy trapdoor function from ABO dual projective hashing

5 Deterministic Encryption from ABO DPH

5.1 Security Definition

Under page limit, we omit the definition of extractors and the left-over hash lemma. Next we give the definition of deterministic encryption.

Definition 3 (Deterministic Encryption). *A deterministic encryption scheme Π is specified by three polynomial-time algorithms, Gen, Enc and Dec.*

- *Gen(1^κ): on input a security parameter κ expressed in the unary representation, the key generation algorithm outputs a public key pk and a secret key sk. The pk includes a description of finite message space $\mathcal{M}$ and a finite ciphertext space $\mathcal{C}$.*
- *Enc(pk, m): on input pk and a message $m \in \mathcal{M}$, the deterministic encryption algorithm outputs a ciphertext $c \in \mathcal{C}$.*
- *Dec(sk, c): on input a secret key sk and a ciphertext c, the decryption algorithm outputs a message $m \in \mathcal{M} \cup \perp$.*

Correctness. For all $\kappa \in \mathbb{N}$, all message $m \in \mathcal{M}$, it holds that

$$\Pr\left[\text{Dec}(sk, \text{Enc}(pk, m)) \neq m : (pk, sk) \leftarrow_\$ \text{Gen}(1^\kappa)\right] \leq \text{negl}(\kappa).$$

Security under chosen-ciphertext attack. We follow the indistinguishability-based security definition of deterministic encryption [7,4]. For simplicity, we only consider security while encrypting a single message, although our proof extends to multiple messages for block-sources. We can also rely on the existing result that for block-sources, single message security equals to multi-message security [7].

Definition 4 (PRIV-CCA). *A deterministic encryption $\Pi := (\text{Gen}, \text{Enc}, \text{Dec})$ is PRIV-CCA-secure for k-source if for any k-source M_0, M_1, the advantage $\text{Adv}_{\Pi, A, M_0, M_1}^{priv\text{-}cca}(\kappa) := 2\Pr[\text{Exp}_{\Pi, A, M_0, M_1}^{priv\text{-}cca}(\kappa) = 1] - 1$ of any PPT adversary A is negligible in κ. The experiment $\text{Exp}_{\Pi, A, M_0, M_1}^{priv\text{-}cca}(\kappa)$ is defined by: 1) $b \leftarrow_\$ \{0, 1\}$; 2) $m_b \leftarrow M_b, (pk, sk) \leftarrow_\$ \text{Gen}(1^\kappa)$; 3) $c := \text{Enc}(pk, m_b)$; 4) $b' \leftarrow A^{\text{Dec}_{\neq c}(sk, \cdot)}(pk, c)$ where the oracle $\text{Dec}_{\neq c}(sk, \cdot)$ decrypts any ciphertext except c; 5) Return $b = b'$.*

5.2   Our Construction

Let $\mathbf{P} := (\mathsf{Setup}, \mathsf{Pub}, \mathsf{Priv}, \mathsf{Tdinv})$, $\mathbf{P}' := (\mathsf{Setup}', \mathsf{Keygen}', \mathsf{Pub}', \mathsf{Priv}', \mathsf{Tdinv}')$ be a dual projective hashing and an ABO dual projective hashing respectively. Let $\mathcal{H} := (\mathcal{K}, H)$ be an ℓ-bit universal and universal one-way hash function with image $\mathcal{R}$. For consistency, $\mathcal{R}$ does not include the default projective tag tag^* of $\mathbf{P}'$. The deterministic encryption Π is shown in Fig. 2. The message space $\mathcal{M}$ is a subset of both $\mathcal{X}$ and $\mathcal{X}'$, and the image $\mathcal{R}$ of the hash function $\mathcal{H}$ is a subset of the set $\mathrm{TAG}'\backslash\{tag^*\}$.

Key Generation: $\mathsf{Gen}(1^\kappa)$ computes as follows.
1. Run $(hp, msk, \mathcal{X}, \mathcal{Y}, \mathcal{P}, \mathcal{U}, \mathcal{W}, \Gamma, \mathbf{H}, \alpha) \leftarrow_\$ \mathsf{Setup}(1^\kappa)$.
2. Run $(hp', msk', \mathrm{TAG}', \mathcal{X}', \mathcal{Y}', \mathcal{P}', \mathcal{U}', \mathcal{W}', \Gamma', \mathbf{H}', \alpha') \leftarrow_\$ \mathsf{Setup}'(1^\kappa)$.
3. Run $(u, \tau) \leftarrow_\$ \mathsf{SampNo}(hp)$, $(u', w', \tau') \leftarrow_\$ \mathsf{Keygen}'(msk', tag^*)$, and $K \leftarrow_\$ \mathcal{K}(1^\kappa)$.
4. Output $pk := hp||u||hp'||u'||K$ and $sk := \tau||\tau'||w'||pk$.

Encryption: $\mathsf{Enc}(pk, m)$ takes input $pk = hp||u||hp'||u'||K$ and message m, and computes as follows.
1. $h := H(K, m)$.
2. $c_1 := \alpha(hp, m)$ and $c_2 := \Lambda_u(m)$. Note that c_2 can be computed using $\mathsf{Priv}(u, m)$.
3. $c_3 := \alpha'(hp', m)$ and $c_4 := \Lambda'_{u'}(h, m)$. Note that c_4 can be computed using $\mathsf{Priv}'(u', h, m)$.
4. Output $h||c_1||c_2||c_3||c_4$.

Decryption: $\mathsf{Dec}(sk, c)$ computes as follows.
1. Parse sk as $\tau||\tau'||w'||pk$ and c as $h||c_1||c_2||c_3||c_4$.
2. $m' \leftarrow \mathsf{Tdinv}(\tau, c_1, c_2)$.
3. $c' := \mathsf{Enc}(pk, m')$.
4. If $c = c'$ then return m'; otherwise return $\perp$.

Fig. 2. Deterministic encryption scheme from (ABO) dual projective hashing

Theorem 2. *Suppose that* $(x, hp) \longmapsto \alpha(hp, x)$ *is an average-case* (k_1, ϵ_1)-*extractor,* $(x, hp') \longmapsto \alpha'(hp', x)$ *is an average-case* (k_2, ϵ_2)-*extractor, the subset membership assumption for* $\mathbf{P}$ *holds, and* $\mathcal{H} := (\mathcal{K}, H)$ *is* ℓ-*bit universal hash function that is also universal one-way. For any adversary* A, *any* k-*sources* $\mathsf{M}_0, \mathsf{M}_1$ *such that* $k \geq \max\{k_1 + \log|\mathcal{R}|, k_2 + \log|\mathcal{R}| + \log|\mathcal{P}|, \log|\mathcal{R}| + 2\log(1/\epsilon_3)\}$, *there exist adversaries* B_{hpt}, B_{uow}, B_{sm} *such that:*

$$\mathsf{Adv}^{priv\text{-}cca}_{\Pi, A, \mathsf{M}_0, \mathsf{M}_1}(\kappa) \leq 2\big(\mathsf{Adv}^{hpt}_{\mathbf{P}, B_{hpt}}(\kappa) + \mathsf{Adv}^{uow}_{\mathcal{H}, B_{uow}}(\kappa) + \mathsf{Adv}^{sm}_{\mathrm{DPH}, B_{sm}}(\kappa) + \epsilon_1 + \epsilon_2 + \epsilon_3\big).$$

Furthermore, the running-time of B_{hpt}, B_{uow}, B_{sm} *are roughly that of* A.

5.3   Extended General Construction

Our security proofs explored the fact that the projective map α acts as an average-case extractor. In specific instantiations, we actually design α as a universal hash function and then apply the generalized leftover hash lemma (LHL) to conclude it is an average-case extractor. This sometimes results in inefficient constructions. Using similar technique of [7], we present an extension of our generic construction, where the extra universality requirement on α is eliminated. We use an invertible, pairwise-independent hash functions, and then showed this extension suffices to provide CCA security by applying a generalized crooked LHL [7].

We say a family of pairwise-independent hash functions $\mathcal{H}_{pi} := (\mathcal{K}_{pi}, H_{pi})$ is *invertible* if there is a PPT algorithm I such that for all K_{pi} output by $\mathcal{K}_{pi}$ and all $m \in \{0,1\}^{\ell}$, $I(K_{pi}, H_{pi}(K_{pi}, m))$ outputs m. Let $\mathbf{P} := (\mathsf{Setup}, \mathsf{Pub}, \mathsf{Priv}, \mathsf{Tdinv})$ be a dual projective hashing. Let $\mathbf{P}' := (\mathsf{Setup}', \mathsf{Keygen}', \mathsf{Pub}', \mathsf{Priv}', \mathsf{Tdinv}')$ be an ABO dual projective hashing. Let $\mathcal{H}_{pi} := (\mathcal{K}_{pi}, H_{pi})$ be a family of ℓ-bit invertible pairwise-independent permutations on $\{0,1\}^{\ell}$. For consistency, $\mathcal{H}_{pi}$ does not map to a default projective tag tag^* of $\mathbf{P}'$. Let $\mathcal{H}_{\mathrm{uow}} := (\mathcal{K}_{\mathrm{uow}}, H)$ be a family of universal one-way hash function with image $\mathcal{R}_{\mathrm{uow}}$. The extended generation construction of deterministic encryption scheme $\Pi := (\mathsf{Enc}^+, \mathsf{Gen}^+, \mathsf{Dec}^+)$ is shown in Fig. 3. The message space $\mathcal{M}$ is $\{0,1\}^{\ell}$. The image of $\mathcal{H}_{pi}$ is a subset of $\mathcal{X}, \mathcal{X}'$, and the domain of $\mathcal{H}_{\mathrm{uow}}$.

Key Generation: $\mathsf{Gen}^+(1^{\kappa})$ computes as follow.
1. Run $(hp, msk, \mathcal{X}, \mathcal{Y}, \mathcal{P}, \mathcal{U}, \mathcal{W}, \Gamma, \mathbf{H}, \alpha) \leftarrow_{\$} \mathsf{Setup}(1^{\kappa})$.
2. Run $(hp', msk', \mathrm{TAG}', \mathcal{X}', \mathcal{Y}', \mathcal{P}', \mathcal{U}', \mathcal{W}', \Gamma', \mathbf{H}', \alpha') \leftarrow_{\$} \mathsf{Setup}'(1^{\kappa})$.
3. Run $(u, \tau) \leftarrow_{\$} \mathsf{SampNo}(hp)$, $(u', w', \tau') \leftarrow_{\$} \mathsf{Keygen}'(msk', tag^*)$, $K_{\mathrm{uow}} \leftarrow_{\$} \mathcal{K}_{\mathrm{uow}}(1^{\kappa})$.
4. For $i = 1$ to 3 do $K_{pi,i} \leftarrow_{\$} \mathcal{K}_{pi}(1^{\kappa})$.
5. Output $pk := hp||u||hp'||u'||K_{\mathrm{uow}}||K_{pi,1}||K_{pi,2}||K_{pi,3}$ and $sk := \tau||\tau'||w'||pk$.
Encryption: $\mathsf{Enc}^+(pk, m)$ takes input $pk = hp||u||hp'||u'||K_{\mathrm{uow}}||K_{pi,1}||K_{pi,2}||K_{pi,3}$ and message m, and computes as follows.
1. For $i = 1$ to 3 do $h_i := H_{pi}(K_{pi,i}, m)$.
2. $h := H(K_{\mathrm{uow}}, h_1)$.
3. $c_1 := \alpha(hp, h_2)$ and $c_2 := \Lambda_u(h_2)$. Note that c_2 can be computed using $\mathsf{Priv}(u, h_2)$.
4. $c_3 := \alpha'(hp', h_3)$ and $c_4 := \Lambda'_{u'}(h, h_3)$. Note that c_4 can be computed using $\mathsf{Priv}'(u', h, h_3)$.
5. Output $h||c_1||c_2||c_3||c_4$.
Decryption: $\mathsf{Dec}^+(sk, c)$ computes as follows.
1. Parse sk as $\tau||\tau'||w'||pk$ and c as $h||c_1||c_2||c_3||c_4$.
2. $h_2' \leftarrow \mathsf{Tdinv}(\tau, c_1, c_2)$.
3. $m' \leftarrow I(K_{pi,2}, h_2')$.
4. $c' := \mathsf{Enc}^+(pk, m')$.
5. If $c = c'$ then return m'; otherwise return $\perp$.

Fig. 3. Deterministic encryption scheme from (ABO) dual projective hashing

---

Using the generalized crooked LHL [7], we are able to show the following.

Theorem 3. *Let* $\Pi := (\mathsf{Enc}^+, \mathsf{Gen}^+, \mathsf{Dec}^+)$ *be as defined in Fig. 3. For any adversary* A, *any* k-*sources* $\mathsf{M}_0, \mathsf{M}_1$ *such that* $k \geq \log|\mathcal{R}_{\mathrm{uow}}| + \log|\mathcal{P}| + \log|\mathcal{P}'| + 2\log(1/\epsilon) - 2$, *there exist adversaries* B_{hpt}, B_{uow}, B_{sm} *such that* $\mathsf{Adv}^{priv-cca}_{\Pi, A, \mathsf{M}_0, \mathsf{M}_1}(\kappa) \leq$

$2\big(\mathsf{Adv}^{hpt}_{\mathbf{P},B_{hpt}}(\kappa)+\mathsf{Adv}^{uow}_{\mathcal{H}_{uow},B_{uow}}(\kappa)+\mathsf{Adv}^{sm}_{\mathrm{DPH},B_{sm}}(\kappa)+3\epsilon\big)$. *Furthermore, the running-time of* B_{hpt}, B_{uow}, B_{sm} *are roughly that of* A.

6   Instantiations

6.1   Instantiations from DDH and DLIN

Let G be a finite cyclic group of prime order q specified by a randomly chosen generator g. The d-LIN assumption asserts that $g_{d+1}^{r_1+\cdots+r_d}$ is pseudorandom given $g_1,\ldots,g_{d+1},g_1^{r_1},\ldots,g_d^{r_d}$ where $g_1,\ldots,g_{d+1}\leftarrow_\$G; r_1,\ldots,r_d\leftarrow_\$\mathbb{Z}_q$.

Here we present the DLIN-based ABO dual projective hashing. When instantiated with our generic transformations, this yields a new DLIN-based $(m, m - d\log q)$-ABO lossy trapdoor functions. It also yields a similar DDH-based ABO lossy trapdoor functions as given in [13]. As the projective map α is a universal hash function, it is also an average-case extractor by applying the generalized LHL [7]. Combining the DLIN-based dual projective hashing [25] and discrete-logarithm based hash function [7] which is universal and collision-resistant, we get a new DLIN-based PRIV-CCA secure deterministic encryption scheme.

- Setup(1^κ): choose G, q, g as above and $\mathbf{P}\leftarrow_\$\mathbb{Z}_q^{d\times m}$. Set $hp := (G, q, g^\mathbf{P})$, $msk := \mathbf{P}$, $\mathcal{X} := \{0,1\}^m$, $\mathcal{Y} := G^m$, $\mathcal{P} := G^d$, $\mathcal{U} := G^{m\times m}$, $\mathcal{W} := \mathbb{Z}_q^m$, TAG $:= \mathbb{Z}_q$. The map α is defined by $\alpha(g^\mathbf{P}, \mathbf{x}) := g^{\mathbf{Px}}$ with $\mathbf{x} \in \{0,1\}^m$.
- Keygen(msk, b^*): choose $\mathbf{W}\leftarrow_\$\mathbb{Z}_q^{m\times d}$, and compute $\mathbf{U} := g^{\mathbf{WP}-b^*\mathbf{I}_m}$. The witness is $\mathbf{W}$. The inversion trapdoor is $(\mathbf{P}, \mathbf{W}, b^*)$. Output $(\mathbf{U}, \mathbf{W}, (\mathbf{P}, \mathbf{W}, b^*))$.
- Priv($\mathbf{U}, b, \mathbf{x}$): Compute $\Lambda_\mathbf{U}(b, \mathbf{x}) := \mathbf{U}^\mathbf{x}*g^{b\mathbf{x}}$, where $*$ indicates the component-wise product of elements of G^m.
- Pub($\mathbf{U}, b^*, g^{\mathbf{Px}}, \mathbf{W}$)): Compute $g^{\mathbf{W}(\mathbf{Px})}$.
- Tdinv($(\mathbf{P}, \mathbf{W}, b^*), b, g^{\mathbf{Px}}, \Lambda_\mathbf{U}(b, \mathbf{x})$) : first compute $\mathbf{A} := \mathbf{WP} + (b - b^*)\mathbf{I}_m$. The trapdoor is $\mathbf{A}^{-1}$. Note that $\Lambda_\mathbf{U}(b, \mathbf{x}) = \mathbf{U}^\mathbf{x} * g^{b\mathbf{x}} = g^{\mathbf{Ax}}$. Given $\mathbf{A}^{-1}$, $\Lambda_\mathbf{U}^*(b, \mathbf{x})$, we can compute $g^\mathbf{x}$ and thus $\mathbf{x}$.

Projectiveness: When $\mathbf{U} = g^{\mathbf{WP}-b^*\mathbf{I}_m}$ and $b = b^*$, let $(\mathbf{U}^\mathbf{x})_i := \Sigma_{j=1}^m \mathbf{U}_{ij}^{x_j}$, we have $\mathsf{Priv}(\mathbf{U}, b^*, \mathbf{x}) = \mathbf{U}^\mathbf{x} * g^{b^*\mathbf{x}} = g^{(\mathbf{WP}-b^*\mathbf{I}_m)\mathbf{x}} * g^{b^*\mathbf{x}} = g^{\mathbf{W}(\mathbf{Px})} = \mathsf{Pub}(\mathbf{U}, b^*, g^{\mathbf{Px}}, \mathbf{W})$.

6.2   Instantiations from DCR

Fix a Blum integer $N := PQ$ for safe primes $P, Q \equiv 3 \pmod 4$ (such that $P := 2p+1$ and $Q := 2q+1$ for sufficiently large primes p, q), where N is a κ-bit string. Let $s \in \mathbb{Z}^+$ be an integer. The multiplicative group $\mathbb{Z}_{N^{s+1}}^*$ is isomorphic to $\mathbb{Z}_{N^s} \times \mathbb{Z}_N^*$. The decisional composite residuosity (DCR) assumption states that any PPT algorithm that receives an input a κ-bit N (generated as above) cannot distinguish a random element in $\mathbb{Z}_{N^{s+1}}^*$ from a random N^s-th power in $\mathbb{Z}_{N^{s+1}}^*$ with non-negligible probability of κ.

First Construction. We present the DCR-based ABO dual projective hashing, extended to the Damgård-Jurik scheme [11]. When instantiated with our generic transformation, this yields the DCR-based $(s \log N, s \log N - \log |\phi(N)|)$-ABO lossy trapdoor functions given in [13] (with slight modifications). As the projective map α is not an average-case extractor, we have to rely on the extended general framework in Section 5.3 to construct PRIV-CCA secure deterministic encryptions. By combining the dual projective hash from DCR [25] and the collision resistant hash function from DCR [7], we get a PRIV-CCA secure deterministic encryption which is as efficient as the DCR-based construction in [7].

- Setup(1^κ): choose a Blum integer $N := PQ$ as above. Pick $g \leftarrow_\$ \mathbb{Z}_{N^{s+1}}^*$. Set $hp := (N, g^{N^s})$, $msk := (g, P, Q)$, $\mathcal{X} := \mathbb{Z}_{N^s}$, $\mathcal{Y} := \mathbb{Z}_{N^{s+1}}^*$, $\mathcal{P} \subseteq \mathbb{Z}_{N^{s+1}}^*$ ($\mathcal{P}$ is isomorphic to $\mathbb{Z}_N^*$), $\mathcal{U} := \mathbb{Z}_{N^{s+1}}^*$, $\mathcal{W} := \mathbb{Z}_{N^s}$, TAG $:= \{0, \ldots, 2^{\kappa/2-1}\}$. The projective map α is defined by $\alpha(g^{N^s}, x) := g^{N^s x}$ where $x \in \mathbb{Z}_{N^s}$.
- Keygen(msk, b^*): choose $w \leftarrow_\$ \mathbb{Z}_{N^s}$, compute public parameter $u := (1 + N)^{-b^*} \cdot g^{N^s w}$. The witness is w. The inversion trapdoor is (P, Q, b^*).
- Priv(u, b, x): compute $\Lambda_u(b, x) := ((1 + N)^b \cdot u)^x$.
- Pub($u, b^*, g^{N^s x}, w$): compute $(g^{N^s x})^w$.
- Tdinv($(P, Q, b^*), b, g^{N^s x}, \Lambda_u(b, x)$): observe that $\Lambda_u(b, x) = ((1 + N)^b \cdot u)^x = ((1 + N)^{b-b^*} \cdot g^{N^s w})^x$. Given the inversion trapdoor (i.e., the factorization of N and the projective tag b^*), we can efficiently compute $(b - b^*)x$. In addition, the restriction $b, b^* \in \{0, \ldots, 2^{\kappa/2} - 1\}$ implies that $(b - b^*)$ is smaller than both P and Q and is therefore relatively prime to N. Thus, we can recover x by computing $(b - b^*)x \cdot (b - b^*)^{-1} \bmod N^s$.

Projectiveness: When $u = (1 + N)^{-b^*} \cdot g^{N^s w}$ and $b = b^*$, we have

$$\mathsf{Priv}(u, b^*, x) = ((1 + N)^{b^*} \cdot u)^x = ((1 + N)^{b^*} \cdot (1 + N)^{-b^*} \cdot g^{N^s w})^x$$
$$= g^{N^s wx} = (g^{N^s x})^w = \mathsf{Pub}(u, b^*, g^{N^s x}, w).$$

The uniform distributions over $\{(1 + N)^{-b} \cdot g^{N^s w} : w \in \mathbb{Z}_{N^s}\}$ and $\{g^{N^s w} : w \in \mathbb{Z}_{N^s}\}$ are computationally indistinguishable following from the DCR assumption [11], which implies the hidden projective tag property.

Second Construction. This is a second DCR-based ABO dual projective hashing which follows the matrix approach [22]. When instantiated with our generic transformation, this yields a DCR-based $(m, m - \log |\phi(N)|)$-ABO lossy trapdoor functions, which is less efficient than [13]. In order to construct a DCR-based deterministic encryption scheme, we still need a universal hash function that is also universal one-way. The projective map in the following construction already satisfies this, and we will discuss more about it after the construction. Combining the instantiation of DCR-based dual projective hashing [25, Second Construction] with the above instantiation and our generic transformation, this yields a new DCR-based PRIV-CCA secure deterministic encryption, which is less efficient than [7].

- Setup(1^κ): choose a Blum integer $N := PQ$ as above. Pick $\mathbf{p} \leftarrow_\$ \mathbb{Z}_N^m, g \leftarrow_\$ \mathbb{Z}_{N^{s+1}}^*$. Set $hp := (N, (g^{N^s})^\mathbf{p})$, $msk := (g, \mathbf{p}, P, Q)$, $\mathcal{X} := \{0,1\}^m$, $\mathcal{Y} := (\mathbb{Z}_{N^{s+1}}^*)^m$, $\mathcal{P} \subseteq \mathbb{Z}_{N^{s+1}}^*$, $\mathcal{U} := (\mathbb{Z}_{N^{s+1}}^*)^{m \times m}$, $\mathcal{W} := \mathbb{Z}_{N^{s+1}}^m$, TAG $:= \{0, \ldots, 2^{\kappa/2-1}\}$. The projective map α is defined by

$$\alpha((g^{N^s})^\mathbf{p}, \mathbf{x}) := (g^{N^s})^{\mathbf{p}^\top \mathbf{x}} \in \mathbb{Z}_{N^{s+1}}^* \text{ where } \mathbf{x} \in \{0,1\}^m, \mathbf{p} \in \mathbb{Z}_N^m.$$

- Keygen(msk, b^*): choose $\mathbf{w} \leftarrow_\$ \mathbb{Z}_{N^{s+1}}^m$, compute public parameter $\mathbf{U} := (1 + N)^{-b^* \mathbf{I}_m} \cdot (g^{N^s})^{\mathbf{w}\mathbf{p}^\top}$. The witness is $\mathbf{w}$. The inversion trapdoor is (P, Q, b^*)
- Priv($\mathbf{U}, b, \mathbf{x}$): compute $\Lambda_\mathbf{U}(b, \mathbf{x}) := ((1 + N)^{b\mathbf{I}_m} \cdot \mathbf{U})^\mathbf{x}$.
- Pub($\mathbf{U}, b^*, (g^{N^s})^{\mathbf{p}^\top \mathbf{x}}, \mathbf{w}$): compute $((g^{N^s})^{\mathbf{p}^\top \mathbf{x}})^\mathbf{w}$.
- Tdinv($(P, Q, b^*), b, (g^{N^s})^{\mathbf{p}^\top \mathbf{x}}, \Lambda_\mathbf{U}(b, \mathbf{x})$) : observe that $\Lambda_\mathbf{U}(b, \mathbf{x}) = ((1+N)^{b\mathbf{I}_m} \cdot \mathbf{U})^\mathbf{x} = (1 + N)^{(b-b^*)\mathbf{x}\mathbf{I}_m} \cdot (g^{N^s})^{\mathbf{w}\mathbf{p}^\top \mathbf{x}} = (1 + N)^{(b-b^*)\mathbf{x}} \cdot (g^{N^s})^{\mathbf{w}\mathbf{p}^\top \mathbf{x}}$.
  Given the inversion trapdoor (i.e., the factorization of N and the projective tag b^*), we can efficiently compute $(b - b^*)\mathbf{x}$. In addition, the restriction $b, b^* \in \{0, \ldots, 2^{\kappa/2} - 1\}$ implies that $(b - b^*)$ is smaller than both P and Q and is therefore relatively prime to N. Thus, we can recover $\mathbf{x}$ by computing $(b - b^*)\mathbf{x}(b - b^*)^{-1} \mod N^s$.

Projectiveness: When $\mathbf{U} = (1 + N)^{-b^* \mathbf{I}_m} \cdot (g^{N^s})^{\mathbf{w}\mathbf{p}^\top}$ and $b = b^*$, we have

$$\mathsf{Priv}(\mathbf{U}, b^*, x) = ((1 + N)^{b^* \mathbf{I}_m} \cdot \mathbf{U})^\mathbf{x} = ((1 + N)^{b^* \mathbf{I}_m} \cdot (1 + N)^{-b^* \mathbf{I}_m} \cdot (g^{N^s})^{\mathbf{w}\mathbf{p}^\top})^\mathbf{x}$$

$$= ((g^{N^s})^{\mathbf{w}\mathbf{p}^\top})^\mathbf{x} = ((g^{N^s})^{\mathbf{p}^\top \mathbf{x}})^\mathbf{w} = \mathsf{Pub}(\mathbf{U}, b^*, (g^{N^s})^{\mathbf{p}^\top \mathbf{x}}, \mathbf{w}).$$

The hidden projective tag property follows from the DCR assumption.

Remark 1. The above projective map α satisfies the universal one-way property and almost universal property. The universal one-way property follows from a similar analysis as that in [7]. Next we show it is almost universal. For any $\mathbf{x} \neq \mathbf{x}' \in \{0,1\}^m$ such that $\alpha((g^{N^s})^\mathbf{p}, \mathbf{x}) = \alpha((g^{N^s})^\mathbf{p}, \mathbf{x}')$, we get $\sum_{i=1}^m p_i x_i \equiv \sum_{i=1}^m p_i x_i' \mod \lambda(N)$, where $\lambda(N)$ is the least common multiple of $P - 1$ and $Q - 1$. Without loss of generality, we assume that $x_1 - x_1' \neq 0$, then $p_1 \equiv \sum_{i=2}^m p_i(x_i' - x_i) \mod \lambda(N)$. This happens with probability $\lceil N/\lambda(N) \rceil / N \leq 2/\lambda = 1/pq$.

6.3 Instantiations from LWE

We present the LWE-based construction, which is based on lossy trapdoor functions in [22]. For a real parameter $0 < \beta < 1$, we denote by Ψ_β the distribution over $\mathbb{R}/\mathbb{Z}$ of a normal variable with means 0 and standard deviation $\beta/\sqrt{2\pi}$ then reduced modulo 1. Denote by $\bar{\Psi}_\beta$ the discrete distribution over $\mathbb{Z}_q$ of the random variable $\lfloor qX \rceil \mod q$ where the random variable X has distribution Ψ_β. In the following, we consider the standard LWE parameters m, n, q as well as additional parameters $\tilde{n}, p$ such that

$$m = O(n \log q), \qquad \beta = \Theta(1/q), \qquad \tilde{n} = m/\log p, \qquad \text{and} \qquad p \leq q/16m\tilde{n}.$$

In particular, let $\gamma < 1$ be a constant. We will set $q = \Theta(n^{1+1/\gamma})$ and $p = \Theta(n^{1/\gamma})$. When instantiated with our generic transformations, this yields the LWE-based ABO lossy trapdoor functions in [22]. The projective map α in the following is in fact a universal hash function which is collision-resistance [16] (under small integer solution assumption which is implied by LWE). Since collision-resistance implies universal one-way, α is also universal one-way. When combining the LWE-based dual projective hashing in [25] with our generic transformations, we get a PRIV-CCA-secure deterministic encryption based on LWE, which is less efficient than that in [7]. In addition, we can give another construction following from the extended general framework which is similar to [7].

Let $r : \{0,1\}^{\tilde{n}} \to \mathbb{Z}_q^{m \times \tilde{n}}$ be a function mapping a branch value to its encoded matrix over $\mathbb{Z}_q$ (see [22, Section 6.4]).

- Setup(1^κ): pick $\mathbf{A} \leftarrow_\$ \mathbb{Z}_q^{n \times m}$. Set $hp := (\mathbf{A})$, $msk := \perp$, $\mathcal{X} := \{0,1\}^m$, $\mathcal{Y} := \mathbb{Z}_q^{\tilde{n}}$, $\mathcal{P} := \mathbb{Z}_q^n$, $\mathcal{U} := \mathbb{Z}_q^{m \times \tilde{n}}$, $\mathcal{W} := \mathbb{Z}_q^{n \times \tilde{n}}$, TAG $:= \{0,1\}^{\tilde{n}}$. The projective map α is defined by $\alpha(\mathbf{A}, \mathbf{x}) := \mathbf{A}\mathbf{x} \in \mathbb{Z}_q^n$ with $\mathbf{x} \in \{0,1\}^m$.
- Keygen($msk, \mathbf{v}^*$): choose $\mathbf{S} \leftarrow_\$ \mathbb{Z}_q^{n \times \tilde{n}}$, $\mathbf{E} \leftarrow_\$ (\bar{\Psi}_\beta)^{m \times \tilde{n}}$. Compute public parameter $\mathbf{U} := \mathbf{A}^\top \mathbf{S} + \mathbf{E} - r(\mathbf{v}^*)$. The witness is $\mathbf{S}$. The inversion trapdoor is $(\mathbf{S}, \mathbf{v}^*)$.
- Priv($\mathbf{U}, \mathbf{v}, \mathbf{x}$): compute $\Lambda_\mathbf{U}(\mathbf{v}, \mathbf{x}) := \mathbf{x}^\top \mathbf{U} + \mathbf{x}^\top r(\mathbf{v}) \in \mathbb{Z}_q^{\tilde{n}}$.
- Pub($\mathbf{U}, \mathbf{v}^*, \mathbf{A}\mathbf{x}, \mathbf{S}$): compute $(\mathbf{A}\mathbf{x})^\top \mathbf{S}$.
- Tdinv($(\mathbf{S}, \mathbf{v}^*), \mathbf{v}, \alpha(\mathbf{A}, \mathbf{x}), \Lambda_\mathbf{U}(\mathbf{v}, \mathbf{x})$) : observe that

$$\Lambda_\mathbf{U}(\mathbf{v}, \mathbf{x}) = \mathbf{x}^\top \mathbf{U} + \mathbf{x}^\top r(\mathbf{v}) = (\mathbf{A}\mathbf{x})^\top \mathbf{S} + \mathbf{x}^\top \mathbf{E} + \mathbf{x}^\top (r(\mathbf{v} - \mathbf{v}^*)).$$

Given the inversion trapdoor $(\mathbf{S}, \mathbf{v}^*)$, we can recover $\mathbf{x}^\top \mathbf{E} + \mathbf{x}^\top (r(\mathbf{v}) - r(\mathbf{v}^*))$. The quantity $\mathbf{x}^\top \mathbf{E}$ has small norm, so we can compute x using the bounded-error decoding to recover $\mathbf{x}^\top (r(\mathbf{v}) - r(\mathbf{v}^*))$ and then $\mathbf{x}$.

Projectiveness: The projective property is approximate, that is when $\mathbf{U} := \mathbf{A}^\top \mathbf{S} + \mathbf{E} - r(\mathbf{v}^*)$ and $\mathbf{v} = \mathbf{v}^*$, we have

$$\begin{aligned}
\mathsf{Priv}(\mathbf{U}, \mathbf{v}^*, \mathbf{x}) &= \mathbf{x}^\top \mathbf{U} + \mathbf{x}^\top r(\mathbf{v}^*) \\
&= \mathbf{x}^\top (\mathbf{A}^\top \mathbf{S} + \mathbf{E} - r(\mathbf{v}^*)) + \mathbf{x}^\top r(\mathbf{v}^*) \\
&= (\mathbf{A}\mathbf{x})^\top \mathbf{S} + \mathbf{x}^\top \mathbf{E} \approx (\mathbf{A}\mathbf{x})^\top \mathbf{S} = \mathsf{Pub}(\mathbf{U}, \mathbf{v}^*, \mathbf{A}\mathbf{x}, \mathbf{S}).
\end{aligned}$$

In fact, for all $\mathbf{x} \in \{0,1\}^m$, with overwhelming probability over $\mathbf{E}$, we have $\mathbf{x}^\top \mathbf{E} \subset [q/p]^{\tilde{n}}$. That is, the projective property holds up to an addictive error term in $[q/p]^{\tilde{n}}$.

The hidden projective tag property follows from the LWE assumption.

ABO Lossy Trapdoor Function. In the lossy mode, we bound the size of the image by $|\mathrm{Img}_\alpha| \cdot (q/p)^{\tilde{n}}$, where $(q/p)^{\tilde{n}}$ accounts for the error incurred by the approximate projective property, then the lossiness is given by $m - (n \log q + \frac{m}{\log p} \log(\frac{q}{p})) = (1 - \gamma)m - n \log q$.

Acknowledgments. Zongyang Zhang is an International Research Fellow of JSPS and his work is in part supported by NSFC under grant No. 61303201. He thanks Shota Yamada for the discussion of lattice-based construction.

Yu Chen is supported by NSFC under grant No. 61303257 and IIE's Cryptography Research Project under Grant No. Y3Z0011102.

Sherman S. M. Chow is supported by the Early Career Scheme and the Early Career Award of the Research Grants Council, Hong Kong SAR (CUHK 439713), and Direct Grant (4055018) of the Chinese University of Hong Kong.

Zhenfu Cao is supported by NSFC under Nos. 61033014, 61161140320, 61371083 and by the Specialized Research Fund for the Doctoral Program of Higher Education under Grant No. 20130073130004.

Yunlei Zhao is supported by NSFC under Grant No.61272012.

References

1. Abdalla, M., Chevalier, C., Pointcheval, D.: Smooth Projective Hashing for Conditionally Extractable Commitments. In: Halevi, S. (ed.) CRYPTO 2009. LNCS, vol. 5677, pp. 671–689. Springer, Heidelberg (2009)
2. Bellare, M., Boldyreva, A., O'Neill, A.: Deterministic and Efficiently Searchable Encryption. In: Menezes, A. (ed.) CRYPTO 2007. LNCS, vol. 4622, pp. 535–552. Springer, Heidelberg (2007)
3. Bellare, M., Brakerski, Z., Naor, M., Ristenpart, T., Segev, G., Shacham, H., Yilek, S.: Hedged Public-Key Encryption: How to Protect against Bad Randomness. In: Matsui, M. (ed.) ASIACRYPT 2009. LNCS, vol. 5912, pp. 232–249. Springer, Heidelberg (2009)
4. Bellare, M., Fischlin, M., O'Neill, A., Ristenpart, T.: Deterministic Encryption: Definitional Equivalences and Constructions without Random Oracles. In: Wagner, D. (ed.) CRYPTO 2008. LNCS, vol. 5157, pp. 360–378. Springer, Heidelberg (2008)
5. Bellare, M., Hofheinz, D., Yilek, S.: Possibility and Impossibility Results for Encryption and Commitment Secure under Selective Opening. In: Joux, A. (ed.) EUROCRYPT 2009. LNCS, vol. 5479, pp. 1–35. Springer, Heidelberg (2009)
6. Blazy, O., Pointcheval, D., Vergnaud, D.: Round-Optimal Privacy-Preserving Protocols with Smooth Projective Hash Functions. In: Cramer, R. (ed.) TCC 2012. LNCS, vol. 7194, pp. 94–111. Springer, Heidelberg (2012)
7. Boldyreva, A., Fehr, S., O'Neill, A.: On Notions of Security for Deterministic Encryption, and Efficient Constructions without Random Oracles. In: Wagner, D. (ed.) CRYPTO 2008. LNCS, vol. 5157, pp. 335–359. Springer, Heidelberg (2008)
8. Brakerski, Z., Segev, G.: Better Security for Deterministic Public-Key Encryption: The Auxiliary-Input Setting. In: Rogaway, P. (ed.) CRYPTO 2011. LNCS, vol. 6841, pp. 543–560. Springer, Heidelberg (2011)
9. Cramer, R., Shoup, V.: A Practical Public Key Cryptosystem Provably Secure Against Adaptive Chosen Ciphertext Attack. In: Krawczyk, H. (ed.) CRYPTO 1998. LNCS, vol. 1462, pp. 13–25. Springer, Heidelberg (1998)
10. Cramer, R., Shoup, V.: Universal Hash Proofs and a Paradigm for Adaptive Chosen Ciphertext Secure Public-Key Encryption. In: Knudsen, L.R. (ed.) EUROCRYPT 2002. LNCS, vol. 2332, pp. 45–64. Springer, Heidelberg (2002)
11. Damgård, I., Jurik, M., Nielsen, J.B.: A generalization of Paillier's public-key system with applications to electronic voting. Int. J. Inf. Sec. 9(6), 371–385 (2010)

12. Dolev, D., Dwork, C., Naor, M.: Nonmalleable Cryptography. SIAM J. Comput. 30(2), 391–437 (2000)
13. Freeman, D.M., Goldreich, O., Kiltz, E., Rosen, A., Segev, G.: More Constructions of Lossy and Correlation-Secure Trapdoor Functions. J. Cryptology 26(1), 39–74 (2013)
14. Fuller, B., O'Neill, A., Reyzin, L.: A Unified Approach to Deterministic Encryption: New Constructions and a Connection to Computational Entropy. In: Cramer, R. (ed.) TCC 2012. LNCS, vol. 7194, pp. 582–599. Springer, Heidelberg (2012)
15. Gennaro, R., Lindell, Y.: A framework for password-based authenticated key exchange. ACM Trans. Inf. Syst. Secur. 9(2), 181–234 (2006)
16. Gentry, C., Peikert, C., Vaikuntanathan, V.: Trapdoors for hard lattices and new cryptographic constructions. In: Dwork, C. (ed.) STOC, pp. 197–206. ACM (2008)
17. Halevi, S., Kalai, Y.T.: Smooth Projective Hashing and Two-Message Oblivious Transfer. J. Cryptology 25(1), 158–193 (2012)
18. Joye, M., Libert, B.: Efficient Cryptosystems from 2^k-th Power Residue Symbols. In: Johansson, T., Nguyen, P.Q. (eds.) EUROCRYPT 2013. LNCS, vol. 7881, pp. 76–92. Springer, Heidelberg (2013)
19. Katz, J., Vaikuntanathan, V.: Smooth Projective Hashing and Password-Based Authenticated Key Exchange from Lattices. In: Matsui, M. (ed.) ASIACRYPT 2009. LNCS, vol. 5912, pp. 636–652. Springer, Heidelberg (2009)
20. Mironov, I., Pandey, O., Reingold, O., Segev, G.: Incremental Deterministic Public-Key Encryption. In: Pointcheval, D., Johansson, T. (eds.) EUROCRYPT 2012. LNCS, vol. 7237, pp. 628–644. Springer, Heidelberg (2012)
21. Naor, M., Segev, G.: Public-Key Cryptosystems Resilient to Key Leakage. In: Halevi, S. (ed.) CRYPTO 2009. LNCS, vol. 5677, pp. 18–35. Springer, Heidelberg (2009)
22. Peikert, C., Waters, B.: Lossy Trapdoor Functions and Their Applications. SIAM J. Comput. 40(6), 1803–1844 (2011)
23. Raghunathan, A., Segev, G., Vadhan, S.P.: Deterministic Public-Key Encryption for Adaptively Chosen Plaintext Distributions. In: Johansson, T., Nguyen, P.Q. (eds.) EUROCRYPT 2013. LNCS, vol. 7881, pp. 93–110. Springer, Heidelberg (2013)
24. Wee, H.: Efficient Chosen-Ciphertext Security via Extractable Hash Proofs. In: Rabin, T. (ed.) CRYPTO 2010. LNCS, vol. 6223, pp. 314–332. Springer, Heidelberg (2010)
25. Wee, H.: Dual Projective Hashing and Its Applications - Lossy Trapdoor Functions and More. In: Pointcheval, D., Johansson, T. (eds.) EUROCRYPT 2012. LNCS, vol. 7237, pp. 246–262. Springer, Heidelberg (2012)
26. Wichs, D.: Barriers in cryptography with weak, correlated and leaky sources. In: Kleinberg, R.D. (ed.) ITCS, pp. 111–126. ACM (2013)

Distributed Smooth Projective Hashing and Its Application to Two-Server Password Authenticated Key Exchange

Franziskus Kiefer and Mark Manulis

Surrey Center for Cyber Security
Department of Computing, University of Surrey, UK
`mail@franziskuskiefer.de`, `mark@manulis.eu`

Abstract. Smooth projective hash functions have been used as building block for various cryptographic applications, in particular for password-based authentication.

In this work we propose the extended concept of *distributed* smooth projective hash functions where the computation of the hash value is distributed across n parties and show how to instantiate the underlying approach for languages consisting of Cramer-Shoup ciphertexts.

As an application of distributed smooth projective hashing we build a new framework for the design of two-server password authenticated key exchange protocols, which we believe can help to "explain" the design of earlier two-server password authenticated key exchange protocols.

Keywords: Smooth Projective Hash Functions, Two-Server PAKE.

1 Introduction

Smooth projective hashing allows to compute the hash value of an element from a set in two different ways: either by using a secret hashing key on the element, or utilising the public projection key and some secret information proving that the particular element is part of a specific subset under consideration. In addition, smooth projective hash values guarantee to be uniformly distributed in their domain as long as the input element is not from a specific subset of the input set. These features make them a quite popular building block in many protocols such as CCA-secure public key encryption, blind signatures, password authenticated key exchange, oblivious transfer, zero-knowledge proofs, commitments and verifiable encryption.

Smooth projective hash functions (SPHF) are due to Cramer and Shoup [10] who used them to construct CCA-secure public key encryption schemes and analyse mechanisms from [9]. The first use of SPHFs in the construction of a password authenticated key exchange (PAKE) protocol is due to Gennaro and Lindell [11], who introduced additional requirements to the SPHF such as pseudorandomness that was later extended in [15]. The SPHF-based approach taken in [11] was further helpful in the "explanation" of the KOY protocol from [14], where those functions were implicitly applied.

I. Boureanu, P. Owesarski, and S. Vaudenay (Eds.): ACNS 2014, LNCS 8479, pp. 199–216, 2014.
© Springer International Publishing Switzerland 2014

Abdalla et al. [1] introduced conjunction and disjunction of languages for smooth projective hashing that were later used in the construction of blind signatures [7,5], oblivious signature-based envelopes [7], and authenticated key exchange protocols for algebraic languages [4]. Blazy et al. [7] demonstrate more general use of smooth projective hashing in designing round-optimal privacy-preserving interactive protocols.

We extend this line of work by considering divergent parametrised languages in one smooth projective hash function that allows multiple parties to jointly evaluate the result of the function. We propose the notion of (distributed) extended smooth projective hashing that enables joint hash computation for special languages. Further, we propose a new two-server password authenticated key exchange framework using the new notion of distributed smooth projective hashing and show how it helps to explain the protocol from [13]. Actually, the authors of [2] already built a group PAKE protocol using smooth projective hashing in a multi-party party protocol. However, they assume a ring structure such that the smooth projective hashing is only used between two parties.

Organisation. We start by recalling smooth projective hash functions and introduce useful definitions in Section 2. Our first contribution is the definition of an extended smooth projective hash function $SPHF^x$ that handles divergent parametrised languages in Section 3. Then we show how to distribute their computation between multiple parties, introducing distributed $SPHF^x$ in Section 3.1 and give a concrete instantiation in Section 3.3. Finally, we propose a two-server PAKE framework in Section 4 and analyse the two-server KOY protocol using a variant of distributed $SPHF^x$ in Section 4.2.

2   Smooth Projective Hash Functions

First, we recall definitions from [5] for classical SPHF with some minor changes. We stick with the framework from [5, Section 3] on cyclic groups $\mathbb{G}$ of prime order and focus on languages of ciphertexts. This seems reasonable since it is the preferred setting and allows a comprehensible description. An extension to graded rings and general languages should be possible and is left open for future work.

A language L_{aux} is indexed by a parameter aux, consisting of global public information and secret variable information aux'. In our setting of languages of ciphertexts the public part of aux is essentially a common reference string crs containing the public key pk of the used encryption scheme. The secret part aux' contains the message that should be encrypted. By π we denote the crs trapdoor, the secret key to pk. We denote $\mathcal{L}$ the encryption scheme used to generate words. Unless stated otherwise we assume that $\mathcal{L}$ is a labelled CCA-secure encryption scheme.

Definition 1 (Languages of Ciphertexts). *Let $L_{\text{aux}} \subseteq \mathcal{S}et$ denote the language of ciphertext under consideration. A ciphertext C is in the language L_{aux} if $C \leftarrow \text{Enc}_{\text{pk}}^{\mathcal{L}}(\ell, \text{aux}'; w)$ for $\text{aux} = (\text{pk}, \text{aux}')$. Formally, a word C is in the language L_{aux} if and only if $\exists \lambda \in \mathbb{Z}_p^{1 \times k}$ such that $\Theta_{\text{aux}}(C) = \lambda \odot \Gamma(C)$, where $\Gamma : \mathcal{S}et \mapsto \mathbb{G}^{k \times n}$ and $\Theta_{\text{aux}} : \mathcal{S}et \mapsto \mathbb{G}^{1 \times n}$ for integers k, n.*

We use the notation $\odot$ and common matrix and vector operations on it from [5]: for $a \in \mathbb{G}$, $r \in \mathbb{Z}_p : a \odot r = r \odot a = a^r \in \mathbb{G}$.

Definition 2 (SPHF [5]). *Let L_{aux} denote a language such that $C \in L_{\text{aux}}$ if there exists a witness w proving so. A smooth projective hash function for ciphertext language L_{aux} consists of the following four algorithms:*

- *$\text{KGen}_{\text{H}}(L_{\text{aux}})$ generates a hashing key $\text{k}_{\text{h}} \in_R \mathbb{Z}_p^{1 \times n}$ for language L_{aux}.*
- *$\text{KGen}_{\text{P}}(\text{k}_{\text{h}}, L_{\text{aux}}, C)$ derives the projection key $\text{k}_{\text{p}} = \Gamma(C) \odot \text{k}_{\text{h}} \in \mathbb{G}^{k \times 1}$, possibly depending on C.*
- *$\text{Hash}(\text{k}_{\text{h}}, L_{\text{aux}}, C)$ outputs the hash value $h = \Theta_{\text{aux}}(C) \odot \text{k}_{\text{h}} \in \mathbb{G}$.*
- *$\text{PHash}(\text{k}_{\text{p}}, L_{\text{aux}}, C, w)$ returns the hash value $h = \lambda \odot \text{k}_{\text{p}} \in \mathbb{G}$, with $\lambda = \Omega(w, C)$ for some $\Omega : \{0,1\}^* \mapsto \mathbb{G}^{1 \times k}$.*

A SPHF has to fulfil the following three properties (formal definitions follow):

- *Correctness*: If $C \in L$, with w proving so, then $\text{Hash}(\text{k}_{\text{h}}, L_{\text{aux}}, C) = \text{PHash}(\text{k}_{\text{p}}, L_{\text{aux}}, C, w)$.
- *Smoothness*: If $C \notin L_{\text{aux}}$, the hash value h is statistically indistinguishable from a random element in $\mathbb{G}$.
- *Pseudorandomness*: If $C \in L_{\text{aux}}$, the hash value h is indistinguishable from a random element in $\mathbb{G}$.[1]

In a nutshell, smoothness ensures that the hash value always looks random in $\mathbb{G}$ when computed on an element not in the language, while pseudorandomness ensures that it looks random in $\mathbb{G}$ when computed on an element in the language. The authors of [6] identify three different SPHF classes: word-independent key and adaptive smoothness (KV-SPHF, first proposed in [15]), word-independent key and non-adaptive smoothness (CS-SPHF, first proposed in [10]), and word-dependent key (GL-SPHF, first proposed in [11]).

In this work we focus on the strongest notion behind KV-SPHF: *word-independent key* with *adaptive smoothness*. Unless stated otherwise all SPHFs in the following are KV-SPHFs where the projection key is independent of the ciphertext. This property enables our construction of extended SPHFs. The corresponding notion of adaptive smoothness with word-independent keys is defined as follows. For any function $f : \mathcal{S}et \setminus L_{\text{aux}} \mapsto \mathbb{G}^{l \times 1}$ the following distributions are statistically ε-close:

---

[1] Note that this is not always a requirement or even possible. But as languages of labelled CCA-secure ciphertexts are hard-on-average problems the corresponding SPHF is also pseudorandom.

$$\{(k_p, h) \mid k_h \overset{R}{\leftarrow} \mathrm{KGen_H}(L_{aux}); k_p \leftarrow \mathrm{KGen_P}(k_h, L_{aux}); h \leftarrow \mathrm{Hash}(k_h, L_{aux}, f(k_p))\}$$
$$\overset{\varepsilon}{=} \{(k_p, h) \mid k_h \overset{R}{\leftarrow} \mathrm{KGen_H}(L_{aux}); k_p \leftarrow \mathrm{KGen_P}(k_h, L_{aux}); h \in_R \mathbb{G}\}$$

Gennaro and Lindell [11] introduced pseudorandomness of SPHFs to show that Hash and PHash are the only way to compute the hash value even though the adversary knows some tuples $(k_p, C, \mathrm{Hash}(k_h, L_{aux}, C))$ for $C \in L_{aux}$. A SPHF is pseudorandom if the hash values produced by Hash and PHash are indistinguishable from random without the knowledge of the uniformly chosen hash key k_h or a witness w, i.e. for all $C \in L_{aux}$ the following distributions are computationally ε-close:

$$\{(k_p, C, h) \mid k_h \overset{R}{\leftarrow} \mathrm{KGen_H}(L_{aux}); k_p \leftarrow \mathrm{KGen_P}(k_h, L_{aux}); h \leftarrow \mathrm{Hash}(k_h, L_{aux}, C)\}$$
$$\overset{\varepsilon}{=} \{(k_p, C, h) \mid k_h \overset{R}{\leftarrow} \mathrm{KGen_H}(L_{aux}); k_p \leftarrow \mathrm{KGen_P}(k_h, L_{aux}); h \in_R \mathbb{G}\}$$

To define pseudorandomness of a SPHF we use an experiment based on those from [11, Corollary 3.3] and [15].

Definition 3 (SPHF Pseudorandomness). *For all PPT algorithms $\mathcal{A}$ there exists a negligible function $\varepsilon(\cdot)$ such that*

$$\left| \Pr[\mathcal{A}^{\mathrm{Enc}_{pk}^{\mathcal{L}}(\cdot), \mathrm{Hash}(\cdot)} = 1] - \Pr[\mathcal{A}^{\mathrm{Enc}_{pk}^{\mathcal{L}}(\cdot), \mathcal{U}(\cdot)} = 1] \right| < \varepsilon(\lambda).$$

- $\mathrm{Enc}_{pk}^{\mathcal{L}}(\ell, \mathrm{aux})$ *with* $\mathrm{aux} = (pk, \mathrm{aux}')$ *returns elements* $C \in L_{aux}$ *encrypting* aux' *using* pk, *label* ℓ *and encryption algorithm* $\mathcal{L}$.
- $\mathrm{Hash}(C)$ *returns* $(\mathrm{KGen_P}(k_h, L_{aux}, C), \mathrm{Hash}(k_h, L_{aux}, C))$ *for fresh* $k_h \leftarrow \mathrm{KGen_H}(L_{aux})$ *if* C *has been output by* $\mathrm{Enc}_{pk}^{\mathcal{L}}$, *nothing otherwise.*
- $\mathcal{U}(C)$ *returns* $(\mathrm{KGen_P}(k_h, L_{aux}, C), h)$ *for fresh* $k_h \leftarrow \mathrm{KGen_H}(L_{aux})$ *and random* $h \in \mathbb{G}$ *if* C *has been output by* $\mathrm{Enc}_{pk}^{\mathcal{L}}$, *nothing otherwise.*

While the authors of [5,6] have skipped the proof of pseudorandomness as it is straightforward, we want to briefly give an intuition why their SPHF framework is pseudorandom. The reasoning for pseudorandomness of SPHFs is actually easy and always follows the same approach given in [11]. By replacing the correct ciphertexts in the simulation with ciphertexts $C \notin L_{aux}$ we can use the smoothness of SPHFs to show their indistinguishability. The replacement itself is covered by the hard-on-average subset membership problem, in the case of ciphertexts their CCA-security. In [15] pseudorandomness in the case of hash key and ciphertext reuse is added. We discuss this extension when defining *concurrent* pseudorandomness of our extended smooth projective hash functions in the next section.

Encryption Schemes and SPHFs. We use SPHFs on labelled *Cramer-Shoup (CS)* encryptions throughout this work as an example, i.e. $\mathcal{L} = \mathrm{CS}$. Thus, we briefly recall its definition. Let $C = (\ell, \boldsymbol{u}, e, v) \leftarrow \mathrm{Enc}_{pk}^{\mathrm{CS}}(\ell, m; r)$ with

$u = (u_1, u_2) = (g_1^r, g_2^r)$, $e = h^r g_1^m$ and $v = (cd^\xi)^r$ with $\xi = H_k(\ell, u, e)$ denote a labelled Cramer-Shoup ciphertext. We assume $m \in \mathbb{Z}_p$ and $\mathbb{G}$ is a cyclic group of prime order p with generators g_1 and g_2 such that $g_1^m \in \mathbb{G}$. The CS public key is defined as $\mathtt{pk} = (p, \mathbb{G}, g_1, g_2, c, d, H_k)$ with $c = g_1^{x_1} g_2^{x_2}, d = g_1^{y_1} g_2^{y_2}, h = g_1^z$ and hash function H_k such that $\mathtt{dk} = (x_1, x_2, y_1, y_2, z)$ denotes the decryption key. Decryption is defined as $g_1^m = \mathtt{Dec}_{\mathtt{dk}}^{\mathrm{CS}}(C) = e/u_1^z$ if $u_1^{x_1+y_1 \cdot \xi'} u_2^{x_2+y_2 \cdot \xi'} = v$ with $\xi' = H_k(\ell, u, e)$. Benhamouda et al. propose a new perfectly smooth SPHF for labelled Cramer-Shoup encryptions in [5]. Note that the witness for $C \in L_{\mathrm{aux}}$ is the used randomness $w = r$. The SPHF is den given by Definition 2 and the following variables: $\Gamma(C) = \begin{pmatrix} g_1 & 1 & g_2 & h & c \\ 1 & g_1 & 1 & 1 & d \end{pmatrix} \in \mathbb{G}^{2 \times 5}$, $\lambda = (r, r\xi) \in \mathbb{Z}_p^{1 \times 2}$ for $\Omega(r, C) = (r, r\xi)$, $\Theta_{\mathrm{aux}}(C) = (u_1, u_1^\xi, u_2, e/m, v) \in \mathbb{G}^{1 \times 5}$ and $\mathtt{k_h} = (\eta_1, \eta_2, \theta, \mu, \nu) \in_R \mathbb{Z}_p^{1 \times 5}$.

We further use *El-Gamal (EG)* encryptions. Let $C = (u, e) \leftarrow \mathtt{Enc}_{\mathtt{pk}}^{\mathrm{EG}}(m; r)$ with $u = g^r$ and $e = h^r g^m$ denote an El-Gamal ciphertext. Note that we assume $m \in \mathbb{Z}_p$ and $\mathbb{G}$ is a cyclic group of prime order p with generator g such that $g^m \in \mathbb{G}$. The El-Gamal public key is defined as $\mathtt{pk} = (p, \mathbb{G}, g, h)$ with $h = g^z$ such that $\mathtt{dk} = z$ denotes the decryption key. Decryption is given by $g^m = \mathtt{Dec}_{\mathtt{dk}}^{\mathrm{EG}}(C) = e/u^z$. A SPHF on El-Gamal ciphertexts can be build from Definition 2 using the following variables: $\Gamma(C) = (g, h)^T \in \mathbb{G}^{2 \times 1}$, $\lambda = r \in \mathbb{Z}_p$ for $\Omega(r, C) = r$, $\Theta_{\mathrm{aux}}(C) = (u, e/m) \in \mathbb{G}^{1 \times 2}$ and $\mathtt{k_h} = (\eta, \theta) \in_R \mathbb{Z}_p^{1 \times 2}$.

3   Extended Smooth Projective Hash Functions (SPHF^x)

We introduce an extended notion of smooth projective hashing that allows us to distribute the computation of the hash value. The new notion of extended SPHF (SPHF^x) is defined in the following setting: The parameter $\mathtt{aux}$, a language is indexed with, allows us to easily describe languages that differ only in the secret part $\mathtt{aux}'$. We consider a language L_{aux} with words (ciphertexts) C that are ordered sets of n ciphertexts $(C_0, \ldots, C_x)$. The secret variable information $\mathtt{aux}'$ is chosen from the additive group $(\mathbb{P}, +) = (\mathbb{Z}_p^+, +)$ with a function $h : \mathbb{P} \mapsto \mathbb{P}^x$. Let $L_{\mathrm{aux}}^{\mathcal{L}}$ denote the language of ciphertexts encrypting the secret part $\mathtt{aux}'$ from $\mathtt{aux}$ with the public key $\mathtt{pk}$ from $\mathtt{aux}$ using encryption scheme $\mathcal{L}$. For all $C_i, i \in \{1, \ldots, x\}$ it must hold that $C_i \in L_{\mathrm{aux}_i}^{\mathcal{L}}$ where $\mathtt{aux}_i = (\mathtt{pk}, \mathtt{aux}_i')$ with $\mathtt{aux}_i' = h(\mathtt{aux}')[i]$. For C_0 it must hold that $C_0 \in L_{\mathrm{aux}}^{\mathcal{L}}$. Furthermore, the ciphertexts must offer certain homomorphic properties such that there exists a modified decryption algorithm $\mathtt{Dec}'$ and a combining function g such that $\mathtt{Dec}_\pi'(C_0) = \mathtt{Dec}_\pi'(g(C_1, \ldots, C_x))$, where π denotes the secret key for the corresponding public key $\mathtt{pk}$ from $\mathtt{crs}$.

The idea of SPHF^x is to be able to use the SPHF functionality not only on a single ciphertext, but on a set of ciphertexts with specific properties. Due to the nature of the words considered in SPHF^x they produce two different hash values. One can think of the two hash values as h_0 for C_0 and h_x for $C_1, \ldots, C_x$. The hash value h_0 can be either computed with knowledge of the hash key $\mathtt{k_{h0}}$ or with the witnesses $w_1, \ldots, w_x$ that $C_1, \ldots, C_x$ are in $L_{\mathrm{aux}_i}^{\mathcal{L}}$ each. The hash value h_x can be computed with knowledge of the hash keys $k_{h1}, \ldots, k_{hx}$ or with the witness w_0 that C_0 is in $L_{\text{aux}}^{\mathcal{L}}$.

Definition 4 (SPHF^x). *Let L_{aux} denote a language such that $C = (C_0, C_1, \ldots, C_x) \in L_{\text{aux}}$ if there exists a witness $w = (w_0, w_1, \ldots, w_x)$ proving so and there exist functions $h(\text{aux}') = (\text{aux}_1', \ldots, \text{aux}_x')$ and $g : \mathbb{G}^l \mapsto \mathbb{G}^{l'}$ as described above. An extended smooth projective hash function for language L_{aux} with $\Gamma \in \mathbb{G}^{k \times n}$ consists of the following six algorithms:*

- $\text{KGen}_H(L_{\text{aux}})$ *generates a hashing key $k_{hi} \in \mathbb{Z}_p^{1 \times n}$ for $i \in \{0, \ldots, x\}$ and language L_{aux}.*
- $\text{KGen}_P(k_{hi}, L_{\text{aux}})$ *derives the projection key $k_{p_i} = \Gamma \odot k_{hi} \in \mathbb{G}^{1 \times k}$ for $i \in \{0, \ldots, x\}$.*
- $\text{Hash}_x(k_{h0}, L_{\text{aux}}, C_1, \ldots, C_x)$ *outputs hash value $h_x = \Theta_{\text{aux}}^x(C_1, \ldots, C_x) \odot k_{h0}$.*
- $\text{PHash}_x(k_{p0}, L_{\text{aux}}, C_1, \ldots, C_x, w_1, \ldots, w_x)$ *returns hash value $h_x = \prod_{i=1}^x (\lambda^i \odot k_{p0})$, where $\lambda^i = \Omega(w_i, C_i)$.*
- $\text{Hash}_0(k_{h1}, \ldots, k_{hx}, L_{\text{aux}}, C_0)$ *outputs hash value $h_0 = \prod_{i=1}^x (\Theta_{\text{aux}}^0(C_0) \odot k_{hi}) = \Theta_{\text{aux}}^0(C_0) \odot \sum_{i=1}^x k_{hi}$.*
- $\text{PHash}_0(k_{p1}, \ldots, k_{p_x}, L_{\text{aux}}, C_0, w_0)$ *returns hash value $h_0 = \prod_{i=1}^x (\lambda^0 \odot k_{p_i})$, with $\lambda^0 = \Omega(w_0, C_0)$.*

The correctness of the scheme can be easily verified by checking that $\text{Hash}_x = \text{PHash}_x$ and $\text{Hash}_0 = \text{PHash}_0$.

Security of SPHF^x. We refine definitions of smoothness and pseudorandomness to account for the two different hash functions. Therefore, we add both hash values to the indistinguishable sets, as well as the vector of projection keys. We start with the smoothness of the described SPHF^x. The smoothness proven in Theorem 1 follows directly from the proof given in [5, Appendix D.3] and follows the same approach for smoothness proofs as in previous works on SPHF [5,11,15]. Recall that we are only concerned with *adaptive smoothness*. Let $\overline{k_p}$ denote the vector of projection keys k_{p_i} for $i = 0, \ldots, x$. For any functions f, f' to $Set \setminus L_{\text{aux}}$ the following distributions are statistically ε-close:

$$\{(\overline{k_p}, h_0, h_x) \mid h_0 \leftarrow \text{Hash}_0(k_{h1}, \ldots, k_{hx}, L_{\text{aux}}, f(k_{p0})); \; h_x \leftarrow \text{Hash}_x(k_{h0}, L_{\text{aux}},$$

$$f'(k_{p1}, \ldots, k_{p_x})); \forall i \in \{0, \ldots, x\} : \; k_{hi} \overset{R}{\leftarrow} \text{KGen}_H(L_{\text{aux}}); k_{p_i} \leftarrow \text{KGen}_P(k_{hi}, L_{\text{aux}})\}$$

$$\overset{\varepsilon}{=} \{(\overline{k_p}, h_0, h_x) \mid h_0 \in_R \mathbb{G}; \; h_x \in_R \mathbb{G}; \forall i \in \{0, \ldots, x\} : \; k_{hi} \overset{R}{\leftarrow} \text{KGen}_H(L_{\text{aux}});$$

$$k_{p_i} \leftarrow \text{KGen}_P(k_{hi}, L_{\text{aux}})\}.$$

Theorem 1 (SPHF^x Smoothness). *The SPHF^x construction from Definition 4 on cyclic groups is statistically smooth.*

Proof. We show that the logarithm of the projection keys $\overline{k_p}$ and the logarithm of the hash values h_0 and h_x are defined by linearly independent equations and thus h_0 and h_x are uniform in $\mathbb{G}$, given $\overline{k_p}$. To show that $(\overline{k_p}, h_0, h_x)$ is uniformly distributed in $\mathbb{G}^{k+2}$ for $C \notin L_{\text{aux}}$, i.e. ε-close to $(\overline{k_p}, g_0, g_x)$ for random $g_0, g_x \in_R \mathbb{G}$, we consider a word $C = (C_0, C_1, \ldots, C_x) \notin L_{\text{aux}}$ and a projection key $k_{p_j} = \Gamma \odot k_{h_j}$ such that one C_j does not fulfill the property $C_j \in L_{\text{aux}_j}$, i.e. $\exists j \in \{0, \ldots, x\}, \forall \lambda^j \in \mathbb{Z}_p^{1 \times k} : \Theta_{\text{aux}_j}(C_j) \neq \lambda^j \odot \Gamma$. From [5, Appendix D.3] it follows directly that $\Theta_{\text{aux}_j}(C_j) \odot k_{h_j}$ is a uniformly distributed element in $\mathbb{G}$, and thus $\Theta_{\text{aux}}^x(C_1, \ldots, C_x) \odot k_{h_0}$ and $\prod_{i=1}^x (\Theta_{\text{aux}}^0(C_0) \odot k_{h_i})$ is uniformly in $\mathbb{G}$. The projection key $\overline{k_p}$ is uniformly at random in $\mathbb{G}^k$ anyway, given the randomness of all k_{h_i}. Note that any violation of $\text{Dec}'_\pi(C_0) = \text{Dec}'_\pi(g(C_1, \ldots, C_x))$ implies the existence of an index j such that $C_j \notin L_{\text{aux}_j}$. $\square$

While smoothness is the foremost property of (extended) smooth projective hash functions, in some cases like password authenticated key exchange pseudorandomness of the produced hash values has to be guaranteed too. Let $\overline{k_p}$ denote the vector of projection keys k_{p_i} for $i = 0, \ldots, x$. A SPHF^x is pseudorandom if its hash values are computationally indistinguishable from random without knowledge of the uniformly chosen hash keys $\overline{k_h}$ or the witnesses $\overline{w}$, i.e. for all $C = (C_0, \ldots, C_x) \in L_{\text{aux}}$ the following distributions are computationally ε-close:

$$\{(\overline{k_p}, C, h_0, h_x) \mid \forall i \in \{0, \ldots, x\} : k_{h_i} \xleftarrow{R} \text{KGen}_H(L_{\text{aux}}); k_{p_i} \leftarrow \text{KGen}_P(k_{h_i}, L_{\text{aux}});$$
$$h_0 \leftarrow \text{Hash}_0(k_{h_1}, \ldots, k_{h_x}, L_{\text{aux}}, C_0); \; h_x \leftarrow \text{Hash}_x(k_{h_0}, L_{\text{aux}}, C_1, \ldots, C_x)\}$$
$$\overset{\varepsilon}{=} \{(\overline{k_p}, C, h_0, h_x) \mid \forall i \in \{0, \ldots, x\} : k_{h_i} \xleftarrow{R} \text{KGen}_H(L_{\text{aux}}); k_{p_i} \leftarrow \text{KGen}_P(k_{h_i}, L_{\text{aux}});$$
$$h_0 \in_R \mathbb{G}; h_x \in_R \mathbb{G}\}$$

To prove pseudorandomness of an SPHF^x we use modified experiments from [11] given in Definition 5. The proof for the pseudorandomness of SPHF^x follows the line of argument from [11].

Definition 5 (SPHF^x Pseudorandomness). *A SPHF^x Π is pseudorandom if for all PPT algorithms $\mathcal{A}$ there exists a negligible function $\varepsilon(\cdot)$ such that*

$$\text{Adv}_{\Pi, \mathcal{A}}^{\text{Pr}} = \left| \Pr[\text{Exp}_{\Pi, \mathcal{A}}^{\text{Pr}} = 1] - \frac{1}{2} \right| \leq \varepsilon(\lambda)$$

$\text{Exp}_{\Pi, \mathcal{A}}^{\text{Pr}}(\lambda)$: *Choose $b \in_R \{0, 1\}$, call $b' \leftarrow \mathcal{A}^{\Omega_{\text{pk}}^{\mathcal{L}}(\cdot)}(\lambda, k_{p_0}, \ldots, k_{p_x})$ with $k_{p_i} \leftarrow \text{KGen}_P(k_{h_i}, L_{\text{aux}}, C_i)$ and $k_{h_i} \leftarrow \text{KGen}_H(L_{\text{aux}})$ for all $i \in 0, \ldots, x$. Return $b = b'$.*

$\Omega_{\text{pk}}^{\mathcal{L}}(\ell, \text{aux})$ *returns elements $C = (C_0, \ldots, C_x) \in L_{\text{aux}}$ with $C_0 \leftarrow \text{Enc}_{\text{pk}}^{\mathcal{L}}(\ell_0, \text{aux}'; r_0)$ and $C_i \leftarrow \text{Enc}_{\text{pk}}^{\mathcal{L}}(\ell_i, \text{aux}'_i; r_i)$ for all $i \in 1, \ldots, x$ and $\text{pk} \in \text{aux}$ using encryption scheme $\mathcal{L}$ and according labels ℓ_i. It additionally returns $\text{Hash}_0(k_{h_1}, \ldots, k_{h_x}, L_{\text{aux}}, C_0), \text{Hash}_x(k_{h_0}, L_{\text{aux}}, C_1, \ldots, C_x)$ if $b = 0$ or $h_0, h_x \in_R \mathbb{G}$ if $b = 1$.*

The following theorem shows pseudorandomness of hash values in SPHF^x.

Theorem 2 (SPHF^x Pseudorandomness). *The SPHF^x construction from Definition 4 on cyclic groups is pseudorandom if $\mathcal{L}$ is a CCA-secure labelled encryption scheme.*

Proof. Pseudorandomness of SPHF^x follows immediately from its smoothness and the CCA-security of the used encryption scheme. First we change $\Omega_{\text{pk}}^{\mathcal{L}}$ such that it returns the encryption of 0 for a random $i \in 0, \ldots, x$. This change is not noticeable by the adversary due to the CCA-security of the encryption scheme. Assuming 0 is not a valid message, i.e. $\text{aux}' \neq 0$ and $\text{aux}_i \neq 0$ for all $i \in 1, \ldots, x$, the pseudorandomness of SPHF^x follows from its smoothness. $\square$

The authors of [15] furthermore highlight that this definition of pseudorandomness is not enough when used in PAKE protocols if the hash values are not bound to a specific session by signatures or MACs. Therefore, they prove pseudorandomness under re-use of hash keys and ciphertexts. Taking into account re-use of SPHF^x values such as ciphertexts and keys we formalise the notion of concurrent pseudorandomness for SPHF^x following the approach from [15]. Let $\overline{k_p}$ denote the vector of projection keys k_{p_i} for $i = 0, \ldots, x$. A SPHF^x is pseudorandom in concurrent execution if the hash values are computationally indistinguishable from random without knowledge of the uniformly chosen hash keys or the witnesses, i.e. for fixed $l = l(\lambda)$ the following distributions are computationally ε-close:

$$\{(\overline{k_{p_1}}, \ldots, \overline{k_{p_l}}, C_1, \ldots, C_l, h_{0,1}, \ldots, h_{0,l}, h_{x,1}, \ldots, h_{x,l}) \mid$$
$$\forall i \in \{0, \ldots, x\}, j \in \{1, \ldots, l\} : k_{hi,j} \xleftarrow{R} \text{KGen}_H(L_{\text{aux}}); k_{p_{i,j}} \leftarrow \text{KGen}_P(k_{hi}, L_{\text{aux}});$$
$$\forall j \in \{1, \ldots, l\} : h_{0,j} \leftarrow \text{Hash}_0(k_{h1,j}, \ldots, k_{hx,j}, L_{\text{aux}}, C_{0,j});$$
$$h_{x,j} \leftarrow \text{Hash}_x(k_{h0,j}, L_{\text{aux}}, C_{1,j}, \ldots, C_{x,j})\}$$
$$\stackrel{\varepsilon}{=} \{(\overline{k_{p_1}}, \ldots, \overline{k_{p_l}}, C_1, \ldots, C_l, h_{0,1}, \ldots, h_{0,l}, h_{x,1}, \ldots, h_{x,l}) \mid$$
$$\forall i \in \{0, \ldots, x\}, j \in \{1, \ldots, l\} : k_{hi,j} \xleftarrow{R} \text{KGen}_H(L_{\text{aux}}); k_{p_{i,j}} \leftarrow \text{KGen}_P(k_{hi}, L_{\text{aux}});$$
$$\forall j \in \{1, \ldots, l\} : h_{0,j} \in_R \mathbb{G}; h_{x,j} \in_R \mathbb{G}\}$$

We extend Definition 5 to capture re-use of hash keys and ciphertexts. The corresponding experiment in Definition 6 generates l hash values to each ciphertext, one for each hash key.

Definition 6 (SPHF^x Concurrent Pseudorandomness). *A SPHF^x Π offers concurrent pseudorandomness if for all PPT algorithms $\mathcal{A}$ and polynomials l there exists a negligible function $\varepsilon(\cdot)$ such that*

$$\text{Adv}_{\Pi,\mathcal{A}}^{\text{Pr}} = \left| \Pr[\text{Exp}_{\Pi,\mathcal{A}}^{\text{Pr}} = 1] - \frac{1}{2} \right| \leq \varepsilon(\lambda)$$

$\text{Exp}_{\Pi,\mathcal{A}}^{\text{Pr}}(\lambda)$: *Choose* $b \in_R \{0,1\}$*, call* $b' \leftarrow \mathcal{A}^{\Omega_{\text{pk}}^{\mathcal{L}}(\cdot)}(\lambda, \overline{k_{p_1}}, \ldots, \overline{k_{p_l}})$ *with* $\overline{k_{p_j}} = (k_{p_0}, \ldots, k_{p_x})$ *where* $k_{p_i} \leftarrow \text{KGen}_P(k_{hi}, L_{\text{aux}}, C_i)$ *and* $k_{hi} \leftarrow \text{KGen}_H(L_{\text{aux}})$ *for all* $i \in 0, \ldots, x$ *and* $j \in 1, \ldots, l$*. Return* $b = b'$*.*

$\Omega_{\text{pk}}^{\mathcal{L}}(\ell, \text{aux})$ *returns elements* $C = (C_0, \ldots, C_x) \in L_{\text{aux}}$ *with* $C_0 \leftarrow \text{Enc}_{\text{pk}}^{\mathcal{L}}(\ell_0, \text{aux}'; r_0)$ *and* $C_i \leftarrow \text{Enc}_{\text{pk}}^{\mathcal{L}}(\ell_i, \text{aux}_i; r_i)$ *for all* $i \in 1, \ldots, x$ *and* $\text{pk} \in \text{aux}$

using encryption algorithm $\mathcal{L}$ and according labels ℓ_i. It additionally returns $\mathtt{Hash}_{0,j}(\mathtt{k_{h1},}_j, \ldots, \mathtt{k_{h}}_x^j, L_{\mathsf{aux}}, C_0), \mathtt{Hash}_{x,j}(\mathtt{k_{h0},}_j, L_{\mathsf{aux}}, C_1, \ldots, C_x)$ *if $b = 0$ or* $h_{0,j}, h_{x,j} \in \mathbb{G}$ *if $b = 1$ for all $j \in 1, \ldots, l$.*

Using Definition 6 we prove the concurrent pseudorandomness of our construction, following the argument from [15, Lemma 1].

Lemma 1 (SPHF^x Concurrent Pseudorandomness). *The SPHF^x construction from Definition 4 on cyclic groups is pseudorandom on re-use of hash and ciphertext values if $\mathcal{L}$ is a CCA-secure labelled encryption scheme.*

Proof. Using a hybrid argument it is enough to show that the adversary can not distinguish between experiment Exp_1 where Ω returns random elements for the first i hash values of the j-th query and all queries $< j$ and correct hashes for all subsequent queries and indices $> i$, and Exp_2 where Ω returns random elements for the first $i + 1$ hash values of the j-th query and all queries $< j$ and correct hashes for all subsequent queries and indices $> i + 1$. Having this in mind the proof follows the same argument as the one for SPHF^x pseudorandomness. We briefly recall the argumentation there. We modify Exp_1 to Exp_1' and Exp_2 to Exp_2' such that Ω returns an encryption of 0 instead of correct encryptions for C_j. Note that we assume 0 is not a valid message such that $C_j \notin L_{\mathsf{aux}}$ in Exp_1'. Due to CCA-security of $\mathcal{L}$ this step is not recognisable by the adversary. Changing Exp_1' to Exp_2' the smoothness of SPHF^x ensures that $\mathcal{A}$ can not distinguish between the two experiments, which proves the lemma. □

3.1 Distributed Computation of SPHF^x

Using SPHF^x is only reasonable in a distributed manner. We therefore consider $n = x + 1$ entities participating in the distributed computation of the SPHF^x hash values h_0, h_x. Let P_i for $i \in \{1, \ldots, x\}$ denote parties, each knowing aux_i and computing the according ciphertext C_i and projection key $\mathtt{k_{p}}_i$. Furthermore, let P_0 denote the participant knowing aux and computing C_0 and $\mathtt{k_{p0}}$. We define protocols in this setting with the purpose that both P_0 and P_1 eventually compute h_0 and h_x.

While P_0 can compute $\mathtt{PHash}_0$ and $\mathtt{Hash}_x$ after receiving all C_i and $\mathtt{k_{p}}_i$, computation of $\mathtt{Hash}_0$ and $\mathtt{PHash}_x$ can not be performed solely by the previously described algorithms in this setting, without disclosing the witness or the hashing key. To compute $\mathtt{PHash}_x$ and $\mathtt{Hash}_0$, parties $P_1, \ldots, P_x$ have to collaborate since they know only part of the input parameters. Distributed SPHF^x defines protocols that allow secure calculation of h_0 and h_x. Intuitively distributed SPHF^x reaches the same security properties as SPHF^x, namely smoothness and pseudorandomness in presence of a passive adversary, by additionally ensuring that no protocol participant alone is able to compute the hash values. Note that while we assume each P_i for $i > 0$ holds a key-pair and knows public keys of all other P_i such that all communication between two P_i is secured by the receivers public key, those keys are not authenticated, i.e. we do not assume a PKI.

A distributed SPHF^x protocol between n participants $P_0, \ldots, P_x$ computing h_x and h_0 consists of three interactive protocols $\texttt{Setup}$, $\texttt{PHash}_x^D$ and $\texttt{Hash}_0^D$. Let Π denote the SPHF^x algorithm that is being distributed.

- $\texttt{Setup}(\textsf{aux}, P_0, \ldots, P_x)$ initialises a new instance for each participant with $(\textsf{aux}, P_0, P_1, \ldots, P_x)$ for P_0 and $(\textsf{aux}_i, P_i, P_0, \ldots, P_x)$ for P_i, $i \in \{1, \ldots, x\}$. Eventually, all participants compute and broadcast projection keys $\textsf{k}_{\textsf{p}_i}$ and encryptions $C_i \leftarrow \texttt{Enc}_{\textsf{pk}}^{\mathcal{L}}(\ell_i, \textsf{aux}_i'; r_i)$ of their secret $\textsf{aux}_i'$ using $\Pi.\texttt{KGen}_\textsf{H}$, $\Pi.\texttt{KGen}_\textsf{P}$ and the associated encryption scheme $\mathcal{L}$. Participants store incoming $\textsf{k}_{\textsf{p}_i}, C_i$ for later use. After receiving $(\textsf{k}_{\textsf{p}_1}, C_1, \ldots, \textsf{k}_{\textsf{p}_x}, C_x)$, P_0 computes $h_0 \leftarrow \Pi.\texttt{PHash}_0(\textsf{k}_{\textsf{p}_1}, \ldots, \textsf{k}_{\textsf{p}_x}, L_\textsf{aux}, C_0, r_0)$ and $h_x \leftarrow \Pi.\texttt{Hash}_x(\textsf{k}_{\textsf{h}0}, L_\textsf{aux}, C_1, \ldots, C_x)$.
- $\texttt{PHash}_x^D$ is executed between parties $P_1, \ldots, P_x$. Each P_i performs $\texttt{PHash}_x^D$ on input $(\textsf{k}_{\textsf{p}0}, \textsf{aux}_i, C_1, \ldots, C_x, r_i)$ such that P_1 eventually holds h_x while all P_i for $i > 1$ do not learn anything about h_x.
- $\texttt{Hash}_0^D$ is executed between parties $P_1, \ldots, P_x$. Each P_i performs $\texttt{Hash}_0^D$ on input $(\textsf{aux}_i', \textsf{k}_{\textsf{h}i}, C_0, \ldots, C_x)$ such that P_1 eventually holds h_0 and all P_i for $i > 1$ do not learn anything about h_0.

A distributed SPHF^x is said to be correct if $\texttt{PHash}_x^D = \texttt{PHash}_x$ and $\texttt{Hash}_0^D = \texttt{Hash}_0$ assuming that all messages are honestly computed and transmitted. The security of the distributed SPHF^x in presence of a passive adversary follows immediately from smoothness and pseudorandomness of the SPHF^x algorithms.

Remark 1. Note that we focus on asymmetric distribution here such that only P_1 computes the hash values. Building symmetric distribution protocols where all parties P_i compute the hash values from this is straightforward but requires a different security model. Likewise, it is possible to build asymmetric distribution protocols where *all* P_i compute *different* hash values (we will see an example of that later).

3.2   Security against Active Adversaries

Smooth projective hashing has not been used in a distributed manner before such that it was not necessary to consider active adversaries. By introducing distributed computation of hash values the $\texttt{Hash}_0^D$ and $\texttt{PHash}_x^D$ protocols are exposed to active attacks. However, the adversary must still not be able to distinguish real hash values from random elements, i.e. smoothness and pseudorandomness must hold. Therefore we introduce a security model for distributed SPHF^x smoothness and pseudorandomness, capturing active attacks in a multi-user and multi-instance setting. Let $\{(P_0^j, P_1^k, \ldots, P_x^l)\}_{P_0^j \in \mathcal{P}_0, P_i^k \in \mathcal{P} \ i \in \{1, \ldots, x\}}$ denote all tuples $(P_0^j, P_1^k, \ldots, P_x^l)$ such that $P_0^j \in \mathcal{P}_0$ knows $\textsf{aux}$ and $P_1^k, \ldots, P_x^l \in \mathcal{P}$ each know according $\textsf{aux}_i$. We say P_0 is *registered* with $(P_1, \ldots, P_x)$. The additional indices j, k, l denote the instance of the respective participant (assigned by oracles and modelled as counters to ensure their uniqueness).

Definition 7 (SPHF^x Security). *A distributed SPHF^x protocol Π is secure (offers adaptive smoothness and concurrent pseudorandomness) if for all PPT adversaries $\mathcal{A}$ there exists a negligible function $\varepsilon(\cdot)$ such that :*

$$\mathsf{Adv}_{\Pi,\mathcal{A}}^{SPHF^x}(\lambda) = \left| \Pr[\mathsf{Exp}_{\Pi,\mathcal{A}}^{SPHF^x}(\lambda) = 1] - \frac{1}{2} \right| \leq \varepsilon(\lambda)$$

$\mathsf{Exp}_{\Pi,\mathcal{A}}^{SPHF^x}(\lambda)$: *Choose $b \in_R \{0,1\}$, call $b' \leftarrow \mathcal{A}^{\mathsf{Setup}(\cdot),\mathsf{Send}(\cdot),\mathsf{Test}(\cdot)}(\lambda, \mathsf{aux}_2, \ldots, \mathsf{aux}_x, \mathcal{L}, \mathtt{crs})$ and return $b = b'$.*

- $\mathsf{Setup}(P_0, \ldots, P_x)$ *initialises new instances with $(\mathsf{aux}, P_1, \ldots, P_x)$ for P_0 registered with $(P_1, \ldots, P_x)$ and $(\mathsf{aux}_1, P_1, P_0, \ldots, P_x)$ for P_1 and returns $((\mathtt{k}_{\mathtt{p}_0}, C_0), (\mathtt{k}_{\mathtt{p}_1}, C_1))$ with $C_i \leftarrow \mathsf{Enc}_{\mathtt{pk}}^{\mathcal{L}}(\ell, \mathsf{aux}_i'; r_i)$ and $\mathtt{k}_{\mathtt{h}_i} \leftarrow \Pi.\mathsf{KGen}_{\mathsf{H}}(L_{\mathsf{aux}})$, $\mathtt{k}_{\mathtt{p}_i} \leftarrow \Pi.\mathsf{KGen}_{\mathsf{P}}(\mathtt{k}_{\mathtt{h}_i}, L_{\mathsf{aux}})$*
- $\mathsf{Send}(P_a, P_b, m)$ *sends message m with alleged originator P_b to P_a and returns P_a's resulting message m' if any.*
- $\mathsf{Test}(P_i^j)$ *for $i \in \{0,1\}$ returns two hash values (h_0, h_x). If the global bit b is 0, the hash values are chosen uniformly at random from $\mathbb{G}$, otherwise the hash values are computed according to protocol specification Π.*

Note that we assume without loss of generality that all participants $P_2, \ldots, P_x$ are corrupted by the adversary, who knows their secrets. Furthermore, note that $\mathcal{A}$ can query the Test oracle only once.

The active security notion for distributed computation of SPHF^x covers smoothness and pseudorandomess as defined before. The experiment is equivalent to the computational smoothness definition when $\mathcal{A}$ computes and forwards all messages honestly but changes at least one aux_i. Note that this is actually a stronger notion than smoothness as we require pseudorandomness of hash values output by the projection function on a word not in the language. This is usually not included in the smoothness definition, which is defined over the hash function. Further, Definition 7 is equivalent to Definition 6 when $\mathcal{A}$ computes and forwards all messages honestly and does *not* change any aux_i.

3.3   Instantiation – Distributed Cramer-Shoup SPHF^x

We exemplify the SPHF^x definition on the previously introduced Cramer-Shoup encryption scheme. The ciphertexts are created as $C_i = (u_{1,i}, u_{2,i}, e_i, v_i) \leftarrow \mathsf{Enc}_{\mathtt{pk}}^{\mathsf{CS}}(\ell_i, \mathsf{aux}_i'; r_i)$ for all $i = 1, \ldots, x$ with $\mathsf{aux}_i' = h(\mathsf{aux}')[i]$ and $C_0 = (u_{1,0}, u_{2,0}, e_0, v_0) \leftarrow \mathsf{Enc}_{\mathtt{pk}}^{\mathsf{CS}}(\ell_0, \mathsf{aux}_0'; r_0)$, where ℓ_i consists of participating parties and the party's projection key. We define modified decryption as $\mathsf{Dec}_\pi'(C) = e \cdot u_1^{-z}$. The combining function g uses the homomorphic property of u_1 and e of the CS ciphertext such that $g(C_1, \ldots, C_x) = (\prod_{i=1}^x u_{1,i}, \prod_{i=1}^x e_i)$ and $\mathsf{aux}' = \sum_{i=1}^x \mathsf{aux}_i'$. The following variables define the Cramer-Shoup SPHF^x:

$$\Gamma = \begin{pmatrix} g_1 & 1 & g_2 & h & c \\ 1 & g_1 & 1 & 1 & d \end{pmatrix} \in \mathbb{G}^{2\times5}, \quad \lambda = (r, r\xi) \in \mathbb{Z}_p^{1\times2}$$

$$\Theta_{\mathrm{aux}}^0(C_0) = (u_1, u_1^\xi, u_2, e/\mathrm{aux}', v) \in \mathbb{G}^{1\times5}$$

$$\Theta_{\mathrm{aux}}^x(C_1, \ldots, C_x) = (\prod_{i=1}^x u_{1,i}, \prod_{i=1}^x u_{1,i}^{\xi_i}, \prod_{i=1}^x u_{2,i}, \prod_{i=1}^x e_i/\mathrm{aux}', \prod_{i=1}^x v_i) \in \mathbb{G}^{1\times5}$$

Using them in the SPHF^x Definition 4 yields the Cramer-Shoup SPHF^x. Instead of aiming for absolute generality we describe the distributed Cramer-Shoup SPHF^x for $x = 2$ such that both participants P_1 and P_2 compute and broadcast $(\mathrm{k}_{\mathrm{P}_i}, C_i)$, while P_0 computes and broadcasts $(\mathrm{k}_{\mathrm{P}_0}, C_0)$. Let $\times$ denote element wise multiplication, e.g., for El-Gamal ciphertexts $C_1 = (u_1, e_1)$, $C_2 = (u_2, e_2)$, $C_1 \times C_2$ is defined as $(u_1 u_2, e_1 e_2)$. PHash$_x^D$ and Hash$_0^D$ protocols are defined as follows:

- PHash$_x^D$ is executed between P_1 and P_2. P_2 computes $h_{x,2} = \lambda \odot \mathrm{k}_{\mathrm{P}_0} = (\mathrm{k}_{\mathrm{P}_0}[1] \cdot \mathrm{k}_{\mathrm{P}_0}[2]^{\xi_2})^{r_2}$ and sends it to P_1. Eventually, P_1 holds $h_x = h_{x,2} \cdot (\lambda \odot \mathrm{k}_{\mathrm{P}_0}) = \mathrm{k}_{\mathrm{P}_0}[1]^{r_1+r_2} \cdot \mathrm{k}_{\mathrm{P}_0}[2]^{\xi_1 \cdot r_1 + \xi_2 \cdot r_2}$. Note that P_1 always performs checks that $\mathrm{k}_{\mathrm{P}_0} \in \mathbb{G}$ and $\mathbb{G} \ni h_2^x \neq 0$.
- Hash$_0^D$ is executed between P_1 and P_2 such that P_1 eventually holds h_0. Let P_i for $i \in \{1,2\}$ denote the participating party knowing $(\mathrm{aux}_i, \mathrm{sk}_i, \mathrm{k}_{\mathrm{h}i} = (\eta_1, \eta_2, \theta, \mu, \nu), \mathrm{pk}_1, \mathrm{pk}_2, C_0 = (u_1, u_2, e, v, \xi))$.
  - P_1 computes $m_0 \leftarrow \mathrm{Enc}_{\mathrm{pk}_1}^{\mathrm{EG}}(g_1^{-\mu}; r)$ and $c_1' \leftarrow \mathrm{Enc}_{\mathrm{pk}_1}^{\mathrm{EG}}(g_1^{\mathrm{aux}_1'}; r')$, and sends (m_0, c_1') to P_2.
  - Receiving (m_0, c_1') from P_1, P_2 computes

$$m_1 \leftarrow (m_0)^{\mathrm{aux}_2'} \times (c_1')^{-\mu} \times \mathrm{Enc}_{\mathrm{pk}_1}^{\mathrm{EG}}(g_1^{-\mu \cdot \mathrm{aux}_2'} \cdot u_1^{\eta_1+\xi\eta_2} \cdot u_2^\theta \cdot e^\mu \cdot v^\nu; r'')$$

  and sends it to P_1.
  - Receiving m_1, P_1 computes the hash value

$$h_0 = g_1^{-\mu \cdot \mathrm{aux}_1'} \cdot \mathrm{Dec}_{\mathrm{sk}_1}^{\mathrm{EG}}(m_1) \cdot u_1^{\eta_1+\xi\eta_2} \cdot u_2^\theta \cdot e^\mu \cdot v^\nu.$$

Security of Distributed Cramer-Shoup SPHF^x. We show now that the proposed distributed Cramer-Shoup SPHF^x is secure. The intuition behind the proof is that the pseudorandomness of h_x can be reduced directly to the DDH problem in $\mathbb{G}$ while pseudorandomness of h_0 value follows from the smoothness and pseudorandomness of the underlying SPHF^x scheme.

Theorem 3 (Cramer-Shoup SPHF^x Security). *The distributed Cramer-Shoup SPHF^x instantiation is secure against active adversaries according to Definition 7 when the DDH assumption in the used group $\mathbb{G}$ holds and $\mathcal{L} = \mathrm{CS}$ is CCA-secure.*

Proof. First, note that the theorem follows immediately from smoothness and pseudorandomness in the passive case if the adversary queries $\mathsf{Test}(P_0)$. We therefore focus on $\mathsf{Test}(P_1)$ queries. We start with the pseudorandomness of h_x, i.e. for all g it holds that $\Pr[h_x = g] = 1/|\mathbb{G}|$. Consider an attacker $\mathcal{A}$ on input $(\lambda, \mathsf{aux}_2, \mathcal{L}, \mathsf{crs})$ and let Exp_0 denote the original SPHF^x experiment.

Exp_1 : We change Test such that a uniformly at random chosen element $g_x \in_R \mathbb{G}$ is returned for h_x.

Claim. $\left| \mathsf{Adv}_{\Pi,\mathcal{A}}^{\mathsf{Exp}_0} - \mathsf{Adv}_{\Pi,\mathcal{A}}^{\mathsf{Exp}_1} \right| \leq \varepsilon(\lambda)$

Proof. The hash value h_x in Exp_0 is computed as $h_x = (\mathrm{k}'_{\mathsf{p}_0}[1] \cdot \mathrm{k}'_{\mathsf{p}_0}[2]^{\xi_1})^{r_1} \cdot h_{x,2}$ with adversarially generated $h_{x,2}$ and $\mathrm{k}'_{\mathsf{p}_0}$. Indistinguishability of h_x and g_x, and thus the claim, follows immediately as long as the DDH assumption in $\mathbb{G}$ holds (using DDH triple $(\mathrm{k}'_{\mathsf{p}_0}[1] \cdot \mathrm{k}'_{\mathsf{p}_0}[2]^{\xi_1}, g^{r_1}, h_x)$ and $(\mathrm{k}'_{\mathsf{p}_0}[1] \cdot \mathrm{k}'_{\mathsf{p}_0}[2]^{\xi_1}, g^{r_1}, g_x)$). Note that P_1 aborts if either $h_{x,2} \notin \mathbb{G}$ or $\mathrm{k}'_{\mathsf{p}_0} \notin \mathbb{G}^2$. □

To show the security (concurrent pseudorandomness and adaptive smoothness) of h_0 we define two Send queries that allow execution of the protocol: $(m_1, c'_1) \leftarrow \mathsf{Send}_1(P_2, P_1, (\mathrm{k}'_{\mathsf{p}_0}, C'_0, \mathrm{k}'_{\mathsf{p}_2}, C'_2))$ starts the protocol execution between P_1 and P_2 and provides the attacker with (m_1, c'_1). Using these messages the adversary (P_2) computes a message m_2 and sends it to P_1 with $\mathsf{Send}_2(P_2, P_1, m_2)$. This reflects the execution of a single protocol run of Hash_0^D such that P_1 eventually computes h_0. In contrast to the passive and classical SPHF proofs we can not replace the ciphertexts with encryptions of words not in the language. However, this is not necessary as t is in fact the Hash computation of the classical Cramer-Shoup SPHF without cancelling the message, i.e. $t = h \cdot m^\mu$.

Exp_2 : We change Test such that a uniformly at random chosen element $g_0 \in_R \mathbb{G}$ is returned for h_0.

Claim. $\left| \mathsf{Adv}_{\Pi,\mathcal{A}}^{\mathsf{Exp}_1} - \mathsf{Adv}_{\Pi,\mathcal{A}}^{\mathsf{Exp}_2} \right| \leq \varepsilon(\lambda)$

Proof. The hash value h_0 in Exp_1 is computed as $h_0 = g^{-\mu_1 \cdot \mathsf{aux}'_1} \cdot \mathsf{Dec}_{\mathsf{sk}_1}^{\mathsf{EG}}(m_2) \cdot t$ with $t = u_{1,0}^{\eta_{1,1} + \xi_0 \eta_{2,1}} u_{2,0}^{\theta_1} e_0^{\mu_1} v_0^{\nu_1}$ where m_2 and $C'_0 = (u_{1,0}, u_{2,0}, e_0, v_0)$ may be adversarially generated. The value t is actually the Hash value of the classical Cramer-Shoup SPHF without cancelled message, or in other words t is the result of a SPHF Hash computation for language $L_{(\mathsf{crs},0)}$ such that any C'_0, encrypting some correct $\mathsf{aux}' \neq 0$, is not in this language. Due to smoothness of the Hash function [6] t is indistinguishable from a uniformly at random chosen element. If the adversary encrypted 0 in C'_0 pseudorandomness of Hash takes effect. Therefore $h_0 = d \cdot t$ is indistinguishable from a random group element for all $d \in \mathbb{G}$. □

In Exp_2 the adversary always gets random group elements in answer to his Test query. Therefore, he can not do better than guessing bit b. □

4   Two-Server PAKE from Distributed SPHF^x

In this section we present a new two-server PAKE framework as an application of our distributed SPHF^x concept. Moreover, we show that the two-server PAKE protocol by Katz et al. [13] can be considered as a variant of our framework using a "mix" of distributed SPHF^x for Cramer-Shoup and El-Gamal ciphertexts.

With a single server storing the password, password authenticated key exchange (PAKE) protocols have an intrinsic single point of failure. As soon as the server's database, storing the client's secrets, gets compromised the attacker can impersonate the client to this server, and most likely also to others considering that users tend to reuse their passwords across multiple services. Mechanisms have been proposed to solve the problem of server compromise [12,19]. However, as long as only one server is used, PAKE protocols are prone to offline dictionary attacks on the server side. Two-server PAKE (2PAKE) protocols can solve this problem by splitting the password in two parts such that a malicious or compromised server can be used to recover only one part of the password. Raimondo and Gennaro [17] proposed a t-out-of-n threshold PAKE, which is not suitable for the 2PAKE setting as it requires $t < n/3$. Another t-out-of-n threshold PAKE was proposed in a PKI-based setting with random oracles [16]. Brainard and Juels [8] proposed two-server password based authentication without security proof. Szydlo and Kaliski [18] later modified constuctions from [8] and proved their security in a simulation-based model. The first two-server PAKE in the password-only setting, i.e. without a PKI, is due to Katz et al. [13], based on the KOY protocol from [14]. We consider the same setting as [13] in which the client computes two independent session keys with the two servers.

4.1   A New Two-Server PAKE Framework

Using distributed SPHF^x we can build efficient 2PAKE protocols. We consider the same setting as 2KOY [13], in particular a client that negotiates independent session keys with both servers that hold $\mathrm{pw}_1 + \mathrm{pw}_2 = \mathrm{pw}$. We omit the second server in the description of the protocol in Figure 1 as the framework is symmetric in the sense that the second server S_2 performs like S_1. The framework follows the same principle as the latest PAKE frameworks from SPHFs. In particular it can be seen as a two-server variant of the PAKE protocol from [15].

You can think of the two-server protocol as the execution of two distributed SPHF^x protocols, one between (C, S_1, S_2) and one between (C, S_2, S_1) where servers S_2 and S_1 swap roles, such that (C, S_1) and (C, S_2) eventually hold common hash values that can be used to generate a shared session key sk_1 and sk_2. The only overlap between the two SPHF^x executions is the Hash_x computation. The reuse of C_1, C_2 in Hash_x functions is covered by the concurrent pseudorandomness.

2PAKE Framework. The servers encrypt their password shares under a public key pk stored in the crs using a CCA-secure labelled encryption scheme and distribute this ciphertext together with two appropriate projection keys for a secure

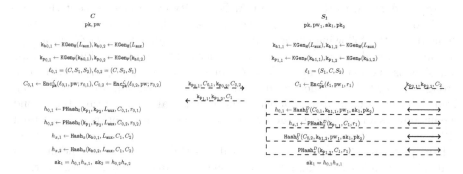

Fig. 1. Two-Server PAKE framework using SPHF^x

Dashed lines denote broadcast messages

distributed SPHF^x, $(k_{p_{1,1}}, k_{p_{1,2}}, C_1)$ and $(k_{p_{2,1}}, k_{p_{2,2}}, C_2)$. The client computes two independent encryptions of the password and generates two independent according projection keys $(k_{p_{0,1}}, C_{0,1}, k_{p_{0,2}}, C_{0,2})$. The previously described SPHF^x allows us to send all k_{p_i}, C_i in one round and therefore reach optimality for this step. Using these values, the client can compute session keys as product of the two hash values $h_{0,1}, h_{x,1}$ for sk_1, which is shared with S_1 and from $h_{0,2}, h_{x,2}$ for sk_2 that is shared with S_2.

Subsequently, the two servers perform the Hash_0^D and PHash_x^D protocols such that S_1 and S_2 eventually hold hash values $h_{0,1}$ and $h_{x,1}$, $h_{0,2}$ and $h_{x,2}$ respectively, to compute sk_1, sk_2 respectively. Eventually, C holds $sk_1 = h_{0,1} \cdot h_{x,1}$ and $sk_2 = h_{0,2} \cdot h_{x,2}$, S_1 holds $sk_1 = h_{0,1} \cdot h_{x,1}$ and S_2 holds $sk_2 = h_{0,2} \cdot h_{x,2}$. An instantiation of the framework using labelled Cramer-Shoup encryption and the aforementioned distributed SPHF^x yields a secure 2PAKE protocol. Note that this actually requires two SPHF^x executions.

Security. We use the well-known game based PAKE model first introduced by Bellare et al. [3] in it's two-server variant from [13]. For a formal description of the model we refer to [13]. The security of the two-server PAKE framework follows directly from the CCA-security of the used encryption scheme and the security of the distributed SPHF^x.

Theorem 4. *Let* $(\mathrm{KGen_H}, \mathrm{KGen_P}, \mathrm{PHash_0}, \mathrm{Hash}_x, \mathrm{Hash}_0^D, \mathrm{PHash}_x^D)$ *be a secure distributed SPHF^x and* $(\mathrm{KGen}, \mathrm{Enc}, \mathrm{Dec})$ *a CCA-secure labelled encryption scheme, then the proposed framework in Figure 1 is a secure two-server PAKE protocol.*

Proof (sketch). Let Π denote a secure instantiation of the 2PAKE framework. To prove security of Π we introduce three experiments such that the adversary in the last experiment Exp_3 can not do better than guessing the password as all messages are password independent, i.e. $\mathrm{Adv}_{\Pi,\mathcal{A}}^{\mathrm{Exp}_3} \leq q/|\mathcal{D}|$ for q active attacks. We initially focus on the AKE-security of sk_1.

Exp_1 is identical to the two-server AKE-security experiment except that the simulator knows π, the decryption key to pk in the crs (only a syntactical change) and the following changes: If $C_{0,1}$ or C_1, handed to S_1 or C are adversarially generated and encrypt the correct password(share), the simulator stops and $\mathcal{A}$ wins the experiment. If $C_{0,1}$, C_1 or C_2, handed to S_1 or C encrypt a wrong password(share), the key for that session is drawn uniformly at random from $\mathbb{G}$. The first change only increases the adversarial advantage and the second one introduces a negligible gap according to the adaptive smoothness of the used SPHF^x.

Exp_2 performs like Exp_1 except that it draws the session key at random from $\mathbb{G}$ if all C_i handed to C and S_1 are oracle generated or encrypt the correct password and no session key has been chosen for the partner in that session (otherwise that previously drawn key is used). This introduces a negligible gap between advantages in Exp_1 and Exp_2 due to the concurrent pseudorandomness of the used SPHF^x.

Exp_3 acts like Exp_2 except that it returns encryptions of 0 for $C_{0,1}$ and C_1 (note that 0 is not a valid password). This step is covered by the CCA-security of the used encryption scheme.

AKE-security of sk_1 follows as all messages are password independent in Exp_3 unless the adversary guesses the correct password. Using the same sequence of experiments but considering C and S_2 instead of C and S_1, AKE-security of sk_2 follows.   □

4.2   2-Server KOY (2KOY) [13]

We can now "explain" the use of SPHF in 2KOY from [13]; similar to [11] that "explained" the original KOY protocol from [14]. We define encryption schemes and distributed SPHF^x used in 2KOY, highlight changes to our framework and discuss implications of this on the security of 2KOY.

The crs contains a public key pk for Cramer-Shoup encryption as well as a public key g_3 for El-Gamal encryption. Since [13] uses El-Gamal encryptions on the server side, we have to use a combination of Cramer-Shoup and El-Gamal based SPHF^x in 2KOY. Instead of using Cramer-Shoup encryptions and SPHF^x, the client computes projection keys for an El-Gamal distributed SPHF^x, which is based on the aforementioned SPHF on El-Gamal ciphertexts.

Likewise, the servers compute projection keys for a Cramer-Shoup distributed $\mathrm{GL\text{-}SPHF}^x$ and El-Gamal encryptions of their password shares.[2] The client sends the projection keys in a third round together with a signature on the session transcript to the servers. Eventually, the client computes hash values using the PHash_0 function of the $\mathrm{GL\text{-}SPHF}^x$ scheme on CS ciphertexts and the Hash_x function of the SPHF^x scheme on El-Gamal ciphertexts. Further, the servers execute the Hash_0^D protocol of the distributed $\mathrm{GL\text{-}SPHF}^x$ scheme on CS ciphertexts and the PHash_x^D protocol of the distributed SPHF^x scheme on El-Gamal ciphertexts.

---

[2] Note that an additional signature on the session transcript in round three ensures "non-malleability" of these ciphertexts.

Security of 2KOY. Security of the protocol against passive adversaries follows immediately from [13, Theorem 1] as we do not change the protocol. However, the authors of [13] need additional mechanisms to prove their protocol secure against an active adversary. They add witness-indistinguishable Σ-protocols to the $\mathtt{PHash}_x^D$ and $\mathtt{Hash}_0^D$ protocols that prove correctness of their messages. Without giving a proof it should be clear that Theorem 4 also holds for the 2KOY instantiation *without* additional mechanisms. Examining the proof of [13, Theorem 2] shows that the additional steps are only necessary to conduct the proof without actually giving additional security. This shows the power of distributed $\mathtt{SPHF}^x$ as they allow for much simpler proofs of multi-party protocols. Furthermore, with our framework the protocol ceomes more efficient than 2KOY as it needs only two rounds instead of three and does not need correctness proofs in the distributed hash and projection protocols.

5 Conclusion

We introduced the notion of extended (distributed) smooth projective hashing and gave an instantiation using Cramer-Shoup ciphertexts. Distributed smooth projective hashing can be used as building block in threshold and multi-party protocols. As an example, we built a two-server PAKE framework using a distributed smooth projective hash function. This two-server PAKE framework yields the most efficient two-server PAKE protocols today. The framework also allows us to explain and simplify the two-server PAKE protocol from [13].

While we focused on two-server password authenticated key exchange as application of distributed SPHF in this work, (distributed) extended smooth projective hash functions is an interesting building block for future work on other multi-party and threshold protocols.

Acknowledgments. This research was supported by the German Science Foundation (DFG) through the project PRIMAKE (MA 4957).

References

1. Abdalla, M., Chevalier, C., Pointcheval, D.: Smooth Projective Hashing for Conditionally Extractable Commitments. In: Halevi, S. (ed.) CRYPTO 2009. LNCS, vol. 5677, pp. 671–689. Springer, Heidelberg (2009)
2. Abdalla, M., Pointcheval, D.: A Scalable Password-Based Group Key Exchange Protocol in the Standard Model. In: Lai, X., Chen, K. (eds.) ASIACRYPT 2006. LNCS, vol. 4284, pp. 332–347. Springer, Heidelberg (2006)
3. Bellare, M., Pointcheval, D., Rogaway, P.: Authenticated key exchange secure against dictionary attacks. In: Preneel, B. (ed.) EUROCRYPT 2000. LNCS, vol. 1807, pp. 139–155. Springer, Heidelberg (2000)
4. Ben Hamouda, F., Blazy, O., Chevalier, C., Pointcheval, D., Vergnaud, D.: Efficient UC-Secure Authenticated Key-Exchange for Algebraic Languages. In: Kurosawa, K., Hanaoka, G. (eds.) PKC 2013. LNCS, vol. 7778, pp. 272–291. Springer, Heidelberg (2013)

5. Benhamouda, F., Blazy, O., Chevalier, C., Pointcheval, D., Vergnaud, D.: New Smooth Projective Hash Functions and One-Round Authenticated Key Exchange. Cryptology ePrint Archive, Report 2013/034 (2013), http://eprint.iacr.org/

6. Benhamouda, F., Blazy, O., Chevalier, C., Pointcheval, D., Vergnaud, D.: New Techniques for SPHFs and Efficient One-Round PAKE Protocols. In: Canetti, R., Garay, J.A. (eds.) CRYPTO 2013, Part I. LNCS, vol. 8042, pp. 449–475. Springer, Heidelberg (2013)

7. Blazy, O., Pointcheval, D., Vergnaud, D.: Round-Optimal privacy-preserving protocols with smooth projective hash functions. In: Cramer, R. (ed.) TCC 2012. LNCS, vol. 7194, pp. 94–111. Springer, Heidelberg (2012)

8. Brainard, J., Juels, A.: A new two-server approach for authentication with short secrets. In: USENIX 2003. SSYM 2003, vol. 12, p. 14. USENIX Association (2003)

9. Cramer, R., Shoup, V.: A practical public key cryptosystem provably secure against adaptive chosen ciphertext attack. In: Krawczyk, H. (ed.) CRYPTO 1998. LNCS, vol. 1462, pp. 13–25. Springer, Heidelberg (1998)

10. Cramer, R., Shoup, V.: Universal Hash Proofs and a Paradigm for Adaptive Chosen Ciphertext Secure Public-Key Encryption. In: Knudsen, L.R. (ed.) EUROCRYPT 2002. LNCS, vol. 2332, pp. 45–64. Springer, Heidelberg (2002)

11. Gennaro, R., Lindell, Y.: A Framework for Password-Based Authenticated Key Exchange. ACM Trans. Inf. Syst. Secur. 9(2), 181–234 (2006)

12. Gentry, C., MacKenzie, P.D., Ramzan, Z.: A Method for Making Password-Based Key Exchange Resilient to Server Compromise. In: Dwork, C. (ed.) CRYPTO 2006. LNCS, vol. 4117, pp. 142–159. Springer, Heidelberg (2006)

13. Katz, J., MacKenzie, P., Taban, G., Gligor, V.: Two-server password-only authenticated key exchange. In: Ioannidis, J., Keromytis, A.D., Yung, M. (eds.) ACNS 2005. LNCS, vol. 3531, pp. 1–16. Springer, Heidelberg (2005)

14. Katz, J., Ostrovsky, R., Yung, M.: Efficient Password-Authenticated Key Exchange Using Human-Memorable Passwords. In: Pfitzmann, B. (ed.) EUROCRYPT 2001. LNCS, vol. 2045, pp. 475–494. Springer, Heidelberg (2001)

15. Katz, J., Vaikuntanathan, V.: Round-optimal password-based authenticated key exchange. In: Ishai, Y. (ed.) TCC 2011. LNCS, vol. 6597, pp. 293–310. Springer, Heidelberg (2011)

16. MacKenzie, P.D., Shrimpton, T., Jakobsson, M.: Threshold password-authenticated key exchange. In: Yung, M. (ed.) CRYPTO 2002. LNCS, vol. 2442, pp. 385–400. Springer, Heidelberg (2002)

17. Raimondo, M.D., Gennaro, R.: Provably secure threshold password-authenticated key exchange. In: Biham, E. (ed.) EUROCRYPT 2003. LNCS, vol. 2656, pp. 507–523. Springer, Heidelberg (2003)

18. Szydlo, M., Kaliski, B.: Proofs for Two-Server Password Authentication. In: Menezes, A. (ed.) CT-RSA 2005. LNCS, vol. 3376, pp. 227–244. Springer, Heidelberg (2005)

19. Wu, T.: RFC 2945 - The SRP Authentication and Key Exchange System (September 2000)

Sakura: A Flexible Coding for Tree Hashing

Guido Bertoni[1], Joan Daemen[1], Michaël Peeters[2], and Gilles Van Assche[1]

[1] STMicroelectronics
[2] NXP Semiconductors

Abstract. We propose a flexible, fairly general, coding for tree hash modes. The coding does not define a tree hash mode, but instead specifies a way to format the message blocks and chaining values into inputs to the underlying function for any topology, including sequential hashing. The main benefit is to avoid input clashes between different tree growing strategies, even before the hashing modes are defined, and to make the SHA-3 standard tree-hashing ready.

Keywords: hash function, tree hashing, indifferentiability, SHA-3.

1 Introduction

A *hashing mode* can be seen as a recipe for computing digests over messages by means of a number of calls to an underlying function. This underlying function may be a fixed-input-length compression function, a permutation or even a hash function in its own right. We use the term *inner function* and symbol f for the underlying function and the term *outer hash function* and symbol F for the function obtained by applying the hashing mode to the inner function.

The hashing mode splits the message into substrings that are assembled into inputs for the inner function, possibly combined with one or more *chaining values* and so-called *frame bits*. Such an input to f is called a *node* [6]. The chaining values are the results of calls to f for other nodes.

Hashing modes serve two main purposes. The first is to build a variable-input-length hash function from a fixed-input-length inner function and the second is to build a tree hash function. In tree hashing, several parts of the message may be processed simultaneously and parallel architectures can be used more efficiently when hashing a single message than in sequential hashing [17,8,22,3,9,6].

The motivation for standardizing a tree hash mode, or to have a tree-hash-ready SHA-3 standard, was discussed at various occasions during the SHA-3 competition on the NIST hash-forum mailing list [18]. A few candidates, like MD6, SANDstorm and Skein, proposed built-in tree hash modes [21,23,10]. At the Third SHA-3 Candidate Conference, Lucks, McGrew and Whiting motivated why the SHA-3 standard should support parallelized tree hashing [15].

Different applications or use cases call for different approaches to tree hashing and different tree topologies. For instance, some environments favor cutting the input message in consecutive pieces and hashing these pieces independently, while others favor to hash interleaved pieces of data, see, e.g., [11]. In his presentation at ESC 2013, Lucks suggested to use a n-ary tree with much potential

I. Boureanu, P. Owesarski, and S. Vaudenay (Eds.): ACNS 2014, LNCS 8479, pp. 217–234, 2014.
© Springer International Publishing Switzerland 2014

parallelism and to let the implementation choose the most appropriate evaluation strategy [14]. As another example, some applications require to keep the intermediate hash values (e.g., to be able to re-compute the digest if only a part of the input changes), whereas the mere exploitation of parallelism does not require it.

Given all this diversity, it seems difficult to agree on a "one-size-fits-all" tree hash mode. Instead, we take the different approach of allowing different tree hash modes to co-exist. However, the co-existence of different modes on top of existing (serial) hash functions calls for caution. While each individual hash mode can be proven secure, the joint use of several modes can become insecure, in particular due to the different coding conventions that could collide into equal inputs to the inner function. This paper proposes a way to bring together different tree hash modes in a secure way and follows ideas presented in [5, Slides 54-59].

We show that it is possible to define a tree hash coding, i.e., a way to format the input to the inner function, that can cover a wide range of tree hash modes. For a carefully designed tree hash coding, one can prove that the union of all tree hash modes compatible with it is *sound*. By sound we mean that it does not introduce any weaknesses on top of the risk of collisions in the inner function. More precisely, a hashing mode is sound if the advantage of differentiating F from a random oracle, assuming f has been randomly selected, is upper bound by $q^2/2^{n+1}$, with q the number of queries to f and n the length of the chaining values [1,16,7,6].

As a result, tree hash modes compatible with the defined coding can be progressively introduced while preserving their joint security. Also, as an additional benefit, a tree hash mode following the coding convention is sound by construction, without the need of additional proofs.

For proving soundness, we use the results of [6], in which we specify a set of conditions for a tree (or sequential) hashing mode to be sound. We assume that to the choice of f is attached a security parameter, like the capacity in the specific case of sponge functions or the security strength [19,2]. We consider this security parameter to be specified together with f and to remain constant for its entire use in a tree hash mode.

The remainder of this paper is structured as follows. In Section 2 we explain the range of possibilities of our proposed sound tree hash coding and illustrate it with some examples. In Section 3 we specify SAKURA, the coding we propose, while in Section 4 we define what it means for a hashing mode to be compatible with SAKURA and prove that any such tree hash mode is sound. In Section 5 we give some examples of modes and in Section 6 we provide a concrete proposal in the context of making the SHA-3 standard tree-hashing ready.

2   Functionality Supported by Sakura

We start by recalling the very general concept of node and tree of nodes. We then capture the functionality of SAKURA with trees of hops and how nodes and hops relate to one another. Finally, some figures illustrate the concepts.

2.1   Modeling tree Hash Modes

We refer to [6, Section 2] for a detailed description of the model. We here give a short summary.

A tree is a directed graph of *nodes*. Informally speaking, each node is hashed with the inner function f and the output is given to its parent node as a chaining value. The exception is for the final node (i.e., the root of the tree), which does not have a parent, and the output of the outer hash function $F(M)$ is the output of f applied to this final node.

A tree hash mode $\mathcal{T}$ specifies a tree of nodes as a function of the input message length $|M|$ and some specific parameters A. In particular, it is up to the mode to define how the tree scales as a function of $|M|$, how the message bits are spread on the nodes, which nodes takes chaining values from which nodes, etc.

For a fixed $|M|$ and A, a tree hashing mode specifies precisely how to format the inputs to the inner function f with bits from the message, chaining values and frame bits. The latter are constant bits for padding or domain separation. The union of tree hash modes is defined in [6, Section 7.3]. The union $\mathcal{T}_{union}$ of k tree hashing modes $\mathcal{T}_i$ simply means that the user has a choice parameter indicating the chosen mode i composed with the tree parameters A_i for the particular mode i. With $\mathcal{T}_{union}$, the user can thus reach any node tree that some $\mathcal{T}_i$ can produce.

2.2   From Generality to Functionality

The model of the tree using nodes is very general and allows modeling even the most cumbersome tree hash mode, e.g., where a node inputs 2 chaining value bits from child #4 then 7 message bits, etc. We now introduce some concepts that restrict this general model to one that can be easily represented and yet is sufficiently flexible to cover all practical cases we can think of.

We represent trees in terms of *hops* that model how message and chaining values are distributed over nodes. Any tree of hops uniquely maps to a tree of nodes, so they are still supported by the model mentioned above. However, not all trees of nodes (such as the cumbersome example above) can be represented in trees of hops.

In SAKURA, any tree of hops is encoded into a tree of nodes. In other words, the functionality supported by SAKURA is exactly that of all possible trees of hops that can be built. SAKURA-compatible tree hash modes are not required to generate all possible hop trees, but instead they can focus on the desired subset of them. In the sequel, we define what the hops are and how they are encoded into nodes.

2.3   Hops and Hop Trees

Unlike a node that may simultaneously contain message bits and chaining values, there are two distinct types of hops: *message hops* that contain only message bits and *chaining hops* that contain only chaining values.

The hops form a tree, with the root of the tree called the *final hop*. Such a hop tree determines the parallelism that can be exploited by processing multiple message hops or chaining hops in parallel.

Each hop has a single outgoing edge. A message hop has no incoming edges. The number of incoming edges of a chaining hop is called its *degree d*. The hops at the other end of these edges are called the *child hops* of that chaining hop. The edges to a hop are labeled with numbers 0 to $d - 1$ and the hop at the end of edge 0 is called the *first child hop*. There is exactly one hop that has no outgoing edge and we call it the *final hop*. There is exactly one path from each hop to the final hop.

We define the position of a hop in a hop tree by an index, that specifies the path to follow to reach this hop starting from the final hop. It consists of a sequence of integers $\alpha = \alpha_0 \alpha_1 \dots \alpha_{n-1}$. Indexing is defined in a recursive way:

- The index of the final hop is the empty sequence, denoted $*$.
- The index of the i-th child of a hop with index α has index $\alpha || i - 1$.

The length of this sequence specifies the distance of the specified hop to the final hop and is called its *height*. The height of the hop tree is the maximum height over all hops.

2.4   Interleaving the Input over Message Hops

In general, message bits are distributed onto message hops from the first to the last child.

In streaming applications, one may wish to divide message substrings over multiple hops as the message becomes available. For this purpose chaining hops have an attribute called *interleaving block size I* that determines how this shall be done. The principle is that a chaining hop distributes the message bits it receives over its child hops. It hands the first I bits to its first child, the second sequence of I bits to its second child and so on. After reaching the last of its child hops, it returns to its first child and so on. When a receiving hop is also a chaining hop, it will distribute the message bits over its child hops according to its own interleaving block size. When this process ends is determined by the hashing mode. For example, it can be when the end of the message is reached or when the hops have reached some maximum size specified in the mode's parameters.

A mode that does not make use of message block interleaving can set the interleaving block size of the chaining hops to a value that is larger than any message that may be presented, and we say $I = \infty$.

The way message bits are distributed is formally captured by the `GetMessage` function in Definition 1 below. For examples with block interleaving, please see Sections 5.2 and 5.3.

2.5   Mapping Hops to Nodes

One can define hashing modes where the concepts of node and hop coincide by imposing that each node contains exactly one hop. With *kangaroo hopping* defined below, however, the first child hop is coded before its parent in the same node.

In a mode without kangaroo hopping, the node tree is constructed from the hop tree using the same topology. A node contains exactly one hop. The nodes are constructed by putting message bits in nodes containing a message hop and by putting chaining values in nodes containing a chaining hop.

The motivation for kangaroo hopping is the following. The length of (a node mapped from) a chaining hop is the number of children multiplied by the length of the chaining value. Compared to sequential hashing, this corresponds to an overhead. Also, there is typically some additional computational overhead per call to f. Kangaroo hopping reduces this overhead by putting multiple hops per node in a way that does not jeopardize the potential parallelism expressed in the hop tree. A chaining hop has an attribute that says whether kangaroo hopping must be applied on it, and if so, the chaining hop is also called a *kangaroo hop*. When encoding a kangaroo hop into a node, the node contains its first child hop itself instead the chaining value (its f-image). For the other child hops it contains the chaining values as usual. Hence, when evaluating $F(M)$, instances of f can process child hops in parallel and then the instance of f for the first child continues processing the parent hop.

Kangaroo hopping can be applied in a recursive way, i.e., the first child hop may also be a kangaroo hop. All in all, a node may contain a message hop followed by zero, one or more chaining hops, or one or more chaining hops. Kangaroo hopping reduces the number of nodes to the total number of hops minus the number of kangaroo hops. It is easy to see that the number of nodes can be reduced to the number of message hops, but not to less.

The result of applying f to the final node is the output of F. The last hop in this node is the final hop. The result of applying f to an inner node is a chaining value.

2.6   Illustrations

We illustrate these concepts with some examples in Figures 1, 2 and 3. These figures depict hop trees with the following conventions. Message hops have sharp corners, chaining hops have rounded corners. The final hop has a grey fill, the others a white fill. An edge between child and parent has an arrow and enters the parent from above if the chaining value obtained by applying f to the child hop is in the parent hop. It has a short dash and enters the parent hop from the left in the case of kangaroo hopping. Hops on the same horizontal line are in the same node.

In Figure 1 there are in total 5 hops: 4 message hops M_0 to M_3 and one chaining hop Z_*. The final node contains both the final hop Z_* and M_0 because of kangaroo hopping. The total number of nodes is 4.

In Figure 2 there are in total 7 hops: 4 message hops M_{00}, M_{01}, M_{10}, M_{11}, and three chaining hops Z_0, Z_1 and Z_*. The final node contains only the final hop Z_*. The hops M_{00} and Z_0 are in a single node. Similarly, M_{10} and Z_1 are in a single node. The total number of nodes is 5.

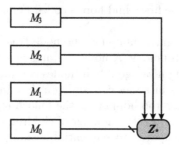

Fig. 1. Example of a hop tree with application of kangaroo hopping. M_0 and Z are in the same node.

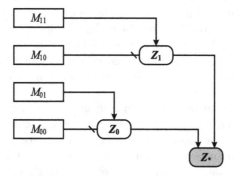

Fig. 2. Another example of a hop tree. M_{00} and Z_0 are in the same node, as well as M_{10} and Z_1.

In Figure 3 there is only a single hop, that is at the same time a message hop and the final hop. Clearly, there is only a single node containing this hop.

Fig. 3. Example of a hop tree with a single node

3 The Sakura Tree Coding

In this section we specify the SAKURA tree coding. The goal of this coding is to allow a tree hash mode to encode a hop tree into the input of f. From this definition, it should be clear how the evaluation of $F(M)$ must be processed.

For a SAKURA-compatible tree hash mode to be sound, the individual parts (e.g., message bits, chaining values) must be unambiguously recovered by parsing the node tree. Of course, such a decoding never occurs in practice but must be ensured for satisfying tree-decodability. The coding adds frame bits for tree-decodability, as well as to ensure domain separation between inner nodes and the final node.

The coding is based on a number of simple principles:

- Nodes, namely inputs to f, can be unambiguously decoded into hops *from the end*. This is done by
  - coding in a trailing frame bit whether it is a chaining hop or a message hop;
  - allowing at most a single message hop per node, and this at the beginning;
  - allowing the parsing of a chaining hop from the end.
- The parsing of a chaining hop from the end is made possible in the following way:
  - it is a series of chaining values followed by an interleaving block size;
  - an interleaving block size consists of 2 bytes;
  - at the end of the chaining values their number is appended in suffix-free coding;
  - the length of the chaining values is determined by the security strength of f.
- We apply simple padding between the hops in a node, so as to allow the alignment of these elements to byte boundaries, 64-bit word boundaries or to any other desired boundaries. (This is up to the mode to define.)
- We apply simple padding at the end of inner nodes. Where appropriate, this can be used by a mode to ensure that different sibling inner nodes have the same length. This may simplify the implementation, e.g., if sibling inner nodes are processed in parallel using SIMD instruction. (Again, this is up to the mode to define.)

3.1   Formal Description of Sakura

We specify the SAKURA tree coding in Figure 4 below. In our specification we use the Augmented Backus-Naur Form (ABNF), which is used for describing the syntax of programming languages or document formats [20]. (We refer to the Wikipedia entries for ABNF.)

In short, an ABNF specification is a set of derivation rules, where a *non-terminal* symbol is assigned a sequence of symbols or a choice of a set of sequences of symbols, separated by |. Symbols that never appear on a left side are terminals. Non-terminal symbols are enclosed between the pair $\langle \rangle$. In our case, the *terminals* are either the frame bits '0' and '1', frame bits whose value is specified in the text (FRAME_BIT), bits coming from the message (MESSAGE_BIT), bits coming from chaining values (CHAINING_BIT), or the empty string ''. The expression $n\langle x \rangle$ denotes a sequence of n elements of type $\langle x \rangle$. In the language of

⟨*final node*⟩ ::= ⟨*node*⟩ '1'

⟨*inner node*⟩ ::= ⟨*node*⟩ ⟨*padSimple*⟩ '0'

⟨*node*⟩ ::= ⟨*message hop*⟩ | ⟨*chaining hop*⟩ | ⟨*kangaroo hopping*⟩

⟨*kangaroo hopping*⟩ ::= ⟨*node*⟩ ⟨*padSimple*⟩ ⟨*chaining hop*⟩

⟨*message hop*⟩ ::= ⟨*message bit string*⟩ '1'

⟨*message bit string*⟩ ::= '' | ⟨*message bit string*⟩ MESSAGE_BIT

⟨*chaining hop*⟩ ::= nrCVs⟨*CV*⟩ ⟨*coded nrCVs*⟩ ⟨*interleaving block size*⟩ '0'

⟨*CV*⟩ ::= nCHAINING_BIT

⟨*coded nrCVs*⟩ ::= ⟨*integer*⟩ ⟨*length of integer*⟩

⟨*integer*⟩ ::= ⟨*frame byte string*⟩

⟨*frame byte string*⟩ ::= '' | ⟨*frame byte string*⟩ 8FRAME_BIT

⟨*length of integer*⟩ ::= 8FRAME_BIT

⟨*interleaving block size*⟩ ::= ⟨*mantissa*⟩ ⟨*exponent*⟩

⟨*mantissa*⟩ ::= 8FRAME_BIT

⟨*exponent*⟩ ::= 8FRAME_BIT

⟨*padSimple*⟩ ::= '1' | ⟨*padSimple*⟩ '0'

Fig. 4. Definition of SAKURA tree hash coding

[6], the produced nodes compose a *tree template*, i.e., a tree with placeholders for message bits and chaining values.

The production rules for ⟨*node*⟩ express which sequences of hops can be encoded in a node. E.g., if the node contains one message hop followed by two chaining hops because of kangaroo hopping, ⟨*node*⟩ expands to ⟨*message hop*⟩ ⟨*padSimple*⟩ ⟨*chaining hop*⟩ ⟨*padSimple*⟩ ⟨*chaining hop*⟩.

The length of the chaining values ⟨*CV*⟩ is n bits, where n is a multiple of 8 to ensure byte-alignment. If the function f has worst-case (or collision resistance) security strength s [19], then we take n equal to s multiplied by two and rounded to a multiple of 8, i.e., $n = 8\lceil s/4 \rceil$. In the case of a sponge function with capacity c, $n = 8\lceil c/8 \rceil$, e.g., if $c = 256$ bits, then a ⟨*CV*⟩ consists of 32 bytes [2]. We assume that the security strength of the inner function is known from the context.

When interpreted as an integer, a byte has the value

$$\sum_{0 \le i < 8} b_i 2^i, \tag{1}$$

where the first bit in a byte has index 0 and the last 7.

The $\langle coded\ nrCVs \rangle$ codes the number of chaining values and is a positive integer. It consists of two fields:

- $\langle integer \rangle$: a byte string that can be decoded to an integer using the function OS2IP(X) specified in the RSA Labs standard PKCS#1[13],
- $\langle length\ of\ integer \rangle$: a single byte that codes the length (in bytes) of the $\langle integer \rangle$ field.

The interleaving block size codes an integer using a floating point representation. Its first byte is the mantissa m and its second byte is the exponent e. The value of the interleaving block size I is then given by $I = 2^e(2m + 1)$. The largest possible value that the interleaving block size can have with this coding is $(2^9 - 1)2^{255}$, obtained by setting all bits in its coding to 1. In practice no message will ever attain this length and we use it to denote that there is no interleaving. This value will be denoted by $I = \infty$ in the remainder of this paper.

Within a node, the chaining bits must come from child nodes with increasing indexes, starting from 0 at the beginning of the node, across all chaining hops of the node. When kangaroo hopping is not used, the node indexing matches the hop indexing, but not in general.

The encoding of the message bits in the tree should allow the reconstruction of the message by applying GetMessage to the final hop according to following definition. Note that reconstructing the message from the nodes is an operation that is relevant in proving soundness rather than something to be used in practice.

Definition 1. *GetMessage is defined by the following recursion:*

- *GetMessage(message hop) is the message hop's message string*
- *GetMessage(chaining hop) = DeInterleave(L, I), where*
  - *L is an ordered list obtained by calling GetMessage() on each child hop,*
  - *I is the input chaining hop's interleaving block size attribute, and*
  - *DeInterleave(L, I) extracts the first I bits from L_0, then the first I bits from L_1, ..., up to the last item of list, then back to L_0, and so on, until all strings in L are empty. Extracting more bits than available reduces to extracting all remaining bits.*

Definition 2. *A tree template is SAKURA-compatible if its nodes are compliant with the coding specified in Figure 4, if the number of $\langle CV \rangle$ and the block interleaving size are coded as explained above, and if the chaining bits and message bits are as defined above.*

3.2 Illustrations

We apply the SAKURA encoding to the examples depicted on Figures 1, 2 and 3. In these examples, we use the following conventions. Bit values are written as 0 or 1, while sequences of 8 bits can be written in hexadecimal notation prefixed with 0x with numerical value following Eq. (1). Spaces are inserted only for reading purposes. If M_α is a message hop, we denote by M_α its message bits. Similarly, if Z_α is a chaining hop, we denote by $\{\mathtt{I}_\alpha\}$ the encoding of its interleaving block size. Then, CV_β is the chaining value resulting from the application of f to the node with index β. Finally, $\mathtt{0}^*$ indicates a non-negative number of bits 0 determined by the tree hash mode, typically inserted for alignment purposes.

The example corresponding to Figure 1 is given in Table 1. In the final node, ⟨*node*⟩ expands to ⟨*message hop*⟩ ⟨*padSimple*⟩ ⟨*chaining hop*⟩, while in all other nodes it simply expands to ⟨*message hop*⟩.

The example corresponding to Figure 2 is given in Table 2. In two inner nodes, ⟨*node*⟩ expands to ⟨*message hop*⟩ ⟨*padSimple*⟩ ⟨*chaining hop*⟩ and in two other inner nodes, ⟨*node*⟩ expands to ⟨*message hop*⟩. In the final node, ⟨*node*⟩ simply expands to ⟨*chaining hop*⟩.

For sequential hashing (Figure 3), this reduces to a single final node containing M11, and the relationship between the inner and outer hash functions reduces to

$$F(M) = f(M\|\mathtt{11}). \tag{2}$$

Table 1. Encoding for the hop tree example depicted in Figure 1

Node index	Encoding
2	$M_3 1\ 10^*\ 0$
1	$M_2 1\ 10^*\ 0$
0	$M_1 1\ 10^*\ 0$
*	$M_0 1\ 10^*\ CV_0\ CV_1\ CV_2\ \text{0x03}\ \text{0x01}\ \{I_*\}0\ 1$

Table 2. Encoding for the hop tree example depicted in Figure 2

Node index	Encoding
10	$M_{11} 1\ 10^*\ 0$
1	$M_{10} 1\ 10^*\ CV_{10}\ \text{0x01}\ \text{0x01}\ \{I_1\}0\ 10^*\ 0$
00	$M_{01} 1\ 10^*\ 0$
0	$M_{00} 1\ 10^*\ CV_{00}\ \text{0x01}\ \text{0x01}\ \{I_0\}0\ 10^*\ 0$
*	$CV_0\ CV_1\ \text{0x02}\ \text{0x01}\ \{I_*\}0\ 1$

4   Sakura-Compatible Tree Hash Modes and Soundness

We define SAKURA-compatible tree hash modes in the following way.

Definition 3. *A tree hash mode is* SAKURA-*compatible if it generates only* SAKURA-*compatible templates.*

We will now prove that any SAKURA-compatible tree hash mode, as well as the union of any set of SAKURA-compatible tree hash modes, is sound by proving a number of lemmas.

We start by defining S as a tree hash mode that can generate all SAKURA-compatible templates. By construction, this mode is SAKURA-compatible. Its parameters A must describe the whole hop tree structure with each hop's attributes, plus the length of all message blocks and the number of zeroes inserted by ⟨*padSimple*⟩. This mode is not meant to be used in practice but only in the scope of this proof.

Lemma 1. *Given a node instance produced by S (i.e., with SAKURA coding) and the knowledge of the security strength of f, one can recover indices of all hops, the message strings of the message hops, the location and indices (relative to the given node instance index) of the chaining values, and the interleaving block size attributes of all chaining hops.*

Proof. From the definition of SAKURA in Figure 4, it is clear that a ⟨*node*⟩, obtained after removing the trailing bit from a ⟨*final node*⟩ or ⟨*inner node*⟩ (and in the latter case, also removing the ⟨*padSimple*⟩ padding), consists of a possible ⟨*message hop*⟩ followed by one or more ⟨*chaining hop*⟩s, with simple padding in between. A ⟨*chaining hop*⟩ in turn consists of a sequence of ⟨*CV*⟩s followed by an encoding of their number and a ⟨*interleaving block size*⟩.

Parsing a ⟨*node*⟩ can be done starting at the end. If the last bit is 1 it simply consists of a single message hop. Otherwise, it ends with a chaining hop. In the latter case, the last two bytes code the interleaving block size of the chaining hop and the byte before that denotes the length of the field coding the number of chaining values and allows localizing it. Decoding this field yields the number of chaining values and together with their lengths uniquely determines their positions in the node, including the start of the chaining hop in the node. This allows continuing the parsing until reaching the beginning of the ⟨*node*⟩ or the end of the ⟨*message hop*⟩ in the beginning of the ⟨*node*⟩.

The interleaving block size of a chaining hop can be computed from the coding in ⟨*interleaving block size*⟩ at its end and the message string of the ⟨*message hop*⟩ (if any) can be obtained by removing the trailing bit 1.

The index of the last ⟨*chaining hop*⟩ is that of the ⟨*node*⟩. Whenever kangaroo hopping is used, the index of a ⟨*chaining hop*⟩ or ⟨*message hop*⟩ is recursively the index of the next ⟨*chaining hop*⟩ with 0 concatenated to it. This is in line with the node indexing specified in Section 3.1.

The indices of the nodes corresponding with the ⟨*CV*⟩s in a ⟨*node*⟩ can be obtained by appending to the last hop index 0 for the first CV, 1 for the second and so on, throughout all the ⟨*chaining hop*⟩s of the node instance from beginning to end.   □

To prove the soundess of S, we use the three conditions that are shown to be sufficient in [6]. We now informally summarize them.

- The mode must be *tree-decodable*. This means that the tree can be parsed to retrieve the frame bits, message bits and chaining bits unambiguously. There must be a decoding algorithm A_{decode} that can parse the tree progressively on subtrees, starting from the final node only, and each time adding a new inner node and pointing at the corresponding chaining value. Also, the process must terminate by requiring that one can distinguish between complete and compliant trees, subtrees that are compliant except for some missing nodes (called *final-subtree-compliant*), and incompliant trees.
- The mode must be *message-complete*. This means that the message can be reconstructed from the complete tree.
- The mode must be *final-node separable*. This essentially means that one can tell the difference between final nodes and inner nodes.

Lemma 2. *The tree hash mode S is tree-decodable.*

Proof. First, there are no tree instances that are both compliant and final-subtree-compliant. Lemma 1 proves that one can always unambiguously decode chaining values and distinguish them from other kind of bits given only one node instance. This means that a final subtree S is a proper final subtree iff there are chaining values pointing to nodes missing in S.

Second, the algorithm A_{decode} can be defined as follows. Given a tree instance S with index set J, it first recursively decodes tree node instances of S as in the proof of Lemma 1. If at any point, the coding does not follow the grammar defined in Figure 4 or when the string is too short to contain the number of $\langle CV \rangle$s coded in $\langle coded\ nrCVs \rangle$, it returns "incompliant".

The algorithm A_{decode} then looks for nodes that have chaining values pointing to nodes missing in S (i.e., whose index is not in J). If there no such chaining values, return "compliant". Otherwise, return "final-subtree-compliant" and the index of such a missing node using a deterministic rule (e.g., the missing node with the first index in lexicographical order).

The algorithm A_{decode} runs in linear time in the number of bits in the tree instance, as can be seen in the proof of Lemma 1.   □

Lemma 3. *The tree hash mode S is message-complete.*

Proof. Given a compliant tree instance S, the algorithm A_{message} can be defined similarly to the `GetMessage` function in Definition 1. From Lemma 1, the necessary hop attributes can be extracted from the tree instance.

Clearly, this algorithm runs in linear time in the number of bits in the tree instance.   □

Lemma 4. *The tree hash mode S is final-node separable.*

Proof. SAKURA enforces domain separation between final and inner nodes, as the trailing bit of a final node is always 1 and that of an inner node is always 0.
    □

Theorem 1. *Any SAKURA-compatible tree hash mode, as well as the union of any set of SAKURA-compatible tree hash modes, is sound.*

Proof. From the previous lemmas and [6, Theorem 1], it follows that $\mathcal{S}$ is sound.

The set $\mathcal{Z}_\mathcal{T}$ of tree templates that a SAKURA-compatible tree hash mode $\mathcal{T}$ produces is included in those produced by $\mathcal{S}$, i.e., $\mathcal{Z}_\mathcal{T} \subseteq \mathcal{Z}_\mathcal{S}$. Therefore, $\mathcal{T}$ can be implemented by running $\mathcal{S}$ as a sub-procedure, after encoding $\mathcal{T}$'s parameters in the format that $\mathcal{S}$ accepts. This only restricts what an attacker can query, so $\mathcal{T}$ is at least as secure as $\mathcal{S}$.

When taking the union of two or more SAKURA-compatible tree hash modes, if the tree instances produced by each of the united modes are SAKURA-compatible, then so are the tree instances produced by the union. It follows that the union of SAKURA-compatible tree hash modes is SAKURA-compatible and the argument above carries over to the union.   □

5   Examples of Tree Hash Modes

In this section we give some examples of tree hash modes that can be realized with the SAKURA coding. In general, specifying a mode mainly comes down to specifying how the tree grows as a function of the size of the input message. These modes are parameterized and the value of the parameters must be known at the time of hashing a message.

For fully specifying a tree hash mode compliant with SAKURA, one has to specify the number of hops and their indices, how the message bits are distributed onto message hops, and for each chaining hop whether kangaroo hopping is applied. In addition, the mode has to specify the length of the padding elements as they appear in the grammar of Figure 4. For the padding between hops, this can be derived from a simple strategy, such as always align on bytes, on 64-bit boundaries or on the input block size (or rate) of the inner hash function f. If desired, the mode can also specify how to use the padding at the end of inner nodes to ensure that sibling nodes executed in parallel branches have the same length.

In our examples, unless otherwise specified, the message is split into B-bit blocks M_i, i.e.,

$$M = M_0 || M_1 || \ldots || M_{n-1},$$

with $n = \lceil |M|/B \rceil$ and where the last block M_{n-1} may be shorter than B bits.

5.1   Final Node Growing

With final node growing, the hop tree has fixed height 1 and the number of leaves increases as a function of the input message length. There is only a single chaining hop, namely the final hop. The indices of the message hops are integers 0 to $n-1$ and the message string in message hop with index i is M_i, hence each message hop has a fixed maximum size B. Interleaving is not applied, so the interleaving block size in the final hop is $I = \infty$.

This mode can be useful to enable a large amount of potential parallelism, namely up to $n = \lceil |M|/B \rceil$ message hops can be processed in parallel if the corresponding message blocks are available at the same time. In practice, a number p of independent processes P_j, $j = 0, \ldots, p - 1$ can be set up, which does not depend on the tree structure other than in the total number of message hops. Each process P_j could take care of message hops with indices $j + kp$.

The drawback of this method is an extra cost proportional to the message length, as n chaining values of length c must be processed in the final node. This extra cost represents approximately a fraction c/B of the nominal work, which can be made arbitrarily small by choosing B large enough.

This mode has two parameters:

- B, the maximum size of message string in message hops, and
- whether or not kangaroo hopping shall be applied in the final hop.

5.2   Leaf Interleaving

With leaf interleaving, the hop tree has a fixed topology, i.e., its height is 1 and it has D message hops, with D a parameter. The size of the message hops depends on the input message length. The message is distributed over the leaves as it arrives in blocks of size B. The message hops have indices $i \in \{0, 1, \ldots, D - 1\}$ and their message string is $M_i \| M_{i+D} \| \ldots \| M_{i+(s_i-1)D}$ with $s_i = \lceil (n - i)/D \rceil$. The interleaving block size in the final hop shall be set to $I = B$. If $|M| < DB$, there are message hops with zero message bits. (Note that an alternate message assignment procedure is proposed later in this section.)

This mode is useful if one wants to hash a message in up to D parallel threads. The drawback is that D represents a limit in the potential parallelism, and this value must be chosen beforehand.

This method has a fixed extra cost, independent of the message length, as the final node has to process D chaining values.

This mode has three parameters:

- B, the interleaving block size,
- D, the number of message hops, and
- whether or not kangaroo hopping shall be applied in the final hop.

Ensuring Equal-Length Inner Nodes. In the implementation, it may be interesting to ensure that all the D nodes processed simultaneously have equal block length w.r.t. the inner function f. For the D (or $D-1$, if kangaroo hopping is applied) inner nodes, this can be achieved by systematically adding bits with value 0 in the ⟨padSimple⟩ padding of the ⟨inner node⟩ production rule. A simple procedure consists in adding padding bits so as to match the length of the longest inner node.

When kangaroo hopping is applied, the final node has the possibility to add padding bits after the message hop, just before the chaining values of the $D - 1$ inner nodes are added, i.e., in the ⟨padSimple⟩ padding of the ⟨kangaroo hopping⟩ production rule. The processing of all D pieces of message can therefore be aligned, even with kangaroo hopping.

Avoiding Systematic Block Alignment. Implementations can also be made easier when the interleaving block size B is equal to, or a multiple of, the input block size (or rate) r of the inner hash function f. This avoids re-shuffling of the input message bytes, in particular for implementations that process less than D nodes in parallel.

But there is a potential efficiency problem in this case if care is not taken in the way the message bits are spread on the D message hops, in particular for the last $|M|$ mod DB bits. If the message bits are cyclically spread by blocks of B bits onto the D message hops until exhaustion, message hops will very often contain a whole number of r-bit blocks. After adding frame and padding bits, the resulting nodes will systematically be just a few bits longer than a whole number of r-bit blocks. This would be unfortunate, as the inner function f would need to process an additional block containing only frame and padding bits and no message payload, and this amounts to quite an extra fixed cost compared to just processing the final hop. E.g., if $B = r = 1024$, $D = 4$ and the message length is 3208 (mod 4096), the last 3208 bits would be split as $1024 + 1024 + 1024 + 136$, causing 3 extra blocks to be absorbed without any payload.

To address this, the mode can simply spread the last $|M|$ mod DB bits as equally as possible (up to, say, bytes) onto the D hops. The mode remains Sakura-compatible since the GetMessage function in Definition 1 simply concatenates the last blocks of each nodes, even if they have less than $I = B$ bits. Taking the same example as above, the last 3208 bits could instead be spread as $800 + 800 + 800 + 808$ and avoid the 3 extra blocks mentioned above. Note that this technique requires to know the end of the message DB bits in advance or to have a buffer of DB bits.

Let us specify a possible alternate procedure, which we illustrate in the case that the message and interleaving block sizes are byte-aligned, i.e., $|M|$ and B are multiples of 8. With $m = |M|/8$ and $b = B/8$, we concentrate on the last m mod Db bytes. If m mod $Db = 0$, message hops all contain whole blocks, and there is nothing to do. If m mod $Db > 0$, we proceed as follows.

- Let M' be the last m mod Db bytes of M.
- For i from 0 to $D - 1$:
  - Move the first $\lfloor \frac{m+i}{D} \rfloor$ remaining bytes from M' to the i-th message hop.

5.3 Macro- and Microscopic Leaf Interleaving

Different orders of magnitudes for the block interleaving size I can be useful depending on the kind of parallelism that one wishes to exploit. At one end of the spectrum is a single-instruction multiple-data (SIMD) unit of a modern processor or core. Such a unit can naturally compute two (or more) instances of the same primitive in parallel. For the processor or core to be able to fetch data in one shot, it is interesting to process simultaneously data blocks that are located close to one another. Suitable I values for addressing this are, e.g., 64 bits or the input block size (or rate) of f.

At the other end of the spectrum is the case of independent processors, cores or even machines that process different parts of the input in parallel. In contrast, it is here important to avoid different processors or cores having to fetch the same memory addresses, or to avoid copying identical blocks of data for two different machines. Suitable I values for addressing this are in the order of kilobytes or megabytes.

The two cases can coexist, for instance, if several cores are used to hash in parallel and each core has a SIMD unit. A suitable tree structure is one with height 2, as depicted in Figure 2. The subtrees rooted by Z_0 and Z_1 are handled by different cores, whereas the leaves are processed together in the SIMD units. The final hop Z_* splits the message to hash into macroscopic blocks (large I), while the intermediate chaining hops Z_0 and Z_1 further split the macroscopic blocks into microscopic blocks suitable for the SIMD unit (small I).

The tree hash mode of Section 5.2 can be generalized to support such mixed interleaving block sizes.

5.4 Binary Tree

With a binary tree, the tree topology evolves as a function of the input message size. All chaining hops have degree 2, and the message strings in the message hops have a fixed maximum size B. The height of the message hops depends on the length of the message and the position of the message string of that message hop in the message. Interleaving is not applied, so the interleaving block size in all chaining hops is $I = \infty$.

This mode is useful if one wants to limit the effort to re-compute the hash when only a small part of the message changes. This requires that the chaining values are stored. Hence, in this application, kangaroo hopping is not interesting.

The hop tree can be defined in the following way. We first arrange the message blocks M_i in a linear array to form the message hops. Each message hop can be seen as a tree with height 0. Then we apply the following procedure iteratively: combine the trees in pairs starting from 0 by adding a chaining hop and connecting the two root hops to it. If the number of trees is odd, the last tree is just kept as such. Applying this $\lceil \log_2 n \rceil$ times will reduce the number of trees to a single one. The most recently added hop is the final hop. The indices of the hops follow directly from the tree topology.

This mode has one parameter: B, the maximum size of message strings in the message hops.

6 Application to Keccak and SHA-3

In the future, one may standardize tree hash modes. By adopting SAKURA coding from the start, any future SAKURA-compatible tree hash mode using KECCAK [4] as inner function can be introduced while guaranteeing soundness of the union of that new mode and any compatible tree hash mode(s) defined up to that point. The sequential hash mode will then simply correspond with the single-hop case of Figure 3. As shown in Eq. (2), this comes down to appending two bits to the message before presenting to the inner function.

As NIST proposed to standardize both arbitrary output length instances (SHAKE128 and SHAKE256) and SHA-2 drop-in replacement instances (SHA3-224 to SHA3-512) with their traditional fixed output length [12], we think that it would not make much sense to combine tree hashing with the latter. The reason is that to carry over the full security of the underlying hash function, one has to set the tree-level chaining value length n equal to the capacity c (or n equal to twice the security strength in general). As for SHA3-n, NIST sets $c = 2n$, so one would need to define some ad-hoc construction on top of it to get two output blocks (like a mask generating function), and this would be absurd given that SHA3-n is obtained by truncating KECCAK's output.

One may additionally require domain separation between SHA-3 and future uses of KECCAK, or even between different instances of SHA-3. For the SHA-3 instances that would foresee tree hashing, domain separation can be applied at the level of the inner function f:

$$f(x) = \text{KECCAK}[r, c](x \| \text{domain separation suffix}).$$

If this additional domain separation is realized by appending sufficiently few bits, there is no performance penalty for messages that consist of byte sequences and rate values that are a multiple of 8. In particular, the multi-rate padding in KECCAK adds at least 2 bits and at most r bits. For byte sequences this becomes at least 1 byte and at most $r/8$ bytes. So up to 6 bits can be appended to the message without impacting these minimum and maximum values.

Acknowledgments. We would like to thank Stefan Lucks, Dan Bernstein and the members of the NIST hash team for useful discussions.

References

1. Bellare, M., Rogaway, P.: Random oracles are practical: A paradigm for designing efficient protocols. In: ACM Conference on Computer and Communications Security 1993, pp. 62–73. ACM (1993)
2. Bertoni, G., Daemen, J., Peeters, M., Van Assche, G.: On the indifferentiability of the sponge construction. In: Smart, N.P. (ed.) EUROCRYPT 2008. LNCS, vol. 4965, pp. 181–197. Springer, Heidelberg (2008), http://sponge.noekeon.org/
3. Bertoni, G., Daemen, J., Peeters, M., Van Assche, G.: Sufficient conditions for sound tree hashing modes, Symmetric Cryptography. In: Handschuh, H., Lucks, S., Preneel, B., Rogaway, P. (eds.) Dagstuhl Seminar Proceedings, no. 09031, Dagstuhl, Germany. Schloss Dagstuhl - Leibniz-Zentrum fuer Informatik, Germany (2009)
4. Bertoni, G., Daemen, J., Peeters, M., Van Assche, G.: The Keccak reference (January 2011), http://keccak.noekeon.org/
5. Bertoni, G., Daemen, J., Peeters, M., Van Assche, G.: Keccak and the SHA3 standardization, presentation at NIST (February 2013), http://csrc.nist.gov/groups/ST/hash/sha-3/documents/Keccak-slides-at-NIST.pdf

6. Bertoni, G., Daemen, J., Peeters, M., Van Assche, G.: Sufficient conditions for sound tree and sequential hashing modes. International Journal of Information Security (2013), http://dx.doi.org/10.1007/s10207-013-0220-y

7. Coron, J.-S., Dodis, Y., Malinaud, C., Puniya, P.: Merkle-damgård revisited: How to construct a hash function. In: Shoup, V. (ed.) CRYPTO 2005. LNCS, vol. 3621, pp. 430–448. Springer, Heidelberg (2005)

8. Damgård, I.: A design principle for hash functions. In: Brassard, G. (ed.) CRYPTO 1989. LNCS, vol. 435, pp. 416–427. Springer, Heidelberg (1990)

9. Dodis, Y., Reyzin, L., Rivest, R.L., Shen, E.: Indifferentiability of permutation-based compression functions and tree-based modes of operation, with applications to MD6. In: Dunkelman, O. (ed.) FSE 2009. LNCS, vol. 5665, pp. 104–121. Springer, Heidelberg (2009)

10. Ferguson, N., Lucks, S., Schneier, B., Whiting, D., Bellare, M., Kohno, T., Callas, J., Walker, J.: The Skein hash function family, Submission to NIST (2008), http://skein-hash.info/

11. Gueron, S.: A j-lanes tree hashing mode and j-lanes SHA-256. Journal of Information Security 4, 4–11 (2013)

12. Kelsey, J.: Moving forward with SHA3, NIST hash forum (November 2013), http://csrc.nist.gov/groups/ST/hash/sha-3/documents/kelsey-email-moving-forward-110113.pdf

13. RSA Laboratories, PKCS # 1 v2.2 RSA Cryptography Standard (2012)

14. Lucks, S.: Tree hashing: A simple generic tree hashing mode designed for SHA-2 and SHA-3, applicable to other hash functions, Early Symmetric Crypto (ESC) (2013)

15. Lucks, S., McGrew, D., Whiting, D.: Batteries included: Features and modes for next generation hash functions. In: The Third SHA-3 Candidate Conference (2012)

16. Maurer, U., Renner, R., Holenstein, C.: Indifferentiability, impossibility results on reductions, and applications to the random oracle methodology. In: Naor, M. (ed.) TCC 2004. LNCS, vol. 2951, pp. 21–39. Springer, Heidelberg (2004)

17. Merkle, R.C.: Secrecy, authentication, and public key systems, PhD thesis. UMI Research Press (1982)

18. NIST, Mailing list on NIST's cryptographic hash workshops and hash algorithm competition, http://csrc.nist.gov/groups/ST/hash/email_list.html

19. Merkle, R.C.: NIST special publication 800-57, recommendation for key management (March 2007) (revised)

20. Overell, P.: Augmented BNF for syntax specifications: ABNF, Internet Request for Comments, RFC 5234 (January 2008)

21. Rivest, R., Agre, B., Bailey, D.V., Cheng, S., Crutchfield, C., Dodis, Y., Fleming, K.E., Khan, A., Krishnamurthy, J., Lin, Y., Reyzin, L., Shen, E., Sukha, J., Sutherland, D., Tromer, E., Yin, Y.L.: The MD6 hash function – a proposal to NIST for SHA-3, Submission to NIST (2008), http://groups.csail.mit.edu/cis/md6/

22. Sarkar, P., Schellenberg, P.J.: A parallelizable design principle for cryptographic hash functions, Cryptology ePrint Archive, Report 2002/031 (2002), http://eprint.iacr.org/

23. Torgerson, M., Schroeppel, R., Draelos, T., Dautenhahn, N., Malone, S., Walker, A., Collins, M., Orman, H.: The SANDstorm hash, Submission to NIST (2008), http://www.sandia.gov/scada/documents/SANDstorm_Submission_2008_10_30.pdf

Reset Indifferentiability from Weakened Random Oracle Salvages One-Pass Hash Functions

Yusuke Naito[1,3], Kazuki Yoneyama[2], and Kazuo Ohta[3]

[1] Mitsubishi Electric Corporation
`Naito.Yusuke@ce.MitsubishiElectric.co.jp`
[2] NTT Secure Platform Laboratories
`yoneyama.kazuki@lab.ntt.co.jp`
[3] The University of Electro-Communications
`kazuo.ohta@uec.ac.jp`

Abstract. Ristenpart et al. (EUROCRYPT 2011) showed that the indifferentiability theorem of Maurer et al. (TCC 2004) does not cover all multi-stage security notions; it only covers single-stage security notions. They defined reset indifferentiability, and proved the reset indifferentiability theorem, which covers all security notions; if a hash function is reset indifferentiable from a random oracle denoted by $\mathcal{RO}$, for any security, any cryptosystem is at least as secure under the hash function as in the $\mathcal{RO}$ model. Unfortunately, they also proved the impossibility of one-pass hash functions such as ChopMD and Sponge; there exists a multi-security notion such that some cryptosystem is secure in the $\mathcal{RO}$ model but insecure when $\mathcal{RO}$ is replaced with a one-pass hash function.

In order to ensure other multi-stage security notions, we propose a new methodology, called the $\mathcal{WRO}$ methodology, instead of the $\mathcal{RO}$ methodology. We consider "Reset Indifferentiability from Weakened Random Oracle" which salvages ChopMD and Sponge. The concrete procedure of the $\mathcal{WRO}$ methodology is as follows:
1. Define a new concept of $\mathcal{WRO}$ instead of $\mathcal{RO}$,
2. Prove that a hash function H is reset indifferentiable from $\mathcal{WRO}$, (here the examples are ChopMD and Sponge), and
3. For multi-stage security $\mathcal{G}$, prove that a cryptosystem C is $\mathcal{G}$-secure in the $\mathcal{WRO}$ model.

As a result, C with H is $\mathcal{G}$-secure by combining the results of Steps 2, 3, and the theorem of Ristenpart et al. Moreover, for a public-key encryption scheme (as C) and the chosen-distribution attack game (as the game of $\mathcal{G}$) we prove that $C(\mathcal{WRO})$ is $\mathcal{G}$-secure, which implies the appropriateness of the new concept of the $\mathcal{WRO}$ methodology.

Keywords: Indifferentiable hash function, reset indifferentiability, multi-stage game, Sponge, ChopMD.

1 Introduction

1.1 Indifferentiability

The Indifferentiability theorem [12] of Maurer, Renner, and Holenstein (MRH), called MRH theorem, covers all single-stage security notions $\mathbf{G}_s$ and all cryptosystems $\mathbf{C}$; for

I. Boureanu, P. Owesarski, and S. Vaudenay (Eds.): ACNS 2014, LNCS 8479, pp. 235–252, 2014.

$\forall \mathcal{G} \in \mathbf{G}_s$ and $\forall C \in \mathbf{C}$, C is at least as $\mathcal{G}$-secure in the F_1 model as in the F_2 model, denoted by $C(F_1) >_{\mathcal{G}} C(F_2)$, if "$F_1$ is indifferentiable from F_2", denoted by $F_1 \sqsubset F_2$. The game of $F_1 \sqsubset F_2$ is a simulation based game where some stateful simulator S is constructed, which represents some adversary in the F_2 model, thereby this game ensures that any adversary in the F_1 model can obtain some information in the F_2 model due to S. Thus, this framework distinguishes interfaces of F which are adversarial and honest interfaces, denoted by $F.adv$ and $F.hon$, respectively. Adversaries are permitted to access to the adversarial interface, and honest parties are permitted to access to the honest interface. The definition of $F_1 \sqsubset F_2$ is that there exists a stateful simulator S such that for any distinguisher $\mathcal{D}$ which interacts with two oracles (L, R), no $\mathcal{D}$ can distinguish real world $(L, R) = (F_1.hon, F_1.adv)$ from ideal world $(L, R) = (F_2.hon, S^{F_2.adv})$ where S has access to $F_2.adv$. MRH proved the following theorem:

MRH Theorem.[12] $F_1 \sqsubset F_2 \Rightarrow \forall C \in \mathbf{C}, \forall \mathcal{G} \in \mathbf{G}_s: C(F_1) >_{\mathcal{G}} C(F_2)$.

1.2 $\mathcal{RO}$ Methodology

Coron, Dodis, Malinaud, and Puniya [7] pointed out that the MRH theorem opened a nice modular approach for security proofs of cryptosystems using hash function $H^{\mathcal{U}}$; $H^{\mathcal{U}} \sqsubset \mathcal{RO} \Rightarrow \forall C \in \mathbf{C}, \forall \mathcal{G} \in \mathbf{G}_s: C(H^{\mathcal{U}}) >_{\mathcal{G}} C(\mathcal{RO})$ where it is assumed that the underlying primitive $\mathcal{U}$ is ideal. Thus designers of hash functions only have to concentrate on designing H such that $H^{\mathcal{U}} \sqsubset \mathcal{RO}$, and ones of cryptosystems concentrate on designing of C such that C is $\mathcal{G}$-secure in the $\mathcal{RO}$ model. This approach is called as the Random Oracle ($\mathcal{RO}$) methodology. In the proof of $H^{\mathcal{U}} \sqsubset \mathcal{RO}$, the real world is $(L, R) = (H^{\mathcal{U}}, \mathcal{U})$ and the ideal world is $(L, R) = (\mathcal{RO}, S^{\mathcal{RO}})$. Hereafter, we call hash function $H^{\mathcal{U}}$ such that $H^{\mathcal{U}} \sqsubset \mathcal{RO}$ an "IFRO (indifferentiable from a $\mathcal{RO}$) hash function" and its construction the "IFRO hash construction".

So far, many IFRO hash constructions have been proposed such as the Chop Merkle-Damgård (ChopMD) construction [7] and the Sponge construction [4]. SHA-512/224 and SHA-512/256, which are standarized in FIPS 180-4 [17], employ the ChopMD construction, and the SHA-3 winner Keccak [16,5] employs the Sponge construction. Therefore, IFRO security is an important criterion of designing hash functions.

1.3 Impossibility of IFRO Security in Multi-Stage Security Games

However, Ristenpart, Shacham, and Shrimpton (RSS) [18] pointed out that the MRH theorem covers all single-stage security notions $\mathbf{G}_s$, while it does not cover all multi-stage security notions $\mathbf{G}_m$.

The impossibility is from a difference of conditions of "state" sizes between indifferentiability and multi-stage security. Indifferentiability deals with a "stateful" simulator, that is, the size of the sate of the simulator is not restricted. On the other hand, in multi-stage games, the size of the state shared among adversaries is restricted.

They gave an example meeting the impossibility. They defined a two party challenge response protocol $C\mathcal{R}$ and multi-stage security, called CRP-security. They showed that $C\mathcal{R}$ is CRP-secure in the $\mathcal{RO}$ model but insecure when using IFRO one-pass hash functions such as the ChopMD hash function and the Sponge hash function.

Note that the RSS result does not always imply that for $\forall G \in \mathbf{G}_m$ and $\forall C \in \mathbf{C}$, C is G-secure in the $\mathcal{RO}$ model and insecure when using $H^{\mathcal{U}}$. So we have the following question:

"Can we prove the G-security of $C(H^{\mathcal{U}})$?"

This paper tackles how to solve this question. The candidate to solve this question is reset indifferentiability of RSS [18].

1.4   Reset Indifferentiability

The reset indifferentiability framework is the extension of the indifferentiability framework and this theorem, called RSS theorem, covers all security notions $\mathbf{G} \ (= \mathbf{G}_s \cup \mathbf{G}_m)$. The RSS theorem ensures that for $\forall G \in \mathbf{G}$ and $\forall C \in \mathbf{C}$, $C(F_1) >_G C(F_2)$ if F_1 is reset indifferentiable from F_2, denoted by $F_1 \sqsubset_r F_2$. The reset indifferentiable game is the same simulation based game as the indifferentiable game [12]. The difference is that indifferentiability deals with a stateful simulator, while reset indifferentiability deals with a *stateless* simulator. The "stateless" setting reflects the settings of multi-stage security games where the state size among adversaries is restricted. So the definition of $F_1 \sqsubset_r F_2$ is that there exists a stateless simulator S such that for any distinguisher $\mathcal{D}$ which interacts with two oracles (L, R), no $\mathcal{D}$ can distinguish a real world $(L, R) = (F_1.hon, F_2.adv)$ from an ideal world $(L, R) = (F_2.hon, S^{F_2.adv})$. RSS proved the following theorem.

RSS Theorem. [18] $F_1 \sqsubset_r F_2 \Rightarrow \forall G \in \mathbf{G}, \forall C \in \mathbf{C} : C(F_1) >_G C(F_2)$.

And, the RSS theorem offers the corollary: $H^{\mathcal{U}} \sqsubset_r \mathcal{RO} \Rightarrow \forall G \in \mathbf{G}, \forall C \in \mathbf{C} : C(H^{\mathcal{U}}) >_G C(\mathcal{RO})$.

Unfortunately, RSS also proved the *impossibility* of $H^{\mathcal{U}} \sqsubset_r \mathcal{RO}$ where H is a one-pass hash construction such as the ChopMD construction and the Sponge construction. Therefore, we have to consider another solution than the $\mathcal{RO}$ methodology.

1.5   Our Contributions – A New Proposal of $\mathcal{WRO}$ Methodology –

We propose a $\mathcal{WRO}$ methodology which is based on "Reset Indifferentiability from Weakened Random Oracle ($\mathcal{WRO}$)" in order to ensure the G-security of $C(H^{\mathcal{U}})$. This paper deals with the ChopMD construction and the fixed output length Sponge (FOL-Sponge) construction as H, because these are employed in important hash functions such as SHA-512/224, SHA-512/256, and SHA-3 winner Keccak.

The concrete proof procedure of the $\mathcal{WRO}$ methodology is as follows:

1. Define a new concept of $\mathcal{WRO}$ instead of $\mathcal{RO}$,
2. Prove that $H^{\mathcal{U}} \sqsubset_r \mathcal{WRO}$ assuming $\mathcal{U}$ is ideal, and
3. Prove that C is G-secure in the $\mathcal{WRO}$ model.

As a result we can ensure that $C(H^{\mathcal{U}})$ is G-secure by combining the results of Steps 2 and 3, and the RSS theorem. Moreover, for public-key encryption (as cryptosystem C) and Chosen Distribution Attack [1,2] (as game G) we prove that $C(\mathcal{WRO})$ is G-secure, which implies the appropriateness of the new concept of the $\mathcal{WRO}$ model.

$\mathcal{D}$'s Procedure 1 (Condition 1)
1. $\mathcal{D}$ makes a query x to R and receives the response y_1.
2. $\mathcal{D}$ makes a query x to R and receives the response y_2.

Fig. 1. Distinguisher's Procedure 1

$\mathcal{D}$'s Procedure 2 (Condition 2)
1. $\mathcal{D}$ makes a query $IV\|M_1$ to R and receives the response y_1
2. $\mathcal{D}$ makes a query $y_1\|M_2$ to R and receives the response y_2

Fig. 2. Distinguisher's Procedure 2

We define $\mathcal{WRO}$ so that one can construct a stateless simulator such that $H^{\mathcal{U}} \sqsubseteq_r \mathcal{WRO}$, that is, an adversary can simulate information of $\mathcal{U}$ ($= H^{\mathcal{U}}.adv$) from $\mathcal{WRO}.adv$. Thus $\mathcal{WRO}$ consists of $\mathcal{RO}$ and sub oracle O^* which leaks information to simulate $\mathcal{U}$, and the interfaces are defined as $\mathcal{WRO}.hon = \mathcal{RO}$ and $\mathcal{WRO}.adv = (\mathcal{RO}, O^*)$.

To our knowledge, our result is the first result to ensure the reducibility from a real model to an ideal model for the important hash constructions, ChopMD and FOLSponge.

How to Define O^*. We explain how to define O^* by basing on the proof of ChopMD$^h \sqsubseteq \mathcal{RO}$, where $h : \{0, 1\}^{m+2n} \to \{0, 1\}^{2n}$ is a random oracle compression function. For two block message $M_1\|M_2$, the output of ChopMD is calculated as ChopMD$^h(M_1\|M_2) = chop_n(h(h(IV\|M_1)\|M_2))$ where $chop_n$ accepts $2n$ bit value $x'\|x^*$ and returns the right n bit value x^*. In this case, the real world is $(L, R) = (\text{ChopMD}^h, h)$. In the indifferentiable game, distinguisher $\mathcal{D}$ tries to distinguish the real world from the ideal world by using query-response values of (L, R). Therefore, the following two points are required to construct a simulator S. The first point is the simulation of h. The second point is the simulation of the relation between L and R in the real world, because L uses R in the real world. We explain the simulations by considering the use of the S's state.

Simulation of h: We explain the simulation of h by using Fig. 1. This example is that $\mathcal{D}$ makes a repeated query. In the real world the responses y_1 and y_2 satisfy the following conditions, since R is a random oracle h,
  – **Condition 1:** y_1 is a random value and $y_2 = y_1$.
  The following demonstrates that S can return responses satisfying the condition by using the S's state.
  – **Constructing S:** In Step 1 S chooses a random value as the response y_1 for the query x. Then S *records* the query response pair (x, y_1). In Step 2 S finds y_1 from the recorded pair (x, y_1), and defines $y_2 := y_1$.
Simulation of the L-R Relation: We explain the simulation of the relation between L and R by using Fig. 2. In the real world, since $(L, R) = (\text{ChopMD}^h, h)$, the query response values in Fig. 2 satisfy the following conditions.
  – **Condition 2:** $chop_n(y_1) = \text{ChopMD}^f(M_1)$ and $chop_n(y_2) = \text{ChopMD}^h(M_1\|M_2)$.
  The following shows that S can return responses satisfying the condition by using the S's state.

- **Constructing** S: In Step 1 S defines $y_1^* := \mathcal{RO}(M_1)$ for the query $IV\|M_1$, chooses a random value y_1', and defines $y_1 := y_1'\|y_1^*$. Then S *records* the pair (M_1, y_1). In Step 2, for the query $y_1\|M_2$, S finds M_1 from the recorded pair (M_1, y_1). Then S chooses a random value y_2', defines $y_2^* := \mathcal{RO}(M_1\|M_2)$, and $y_2 := y_2'\|y_2^*$. This procedure ensures that $chop_n(y_1) = \mathcal{RO}(M_1)$ and $chop_n(y_2) = \mathcal{RO}(M_1\|M_2)$.

Thus, we can construct a stateful simulator S which ensures the two points. On the other hand, we cannot construct a stateless simulator S which ensures the two points. So we compensate the stateless setting by using sub oracle O^*. We define the sub oracle as follows.

Sub Oracle for Simulation of h: In order to ensure the condition 1, we add random oracle $\mathcal{RO}^*$ to O^*. Then we can construct a stateless simulator S which ensures the condition 1: In Step 1 S defines $y_1 := \mathcal{RO}^*(x)$. In Step 2 S defines $y_2 := \mathcal{RO}^*(x)$. This procedure ensures that $y_1 = y_2$.

Sub Oracle for Simulation of $L\text{-}R$ Relation: In order to ensure the condition 2, we add random oracle $\mathcal{RO}^\dagger$ and trace oracle $\mathcal{TO}$ to O^*. The definition of $\mathcal{TO}$ is that for query y_1' to $\mathcal{TO}$, $\mathcal{TO}$ returns M_1 if a query M_1 to $\mathcal{RO}^\dagger$ was made such that $y_1' = \mathcal{RO}^\dagger(M_1)$, otherwise $\mathcal{TO}$ returns $\perp$. Then we can construct a stateless simulator S which ensures the condition 2: In Step 1, for query $IV\|M_1$, S defines $y_1' := \mathcal{RO}^\dagger(M_1)$ and $y_1^* := \mathcal{RO}(M_1)$, and $y_1 := y_1'\|y_1^*$. In Step 2, for query $y_1\|M_2$, S obtains y_1' from y_1 and makes a query y_1' to $\mathcal{TO}$. Then M_1 is returned from $\mathcal{TO}$. Finally S defines $y_2^* := \mathcal{RO}(M_1\|M_2)$ and $y_2' := \mathcal{RO}^\dagger(M_1\|M_2)$, and $y_2 := y_2'\|y_2^*$. This procedure ensures that $chop_n(y_1) = \mathcal{RO}(M_1)$ and $chop_n(y_2) = \mathcal{RO}(M_1\|M_2)$.

We thus define $O^* := (\mathcal{RO}^*, \mathcal{RO}^\dagger, \mathcal{TO})$, thereby we can construct a stateless simulator which ensures the above two conditions, and can prove ChopMD$^h \sqsubseteq_r \mathcal{WRO}$ (Theorem 2).

Similarly, for the FOLSponge construction, we define $O^* := (\mathsf{IC}, \mathcal{RO}^\dagger, \mathcal{TO})$, thereby we can construct a stateless simulator which ensures the above two simulations, and can prove FOLSponge $\sqsubseteq_r \mathcal{WRO}$ (Theorem 3) where $\mathsf{IC} = (E, D)$ is an ideal cipher. E is an encryption oracle and D is a decryption oracle.

Consequently, we define the sub oracle as $O^* := (\mathcal{RO}^*, \mathcal{RO}^\dagger, \mathcal{TO}, \mathsf{IC})$ in order to evaluate the ChopMD and the FOLSponge constructions by the single $\mathcal{WRO}$. Thus, $\mathcal{WRO}$ consists of $(\mathcal{RO}, \mathcal{RO}^*, \mathcal{RO}^\dagger, \mathcal{TO}, \mathsf{IC})$, and the interfaces are defined as $\mathcal{WRO}.hon = \mathcal{RO}$ and $\mathcal{WRO}.adv = (\mathcal{RO}, \mathcal{RO}^*, \mathcal{RO}^\dagger, \mathcal{TO}, \mathsf{IC})$.

Appropriateness of $\mathcal{WRO}$. We succeed to bypass the impossible result in [18] by introducing the $\mathcal{WRO}$ model; however, it is non-trivial if previous cryptosystems that are secure for multi-stage games in the $\mathcal{RO}$ model are still secure in the $\mathcal{WRO}$ model. Thus, the next step is to show that there exists a secure cryptosystem for a multi-stage game in the $\mathcal{WRO}$ model. We consider public-key encryption (PKE) (as cryptosystem C) for the Chosen Distribution Attack (CDA) game [1,2] (as game $\mathcal{G}$). Roughly, we say a PKE scheme is CDA secure if message privacy is preserved even if an adversary can control distributions of messages and randomness in generating the challenge ciphertext. The CDA game captures several flavors of PKE settings (e.g., deterministic PKE

(DPKE) [1,3,6,10,13], hedged PKE (HPKE) [2], and message-locked PKE (MLPKE)), and such PKE settings are tools for many practical applications. Thus, our target is to find a CDA secure cryptosystem in the $\mathcal{WRO}$ model.

First, we start with the result in [18]. They showed that any CPA secure PKE scheme in the $\mathcal{RO}$ model can be (redundancy-freely) transformed to an IND-SIM secure PKE scheme in the $\mathcal{RO}$ model via conversion REwH1 [2]. The IND-SIM security is a very weak property that an adversary cannot distinguish between encryptions of chosen messages under chosen randomness and the output of a simulator.[1] We show that any IND-SIM secure [18] PKE scheme in the $\mathcal{RO}$ model is also CDA secure in the $\mathcal{WRO}$ model (Theorem 4). The combination of our theorem and the previous result implies that a CDA secure PKE scheme in the $\mathcal{WRO}$ model can be obtained from any CPA secure PKE scheme in the $\mathcal{RO}$ model.[2]

To prove the CDA security in the $\mathcal{WRO}$ model, we must ensure that the sub oracle O^* gives no advantage to an adversary in the CDA game. The CDA game consists of two stages, where a first stage adversary $\mathcal{A}_1$ sends no value to a second stage adversary $\mathcal{A}_2$.[3] First, the challenge ciphertext c_β does not leak any information of messages (m_0, m_1) and r even with access to $\mathcal{RO}$. This property is guaranteed by the IND-SIM security. Next, if $\mathcal{RO}^\dagger$ and $\mathcal{RO}^*$ are ideal primitives whose outputs do not leak no information for the inputs, these oracles give no advantage to the adversary. Finally, $\mathcal{A}_1$ might deliver some information about (m_0, m_1) or r via interfaces of IC, $\mathcal{TO}$ and $\mathcal{RO}^\dagger$. $\mathcal{A}_1$ can pose (m_0, m_1) or r (or a related value) to $\mathcal{RO}^\dagger$, E, and D, where E and D are an encryption oracle and a decryption oracle of IC. If $\mathcal{A}_2$ could pose the corresponding output value of $\mathcal{RO}^\dagger$, E, or D to $\mathcal{TO}$, D, or E, $\mathcal{A}_2$ would obtain information from $\mathcal{A}_1$. However, indeed, $\mathcal{A}_2$ cannot find the corresponding output value except negligible probability because of following two reasons: 1) Any meaningful information from $\mathcal{A}_1$ is not obtained from any of c_β, $\mathcal{RO}$, $\mathcal{RO}^\dagger$ and $\mathcal{RO}^*$ as discussed above. 2) Outputs of $\mathcal{RO}^\dagger$, E, and D are uniformly random, and then a possible action of $\mathcal{A}_2$ is randomly guessing these values. Therefore, $\mathcal{TO}$ and IC also give no advantage to the adversary.

1.6   Related Works

RSS gave a "from scratch" proof where REwH1 using the NMAC hash function [9] is CDA secure. This approach has to consider structures of hash functions, while our approach does not have to consider them. We only have to deal with the handy tool $\mathcal{WRO}$. Moreover, the NMAC hash construction does not cover important hash constructions ChopMD and Sponge.

---

[1] This definition is meaningless in the standard model because the encryption algorithm uses no further randomness beyond that input.

[2] From Theorem 2 and 3, the CDA security in the $\mathcal{WRO}$ model is preserved if $\mathcal{WRO}$ is replaced with the ChopMD construction and the FOLSponge construction. Therefore, our result achieves that a CDA secure PKE scheme with such practical hash functions can be obtained from any CPA secure PKE scheme in the $\mathcal{RO}$ model.

[3] In the first stage, an adversary $\mathcal{A}_1$ outputs two messages (m_0, m_1) and a random value r such that the jointed values $m_i\|r$ have sufficient min-entropy. In the second stage, an adversary $\mathcal{A}_2$ receives the challenge ciphertext $c_\beta = \mathcal{E}(m_\beta; r)$ from the game where β is a random value of a single bit, and outputs a bit b, where $\mathcal{E}$ is an encryption function. The adversary wins if $b = \beta$.

Two papers [8,11] independently show that for any domain extender H it is impossible to prove $H^{\mathcal{U}} \sqsubset_r \mathcal{RO}$. Because of the impossibility result, it cannot be guaranteed to securely instantiate $\mathcal{RO}$ by $H^{\mathcal{U}}$ via the reset indifferentiability. Thus, they try to salvage H by relaxing limitations of S and/or $\mathcal{D}$. Conversely, we salvage H by showing instantiability from $\mathcal{WRO}$.

Demay et al. [8] propose a relaxed model that is called *resource-restricted indifferentiability*. This model allows simulator S to have a fixed size state while the reset indifferentiability restrict S to be stateless. That means, adversaries in a multi-stage game can share a fixed size (denoted by parameter s) state. They show that it is possible to securely instantiate $\mathcal{RO}$ by $H^{\mathcal{U}}$ via the resource-restricted indifferentiability. Specifically, they define that F_1 is s-resource-restricted indifferentiable from F_2 (denoted by $F_1 \sqsubset_{rr,s} F_2$) if $\exists S$ with the state size s bit s.t. no $\mathcal{D}$ distinguishes the real world $(F_1.hon, F_1.adv)$ from the ideal world $(F_2.hon, S^{F_2.adv})$. They prove that for any multi-stage game security $\mathcal{G}$ that the size of shared state between adversaries in multi-stage is restricted to equal or lower than s bit, $F_1 \sqsubset_{rr,s} F_2 \Rightarrow \forall C \in \mathbf{C}\ C(F_1) >_{\mathcal{G}} C(F_2)$.

They also show a necessary condition of parameter s (i.e., $s = l - m - \log q > 0$) to prove $H^{\mathcal{U}} \sqsubset_{rr,s} \mathcal{RO}$ for any domain extender H, where l is the maximal input length of H, m is the input length of the ideal primitive of H (e.g., compression function) and q is the number of query of S. Their theorem is only valid for the case $s > 0$; that is, their result is still restricted to *specific* multi-stage games. Indeed, unfortunately, their approach *cannot* cover security games that shared state between adversaries in multi-stage is restricted to zero (i.e., $s = 0$). Because the CDA game is the case $s = 0$, they cannot salvage H for the CDA game while our result can do that.

Luykx et al. [11] propose a relaxed model that is called *i-reset indifferentiability*. This model restricts distinguisher $\mathcal{D}$ so that $\mathcal{D}$ is allowed to reset the memory of simulator S only i times while the reset indifferentiability allows $\mathcal{D}$ to reset any times. That means, the number of stages in multi-stage games is equal or lower than i. They define that F_1 is i-reset indifferentiable from F_2 (denoted by $F_1 \sqsubset_{r,i} F_2$) if $\exists S$ which is stateful s.t. no $\mathcal{D}$ distinguishes the real world $(F_1.hon, F_1.adv)$ from the ideal world $(F_2.hon, S^{F_2.adv})$, where $\mathcal{D}$ can reset S up to i times. They prove that for any i'-stage ($1 \leq i' \leq i$) game security $\mathcal{G}$, $F_1 \sqsubset_{r,i} F_2 \Rightarrow \forall C \in \mathbf{C}\ C(F_1) >_{\mathcal{G}} C(F_2)$.

Unfortunately, they show the impossibility that $H^{\mathcal{U}} \sqsubset_{r,i} \mathcal{RO}$ cannot be proved for *any one-pass hash construction* even if $i = 1$, and Baecher et al. clarifies that 1-reset indifferentiability is equivalent to the reset indifferentiability. Hence, their approach *cannot* salvage practical H. On the other hand, our result can salvage important and practical one-pass H such as ChopMD and FOLSponge (Theorems 2 and 3); therefore, our methodology with $\mathcal{WRO}$ is more suitable in a practical sense.

Recently, an independent paper from this paper was accepted at EUROCRYPT 2014 [14]. This independent paper proposed the unsplittability approach and showed that this approach salvages some cryptosystems using Merkle-Damgård type hash constructions in some multi-stage security games. Note that the unsplittability approach is different from the $\mathcal{WRO}$ methodology. Moreover, these hash constructions do not include Sponge, while these include ChopMD.

2 Preliminaries

Notations. Given two strings x and y, we use $x\|y$ to denote the concatenation of x and y. Given a value y, $x \leftarrow y$ means assigning y to x. When X is a non-empty finite set, we write $x \overset{\$}{\leftarrow} X$ to mean that a value is sampled uniformly at random from X and assign to x. $\oplus$ is bitwise exclusive or. $|x|$ is the bit length of x. Given two sets A and C, $C \overset{\cup}{\leftarrow} A$ means assign $A \cup C$ to C. For any $l \times r$-bit value M, $div(r, M)$ divides M into r-bit values $(M_1, \ldots, M_l)$ and outputs them where $M_1\|\cdots\|M_l = M$. For a b-bit value x, $x[i, j]$ is the value from (left) i-th bit to (left) j-th bit where $1 \le i \le j \le b$. For example, let $x = 01101001$, $x[3, 5] = 101$. For a Boolean function F, we denote by "$\exists_1 M$ s.t. $F(M)$ is true" "there exists just a value M such that $F(M)$ is true". Vectors are written in boldface, e.g., $\mathbf{x}$. If $\mathbf{x}$ is a vector then $|\mathbf{x}|$ denotes its length and $\mathbf{x}[i]$ denotes its i-th component for $1 \le i \le |\mathbf{x}|$. $bit_j(\mathbf{x})$ is the left j-th bit of $\mathbf{x}[1]\|\ldots\|\mathbf{x}[|\mathbf{x}|]$.

Throughout this paper, we assume that any algorithm and game is implicitly given a security parameter as input if we do not explicitly state.

Indifferentiability Frameworks [12,18]. The indifferentiability framework [12] ensures reducibility from one system F_1 to another system F_2 in any single-stage security game, where an adversary uses a single state; for any single-stage security, any cryptosystem is at least as secure in F_1 model as in F_2 model. This framework considers two interfaces of system F. One is an adversarial interface, denoted by $F_i.adv$ to which adversaries have access. The other is an honest interface, denoted by $F_i.hon$ to which honest parties have access. In this framework, the reducibility reflects in a simulation based game, called an indifferentiability game. When considering the reducibility from F_1 to F_2, the advantage of this game is defined as follows.

$$\mathsf{Adv}^{\mathsf{indiff}}_{F_1,F_2,S}(A) = |\Pr[\mathcal{D}^{F_1.hon,F_1.adv} \Rightarrow 1] - \Pr[\mathcal{D}^{F_2.hon,S^{F_2.adv}} \Rightarrow 1]|$$

where S is a simulator which has access to $F_2.adv$ and $\mathcal{D}$ is a distinguisher which has access to left oracle L and right oracle R. The F_1 case is that $(L, R) = (F_1.hon, F_1.adv)$, called Real World. The F_2 case is that $(L, R) = (F_2.hon, S^{F_2.adv})$, called Ideal World. The reducibility from F_1 to F_2 is ensured if F_1 is indifferentiable from F_2; there exists a stateful simulator S such that for any $\mathcal{D}$ the indifferentiable advantage is negligible in the security parameter [12].

The reset indifferentiability framework [18] is the extension of the indifferentiability framework and covers any multi-stage security game in addition to any single-stage security game. A multi-stage game is that the size of the state shared among adversaries are restricted. The restricted situation is covered by dealing with a *stateless* simulator. When considering the reducibility from F_1 to F_2, the advantage of this game is defined as follows.

$$\mathsf{Adv}^{\mathsf{r\text{-}indiff}}_{F_1,F_2,S}(A) = |\Pr[\mathcal{D}^{F_1.hon,F_1.adv} \Rightarrow 1] - \Pr[\mathcal{D}^{F_2.hon,S^{F_2.adv}} \Rightarrow 1]|$$

The reducibility from F_1 to F_2 is ensured if F_1 is reset indifferentiable from F_2; there exists a *stateless* simulator S such that for any $\mathcal{D}$ the indifferentiable advantage is negligible in the security parameter [18]. More precisely, RSS gave the following theorem.

ChopMD^h(M)
___
1 $M' \leftarrow \text{pad}_c(M)$;
2 $(M_1, \ldots, M_i) \leftarrow div(d, M')$;
3 $x \leftarrow IV$;
4 for $j = 1, \ldots, i$ do $x \leftarrow h(x \| M_j)$;
5 **return** $x[s + 1, s + n]$;

FOLSponge^P(M)
___
1 $M' \leftarrow \text{pad}_S(M)$;
2 $(M_1, \ldots, M_i) \leftarrow div(n, M')$;
3 $s = IV$;
4 for $i = 1, \ldots, i$ do $s = P(s \oplus (M_i \| 0^c))$;
5 **return** $s[1, n]$;

$\mathcal{RO}_w^\dagger$(M)
___
1 if $F^\dagger[M] = \perp$ then $F^\dagger[M] \xleftarrow{\$} \{0, 1\}^w$;
2 **return** $F^\dagger[M]$;

$\mathcal{TO}(y)$
___
1 if $\exists_1 M$ s.t. $F^\dagger[M] = y$ then **return** M;
2 **return** $\perp$;

Fig. 4. $\mathcal{RO}_w^\dagger$ and $\mathcal{TO}$ where $F^\dagger$ is a (initially everywhere $\perp$) table

Fig. 3. Chop Merkle-Damgård and Sponge

Theorem 1 (RSS Theorem [18]). *Let G be any game. Let F_1 and F_2 be cryptographic systems. Let S be a stateless simulator. For any adversary $\mathcal{A} = (\mathcal{A}_1, \ldots, \mathcal{A}_m)$, there exist an adversary $\mathcal{B} = (\mathcal{B}_1, \ldots, \mathcal{B}_m)$ and a distinguisher $\mathcal{D}$ such that*

$$\Pr[\mathcal{A} \text{ wins in } F_1 \text{ model in } G] \leq \Pr[\mathcal{B} \text{ wins in } F_2 \text{ model in } G] + \text{Adv}_{F_1, F_2, S}^{r\text{-indiff}}(\mathcal{D}).$$

Moreover, $t_{\mathcal{B}_i} \leq t_{\mathcal{A}_i} + q_{\mathcal{A}_i} t_S, q_{\mathcal{B}_i} \leq q_{\mathcal{A}_i} q_S, t_A \leq m + t_G + \sum_{i=1}^m q_{G,i} t_{\mathcal{A}_i}, q_A \leq q_{G,0} + \sum_{i=1}^m q_{G,i} t_{\mathcal{A}_i}$ where $t_{\mathcal{A}}, t_{\mathcal{B}}, t_{\mathcal{D}}$ are the maximum running times of $\mathcal{A}, \mathcal{B}, \mathcal{D}$; $q_{\mathcal{A}}, q_{\mathcal{B}}$ are the maximum number of queries made by $\mathcal{A}$ and $\mathcal{B}$ in a single execution; and $q_{G,0}, q_{G,1}$ are the maximum number of queries made by G to the private interface and to the adversary.

Definitions of Hash Functions. We give the description of the ChopMD construction [7]. Let h be a compression function which maps a value of $d + n + s$ bits to a value of $n + s$ bits. The ChopMD ChopMD^h : $\{0, 1\}^* \rightarrow \{0, 1\}^n$ is defined in Fig. 3. pad_c : $\{0, 1\}^* \rightarrow (\{0, 1\}^d)^*$ is an injective padding function such that its inverse is efficiently computable. IV is a constant value of $n + s$ bits.

We give the description of the FOLSponge construction [4]. Let P be a permutation of d bits. The FOLSonge FOLSponge^P : $\{0, 1\}^* \rightarrow \{0, 1\}^n$ is defined in Fig. 3 such that $n < d$.[4] Let $c = d - n$. pad_S : $\{0, 1\}^* \rightarrow (\{0, 1\}^n)^*$ is an injective padding function such that the last n-bit value is not 0. IV is a constant value of d bits. $IV_1 = IV[1, n]$ and $IV_2 = IV[n + 1, d]$. For example, $\text{pad}_S(M) = M \| 1 \| 0^i$ where i is a smallest value such that $|M \| 1 \| 0^i|$ is a multiple of n.

3 Reset Indifferentiability from $\mathcal{WRO}$

RSS [18] proved the impossibility of proving that the ChopMD and the FOLSponge are reset indifferentiable from random oracles. To compensate the impossibility, we change

---

[4] Note that if the output length (denoted by l) is smaller than n, the output length is achieved by returning $s[1, l]$.

the ideal world from a random oracle to a weakened random oracle ($\mathcal{WRO}$). We define $\mathcal{WRO}$ such that both of the ChopMD and the FOLSponge are reset indifferentiable from $\mathcal{WRO}$s.

We define $\mathcal{WRO}$ as ($\mathcal{RO}_n, \mathcal{RO}_v^*, \mathcal{RO}_w^\dagger, \mathcal{TO}, \mathsf{IC}_{a,b}$), where $\mathcal{RO}_n, \mathcal{RO}_v^*$, and $\mathcal{RO}_w^\dagger$ are arbitrary input length random oracles whose output lengths are n bit, v bit, and w bit, respectively, $\mathcal{TO}$ is a trace oracle, and $\mathsf{IC}_{a,b}$ is an ideal cipher with key length a and block length b. The definition of $\mathcal{TO}$ is that for query y to $\mathcal{TO}$, it returns M if $\exists_1 M$ such that a query M to $\mathcal{RO}_w^\dagger$ such that $y = \mathcal{RO}_w^\dagger(M)$ was made, and otherwise it returns $\perp$. Fig. 4 shows the method of implementing a $\mathcal{RO}_w^\dagger$ and a $\mathcal{TO}$. $E : \{0,1\}^a \times \{0,1\}^b \rightarrow \{0,1\}^b$ denotes the encryption oracle of $\mathsf{IC}_{a,b}$, and $D : \{0,1\}^a \times \{0,1\}^b \rightarrow \{0,1\}^b$ denotes the decryption oracle. The interfaces are defined by $\mathcal{WRO}.hon = \mathcal{RO}_n$ and $\mathcal{WRO}.adv = (\mathcal{RO}_n, \mathcal{RO}_v^*, \mathcal{RO}_w, \mathcal{TO}, \mathsf{IC}_{a,b})$. Note that the parameters (n, v, w, a, b) are defined in each hash function.

For a hash function $H^{\mathcal{U}}$ using an ideal primitive $\mathcal{U}$, the advantage of reset indifferentiability from $\mathcal{WRO}$ is defined as follows.

$$\mathsf{Adv}^{\text{r-indiff}}_{H^{\mathcal{U}},\mathcal{WRO},S}(\mathcal{D}) = |\Pr[\mathcal{D}^{H^{\mathcal{U}},\mathcal{U}} \Rightarrow 1] - \Pr[\mathcal{D}^{\mathcal{WRO}.hon,S^{\mathcal{WRO}.adv}} \Rightarrow 1]|.$$

The RSS theorem ensures that if $H^{\mathcal{U}}$ is reset indifferentiable from a $\mathcal{WRO}$, any security of any cryptosystem is preserved when a $\mathcal{WRO}$ is replaced by $H^{\mathcal{U}}$, where in the $\mathcal{WRO}$ model adversaries have access to $\mathcal{WRO}.adv$ and the cryptosystem has access to $\mathcal{WRO}.hon$, and for the $H^{\mathcal{U}}$ case, adversaries have access to $\mathcal{U}$ and the cryptosystem has access to $H^{\mathcal{U}}$.

3.1   Reset Indifferentiability for ChopMD

In this proof, we define the parameter of $\mathcal{WRO}$ as $w = s$ and $v = n + s$. Note that $\mathsf{IC}_{a,b}$ is not used. Therefore, $\mathcal{WRO} = (\mathcal{RO}_n, \mathcal{RO}_{n+s}^*, \mathcal{RO}_s^\dagger, \mathcal{TO})$.

Theorem 2. *Let the compression function h be a random oracle. There exists a stateless simulator S such that for any distinguisher $\mathcal{D}$,*

$$\mathsf{Adv}^{\text{r-indiff}}_{\text{ChopMD}^h,\mathcal{WRO},S}(\mathcal{D}) \leq \frac{q_R(q_R - 1) + 2\sigma(\sigma + 1)}{2^s}$$

where $\mathcal{D}$ can make queries to left oracle $L = \text{ChopMD}^h/\mathcal{RO}_n$ and right oracle $R = h/S$ at most q_L, q_R times, respectively, and l is a maximum number of blocks of a query to L. $\sigma = lq_L + q_R$. S makes at most $4q_R$ queries and runs in time $O(q_R)$. ♦

An intuition of this proof is shown in Subsection 1.5. This proof is given in Section 4.

3.2   Reset Indifferentiability for FOLSponge

We define the parameter of $\mathcal{WRO}$ as $w = c$ and $b = d$. We don't care the key size a, since $\mathsf{IC}_{a,b}$ can be regarded as random permutation by fixing a key k^*. We denote $E(k^*, \cdot)$ by a random permutation $\mathcal{P}(\cdot)$ of d bit and $D(k^*, \cdot)$ by its inverse oracle $\mathcal{P}^{-1}(\cdot)$. Note that in this proof, $\mathcal{RO}_v^*$ are not used. Therefore, $\mathcal{WRO} = (\mathcal{RO}_n, \mathcal{RO}_c^\dagger, \mathcal{TO}, \mathcal{P}, \mathcal{P}^{-1})$.

Theorem 3. *Assume that the underlying permutation P is a random permutation and P^{-1} is its inverse oracle. There exists a stateless simulator $S = (S_F, S_I)$ such that for any distinguisher $\mathcal{D}$,*

$$\mathsf{Adv}^{r\text{-indiff}}_{\mathrm{FOLSponge}^P, \mathcal{WRO}, S}(\mathcal{D}) \leq \frac{2\sigma(\sigma+1) + q(q-1)}{2^c} + \frac{\sigma(\sigma-1) + q(q-1)}{2^{d+1}}$$

where $\mathcal{D}$ can make at most q_L, q_F and q_I queries to left $L = \mathrm{FOLSponge}^P/\mathcal{RO}_n$ and right oracles $R_F = P/S_F$, $R_I = P^{-1}/S_I$. l is a maximum number of blocks of a query to L. $\sigma = lq_L + q_F + q_I$ and $q = q_F + q_I$. S makes at most $4q$ queries and runs in time $O(q)$. ♦

In the following, we outline why a stateless simulator can be constructed. To simplify the explanation, we omit the padding function of $\mathrm{FOLSponge}^P$. Therefore, queries to L are in $(\{0,1\}^n)^*$. Since $\mathcal{D}$ interacts with (L, R_F, R_I), helpful information for $\mathcal{D}$ is obtained from these oracles. Thus, the S's tasks are to simulate the following two points.

- Simulation of P and P^{-1}: Since in the real world $R_F = P$ and $R_I = P^{-1}$, S must simulate P and P^{-1}.
- Simulation of L-R relation: Since there is a relation based on the FOLSponge construction among query-response values of L and of R_F in the real world, S must simulate such relation.

Using $\mathcal{WRO}$, we can construct a stateless simulator which succeeds in these simulations.

- Simulation of P and P^{-1}: S succeeds in this simulation by using $\mathcal{P}$ and $\mathcal{P}^{-1}$; S returns the response of $\mathcal{P}(x)$ for query x, and returns the response of $\mathcal{P}^{-1}(y)$ for query y.
- Simulation of L-R relation: S succeeds in this simulation by using $\mathcal{RO}^\dagger_c$ and $\mathcal{TO}$. We explain this simulation by using the following example.
  - $\mathcal{D}$ makes query X_1 $(:= IV \oplus (M_1 \| 0^c))$ to R_F and receives the response Y_1.
  - $\mathcal{D}$ makes query X_2 $(:= Y_1 \oplus (M_2 \| 0^c))$ to R_F and receives the response Y_2.

In the real world, there are the relations $Y_1[1, n] = L(M_1)$ and $Y_2[1, n] = L(M_1 \| M_2)$. Then S succeeds in this simulation by the following procedures.

  - For query X_1 to S_F, S_F parses $X_1 = W_1 \| IV_2$, $M_1 = W_1 \oplus IV_1$, $Y_1^* := \mathcal{RO}_n(M_1)$, $Y_1' := \mathcal{RO}^\dagger_c(M_1)$ and $Y_1 = Y_1^* \| Y_1'$.
  - For query X_2 S_F parses $X_2 = W_2 \| Y_1'$, $M_1 = \mathcal{TO}(Y_1')$, $Y_1^* = \mathcal{RO}_n(M_1)$, $M_2 = W_2 \oplus Y_1^*$ and $Y_2 := \mathcal{RO}_n(M_1 \| M_2) \| \mathcal{RO}^\dagger_c(M_1 \| M_2)$.

These procedures ensure that in the ideal world, $Y_1[1, n] = L(M_1)$ and $Y_2[1, n] = L(M_1 \| M_2)$.

As a result, we can construct a stateless simulator S which succeeds in the simulations of (P, P^{-1}) and of the L-R relation. Thus we can prove Theorem 3. The proof is given in the full version of this paper [15].

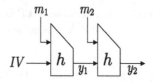

Fig. 5. Figure of Merkle-Damgård

$S(x\|m)$ where $x_1 = x[1, s], x_2 = x[s + 1, n]$ and $|m| = d$
1 $M \leftarrow \mathcal{TO}(x_1)$;
2 if $x = IV$ then $z \leftarrow \mathcal{RO}_n(m)$; $w \leftarrow \mathcal{RO}_s^\dagger(m)$;
3 else if $M \neq\perp$ and $x_2 \neq \mathcal{RO}_n(M)$ then $z \leftarrow \mathcal{RO}_n(M\|m)$; $w \leftarrow \mathcal{RO}_s^\dagger(M\|m)$;
4 else $w\|z \leftarrow \mathcal{RO}_{n+s}^*(x\|m)$;
5 **return** $w\|z$;

Fig. 6. Simulator S

4   Proof of Theorem 2

First we define a graph G_{MD}, which is initialized with a single node IV. Edges and nodes in this graph are defined by query-response values to R, which follow the MD structure. The nodes are chaining values and the edges are message blocks. For example, if $(IV, m_1, y_1), (y_1, m_2, y_2)$ are query response values of R, (IV, y_1, y_2) are the nodes of the graph and (m_1, m_2) are the edges. We denote the MD path by $IV \xrightarrow{m_1} y_1 \xrightarrow{m_2} y_2$ or $IV \xrightarrow{m_1\|m_2} y_2$ (Fig. 5 may help to understand this path).

To simplify this proof, we omit the padding function pad_c. Thus queries to L are in $(\{0, 1\}^d)^*$. Note that ChopMD with pad_c is the special case of that without pad_c, thereby the security of ChopMD without pad_c ensures one with pad_c.

We define a stateless simulator S in Fig. 6. Step 4 ensures the simulation of h and Steps 2 and 3 ensure the simulation of the L-R relation.

Detail. In the following, for the simulator S in Fig. 6 and any distinguisher $\mathcal{D}$, we evaluate the bound of the reset indifferentiable advantage of ChopMD^h from $\mathcal{WRO}$. To evaluate the bound we consider the following five games. In each game, $\mathcal{D}$ has access to (L, R).

- Game 1 is the ideal world, that is, $(L, R) = (\mathcal{RO}_n, S)$.
- Game 2 is $(L, R) = (\mathcal{RO}_n, S_1)$, where S_1 keeps all query-response pairs. For a query $x\|m$ to S_1, if there is $(x\|m, w\|z)$ in the query response history, then S_1 returns $w\|z$, otherwise, S_1 returns the output of $S(x\|m)$.
- Game 3 is $(L, R) = (L_1, S_1)$, where for a query M to L_1 L_1 makes S_1 queries corresponding with ChopMD$^{S_1}(M)$ and returns the response of $\mathcal{RO}_n(M)$.
- Game 4 is $(L, R) = (\text{ChopMD}^{S_1}, S_1)$.
- Game 5 is the real world, that is, $(L, R) = (\text{ChopMD}^h, h)$.

Let G_i be an event that $\mathcal{D}$ outputs 1 in Game i. We thus have that

$$\mathsf{Adv}^{\text{r-indiff}}_{\text{ChopMD}^h, \mathcal{WRO}, S}(\mathcal{D}) \leq \sum_{i=1}^{4} |\Pr[G_i] - \Pr[G_{i+1}]| \leq \frac{q_R(q_R - 1) + 2\sigma(\sigma + 1)}{2^s}.$$

In the following, we justify the above bound by evaluating each difference.

Game 1 $\Rightarrow$ Game 2. From Game 1 to Game 2, we change R from S to S_1 where S_1 records query response values, while S does not record them. The query-response history ensures that in Game 2 if a query $x\|m$ to S_1 was made and y was responded, for the repeated query $x\|m$ to S_1 the same value y is responded, while in Game 1 there is a case that for some repeated query $x\|m$ to S_1 where y was responded, a distinct value y^* ($\neq y$) is responded. The difference $|\Pr[G_1] - \Pr[G_2]|$ is thus bounded by the probability that in Game 1 the distinct value is responded. We call the event "**Diff**". Since the procedure of S to define outputs is controlled by $\mathcal{TO}$ (See the steps 2-4), the event **Diff** relies on outputs of $\mathcal{TO}$. Thus, if **Diff** occurs, for some repeated query to $\mathcal{TO}$ the distinct value is responded. More precisely, if **Diff** occurs, the following event occurs.

- For a query y to $\mathcal{TO}$, w was responded, and then for the repeated query a different value w^* is responded. From the definition of $\mathcal{TO}$, there are two cases for (w, w^*); **Diff**$_1$: $w = \perp$ and $w^* \neq \perp$, **Diff**$_2$: $w \neq \perp$ and $w^* = \perp$.

We thus have that

$$|\Pr[G_1] - \Pr[G_2]| \leq \Pr[\textbf{Diff}_1] + \Pr[\textbf{Diff}_2] \leq \frac{q_R(q_R - 1)}{2^s}.$$

We justify the bound as follows.

First we bound the probability of $\Pr[\textbf{Diff}_1]$. Since the response w of the first query is $\perp$, when the first query is made, the query w^* to $\mathcal{RO}^{\dagger}_s$ such that $y = \mathcal{RO}^{\dagger}_s(w^*)$ was not made. Since the response w^* of the repeated query is not $\perp$, when the repeated query is made, the query w^* to $\mathcal{RO}^{\dagger}_s$ was made such that $y = \mathcal{RO}^{\dagger}_s(w^*)$. Therefore, first y is defined. Second, the output of $\mathcal{RO}^{\dagger}_s(w^*)$ is defined. Thus, $\Pr[\textbf{Diff}_1]$ is bounded by the probability that the response of $\mathcal{RO}^{\dagger}_s(w^*)$, which is an s-bit random value, collides with the value y. Since the numbers of queries to $\mathcal{RO}^{\dagger}_s$ and $\mathcal{TO}$ are at most q_R times, respectively, we have that

$$\Pr[\textbf{Diff}_1] \leq \sum_{i=1}^{q_R} \frac{i-1}{2^s} \leq \frac{q_R(q_R - 1)}{2^{s+1}}.$$

Next we bound the probability of $\Pr[\textbf{Diff}_2]$. Since the response w of the first query is not $\perp$, when the first query is made, the query w to $\mathcal{RO}^{\dagger}_s$ was made such that $y = \mathcal{RO}^{\dagger}_s(w)$. Since the response w^* of the repeated query is $\perp$, when the repeated query is made, a query w' to $\mathcal{RO}^{\dagger}_s$ was made such that $w \neq w'$ and $\mathcal{RO}^{\dagger}_s(w) = \mathcal{RO}^{\dagger}_s(w')$. Therefore, $\Pr[\textbf{Diff}_2]$ is bounded by the collision probability of $\mathcal{RO}^{\dagger}_s$. We thus have that

$$\Pr[\textbf{Diff}_2] \leq \sum_{i=1}^{q_R} \frac{i-1}{2^s} \leq \frac{q_R(q_R - 1)}{2^{s+1}}.$$

Game 2 $\Rightarrow$ Game 3. From Game 2 to Game 3, we change L from $\mathcal{RO}_n$ to L_1 where in Game 3 L makes additional queries to R corresponding with the calculation of ChopMD$^{S_1}(M)$. Note that $\mathcal{D}$ cannot directly observe the additional query response values but can observe those by making the queries to R. So we have to show that in Game 3 the additional queries by L don't affect $\mathcal{D}$'s behavior. We ensure this by Lemma 1 where in Game j, for any MD path $IV \xrightarrow{M} z$, $z = \mathcal{RO}_s^{\dagger}(M)\|\mathcal{RO}_n(M)$ unless Bad_j occurs. By Lemma 1, in both games, unless the bad event occurs, all responses to R are defined by the same queries to $\mathcal{RO}_s^{\dagger}$ and to $\mathcal{RO}_n$. Namely, in Game 3, the responses of the additional queries to R which $\mathcal{D}$ observes are chosen from the same distribution as in Game 2 unless the bad event occurs. Thus, the difference $|\text{Pr}[G_2] - \text{Pr}[G_3]|$ is bounded by the probability of occurring the bad event.

First we define the bad event. Let T_i be a list which records $(x_t[1, s], y_t[1, s])$ for $t = 1, \ldots, i - 1$ where $(x_t\|m_t, y_t)$ is a t-th query response pair of S where $y_t = S(x_t\|m_t)$.

- Bad_j is that in Game j for some i-th query $x_i\|m_i$ to S, the response y_i is such that $y_i[1, s]$ collides with some value in $T_i \cup \{x_i[1, s]\} \cup \{IV[1, s]\}$.

Note that since all outputs of S_1 are defined by using S, we deal with S instead of S_1.

Next we give Lemma 1 as follows. Note that Lemma 1 is also used when evaluating the difference between Game 3 and Game 4.

Lemma 1. *In Game j, for any MD path $IV \xrightarrow{M} y$ $y = \mathcal{RO}_s^{\dagger}(M)\|\mathcal{RO}_n(M)$ unless Bad_j occurs.* ◆

Proof of Lemma 1. Assume that Bad_j does not occur. We show that for any MD path $IV \xrightarrow{M} y$, $y = \mathcal{RO}_s^{\dagger}(M)\|\mathcal{RO}_n(M)$. Let $(x_1\|m_1, y_1), \ldots, (x_t\|m_t, y_t)$ be query response pairs to S which correspond with the MD path where $x_1 = IV$, $x_i = y_{i-1}$ $(i = 2, \ldots, t)$, $y_t = y$, and $M = m_1\|\ldots\|m_t$.

When $t = 1$, $y = \mathcal{RO}_s^{\dagger}(M)\|\mathcal{RO}_n(M)$ (see Step 2).

We consider the case that $t \geq 2$.

Since Bad_j does not occur, the following case does not occur; for some $i \in \{1, \ldots, t-1\}$, $(x_i\|m_i, y_i)$ is defined after $(x_{i+1}\|m_{i+1}, y_{i+1})$ was defined. So $(x_1\|m_1, y_1), \ldots, (x_t\|m_t, y_t)$ are defined by this order.

Since Bad_j does not occur, no collision of outputs of $\mathcal{RO}_s^{\dagger}$ occurs. Therefore, when the query $S_1(x_t\|m_t)$ is made, the pair $(m_1\|\ldots\|m_{j-1}, y_{t-1})$ has been recorded in the table $\mathsf{F}^{\dagger}$ of $\mathcal{RO}_s^{\dagger}$, that is, $\mathsf{F}^{\dagger}[m_1\|\ldots\|m_{t-1}] = y_{t-1} = x_t$.

Since Bad_j does not occur, no collision of outputs of $\mathcal{RO}_s^{\dagger}$ occurs. Therefore, there is no value M^* such that $M^* \neq m_1\|\ldots\|m_{t-1}$ and $\mathsf{F}^{\dagger}[M^*] = x_t$.

Thus, for the query $x_t\|m_t$ to S, S makes the query $x_t[1, s]$ to $\mathcal{TO}$, receives $m_1\|\ldots\|m_{t-1}$ (Step 1), and returns the response y_t such that $y_t = \mathcal{RO}_s^{\dagger}(M)\|\mathcal{RO}_n(M)$ (Step 3). □

By Lemma 1, the difference $|\text{Pr}[G_2] - \text{Pr}[G_3]|$ is bounded by

$$\max\{\text{Pr}[Bad_2], \text{Pr}[Bad_3]\} \leq \frac{\sigma(\sigma + 1)}{2^s}.$$

Finally we justify the bound. The left s-bit values of all outputs of S_1 are uniformly chosen at random from $\{0, 1\}^s$. The probability of occurring the bad event is that for some i-th query to S the left s-bit value of the response, which is a random value, hits some of $T_i \cup \{x_i[1, s]\} \cup \{IV[1, s]\}$. We thus have

$$\Pr[Bad_2] \leq \sum_{i=1}^{q_R} \frac{2(i-1) + 2}{2^s} = \frac{q_R(q_R + 1)}{2^s}, \ \Pr[Bad_3] \leq \sum_{i=1}^{\sigma} \frac{2(i-1) + 2}{2^s} = \frac{\sigma(\sigma + 1)}{2^s}$$

where S_1 is called at most q_R times in Game 2 and σ times in Game 3.

Game 3 $\Rightarrow$ Game 4. From Game 3 to Game 4, we change L where in Game 3 $L(M) = RO_n(M)$, while in Game 4 $L(M) = \mathsf{ChopMD}^{S_1}(M)$. Therefore, the modification does not change $\mathcal{D}$'s behavior iff in Game 4 $\mathsf{ChopMD}^{S_1}(M) = RO_n(M)$. Since Lemma 1 ensures that for any MD path $IV \xrightarrow{M} z$, $z = RO_s^\dagger(M) \| RO_n(M)$ unless the bad event Bad_4 occurs, the modification does not change $\mathcal{D}$'s behavior. Thus the difference $|\Pr[G_3] - \Pr[G_4]|$ is bounded by the probability of occurring Bad_4. Since S_1 is called at most σ times, we have

$$|\Pr[G_3] - \Pr[G_4]| \leq \Pr[Bad_4] \leq \frac{\sigma(\sigma + 1)}{2^s}.$$

Game 4 $\Rightarrow$ Game 5. From Game 4 to Game 5, we change R from S_1 to h. Since outputs of S_1 are uniformly chosen at random from $\{0, 1\}^{n+s}$, the modification of R does not affect $\mathcal{D}$'s behavior. We thus have that $\Pr[G_4] = \Pr[G_5]$.   □

5 Multi-Stage Security in the $\mathcal{WRO}$ Model

In this section, we show appropriateness of our $\mathcal{WRO}$ methodology. We construct a (non-adaptive) CDA secure [2] PKE scheme in the $\mathcal{WRO}$ model. Specifically, we show that if a PKE scheme satisfies an weak security (i.e., IND-SIM security [18]) in the $\mathcal{RO}$ model, then it is also CDA secure in the $\mathcal{WRO}$ model.

An IND-SIM secure PKE in the $\mathcal{RO}$ model is easily obtained by applying a known technique [18] that any CPA secure PKE scheme can be converted into IND-SIM secure by using EwH [1] and REwH1 [2] in the $\mathcal{RO}$ model. Therefore, our result implies that a very large class of PKE schemes is CDA secure in the $\mathcal{WRO}$ model (e.g., factoring-based, Diffie-Hellman-based, lattice-based, etc.).

Furthermore, our result in Section 3 guarantees to instantiate $\mathcal{WRO}$ by ChopMD or FOLSponge. Hence, finally, we have that any CPA secure PKE in the $\mathcal{RO}$ model can be converted into CDA secure with ChopMD or FOLSponge. While the previous work [18] showed CDA secure PKE schemes only with the specific NMAC hash function, our work achieves CDA secure PKE schemes with large class of hash functions (i.e., ChopMD and FOLSponge).

5.1 CDA Secure PKE in the $\mathcal{WRO}$ Model

Public Key Encryption (PKE). A public key encryption scheme $\mathcal{AE} = (\mathsf{Gen}, \mathsf{Enc}, \mathsf{Dec})$ consists of three algorithms. Key generation algorithm Gen outputs public key

$$\begin{array}{|l|}
\hline
\text{CDA}_{\mathcal{AE},F}^{\mathcal{A}_1,\mathcal{A}_2} \\
\hline
\beta \xleftarrow{\$} \{0,1\} \\
(pk, sk) \xleftarrow{\$} \text{Gen} \\
(\mathbf{m}_0, \mathbf{m}_1, \mathbf{r}) \leftarrow \mathcal{A}_1^{F.adv} \\
\mathbf{c} \leftarrow \text{Enc}^{F.hon}(pk, \mathbf{m}_\beta; \mathbf{r}) \\
\beta' \leftarrow \mathcal{A}_2^{F.adv}(pk, \mathbf{c}) \\
\mathbf{return}\ (\beta = \beta') \\
\hline
\end{array}$$

$$\begin{array}{|ll|}
\hline
\text{IND-SIM}_{\mathcal{AE},S,F}^{\mathcal{B}} & \text{RoS}(m, r) \\
\hline
\beta \xleftarrow{\$} \{0,1\} & \text{If } \beta = 1 \text{ then } \mathbf{return}\ \text{Enc}^{F.hon}(pk, m; r) \\
(pk, sk) \xleftarrow{\$} \text{Gen} & \text{Otherwise } \mathbf{return}\ \mathcal{S}^{F.hon}(pk, |m|) \\
\beta' \leftarrow \mathcal{B}^{\text{RoS},F.adv}(pk) & \\
\mathbf{return}\ (\beta = \beta') & \\
\hline
\end{array}$$

Fig. 7. CDA game and IND-SIM game

pk and secret key sk. Encryption algorithm Enc takes public key pk, plaintext m, and randomness r, and outputs ciphertext c. Decryption algorithm Dec takes secret key sk and ciphertext c, and outputs plaintext m or distinguished symbol $\perp$. For vectors $\mathbf{m}, \mathbf{r}$ with $|\mathbf{m}| = |\mathbf{r}| = l$ which is the size of vectors, we denote by $\text{Enc}(pk, \mathbf{m}; \mathbf{r})$ the vector $(\text{Enc}(pk, \mathbf{m}[1]; \mathbf{r}[1]), \ldots, \text{Enc}(pk, \mathbf{m}[l]; \mathbf{r}[l]))$. We say that $\mathcal{AE}$ is deterministic if Enc is deterministic.

CDA Security. We explain the CDA security (we quote the explanation of the CDA security in [18]). Fig. 7 illustrates the non-adaptive CDA game for a PKE scheme $\mathcal{AE}$ using a functionality F. This notion captures the security of a PKE scheme when randomness $\mathbf{r}$ used in encryption may not be a string of uniform bits. For the remainder of this section, fix a randomness length $\rho \geq 0$ and a plaintext length $\omega > 0$. An (μ, ν)-mmr-source M is a randomized algorithm that outputs a triple of vector $(\mathbf{m}_0, \mathbf{m}_1, \mathbf{r})$ such that $|\mathbf{m}_0| = |\mathbf{m}_1| = |\mathbf{r}| = \nu$, all components of $\mathbf{m}_0$ and $\mathbf{m}_1$ are bit strings of length ω, all components of $\mathbf{r}$ are bit strings of length ρ, and $(\mathbf{m}_\beta[i], \mathbf{r}[i]) \neq (\mathbf{m}_\beta[j], \mathbf{r}[j])$ for all $1 \leq i < j \leq \nu$ and all $\beta \in \{0,1\}$. Moreover, the source has min-entropy μ, meaning $\Pr[(\mathbf{m}_\beta[i], \mathbf{r}[i]) = (m', r')|(\mathbf{m}_0, \mathbf{m}_1, \mathbf{r}) \leftarrow M] \leq 2^{-\mu}$ for all $\beta \in \{0,1\}$, all $1 \leq i \leq \nu$, and all (m', r'). A CDA adversary $\mathcal{A}_1, \mathcal{A}_2$ is a pair of procedures, the first of which is a (μ, ν)-mmr-source. The CDA advantage for a CDA adversary $\mathcal{A}_1, \mathcal{A}_2$ against scheme $\mathcal{AE}$ using a functionality F is defined by

$$\text{Adv}_{\mathcal{AE},F}^{\text{cda}}(\mathcal{A}_1, \mathcal{A}_2) = 2 \cdot \Pr[\text{CDA}_{\mathcal{AE},F}^{\mathcal{A}_1,\mathcal{A}_2} \Rightarrow \text{true}] - 1.$$

As noted in [2], in the RO model, mmr-sources have access to the RO. In this setting, the min-entropy requirement is independent of the coins used by the RO, meaning the bound must hold for any fixed choice of function as the RO. If this condition is removed, one can easily break the CDA security (i.e., $\mathcal{A}_1$ and $\mathcal{A}_2$ can easily share the messages $(\mathbf{m}_1, \mathbf{m}_2, \mathbf{r})$) for any cryptosystem using any indifferentiable hash function.

IND-SIM Security. The IND-SIM security is a special notion for PKE schemes. It captures that an adversary cannot distinguish outputs from the encryption algorithm and from a simulator S even if the adversary can choose plaintext and randomness. Fig. 7 shows the IND-SIM game. We define the IND-SIM advantage of an adversary $\mathcal{B}$ by

$$\text{Adv}_{\mathcal{AE},S,F}^{\text{ind-sim}}(\mathcal{B}) = 2 \cdot \Pr[\text{IND-SIM}_{\mathcal{AE},F}^{\mathcal{B}} \Rightarrow \text{true}] - 1.$$

As noted in [18], in the standard model this security goal is not achievable because $\mathcal{AE}$ uses no randomness beyond that input. In the RO model, we will use it when the adversary does not make any RO queries. A variety of PKE schemes is shown to satisfy IND-SIM security in the RO model.

CDA Security in the $\mathcal{WRO}$ Model. The following theorem shows that for any PKE scheme the non-adaptive CDA security in the $\mathcal{WRO}$ model is obtained from IND-SIM security in the RO model.

Theorem 4. *Let $\mathcal{AE}$ be a PKE scheme. Let $(\mathcal{A}_1, \mathcal{A}_2)$ be a CDA adversary in the $\mathcal{WRO}$ model making at most $q_{RO}, q_{RO^*}, q_{RO^\dagger}, q_{TO}, q_E, q_D$ queries to $RO_n, RO_v^*, RO_w^\dagger, TO, IC_{a,b} = (E, D)$. For any simulator S there exists an IND-SIM adversary $\mathcal{B}$ such that*

$$\mathrm{Adv}^{cda}_{\mathcal{AE}, \mathcal{WRO}}(\mathcal{A}_1, \mathcal{A}_2) \leq \mathrm{Adv}^{ind\text{-}sim}_{\mathcal{AE}, S, RO_n}(\mathcal{B}) + q_{RO} \cdot \mathrm{maxpk}_{\mathcal{AE}} + \frac{q_{RO} + 4q^2_{RO^*}}{2^\mu}$$

$$+ \max\left\{\frac{4q^2_{RO^\dagger} + 4q^2_{TO}}{2^\mu}, \frac{q_{TO}}{2^{w-\log q_{RO^\dagger}}}\right\} + \max\left\{\frac{4q^2_E + 4q^2_D}{2^\mu}, \frac{q_D}{2^{b-\log q_E}}, \frac{q_E}{2^{b-\log q_D}}\right\}.$$

$\mathcal{B}$ makes no RO queries, makes v RoS-queries, and runs in time that of $(\mathcal{A}_1, \mathcal{A}_2)$ plus $O(q_{RO} + q_{RO^*} + q_{RO^\dagger} + q_{TO} + q_E + q_D)$. $\mathrm{maxpk}_{\mathcal{AE}}$ is the maximum public key collision probability defined as $\mathrm{maxpk}_{\mathcal{AE}} = \max_{\gamma \in \{0,1\}^*} \Pr[pk = \gamma : (pk, sk) \xleftarrow{\$} \mathrm{Gen}]$. μ is min-entropy of the mmr-source. ♦

The proof outline is as follows: First, we start with game $\mathbf{G}_0$ which is exactly the same game as the CDA game in the $\mathcal{WRO}$ model. Secondly, we transform $\mathbf{G}_0$ to game $\mathbf{G}_1$ so that RO_n returns a random value when $\mathcal{A}_1$ poses a message that is posed to RO_n by Enc to generate the challenge ciphertext. In game $\mathbf{G}_1$, outputs of RO_n does not contain any information about computations to generate the challenge ciphertext for $\mathcal{A}_1$. Thirdly, we transform $\mathbf{G}_1$ to game $\mathbf{G}_2$ so that the table of inputs and outputs of each oracle in $\mathcal{WRO}$ (except RO_n) for $\mathcal{A}_1$ is independent of the table for $\mathcal{A}_2$ according to the output of $\mathcal{A}_1$. In game $\mathbf{G}_2$, queries to sub-oracles for $\mathcal{A}_2$ does not contain any information about the output of $\mathcal{A}_1$, and $\mathcal{A}_1$ cannot hand over any information to $\mathcal{A}_2$ with sub-oracles. Fourthly, we transform $\mathbf{G}_2$ to game $\mathbf{G}_3$ so that ciphertext $\mathbf{c}$ is generated from a simulator S in the IND-SIM game. In game $\mathbf{G}_3$, ciphertext $\mathbf{c}$ does not contain any information about outputs of $\mathcal{A}_1$. Thus, $\mathcal{A}_1$ cannot hand over any information to $\mathcal{A}_2$ with $\mathbf{c}$. Finally, we transform $\mathbf{G}_3$ to game $\mathbf{G}_4$ so that RO_n returns a random value when $\mathcal{A}_2$ poses a message that is posed to RO_n by Enc to generate the challenge ciphertext. In game $\mathbf{G}_4$, outputs of RO_n does not contain any information about computations to generate the challenge ciphertext for $\mathcal{A}_2$. Thus, the advantage of $\mathcal{A}_2$ in $\mathbf{G}_4$ is nothing.

The proof of Theorem 4 is shown in the full version of this paper [15].

References

1. Bellare, M., Boldyreva, A., O'Neill, A.: Deterministic and Efficiently Searchable Encryption. In: Menezes, A. (ed.) CRYPTO 2007. LNCS, vol. 4622, pp. 535–552. Springer, Heidelberg (2007)

 2. Bellare, M., Brakerski, Z., Naor, M., Ristenpart, T., Segev, G., Shacham, H., Yilek, S.: Hedged public-key encryption: How to protect against bad randomness. In: Matsui, M. (ed.) ASIACRYPT 2009. LNCS, vol. 5912, pp. 232–249. Springer, Heidelberg (2009)
 3. Bellare, M., Fischlin, M., O'Neill, A., Ristenpart, T.: Deterministic Encryption: Definitional Equivalences and Constructions without Random Oracles. In: Wagner, D. (ed.) CRYPTO 2008. LNCS, vol. 5157, pp. 360–378. Springer, Heidelberg (2008)
 4. Bertoni, G., Daemen, J., Peeters, M., Van Assche, G.: On the Indifferentiability of the Sponge Construction. In: Smart, N.P. (ed.) EUROCRYPT 2008. LNCS, vol. 4965, pp. 181–197. Springer, Heidelberg (2008)
 5. Bertoni, G., Daemen, J., Peeters, M., Van Assche, G.: The Keccak SHA-3 submission. Submission to NIST, Round 3 (2011)
 6. Boldyreva, A., Fehr, S., O'Neill, A.: On Notions of Security for Deterministic Encryption, and Efficient Constructions without Random Oracles. In: Wagner, D. (ed.) CRYPTO 2008. LNCS, vol. 5157, pp. 335–359. Springer, Heidelberg (2008)
 7. Coron, J.-S., Dodis, Y., Malinaud, C., Puniya, P.: Merkle-Damgård Revisited: How to Construct a Hash Function. In: Shoup, V. (ed.) CRYPTO 2005. LNCS, vol. 3621, pp. 430–448. Springer, Heidelberg (2005)
 8. Demay, G., Gaži, P., Hirt, M., Maurer, U.: Resource-restricted indifferentiability. In: Johansson, T., Nguyen, P.Q. (eds.) EUROCRYPT 2013. LNCS, vol. 7881, pp. 664–683. Springer, Heidelberg (2013)
 9. Dodis, Y., Ristenpart, T., Shrimpton, T.: Salvaging Merkle-Damgård for Practical Applications. In: Joux, A. (ed.) EUROCRYPT 2009. LNCS, vol. 5479, pp. 371–388. Springer, Heidelberg (2009); Full Version in ePrint 2009/177
10. Fuller, B., O'Neill, A., Reyzin, L.: A Unified Approach to Deterministic Encryption: New Constructions and a Connection to Computational Entropy. In: Cramer, R. (ed.) TCC 2012. LNCS, vol. 7194, pp. 582–599. Springer, Heidelberg (2012)
11. Luykx, A., Andreeva, E., Mennink, B., Preneel, B.: Impossibility results for indifferentiability with resets. ePrint 2012/644 (2012)
12. Maurer, U.M., Renner, R.S., Holenstein, C.: Indifferentiability, Impossibility Results on Reductions, and Applications to the Random Oracle Methodology. In: Naor, M. (ed.) TCC 2004. LNCS, vol. 2951, pp. 21–39. Springer, Heidelberg (2004)
13. Mironov, I., Pandey, O., Reingold, O., Segev, G.: Incremental Deterministic Public-Key Encryption. In: Pointcheval, D., Johansson, T. (eds.) EUROCRYPT 2012. LNCS, vol. 7237, pp. 628–644. Springer, Heidelberg (2012); Full Version in ePrint 2012/047
14. Mittelbach, A.: Salvaging indifferentiability in a multi-stage setting. In: Nguyen, P.Q., Oswald, E. (eds.) EUROCRYPT 2014. LNCS, vol. 8441, pp. 603–621. Springer, Heidelberg (2014)
15. Naito, Y., Yoneyama, K., Ohta, K.: Reset Indifferentiability from Weakened Random Oracle Salvages One-pass Hash Functions. In: ePrint 2012/014 (2012); Full Version of this Paper
16. National Institute of Standards and Technology. Cryptographic Hash Algorithm Competition. http://csrc.nist.gov/groups/ST/hash/sha-3/winner_sha-3.html
17. National Institute of Standards and Technoloty. FIPS PUB 180-4 Secure Hash Standard. In: FIPS PUB (2012)
18. Ristenpart, T., Shacham, H., Shrimpton, T.: Careful with Composition: Limitations of the Indifferentiability Framework. In: Paterson, K.G. (ed.) EUROCRYPT 2011. LNCS, vol. 6632, pp. 487–506. Springer, Heidelberg (2011); Full Version: ePrint 2011/339

Memoryless Unbalanced Meet-in-the-Middle Attacks: Impossible Results and Applications

Yu Sasaki

NTT Secure Platform Laboratories
3-9-11 Midori-cho, Musashino-shi, Tokyo 180-8585 Japan
sasaki.yu@lab.ntt.co.jp

Abstract. A meet-in-the-middle (MitM) attack is a popular tool for cryptanalysis. It independently computes two functions $\mathcal{F}$ and $\mathcal{G}$, and finds a match of their outputs. When the cost of computing $\mathcal{F}$ and $\mathcal{G}$ are different, the problem is called unbalanced MitM attack. It is known that, for the balanced case, the MitM attack can be performed only with a negligible memory size without significantly increasing the computational cost by using the Floyd's cycle-finding algorithm. It is also widely believed that the same technique can be applied to the unbalanced case, while no one has shown the evidence of its possibility yet. This paper contains two contributions. Firstly, we show an impossibility of the memoryless unbalanced MitM attack without significantly increasing the computational cost. The conversion to the memoryless attack with the Floyd's cycle-finding algorithm always requires additional computational cost. Secondly, we find applications of the memoryless unbalanced MitM attack to show that it is still meaningful even with some additional computational cost. It can be used to generate multi-collisions of hash functions by using a dedicated collision attack algorithm. Our method finds 3-collisions of SHA-1 with 2^{142} computations and negligible memory size, while the known best attack requires $2^{106.6}$ computations and $2^{53.3}$ memory size. The memoryless unbalanced MitM attack can also be applied to the limited-birthday distinguisher for hash functions.

Keywords: unbalanced meet-in-the-middle, memoryless attack, Floyd's cycle-finding algorithm, hash function, SHA-1, 3-collision, limited-birthday distinguisher.

1 Introduction

A meet-in-the-middle (MitM) attack is a tool for cryptanalysis on symmetric-key primitives. It was introduced by Diffie and Hellman [1]. Then, Chaum and Evertse applied it to the key recovery attack on reduced-round DES [2]. Since then, it has been applied to many block-ciphers, hash functions and MACs for various purposes. Showing all references is hard. Several examples are [3–13]. The MitM attack separates the target function to be analyzed into two independent subfunctions $\mathcal{F}$ and $\mathcal{G}$ so that the original function is represented by $\mathcal{G} \circ \mathcal{F}$. The goal of the attack is

I. Boureanu, P. Owesarski, and S. Vaudenay (Eds.): ACNS 2014, LNCS 8479, pp. 253–270, 2014.
© Springer International Publishing Switzerland 2014

finding a pair (x, y) such that $\mathcal{F}(x) = \mathcal{G}(y)$. Because $\mathcal{F}$ and $\mathcal{G}$ are independent, the attack can be efficiently performed.

Let n be the size of the two functions output, let N_F and N_G be two values satisfying $N_F \times N_G = 2^n$ and let C_F and C_G be the computational cost to compute $\mathcal{F}$ and $\mathcal{G}$, respectively. The attack is processed as follows.

1. $\mathcal{F}$ is computed for N_F distinct input values $x_1, x_2 \ldots, x_{N_F}$, and $(x_i, \mathcal{F}(x_i))$ for $i = 1, 2, \ldots, N_F$ are stored in a list L_F.
2. $\mathcal{G}$ is computed for N_G distinct input values $y_1, y_2 \ldots, y_{N_G}$, and $(y_j, \mathcal{G}(y_j))$ for $j = 1, 2, \ldots, N_G$ are stored in a list L_G.
3. Find a match between $\mathcal{F}(x_i)$ and $\mathcal{G}(y_j)$ stored in L_F and L_G.

If a match is found, the adversary can obtain some important information depending on the attack scenario, *i.e.*, secret-key candidates in key recovery attacks for block-ciphers or preimage candidates in preimage attacks for hash functions. With the simple method, the above procedure requires $N_F \times C_F + N_G \times C_G$ computations. Therefore, N_F and N_G are chosen so that $N_F \times C_F$ and $N_G \times C_G$ are balanced. The memory to store N_F pairs of $(x_i, \mathcal{F}(x_i))$ and N_G pairs of $(y_j, \mathcal{G}(y_j))$ is also required. Here, one of L_F and L_G can be omitted by checking the match online as soon as each pair is obtained. The attack is called a (balanced) MitM attack when the cost of computing $\mathcal{F}$ and $\mathcal{G}$ are the same, *i.e.* $C_F = C_G$, and called an unbalanced MitM attack when $C_F \neq C_G$. For the balanced case, the computational cost is $2^{n/2} \times C_F (= 2^{n/2} \times C_G)$, and the memory size is also $2^{n/2}$. For the unbalanced case, the computational cost is $N_F \times C_F (= N_G \times C_G)$, and the memory size is $\min\{N_F, N_G\}$. Note that the terminology of "MitM" is often used even if $\mathcal{F}$ and $\mathcal{G}$ are not subfunctions of the original attack target, but simply two independent functions. In this paper, we also use the terminology of "MitM" to describe a match of two independent function outputs.

It is well-known that the balanced case can be performed only with a negligible memory size by using the Floyd's cycle-finding algorithm [14] with keeping almost the same computational complexity as the sufficient memory case. The idea is computing $\mathcal{F}$ or $\mathcal{G}$ $2^{n/2}$ times in a sequential form to make a long chain so that the output value of the previous evaluation of $\mathcal{F}$ or $\mathcal{G}$ is used as an input value to the next evaluation of $\mathcal{F}$ or $\mathcal{G}$. In the below, we firstly explain the MitM attack with the Floyd's cycle-finding algorithm with $2^{n/2}$ memory size. The idea is also illustrated in Fig. 1.

1. Set a start value of the chain, v_0, to an arbitrary value.
2. For $i = 1, 2, 3, \cdots$ do as follows.

$$\begin{cases} v_i \leftarrow \mathcal{F}(v_{i-1}) & \text{if a selecting bit } (e.g. \text{ LSB}) \text{ of } v_{i-1} \text{ is } 0, \\ v_i \leftarrow \mathcal{G}(v_{i-1}) & \text{if a selecting bit } (e.g. \text{ LSB}) \text{ of } v_{i-1} \text{ is } 1. \end{cases}$$

   Store v_i in a list L.
3. If a match between v_i and previously stored $v_{i'}$ in L is found, check if v_i and $v_{i'}$ are computed with different choices of $\mathcal{F}$ and $\mathcal{G}$.

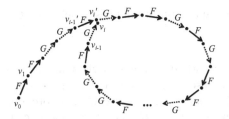
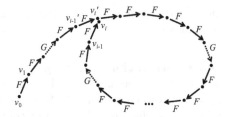

Fig. 1. MitM Attack with the Floyd's Cycle-Finding Algorithm ($\#\mathcal{F} : \#\mathcal{G} = 1 : 1$). v_{i-1} and v'_{i-1} are the solution

Fig. 2. Idea for the Unbalanced MitM Attack ($\#\mathcal{F} > \#\mathcal{G}$). The solution is not obtained from this cycle.

4. If so, output v_{i-1} and $v_{i'-1}$ as a solution of the MitM attack. Otherwise, go back to step 1, and repeat the attack until a solution is found.

Because the attack needs to find a match of different functions' outputs, the function must be switched between $\mathcal{F}$ and $\mathcal{G}$ with probability $1/2$ when the cycle is constructed. At Step 2, a selecting bit is introduced for this purpose. Not only the value of LSB of v_{i-1}, but also any choice of an event that occurs with probability $1/2$ can be used, as long as the selecting rule is fixed. At Step 4, the probability that v_i and $v_{i'}$ are computed with different choices of $\mathcal{F}$ and $\mathcal{G}$ is $1/2$. Therefore, the cycle construction is iterated 2 times on average. Finally, a match between v_i and $v_{i'}$ is found with $O(2^{n/2})$ evaluations, and thus the size of L is also $O(2^{n/2})$. To perform the above procedure with a negligible memory size, instead of all v_i, only a very small fraction of v_i are stored in L. Due to the sequential computational structure, a match between v_i and $v_{i'}$ indicates that the chain becomes a cycle of size $O(2^{n/2})$. Therefore, even if a match between v_i and all previous $v_{i'}$ cannot be checked immediately, sooner or later, the computation reaches one of the values stored in L with at most $O(2^{n/2})$ additional computational cost. If a match is found, by recomputing the cycle from previously stored point, the match between v_{i-1} and $v_{i'-1}$ can be detected. The attack smartly reduces the memory size of the balanced MitM attack only with a small (constant time) increasing computational cost.

It raises a natural question: *can the unbalanced MitM attack also be performed with a negligible memory size only with a small increased computational cost?* Although no one has discussed its possibility in details yet, it is often believed to be possible.

Without losing the generality, throughout the paper, we suppose that C_G is much bigger than C_F, and thus N_G is much smaller than N_F. Obviously, by using the Floyd's cycle-finding algorithm in Fig. 1, *i.e.* by computing $\mathcal{F}$ and $\mathcal{G}$ for the same quantity, the attack can be memoryless. However, this requires $2^{n/2} \times C_G$ computational cost, which is much more than the standard attack (with a sufficient memory size) of $N_G \times C_G$. So far, no other attempt is known for the memoryless unbalanced MitM attack. Consequently, the possibility of the memoryless attack with negligible additional computational cost from $N_G \times C_G$ is unknown.

Our Contributions. In this paper, we investigate the memoryless unbalanced MitM attack. The fact that the balanced case computes $\mathcal{F}$ and $\mathcal{G}$ in the same ratio seems to come from the fact that C_F and C_G are identical. Therefore, our approach is changing the ratio of computing $\mathcal{F}$ and $\mathcal{G}$ when the cycle is constructed. The idea is illustrated in Fig. 2. Because $C_F < C_G$, we compute $\mathcal{F}$ much more than $\mathcal{G}$. This raises a new difficulty: when a match between v_i and $v_{i'}$ are obtained, the probability that v_i and $v_{i'}$ are computed with different functions becomes lower. Both are likely to be generated by $\mathcal{F}$. Hence, the number of iterations of the cycle construction will increase.

In this paper, we begin with summarizing the computational cost of the unbalanced MitM attack with a sufficient memory size when the cost of two functions are given in variables C_F and C_G. Most of previous work analyzed the case that $C_F = 1$. We extend it to a two-variable case.

Then, we evaluate the computational cost of the memoryless unbalanced MitM attack described in Fig. 2, and show that improving $2^{n/2} \times C_G$, which is the simple application of the Floyd's cycle-finding algorithm, is impossible for any values of C_F and C_G, and any choice of the ratio of computing $\mathcal{F}$ and $\mathcal{G}$.

Finally, we show an application of the memoryless unbalanced MitM attack. That is to say, the simple application of the Floyd's cycle-finding algorithm is still meaningful. As the first application, we show that it can be used to generate 3-collisions of hash functions by using a dedicated collision attack algorithm. The current best generic 3-collision attack against an n-bit hash function is the one proposed by Joux and Lucks [17], which requires a computational cost of $O(2^{2n/3})$ and a memory size of $O(2^{n/3})$. Although the computational cost of this attack matches the information theoretic lower-bound, preparing a memory of $O(2^{n/3})$ size is hard for a large n. For example, SHA-1 [18] produces 160-bit hash digests, and the generic attack by [17] requires $2^{106.6}$ computational cost and $2^{53.3}$ memory size. We point out that if a collision attack exists for a hash function, it can be converted to a memoryless[1] 3-collision attack with some additional computational cost. For SHA-1, a (memoryless) collision attack was proposed by Wang et al. [19] which claimed 2^{69} computational cost. Although many papers claim the improved computational cost [21–26], the current best complexity is unclear. Because our purpose is showing a generic conversion framework, the current exact computational cost is not a main issue. Suppose that collisions of SHA-1 can be generated with 2^{61} computational cost [25]. Then, our conversion method can find 3-collisions of SHA-1 with 2^{142} computational cost and negligible memory size. We do not claim that this is better than the generic attack by [17]. However, we believe that the possibility of memoryless 3-collision attack is worth noting, and if the attack is measured by a product of a computational cost and a memory size, our result ($2^{142} \times 1 = 2^{142}$) becomes better than [17]

---

[1] Here, we suppose that the collision attack itself is memoryless. In fact, many collision attacks based on the ones by Wang et al. [19, 20] require few memory.

$(2^{106.6} \times 2^{53.3} = 2^{160})$. We also apply the memoryless 3-collision attack to hash function HAVAL [27] by exploiting the existing collision attack presented by [28]. The comparison of the complexity is given in Table 1.

Table 1. Comparison of 3-collision Attacks

Target	Attack Method	Computational Cost	Memory Size	Reference
SHA-1	Generic Attack	$2^{106.6}$	$2^{106.6}$	[29]
	Improved Generic Attack	$2^{106.6}$	$2^{53.3}$	[17]
	Memoryless Attack	2^{142}	negl.	Sect. 4.3
4-pass HAVAL	Generic Attack	$2^{170.6}$	$2^{170.6}$	[29]
	Improved Generic Attack	$2^{170.6}$	$2^{85.3}$	[17]
	Memoryless Attack	2^{165}	negl.	Sect. 4.3
5-pass HAVAL	Generic Attack	$2^{170.6}$	$2^{170.6}$	[29]
	Improved Generic Attack	$2^{170.6}$	$2^{85.3}$	[17]
	Memoryless Attack	2^{252}	negl.	Sect. 4.3

As the second application, we show that the memoryless unbalanced MitM can be applied to the limited-birthday distinguisher on a hash function which has been recently proposed by Iwamoto *et al.* [30].

Paper Outline. The organization of this paper is as follows. In Sect. 2, we generalize the cost of the unbalanced MitM attack in which the computational cost of $\mathcal{F}$ and $\mathcal{G}$ are given in variables. In Sect. 3, we show the impossibility of improving the simple application of the Floyd's cycle-finding algorithm for the memoryless unbalanced MitM attack. In Sect. 4, we show the application of the memoryless unbalanced MitM attack. Finally, we conclude this paper in Sect. 5.

2   Generalizing the Computational Cost of Unbalanced MitM Attacks

In this section, we evaluate the cost of the unbalanced MitM attack when a sufficient memory size is given. The goal of the attack is finding a match between two functions of n-bit output $\mathcal{F}$ and $\mathcal{G}$, where one execution of $\mathcal{F}$ and $\mathcal{G}$ require C_F and C_G computational cost, respectively. To make the discussion easy, we discuss the cost in exponential forms. Hence, we suppose that $C_F = 2^\alpha$ and $C^G = 2^\beta$. Without losing the generality, we suppose that $\alpha < \beta$.

2.1   Previous Work for $C_F = 1$

There are several previous work, *e.g.* [3, 31], which performs the unbalanced MitM attack when the cost for the cheaper function is 1, *i.e.* $C_F = 1$ and $C_G = 2^\beta$. The attack procedure for this case is described as follows.

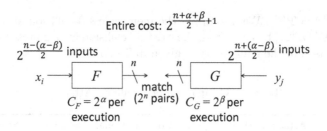

Fig. 3. Sketch of the Unbalanced MitM Attack with Sufficient Memory

1. Set $N_G \leftarrow 2^{(n-\beta)/2}$. For $j = 1, 2, \cdots, N_G$, choose a value of y_j, compute $\mathcal{G}(y_j)$, and store the result in a list L where the data is indexed by $\mathcal{G}(y_j)$.
2. Set $N_F \leftarrow 2^{(n+\beta)/2}$. For $i = 1, 2, \cdots, N_F$, choose a value of x_i, compute $\mathcal{F}(x_i)$, and search for a match with $\mathcal{G}(y_j)$ in the list L.

Because $N_F \times N_G = 2^n$, one match is expected on average. The memory size for Step 1 is N_G, which is $2^{(n-\beta)/2}$. N_F and N_G are chosen so that the computational cost for Step 1 and Step 2 are balanced. The computational cost for Step 1 is $2^{(n-\beta)/2} \times 2^\beta = 2^{(n+\beta)/2}$. The computational cost for Step 2 is $2^{(n+\beta)/2} \times 1 = 2^{(n+\beta)/2}$. In the end, the attack is performed with $2^{((n+\beta)/2)+1}$ computational cost and $2^{(n-\beta)/2}$ memory size.

2.2 Generalization for $C_F = 2^\alpha$

We generalize the attack in Sect. 2.1 so that the cost of computing $\mathcal{F}$ is given by 2^α. The only difference from Sect. 2.1 is the choice of N_F and N_G. The attack procedure is as follows, which is also depicted in Fig. 3.

1. Set $N_G \leftarrow 2^{(n+(\alpha-\beta))/2}$. For $j = 1, 2, \cdots, N_G$, choose a value of y_j, compute $\mathcal{G}(y_j)$, and store the result in a list L where the data is indexed by $\mathcal{G}(y_j)$.
2. Set $N_F \leftarrow 2^{(n-(\alpha-\beta))/2}$. For $i = 1, 2, \cdots, N_F$, choose a value of x_i, compute $\mathcal{F}(x_i)$, and search for a match with $\mathcal{G}(y_j)$ in the list L.

Because $N_F \times N_G = 2^n$, one match is expected on average. The memory size for Step 1 is N_G, which is $2^{(n+(\alpha-\beta))/2}$. The computational cost for Step 1 is $N_G \times 2^\beta = 2^{(n+\alpha+\beta)/2}$. The computational cost for Step 2 is $N_F \times 2^\alpha = 2^{(n+\alpha+\beta)/2}$. In summary, the unbalanced MitM attack can be performed with $2^{((n+\alpha+\beta)/2)+1}$ computational cost and $2^{(n+(\alpha-\beta))/2}$ memory size.

Note that by setting $C_F = 1$, i.e. $\alpha = 0$, the complexity becomes $2^{((n+\beta)/2)+1}$ computational cost and $2^{(n-\beta)/2}$ memory size, which matches in Sect. 2.1.

The generalization in this section is quite straight-forward. We showed the generalization as a tool for the future usage. Indeed, the discussion from the next section uses this result.

3 Impossibility of Efficient Memoryless Unbalanced MitM Attacks

In this section, we aim to convert the unbalanced MitM attack in Sect. 2 to the memoryless attack by using the Floyd's cycle-finding algorithm. Firstly, we explain the simple application of the Floyd's cycle-finding algorithm in Sect. 3.1. We then explain that it is impossible to improve the computational cost by changing the ratio of computing $\mathcal{F}$ and $\mathcal{G}$ in Sect. 3.2. We give some remarks in Sect. 3.3.

3.1 Simple Application of the Floyd's Cycle-Finding Algorithm

In this section, we simply apply the memoryless attack on the balanced case even though the cost of two functions $\mathcal{F}$ and $\mathcal{G}$ are unbalanced. We again suppose that $C_F = 2^\alpha$, $C^G = 2^\beta$ and $\alpha < \beta$. Because $\mathcal{F}$ and $\mathcal{G}$ are computed in the same ratio, we choose an event of probability $1/2$ as a selection rule of the choice of $\mathcal{F}$ and $\mathcal{G}$. Here, we simply use the LSB of previous chaining value.

To find a match, both $\mathcal{F}$ and $\mathcal{G}$ are computed about $2^{n/2}$ times, which requires the computational cost of $2^{\alpha+(n/2)}$ and $2^{\beta+(n/2)}$, respectively. If a match between v_i and v_i' is found, we check if they are generated from different choices of $\mathcal{F}$ and $\mathcal{G}$. Because $\mathcal{F}$ and $\mathcal{G}$ are switched with probability $1/2$, they are generated from different functions with probability $1/2$. Therefore, we need to iterate the attack 2 times on average, which requires the computational cost of $2^{\alpha+(n/2)+1} + 2^{\beta+(n/2)+1}$. Considering that $\alpha < \beta$, the entire computational cost is

$$2^{\beta+(n/2)+1}. \tag{1}$$

The evaluation is summarized in Table 2.

Table 2. Complexity for the simple application of the Floyd's cycle-finding algorithm

Functions	#computed times per match	Computational cost per match	#iterations of cycle constructions	Dominant computational cost
$\mathcal{F}$	$2^{n/2}$	$2^{\alpha+(n/2)}$		
$\mathcal{G}$	$2^{n/2}$	$2^{\beta+(n/2)}$	2	$2^{\beta+(n/2)+1}$

Note that the computational cost with a sufficient memory size is $2^{((n+\alpha+\beta)/2)+1}$ as shown in Sect. 2.2. Compared to it, the simple application of the Floyd's cycle-finding algorithm increases the computational cost by a factor of $2^{(\beta-\alpha)/2}$.

3.2 Unbalanced Selecting Bits: Changing the Ratio of $\mathcal{F}$ to $\mathcal{G}$

To make the computational cost of computing $\mathcal{F}$ and $\mathcal{G}$ balanced, we use an event with probability $2^{-(\beta-\alpha)}$ as a selection rule of the choice of $\mathcal{F}$ and $\mathcal{G}$. Therefore, if the $(\beta - \alpha)$ LSBs of v_{i-1} are all 0, we compute $v_i \leftarrow \mathcal{G}(v_{i-1})$. Otherwise, we compute $v_i \leftarrow \mathcal{F}(v_{i-1})$. Then, the ratio of $\mathcal{F}$ to $\mathcal{G}$ becomes $2^{\beta-\alpha}$ to 1. To be more precise, the chain is computed as follows.

$$\begin{cases} v_i \leftarrow \mathcal{F}(v_{i-1}) & \text{if } (\beta - \alpha) \text{ LSBs of } v_{i-1} \text{ are all 0,} \\ v_i \leftarrow \mathcal{G}(v_{i-1}) & \text{otherwise.} \end{cases}$$

The number of computations of $\mathcal{F}$ and $\mathcal{G}$ become $2^{n/2+(\beta-\alpha)/2}$ and $2^{n/2-(\beta-\alpha)/2}$ respectively. The corresponding computational cost is obtained by multiplying 2^α and 2^β respectively, which result in $2^{(n+\alpha+\beta)/2}$ for both. Because $\mathcal{F}$ and $\mathcal{G}$ is computed in the ratio $2^{\beta-\alpha}$ to 1, the probability that a match is obtained from different choice of $\mathcal{F}$ and $\mathcal{G}$ is about $2^{-(\beta-\alpha)}$. Therefore, the cycle construction must be iterated $2^{\beta-\alpha}$ times on average. The entire computational cost becomes $2^{(n+3\beta-\alpha)/2+1}$. The evaluation is summarized in Table 3.

Table 3. Complexity using the unbalanced ratio of $\mathcal{F}$ to $\mathcal{G}$

Functions	#computed times per match	Computational cost per match	#iterations of cycle constructions	Dominant computational cost
$\mathcal{F}$	$2^{n/2+(\beta-\alpha)/2}$	$2^{(n+\alpha+\beta)/2}$	$2^{\beta-\alpha}$	$2^{(n+\alpha+\beta)/2+1} \times 2^{\beta-\alpha}$
$\mathcal{G}$	$2^{n/2-(\beta-\alpha)/2}$	$2^{(n+\alpha+\beta)/2}$		$= 2^{(n+3\beta-\alpha)/2+1}$

Let us compare the computational cost of this case with the one in Sect. 3.1. The condition that the computational cost of this attack can be smaller than the one in Sect. 3.1 is

$$2^{\beta+(n/2)+1} > 2^{(n+3\beta-\alpha)/2+1},$$

which is converted into

$$\alpha > \beta.$$

This clearly contradicts to the assumption of $\alpha < \beta$, thus regardless of the values of α and β, the attack in Sect. 3.1 is better.

Results do not change even if we consider the other ratio. Let us set the ratio of the number of $\mathcal{F}$ and $\mathcal{G}$ to 2^z to 1. The evaluation is similar. $\mathcal{F}$ is computed $2^{n/2+z/2}$ times in a cycle, and its computational cost is $2^{n/2+z/2+\alpha}$. $\mathcal{G}$ is computed $2^{n/2-z/2}$ times in a cycle, and its computational cost is $2^{n/2-z/2+\beta}$. The probability that a match is obtained from different choices of $\mathcal{F}$ and $\mathcal{G}$ is about 2^{-z}. Therefore, the cycle construction will be iterated 2^z times on average. Hence, the total computational cost is $2^{n/2+z/2+\alpha} + 2^{n/2+z/2+\beta}$. The results are summarized in Table 4.

Table 4. Complexity evaluation by setting the ratio of $\mathcal{F}$ to $\mathcal{G}$ as a variable

Func.	#computed times per match	Computational cost per match	#iterations of cycle constructions	Dominant computational cost
$\mathcal{F}$	$2^{n/2+z/2}$	$2^{n/2+z/2+\alpha}$		
$\mathcal{G}$	$2^{n/2-z/2}$	$2^{n/2-z/2+\beta}$	2^z	$2^{n/2+3z/2+\alpha} + 2^{n/2+z/2+\beta}$

Compared to $2^{\beta+(n/2)+1}$ for the simple application in Sect. 3.1, the second term of the dominant computational cost in Table 4, which is $2^{n/2+z/2+\beta}$, is always higher by a factor of $2^{z/2-1}$.

3.3 Summary and Remarks

We showed that as long as the Floyd's cycle-finding algorithm is used, the simple application that computes $\mathcal{F}$ and $\mathcal{G}$ in the same ratio is the best, and the attack increases the computational cost by a factor of $2^{(\beta-\alpha)/2}$ compared to the one with a sufficient memory size.

We like to note that without using the Floyd's cycle-finding algorithm, the trivial time-memory tradeoff exists for both balanced and unbalanced MitM attacks. In the MitM attack, N_G outputs are stored for $\mathcal{G}$, and N_F outputs are generated online for $\mathcal{F}$, where $N_G \times N_F = 2^n$. Usually, N_G and N_F are chosen so that the computational cost $N_G \times C_G$ and $N_F \times C_F$ are balanced. In order to reduce the memory size, instead of storing N_G outputs for $\mathcal{G}$, we only store $\mathcal{G}/w$ results. When N_F are computed later, we generate $w \times N_F$ results so that a match is still expected. This reduces a memory size by a factor of w and increases the computational cost by a factor of w. This is a tradeoff such that Time $\times$ Memory = constant. If the memory size needs to be reduced only by a small factor, using this trivial time-memory tradeoff may be more convenient than using the fully memoryless cycle-finding algorithm which always increases the computational cost by a factor of $2^{(\beta-\alpha)/2}$.

4   Applications of the Memoryless Unbalanced MitM Attacks

In the previous section, we showed a negative result, *i.e.* the computational cost of the memoryless unbalanced MitM attack cannot be faster than the simple application in Sect. 3.1. In this section, we show that the memoryless unbalanced MitM attack in Sect. 3.1 is still meaningful. Firstly in Sect. 4.1, we explain the generic condition that the memoryless unbalanced MitM attack can be applied. Secondly in Sect. 4.2, we explain that several claims of the previous memoryless MitM preimage attacks, *e.g.* [15], is incorrect. Thirdly in Sect. 4.3, as a concrete example, we show that it can be used to generate 3-collisions for hash functions by exploiting a dedicated collision attack algorithm. Finally in Sect. 4.4, as another example, we show the applications to the limited-birthday distinguisher recently proposed by Iwamoto *et al.* [30].

4.1   Conditions to Apply Memoryless Unbalanced MitM Attack

From eq. (1), the computational cost of the memoryless unbalanced MitM is given by $2^{\beta+(n/2)+1}$, where 2^{β} is the cost to execute the heavier function $\mathcal{G}$. In order to be faster than 2^n computational cost, we obtain the condition $2^{\beta+(n/2)+1} < 2^n$, which is converted to

$$C_G = 2^{\beta} < 2^{(n/2)-1}. \tag{2}$$

Therefore, to be converted to the memoryless attack, the computational cost of $\mathcal{G}$ must be smaller than the birthday attack complexity.

4.2   Incorrectness of Previous Memoryless MitM Preimage Attack

Recently, various preimage attacks based on the MitM attack have been proposed against narrow-pipe Merkle-Damgård hash functions [7, 11, 13, 15, 16]. In those hash functions, the hash digest is computed by iteratively computing the compression function $H_i \leftarrow \mathrm{CF}(H_{i-1}, M_{i-1})$, where M_i is the message value and H_0 is an initial value defined in the hash function specification.

Those attacks, for a given hash digest, aim to generate a preimage consisting of two message blocks. The attack is depicted in Fig. 4. It firstly generates pseudo-preimages, which are a pair of (H_1, M_1) such that $H_1 \neq \mathrm{IV}$ and the corresponding compression function output, H_2, is a given digest. In many cases, the cost of the pseudo-preimage generation is much higher than $2^{n/2}$. After that, generated pseudo-preimages are converted into a preimage by applying the unbalanced MitM attack for the first message block. In details, the pseudo-preimage attack is regarded as function $\mathcal{G}$ and the random message generation for the first message block is regarded as function $\mathcal{F}$ whose computational cost is 1 per execution.

Several (but not all) previous work claim that the unbalanced MitM part can be performed with negligible memory size by using the Floyd's cycle-finding algorithm, e.g. [15, Section 4.5].

However, the conversion from pseudo-preimages to preimages is an example that the unbalanced MitM attack part cannot be memoryless by using the Floyd's cycle-finding algorithm. If the conversion is applied, the computational cost of the memoryless preimage attack becomes more than 2^n, which is worse than the generic attack. This result immediately indicates the incorrectness of the claim in previous work about the memoryless preimage attack. We would like to stress that, with a sufficient amount of memory, the previous attack can work correctly.

4.3   Application to 3-Collisions

The first application of the memoryless unbalanced MitM attack is a 3-collision attack on hash functions. A 3-collision on a hash function $\mathcal{H}$ is a triplet of distinct input values (I_1, I_2, I_3) such that $\mathcal{H}(I_1) = \mathcal{H}(I_2) = \mathcal{H}(I_3)$.

In general, it is known that a t-collision can be generated with a computational cost of $O(2^{(t-1)n/t})$ and $O(2^{(t-1)n/t})$ memory size [29]. For $n = 3$, the

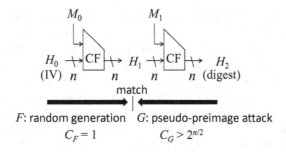

Fig. 4. Previous preimage attacks using unbalanced MitM attack

computational cost is $O(2^{2n/3})$ and the memory size is $O(2^{2n/3})$. At Asiacrypt 2009, Joux and Lucks showed a generic 3-collision attack on an n-bit narrow-pipe Merkle-Damgård hash function [17], which requires a computational cost of $O(2^{2n/3})$ and a memory size of $O(2^{n/3})$. One drawback of this attack is a memory size of $O(2^{n/3})$. For a relatively large n, preparing a memory of size $O(2^{n/3})$ is infeasible.

We point out that a memoryless 3-collision attack on $\mathcal{H}$ can be achieved from a (memoryless) collision attack on $\mathcal{H}$. In short, the strategy is as follows, which is also illustrated in Fig. 5. A collision attack produces a pair of input messages (I_1, I_2) such that $\mathcal{H}(I_1) = \mathcal{H}(I_2)$ with a computational cost of $C_G = 2^\beta$, where $\beta < n/2$. This operation is regarded as function $\mathcal{G}$, namely, $\mathcal{G}$ produces an n-bit value $\mathcal{H}(I_1) = \mathcal{H}(I_2)$ at a computational cost of $C_G = 2^\beta$. To find the third colliding input message I_3, we simply test randomly generated messages. Therefore, $\mathcal{F}$ produces an n-bit value $\mathcal{H}(I_3)$ at a computational cost of $C_F = 1$. A 3-collision is generated by observing a match of the output values between $\mathcal{F}$ and $\mathcal{G}$. This is exactly the unbalanced MitM attack. Hence the 3-collision attack

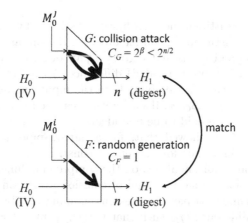

Fig. 5. Memoryless 3-collision Attack with Memoryless Unbalanced MitM Attack

can be memoryless by following the strategy in Sect. 3.1, which results in the computational cost of $2^{\beta+(n/2)+1}$ and a negligible memory size.

For example, SHA-1 [18] is a 160-bit narrow-pipe hash function. On one hand, the generic attack by [17] requires $2^{106.6}$ computational cost and $2^{53.3}$ memory size to find a 3-collision. On the other hand, [25] showed that collisions of SHA-1 can be generated with 2^{61} computational cost and negligible memory size. Then, the conversion in Sect. 3.1 can find 3-collisions of SHA-1 with $2^{142}(= 2^{61+(160+/2)+1})$ computational cost and negligible memory size. Other two examples are 4-pass HAVAL and 5-pass HAVAL [27], each is a 256-bit narrow-pipe hash function. A collision attack was proposed by Yu *et al.*, which finds collisions of 4-pass HAVAL with 2^{36} computational cost and negligible memory and collisions of 5-pass HAVAL with 2^{123} computational cost and negligible memory [28]. The generic 3-collision attack by [17] requires $2^{170.6}$ computational cost and $2^{85.3}$ memory size for both of 4-pass and 5-pass HAVAL. Preparing a memory of size $2^{85.3}$ seems almost infeasible. The conversion in Sect. 3.1 can find 3-collisions of 4-pass HAVAL with $2^{165}(= 2^{36+(256/2)+1})$ computational cost and negligible memory size and 3-collisions of 5-pass HAVAL with $2^{252}(= 2^{123+(256/2)+1})$ computational cost and negligible memory size.

Strictly speaking, we need to be more careful about the details of collision finding algorithm $\mathcal{G}$ to generate a Floyd's cycle. The collision attack on SHA-1 [19, 25], to achieve the claimed computational cost, involves various analytic techniques such as message modification technique and early aborting technique. To make the cycle, $\mathcal{G}$ must be solely dependent on the value of v_{i-1}. Besides, for the same v_{i-1} received in different timings, $\mathcal{G}$ must reproduce the same output value v_i. In short, this can be achieved by fixing the search rule *i.e.* in which order the freedom degrees are used and the conditions to apply the techniques. We show the detailed analysis specific to the SHA-1 collision search in Appendix.

4.4   Application to Limited-Birthday Distinguisher

The limited-birthday distinguisher was firstly mentioned by Gilbert and Peyrin at FSE 2010 [32] to distinguish a target function $\mathcal{H}$ from an ideal one. In this framework, the distinguisher is firstly given a pair of an input (truncated) difference Δ_{IN} and an output (truncated) difference Δ_{OUT}. The goal of the distinguisher is finding a value x satisfying both the input and output differences, *i.e.*, $\mathcal{H}(x) \oplus \mathcal{H}(x \oplus \Delta_{IN}) = \Delta_{OUT}$. If such a value can be found for $\mathcal{H}$ faster than for an ideal function, $\mathcal{H}$ is said to be non-ideal.

Then, Iwamoto *et al.* showed that, for a narrow-pipe hash function, the limited-birthday distinguisher for the entire construction can be constructed from a semi-free-start collision attack on the compression function [30]. Here, a semi-free-start collision attack is a kind of collision attack on the compression function CF, which finds a triplet of a previous chaining variable H_{i-1}, a message x, and a message difference δ_{IN} such that $CF(H_{i-1}, x) = CF(H_{i-1}, x \oplus \delta_{IN})$. Iwamoto *et al.* point out that in many of previous semi-free-start collision attacks, δ_{IN} can be fixed before x is searched. Then, their framework of the conversion to the limited-birthday distinguisher on $\mathcal{H}$ is as follows, which is also illustrated in Fig. 6.

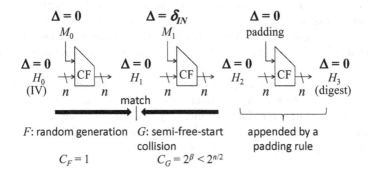

Fig. 6. Framework of the Limited-birthday Distinguisher on $\mathcal{H}$ from a Semi-free-start Collision Attack on CF. An input difference is fixed to $(0\|\delta_{IN})$, and an output difference is fixed to 0.

1. Find a semi-free-start-collision attack on CF, which can work for a pre-specified message difference δ_{IN}. Set an input difference for $\mathcal{H}$ to $(0\|\delta_{IN})$ and set an output difference of $\mathcal{H}$ to 0.
2. For the second message block, perform the semi-free-start-collision attack to find many triplets of $(H_1, M_1, M_1 \oplus \delta_{IN})$. The results are stored in a list L.
3. For the first message block, compute $H_1 \leftarrow (H_0, M_0)$ for many randomly generated messages M_0, and find a match with one of the H_1 in L.
4. For a matched $M_0\|M_1$ and $M_0\|M_1\oplus\delta_{IN}$, a padding block is often appended inside the computation of $\mathcal{H}$. Because all input information for the third message block has no difference, the output difference is ensured to be 0.

The match between the first message block and the second message block is an unbalanced MitM attack. Suppose that the cost of semi-free-start collision attack is 2^β, and $\beta < n/2$. It generates $2^{(n-\beta)/2}$ semi-free-start collisions with a computational cost of $2^{(n-\beta)/2} \times 2^\beta = 2^{(n+\beta)/2}$ and the results are stored in a list L with $2^{(n-\beta)/2}$ memory size. It also tests $2^{(n+\beta)/2}$ random messages in the first message block. In the end, the total computational cost is $2^{((n+\beta)/2)+1}$.

As discussed in Sect. 3.1, the attack can be memoryless, which results in the computational cost of $2^{\beta+(n/2)+1}$ and negligible memory size.

5   Concluding Remarks

In this paper, we studied the memoryless unbalanced MitM attack with the Floyd's cycle-finding algorithm. On the contrary to the previous belief, the unbalanced MitM attack cannot be memoryless without significantly increasing the computational cost compared to the sufficient-memory case. We showed that among any ratio of the numbers of computing $\mathcal{F}$ and $\mathcal{G}$, 1 to 1 leads to the best computational cost. We then searched for the applications in which the memoryless unbalanced MitM attack with the Floyd's cycle-finding algorithm is still useful. The condition to apply the Floyd's cycle-finding algorithm is that the computational cost for the heavier function $\mathcal{G}$ must be below $2^{(n/2)-1}$. We showed that the application to the MitM preimage attack is impossible. We also showed that a 3-collision attack and a limited-birthday distinguisher on a hash function are good examples of applications.

Our research is the first-step to discuss the unbalanced memoryless MitM attack. A possible future research direction is finding alternatives of the Floyd's cycle-finding algorithm to reduce the memory size. In particular, it is interesting to investigate the memoryless attack when the computational cost of the heavier function $\mathcal{G}$ is bigger than the birthday attack cost.

Acknowledgments. The author would like to appreciate Takanori Isobe for insightful discussions.

References

1. Diffie, W., Hellman, M.E.: Exhaustive Cryptanalysis of the NBS Data Encryption Standard. Computer Issue 6(10) (1977)
2. Chaum, D., Evertse, J.-H.: Crytanalysis of DES with a Reduced Number of Rounds: Sequences of Linear Factors in Block Ciphers. In: Williams, H.C. (ed.) CRYPTO 1985. LNCS, vol. 218, pp. 192–211. Springer, Heidelberg (1986)
3. Aoki, K., Sasaki, Y.: Preimage Attacks on One-Block MD4, 63-Step MD5 and More. In: Avanzi, R.M., Keliher, L., Sica, F. (eds.) SAC 2008. LNCS, vol. 5381, pp. 103–119. Springer, Heidelberg (2009)
4. Bogdanov, A., Khovratovich, D., Rechberger, C.: Biclique Cryptanalysis of the Full AES. In: Lee, D.H., Wang, X. (eds.) ASIACRYPT 2011. LNCS, vol. 7073, pp. 344–371. Springer, Heidelberg (2011)
5. Bogdanov, A., Rechberger, C.: A 3-Subset Meet-in-the-Middle Attack: Cryptanalysis of the Lightweight Block Cipher KTANTAN. In: Biryukov, A., Gong, G., Stinson, D.R. (eds.) SAC 2010. LNCS, vol. 6544, pp. 229–240. Springer, Heidelberg (2011)
6. Canteaut, A., Naya-Plasencia, M., Vayssière, B.: Sieve-in-the-Middle: Improved MITM Attacks. In: Canetti, R., Garay, J.A. (eds.) CRYPTO 2013, Part I. LNCS, vol. 8042, pp. 222–240. Springer, Heidelberg (2013)
7. Guo, J., Ling, S., Rechberger, C., Wang, H.: Advanced Meet-in-the-Middle Preimage Attacks: First Results on Full Tiger, and Improved Results on MD4 and SHA-2. In: Abe, M. (ed.) ASIACRYPT 2010. LNCS, vol. 6477, pp. 56–75. Springer, Heidelberg (2010)
8. Isobe, T.: A Single-Key Attack on the Full GOST Block Cipher. In: Joux, A. (ed.) FSE 2011. LNCS, vol. 6733, pp. 290–305. Springer, Heidelberg (2011)
9. Isobe, T., Shibutani, K.: All Subkeys Recovery Attack on Block Ciphers: Extending Meet-in-the-Middle Approach. In: Knudsen, L.R., Wu, H. (eds.) SAC 2012. LNCS, vol. 7707, pp. 202–221. Springer, Heidelberg (2013)

10. Isobe, T., Shibutani, K.: Generic Key Recovery Attack on Feistel Scheme. In: Sako, K., Sarkar, P. (eds.) ASIACRYPT 2013, Part I. LNCS, vol. 8269, pp. 464–485. Springer, Heidelberg (2013)
11. Knellwolf, S., Khovratovich, D.: New Preimage Attacks against Reduced SHA-1. In: Safavi-Naini, R., Canetti, R. (eds.) CRYPTO 2012. LNCS, vol. 7417, pp. 367–383. Springer, Heidelberg (2012)
12. Khovratovich, D., Nikolić, I., Weinmann, R.P.: Meet-in-the-Middle Attacks on SHA-3 Candidates. In: Dunkelman, O. (ed.) FSE 2009. LNCS, vol. 5665, pp. 228–245. Springer, Heidelberg (2009)
13. Sasaki, Y., Aoki, K.: Finding Preimages in Full MD5 Faster Than Exhaustive Search. In: Joux, A. (ed.) EUROCRYPT 2009. LNCS, vol. 5479, pp. 134–152. Springer, Heidelberg (2009)
14. Floyd, R.W.: Nondeterministic Algorithms. Journal of the ACM 14(4), 636–644 (1967)
15. Aoki, K., Sasaki, Y.: Meet-in-the-Middle Preimage Attacks Against Reduced SHA-0 and SHA-1. In: Halevi, S. (ed.) CRYPTO 2009. LNCS, vol. 5677, pp. 70–89. Springer, Heidelberg (2009)
16. Sasaki, Y., Wang, L., Wu, S., Wu, W.: Investigating Fundamental Security Requirements on Whirlpool: Improved Preimage and Collision Attacks. In: Wang, X., Sako, K. (eds.) ASIACRYPT 2012. LNCS, vol. 7658, pp. 562–579. Springer, Heidelberg (2012)
17. Joux, A., Lucks, S.: Improved Generic Algorithms for 3-Collisions. In: Matsui, M. (ed.) ASIACRYPT 2009. LNCS, vol. 5912, pp. 347–363. Springer, Heidelberg (2009)
18. U.S. Department of Commerce, National Institute of Standards and Technology: Secure Hash Standard (SHS) (Federal Information Processing Standards Publication 180-3) (2008),
http://csrc.nist.gov/publications/fips/fips180-3/fips180-3_final.pdf
19. Wang, X., Yin, Y.L., Yu, H.: Finding Collisions in the Full SHA-1. In: Shoup, V. (ed.) CRYPTO 2005. LNCS, vol. 3621, pp. 17–36. Springer, Heidelberg (2005)
20. Wang, X., Yu, H., Yin, Y.L.: Efficient Collision Search Attacks on SHA-0. In: Shoup, V. (ed.) CRYPTO 2005. LNCS, vol. 3621, pp. 1–16. Springer, Heidelberg (2005)
21. Chen, R.: New Techniques for Cryptanalysis of Cryptographic Hash Functions. Ph.D. thesis, Technion (2011)
22. Cochran, M.: Notes on the Wang et al. 2^{63} SHA-1 Differential Path. Cryptology ePrint Archive, Report 2007/474 (2007)
23. Joux, A., Peyrin, T.: Hash Functions and the (Amplified) Boomerang Attack. In: Menezes, A. (ed.) CRYPTO 2007. LNCS, vol. 4622, pp. 244–263. Springer, Heidelberg (2007)
24. Rijmen, V., Oswald, E.: Update on SHA-1. In: Menezes, A. (ed.) CT-RSA 2005. LNCS, vol. 3376, pp. 58–71. Springer, Heidelberg (2005)
25. Stevens, M.: New Collision Attacks on SHA-1 Based on Optimal Joint Local-Collision Analysis. In: Johansson, T., Nguyen, P.Q. (eds.) EUROCRYPT 2013. LNCS, vol. 7881, pp. 245–261. Springer, Heidelberg (2013)
26. Wang, X.: Cryptanalysis of SHA-1 Hash Function. Keynote Speech at The First Cryptographic Hash Workshop conducted by NIST (2005), http://csrc.nist.gov/groups/ST/hash/first_workshop.html

27. Zheng, Y., Pieprzyk, J., Seberry, J.: HAVAL — One-Way Hashing Algorithm with Variable Length of Output. In Seberry, J., Zheng, Y., eds.: AUSCRYPT'92. In: Zheng, Y., Seberry, J. (eds.) AUSCRYPT 1992. LNCS, vol. 718, pp. 83–104. Springer, Heidelberg (1993)

28. Yu, H., Wang, X., Yun, A., Park, S.: Cryptanalysis of the Full HAVAL with 4 and 5 Passes. In: Robshaw, M. (ed.) FSE 2006. LNCS, vol. 4047, pp. 89–110. Springer, Heidelberg (2006)

29. Suzuki, K., Tonien, D., Kurosawa, K., Toyota, K.: Birthday Paradox for Multi-Collisions. IEICE Transactions on Fundamentals of Electronics, Communications and Computer Sciences E91-A(1), 39–45 (2008)

30. Iwamoto, M., Peyrin, T., Sasaki, Y.: Limited-birthday Distinguishers for Hash Functions: Collisions Beyond the Birthday Bound can be Meaningful. In: Sako, K., Sarkar, P. (eds.) ASIACRYPT 2013, Part II. LNCS, vol. 8270, pp. 504–523. Springer, Heidelberg (2013)

31. Leurent, G.: MD4 is Not One-Way. In: Nyberg, K. (ed.) FSE 2008. LNCS, vol. 5086, pp. 412–428. Springer, Heidelberg (2008)

32. Gilbert, H., Peyrin, T.: Super-Sbox Cryptanalysis: Improved Attacks for AES-Like Permutations. In: Hong, S., Iwata, T. (eds.) FSE 2010. LNCS, vol. 6147, pp. 365–383. Springer, Heidelberg (2010)

33. De Cannière, C., Mendel, F., Rechberger, C.: Collisions for 70-Step SHA-1: On the Full Cost of Collision Search. In: Adams, C., Miri, A., Wiener, M. (eds.) SAC 2007. LNCS, vol. 4876, pp. 56–73. Springer, Heidelberg (2007)

34. Grechnikov, E.A.: Collisions for 72-step and 73-step SHA-1: Improvements in the Method of Characteristics. Cryptology ePrint Archive, Report 2010/413 (2010)

35. Grechnikov, E., Adinetz, A.: Collision for 75-step SHA-1: Intensive Parallelization with GPU. Cryptology ePrint Archive, Report 2011/641 (2011)

A   Cycle Construction with SHA-1 Collision Attack

The core idea of the Floyd's cycle-finding algorithm is that, for a previous chain value v_{i-1}, a function $\mathcal{G}$ (and $\mathcal{F}$) must reproduce an identical value v_i as the next chain value. Because the collision attack requires a complicated attack procedure, the detailed operations in $\mathcal{G}$ must be carefully determined. In this section, we explain the following three points that require special attention.

- How to ensure sufficient freedom degrees to find a collision of SHA-1.
- How to reproduce the same colliding value for the same input v_{i-1} received in different timings.
- How to apply advanced collision-search techniques by ensuring the reproduction of the same colliding value.

Ensuring Sufficient Freedom Degrees. Collision attack on SHA-1 [19] generates a collision of 2-blocks long. From several experimental researches on reduced rounds [33–35], we can see that the available freedom degrees for the collision search within the first message block may not be sufficient. This is because most of the message bits must be fixed to control the differential propagation. Therefore, embedding a previous 160-bit chain value v_{i-1} inside the first message block gives a critically bad impact.

In our method, $\mathcal{G}$ generates a collision consisting of four message blocks, where the size of each message block is 512 bits. The overview is given in Fig. 7. We

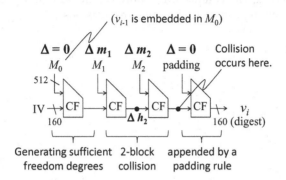

Fig. 7. Construction of $\mathcal{G}$ with SHA-1 Collision Attack

add another message block M_0 before the 2-block collision. The size of M_0 is 512 bits. We set 160 bits of M_0 to v_{i-1}. The other 352 bits can be fixed to any value as long as the rule is uniquely fixed for the reproduction. The simplest way is fixing the other 352 bits to 0. This reproduces the same output value of the first message blocks for the same v_{i-1}. Then, the 2-block collision is located in the second and third message blocks. Note that the third message blocks are also heavily fixed to control the differential propagation. Hence, we cannot embed the padding string inside the third message block. This is the reason why we need the fourth message block.

Because no limitation exists for the second and third message blocks, sufficient freedom degrees can be ensured for generating a 2-block collision.

Reproducing the Same Colliding Value. Collision search algorithm is usually a random algorithm. Messages to be tested are generated randomly from uniformly distributed space. However, this way cannot be used in our case due to the problem of reproduction.

The problem can be simply avoided by stopping using the random algorithm but choose messages to be tested in a specific rule. An example is pre-determining the message-bit positions to be modified during the collision search. If 2^β messages need to be tested, we can choose particular β-bit position. Whenever we change the message, we take the message by modifying the chosen β-bit position. In addition, we set the rule of the order of the modification. For example, we modify the message from the least significant bit. The rule enables us to reproduce the same message when the same situation occurs. Note that not only inside M_1 but also the 352 bits of M_0 can be modified as long as the modification rule is uniquely fixed.

Application of Advanced Collision-Search Techniques. Complicated collision-search techniques such as the message modification technique and the early aborting technique can also be applied with ensuring the reproductivity by pre-determining the application rule. The important thing is that the collision-search algorithm must behave in the same way when the same situation occurs. Therefore, by setting the condition to apply the message modification or early aborting technique, reproducing the same result is possible.

On the (In)Equivalence of Impossible Differential and Zero-Correlation Distinguishers for Feistel- and Skipjack-Type Ciphers

Céline Blondeau[1], Andrey Bogdanov[2], and Meiqin Wang[3]

[1] Department of Information and Computer Science, Aalto University School of Science, Finland
celine.blondeau@aalto.fi
[2] Technical University of Denmark, Denmark
anbog@dtu.dk
[3] Key Laboratory of Cryptologic Technology and Information Security, Ministry of Education, Shandong University, Jinan 250100, China
mqwang@sdu.edu.cn

Abstract. For many word-oriented block ciphers, impossible differential (ID) and zero-correlation linear (ZC) cryptanalyses are among the most powerful attacks. Whereas ID cryptanalysis makes use of differentials which never occur, the ZC cryptanalysis relies on linear approximations with correlations equal to zero. While the key recovery parts of ID and ZC attacks may differ and are often specific to the target cipher, the underlying distinguishing properties frequently cover the same number of rounds. However, in some cases, the discrepancy between the best known IDs and ZC approximations is rather significant.

At EUROCRYPT'13, a link between these two distinguishers has been presented. However, though being independent of the underling structure of the cipher, it is usually not useful for most known ID or ZC distinguishers. So despite the relevance of those attacks, the question of their equivalence or inequivalence has not been formally addressed so far in a constructive practical way.

In this paper, we aim to bridge this gap in the understanding of the links between the ID and ZC properties. We tackle this problem at the example of two wide classes of ciphers, namely, Feistel- and Skipjack-type ciphers. As our major contribution, for those ciphers, we derive conditions for impossible differentials and zero-correlation approximations to cover the same number of rounds. Using the conditions, we prove an equivalence between ID and ZC distinguishers for type-I and type-II Feistel-type ciphers, for Rule-A and Rule-B Skipjack-type ciphers, as well as for TWINE and LBlock. Moreover, we show this equivalence for the Extended Generalised Feistel construction presented at SAC'13. We also use our theoretical results to argue for an inequivalence between ID and ZC distinguishers for a range of Skipjack-type ciphers.

Keywords: impossible differential, zero-correlation, Feistel-type ciphers, Skipjack-type ciphers.

I. Boureanu, P. Owesarski, and S. Vaudenay (Eds.): ACNS 2014, LNCS 8479, pp. 271–288, 2014.

1   Introduction

Differential and linear cryptanalyses [3,14] definitely belong to the most essential types of attacks on block ciphers and have known numerous generalizations and extensions. Among those are impossible differential (ID) cryptanalysis [2,12] and zero-correlation (ZC) cryptanalysis [8,9] which have been proven efficient when applied to word-oriented block ciphers – block ciphers with strong local diffusion.

Classically, *ID distinguishers* take advantage of differentials which never occur for the studied permutations. This technique has been the subject of many research publications. The security of new and old primitives has been evaluated with respect to this attack. For instance, an early ID attack still remains the best known key-recovery for Skipjack [2]. Also automated methods to find IDs have been proposed [13, 25].

In *ZC cryptanalysis*, attackers rather take advantage of linear approximations that have probability 1/2 to hold. This new attack which can be seen as multidimensional linear attack with capacity equal to zero [7], has also been applied to many word-oriented block ciphers [6, 7, 9, 18, 23, 24] to evaluate their security and often improve upon the state-of-the-art cryptanalysis.

Usually techniques similar to the $\mathcal{U}$-method or a generalization thereof are used to identify ID distinguishers for word-oriented construction. In the following, we refer to these various methods as *matrix methods*. Recently, it has been shown in [18] that this method can be applied to find ZC distinguishers in particular for the block cipher LBlock [26].

While for many of these ciphers the discovered ZC distinguishers cover the same number of rounds as the ID distinguishers, the numbers of rounds covered by the properties can be sometimes rather distinct. In [7], there is a ZC distinguisher for a 30-round Skipjack variant for which only a 21-round ID distinguisher is known to exist. This discrepancy raises the *question of equivalence between ZC and ID distinguishers*. As a first attempt to formalize this problem, at EUROCRYPT'13 [4], using a mathematical link between linear and differential cryptanalysis, this question has been shown to have a positive answer in the special case of multidimensional linear spaces of specific size. The link of [4] can be outlined as follows:

For a given n-bit block cipher, we have an ID distinguisher $(0, \delta) \nrightarrow (0, \gamma)$ with $\delta \in \mathbb{F}_2^t \setminus \{0\}$ and $\gamma \in \mathbb{F}_2^{n-t} \setminus \{0\}$ if and only if we have a ZC distinguisher $(u, 0) \nrightarrow (v, 0)$ with $u \in \mathbb{F}_2^{n-t} \setminus \{0\}$ and $v \in \mathbb{F}_2^t \setminus \{0\}$. Though this relation is independent of the underlying cipher and its specific structure, it has the limitation of involving $(2^t - 1)(2^{n-t} - 1) \approx 2^n$ differentials or linear approximations. However, for many ciphers, fewer differentials are involved, which poses a limitation to the practical application of this general theoretical result.

In this paper, with matrix techniques for IDs and ZC approximations, we address this question for many more relevant constructions including Feistel-type and Skipjack-type ciphers. A major difference of this paper with the link of [4] is that the results presented here depend of the structure of the underlying ciphers, thus, being both less general and more practical.

Our Contributions. The contributions of this paper are as follows.

- **Condition of equivalence between ZC and ID distinguishers:** As our main contribution, we show that for many constructions, once we have an ID distinguisher on r rounds involving M differentials, we obtain a ZC distinguisher on the same r rounds involving M linear approximations, and vise versa. This yields a necessary and sufficient condition of equivalence between ZC and ID distinguishers. We point out that the key recovery procedures on top of those distinguishers may be quite different and may result in different number of rounds cryptanalyzed in the actual attacks. While for most Feistel constructions, the inverse of the internal function is not required for deciphering, for ciphers like Skipjack the deciphering is obtained thanks to the inverse of the internal function. We refer to the first type as *Feistel-type* ciphers and to the second type as *Skipjack-type* ciphers. Understanding the relation between these distinguishers, ID and ZC, will help designers check if a separate study of ZC and ID distinguishers is necessary for a security evaluation. Representation of the different constructions can be found in the different part of this paper. For instance, in Fig. 1, Feistel-type ciphers are represented, and in Fig. 3 and Fig. 4 Skipjack-type ciphers are represented.
- **Inequivalence considerations for ZC and ID distinguishers:** The necessary and sufficient equivalence condition also allows us to reason about cases of inequivalence for Feistel- and Skipjack-type ciphers. We consider inequivalence between ZC and ID distinguishers for several interesting examples including the Feistel-type constructions of FSE'10 [19] featuring optimal branch shuffles as well as for the construction proposed at SAC'13 [1]. We also explain the type of inequivalence between ID and ZC distinguishers observed for Skipjack variants in ASIACRYPT'12 [7].

Organization of the Paper. The remainder of this paper is organized as follows. In Section 2, we define what we call a Feistel-type cipher and recall how a matrix representation of the round function can be used to find ID distinguishers or to compute the differential diffusion of such constructions. In the same section, we also reconsider the recent method proposed in [18] to find ZC distinguishers on a Feistel-type cipher. Based on this method, in Section 3, we present conditions under which ID distinguishers involving M differentials and ZC ones involving M linear approximations can be applied on the same number of rounds of a Feistel-type cipher. Section 4 is dedicated to the Skipjack-type ciphers. In this section, we discuss the equivalence/inequivalence between ZC and ID distinguishers on Skipjack variants. In Section 5, we discuss the adaption of the results of Section 3 and Section 4 to other types of word-oriented ciphers. In particular, we discuss the Extended Generalised Feistel construction presented at SAC'13 [1] and constructions similar to MARS and GF-NLFSR such as Four-Cell. Section 6 concludes this paper.

2   Preliminaries

In this paper we assume word-oriented block ciphers with b words. The state of a n-bit word-oriented block cipher with $n = b \cdot s$ is represented by $X = (X_1, X_2, \cdots, X_b)$ where the X_i, $1 \leq i \leq b$ are blocks or words of s bits.

As recalled in the introduction, different constructions make use of this block decomposition of the state, to apply at each round non-linear operations on a subset of these blocks. Impossible differential cryptanalysis and zero-correlation linear cryptanalysis are among the best attacks on this type of construction. In this section, we describe these two distinguishers and their relation on what we call a Feistel-type cipher.

2.1   Feistel-Type Cipher and Matrix Representation

At FSE'10 [19], Suzaki and Minematsu proposed a general framework to describe what we call in this paper a Feistel-type cipher. This framework covers the well known type-I (see Fig. 1), type-II, type-III (similar to type-I) constructions as well as constructions such as the one proposed by Nyberg in [16]. The round function of Feistel-type cipher is such that a branch (word) can at each round be the input of a non-linear function or be linearly affected by the output of such non-linear function. As represented[1] in Fig. 1, a branching operation is done on the branches corresponding of the input of a non-linear function, and an exclusive-or addition (Xor) is done on the branches modified by the output of these non-linear functions. The number I of non-linear layers depends on the construction and can vary from 1 to $b/2$. Part of the diffusion is then provided by a permutation of the branches. For such constructions, a key is usually Xor-ed

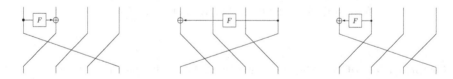

Fig. 1. A type-I Feistel with 4 branches: On the left the round function, in the middle the inverse of the round function and on the right the mirror of the round function as described in Def. 2.

to the partial state. As the distinguishers presented in this paper do not depend on this operation, this part will not be described.

Notice that given the round function of a Feistel-type cipher, as for a SPN constructions, one can distinguish the non-linear part consisting of the application of the non-linear functions to the linear part, consisting on the permutation of the branches. Similarly to what has been done in [1], the round function of a

---

[1] While depending on the construction, the number of branches of a word-oriented cipher can varies, for illustration purposes the pictures presented in this paper concentrate on ciphers with 4 branches.

Feistel-type cipher can be matricially represented. This description can be split in regard to the different layers which are F-layer and P-layer.

Definition 1. *Omitting key and constant addition, the round function of a Feistel-type cipher with b branches can be matricially represented as a combination of two $b \times b$ matrices $\mathcal{F}$, $\mathcal{P}$ with coefficients $\{0, 1, F_i\}$ where the $\{F_i\}_{i \leq I}$ denote the internal non-linear functions.*

- *Representing the non-linear layer (F-layer), the non-zero coefficients of the matrix $\mathcal{F}$ are equal to 1 in the diagonal and have coefficient F_i in row j and column k if the input of the function F_i is given by the k-th branch and the output is Xor-ed to the j-th branch. Meaning that $\mathcal{F}$ can have up to one F_i on each row and column.*
- *Representing the permutation of the branches (P-layer), the matrix $\mathcal{P}$ is a permutation matrix with only one non-zero coefficient per line and column.*

From these two matrices, a Feistel-type round function can be represented by a $b \times b$ matrix $\mathcal{R}$ as $\mathcal{R} = \mathcal{P} \cdot \mathcal{F}$.

Example 1. The round function of the Type-I Feistel with 4 branches depicted in Fig. 1 can be represented from $\mathcal{F}$ and $\mathcal{P}$ as follows:

$$\mathcal{F} = \begin{pmatrix} 1 & 0 & 0 & 0 \\ F & 1 & 0 & 0 \\ 0 & 0 & 1 & 0 \\ 0 & 0 & 0 & 1 \end{pmatrix}, \quad \mathcal{P} = \begin{pmatrix} 0 & 1 & 0 & 0 \\ 0 & 0 & 1 & 0 \\ 0 & 0 & 0 & 1 \\ 1 & 0 & 0 & 0 \end{pmatrix} \quad \text{and } \mathcal{R} = \mathcal{P} \cdot \mathcal{F} = \begin{pmatrix} F & 1 & 0 & 0 \\ 0 & 0 & 1 & 0 \\ 0 & 0 & 0 & 1 \\ 1 & 0 & 0 & 0 \end{pmatrix}.$$

In this paper, we assume that the internal non-linear functions $F_i : \mathbb{F}_2^s \to \mathbb{F}_2^s$, are bijective. When it is not necessary, to make a distinction between the different non-linear functions, we denote them as F instead of F_i.

In this paper, -1 and $-F$ are identified with respectively 1 and F. The matrix representation of the inverse round function is $\mathcal{R}^{-1} = \mathcal{F}^{-1} \cdot \mathcal{P}^{-1}$.

2.2 Matrix Method for Impossible Differential Distinguisher

Through this paper, we express a truncated input (resp. output) difference as a vector Δ (resp. Γ) of size b.

Impossible differential distinguishers are often derived from a miss-in-the-middle or inconsistency between two intermediate differences. More precisely, cryptanalysts are interested in finding truncated differences Δ and Γ and some integers ℓ and m such that we have an inconsistency between the intermediate differences $\mathcal{R}^\ell \cdot \Delta$ and $\mathcal{R}^{-m} \cdot \Gamma$.

To study the propagation of differences thought this type of construction, the rules depicted in Fig. 2 and the matrix representation of the round function of a Feistel-type cipher are used. In particular one can find ID by computing the values $\mathcal{R}^\ell \cdot \Delta$ and $\mathcal{R}^{-m} \cdot \Gamma$ and detecting an inconsistency between the intermediate differences. This method has been described in [11, 13] and used to analyse the security of many ciphers.

Context	Branching	Xor	F-function

Differential:

δ_1 → δ_2, δ_3 $\delta_3 = \delta_1 = \delta_2$

$\delta_1 \oplus \delta_2$, δ_3 $\delta_3 = \delta_1 \oplus \delta_2$

δ_1, F, δ_2 $\delta_1 = \delta_2 = 0$; $\delta_1 \neq 0$ and $\delta_2 \neq 0$

Linear:

u_1 → u_2, u_3 $u_3 = u_1 \oplus u_2$

$u_1 \oplus u_2$, u_3 $u_3 = u_1 = u_2$

u_1, F, u_2 $u_1 = u_2 = 0$; $u_1 \neq 0$ and $u_2 \neq 0$

Fig. 2. Propagation of differences and linear masks through the basic operations. δ_1, δ_2, δ_3 denote differences and u_1, u_2, u_3 linear masks. The conditions correspond to the case where the probabilities/correlations are non-zero.

2.3 Matrix Method for Zero-Correlation Distinguishers

While ID cryptanalysis has been defined at the end of the 90's, the first attack using linear approximations with no-correlation has been published in 2012 [9].

Through this paper, we denote a truncated input (resp. output) mask as a vector U (resp. V) of size b. As for ID cryptanalysis, the classical method used to find ZC approximations consists in detecting an inconsistency, a difference, between two intermediate masks.

In [18] a generic method to find zero-correlation linear approximations on Feistel-type ciphers is described. This method is similar to the matrix method used for finding impossible differentials. Nevertheless, as depicted in Fig. 2, the branching and Xor operations in the linear context and then a fortiori for ZC distinguishers are converse to the ones in the differential context.

From these simple observations, we deduce that the matrix representation of the round function can not be used directly to find ZC distinguishers. Instead, as in [18] it seems natural to define what we will call the mirror round function. In this mirror function as illustrated in Fig. 1 the role played by the input and output of the non-linear functions are swapped meaning that the branching and Xor operations are swapped.

The matrix representation of what we call mirror function of a Feistel-type cipher can be defined easily from the matrix representation of the original function.

Definition 2. *For a Feistel-type cipher given the matrix representation of the round function $\mathcal{R} = \mathcal{P} \cdot \mathcal{F}$, we call mirror function the round function described by the matrix $\mathcal{M} = \mathcal{P} \cdot \mathcal{F}^T$, where $\mathcal{F}^T$ denotes the transposition of the matrix $\mathcal{F}$.*

Example 2. The mirror function of the Feistel-type function of Fig. 1 can be represented by the matrix

$$\mathcal{M} = \begin{pmatrix} 0 & 1 & 0 & 0 \\ 0 & 0 & 1 & 0 \\ 0 & 0 & 0 & 1 \\ 1 & F & 0 & 0 \end{pmatrix} \text{ with inverse } \mathcal{M}^{-1} = \begin{pmatrix} F & 0 & 0 & 1 \\ 1 & 0 & 0 & 0 \\ 0 & 1 & 0 & 0 \\ 0 & 0 & 1 & 0 \end{pmatrix}.$$

Description of the matrix method in the ZC context [18] is given from the mirror of the round function of the LBlock cipher. In a general matter, as in the differential context, we can use this method to determine the linear diffusion of the cipher or to find ZC distinguishers on a Feistel-type cipher.

3   Equivalence for Feistel-Type Ciphers

3.1   Condition of Equivalence

In the previous section, we explain how ID and ZC distinguishers on a Feistel-type cipher can be found using a matrix method. However, the provided discussion shows that the matrices used in both context are different. While in the differential context the matrix $\mathcal{R}$ representing the round function can be used directly, in the linear context one should use the matrix $\mathcal{M}$ refereed as mirror matrix. Based on these remarks and on the fact that ZC distinguishers and ID distinguishers threaten usually the same number of rounds of many Feistel-type ciphers, we study in this section, the relation between these attacks. In particular we analyze the conditions which allow us to state that we have an ID distinguisher involving M differentials on $r = \ell + m$ rounds of the cipher if and only if we have a ZC distinguisher involving M linear approximations on the same $r = \ell + m$ rounds.

Theorem 1. *Let $\mathcal{R}$ be the matrix representation of the round function of a generalized Feistel Network as presented in Sect. 2 and $\mathcal{M}$ be the matrix representation of its mirror function. If it exists a $b \times b$ permutation matrix $\mathcal{Q}$ such that*

$$\mathcal{R} = \mathcal{Q} \cdot \mathcal{M} \cdot \mathcal{Q}^{-1} \text{ or } \mathcal{R} = \mathcal{Q} \cdot \mathcal{M}^{-1} \cdot \mathcal{Q}^{-1}, \tag{1}$$

we deduce that:
It exists an impossible differential distinguisher on r rounds involving M differentials if and only if it exists a zero-correlation linear distinguisher on r rounds involving M linear masks.

Proof. As the second condition of (1) seems to be the most likely in practice, we assume in this proof that we have $\mathcal{R} = \mathcal{Q} \cdot \mathcal{M}^{-1} \cdot \mathcal{Q}^{-1}$. The other case can be proved in a similar way.
We assume that we have an ID on $\ell + m$ rounds meaning that we know some Δ and Γ such that we have an inconsistency between $\mathcal{R}^{\ell} \cdot \Delta$ and $\mathcal{R}^{-m} \cdot \Gamma$.
As we have $\mathcal{R}^{\ell} = \mathcal{Q} \cdot \mathcal{M}^{-\ell} \cdot \mathcal{Q}^{-1}$ and $\mathcal{R}^{-m} = \mathcal{Q}^{-1} \cdot \mathcal{M}^{m} \cdot \mathcal{Q}$, we deduce that we have an inconsistency between $\mathcal{R}^{\ell} \cdot \Delta$ and $\mathcal{R}^{-m} \cdot \Gamma$, if and only if we have an inconsistency between $\mathcal{Q} \cdot \mathcal{M}^{-\ell} \cdot \mathcal{Q}^{-1} \cdot \Delta$ and $\mathcal{Q}^{-1} \cdot \mathcal{M}^{m} \cdot \mathcal{Q} \cdot \Gamma$. Given the masks $U = \mathcal{Q}^{-1} \cdot \Delta$ and $V = \mathcal{Q} \cdot \Gamma$, we deduce an inconsistency between $\mathcal{Q} \cdot \mathcal{M}^{-\ell} \cdot U$ and $\mathcal{Q}^{-1} \cdot \mathcal{M}^{m} \cdot V$.
Notice that the intermediate masks correspond to a linear permutation of the intermediate differences and that we have transformed the inconsistency in the differential context to an inconsistency in the linear context.

More precisely, we have shown that if it exists a permutation matrix Q such that $\mathcal{R} = Q \cdot \mathcal{M}^{-1} \cdot Q^{-1}$, and if we have an ID distinguisher on $\ell + m$ rounds of a Feistel-type cipher, we have a ZC distinguisher on $m + \ell$ rounds of the same cipher. The converse proof is obtained by inverting the role played by $\mathcal{R}$ and $\mathcal{M}$. From the details provided in the proof, one can notice that since Q is a permutation matrix, the truncated masks and differences, U and Δ as well as V and Γ, are similar and the number of differences corresponds to the number of masks.   □

Similarly one can prove that the linear and differential diffusion of a Feistel-type cipher are equal if the round function respect one of the conditions given in (1).

3.2   Example of Equivalence

In practice many Feistel-type ciphers respect the condition given in Th. 1. In this section, we discuss some of the well-known constructions.

For instance for the type-I Feistel-type cipher of Ex. 1 we have

$$
Q = \begin{pmatrix} 1\,0\,0\,0 \\ 0\,0\,0\,1 \\ 0\,0\,1\,0 \\ 0\,1\,0\,0 \end{pmatrix} \text{ and } \mathcal{R} = Q \cdot \mathcal{M}^{-1} \cdot Q^{-1}.
$$

Using this method, we can also show that any type-II Feistel-type ciphers have the same linear and differential diffusion.

The construction proposed by Nyberg [16] is, at the difference of the type-I and type-II one non-alternating, meaning that over the rounds the same branch can affected by many branching operations before being affected by a Xor. As this construction fulfills the condition given in Th 1, from the model proposed in this paper, one can easily adapt the security analysis provided against ID cryptanalysis to the linear context.

In [19], Suzaki and Minematsu proposed a general framework for all these Feistel-type ciphers. Based on this analysis, they later design the block cipher TWINE [21]. While the security of this cipher in regard to ID cryptanalysis has been analysed by the designers, up to our knowledge no analysis of the security/insecurity of this cipher in regard to ZC cryptanalysis has been done. In [20], the authors explain the similarity between TWINE and LBlock. From our framework, we can check that the 14-round ID distinguisher of LBlock or TWINE [21] can be converted directly to a 14-round zero-correlation one. As this distinguisher was considered in the security analysis performed by the designers and the round function of these ciphers fulfilled to conditions of Th. 1, one can question the relevance of, for instance, the zero-correlation attack of [18] on LBlock.

The next section is dedicated to the analysis of the results of [19].

3.3   Example of Non-Equivalence

In Appendix of [19], many Feistel-type round functions with different diffusion layers are proposed. Among other, the security in regards to ID cryptanalysis is analyzed for different permutations, π, of the 6, 8, 10, 12, 14 or 16 branches.

We checked the framework proposed in Th. 1 on these constructions. In particular, for each permutation π proposed in [19], using the matrix representation, we checked if it exists a permutation matrix Q, such that one of the conditions given in (1) is satisfied. As no security analysis against zero-correlation linear attack is provided in [19], we compare our result (existence or non-existence of such matrix) with the differential and linear diffusion provided in [19]. While for most of them we can prove that the existence of an ID distinguisher implies the existence of a ZC distinguisher, for illustration purpose, we present here two cases where the condition given in Th. 1 is not satisfied. In Tables 1 and 2 both ciphers have an impossible distinguisher on 14 rounds and after 8 rounds 38, 40 or 35 Sboxes are active in the differential or linear context.

Table 1. Case No.12 of Table 5 of [19] ($b = 14$).

π	Number of rounds		Number of active Sboxes	
	impossible	diffusion	diff. context	linear context
$\{1, 2, 9, 4, 11, 6, 7, 8, 5, 12, 13, 10, 3, 0\}$	14	8	38	40

The permutation defined Table 1 is such that the minimal number of active Sboxes after 8 rounds in the differential context is smaller than the one in the linear context, this results is confirmed by the fact that we can prove that there exists no-matrix Q verifying the condition given in Th. 1. The diffusion (number

Table 2. Case No.5 of Table 4 of [19] ($b = 12$).

π	Number of rounds		Number of active Sboxes	
	impossible	diffusion	diff. context	linear context
$\{5, 0, 7, 2, 1, 6, 11, 8, 3, 10, 9, 4\}$	14	8	35	35

of active Sboxes) in the linear and differential context of the Feistel-type function given in Table 2 has been computed as equal. With the method described in this paper, we can show that the condition of Th. 1 is not fulfilled. This example illustrates the possibility that the conditions given in Th. 1 are sufficient but not necessary to have the same linear and differential diffusion.

4   Equivalence for Skipjack-Type Ciphers

4.1   Skipjack-Type Ciphers

Some word-oriented ciphers, which are also vulnerable to ID and ZC do not fulfill the conditions given in Sect. 3. This is for instance the case of the cipher Skipjack and its two different round functions known as Rule-A and Rule-B.

Fig. 3. Rule-A (left) and Rule-B (right) as in Skipjack

For these functions represented in Fig. 3, the internal non-linear functions should be bijective to allow the decryption.

In this section, a Skipjack-type cipher is defined as an iteration of Skipjack-type round functions. For such round function the input and output of a non-linear function are on the same branch. Such round function can have one non-linear bijective function in each of its branch. We assume that the linear operations consisting at mixing the information of the different branches are executed after the F-layer. We call this step X-layer. In this section, we assume that only one branching or exclusive-or operation is allowed on each branches. The permutation of the branches, P-layer, is the last operation performed in this round function. More precisely, using a matrix representation, a Skipjack-type round function can be described as follows.

Definition 3. *A Skipjack-type round function with b branches can be matricially represented as a combination of three $b \times b$ matrices $\mathcal{G}$, $\mathcal{X}$, $\mathcal{P}$ with coefficients $\{0, 1, F\}$, where F denotes a non-linear layer operation.*

- *Representing the F-layer, the matrix $\mathcal{G}$ is diagonal with 1 or F in the diagonal. The j-th element of the diagonal is equal to F if a non-linear function is applied to the branch j.*
- *Representing the X-layer, the matrix $\mathcal{X}$ has 1's in the diagonal and at maximum two 1 per row and column.*
- *Representing the P-layer, the matrix $\mathcal{P}$ is a permutation matrix with only one non-zero element per line and column.*

From these three matrices, a Skipjack-type round function can be represented by a $b \times b$ matrix $\mathcal{R}$ defined as $\mathcal{R} = \mathcal{P} \cdot \mathcal{X} \cdot \mathcal{G}$.

Example 3. Rule-A of Skipjack depicted in Fig. 3 can be represented as

$$\mathcal{R}_A = \mathcal{P} \cdot \mathcal{X}_A \cdot \mathcal{G} = \begin{pmatrix} F & 1 & 0 & 0 \\ 0 & 0 & 1 & 0 \\ 0 & 0 & 0 & 1 \\ F & 0 & 0 & 0 \end{pmatrix},$$

with $\mathcal{X}_A = \begin{pmatrix} 1 & 0 & 0 & 0 \\ 1 & 1 & 0 & 0 \\ 0 & 0 & 1 & 0 \\ 0 & 0 & 0 & 1 \end{pmatrix}$, $\mathcal{G} = \begin{pmatrix} F & 0 & 0 & 0 \\ 0 & 1 & 0 & 0 \\ 0 & 0 & 1 & 0 \\ 0 & 0 & 0 & 1 \end{pmatrix}$ and $\mathcal{P} = \begin{pmatrix} 0 & 1 & 0 & 0 \\ 0 & 0 & 1 & 0 \\ 0 & 0 & 0 & 1 \\ 1 & 0 & 0 & 0 \end{pmatrix}$.

Def. 3 covers more constructions than just the Rule-A of the Skipjack. In Fig. 4 an other example of Skipjack-type function with two non-linear functions and different P-layer is represented.

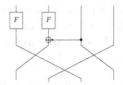

Fig. 4. A Skipjack-type round function with two internal non-linear layers

ID distinguishers can be found using this matrix representation. The inconsistency rules and the properties defined in Fig. 2 remains the same than for a Feistel-type cipher.

As in Sect. 3, we identify -1 as 1, $-F$ as F but also in this section, we identify $1/F$ and F^{-1} as F.

Definition 4. *Given* $\mathcal{R} = \mathcal{P} \cdot \mathcal{X} \cdot \mathcal{G}$ *the matrix representation of a Skipjack-type round function (see. Def. 3), we call mirror function the round function described by the matrix* $\mathcal{M} = \mathcal{P} \cdot \mathcal{X}^T \cdot \mathcal{G}$.

Example 4. The mirror of the Skipjack Rule-A round function given in Fig. 3 is:

$$\text{with } \mathcal{M} = \begin{pmatrix} 0 & 1 & 0 & 0 \\ 0 & 0 & 1 & 0 \\ 0 & 0 & 0 & 1 \\ F & 1 & 0 & 0 \end{pmatrix}.$$

Similarly to the description provided in Sect. 2.3 for Feistel-type ciphers, this mirror representation can be use find ZC distinguishers on a cipher defined as an iteration of a unique Skipjack-type round function.

4.2 Condition of Equivalence

In this section, before describing in Th. 2 under which condition, the existence of an ID distinguisher involving M differences is equivalent to the existence of a ZC distinguisher involving M linear masks, we explain why the Rule-B of Skipjack depicted in Fig. 3, can be represented in our model.

Rule-B of Skipjack depicted in Fig. 3 can be represented using the matrices $\mathcal{G}$ and $\mathcal{P}$ of Ex. 3 as

$$\mathcal{R}_B = \mathcal{P} \cdot \mathcal{G} \cdot \mathcal{X}_B = \begin{pmatrix} F & 1 & 0 & 0 \\ 0 & 0 & 1 & 0 \\ 0 & 0 & 0 & 1 \\ 1 & 0 & 0 & 0 \end{pmatrix} \text{ with } \mathcal{X}_B = \begin{pmatrix} 1 & 0 & 0 & 0 \\ 0 & 1 & 0 & 0 \\ 0 & 0 & 1 & 0 \\ 1 & 0 & 0 & 1 \end{pmatrix}.$$

Notice that for $\mathcal{R}_B$ at contrary to $\mathcal{R}_A$ the X-layer is performed before the F-layer. Nevertheless, when it comes at computing the differential and linear diffusion but also at finding ID or ZC distinguishers of a cipher defined as an iteration of Rule-B, the first and or last linear layer can be omitted or interchanged. More explicitly we can define new round function with matrix representation: $\mathcal{R}_* = \mathcal{X}_B \cdot \mathcal{P} \cdot \mathcal{G} = \mathcal{P} \cdot (\mathcal{P}^{-1} \cdot \mathcal{X}_B \cdot \mathcal{P}) \cdot \mathcal{G}$. This transformed function corresponds to the mirror of Rule-A given in Ex. 4.

Remark 1. In a general matter, if the X-layer is performed before the F-layer, meaning if the round function is represented as $\mathcal{R} = \mathcal{P} \cdot \mathcal{G} \cdot \mathcal{X}$ with $\mathcal{P}, \mathcal{X}, \mathcal{G}$ as in Def. 3, for studying the differential and linear properties, we can transform of this round function to fulfill the Def. 3 of a Skipjack-type cipher. The matrix representation of this transformed round function can be computed as $\mathcal{R}_* = \mathcal{X} \cdot \mathcal{P} \cdot \mathcal{G} = \mathcal{P} \cdot (\mathcal{P}^{-1} \cdot \mathcal{X} \cdot \mathcal{P}) \cdot \mathcal{G}$.

While the number of differences (resp. masks) considered in an ID (resp. ZC) distinguisher remain the same for the transformed round function than for the original one, the input/output differences (resp. masks) pattern can be different for the transformed cipher than for the original one. For instance, as illustrated in Table 3, when iterating only Rule-B the input differences of the ID distinguisher are equal in two of the branches, while when iterating only Rule-A the input differences are non-zero in only one of the branches.

In this section we assume a cipher with identical round functions. Discussion for construction with different rules will be provided in Sect. 4.3.

Theorem 2. *Let $\mathcal{R}$ be the matrix representation of a Skipjack-type round function as in Def. 3 and $\mathcal{M}$ be its mirror function. If it exists a $b \times b$ permutation matrix $\mathcal{Q}$ such that*

$$\mathcal{R} = \mathcal{Q} \cdot \mathcal{M} \cdot \mathcal{Q}^{-1} \ or \ \mathcal{G} \cdot \mathcal{P} \cdot \mathcal{X} = \mathcal{Q} \cdot \mathcal{M}^{-1} \cdot \mathcal{Q}^{-1}, \tag{2}$$

we deduce that:
It exists an impossible differential distinguisher on r rounds involving M differentials if and only if it exists a zero-correlation linear distinguisher on r rounds involving M linear masks.

Proof. The proof is similar to the one of Th. 1. While the proof is easy for the first condition of (2), we assume here that $\mathcal{G} \cdot \mathcal{P} \cdot \mathcal{X} = \mathcal{Q} \cdot \mathcal{M}^{-1} \cdot \mathcal{Q}^{-1}$. The different steps of the proof for the Rule-A of Skipjack are illustrated in Fig. 5.

From Def. 3, we have $\mathcal{R}^{-1} = \mathcal{G}^{-1} \cdot \mathcal{X}^{-1} \cdot \mathcal{P}^{-1}$ or equivalently $\mathcal{R}^{-1} = \mathcal{P}^{-1} \cdot (\mathcal{P} \cdot \mathcal{G}^{-1} \cdot \mathcal{P}^{-1}) \cdot (\mathcal{P} \cdot \mathcal{X}^{-1} \cdot \mathcal{P}^{-1})$. One can notice that the order of the operations of the inverse of the round function does not match the order of the mirror function or even the one of the round function. From Rem. 1, we can modify the round function to obtain the transformed function $\mathcal{R}_*^{-1} = \mathcal{P} \cdot \mathcal{X}^{-1} \cdot \mathcal{P}^{-1} \cdot \mathcal{G}^{-1} \cdot \mathcal{P}^{-1} = \mathcal{P} \cdot (\mathcal{R}_*)^{-1} \cdot \mathcal{P}^{-1}$.

We have an inconsistency between $\mathcal{R}^{\ell} \cdot \Delta$ and $\mathcal{R}^{-m} \cdot \Gamma$ if and only if we have an inconsistency between $\mathcal{R}_*^{\ell} \cdot \Delta_*$ and $\mathcal{R}_*^{-m} \cdot \Gamma_*$, where Δ_* and Γ_* are linear combinations of Δ and Γ and where $\mathcal{R}_* = (\mathcal{R}_*^{-1})^{-1}$. More explicitly, if and only if we have an inconsistency between $[\mathcal{P} \cdot (\mathcal{G} \cdot \mathcal{P} \cdot \mathcal{X})^l \cdot \mathcal{P}^{-1}] \cdot \Delta_*$ and $[\mathcal{P} \cdot (\mathcal{X}^{-1} \cdot \mathcal{P}^{-1} \cdot \mathcal{G}^{-1})^m \cdot \mathcal{P}^{-1}] \cdot \Gamma_*$.

Assuming representatives of the linear masks U and V similar to Δ_* and Γ_* this means that we have an inconsistency between $[\mathcal{P} \cdot (\mathcal{Q} \cdot \mathcal{M}^{-1} \cdot \mathcal{Q}^{-1})^l \cdot \mathcal{P}^{-1}] \cdot V$ and $[\mathcal{P} \cdot (\mathcal{Q} \cdot \mathcal{M} \cdot \mathcal{Q}^{-1})^m \cdot \mathcal{P}^{-1}] \cdot U$.

And we deduce an inconsistency between $\mathcal{S} \cdot \mathcal{M}^{-\ell} \cdot \mathcal{S}^{-1} \cdot V$ and $\mathcal{S} \cdot \mathcal{M}^m \cdot \mathcal{S}^{-1} \cdot U$ where $\mathcal{S} = \mathcal{P} \cdot \mathcal{Q}$ is a permutation matrix. Meaning that we have transformed an ID distinguisher on $\ell + m$ rounds to a ZC distinguisher on $m + \ell$ rounds. □

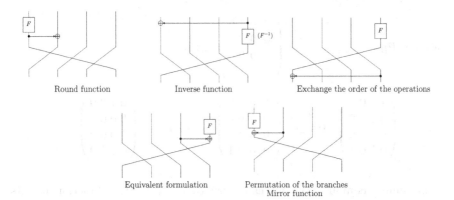

Round function   Inverse function   Exchange the order of the operations

Equivalent formulation   Permutation of the branches
                                Mirror function

Fig. 5. Illustration of the different steps in the proof of Th. 2 for Rule-A of Skipjack

4.3 Example of Skipjack-Type Ciphers

While Skipjack is defined as a 32-round cipher where 8 rounds of Rule-A are followed by 8 rounds of Rule-B, analysis of different variants using different combination of these rules can be found in the literature. In this section, we discuss these different variants.

Taken independently, Rule-A and Rule-B fulfill the condition given in Th. 2 and a cipher using only one of these rules will have ZC and ID distinguishers on the same number of rounds.

But using a combination of theses rules, we know [7] that ZC and ID distinguishers are inequivalent (see Table 3). In particular, the number of rounds on which the distinguisher can be applied depends on the alternation. For instance the original Skipjack where 8 rounds of Rule-A are followed by 8 rounds of Rule-B is more resistant to ZC cryptanalysis than to ID cryptanalysis [7].

Table 3. ID and ZC for different variants of Skipjack

Structure	Impossible Differential		Zero-Correlation Linear Hull	
	rounds	pattern	rounds	pattern
Original	24	$(0, \delta, 0, 0) \nrightarrow (\gamma, 0, 0, 0)$	17	$(u, 0, 0, 0) \nrightarrow (v, v, 0, 0)$
(4 Rule-A, 4 Rule-B)	21	$(0, \delta, 0, 0) \nrightarrow (\gamma, 0, 0, 0)$	30	$(u, u, 0, 0) \nrightarrow (v, v, 0, 0)$
(only Rule-A)	16	$(0, \delta, 0, 0) \nrightarrow (\gamma, \gamma, 0, 0)$	16	$(u, 0, 0, 0) \nrightarrow (v, v, 0, 0)$
(only Rule-B)	16	$(\delta, \delta, 0, 0) \nrightarrow (\gamma, 0, 0, 0)$	16	$(u, u, 0, 0) \nrightarrow (0, v, 0, 0)$

This example illustrates that when designing a cipher using a combination of different round functions, a more precise analysis than the one proposed in this paper may be required. Below we describe an analysis for a variant where a round with Rule-B is followed directly by a round with Rule-A.

After analysis we can show that when Rule-B is followed by Rule-A the two rounds are equivalent, in the sense of Rem. 1, to the round function given in Fig. 4. The matrix representation of this round function is:

$$
\mathcal{R}_{BA} = \mathcal{P}_{BA} \cdot \mathcal{X}_{BA} \cdot \mathcal{G}_{BA} = \begin{pmatrix} 0 & F & 1 & 0 \\ 0 & 0 & 0 & 1 \\ F & 0 & 0 & 0 \\ 0 & 0 & 1 & 0 \end{pmatrix} \text{ with}
$$

$$
\mathcal{X}_{BA} = \begin{pmatrix} 1 & 0 & 0 & 0 \\ 0 & 1 & 1 & 0 \\ 0 & 0 & 1 & 0 \\ 0 & 0 & 0 & 1 \end{pmatrix}, \mathcal{G}_{BA} = \begin{pmatrix} F & 0 & 0 & 0 \\ 0 & F & 0 & 0 \\ 0 & 0 & 1 & 0 \\ 0 & 0 & 0 & 1 \end{pmatrix} \text{ and } \mathcal{P}_{BA} = \begin{pmatrix} 0 & 1 & 0 & 0 \\ 0 & 0 & 0 & 1 \\ 1 & 0 & 0 & 0 \\ 0 & 0 & 1 & 0 \end{pmatrix}.
$$

From simple computation, we can show that neither this function nor its inverse are equivalent to its mirror function. This observation can most probably explain why ID and ZC distinguishers can not be applied of the same numbers of rounds for different variants of Skipjack.

5   Other Constructions

5.1   Generalized Feistel-Type Ciphers

For some constructions such as the one proposed by Berger, Minier, Thomas in [1], the round function can be decomposed into a non-linear layer, F-layer, similar to the one of Feistel-type cipher (see Sect. 2), a X-layer similar to the one described for the Skipjack-type cipher (see Sect. 4) and a permutation layer (P-layer). A full description of these layers can be found in [1]. An example with 4 branches of the construction proposed in [1] is depicted in Fig. 6.

In this section we denote by $\mathcal{F}, \mathcal{X}, \mathcal{P}$, the matrix representation of the different layers, where $\mathcal{F}$ and $\mathcal{P}$ are defined as in Def. 1, and $\mathcal{X}$ is defined as in Def. 3. The round function of the construction described in this section can be represented by the product of these three matrices $\mathcal{R} = \mathcal{P} \cdot \mathcal{X} \cdot \mathcal{F}$.

For such constructions, one can see that ZC distinguishers can be found thanks to the matrix $\mathcal{M} = \mathcal{P} \cdot \mathcal{X}^T \cdot \mathcal{F}^T$, which corresponds to the representation of the mirror round function.

Similarly than for Th. 1 and 2 we derive conditions on the equivalence between ID and ZC distinguishers with same number of differences and masks.

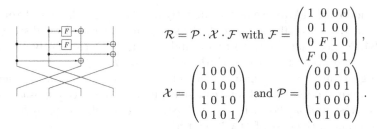

$$\mathcal{R} = \mathcal{P} \cdot \mathcal{X} \cdot \mathcal{F} \text{ with } \mathcal{F} = \begin{pmatrix} 1 & 0 & 0 & 0 \\ 0 & 1 & 0 & 0 \\ 0 & F & 1 & 0 \\ F & 0 & 0 & 1 \end{pmatrix},$$

$$\mathcal{X} = \begin{pmatrix} 1 & 0 & 0 & 0 \\ 0 & 1 & 0 & 0 \\ 1 & 0 & 1 & 0 \\ 0 & 1 & 0 & 1 \end{pmatrix} \text{ and } \mathcal{P} = \begin{pmatrix} 0 & 0 & 1 & 0 \\ 0 & 0 & 0 & 1 \\ 1 & 0 & 0 & 0 \\ 0 & 1 & 0 & 0 \end{pmatrix}.$$

Fig. 6. Round function proposed in Fig. 3 of [1] and its matrix representation (Example with 4 branches)

Theorem 3. *Let $\mathcal{R} = \mathcal{P} \cdot \mathcal{X} \cdot \mathcal{F}$ be the matrix representation of a generalized Feistel-type round function and $\mathcal{M} = \mathcal{P} \cdot \mathcal{X}^T \cdot \mathcal{F}^T$ be its mirror function. If it exists a permutation matrix $\mathcal{Q}$ such that*

$$\mathcal{R} = \mathcal{Q} \cdot \mathcal{M} \cdot \mathcal{Q}^{-1} \text{ or } \mathcal{R} = \mathcal{Q} \cdot \mathcal{M}^{-1} \cdot \mathcal{Q}^{-1}, \text{ or } \mathcal{F} \cdot \mathcal{P} \cdot \mathcal{X} = \mathcal{Q} \cdot \mathcal{M}^{-1} \cdot \mathcal{Q}^{-1}, \quad (3)$$

we deduce that:
It exists an impossible differential distinguisher on r rounds involving M differentials if and only if it exists a zero-correlation linear distinguisher on r rounds involving M linear masks.

The round functions of Sect. 2.2 of [1] fulfill the model presented in this section. In particular, one can check that $\mathcal{R} = \mathcal{M}^{-1}$. While in the original paper, the security in regard to ZC cryptanalysis is not measured, thanks to the analysis presented in this paper we are able to prove the existence of ZC distinguishers on the same number of rounds than the ID distinguishers.

5.2   Constructions Similar to MARS and Four-Cell

For some of the constructions depicted in Fig. 7, the output of the round function can in the same round influence many branches (i.e. MARS [15]) or many branches can be used to determine the input of a non-linear function (i.e. SMS4 [17]). While the round function of MARS can be represented using the following matrices,

$$\mathcal{R} = \mathcal{P} \cdot \mathcal{F} \text{ with } \mathcal{F} = \begin{pmatrix} 1 & 0 & 0 & 0 \\ F & 1 & 0 & 0 \\ F & 0 & 1 & 0 \\ F & 0 & 0 & 1 \end{pmatrix} \text{ and } \mathcal{P} = \begin{pmatrix} 0 & 1 & 0 & 0 \\ 0 & 0 & 1 & 0 \\ 0 & 0 & 0 & 1 \\ 1 & 0 & 0 & 0 \end{pmatrix},$$

one can see that this decomposition does not correspond to the one of the round function of a Feistel-type cipher.

In [13], the authors show the existence of an ID distinguisher on 11 rounds on MARS: $(0,0,0,\delta) \nrightarrow (\delta,0,0,0)$, $\delta \in \mathbb{F}_2^s$, and the existence of a 11-round ID distinguisher on SMS4: $(\delta,\delta,\delta,0) \nrightarrow (0,\delta,\delta,\delta)$, $\delta \in \mathbb{F}_2^s$. As we can easily see from Fig. 7 that the round function of SMS4 is the mirror function of the round function of MARS, we deduce directly a ZC distinguisher on 11 rounds of MARS: $(u, u, u, 0) \nrightarrow (0, u, u, u)$, $u \in \mathbb{F}_2^s$ as well as a 11-round ZC distinguisher on SMS4. Notice that for these two round functions we can easily see that it exists a permutation matrix $\mathcal{Q}$ such that $\mathcal{R}^{-1} = \mathcal{Q} \cdot \mathcal{R} \cdot \mathcal{Q}^{-1}$.

More generally, to perform a similar analysis on this construction than the analysis presented in Sect. 5.1, one can give a more precise decomposition of the matrix representation. For a better understanding, we illustrate in Fig. 7 this decomposition in the case of MARS and SMS4.

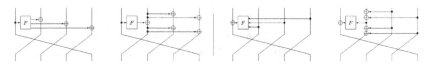

Fig. 7. Left: Round function of MARS and equivalent representation. Right: Round function of SMS4 and equivalent representation.

Let $\mathcal{Y}$ represent the first X-layer and be defined as the matrix $\mathcal{X}$ of Def. 3, a round function of a MARS-type cipher can be decomposed as $\mathcal{R} = \mathcal{P} \cdot \mathcal{X} \cdot \mathcal{F} \cdot \mathcal{Y}$. Based on Rem. 1, we can analyze the transformed function: $\mathcal{R}_* = \mathcal{Y} \cdot \mathcal{P} \cdot \mathcal{X} \cdot \mathcal{F} = \mathcal{P} \cdot (\mathcal{P}^{-1} \cdot \mathcal{Y} \cdot \mathcal{P} \cdot \mathcal{X}) \cdot \mathcal{F}$. If we denote $\mathcal{X}'_* = \mathcal{P}^{-1} \cdot \mathcal{Y} \cdot \mathcal{P} \cdot \mathcal{X}$ we have $\mathcal{R}_* = \mathcal{P} \cdot \mathcal{X}'_* \cdot \mathcal{F}$.

For this type of construction where the X-layer is represented by a matrix $\mathcal{X}'$ similar to the matrix $\mathcal{X}$ of Def. 3 but where we can have more than two "1" per row or column, another arithmetic is required. In particular, one should assume that $F(\delta_1) \oplus F(\delta_2) = F(\delta_1 + \delta_2)$ meaning that F is linear when it comes to analyze the differential and linear properties of the cipher.

By noticing that this transformed round function corresponds to the description of the Generalized Feistel-type cipher of Sect. 5.1, one can verify that for both MARS and SMS4, none of the conditions described in (3) are satisfied.

In ASISP 2009 [10] a construction called GF-NLFSR was proposed. For this construction which is a generalization of the Skipjack-type construction, many operations on the branches can be performed in the same rounds. The four branches instance of this construction is known as Four-Cell.

Similarly than for ciphers of the previous type one can determine under which condition we can convert an ID distinguisher using M differences to a ZC distinguisher using M linear masks. This simple analysis show that the mirror round function of Four-Cell is not equivalent to the function or its function, and while the best known ID distinguisher is on 18 rounds [22], we were only able to find a ZC distinguisher on 12 rounds.

6   Conclusion

Understanding the relations between ID and ZC is of great importance to simplify the analysis by designers and cryptanalysts. In this paper, we show that for some constructions based on the generalizations of the well-known Feistel and Skipjack constructions, ZC distinguishers and ID distinguishers can be derived from each other. In particular, we show that, if a round function and its mirror representation are related, both distinguishers cover the same number of rounds. Examples of ciphers for which we can prove such an equivalence are provided, along with a discussion of inequivalent cases. While we do not claim to have considered all types of word-oriented ciphers, this work is bridging the gap between these two attacks and allows for a better understanding of how to design ciphers with similar ID and ZC properties. The question of equivalence between corresponding key-recovery attacks – applied on top of those distinguishers – has been tackled in [5] and remains dependent on the outer rounds.

Acknowledgements. This work has been supported by the National Basic Research 973 Program of China under Grant No. 2013CB834205, National Natural Science Foundation of China under Grant No. 61133013, Program for New Century Excellent Talents in University of China under Grant No. NCET-13-0350, as well as the Interdisciplinary Research Foundation of Shandong University of China under Grant No. 2012JC018.

References

1. Berger, T.P., Minier, M., Thomas, G.: Extended Generalized Feistel Networks using Matrix Representation. In: SAC 2013 (to appear)
2. Biham, E., Biryukov, A., Shamir, A.: Cryptanalysis of Skipjack Reduced to 31 Rounds Using Impossible Differentials. In: Stern, J. (ed.) EUROCRYPT 1999. LNCS, vol. 1592, pp. 12–23. Springer, Heidelberg (1999)
3. Biham, E., Shamir, A.: Differential Cryptanalysis of DES-like Cryptosystems. In: Menezes, A., Vanstone, S.A. (eds.) CRYPTO 1990. LNCS, vol. 537, pp. 2–21. Springer, Heidelberg (1991)
4. Blondeau, C., Nyberg, K.: New Links between Differential and Linear Cryptanalysis. In: Johansson, T., Nguyen, P.Q. (eds.) EUROCRYPT 2013. LNCS, vol. 7881, pp. 388–404. Springer, Heidelberg (2013)
5. Blondeau, C., Nyberg, K.: Links Between Truncated Differential and Multidimensional Linear Properties of Block Ciphers and Underlying Attack Complexities. In: Oswald, E., Nguyen, P.Q. (eds.) EUROCRYPT 2014. LNCS, vol. 8441, pp. 165–182. Springer, Heidelberg (2014)
6. Bogdanov, A., Geng, H., Wang, M., Wen, L., Collard, B.: Zero-Correlation Linear Cryptanalysis with FFT and Improved Attacks on ISO Standards Camellia and CLEFIA. In: SAC 2013. LNCS. Springer (2014)
7. Bogdanov, A., Leander, G., Nyberg, K., Wang, M.: Integral and Multidimensional Linear Distinguishers with Correlation Zero. In: Wang, X., Sako, K. (eds.) ASIACRYPT 2012. LNCS, vol. 7658, pp. 244–261. Springer, Heidelberg (2012)
8. Bogdanov, A., Rijmen, V.: Linear hulls with correlation zero and linear cryptanalysis of block ciphers. Designs, Codes and Cryptography 70(3), 369–383 (2014)
9. Bogdanov, A., Wang, M.: Zero Correlation Linear Cryptanalysis with Reduced Data Complexity. In: Canteaut, A. (ed.) FSE 2012. LNCS, vol. 7549, pp. 29–48. Springer, Heidelberg (2012)
10. Choy, J., Chew, G., Khoo, K., Yap, H.: Cryptographic Properties and Application of a Generalized Unbalanced Feistel Network Structure. In: Boyd, C., González Nieto, J. (eds.) ACISP 2009. LNCS, vol. 5594, pp. 73–89. Springer, Heidelberg (2009)

11. Kim, J., Hong, S., Lim, J.: Impossible differential cryptanalysis using matrix method. Discrete Mathematics 310(5), 988–1002 (2010)
12. Knudsen, L.R.: DEAL- A 128-bit Block-Cipher. NIST AES Proposal (1998)
13. Luo, Y., Lai, X., Wu, Z., Gong, G.: A unified method for finding impossible differentials of block cipher structures. Inf. Sci. 263, 211–220 (2014)
14. Matsui, M.: Linear Cryptanalysis Method for DES Cipher. In: Helleseth, T. (ed.) EUROCRYPT 1993. LNCS, vol. 765, pp. 386–397. Springer, Heidelberg (1994)
15. Moriai, S., Vaudenay, S.: On the pseudorandomness of Top-Level schemes of block ciphers. In: Okamoto, T. (ed.) ASIACRYPT 2000. LNCS, vol. 1976, pp. 289–302. Springer, Heidelberg (2000)
16. Nyberg, K.: Generalized Feistel Networks. In: Kim, K.-c., Matsumoto, T. (eds.) ASIACRYPT 1996. LNCS, vol. 1163, pp. 91–104. Springer, Heidelberg (1996)
17. SMS4. Specication of SMS4, block cipher for WLAN products SMS4 (in Chinese)
18. Soleimany, H., Nyberg, K.: Zero-Correlation Linear Cryptanalysis of Reduced-Round LBlock. In: International Workshop on Coding and Cryptography, WCC 2013, pp. 329–343 (2013)
19. Suzaki, T., Minematsu, K.: Improving the Generalized Feistel. In: Hong, S., Iwata, T. (eds.) FSE 2010. LNCS, vol. 6147, pp. 19–39. Springer, Heidelberg (2010)
20. Suzaki, T., Minematsu, K., Morioka, S., Kobayashi, E.: TWINE: A Lightweight, Versatile Block Cipher. In: Leander, G., Standaert, F.-X. (eds.) ECRYPT Workshop on Lightweight Cryptography (2011)
21. Suzaki, T., Minematsu, K., Morioka, S., Kobayashi, E.: TWINE: A Lightweight Block Cipher for Multiple Platforms. In: Knudsen, L.R., Wu, H. (eds.) SAC 2012. LNCS, vol. 7707, pp. 339–354. Springer, Heidelberg (2013)
22. Wu, W., Zhang, L., Zhang, L., Zhang, W.: Security analysis of the GF-NLFSR structure and Four-Cell block cipher. In: Qing, S., Mitchell, C.J., Wang, G. (eds.) ICICS 2009. LNCS, vol. 5927, pp. 17–31. Springer, Heidelberg (2009)
23. Wen, L., Wang, M., Bogdanov, A.: Multidimensional zero-correlation linear cryptanalysis of E2. In: Pointcheval, D., Vergnaud, D. (eds.) AFRICACRYPT 2014. LNCS, vol. 8469, pp. 147–164. Springer, Heidelberg (2014)
24. Wen, L., Wang, M., Bogdanov, A., Chena, H.: Multidimensional Zero-Correlation Attacks on Lightweight Block Cipher HIGHT: Improved Cryptanalysis of an ISO Standard. Information Processing Letters 114(6), 322–330 (2014)
25. Wu, S., Wang, M.: Automatic Search of Truncated Impossible Differentials for Word-Oriented Block Ciphers. In: Galbraith, S., Nandi, M. (eds.) INDOCRYPT 2012. LNCS, vol. 7668, pp. 283–302. Springer, Heidelberg (2012)
26. Wu, W., Zhang, L.: LBlock: A Lightweight Block Cipher. In: Lopez, J., Tsudik, G. (eds.) ACNS 2011. LNCS, vol. 6715, pp. 327–344. Springer, Heidelberg (2011)

Improved Cryptanalysis on Reduced-Round GOST and Whirlpool Hash Function[*]

Bingke Ma[1,2,3], Bao Li[1,2], Ronglin Hao[1,2,4], and Xiaoqian Li[1,2,3]

[1] State Key Laboratory of Information Security, Institute of Information Engineering, Chinese Academy of Sciences, Beijing, 100093, China
[2] Data Assurance and Communication Security Research Center, Chinese Academy of Sciences, Beijing, 100093, China
{bkma,lb,xqli}@is.ac.cn
[3] University of Chinese Academy of Sciences, Beijing, China
[4] Department of Electronic Engineering and Information Science, University of Science and Technology of China, Hefei, 230027, China
haorl@mail.ustc.edu.cn

Abstract. The GOST hash function family has served as the new Russian national hash standard (GOST R 34.11-2012) since January 1, 2013, and it has two members, *i.e.*, GOST-256 and GOST-512 which correspond to two different output lengths. Most of the previous analyses of GOST emphasize on the compression function rather than the hash function. In this paper, we focus on security properties of GOST under the hash function setting. First we give two improved preimage attacks on 6-round GOST-512 compared with the previous preimage attack, *i.e.*, a time-reduced attack with the same memory requirements and a memoryless attack with almost identical time. Then we improve the best collision attack on reduced GOST-256 (resp. GOST-512) from 5 rounds to 6.5 (resp. 7.5) rounds. Finally, we construct a limited-birthday distinguisher on 9.5-round GOST using the limited-birthday distinguisher on hash functions proposed at ASIACRYPT 2013. An essential technique used in our distinguisher is the carefully chosen differential trail, which can further exploit freedom degrees in the inbound phase when launching rebound attacks on the GOST compression function. This technique helps us to reduce the time complexity of the distinguisher significantly. We apply this strategy to Whirlpool, an ISO standardized hash function, as well. As a result, we construct a limited-birthday distinguisher on 9-round Whirlpool out of 10 rounds, and reduce the time complexity of the previous 7-round distinguisher. To the best of our knowledge, all of our results are the best cryptanalytic results on GOST and Whirlpool in terms of the number of rounds analyzed under the hash function setting.

Keywords: hash function, GOST, Whirlpool, multicollision, preimage, collision, limited-birthday distinguisher.

[*] This work was supported by the National Basic Research Program of China (973 Project, No.2013CB338002), the National High Technology Research and Development Program of China (863 Program, No.2013AA014002), the National Natural Science Foundation of China (No.61379137), and the Strategic Priority Research Program of Chinese Academy of Sciences under Grant XDA06010702.

I. Boureanu, P. Owesarski, and S. Vaudenay (Eds.): ACNS 2014, LNCS 8479, pp. 289–307, 2014.

1   Introduction

A hash function takes a message of arbitrary length and produces a bit string of fixed length. For a hash function, three classical security notions are mainly considered: collision resistance, second preimage resistance, and preimage resistance. Many nowaday hash functions divide messages into many blocks and process each block with a compression function iteratively, such as the Merkle-Damgård [5,25] based hash functions. Security properties of the underlying compression functions are also considered by cryptanalysts, and sometimes they do have impacts on the security properties of the hash functions. An example was shown in a recent work [13] by Iwamoto et al., in which a semi-free-start collision attack on the compression function can be turned into a limited-birthday distinguisher on the hash function.

The old GOST R 34.11-94 hash function [10] was theoretically broken in 2008 [21,22]. As a consequence, the new GOST R 34.11-2012 hash function [6,11,15] has replaced GOST R 34.11-94 as the new Russian national hash standard since January 1, 2013. GOST R 34.11-2012 shares a lot of its structure with the broken GOST R 34.11-94, while its internal compression function is very similar to the one of the ISO standardized hash function Whirlpool [3,12]. The main differences between GOST and Whirlpool are the number of rounds and the transposition operations.

Several cryptanalytic results [1,2,30] have been presented for the new GOST hash function, but most of them only focus on the GOST compression function rather than the hash function, except for a recent work by Zou et al. [32]. They presented collision attacks on 5 rounds of all variants of GOST and a preimage attack on 6-round GOST-512 out of 12 rounds. For Whirlpool, there are several cryptanalytic results concerning the compression function [23,18,19,29]. While at the hash function level, the best collision [19] and preimage [29] attacks only reach 5.5 and 6 rounds out of 10 rounds, and a 7-round limited-birthday distinguisher on Whirlpool was given in [13] recently.

Our Contributions. In this paper, we look into the similarities and differences of GOST and Whirlpool, and improve previous attacks on GOST and Whirlpool under the hash function setting. First we give two improved preimage attacks on 6-round GOST-512 compared to [32], i.e., a time-reduced attack with the same memory requirements and a memoryless attack with almost identical time. Then by discovering the weakness of the transposition operation of GOST, we present a 6.5-round collision attack on GOST-256 and a 7.5-round attack on GOST-512, while previous results only reach 5 rounds. Finally, we construct a limited-birthday distinguisher [13] on 9.5-round GOST. A very essential part of our distinguisher is the carefully chosen truncated differential trail, which reduces the time complexity of the distinguisher significantly. We apply similar strategy to Whirlpool, and achieve a 9-round limited-birthday distinguisher. The time complexity of the previous 7-round distinguisher [13] is reduced as well. As far as we know, these are the best results on GOST and Whirlpool in terms of the number of rounds analyzed under the hash function setting. Our results and some representative previous works are summarized in Table 1.

The rest of this paper is organized as follows: In Section 2, we give brief description of the GOST hash function and the tools used in this paper. In Section 3, we present improved preimage attacks on 6-round GOST-512. In Section 4, we show collision attacks on both GOST variants. In Section 5, a limited-birthday distinguisher on 9.5-round GOST is given. Due to the space limitation, details of the limited-birthday distinguishers on reduced-round Whirlpool are provided in the full version of this paper [20]. We conclude and summarize the paper in Section 6.

Table 1. Comparison of Previous and Ours Results on GOST and Whirlpool

Target	Attack Type	Rounds	Time	Memory	Ideal	Reference
GOST-256	Collision Attack	5	2^{122}	2^{64}	2^{128}	[32]
(12 Rounds)		6.5	2^{125}	2^{64}		Section 4.1
GOST-512 (12 Rounds)	Preimage Attack	6	2^{505}	2^{64}	2^{512}	[32]
		6	2^{496}	2^{64}		Section 3
		6	2^{504}	2^{11}		Section 3
	Collision Attack	5	2^{122}	2^{64}	2^{256}	[32]
		7.5	2^{181}	2^{64}		Section 4.2
	Limited-birthday Distinguisher	9.5	2^{441}	2^{136}	2^{449}	Section 5.1
Whirlpool (10 Rounds)	Collision Attack	5.5	2^{120}	2^{64}	2^{256}	[19]
	Preimage Attack	6	2^{481}	2^{256}	2^{512}	[29]
	Limited-birthday Distinguisher	7	2^{440}	2^{128}	2^{505}	[13]
		7.5	2^{368}	2^{144}	2^{497}	Full Version [20]
		9	2^{354}	2^{158}	2^{385}	Full Version [20]

2   Preliminaries

2.1   The GOST Hash Function

The GOST hash function takes any message up to 2^{512} bits as input, and outputs a 256- or 512-bit hash value, *i.e.*, GOST-256 and GOST-512. GOST-512 and GOST-256 are almost the same, except that they have different initial values, and GOST-256 truncates the final 512-bit chaining value into a 256-bit digest. As depicted in Fig. 1, the GOST hash function family adopts the Merkle-Damgård structure with a unique output transformation. The hash computation contains three stages. Before we give specific descriptions of each stage, we define several notations.

$A\|B$ The concatenation of two bit strings A and B.

M The input message, which is divided into 512-bit blocks.

M_i The i-th 512-bit message block of M.

$|M|$ The bit length of M.

Len The bit length of the last message block of M.

Σ The 512-bit checksum of all message blocks.

CF The compression function.

h_i The i-th 512-bit chaining variable.

CT_i The i-th 512-bit counter which denotes the total message bits processed before the i-th CF call.

In the initialization stage, M is padded into a multiple of 512 bits, *i.e.*, $M\|1\|0^*$ is the padded message, which is then divided into N 512-bit blocks $M_0\|M_1\|...\|M_{N-1}$. h_0 is assigned to the predefined IV of GOST-256 or GOST-512. $|M|$, Σ and CT_0 are assigned to 0. In the compression stage, each block M_i is processed iteratively, *i.e.*, $h_{i+1} = CF(h_i, M_i, CT_i)$ for $i = 0, 1, ..., N - 1$. After each compression function computation, $|M|,\Sigma$ and CT_{i+1} are updated accordingly. In the finalization stage, the immediate chaining value of the last message block h_N goes through the output transformation, *i.e.*, $h_{N+1} = CF(h_N, |M|, 0)$, $h_{N+2} = CF(h_{N+1}, \Sigma, 0)$. For GOST-256 (resp. GOST-512), $MSB_{256}(h_{N+2})$ (resp. h_{N+2}) is the hash value of M.

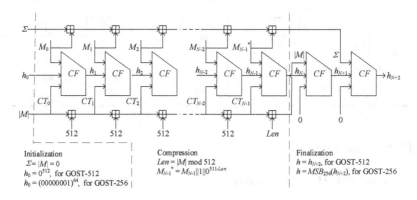

Fig. 1. Three Stages of the GOST Hash Function

The compression function $CF(h_i, M_i, CT_i)$ can be seen as an AES-like block cipher E_K used in a Miyaguchi-Preneel-like mode, *i.e.*, $CF(h_i, M_i, CT_i) = E_{h_i \oplus CT_i}(M_i) \oplus M_i \oplus h_i$. As for the block cipher E_K, a 512-bit internal state is denoted as an 8×8 byte matrix. For the key schedule part, $h_i \oplus CT_i$ is assigned as the key K, then K_0 is computed from K as follows:

$$K_0 = L \circ P \circ S(K)$$

The round keys $K_1, K_2, ..., K_{12}$ are generated as follows:

$$K_{j+1} = L \circ P \circ S \circ XC(K_j) \; for \; j = 0, 1, 2, ...11,$$

where K_{12} is used as the post-whitening key:

- **AddRoundConstant(XC):** XOR a 512-bit constant predefined by the designers.
- **SubBytes(S):** process each byte of the state through the SBox layer.
- **Transposition(P):** transpose the k-th column to be the k-th row for $k = 0, 1, 2, ..., 7$, $i.e.$, transposition of the state matrix.
- **MixRows(L):** multiply each row of the state matrix by an MDS matrix.

For the data processing part, M_i is the plaintext, and is assigned to the initial state S_0. Then the state is updated 12 times with the round function as follows:

$$S_{j+1} = L \circ P \circ S \circ X(S_j), \; for \; j = 0, 1, 2, ...11,$$

where **AddRoundKey(X)** XOR the state with the round key K_j. Finally, the ciphertext $E_K(M_i)$ is computed with $S_{12} \oplus K_{12}$.

Notations. The round indexes of GOST are denoted with $r_0, r_1, r_2, ..., r_{11}$. The input state of round r_j is denoted as S_j, and S_j^X, S_j^S, S_j^P, S_j^L denote the corresponding state after the **X, S, P, L** operation of round r_j respectively, $i.e.$, $S_{j+1} = S_j^L$.

2.2 The Multicollision Attack and Its Applications

The t-multicollisions are t-tuples of messages which all hash to the same value. In [14], Joux gave the multicollision attack on iterated hash functions. He shows that constructing 2^t-collisions costs only t times as much as building ordinary 2-collisions.

The multicollision attack has been used in many occasions. A variant of the multicollision attacks, known as the expandable messages [16], was applied in second preimage attacks. Moreover, the expandable messages were also used to construct long preimages [31,29]. Another application of the multicollision attacks was given in [8] to attack Merkle-Damgård-like hash functions with linear-XOR or additive checksum operations.

2.3 Limited-Birthday Distinguisher on Hash Functions

The limited-birthday problem was first proposed by Gilbert and Peyrin in [9], and they also presented a generic procedure to solve this problem. In [13], Iwamoto et al. proved that the generic attack given in [9] is actually the best generic attack possible. Moreover, they proposed a new generic distinguisher for Merkle-Damgård-like hash functions based on the limited-birthday problem. Now we give brief descriptions of the limited-birthday problem for hash functions and the new distinguisher derived.

The Limited-Birthday Problem. [13] *"Let h be an n-bit output hash function, and process any input messages of fixed size, m bits where $m \geq n$. Let IN be a set of admissible input differences and OUT be a set of admissible output differences, with the property that IN and OUT are closed sets with respect to $\oplus$*[1]*. Then for the limited-birthday problem, the goal of the adversary is to generate a message pair (M, M'), such that $M \oplus M' \in IN$ and $h(M) \oplus h(M') \in OUT$"* *for a randomly chosen instance of h."*

Note that IN and OUT can be freely chosen by the adversary, let 2^I and 2^O denote the sizes of IN and OUT respectively, it is proved in [13] that the lower bound of the time complexity of the limited-birthday problem for a one-way function is

$$max\{2^{\frac{n-O+1}{2}}, 2^{n-I-O+1}\}.$$

The Limited-Birthday Distinguisher on Hash Functions. Let h be an n-bit hash function which iteratively calls CF to process each fixed length message block, where CF is a compression function which takes an m-bit message and a k-bit ($k \geq n$) chaining variable as inputs, and outputs a k-bit chaining value. A semi-free-start collision for CF is a pair $((CV, M), (CV, M'))$ with $M \neq M'$ and a freely chosen CV, such that $CF(CV, M) = CF(CV, M')$. Assume that the adversary is able to find 2^s distinct semi-free-start collisions of CF in 2^c time, with $s \leq k/2$ and $s \leq c$. IN corresponds to the set of all possible differences for all the colliding messages, a limited-distinguisher on h can be derived as follows:

1. Generate 2^s semi-free-start collisions $\{(CV_j, M_j), (CV_j, M'_j)\}$ on CF with 2^c operations, and store all 2^s CV_j values in a list TL_1.
2. From IV, pick 2^{k-s} random message blocks $\{M_i\}$, and compute the corresponding chaining values $\{h_i\}$.
3. For each h_i, check whether it is in the list TL_1. If so, the message couple $((M_i||M_j), (M_i||M'_j))$ is a collision pair of the hash function.

The above procedure needs $2^c + 2^{k-s}$ computations. The adversary outputs the collision couple, whose input difference mask lies in a space IN of size 2^I, and output difference mask lies in a space OUT of size 1 (due to the collision). The limited-birthday problem tells us that this should require $max\{2^{n/2}, 2^{n-I+1}\}$ queries in the ideal case. Since $2^c + 2^{k-s} \geq 2^s + 2^{k-s} \geq 2^{k/2} \geq 2^{n/2}$, the above procedures can be seen as a valid distinguisher if and only if

$$2^c + 2^{k-s} < 2^{n-I+1}.$$

It is also described in [13] that one can even derive a valid limited-birthday distinguisher from a semi-free-start near-collision attack, when the near-collision is located in the last message block and padding can be satisfied.

---

[1] The $\oplus$ operation can be replaced by any other group operation, we use $\oplus$ for a simple specification.

3   Improved Preimage Attack on 6-Round GOST-512

In this section, we improve the preimage attack on 6-round GOST-512 in [32]. First we reduce the time complexity from 2^{505} to 2^{496} by removing the unnecessary MitM (Meet-in-the-Middle) step. Then we show a memoryless attack with time complexity 2^{504}. Moreover, by using the technique in [8] to build more complicate multicollisions, we deal with the checksum straightforwardly with success probability 1 while Zou's attack deals with it probabilisticly. Before describing our attacks, we clarify that a single compression function computation (resp. a 512-bit storage which is the bit size of the state) is used as the basic unit of time (resp. memory) in this paper.

The MitM preimage attack on GOST-like compression functions has been well studied [28,31,29,32], thus we use the results without providing more details. As depicted in Fig. 2, our preimage attack is divided into three steps. The specific procedures of each step are described as follows:

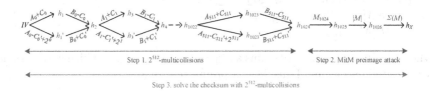

Step 1. 2^{512}-multicollisions   Step 2. MitM preimage attack

Step 3. solve the checksum with 2^{512}-multicollisions

Fig. 2. 3 Steps of the Preimage Attacks on 6-round GOST-512

Step 1.   From IV, use the technique of [8] to build 2^{512}-multicollisions. The exact steps are as follows:

1. Let $h_0 = IV$.
2. For $i = 0$ to 511:
   (a) Let A_i, B_i be two random blocks.
   (b) For $j = 0$ to $2^{256} - 1$:
      i. $X[j] = (A_i + j)\|(B_i - j)$.
      ii. $X'[j] = (A_i - j + 2^i)\|(B_i + j)$.
      iii. Let $Y_i[j]$ denote immediate hash value of $X[j]$ from h_{2i}, store it in the list Y_i.
      iv. Let $Y_i'[j]$ denote immediate hash value of $X'[j]$ from h_{2i}, store it in the list Y_i'.
   (c) Search for a collision in Y_i and Y_i'. Let $M_{2i}\|M_{2i+1} = (A_i + C_i)\|(B_i - C_i)$ and $M_{2i}'\|M_{2i+1}' = (A_i - C_i' + 2^i)\|(B_i + C_i')$ denote the collision pair, and $h_{2(i+1)}$ denote the collision hash value.

In the end, h_{1024} is the hash value of the 2^{512}-multicollisions.

Step 2.   We randomly choose the value of an additional message block M_{1024}, and make sure M_{1024} satisfy padding. Without loss of generality, we fix the last bit of M_{1024} to '1', then the bit length of the message can be denoted as $|M| = 1024 \times 512 + 511 = 524799$. From h_{1024}, we compute the immediate chaining value h_{1026} with M_{1024} and $|M|$. Suppose that h_X is the target value. We find a preimage $\Sigma(M)$ using the MitM preimage attack with a probability $1 - e^{-1}$. If no candidate for $\Sigma(M)$ is found, we just choose another value of M_{1024} and repeat Step 2.

Step 3. Step 2 will eventually succeed, thus we get the checksum value $\Sigma(M)$, and need to find a combination of the first 1025 message blocks to satisfy $\Sigma(M)$. This problem has already been well studied in [8], and the exact steps are as follows:

1. Let $CCS = h_X - M_{1024}$ denote the checksum which is desired.
2. Compute $Q = \sum_{i=0}^{511}(A_i + B_i)$.
3. Compute $D = CCS - Q = \sum_{i=0}^{511} k_i 2^i$, the k_i sequence is the binary representation of D.
4. Set M to an empty message.
5. For $i = 0$ to 511:
   (a) If $k_i = 0$, then $M = M||M_{2i}||M_{2i+1}$.
   (b) Else $M = M||M'_{2i}||M'_{2i+1}$.
6. $M = M||M_{1024}$.

At the end of this phase, M contains a sequence of 1025 blocks which corresponds to the desired checksum. Thus M is a preimage of h_X.

Memoryless Collision Search. In Step 1, we need to launch the collision search 512 times, and a common birthday attack would require 2^{256} memory. Thanks to the memoryless MitM (collision) attacks[2] [27,26] [24, Remark 9.93], the memory requirement can be reduced to 2^{11} (since the collision pairs and the immediate hash values need to be stored). The specific steps for each collision search are as follows:

1. Denote h_{2i} as the initial hash value of the i-th collision search.
2. Randomly choose two message blocks A_i, B_i.
3. Let s_0 denote the immediate hash value of $A_i||B_i$ from h_{2i}.
4. For $j = 0$ to 2^{256}
   (a) If the least significant bit of s_j is 0, compute s_{j+1}, which is the immediate hash value of $(A_i + s_j)||(B_i - s_j)$ from h_{2i}.
   (b) Else compute s_{j+1}, which is the immediate hash value of $(A_i - s_j + 2^i)||(B_i + s_j)$ from h_{2i}.

Finally, the attacker detects the cycle of the above procedure, and finds intersection point of the cycle. We denote s_α and s_β as the two points before the intersection point. If the least significant bit of s_α and s_β are distinct, without loss of generality, we suppose the least significant bit of s_α is 0 and the least significant bit of s_β is 1, then $(A_i + s_\alpha)||(B_i - s_\alpha)$ and $(A_i - s_\beta + 2^i)||(B_i + s_\beta)$ are the collision

---

[2] The memoryless attacks are based on cycle detection techniques such as Floyd's cycle-finding algorithm [7] or Brent's algorithm [4].

message blocks desired. The time complexity is at most 2^3 times[3] more than the generic birthday attack. Thus we need a total $1024 \times 2^3 \times 2^{256} = 2^{269}$ compression function computations and 2^{11} memory to generate the 2^{512}-multicollisions.

Memoryless Meet-in-the-Middle Preimage Attack.   The memoryless MitM preimage attack, explored by Khovratovich *et al* in [17], is based on the classical memoryless MitM technique [26]. Similar to the memoryless MitM preimage attack on Whirlpool in [29], we can launch a memoryless MitM preimage attack on the GOST compression function with 2^{504} computations. Please refer to [29,32] for more details.

Now we consider the overall complexity of our attack. Step 1 can be done with 2^{269} compression function calls and 2^{11} memory. As for step 2, we need 2^{496} time and 2^{64} memory to minimize the time complexity or 2^{504} time to launch the memoryless attack. There are only a few simple operations in step 3, both time and memory are negligible. So it takes 2^{496} time and 2^{64} memory or 2^{504} time and 2^{11} memory to find a single preimage of 6-round GOST-512.

Remarks.   An improved preimage attack on the compression function of GOST is likely to work for the preimage attack on the hash function using the generic procedures above.

4   Improved Collision Attacks on Reduced-Round GOST

As far as we know, the 5-round attacks [32] are the best collision attacks on GOST-256 and GOST-512 in terms of rounds attacked. In this section, we present improved collision attacks on both variants of GOST. The improved collision attacks mainly come from a direct observation of the transposition operation of GOST. First, we describe a collision attack on 6.5-round GOST-256. Then by further exploiting freedom degrees in the chaining values, we present a collision attack on 7.5-round GOST-512.

4.1   Collision Attack on 6.5-Round GOST-256

We first show collision attack on the compression function of GOST-256 by using the rebound attack [23] and the SuperSBox technique [9,18]. Then we show how to convert it to a collision attack on the GOST-256 hash function.

Attack on the Compression Function.   The truncated differential trail used in our attack is depicted in Fig. 3. Since the transposition operation P has the involution property, the active columns of S_0 and S_6^P will both locate at the first

---

[3] The success possibility is $1/2$, and using Brent's algorithm [4] to detect the cycle and find the intersection point costs at most 2^2 times more than the generic birthday attack.

column. Thus, if they cancel each other, we would achieve a collision attack on the compression function. Note that the involution property of P is originally exploited in [30], and will also be used in our later analyses. The whole attack can be divided into the inbound phase (in red), and the outbound phase (in blue). In the following part we describe each phase in detail.

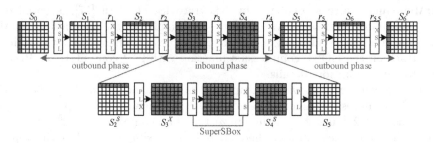

Fig. 3. Collision Attack on 6.5-Round GOST-256 Compression Function

Inbound Phase. We need to find two states which follow the two middle rounds from S_2^S to S_5. It can be summarized as follows.

1. We start from picking a random nonzero difference of S_2^S at the 8-byte active positions indicated in Fig. 3. Since all the operations between S_2^S and S_3^X are linear, we can propagate the difference forwards to S_3^X. The states between S_3^X and S_4^S can be seen as eight parallel SuperSBoxes, and the input to each SuperSBox is the corresponding row of S_3^X. For each SuperSBox, we enumerate all 2^{64} pairs of inputs according to the difference of S_3^X, and calculate the corresponding output differences of the SuperSBox. Store all the output differences and corresponding pairs of values in a table for each SuperSBox. This step requires 2^{64} time and 2^{64} memory.

2. Pick a random nonzero difference of S_5 at the 8-byte active positions, and propagate the difference backwards to S_4^S. Note that this can be repeated for all $255 = 2^8 - 1$ nonzero differences of each active byte in each row independently.

3. Now we have to connect the states S_3^X and S_4^S such that the differential trail holds, and this can be done for each row independently. For each SuperSBox, we search the corresponding difference of S_4^S in the table built in step 1. Since we have 2^{64} values in each table, and we need to match a 64-bit difference value, the expected number of solutions is 1.

4. We can repeat step 2 and step 3 with another nonzero difference of S_5. After enumerating all 2^{64} differences of S_5, we expect to get 2^{64} solutions. Combining with the complexity of step 1, the above procedures require 2^{64} time and 2^{64} memory to generate 2^{64} solutions. In other words, the expected time needed to get one solution is only 1.

If the number of solutions of the inbound phase is insufficient, we can repeat step 1-4 with another difference of S_2^S. Since there are 2^{64} differences for S_2^S, we can generate at most $2^{64+64} = 2^{128}$ solutions for the inbound phase.

Outbound Phase. We use the solutions of the inbound phase and propagate them forwards and backwards. The outbound phase has one $8 \rightarrow 1$ transition, and we need to match a 64-bit difference between S_0 and S_6^P, so it requires $2^{56+64} = 2^{120}$ computations to find one collision for the 6.5-round compression function.

Impact of the DDT of the GOST SBox. The DDT (Difference Distribution Table) of the SBox is the core of the rebound attack. The SBox of GOST is not as balanced as the AES SBox. In fact, its maximal differential probability reaches 2^{-5} while the one of the AES SBox is 2^{-6}. Thus, the matching probability of the GOST SBox is lower than the AES SBox, which might introduce some small biases. However, as discussed in [29], the DDT has no impacts on the expected number of solutions for a random difference pair of an SBox. Hence, the time complexity is not increased if we need to find many solutions from the inbound phase.

Attack on the Hash Function. Similar to the technique of [32], we extend the attack on the compression function to the hash function. Since we aim to construct two collision messages with identical length, we only need to deal with the final checksums. As depicted in Fig. 4, we first build 2^{32}-multicollisions, then find two message chains with an identical checksum. The exact steps are as follows:

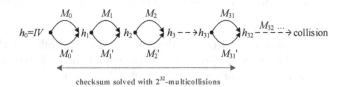

Fig. 4. Collision Attack on 6.5-round GOST-256

1. Start from the initial value $h_0 = IV$:
   For $j = 0$ to 31,
   - Find two messages M_j and M'_j using the compression function collision attack above, such that $CF(h_j, M_j) = CF(h_j, M'_j)$, and let $h_{j+1} = CF(h_j, M_j)$. Notice that (M_j, M'_j) differs only in the first column.
2. After step 1, we build 2^{32}-multicollisions from h_0 to h_{32}. Since each collision pair only differs in the first column, besides the identical parts of the 2^{32}-multicollisions always have identical sums including carries, the difference of their checksums lies in a space whose size is at most 2^{64}. We can generate 2^{32} checksums with the 2^{32}-multicollisions. According to the birthday paradox, we expect to find one collision among these checksums. Then we append any identical message blocks which satisfy padding, and finally construct a collision on the GOST-256 hash function.

In the above procedures, collision attack on the compression function is repeated 32 times, so the overall time complexity of the collision attack on GOST-256 is $32 \times 2^{120} = 2^{125}$ which is lower than the birthday bound 2^{128}. The memory requirement stays 2^{64} due to the SuperSBox technique.

4.2 Collision Attack on 7.5-Round GOST-512

The collision attack on GOST-256 can be directly applied to GOST-512 with the same complexity, but in this part we show how to extend one more round for GOST-512. The differential trail of the 7.5-round attack on the compression function is depicted in Fig. 5. Again the inbound phase can provide at most 2^{128} solutions with 2^{128} time and 2^{64} memory. But there are two $8 \rightarrow 1$ transitions in the outbound phase, and we need to match a 64-bit difference between S_0 and S_7^P in order to get a collision, thus we need at least $2^{56+56+64} = 2^{176}$ solutions from the inbound phase. The freedom degree of the inbound phase is obviously insufficient, and the attack will only succeed with a very low probability $2^{128-176} = 2^{-48}$.

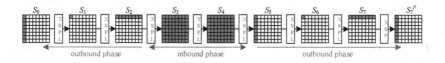

Fig. 5. Collision Attack on 7.5-round GOST-512 Compression Function

Luckily, we can exploit more freedom degrees by choosing different chaining values as depicted in Fig. 6. More precisely, we launch a two-block attack on the compression function. First, from a chaining value h_{2i}, we randomly choose a message block M_{2i} and compute the corresponding chaining variable h_{2i+1}. Then we launch the rebound attack with the value of h_{2i+1} and check if a collision pair (M_{2i+1}, M'_{2i+1}) is obtained. If no collision is achieved, we choose another value for M_{2i} and repeat this procedure. Since the collision attack succeeds with probability 2^{-48}, we expect to get one collision after we randomly choose 2^{48} different values for M_{2i}. Hence, the rebound attack needs to be repeated 2^{48} times, and the time and memory required are $2^{48+128} = 2^{176}$ and 2^{64} respectively.

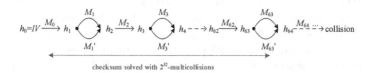

Fig. 6. Collision Attack on 7.5-round GOST-512

As depicted in Fig. 6, we build 2^{32}-multicollisions by repeating the compression function attack 32 times. According to the birthday paradox, we expect to get two messages with identical checksum from the 2^{32}-multicollisions, and derive a collision for the GOST-512 hash function. Thus the time complexity is $32 \times 2^{176} = 2^{181}$, while the memory requirement remains 2^{64}. Note that when the same strategy is applied to GOST-256, the time complexity is beyond the birthday attack bound 2^{128}.

5   Limited-Birthday Distinguishers on GOST-512 and Whirlpool

In this section, we build limited-birthday distinguishers for reduced-round GOST-512 and Whirlpool. It is indicated in [13] that if a better balance is achieved between the total number of semi-free-start collisions one can generate and the average complexity to generate one collision, a better limited-birthday distinguisher can be derived. Therefore, we try to achieve a better balance between attack parameters by choosing the differential trails used in the inbound phase carefully. This is actually a very essential idea of our distinguishers. We launch a 9.5-round semi-free-start collision attack on GOST-512 compression function with a differential trail, which is different from previous trails for collision-like attacks. As a result, we build a valid limited-birthday distinguisher on 9.5-round GOST-512.

The very same strategy can be applied to Whirlpool as well. With the expandable messages [16], we are able to convert a semi-free-start near-collision attack on 9-round Whirlpool compression function into a valid distinguisher for 9-round Whirlpool hash function. We also reduce the time complexity of the previous distinguisher on 7-round Whirlpool [13]. Due to the space limitations, specific descriptions of the limited-birthday distinguishers on Whirlpool are provided in the full version of this paper [20].

5.1   Limited-Birthday Distinguisher on 9.5-Round GOST-512

Semi-Free-Start Collision Attack on the GOST Compression Function. The differential trail used in the 9.5-round semi-free-start collision attack on the GOST-512 compression function conforms to the following form:

$$8 \xrightarrow{r_0} 1 \xrightarrow{r_1} 8 \xrightarrow{r_2} 64 \xrightarrow{r_3} 8x \xrightarrow{r_4} 8x \xrightarrow{r_5} 64 \xrightarrow{r_6} 8 \xrightarrow{r_7} 1 \xrightarrow{r_8} 8 \xrightarrow{r_{8.5}} 8$$

where $x = 1, 2, ..., 8$ and denotes the number of active rows (columns) in the middle rounds. Fig. 7 depicts the trail when $x = 3$. Suppose there are $8x$ active bytes in the middle parts of the trail, we describe the attack in detail.

Inbound Phase. We aim to connect both differences and actual values between S_2^S and S_7. The inbound phase is divided into two subinbound phases, and the merge inbound phase merges the two subinbound phases.

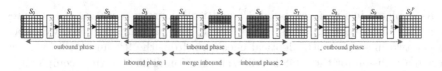

Fig. 7. Semi-free-start Collision Attack on 9.5-Round GOST-512 Compression Function

1. **Phase 1.** We find states connecting S_3^X and S_4.
   (a) We start with a random difference of S_4, and propagate the difference backwards to S_3^S.
   (b) Choose a random difference of S_2^S. Since all the operations between S_2^S and S_3^X are linear, we can propagate the difference forwards to S_3^X, and match it with the difference of step 1(a) through the SBox layer. Notice the match can be done for each row independently. We have 255 different values for each active byte S_2^S, and expect to get one difference match and each match provides 2^8 solutions. So it takes 2^9 operations to find 2^8 solutions of S_3^X and S_4 for each row. After enumerating all 2^{64} differences of S_2^S for each row independently, we expect to get 2^{64} solutions in 2^9 computations.

2. **Subinbound Phase 2.** We find states connecting S_6^X and S_7.
   (a) Start with a random difference of S_5^S. Since all the operations between S_5^S and S_6^X are linear, we can propagate the difference forwards to S_6^X.
   (b) Choose a random difference of S_7 and propagate the difference backwards to S_6^S, match it with the difference of step 2(a) through the SBox layer. Again, we expect to get 2^{64} solutions of S_6^X and S_7 after enumerating all 2^{64} differences of S_7 in 2^9 computations.

3. **Merge Inbounds.** We need to connect the actual values of S_4 and S_6^X obtained from the two subinbound phases. That is, we need to find solutions for the following equation using the freedom degrees of the key:

$$L \circ P \circ S(L \circ P \circ S(S_4 \oplus K_4) \oplus K_5) \oplus K_6 = S_6^X, \qquad (1)$$

where $K_4, K_5 = L \circ P \circ S(K_4 \oplus C_4), K_6 = L \circ P \circ S(K_5 \oplus C_5)$ denote the round keys, and C_4, C_5 denote the round constants in the key schedule. Equation (1) can be rewritten as:

$$S(L \circ P \circ S(S_4 \oplus K_4) \oplus K_5) \oplus S(K_5 \oplus C_5) = P^{-1} \circ L^{-1}(S_6^X). \qquad (2)$$

Notice equation (2) can be solved column by column independently. We denote the left half and the right half of equation (2) with V_L and V_R respectively. The merge inbounds phase is then as follows:

(a) Enumerate all 2^{64} values of each column of S_4 and all 2^{64} values of the corresponding column of K_4, propagate forwards to get the corresponding values of V_L. Store all the pairs in tables and sort them by the value of $S_4 \| V_L$. The size of the tables is 2^{128}. This step requires 2^{128} time and 2^{128} memory, and the precomputed tables can be reused in later attacks. Notice that we omit the precomputation part in the complexity analysis of our distinguishers, since the precomputation part is not the dominated part.

(b) For each pair (S_4, S_6^X), we compute the value of V_R with S_6^X and check whether $S_4 || V_R$ is in the tables built in step 3(a). Notice that K_4 provides 2^{64} freedom degrees per column in the matching part. For each active column of S_4, we need to match two 64-bit values with probability $2^{64-128} = 2^{-64}$. For each non-active column, we need to match one 64-bit value and expect to find one match. Hence, if there are x active columns in S_4, the matching probability is 2^{-64x}. Notice that we have generated 2^{64} pairs of S_4 in step 1, and 2^{64} pairs of S_6^X in step 2, thus we expect to get $2^{64+64-64x} = 2^{64(2-x)}$ solutions. This step requires 2^{64} table lookups, and the average complexity to find one solution is $2^{64-64(2-x)} = 2^{64(x-1)}$.

(c) After we connect the values of S_4 and S_6^X for each column of S_4 independently, we propagate both forwards and backwards to S_2^S and S_7, thus derive a solution for the inbound phase.

4. If the solutions of the inbound phase are not enough, we can repeat the above steps from step 1(a) with another difference of S_4. If the solutions are still insufficient, we can repeat the above steps from step 2(a) with another difference of S_5^S. Since there are x active columns in S_4 and x active rows in S_5^S, we can repeat the above steps $2^{64(x+x)} = 2^{128x}$ times. Each time we obtain $2^{64(2-x)}$ solutions with 2^{64} time. So the maximum number of solutions we can generate is $2^{128x+64(2-x)} = 2^{128+64x}$. The average complexity to find one solution remains $2^{64(x-1)}$.

Outbound Phase.   The outbound phase has two $8 \rightarrow 1$ transitions, and we need to match a 64-bit difference, so it requires $2^{56 \times 2+64} = 2^{176}$ computations to find one collision for the 9.5-round compression function.

Combining the results of the inbound phase and the outbound phase together, we deduce that we can generate at most $2^{128+64x-176} = 2^{64x-48}$ semi-free-start collisions, and the average complexity to find one collision is $2^{64(x-1)+176} = 2^{64x+112}$.

The Limited-Birthday Distinguisher on 9.5-Round GOST-512.   In order to apply the limited-birthday distinguisher on GOST-like hash functions, we have to deal with the message checksums, *i.e.*, we need to find two message chains with identical length and checksum. As depicted in Fig. 8, we can solve this problem with two MitM procedures. The specific steps are as follows:

1. We find 2^y semi-free-start collisions, and store the corresponding chaining variables $h_{1,i}$ and message pairs $(M_{1,i}, M'_{1,i})$ in a table TL_1. Notice there are only 8 active bytes in the colliding pairs, thus the difference of the colliding pairs lies in a space whose size is at most 2^{64}.

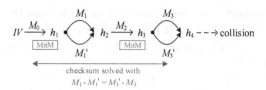

Fig. 8. Limited-Birthday Distinguisher on 9.5-Round GOST-512

2. Start from IV, randomly choose 2^{512-y} different values of $M_{0,j}$, and compute the corresponding chaining value $h'_{1,j}$, check whether it is in TL_1. There is a high probability that we can find a match. We denote the corresponding message pairs as $((M_0||M_1),(M_0||M'_1))$, and the immediate hash value as h_2.
3. Find all entries in TL_1 which satisfy $M_k - M'_k = M'_1 - M_1$, and store all (M_k, M'_k) pairs in a table TL_2. The equation holds with a probability 2^{-64}, since the difference space of the colliding pairs is at most 2^{64}. There are 2^y entries in TL_1, so the expected number of entries in TL_2 is 2^{y-64}.
4. Start from h_2, randomly choose $2^{512-(y-64)}$ different values of $M_{2,j}$, and compute the corresponding chaining value $h'_{2,j}$, check whether it is in TL_2. There is a high probability that we can find a match. We denote the corresponding message pairs as $((M_2||M_3),(M_2||M'_3))$, and the immediate hash value as h_4.
5. Since $M_1 - M'_1 = M'_3 - M_3$, if we append any identical messages which satisfy padding to the message pairs $((M_0||M_1||M_2||M_3),(M_0||M'_1||M_2||M'_3))$, we get a collision pair of the hash function.

Suppose the time needed to find one semi-free-start collision is 2^{T_1}, then the time complexity of the above procedure is

$$T = 2^{y+T_1} + 2^{512-y} + 2^{512-(y-64)} = 2^{y+T_1} + 2^{512-y} + 2^{576-y}.$$

Although there are two different positions in the two message chains, $i.e.$, (M_1, M_3) and (M'_1, M'_3), but their values are restrained by $M_1 - M'_1 = M'_3 - M_3$, so we know that $2^I = 2^{64}$, and $2^O = 1$. For an ideal one-way function, find two such messages would require $2^{n-I-O+1} = 2^{449}$ computations. If $T < 2^{449}$, the above procedure can be seen as a valid distinguisher on 9.5-round GOST-512.

As we mentioned above, the average time complexity to find one semi-free-start collision is $2^{T_1} = 2^{64x+112}$, and we can generate at most $2^{N_1} = 2^{64x-48}$ semi-free-start collisions. Now we show how to choose the values of y and T_1 which minimize the time complexity.

Two different occasions need to be considered. In the first occasion, if we can generate enough collisions, we can balance T by letting $y + T_1 = 576 - y$, $i.e.$, $y = (576 - T_1)/2 = 232 - 32x$. In this occasion, we need to ensure $N_1 \geq y$. Since both T_1 and N_1 can be denoted with x, we solve this inequality and get that $x > 2$. Then T can be rewritten as:

$$T = 2^{y+T_1+1} = 2^{232-32x+64x+112+1} = 2^{345+32x}, \; for \; x = 3,4,5,6,7,8.$$

On the other hand, when $x \leq 2$, we can't generate enough collisions, so T is dominated by 2^{576-y} and we need to find all the semi-free-start collisions in order to maximize y. In this occasion, we find all the collisions, *i.e.*, let $y = N_1 = 64x - 48$, then T can be rewritten as:

$$T = 2^{576-y} = 2^{576-64x+48} = 2^{624-64x}, \; for \; x = 1, 2.$$

Finally, we consider both occasions, and find out that the lowest complexity is 2^{441} when $x = 3$. Notice $2^{441} < 2^{449}$, thus we build a valid limited-birthday distinguisher on 9.5-round GOST-512. Since we need to store all the collision pairs, the memory requirement is $2^y = 2^{136}$.

6   Conclusion

In this paper, we have first investigated fundamental security requirements of reduced-round GOST, including improved preimage attacks on GOST-512 and improved collision attacks on both GOST-256 and GOST-512. Then, using the newly proposed limited-birthday distinguisher on hash functions, we construct a 9.5-round distinguisher on GOST-512 by choosing the differential trail discreetly. Finally, we apply this strategy to Whirlpool, and achieve a new 9-round distinguisher. We also reduce the time complexity of the previous 7-round distinguisher. As far as we know, all of our results are the best cryptanalytic results on GOST and Whirlpool in terms of the number of rounds analyzed under the hash function setting.

A notable implication of our collision attack and distinguisher on GOST is the importance of a proper transposition operation such as the AES ShiftRow. More attention is paid to construct secure SBoxes or MDS matrices in designing AES-like primitives, but a misbehaviour of a transposition operation might bring security problems. As in the GOST case, the transposition operation which transposes the state matrix seems not an optimal selection to achieve transposition, since compared to the ShiftColumn operation of Whirlpool, the transposition operation of GOST facilitates our collision and distinguisher attacks with more rounds.

Acknowledgements. We would like to thank the anonymous reviewers of ACNS 2014 for their valuable comments and suggestions.

References

1. AlTawy, R., Kircanski, A., Youssef, A.M.: Rebound Attacks on Stribog. In: ICISC 2013. LNCS. Springer (2013) (to appear)
2. AlTawy, R., Kircanski, A., Youssef, A.M.: Rebound Attacks on Stribog. Cryptology ePrint Archive, Report 2013/539 (2013), http://eprint.iacr.org/2013/539.pdf
3. Barreto, P., Rijmen, V.: The Whirlpool Hashing Function. Submitted to NESSIE (2000), http://www.larc.usp.br/~pbarreto/WhirlpoolPage.html

4. Brent, R.P.: An Improved Monte Carlo Factorization Algorithm. BIT Numerical Mathematics 20(2), 176–184 (1980)
5. Damgård, I.: A Design Principle for Hash Functions. In: Brassard, G. (ed.) CRYPTO 1989. LNCS, vol. 435, pp. 416–427. Springer, Heidelberg (1990)
6. Dolmatov, V., Degtyarev, A.: GOST R 34.11-2012 Hash Function (2013)
7. Floyd, R.W.: Nondeterministic Algorithms. J. ACM 14(4), 636–644 (1967)
8. Gauravaram, P., Kelsey, J.: Linear-XOR and Additive Checksums Don't Protect Damgård-Merkle Hashes from Generic Attacks. In: Malkin, T. (ed.) CT-RSA 2008. LNCS, vol. 4964, pp. 36–51. Springer, Heidelberg (2008)
9. Gilbert, H., Peyrin, T.: Super-Sbox Cryptanalysis: Improved Attacks for AES-like Permutations. In: Hong, S., Iwata, T. (eds.) FSE 2010. LNCS, vol. 6147, pp. 365–383. Springer, Heidelberg (2010)
10. Information Protection and Special Communications of the Federal Security Service of the Russian Federation: GOST R 34.11-94, Information Technology Cryptographic Data Security Hashing Function (1994) (in Russian)
11. Information Protection and Special Communications of the Federal Security Service of the Russian Federation: GOST R 34.11-2012, Information Technology Cryptographic Data Security Hashing Function (2012), https://www.tc26.ru/en/GOSTR3411-2012/GOST_R_34_11-2012_eng.pdf
12. International Organization for Standardization: ISO/IEC 10118-3:2004: Information technology - Security techniques - Hash-functions - Part 3: Dedicated hash-functions (2004)
13. Iwamoto, M., Peyrin, T., Sasaki, Y.: Limited-Birthday Distinguishers for Hash Functions. In: Sako, K., Sarkar, P. (eds.) ASIACRYPT 2013, Part II. LNCS, vol. 8270, pp. 504–523. Springer, Heidelberg (2013)
14. Joux, A.: Multicollisions in Iterated Hash Functions. Application to Cascaded Constructions. In: Franklin, M. (ed.) CRYPTO 2004. LNCS, vol. 3152, pp. 306–316. Springer, Heidelberg (2004)
15. Kazymyrov, O., Kazymyrova, V.: Algebraic Aspects of the Russian Hash Standard GOST R 34.11-2012. Cryptology ePrint Archive, Report 2013/556 (2013), http://eprint.iacr.org/2013/556.pdf
16. Kelsey, J., Schneier, B.: Second Preimages on n-Bit Hash Functions for Much Less than 2^n Work. In: Cramer, R. (ed.) EUROCRYPT 2005. LNCS, vol. 3494, pp. 474–490. Springer, Heidelberg (2005)
17. Khovratovich, D., Nikolić, I., Weinmann, R.-P.: Meet-in-the-Middle Attacks on SHA-3 Candidates. In: Dunkelman, O. (ed.) FSE 2009. LNCS, vol. 5665, pp. 228–245. Springer, Heidelberg (2009)
18. Lamberger, M., Mendel, F., Rechberger, C., Rijmen, V., Schläffer, M.: Rebound Distinguishers: Results on the Full Whirlpool Compression Function. In: Matsui, M. (ed.) ASIACRYPT 2009. LNCS, vol. 5912, pp. 126–143. Springer, Heidelberg (2009)
19. Lamberger, M., Mendel, F., Schläffer, M., Rechberger, C., Rijmen, V.: The Rebound Attack and Subspace Distinguishers: Application to Whirlpool. J. Cryptology, 1–40 (2013)
20. Ma, B., Li, B., Hao, R., Li, X.: Improved Cryptanalysis on Reduced-Round GOST and Whirlpool Hash Function (Full Version). Cryptology ePrint Archive (2014)
21. Mendel, F., Pramstaller, N., Rechberger, C.: A (Second) Preimage Attack on the GOST Hash Function. In: Nyberg, K. (ed.) FSE 2008. LNCS, vol. 5086, pp. 224–234. Springer, Heidelberg (2008)
22. Mendel, F., Pramstaller, N., Rechberger, C., Kontak, M., Szmidt, J.: Cryptanalysis of the GOST Hash Function. In: Wagner, D. (ed.) CRYPTO 2008. LNCS, vol. 5157, pp. 162–178. Springer, Heidelberg (2008)

23. Mendel, F., Rechberger, C., Schläffer, M., Thomsen, S.S.: The Rebound Attack: Cryptanalysis of Reduced Whirlpool and Grøstl. In: Dunkelman, O. (ed.) FSE 2009. LNCS, vol. 5665, pp. 260–276. Springer, Heidelberg (2009)
24. Menezes, A.J., Van Oorschot, P.C., Vanstone, S.A.: Handbook of Applied Cryptography. CRC Press (2010)
25. Merkle, R.: One Way Hash Functions and DES. In: Brassard, G. (ed.) CRYPTO 1989. LNCS, vol. 435, pp. 428–446. Springer, Heidelberg (1990)
26. Morita, H., Ohta, K., Miyaguchi, S.: A Switching Closure Test to Analyze Cryptosystems. In: Feigenbaum, J. (ed.) CRYPTO 1991. LNCS, vol. 576, pp. 183–193. Springer, Heidelberg (1992)
27. Quisquater, J.-J., Delescaille, J.-P.: How Easy Is Collision Search? Application to DES. In: Quisquater, J.-J., Vandewalle, J. (eds.) EUROCRYPT 1989. LNCS, vol. 434, pp. 429–434. Springer, Heidelberg (1990)
28. Sasaki, Y.: Meet-in-the-Middle Preimage Attacks on AES Hashing Modes and an Application to Whirlpool. In: Joux, A. (ed.) FSE 2011. LNCS, vol. 6733, pp. 378–396. Springer, Heidelberg (2011)
29. Sasaki, Y., Wang, L., Wu, S., Wu, W.: Investigating Fundamental Security Requirements on Whirlpool: Improved Preimage and Collision Attacks. In: Wang, X., Sako, K. (eds.) ASIACRYPT 2012. LNCS, vol. 7658, pp. 562–579. Springer, Heidelberg (2012)
30. Wang, Z., Yu, H., Wang, X.: Cryptanalysis of GOST R Hash Function. Cryptology ePrint Archive, Report 2013/584 (2013), http://eprint.iacr.org/2013/584.pdf
31. Wu, S., Feng, D., Wu, W., Guo, J., Dong, L., Zou, J.: (Pseudo) Preimage Attack on Round-Reduced Grøstl Hash Function and Others. In: Canteaut, A. (ed.) FSE 2012. LNCS, vol. 7549, pp. 127–145. Springer, Heidelberg (2012)
32. Zou, J., Wu, W., Wu, S.: Cryptanalysis of the Round-Reduced GOST Hash Function. In: Inscrypt 2013. LNCS. Springer (2013) (to appear)

Differential Cryptanalysis and Linear Distinguisher of Full-Round Zorro

Yanfeng Wang[1,3] , Wenling Wu[1,2], Zhiyuan Guo[1,3], and Xiaoli Yu[1,3]

[1] Trusted Computing and Information Assurance Laboratory, Institute of Software,
Chinese Academy of Sciences, Beijing 100190, P.R. China
[2] State Key Laboratory of Computer Science, Institute of Software,
Chinese Academy of Sciences, Beijing 100190, P.R. China
[3] Graduate University of Chinese Academy of Sciences, Beijing 100049, P.R. China
{wwl,wangyanfeng}@tca.iscas.ac.cn

Abstract. Zorro is an AES-like lightweight block cipher proposed in
CHES 2013, which only uses 4 S-boxes per round. The designers showed
the resistance of the cipher against various attacks and concluded the
cipher has a large security margin. Recently, Guo et. al [1] have given a
key recovery attack on full-round Zorro by using the internal differential
characteristics. However, the attack only works for 2^{64} out of 2^{128} keys.
In this paper, the secret key selected randomly from the whole key space
can be recovered much faster than the brute-force attack. We first observe
that the fourth power of the MDS matrix used in Zorro(or AES) equals
to the identity matrix. Mooveover, several iterated differential characteristics and iterated linear trails are found due to the interesting property.
We select three characteristics with the largest probability to give the
key recovery attack on Zorro and a linear trail with the largest correlation to show a linear distinguishing attack with $2^{105.3}$ known plaintexts.
The results show that the security of Zorro against linear and differential cryptanalysis evaluated by designers is insufficient and the security
margin of Zorro is not enough.

Keywords: Zorro, block cipher, differential cryptanalysis, linear distinguisher.

1 Introduction

Block ciphers are used as building blocks for many symmetric cryptographic
primitives for encryption, authentication, pseudo-random number generation,
and hash functions. Security of these primitives is evaluated in regard to known
attacks against block ciphers. Among the different types of attacks, the statistical
ones exploit non-uniform behavior of the data extracted from the cipher to distinguish the block cipher from random permutations. Differential cryptanalysis[2]
and linear cryptanalysis[3] are the most prominent statistical attacks against
block ciphers.

Differential cryptanalysis has been introduced in 1990 by Biham and Shamir
in order to break the DES block cipher. This statistical cryptanalysis exploits

I. Boureanu, P. Owesarski, and S. Vaudenay (Eds.): ACNS 2014, LNCS 8479, pp. 308–323, 2014.
© Springer International Publishing Switzerland 2014

the existence of a differential, i.e., a pair $(\triangle_{in}, \triangle_{out})$ of differences such that for a given input difference $\triangle_{in}$, the output difference after encryption equals $\triangle_{out}$ with a high probability. For a b-bit random permutation, the probability is about 2^{-b}. The gap of the probability results in a distinguisher between the cipher and the random permutation, which is often extended to distinguish the correct key and the wrong keys. In 1993, the iterated differentials are proposed to analyze DES and s2-DES[4]. Since then, the differential cryptanalysis is always a hot topic of cryptanalysis[5,6,7]. The problem of estimating the data complexity, time complexity and success probability of a differential cryptanalysis is far from being simple. In 2011, [8] presented a general method (Algorithm 1) for finding an accurate number of samples to reach given error probabilities which can be applied to the differential cryptanalysis.

Linear cryptanalysis[9,10] is a known-plaintext attack proposed in 1993 by Matsui to break DES. It exploits the correlation between linear combinations of input bits and linear combinations of output bits of the block cipher. If the correlation between input and output equals C, the required amount of known plaintexts is about C^{-2} if we want to distinguish the block cipher from the random permutation with a high success probability.

The large development of low resource devices such as RFID tags and sensor nodes increases the need to provide security among such devices. The implementation costs should be taken into account when choosing security algorithms for resource-limited devices. Symmetric-key algorithms, especially block ciphers, still play an important role in the security of embedded systems. Recently, a lot of block ciphers and authenticated encryption ciphers suitable for these environments have been designed, such as PRESENT[11], KATAN & KTANTAN[12], PRINT[13], LBlock[14], FIDES[15], Piccolo[16], LED[17] etc.

Zorro[18] is a new lightweight block cipher proposed at CHES 2013. It is an AES-like block cipher and is designed to improve the side-channel resistance of AES[19]. The secret key is added to the state only after each 4 rounds as in the block cipher LED-64. The S-box layer of Zorro only applies four same S-boxes to the first row per round and the S-box is different from that of AES. Besides, the MC operation is the same as AES. The designers have evaluated the security of the cipher against various methods. For differential/linear cryptanalysis, authors found a balance between the number of inactive S-boxes and degrees of freedom for the differential (or linear) paths. Considering the average number of conditions imposed at each round, designers concluded that 14(or 16) rounds are the upper bound for building a classical differential(or linear) path. Finally, a 12-round meet-in-the-middle attack was shown as the best powerful attack on Zorro in the single key model. Recently, Guo et. al[1] have given a key recovery attack on full-round Zorro by using the internal differential characteristics, while it only works for 2^{64} keys of the whole key space.

In this paper, we revaluated the security of Zorro against differential cryptanalysis and linear cryptanalysis. As mentioned in [1], the main weakness of Zorro includes defining a new S-box and applying only four S-boxes to the first row per round. Besides, we observed that the fourth power of the MDS matrix of

Zorro(or AES) is equal to the identity matrix. Coincidentally, one step of Zorro consists of four rounds with four MDS matrix transformations. Interestingly, there exist several iterated differential characteristics with a high probability and iterated linear trails with a high correlation for one step of Zorro. Furthermore, we can recover the secret key of the full-round Zorro based on a 23-round differential characteristic with a time complexity of 2^{106} full-round Zorro encryptions. Interestingly, no matter how many plaintext-ciphertext pairs are given, the time complexity of filtering the right key is at least 2^{96} full-round encryptions based on the 23-round distinguisher. In order to clarify the special property of the structure used in Zorro, another TMTO attack based on a 22-round differential characteristic is also shown and it only costs about 2^{64} full-round Zorro encryptions to filter out the right key. Meanwhile, $1/C^2$ of some linear trails of full-round Zorro is also lower than the size of the plaintext space 2^{128}. Thus, we can obtain a full-round linear distinguisher for Zorro with $1/C^2$ known plaintexts. All in all, the above results have threatened the theoretical security of the full-round Zorro.

The remainder of this paper is organized as follows. Section 2 gives a brief description of Zorro block cipher. Section 3 proposes some iterated differential characteristics for one step of Zorro and shows two key recovery attacks on full-round Zorro. Section 4 presents a linear distinguisher of full-round Zorro based on the theory of correlation matrix. Finally, Section 5 concludes this paper.

2   A Brief Description of Zorro

The block cipher Zorro has 128-bit key and 128-bit state. It iterates 24 rounds and the 24 rounds are divided into 6 steps of 4 rounds each.

Encryption Algorithm. As in AES-128, the state in Zorro is regarded as 4×4 matrix of bytes, and one round consists of four distinct transformations: SB^*, AC, SR and MC. SB^* is the S-box layer where only 4 same S-boxes are applied to the 4 bytes of the first row in the state matrix. The S-box used in Zorro is different from the one of AES and the definition of S-box is referred to Appendix A. Next, AC is the addition of round constants in round i. Specifically, the four constants $(i, i, i, i<<3)$ are added to the four bytes of the first row. Finally, the last two transformations, SR and MC, are the AES's ShiftRows and MixColumns.

Key Schedule Algorithm. The key schedule algorithm of Zorro is similar to that of LED. Before the first and after each step, the master key is bitwisely added to the state and the same addition is done after the last step.

Let us focus on MC(MixColumn) used in Zorro which is a permutation operation on the state column by column. The matrix multiplication can be shown as:

$$M = \begin{pmatrix} 02\ 03\ 01\ 01 \\ 01\ 02\ 03\ 01 \\ 01\ 01\ 02\ 03 \\ 03\ 01\ 01\ 02 \end{pmatrix}, \qquad M^{-1} = \begin{pmatrix} 0E\ 0B\ 0D\ 09 \\ 09\ 0E\ 0B\ 0D \\ 0D\ 09\ 0E\ 0B \\ 0B\ 0D\ 09\ 0E \end{pmatrix}.$$

Interestingly, the following equation is true:

$$M^4 = \begin{pmatrix} 01\ 00\ 00\ 00 \\ 00\ 01\ 00\ 00 \\ 00\ 00\ 01\ 00 \\ 00\ 00\ 00\ 01 \end{pmatrix}.$$

Combined with the fact that only 4 S-boxes are applied to the first row for every round, iterated differential characteristics and linear trails are found for four rounds(one step) of Zorro.

3 Differential Cryptanalysis of Full-Round Zorro

Differential cryptanalysis defines characteristics that describe possible evolvements of the differences through the cipher. For non-linear operations (such as S-boxes), it is possible to predict statistical information on the output difference given the input difference by generating the differential distribution table (DDT). If the expected difference for the intermediate data before the last few rounds is given, it may be possible to deduce the unknown key by a statistical analysis. The attack is a chosen plaintext attack that is performed in two phases: In the data collection phase the attacker requests encryption of a large number of pairs of plaintexts, where the differences of all the plaintext pairs are selected to have the input difference of the characteristic. In the data analysis phase the attacker then recovers the key from the collected ciphertexts.

Generally, the total probability of a differential characteristic is the product of the probabilities of each round assuming that the round functions are independent. For Zorro, the secret key is added to the data every four rounds. If we add one value to the input and one at the output of the step, 4 rounds of Zorro can be seen as a step that has no constants in the rounds[1]. As a result, the assumption that the step functions are independent is more rational than the one that round functions are independent for Zorro. In this section, we will present two key recovery attacks on full-round Zorro. The basic one uses a 23-round distinguisher to give an attack with a time complexity of 2^{106} and a memory complexity of 2^{32}. In order to clarify the special structure used in Zorro, another attack with a key searching time complexity of 2^{64} and a memory complexity of 2^{64} is also described.

3.1 Iterated Differential Characteristic

As mentioned by designers, the most damaging differential patterns are those that would exclude active bytes affected by non-linear operations. This kind of differential characteristic with probability 1 exists for at most two rounds. We extend one type of the differential pattern to 4 rounds by adding 4 active bytes. In order to keep the high differential probability for one step, we aim to build iterated differential trails taking advantage of the fact that $M^4 = I$. In order to reduce the searching cases and remove the influence of ShiftRow, we set the original four-byte differences in each row all equal and the first row all zero. The obtained active model is shown in Figure 1. The big squares represent states, small squares represent bytes, white bytes are the ones with zero difference, gray bytes are the ones with a non-zero difference and the letters in gray bytes present the values of difference. As shown in Figure 1, the probability of the path from #1 to #7 is always 1 as the S-boxes are all inactive. If the output differences of all the 4 active S-boxes in the fourth round are equal to the input differences, then the differences of #1 are equal to those of #9 because $M^4 = I$.

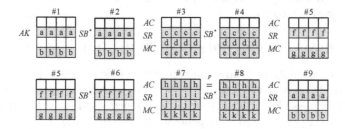

Fig. 1. Iterated differential characteristic of four rounds Zorro

Firstly, we find that 255 different values of (a, b) make the path from #1 to #7 with probability 1. After searching the differential distribution table (DDT) of the S-box used in Zorro, 101 original differences make the path from #7 to #9 possible. The probability of the differential characteristic from #1 to #9(four rounds) is determined by the value of (h, h) in DDT. Specifically, if the value of (h, h) in DDT of S-box is m, then there are m different solutions with the equation $S(x) \oplus S(x \oplus h) = h$. Thus, the probability of the differential characteristic p shown in Figure 1 is $(m/256)^4$. Obviously, the largest m means the highest probability of the characteristic. We find that the maximum m is equal to 6 and 3 options of h make the probability of the differential characteristic be $(6/256)^4 \approx 2^{-21.66}$. The corresponding values of differences expressed in decimal are shown in Table 1. Furthermore, if the state of #1 is replaced by #3, #5 or #7, we can obtain another three iterated differential characteristics with the same probability.

3.2   Basic Key Recovery Attack on Full-Round Zorro

In order to recover the secret key of Zorro, three iterated differential characteristics of 23-round Zorro are used to distinguish the right key and the wrong keys. With the assumption that the step functions of Zorro are independent, we can

Table 1. Three kinds of iterated differential characteristics on one step

NO	a	b	c	d	e	f	g	h	i	j	k
1	22	58	22	88	98	166	138	123	221	35	169
2	107	189	107	183	10	30	200	234	244	93	149
3	88	232	88	123	147	174	30	247	89	140	146

extend the iterated characteristics to 5 steps of Zorro. The probability becomes $2^{-21.66 \times 5} = 2^{-108.3}$ which is much lower than 2^{-128} for the random permutation. Meanwhile, the 23-round differential characteristics shown in Figure 2 have the same probability $2^{-108.3}$ as the path from #1 to #7 with probability 1, where the values of a and b are referred to Table 1. With another assumption that the secret key is randomly chosen from the whole key space, we can give a key recovery attack on the full-round Zorro.

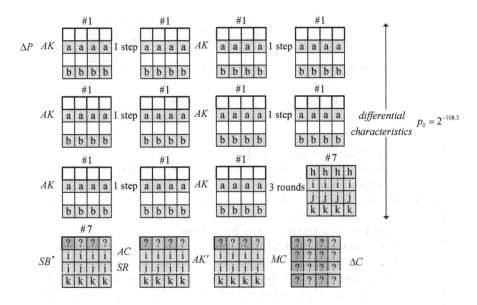

Fig. 2. Key recovery attack on full-round Zorro

Outline. In order to recover the secret key of Zorro efficiently, we combine 3 iterated differential trails to give a structure attack. If we denote the secret key by K, we can change the order of MC and AK in the last round by adding the equivalent key $K' = MC^{-1}(K)$ before MC. Meanwhile, recovering the equivalent key means that the secret key is found. Note that it is impossible to distinguish equivalent keys that share the same values in the last three rows based on the above distinguisher. Therefore, we focus on the 4 bytes of the first row of K'. We first reduce the size of guessing key space from 2^{32} to 1 and then exhaustively search the remaining key candidates for the whole 128-bit key.

1. Choice of Plaintext Pairs
   The chosen plaintexts structure is shown as Figure 3. It is easy to see that in such a structure each difference appears three times. Thus, a total of 9 pairs are contained in a structure of 7 plaintexts. Choose n structures and ask all the $7n$ plaintexts for the corresponding ciphertexts, we can obtain $9n$ plaintext-ciphertext pairs.

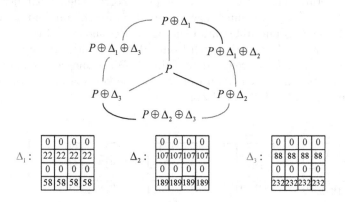

Fig. 3. Chosen plaintexts structure

2. Filtration of Plaintext-Ciphertext Pairs
   Choose ciphertext pairs so that the differences of the input of 24-round satisfy the condition in #7. About 2^{32} among 2^{128} pairs can satisfy the differential condition. Therefore, it remains about $9n \times 2^{-96}$ plaintext-ciphertext pairs to distinguish the right key from wrong keys.
3. Reduction of Key Candidates in the First Row
   Guess the four bytes of the first row of K' (2^{32}), and decrypt the remaining pairs to get the differences of the bytes which fall in the first row of the output of 23-round. If the differences satisfy the condition in the first row of the output of distinguisher, increase the corresponding counter of the guessed key.
4. Extraction from Key Candidates
   Up to now, $9n \times 2^{-96}$ plaintext-ciphertext pairs are left to distinguish the right key from wrong keys. The correct key is suggested with a probability of $2^{-108.3}/2^{-96} = 2^{-12.3}$ while it is about $2^{-128}/2^{-96} = 2^{-32}$ for the incorrect keys. Utilizing the probability differences between the correct key and incorrect keys, we can extract the correct key. We use the ranking paradigm to filter out the key in the first position as the right key candidate.
5. Recovery the Right Key
   Exhaustively test the remaining key candidates(2^{96} keys) to find the correct 128-bit key.

Complexities

1. Data Complexity
   As mentioned in the first step of attack, $7n$ chosen plaintexts are needed to process the attack.
2. Time Complexity
   One computational complexity is checking whether the differences of cipher-text pairs satisfy the differences of last three rows of #7 or not. It can be processed column by column. As is known to us, having known arbitrary 4 bytes in the input and output of MC in AES, the other 4 bytes can be determined. Thus, we can pre-compute all the 2^8 possible outputs of MC with knowing last three input bytes (i, j, k) and store them in a table with the last output byte as the index. Given the difference in the last byte of arbitrary column, the only possible differences in the other three bytes can be obtained from the table. Thus, a pair can be verified after looking up the table at most 4 times, which is much less than $1/4$ one-round encryption. Checking all pairs spend about $9n \times 2^{-6.6}$ full-round Zorro encryptions.
   Another computational complexity is incrementing counters for correct key candidates from the tuples of guessed 32-bit keys and plaintext-ciphertext pairs. It is smaller than $9n \times 2^{-96} \times 2^{32}$ one round encryption. Finally, we need about 2^{96} full-round Zorro encryptions to exhaustively test the remaining key candidates.
3. Memory Complexity
   Since attackers must choose the correct key among the 32-bit keys, it is necessary for the attacker to have enough memory for each 2^{32} keys, which is independent of n.

Given the probabilities (p_0, p), the authors provided a general method for finding an accurate number of samples to reach given error probabilities in [8](Algorithm 1 shown in Appendix B), where p(resp. p_0) is the probability suggested for a wrong key(resp. for the right key). We first denote the type-I error probability (the probability to wrongfully discard the right key) with α and the type-II error probability (the probability to wrongfully accept a random key as the right key) with β. In our attack, we want to determine the number of sample $9n \times 2^{-96}$ with $p_0 = 2^{-12.3}$ and $p = 2^{-32}$. If $\alpha = 10\%$ and $\beta = 2^{-32}$, about $2^{16.85}$ samples($9n \times 2^{-96}$ pairs) can reduce 2^{32} keys to 1 candidate. That is to say, the data complexity of our attack is about $2^{112.5}$ chosen plaintexts. Therefore, the number of remaining key candidates for 128-bit key is about 2^{96} and we exhaustively check the key candidates to filter out the right key. All in all, the time complexity is about $2^{112.85} \times 2^{-6.6} + 2^{16.85} \times 2^{32} \times 1/24 + 2^{96} \approx 2^{106}$ full-round Zorro encryptions.

As mentioned before, it is impossible to distinguish the wrong keys that share the same values in the last three rows with the right key based on the above 23-round distinguisher. Thus, the number of key candidates after the distinguishing process is no less than 2^{96}. In other words, the time complexity for searching the right key is 2^{96} full-round encryptions at least no matter how many plaintext-ciphertext pairs are given. In order to reduce the time complexity of key filtering process, we will show a TMTO attack in the next section.

3.3 TMTO Key Recovery Attack on Full-Round Zorro

In this section, three iterated differential characteristics of 22-round Zorro are used to filter out the right key from the whole key space. The 22-round differential characteristics shown in Figure 4 also have the probability of $2^{-108.3}$, where the values of c, d and e are referred to Table 1. With the assumption that the secret key is randomly chosen from the whole key space, we can also give a full-round key recovery attack on Zorro with a less time complexity for key filtering process. We first consider 64-bit equivalent key and then use the ranking paradigm to filter out the correct one as the right 64-bit key candidate. Finally, exhaustively test the remaining 2^{64} key candidates to find the correct 128-bit key.

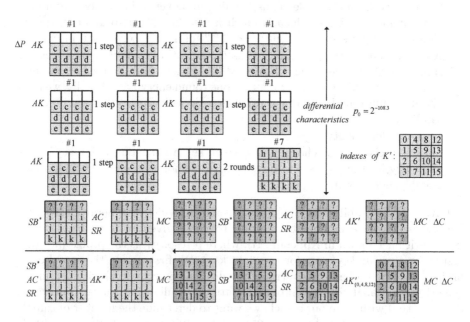

Fig. 4. TMTO key recovery attack on full-round Zorro

Outline. As before, we combine 3 iterated differential trails to give a structure attack and recover the equivalent key $K' = MC^{-1}(K)$ before MC. We divide the 128-bit K' to 16 bytes and denote them as shown in Figure 4. As we know, the key addition can be removed through the linear function with the corresponding operation. Because the S-box layer of Zorro only consists of four S-boxes, we divide the 128-bit K' into two parts, the first row after and the last three rows before the 24-round S-box layer. The following three rows of K' can be removed before the 23-round MC operation and a new 128-bit key K'' generated from 12 bytes of K' appears. Meanwhile,

$$K'' = \begin{pmatrix} K_0'' & K_4'' & K_8'' & K_{12}'' \\ K_1'' & K_5'' & K_9'' & K_{13}'' \\ K_2'' & K_6'' & K_{10}'' & K_{14}'' \\ K_3'' & K_7'' & K_{11}'' & K_{15}'' \end{pmatrix} = MC^{-1} \times \begin{pmatrix} 0 & 0 & 0 & 0 \\ K_{13}' & K_1' & K_5' & K_9' \\ K_{10}' & K_{14}' & K_2' & K_6' \\ K_7' & K_{11}' & K_{15}' & K_3' \end{pmatrix}.$$

The 128-bit K'' is independent with $K_{\{0,4,8,12\}}'$ and they together determine the equivalent 128-bit key K'. We can replace the operation AK' by respectively adding K'' after the 23-round SR and adding $K_{\{0,4,8,12\}}'$ after the 24-round SR. Similarly, it is impossible to distinguish the keys located in the last three rows of K'' based on the distinguisher(Figure 4). As a result, we first use the plaintext-ciphertext pairs and distinguisher to filter out the correct 64-bit equivalent key($K_{\{0,4,8,12\}}'$ and $K_{\{0,4,8,12\}}''$). Finally, exhaustively test the remaining 2^{64} key candidates to find the right 128-bit key.

1. Choice of Plaintext Pairs

   The chosen plaintexts structure is similar to that of the basic attack. Three kinds of differences are used to construct each structure and their values are given in Figure 5. Thus, we can obtain $9n$ differential pairs with $7n$ plaintext-ciphertext pairs.

$\Delta_1:$

0	0	0	0
22	22	22	22
88	88	88	88
98	98	98	98

$\Delta_2:$

0	0	0	0
107	107	107	107
183	183	183	183
10	10	10	10

$\Delta_3:$

0	0	0	0
88	88	88	88
123	123	123	123
147	147	147	147

Fig. 5. Three differences in the chosen plaintexts structure

2. Filtration of Plaintext-Ciphertext Pairs

   Considering one column MC transformation used in AES, if we have known arbitrary four bytes among the 8 bytes in the input and output, then the other four bytes can be determined with probability 1. Given a ciphertext pair, we can obtain the differences in the last three rows after the MC operation of 23-round with probability 1. Meanwhile, if a pair may suggest some keys, then the differences in the last three rows before the MC are equal to that of the output of the distinguisher. As a result, 6 bytes are known for each column and the matching between four columns occurs with a probability of $2^{-16\times 4} = 2^{-64}$. Choose ciphertext pairs that the differences of the last three rows successfully match between the MC operation of the 23-round. About 1 among 2^{64} pairs can satisfy the above condition. Therefore, it remains about $9n \times 2^{-64}$ plaintext-ciphertext pairs to distinguish the right 64-bit key from wrong keys.

3. Reduction of Key Candidates

To reduce the time complexity, we compute the values of suggested keys from the remaining ciphertext pairs instead of exhaustively guessing the corresponding keys. The procedure can be described as follows:

(a) Given a remaining pair, we can easily get the differences before and after the MC of 23-round as explained above. Thus, the input and the output differences of the S-box layers in the 23-round and 24-round are known.

(b) After looking up the difference table of S-box, we can obtain the corresponding input and output values of the 8 S-boxes(4 in 23-round and 4 in 24-round).

(c) Up to now, we have known the output values of the 4 S-boxes in the 24-round. Furthermore, we can easily get the suggested values $K'_{\{0,4,8,12\}}$. On the average, only one key is suggested because given the input and output difference of the S-box in Zorro, one solution is averagely obtained.

(d) Meanwhile, we have known all the values before the 23-round MC and the values in the first row after the 23-round SR. Easily, the possible values of $K''_{\{0,4,8,12\}}$ are also obtained.

(e) Increase the corresponding counters of the computed 64-bit keys.

The above steps are repeated at most $9n \times 2^{-64}$ times. If there exists impossible input-output difference pair of S-box in Step (b), skip the following three steps and go to the next remaining pair.

4. Extraction from Key Candidates

There are $9n \times 2^{-64}$ plaintext-ciphertext pairs to distinguish the right 64-bit key from wrong keys. The incorrect key is suggested with a probability of $2^{-128}/2^{-64} = 2^{-64}$ while it is about $2^{-108.3}/2^{-64} = 2^{-44.3}$ for the right key. We also use the ranking paradigm to filter out the correct key.

5. Recovery the Right Key

Exhaustively test the remaining 2^{64} key candidates to find the correct 128-bit key.

Similarly, we want to determine the number of samples $9n \times 2^{-64}$ with $p_0 = 2^{-44.3}$ and $p = 2^{-64}$. If $\alpha = 10\%$ and $\beta = 2^{-64}$, about $2^{49.81}$ samples($9n \times 2^{-64}$ pairs) can reduce 2^{64} keys to 1 candidates. That is to say, the data complexity of our attack is about $2^{113.5}$ chosen plaintexts. To clarify the special structure of Zorro, we only focus on the time complexity for searching the right key after filtering out wrong pairs. For a remaining pair, the suggested 64-bit keys can be computed by looking up table 8 times. All in all, it costs much smaller than $9n \times 2^{-64}$ one round encryption to reduce the key space to 2^{64}. Finally, we need about 2^{64} full-round Zorro encryptions to exhaustively test the remaining key candidates. Thus, the time complexity of searching keys is about $2^{49.81} \times 1/24 + 2^{64} \approx 2^{64}$ full-round Zorro encryptions with 2^{64} memory.

4 Linear Distinguishing Attack on Full-Round Zorro

Consider an n-bit block cipher F and let the input of the function be $x \in F_2^n$. A linear approximation (u, v) with an input mask u and an output mask v has probability

$$p(u, v) = Pr_{x \in F_2^n}(u \cdot x \oplus v \cdot F(x) = 0).$$

The value $C_F(u, v) = 2p(u, v) - 1$ is called the correlation of linear approximation (u, v).

Consider a mapping $F : \mathbb{F}_2^n \to \mathbb{F}_2^n$ given as a key-alternating iterative block cipher, i.e. $F = F_r \circ F_{r-1} \circ ... \circ F_1$. A linear trail consists of an input mask u and output mask v and a vector $U = (u_1, ..., u_{r-1})$ with $u_i \in \mathbb{F}_2^n$. The correlation of the trail is defined as

$$C_F(u, v, U) = C_{F_1}(u, u_1)C_{F_2}(u_1, u_2)...C_{F_{r-1}}(u_{r-2}, u_{r-1})C_{F_r}(u_{r-1}, v).$$

In contrary to the piling-up lemma[3], no assumption of any kind has to be made for this equation to hold. The characteristics of the correlation matrices of some special boolean functions are summarized as follows[19]:

Lemma 1 *(XOR with a Constant): Consider the function that consists of the bitwise XOR with a constant vector k: $F(x) = x \oplus k$, the correlation matrix is a diagonal matrix with*

$$C_F(u, u) = (-1)^{u^T k}.$$

Lemma 2 *(Linear functions): Consider a linear function $F(x) = Mx$, with M an $m \times n$ binary matrix. The elements of the corresponding correlation matrix are given by*

$$C_F(u, v) = \delta(M^T v \oplus u),$$

where

$$\delta(w) = \begin{cases} 1, & \text{when } w = 0 \\ 0, & \text{when } w \neq 0 \end{cases}.$$

Lemma 3 *(Bricklayer Functions): Consider a bricklayer function $y = F(x)$ that is defined by the following component functions: $y_{(i)} = F_{(i)}(x_{(i)})$ for $1 \leq i \leq l$. For every component function $F_{(i)}$ there is a corresponding correlation matrix denoted by $C_{F_{(i)}}$. The elements of the correlation matrix of F are given by*

$$C_F(u, v) = \prod_i C_{F_{(i)}}(u_{(i)}, v_{(i)}),$$

where $u = (u_{(1)}, u_{(2)}, ..., u_{(l)})$ and $v = (v_{(1)}, v_{(2)}, ..., v_{(l)})$.

In this section, we will give a linear distinguishing attack for full-round Zorro according to the above three rules. F represents the 24-round Zorro, and F_i represents the corresponding i-th step function. Note that the fact $M^4 = I$ implies that $(M^T)^4 = I$, where M^T means the transpose of matrix M.

4.1   Iterated Linear Trail

There exists some iterated linear trails for 4 rounds of Zorro and the pattern can also be shown as Figure 1, where the gray bytes are the ones with a non-zero mask. We compute the correlation of the linear trail using the theory of the correlation matrix with $u = v = u_i (i \leq 6)$. There are 255 different (a, b)

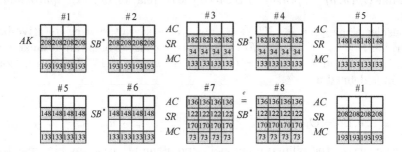

Fig. 6. Iterated linear trail of one-step Zorro

which result in the path from #1 to #7 with the absolute of correlation to be 1. After searching the linear approximation table(LAT) of the S-box used in Zorro, only 210 original linear masks make the path from #7 to #8 with a non-zero correlation. The largest linear correlation occurs when $a = 208$ and $b = 193$ and the absolute value of the corresponding correlation $|c| = (28/128)^4 \approx 2^{-8.77}$. If we change the relative location of #1 with #3, #5 or #7, $|c|$ remains equal. Meanwhile, if the input mask and the output mask of one step are both $(0, 0, 0, 0, 208, 208, 208, 208, 0, 0, 0, 0, 193, 193, 193, 193)$, the linear trail is determined as Figure 6.

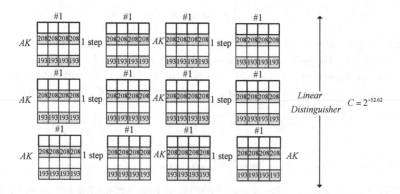

Fig. 7. Linear distinguisher on full-round of Zorro

4.2 Linear Distinguisher of the Full-Round Zorro

If we fix the input linear mask of every step to be the pattern of #1 with $a = 208$ and $b = 193$, we can get a linear trail of full-round Zorro. The absolute value of the correlation of the linear trail can be computed as $|C| = 2^{-8.77 \times 6} = 2^{-52.62}$ without any assumption. Thus we can distinguish the full-round Zorro from random permutation by using $1/C^2 \approx 2^{105.3}$ known plaintexts and the distinguisher is shown as Figure 7.

5 Conclusion

In this paper, we evaluated the security of Zorro against differential cryptanalysis and linear cryptanalysis. Two different key recovery attacks were described in Section 3. The basic one recovered the secret key with a data complexity of $2^{112.4}$ chosen plaintexts, a time complexity of 2^{106} full-round Zorro encryptions and a memory complexity of 2^{32}. The TMTO attack required $2^{113.9}$ chosen plaintexts, a key filtering complexity of 2^{64} full-round Zorro encryptions and 2^{64} memory. Meanwhile, we gave a linear distinguishing attack on the full-round Zorro with $2^{105.3}$ known plaintexts.

For convenience, we fix that the differences of four bytes in each row are all the same. If we exhaustively search the characteristics covering three rounds with probability 1, we may obtain some trails for one step of Zorro with a probability higher than $2^{-21.66}$. Thus the complexity of our key recovery attacks can be improved. The similar cases may occur for the linear distinguishing attack. In summary, the results show that only four S-boxes located in the first row and an iterated structure as AES produce a theoretical weak block cipher. Designers should carefully reduce the non-linear operations when designing a lightweight block cipher based on AES block cipher.

Acknowledgments. We thank the anonymous reviewers for their useful comments that help to improve the paper. The research presented in this paper is supported by the National Basic Research Program of China (No. 2013CB338002) and National Natural Science Foundation of China (No. 61272476, No.61232009 and No. 61202420).

References

1. Guo, J., Nikolic, I., Peyrin, T., Wang, L.: Cryptanalysis of Zorro. Cryptology ePrint Archive, Report 2013/713 (2013), http://eprint.iacr.org/
2. Biham, E., Shamir, A.: Differential cryptanalysis of DES-like cryptosystems. In: Menezes, A., Vanstone, S.A. (eds.) CRYPTO 1990. LNCS, vol. 537, pp. 2–21. Springer, Heidelberg (1991)
3. Matsui, M.: Linear cryptanalysis method for DES cipher. In: Helleseth, T. (ed.) EUROCRYPT 1993. LNCS, vol. 765, pp. 386–397. Springer, Heidelberg (1994)
4. Knudsen, L.R.: Iterative characteristics of DES and s2-DES. In: Brickell, E.F. (ed.) CRYPTO 1992. LNCS, vol. 740, pp. 497–511. Springer, Heidelberg (1993)

5. Knudsen, L.: Truncated and higher order differentials. In: Preneel, B. (ed.) FSE 1994. LNCS, vol. 1008, pp. 196–211. Springer, Heidelberg (1995)
6. Sugita, M., Kobara, K., Imai, H.: Security of reduced version of the block cipher Camellia against truncated and impossible differential cryptanalysis. In: Boyd, C. (ed.) ASIACRYPT 2001. LNCS, vol. 2248, pp. 193–207. Springer, Heidelberg (2001)
7. Wang, M.: Differential cryptanalysis of reduced-round Present. In: Vaudenay, S. (ed.) AFRICACRYPT 2008. LNCS, vol. 5023, pp. 40–49. Springer, Heidelberg (2008)
8. Blondeau, C., Gérard, B., Tillich, J.P.: Accurate estimates of the data complexity and success probability for various cryptanalyses. Designs, Codes and Cryptography 59(1-3), 3–34 (2011)
9. Biham, E.: On Matsui's linear cryptanalysis. In: De Santis, A. (ed.) EUROCRYPT 1994. LNCS, vol. 950, pp. 341–355. Springer, Heidelberg (1995)
10. Baignères, T., Junod, P., Vaudenay, S.: How far can we go beyond linear cryptanalysis? In: Lee, P.J. (ed.) ASIACRYPT 2004. LNCS, vol. 3329, pp. 432–450. Springer, Heidelberg (2004)
11. Bogdanov, A.A., Knudsen, L.R., Leander, G., Paar, C., Poschmann, A., Robshaw, M., Seurin, Y., Vikkelsoe, C.: Present: An ultra-lightweight block cipher. In: Paillier, P., Verbauwhede, I. (eds.) CHES 2007. LNCS, vol. 4727, pp. 450–466. Springer, Heidelberg (2007)
12. De Cannière, C., Dunkelman, O., Knežević, M.: KATAN and KTANTAN — A family of small and efficient hardware-oriented block ciphers. In: Clavier, C., Gaj, K. (eds.) CHES 2009. LNCS, vol. 5747, pp. 272–288. Springer, Heidelberg (2009)
13. Knudsen, L., Leander, G., Poschmann, A., Robshaw, M.J.B.: PRINT cipher: A block cipher for ic-printing. In: Mangard, S., Standaert, F.-X. (eds.) CHES 2010. LNCS, vol. 6225, pp. 16–32. Springer, Heidelberg (2010)
14. Wu, W., Zhang, L.: LBlock: A lightweight block cipher. In: Lopez, J., Tsudik, G. (eds.) ACNS 2011. LNCS, vol. 6715, pp. 327–344. Springer, Heidelberg (2011)
15. Bilgin, B., Bogdanov, A., Knežević, M., Mendel, F., Wang, Q.: FIDES: Lightweight authenticated cipher with side-channel resistance for constrained hardware. In: Bertoni, G., Coron, J.-S. (eds.) CHES 2013. LNCS, vol. 8086, pp. 142–158. Springer, Heidelberg (2013)
16. Shibutani, K., Isobe, T., Hiwatari, H., Mitsuda, A., Akishita, T., Shirai, T.: Piccolo: An ultra-lightweight blockcipher. In: Preneel, B., Takagi, T. (eds.) CHES 2011. LNCS, vol. 6917, pp. 342–357. Springer, Heidelberg (2011)
17. Guo, J., Peyrin, T., Poschmann, A., Robshaw, M.: The LED block cipher. In: Preneel, B., Takagi, T. (eds.) CHES 2011. LNCS, vol. 6917, pp. 326–341. Springer, Heidelberg (2011)
18. Gérard, B., Grosso, V., Naya-Plasencia, M., Standaert, F.-X.: Block ciphers that are easier to mask: How far can we go? In: Bertoni, G., Coron, J.-S. (eds.) CHES 2013. LNCS, vol. 8086, pp. 383–399. Springer, Heidelberg (2013)
19. Daemen, J., Rijmen, V.: The Design of Rijndael. Springer-Verlag New York, Inc., Secaucus (2002)

Appendix A: S-box of Zorro

	0	1	2	3	4	5	6	7	8	9	A	B	C	D	E	F
00	B2	E5	5E	FD	5F	C5	50	BC	DC	4A	FA	88	28	D8	E0	D1
10	B5	D0	3C	B0	99	C1	E8	E2	13	59	A7	FB	71	34	31	F1
20	9F	3A	CE	6E	A8	A4	B4	7E	1F	B7	51	1D	38	9D	46	69
30	53	E	42	1B	F	11	68	CA	AA	6	F0	BD	26	6F	0	D9
40	62	F3	15	60	F2	3D	7F	35	63	2D	67	93	1C	91	F9	9C
50	66	2A	81	20	95	F8	E3	4D	5A	6D	24	7B	B9	EF	DF	DA
60	58	A9	92	76	2E	B3	39	C	29	CD	43	FE	AB	F5	94	23
70	16	80	C0	12	4C	E9	48	19	8	AE	41	70	84	14	A2	D5
80	B8	33	65	BA	ED	17	CF	96	1E	3B	B	C2	C8	B6	BB	8B
90	A1	54	75	C4	10	5D	D6	25	97	E6	FC	49	F7	52	18	86
A0	8D	CB	E1	BF	D7	8E	37	BE	82	CC	64	90	7C	32	8F	4B
B0	AC	1A	EA	D3	F4	6B	2C	FF	55	A	45	9	89	1	30	2B
C0	D2	77	87	72	EB	36	DE	9E	8C	DB	6C	9B	5	2	4E	AF
D0	4	AD	74	C3	EE	A6	F6	C7	7D	40	D4	D	3E	5B	EC	78
E0	A0	B1	44	73	47	5C	98	21	22	61	3F	C6	7A	56	DD	E7
F0	85	C9	8A	57	27	7	9A	3	A3	83	E4	6A	A5	2F	79	4F

Appendix B: Computation of the exact number of samples required for a statistical attack

---

Input: Given error probabilities (α, β) and probabilities (p_0, p).

Output: N and τ : the minimum number of samples and the corresponding relative threshold to reach error probabilities less than (α, β).

Set τ_{min} to p and τ_{max} to p_0.
repeat
    Set τ to $(\tau_{min} + \tau_{max})/2$.
    Compute N_{nd} such that $\forall N > N_{nd}$, $G_{nd}(N, \tau) \leq \alpha$.
    Compute N_{fa} such that $\forall N > N_{fa}$, $G_{fa}(N, \tau) \leq \beta$.
    if $N_{nd} > N_{fa}$ **then**
        $\tau_{max} = \tau$.
    else
        $\tau_{min} = \tau$.
    end if
until $N_{nd} = N_{fa}$.
Return $N = N_{nd} = N_{fa}$ and τ.

Detecting Hidden Leakages

Amir Moradi[1], Sylvain Guilley[2,3], and Annelie Heuser[2,*]

[1] Horst Görtz Institute for IT Security, Ruhr University Bochum, Germany
amir.moradi@rub.de
[2] TELECOM-ParisTech, Crypto Group (COMELEC dpt), Paris, France
firstname.lastname@telecom-paristech.fr
[3] Secure-IC S.A.S., Rennes, France

Abstract. Reducing the entropy of the mask is a technique which has been proposed to mitigate the high performance overhead of masked software implementations of symmetric block ciphers. Rotating S-box Masking (RSM) is an example of such schemes applied to AES with the purpose of maintaining the security at least against univariate first-order side-channel attacks. This article examines the vulnerability of a realization of such technique using the side-channel measurements publicly available through DPA contest V4. Our analyses which focus on exploiting the first-order leakage of the implementation discover a couple of potential attacks which can recover the secret key. Indeed the leakage we exploit is due to a design mistake as well as the characteristics of the implementation platform, none of which has been considered during the design of the countermeasure (implemented in naive C code).

Keywords: Side-channel analysis, leakage detection, variance test, NICV, correlation-collision, CPA, hidden models, linear regression.

1 Introduction

Counteracting side-channel analysis attacks, as a major concern for embedded cryptographic solutions, is a must for today's both software- and hardware-based applications. One of the most studied countermeasures is masking [9,12,25,35], which by randomizing the secret internals aims at cutting the relation between the side-channel leakages and predictable processes. Realization of masking in hardware platforms faces many challenges due to the uncontrolled glitches happening inside the masked circuits. Since these issues are out of scope of this article, the interested reader is referred to [26,29,32,38]. Although there exist a couple of different masking techniques, the focus of this work is on Boolean masking for software-based platforms, where the challenges are mainly due to their significant overhead.

If masking is correctly realized in software, it can significantly increase the complexity of a successful attack. The goal of most of the techniques is to prove

---

* Annelie Heuser is a Google European fellow in the field of privacy and is partially founded by this fellowship.

I. Boureanu, P. Owesarski, and S. Vaudenay (Eds.): ACNS 2014, LNCS 8479, pp. 324–342, 2014.
© Springer International Publishing Switzerland 2014

the impossibility of first-order attacks if the implementation as well as the leakage models follow the corresponding assumptions. As stated, the significant overhead needed to realize the masking schemes is amongst their major drawbacks. This overhead is due to two main issues:

- processing the mask and the masked data. For example, the linear operations (e.g., MixColumns of AES) must be performed on the masked data as well as on the mask, and
- on-the-fly recomputation of the masked look-up tables which are responsible to realize the non-linear operations, e.g., AES S-box.

The first issue is usually not the most dominant part and stays as is for most of the masking schemes. However, many solutions have been proposed to relax the second problem. Some focused on avoiding look-up tables for non-linear operations (like with secure multiplication — the interested reader is referred to [39,17]). It is worth to mention that masking schemes usually assume uniformly distributed random masks. Therefore, on-the-fly recomputation of the S-box is unavoidable unless a huge memory is available to precompute all the necessary tables [36]. Since dealing with this overhead is challenging, a couple of heuristic scenarios, e.g., reusing the mask for certain S-boxes, have been used mainly by industry sector[1]. However, each of these heuristics has a drawback which may lead to a seriously vulnerable implementation (see [10]). Instead, reducing the entropy of the mask is the idea followed by [30,31]. Use of fewer mask values allows precomputing all masked look-up tables and fit them to the small-size platforms, e.g., smartcards or microcontrollers with a few Kilobytes of flash memory. These schemes claim to provide the first-order security, which is defined as follows:

> For all possible mask values, mean of the side-channel leakages based on the predictable secret internals, e.g., one S-box output, is independent of the selected internal, i.e., $\mathbb{E}(l|v)$ is constant, where l and v denote leakage and a secret internal respectively.

In this work we mainly concentrate on a software implementation of Rotating S-boxes Masking (RSM) as a low-entropy masking scheme for AES [31]. We first in Section 2 restate the scheme and provide the necessary notations for formal discussions. Next we focus on an implementation which is publicly available through the *DPA Contest V4* [43]. We also use the corresponding side-channel measurements (of DPA Contest V4) to perform our security evaluations. The practical analyses, which are given in Section 3, aim at examining the existence of a first-order leakage. Two attacks are detailed: one correlation-collision (without a model) and then one correlation attack (with a model). Despite the claims of the original scheme as well as the security proofs, our analysis exploits a strong first-order leakage allowing us to recover the first 128-bit round key using less than 200 measurements. We also provide theoretical reasoning behind the exploitable leakage as well as a solution to prevent it in Section 4.

---

[1] Based on the authors' observations.

As related works we should address three recently published articles [3,23,46] which made use of DPA Contest V4 measurements. Although all of these articles provide many useful discussions and analysis tools, none of them exploits the first-order leakage that we present here. We give more detailed comparison between these works and our contribution in Section 4.

2   Masking in Software

Cryptographic software can be protected against differential side-channel attacks by having the sensitive intermediate variables depend on some random numbers. This strategy is called masking. The procedure consists in splitting every sensitive intermediate variable into several shares randomly, with the property that there exists a way to constructively recombine them to recover the sensitive variable. A classical sharing is the first-order Boolean additive masking, where a sensitive variable X is split in two shares S_0 and S_1 in such a way $X = S_0 \oplus S_1$. Typically, in this scheme, S_1 can be drawn *uniformly* randomly, and will be called the mask. Then S_0 is computed as $X \oplus S_1$. It is well known that any linear operation l is easy to evaluate in this paradigm: it is indeed sufficient to compute l on each share individually. The reason is that $S_0' = l(S_0)$ and $S_1' = l(S_1)$ is a sharing of $l(X)$. However, this does not apply to non-linear operations, such as the computation of a substitution box (S-box). Most of the research effort in the field of masking has thus been spent on this topic.

As we shall detail in the sequel, variants of masking schemes have been put forward. Their motivations are manifold:

- *first-order* masking might not be secure enough, i.e., more shares are required;
- some cryptographic functions are not *Boolean* (e.g., RSA is based on modular arithmetic, hence is preferably masked in some ring $\mathbb{Z}_N$);
- there are situations where the mask cannot be injected *additively* (which has the merit of being compatible with the key addition stage), but rather multiplicatively [19] or via a homographic function [14].

2.1   Traditional Scheme

Historically, the initial masking strategy was called the "S-box precomputation". We illustrate in the sequel such masking on a substitution permutation network (SPN) such as the AES, where the S-box is called SubBytes. For each unique S-box table in the design (e.g., one in case of AES and eight in case of DES), two random variables S_1 and S_1' are drawn, in order to mask respectively its input and its output. Using them, a so-called masked S-box MaskedSubBytes is computed [27]. For every input Y, MaskedSubBytes evaluates MaskedSubBytes$(Y) = $ SubBytes$(Y \oplus S_1) \oplus S_1'$. This table can be used to securely traverse the S-box of the first share $S_0 = X \oplus S_1$, since MaskedSubBytes(S_0) is equal to SubBytes$(X) \oplus S_1'$, and thus this new share combined with S_1' is a valid sharing of SubBytes(X). Nevertheless, in this operation, neither X nor SubBytes(X) appears unmasked, hence the security. So to protect a complete algorithm, the procedure is as follows; each plaintext byte P is first masked with S_1. Then, usually, the first operation is the addition with a key k. This operation is *on purpose* compatible with the masking, meaning that it is secure to add k to $P \oplus S_1$: indeed, it yields $(P \oplus k) \oplus S_1$, which together with S_1 is a sharing of $P \oplus k$. The share $(P \oplus k) \oplus S_1$ can now enter the precomputed MaskedSubBytes as already discussed. The computation goes on this way until the end of the algorithm, where it is eventually secure to demask the masked ciphertext with S_1' (after the last key addition).

Such a protection is especially efficient for algorithms such as AES that uses several instances of the same S-box. Indeed, the precomputation of MaskedSubBytes (which will consist in 2×256 XORs and 256 copies of bytes) is factored for each invocation of the S-box (16 times per round, for all the 14 rounds in the case of AES-256). Since MixColumns is linear and hence transparent to Boolean masking, it should generally be performed on both shares. However, since MixColumns(S_1', S_1', S_1', S_1') $=S_1'$, it is sufficient to perform MixColumns on only one share.

2.2 Problems

The "S-box precomputation" has two types of contradictory drawbacks:

1. First of all, it has an inherently low security level, because some efficient attacks have reported, such as second-order attacks (that combine two leaking samples in a view to remove their common mask) are very practical. Moreover, there exist efficient techniques, e.g., [34,44], which target the precomputation of MaskedSubBytes.
2. Second, it is already costly in practice, both in terms of cycle count (owing to the long S-box precomputation), and in terms of mask "entropy" budget. We recall that producing random numbers is difficult and costly; indeed, in theory, the modelization of masking requires independent and uniformly distributed masks. Even if masks are practically produced by an algorithmic pseudo-random generator (e.g., a stream cipher), this operation is obviously consuming resources.

Therefore researches have been carried out in these two directions. Without surprise, increasing the number of shares does impact negatively the performances. At the opposite, it is interesting to note that some simplifications successfully managed to maintain a notion of security while avoiding the precomputation stage and reducing the required pool of entropy.

2.3 Multi-mask FEMS vs Mono-Mask LEMS

Systematic countermeasures aim at fixing the problem of the masks reuse. Indeed, this can be exploited by a combination of the two leakage samples using the same mask to cancel or bias it. If the two leaking operations are similar, e.g., two computations of S-box, then the attack is referred to as a *collision attack* [6]. Otherwise, the attack is generally termed bivariate, and can consist in second-order CPA [28], multivariate MIA [18], or any other variant (e.g., [15]). For this reason, every intermediate variable is masked independently (e.g., the same masked S-box cannot be used twice), and the sharing is done with strictly more than two shares. Hence the name multi-mask fully entropic masking scheme (FEMS, as coined in [46]). However, this generalization is not trivial. For example, the first attempt to adapt the *precomputation S-box* scheme to d masks (i.e., $d+1$ shares) by [41] happened to be flawed. Indeed, a dependence with the sensitive variable could be exhibited by combining only two shares [13]. The design error was that only one masked table was used. A repaired version has been presented recently at [11]; it employs $d+1$ tables that need each to be precomputed d times (hence a quadratic complexity overhead in the number of masks). Other provably secure schemes have been promoted, such as the computation of the S-box in a Galois field; refer for instance to [39]. In some contexts (e.g., AES), it is the most efficient scheme, but still with roughly d^2 complexity.

At the opposite direction, some masking schemes have been designed to limit the amount of entropy. They are referred to as LEMS (low-entropy masking schemes) in [46]. Specifically, the masking scheme requires only one mask, that can take only a small number of values. This allows to precompute once for all possible masked S-boxes, and to store them *hardwired* in memory. This strategy is winning in terms of performance (albeit at the expense of more ROM). Security-wise, as the mask S_1 is no longer uniformly distributed, zero-offset [45] or mutual information attacks [2] become possible. But the degree to which the leakage shall be raised for a CPA attack – on a platform with a linear leakage function – to be successful can be made strictly larger than three (see next section), and thus becomes the relevant security parameter.

2.4 RSM

Rotating S-box Masking (RSM) is an example of such low entropy masking schemes [31]. The mask values are chosen in such a way that the leakage caused by the masked variable $X \oplus S_1$ depends on X only at degree 4. It is explained in [4] that such security can be reached if the masks are distributed as the 16 codewords of the $[8, 4, 4]$ linear code, extension with one parity bit of the $[7, 4, 3]$ Hamming code.

3 Practical Realization

3.1 DPA Contest V4

How the Scheme is Implemented. The investigated cipher is AES-256 in encryption (Electronic Code Book) mode. It complies with the NIST FIPS standard [33]. In the notations that will follow, some minor adjustments are done with respect to the standard; for instance, depending on the context, SubBytes (resp. MixColumns) can be considered on the whole state or on individual bytes (resp. individual columns). It is mainly coded in the C language, and is compiled by avr-gcc; only some constants to be stored in Flash memory are given in an assembly code. The implementation realizing the RSM scheme is supposed to provide security against *univariate* side-channel attacks up to order 3 if the leakage model is linear.

It can be considered that the protection by masking is added on top of an unprotected AES. This "base AES" has those features:

- The key schedule is precomputed.
- The sixteen substitution boxes (S-boxes) are called in this order:

$$0,\ 2,\ 4,\ 6,\ 8,\ 10,\ 12,\ 14,\ \ //\ \text{Even S-boxes first}$$
$$1,\ 3,\ 5,\ 7,\ 9,\ 11,\ 13,\ 15.\ \ //\ \text{Odd S-boxes second}$$

- The MixColumns operation is computed on a byte-by-byte basis, using an xtime table.

The masking protection is an additive Boolean masking scheme, with statically masked S-boxes (as introduced in Section 2.4). It adds to the "base AES" those features:

- Sixteen values of the mask (noted S_1 in Section 2), are noted as $M_i, i = [\![0, 15]\!]$. Those values are incorporated in the computation. They constitute a space vector, defined as {0x00, 0x0f, 0x36, 0x39, 0x53, 0x5c, 0x65, 0x6a, 0x95, 0x9a, 0xa3, 0xac, 0xc6, 0xc9, 0xf0, 0xff}, and are public information. They are precomputed as state-wide masks, called $\mathsf{Mask_{offset}}$ and defined as:

$$\begin{aligned}
\mathsf{Mask_{offset}} = ((&M_{\mathsf{offset}+0},\ M_{\mathsf{offset}+1},\ M_{\mathsf{offset}+2},\ M_{\mathsf{offset}+3}),\\
&(M_{\mathsf{offset}+4},\ M_{\mathsf{offset}+5},\ M_{\mathsf{offset}+6},\ M_{\mathsf{offset}+7}),\\
&(M_{\mathsf{offset}+8},\ M_{\mathsf{offset}+9},\ M_{\mathsf{offset}+10}, M_{\mathsf{offset}+11}),\\
&(M_{\mathsf{offset}+12}, M_{\mathsf{offset}+13}, M_{\mathsf{offset}+14}, M_{\mathsf{offset}+15}))\ .
\end{aligned}$$

Notice that in the equation above, the layout of the bytes is *transposed* with respect to the canonical representation of the state (i.e., lines represent columns).

- A random offset, noted offset, is drawn randomly in $[\![0, 15]\!]$ at the beginning of the computation; it determines the allocation of the masks for each byte of the state. Explicitly, the state byte i is masked by mask $M_{\mathsf{offset}+i}$. In this equation, offset $+ i$ is to be understood "modulo 16". We do the same assumption in the sequel concerning indices of bytes in a state.
- The S-box is replaced by sixteen masked S-boxes, that are stored precomputed; their equation is $\mathsf{MaskedSubBytes}_i(X) = \mathsf{SubBytes}(X \oplus M_i) \oplus M_{i+1}$, where X is a byte. This means that the output mask of each S-box is the *successor* of the input mask. This also explains why S-boxes are not called in the natural order; the goal is to prevent unfortunate demasking that might occur otherwise.

- To pass through the linear layer, the mask bytes are *compensated* (by exclusive-or), thanks to sixteen 128-bit precomputed constants, that are equal to:

$$\mathsf{MaskCompensation}_{\mathsf{offset}} = \mathsf{Mask}_{\mathsf{offset}} \oplus \mathsf{MixColumns}(\mathsf{ShiftRows}(\mathsf{Mask}_{\mathsf{offset}}))$$

$$= \mathsf{Mask}_{\mathsf{offset}} \oplus ($$

$$\mathsf{MixColumns}(M_{\mathsf{offset}+0},\ M_{\mathsf{offset}+5},\ M_{\mathsf{offset}+10}, M_{\mathsf{offset}+15}),$$

$$\mathsf{MixColumns}(M_{\mathsf{offset}+4},\ M_{\mathsf{offset}+9},\ M_{\mathsf{offset}+14}, M_{\mathsf{offset}+3}),$$

$$\mathsf{MixColumns}(M_{\mathsf{offset}+8},\ M_{\mathsf{offset}+13}, M_{\mathsf{offset}+2},\ M_{\mathsf{offset}+7}),$$

$$\mathsf{MixColumns}(M_{\mathsf{offset}+12}, M_{\mathsf{offset}+1},\ M_{\mathsf{offset}+6},\ M_{\mathsf{offset}+11}))\ .$$

This operation can be termed a "trans-masking", insofar as it simultaneously removes the mask used to protect the linear part of the current round and remasks with the new mask suitable for the S-boxes at the next round, and so without revealing any sensitive variable unmasked.
- For the last round, the compensation is slightly different, because there is no MixColumns. Instead of $\mathsf{MaskCompensation}_{\mathsf{offset}}$, the following constant is added by exclusive-or to the state to remove the mask and generate the ciphertext:

$$\mathsf{MaskCompensationLastRound}_{\mathsf{offset}} = \mathsf{ShiftRows}(\mathsf{Mask}_{\mathsf{offset}})\ .$$

The protected AES can thus be represented by the algorithm 1. The unprotected version of this algorithm can be recovered by erasing the lines in blue, and by trading MaskedSubBytes for SubBytes. This algorithm runs in constant time (the test at line 10 does not depend either on plaintext or roundkeys), so timing attacks [16] do not apply.

How the Measurement Is Performed. The information related to experimental setup is as mentioned on the DPA contest V4 website [43]. The whole design is loaded into an ATMega163 8-bit smartcard, and evaluated on a SASEBO-W platform. The measurements were taken using a LeCroy wave-runner 6100A oscilloscope by means of a Langer EMV 0–3 GHz EM probe. The acquisition bandwidth is 200 MHz and the sampling rate $F_S = 500$ MS/s. The smartcard is powered at 2.5 V and clocked at 3.57 MHz by the on-board Xilinx Spartan-6 FPGA.

3.2 Analysis

Before doing the analysis it is worth to have a look at the mean of the traces and specify the operations performed at different time periods. Figure 1 shows a mean trace (obtained using 1 000 traces) where the operations of the first round of the underlying AES encryption are marked. The following parts of this section deal with different schemes and methods we used to analyze the vulnerability of the implementation.

Algorithm 1. AES-256 used for the DPA contest V4 [43].

Input : Plaintext X, seen as 16 bytes X_i, $i \in [\![0,15]\!]$,
                Key schedule, 15 128-bit constants $\mathsf{RoundKey}_r$, $r \in [\![0,14]\!]$
Output: Ciphertext X, seen as 16 bytes X_i, $i \in [\![0,15]\!]$

1 Draw a random offset, uniformly in $[\![0,15]\!]$
2 $X = X \oplus \mathsf{Mask_{offset}}$ /* Plaintext blinding */
3
4 **for** $r \in [\![0,13]\!]$ **do**
5      $X = X \oplus \mathsf{RoundKey}_r$ /* AddRoundKey */
6   **for** $i \in [\![0,15]\!]$ **do**
7        $X_i = \mathsf{MaskedSubBytes_{offset}}_{+i+r}(X_i)$
8   **end**
9      $X = \mathsf{ShiftRows}(X)$
10   **if** $r \neq 13$ **then**
11       $X = \mathsf{MixColumns}(X)$
12       $X = X \oplus \mathsf{MaskCompensation_{offset}}_{+1+r}$
13   **end**
14 **end**
15
16 $X = X \oplus \mathsf{RoundKey}_{14}$ /* Last AddRoundKey */
17 $X = X \oplus \mathsf{MaskCompensationLastRound_{offset}}_{+14}$ /* Ciphertext demasking */

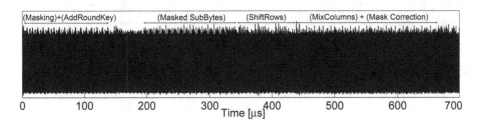

Fig. 1. A mean trace covering the first round of the AES encryption, using 1 000 traces

Examining the First-Order Leakage. Back to the original correlation-collision attack [29], which is shortly restated later, the authors proposed a *variance test approach* which can identify the time instances when a first-order leakage is exhibited by the traces. It is worth to mention that relatively-similar approaches were previously introduced in [1,42] as *inter cluster separation* and *variance test*. In order to follow this approach we first need to estimate the mean of the traces classified by the plaintext bytes. To express it formally let us denote the number of traces by N, the plaintexts by $p^0, \ldots, p^{N-1}$, the plaintext bytes by $p_{j \in \{0,\ldots,15\}}^{n \in \{0,\ldots,N-1\}}$, and the traces by $t^0, \ldots, t^{N-1}$. We also express the corresponding random variables as P, $P_{j \in \{0,\ldots,15\}}$, and T. We now estimate the mean traces, denoted by $m_{j=\{0,\ldots,15\}}^{i=\{0,\ldots,255\}}$, as follows:

$$m_j^i = \mathbb{E}(T | P_j = i) \ .$$

According to [29] a variance trace over the mean traces, e.g., $v_{j\in\{0,...,15\}} = \mathrm{Var}(m_j^i; \forall i)$ should indicate the time samples in which the mean traces depend on the plaintext byte, i.e., j. For example, Fig. 2 shows two variance traces v_0 and v_2 obtained using 100 000 traces. Note that according to the realization of the scheme expressed in Section 3.1, the corresponding plaintext bytes of these two variance traces, i.e., 0 and 2, are processed consequently during the SubBytes operation. As clearly shown by the graphics, there is an unambiguous dependency between the mean traces $m_0^{i\in\{0,...,255\}}$ and the value of the first plaintext byte when the relevant S-box is computed. Therefore, due to the initial AddRoundKey and the AES S-box as a bijection, the same dependency holds for the S-box input as well as its output. As a result, back to the definition of a first-order leakage illustrated in Section 1 we conclude that there is a first-order leakage available in the traces. In the next parts of this section we show how to extract this leakage thereby recovering the secrets. We should note that the big peaks shown by Fig. 2 before 50 μs are related to the initial masking of plaintext bytes before the key addition.

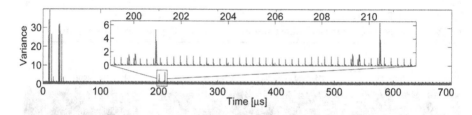

Fig. 2. Two variance traces v_0 and v_2, using 100 000 traces, i.e., around 390 traces per mean trace

Correlation-Collision Attack In order to perform a correlation-collision attack which aims at recovering the linear difference between the targeted key bytes (see AES linear collision attack [7]) the mean traces, e.g., m_0^i and m_2^i, should be first aligned based on the time instances of leaking parts discovered by the variance check approach restated above. Suppose that $m_2^{\prime i}$ indicate the mean traces m_2^i which are aligned to the mean traces m_0^i, i.e., by shifting each mean trace m_2^i 9.524 μs (4762 sample points) to the left (see Fig. 2). For a specific key difference guess $\Delta k = k_0 \oplus k_2$, computing the correlation between m_0^i and $m_2^{\prime i \oplus \Delta k}$ (series of 256 values indexed by i) at each sample point individually leads to a correlation trace $c^{\Delta k}$. Repeating the same scenario for all possible Δk guesses we obtain 256 correlation traces which are shown by Fig. 3. The correct Δk can be clearly distinguished from the other candidates. We repeated this scheme targeting different key bytes, and the difference between all key bytes can be recovered similarly. Moreover, the number of required traces for a successful Δk recovery, reported as 2500 traces by Fig. 3(b), is approximately the same for other key bytes. The achieved correlation is almost reaching one (its maximal value), which is consistent with the reuse of exactly the same code for the evaluation of all the sixteen S-boxes.

We now seek for a faster attack, namely a CPA with a relevant leakage model.

CPA by Bit Model. According to the property of the underlying masking scheme and the specific way the mask list is selected [31] (also restated in Section 2), there should not exist any first-order leakage. However, the results shown above somehow contradict with the security proofs. Therefore, we tried to *pinpoint* the leakage source by performing CPA attacks with different hypothetical power models. The straightforward models like the Hamming weight (HW) of the S-box input or its output failed to recover any secret. The same holds for all bit-wise models, e.g., the most significant bit (MSB) of the S-box output. However, our analysis showed a clear dependency between the traces and bit-wise Hamming distance (HD) of the S-box input and output. In other words, when the power model is selected as

$$hp(x, k, b) = (x \oplus k \oplus \mathsf{SubBytes}\,(x \oplus k))\ \&\ 2^b\ , \tag{1}$$

where x denotes the plaintext byte value, k the key byte candidate, and $b \in \{0, \ldots, 7\}$ the bit position within the byte, the CPA attack is able to recover the correct key candidate. Figure 4 shows the CPA attack results for all 8 bit-wise models targeting the first key byte. As shown by the graphics, the attacks are successful not for all the selected models, and the polarity of the relation between the model and the traces differs from a model to another. For example, the polarity of correlation value for the correct key candidate related to the bits 0 and 3 is the inverse of that of the bits 6 and 7. We should mention that the shape of the graphics and the attack results look similar when targeting other key bytes. Another issue is related to the low number of required traces, i.e., around 500, to successfully mount the attack.

Leakage Source. In order to find the reason behind such leakage we carefully followed the operations performed during the SubBytes operation. As illustrated

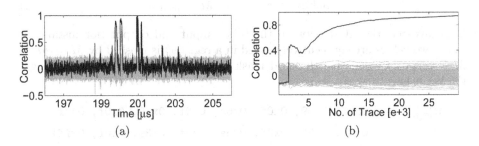

Fig. 3. Result of a correlation collision attack targeting the difference between the first and the third key bytes $\Delta k = k_0 \oplus k_2$, (a) using 100 000 traces, (b) at time instance 200.968 μs over number of traces

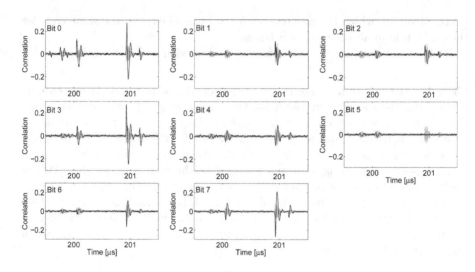

Fig. 4. The CPA attack results, bit-wise HD model of S-box input:output, using 100 000 traces

before the i-th masked S-box, which gets the input masked by M_i, issues the S-box output masked by $M_{i+1 \bmod 16}$. It means,

$$\mathsf{MaskedSubBytes}_i(x') = \mathsf{SubBytes}(x' \oplus M_i) \oplus M_{i+1 \bmod 16},$$

where x' denotes the masked input as $x \oplus M_i$. Since during the SubBytes operation the cipher state is replaced by its substituted one using the S-box, the XOR of the S-box input and output usually influences the power consumption. Following the given formula above, the XOR of a masked S-box input and output yields to

$$
\begin{aligned}
x' \oplus \mathsf{SubBytes}(x' \oplus M_i) \oplus M_{i+1 \bmod 16} &= \\
x \oplus M_i \oplus \mathsf{SubBytes}(x) \oplus M_{i+1 \bmod 16} &= \\
x \oplus \mathsf{SubBytes}(x) \oplus M_i \oplus M_{i+1 \bmod 16}. &
\end{aligned}
\tag{2}
$$

It means that the XOR between the S-box input and output (for instance if these two values are consecutively saved in a register) is masked by $M_i' = M_i \oplus M_{i+1 \bmod 16}$. Considering the used mask table (see Section 2), M_i' is amongst the list below:

$$
\begin{aligned}
M_{i \in [\![0,15]\!]}' = \{ \ & \texttt{0x0f, 0x39, 0x0f, 0x6a, 0x0f, 0x39, 0x0f, 0xff,} \\
& \texttt{0x0f, 0x39, 0x0f, 0x6a, 0x0f, 0x39, 0x0f, 0xff} \} \ .
\end{aligned}
$$

First, this mask list does belong to the codewords ($[8, 4, 4]$ code) defined in Section 2.4, since they are obtained by the composition with a XOR (the internal law) of pairs of codewords. Second, the distribution of the list does not seem to

Table 1. Probabilities of $M'^{(b)}$ being equal to one

$M'^{(b)}$	$M'^{(0)}$	$M'^{(1)}$	$M'^{(2)}$	$M'^{(3)}$	$M'^{(4)}$	$M'^{(5)}$	$M'^{(6)}$	$M'^{(7)}$
$\mathbb{P}(M'^{(b)} = 1)$	0.875	0.750	0.625	1.000	0.375	0.500	0.250	0.125

be a suitable mask list as it consists of 8 times `0x0f`, 4 times `0x39`, 2 times `0x6a`, and 2 times `0xff`. This code M' is not balanced, hence inefficient against first-order attacks. Therefore, the leakage observed by the correlation-collision attack as well as the CPA with bit-wise HD model is due to this fact that the XOR of the S-box input and output is not suitably masked.

CPA by Optimal Model. In order to understand the results in Fig. 4, which show very distinct correlation coefficients for each bit, and to identify an optimal model for CPA, we further investigate in the code M'. As in Eq. (1), let $z = x \oplus k \oplus \mathsf{SubBytes}\,(x \oplus k)$ and $y = \mathrm{HW}(z \oplus m') + N$, with random mask $m' \in M'$ and additive noise N. It is known [37] that, if the noise N is Gaussian, the optimal model is given by $f_{\mathrm{opt}}(Z) = \mathbb{E}(Y|Z)$. We note that m' is uniformly distributed in M', that is a *code with duplicated codewords* (i.e., it is not a *simple* code as M). By linearity of the Hamming weight, we gain the following: (by $z^{(b)}$ and $m'^{(b)}$ we denote the right most b-th bit of z and m' respectively)

$$
\begin{aligned}
f_{\mathrm{opt}}(z) &= \textstyle\sum_{b=0}^{7} \mathbb{E}(z^{(b)} \oplus m'^{(b)}) \\
&= \textstyle\sum_{b=0}^{7} z^{(b)} \times \mathbb{P}(m'^{(b)} = 0) + (1 - z^{(b)}) \times \mathbb{P}(m'^{(b)} = 1) \\
&= \underbrace{\textstyle\sum_{b=0}^{7} \mathbb{P}(m'^{(b)} = 1)}_{:=\alpha} + \textstyle\sum_{b=0}^{7} z^{(b)} \times 2\left(\mathbb{P}(m'^{(b)} = 0) - \tfrac{1}{2}\right) \ .
\end{aligned} \tag{3}
$$

Further, according to M' we can compute the probabilities for each $m'^{(b)}$ equal to 1 as given in Tab. 1, and of course, $\mathbb{P}(m'^{(b)} = 1) = 1 - \mathbb{P}(m'^{(b)} = 0)$.

We can ignore the constant $\alpha = 4.5$ in Eq. (3), as it is not relevant for CPA. Similarly, we can multiply f_{opt} by a constant (e.g., -4) to make all the coefficients be integers. After these transformations, the optimal model is:

$$
f_{\mathrm{opt}}(z) = 3\,z^{(0)} + 2\,z^{(1)} + z^{(2)} + 4\,z^{(3)} - z^{(4)} - 2\,z^{(6)} - 3\,z^{(7)} \ . \tag{4}
$$

Note that, we removed the factor for $z^{(5)}$ as the probabilities for both states are 0.5 and thus bit 5 is perfectly masked.

However, the model for CPA given in Eq. (4) is only valid if the assumption $y = \mathrm{HW}(z \oplus m') + N$ is true. Or in other words, if the power consumption is not composed of a weighted sum of bits with different weights, otherwise the probabilities from Tab. 1 have to be adjusted with the weights of the bits. Thus, in order to identify the weights, we performed a linear regression [22,40] using the model

$$
hp(x, b) = (x \oplus k^* \oplus \mathsf{SubBytes}\,(x \oplus k^*) \oplus m') \ \& \ 2^b \ , \tag{5}
$$

where the mask m' and the correct key k^* are known. Figure 5(a) shows the weights (β-coefficients) estimated by linear regression for each bit $b = \{0, \ldots, 7\}$. Interestingly, one can clearly identify similar β-coefficients for each bit and thus a clear Hamming weight leakage at the last two leakage moments. Note that, these are the same moments as in Fig. 4. Therefore, the assumption on y is valid and we can directly use the weights as in Eq. (4).

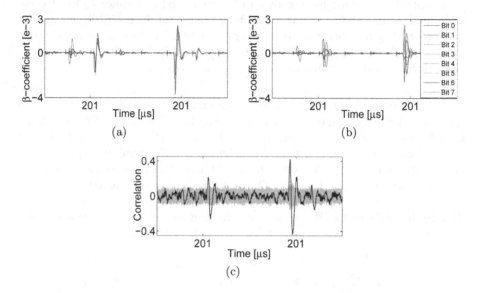

Fig. 5. (a) β-coefficients for bit $b = \{0, \ldots, 7\}$ when the mask and the correct key are known, showing a clear HW leakage at the main leakage moments, (b) β-coefficients when the mask is unknown (c) CPA result using the optimal model Eq. (4) using 1 000 traces

The CPA attack result when using the optimal model (Eq. (4)) is depicted in Fig. 5(c). The graphics show the suitability of the model as the correlation of the correct key candidate is much higher compared to that of Fig. 4 indicating less than 200 traces for a successful attack. Interestingly, the "investment" of 100 000 traces required for the leakage detection (recall Fig. 2) allows a considerable speed-up in the leakage exploitation.

Additionally, the probabilities given in Tab. 1 also explain the results of the bitwise CPA. As explained above bit 5 is perfectly masked, which is also reflected in Fig. 4. Additionally, the greater $|\mathbb{P}(M'^{(b)} = 1) - 0.5|$ the easier the bit is to attack, since it is not well masked. For example, the bits with the highest distance are $b = \{0, 3, 7\}$, which also show the highest correlation coefficient in Fig. 4.

Moreover, we perform a linear regression without considering the mask using the model

$$hp(x, b) = \left((x \oplus k^* \oplus \mathsf{SubBytes}\,(x \oplus k^*))\ \&\ 2^b\right). \tag{6}$$

The β-coefficients are displayed in Fig. 5(b). When looking at the highest leakage moment around $201\mu s$, we can see that coefficient of bit 5 is nearly zeros, thus has no influence as explained before. Furthermore, the other bits follow the same tendency as in Fig. 4 and in Tab. 1. Thus, using the optimal model in Eq. (4) is "equivalent" to the use of a profiled model.

4   Discussion

4.1   Attack and Leakage Orders

The leakage we discovered in the specific implementation of RSM on the ATMega smartcard is based on Hamming distance. Indeed by Hamming distance between a and b we recover the bits of $a \oplus b = (a \wedge \neg b) \vee (\neg a \wedge b)$. Therefore, the execution platform itself is realizing the multiplication between several values, that happen to be $x \oplus k \oplus M_i$ on the one hand and $\mathsf{SubBytes}(x \oplus k) \oplus M_{i+1 \bmod 16}$ on the other. So, as noted in Eq. (2), a first-order leakage is created by the device itself by artificially multiplying the bits of the S-box input and output. This leakage is subtle in that it is not a trivial unmasking, as if $X \oplus S_0$ would be overwritten by S_0.

Strictly speaking, the *rot is already set in*, meaning that the implementation on the smartcard actually prepares a leakage that can be exploited at first order by an attacker.

4.2   Comparison with other Attacks on the DPA Contest V4 AES Traces

Ye and Eisenbarth implemented several distribution-based attacks [46]. They exploit the fact that even though the implementation of RSM manages to cancel the moments of order 1, 2 and 3 of the leakage conditioned by a sensitive byte, the moments of order greater than 3 do depend on the sensitive byte. Therefore, the information-theoretic study of the leakage will without doubt allow to put forward biases exploitable in key recovery attacks. In this sense, RSM is not a first-order masking scheme according to the definition that can be found in [11] for instance. A couple of nice and interesting tools, e.g., detecting the collisions due to the complimentary mask lists, are provided in [46] to make use of the leakage distributions. As underlined at [21], the common protection strategy behind *leakage squeezing* [24] and RSM [31], namely the cancellation of leakage moments, indeed conveys an increased security. This explains why the attacks of Ye and Eisenbarth require many more traces (around 10 000), where a first-order attack knowing the mask requires only about 12 traces.

Lerman et al. have developed a profiling attack that consists in recovering the masks [23]. They used supervised learning to recognize the mask offset, that leaks strongly. This is illustrated in Fig. 6, which shows that the normalized inter-class variance (i.e., $\mathrm{NICV} = \mathrm{Var}(\mathbb{E}(T|\mathsf{offset}))/\mathrm{Var}(T)$ [5], also known as the *coefficient*

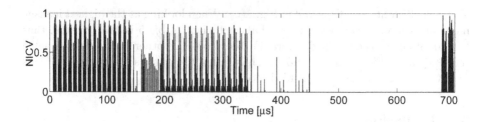

Fig. 6. Normalized inter-class variance for the mask offset of the RSM countermeasure

of determination) reaches almost its maximal value '1' at many points in the trace. The idea behind the attack is to make profiles based on the mask value (which has a low entropy), and use these profiles to detect the randomly selected mask during the attack phase and finally run a CPA [8] knowing the mask.

Belgarric et al. prove in [3] that an straightforward second-order correlation attack using the centered product as a combination function [37] needs 300 traces to retrieve the key with probability greater than 80%. Then, the authors assume that the attacker does not know exactly the two leakage points to be combined. Using time-frequency techniques, such as the discrete Hartley transform, the attack remains feasible within about 550 traces even if the investigated window sizes around the leaking samples is of width 2000.

Our Attack is particular, in that it requires neither a learning nor a profiling phase. It also does not make use of either the higher-order moments or the leakage distributions. It simply consists in launching a standard attack of lowest possible degree, namely one, with a regular distinguisher (the Pearson correlation coefficient). Our attack, and more precisely the methodology that led to the attack, is *constructive*, in that it allows to point out the leakage cause, which allowed us to fix it (refer to the next Section 4.3).

Summing up, none of the other three attacks referred in this section are specific to RSM, except that of Ye and Eisenbarth (but they require much more traces than a regular second-order attack). Indeed, the attacks of Lerman et al., and Belgarric et al. could as well apply on an FEMS. Since there exists first-order leakage in particular points of the traces, it is not clear whether this leakage was beneficial in the work by Ye and Eisenbarth as well as by Belgarric et al.It is uncertain whether these works are still efficient if the aforementioned first-order leakage is avoided. Our attack is specific to the mask distributions, but what it exploits is an unexpected leakage provided by the implementation platform. Concluding, even if all assumptions including the leakage models are hold, the RSM can be insecure *if implemented improperly*.

Table 2. Reordering of the sixteen codewords of $[8, 4, 4]$ linear code so that the Hamming distance between two consecutive codewords is balanced

i	0	1	2	3	4	5	6	7
M_i	0x00	0x0f	0x36	0x39	0x53	0x95	0x5c	0xc9
M_{i+1}	0x0f	0x36	0x39	0x53	0x95	0x5c	0xc9	0xff
$M_i' = M_i \oplus M_{i+1}$	0x0f	0x39	0x0f	0x6a	0xc6	0xc9	0x95	0x36

i	8	9	10	11	12	13	14	15
M_i	0xff	0xc6	0xac	0x9a	0x6a	0xa3	0x65	0xf0
M_{i+1}	0xc6	0xac	0x9a	0x6a	0xa3	0x65	0xf0	0x00
$M_i' = M_i \oplus M_{i+1}$	0x39	0x6a	0x36	0xf0	0xc9	0xc6	0x95	0xf0

4.3 Plugging the First-Order Leakage

There are various ways to plug the first-order leakage. We mention hereafter two of them.

- First of all, the masks sequence (S-box input:output relationship) can be tuned, so as to make the HD leakage of Eq. (2) leak-free at first order (which is lower than claimed for RSM, i.e., order 1 versus order 3). We found that there exist several reordering functions $f : \{0, 15\} \to \{0, 15\}$ of the masks such that $M_i \oplus M_{i+1}$ is balanced. One example of such order is shown in Tab. 2.
- Second, it is easy to identify in the ASM generated by `avr-gcc` the register transfers that are leaking. The leakage source happens to be an instruction `lpm` (Load Program Memory, i.e., read from FLASH) that overwrites its input with its output. We have implemented a secure `lpm` (as an ASM macro) that clears the destination register before it is written to when we access FLASH (where the MaskedSubBytes tables are stored). Still, this implementation (as any implementation of masking) deserves a verification, either with formal methods or with real-world leakage measurements.

5   Conclusions

This paper has highlighted a systematic methodology to detect and then to attack side-channel leakages on cryptographic implementations. The first stage consists in the *identification*. It can be realized by many tools, such as variance-based tests or NICV [5]. Generally these approaches only detect leakages that involve one or a few bytes of known data (typically plaintext or ciphertext). Indeed, the more bytes, the more traces for the partitioning, and also the more memory for the conditional traces averaging. Another approach, based on pair-wise comparison of traces, has been suggested [20]; however, it requires chosen plaintexts. Second, the attacker will try to turn this leakage into a bias that can yield to a key recovery. The second stage is referred to as the *exploitation*. This step is illustrated in the paper by the intuition that a timely leakage occurring during the S-boxes is likely to have a given expression. A naturally expression (namely the overwriting of a look-up table address by the result) is indeed shown to leak, at first-order (despite the masks that are still there). The efficiency of such an attack is contrasted to second-order attacks [3]. In summary, this paper has shown that a universal verification of the implementation in practice is necessary due diligence, even for provable masking scheme (that are based on hypotheses that must be checked).

Acknowledgements. The authors would like to thank Nicolas Bruneau, from STMicroelectronics Rousset & TELECOM-ParisTech, for the computation of the normalized inter-class variance (NICV) on the offset, and for the research of the masks reordering.

References

1. Batina, L., Gierlichs, B., Lemke-Rust, K.: Differential Cluster Analysis. In: Clavier, C., Gaj, K. (eds.) CHES 2009. LNCS, vol. 5747, pp. 112–127. Springer, Heidelberg (2009)
2. Batina, L., Gierlichs, B., Prouff, E., Rivain, M., Standaert, F.-X., Veyrat-Charvillon, N.: Mutual Information Analysis: a Comprehensive Study. J. Cryptology 24(2), 269–291 (2011)
3. Belgarric, P., Bhasin, S., Bruneau, N., Danger, J.-L., Debande, N., Guilley, S., Heuser, A., Najm, Z., Rioul, O.: Time-Frequency Analysis for Second-Order Attacks. In: CARDIS 2013. LNCS. Springer (2013)
4. Bhasin, S., Carlet, C., Guilley, S.: Theory of masking with codewords in hardware: low-weight dth-order correlation-immune Boolean functions. Cryptology ePrint Archive, Report 2013/303 (2013), http://eprint.iacr.org/2013/303/
5. Bhasin, S., Danger, J.-L., Guilley, S., Najm, Z.: NICV: Normalized Inter-Class Variance for Detection of Side-Channel Leakage. In: International Symposium on Electromagnetic Compatibility (EMC 2014), Tokyo, May 12-16. IEEE (2014); Session OS09: EM Information Leakage. Hitotsubashi Hall (National Center of Sciences), Chiyoda, Tokyo, Japan
6. Bogdanov, A.: Improved Side-Channel Collision Attacks on AES. In: Adams, C., Miri, A., Wiener, M. (eds.) SAC 2007. LNCS, vol. 4876, pp. 84–95. Springer, Heidelberg (2007)
7. Bogdanov, A.: Multiple-Differential Side-Channel Collision Attacks on AES. In: Oswald, E., Rohatgi, P. (eds.) CHES 2008. LNCS, vol. 5154, pp. 30–44. Springer, Heidelberg (2008)
8. Brier, É., Clavier, C., Olivier, F.: Correlation Power Analysis with a Leakage Model. In: Joye, M., Quisquater, J.-J. (eds.) CHES 2004. LNCS, vol. 3156, pp. 16–29. Springer, Heidelberg (2004)
9. Chari, S., Jutla, C.S., Rao, J.R., Rohatgi, P.: Towards Sound Approaches to Counteract Power-Analysis Attacks. In: Wiener, M. (ed.) CRYPTO 1999. LNCS, vol. 1666, pp. 398–412. Springer, Heidelberg (1999)
10. Clavier, C., Feix, B., Gagnerot, G., Roussellet, M., Verneuil, V.: Improved Collision-Correlation Power Analysis on First Order Protected AES. In: Preneel, B., Takagi, T. (eds.) CHES 2011. LNCS, vol. 6917, pp. 49–62. Springer, Heidelberg (2011)

11. Coron, J.-S.: Higher Order Masking of Look-up Tables. Cryptology ePrint Archive, Report 2013/700 (2013), http://eprint.iacr.org/

12. Coron, J.-S., Goubin, L.: On Boolean and Arithmetic Masking against Differential Power Analysis. In: Paar, C., Koç, Ç.K. (eds.) CHES 2000. LNCS, vol. 1965, pp. 231–237. Springer, Heidelberg (2000)

13. Coron, J.-S., Prouff, E., Rivain, M.: Side Channel Cryptanalysis of a Higher Order Masking Scheme. In: Paillier, P., Verbauwhede, I. (eds.) CHES 2007. LNCS, vol. 4727, pp. 28–44. Springer, Heidelberg (2007)

14. Courtois, N., Goubin, L.: An Algebraic Masking Method to Protect AES Against Power Attacks. In: Won, D.H., Kim, S. (eds.) ICISC 2005. LNCS, vol. 3935, pp. 199–209. Springer, Heidelberg (2006)

15. Dabosville, G., Doget, J., Prouff, E.: A New Second-Order Side Channel Attack Based on Linear Regression. IEEE Trans. Computers 62(8), 1629–1640 (2013)

16. Dhem, J.-F., Koeune, F., Leroux, P.-A., Mestré, P., Quisquater, J.-J., Willems, J.-L.: A practical implementation of the timing attack. In: Schneier, B., Quisquater, J.-J. (eds.) CARDIS 1998. LNCS, vol. 1820, pp. 167–182. Springer, Heidelberg (2000)

17. Genelle, L., Prouff, E., Quisquater, M.: Thwarting Higher-Order Side Channel Analysis with Additive and Multiplicative Maskings. In: Preneel, B., Takagi, T. (eds.) CHES 2011. LNCS, vol. 6917, pp. 240–255. Springer, Heidelberg (2011)

18. Gierlichs, B., Batina, L., Preneel, B., Verbauwhede, I.: Revisiting Higher-Order DPA Attacks: Multivariate Mutual Information Analysis. In: Pieprzyk, J. (ed.) CT-RSA 2010. LNCS, vol. 5985, pp. 221–234. Springer, Heidelberg (2010)

19. Golic, J.D., Tymen, C.: Multiplicative Masking and Power Analysis of AES. In: Kaliski Jr., B.S., Koç, Ç.K., Paar, C. (eds.) CHES 2002. LNCS, vol. 2523, pp. 198–212. Springer, Heidelberg (2003)

20. Goodwill, G., Jun, B., Jaffe, J., Rohatgi, P.: A testing methodology for side-channel resistance validation. In: NIST Non-Invasive Attack Testing Workshop (September 2011),
    http://csrc.nist.gov/news_events/non-invasive-attack-testing-workshop/papers/08_Goodwill.pdf

21. Grosso, V., Standaert, F.-X., Prouff, E.: Leakage Squeezing, Revisited. In: CARDIS 2013. LNCS. Springer (2013)

22. Kardaun, O.: Classical Methods of Statistics. Springer (2005)

23. Lerman, L., Medeiros, S.F., Bontempi, G., Markowitch, O.: A Machine Learning Approach Against a Masked AES. In: CARDIS 2013. LNCS, Springer (2013)

24. Maghrebi, H., Guilley, S., Danger, J.-L.: Leakage Squeezing Countermeasure Against High-Order Attacks. In: Ardagna, C.A., Zhou, J. (eds.) WISTP 2011. LNCS, vol. 6633, pp. 208–223. Springer, Heidelberg (2011), doi:10.1007/978-3-642-21040-2_14.

25. Mangard, S., Oswald, E., Popp, T.: Power Analysis Attacks: Revealing the Secrets of Smart Cards. Springer (2007)

26. Mangard, S., Pramstaller, N., Oswald, E.: Successfully Attacking Masked AES Hardware Implementations. In: Rao, J.R., Sunar, B. (eds.) CHES 2005. LNCS, vol. 3659, pp. 157–171. Springer, Heidelberg (2005)

27. Messerges, T.S.: Power Analysis Attacks and Countermeasures for Cryptographic Algorithms. PhD thesis, University of Illinois at Chicago, USA, 468 pages (2000)

28. Messerges, T.S.: Using Second-Order Power Analysis to Attack DPA Resistant Software. In: Paar, C., Koç, Ç.K. (eds.) CHES 2000. LNCS, vol. 1965, pp. 238–251. Springer, Heidelberg (2000)

29. Moradi, A., Mischke, O., Eisenbarth, T.: Correlation-Enhanced Power Analysis Collision Attack. In: Mangard, S., Standaert, F.-X. (eds.) CHES 2010. LNCS, vol. 6225, pp. 125–139. Springer, Heidelberg (2010)
30. Nassar, M., Guilley, S., Danger, J.-L.: Formal Analysis of the Entropy / Security Trade-off in First-Order Masking Countermeasures against Side-Channel Attacks. In: Bernstein, D.J., Chatterjee, S. (eds.) INDOCRYPT 2011. LNCS, vol. 7107, pp. 22–39. Springer, Heidelberg (2011)
31. Nassar, M., Souissi, Y., Guilley, S., Danger, J.-L.: RSM: A small and fast countermeasure for AES, secure against 1st and 2nd-order zero-offset SCAs. In: DATE 2012, pp. 1173–1178. IEEE (2012)
32. Nikova, S., Rijmen, V., Schläffer, M.: Secure Hardware Implementation of Nonlinear Functions in the Presence of Glitches. J. Cryptology 24(2), 292–321 (2011)
33. NIST/ITL/CSD. Advanced Encryption Standard (AES). FIPS PUB 197 (November 2001), http://csrc.nist.gov/publications/fips/fips197/fips-197.pdf
34. Pan, J., den Hartog, J.I., Lu, J.: You Cannot Hide behind the Mask: Power Analysis on a Provably Secure S-Box Implementation. In: Youm, H.Y., Yung, M. (eds.) WISA 2009. LNCS, vol. 5932, pp. 178–192. Springer, Heidelberg (2009)
35. Prouff, E., Giraud, C., Aumônier, S.: Provably Secure S-Box Implementation Based on Fourier Transform. In: Goubin, L., Matsui, M. (eds.) CHES 2006. LNCS, vol. 4249, pp. 216–230. Springer, Heidelberg (2006)
36. Prouff, E., Rivain, M.: A Generic Method for Secure SBox Implementation. In: Kim, S., Yung, M., Lee, H.-W. (eds.) WISA 2007. LNCS, vol. 4867, pp. 227–244. Springer, Heidelberg (2008)
37. Prouff, E., Rivain, M., Bevan, R.: Statistical Analysis of Second Order Differential Power Analysis. IEEE Trans. Computers 58(6), 799–811 (2009)
38. Prouff, E., Roche, T.: Higher-Order Glitches Free Implementation of the AES Using Secure Multi-party Computation Protocols. In: Preneel, B., Takagi, T. (eds.) CHES 2011. LNCS, vol. 6917, pp. 63–78. Springer, Heidelberg (2011)
39. Rivain, M., Prouff, E.: Provably Secure Higher-Order Masking of AES. In: Mangard, S., Standaert, F.-X. (eds.) CHES 2010. LNCS, vol. 6225, pp. 413–427. Springer, Heidelberg (2010)
40. Schindler, W., Lemke, K., Paar, C.: A Stochastic Model for Differential Side Channel Cryptanalysis. In: Rao, J.R., Sunar, B. (eds.) CHES 2005. LNCS, vol. 3659, pp. 30–46. Springer, Heidelberg (2005)
41. Schramm, K., Paar, C.: Higher Order Masking of the AES. In: Pointcheval, D. (ed.) CT-RSA 2006. LNCS, vol. 3860, pp. 208–225. Springer, Heidelberg (2006)
42. Standaert, F.-X., Gierlichs, B., Verbauwhede, I.: Partition vs. Comparison Side-Channel Distinguishers: An Empirical Evaluation of Statistical Tests for Univariate Side-Channel Attacks against Two Unprotected CMOS Devices. In: Lee, P.J., Cheon, J.H. (eds.) ICISC 2008. LNCS, vol. 5461, pp. 253–267. Springer, Heidelberg (2009)
43. TELECOM ParisTech SEN research group, 4th edn. DPA Contest (2013-2014), http://www.DPAcontest.org/v4/
44. Tunstall, M., Whitnall, C., Oswald, E.: Masking Tables - An Underestimated Security Risk. In: FSE 2013. LNCS, vol. 8424, Springer (2014), http://eprint.iacr.org/2013/735
45. Waddle, J., Wagner, D.: Towards Efficient Second-Order Power Analysis. In: Joye, M., Quisquater, J.-J. (eds.) CHES 2004. LNCS, vol. 3156, pp. 1–15. Springer, Heidelberg (2004)
46. Ye, X., Eisenbarth, T.: On the Vulnerability of Low Entropy Masking Schemes. In: CARDIS 2013. LNCS. Springer (2013)

Improving Intrusion Detection Systems
for Wireless Sensor Networks

Andriy Stetsko, Tobiáš Smolka, Vashek Matyáš, and Martin Stehlík

Masaryk University, Brno, Czech Republic
{stetsko,xsmolka,matyas,xstehl2}@fi.muni.cz

Abstract. A considerable amount of research has been undertaken in the field of intrusion detection in wireless sensor networks. Researchers proposed a number of relevant mechanisms, and it is not an easy task to select the right ones for a given application scenario. Even when a network operator knows what mechanism to use, it remains an open issue how to configure this particular mechanism in such a way that it is efficient for the particular needs. We propose a framework that optimizes the configuration of an intrusion detection system in terms of detection accuracy and memory usage. There is a variety of scenarios, and a single set of configuration values is not optimal for all of them. Therefore, we believe, such a framework is of a great value for a network operator who needs to optimize an intrusion detection system for his particular needs, e.g., attacker model, environment, node parameters.

Keywords: Intrusion detection, optimization, wireless sensor networks.

1 Introduction

A wireless sensor network (WSN) consists of sensor nodes – small devices equipped with sensors, microcontroller, wireless transceiver and battery. Each node monitors a physical phenomenon and sends the measurements to a base station. Since a node communication range is limited to tens of meters and it is not always feasible for the node to directly communicate with the base station, data are usually sent hop-by-hop from one node to another until they reach the base station. WSNs can support various applications for ecology and wildlife monitoring, military, building and industrial automation, energy management, agriculture, etc.

Sensor nodes are constrained in *processing power*, *memory* and mainly in *energy*. A MICAz sensor node is a typical sensor node. It is equipped with the 8 MHz Atmel Atmega128L microcontroller, 512 KB flash memory, 802.15.4 compliant Texas Instruments CC2420 transceiver and two AA batteries. The transceiver consumes 18.8 mA (with 3.3 V power supply) in the receiving mode [1], which is the most energy consuming mode. If we use two NiZn AA batteries with a nominal voltage of 1.65 V and a capacity of 1800 mAh, the estimated lifetime of a constantly receiving node is approximately 96 hours, i.e., 4 days. However, in general for WSNs one expects a functional network for the duration of time that ranges from several days to several years.

I. Boureanu, P. Owesarski, and S. Vaudenay (Eds.): ACNS 2014, LNCS 8479, pp. 343–360, 2014.

In this paper, we propose a *framework that semi-automatically optimizes the configuration of an intrusion detection system* (IDS) in terms of detection accuracy and memory usage for any given scenario, e.g., a network topology, the network stack of benign sensor nodes, and anticipated attacks. We do not aim to propose particular novel techniques for intrusion detection (as such) in sensor networks and our ultimate long-term aim is to provide a framework that does not depend on a particular attacker model (or a group of models). We focus on intrusion detection since it is an essential mechanism to protect a network against internal attacks that are relatively easy and not expensive to mount in WSNs. In comparison to conventional wired and wireless networks, an attacker can often easily access the deployment area of a WSN, capture some nodes, and launch a wide range of attacks (for the list of possible attacks, see [18]).

The paper roadmap is as follows. The conceptual architecture of our framework is described in Section 2. Section 3 contains high-level technical details of our proof-of-concept implementation. In Section 4, we describe our test case. We tested the framework using a static topology in three different scenarios – these scenarios were selected to illustrate the framework merits, Section 5 describes these scenarios and test results. We compare our approach to related work in Section 6. Finally, Section 7 concludes the paper and presents plans for our future work. Particular details of evolutionary algorithms that we used for optimization are then provided in our technical report [7].

2   Conceptual Architecture of the Framework

In this section, we present the conceptual architecture of our framework that semi-automatically optimizes the configuration of an IDS for a given application scenario. The framework includes an *optimization engine* and a general-purpose *network simulator* (see Figure 1). The whole process consists of five main steps. In the first step, a network operator defines a fitness function for the evaluation of an IDS configuration. We define a reasonable fitness function in Subsection 3.3. It integrates evaluation metrics from [2] such as true positives, true negatives and memory usage. In the second step, the network operator configures the network simulator in such way that it simulates a scenario in which an IDS should be deployed. This step is described in Subsection 2.1 in more detail. The remaining three steps are completely automatic. The third and fourth steps take place in an iterative manner. The optimization engine provides a candidate configuration of an IDS to the simulator. The simulator evaluates it according to predefined metrics, e.g., detection accuracy, memory usage, and returns information required to compute the fitness function back to the optimization engine. Based on the evaluation, the optimization engine changes the values of parameters and repeats the procedure until a predefined condition holds, e.g., parameters become optimal for a given scenario, or the maximum number of iterations is exceeded. Finally, in the fifth step, the optimization engine outputs the best found (hopefully, the optimal) IDS configuration.

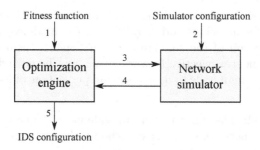

Fig. 1. Conceptual architecture. The arrows depict input (output) to (from) the components of our framework.

2.1   Simulator Configuration

The network operator provides a complete network model, which among others, includes a *network topology, models of benign and malicious nodes, wireless channel and energy consumption models* (see Figure 1).

Network Topology: The simulator provides a possibility to set a topology manually or to generate it automatically. In case the network operator knows the precise topology of the network, he can use the first option, and optimize the IDS for this particular topology. In case the topology is not known in advance, the network operator can use the second option, generate several random topologies, and optimize the IDS for all of them simultaneously. For more details, see the discussion on robustness of a found solution in Subsection 2.2.

Benign Sensor Node: Models of the node hardware and software should be provided, i.e., radio, IDS, medium access control (MAC) layer, network layer, and application layer models. There could be several types of a benign node in the network (e.g., a cluster head, a base station, a general-purpose sensor node), and they might have a different network stack. The network operator composes a benign node model from the available protocols (distributed within the simulator, or implemented by a third party). If the required protocol at a certain network layer is not available, the network operator should implement it. Further, the network operator configures the parameters of the models.

Malicious Sensor Node: Similarly, models of the node hardware and software should be provided. There could be several types of a malicious node in the network (e.g., internal/external [18], passive/active [21]). Usually, it is known to a network operator where the network will be deployed, and what the purpose of the network is. Based on this information, the network operator can estimate the risks of different attacks (e.g., selective forwarding, jamming, hello flood), and include into a simulation only those that pose a serious threat. The network operator composes a malicious node model from the modified models available within the distribution of the simulator, or implements them by himself. For example, to implement a selective forwarder, it might be enough to modify the network layer of a benign node to drop a certain percentage of incoming packets.

Wireless Channel: The simulator can provide more than one model for radio propagation, and a network operator can choose the one that is more suitable for the environment where a network will be deployed.

Energy Consumption: The simulator can provide more than one energy consumption model.

2.2   Discussion

In this subsection, we discuss several issues related to the framework design choices and framework usage.

Simulator Versus Testbed: We decided to use a simulator since a testbed is slow for comparison of considered alternative configurations, labour-intensive and it does not produce comparable results due to the uncontrollable factors (e.g., wireless channel effects). Candidate configurations should be tested under the same network conditions, otherwise they cannot be compared. In a testbed, we are not able to *reproduce* the same environment each time a candidate configuration is tested because of the wireless channel effects. The simulator provides us with such a possibility. The usage of a simulator, however, does not mean that different wireless channel effects (similar to those in a real network) cannot be modelled in the simulator (see wireless channel models in [9]).

Simulator Calibration: In order to get realistic results, the operator needs to calibrate an energy consumption model and a wireless channel model in accordance to the environment where a network will be deployed (we calibrated the wireless channel for two specific environments in [4]). Their calibration can be done manually or automatically by the integration of a simulator and a testbed [5]. The calibration should take place before the optimization. The carefully calibrated wireless channel model (energy consumption model) can statistically reflect the wireless channel behaviour (energy consumption) in a real network.

Solution Robustness: A wireless environment is dynamic. It can change in an unexpected way which may result into conditions that were not observed during the calibration. The framework, however, should cope with that, i.e., a found solution should keep working (preferably decreasing its effectiveness only gradually) even if some network characteristics change in the network. In order to achieve this, a candidate solution should be evaluated on networks with different topologies and a wireless channel model should be calibrated for different environments (e.g., network congestion, network maximum throughput). Moreover, the network operator can calibrate a wireless channel model for some pessimistic scenario (even though it has not been observed yet in a given environment). For example, he can deliberately increase the noise level in the noise model, increase the path loss or variation in the log-normal shadowing model. For more information on the log-normal shadowing model, see [9]. The evaluations obtained from different networks can be combined into a single evaluation score.

Framework Generality: The framework is generic, and it could be used to optimize different types of an IDS (misuse-based or anomaly-based, centralized or distributed). Further, we list several examples.

In [15], the authors proposed a scheme that activates IDS agents preloaded in sensor nodes with a certain probability. Our framework can be used to find an optimal value of the probability for a given application scenario, i.e., to solve the trade-off between the number of packets (links) left unmonitored (influences a detection accuracy) and the number of IDS agents being activated (influences energy consumption).

In [17], the authors proposed a distributed IDS that involves a set of rules to detect different types of an attack. Our framework can be used to automatically select the appropriate rules and optimize (among others) their detection thresholds.

In [16], the authors proposed an IDS to detect packet reception rate and receive power anomalies. The authors demonstrated that there is a trade-off between detection probability, detection delays and false positives for their technique. Our framework can help a network operator to find the optimal values of the IDS parameters for his/her application scenario.

3   Implementation of the Framework

Relevant high-level implementation details are provided in this section.

3.1   Optimization Engine

There are two classes of optimization algorithms – exact and approximate (heuristic) algorithms. Since the evaluation of candidate solutions cannot be done analytically in our case, the exact algorithms can hardly be applied. The heuristics are divided into population-based and single-solution based algorithms. We use a population-based algorithm because in comparison to a single-solution based algorithm it provides us with the ability to evaluate multiple candidate solutions in parallel and hence to speed up the convergence of an optimization.

There is a variety of population-based algorithms, e.g., evolutionary algorithms (EAs), particle swarm optimization, immune networks. We use EAs as we already have successfully applied these algorithms for the automatic generation of secrecy amplification protocols in WSNs [3].

EAs work with a population of candidate solutions (*individuals* in terms of EAs) and *evaluate* them using a *fitness function*. EAs generate new candidate solutions applying genetic operators of crossover and mutation to the solutions in the population. In each *generation*, EAs update the population with new candidate solutions. The process repeats until an optimal solution is found or the maximum number of iterations is exceeded. For more information on EAs, see [8].

The optimization engine is based on Evolving Objects [10], an advanced component-based framework with a high number of already implemented optimization algorithms. For the purpose of this work, we used a basic evolutionary algorithm *eoEasyEA* that is highly configurable and suits our needs. We reused existing operators for selection, replacement, termination and statistics collection, and implemented only problem specific parts of initialization, mutation, crossover, and evaluation. More details on the settings of EAs can be found in our technical report [7].

3.2   Network Simulator

We use the MiXiM network simulator [11], which is based on the OMNeT++ simulation framework [12]. MiXiM has a modular architecture with a high number of already implemented models for a WSN simulation. It inherits many advanced features from OMNeT++ and thus is very adaptable and configurable. The whole simulation is configured via a dedicated OMNeT++ configuration file. A candidate solution (an individual) is represented as a list of configuration values stored in a separate configuration file. Before the evaluation (simulation) starts, the file is included in the main configuration file.

The choice of a general-purpose WSN simulator allowed us to move one step forward towards more realistic simulations, since MiXiM provides more accurate simulation models, e.g., for wireless channel, radio, and MAC layers, in comparison to a very fast purpose-built simulator we used in our previous work [3]. However, the accuracy comes at the price of speed. We simulated a network operating for one hour, and it took about 5 minutes to simulate such network on a single CPU core. In order to get a solution in acceptable time, we decided to utilize distributed computing.

We chose the BOINC distributed computing platform [13] for our experiments. In cooperation with the Institute of Computer Science at Masaryk University, we attached about 200 CPU cores from the campus to our BOINC infrastructure and used them when they were idle. Other 700 cores were available from the National Grid Infrastructure project MetaCentrum.

3.3 Configuration Evaluation

A candidate configuration of an IDS is evaluated based on its *accuracy* and *memory usage*. In this paper, two terms IDS and monitoring node are used interchangeably.

Notation 1. *The set $A = \{a_1, ..., a_{n_m}\}$ is a set of malicious nodes in a network.*

Notation 2. *The set $C = \{c_1, ..., c_{n_b}\}$ is a set of all benign nodes in a network.*

Notation 3. *The function $x : \mathbb{N} \to \mathbb{N}$ takes a sensor node index as an argument, and returns a number of the neighbours that consider this node benign.*

Notation 4. *The function $y : \mathbb{N} \to \mathbb{N}$ takes a sensor node index as an argument, and returns a number of the neighbours that consider this node malicious.*

Notation 5. *The function $n : \mathbb{N} \to \mathbb{N}$ takes a sensor node index as an argument, and returns a number of the neighbours of this node.*

Notation 6. *The function $m : \mathbb{N} \to \mathbb{N}$ takes a sensor node index as an argument, and returns the amount of memory (in bytes) used by an IDS on this node.*

Accuracy: We measured accuracy based on the number of true positives and true negatives:

- A true positive occurs when a monitoring node $c \in C$ correctly considers its neighbour $a \in A$ malicious.
- A true negative occurs when a monitoring node $c_i \in C$ correctly considers its neighbour $c_j \in C$ $(i \neq j)$ benign.

A node $k \in C \cup A$ considers the node $l \in C \cup A$ as a neighbour if it received at least one packet from l during the simulation. We assume that sensor nodes are distributed in such a way, that every node in the network has at least one neighbour.

For a benign node c_i, we calculated the percentage of the neighbours that considered the node benign. Further, we found the average of such values over all benign nodes in the network and denoted the result as tn. Similarly, for a malicious node a_i, we calculated the percentage of the neighbours that considered the node malicious. Further, we found the average of such values over all malicious nodes in the network and denoted the result as tp.

The accuracy function is the weighted mean of tn and tp:

$$\frac{w_1 * tn + w_2 * tp}{(w_1 + w_2)}, \text{ where } tn = \frac{1}{|C|} * \sum_{c_i \in C} \frac{x(c_i)}{n(c_i)}, tp = \frac{1}{|A|} * \sum_{a_i \in A} \frac{y(a_i)}{n(a_i)}.$$

We assume that $|C| > 0$ and $|A| > 0$.

The function values range from 0 to 1. If every malicious node in the network is detected by all of its neighbours, and every benign node in the network is not considered malicious by any of its neighbours, the accuracy function is equal to 1, i.e., the maximum possible value. On the other hand, if none of malicious nodes is detected by at least one of its neighbours, and every benign node is considered malicious by all of its neighbours, the accuracy function is equal to 0, i.e., the minimum possible value.

The proposed function does not take the distribution of $\frac{x(c_i)}{n(c_i)}$ and $\frac{y(b_i)}{n(b_i)}$ into account. In certain cases, e.g., when a base station uses a majority voting scheme to make a final decision whether a node is benign or not, it might be preferable to have more values of $\frac{x(c_i)}{n(c_i)}$ and $\frac{y(b_i)}{n(b_i)}$ that are slightly above 0.5 instead of a few values that are extremely high.

Memory Usage: The effectiveness of memory usage by the IDS on a node $c_i \in C$ was evaluated using the formula: $\frac{1}{1+m(c_i)}$.

If the IDS is switched off at the node c_i, then $m(c_i) = 0$ and $\frac{1}{1+m(c_i)} = 1$. Furthermore, if $m(c_i)$ increases, then the effectiveness of memory usage decreases towards zero.

Further, we calculated the average value of $\frac{1}{1+m(c_i)}$ over all benign nodes in the network. More formally, it can be written as: $\frac{1}{|C|} * \sum_{c_i \in C} \frac{1}{1+m(c_i)}$. We assume that $|C| > 0$.

The designed function provides values that are not correlated to accuracy values. In certain cases, however, it might be useful to take into account that even a small amount of memory is a waste if the accuracy of an IDS is low. Yet a higher amount of used memory can be justified if the IDS is highly accurate.

Fitness Function: For the purpose of this work, we added both accuracy and memory usage metrics together, making the accuracy metric to contribute more to the value of the sum than the memory metric by introducing weights. The weight was set to 1 for the accuracy metric, and it was set to 0.1 for the memory usage metric. The weight for the memory usage should be carefully selected – if it is too high (i.e., it is more important to save memory than to detect attacks), the optimal solution is to switch all IDSs off, or set a maximum number of monitored nodes and buffer size to zero. We set $w_1 = w_2 = 1$ in the accuracy metric. The resulting fitness function is:

$$\frac{1}{2|C|} * \sum_{c_i \in C} \frac{x(c_i)}{n(c_i)} + \frac{1}{2|A|} * \sum_{a_i \in A} \frac{y(a_i)}{n(a_i)} + 0.1 \frac{1}{|C|} * \sum_{c_i \in C} \frac{1}{1+m(c_i)}.$$

4   Our Test Case

In this section, we describe the scenario for which we would like to test the framework on. The framework is used to find optimal parameters of an IDS (we implemented it in the MiXiM simulator for purposes of our previous work [6]) for a given scenario. A network operator (a person who uses our framework) knows behavior of benign nodes and assumes behavior of malicious nodes.

If another than assumed type of an attack appears in the deployed network, the parameters found by the framework might not be optimal for such network.

4.1 Topology

We generated a topology of 250 static sensor nodes uniformly randomly distributed over an 200 m × 200 m area. A single base station is placed in the center of the area. The topology together with a routing tree is depicted in Figure 2. There are 246 benign sensor nodes (white) including the base station, and 5 malicious nodes (black filled). According to [14], the terrestrial WSNs typically consist of hundreds to thousands of inexpensive sensor nodes. However, the purchase of a large network is not always feasible due to the current price of sensor nodes. A MICAz sensor node costs about €80. Therefore, we believe that medium-sized networks that consist of hundreds of nodes are more reasonable to consider.

In order to make the analysis of results (w.r.t. their optimality) from the framework simpler and more intuitive, we focus on static sensor nodes. However, more dynamic network scenarios can be modeled as well. MiXiM provides a variety of node mobility models [11].

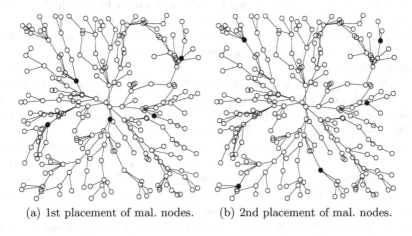

(a) 1st placement of mal. nodes.   (b) 2nd placement of mal. nodes.

Fig. 2. Topology, routing tree, and placement of malicious nodes

4.2 Benign Node

We assume a benign node uses a network stack that consists of application, routing protocol, MAC protocol, and intrusion detection system.

Application Layer: We consider a standard application for a WSN, where every node sends one packet to a base station every 30 seconds. The application runs for one hour. In order to avoid collisions (due to node synchronization), the whole time-frame is divided into intervals of length 30 seconds. For every interval i, a node generates a random number r ($0 \leq r \leq 30$) and starts transmitting at $i + r$. The size of a packet is 152 B.

Network Layer: We assume that the network layer uses static routing. The routing tree was generated as follows. A base station broadcasts a packet containing its identification together with the value h set to 0. A node waits until it receives a packet from a neighbour that is the closest one (has the highest signal strength). Then the node sets the neighbour as its parent, increases value h by 1 and broadcasts the value together with its identification. Value h represents number of hops to the base station.

Medium Access Layer: We use CSMA-CA at this layer.

Physical Layer: We use a model for CC2420 radio that is commonly used in sensor nodes, e.g., TELOSB, MICAz sensor nodes.

Intrusion detection system: We use a simple IDS that we implemented in the MiXiM simulator for the purpose of our previous work [6]. The IDS uses a detection rule (more specifically, a retransmission rule) from [17]. It is not the goal of this paper to propose a complex IDS, but rather to test the framework as such. In the conventional networks, one can use a commercial IDS, to run the framework on, and compare the IDS before and after the optimization to see the improvement. For WSNs, however, to our best knowledge, there are no commercial IDSs available.

An IDS is running on a sensor node and it continuously analyzes sent and overheard packets. The IDS does not include responsive and collaborative components (see [20] for the conceptual architecture of an IDS in WSNs). Therefore, the IDS does not generate any additional traffic.

A monitoring node overhears to some extent both incoming and outgoing packets of a close enough monitored neighbour. An IDS stores a table, where each row corresponds to a certain monitored node. The table contains the number of packets received (PR) and forwarded (PF) by a monitored node. The number of rows is limited to a *number of monitored nodes*.

The detection exploits the fact that a monitoring node overhears (to some extent) both incoming and outgoing packets of a close enough monitored neighbour. If the IDS on a node $c_i \in C$ overhears a packet P sent to a node $b_j \in C \cup A$, b_j is close enough and b_j should forward the packet (e.g., b_j is not a base station), then the IDS stores P in the buffer and increments the PR counter of the monitored node b_j. The number of packets is limited by a *buffer size*. If a new packet arrives but the buffer is full, the oldest packet is removed from the buffer. When the IDS overhears the packet P being forwarded by the node b_j, it removes P from the buffer (if it is still there) and increments the PF counter of the node b_j. Since both the table and the buffer are limited, the IDS monitors only the closest nodes and the newest packets.

The detection is done at the end of the simulation based on the collected statistics. The node c_i considers the node b_j as a selective forwarder if the dropping ratio of b_j, i.e., ratio of a number of packets dropped to a number of packets received, is higher than a predefined *detection threshold*. If the node c_i overheard less than the predefined *number of packets received* by b_j as overheard by c_i, c_i does not consider b_j malicious as the number of overheard packets is small and there is a high level of uncertainty. We cannot influence the number of overheard packet, but we can change our decision making process based on this value and potentially decrease a number of false positives.

The IDS running on a node c_i consumes $m(c_i) = p_1 * 8 + p_2 * 16$ B of memory. Each record in the table occupies 8 B (4 B for node ID, 2 B for PR, 2 B for PF), and there are p_1 such records. Each record in the buffer occupies 16 B (4 B for MAC source ID, 4 B for MAC destination ID, 4 B for MAC intermediate node ID, and 4 B for packet counter), and there are p_2 such records.

We would like to optimize the following four parameters: p_1 (number of nodes to be monitored), p_2 (a number of packets stored in a buffer), p_3 (number of packets received) and p_4 (detection threshold). The value of p_1 ranges from 0 to 54 (the maximum number of neighbours in our simulation scenario), p_2 – from 0 to 100, p_3 – from 0 to 2000, and p_4 from 0 to 100.

4.3   Malicious Node

Currently, for our proof-of-concept implementation of the framework, we assume a single type of malicious node – a selective forwarder, i.e., a node that drops a certain percentage of received packets. We assume the model is the same as the model of a benign node, except for the network layer that is modified to drop a certain percentage of received packets (in our case 50%), and an IDS that is omitted.

5   Testing Results

We tested our prototype on three optimization scenarios, each with the different size of the search space. Their description together with the obtained results are presented in the following subsections. The settings of EAs for each optimization scenario are described in the corresponding subsections of our technical report [7]. For the evaluation of a candidate configuration, we used the fitness function defined in Subsection 3.3. Time needed to complete the optimization is indicated in terms of a number of EA generations and evaluations.

5.1   Optimization Scenario No. 1

In this scenario, we assume that every benign node in the network runs an IDS, and the IDS is configured in the same way for these nodes. The goal is to optimize the configuration (p_1, p_2, p_3 and p_4), common for all sensor nodes, using our framework.

We performed both an exhaustive search and an EA-based search, and compared the results. In order to make the exhaustive search timely acceptable, we fixed $p_2 = 100$ and $p_3 = 0$. The reduced search space contained 5555 possible configurations (see the description of an IDS in Subsection 4.2).

Exhaustive Search: Fitness values for each possible combination of p_1 and p_4 are depicted in Figure 3. The maximum fitness value (0.8249276442) was achieved for the configuration with $p_1 = 27$ and $p_4 = 0.45$. The threshold is below 0.5 (the dropping rate of a malicious node, see Subsection 4.3), because a monitoring node cannot reliably overhear all packets sent to a malicious node, and hence the dropping rate of the malicious node as observed by the monitoring node may be lower than 0.5.

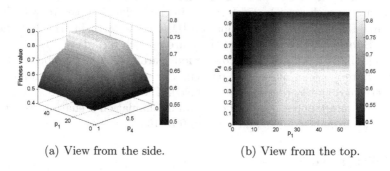

(a) View from the side.   (b) View from the top.

Fig. 3. Fitness values for all possible combinations of p_1 and p_4

Evolutionary Algorithm: We ran the optimization process 30 times. The EA was able to find the best configuration (found by the exhaustive search) using 19 generations on average. The standard deviation was 9.64. On average, the EA required 144.87 evaluations. The standard deviation was 67.37. In the worst case, the EA required 271 evaluations, while the exhaustive search required 5400 evaluations.

5.2 Optimization Scenario No. 2

In this scenario, we assume that only a subset of benign nodes runs IDSs, which are configured in the same way on all selected nodes. As opposed to the node (IDS) placement problem, the framework should find the optimal placement as well as the optimal configuration of the IDSs.

There are 250 parameters to optimize: p_1, p_2, p_3, p_4, and 246 Boolean parameters, each indicating whether the IDS should be enabled or disabled on a given node. We fixed two parameters ($p_2 = 100$ and $p_3 = 0$). The search space contained $55 * 101 * 2^{246}$ possible configurations.

We ran the optimization process on two networks with the same topology but with the different placement of malicious nodes (see Figure 4(a) and Figure 4(b)). The malicious nodes are depicted with black filling. We repeated the optimization process 30 times for both placements of malicious nodes.

First Placement of Malicious Nodes: The best configuration found by the EA had the fitness value equal to 0.8940953359, $p_1 = 27$, and $p_4 = 0.45$ (the same values were found for the first optimization scenario). The switched on/off IDSs are depicted in Figure 4(a). Nodes that ran an IDS are depicted with grey filling. The configuration generated 1723 false positives and 33 false negatives, i.e., 7.03 false positives per benign node, and 6.6 false negatives per malicious node. The configuration was found using 581.77 generations on average. The standard deviation was 88.59. On average, the EA required 10600.17 evaluations. The standard deviation was 1603.29. In the worst case, the EA required 13349 evaluations.

Although we did not perform an exhaustive search, we believe that the found configuration was optimal. The intuition behind this is as follows. If an IDS running on a node $c_i \in C$ detects a malicious neighbour $a_j \in A$, then switching it off reduces a number of false positives, increases memory usage effectiveness, but causes a false negative. As we discovered, it is natural for the EA to switch such an IDS on since the benefit (according to the designed evaluation function, see Subsection 3.3) is higher than from switching the IDS off. We verified (by setting $p_4 = 0$ and $p_1 = 54$) that the EA achieved the minimum possible number of false negatives, and the minimum number of false positives for the given number of false negatives.

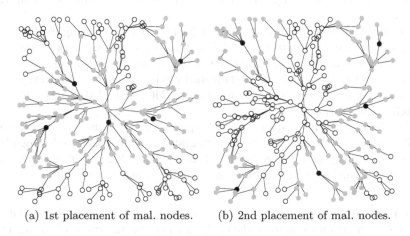

(a) 1st placement of mal. nodes.   (b) 2nd placement of mal. nodes.

Fig. 4. The best found placements of IDSs in the network

Second Placement of Malicious Nodes: The best configuration found by the EA had the fitness value equal to 0.8780288967, $p_1 = 24$, and $p_4 = 0.5$. The switched on/off IDSs are depicted in Figure 4(b). The configuration generated 1173 false positives and 42 false negatives. We believe that the found configuration was optimal. The intuition behind this is the same as for the first placement of malicious nodes. We verified (by setting $p_4 = 0$ and $p_1 = 54$) that the achieved number of false negatives was the lowest possible, and the achieved number of false positives was the lowest possible for the given number of false negatives.

The best configuration was found by 14 optimization runs. The average number of generations was 499.57. The standard deviation was 82.185. On average, the EA required 9096.1 evaluations. The standard deviation was 1501.5. Other 8 runs ended up with the configuration where the fitness value was equal to 0.8764108606. The rest of the runs found configurations with fitness values equal to or higher than 0.8656972029.

When comparing the best configurations found for both placements, an average number of false events per node (an average number of false positives per node added together with an average number of false negatives per node) was higher for the first placement (13.6 versus 13.17), but the fitness value was higher for the second one (0.8940953359 versus 0.8780288967). That might be caused by the fact that nodes falsely accused or falsely not detected in the first placement had a higher number of neighbours, which is also reflected in the selected value of p_1 (27 versus 24).

5.3   Optimization Scenario No. 3

In this scenario, we again assume that only a subset of benign nodes runs IDSs. In comparison to the previous optimization scenario, here each IDS may be configured in a different way. As opposed to the node (IDS) placement problem, the framework should find the optimal placement as well as the optimal configuration of each IDS.

The search space contained $(55 * 101 * 2001 * 101 * 2)^{246}$ configurations. The IDS implemented in our test case did not influence the network traffic, and hence did not influence other IDSs. Therefore, configurations of any two IDSs were independent of each other. We launched 246 independent optimizations and significantly reduced the search space, i.e., to $246 * (55 * 101 * 2001 * 101 * 2)$ possible configurations.

We did two experiments. In the first experiment, we launched a single optimization that searched for the best configuration for all sensor nodes together. In the second experiment, we launched 246 independent optimizations, each searching for the best configuration for a particular sensor node only.

First Experiment: We started with a randomly generated initial population. The evolution began to improve the configuration, but the speed of convergence was too slow. Therefore, we decided to start the optimization process again, using the population of the best configurations from the second optimization scenario (see Subsection 5.2). This optimization was gradually improving the configuration and reached the fitness value of 0.955133 after 136'765 evaluations in the $21'439^{th}$ generation. The evolution was stopped when no improvement was found during next 500 generations.

Second Experiment: All 246 optimizations started with the initial population that contained the best configurations for the second optimization scenario. By combining optimized parameters from these optimizations, a configuration that reached the fitness value of 0.9604364302 was found. When compared to the second optimization scenario, this approach was able to significantly improve the resulting IDS configuration by tweaking the parameters independently for each node. A configuration found in each independent optimization required 422.63 generations on average. The standard deviation was 63.84. On average, the EA required 2811.68 evaluations to find a configuration in each independent optimization. The standard deviation was 427.05. In the worst case, the EA required 5365 evaluations.

We ran another experiment to verify whether the configuration found by the EA was optimal. The experiment was based on the intuition we mentioned in Subsection 5.2. For an IDS, we fixed the parameters in such a way that it could detect as many malicious nodes as possible ($p_1 = 54$, $p_2 = 100$, $p_3 = 0$, $p_4 = 0$). Further, we found the minimum value of p_1 such that all malicious nodes can still be detected by the IDS. The same procedure was repeated for other three parameters. We confirmed that p_1, p_2 and the placement of IDSs were optimal. However, p_3 and p_4, as we discovered, could be further improved.

6   Related Work

The placement of nodes (IDSs) can be considered as a subproblem of a more general node (IDS) configuration problem where one of the node (IDS) configuration parameters may indicate where the node is placed (whether an IDS is enabled/disabled at this node).

The placement problem received high attention from research community. For example, [22,23,24] proposed techniques for IDS placement problem in WSNs. [19] surveyed 46 techniques that help to find optimal node placement in WSNs. In contrast, our framework is more generic and additionally provides a possibility to find optimal configuration of IDS parameters (e.g., detection threshold, buffer size). For more information, see Sections 4 and 5. To the best of our knowledge, we are the first optimizing IDS parameters in WSNs.

[22] proposed an algorithm finding a minimum number of activated IDSs such that every packet forwarded from a source towards the base station was analyzed at least once on its path. In comparison to our work, the authors did not consider IDS configuration. Furthermore, the algorithm considers only packets forwarded by the monitoring nodes and not packets overheard in a promiscuous mode.

[26] aimed at multi-objective optimization using an EA for deployment of a homogeneous WSN with the coverage and lifetime of the network as objectives. [25] presented a methodology of multi-objective optimization for self-organizing WSNs using an EA. Their fitness function took application-specific, connectivity and energy-related metrics into account. The goal was to find out optimized operation mode for each node in the network. The authors did not consider any IDS. Furthermore, they did not consider node parametrization.

Methodology how a multi-objective evolutionary algorithm for design-space exploration could be configured was presented in [27]. Lifetime, latency and reliability are used as three QoS (Quality of Service) metrics with several trade-offs. In our work, we used a different set of metrics. The authors used multi-objective optimization.

[28,29,30] used EAs for several optimization issues in WSNs.

[30] incorporated *local monitoring nodes* (LMNs) into the WSN. These nodes observe suspicious behavior and monitor data message patterns, message collisions, route traffic activity trends and sensor positioning in their neighbourhood. The fitness function measures optimality of the LMN positioning and accurate identification of malicious nodes. The authors do not consider optimization of IDSs parameters in this work.

More detailed treatment of related work is provided in our tech. report [7].

7   Conclusion and Future Work

To our best knowledge, there is no work that focuses on (semi) automatic and systematic configuration of intrusion detection systems for wireless sensor networks, which we believe is an important area to explore.

In this work, we describe procedures to optimize the configuration of an intrusion detection system for a given application of a wireless sensor network. Also, we discusses how solution robustness and solution realism can be achieved.

We presented a prototype of our framework that optimizes the configuration of an intrusion detection system in wireless sensor networks. The design and implementation of the framework leveraged our previous results in the field of simulators (particularly realism of simulators for wireless sensor networks), optimization and evaluation metrics.

We tested our framework on three carefully selected scenarios with a different size of their search space. Our results demonstrated that evolutionary algorithms can be potentially used to search for a solution of the given problem more effectively. However, this conclusion is not valid in general (since the hypothesis was tested only on three selected scenarios). More general conclusion can be made if the community use evolutionary algorithms on a bigger set of different scenarios (different application, routing, medium access control and physical layer, different topologies, different attacker models).

Our framework can find reasonable (if not optimal) configuration of an intrusion detection system for a given (arbitrary but specified in advance) scenario. Values found by our framework may not be reasonable if these values are used in a different scenario, i.e., intrusion detection system, topology, attacker behavior.

The obtained results, we believe, are more than promising. Hence, we plan to use our framework to optimize different techniques for detection of different attackers. Also, we plan to use our framework to optimize an intrusion detection system for our laboratory testbed, configure the intrusion detection system according to the output provided by the framework, deploy it, and analyze the results collected from the testbed.

The future version of our framework will also use multi-objective evolutionary algorithms.

While we focused on the optimization of an intrusion detection system (other layers were fixed), we believe that such a framework can be easily extended to optimize the whole network stack. This can be explored in the future.

Acknowledgment. This work was supported by the project GAP202/11/0422 of the Czech Science Foundation. We thank the National Grid Infrastructure project MetaCentrum and Institute of Computer Science at Masaryk University for the provided computational resources. Our thanks also belong to anonymous reviewers.

References

1. Texas Instruments. CC2420 – 2.4 GHz IEEE 802.15.4 / ZigBee-ready RF transceiver, http://focus.ti.com/
2. Stetsko, A., Matyas, V.: Effectiveness metrics for intrusion detection in wireless sensor networks. In: European Conference on Computer Network Defense, pp. 21–28 (2009)
3. Svenda, P., Sekanina, L., Matyas, V.: Evolutionary design of secrecy amplification protocols for wireless sensor networks. In: ACM Conference on Wireless Network Security, pp. 225–236 (2009)
4. Stetsko, A., Stehlik, M., Matyas, V.: Calibrating and comparing simulators for wireless sensor networks. In: IEEE Conference on Mobile Adhoc and Sensor Systems, pp. 733–738 (2011)
5. Wen, Y., Zhang, W., Wolski, R., Chohan, N.: Simulation-based augmented reality for sensor network development. In: ACM Conference on Embedded Networked Sensor Systems, pp. 275–288 (2007)
6. Stetsko, A., Smolka, T., Jurnecka, F., Matyas, V.: On the credibility of wireless sensor network simulations: evaluation of intrusion detection system. In: Conference on Simulation Tools and Techniques, pp. 75–84 (2012)
7. Stetsko, A., Smolka, T., Matyas, V., Stehlik, M.: Improving intrusion detection systems for wireless sensor networks. Technical report FIMU-RS-2014-01: Masaryk University, Faculty of Informatics, Brno, Czech Republic (March 2014)
8. Talbi, E.-G.: Metaheuristics – From Design to Implementation. John Wiley & Sons, Inc. (2009)
9. Rappaport, T.: Wireless communications: Principles and practice, 2nd edn. Prentice Hall PTR (2001)
10. Keijzer, M., Merelo, J.J., Romero, G., Schoenauer, M.: Evolving objects: A general purpose evolutionary computation library. In: Conference on Evolution Artificielle, pp. 231–242 (2002)
11. Kopke, A., Swigulski, M., Wessel, K., Willkomm, D., Haneveld, P.T.K., Parker, T.E.V., Visser, O.W., Lichte, H.S., Valentin, S.: Simulating wireless and mobile networks in OMNeT++ the MiXiM vision. In: Conference on Simulation Tools and Techniques for Communications, Networks and Systems & Workshops (2008)
12. OMNeT++ Community, http://www.omnetpp.org/
13. Anderson, D.P.: BOINC: a system for public-resource computing and storage. In: IEEE/ACM Workshop on Grid computing, pp. 4–10 (2004)
14. Yick, J., Mukherjee, B., Ghosal, D.: Wireless sensor network survey. Computer Networks 52(12), 2292–2330 (2008)
15. Roman, R., Zhou, J., Lopez, J.: Applying intrusion detection systems to wireless sensor networks. In: IEEE Consumer Communications and Networking Conference, pp. 640–644 (2006)
16. Onat, I., Miri, A.: An intrusion detection system for wireless sensor networks. In: IEEE Conference on Wireless and Mobile Computing, Networking and Communications, pp. 253–259 (2005)

17. da Silva, A.P.R., Martins, M.H.T., Rocha, B.P.S., Loureiro, A.A.F., Ruiz, L.B., Wong, H.C.: Decentralized intrusion detection in wireless sensor networks. In: ACM International Workshop on Quality of Service & Security in Wireless and Mobile Networks, pp. 16–23 (2005)
18. Karlof, C., Wagner, D.: Secure routing in wireless sensor networks: attacks and countermeasures. Ad Hoc Networks 1(23), 293–315 (2003)
19. Younis, M., Akkaya, K.: Strategies and techniques for node placement in wireless sensor networks: A survey. Ad Hoc Networks 6(4), 621–655 (2008)
20. Zhang, Y., Lee, W.: Intrusion detection in wireless ad-hoc networks. In: Conference on Mobile Computing and Networking, pp. 275–283 (2000)
21. Roosta, T., Pai, S., Chen, P., Sastry, S., Wicker, S.: Inherent security of routing protocols in ad-hoc and sensor networks. In: Global Telecommunications Conference, pp. 1273–1278 (2007)
22. Anjum, F., Subhadrabandhu, D., Sarkar, S., Shetty, R.: On optimal placement of intrusion detection modules in sensor networks. In: Conference on Broadband Networks, pp. 690–699 (2004)
23. Liu, C., Cao, G.: Distributed monitoring and aggregation in wireless sensor networks. In: Conference on Computer Communications, pp. 1–9 (2010)
24. Hassanzadeh, A., Stoleru, R.: Towards optimal monitoring in cooperative IDS for resource constrained wireless networks. In: Conference on Computer Communications and Networks, pp. 1–8 (2011)
25. Ferentinos, K.P., Tsiligiridis, T.A.: Adaptive design optimization of wireless sensor networks using genetic algorithms. Computer Networks 51(4), 1031–1051 (2007)
26. Jourdan, D.B., de Weck, O.L.: Layout optimization for a wireless sensor network using a multi-objective genetic algorithm. In: IEEE Vehicular Technology Conference, pp. 2466–2470 (2004)
27. Nabi, M., Blagojevic, M., Basten, T., Geilen, M., Hendriks, T.: Configuring multi-objective evolutionary algorithms for design-space exploration of wireless sensor networks. In: ACM Workshop on Performance Monitoring and Measurement of Heterogeneous Wireless and Wired Networks, pp. 111–119 (2009)
28. Khanna, R., Liu, H., Chen, H.H.: Self-organization of sensor networks using genetic algorithms. In: IEEE Conference on Communications, pp. 3377–3382 (2006)
29. Khanna, R., Liu, H., Chen, H.H.: Dynamic optimization of secure mobile sensor networks: A genetic algorithm. In: IEEE Conference on Communications, pp. 3413–3418 (2007)
30. Khanna, R., Liu, H., Chen, H.H.: Reduced complexity intrusion detection in sensor networks using genetic algorithm. In: IEEE Conference on Communications, pp. 1–5 (2009)

MoTE-ECC: Energy-Scalable Elliptic Curve Cryptography for Wireless Sensor Networks

Zhe Liu[1], Erich Wenger[2], and Johann Großschädl[1]

[1] University of Luxembourg,
Laboratory of Algorithmics, Cryptology and Security (LACS),
6, rue Richard Coudenhove-Kalergi, L–1359 Luxembourg
{zhe.liu,johann.groszschaedl}@uni.lu
[2] Graz University of Technology,
Institute for Applied Information Processing and Communications,
Inffeldgasse 16a, A–8010 Graz, Austria
erich.wenger@iaik.tugraz.at

Abstract. Wireless Sensor Networks (WSNs) are susceptible to a wide range of malicious attacks, which has stimulated a body of research on "light-weight" security protocols and cryptographic primitives that are suitable for resource-restricted sensor nodes. In this paper we introduce MoTE-ECC, a highly optimized yet scalable ECC library for Memsic's MICAz motes and other sensor nodes equipped with an 8-bit AVR processor. MoTE-ECC supports scalar multiplication on Montgomery and twisted Edwards curves over Optimal Prime Fields (OPFs) of variable size, e.g. 160, 192, 224, and 256 bits, which allows for various trade-offs between security and execution time (resp. energy consumption). OPFs are a special family of "low-weight" prime fields that, in contrast to the NIST-specified fields, facilitate a parameterized implementation of the modular arithmetic so that one and the same software function can be used for operands of different length. To demonstrate the performance of MoTE-ECC, we take (ephemeral) ECDH key exchange between two nodes as example, which requires each node to execute two scalar multiplications. The first scalar multiplication is performed on a fixed base point (to generate a key pair), whereas the second scalar multiplication gets an arbitrary point as input. Our implementation uses a fixed-base comb method on a twisted Edwards curve for the former and a simple ladder approach on a birationally-equivalent Montgomery curve for the latter. Both scalar multiplications require about $9 \cdot 10^6$ clock cycles in total and occupy only 380 bytes in RAM when the underlying OPF has a length of 160 bits. We also describe our efforts to harden MoTE-ECC against side-channel attacks (e.g. simple power analysis) and introduce a highly regular implementation of the comb method.

1 Introduction

Some ten years ago, an article in MIT's Technology Review magazine identified Wireless Sensor Networks (WSNs) as one of the technologies that will change

I. Boureanu, P. Owesarski, and S. Vaudenay (Eds.): ACNS 2014, LNCS 8479, pp. 361–379, 2014.
© Springer International Publishing Switzerland 2014

the world in the 21st century [6]. This prediction could not have been more true given today's omnipresence of wireless sensors in various kinds of applications ranging from medical monitoring over home automation to environmental surveillance [1]. All these applications rely on distributed sensor nodes being able to collect, process and transmit data correctly and reliably, which has initiated a large body of research on the security of WSNs. Unfortunately, a WSN is, in general, harder to protect than a "traditional" (i.e. wired) network like e.g. an Ethernet-based LAN, which has two major reasons. First, the wireless nature of communication within a WSN makes eavesdropping fairly easy. Second, the nodes themselves can be subject to an attack since WSNs are often deployed in unattended areas. An attacker could, for example, capture one or more nodes and compromise them to obtain all stored data, or he may even reprogram the nodes and inject them into the WSN to conduct malicious activities [25].

Similar to conventional networks (e.g. the Internet), Public-Key Cryptography (PKC) can play a vital role in the security arena of WSNs [25]. The main problem with the practical use of PKC are the extremely constrained resources of battery-powered sensor nodes. For example, the prevalent MICAz mote from Memsic [8] is equipped with an 8-bit AVR processor (the ATmega128 [3]) and features only 4 kB of RAM and 128 kB flash memory. Gura et al [13] were the first to demonstrate that Elliptic Curve Cryptography (ECC) [15] is feasible on such restricted 8-bit platforms. Thanks to their so-called hybrid multiplication technique (a smart optimization of long-integer multiplication by exploiting the large register file of the ATmega128), they managed to reach an execution time of just $6.4 \cdot 10^6$ clock cycles for a full scalar multiplication on a SECG-specified elliptic curve over a 160-bit generalized-Mersenne prime field. TinyECC [23] is the currently most-widely used ECC library for WSNs; it is highly configurable and features a number of optimizations for "standardized" curves over 160 and 192-bit prime fields. Other examples of highly-optimized ECC implementations for 8-bit AVR processors are WM-ECC [33], Nano-ECC [31], MIRACL [7], and RELIC [2]. Very recently, it was shown that even high-security ECC using an elliptic curve over a 255-bit pseudo-Mersenne prime field is feasible on the ATmega128 [17]. However, as noted in [31], the feasibility of ECC on constrained devices does not automatically imply that it is attractive to use ECC since the state-of-the-art in terms of performance is still not satisfactory for many kinds of application. Therefore, the efficient implementation of ECC on sensor nodes remains an active research topic and approaches to further reduce the execution time (i.e. energy cost) and memory footprint are still eagerly sought.

In this paper we introduce MoTE-ECC, a light-weight ECC implementation for Memsic's MICAz motes and other 8-bit AVR-based sensor nodes (or, more generally, embedded devices equipped with an 8-bit AVR processor). The main goal we aimed to achieve with the design and implementation of MoTE-ECC was to find a suitable compromise between the following four requirements: (1) short execution times, (2) high flexibility and scalability (i.e. support of curves providing different levels of security), (3) low memory (i.e. RAM) footprint, and (4) some basic protection against passive implementation attacks. Energy is, in general, the most precious resource of a battery-powered sensor node. Therefore, it is important to optimize the performance of ECC software because the energy consumption of scalar multiplication grows linearly with the execution time. Another essential requirement of an ECC implementation for WSNs is to support curves of different order (i.e. different cryptographic "strength") since the various tasks a sensor node performs during its lifetime have very different security needs [30,22]. For example, a multi-tier security framework for WSNs can permit lower security levels (i.e. shorter keys) for some less-critical tasks in order to save energy. High flexibility at the field-arithmetic layer is difficult to achieve with the NIST-specified generalized Mersenne primes as each of them requires a different reduction routine (see [15, Section 2.2.6]). Consequently, an implementation supporting all five NIST fields needs five different modular reduction functions, which massively bloats code size. MoTE-ECC uses so-called *Optimal Prime Fields (OPFs)*, a special family of fields that allows for flexible yet efficient modular arithmetic [24,34]. Formally, an OPF is defined through a prime of the form $p = u \cdot 2^k + 1$ where u is "small" in relation to 2^k (e.g. u is a 16-bit integer). All arithmetic functions of our OPF library get the factor u as well as the length of p as parameter and can process operands of arbitrary size (e.g. from 160 to 512 bits) without the need to re-compile the library. Thus, we can easily trade security versus performance and energy efficiency, which means MoTE-ECC is an energy-scalable ECC implementation.

The version of MoTE-ECC we describe in this paper supports two families of elliptic curves, namely Montgomery [27] and twisted Edwards [5] curves. An outstanding feature of elliptic curves in Montgomery form is the existence of a differential addition law that involves only the x-coordinate of the points. The so-called Montgomery ladder for scalar multiplication can use such differential additions in an efficient way and has the further benefit of a regular execution profile, which naturally protects against Simple Power Analysis (SPA) attacks [20]. Montgomery curves excel in settings where run-time memory (i.e. RAM) is scarce and scalar multiplication has to be performed with an arbitrary base point that is not known a priori. On the other hand, twisted Edwards curves provide the currently fastest formulas for general (i.e. non-differential) addition of points. Furthermore, the addition law presented in [5, Section 6] is complete if the curve parameters fulfill certain conditions. These properties make twisted Edwards curves attractive for applications that perform scalar multiplications by a fixed base point using e.g. the comb method [15]. In this paper, we take ephemeral ECDH key exchange as example[1] to evaluate the performance and memory consumption of MoTE-ECC. Ephemeral ECDH has one big advantage over static ECDH, namely *forward secrecy*, which is a highly desirable feature

---

[1] In accordance with previous work on ECC for WSNs (e.g. [23]), we use a straight-forward (i.e. unauthenticated) variant of the ECDH protocol for our performance evaluation. However, a real-world application of (ephemeral) ECDH key exchange would require protection against Man-in-the-Middle (MitM) attacks, which can be achieved by signing the messages sent in each run of the protocol, or by using an advanced version of ECDH with "implicit" authentication, e.g. ECMQV.

for any kind of network, including WSNs. Our ECDH implementation combines the individual advantages of the Montgomery form and twisted Edwards form by exploiting the fact that every twisted Edwards curve is birationally equivalent to a Montgomery curve [5]. Ephemeral ECDH key exchange between two sensor nodes requires each node to execute two scalar multiplications; the first is performed with a fixed base point (namely the generator of an elliptic curve group) to generate a key pair, whereas the second scalar multiplication gets an arbitrary point as input and yields the shared secret key. Our implementation uses a fixed-base comb method on a twisted Edwards curve for the former and a Montgomery ladder on a Montgomery curve that is birationally equivalent to the Edwards curve for the latter, thereby combining the specific computational advantages of the two curve shapes in an optimal way[2].

We also made an effort to protect MoTE-ECC against passive, non-invasive implementation attacks. In the case of our ephemeral ECDH, this boils down to protecting the two scalar multiplications against Simple Power Analysis (SPA) attacks since, in each run of the protocol, a freshly generated random scalar is used, i.e. Differential Power Analysis (DPA) is not possible. All field-arithmetic operations are implemented in a highly regular fashion (i.e. without conditional statements such as if-then-else constructs) so that always exactly the same sequence of instructions is executed, independent of the value of the operands [24]. Furthermore, we developed a new approach for performing the fixed-base comb method with the goal of reducing SPA-leakage in relation to a standard implementation. It should be noted, however, that WSN applications have less stringent demands regarding side-channel resistance than e.g. smart cards. The integration of countermeasures against all known forms of side-channel attacks would introduce unfeasible overheads for most WSN applications. Instead, we aimed to protect our ECDH implementation against a so-called stealthy node compromise (i.e. a side-channel attack mounted "in the field" without physically capturing a node) as described in [9]. Since such in-field attacks are carried out under sub-optimal conditions (e.g. large noise levels), it normally suffices to have some basic countermeasures in place.

2   Arithmetic in Optimal Prime Fields

The prime fields we use in MoTE-ECC belong to a special class of finite fields known as Optimal Prime Fields (OPFs) [11]. These fields are defined by primes that can be written as $p = u \cdot 2^k + v$ whereby u and v are "small" compared to 2^k so that they fit into one or two registers of the target platform. MoTE-ECC supports OPFs with $2^{15} \leq u < 2^{16}$ (i.e. u is 16 bits long) and $v = 1$. A concrete example is $p = 65356 \cdot 2^{144} + 1$ (i.e. $u = 65356$ and $k = 144$), which happens to be a 160-bit prime that looks as follows in hex notation.

$$p = \text{0xFF4C0000000000000000000000000000000000001}$$

---

[2] MoTE-ECC is an abbreviation for Montgomery and Twisted Edwards based ECC.

Primes of such form are characterized by a low Hamming weight since only the two most significant bytes and the least significant byte are non-zero; all bytes in between are zero. The low weight of p allows for specific optimization of the modular arithmetic because only the non-zero bytes of p need to be processed in the reduction operation. For example, Montgomery's algorithm [26] can be simplified for these primes so that the modular reduction has only linear complexity, similar to generalized-Mersenne or pseudo-Mersenne primes [15].

2.1   Parameterized OPF Library

Our implementation of arithmetic operations in OPFs is largely based upon the OPF library for 8-bit AVR processors described in [24]. This library provides the full spectrum of arithmetic functionality required for scalar multiplication on Montgomery and twisted Edwards curves (i.e. addition, subtraction, multiplication, squaring and inversion), whereby each operation includes a reduction modulo a low-weight prime of the form $p = u \cdot 2^k + 1$. Both multiplication and squaring employ a special variant of the Montgomery reduction method [26] so that only the non-zero bytes of p are processed. All functions of the library are written in assembly language and optimized to yield a good trade-off between performance and (binary) code size. Furthermore, the arithmetic functions are parameterized, which means the operand length is not fixed (i.e. hard-coded) but passed as parameter to the function. In this way, the OPF library provides a high degree of flexibility as one and the same function can process operands of any length. Another important feature of the library is its resilience against SPA attacks as all arithmetic operations are implemented in a regular fashion and execute always the same sequence of instructions, regardless of the actual value of the operands. Only the inversion from [24] has a non-regular execution profile; therefore, we implemented a Fermat-based inversion from scratch (see below). A detailed description of the OPF library can be found in [24].

2.2   Fermat-Based Inversion in OPFs

Unlike to field addition and multiplication, inversion in $\mathbb{F}_p$ is not executed during the scalar multiplication when using projective coordinates [15]. In fact, the inversion operation is only needed to convert the result from projective back to affine coordinates. Two well-known techniques for computing the inverse of an element of $\mathbb{F}_p$ are the Extended Euclidean Algorithm (EEA) [15] and Fermat's little theorem. However, the EEA is highly irregular and may leak information about the input value that could be exploited to mount an attack as described in [28] to recover a few bits of the secret scalar. Therefore, it is mandatory to use an inversion algorithm that executes in a regular way and is not vulnerable to SPA and SPA-like attacks. Our implementation of the inversion in OPFs is based on Fermat's little theorem $a^{p-2} \equiv a^{-1} \bmod p$, i.e. we perform inversion via exponentiation. Unfortunately, the conventional square-and-multiply exponentiation method with an exponent of the form $u \cdot 2^k - 1$ requires n squarings and almost n multiplications, whereby n denotes the bit-length of p. To reduce

---

Algorithm 1. Optimized exponentiation-based inversion for OPFs

---

Input: Element a of $\mathbb{F}_p$ with $p = u \cdot 2^k + 1$.

Output: $r \equiv a^{u \cdot 2^k - 1} \equiv a^{-1} \bmod p$.

1: $u' \leftarrow u - 1$	16: $t \leftarrow r \cdot a$
2: $r \leftarrow a$, $b \leftarrow \lceil ld(k) - 2 \rceil$, $i \leftarrow 1$	17: $b \leftarrow 1$
3: **while** $b > 0$ **do**	18: **while** $b < 0x8000$ **do**
4: $t \leftarrow r^2$	19: **if** u' & $b > 0$ **then**
5: **for** $j = 1$ **to** $i - 1$ **do**	20: $r \leftarrow r \cdot t$
6: $t \leftarrow t^2$	21: **end if**
7: **end for**	22: $t \leftarrow t^2$
8: $r \leftarrow r \cdot t$	23: $b \leftarrow b \ll 1$
9: $i \leftarrow i \ll 1$	24: **end while**
10: **if** k & $b > 0$ **then**	25: **if** u' & $b > 0$ **then**
11: $r \leftarrow r^2 \cdot a$	26: $r \leftarrow r \cdot t$
12: $i \leftarrow i + 1$	27: **end if**
13: **end if**	
14: $b \leftarrow b \gg 1$	
15: **end while**	

---

execution time, we developed an inversion technique that is specifically crafted for OPFs (specified in Algorithm 1). Thanks to this algorithm, it is possible to nearly halve the overall number of operations to n squarings plus only $HW(k)$ $+ HW(u - 1) + 1$ multiplications, where $HW(x)$ denotes the Hamming weight of x. In practice, this optimization almost doubles the performance compared to a straightforward square-and-multiply exponentiation. Algorithm 1 operates in two phases; in the first phase, $a^{2^k - 1}$ is calculated using the exponentiation method of Itoh and Tsujii [18], which was originally proposed for binary extension fields. In the second phase, a right-to-left square-and-multiply algorithm is carried out. Note that, for our primes, this second phase is much shorter since u is (at most) 16 bits long. In step 16, the multiplication $r \cdot a = a^{2^k - 1} \cdot a$ yields $t = a^{2^k}$, which is needed for the right-to-left square-and-multiply algorithm.

3   Scalar Multiplication for Ephemeral ECDH

Performing ephemeral ECDH key exchange between two sensor nodes requires each node to execute two scalar multiplications; one to generate an ephemeral key pair and the second to obtain the shared secret. MoTE-ECC uses a twisted Edwards curve [5] for the former and a Montgomery curve [27] for the latter. In fact, it is more correct to say that both scalar multiplications are computed on the same elliptic curve; in one case we adopt the twisted Edwards form of this curve and in the second case its Montgomery form. We describe both forms in the next subsection and also discuss the execution time of scalar multiplication algorithms by counting the number of underlying field operations, whereby we adhere to the following notation: M (multiplication), S (squaring), A (addition or subtraction), I (inversion), and D (multiplication by a curve constant).

3.1 Montgomery and Twisted Edwards Curves

Montgomery Curve. In 1987, Peter Montgomery introduced a special model of elliptic curves, today known as Montgomery model [27]. An elliptic curve in Montgomery form over a prime field $\mathbb{F}_p$ is defined through the equation

$$E_M : \ Bv^2 = u^3 + Au^2 + u \tag{1}$$

where $A \in \mathbb{F}_p \setminus \{-2, 2\}$ and $B \in \mathbb{F}_p \setminus \{0\}$. The major attraction of these curves is the possibility to perform point arithmetic with the x-coordinate only. More precisely, when using projective coordinates to represent curve points, just the X and Z coordinate are needed to perform point addition and doubling. A so-called "differential" point addition requires exactly $3M + 2S + 6A$, whereas the doubling of a point costs $2M + 2S + 1D + 4A$. The Montgomery ladder is well known for being a *per se* highly regular algorithm for scalar multiplication on Montgomery curves [29]. Its regularity is simply due to the fact that it always executes both a point addition and a point doubling per scalar bit, irrespective of whether said bit is 0 or 1. Therefore, given a scalar k and base point P, the cost of computing $k \cdot P$ amounts to $5M + 4S + 1D + 10A$ per bit of k.

Normally, the parameter A is chosen so that multiplication by $(A + 2)/4$ is fast. However, in our case this means the Montgomery image of $(A + 2)/4$ has to be small since, as stated in Section 2.1, the OPF library uses Montgomery's reduction technique [26] for the modular multiplication.

Twisted Edwards Curve. Currently, elliptic curves in twisted Edwards form offer the most efficient formulae for general (i.e. non-differential) point addition [16], which makes them attractive for practical implementations. According to Bernstein et al [5], a twisted Edwards curve over a non-binary field $\mathbb{F}_q$ is given by an equation of the form

$$E_E : \ ax^2 + y^2 = 1 + dx^2y^2 \tag{2}$$

whereby a and d are distinct, non-zero elements of $\mathbb{F}_q$. The authors of [5] also introduced formulae for addition and doubling on such a curve using standard projective coordinates. Thereafter, Hişil et al proposed an extended coordinate system that includes an auxiliary coordinate $t = xy$ [16]. Instead of representing a point on a twisted Edwards curve E_E by its x and y coordinate only, one can use the extended affine coordinates (x, y, t). The corresponding projective coordinates of that point are $(X : Y : T : Z)$, whereby the auxiliary coordinate T has the property $T = XY/Z$ with $Z \neq 0$. Thanks to these coordinates, Hişil et al were able to devise very efficient point addition formulae, especially if the parameter $a = -1$. After applying some straightforward optimizations [14], the computational cost of a mixed point addition on a curve with $a = -1$ amounts to $7M + 6A$, while a doubling requires $3M + 4S + 6A$.

Birational Equivalence. Bernstein et al proved in [5] that the set of twisted Edwards curves over a non-binary field $\mathbb{F}_q$ is equivalent to the set of Montgomery curves over $\mathbb{F}_q$. In particular, they showed that the twisted Edwards curve E_E over $\mathbb{F}_q$ with non-zero parameters a, d is birationally equivalent over $\mathbb{F}_q$ to the Montgomery curve E_M given by

$$A = 2(a + d)/(a - d), \quad B = 4/(a - d) \tag{3}$$

For an arbitrary point (x, y) on the twisted Edwards curve E_E, we can get the related point (u, v) on the equivalent Montgomery curve E_M as follows

$$u = (1 + y)/(1 - y), \quad v = (1 + y)/((1 - y)x) \tag{4}$$

Conversely, given the curve parameters $A \in \mathbb{F}_q \setminus \{-2, 2\}$ and $B \in \mathbb{F}_q \setminus \{0\}$, the corresponding Montgomery curve E_M is birationally equivalent over $\mathbb{F}_q$ to the twisted Edwards curve E_E with the parameters

$$a = (A + 2)/B, \quad d = (A - 2)/B \tag{5}$$

and the point (x, y) corresponding to (u, v) can be obtained as follows

$$x = u/v, \quad y = (u - 1)/(u + 1) \tag{6}$$

3.2 Generation of Curves

The security of elliptic curve cryptosystems is based on the intractability of the underlying Elliptic Curve Discrete Logarithm Problem (ECDLP). To date, the most efficient algorithm for solving a generic instance of the ECDLP in a given elliptic curve group $E(\mathbb{F}_p)$ has complexity $\mathcal{O}(\sqrt{n})$ where n is the largest prime divisor of $\#E(\mathbb{F}_p)$ [15]. Therefore, one must be careful to choose a field $\mathbb{F}_p$ and a curve E over $\mathbb{F}_p$ so that $E(\mathbb{F}_p)$ has prime order or contains a large subgroup of prime order. More concretely, when writing $\#E(\mathbb{F}_p)$ as a product of a prime n and a co-factor h, then n should have a length of approximately 160 bits and h should be small, e.g. $h \leq 4$ [15]. Furthermore, one has to ensure that E does not belong to a class of curves for which the ECDLP can be solved in less than $\sqrt{n}$ steps. Examples for such "weak" curves over $\mathbb{F}_p$ are anomalous curves and curves with small embedding degree (e.g. supersingular curves). Depending on the application, further security criteria not directly related to the ECDLP in $E(\mathbb{F}_p)$ may need to be considered. One example is *twist security*, which means that not only the curve E itself, but also the quadratic twist E' of E meets all criteria for hardness of the ECDLP. Using a curve with a secure twist thwarts certain implementation attacks (e.g. [10]) and allows for a simplification of the ECDH protocol when only the x-coordinates of points are exchanged [4].

Besides the security requirements from above, our curve generation process also takes certain efficiency criteria into account to ensure the point arithmetic on both the twisted Edwards curve and its Montgomery equivalent can achieve the best possible execution times. When generating a Montgomery curve, it is common practice to choose the curve parameter A such that $(A + 2)/4$ is small (as suggested in [27]). In our case, this actually means the Montgomery image of $(A+2)/4$ has to be small since our OPF library uses Montgomery reduction for the multiplication in $\mathbb{F}_p$. The second curve parameter B does not appear in the addition/doubling formulae and, therefore, has no impact on the execution time. On the other hand, the point arithmetic on a twisted Edwards curve is most efficient when the parameter a is fixed to -1 as in this case Hisil et al's fast and complete $7M$ formula for mixed addition can be used [16]. The second parameter d appears as operand in the complete addition formula described in Section 3.1 of [16], but not in the dedicated addition from [16, Section 3.2]. In our case, we can still use the complete addition formula without loss of performance since the comb method always adds a fixed base point P (or a multiple of P), which allows us to pre-compute $2d\,T_2$ as suggested in [16]. Another issue to consider is that the addition formula from [16, Section 3.1] is only complete when a is a square and d a non-square in $\mathbb{F}_p$. Fortunately, $a = -1$ is always a square in an OPF defined by a prime of the form $p = u \cdot 2^k + 1$; this becomes immediately evident by an evaluation of the Legendre symbol $\left(\frac{-1}{p}\right)$ taking into account that $(p-1)/2$ is highly even for all our primes.

As pointed out in Subsection 3.1, every twisted Edwards curve over a non-binary finite field $\mathbb{F}_q$ is birationally equivalent over $\mathbb{F}_q$ to a Montgomery curve and, conversely, every Montgomery curve is birationally equivalent to a twisted Edwards curve [5]. However, this does not imply that every Montgomery curve is birationally equivalent to a twisted Edwards curve with a fast and complete addition law. The goal of our curve generation procedure is to find a Montgomery curve along with its twisted Edwards counterpart so that both satisfy the security and efficiency criteria outlined above. To achieve this, we used the computer algebra system Magma. Magma provides an extensive pool of functions for computations on elliptic curves given in both short and long (non-simplified) Weierstraß form, but does not directly support the twisted Edwards from. However, a twisted Edwards curve with the parameters $a, d \in \mathbb{F}_q$ can be expressed via a non-simplified Weierstraß equation as follows.

$$a_2 = \frac{a+d}{2}, \; a_4 = \left(\frac{a-d}{4}\right)^2, \text{ and } a_1 = a_3 = a_6 = 0 \qquad (7)$$

The above formulas were derived by simply exploiting the fact that any twisted Edwards curve over a non-binary field $\mathbb{F}_q$ is birationally equivalent to a Montgomery curve, which was formally proven in [5]. We fixed the parameter a to -1 to take advantage of the fast formulas for point addition and doubling presented in [16]. Furthermore, we only consider values of d that are non-square so as to ensure completeness of the addition formula.

3.3 Regular Digit-Set Conversion for Comb Method

When performing a scalar multiplication $k \cdot P$ on a fixed base point P, one can take advantage of the so-called comb method to reduce execution time [15]. In general, the comb method processes $w \geq 2$ bits of the scalar k at once and requires pre-computation and storage of (up to) 2^w curve points, all of which are linear combinations of w multiples of P. An n-bit scalar multiplication consists of exactly $d = \lceil n/w \rceil$ point doublings and at most d point additions. Thus, the w-bit comb method cuts the number of point doublings by a factor of w versus the binary (i.e. "double-and-add") technique. The number of point additions is not constant but depends on the scalar since, similar to the binary method, the addition step is simply omitted if the corresponding w bits of k are all 0. It is possible to reduce the number of pre-computed points to 2^{w-1} at the expense of point negation operations to be carried out "on-the-fly," resulting in a slight performance degradation. Our implementation of the comb method follows this avenue; in each step we process $w = 4$ bits of the scalar at once using $2^{w-1} = 8$ pre-computed points, which are negated on-the-fly if necessary.

A conventional implementation of the comb technique can leak information related to the scalar k since, as explained above, the number of point additions is not constant but depends on k. MoTE-ECC uses the comb method for fixed-point scalar multiplication on a twisted Edwards curve, which means we could exploit the completeness of the Edwards addition law and just add the neutral element $\mathcal{O}$ to achieve a (more) regular execution profile. Even though such an approach would foil timing attacks, it may still leak SPA-relevant information since the coordinates of $\mathcal{O}$ consist of the field elements 0 and 1. Multiplying an arbitrary field element by 0 or 1 causes less bit flips in the multiplier hardware and register file than a multiplication of two random elements of $\mathbb{F}_p$. Thus, we opted to not add $\mathcal{O}$ but represent the 4-bit digits processed in each step of the comb method using a signed digit-set that does not contain 0.

To foil SPA attacks, all operations involving bits of the secret scalar k need to be implemented in a highly regular way without conditional statements. In our case, this requirement boils down to the demand for a regular algorithm to convert a radix-2^4 integer with digits from the set $D = \{0, 1, 2, \ldots, 14, 15\}$ into an equivalent radix-2^4 representation using a "zero-free" digit set of the form $D' = \{\pm 1, \pm 3, \ldots, \pm 13, \pm 15\}$. Algorithms for this kind of digit-set conversion were proposed in e.g. [19,14]. However, we use a different conversion technique that is more regular and easier to implement than the state-of-the-art. Our algorithm for digit-set conversion is based on the following observation: Any odd n-bit integer k given by $k = \sum_{i=0}^{n-1} k_i \cdot 2^i$ with $k_i \in \{0,1\}$ for $0 < i < n-1$ and $k_{n-1} = k_0 = 1$ can be written in standard Binary Signed-Digit (BSD) form as $k = 2^{n-1} + \sum_{i=0}^{n-2}(2k_{i+1} - 1) \cdot 2^i$. The expression $2k_{i+1} - 1$ yields either 1 (when $k_{i+1} = 1$) or -1 (if $k_{i+1} = 0$), i.e. all digits of our BSD representation of k are non-zero. One can verify the correctness of this conversion as follows.

$$k = 2^{n-1} + \sum_{i=0}^{n-2}(2k_{i+1} - 1) \cdot 2^i = 2^{n-1} - \sum_{i=0}^{n-2} 2^i + \sum_{i=0}^{n-2} 2k_{i+1} \cdot 2^i =$$

$$= 1 + \sum_{i=0}^{n-2} k_{i+1} \cdot 2^{i+1} = 1 + \sum_{i=1}^{n-1} k_i \cdot 2^i = \sum_{i=0}^{n-1} k_i \cdot 2^i \text{ with } k_0 = 1 \quad (8)$$

Equation (8) leads to a simple technique to convert an odd integer given in conventional binary form into a BSD representation consisting of only non-zero

Algorithm 2. Regular w-bit comb method for fixed-base scalar multiplication

Input: n-bit scalar $k = (k_{n-1}, \ldots, k_1, k_0)_2$ with $k_0 = 1$, point $P \in E(\mathbb{F}_p)$.

Output: $Q = k \cdot P$

1: Pre-compute $R[j] = R[a_{w-2}, \ldots, a_1, a_0] = 2^{dw}P + (2a_{w-2} - 1)2^{(d-1)w}P + \ldots + (2a_1 - 1)2^w P + (2a_0 - 1)P$ for all bit-strings $j = (a_{w-2}, \ldots, a_1, a_0)$ of length $w - 1$

2: $Q \leftarrow R[k_{dw}, \ldots, k_{2d}, k_d]$

3: **for** $i = d - 1$ **downto** 1 **do**

4: $\quad Q \leftarrow 2Q$

5: $\quad Q \leftarrow Q + (2k_{(w-1)d+i} - 1) \cdot R[k_{(w-2)d+i}, \ldots, k_{d+i}, k_i]$

6: **end for**

digits, namely -1 and 1. We just have to shift the whole binary representation of k one bit to the right and insert a "1" at the vacant MSB position. Now this shifted bit-string is already exactly the BSD-form of k when we interpret all 0 bits as -1. A radix-2^4 representation can be obtained by dividing the bit-string into groups of 4-bit digits, each of which corresponds to an odd number in the range $[-15, 15]$. In this way, we get a signed radix-2^4 representation that does not contain zero digits. Similar to Joye et al's signed-digit recoding algorithm from [19, Sect. 3.2], our conversion technique requires k to be odd as otherwise the result will be off by 1. More precisely, when performing a scalar multiplication using the proposed digit-set conversion with an even k, the actual result is $(k - 1) \cdot P$ instead of $k \cdot P$, which means a final addition of P is required. However, such a final addition does not necessarily introduce an irregularity in the comb method since we can define private keys to be odd (or even) so that the final addition is either never or always executed. Unlike the recoding technique from [19], the execution time and power consumption profile of our conversion is independent of the position of the MSB of k since a leading bit-string of the form $000 \cdots 001$ becomes $1\bar{1}\bar{1} \cdots \bar{1}\bar{1}\bar{1}$ where $\bar{1}$ denotes -1. Hence, short scalars (i.e. scalars having less than n bits) are processed in precisely the same way as an n-bit scalar, which is not the case for the conversion proposed in [19].

Algorithm 2 shows a highly regular variant of the fixed-base comb method for point multiplication. We use the same notation as Sect. 3.3.2 in [15], which means w denotes the number of bits (i.e. length of the bit-string) processed in each iteration of the loop and $d = \lceil n/w \rceil$. Similar to the straightforward comb method specified in [15, Algorithm 3.44], our variant comprises an offline phase (Step 1) and an online phase. In the first phase, 2^{w-1} points are pre-computed and stored, all of which are linear combinations of P. Our implementation pre-computes eight points as we use $w = 4$ to achieve a balance between execution time and storage requirements. Note that an expression of the form $(2a_i - 1)$ in Step 1 yields either 1 (when $a_i = 1$) or -1 (if $a_i = 0$), thereby performing the digit-set conversion described above. The online phase consists of a simple loop that executes a doubling followed by an addition in each iteration. However, in contrast to the standard comb method, $w - 1$ bits (instead of w bits) of k are used to determine which of the 2^{w-1} pre-computed points is to be added, while a further bit (namely $k_{(w-1)d+i}$ in Step 5 of Algorithm 2) defines whether this point is actually added or subtracted. To achieve a regular execution, we need a function that, depending on the value of a bit, assigns either a point R or the negative of that point (i.e. $-R$) to a destination. The negative of a point R in extended affine coordinates is $-R = (-x, y, -t)$ [16]; consequently, the problem of negating a point boils down to the negation of elements of $\mathbb{F}_p$, which can be realized through subtractions from p. MoTE-ECC performs the negation of an element $x \in \mathbb{F}_p$ depending on the value of a bit b as follows. First, we compute $x' = p - x$ via subtraction. Then, we use the bit b to derive a mask m, which is either an "all-1" byte (if $b = 1$) or an "all-0" byte (if $b = 0$), in the same way as described in [24]. Furthermore, we need a second mask m' that is the bit-wise complement of m, i.e. m' is 0 if m is an "all-1" byte and vice versa. After these preparations, we compute $(x_i' \& m) \mid (x_i \& m')$ for all bytes of x' and x (where $\&$ and $\mid$ denote the bit-wise *and* and *or* operation, respectively) and assign the result to the corresponding byte of the destination. The field element we get in this way is either $-x = p - x$ (if $b = 1$, i.e. the negation is actually carried out) or simply x (if $b = 0$, i.e. no negation). In summary, our regular comb method executes always exactly $d - 1$ point additions and $d - 1$ doublings, irrespective of the actual value of the scalar bits and the index of the MSB.

4   Implementation and Evaluation

We implemented MoTE-ECC for the 8-bit AVR platform (e.g. ATmega128 [3]) and assessed its execution time and memory footprint using ephemeral ECDH key exchange as example. The main idea of our ECDH protocol is to exploit the birational equivalence between Montgomery and twisted Edwards curves [5] to improve the overall performance. Assume two sensor nodes, named $\mathcal{A}$ and $\mathcal{B}$ in the following, want to establish a shared secret key, whereby the set of domain parameters (a, d, A, B, G, p) has already been agreed upon. Here, a and d are the parameters of a twisted Edwards curve E_E, while A and B characterize the birationally-equivalent Montgomery curve E_M. G is a point of prime order on E_E, and p defines the underlying OPF. One round of our ECDH key exchange protocol can be divided into two stages as follows:

1. Node $\mathcal{A}$ generates a private key d_A and computes the corresponding public key $Q = d_A \cdot G$. This scalar multiplication is done on the twisted Edwards curve E_E using generator G. Then, node $\mathcal{A}$ converts the point $Q = (x_q, y_q)$ to a point $M = (x_m, y_m)$ on the birationally equivalent Montgomery curve E_M and sends the x-coordinate x_m of M to node $\mathcal{B}$. Node $\mathcal{B}$ performs the same steps with private key d_B and sends its x-coordinate to $\mathcal{A}$.
2. After node $\mathcal{A}$ has received the x-coordinate from $\mathcal{B}$, it computes the scalar multiplication $S = d_A \cdot M$ (whereby M consists of only an x coordinate) on the Montgomery curve E_M. Node $\mathcal{B}$ does the same with the x coordinate it received from node $\mathcal{A}$.

Both node $\mathcal{A}$ and node $\mathcal{B}$ have to carry out two scalar multiplications to obtain the shared secret key $S = d_A \cdot d_B \cdot G$. Since the base point G is fixed and known

Table 1. Execution time (in clock cycles) of field arithmetic operations for operands of a length of 160, 192, 224, and 256 bits

Operation	160 bits	192 bits	224 bits	256 bits
mod_add	530	631	732	833
mod_sub	530	631	732	833
mod_mul	3237	4500	5971	7650
mod_sqr	2901	3909	5058	6347
mod_inv	571916	830823	1163655	1491839

in advance, we can speed up the execution of the first scalar multiplication with help of the fixed-base comb method using a window width of $w = 4$ and eight pre-computed points as described in Section 3.3.

MoTE-ECC adopts the "extended" coordinate system for twisted Edwards curves introduced in [16], which means we obtain the point Q resulting from the first scalar multiplication in extended projective coordinates. A straightforward conversion of a point Q on a twisted Edwards curve E_E into a point M on the birationally-equivalent Montgomery curve E_M can be executed in the following way. We firstly convert the projective point $Q = (X_q, Y_q, T_q, Z_q)$ on E_E to its affine representation $Q = (x_q, y_q)$ and then calculate the equivalent point $M = (x_m, y_m)$ on E_M via $x_m = (1 + y_q)/(1 - y_q)$ and $y_m = (1 + y_q)/((1 - y_q) \cdot x_q)$ as specified in [5]. However, when doing so, we have to execute an inversion in the affine-to-projective conversion to get $1/Z_q$ and another inversion as part of the Edwards-to-Montgomery transformation (to obtain $1/[(1 - y_t) \cdot x_t]$). To reduce the computational overhead caused by two inversions, we directly transform the point $Q = (X_q, Y_q, T_q, Z_q)$ to the point $M = (x_m, y_m)$ as follows.

$$x_m = (1 + y_q)/(1 - y_q) = (1 + Y_q/Z_q)/(1 - Y_q/Z_q) = (Z_q + Y_q)/(Z_q - Y_q) \quad (9)$$
$$y_m = (1 + y_q)/(x_q \cdot (1 - y_q)) = (Z_q^2 + Y_q Z_q)/(X_q Z_q - X_q Y_q) \quad (10)$$

In this way, we only need one inversion to compute $1/(X_q Z_q - X_q Y_q)$, which we just have to multiply by X_q to get $1/(Z_q - Y_q)$.

4.1   Execution Time

As explained in Section 2, we implemented the OPF inversion from scratch and used the OPF library from [24] for all other arithmetic operations. Table 1 lists the simulated execution times for the ATmega128. The modular multiplication only takes 3237, 4500, 5971 and 7650 clock cycles for 160, 192, 224 and 256-bit operands, respectively. As stated in [24], these timings represent speed records for modular multiplication on an 8-bit AVR processor. For 256-bit operands, the OPF multiplication is even faster than the multiplication of the NaCl software for AVR [17]. As also shown in Table 1, our regular Itoh-Tsujii inversion needs 571916 clock cycles (in a 160-bit OPF), which is about 1.36 times faster than the unprotected inversion of the well-known TinyECC library [23].

Table 2. Execution time (in clock cycles) of point arithmetic operations over 160, 192, 224, and 256-bit OPFs

Operation	160 bits	192 bits	224 bits	256 bits
Mo point add	19479	25890	33207	41428
Mo point dbl	15950	21072	26884	33390
TE point add	27355	36903	47907	60367
TE point dbl	25421	33848	43463	54262

We wrote the functions for point arithmetic in ANSI C and determined the execution time of point addition and point doubling on both twisted Edwards and Montgomery curves. The timings are reported in Table 2 for OPFs of sizes ranging between 160 and 256 bits. Taking the 160-bit OPF as example, it turns out that addition and doubling on a Montgomery curve require exactly $19,479$ and $15,950$ clock cycles, respectively. On the other hand, adding two points on a twisted Edwards curve needs $27,355$ clock cycles, while a doubling operation costs $25,421$ cycles. Our simulation results are exactly in line with the analysis in Section 3. For example, the point addition on a Montgomery curve requires only $3M + 2S$, which is clearly more efficient than the $7M$ for adding points on a twisted Edwards curve. Thus, it is not surprising that the point arithmetic on the Montgomery curve is much faster than on the twisted Edwards curve. The addition and doubling operation of our implementation for Montgomery curves outperform that of the TinyECC library by a factor of more than three. On the other hand, the point addition and doubling on the twisted Edwards curve are roughly 2.1 and 1.9 times faster than TinyECC, respectively.

Table 3. Execution time (in clock cycles) of scalar multiplication over 160, 192, 224 and 256-bit OPFs

Operation	160 bits	192 bits	224 bits	256 bits
Scalar mul. Mo curve	6276630	9964549	14856446	21118778
Scalar mul. TE curve	2767454	4412519	6603888	9420788
Full MoTE-ECDH	9044084	14377068	21460334	30539566

The execution times of a full scalar multiplication using the two curve shapes over 160, 192, 224 and 256-bit OPFs are summarized in Table 3. Each run of our ECDH key exchange protocol consists of two scalar multiplications; the first one is performed on a twisted Edwards curve, while the second is carried out on the birationally-equivalent Montgomery curve. When using a fixed-base comb method as described in Section 3.3, the first stage of the ECDH protocol can be executed in about $2.76 \cdot 10^6$ clock cycles over a 160-bit OPF (i.e. 0.37 s at the typical sensor-node frequency of 7.37 MHz), which already includes the Edwards-to-Montgomery conversion. The second stage of the ECDH protocol is more expensive than the first one since it involves a scalar multiplication by an elliptic-curve point that is neither fixed nor known a priori. MoTE-ECC uses a simple ladder on a Montgomery curve for this second scalar multiplication and achieves an execution time of roughly $6.27 \cdot 10^6$ cycles in the 160-bit case. The complete computational cost of an ephemeral ECDH key exchange amounts to about $9.04 \cdot 10^6$ clock cycles when using a 160-bit OPF as underlying algebraic structure, which corresponds to an execution time of 1.22 s at 7.37 MHz.

4.2   Memory Footprint and Code Size

Besides performance, run-time memory consumption is an important criterium for WSN applications since a typical AVR-based sensor node features only 4 kB RAM. Our comb method for scalar multiplication on a twisted Edwards curve requires to store eight points given in extended affine coordinates. However, as these points are pre-computed "off-line," we can store them in ROM or in flash memory. In this way, we only need to transfer the point that is required for the current iteration of the comb method from ROM or flash memory to RAM. As a consequence, a full ephemeral ECDH key exchange supporting elliptic curves over 160, 192, 224, and 256-bit OPFs (without re-compilation) occupies a mere 556 bytes in RAM, which includes besides all global and local variables also the stack. A stripped-down variant of MoTE-ECC supporting only fields of a size of up to 160 bits has a RAM footprint of just 380 bytes.

Even though ROM (resp. flash) usage is, in general, less critical than RAM footprint, it is still important to analyze the (binary) code size. The arithmetic library for OPFs used by MoTE-ECC is implemented in a parameterized form with rolled loops (so as to support operands of varying length [24]), which has the side-benefit of compact code size. Besides the field arithmetic, also the concrete implementation of the fixed-base comb method has a large impact on the ROM (resp. flash) requirements of MoTE-ECC. Our choice of $w = 4$ with eight pre-computed points represents a fair trade-off between performance and code size. The total ROM/flash footprint of MoTE-ECC supporting Montgomery as well as twisted Edwards curves is 14.7 kB, which constitutes some 11.5% of the 128 kB flash memory that is available on a typical AVR-based sensor node.

4.3   Comparison with Related Work

Many ECC implementations for the 8-bit AVR platform have been reported in the literature. However, most of them were solely optimized for speed and did not properly consider the limited resources of 8-bit sensor nodes. We compare our MoTE-ECC library with previous work in three main aspects: performance (i.e. execution time of fixed-point and variable-point scalar multiplication, and execution time of both together), RAM footprint, and ROM requirements. The key figures of MoTE-ECC and previous ECC implementations can be found in Table 4, whereby all timings are specified for an ATmega128 processor clocked at a frequency of 7.37 MHz. We take the implementations using a 160-bit field as example to demonstrate the advantages of MoTE-ECC. Our implementation achieves the best execution time for ephemeral ECDH key exchange among all

Table 4. Comparison of ECC libraries for 160, 192, 224, and 256-bit prime fields

Reference	Field	Fixed P.	Rand. P.	RAM	ROM	ECDH
Liu [23]	160 bit	2.05 s	2.30 s	1174 B	19.0 kB	4.35 s
Wang [33]	160 bit	1.24 s	1.35 s	3200 B	15.8 kB	2.59 s
Szczech. [31]	160 bit	1.27 s	1.27 s	1800 B	46.1 kB	2.54 s
Gura [13]	160 bit	0.88 s	0.88 s	282 B	3.7 kB	1.76 s
Ugus [32]	160 bit	0.57 s	1.03 s	543 B	3.6 kB	1.60 s
Großschädl [12]	160 bit	0.74 s	0.74 s	n/a	n/a	1.48 s
MoTE-160	160 bit	0.37 s	0.85 s	556 B	14.7 kB	1.22 s
Liu [23]	192 bit	2.90 s	2.90 s	1510 B	19.0 kB	5.80 s
Gura [13]	192 bit	1.35 s	1.35 s	336 B	4.0 kB	2.70 s
Lederer [21]	192 bit	0.71 s	1.67 s	1398 B	23.0 kB	2.38 s
MoTE-192	192 bit	0.60 s	1.35 s	556 B	14.7 kB	1.95 s
Gura [13]	224 bit	2.38 s	2.38 s	422 B	4.8 kB	4.76 s
MoTE-224	224 bit	0.90 s	2.01 s	556 B	14.7 kB	2.91 s
Hutter [17]	255 bit	3.80 s	3.80 s	922 B	17.4 kB	7.60 s
Hutter [17]	255 bit	3.11 s	3.11 s	681 B	28.9 kB	6.22 s
MoTE-256	256 bit	1.28 s	2.86 s	556 B	14.7 kB	4.14 s

prime-field based ECC libraries documented in the literature. In particular, we require just about 28% of the execution time of TinyECC [23]. However, since MoTE-ECC supports two curve shapes, it occupies slightly more RAM and is larger in terms of code size than the implementations from [13] and [32]. When compared with all known implementations using 160-bit fields (including also binary-field libraries, which are not specified in Table 4), our implementation is only slower than the work of Aranha et al [2]. However, their software employs a carefully-optimized multiplication technique for binary fields, which achieves high performance at the expense of a RAM footprint of 2.8 kB and a code size of 32.0 kB. Furthermore, it should be noted that MoTE-ECC contains counter-measures against SPA attacks, which is not the case for all other ECC libraries listed in Table 4 except NaCl [17] and the work introduced in [21]. NaCl is the only implementation with a high level of SPA resistance similar to ours. While NaCl is fast and small in terms of code size, it supports only a single curve. In contrast, our implementation is highly scalable as it supports fields and curves of various size (e.g. from 160 to 256 bits) without re-compilation.

5   Conclusions

The main contributions of this paper can be recapitulated as follows: First, we extended Liu et al's [24] parameterized yet efficient arithmetic library for OPFs with a Fermat-based inversion that is robust against SPA attacks. Second, we presented a highly regular implementation of the comb method so as to reduce the SPA-leakage of fixed-base scalar multiplication. Third, we described a new way of performing ephemeral ECDH key exchange by combining the individual computational benefits of Montgomery and twisted Edwards curves. Fourth, we discussed how these curves have to be generated to satisfy both efficiency and security criteria. The former three contributions have been implemented and evaluated in MoTE-ECC, an efficient, scalable, and SPA-resistant ECC library for AVR processors such as the ATmega128. MoTE-ECC is able to perform the two scalar multiplications of an ephemeral ECDH key exchange in a little more than $9 \cdot 10^6$ clock cycles altogether when the underlying OPF has a size of 160 bits, which significantly advances the state-of-the-art in prime-field based ECC on an 8-bit processor. Another advantage of MoTE-ECC is its scalability since it supports fields and curves of different size (e.g. 160, 192, 224, and 256 bits) without re-compilation. The RAM footprint of MoTE-ECC for OPFs of up to 256 bits is 556 bytes, which is less than 15% of the available RAM of a typical AVR-based sensor node. A stripped-down variant of MoTE-ECC that supports OPFs of a size of up to 160 bits occupies only 380 bytes in RAM.

Acknowledgements. We thank the anonymous reviewers of CHES 2013 and ACNS 2014 for their valuable comments and suggestions.

The research described in this paper was supported in part by the Austrian Research Promotion Agency (FFG) under grant 836628 (SeCoS) and the Fonds National de la Recherche (FNR) Luxembourg under AFR grant 1359142.

References

1. Akyildiz, I.F., Vuran, M.C.: Wireless Sensor Networks. John Wiley and Sons (2010)
2. Aranha, D.F., Dahab, R., López, J.C., Oliveira, L.B.: Efficient implementation of elliptic curve cryptography in wireless sensors. Advances in Mathematics of Communications 4(2), 169–187 (2010)
3. Atmel Corporation. 8-bit ARV® Microcontroller with 128K Bytes In-System Programmable Flash: ATmega128, ATmega128L, Datasheet, available for download at http://www.atmel.com/dyn/resources/prod_documents/doc2467.pdf (June 2008)
4. Bernstein, D.J.: Curve25519: New diffie-hellman speed records. In: Yung, M., Dodis, Y., Kiayias, A., Malkin, T. (eds.) PKC 2006. LNCS, vol. 3958, pp. 207–228. Springer, Heidelberg (2006)
5. Bernstein, D.J., Birkner, P., Joye, M., Lange, T., Peters, C.: Twisted edwards curves. In: Vaudenay, S. (ed.) AFRICACRYPT 2008. LNCS, vol. 5023, pp. 389–405. Springer, Heidelberg (2008)
6. Brody, H.: 10 emerging technologies that will change the world. Technology Review 106(1), 33–49 (2003)
7. CertiVox Corporation. CertiVox MIRACL SDK. Source code (June 2012), available for download at http://www.certivox.com
8. Crossbow Technology, Inc. MICAz Wireless Measurement System (2006), Data sheet, available for download at
http://www.xbow.com/Products/Product_pdf_files/
Wireless_pdf/MICAz_Datasheet.pdf

9. de Meulenaer, G., Standaert, F.-X.: Stealthy compromise of wireless sensor nodes with power analysis attacks. In: Chatzimisios, P., Verikoukis, C., Santamaría, I., Laddomada, M., Hoffmann, O. (eds.) MOBILIGHT 2010. LNICST, vol. 45, pp. 229–242. Springer, Heidelberg (2010)
10. Fouque, P.-A., Lercier, R., Réal, D., Valette, F.: Fault attack on elliptic curve Montgomery ladder implementation. In: Breveglieri, L., Gueron, S., Koren, I., Naccache, D., Seifert, J.-P. (eds.) Proceedings of the 5th International Workshop on Fault Diagnosis and Tolerance in Cryptography (FDTC 2008), pp. 92–98. IEEE Computer Society Press (2008)
11. Großschädl, J.: TinySA: A security architecture for wireless sensor networks. In: Diot, C., Ammar, M., Sá da Costa, C., Lopes, R.J., Leitão, A.R., Feamster, N., Teixeira, R. (eds.) Proceedings of the 2nd International Conference on Emerging Networking Experiments and Technologies (CoNEXT 2006), pp. 288–289. ACM Press (2006)
12. Großschädl, J., Hudler, M., Koschuch, M., Krüger, M., Szekely, A.: Smart elliptic curve cryptography for smart dust. In: Zhang, X., Qiao, D. (eds.) QShine 2010. LNICST, vol. 74, pp. 623–634. Springer, Heidelberg (2012)
13. Gura, N., Patel, A., Wander, A., Eberle, H., Shantz, S.C.: Comparing elliptic curve cryptography and RSA on 8-bit cPUs. In: Joye, M., Quisquater, J.-J. (eds.) CHES 2004. LNCS, vol. 3156, pp. 119–132. Springer, Heidelberg (2004)
14. Hamburg, M.: Fast and compact elliptic-curve cryptography. Cryptology ePrint Archive, Report 2012/309 (2012), http://eprint.iacr.org
15. Hankerson, D.R., Menezes, A.J., Vanstone, S.A.: Guide to Elliptic Curve Cryptography. Springer (2004)
16. Hisil, H., Wong, K.K.-H., Carter, G., Dawson, E.: Twisted Edwards curves revisited. In: Pieprzyk, J. (ed.) ASIACRYPT 2008. LNCS, vol. 5350, pp. 326–343. Springer, Heidelberg (2008)
17. Hutter, M., Schwabe, P.: NaCl on 8-bit AVR microcontrollers. In: Youssef, A., Nitaj, A., Hassanien, A.E. (eds.) AFRICACRYPT 2013. LNCS, vol. 7918, pp. 156–172. Springer, Heidelberg (2013)
18. Itoh, T., Tsujii, S.: A fast algorithm for computing multiplicative inverses in $GF(2^m)$ using normal bases. Information and Computation 78(3), 171–177 (1988)
19. Joye, M., Tunstall, M.: Exponent recoding and regular exponentiation algorithms. In: Preneel, B. (ed.) AFRICACRYPT 2009. LNCS, vol. 5580, pp. 334–349. Springer, Heidelberg (2009)
20. Joye, M., Yen, S.-M.: The Montgomery Powering Ladder. In: Kaliski Jr., B.S., Koç, Ç.K., Paar, C. (eds.) CHES 2002. LNCS, vol. 2523, pp. 291–302. Springer, Heidelberg (2003)
21. Lederer, C., Mader, R., Koschuch, M., Großschädl, J., Szekely, A., Tillich, S.: Energy-efficient implementation of ECDH key exchange for wireless sensor networks. In: Markowitch, O., Bilas, A., Hoepman, J.-H., Mitchell, C.J., Quisquater, J.-J. (eds.) Information Security Theory and Practice. LNCS, vol. 5746, pp. 112–127. Springer, Heidelberg (2009)
22. Lee, J., Son, S.H., Singhal, M.: Design of an architecture for multiple security levels in wireless sensor networks. In: Proceedings of the 7th International Conference on Networked Sensing Systems (INSS 2010), pp. 107–114. IEEE (2010)
23. Liu, A., Ning, P.: TinyECC: A configurable library for elliptic curve cryptography in wireless sensor networks. In: Proceedings of the 7th International Conference on Information Processing in Sensor Networks (IPSN 2008), pp. 245–256. IEEE Computer Society Press (2008)

24. Liu, Z., Großschädl, J., Wong, D.S.: Low-weight primes for lightweight elliptic curve cryptography on 8-bit AVR processors. In: Lin, D., Xu, S., Yung, M. (eds.) Information Security and Cryptology — INSCRYPT 2013. LNCS (2014)
25. Lopez, J., Zhou, J.: Wireless Sensor Network Security. Cryptology and Information Security Series, vol. 1. IOS Press (2008)
26. Montgomery, P.L.: Modular multiplication without trial division. Mathematics of Computation 44(170), 519–521 (1985)
27. Montgomery, P.L.: Speeding the Pollard and elliptic curve methods of factorization. Mathematics of Computation 48(177), 243–264 (1987)
28. Naccache, D., Smart, N.P., Stern, J.: Projective coordinates leak. In: Cachin, C., Camenisch, J.L. (eds.) EUROCRYPT 2004. LNCS, vol. 3027, pp. 257–267. Springer, Heidelberg (2004)
29. Okeya, K., Kurumatani, H., Sakurai, K.: Elliptic curves with the montgomery-form and their cryptographic applications. In: Imai, H., Zheng, Y. (eds.) PKC 2000. LNCS, vol. 1751, pp. 238–257. Springer, Heidelberg (2000)
30. Slijepcevic, S., Potkonjak, M., Tsiatsis, V., Zimbeck, S., Srivastava, M.B.: On communication security in wireless ad-hoc sensor networks. In: Proceedings of the 11th IEEE International Workshops on Enabling Technologies: Infrastructure for Collaborative Enterprises (WET ICE 2002). IEEE Computer Society Press (2002)
31. Szczechowiak, P., Oliveira, L.B., Scott, M., Collier, M., Dahab, R.: NanoECC: Testing the limits of elliptic curve cryptography in sensor networks. In: Verdone, R. (ed.) EWSN 2008. LNCS, vol. 4913, pp. 305–320. Springer, Heidelberg (2008)
32. Ugus, O., Westhoff, D., Laue, R., Shoufan, A., Huss, S.A.: Optimized implementation of elliptic curve based additive homomorphic encryption for wireless sensor networks. In: Wolf, T., Parameswaran, S. (eds.) Proceedings of the 2nd Workshop on Embedded Systems Security (WESS 2007), pp. 11–16 (2007), http://arxiv.org/abs/0903.3900
33. Wang, H., Li, Q.: Efficient implementation of public key cryptosystems on mote sensors (Short paper). In: Ning, P., Qing, S., Li, N. (eds.) ICICS 2006. LNCS, vol. 4307, pp. 519–528. Springer, Heidelberg (2006)
34. Zhang, Y., Großschädl, J.: Efficient prime-field arithmetic for elliptic curve cryptography on wireless sensor nodes. In: Proceedings of the 1st International Conference on Computer Science and Network Technology (ICCSNT 2011), vol. 1, pp. 459–466. IEEE (2011)

BackRef: Accountability in Anonymous Communication Networks

Michael Backes[1,3], Jeremy Clark[2], Aniket Kate[1], Milivoj Simeonovski[1], and Peter Druschel[3]

[1] Saarland University, Germany
[2] Concordia University, Canada
[3] Max Planck Institute for Software Systems (MPI-SWS), Germany

Abstract. Many anonymous communication networks (ACNs) rely on routing traffic through a sequence of proxy nodes to obfuscate the originator of the traffic. Without an accountability mechanism, exit proxy nodes may become embroiled in a criminal investigation if originators commit criminal actions through the ACN. We present BACKREF, a generic mechanism for ACNs that provides practical repudiation for the proxy nodes by tracing back the selected outbound traffic to the predecessor node (but not in the forward direction) through a cryptographically verifiable chain. It also provides an option for full (or partial) traceability back to the entry node or even to the corresponding originator when all intermediate nodes are cooperating. Moreover, to maintain a good balance between anonymity and accountability, the protocol incorporates whitelist directories at exit proxy nodes. BACKREF offers improved deployability over the related work, and introduces a novel concept of pseudonymous signatures that may be of independent interest.

We exemplify the utility of BACKREF by integrating it into the onion routing (OR) protocol, and examine its deployability by considering several system-level aspects. We also present the security definitions for the BACKREF system (namely, anonymity, backward traceability, no forward traceability, and no false accusation) and conduct a formal security analysis of the OR protocol with BACKREF using ProVerif, an automated cryptographic protocol verifier, establishing the aforementioned security properties against a strong adversarial model.

Keywords: anonymity, malicious users, accountability, repudiation, traceability, formal verification.

1 Introduction

Anonymous communication networks (ACNs) are designed to hide the originator of each message within a larger set of users. In some systems, like DC-Nets [1] and Dissent [2], the message emerges from aggregating all participants' messages. In other systems, like onion routing [3], mix networks [4], and peer-to-peer anonymous communication networks [5], messages are routed through volunteer nodes

I. Boureanu, P. Owesarski, and S. Vaudenay (Eds.): ACNS 2014, LNCS 8479, pp. 380–400, 2014.

that act as privacy-preserving proxies for the users' messages. We call this latter class proxy-based ACNs and concentrate on it henceforth.

Proxy-based ACNs provide a powerful service to their users, and correspondingly they have been the most successful ACNs so far [6,7]. However the nature of the properties of the technology can sometimes be harmful for the nodes serving as proxies. If a network user's online communication results in a criminal investigation or a cause of action, the last entity to forward the traffic may become embroiled in the proceedings [8,9], whether as the suspect/defendant or as a third party with evidence. While repudiation in the form of a partial or full traceability has never been a component of any widely-deployed ACN, it may become the case that new anonymity networks, or a changing political climate, initiate an interest in providing a verifiable trace to users who misuse anonymity networks according to laws or terms of service.

While several proposals [10,11,12,13,14,15,16] have been made to tackle or at least to mitigate this problem under the umbrella term of *accountable anonymity*, as we discuss in the next section some of them are broken, while others are not scalable enough for deploying in low latency ACNs.

Our Contributions. In this work, we design BACKREF, a novel practical repudiation mechanism for anonymous communication, which has advantages in terms of deployability and efficiency over the literature. To assist in the design of BACKREF, we propose a concept of pseudonymous signatures (§3), which employ pseudonyms (or half Diffie-Hellman exponents) as temporary public keys (and corresponding temporary secrets) employed or employable in almost all ACNs for signing messages. These pseudonym signatures are used to create a verifiable *pseudonym-linkability* mechanism where any proxy node within the route or path, *when required*, can verifiably reveal its predecessor node in time-bound manner. We use this property to design a novel repudiation mechanism (§4), which allows each proxy node, in cooperation with the network, to issue a cryptographic guarantee that a selected traffic flow can be traced back to its originator (*i.e.*, predecessor node) while maintaining the eventual forward secrecy of the system. Unlike the related work, which largely relies on group signatures and/or anonymous credentials, BACKREF avoids the logistical difficulties of organizing users into groups and arranging a shared group key, and does not require access to a trusted party to issue credentials. While BACKREF is applicable to all proxy-based ACNs, we illustrate its utility by applying it to the onion routing (OR) protocol. We observe that it introduces a small computational overhead and does not affect the performance of the underlying OR protocol (§5). BACKREF also includes a *whitelisting* option; *i.e.*, if an exit node considers traceability to one or more web-services unnecessary, then it can include those services in a *whitelist* directory such that accesses to those are not logged.

We formally define the important security properties of the BACKREF network (§6). In particular, we formalize anonymity and no forward traceability as observational equivalence relations, and backward traceability and no false accusation as trace properties. We conduct a formal security analysis of BACKREF using ProVerif, an automated cryptographic protocol verifier, establishing the aforementioned security and privacy properties against a strong adversarial model. We believe both the definitions and the security analysis are of independent interest, since they are the first for the OR protocol.

2   Background and Related Work

Anonymous communication networks (ACNs) aim at protecting personally identifiable information (PII), in particular the network addresses of the communicating parties by hiding correlation between input and output messages at one or more network entities. For this purpose, the ACN protocols employ techniques such as using a series of intermediate routers and layered encryptions to obfuscate the source of a communication, and adding fake traffic to make the 'real' communication difficult to extract.

Anonymous Communication Protocols. Single-hop proxy servers, which relay traffic flows, enable a simple form of anonymous communication. However anonymity in this case requires, at a minimum, that the proxy is trustworthy and not compromised, and this approach does not protect the anonymity of senders if the adversary inspects traffic through the proxy [17]. Even with the use of encryption between the sender and proxy server, timing attacks can be used to correlate flows.

Starting with Chaum [4], several ACN technologies have been developed in the last thirty years to provide stronger anonymity not dependent on a single entity [6,3,7,2,1,18,19,20,21]. Among these, mix networks [4,7] and onion routing [6] have arguably been most successful. Both offer user anonymity, relationship anonymity and unlinkability [22], but they obtain these properties through differing assumptions and techniques.

An onion routing (OR) infrastructure involves a set of *routers* (or *OR nodes*) that relay traffic, a *directory service* providing status information for OR nodes, and *users*. Users benefit from anonymous access by constructing a *circuit*—a small ordered subset of OR nodes—and routing traffic through it sequentially. The crucial property for anonymity is that an OR node within the built circuit is not able to identify any portion of the circuit other than its predecessor and successor. The user sends messages (to the first OR node in the circuit) in a form of an *onion*—a data structure multiply encrypted by symmetric session keys (one encryption layer per node in the circuit). The symmetric keys are negotiated during an initial *circuit construction* phase. This is followed by a second phase of *low latency* communication (opening and closing streams) through the constructed circuit for the session duration. An OR network does not aim at providing anonymity and unlinkability against a global passive observer, which in theory can analyze end-to-end traffic flow. Instead, it assumes an adversary that adaptively compromises a small fraction of OR nodes and controls a small fraction of the network.

A mix network achieves anonymity by relaying messages through a path of mix nodes (or mixes) in a latency-tolerant manner. The user encrypts a message to be partially decrypted by each mix along the path. Mixes accept a batch of encrypted messages, which are partially decrypted, randomly permuted, and forwarded. Unlike onion routing, an observer is unable to correlate incoming and outgoing messages at the mix; thus, mix networks provide anonymity against a powerful global passive adversary. In fact, as long as a single mix in the user's path remains uncompromised, the message will maintain some anonymity.

Accountable Anonymity Mechanisms. The literature has examined several approaches for adding accountability to ACN technologies, allowing misbehaving users to be selectively traced [10,11,12], exit nodes to deny originating traffic it forwards [13,14], misbehaving users to be banned [15,16], and misbehaving participants to be discovered [2,23,24]. All of these approaches either require users to obtain credentials or do not extend to interactive, low-latency, internet-scale ACNs. A number also partition users into subgroups, which reduces anonymity and requires a group manager. BACKREF does not require credentials, subgroups, and is compatible with low-latency ACNs like onion routing, adding minimal overhead.

Kopsell et al. [10] propose traceability through threshold group signatures. A user logs into the system to join a group, signs messages with a group signature, and a group manager is empowered to revoke anonymity. The system also introduces an external proxy to inspect all outbound traffic for correct signatures and protocol compliance. The inspector has been criticized for centralizing traffic flows, which enables DOS, censorship, and increases observability [25].

Von Ahn et al. [11] also use group signatures as the basis for a general transformation for traceability in ACNs and illustrate it with DC networks. Users are required to register as members of a group capable of sending messages through the network. Our solution can be viewed as a follow-up to this paper, with a concentration on deployability: we do not require users to be organized into groups or introduce new entities, and we concentrate on onion routing.

Diaz and Preneel [12] achieve traceability through issuing anonymous credentials to users and utilizing a traitor tracing scheme to revoke anonymity. It is tailored to high-latency mix networks and requires a trusted authority to issue credentials—both impede deployability. Danezis and Sassaman [25] demonstrate a bypass attack on this and the Kopsell et al. scheme [10]. The attack is based on the protocols' assumption that there can be no leakage of information from inside the channel to the world unless it passes through the verification step. Our protocol does not rely on such a strong assumption, namely any exit node (or any node who leaks the information) with enabled BACKREF can always activate the repudiation mechanism and shift liability to its predecessor node.

Short of revoking the anonymity of misbehaving users, techniques have been proposed to at least allow exit nodes to deny originating the traffic. Golle [13] and Clark et al. [14] pursue this goal, with the former being specific to high-latency mix networks and the latter requiring anonymous credentials. Tor offers a service called ExoneraTor [26] that provides a record of which nodes were online at a given time, but it does not explicitly prove that a given traffic flow originated from Tor. Other techniques, such as Nymble [15] and its successors (see a survey [16]), enable users to be banned. However these systems inherently require some form of credential or pseudonym infrastructure for the users, and also require web-servers to verify user requests. Finally, Dissent [2] and its successors [23,24] presents an interesting approach for accountable anonymous communication for DC Nets [1], however even when highly optimized [23], DC Nets are not competitive for internet-scale application.

3   Design Overview

In this section we describe our threat model and system goals, and present our key idea and design rationale.

3.1   Threat Model and System Goals

We consider the same threat model as the underlying ACN in which we wish to incorporate the BACKREF mechanism. Our active adversary $\mathcal{A}$ aims at breaking some anonymity property by determining the ultimate source and/or destination of a communication stream or breaking unlinkability by linking two communication streams of the same user. We assume that some, but not all, of the nodes in the path of the communication stream are compromised by the adversary $\mathcal{A}$, who knows all their secret values, and is able to fully control their functionalities. For high latency ACNs like mix networks, we assume that the adversary can also observe all traffic in the network, as well as intercept and inject arbitrary messages, while for low latency ACNs like onion routing, we assume the adversary can observe, intercept, and inject traffic in some parts of the network.

While maintaining the anonymity and unlinkability properties of an ACN, we wish to achieve the following goals when incorporating BACKREF in the ACN:

Repudiation: For a communication stream flowing through a node, the node operator should be able to prove that the stream is coming from another predecessor node or user.

Backward traceability: Starting from an exit node of a path (or circuit), it should be possible to trace the source of a communication stream back to the entry node when all nodes in the path verifiably reveal their predecessors.

No forward traceability: For a compromised node, it should not be possible for the adversary $\mathcal{A}$ to use BACKREF to verifiably trace its successor in any completed anonymous communication session through it.

No false accusation: It should not be possible for a compromised node to corrupt the BACKREF mechanism to trace a communication stream:

   1. to a path different from the path employed for the stream, and
   2. to a node other than its predecessor in the path.

Non-goals. We expect our accountability notion to be reactive in nature. We do not aim at proactive accountability and do not try to stop an illegal activity in an ACN in a proactive manner, as we believe perfect black-listing of web urls and content to be an infeasible task. Moreover, some nodes may choose not to follow the BACKREF mechanism locally (e.g., they may not maintain

Fig. 1. Backward Traceability Verification

or share the required evidence logs), and full backward traceability cannot be ensured in those situations; nevertheless, the cooperating nodes can still prove their innocence in a verifiable manner.

Due to its reactive nature, our repudiation mechanism inherently requires evidence logs containing verifiable routing information. Encrypting these logs and regularly rotating the corresponding keys can provide us eventual forward secrecy [27]. However, we cannot aim for *immediate* forward secrecy due to the inherently *eventual* forward secret nature of the encryption mechanism.

3.2 Design Rationale and Key Idea

Fig. 1 presents a general expected architecture to achieve the above mentioned goals. It is clear the network level logs and the currently cryptographic mechanism in the ACNs cannot be used for verifiably backward traceability purpose as they cannot stop false accusations (or traceability) by compromised nodes: a compromised node can tamper with its logs to intermix two different ACN paths as there is no cryptographic association between different parts of an ACN path.

We observe that almost all OR protocols [19,27,28,29,30,31] (except TAP) and mix network protocols [32,33,34,20,7,21] employ (or can employ[1]) an element of a cyclic group of prime order satisfying some (version of) Diffie-Hellman assumption as an authentication challenges or randomization element per node in the path. In particular, it can be represented as $X = g^x$, where g is a generator of a cyclic group $\mathbb{G}$ of prime order p with the security parameter κ and $x \in_R \mathbb{Z}_p$ is a random secret value known only to the user. This element is used by each node on the path to derive a secret that is shared with the user and is used to extract a set of (session) keys for encryption and integrity protection. In the anonymity literature, these authentication challenges X are known as user *pseudonyms*.

The key idea of our BACKREF mechanism is to use these pseudonyms $X = g^x$ and the corresponding secret keys x as signing key pairs to sign pseudonym's for successor nodes at entry and middle nodes, and to sign the communication stream headers at the exit nodes. Signatures that use (x, g^x) as the signing key pair are referred to as *pseudonym signatures*. As pseudonyms are generated independently for every single node, and the corresponding secret exponents are random elements of $\mathbb{Z}_p$, they do not reveal the user's identity. Moreover, it also is not possible to link two or more pseudonyms to a single identity. Therefore,

---

[1] Although some these have been defined using RSA encryptions, as discussed in [20] they can be modified to work in the discrete logarithm (DL) setting.

pseudonym signatures become particularly useful in our BACKREF mechanism, where users utilize them to sign messages without being identified by the verifier.

We can employ a CMA-secure [35] signature scheme against a computationally bounded adversary (with the security parameter κ) such that, along with the usual existential unforgeability, the resultant pseudonym signature scheme satisfies the following property:

Unconditional Signer Anonymity: The adversary cannot determine a signer's identity, even if it is allowed to obtain signatures on an unbounded number of messages of its choice.

We use such temporary signing key pairs (or pseudonym signatures) to sign consecutively employed pseudonyms in an ACN path and the web communication requests leaving the ACN path. Pseudonym signatures provide linkability between the employed pseudonyms and the communicated message on an ACN path. However, these pseudonyms are not sufficient to link the node employed in the ACN path: for a pseudonym received by a node, its predecessor node can always deny sending the pseudonym in the first place. We solve this problem by introducing *endorsement signatures*: We assume that every node signs the pseudonym while sending it to the successor so that it cannot plausibly deny this transfer during backward tracing.

3.3   Scope of Solution

To understand the scope of BACKREF, first consider traceability in the context of the simplest ACN: a single-hop proxy. Any traceability mechanism from the literature implicitly assumes a solution to the problem of how users can be traced through a simple proxy. We dub this the 'last mile' problem. The proxy can keep logs, but this requires a trusted proxy. Alternatively the ISP could observe and log relevant details about traffic to the proxy, requiring trust in the ISP. The solution more typically used in the literature is to assume individual users have digital credentials or signing keys—essentially some form of PKI is in place to certify the keys of individual users. [10,11,12,13,14]

None of these last mile solutions are particularly attractive. The assumption of a PKI provides the best distribution of trust but short-term deployment appears infeasible. We believe the involvement of ISPs is the most readily deployable. Such a solution involves an ISP with a packet attestation mechanism [36] which acts as a trusted party capable of proving the existence of a particular communication. We discuss the packet attestation mechanism further in §5.

For selected traffic flows, BACKREF provides traceability to the entrance node. This is effectively equivalent to reducing the strong anonymity of a distributed cryptographic ACN to the weak anonymity of a single hop proxy. For full traceability, we then must address the 'last mile' problem: tracing the flow back to the individual sender. Thus BACKREF is not a full traceability mechanism, but rather an essential component that can be composed with any *systems* solution to the last mile problem. While we later discuss a solution that involves ISPs, we emphasize that BACKREF itself is concentrated on, arguably, the more difficult problem of offering ensured traceability within the ACN.

4 Repudiation (or Traceability)

In this section, we present our BACKREF repudiation scheme. For ease of exposition, we include our scheme in an OR protocol instead of including it in the generic ACN protocol. Nevertheless, our scheme is applicable to almost all ACNs mentioned in §3.2. We start our discussion with a brief overview of the OR protocol in the Tor notions [37]. We then discuss the protocol flow for BACKREF and describe our cryptographic components.

4.1 The OR Protocol: Overview

The OR protocol is defined in two phases: circuit construction and streams relay.

OR Circuit Construction. The circuit construction phase involves the user onion proxy (OP) randomly selecting a short circuit of (*e.g.*, 3) OR nodes, and negotiating a session key with each selected OR node using one-way authenticated key exchange (1W-AKE) [31] such as the ntor protocol. When a user wants to create a circuit with an OR node N_1, she runs the *Initiate* procedure of the ntor protocol to generate and send an authentication challenge to N_1. Node N_1 then runs the respond procedure and returns the authentication response. Finally, the user uses the *ComputeKey* procedure of ntor along with the response to authenticate N_1 and to compute a session key with it. To extend the circuit further, the user sends an extend request to N_1 specifying the address of the next node N_2 and a new ntor authentication challenge for N_2. The process continues until the user exchanges the key with the exit node N_3.

Relaying Streams. Once a circuit (denoted as $\langle U \leftrightarrow N_1 \leftrightarrow N_2 \leftrightarrow N_3 \rangle$) has been constructed through N_1, N_2 and N_3, the user-client U routes traffic through the circuit using onion-wrapping *WrOn* and onion-unwrapping *UnwrOn* procedures. *WrOn* creates a layered encryption of a payload (plaintext or onion) given an ordered list of (three) session keys. *UnwrOn* removes one or more layers of encryptions from an onion to output a plaintext or an onion given an input onion and a ordered list of one or more session keys. To reduce latency, many of the user's communication streams employ the same circuit [6].

The structure and components of communication streams may vary with the network protocol. For ease of exposition, we assume the OR network uses TCP-based communication in the same way as Tor, but our schemes can easily be adapted for other types of communication streams.

In Tor, the communication between the user's TCP-based application and her Tor proxy takes place via SOCKS. To open a communication stream (i.e., to start a TCP connection to some web server and port), the user proxy sends a *relay begin* cell (or packet) over the circuit to the exit node N_3. When N_3

receives the TCP request, it makes a standard TCP handshake with the web server. Once the connection is established, N_3 responds to the user with a *relay connected* cell. The user then forwards all TCP stream requests for the server as *relay data* cells to the circuit. (See [6,37] for a detailed explanation.)

4.2   The BackRef Protocol Flow

Consider a user U who wishes to construct an OR circuit $\langle U \leftrightarrow N_1 \leftrightarrow N_2 \leftrightarrow N_3 \rangle$, and use it to send communication stream m. BACKREF adds the repudiation mechanism as a layer on the top of the existing OR protocol. We assume that every OR node possesses a signing (private) key for which the corresponding verification (public) key is publicly available through the OR directory service.

The corresponding OR protocol with the BACKREF scheme works according to the following five steps:

1. Circuit Construction with an Entry Node: The user U creates a circuit with the entry node N_1 using the ntor protocol. If the user is an OR node, then it endorses its pseudonym X_1 by signing it with its public key and sending the signature along with X_1.

However, if the user U is not an OR node, it cannot endorse the pseudonym X_1 as no public-key infrastructure (PKI) or credential system is available to him. We solve this systems problem by entrusting the ISP with a packet attestation mechanism [36] such that the ISP can prove that a pseudonym was sent by U to N_1. We discuss the packet attestation mechanism in §5.

2. Circuit Extension: To extend a circuit to N_2, U generates a new pseudonym X_2 of an ntor instance, signs X_2 and the current timestamp with the secret value x_1 associated with X_1, and sends an extend request to N_1 along with the identifier for N_2, $\{X_2 \| \mathrm{ts}_{x_2}\}_{\sigma_{X_1}}$ and a timestamp ts_{x_2}. Notice that the extension request is encrypted by a symmetric session key negotiated between U and N_1.

Upon receiving a message, N_1 decrypts and verifies $\{X_2 \| \mathrm{ts}_{x_2}\}_{\sigma_{X_1}}$ using the previously received pseudonym X_1 and timestamp. We call this verification *pseudonyms linkability verification*. If the signature is valid, it creates an evidence record as discussed in Step 4, signs X_2 using its private key to generate $\{X_2 \| \mathrm{ts}_2\}_{\sigma_{sk_1}}$ and sends a circuit create request to the node N_2 with $\{X_2 \| \mathrm{ts}_2\}_{\sigma_{sk_1}}$.

Node N_2, upon receiving a circuit creation request along with $\{X_2 \| ts_2\}_{\sigma_{sk_1}}$, verifies the signature. Upon a successful verification, it replies to N_1 with an ntor authentication response for the OR key agreement and generates the OR session key for its session with (unknown) user U. N_1 sends the authentication response back to U using their OR session, who then computes the session key with N_2 and continues to build its circuit to N_3 in a similar fashion.

Notice that we carefully avoid any conceptual modification of the OR circuit construction protocol; the above signature generation and verification steps are the only adjustments that BACKREF makes to this protocol.

3. Stream Verification: Once a circuit $\langle U \leftrightarrow N_1 \leftrightarrow N_2 \leftrightarrow N_3 \rangle$ has been established, the user U can utilize it to send her web stream requests. To open a

TCP connection, the user sends a *relay begin* cell to the exit node N_3 through the circuit. The user U includes a pseudonym signature (or stream request signature) on the cell contents signed with the secret exponent x_3 of X_3. The user also includes a timestamp in her stream request. When the *relay* cell reaches the exit node N_3, the exit node verifies the pseudonym signature with X_3. Once the verification is successful and the timestamp is current, N_3 creates the evidence log (Step 4) and proceeds with the TCP handshake to the destination server. The *relay* stream request is discarded otherwise.

This stream verification helps N_3 to prove linkability between its handshakes with the destination server and the pseudonym X_3 it has received from N_2. When a whitelist directory exists, the exit node first consults the directory and if the request (*i.e.*, web stream request) is whitelisted, the exit node just forwards it to the destination server. In such a case, the exit node does not require any signature verification and also does not create an evidence log. We further discuss the server whitelisting in §4.4.

4. Log Generation: After every successful pseudonym linkability or stream verification, the evidence record is created. A pseudonym linkability verification evidence record associates linkability between two pseudonyms X_i and X_{i+1} and an endorsement signature on X_i, while a stream verification evidence record associates a stream verification with an endorsement signature on X_3 for N_3.

5. Repudiation or Traceability: The verifier contacts the exit node N_3 with the request information (e.g., IP address, port number, and timestamp) for a malicious stream coming out of the exit node N_3. The operator of N_3 can determine a record using the stream request information. This evidence record verifiably reveals the identity of the middle node N_2.

As an *optional* next step, using the evidence records, it is possible for N_2 to verifiably reveal the identity of its predecessor N_1. Then, the last mile of a full traceability is to reach from N_1 to the user U in a verifiable manner using the record on N_1 and the request information on the ISP [36]. When the user U is an OR node a record at N_1 is sufficient and the last mile problem does not exist.

4.3 Cryptographic Details

BLS Signatures. For pseudonym and endorsement signatures, we use the short signature scheme of Boneh, Lynn and Shacham (BLS) [38]. Consider two Gap co-Diffie-Hellman groups (or co-GDH group) $\mathbb{G}_1$ and $\mathbb{G}_2$ and a multiplicative cyclic group $\mathbb{G}_T$, all of the same prime order p, associated by a bilinear map [39] $e : \mathbb{G}_1 \times \mathbb{G}_2 \to \mathbb{G}_T$.

Let g_1, g_2, and g_T be generators for $\mathbb{G}_1$, $\mathbb{G}_2$, and $\mathbb{G}_T$ respectively and let a full-domain hash function $H : \{0,1\}^* \to \mathbb{G}_1$. The BLS signature scheme [38] comprises following three algorithms:

Key Generation: Choose random $sk \in_R \mathbb{Z}_p$ and compute $pk = g_2^{sk}$. The private key is sk, and the public key is pk.

Signing: Given a private key $pk \in \mathbb{Z}_p$, and a message $m \in \{0,1\}^*$, compute $h = H(m) \in \mathbb{G}_1$ and signature $\sigma = h^{sk}$, where $\sigma \in \mathbb{G}_1$.

Verification: Given a public key $pk \in \mathbb{G}_2$, message $m \in \{0,1\}^*$, and signature $\sigma \in \mathbb{G}_1$, compute $h = H(m) \in \mathbb{G}_1$ and verify that (g_2, pk, h, σ) is a valid co-Diffie-Hellman tuple.

We choose the BLS signature scheme due to the shorter size of their signatures; however, if signing and verification efficiency is more important, we can choose faster signature schemes such as [40].

Circuit Extension. To extend the circuit $\langle U \leftrightarrow N_1 \rangle$ to the next hop N_2, the user U chooses $x_2 \in_R \mathbb{Z}_p$ and generates a pseudonym $X_2 = g_2^{x_2}$, where $g_2 \in \mathbb{G}_2$. U then signs the pseudonym X_2 and the current timestamp[2] value ts_{x_2} with pseudonym X_1 as public key to obtain a signature $\sigma_{X_1} = H(X_2\|\text{ts}_{x_2})^{x_1}$. Upon receiving the signed pseudonym $\{X_2\|\text{ts}_{x_2}\}_{\sigma_{X_1}}$ along with the timestamp ts_{x_2}, the node N_1 checks if the timestamp is current and verifies it as follows:

$$e(H(X_2\|\text{ts}_{x_2}), X_1) \stackrel{?}{=} e(\sigma_{X_1}, g_2)$$

Pseudonym Endorsement. After successful verification, N_1 creates an endorsement signature $\sigma_1 = H(X_2\|\text{ts}_2)^{sk_1}$ for pseudonym X_2 and current timestamp ts_2 using its signing key sk_1 and sends it along with X_2 and ts_2 to N_2.

The node N_2 then follows the pseudonym endorsement step. Upon receiving the signed pseudonym $\{X_2\|\text{ts}_2\}_{\sigma_1}$, N_2 verifies it as follows:

$$e(H(X_2\|\text{ts}_2), pk_1) \stackrel{?}{=} e(\sigma_1, g_2).$$

On a successful verification, N_2 continues with the OR protocol.

Stream Verification. To generate a stream request signature, the user signs the stream request (*i.e.,* selected contents of the *relay begin* cell) using the pseudonym $X_3 = g_2^{x_3}$ where x_3 is the secret corresponding to X_3. For contents of the *relay* cell $m = \{\text{address}\|\text{port}\|\text{ts}_{x_m}\}$, the stream request signature σ_{X_3} is defined as $\sigma_{X_3} = H(m)^{x_3}$. The user sends the signature along with the *relay* cell and the current timestamp ts_{x_m} to the exit node through the already-built circuit.

Once the signed stream request reaches N_3, it verifies the signature as follows:

$$e(H(m), X_3) \stackrel{?}{=} e(\sigma_{X_3}, g_2).$$

Upon a successful verification, the exit node N_3 proceeds with the TCP handshake. A verified request allows the node to link X_3 and the request.

Note that when the destination server ensures an authenticated end-to-end connection with the user, stream verification of the stream request (*relay begin*) suffices; otherwise, the user should sign and the exit node should verify each *relay data* cell to avoid any content modification attack by the exit node.

Log Generation. After every successful pseudonym or stream verification, an evidence record is added to the evidence log. The evidence records differ with nodes' positions within a circuit, and we define two types of evidence logs.

---

[2] Here, in presence of evidence records, we require only coarse-grained timestamps (e.g., dd/mm/yyyy:hh) for replay prevention. Moreover, in the low-latency ACNs, we avoid fine-grained timestamps as they may lead to (offline) traffic-analysis attacks.

Exit node log: For every successful stream verification, an evidence record is added to the evidence log at the exit node. A single evidence record consists of the signature on X_3 (i.e., $\{X_3\|ts_3\}_{\sigma_2}$), and the stream request $H(m)$ coupled by the pseudonym signature $\{m\}_{\sigma_{X_3}}$ and the timestamp ts_{x_m}.

Middle and entry node log: The middle and entry node evidence record comprises two pseudonyms X_i, X_{i+1}, and a timestamp value $ts_{x_{i+1}}$ coupled with the appropriate signatures and the IP address of N_{i-1}. The pseudonym X_i is coupled with an endorsement signature $\{X_i\|ts_i\}_{\sigma_{i-1}}$ from node N_{i-1}, and the pseudonym X_{i+1} is coupled by a pseudonym signature $\{X_{i+1}\|ts_{x+1}\}_{\sigma_{X_i}}$. When the user is not an OR node and does not posse a verifiable signature key pair, the corresponding record at N_1 consists of a signed pseudonym $\{X_2\|ts_{x_2}\}_{\sigma_{X_1}}$, pseudonym X_1, timestamp value ts_{x_2}, and the IP of the user.

Repudiation or Traceability. Given the server logs of a stream request, an evidence record corresponding to the stream request can be obtained. In the first step, it is checked whether the timestamp matches the stream request under observation. In the next step, the association between the stream request and the pseudonym of the exit node X_3 is verified using the pseudonym signature. Then, the association of the pseudonym X_3 and N_2 is checked using the pseudonym endorsement signature. Given the pseudonym X_3 and a timestamp ts_{x_m}, the backward traceability verification at node N_2 is carried out as follows:

1. Do a lookup in the evidence log to locate the signed pseudonym $\{X_3\|ts_{x_3}\}_{\sigma_{X_2}}$ and the timestamp ts_{x_3}, where X_3 is the lookup index.
2. Compare the timestamps (ts_{x_m} and ts_{x_3}) under observation and prove the linkability between X_2 and X_3 by verifying the signature $\{X_3\|ts_{x_3}\}_{\sigma_{X_2}}$.
3. If verification succeeds, reveal the IP address of the node N_1 who has forwarded X_2 and verify $\{X_2\|ts_2\}_{\sigma_1}$ with pk_1.

The above three steps can be used repeatedly to reach the entry node. However, they cannot be used to verifiably reach the user if we do not assume any public key and credential infrastructure for the users. Instead, our protocol relies on the ISP between user U and N_1 to use packet attestation [36] to prove that the pseudonym X_1 was sent from U to N_1.

4.4   Exit Node Whitelisting Policies

To provide a good balance between anonymity and accountability, we include a whitelisting option for exit nodes. This option allows a user to avoid the complete verification and logging mechanisms if her destination is in the whitelist directory of her exit node. In particular, we categorize the destinations into two groups:

Whitelisted Destinations: For several destinations such as educational .edu websites, an exit node may find traceability to be unnecessary. The exit node includes such destinations in a whitelist directory such that, for these destinations, it does not require any endorsement and pseudonym signatures. Traffic sent to these whitelisted destinations through the circuit remains anonymous in the current ACNs sense as the sender does not have to employ BACKREF. In that case, to protect malicious user's access, such destinations may use end-to-end blacklisting systems such as Nymble [15] and its successors [16].

Non-listed Destinations: For destinations that are not listed in the exit-node whitelist directory, the user has to use BACKREF while building the circuit to it; otherwise, the exit node will drop her requests to the non-listed destinations.

We emphasize that BACKREF is *not* an "all-or-nothing" design alternative: it allows an ACN to conveniently disable the complete verification and logging mechanisms for some pre-selected destinations. In particular, an exit node with "Sorry, it is an anonymity network, no logs" opinion can still whitelist the whole Internet, while others employ BACKREF for non-whitelisted sites. The use of BackRef is transparent, and users can choose if they wish to use a BackRef node for their circuits.

5   Systems Aspects and Discussion

Communication Overhead. Communication overhead for BACKREF is minimal: every circuit creation, circuit extension, and stream request carries a 32 byte BLS signature and additional 4 byte timestamp.

Computation Overhead. In a system with BACKREF, every node has to verify a signature and generate another. Using the pairing-based cryptography (PBC) library, a BLS signature generation takes less than $1ms$ while a verification requires nearly $3ms$ for 128-bit security on a commodity PC with an Intel i5 quad-core processor with 3.3 GHz and 8 GB RAM. Signing and verification time (and correspondingly system load) can be further reduced using faster signature schemes (*e.g.,* [40]).

Log Storage. BACKREF requires nodes to maintain logs of cryptographic information for potential use by law enforcement. These logs are not innocuous, and the implications of publicly disclosing a record need to be considered. The specificity of the logs should be carefully designed to balance minimal disclosure of side-information (such as specific timings) while allowing flows to be uniquely identified. It must also be possible to reconstruct the logged data from the types of information available to law enforcement. The simplest entry would contain the destination IP, source (exit node) IP, a coarse timestamp, as well as the signature. Logs should be maintained for a pre-defined period and then erased.

No single party can hold the logs without entrusting this entity with the anonymity of all users. The OR nodes can retain the logs themselves. This, however, would require law enforcement to acquire the logs from every such node and consequently involve the nodes in the investigation—a scenario that may not be desirable. Furthermore, traceability exposes nodes of all types, not just exit nodes, to investigation. We are aware of a number of entities who deliberately run middle nodes in Tor to avoid this exposure. An alternative is to publish encrypted logs, where a distributed set of trustees share a decryption key and act as a liaison to law enforcement, while holding each other accountable by refusing to decrypt logs of users who have not violated the traceability policy. Such an entity acts in a similar fashion to the group manager schemes based on group signatures [11].

Non-cooperating Nodes. Given the geographic diversity of the ACNs, it is always possible that some proxy nodes will cooperate with the BACKREF mechanism, while others will not. The repudiation property of BACKREF ensures that a cooperating node always at least correctly shift liability to a non-cooperating node. Moreover, such a cooperating node may also *reactively* decide to block any future communication from the non-cooperating node as a policy.

Venturing the Last Mile. In the scenarios where full traceability is required, we need a mechanism for solving the last mile problem addressed in the previous sections. BACKREF does not introduce any PKI for the users, therefore our protocol has to rely on some trust mechanism to prove the linkability between the IP address of the user and the entry node pseudonym. For this purpose, we consider an ISP with a packet attestation mechanism [36] to be a proper solution that adds a small overhead for the existing ISP infrastructure and at the same time does not harm any of the properties provided by the ACN. In some countries there is an obligation for the ISPs to retain data that identify the user. In other countries the ISPs are not obligated by law, but it is nevertheless common practice. The protocol is designed in a way that the ISP has to attest only to the *ClientKeyExchange* message (this message is a part of the TLS establishing procedure, and also is public and not encrypted message) which is used to establish the initial TLS communication. This message does not reveal any sensitive information related to the identity of the user. By its design, we reuse this message as a pseudonym for the entry OR node.

6   Security Analysis

We conduct a formal security analysis of BACKREF. We model our protocol from §4 (in a restricted form) in the applied pi calculus [41] and verify its important properties, *i.e.*, anonymity, backward traceability, no forward traceability, and no false accusation with ProVerif [42], a state-of-the-art automated theorem prover that provides security guarantees for an unbounded number of protocol sessions.

We model backward traceability and no false accusation as trace properties, and anonymity and no forward traceability as observational equivalence relations. The employed ProVerf scripts as well as an extended version of the paper are available online [43],[44].

Basic Model. We model the OR protocol in the applied pi calculus to use circuits of length three (*i.e.*, one user and three nodes); the extension to additional nodes is straightforward. To prove different security properties we upgrade the model to use additional processes and events. To solve the last mile problem, our model involves an honest ISP which can prove the existence of a communication channel between the user and the entry node. This channel is modeled as private, preventing any ISP log forgeries. The cryptographic log collection model is designed in a decentralized way such that nodes retain the logs themselves in a table that is inaccessible to the adversary.

We model the flow of the pseudonyms and the onion, together with the corresponding verification. However, we do not model the underlying, crypto-graphically verified 1W-AKE ntor [31] protocol, and assume that the session key between the user and the selected OR process is exchanged securely. The attacker is a standard Dolev-Yao active adversary with full control over the public channels: It learns everything ever send on the network, and can create and insert messages on the public channels. It also controls network scheduling.

Backward Traceability. The goal of our protocol is to trace the source of the communication stream starting from an exit node. We verify that the property of backward traceability arrives from the correctness of the (backward) verification mechanism. The correctness property can be formalized in ProVerif as follows:

$$TraceUser(IP) \implies (LookupISP(X_1, IP) \implies (RevealPred(IP)) \implies$$
$$(RevealPred(ipN1)) \implies (RevealPred(ipN2)) \land CheckSig \land LookupN3(m))), \quad (1)$$

where the notation A $\implies$ B denotes the requirement that the event A must be preceded by a event B. In our protocol, the property says that the user U is traced if all nodes in the circuit verifiably trace their predecessors and the ISP solves the last mile problem. The traceability protocol P starts with the event $LookupN3(m)$ which means that for a given message m (stream request) the verifier consults the log, and if such a request exists, it checks the signature $CheckSig$. Finally, when all conditions are fulfilled, the verifier reveals the identity of the predecessor node $RevealPred(ipN2)$. This completes the nested correspondence $(CheckSig \land LookupN3(m) \land RevealPred(ipN2))$ which verifiably traces N_2. In a similar fashion, the verifier traces N_1 and U.

To solve the last mile problem, after the identity of U is revealed the verifier lookup into the evidence table of the ISP $(LookupISP)$ to prove the connection between the identity of the user IP and the pseudonym of the entry node X_1. If such a record exists, the event $TraceUser(IP)$ is executed.

Theorem: The trace property defined in equation (1) holds true for all possible executions of process P.

Proof. Automatically proven by ProVerif.   □

No False Accusation. There are two aspects associated with false accusations:
1. It should not be possible for a malicious node N_A to trace a communication stream to an OR node N_C other than to its predecessor in the corresponding circuit. Informally, to break this property, N_A has to be obtain a signature of N_C on a particular pseudonym associated with the circuit. This requires N_A to forge a signature for N_C, which is not possible due to the unforgeability property of the signature scheme.
2. It should not be possible for a malicious node N_A to trace a communication stream to a circuit C_1 other than the circuit C_2 employed for the communication stream. Consider a scenario where two concurrent circuits (C_1 and

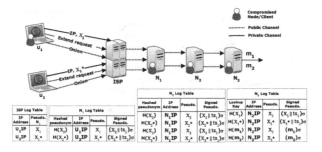

Fig. 2. No False Accusation adversarial model

C_2), established by two different users U_1 and U_2, pass through a malicious node N_A. Suppose that N_A collaborates with U_2 who is misbehaving and has used the OR network for criminal activities. To help U_2 by falsely accusing a different predecessor, N_A must forge two signatures: To link two pseudonyms X_{1i-1} and X_{2i} from circuits C_1 and C_2 respectively, N_A has to forge the pseudonym signature on X_{2i} with X_{1i-1} as a public key, or he has to know the temporal signing key pair for the predecessor in C_1.

Intuitively, the first case is ruled out by the unforgeability property of the signature scheme. We model the later case as a trace property. Here, even when N_A collaborates with U_2, it cannot forge the signed pseudonym received from its predecessor. The property remains intact as long as one of the nodes on C_1 and the packet attesting ISP [36] remain uncompromised. In the absence of a PKI or credential system for users, the last condition is unavoidable.

We formalize and verify the latter case of the property in an adversarial model where the attacker has compromised one user (U_1 or U_2). Figure 2 provide a graphical representation of the protocol P. We upgrade the basic model involving additional user U_2 who sends additional message m_2. As mentioned before, to simulate the packet attesting mechanism [36] we involve a honest ISP between the user and the entry node. The ISP only collects data that identifies the user (IP address of the user) and the pseudonym for the entry node (X_1), which is send in plain-text. The adversary does not have access to the log stored by the ISP. We want to verify that for all protocol executions the request m_i cannot be associated with any user U_i other than the originator. To formalize the property in ProVerif, we model security-related protocol events with logical predicates. The event CorrISP defines the point of the protocol where the ISP is corrupted. In absence of support for timestamp in ProVerif, we model timestamp values ts for circuits as fresh *nonces*. The property can be formalized as follows:

$$Accuse(IP, m) \implies CorrISP. \tag{2}$$

It says that if a user with address IP is falsely accused for a message m, i.e. $Accuse(IP, m)$, then indeed the ISP has to be corrupted.

Theorem: The trace property defined in equation (2) holds true for all possible executions of process P.

Proof. Automatically proven by ProVerif.   □

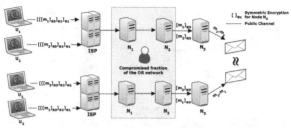

Fig. 3. Anonymity Game

Anonymity. We use observational equivalence to formalize privacy related properties such as in [45], [46]. We model anonymity as an equivalence relation between two processes that are replicated an unbounded number of times and execute in parallel. In the first process P, users U_1 and U_2 send two messages m_1 and m_2, respectively. While in the second process Q the two messages are swapped. If the two defined processes are observationally equivalent ($P \approx Q$), then we say that the attacker cannot distinguish between m_1 and m_2 i.e. cannot learn which message is sent by which user. In our scenario we assume that the attacker can compromise some fraction of the OR nodes, but not all of them. Figure 3 provides a graphical representation of the anonymity game where the exit node N_3 is honest. The game works as follows:

1. U_1 and U_2 create an onion data structure O_1 and O_2, respectively, intended for N_3 and send via previously built circuits C_1 ($U_1 \leftrightarrow N_1 \leftrightarrow N_2 \leftrightarrow N_3$) and C_2 ($U_2 \leftrightarrow N_1 \leftrightarrow N_2 \leftrightarrow N_3$). Nodes communicate between each other through public channels. 2. Two of the intermediate nodes are corrupted and the attacker has full control over them. The intermediate compromised nodes (in our case N_1 and N_2) remove one layer of encryption from O_1 and O_2 and send the onion to the exit node N_3. 3. After receiving these two onions from the users U_1 and U_2 and possibly other onions from compromised users, the exit OR node N_3 removes the last layer of the encryption and publishes the message on a public channel.

Note that the ISP does not affect the anonymity game and only acts as a proxy between the users and the outside world. For the verification, we assume that U_1 and U_2 are honest and they follow the protocol. Nevertheless, the action of any compromised user and honest users can be interleaved in any order.

Theorem: The observational equivalence relation $P \approx Q$ holds true.

Proof. Automatically proven by ProVerif.   □

No Forward Traceability. The evidence log of the backward traceability protocol in BACKREF does not store any information (*i.e.*, IP addresses) that can identify or verifiably reveal the identity of a node's successor. The log contains only the pseudonym for the successor node which does not reveal anything about the identity of the node.

We formalize this property as an observational equivalence relation between two distinct processes and verify that an adversary cannot distinguish them. Figure 4 provides a graphical representation of the game. To prove the observational equivalence, we model a scenario with concurrent circuit executions.

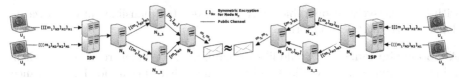

Fig. 4. No Forward Traceability

In this game, the adversary can corrupt parties and extract their secrets only after the message transmission over the circuit has completed. For this game, our model involves an additional middle node and user U_2. Two users U_1 and U_2 send two different messages m_1 and m_2 via two circuits. We verify that it is impossible for an attacker to deduce any meaningful information about the successor node for a particular request. Our game works as follows: 1. U_1 and U_2 start the protocol and construct two different circuits, $C_1(U \leftrightarrow N_1 \leftrightarrow N_2 \leftrightarrow N_3)$ and $C_2(U \leftrightarrow N_1 \leftrightarrow N_2^* \leftrightarrow N_3)$ respectively, with adequate values (x_1, x_2, x_3) for a circuit C_1 and (x_1', x_2', x_3') for C_2. 2. U_1 and U_2 create an onion data structure O_1 and O_2 and send to the exit node N_3 via previously built circuits C_1 and C_2. Nodes communicate with each other through public channels. 3. After receiving the two onions from the users and possibly other onions from compromised users, N_3 removes the last layer of the encryption and publishes the messages on a public channel. 4. After protocol completion, the entry node N_1 is compromised and the adversary obtains the evidence log.

In the first process P, U_1 sends m_1 and U_2 sends m_2, while the process Q is reversed process P. For the no forward traceability verification, we assume that all other parties in the protocol remain honest, except the compromised N_1. For example, if two neighbor nodes are compromised, the no forward traceability can be easily broken by activating the backward traceability mechanism.

Theorem: The observational equivalence relation $P \approx Q$ holds true.

Proof. Automatically proven by ProVerif.   □

Finally, to the best of our knowledge, our formal analysis is the first ProVerif-based analysis of the OR protocol; it can be of independent interest towards formalizing and verifying other properties of the OR protocol.

7   Conclusion

We presented BACKREF, an accountability mechanism for ACNs that provides practical repudiation for the proxy nodes, allowing selected outbound traffic flows to be traced back to the predecessor node. It also provides a full traceability option when all intermediate nodes are cooperating. While traceability mechanisms have been proposed in the past, BACKREF is the first that is both compatible with low-latency, interactive applications (such as anonymous web browsing) and does not require group managers or credential issuers. BACKREF is provably secure, requires little overhead, and can be adapted to a wide range of anonymity systems. We also analyzed some important systems issues (namely, white-listing, log storage, non-cooperating nodes, and the last mile problem) with any reactively accountable ACN, and presented plausible options towards deploying BACKREF in practice.

Acknowledgments. We would like to thank the anonymous reviewers for their valuable comments. We would also like to thank Kim Pecina for his assistance with ProVerif proofs. This work was supported by the German Ministry for Education and Research through funding for the Center for IT-Security, Privacy and Accountability and the German Universities Excellence Initiative.

References

1. Chaum, D.: The dining cryptographers problem: Unconditional sender and recipient untraceability. J. Cryptology 1(1) (1988)
2. Corrigan-Gibbs, H., Ford, B.: Dissent: accountable anonymous group messaging. In: CCS, pp. 340–350 (2010)
3. Syverson, P.F., Goldschlag, D.M., Reed, M.G.: Anonymous connections and onion routing. In: IEEE Symposium on Security and Privacy (1997)
4. Chaum, D.: Untraceable electronic mail, return addresses, and digital pseudonyms. CACM 24(2) (1981)
5. Mittal, P., Borisov, N.: Shadowwalker: peer-to-peer anonymous communication using redundant structured topologies. In: CCS, pp. 161–172 (2009)
6. Dingledine, R., Mathewson, N., Syverson, P.: Tor: the second-generation onion router. In: USENIX Security (2004)
7. Möller, U., Cottrell, L., Palfrader, P., Sassaman, L.: Mixmaster Protocol— Version 2. IETF Internet Draft (2003), http://mixmaster.sourceforge.net/
8. Janssen, A.W.: Tor madness reloaded (2007), http://itnomad.wordpress.com/2007/09/16/tor-madness-reloaded/ (accessed January 2014)
9. AccusedOperator: Raided for operating a Tor exit node (2012), http://raided4tor.cryto.net/
10. Köpsell, S., Wendolsky, R., Federrath, H.: Revocable anonymity. In: Müller, G. (ed.) ETRICS 2006. LNCS, vol. 3995, pp. 206–220. Springer, Heidelberg (2006)
11. von Ahn, L., Bortz, A., Hopper, N.J., O'Neill, K.: Selectively traceable anonymity. In: Danezis, G., Golle, P. (eds.) PET 2006. LNCS, vol. 4258, pp. 208–222. Springer, Heidelberg (2006)
12. Diaz, C., Preneel, B.: Accountable anonymous communication. In: Security, Privacy, and Trust in Modern Data Management (2007)
13. Golle, P.: Reputable mix networks. In: Martin, D., Serjantov, A. (eds.) PET 2004. LNCS, vol. 3424, pp. 51–62. Springer, Heidelberg (2005)
14. Clark, J., Gauvin, P., Adams, C.: Exit node repudiation for anonymity networks. In: On the Identity Trail: Privacy, Anonymity and Identity in a Networked Society. Oxford University Press (2009)
15. Johnson, P.C., Kapadia, A., Tsang, P.P., Smith, S.W.: Nymble: Anonymous IP-address blocking. In: Borisov, N., Golle, P. (eds.) PET 2007. LNCS, vol. 4776, pp. 113–133. Springer, Heidelberg (2007)
16. Henry, R., Goldberg, I.: Formalizing anonymous blacklisting systems. In: IEEE Symposium on Security and Privacy, pp. 81–95 (2011)
17. Goldberg, I., Wagner, D., Brewer, E.: Privacy-enhancing technologies for the internet. In: IEEE Compcon. (1997)

18. Goldberg, I., Shostack, A.: Freedom network 1.0 architecture and protocols. Technical report, Zero-Knowledge Systems (2001)
19. Kate, A., Zaverucha, G.M., Goldberg, I.: Pairing-based onion routing with improved forward secrecy. ACM Trans. Inf. Syst. Secur. 13(4) (2010)
20. Danezis, G., Goldberg, I.: Sphinx: A compact and provably secure mix format. In: IEEE Symposium on Security and Privacy (2009)
21. Danezis, G., Dingledine, R., Mathewson, N.: Mixminion: design of a type iii anonymous remailer protocol. In: IEEE Symposium on Security and Privacy (2003)
22. Pfitzmann, A., Hansen, M.: A terminology for talking about privacy by data minimization v0.34, http://dud.inf.tu-dresden.de/literatur/Anon_Terminology_v0.34.pdf (August 2010)
23. Wolinsky, D.I., Corrigan-Gibbs, H., Ford, B., Johnson, A.: Dissent in numbers: making strong anonymity scale. In: OSDI (2012)
24. Corrigan-Gibbs, H., Wolinsky, D.I., Ford, B.: Proactively accountable anonymous messaging in verdict. In: USENIX Security (2013)
25. Danezis, G., Sassaman, L.: How to bypass two anonymity revocation schemes. In: Borisov, N., Goldberg, I. (eds.) PETS 2008. LNCS, vol. 5134, pp. 187–201. Springer, Heidelberg (2008)
26. TorProject: Exonerator Service (2012), https://exonerator.torproject.org/ (accessed January 2014)
27. Øverlier, L., Syverson, P.F.: Improving efficiency and simplicity of tor circuit establishment and hidden services. In: Borisov, N., Golle, P. (eds.) PET 2007. LNCS, vol. 4776, pp. 134–152. Springer, Heidelberg (2007)
28. Kate, A., Goldberg, I.: Using sphinx to improve onion routing circuit construction. In: Sion, R. (ed.) FC 2010. LNCS, vol. 6052, pp. 359–366. Springer, Heidelberg (2010)
29. Backes, M., Kate, A., Mohammadi, E.: Ace: an efficient key-exchange protocol for onion routing. In: WPES (2012)
30. Catalano, D., Fiore, D., Gennaro, R.: Certificateless onion routing. In: CCS (2009)
31. Goldberg, I., Stebila, D., Ustaoglu, B.: Anonymity and one-way authentication in key exchange protocols. Designs, Codes and Cryptography (2012)
32. Camenisch, J.L., Lysyanskaya, A.: A formal treatment of onion routing. In: Shoup, V. (ed.) CRYPTO 2005. LNCS, vol. 3621, pp. 169–187. Springer, Heidelberg (2005)
33. Danezis, G., Diaz, C., Troncoso, C., Laurie, B.: Drac: An architecture for anonymous low-volume communications. In: Atallah, M.J., Hopper, N.J. (eds.) PETS 2010. LNCS, vol. 6205, pp. 202–219. Springer, Heidelberg (2010)
34. Shimshock, E., Staats, M., Hopper, N.: Breaking and provably fixing minx. In: Borisov, N., Goldberg, I. (eds.) PETS 2008. LNCS, vol. 5134, pp. 99–114. Springer, Heidelberg (2008)
35. Goldwasser, S., Micali, S., Rivest, R.L.: A digital signature scheme secure against adaptive chosen-message attacks. SIAM J. Comput. 17(2), 281–308 (1988)
36. Haeberlen, A., Fonseca, P., Rodrigues, R., Druschel, P.: Fighting cybercrime with packet attestation. Technical report, MPI-SWS (2011)
37. Dingledine, R., Mathewson, N.: Tor Protocol Specification (2008), https://gitweb.torproject.org/torspec.git/tree/HEAD (accessed January 2014)
38. Boneh, D., Lynn, B., Shacham, H.: Short signatures from the weil pairing. In: Boyd, C. (ed.) ASIACRYPT 2001. LNCS, vol. 2248, p. 514. Springer, Heidelberg (2001)

39. Blake, I., Seroussi, G., Smart, N., Cassels, J.W.S.: Advances in Elliptic Curve Cryptography. Cambridge University Press (2005)
40. Bernstein, D.J., Duif, N., Lange, T., Schwabe, P., Yang, B.-Y.: High-speed high-security signatures. In: Preneel, B., Takagi, T. (eds.) CHES 2011. LNCS, vol. 6917, pp. 124–142. Springer, Heidelberg (2011)
41. Abadi, M., Fournet, C.: Mobile values, new names, and secure communication. In: POPL (2001)
42. Blanchet, B.: An efficient cryptographic protocol verifier based on prolog rules. In: CSFW (2001)
43. BackRef: Introducing accountability to anonymity networks (proverif scripts), http://crypsys.mmci.uni-saarland.de/projects/BackRef/
44. Backes, M., Clark, J., Kate, A., Simeonovski, M., Druschel, P.: Backref: Introducing accountability to anonymity networks, http://arxiv.org/abs/1311.3151
45. Delaune, S., Kremer, S., Ryan, M.: Verifying privacy-type properties of electronic voting protocols, 435–487 (2009)
46. Chothia, T.: Analysing the MUTE anonymous file-sharing system using the pi-calculus. In: Najm, E., Pradat-Peyre, J.-F., Donzeau-Gouge, V.V. (eds.) FORTE 2006. LNCS, vol. 4229, pp. 115–130. Springer, Heidelberg (2006)

WebTrust – A Comprehensive Authenticity and Integrity Framework for HTTP

Michael Backes[1], Rainer W. Gerling[2], Sebastian Gerling[1], Stefan Nürnberger[1], Dominique Schröder[1], and Mark Simkin[1]

[1] CISPA, Saarland University
[2] University of Applied Sciences Munich

Abstract. HTTPS is *the* standard for confidential and integrity-protected communication on the Web. However, it authenticates the server, not its content. We present WebTrust, the first comprehensive authenticity and integrity framework that allows on-the-fly verification of static, dynamic, and real-time streamed Web content from untrusted servers. Our framework seamlessly integrates into HTTP and allows to validate streamed content progressively at arrival. Our performance results demonstrate both the practicality and efficiency of our approach.

Keywords: HTTP, Integrity, Authenticity, Verifiable Data Streaming.

1 Introduction

The *Hypertext Transfer Protocol* (HTTP) is the standard protocol in the World Wide Web that allows clients to request and receive any type of content from a server such as static, dynamically created, or even live streamed content [9]. HTTP is a pure transfer protocol that does not provide any state information or security guarantees by itself. For many applications, however, security guarantees are strictly necessary and various extensions haven been proposed. The standard protocol to provide security guarantees is HTTPS (HTTP over TLS [31]), which establishes a secure channel between the client and the server. Although a secure channel guarantees that the transferred content has not been modified during the transmission, it *neither* guarantees the authenticity *nor* the integrity of the delivered document itself. Moreover, if an attacker gained access to the server, any content the attacker would put on the server would be authenticated at the client's side, since HTTPS only authenticates the connection. This situation is completely unsatisfactory, since one can neither rely on the information in published documents nor prove their correctness to third parties (non-repudiation). Consider for example news aggregators that mainly serve information generated by news agencies: An established HTTPS connection to a news aggregator or social network cannot guarantee anything about the authenticity and integrity of the delivered content itself. The problem becomes even more challenging when we want to ensure the authenticity and integrity of live streamed content.

One intuitive approach to ensure the authenticity and integrity of content would be to append a digital signature. However, signatures need to be downloaded

I. Boureanu, P. Owesarski, and S. Vaudenay (Eds.): ACNS 2014, LNCS 8479, pp. 401–418, 2014.

separately and there is no unified solution that integrates into the existing infrastructure. Moreover, in case of large files, a single signature can only be verified after the content has been downloaded completely. Individual signatures also do not fulfill the requirements defined by today's Web resources that embed other resources such as images and scripts. Especially for (live) streamed content, this calls for a flexible and efficient solution that allows to verify content on-the-fly. In order to prevent an attacker from being able to replace partial content with other, also signed, content, all relevant interconnected documents need to be verified together. Mobile broadband providers replace embedded pictures with their compressed versions in order to save bandwidth [10]. Certain Internet providers even go as far as to inject advertisements into foreign websites [30].

1.1 Contribution

In this paper we present WebTrust, a comprehensive integrity and authenticity framework for static, dynamic, and live streamed Web content that seamlessly integrates into the existing infrastructure. Our framework allows content generators to publish authenticity- and integrity-protected content (from now on referred to as *WebTrust protected content*) on untrusted servers. In addition, WebTrust offers protection against active network attackers. The integrity and authenticity of downloaded HTTP documents can further be proven to third parties in an offline setting (non-repudiation). The verification of documents takes place on-the-fly (progressive content verification (PCV)) while the document is still being downloaded. In particular, WebTrust enables the client to detect any modified data packet upon arrival without downloading the entire document. Our solution adapts recent cryptographic primitives and profits from the lessons learned in previous approaches that focus on subsets of the aforementioned problems to realize our comprehensive integrity and authenticity framework [32,2,12,23,37,14]. WebTrust further supports efficient data updates and enables the usage of Web caches (the latter only, if confidentiality is not needed). Finally, our concept and implementation supports individual verifiability of content aggregated from different authors via IFrames.

1.2 Related Work

We discuss related frameworks that also provide authenticity and integrity guarantees and we compare them to WebTrust in Table 1. In that table, we compare the approaches w.r.t. the following features: The 1st column indicates if the framework supports *verifiable authorship* meaning that the content can be verified against the author and not (only) against the server. The 2nd column shows if documents can be *revoked*, i.e., the author can enforce and immediate expiration. The property of *non-repudiation* is compared in the 3rd column and allows proving the authorship to third parties. The 4th column indicates if the content can be *updated*, i.e., updating parts of the content is possible without re-signing the entire dataset. The 5th column shows if caches resp. content distribution networks (CDN) are supported, i.e., the content can be distributed to

Table 1. Comparison of approaches to protect the integrity of HTTP transferred data

Feature	1	2	3	4	5	6	7
SHTTP [32]	–	–	–	–	–	S/D/L	–
HTTPS [31]	–	–	–	–	–	S/D/L	–
SSL Splitting [18,19]	–	–	–	–	✓	S/D/L	–
Bayardo and S. [2]	✓	–	✓	–	✓	S/D/–	✓
Sine [12]	–	–	✓	–	✓	S/D/–	✓
HTTPI [6]	–	–	–	–	✓	S/D/L	–
Spork [23]	–	–	✓	–	✓	S/D/–	–
HTTPi [37]	–	–	✓	–	✓	S/D/–	✓
iHTTP [14]	–	–	✓	–	✓	S/–/–	✓
WebTrust	✓	✓	✓	✓	✓	S/D/L	✓

Legend: 1. Verifiable Authorship 2. Document Revocation 3. Non-repudiation 4. Data updates 5. Caching/CDN-Support 6. Content types (**S**tatic, **D**ynamic, **L**ive Streaming) 7. Progressive Verification ✓: yes/full support, – no support.

different servers without harming the verifiability. In the 6th column the different supported content types are listed such as static, dynamic, and streamed live content. Handling streamed content is particularly challenging as full precomputation is generally not possible. Static content is a mere copy of the file to the client, while dynamic content is generated on demand, and (live) streamed content is a stream of data that has an infinite size and is not known in advance. The 7th column compares the approaches w.r.t. progressive verification meaning that the content can be verified while loading. Progressive verification is desired in setting where the clients do not want to wait until the end of a stream to verify any of the security properties. Due to space constrains we cannot discuss each approach in detail, but the chart already shows that none of the existing approaches provides a comprehensive solution to all common usage scenarios of HTTP. Further approaches exist that focus on efficient methods for a specific data type (cf. [20,8,29]), or focus on the data transmission of files on the Internet, or focus on streams such as [13,28] (not in real-time) or [27] for multicast streams over lossy channels with real-time support. Two less closely related approaches [11,30] also consider the problem of providing integrity for HTTP, however, they do not provide security guarantees in a cryptographic sense. Therefore we omit a more detailed discussion of these papers.

2   System Model

In the following we provide a high-level overview of WebTrust and discuss the attacker model as well as the underlying assumptions of our system. The global setup of WebTrust consists of three parties: the *client* with a Web browser, the HTTP-based Web *server*, and the *content generator* (cf. Figure 1).

The content generator either creates WebTrust-protected documents a priori and uploads them to the Web server (static content), or the content is created

Fig. 1. WebTrust system overview

on-the-fly by the content-generator and merely relayed by the server to the client (dynamic content). The client is then able to request protected resources based on the Unified Resource Identifier (URI) from the Web server and to progressively verify their integrity and authenticity with the help of the content generator's public key during the arrival. Depending on the scenario, the Web server can also fetch dynamic content from the content generator. The content generator and the Web server do not have to be different entities. However, we recommend them to be different whenever possible to mitigate the risks of key exposure through Web server breaches. Splitting these entities also allows us to assume an untrusted Web server which is accessible from the Web and potentially vulnerable.

2.1 Security Objectives

The goal of WebTrust is to provide robust security guarantees to users. In particular, our system needs to fulfill the following security objectives: *authenticity*, *integrity*, *validity*, and *freshness* of Web documents with respect to their author:

- **Authenticity** ensures that content indeed stems from the alleged author.
- **Integrity** ensures that content cannot be altered after its generation without being detected.
- **Freshness** ensures that a client always receives the *latest* version of a document, i.e., a man in the middle cannot replace a response with an integrity-protected and authentic, *but old* copy of a requested document.
- **Document revocation** ensures that a document was not actively revoked by its author.
- **Non repudiation** allows to proof the authenticity of documents to third parties.

Depending on the scenario, confidentiality of the transmission needs to be provided as well. This is not explicitly stated as an security objective, since this is orthogonal to our solution and can be achieved by transmitting WebTrust protected documents via HTTPS.

2.2 Attacker Model

We assume an active adversary that is able to eavesdrop and arbitrarily modify all network traffic. Such an adversary could be, for instance, the Internet service provider that is in control of the network connection. In addition, we assume that the adversary is able to fully compromise the Web servers in our scenario (including the servers of a content distribution network (CDN)).

This effectively grants the attacker access to all files stored on such server and allows to manipulate all requests and responses processed by them.

2.3 Assumptions

To provide robust security guarantees, it is central for WebTrust that the cryptographic keys used to sign content cannot be accessed by an attacker. Therefore, WebTrust has the following requirements to achieve its goals:

1. The content generator stores sensitive keys to sign content locally. We assume that these keys cannot be accessed by an attacker.
2. In case the content generator and the Web server are the same entity (implies that keys are stored locally on the Web server), we assume that the Web server cannot be compromised by an attacker. Otherwise, we consider the Web server untrusted without further assumptions.
3. We assume a standard trusted PKI that provides additional support for WebTrust content revocation lists (WT-CRLs) (cf. Section 4).

3 Theoretical Foundations

In the following we introduce the cryptographic primitives required by WebTrust, namely *elliptic curve cryptography* [22], *collision-resistant hash functions* [16], *chameleon hash functions* [17], *digital signatures* [16], and *verifiable data streaming* [34]. We use the following notation: By $y \leftarrow A(x)$ we denote the execution of a probabilistic polynomial time (PPT) algorithm on input x with output y.

3.1 Hash Functions

Collision-Resistant Hash Functions. We assume the existence of compressing collision-resistant hash functions. Roughly speaking, a function H is called collision-resistant if the probability that an efficient adversary finds two distinct pre-images $m_0 \neq m_1$ that map to the same image $H(m_0) = H(m_1)$ is negligible. WebTrust supports any state of the art collision-resistant hash function.

Chameleon Hash Functions. A chameleon hash (CH) function is similar to regular collision-resistant hash functions that are based on number theoretic assumptions and it provides additionally a trapdoor. Invertible chameleon hash functions are defined through the tuple $\mathcal{CH} = (\mathsf{chGen}, \mathsf{ch}, \mathsf{col}, \mathsf{scol})$ [17]. Its key generation algorithm $\mathsf{chGen}(1^\lambda)$ returns a key pair (sk_{ch}, pk_{ch}). The function $\mathsf{ch}(x; r)$ is parametrized by the public key pk_{ch} and outputs a hash value $h \in \{0, 1\}^{\mathrm{out}}$ for a input message $x \in \{0, 1\}^{\mathrm{in}}$ and a randomness $r \in \{0, 1\}^\lambda$. The trapdoor sk_{ch} allows us to efficiently find collisions, i.e., a randomness r' such that both (x, r) and (x', r') will be mapped to the same hash value. CH functions can be instantiated from many number theoretic assumptions, such as the discrete logarithm assumption [17,1], the factoring assumption [35], and the RSA assumption [1,15]. We use the scheme introduced by Nyberg and Rueppel [1].

Its security is proven in the generic group model assuming the hardness of some variant of the discrete logarithm problem in the cyclic group $\mathbb{Z}_p$. Our framework uses the elliptic curve variant of the Nyberg and Rueppel chameleon hash function. The advantage of using elliptic curves is that the chameleon hash values become smaller in size. For our choice of the curve, please refer to Section 7.

Merkle Trees. A Merkle Tree is a binary tree that allows an efficient verification of distinct elements from larger data sets. Data is stored in the tree's leafs and all inner nodes are computed recursively as the hash value of its concatenated children. The root node's value is published as the public key and can be used to verify each leaf individually. The authentication of a certain leaf requires all hash values that are adjacent to the nodes on the path from this leaf node to the root node, hence all proofs are logarithmic with respect to the amount of leafs.

3.2   Verifiable Data Streaming (VDS)

The verifiable data streaming (VDS) protocol [34] allows to authenticate data streams. VDS is based on a variant of Merkle Trees [21], so-called chameleon authentication trees (CAT), which have the following additional capabilities: New elements can be inserted into the tree without updating the root and already inserted elements can be updated efficiently. The correctness of each single element in the tree is publicly verifiable and can be proven to third parties. In essence, the security of VDS says that only the data owner can insert elements to and modify exiting elements in the CAT.

VDS Adaptation for WebTrust. The original VDS protocol [34] was designed to allow a computationally weak client to stream its entire data to a seemingly all-powerful server. In our scenario, the content generator is the client of the VDS setting. It streams content to an untrusted server, which is later received and publicly verified by other clients.

Consider the tree as depicted in Figure 2.

The root $v_{1,0}$ of the tree is a hash, which is part of the content generator's public key. In the following, we denote the root value by ρ. Each left node of the tree is computed by a collision-resistant hash function and every right node is computed via a CH function. Since the CH function takes a randomness as additional input, it is necessary to store it in the right nodes. To verify a leaf in the tree, one has to compute an authentication path as in a traditional Merkle Tree (cf. Figure 3): To verify L_0 in the tree, the algorithm computes $v_{0,0} \leftarrow H(L_0\|v_{-1,1})$ and checks if $\rho = H(v_{0,0}\|v_{0,1})$.

Now, let us assume that the client requests a video stream of a press conference and the client would like to verify the authenticity and integrity of the streamed content on-the-fly. The basic idea is to chop the stream in chunks of data such that a hash of each chunk is stored in a leaf. We illustrate this idea with a tree of small depth, but our data structure supports a binary tree of polynomial depth that can authenticate an exponential number of leaves. For an easier exposition of the main idea, we assume that the first two leaves L_0, L_1 are known in advance. To set up the tree, the algorithm picks two dummy elements for the part of the

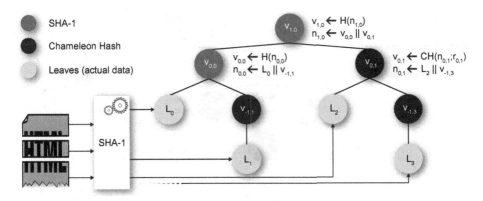

Fig. 2. CAT for four leaves (L_0 to L_3) with vertices named $v_{height,index}$

stream that is unknown. In our case, it chooses elements $(n_{0,1}, r_{0,1})$ uniformly at random. The element $n_{0,1}$ is the input to the chameleon hash functions stored at node $v_{0,1}$ and $r_{0,1}$ is the corresponding randomness. Now, suppose that another element is streamed to the client that will be stored in the leave L_2. To add this elements to the tree, the server picks a dummy value for $v_{-1,3}$ and computes the collision with help of the algorithm $r'_{0,1} \leftarrow \mathsf{col}(sk_{ch}, n_{0,1}, r_{0,1}, (L_2 \| v_{-1,3}))$ and sends $(L_2, v_{-1,3}, r'_{0,1})$ to the client.

3.3   Digital Signature Schemes

Digital signature schemes allow to compute a signature σ on a document m using a private key sk, such that any party in possession of the corresponding public key pk can verify the validity of σ. Our construction requires a digital signature scheme that is secure against the standard notion of existential forgery under chosen message attacks [16]. WebTrust uses the RSA [33] signature scheme. It is provable secure in the random oracle model [3] and its underlying mathematical structure are composite order groups.

4   System Details

WebTrust leverages the previously described cryptographic primitives to achieve robust progressive integrity and authenticity verification of different content types with respect to their authors. In the following we describe our framework in detail and discuss how our security objectives (cf. Section 2.1) can be achieved. Moreover, we show that WebTrust is backwards compatible and supports caches as well as CDNs. WebTrust splits all content types into individual segments and processes them in the *signature provider* (Sign in the following figures) of the content generator (cf. Figure 4 for static content and Figure 5 for dynamic content). Our system currently supports two different signature providers, namely VDSECC and RSA-Chaining.

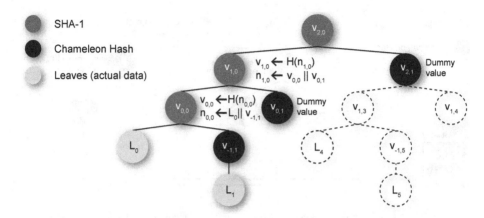

Fig. 3. CAT of depth 5 that authenticates the leaves L_0 and L_1. Root node and left nodes are computed by a collision-resistant hash function, right nodes by a chameleon hash. The leaves $L_2, \ldots L_7$ are unknown. Appending the leaves L_4 and L_5 to the CAT (dotted in gray), requires the computation of a collision in nodes $v_{2,1}$ and $v_{-1,5}$.

VDSECC. VDSECC combines the VDS protocol with the elliptic curve variant of the Nyberg and Rueppel chameleon hash. It generates one CAT for each content object. For each content object its individual segments are hashed and added to the CAT. The first segment of a content object always includes metainformation such as the content URI, the creation date, and the expiration date. The ordering of segments is implicitly ensured through the CAT itself. Once a segment has been processed by the VDSECC signature provider, the returned proof is attached to the segment. The verification of each segment is done as previously described in Section 3.2.

RSA-Chaining. RSA-Chaining produces a signature chain by creating one signature for each pair of adjacent segments. For each incoming content object all

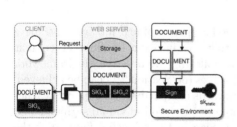

Fig. 4. Static content: Data and signatures are broken into segments and are delivered interleaved

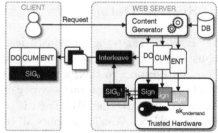

Fig. 5. Dynamic content (Web server and content generator as a single entity): Signatures SIG_B^1, $SIG_B^2, \ldots$ are calculated during dynamic document creation

its individual segments are first prepended by the same meta-information that we add to the first packet in the CAT and we additionally add the segments position in the chain. Afterwards, each segments is hashed and finally signed using RSA with the content generator's secret key. Once a segment has been processed by the RSA signature provider, each signature is attached to the segment. The client-side verification is based on a classical RSA signature verification against the content generator's public key. The chaining ensures that ordering of segments in the stream cannot be altered.

In order to achieve a seamless integration into the existing Web infrastructure, we now need to embed the signatures either created by the VDSECC or the RSA-Chaining signature provider into the data transmission in a backwards compatible manner. We achieve this by leveraging the existing HTTP/1.1 chunked mode. HTTP chunking ([9] section 3.6.1) is designed for documents whose size is unknown a priori and which are generated and transferred piecemeal to the client. Since HTTP chunking is a transfer encoding, it does not modify the content but merely the way it is transported to the client and thus perfectly meets our requirements. Clients that do not support WebTrust will simply ignore the attached signatures. Clients with WebTrust support will extract the embedded signatures for incoming segments, compute the hash of each segment, and finally verify whether the signatures are valid or not.

4.1 Progressive Content Processing

The progressive verification of WebTrust is enabled by splitting content into segments in combination with the particular design of the signature providers. Due to the content splitting, every segment is sent to the client with its own authenticity and integrity protection that can be verified immediately after arrival. Both signature providers are designed to allow the signing of a segment i without yet knowing the segment $i + 1$. VDSECC and RSA-Chaining allow the client to verify content object partially (e.g., media sub streams) without requiring the client to know the start, the end, or the file as a whole. WebTrust allows the progressive verification of all content types.

4.2 Individual Verifiability

Since WebTrust is supposed to be used by authors of content to protect their data, it allows to combine content of different authors in one website with individual verifiability. Our framework realizes this by loading each author's content into an individual IFrame of a website. Each IFrame triggers a separate WebTrust protected HTTP request. The user gets visual feedback about the verification result of each IFrame as shown in Figure 6.

In certain scenarios it may be desirable to ensure that an attacker cannot substitute any of the IFrames with a different signed resource. Consider the following scenario: A client requests the document www.example.com/a.html, which explicitly references a JavaScript file www.example.com/script.js. Assume that another script file signed by the same author with the same key exists

Fig. 6. The WebTrust Chrome Extension showing the verified authorship of an embedded tweet in our modified Twitter page

at `www.example.com/anotherscript.js`. In this scenario, an attacker may replace `script.js` with `anotherscript.js` in the web response. To prevent this, WebTrust supports the incorporation of the content's full URI into the signature. This allows the detection of maliciously replaced files. Furthermore, WebTrust can be configured to include arbitrary HTTP headers in the signature. This may be particularly useful for critical headers such as cookies.

4.3   Content Updates

CATs allow content updates by design and our RSA signature chains can achieve the same functionality with the help of WT-CRLs. However, their update algorithms differ fundamentally. In particular, when using a CAT each update requires an update of the public key and involves updating a logarithmic amount of nodes in the tree. Instead, we introduce a second CAT which aggregates the roots of all the content object CATs as its leaf nodes. This method allows us to verify several content objects against only one public key, which is the root of the second CAT. When using RSA-Chaining, the update algorithm computes signatures for the new segment and adds the old segment to the WT-CRL. Hence, the size of the WT-CRL is linear with respect to the amount of updates.

4.4   Caching and CDN-Support

WebTrust content can be cached by proxies, cache servers, or CDNs, since the signature of static content is also static. Outsourcing content to CDNs is common practice to reduce load on a single server. In addition, CDNs equalize latencies around the globe by mirroring content at locations with a large distance to the central server. Dynamic content could also be cached from a technical point of view, but usually this content would have a `no-cache` directive set because caching does not make sense from a logical point of view.

4.5 Key Security

Content generators use secret keys to generate WebTrust protected content. These keys need to be protected against malicious access. In particular, in the case where the Web server and the content generator are the same entity, keys should be protected by a Hardware Security Module (HSM) as shown in Figure 5. With an HSM in place, an attacker that breaks into the Web server could still forge signed content by using the HSM as a signing oracle. However, he would never get hold of the key itself. This achieves the same level of security as storing HTTPS/TLS certificate private keys in an HSM.

5 Implementation

5.1 Server

We implemented the WebTrust server extension as a patch to the Apache Tomcat Web server 7.0.39. Our patch extends the existing processing routines for the HTTP chunked transfer encoding using a filter in the HTTP chunking driver of Tomcat. The HTTP 1.1 chunked mode allows so-called chunk-extensions that can be embedded into a chunk's header. The specification starts with the number of bytes in hexadecimal format, which can be followed by extensions of the format `;key=value,key=value,....` The extensions are then followed by a line break before the actual chunk data. This overall format is repeated for every chunk. We attach the base64-encoded WebTrust protection as extension in the requested format (the example has a chunk size of 2761 bytes, `0xAC9` bytes in hex):

```
AC9;SIG=8CD3ABU8ULS2KMDN4HW3NK6A5BPP84HB6A7CC
```

Since the transmitted bytes are still well-formed HTTP, legacy clients will only extract the unmodified content. We successfully verified this compatibility of HTTP chunking extensions with Firefox, Chrome, Safari, Internet Explorer, wget, curl and Java. The public key for the overall verification is specified in the HTTP header itself, since it does not change for a single request. For that purpose, we added two additional HTTP headers to indicate the used WebTrust algorithm (here, VDS with SHA-1) and the corresponding public key:

```
Content-Verification-Scheme: 1.0/SHA1-VDSECC
Content-Verification-Key: 61KJHQ1J4NED97NBP2SJ44FP0
```

Similarly, chained hashes that are signed with RSA are implemented (1.0/SHA1-RSA).

The signature cache for static content is implemented using the `default` servlet of Tomcat. The `default` servlet is used when there is no dynamic servlet to generate content and the URI points to an actual file on the server. For each such file, we keep a list of chunk sizes and attached signatures. The `default` servlet implementation ensures that every response uses the same chunk size and hence can benefit from the stored signature chain. For the dynamic case, the implementation is slightly more complex: Servlets decide on their own how many bytes to flush to the network. For example, every time they call `flush()`, the bytes written so far are sent to the WebTrust filter which takes care of accumulating them and eventually adding the signature. This ensures that if the servlet generates exactly the same output over two different runs, we generate exactly the same chunks. As those chunks appear to be static, we can cache them. The look-up procedure is realized using a hash map that is indexed by a tuple consisting of the SHA-1 hash of the content and the preceding signature.

To further reduce the server load we enable the WebTrust extension only if the client has requested its usage by sending the `'Accept-Content-Verification: SHA1-RSA'` header, where `SHA1-RSA` defines one of the supported schemes. Depending on the flag set by the client, the server responds using the requested scheme. The implementation of the cryptographic primitives on the server side is based on the `SunRsaSign` and `Sun` cryptography providers for non elliptic curve primitives as delivered with Oracle's Java [26], and based on Bouncycastle [4] for the elliptic curve primitives, and our own Java implementation for the CAT.

5.2   Client

We implemented the client-side prototype as a patch to the open source Chromium browser 29 [7] in combination with a browser extension. The patch targets the chunked-mode handling of Chromium and is used to parse and verify the WebTrust integrity and authenticity proof of incoming documents. Moreover, it includes the routines for adding the WebTrust headers into Web requests, which can be switched on and off. The required cryptographic primitives build upon the OpenSSL library [25] and include our own implementation for CATs in C++. The browser extension is used to prototype the UI for providing the user with feedback about the verification result. It also supports to give feedback for the individual verifiability of documents loaded inside of IFrames as described in Section 4.1. We would like to stress that this approach is merely used for prototyping the client application. A future release of the system is supposed to directly integrate the individual verifiability into Web browsers instead of an extension to optimize usability and performance. We would like to point out that although our concept leverages a PKI for freshness and revocation, our client-side prototype focuses primarily on the implementation and evaluation of our new signature providers and hence does not have an implementation for revocation.

6   Security Evaluation

In the following, we discuss how WebTrust fulfills the security objectives defined in Section 2.1 and how WebTrust is protected against attacks.

6.1   Integrity, Authenticity, and Non Repudiation

Our integrity check is based on hashing content segments with a collision resistant hash function. The property of collision resistance guarantees that an attacker cannot find a second chunk that maps to the same hash value. To ensure that content segments cannot be replaced, all hashes are authenticated by one of the signature providers. Since the attacker can neither access the author's secret keys, nor forge valid signatures for RSA-Chaining or VDSECC without the secret key, the hash as proof of integrity cannot be replaced or modified. Since the proofs of integrity are verified against a specific user's public key, this immediately provides authenticity. Therefore, the integrity and authenticity of data is guaranteed and our signature providers allow to prove the correctness of the WebTrust protected segments to third parties (non repudiation). Whenever embedded content or a client-side script fetches another resource, this triggers another HTTP request, which is then also verified by WebTrust.

6.2   Freshness and Content Revocation

Our framework supports freshness, i.e. the user always obtains the latest version of the requested content object. This is achieved by incorporating an expiry date into the content object. If content is replaced before it is expired, the old version is revoked and does no longer verify successfully. In the case of RSA-Chaining this revocation is achieved by adding the old version to the WT-CRL at the PKI. This explicit revocation is not needed for the VDS protocol, which updates the public key on every update thereby rendering old versions invalid.

6.3   Active Network Attacker

The active network attacker can modify or replace data packets containing documents or signatures. However, any modification or replacement would either result in an invalid signature since the document and its corresponding signature would no longer match, or result in a document signed with the untrusted key of the attacker. The attacker cannot access the secret key that was used by the content author to sign the original data and hence cannot re-compute the signature. The attacker can also try to substitute the response with a valid response of another or older document. Replacement with another document is prevented by the embedded absolute URI as part of the signature chain, which reveals the substitution. The older document is prevented by the previously described freshness properties. Since HTTP is per se stateless, session cookies are often deployed to transfer state information. This way, the same URI can transfer different Web resources. WebTrust allows to uniquely identify these different documents, since the session information is part of the signed HTTP header.

6.4   Active Attacker against CDN and Web Server

Our solution successfully protects against the CDN Attacker. The CDN stores solely documents that are already WebTrust protected. If an attacker exploits a known vulnerability in the CDN server, documents can be replaced. However, the attacker cannot forge valid signatures for this malicious content since there

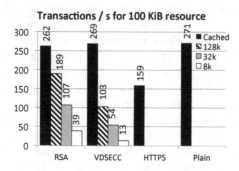

Fig. 7. Average transactions per second under maximum load

is no possibility to access the required secret key. Hence, our solution preserves the authenticity and integrity of documents. Since we assume that static and dynamic content signing takes place at the content generator where an attacker cannot gain access, content can only be manipulated after it has left the content generation server. In this stage, it is already digitally signed and can no longer be manipulated without detection.

7   Experimental Evaluation

In the following, we provide the experimental evaluation of our prototypical Web-Trust implementation. The evaluation encompasses the computational overhead at the client and the content generator as well as the network overhead. However, the measured overhead does not include any processing of or communication with the PKI, which may slightly skew the measured performance. Moreover, we discuss usability issues of the current implementation.

7.1   Performance Evaluation

We conducted a comprehensive performance evaluation to measure the runtime and network overhead induced by WebTrust. The server side evaluation was performed with our patched Apache Tomcat version running on a Dell Opti-plex 9010 Workstation equipped with an Intel Core i7 CPU and 32 GB of Ram. The client side evaluation was performed on an identical machine with 16 GB of Ram instead. We chose the security parameters of the cryptographic schemes according to the latest NIST recommendations [24], i.e. 2048 bit for RSA. To achieve a comparable level of security, we chose the elliptic curve P-224 for the chameleon hashes inside the CAT.

The performance and network overhead depends on the total amount of signatures that are sent over the network, i.e. the ratio between transmitted bytes of data and transmitted bytes used for signatures. The smaller the size of each chunk, the more signatures are need for the same amount of data. In our proto-type, we evaluated different chunk sizes, namely 8 KB, 32 KB and 128 KB. If we

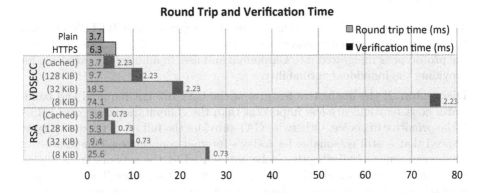

Fig. 8. Round trip times for a 100 KB document

consider a video stream of moderate standard definition quality with 2 Mbit/s data rate, then 128 KB chunks would correspond to one second of video – which seems to be an acceptable frequency for content verification. The experiments were conducted using the Siege [36] benchmark tool that downloaded a 100 KB file 10,000 times while simulating 100 concurrent users accessing the server. The server and the client were both connected to the Internet via a 1 Gbit/s uplink and they are 11 hops apart. We measured the maximum transactions that the server was capable of delivering without WebTrust, with WebTrust RSA and VDSECC and over HTTPS (see in Figure 7).

This number of transactions is limited by the computational burden on the server side. The client-side verification adds an additional delay for verifying each chunk. This delay is $121\mu s$ for one RSA signature verification and $371\mu s$ for one CAT node verification. The resulting round trip times are depicted in Figure 8. Our results show that in the case of static content, the cached versions have a negligible overhead compared to plain HTTP connections. Without server-side caching, i.e. the server has to calculate the corresponding RSA signatures or CAT trees for each chunk, the computational load on the server side increases. However, RSA signature chaining still outperforms HTTPS with RSA 2048 bit Diffie-Hellman key exchange and AES-256-CBC encryption. Even though the VDSECC-based authentication without caching provides less throughput than HTTPS, VDSECC is the only primitive whose revocation mechanism does not need to keep a list for each revoked document (see section 4).

Network Overhead. WebTrust introduces a small overhead in size for every signature that is transmitted from the Web server to the client. The overhead for a single signature depends on the signature scheme and its security parameter. The signature size of RSA 2048 bit is 344 bytes. The size of one VDSECC data structure is 167 bytes. These sizes resemble a space overhead of 4% (RSA) and 2% (VDSECC) in the worst case of very small 8 KiB sized chunks. For more realistic sizes of 128 KB chunks, the overhead is a mere 0.3% for RSA and 0.1% for VDSECC, respectively.

7.2   Usability

The prototypical implementation seamlessly integrates into HTTP's chunked transfer encoding, which provides full backward compatibility. At the client-side, the prototype is integrated into Chromium and uses in addition an extension for providing the individual verifiability.

Discussion. If the distinctive features of the CAT are not required and bandwidth considerations are less important than the computational overhead RSA is the primitive of choice. Otherwise CAT provides the full set of functionality at a speed that is still reasonable for today's Internet connections. Our round-trip time measurement indicates that delay introduced by the network transmission still dominates the computation times the client and the server. The CAT-based solution leaves still room for performance optimizations. Depending on the use-case one could pre-calculate several keys to further reduce the computational load [5], especially on the client side. Moreover, we did not use multi-threading for verifying chunks simultaneously. Depending on the scenario one could also reduce both the computational and the network overhead can be tweaked by changing the verification ratio via the chunk size.

8   Conclusion

Verifying the integrity and authenticity of dynamic Web content and real-time Web streams on-the-fly is infeasible with existing solutions. Motivated by this lack of solutions, we developed WebTrust, the first comprehensive solution to provide integrity in all major Web scenarios. WebTrust allows to verify integrity and authenticity of static, dynamic, and streamed Web content and integrates seamlessly into the existing Web infrastructure. Our performance results demonstrate both its practicality and efficiency, even in the mobile setting. The results of our evaluation show that there is not one primitive for all scenarios that clearly outperforms all others. Which technique and which cryptographic primitive to use highly depends on the task since no primitive provides all security features, a small overhead in size, enables caching, and provides a high performance both on the client and the server side.

Acknowledgement. We thank the anonymous reviewers for their comments and Oliver Schranz for his assistance with the implementation. This work was supported by the German Ministry for Education and Research (BMBF) through funding for the Center for IT-Security, Privacy and Accountability (CISPA).

References

1. Ateniese, G., de Medeiros, B.: On the Key Exposure Problem in Chameleon Hashes. In: Blundo, C., Cimato, S. (eds.) SCN 2004. LNCS, vol. 3352, pp. 165–179. Springer, Heidelberg (2005)

2. Bayardo, R.J., Sorensen, J.S.: Merkle tree authentication of HTTP responses. In: Proc. of the 14th International Conference on World Wide Web (WWW 2005), pp. 1182–1183. ACM (2005)
3. Bellare, M., Rogaway, P.: Random Oracles are Practical: A Paradigm for Designing Efficient Protocols. In: Proc. of the 1st ACM Conference on Computer and Communication Security (CCS 1993), pp. 62–73. ACM (1993)
4. bouncycastle.org: The Legion of the Bouncy Castle (2013), http://www.bouncycastle.org/
5. Catalano, D., Fiore, D., Gennaro, R.: Certificateless onion routing. In: Proc. of the 16th ACM Conference on Computer and Communication Security (CCS 2009), pp. 151–160. ACM (2009)
6. Choi, T., Gouda, M.G.: HTTPI: An HTTP with Integrity. In: Proc. of the 20th International Conference on Computer Communications and Networks (ICCCN 2011), pp. 1–6. IEEE Computer Society (2011)
7. The Chromium Projects (2014), http://www.chromium.org/
8. Devanbu, P., Gertz, M., Kwong, A., Martel, C., Nuckolls, G., Stubblebine, S.G.: Flexible Authentication Of XML documents. In: Proc. of the 8th ACM Conference on Computer and Communication Security (CCS 2001), pp. 136–145. ACM (2001)
9. Fielding, R., Gettys, J., Mogul, J., Frystyk, H., Masinter, L., Leach, P., Berners-Lee, T.: RFC 2616 - Hypertext Transfer Protocol – HTTP/1.1 (1999), http://tools.ietf.org/html/rfc2616
10. Fox, A., Brewer, E.A.: Reducing WWW Latency and Bandwidth Requirements by Real-Time Distillation. In: Proc. of the 5th International Conference on World Wide Web (WWW 1996), pp. 1445–1456. Elsevier (1996)
11. Franks, J., Hallam-Baker, P., Hostetler, J., Lawrence, S., Leach, P., Luotonen, A., Stewart, L.: RFC 2617 - HTTP Authentication: Basic and Digest Access Authentication (1999), http://tools.ietf.org/html/rfc2617
12. Gaspard, C., Goldberg, S., Itani, W., Bertino, E., Nita-Rotaru, C.: Sine: Cache-friendly integrity for the web. In: Proc. of the 5th IEEE Workshop on Secure Network Protocols (NPSec 2009), pp. 7–12. IEEE Computer Society (2009)
13. Gennaro, R., Rohatgi, P.: How to sign digital streams. In: Kaliski Jr., B.S. (ed.) CRYPTO 1997. LNCS, vol. 1294, pp. 180–197. Springer, Heidelberg (1997)
14. Gionta, J., Ning, P., Zhang, X.: iHTTP: Efficient Authentication of Non-confidential HTTP Traffic. In: Bao, F., Samarati, P., Zhou, J. (eds.) ACNS 2012. LNCS, vol. 7341, pp. 381–399. Springer, Heidelberg (2012)
15. Hohenberger, S., Waters, B.: Realizing Hash-and-Sign Signatures under Standard Assumptions. In: Joux, A. (ed.) EUROCRYPT 2009. LNCS, vol. 5479, pp. 333–350. Springer, Heidelberg (2009)
16. Katz, J., Lindell, Y.: Introduction to Modern Cryptography (Chapman & Hall/Crc Cryptography and Network Security Series). Chapman and Hall/CRC (2007)
17. Krawczyk, H., Rabin, T.: Chameleon Signatures. In: Proc. of the 7th Annual Network and Distributed System Security Symposium (NDSS 2000). The Internet Society (2000)
18. Lesniewski-Laas, C., Kaashoek, M.F.: SSL Splitting: Securely Serving Data from Untrusted Caches. In: Proc. of the 12th Usenix Security Symposium, pp. 187–199. Usenix Association (2003)
19. Lesniewski-Laas, C., Kaashoek, M.F.: SSL splitting: Securely serving data from untrusted caches. Computer Networks 48(5), 763–779 (2005)
20. Lin, C.Y., Chang, S.F.: Generating robust digital signature for image/video authentication. In: Proc. of the 1st Workshop on Multimedia and Security at ACM Multimedia 1998, vol. 98, pp. 94–108. ACM (1998)

21. Merkle, R.C.: Method of Providing Digital Signatures (US Patent: US4309569A) (1979)
22. Miller, V.S.: Use of Elliptic Curves in Cryptography. In: Williams, H.C. (ed.) CRYPTO 1985. LNCS, vol. 218, pp. 417–426. Springer, Heidelberg (1986)
23. Moyer, T., Butler, K.R.B., Schiffman, J., McDaniel, P., Jaeger, T.: Scalable Web Content Attestation. IEEE Transactions on Computers 61(5), 686–699 (2012)
24. NIST: Recommendation for Key Management. Special Publication 800-57 Part 1 Rev. 3 (2012)
25. OpenSSL. (2014), http://www.openssl.org/
26. Oracle: Java Cryptography Architecture – Oracle Providers Documentation (2013),
    http://docs.oracle.com/javase/7/docs/technotes/guides/security/SunProviders.html
27. Pannetrat, A., Molva, R.: Efficient Multicast Packet Authentication. In: Proc. of the 10th Annual Network and Distributed System Security Symposium (NDSS 2003). The Internet Society (2003)
28. Perrig, A., Canetti, R., Tygar, D., Song, D.: Efficient authentication and signing of multicast streams over lossy channels. In: Proc. of the 2000 IEEE Symposium on Security and Privacy (Oakland 2000), pp. 56–73. IEEE Computer Society (2000)
29. Ray, I., Kim, E.: Collective Signature for Efficient Authentication of XML Documents. In: Deswarte, Y., Cuppens, F., Jajodia, S., Wang, L. (eds.) Security and Protection in Information Processing Systems. IFIP, vol. 147, pp. 411–424. Springer, Boston (2004)
30. Reis, C., Gribble, S.D., Kohno, T., Weaver, N.C.: Detecting In-Flight Page Changes with Web Tripwires. In: Proc. of the 5th Usenix Symposium on Networked Systems Design and Implementation (NSDI 2008), pp. 31–44. Usenix Association (2008)
31. Rescorla, E.: RFC 2818 - HTTP Over TLS (2000),
    http://tools.ietf.org/html/rfc2818
32. Rescorla, E., Schiffman, A.: RFC 2660 - The Secure HyperText Transfer Protocol (1999), http://tools.ietf.org/html/rfc2660
33. Rivest, R.L., Shamir, A., Adleman, L.M.: A Method for Obtaining Digital Signatures and Public-Key Cryptosystems. Communications of the ACM (CACM) 21(2), 120–126 (1978)
34. Schröder, D., Schröder, H.: Verifiable data streaming. In: Proc. of the 19th ACM Conference on Computer and Communication Security (CCS 2012), pp. 953–964. ACM (2012)
35. Shamir, A., Tauman, Y.: Improved Online/Offline Signature Schemes. In: Kilian, J. (ed.) CRYPTO 2001. LNCS, vol. 2139, pp. 355–367. Springer, Heidelberg (2001)
36. Siege Home (2014), http://www.joedog.org/siege-home/
37. Singh, K., Wang, H.J., Moshchuk, A., Jackson, C., Lee, W.: Practical End-to-End Web Content Integrity. In: Proc. of the 21st International Conference on World Wide Web (WWW 2012), pp. 659–668. ACM (2012)

A Revocable Group Signature Scheme from Identity-Based Revocation Techniques: Achieving Constant-Size Revocation List

Nuttapong Attrapadung[1], Keita Emura[2], Goichiro Hanaoka[1], and Yusuke Sakai[1,*]

[1] National Institute of Advanced Industrial Science and Technology (AIST), Japan
{n.attrapadung,hanaoka-goichiro,yusuke.sakai}@aist.go.jp
[2] National Institute of Information and Communications Technology (NICT), Japan
k-emura@nict.go.jp

Abstract. Any multi-user cryptographic primitives need revocation since a legitimate user may quit the organization, or may turn to be malicious, or the key may be leaked. In the group signature context, usually group manager publishes the revocation list that contains revocation tokens. Since signers/verifiers need to obtain the revocation list in *each revocation epoch* for generating/verifying a group signature, a small-size revocation list is really important in practice. However, all previous revocable group signatures require at least $O(r)$-size revocation list, where r is the number of revoked users. In this paper, we propose the first revocable group signature scheme with the constant size revocation list from identity-based revocation (IBR) techniques. We use an IBR scheme proposed by Attrapadung-Libert-Panafieu (PKC2011) as a building block. Although the maximum number of the revoked users needs to be fixed in the setup phase, however, the maximum number of group members is potentially unbounded (as in IBR). This property has not been achieved in the recent scalable revocable group signature schemes, and seems to be of independent interest.

Keywords: Revocable Group Signature, Identity-Based Revocation.

1 Introduction

1.1 Group Signature and Revocation

Group signature, proposed by Chaum and van Heyst [12], is a famous cryptographic primitive that enables signer anonymity. The group manager (GM) issues a signing key to a user, and the user makes a group signature on a certain message. A verifier can verify the signature by a group public key only, i.e., without using any user-dependent value. Therefore, no verifier can identify who the actual signer is, though the validity of signatures can be verified.

---

* The fourth author is supported by a JSPS Fellowship for Young Scientists.

I. Boureanu, P. Owesarski, and S. Vaudenay (Eds.): ACNS 2014, LNCS 8479, pp. 419–437, 2014.

Any multi-user cryptographic primitives need revocation since a legitimate user may quit the organization, or may turn to be malicious, or the key may be leaked. In the group signature context, usually GM publishes the revocation list that contains revocation tokens.[1] Nakanishi et al. [28] proposed the first (pairing-based) group signature schemes with constant signing/verification costs in the random oracle model. However, their scheme requires $O(\sqrt{N})$-size public key, where N is the maximum number of users. Fan et al. [15] also proposed a group signature scheme with constant signing/verification costs in the random oracle model. Though they achieve constant-size group public keys, GM needs to publish $O(N)$ size values at each revocation. Therefore, the revocation list size of the Fan et al. scheme is $O(N)$.

Libert, Peters, and Yung (LPY) [25] proposed scalable group signature schemes with revocation in the standard model by applying broadcast encryption (BE) techniques, where no signing key update is required, the verification cost does not depend on the number of (revoked) users, and the size of public key is also small. Their main idea for implementing the revocation functionality in an efficient way is to apply subset cover framework (proposed by Naor, Naor, and Lotspiech (NNL) [30]) which is explained as follows. The set of authorized users S is partitioned into disjoint subsets $S_1, \ldots, S_m$, and an encryption key is associated with each subset. There are mainly two ways for making partitions called Complete Subtree (CS) and Subset Difference (SD). Here, $m = O(r)$ (SD) and $m = O(r \cdot \log(N/r))$ (CS). A public key setting of subset cover framework is proposed in [14], where CS and SD settings can be implemented by using identity-based encryption (IBE) and hierarchical IBE (HIBE), respectively. In the LPY schemes [25], denoted as the LPY1(SD) scheme and the LPY2(CS) scheme, respectively, each user has a decryption key of IBE(CS) or HIBE(SD) issued by GM in the join phase. Moreover, in each revocation epoch, GM publishes the revocation list which contains m NNL ciphertexts as revocation tokens. In the signature generation phase, a signer proves the decryption ability of a NNL ciphertext in order to prove that the signer has not been revoked. They use the Boneh-Boyen-Goh (BBG) HIBE [8] for SD and the Boneh-Boyen IBE [6] for CS as building blocks. One may think that the Boneh-Gentry-Waters (BGW) BE scheme [10] should be applied, since the BGW scheme supports the constant-size ciphertext and it may lead to an efficient construction. It might be true, but the size of public key becomes linear of N, and therefore there is no improvement form the Nakanishi et al. scheme [28] though random oracles can be removed.

Libert, Peters, and Yung also proposed another SD-based revocable group signature scheme with the constant-size certificate [24] by applying concise vector commitments [27] instead of HIBE. We denote this scheme the LPY3 scheme. In order to show that a signer belongs to one of the SD subsets, the signer proves that certain equality and inequality relations of identities against primary/secondary roots of the corresponding SD subset. See [24] for scheme

---

[1] Actually, the revocation list contains a set of the revoked users, however, this can be represented as at most N bits. So, we estimate the overhead size of the revocation list, i.e., the size of tokens, as in [24] and BE schemes.

details, but the crucial point is the revocation list contains m structure-preserving signatures (such as the Abe-Haralambiev-Ohkubo (AHO) signature [1,2]) for anonymously proving the equality and inequality relations.

Problem Statement: Though three LPY schemes [25,24] achieve not only efficient signing/verification costs but also small-size group public key and user certificate, the group public key and certificates need to be obtained only once. Whereas signers and verifiers need to obtain the revocation list in *each revocation epoch* for generating/verifying a group signature, and therefore a small-size revocation list is desired in practice. That is, there is room for argument on the size of the revocation list. However, as explained before, the set of authorized users is partitioned into disjoint subsets $S_1, \ldots, S_m$, and revocation list contains NNL ciphertexts/signatures in the LPY schemes, since m subsets are required for covering all non-revoked users.

It is to be noted that the efficiency of the LPY schemes, in terms of the public key size and signing/verification costs, are realized from the BE technique, but this technique itself brings on $O(r)$-size revocation list. So, for reducing the size of revocation list without detracting benefit points taken from BE, we need to not only investigate another methodology of BE but also this methodology also covers the above outcome of the BE technique.

1.2   Our Contribution

In this paper, we propose the first revocable group signature scheme in the standard model with the constant-size revocation list. We compare our schemes and (pairing-based) revocable group signature schemes which are secure in the standard model [26,24,25,29] in Table 1. As the underlying one-time signature (OTS) scheme of these group signature schemes, we use the Groth OTS scheme [17] (which is existential unforgeable under the discrete logarithm assumption in the standard model), where the verification key consists of 3 group elements and the signature consists of 2 group elements.

Our Main Idea: Revocable Group Signatures from IBR Techniques:
In Identity-Based BE (IBBE), a user with ID can decrypt a ciphertext if $\mathsf{ID} \in S$, where S is the set of authorized users. In contrary, in Identity-Based Revocation (IBR) [23], a user with ID can decrypt a ciphertext if $\mathsf{ID} \notin S$. In the group signature context, the set S can be seen as IDs of revoked users, say $\mathcal{R}$, and only a non-revoked user can prove that $\mathsf{ID} \notin \mathcal{R}$ by showing the decryption ability of a ciphertext associated with $\mathcal{R}$. We apply the Attrapadung-Libert-Panafieu IBR (ALP-IBR) scheme [4,3] as a building block.

It is particularly worth noting that only one ciphertext (corresponding to $\mathcal{R}$) needs to be contained into the revocation list, whereas m ciphertexts for each subset $S_1, \ldots, S_m$ and signatures thereof needs to be contained in the LPY1(SD)/LPY2(CS) schemes [25]. That is, revocation tokens contained in the revocation list can be described as in informally for now:

Table 1. Comparison between Pairing-based Revocable Group Signatures in the Standard Model. Let N be the maximum number of users, T be the maximum number of revocation epochs, T' be the parameter of the accumulated value in [29], r be the number of revoked users, and R be the maximum number of revoked users. We denote the number of group elements contained in a group signature on () in Signature size. $\Diamond$ stands for this scheme can be modified to have $O(1)$-size group public keys. † stands for this complexity is only invoked at the first signature of each revocation epoch. Bounded means that the maximum number of users N needs to be fixed in the setup phase.

Schemes	Group PK size	Sig. size	Membership cert size	Rev. list size
LV [26]	$O(T)^\Diamond$	$O(1)$ (47)	$O(1)$	$O(r)$
LPY1(SD) [25]	$O(\log N)^\Diamond$	$O(1)$ (96)	$O(\log^3 N)$	$O(r)$
LPY2(CS) [25]	$O(1)$	$O(1)$ (96)	$O(\log N)$	$O(r \cdot \log(N/r))$
LPY3 [24]	$O(\log N)$	$O(1)$ (144)	$O(1)$	$O(r)$
NF [29]	$O(T' \log N)$	$O(1)$ (143)	$O(T')$	$O(r/T')$
This work	$O(1)$	$O(1)$ (98)	$O(R)$	$O(1)$

Schemes	Sig. cost	Verif. cost	Rev. cost	Num. of Max. Users
LV [26]	$O(1)$	$O(r)$	$O(r)$	Bounded
LPY1(SD) [25]	$O(\log N)^\dagger$	$O(1)$	$O(r \cdot \log N)$	Bounded
LPY2(CS) [25]	$O(1)$	$O(1)$	$O(r \cdot \log(N/r))$	Bounded
LPY3 [24]	$O(1)$	$O(1)$	$O(r)$	Bounded
NF [29]	$O(T')^\dagger$	$O(1)$	$O(r \cdot \log N)$	Bounded
This work	$O(r)^\dagger$	$O(1)$	$O(r)$	Unbounded

LPY1(SD)/LPY2(CS): $RL = \{(\mathsf{Enc}(S_1), \ldots, \mathsf{Enc}(S_m)\}$, where Enc is IBE or HIBE, $S_1, \ldots, S_m$ are subsets, and $m = O(r)$ (SD) and $m = O(r \cdot \log(N/r))$ (CS). More precisely, RL contains m (structure-preserving) signatures on each $\mathsf{Enc}(S_i)$ for $i \in [1, m]$.

Ours: $RL = \{\mathsf{Enc}(\mathcal{R})\}$, where Enc is IBR of ALP and $\mathcal{R}$ is the set of revoked users. More precisely, RL contains a signature on $\mathsf{Enc}(\mathcal{R})$. Note that no structure-preserving signature is required here.

Since the ALP-IBR ciphertext is constant size, we can achieve the revocation list containing the $O(1)$-size revocation token. Moreover, in our scheme, a signer is not required to hide such information since all signers share one ciphertext, whereas in the LPY1(SD)/LPY2(CS) schemes, a signer needs to hide which subset is chosen, so as to achieve anonymity. This is the reason why no structure-preserving signature is required for establishing RL, and a structure preserving signature is used for hiding a membership certificate only in our scheme.

As another benefit point to apply IBR, the maximal number of group members is potentially unbounded (as in IBR). Though this property has been achieved in the (non-revocable) dynamic group signature context and revocable group signature scheme applying the revocation methodology introduced in [9],[2] whereas scalable revocable group signature schemes (introduced in Table 1) do not achieve this property, since these schemes apply BEs, vector commitments, or accumulators.

Moreover, a revocable group signature with constant-size public key can be constructed, though it is required to be obtained only once. That is, in IBR context, R-size public key is published in order to compute a ciphertext, whereas in group signature context, ciphertexts need to be computed by GM only,[3] and signers/verifiers do not use the IBR public key for signing/verification algorithms. So, the IBR public key can be contained into the GM secret key, and can be removed from the group public key.

We achieve the constant-size revocation list as expense of the size of membership certificate. Our scheme can be viewed as pre-computing *offline* components (certificate) so as to achieving optimal-size *online* components (revocation token). Though a signer is required $O(r)$ computations for signing, however, this procedure is only invoked at the first signature of each revocation epoch as in [25],[4] and no signing key update is required.

Concurrent Work: Independent of our work, recently Nakanishi and Funabiki (NF) [29] also consider to reduce the revocation list size by using a completely different method, namely extended accumulators based on [5]. Briefly, they reduce the number of structure-preserving signatures of the LPY3 scheme [24] from m to $\lceil m/T' \rceil$, where GM accumulates T' subsets in the SD method, and makes $\lceil m/T' \rceil$ signatures. Their scheme can be seen as a trade-off scheme, where they can reduce the revocation size as expense of the size of public key and membership certificate.

Improvement of the NF Scheme: We observe that the NF scheme also can achieve the constant size revocation list by setting $T' \geq R$ though this fact is not mentioned in the NF paper [29]. However, the signature size is longer than that of our scheme (see Table 1). That is, our scheme is more efficient than this variant of the NF scheme.

---

[2] RL contains signing keys of revoked users, and non-revoked users update their signing keys using these values. Moreover, GM also updates gpk according to the current RL. This methodology can be used for [13,16].

[3] The same thing occurs in the LPY1(SD) scheme [25], where the HIBE public key, say mpk_{BBG} in their notation, can be removed from the group public key. Note that the LPY3 scheme [25] requires $O(\log N)$-size group public key since signers need to compute vector commitments. Similarly, the NF scheme [29] requires $O(T' \cdot \log N)$-size group public key since signers need to compute accumulators. Moreover, even if a revocable group signature scheme is constructed from the BGW-BE scheme whose public key size is $O(N)$, it seems hard to reduce the public key size since a decryptor of a BE ciphertext needs to use the public key.

[4] Similarly, in the LPY1(SD) scheme [25], signers need to derive their HIBE secret key before computing a group signature.

2   Preliminaries

In this section, we give definitions of complexity assumptions, and introduce cryptographic tools which are applied in our construction. Let PPT means probabilistic polynomial time, and $x \xleftarrow{\$} X$ means that an element x is chosen at uniformly random from a set X. We use bilinear maps $e : \mathbb{G} \times \mathbb{G} \to \mathbb{G}_T$ over groups of prime order p, where $e(g,h) \neq 1_{\mathbb{G}_T}$ iff $g,h \neq 1_{\mathbb{G}}$.

2.1   Complexity Assumptions

Definition 1 (The Decision Linear (DLIN) assumption [9]). *We say that the DLIN assumption holds in $\mathbb{G}$ if for all PPT adversary $\mathcal{A}$, $\mathsf{Adv}_{\mathcal{A}}^{\mathsf{DLIN}}(\lambda) :=$ $|\Pr[\mathcal{A}(g,g^a,g^b,g^{ac},g^{bd},g^{c+d}) = 0] - \Pr[\mathcal{A}(g,g^a,g^b,g^{ac},g^{bd},g^z) = 0]|$ is negligible, where $g \xleftarrow{\$} \mathbb{G}$ and $a,b,c,d,z \xleftarrow{\$} \mathbb{Z}_p^*$.*

Definition 2 (The q-Strong Diffie-Hellman (SDH) assumption [7]). *We say that the q-SDH assumption holds in $\mathbb{G}$ if for all PPT adversary $\mathcal{A}$, $\mathsf{Adv}_{\mathcal{A}}^{q\text{-SDH}}(\lambda)$ $:= \Pr[\mathcal{A}(g,g^a,g^{a^2},\ldots,g^{a^q}) = (g^{\frac{1}{a+x}},x)]$ is negligible, where $g \xleftarrow{\$} \mathbb{G}$, $a \xleftarrow{\$} \in \mathbb{Z}_p^*$, and $x \in \mathbb{Z}_p$.*

Definition 3 (The q-Simultaneous Flexible Pairing (SFP) assumption [2]). *We say that the q-SFP assumption holds in $\mathbb{G}$ if for all PPT adversary $\mathcal{A}$, $\mathsf{Adv}_{\mathcal{A}}^{q\text{-SFP}}(\lambda) := \Pr[\mathcal{A}(g_z,h_z,g_r,h_r,a,\tilde{a},b,\tilde{b},\{(z_j,r_j,s_j,t_j,u_j,v_j,w_j)\}_{j=1}^q) = (z^*,r^*,s^*,t^*,u^*,v^*,w^*)]$ is negligible, where $g_z,h_z,g_r,h_r,a,\tilde{a},b,\tilde{b} \xleftarrow{\$} \mathbb{G}$, $z^* \neq 1_{\mathbb{G}}$, and $z^* \neq z_j$ for all $j = 1,\ldots,q$. Note that for all $j = 1,\ldots,q$, $e(a,\tilde{a}) = e(g_z,z_j)$ $e(g_r,r_j)e(s_j,t_j)$ and $e(b,\tilde{b}) = e(h_z,z_j)e(h_r,u_j)e(v_j,w_j)$ hold, and $(z^*,r^*,s^*,t^*,u^*,v^*,w^*)$ also satisfies these equations.*

Next, we newly define a static complexity assumption (flexible Parallel Bilinear Diffie-Hellman, flexible PBDH) as follows. The flexible PBDH assumption can be considered as a variant of the Bilinear Diffie-Hellman Exponent (BDHE) assumption [8,10]. We give the analysis of the flexible PBDH assumption over bilinear generic group model in the full version of this paper due to the page limitation, where it belongs to the uber-assumption family [8,11].

Definition 4 (The q-Computation Flexible PBDH assumption). *We say that the flexible q-Flexible Parallel Bilinear Diffie-Hellman (q-flexible PBDH) assumption holds in $(\mathbb{G},\mathbb{G}_T)$ if for all PPT adversary $\mathcal{A}$, $\mathsf{Adv}_{\mathcal{A}}^{q\text{-F-PBDH}}(\lambda) :=$ $\Pr[\mathcal{A}(g,\{g^{\frac{a}{b_i}},g^{b_i}\}_{i\in[1,q]},\{g^{\frac{ab_i}{b_j}}\}_{i,j\in[1,q],i\neq j}) = (g^y,g^{y(\frac{a}{b_i}(b_1+\cdots+b_q))}) \wedge i \in [1,q] \wedge y \in \mathbb{Z}_p^*]$ is negligible, where $g \xleftarrow{\$} \mathbb{G}$ and $a,b_1,\ldots,b_q \xleftarrow{\$} \mathbb{Z}_p$.*

2.2   Groth-Sahai Proof Systems

Here, we introduce Groth-Sahai proof systems [19] as follows. Let A,B be equal-dimension vectors or matrices containing group elements. Then $A \odot B$ denotes their entry-wise product. Let $\mathbf{f} := (\mathbf{f_1}, \mathbf{f_2}, \mathbf{f_3}) \in \mathbb{G}^3 \times \mathbb{G}^3 \times \mathbb{G}^3$ be a common reference string (CRS) s.t. $\beta_1, \beta_2, \xi_1, \xi_2 \xleftarrow{\$} \mathbb{Z}_p^*$, $f_1 = g^{\beta_1}$, $f_2 = g^{\beta_2}$, $\mathbf{f_1} = (f_1, 1, g)$ and $\mathbf{f_2} = (1, f_2, g)$. In the perfectly sound proof setting, $\mathbf{f_3} = \mathbf{f_1}^{\xi_1} \odot \mathbf{f_2}^{\xi_2}$ where $\xi_1, \xi_2 \in \mathbb{Z}_p^*$. To commit a group element $X \in \mathbb{G}$, compute commitments $C = (1, 1, X) \odot \mathbf{f_1}^r \odot \mathbf{f_2}^s \odot \mathbf{f_3}^t$ with $r, s, t \xleftarrow{\$} \mathbb{Z}_p^*$, which is a ciphertext of the Boneh-Boyen-Shacham linear encryption scheme. In the witness indistinguishability (WI) setting, $\mathbf{f_1}, \mathbf{f_2}, \mathbf{f_3}$ are linearly independent. Then, C is a perfectly hiding commitment. To commit a scalar $x \in \mathbb{Z}_p$, compute $C = \boldsymbol{\varphi}^x \odot \mathbf{f_1}^r \odot \mathbf{f_2}^s$ with $r, s \xleftarrow{\$} \mathbb{Z}_p^*$. In the perfectly sound proof setting, $\boldsymbol{\varphi} = \mathbf{f_3} \odot (1, 1, g)$ where $\mathbf{f_3} = \mathbf{f_1}^{\xi_1} \odot \mathbf{f_2}^{\xi_2}$ for $\xi_1, \xi_2 \in \mathbb{Z}_p^*$. Then, $\boldsymbol{\varphi}, \mathbf{f_1}, \mathbf{f_2}$ are linearly independent. In the WI setting, $\boldsymbol{\varphi} = \mathbf{f_1}^{\xi_1} \odot \mathbf{f_2}^{\xi_2}$ for $\xi_1, \xi_2 \in \mathbb{Z}_p^*$.

Groth-Sahai proofs prove that the committed values satisfy pairing-product equations $\prod_{i=1}^n e(\mathcal{A}_i, \mathcal{X}_i) \cdot \prod_{i=1}^n \cdot \prod_{j=1}^n e(\mathcal{X}_i, \mathcal{X}_j)^{a_{i,j}} = t_T$ for variables $\mathcal{X}_1, \dots, \mathcal{X}_n \in \mathbb{G}$, constants $t_T \in \mathbb{G}_T$, $\mathcal{A}_1, \dots, \mathcal{A}_n \in \mathbb{G}$, $a_{i,j} \in \mathbb{Z}_p$ for $i, j \in \{1, \dots, n\}$. Groth-Sahai proofs also follow multi-exponentiation equations $\prod_{i=1}^m \mathcal{A}_i^{y_i} \cdot \prod_{i=1}^n \mathcal{X}_j^{b_j} \cdot \prod_{i=1}^m \cdot \prod_{i=1}^n \mathcal{X}_j^{y_i \gamma_{ij}} = T$ for variables $\mathcal{X}_1, \dots, \mathcal{X}_n \in \mathbb{G}$, $y_1, \dots, y_m \in \mathbb{Z}_p$, and constants $T, \mathcal{A}_1, \dots, \mathcal{A}_m \in \mathbb{G}$, $b_1, \dots, b_n \in \mathbb{Z}_p$ and γ_{ij} for $i \in \{1, \dots, m\}$ and $j \in \{1, \dots, n\}$. Proofs for quadratic equations require 9 group elements, proofs for linear equations require 3 group elements, and proofs for linear multi-exponentiation equations require 2 group elements.

2.3   The Abe-Haralambiev-Ohkubo Structure-preserving Signatures

In this section, we introduce the AHO signature [2]. Let $pp = ((\mathbb{G}, \mathbb{G}_T), g)$ and $n \in \mathbb{N}$ be an upper bound on the number of group elements that can be signed altogether. In our group signature, we set $n = 3$.

KeyGen(pp, n) : Choose $G_r, H_r \xleftarrow{\$} \mathbb{G}$, $\gamma_z, \delta_z \xleftarrow{\$} \mathbb{Z}_p$, and $\gamma_i, \delta_i \xleftarrow{\$} \mathbb{Z}_p$ for $i = 1, \dots, n$. Compute $G_z = G_r^{\gamma_z}$, $H_z = H_r^{\delta_z}$, $G_i = G_r^{\gamma_i}$, and $H_i = H_r^{\delta_i}$ for $i = 1, \dots, n$, and compute $\alpha_a, \alpha_b \xleftarrow{\$} \mathbb{Z}_p$, $A = e(G_r, g^{\alpha_a})$, and $B = e(H_r, g^{\alpha_b})$. Output $pk = (G_r, H_r, G_z, H_z, \{G_i, H_i\}_{i=1}^n, A, B) \in \mathbb{G}^{2n+4} \times \mathbb{G}_T^2$ and $sk = (\alpha_a, \alpha_b, \gamma_z, \delta_z, \{\gamma_i, \delta_i\}_{i=1}^n)$.

Sign($sk, (M_1, \dots, M_n)$) : Choose $\zeta, \rho, \tau, \nu, \omega \xleftarrow{\$} \mathbb{Z}_p$, and output a signature $\sigma = (\theta_1, \dots, \theta_7)$ where $\left(\theta_1 = g^\zeta, \theta_2 = g^{\rho - \gamma_z \xi} \cdot \prod_{i=1}^n M_i^{-\gamma_i}, \theta_3 = G_r^\tau, \theta_4 = g^{(\alpha_a - \rho)/\tau},\right.$

$\left.\theta_5 = g^{\nu - \delta_z \xi} \cdot \prod_{i=1}^n M_i^{-\delta_i}, \theta_6 = H_r^\omega, \theta_7 = g^{(\alpha_b - \nu)/\omega}\right).$

Verify($pk, \sigma, (M_1, \dots, M_n)$) : Check the equations $A = e(G_z, \theta_1)e(G_r, \theta_2)e(\theta_3, \theta_4)$ $\prod_{i=1}^n e(G_i, M_i)$ and $B = e(H_z, \theta_1)e(H_r, \theta_5)e(\theta_6, \theta_7) \prod_{i=1}^n e(H_i, M_i)$. If both equations hold, then output 1, and 0 otherwise.

The AHO signature is existential unforgeable under the q-SFP assumption.

3   Definitions of Revocable Group Signature

In this section, we give the syntax and correctness definitions of revocable group signature. We use the LPY definitions [24,25] which are modified from the Kiayias-Yung (KY) model [21,20] to match the revocation functionality. We use R to the Setup algorithm as its input, instead of the maximal number of group members N, due to our construction. Though we need to fix R in the setup phase, however, the maximal number of group members is potentially unbounded (as in IBR).

A revocable group signature scheme $\mathcal{R}\text{-}\mathcal{GS}$ consists of 6 algorithms (Setup, Join, Revoke, Sign, Verify, Open) as follows:

Definition 5 (Revocable Group Signature).

Setup(λ, R) : *This algorithm takes as inputs a security parameter $\lambda \in \mathbb{N}$ and a maximal number of revoked users $R \in \mathbb{N}$, and outputs a group public key $\mathcal{Y}$, the group manager (GM) private key for revocation $\mathcal{S}_{GM}$, and the opening authority (OA) private key for opening $\mathcal{S}_{OA}$. Moreover, the algorithm initializes a public state St comprising a set data structure $St_{users} = \emptyset$ and a string data structure $St_{trans} = \epsilon$.*

Join$^{GM, \mathcal{U}_i}$: *This interactive protocol between GM and a user $\mathcal{U}_i$ (whose identity is ID_i) involves two interactive Turing machines J_{user} and J_{GM} which execution is denoted as $[J_{user}(\lambda, \mathcal{Y}), J_{GM}(\lambda, St, \mathcal{Y}, \mathcal{S}_{GM})]$. $\mathcal{U}_i$ obtains a membership secret sec_i and a membership certificate $cert_i$ which contains ID_i. If the protocol is successful, GM updates $St_{users} \leftarrow St_{users} \cup \{ID_i\}$ and $St_{trans} \leftarrow St_{trans} || \langle i, transcript_i \rangle$.*

Revoke$(\mathcal{Y}, \mathcal{S}_{GM}, t, \mathcal{R}_t \subset St_{users})$: *This algorithm takes as input $\mathcal{Y}$, $\mathcal{S}_{GM}$, a revocation epoch t, and a set of revoked users $\mathcal{R}_t \subset St_{users}$, and outputs an updated revocation list RL_t which contains $\mathcal{R}_t$.*

Sign$(t, RL_t, cert, sec, M)$: *This algorithm takes as input a time t, RL_t, cert, sec, and a message M to be signed, and outputs $\bot$ if $ID \in \mathcal{R}_t$, and a group signature Σ, otherwise.*

Verify$(\Sigma, t, RL_t, M, \mathcal{Y})$: *This algorithm takes as input Σ, t, RL_t, M, and $\mathcal{Y}$, and outputs 1 or 0 which mean valid or invalid, respectively.*

Open$(M, \Sigma, \mathcal{Y}, t, \mathcal{S}_{OA}, St)$: *This algorithm takes as input M, Σ, $\mathcal{Y}$, t, $\mathcal{S}_{OA}$, and $St := (St_{users}, St_{trans})$, and outputs i such that $ID_i \in St_{users} \cup \{\bot\}$, where $\bot$ is a symbol indicating an opening failure.*

Next, we define correctness. Let St be a public state, and St is said to be valid if it can be reached from $St = (\emptyset, \epsilon)$ by a Turing machine having oracle access to J_{GM}. A state St' is said to be extended anther state St if it can be reached from St. As in [21,20,24,25] we use $cert_i \rightleftharpoons_{\mathcal{Y}} sec_i$ to express that there exist coin tosses ϖ for J_{GM} and J_{user} s.t., for some valid state St', the execution of $[J_{user}(\lambda, \mathcal{Y}), J_{GM}(\lambda, St, \mathcal{Y}, \mathcal{S}_{GM})](\varpi)$ provides J_{user} with $\langle i, cert_i, sec_i \rangle$.

Definition 6 (Correctness).   *A revocable group signature scheme $\mathcal{R}\text{-}\mathcal{GS}$ is said to be correct if:*

1. *In a valid state* $St = (St_{\mathsf{users}}, St_{\mathsf{trans}})$, *the condition* $|St_{\mathsf{users}}| = |St_{\mathsf{trans}}|$ *holds, and no two entries of* St_{trans} *can contain certificates with the same tag. Note that in our scheme, tag is* (ID, X).
2. *If* $[\mathsf{J}_{\mathsf{user}}(\lambda, \mathcal{Y}), \mathsf{J}_{\mathsf{GM}}(\lambda, St, \mathcal{Y}, \mathcal{S}_{\mathsf{GM}})]$ *is honestly run by both parties and* $\langle i, \mathsf{cert}_i, \mathsf{sec}_i \rangle$ *is obtained by* $\mathsf{J}_{\mathsf{user}}$, *then* $\mathsf{cert}_i \rightleftharpoons_{\mathcal{Y}} \mathsf{sec}_i$ *holds.*
3. *For each* t *and any* $\langle i, \mathsf{cert}_i, \mathsf{sec}_i \rangle$ *satisfying condition 2,* $\mathsf{Verify}(\mathsf{Sign}(t, RL_t, \mathsf{cert}_i, \mathsf{sec}_i, M), t, RL_t, M, \mathcal{Y}) = 1$ *holds if* $\mathsf{ID}_i \notin \mathcal{R}_t$.
4. *For any* $\langle i, \mathsf{cert}_i, \mathsf{sec}_i \rangle$ *resulting from the interaction* $[\mathsf{J}_{\mathsf{user}}(\cdot, \cdot), \mathsf{J}_{\mathsf{GM}}(\cdot, St, \cdot, \cdot)]$ *for some valid state* St, *any* t *s.t.* $\mathsf{ID}_i \notin \mathcal{R}_t$, $\mathsf{Open}(M, \Sigma, \mathcal{Y}, t, \mathcal{S}_{\mathsf{OA}}, St) = i$ *holds where* $\Sigma = \mathsf{Sign}(t, RL_t, \mathsf{cert}_i, \mathsf{sec}_i, M)$.

Next we introduce three security definitions, misidentification, non-frameability, and anonymity. Before that, we introduce variables and oracles as follows:

$\mathsf{state}_{\mathcal{I}}$: This is a data structure which is initialized as $\mathsf{state}_{\mathcal{I}} = (St, \mathcal{Y}, \mathcal{S}_{\mathsf{GM}}, \mathcal{S}_{\mathsf{OA}})$ $\leftarrow \mathsf{Setup}(\lambda, R)$. This structure represents the state of the interface as the adversary invokes the various oracles, and includes a counter t which indicates the number of user revocation queries so far (i.e., the current revocation epoch).

$n = |St_{\mathsf{users}}|$: This is the current cardinality of the group.

Sigs : This is a set of signatures Sigs created by the signing oracle. Each entry is represented as $(\mathsf{ID}_i, t, M, \Sigma)$, where Σ is a group signature on M signed by $\mathcal{U}_i$ on t.

U^a : This is the set of corrupted users who were introduced by the adversary $\mathcal{A}$ via an execution of the join protocol.

U^b : This is the set of honest users who were added in the system by the join protocol with the adversary $\mathcal{A}$ who acts a dishonest GM. $\mathcal{A}$ can obtain the transcript of the join protocol, but $\mathcal{A}$ cannot obtain sec.

Q_{pub}, Q_{keyGM}, **and** Q_{keyOA} : When these oracles are invoked, the interface looks up $\mathsf{state}_{\mathcal{I}}$, and returns $\mathcal{Y}$, $\mathcal{S}_{\mathsf{GM}}$, or $\mathcal{S}_{\mathsf{OA}}$, respectively.

$Q_{\mathsf{a\text{-}join}}$: This is the join oracle for a corrupted user. On behalf of GM, the interface runs J_{GM} in interaction with $\mathsf{J}_{\mathsf{user}}$ which is run by the adversary. If this protocol successfully ends, the interface increments $n \leftarrow n + 1$, add ID_n to U^a, and updates St s.t. $St_{\mathsf{users}} \leftarrow St_{\mathsf{users}} \cup \{\mathsf{ID}_n\}$ and $St_{\mathsf{trans}} \leftarrow St_{\mathsf{trans}} || \langle n, \mathsf{transcript}_n \rangle$.

$Q_{\mathsf{b\text{-}join}}$: This is the join oracle for an honest user. On behalf of a user, the interface runs $\mathsf{J}_{\mathsf{user}}$ in interaction with J_{GM} which is run by the adversary. If this protocol successfully ends, the interface increments $n \leftarrow n + 1$, add ID_n to U^b, and updates St s.t. $St_{\mathsf{users}} \leftarrow St_{\mathsf{users}} \cup \{\mathsf{ID}_n\}$ and $St_{\mathsf{trans}} \leftarrow St_{\mathsf{trans}} || \langle n, \mathsf{transcript}_n \rangle$. Moreover, the interface stores cert_n and sec_n in a private part of $\mathsf{state}_{\mathcal{I}}$.

Q_{sig} : This is the signing oracle. Given (i, M), the interface checks whether the private area of $\mathsf{state}_{\mathcal{I}}$ contains $(\mathsf{cert}_i, \mathsf{sec}_i)$ or not, and also checks $\mathsf{ID}_i \notin \mathcal{R}_t$, where t is the current revocation epoch. In no such $(\mathsf{cert}_i, \mathsf{sec}_i)$ with $\mathsf{ID}_i \notin \mathcal{R}_t$ exist or $\mathsf{ID}_i \notin U^b$, then return $\perp$. Otherwise, the interface runs $\Sigma \leftarrow \mathsf{Sign}(t, RL_t, \mathsf{cert}_i, \mathsf{sec}_i, M)$, updates $\mathsf{Sigs} \leftarrow \mathsf{Sigs} || (\mathsf{ID}_i, t, M, \Sigma)$, and returns Σ.

Q_{open} : This is the opening oracle. Given (M, Σ), the interface runs $\mathsf{Open}(M, \Sigma,$ $\mathcal{Y}, t, \mathcal{S}_{\mathsf{OA}}, St)$ using the current state St, and returns its output result.

$Q_{\mathsf{open}}^{\neg S}$: This is the restricted opening oracle. Let S be a set with the form (M, Σ, t). Given (M, Σ, t) the oracle returns the result of $\mathsf{Open}(M, \Sigma, \mathcal{Y}, t,$ $\mathcal{S}_{\mathsf{OA}}, St)$ if $(M, \Sigma, t) \notin S$.

Q_{read} **and** Q_{write} : These are reading and writing oracles, respectively, in order to read/write $\mathsf{state}_{\mathcal{I}}$. Q_{read} outputs the whole $\mathsf{state}_{\mathcal{I}}$ but the public/private keys and the private part of $\mathsf{state}_{\mathcal{I}}$ where membership secrets are stored after $Q_{\mathsf{b\text{-}join}}$ queries. The adversary can modify $\mathsf{state}_{\mathcal{I}}$ via Q_{write} at will as long as it does not remove or alter elements of St_{users}, St_{trans}, or invalidate the public state St.

Q_{revoke} : This is the revocation oracle. Given an index $i \in \mathbb{N}$ such that $\mathsf{ID}_i \in St_{\mathsf{users}}$, the interface checks whether ID_i is contained in the appropriate user set (i.e., either U^a or U^b) or not, and whether $\langle i, \mathsf{transcript}_i \rangle$ s.t. $\mathsf{ID}_i \notin \mathcal{R}_t$ is contained in St_{trans} or not, where t is the current revocation epoch. If not, then return $\bot$. Otherwise, the interface increments $t \leftarrow t+1$, adds ID_i to $\mathcal{R}_t$, and updates RL_t. We assumed that the adversary only revokes one user per query to Q_{revoke}. However, it can be easily extended to allow multiple users revocation at once.

Moreover, we define the $\mathsf{IsRevoked}$ algorithm. This algorithm takes as input $(\mathsf{sec}, \mathsf{cert}, RL_t)$, and outputs 1 if a user who has $(\mathsf{sec}, \mathsf{cert})$ is contained in RL_t, and 0 otherwise.

Next we introduce three security definitions, misidentification, non-frameability, and anonymity. Briefly, misidentification guarantees that no adversary (who does not have $\mathcal{S}_{\mathsf{GM}}$) can produce a valid group signature whose opening result is in outside of the set of non-revoked adversarially-controlled users. Non-frameability guarantees that no adversary (who can corrupt GM and OA) can produce a group signature whose opening result is an honest user. Anonymity guarantees that no adversary (who does not have $\mathcal{S}_{\mathsf{OA}}$) can distinguish whether signers of two group signatures are the same or not.

Definition 7 (Misidentification). *Let $\mathcal{A}$ be an adversary and $\mathcal{C}$ be the challenger. $\mathcal{C}$ runs $\mathsf{state}_{\mathcal{I}} = (St, \mathcal{Y}, \mathcal{S}_{\mathsf{GM}}, \mathcal{S}_{\mathsf{OA}}) \leftarrow \mathsf{Setup}(\lambda, R)$. $\mathcal{A}$ is allowed to access Q_{pub}, $Q_{\mathsf{a\text{-}join}}$, Q_{revoke}, Q_{read}, and Q_{keyOA}. Finally, $\mathcal{A}$ outputs (M^*, Σ^*). We say that $\mathcal{A}$ wins if (1) $\mathsf{Verify}(\Sigma^*, t^*, RL_{t^*}, M^*, \mathcal{Y}) = 1$, where t^* is the challenge revocation epoch, and (2) for $\mathsf{ID} \leftarrow \mathsf{Open}(M^*, \Sigma^*, \mathcal{Y}, t^*, \mathcal{S}_{\mathsf{OA}}, St')$, $\mathsf{ID} \notin U^a \setminus \mathcal{R}_{t^*}$. Let $\mathsf{Adv}_{\mathcal{A}}^{\mathsf{mis\text{-}id}}(\lambda) := \Pr[\mathcal{A}\ wins]$. We say that $\mathcal{R}\text{-}\mathcal{GS}$ is secure against misidentification attack if for all PPT $\mathcal{A}$, $\mathsf{Adv}_{\mathcal{A}}^{\mathsf{mis\text{-}id}}(\lambda)$ is negligible.*

Definition 8 (Non-frameability). *Let $\mathcal{A}$ be an adversary and $\mathcal{C}$ be the challenger. $\mathcal{C}$ runs $\mathsf{state}_{\mathcal{I}} = (St, \mathcal{Y}, \mathcal{S}_{\mathsf{GM}}, \mathcal{S}_{\mathsf{OA}}) \leftarrow \mathsf{Setup}(\lambda, R)$. $\mathcal{A}$ is allowed to access Q_{pub}, Q_{KeyGM}, Q_{keyOA}, $Q_{\mathsf{b\text{-}join}}$, Q_{revoke}, Q_{sig}, Q_{read}, and Q_{write}. Finally, $\mathcal{A}$ outputs $(M^*, \Sigma^*, t^*, RL_{t^*})$. We say that $\mathcal{A}$ wins if (1) $\mathsf{Verify}(\Sigma^*, t^*, RL_{t^*}, M^*, \mathcal{Y}) = 1$, and (2) for $\mathsf{ID} \leftarrow \mathsf{Open}(M^*, \Sigma^*, \mathcal{Y}, t^*, \mathcal{S}_{\mathsf{OA}}, St')$, $\mathsf{ID} \in U^b$ and $(\mathsf{ID}, t^*, M^*, *) \notin \mathsf{Sigs}$. Let $\mathsf{Adv}_{\mathcal{A}}^{\mathsf{nf}}(\lambda) := \Pr[\mathcal{A}\ wins]$. We say that $\mathcal{R}\text{-}\mathcal{GS}$ is secure against misidentification attack if for all PPT $\mathcal{A}$, $\mathsf{Adv}_{\mathcal{A}}^{\mathsf{nf}}(\lambda)$ is negligible.*

Definition 9 (Anonymity). *Let $\mathcal{A}$ be an adversary and $\mathcal{C}$ be the challenger. $\mathcal{C}$ runs $\mathsf{state}_{\mathcal{I}} = (St, \mathcal{Y}, \mathcal{S}_{\mathsf{GM}}, \mathcal{S}_{\mathsf{OA}}) \leftarrow \mathsf{Setup}(\lambda, R)$. $\mathcal{A}$ is allowed to access Q_{pub}, Q_{KeyGM}, Q_{revoke}, Q_{open}, Q_{read}, and Q_{write}. $\mathcal{A}$ outputs $(aux, M^*, t^*, RL_{t^*}, (\mathsf{cert}_0^*,$ $\mathsf{sec}_0^*), (\mathsf{cert}_1^*, \mathsf{sec}_1^*))$. For $d \in \{0,1\}$, if $(\mathsf{cert}_d^* \rightleftharpoons_{\mathcal{Y}} \mathsf{sec}_d^*)$, $\mathsf{IsRevoked}(\mathsf{sec}_d^*, \mathsf{cert}_d^*,$ $RL_{t^*}) = 0$, and $\mathsf{cert}_0^* \neq \mathsf{cert}_1^*$, then $\mathcal{C}$ chooses $b \xleftarrow{\$} \{0,1\}$, computes $\Sigma^* \leftarrow$ $\mathsf{Sign}(t^*, RL_{t^*}, \mathsf{cert}_b^*, \mathsf{sec}_b^*, M^*)$, and sends Σ^* to $\mathcal{A}$. Then $\mathcal{A}$ is allowed to access $Q_{\mathsf{pub}}, Q_{\mathsf{KeyGM}}, Q_{\mathsf{open}}, Q_{\mathsf{read}},$ and Q_{write}, with one exception that $\mathcal{A}$ is not allowed to send (M^*, Σ^*, t^*) to Q_{open}. Finally, $\mathcal{A}$ outputs $b' \in \{0,1\}$. Let $\mathsf{Adv}_{\mathcal{A}}^{\mathsf{anon}}(\lambda) :=$ $|\Pr[b = b'] - \frac{1}{2}|$. We say that $\mathcal{R}\text{-}\mathcal{GS}$ is anonymous if all PPT $\mathcal{A}$, $\mathsf{Adv}_{\mathcal{A}}^{\mathsf{anon}}(\lambda)$ is negligible.*

4 Attrapadung-Libert-Panafieu Identity-Based Revocation

For the sake of clarity, in this section we introduce the Attrapadung-Libert-Panafieu Identity-Based Revocation (ALP-IBR) scheme [4,3]. Before that, we introduce the underlying idea for constructing ALP-IBR as follows: Let $\mathcal{R} = (\mathsf{ID}_1, \ldots, \mathsf{ID}_r)$ be the set of unauthorized users, and then the polynomial $f_{\mathcal{R}}(Z) = (Z - \mathsf{ID}_1) \cdots (Z - \mathsf{ID}_r) = a_0 + a_1 Z + \cdots a_{r-1} Z^{r-1} + Z^r$ and its coefficients $\boldsymbol{y}_{\mathcal{R}} = (a_0, a_1, \ldots, a_{r-1}, 1)$ are uniquely determined. Let $\boldsymbol{X}_{\mathsf{ID}} := (1, \mathsf{ID}, \mathsf{ID}^2, \ldots, \mathsf{ID}^r)$. Then, $\mathsf{ID} \notin \mathcal{R} \iff f_{\mathcal{R}}(\mathsf{ID}) \neq 0 \iff \boldsymbol{y}_{\mathcal{R}} \cdot \boldsymbol{X}_{\mathsf{ID}} \neq 0$ hold. Let $(r+1) \times r$ matrix M_{ID} be

$$M_{\mathsf{ID}} := \begin{pmatrix} -\mathsf{ID} & -\mathsf{ID}^2 & \cdots & -\mathsf{ID}^r \\ 1 & 0 & \cdots & 0 \\ 0 & 1 & \cdots & 0 \\ \vdots & \vdots & \ddots & \vdots \\ 0 & 0 & \cdots & 1 \end{pmatrix} = \begin{pmatrix} -\mathsf{ID} & -\mathsf{ID}^2 & \cdots & -\mathsf{ID}^r \\ & I_r & \end{pmatrix}$$

where I_r is the $r \times r$ identity matrix, and let M_1 be the first row of M_{ID}, i.e., $(-\mathsf{ID}, -\mathsf{ID}^2, \ldots, -\mathsf{ID}^r)$. Let $\boldsymbol{\omega} = (a_1, \ldots, a_{r-1}, 1)$. Then, $\boldsymbol{\omega} M_1^{\mathsf{T}} = -(a_1 \mathsf{ID} + a_2 \mathsf{ID}^2 + \cdots + a_{r-1} \mathsf{ID}^r + \mathsf{ID}^r)$. Now $f_{\mathcal{R}}(\mathsf{ID}) \neq 0 \iff -(a_1 \mathsf{ID} + a_2 \mathsf{ID}^2 + \cdots + a_{r-1} \mathsf{ID}^r + \mathsf{ID}^r) \neq a_0$ holds. That is, $\mathsf{ID} \notin \mathcal{R} \iff \boldsymbol{\omega} M_1^{\mathsf{T}} \neq a_0$ holds. The ALP-IBR scheme is constructed by using this relation.

Next, we introduce the ALP-IBR scheme. An IBR scheme $\mathcal{IBR}$ consists of 4 algorithms (Setup, KeyGen, Encrypt, Decrypt). Briefly, a user whose identity is ID has a secret key sk_{ID}. A ciphertext which is associated with a set of revoked user $\mathcal{R}$ can be decrypted by sk_{ID} if $\mathsf{ID} \notin \mathcal{R}$. In the following scheme, $g^{\boldsymbol{\alpha}} := (g^{\alpha_1}, \ldots, g^{\alpha_{R+1}})$ for $\boldsymbol{\alpha} = (\alpha_1, \ldots, \alpha_{R+1})$ and for $\boldsymbol{A} = g^{\boldsymbol{\alpha}}$, $\boldsymbol{A}^z = (g^{\boldsymbol{\alpha}})^z = g^{\langle \boldsymbol{a}, z \rangle}$, where $\langle \cdot, \cdot \rangle$ is the inner product.

$\mathsf{Setup}(1^{\lambda}, R)$: Here λ is a security parameter and R is the maximum number of revoked users. Choose a bilinear group $\mathbb{G}$ of prime order $p > 2^{\lambda}$ with a random generator $g \xleftarrow{\$} \mathbb{G}$. Choose $\alpha, \alpha_1, \ldots, \alpha_{R+1} \xleftarrow{\$} \mathbb{Z}_p^*$, and set $\boldsymbol{\alpha} := (\alpha_1, \ldots, \alpha_{R+1})$. Output $pk_{\mathsf{ALP}} = (g, g^{\boldsymbol{\alpha}}, \mathsf{A} = e(g,g)^{\alpha})$ and $msk_{\mathsf{ALP}} = \alpha$.

KeyGen(ID, msk, pk) : Let M_{ID} be a $(R+1) \times R$ matrix defined as in the above. Choose $u \overset{\$}{\leftarrow} \mathbb{Z}_p^*$, and compute $D_0 = g^u$, $D_1 = g^{\alpha+u\alpha_1}$, and $\boldsymbol{K} = g^{uM_{\mathsf{ID}}^{\mathrm{T}}\boldsymbol{\alpha}}$, and output $sk_{\mathsf{ID}} = (D_0, D_1, \boldsymbol{K})$, where $\boldsymbol{K} = g^{uM_{\mathsf{ID}}^{\mathrm{T}}\boldsymbol{\alpha}} = (g^{u(-\mathsf{ID}\alpha_1+\alpha_2)}, \ldots, g^{u(-\mathsf{ID}^R\alpha_1+\alpha_{R+1})}) \in \mathbb{G}^R$.

Encrypt($\mathcal{R}, M, pk$) : For a set of revoked user $\mathcal{R} = (\mathsf{ID}_1, \ldots, \mathsf{ID}_r)$, let $\boldsymbol{y}_{\mathcal{R}} = (a_0, a_1, \ldots, a_{r-1}, 1)$ is the vector of coefficients of $f_{\mathcal{R}}(Z) = (Z - \mathsf{ID}_1) \cdots (Z - \mathsf{ID}_r)$, where $\mathcal{R} = \{\mathsf{ID}_1, \ldots, \mathsf{ID}_r\}$ is the set of identities of revoked users. Choose $s \overset{\$}{\leftarrow} \mathbb{Z}_p^*$, and compute $C_0 = M \cdot \mathsf{A}^s$, $C_1 = g^s$, and $C_2 = g^{s\langle \boldsymbol{y}_{\mathcal{R}}, \boldsymbol{\alpha}\rangle}$. Note that $C_2 = g^{s\langle \boldsymbol{y}_{\mathcal{R}}, \boldsymbol{\alpha}\rangle}$ can be computed without knowing $\boldsymbol{\alpha}$ from g^α and $\boldsymbol{y}_{\mathcal{R}}$. Output a ciphertext $C = (C_0, C_1, C_2)$.

Decrypt($C, \mathcal{R}, sk_{\mathsf{ID}}, pk$) : Let M_1 be the vector of the first row of M_{ID}. Let $\boldsymbol{y}_{\mathcal{R}} = (a_0, a_1, \ldots, a_{r-1}, 1)$ as in the Encryption algorithm. If $\mathsf{ID} \in \mathcal{R}$, then $\boldsymbol{\omega}M_1^{\mathrm{T}} = a_0$ holds, where $\boldsymbol{\omega} = (a_1, \ldots, a_r, 1)$, and output $\perp$. Otherwise, if $\mathsf{ID} \notin \mathcal{R}$, then $\boldsymbol{\omega}M_1^{\mathrm{T}} \neq a_0$ holds. Let $\boldsymbol{K}_r$ be the vector of the first r components of $\boldsymbol{K}$, i.e., $\boldsymbol{K}_r := (g^{u(-\mathsf{ID}\alpha_1+\alpha_2)}, \ldots, g^{u(-\mathsf{ID}^r\alpha_1+\alpha_{r+1})}) \in \mathbb{G}^r$. Then,

$$\boldsymbol{K}_r^{\boldsymbol{\omega}} = g^{u(\alpha_1\boldsymbol{\omega}M_1^{\mathrm{T}}+\langle\boldsymbol{y}_{\mathcal{R}},\boldsymbol{\alpha}\rangle-\alpha_1 a_0)} = g^{u\alpha_1(\boldsymbol{\omega}M_1^{\mathrm{T}}-a_0)}g^{u\langle\boldsymbol{y}_{\mathcal{R}},\boldsymbol{\alpha}\rangle},$$

$$\frac{e(C_2, D_0)}{e(\boldsymbol{K}_r^{\boldsymbol{\omega}}, C_1)} = \frac{e(g^{s\langle\boldsymbol{y}_{\mathcal{R}},\boldsymbol{\alpha}\rangle}, g^u)}{e(g^{u\alpha_1(M_1\boldsymbol{\omega}-a_0)}g^{u\langle\boldsymbol{y}_{\mathcal{R}},\boldsymbol{\alpha}\rangle}, g^s)}$$

$$= \frac{e(g^{u\langle\boldsymbol{y}_{\mathcal{R}},\boldsymbol{\alpha}\rangle}, g^s)}{e(g^{u\alpha_1(M_1\boldsymbol{\omega}-a_0)}, g^s)e(g^{u\langle\boldsymbol{y}_{\mathcal{R}},\boldsymbol{\alpha}\rangle}, g^s)}$$

$$= e(g, g)^{-su\alpha_1(M_1\boldsymbol{\omega}-a_0)}, \text{ and}$$

$e(D_1, C_1) = e(g^{\alpha+u\alpha_1}, g^s) = e(g, g)^{\alpha s}e(g, g)^{su\alpha_1}$ holds. Therefore,

$$\frac{C_0}{e(D_1, C_1)\left(\frac{e(C_2,D_0)}{e(\boldsymbol{K}_r^{\boldsymbol{\omega}},C_1)}\right)^{\frac{1}{M_1\boldsymbol{\omega}-a_0}}} = M \cdot \mathsf{A}^s/e(g, g)^{\alpha s} = M \text{ holds.}$$

5   Proposed Revocable Group Signature Scheme from Identity-Based Revocation

General Idea: In this section, we give our revocable group signature. In order to explain our construction methodology, first we give a big picture which gives our intuitive idea as follows. Assume that GM has a (long term) signature signing/verification key (gsk, gpk), and a (structure preserving) signature signing/verification key $(sk_{\mathsf{GM}}, vk_{\mathsf{GM}})$. Let (upk, usk) be a public/secret key pair of a user, $\mathcal{OTS} = (\mathcal{G}, \mathcal{S}, \mathcal{V})$ be an OTS scheme, $(\mathsf{Sign}^{(i)}, \mathsf{Verify}^{(i)})$ for $i = 1, 2$ be signature schemes, IBR be an IBR scheme, and Tag be a tag-based encryption scheme [22]. For an element X, we denote by $\overline{X}$ as its corresponding variable in the proof system, and denote com_X as the corresponding commitment.

User Signing Key: cert $= (\mathsf{ID}, upk, \mathsf{IBR}.sk_{\mathsf{ID}}, \sigma = \mathsf{Sign}_{sk_{\mathsf{GM}}}^{(1)}(upk, \mathsf{IBR}.sk_{\mathsf{ID}}))$ and $\sec_i = usk$.

Revocation Token: $\mathsf{IBR.Enc}(\mathcal{R}, M)$ and $\sigma_{\text{revoke}} = \mathsf{Sign}^{(2)}_{\text{gsk}}(\mathsf{IBR.Enc}(\mathcal{R}, M))$.

Group Signature: $(\mathsf{SK}, \mathsf{VK}) \leftarrow \mathcal{G}(\lambda)$. Commit upk, $\mathsf{IBR}.sk_{\mathsf{ID}}$, and σ to $\mathbf{com} = (com_{upk}, com_{\mathsf{IBR}.sk_{\mathsf{ID}}}, com_\sigma)$. Compute a proof $\mathbf{\Pi}$ that the committed values satisfying the following:

$$\mathsf{IBR.Dec}\big(\overline{\mathsf{IBR}.sk_{\mathsf{ID}}}, \mathsf{IBR.Enc}(\mathcal{R}, M)\big) = M \tag{1}$$

$$\mathsf{Verify}^{(1)}_{vk_{\mathsf{GM}}}\big((\overline{upk}, \overline{\mathsf{IBR}.sk_{\mathsf{ID}}}), \overline{\sigma}\big) = 1 \tag{2}$$

$$\mathsf{Tag.Enc}\big(pk_{\mathsf{OA}}, \mathsf{VK}, \overline{upk}\big) = C \tag{3}$$

Compute $\mathcal{S}_{\mathsf{SK}}(C, \mathbf{com}, \mathbf{\Pi}) = \sigma_{\mathsf{OTS}}$. A group signature is $\Sigma = (\mathsf{VK}, \sigma_{\mathsf{OTS}}, C, \mathbf{com}, \mathbf{\Pi})$.

Verification : Verify proof $\mathbf{\Pi}$, σ_{OTS}, and $\mathsf{Verify}^{(2)}_{\text{gpk}}(\mathsf{IBR.Enc}(\mathcal{R}, M), \sigma_{\text{revoke}}) = 1$.

Open : $\mathsf{Tag.Dec}\big(sk_{\mathsf{OA}}, \mathsf{VK}, C\big) = upk$.

That is, a signer (whose identity is ID) has (upk, usk), and has a decryption key of IBR $\mathsf{IBR}.sk_{\mathsf{ID}}$ which is issued by GM. GM also issues a signature σ of $(upk, \mathsf{IBR}.sk_{\mathsf{ID}})$. The signer proves that (1) ID $\notin \mathcal{R}$ by showing that $\mathsf{IBR.Enc}(\mathcal{R}, M)$ can be decrypted by $\mathsf{IBR}.sk_{\mathsf{ID}}$, (2) $(upk, \mathsf{IBR}.sk_{\mathsf{ID}})$ are issued by GM by showing the possession of σ on $(upk, \mathsf{IBR}.sk_{\mathsf{ID}})$, and (3) C is a ciphertext (with tag VK) of upk.

Techniques Towards Our Construction: In the actual scheme, $usk = x$ and $upk = X := g^x$ and $(sk_{\mathsf{GM}}, vk_{\mathsf{GM}})$ is a key pair of the AHO signature scheme. Moreover, we use the Kiltz tag-based encryption [22] for $\mathsf{Tag.Enc}$. Note that we do not have to prepare a full IBR ciphertext. Actually, for each revocation epoch t, GM computes a (de-randomized) ALP-IBR ciphertext $C_t = g^{\langle \mathbf{y}_{\mathcal{R}}, \boldsymbol{\alpha} \rangle}$ instead of $\mathsf{IBR.Enc}(\mathcal{R}_t, M)$, where $\mathcal{R}_t := (\mathsf{ID}_1, \ldots, \mathsf{ID}_r)$ is the set of current revoked users. GM signs C_t as an evidence that C_t is made by GM ($\mathsf{Sign}^{(2)}$ in the big picture). Unlike the LPY schemes, the signer does not have to hide C_t, since it is shared by all signers, and therefore GM does not have to use any structure preserving signature for signing C_t (this is the reason why we need to setup just one AHO signature key pair whereas the LPY schemes require two AHO signature key pairs), and a signer does not have to compute a commitment of C_t and the corresponding Groth-Sahai proof.

For proving the decryption ability, we use the following (modified) decryption equation. Let $y := M_1\boldsymbol{\omega}$, $\mathsf{A} := e(g,g)^\alpha$, $\Gamma_1 := g^{u\boldsymbol{\omega}^\mathsf{T} M_{\mathsf{ID}}^\mathsf{T}\alpha}$, $\Gamma_2 = g^y$, $\Gamma_3 := g^u$, and $\Gamma_4 := g^\alpha \cdot g^{u\alpha_1}$. Here, $\mathsf{IBR}.sk_{\mathsf{ID}} = (\Gamma_3, \Gamma_4)$, and Γ_1 can be computed from $\mathbf{K} = g^{uM_{\mathsf{ID}}^\mathsf{T}\alpha}$ and $\boldsymbol{\omega}$ as in the ALP-IBR scheme. Then, from the equation $e(g^\alpha \cdot g^{u\alpha_1}, g) = e(g,g)^\alpha \left(\frac{e(\mathbf{K}^{\boldsymbol{\omega}}, g)}{e(g^{\langle \mathbf{y}_{\mathcal{R}}, \boldsymbol{\alpha} \rangle}, g^u)}\right)^{\frac{1}{y-a_0}}$, we have

$$e(\Gamma_4, g) = \mathsf{A} \cdot \left(\frac{e(\Gamma_1, g)}{e(C_t, \Gamma_3)}\right)^{\frac{1}{y-a_0}} = \mathsf{A} \cdot \frac{e(\Gamma_1^{\frac{1}{y-a_0}}, g)}{e(C_t, \Gamma_3^{\frac{1}{y-a_0}})} = \mathsf{A} \cdot \frac{e(\sigma_{y,1}, g)}{e(C_t, \sigma_{y,2})} \tag{4}$$

where $\sigma_{y,1} = \Gamma_1^{\frac{1}{y-a_0}}$ and $\sigma_{y,2} = \Gamma_3^{\frac{1}{y-a_0}}$ are Boneh-Boyen short signatures [7]. In order to prove that these are valid short signatures on y with the verification key g^{a_0}, we use the following equations

$$e(\sigma_{y,1}, \Gamma_2/g^{a_0}) = e(\Gamma_1, g), \ e(\sigma_{y,2}, \Gamma_2/g^{a_0}) = e(\Gamma_3, g)$$

From these equations, $y \neq a_0$ is guaranteed. This technique has been considered in the LPY3 paper [24] for proving an inequality relation. Note that Γ_3 and Γ_4 (and $upk = X$ also) are signed by GM by using the AHO signature, and the signer also proves that the possession of an AHO signature on (X, Γ_3, Γ_4). One may think that $g^{\frac{1}{y-a_0}}$ and $C_t^{\frac{1}{y-a_0}}$ are enough to prove the decryption ability. As the reason, the equation (4) is linear since g and C_t are constant values. This helps to reduce the signature size since the corresponding Groth-Sahai proof contains just 3 group elements, whereas for a quadratic equation the corresponding Groth-Sahai proof contains 9 group elements.

As another part of a group signature, a signer encrypts its identifier X, and prove that a plaintext X is signed by GM. To do so, the signer makes a commitment of X and also makes commitments of the AHO signature of X, and make Groth-Sahai proofs that a plaintext X is signed by GM. For achieving CCA - anonymity, where an adversary is allowed to issue open queries in the anonymity game, we use the Kiltz tag-based encryption scheme [22], as in the Groth group signature scheme [18] and the LPY schemes.

Note that all components of an AHO signature do not have to be committed by applying the ReRand algorithm [2]. That is, for an AHO signature σ, let $\{\theta_i'\}_{i=1}^7 \leftarrow$ ReRand(pk_{AHO}, σ) be a result of re-randomization. Then, $\{\theta_i'\}_{i \in \{3,4,6,7\}}$ are independent of the corresponding signed message, and therefore $\{\theta_i'\}_{i \in \{3,4,6,7\}}$ can be directly included into a part of a group signature. That is, the size of group signature can be reduced by avoiding to compute commitments of $\{\theta_i'\}_{i \in \{3,4,6,7\}}$ thanks to the ReRand algorithm. This technique also has been considered in LPY schemes [25,24].

Our Proposed Scheme: Each user $\mathcal{U}_i$ has a long term signature signing/verification key (usk[i], upk[i]) which is registered in some PKI. Moreover, GM also has a long term signature signing/verification key (gsk, gpk) which is also registered in some PKI. We assume that each user has a unique identity ID $\in \mathbb{Z}_p$ (chosen by GM), and ID$_i \neq$ ID$_j$ for all $i \neq j$.

Construction 1 (Revocable Group Signature from IBR).

Setup(λ, R):
1. *Choose* $(\mathbb{G}, \mathbb{G}_T)$ *of prime order* $p > 2^\lambda$, *where* $\langle g \rangle = \mathbb{G}$.
2. *Generate a key pair* (sk_{AHO}, pk_{AHO}) *for the AHO signature in order to sign three group elements.*
   - $pk_{AHO} = (G_r, H_r, G_z, H_z, \{G_i, H_i\}_{i=1}^3, A, B)$
   - $sk_{AHO} = (\alpha_a, \alpha_b, \gamma_z, \delta_z, \{\gamma_i, \delta_i\}_{i=1}^3)$
3. *Setup the ALP-IBR scheme, and obtain* (pk_{ALP}, msk_{ALP}). *Parse* $pk_{ALP} = (g, g^\alpha, A = e(g, g)^\alpha)$.

4. *Select a CRS for NIWI proof system:* $\mathbf{f} := (\mathbf{f_1}, \mathbf{f_2}, \mathbf{f_3}) \in \mathbb{G}^3 \times \mathbb{G}^3 \times \mathbb{G}^3$ *s.t.*
   $\beta_1, \beta_2, \xi_1, \xi_2 \overset{\$}{\leftarrow} \mathbb{Z}_p^*$, $f_1 = g^{\beta_1}$, $f_2 = g^{\beta_2}$, $\mathbf{f_1} = (f_1, 1, g)$, $\mathbf{f_2} = (1, f_2, g)$,
   and $\mathbf{f_3} = \mathbf{f_1}^{\xi_1} \odot \mathbf{f_2}^{\xi_2}$. $\varphi = \mathbf{f_3} \odot (1, 1, g)$ *is also defined.*

5. *Choose* $U, V \overset{\$}{\leftarrow} \mathbb{G}$ *(for the Kiltz Tag-based encryption scheme).*

6. *Choose a strongly unforgeable OTS scheme* $\mathcal{OTS} = (\mathcal{G}, \mathcal{S}, \mathcal{V})$.

Output $\mathcal{Y} = (g, \mathsf{A}, pk_{\mathsf{AHO}}, \mathsf{gpk}, \mathbf{f}, \varphi, (U, V), \mathcal{OTS})$, $\mathcal{S}_{\mathsf{GM}} = (pk_{\mathsf{ALP}}, msk_{\mathsf{ALP}},$
$(sk_{\mathsf{AHO}}, \mathsf{gsk}))$, *and* $\mathcal{S}_{\mathsf{OA}} = (\beta_1, \beta_2)$. *Note that* (g, A) *is a part of* pk_{ALP}.

Join$^{\mathsf{GM}, \mathcal{U}_i}$:

User : *Choose* $x \overset{\$}{\leftarrow} \mathbb{Z}_p$, *compute* $X = g^x$, *and send* X *to GM.*

GM :

1. *If* X *already appears in some entry* transcript$_j$, *then abort and return* $\perp$. *Otherwise, choose* $\mathsf{ID}_i \in \mathbb{Z}_p$.

2. *Choose* $u \overset{\$}{\leftarrow} \mathbb{Z}_p^*$, *and compute* g^u, $g^\alpha \cdot g^{u\alpha_1}$ *and* $g^{u M_{\mathsf{ID}_i}^{\mathsf{T}} \alpha}$, *where*

$$M_{\mathsf{ID}_i} := \begin{pmatrix} -\mathsf{ID}_i & -\mathsf{ID}_i^2 & \cdots & -\mathsf{ID}_i^R \\ & I_R & \end{pmatrix}$$

is a $(R+1) \times R$ *matrix,* I_R *is the* $R \times R$ *identity matrix, and* T *is transpose of matrix.*

3. *Generate an AHO signature* $\sigma = (\theta_1, \ldots, \theta_7)$ *on* $(X, g^u, g^\alpha \cdot g^{u\alpha_1})$ *by using* sk_{AHO}.

4. *Send* $(g^u, g^\alpha \cdot g^{u\alpha_1}, g^{u M_{\mathsf{ID}_i}^{\mathsf{T}} \alpha})$ *to User.*

User : *If these keys are well-formed, then compute* $sig_i = \mathsf{Sign}_{\mathsf{usk}[i]}(X || (g^u, g^\alpha \cdot g^{u\alpha_1}, g^{u M_{\mathsf{ID}_i}^{\mathsf{T}} \alpha}))$ *by using the long-term key, and send* sig_i *to GM.*

GM : *If* $\mathsf{Verify}_{\mathsf{upk}[i]}(X || g^u, g^\alpha \cdot g^{u\alpha_1}, g^{u M_{\mathsf{ID}_i}^{\mathsf{T}} \alpha}), sig_i) = 1$, *then send* σ *to User, and store* transcript$_i$ = $(\mathsf{ID}_i, X, \sigma)$ *in* St_{trans}. *Moreover, update* $St_{\mathsf{users}} \leftarrow St_{\mathsf{users}} \cup \{\mathsf{ID}_i\}$.

User : *Set* cert$_i$ = $(\mathsf{ID}_i, \sigma, X, (g^u, g^\alpha \cdot g^{u\alpha_1}, g^{u M_{\mathsf{ID}_i}^{\mathsf{T}} \alpha}))$ *and* sec$_i$ = x.

Revoke$(\mathcal{Y}, \mathcal{S}_{\mathsf{GM}}, t, \mathcal{R}_t \subset St_{\mathsf{users}})$:

1. *Let* $\mathcal{R}_t := (\mathsf{ID}_1, \ldots, \mathsf{ID}_r) \subset St_{\mathsf{users}}$ *be the revocation list on time* t. *For a variant Z, define the revocation polynomial* $f_{\mathcal{R}_t}(Z) := (Z - \mathsf{ID}_1) \cdots (Z - \mathsf{ID}_R) = a_0 + a_1 Z + a_2 Z^2 + \cdots + a_{r-1} Z^{r-1} + Z^r$, *and let* $\mathbf{y}_{\mathcal{R}_t}$ *be a set of coefficients* $(a_0, a_1, \ldots, a_{r-1}, 1)$.

2. *Compute a (part of) de-randomized IBR ciphertext* $C_t = g^{\langle \mathbf{y}_{\mathcal{R}}, \alpha \rangle}$ *from* $\mathbf{y}_{\mathcal{R}_t}$ *and* $g^\alpha = (g^{\alpha_1}, \ldots, g^{\alpha_{r+1}})$.

3. *Generate a signature* Θ_t *on* (C_t, g^t) *by using* gsk.

Output $RL_t = (t, \mathcal{R}_t, C_t, \Theta_t)$. *Note that we estimate the size of* RL_t *without considering IDs as in the estimation of the certificate-size in [24].*

Sign$(t, RL_t, \mathsf{cert}, \mathsf{sec}, M)$:

1. *Parse* cert = $(\mathsf{ID}, \sigma, X, (g^u, g^\alpha \cdot g^{u\alpha_1}, g^{u M_{\mathsf{ID}}^{\mathsf{T}} \alpha}))$ *and* sec = x.

2. $(\mathsf{SK}, \mathsf{VK}) \leftarrow \mathcal{G}(\lambda)$ *(OTS).*

3. Let $\boldsymbol{\omega} := (a_1, \ldots, a_{r-1}, 1)$ and $M_1 = (-\mathsf{ID}, -\mathsf{ID}^2, \ldots, -\mathsf{ID}^r)$ (the first row of M_{ID}). Set $y := \boldsymbol{\omega} M_1^{\mathsf{T}}$ and compute $\Gamma_1 = g^{u\boldsymbol{\omega}^{\mathsf{T}} M_{\mathsf{ID}}^{\mathsf{T}} \boldsymbol{\alpha}}$ and $\Gamma_2 = g^y$, set $\Gamma_3 = g^u$, and $\Gamma_4 = g^{\alpha} \cdot g^{u\alpha_1}$, and compute $\sigma_{y,1} = \Gamma_1^{\frac{1}{y-a_0}}$ and $\sigma_{y,2} = \Gamma_3^{\frac{1}{y-a_0}}$.

4. Compute $\{\theta_i'\}_{i=1}^7 \leftarrow \mathsf{ReRand}(pk_{\mathsf{AHO}}, \sigma)$.

5. Compute Groth-Sahai commitments com_X and $\{com_{\theta_i'}\}_{i \in \{1,2,5\}}$, and compute a NIWI proof π_σ which provides evidence that

$$A = e(G_z, \theta_1')e(G_r, \theta_2')e(\theta_3', \theta_4')e(G_1, X)e(G_2, \Gamma_3)e(G_3, \Gamma_4)$$
$$B = e(H_z, \theta_1')e(H_r, \theta_5')e(\theta_6', \theta_7')e(H_1, X)e(H_2, \Gamma_3)e(H_3, \Gamma_4)$$

Since $\{\theta_i'\}_{i \in \{3,4,6,7\}}$ are constants, the above equations are both linear and require 3 elements each. That is, π_σ contains 6 group elements.

6. Compute Groth-Sahai commitments $\{com_{\sigma_{y,i}}\}_{i=1}^2$ and $\{com_{\Gamma_i}\}_{i=1}^4$, and compute a NIWI proof π_Γ which provides evidence that $A \cdot \frac{e(\sigma_{y,1}, g)}{e(C_t, \sigma_{y,2})} = e(g, \Gamma_4)$, $e(\sigma_{y,1}, \Gamma_2/g^{a_0}) = e(\Gamma_1, g)$, and $e(\sigma_{y,2}, \Gamma_2/g^{a_0}) = e(\Gamma_3, g)$. Since the first equation is linear, and the second and third equations are quadratic, π_Γ requires 21 group elements.

7. Encrypt X by the Kiltz tag-based encryption scheme [22] (tag: VK), where $z_1, z_2 \overset{\$}{\leftarrow} \mathbb{Z}_p$ and $(\Psi_1, \Psi_2, \Psi_3, \Psi_4, \Psi_5) = (f_1^{z_1}, f_2^{z_2}, X \cdot g^{z_1+z_2}, (g^{\mathsf{VK}} \cdot U)^{z_1}), (g^{\mathsf{VK}} \cdot V)^{z_2}))$.

8. Generating a NIZK proof that com_X and (Ψ_1, Ψ_2, Ψ_3) are Boneh-Boyen-Shacham linear encryptions of the same value X. $com_X \odot (\Psi_1, \Psi_2, \Psi_3)^{-1}$ can be represented as $com_X \odot (\Psi_1, \Psi_2, \Psi_3)^{-1} = (f_1^{\tau_1} f_{3,1}^{\tau_3}, f_2^{\tau_2} f_{3,2}^{\tau_3}, g^{\tau_1+\tau_2} f_{3,3}^{\tau_3})$. Compute Groth-Sahai commitments $\{com_{\tau_j}\}_{j=1}^3$ and proofs $\{\pi_{eq-com_j}\}_{j=1}^3$ that (τ_1, τ_2, τ_3) satisfies the above three relations. Since these are linear equations, each π_{eq-com_j} requires 2 group elements, and $\{\pi_{eq-com_j}\}_{j=1}^3$ requires 6 group elements in total.

9. Compute $\sigma_{\mathsf{VK}} = g^{1/(x+\mathsf{VK})}$ and compute a Groth-Sahai commitment $com_{\sigma_{\mathsf{VK}}}$ and compute a NIWI proof $\pi_{\sigma_{\mathsf{VK}}}$ that the committed value σ_{VK} and X satisfy $e(\sigma_{\mathsf{VK}}, X \cdot g^{\mathsf{VK}}) = e(g, g)$. Since this equation is quadratic, $\pi_{\sigma_{\mathsf{VK}}}$ requires 9 group elements.

10. Compute $\sigma_{\mathsf{OTS}} = \mathcal{S}_{\mathsf{SK}}(M, RL_t, \Psi_1, \Psi_2, \Psi_3, \Psi_4, \Psi_5, \Omega, \mathbf{com}, \mathbf{\Pi}))$, where $\Omega = \{\theta_i'\}_{i \in \{3,4,6,7\}}$, $\mathbf{com} = (\{com_{\Gamma_i}\}_{i=1}^4, com_X, \{com_{\sigma_{y,i}}\}_{i=1}^2, \{com_{\theta_i'}\}_{i \in \{1,2,5\}}, \{com_{\tau_i}\}_{i=1}^3, com_{\sigma_{\mathsf{VK}}})$, and $\mathbf{\Pi} = (\pi_\Gamma, \pi_\sigma, \pi_{eq-com_1}, \pi_{eq-com_2}, \pi_{eq-com_3}, \pi_{\sigma_{\mathsf{VK}}})$.

Output the group signature $\Sigma = (\mathsf{VK}, \Psi_1, \Psi_2, \Psi_3, \Psi_4, \Psi_5, \Omega, \mathbf{com}, \mathbf{\Pi}, \sigma_{\mathsf{OTS}})$.

Verify$(\Sigma, t, RL_t, M, \mathcal{Y})$:

1. If $\mathcal{V}(\mathsf{VK}, (M, RL_t, \Psi_1, \Psi_2, \Psi_3, \Psi_4, \Psi_5, \Omega, \mathbf{com}, \mathbf{\Pi}), \sigma_{\mathsf{OTS}}) = 0$, then return 0.

2. Return 0 if $e(\Psi_1, g^{\mathsf{VK}}) \neq e(f_1, \Psi_4)$ or $e(\Psi_2, g^{\mathsf{VK}}) \neq e(f_2, \Psi_5)$.

3. Return 1 if all proofs properly verify. Otherwise, return 0.

In the verification, a verifier uses (C_t, g^t) which is signed by GM. This can be checked by Θ_t and gpk. *We assume that the verifier always uses (C_t, g^t) certified by GM.*

Open($M, \Sigma, \mathcal{Y}, t, \mathcal{S}_{OA}, St$):

1. *Return $\perp$ if* Verify($\Sigma, t, RL_t, M, \mathcal{Y}$) = 0.
2. *Otherwise, compute $\tilde{X} = \Psi_3 \cdot \Psi_1^{1-/\beta_1} \Psi_2^{-1/\beta_2}$.*
3. *Find a record* (ID, X, σ) *in* St_{trans} *such that $X = \tilde{X}$. If no record exists, return $\perp$. Otherwise, return* ID.

Duo to the page limitation, we give the security proofs of the following theorems in the full version of this paper.

Theorem 1 (Misidentification). *The proposed group signature scheme is secure against misidentification attack under the q_a-SFP assumption and the q_a-flexible PBDH assumption, where q_a is the maximal numbers of $Q_{\text{a-join}}$ queries.*

Theorem 2 (Non-frameability). *The proposed group signature scheme is secure against framing attack under the q_b-SDH assumption and $\mathcal{OTS}$ is a strongly unforgeable one-time signature scheme, where q_b is the maximal numbers of $Q_{\text{b-join}}$ queries.*

Theorem 3 (Anonymity). *The proposed group signature scheme is anonymous under the DLIN assumption and $\mathcal{OTS}$ is a strongly unforgeable one-time signature scheme.*

Acknowledgement. We thank the members of Shin-Akarui-Angou-Benkyou-Kai and Prof. Toru Nakanishi for their helpful comments.

References

1. Abe, M., Fuchsbauer, G., Groth, J., Haralambiev, K., Ohkubo, M.: Structure-preserving signatures and commitments to group elements. In: Rabin, T. (ed.) CRYPTO 2010. LNCS, vol. 6223, pp. 209–236. Springer, Heidelberg (2010)
2. Abe, M., Haralambiev, K., Ohkubo, M.: Signing on elements in bilinear groups for modular protocol design. IACR Cryptology ePrint Archive 133 (2010)
3. Attrapadung, N., Herranz, J., Laguillaumie, F., Libert, B., de Panafieu, E., Ràfols, C.: Attribute-based encryption schemes with constant-size ciphertexts. Theor. Comput. Sci. 422, 15–38 (2012)
4. Attrapadung, N., Libert, B., de Panafieu, E.: Expressive key-policy attribute-based encryption with constant-size ciphertexts. In: Catalano, D., Fazio, N., Gennaro, R., Nicolosi, A. (eds.) PKC 2011. LNCS, vol. 6571, pp. 90–108. Springer, Heidelberg (2011)
5. Begum, N., Nakanishi, T., Funabiki, N.: Efficient proofs for CNF formulas on attributes in pairing-based anonymous credential system. In: Kwon, T., Lee, M.-K., Kwon, D. (eds.) ICISC 2012. LNCS, vol. 7839, pp. 495–509. Springer, Heidelberg (2013)

6. Boneh, D., Boyen, X.: Efficient selective-ID secure identity-based encryption without random oracles. In: Cachin, C., Camenisch, J.L. (eds.) EUROCRYPT 2004. LNCS, vol. 3027, pp. 223–238. Springer, Heidelberg (2004)

7. Boneh, D., Boyen, X.: Short signatures without random oracles and the SDH assumption in bilinear groups. J. Cryptology 21(2), 149–177 (2008)

8. Boneh, D., Boyen, X., Goh, E.-J.: Hierarchical identity based encryption with constant size ciphertext. In: Cramer, R. (ed.) EUROCRYPT 2005. LNCS, vol. 3494, pp. 440–456. Springer, Heidelberg (2005)

9. Boneh, D., Boyen, X., Shacham, H.: Short group signatures. In: Franklin, M. (ed.) CRYPTO 2004. LNCS, vol. 3152, pp. 41–55. Springer, Heidelberg (2004)

10. Boneh, D., Gentry, C., Waters, B.: Collusion resistant broadcast encryption with short ciphertexts and private keys. In: Shoup, V. (ed.) CRYPTO 2005. LNCS, vol. 3621, pp. 258–275. Springer, Heidelberg (2005)

11. Boyen, X.: The Uber-assumption family. In: Galbraith, S.D., Paterson, K.G. (eds.) Pairing 2008. LNCS, vol. 5209, pp. 39–56. Springer, Heidelberg (2008)

12. Chaum, D., van Heyst, E.: Group signatures. In: Davies, D.W. (ed.) EUROCRYPT 1991. LNCS, vol. 547, pp. 257–265. Springer, Heidelberg (1991)

13. Delerablée, C., Pointcheval, D.: Dynamic fully anonymous short group signatures. In: Nguyên, P.Q. (ed.) VIETCRYPT 2006. LNCS, vol. 4341, pp. 193–210. Springer, Heidelberg (2006)

14. Dodis, Y., Fazio, N.: Public key broadcast encryption for stateless receivers. In: Feigenbaum, J. (ed.) DRM 2002. LNCS, vol. 2696, pp. 61–80. Springer, Heidelberg (2003)

15. Fan, C.-I., Hsu, R.-H., Manulis, M.: Group signature with constant revocation costs for signers and verifiers. In: Lin, D., Tsudik, G., Wang, X. (eds.) CANS 2011. LNCS, vol. 7092, pp. 214–233. Springer, Heidelberg (2011)

16. Furukawa, J., Imai, H.: An efficient group signature scheme from bilinear maps. IEICE Transactions 89(5), 1328–1338 (2006)

17. Groth, J.: Simulation-sound NIZK proofs for a practical language and constant size group signatures. In: Lai, X., Chen, K. (eds.) ASIACRYPT 2006. LNCS, vol. 4284, pp. 444–459. Springer, Heidelberg (2006)

18. Groth, J.: Fully anonymous group signatures without random oracles. In: Kurosawa, K. (ed.) ASIACRYPT 2007. LNCS, vol. 4833, pp. 164–180. Springer, Heidelberg (2007)

19. Groth, J., Sahai, A.: Efficient non-interactive proof systems for bilinear groups. In: Smart, N.P. (ed.) EUROCRYPT 2008. LNCS, vol. 4965, pp. 415–432. Springer, Heidelberg (2008)

20. Kiayias, A., Yung, M.: Group signatures: Provable security, efficient constructions and anonymity from trapdoor-holders. IACR Cryptology ePrint Archive 76 (2004)

21. Kiayias, A., Yung, M.: Secure scalable group signature with dynamic joins and separable authorities. IJSN 1(1/2), 24–45 (2006)

22. Kiltz, E.: Chosen-ciphertext security from tag-based encryption. In: Halevi, S., Rabin, T. (eds.) TCC 2006. LNCS, vol. 3876, pp. 581–600. Springer, Heidelberg (2006)

23. Lewko, A.B., Sahai, A., Waters, B.: Revocation systems with very small private keys. In: IEEE Symposium on Security and Privacy, pp. 273–285 (2010)

24. Libert, B., Peters, T., Yung, M.: Group signatures with almost-for-free revocation. In: Safavi-Naini, R., Canetti, R. (eds.) CRYPTO 2012. LNCS, vol. 7417, pp. 571–589. Springer, Heidelberg (2012)

25. Libert, B., Peters, T., Yung, M.: Scalable group signatures with revocation. In: Pointcheval, D., Johansson, T. (eds.) EUROCRYPT 2012. LNCS, vol. 7237, pp. 609–627. Springer, Heidelberg (2012)
26. Libert, B., Vergnaud, D.: Group signatures with verifier-local revocation and backward unlinkability in the standard model. In: Garay, J.A., Miyaji, A., Otsuka, A. (eds.) CANS 2009. LNCS, vol. 5888, pp. 498–517. Springer, Heidelberg (2009)
27. Libert, B., Yung, M.: Concise mercurial vector commitments and independent zero-knowledge sets with short proofs. In: Micciancio, D. (ed.) TCC 2010. LNCS, vol. 5978, pp. 499–517. Springer, Heidelberg (2010)
28. Nakanishi, T., Fujii, H., Hira, Y., Funabiki, N.: Revocable group signature schemes with constant costs for signing and verifying. In: Jarecki, S., Tsudik, G. (eds.) PKC 2009. LNCS, vol. 5443, pp. 463–480. Springer, Heidelberg (2009)
29. Nakanishi, T., Funabiki, N.: Revocable group signatures with compact revocation list using accumulators. In: ICISC (to appear, 2013)
30. Naor, D., Naor, M., Lotspiech, J.: Revocation and tracing schemes for stateless receivers. In: Kilian, J. (ed.) CRYPTO 2001. LNCS, vol. 2139, pp. 41–62. Springer, Heidelberg (2001)

Faster Batch Verification of Standard ECDSA Signatures Using Summation Polynomials

Sabyasachi Karati and Abhijit Das

Department of Computer Science and Engineering
Indian Institute of Technology Kharagpur, India
{skarati,abhij}@cse.iitkgp.ernet.in

Abstract. Several batch-verification algorithms for original ECDSA signatures are proposed for the first time in AfricaCrypt 2012. Two of these algorithms are based on the naive idea of taking square roots in the underlying fields, and the others perform symbolic manipulation to verify small batches of ECDSA signatures. In this paper, we use elliptic-curve summation polynomials to design a new ECDSA batch-verification algorithm which is theoretically and experimentally much faster than the symbolic algorithms of AfricaCrypt 2012. Our experiments on NIST prime and Koblitz curves demonstrate that our proposed algorithm increases the optimal batch size from seven to nine. We also mention how our algorithm can be adapted to Edwards curves.

Keywords: Elliptic Curve, ECDSA, Batch Verification, Summation Polynomial, Koblitz Curve, Edwards Curve, EdDSA.

1 Introduction

When multiple signatures sharing common system parameters need to be verified, the concept of batch verification turns out to be useful. The basic incentive is a reduction in the running time of individually verifying the signatures. The elliptic-curve digital signature algorithm (ECDSA) [12] has been accepted as a standard signature scheme. An ECDSA signature on a message M is a pair (r, s), where r is x-coordinate of an elliptic-curve point $R = (r, y)$, and s absorbs the hash of M and the private key of the signer. The absence of the y-coordinate of the point R in an ECDSA signature resists a straightforward adaptation of the previously proposed batch-verification methods [16,11]. There exist two y-coordinates corresponding to the x-coordinate r. This results in an ambiguity in identifying the correct y-coordinate and leads to a sizable overhead for eliminating the y-coordinate from the batch-verification equation. In a variant ECDSA* [7], the entire point R replaces r in the signature. As a result, batch verification of ECDSA* signatures is straightforward. However, since ECDSA* is not standardized and leads to an expansion in the signature size without any increase in security, batch verification of standard ECDSA signatures continues to remain a problem of both theoretical and practical importance in cryptography.

I. Boureanu, P. Owesarski, and S. Vaudenay (Eds.): ACNS 2014, LNCS 8479, pp. 438–456, 2014.

Karati et al. [13] propose several batch-verification algorithms for standard ECDSA signatures. Their naive algorithm N is based upon the computation of the y-coordinate by taking a square root in the underlying field. The algorithms S1 and S2 of [13] trades the square-root computation time by symbolic manipulations that treat the y-coordinates as symbols satisfying the elliptic-curve equation. Algorithm S1 performs linearization during the elimination of the unknown y-coordinates. Algorithms S2 adopts a separate and more efficient elimination method. Both S1 and S2 outperform the naive method N for small batch sizes. For a batch of size t, S1 runs is $O(m^3)$ time and S2 runs in $O(mt^2)$ time, where $m = 2^t$, and the running times are measured in the number of field operations. Since m is already an exponential function in t, these algorithms become impractical except only for small batch sizes. Reducing the running time to below $O(mt^2)$ is stated as an open problem in [13].

In this paper, we address this open problem. We propose a new batch-verification algorithm (we call it SP) which is theoretically more efficient and experimentally faster than the symbolic-computation algorithms of [13]. Our proposed algorithm uses a separate elimination technique which is based on Semaev's elliptic-curve summation polynomials [21]. Algorithm SP has a running-time complexity of $O(m)$ and so is theoretically superior than the earlier symbolic algorithms. Practically, Algorithm SP can handle batches of size up to ten, whereas the earlier symbolic algorithms are effective for batch sizes $t \leqslant 8$ only. We show that Algorithm SP (like S1 and S2) supplies security guarantees equivalent to the standard batch-verification algorithm for ECDSA* [7].

Algorithms S1 and S2 proceed in two phases. In the first phase, a sum of the elliptic-curve points (r_i, y_i) is computed. In this phase, r_i are known and y_i are treated as symbols. The second phase eliminates all y_i values using more symbolic manipulations. The elimination phase effectively determines the running times of S1 and S2 as $O(m^3)$ and $O(mt^2)$, respectively. Algorithm SP, on the contrary, completely avoids the symbolic addition phase, and manages the elimination of all y_i values in $O(m)$ time only.

The rest of the paper is organized as follows. Section 2 introduces the notations and a quick overview of the ECDSA scheme and the batch-verification algorithms of [13]. In section 3, we propose the new Algorithm SP. Section 4 contains the complexity analysis and the security analysis of Algorithm SP. NIST Koblitz curves are dealt with in Section 5. We provide our experimental results for NIST prime and Koblitz curves in Section 6. Section 7 deals with the adaptation of Algorithm SP to Edwards curves. The security of Algorithm SP depends on the structures of the elliptic-curve groups over quadratic extensions of the base fields. These structures are studied in Section 8 for some of the NIST curves. Section 9 concludes the paper after highlighting some pertinent open problems.

2   Notations and Background

In the rest of this paper, we plan to verify a batch of t ECDSA signatures $(M_1, r_1, s_1), (M_2, r_2, s_2), \ldots, (M_t, r_t, s_t)$.

2.1 ECDSA over NIST Prime Fields

Let
$$E : y^2 = x^3 + ax + b \tag{1}$$
be an elliptic curve defined over the prime field $\mathbb{F}_p$. The size of the group $E(\mathbb{F}_p)$ is assumed to be a prime n close to p. Let P be a fixed generator of $E(\mathbb{F}_p)$.

An ECDSA private key d is randomly chosen from $\{1, 2, \ldots, n-1\}$. The public key is computed as $Q = dP$.

The ECDSA signature (r, s) on a message M is generated as follows. A random session key $k \in \{1, 2, \ldots, n-1\}$ is selected. The point $R = kP$ is computed, and r is taken as the x-coordinate $x(R)$ of R reduced modulo n. Finally, s is computed as $s = k^{-1}(H(M) + dr) \pmod{n}$, where H is a cryptographic hash function like SHA-1 [18].

By Hasse's theorem, we have $|n - p - 1| \leqslant 2\sqrt{p}$. If $n \geqslant p$, then r as an element of $\mathbb{Z}_n$ has a unique representation in $\mathbb{Z}_p$, otherwise it has two representations. The density of elements of $\mathbb{Z}_n$ having two representations in $\mathbb{Z}_p$ is $\leqslant 2/\sqrt{p}$ which is close to zero if p is large. Consequently, we ignore the cases where the modulo n and the modulo p values of r may be different.

To verify an ECDSA signature (M, r, s), we compute $w = s^{-1} \pmod{n}$, $u = H(M)w \pmod{n}$ and $v = rw \pmod{n}$. The point R is reconstructed as
$$R = uP + vQ. \tag{2}$$

The signature is accepted if and only if $x(R) = r \pmod{n}$.

As mentioned before, an ECDSA* signature on M is the pair (R, s). Verification proceeds as in the case of ECDSA signatures, and the validity of Eqn(2) is used as the acceptance criterion.

For a given x-coordinate r, there are in general two y-coordinates $\pm y$. The point R is one of (r, y) and $(r, -y)$. In another variant of ECDSA, henceforth referred to as ECDSA#, an extra bit is appended to a standard ECDSA signature in order to identify which of $(r, \pm y)$ is equal to R. Unlike ECDSA*, ECDSA#—although not accepted as a standard—does not suffer from an unacceptable expansion in the signature size. Since ECDSA# has important bearings on the naive batch-verification algorithm of [13], we refer to it in Section 6. ECDSA* is considered only in the security proof of Algorithm SP.

2.2 Batch Verification of ECDSA Signatures

We assume that all of the t signatures (M_i, r_i, s_i) come from the same signer with public key Q (an adaptation to the case of multiple signers being straightforward). A batch-verification attempt aggregates the t signatures as
$$\sum_{i=1}^{t} R_i = \left(\sum_{i=1}^{t} u_i \right) P + \left(\sum_{i=1}^{t} v_i \right) Q. \tag{3}$$

The right side of Eqn(3) can be computed numerically using two scalar multiplications (or one double scalar multiplication). Let this point be (α, β). If R_i

are reconstructed as $u_i P + v_i Q$, the effort is essentially the same as individual verification. The algorithms of [13] get around this difficulty in several ways.

The naive method N computes y_i by taking the square root of $r_i^3 + ar_i + b$. Since there are two square roots (in general) for each r_i, the ambiguity in the *sign* of y_i can be removed by trying all of the $m = 2^t$ combinations. If Eqn(3) holds for any of these choices, the batch of signatures is accepted. If we use ECDSA#, then the y_i values can be uniquely identified, and we can avoid trying all the $m = 2^t$ combinations. This variant of the naive algorithm is referred to as N'. The computation of the square roots of $r_i^3 + ar_i + b$ cannot be avoided in Algorithms N and N'. If the underlying field is large, this overhead may be huge.

The symbolic-manipulation algorithms S1 and S2 avoid computing these square roots altogether. They instead compute the left side of Eqn(3) symbolically. Each y_i is treated as a symbol satisfying $y_i^2 = r_i^3 + ar_i + b$. This symbolic addition gives an equality of the form

$$(g(y_1, y_2, \ldots, y_t), h(y_1, y_2, \ldots, y_t)) = (\alpha, \beta), \qquad (4)$$

where g and h are polynomials in y_i with each y_i-degree $\leqslant 1$.

Algorithm S1 makes a linearization by repeatedly squaring $g(y_1, y_2, \ldots, y_t) = \alpha$ (or multiplying by even-degree monomials). At this stage too, the equations $y_i^2 = r_i^3 + ar_i + b$ are used in order to keep the y_i-degrees $\leqslant 1$ in each generated equation. The linearized system has $2^{t-1} - 1 = \frac{m}{2} - 1$ variables standing for the square-free monomials in $y_1, y_2, \ldots, y_t$ of even degrees. The linearized system is in general dense, and is solved by Gaussian elimination in $O(m^3)$ time. The equation $h(y_1, y_2, \ldots, y_t) = \beta$ is subsequently used to solve for each y_i. Finally, it is verified whether $y_i^2 = r_i^3 + ar_i + b$ for all i.

Algorithm S2 avoids the massive $O(m^3)$ overhead of Gaussian elimination as follows. The equation $g(y_1, y_2, \ldots, y_t) = \alpha$ is rewritten as $\gamma(y_2, y_3, \ldots, y_t)y_1 + \delta(y_2, y_3, \ldots, y_t)$. Multiplying this by $\gamma y_1 - \delta$ and using $y_1^2 = r_1^3 + ar_1 + b$ gives an equation free from y_1. The other variables $y_2, y_3, \ldots, y_t$ are eliminated one by one in the same way. Eventually, the batch is accepted if we obtain the zero polynomial after all y_i are eliminated. This elimination phase takes $O(mt^2)$ time.

An improved variant of S1 and S2 significantly speeds up the symbolic-addition phase. Let $\tau = \lceil t/2 \rceil$. Eqn(3) is rewritten as $\sum_{i=1}^{\tau} R_i = (\alpha, \beta) - \sum_{i=\tau+1}^{t} R_i$. The two sides are individually computed symbolically. This reduces the running time of the symbolic-addition phase from $O(mt^2)$ to $O(\sqrt{m}t^2)$. These variants of S1 and S2 are referred to as S1' and S2'. The elimination phases of S1' and S2' run in $O(m^{3/2})$ and $O(mt^2)$ times, respectively.

2.3   Randomization of Batch Verification

Bernstein et al. [2] propose two attacks on these batch-verification algorithms. They also suggest that these attacks can be largely eliminated by randomizing the batch-verification process (see [1,16]). For randomly chosen non-zero multipliers $\xi_1, \xi_2, \ldots, \xi_t$, the individual verification equations are now combined as

$$\sum_{i=1}^{t} \xi_i R_i = \left(\sum_{i=1}^{t} \xi_i u_i \right) P + \left(\sum_{i=1}^{t} \xi_i v_i \right) Q. \qquad (5)$$

The right side can again be computed numerically. The x-coordinates of $\xi_i R_i$ can be computed from $x(R_i)$ [15,14], and are supplied as inputs to the batch-verification algorithms. The randomization process is external to batch verification. However, individual verification does not require randomization. Although randomized batch verification is the cryptographically meaningful implementation of the algorithms, we also study batch verification without randomization in order to compare the raw performances of various batch-verification algorithms.

It is worthwhile to note that Eqns(3) and (5) can be readily modified to the case when the t signatures come from different signers having different public keys Q_i. For example, the sum $\left(\sum_{i=1}^{t} \xi_i v_i\right) Q$ in Eqn(5) should be replaced by $\sum_{i=1}^{t} (\xi_i v_i Q_i)$. But then, the number of scalar multiplications increases from two to $t+1$. Since randomization incurs additional overheads similar to several scalar multiplications, randomized batch verification using the algorithms S2′ or SP is expected to be slower than individual verification. Consequently, we do not study the case of multiple signers in this paper.

3   A New Batch-Verification Algorithm (SP) for ECDSA

The new batch-verification algorithm we propose in this paper is based on elliptic-curve summation polynomials introduced by Semaev [21] in the context of improving the known bounds of the index-calculus method for solving the elliptic-curve discrete-logarithm problem.

Let E be the elliptic curve defined over a prime field $\mathbb{F}_p$ by Eqn(1). Let $x_1, x_2, \ldots, x_t$ be $t \geqslant 2$ elements of $\mathbb{F}_p$. The t-variable summation polynomial f_t is defined by the following recurrences:

$$f_2(x_1, x_2) = x_1 - x_2, \tag{6}$$

$$\begin{aligned} f_3(x_1, x_2, x_3) = (x_1 - x_2)^2 x_3{}^2 - 2((x_1 + x_2)(x_1 x_2 + a) + 2b)x_3 + \\ ((x_1 x_2 - a)^2 - 4b(x_1 + x_2)), \end{aligned} \tag{7}$$

$$f_t(x_1, x_2, \ldots, x_t) = \mathrm{Res}_X\left(f_{t-k}(x_1, \ldots, x_{t-k-1}, X), f_{k+2}(x_{t-k}, \ldots, x_t, X)\right)$$
$$\text{for } t \geqslant 4 \text{ and for any } k \text{ in the range } 1 \leqslant k \leqslant t - 3. \tag{8}$$

Here, Res_X stands for the resultant of two polynomials with respect to the variable X. Semaev proves that $f_t(x_1, x_2, \ldots, x_t) = 0$ if and only if there exist $y_1, y_2, \ldots, y_t \in \overline{\mathbb{F}}_p$ with (x_i, y_i) satisfying Eqn(1) for all $i = 1, 2, \ldots, t$ such that we have the following sum in the elliptic-curve group $E(\overline{\mathbb{F}}_p)$:

$$(x_1, y_1) + (x_2, y_2) + \cdots + (x_t, y_t) = \mathcal{O}, \tag{9}$$

where $\mathcal{O}$ is the point at infinity on E, and $\overline{\mathbb{F}}_p$ is the algebraic closure of $\mathbb{F}_p$.

For the batch verification of t ECDSA signatures (M_i, r_i, s_i), we first compute the numeric sum R on the right side of Eqn(5). In the non-randomized case of Eqn(3), we have $\xi_1 = \xi_2 = \cdots = \xi_t = 1$. Let $R = (\alpha, \beta)$, where $\alpha, \beta \in \mathbb{F}_p$. Let $\xi_i(r_i, y_i) = (r_i', y_i')$. Eqn(5) can be rewritten as

$$(r_1', y_1') + (r_2', y_2') + \cdots + (r_t', y_t') + (\alpha, -\beta) = \mathcal{O}. \tag{10}$$

By Eqn(9), this is equivalent to the condition $f_{t+1}(r'_1, r'_2, \ldots, r'_t, \alpha) = 0$. Algorithm 1 incorporates this idea to verify a batch of t ECDSA signatures.

Algorithm 1. ECDSA Batch-verification Algorithm SP for NIST Prime Curves

---

INPUT: Domain Parameters, ECDSA signatures (M_1, r_1, s_1), (M_2, r_2, s_2), $\ldots$,
$\qquad (M_t, r_t, s_t)$ and public keys $Q_1, Q_2, \ldots, Q_t$ of the signers.
OUTPUT: Accept/Reject the batch of t signatures.

1. Optional sanity check: For each $i = 1, 2, \ldots, t$, check whether $r_i^3 + ar_i + b$ is a quadratic residue modulo p. If not, reject the i-th signature and remove it from the batch. Let us assume that all the signatures in the batch pass the sanity check. (Also see Section 4.5.)
2. Compute $w_i = s_i^{-1} \pmod{n}$ for all $i = 1, 2, \ldots, t$.
3. Compute $u_i = H(M_i)w_i \pmod{n}$ for all $i = 1, 2, \ldots, t$.
4. Compute $v_i = r_i w_i \pmod{n}$ for all $i = 1, 2, \ldots, t$.
5. Choose t random integers $\xi_1, \xi_2, \ldots, \xi_t \in \{1, 2, \ldots, n-1\}$, where n is the order of the base point of the elliptic curve. For the non-randomized version, we take $\xi_1 = \xi_2 = \cdots = \xi_t = 1$.
6. Compute $R = (\sum_{i=1}^{t} \xi_i u_i)P + (\sum_{i=1}^{t} \xi_i v_i)Q = (\alpha, \beta)$.
7. For the randomized version, compute $r'_i = x(\xi_i(r_i, y_i))$ using Montgomery ladders or seminumeric scalar multiplication of [14,15]. For the non-randomized version, take $r'_i = r_i$.
8. Compute the value of the summation polynomial $\phi = f_{t+1}(r'_1, r'_2, \ldots, r'_t, \alpha)$.
9. Accept the batch of signatures if and only if $\phi = 0$.

---

4 Analysis of Algorithm SP

4.1 Properties of Summation Polynomials

For $t = 2$ or 3, we straightaway use the formulas given in Eqn(6) or (7). For $t \geqslant 4$, we make two recursive calls as given in Eqn(8). In order to optimize efficiency, the number of variables in each recursive call should be about $t/2$. More precisely, we always choose $k = \lceil t/2 \rceil$ (this is in the allowed range of values of k), so the first recursive call computes $f_{\lceil t/2 \rceil + 1}$ and the second recursive call computes $f_{\lfloor t/2 \rfloor + 1}$. The leaves of the recursion tree deal with the base cases of Eqns(6) and (7).

Theorem 1: Let $t = 2^h + 2$ for some $h \geqslant 0$. Then, the recursion tree for the computation of f_t is a complete binary tree of height h, and all the leaves correspond to the computation of f_3 by Eqn(7).

Proof We proceed by induction on h. For $h = 0$, we compute f_3 straightaway from Eqn(7) without making any recursive call, that is, the recursion tree is of height zero. For $h \geqslant 1$, suppose that the assertion holds for the computation of $f_{2^{h-1}+1}$. The computation of f_t proceeds as

$$f_t(x_1, x_2, \ldots, x_t) = \mathrm{Res}_X(f_{\frac{t}{2}+1}(x_1, \ldots, x_{\frac{t}{2}}, X), f_{\frac{t}{2}+1}(x_{\frac{t}{2}+1}, \ldots, x_t, X)).$$

Here, t is even, so $\lceil t/2 \rceil = \lfloor t/2 \rfloor = t/2$. Moreover, $t/2 = 2^{h-1} + 1$, so by the induction hypothesis, the sub-trees for the two recursive calls are complete binary trees with each leaf computing f_3.   ●

In general, let h be the height of the recursion tree for the computation of f_t. By Theorem 1, we have $2^{h-1} + 2 < t \leqslant 2^h + 2$, that is, $\log_2(t-2) \leqslant h < 1 + \log_2(t-2)$, that is, the height of the recursion tree is $\Theta(\log t)$.

Theorem 2:   Let $t = 2^h + 2$ with $h \geqslant 1$. If we compute f_t recursively as

$$f_t(x_1, x_2, \ldots, x_t) = \operatorname{Res}_X \left(f_{\frac{t}{2}+1}\left(x_1, \ldots, x_{\frac{t}{2}}, X\right), f_{\frac{t}{2}+1}\left(x_{\frac{t}{2}+1}, \ldots, x_t, X\right)\right), \quad (11)$$

then we take the resultant of two polynomials in X of degrees equal to $2^{\left(\frac{t-2}{2}\right)}$.

Proof.   We first supply a direct proof based upon induction on h. For the base case $h = 1$, we have four elements x_1, x_2, x_3, x_4. We compute $f_4(x_1, x_2, x_3, x_4) = \operatorname{Res}_X(f_3(x_1, x_2, X), f_3(x_3, x_4, X))$. By Eqn(7), the X-degree of each of the two arguments of Res_X is $2 = 2^{\left(\frac{4-2}{2}\right)}$.

Now, let $h \geqslant 2$ and $t' = \frac{t}{2} + 1 = 2^{h-1} + 2$. We have $f_{t'}(x_1, x_2, \ldots, x_{t'-1}, X) = \operatorname{Res}_Y \left(f_{\frac{t'}{2}+1}\left(x_1, \ldots, x_{\frac{t'}{2}}, Y\right), f_{\frac{t'}{2}+1}\left(x_{\frac{t'}{2}+1}, \ldots, x_{t'-1}, X, Y\right)\right)$. We inductively assume that this computation of $f_{t'}$ involves the resultant calculation of two polynomials of Y-degree $\delta = 2^{\left(\frac{t'-2}{2}\right)}$ each. But each summation polynomial is symmetric about its arguments. Therefore, the X-degree of the second argument is again $\delta = 2^{\left(\frac{t'-2}{2}\right)}$. Let us write

$$f_{\frac{t'}{2}+1}\left(x_1, \ldots, x_{\frac{t'}{2}}, Y\right) = a_\delta Y^\delta + a_{\delta-1}Y^{\delta-1} + \cdots + a_0, \quad (12)$$

$$f_{\frac{t'}{2}+1}\left(x_{\frac{t'}{2}+1}, \ldots, x_{t'-1}, X, Y\right) = b_\delta Y^\delta + b_{\delta-1}Y^{\delta-1} + \cdots + b_0. \quad (13)$$

Here, the coefficients a_i do not involve X, whereas the coefficients b_i are polynomials in X. Since the X-degree of the second polynomial is δ, and the polynomial is symmetric about X and Y, we conclude that the X-degree of b_δ is δ. The X-degrees of the other coefficients b_i are $\leqslant \delta$.

The $(2\delta) \times (2\delta)$ Sylvester matrix of the polynomials in Eqns(12) and (13) is

$$S = \begin{pmatrix} a_\delta & a_{\delta-1} & \cdots & a_0 & 0 & \cdots & 0 \\ 0 & a_\delta & a_{\delta-1} & \cdots & a_0 & \cdots & 0 \\ \vdots & \vdots & \vdots & \vdots & \vdots & \vdots & \vdots \\ 0 & \cdots & 0 & a_\delta & a_{\delta-1} & \cdots & a_0 \\ b_\delta & b_{\delta-1} & \cdots & b_0 & 0 & \cdots & 0 \\ 0 & b_\delta & b_{\delta-1} & \cdots & b_0 & \cdots & 0 \\ \vdots & \vdots & \vdots & \vdots & \vdots & \vdots & \vdots \\ 0 & \cdots & 0 & b_\delta & b_{\delta-1} & \cdots & b_0 \end{pmatrix}$$

The X-degree of $\det S$ is the X-degree of b_δ^δ, that is, $\delta^2 = 2^{t'-2} = 2^{\left(\frac{t-2}{2}\right)}$. Similarly, the X-degree of $f_{\frac{t}{2}+1}\left(x_{\frac{t}{2}+1}, \ldots, x_t, X\right)$ is again $2^{\left(\frac{t-2}{2}\right)}$.   •

Alternative proof In [21], Semaev proves that the summation polynomial f_k, $k \geqslant 3$, is of the form

$$f_k(x_1, x_2, \ldots, x_k) = f_{k-1}^2(x_1, x_2, \ldots, x_{k-1}) x_k^{2^{k-2}} + \cdots. \tag{14}$$

Now, we put $k = \frac{t}{2} + 1$ and $x_k = X$, and rewrite Eqn(14) as

$$f_{\frac{t}{2}+1}\left(x_1, \ldots, x_{\frac{t}{2}}, X\right) = f_{\frac{t}{2}}^2\left(x_1, x_2, \ldots, x_{\frac{t}{2}}\right) X^{2^{\left(\frac{t-2}{2}\right)}} + \cdots,$$

that is, $f_{\frac{t}{2}+1}\left(x_1, \ldots, x_{\frac{t}{2}}, X\right)$ is a polynomial of degree $2^{\left(\frac{t-2}{2}\right)}$ in X. Likewise, $f_{\frac{t}{2}+1}\left(x_{\frac{t}{2}+1}, \ldots, x_n, X\right)$ too is a polynomial of degree $2^{\left(\frac{t-2}{2}\right)}$ in X.   •

Theorem 2 can be generalized to any value of t (that is, values not only of the form $2^h + 2$). However, the resulting formulas involve many floor and ceiling expressions. For the sake of simplicity, we restrict only to the special case which already portrays the performance of SP as a function of t.

4.2   A Strategy to Handle the Variables in the Recursion Tree

Let r_i denote the known x-coordinates, and X_j the variables used in the recursion of Eqn(8). For achieving good performance, we reduce the number of variables in each node of the recursion tree. Each child of the root has one variable. Now, let some node compute the summation polynomial of $r_i, r_{i+1}, \ldots, r_{i+k-1}, X_j$ (the case of one variable). Its two child nodes compute the summation polynomials of $r_i, r_{i+1}, \ldots, r_{i+\lceil k/2 \rceil - 1}, X_{j'}$ and $r_{i+\lceil k/2 \rceil}, \ldots, r_{i+k-1}, X_j, X_{j'}$. On the other hand, if a node computes the summation polynomial of $r_i, r_{i+1}, \ldots, r_{i+k-1}, X_j, X_{j'}$ (the case of two variables), then its two child nodes compute the summation polynomials of $r_i, r_{i+1}, \ldots, r_{i+\lceil k/2 \rceil - 1}, X_j, X_{j''}$ and $r_i, r_{i+1}, \ldots, r_{i+k-1}, X_{j'}, X_{j''}$. This is allowed since summation polynomials are symmetric about its arguments. It is thus ensured that the number of variables in each node never exceeds two. At each node of the leftmost paths in the two subtrees of the root, the number of variables is $\leqslant 1$. At every other node in the tree, the number of variables is exactly two. Figure 1 shows the recursive construction of $f_{10}(r_1, r_2, \ldots, r_{10})$. Only the nodes on the paths from the root to the leaves (r_1, r_2, X_4) and (r_6, r_7, X_6) have numbers of variables $\leqslant 1$.

4.3   Running Time of SP

Let $C(t)$ denote the running time of Algorithm SP in the number of field operations on a batch of size t. In view of Eqn(10), we need to compute f_{t+1}. If $t = 2$, we use the base case which return in constant time. For $t \geqslant 3$, we use the

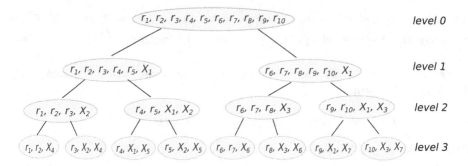

Fig. 1. Recursion tree for computing the summation polynomial of ten variables

recursive strategy of Eqn(11). Recursion stops in all cases at the base case of the computation of f_3. By Theorem 2, we need to take the resultant of two polynomials of degree $2^{\left(\frac{t-1}{2}\right)}$ each. The time complexity of resultant computation for two k-degree polynomials by the subresultant PRS algorithm [6,9] is $O(k^2)$.

The running time of SP is dominated by the times for the computation of the resultants. The degrees of the polynomials, of which the resultant is computed, is a function of the level λ in the tree. In addition, the resultant-computation time depends on how many variables are involved at that node, call it ν. We can have $\nu = 0, 1, 2$ only. Let $C_\nu^{(\lambda)}$ denote the time for resultant computation for a given λ and ν. The case of $C_0^{(\lambda)}$ occurs at level $\lambda = 0$ only. The case of $C_1^{(\lambda)}$ occurs on the leftmost paths of the two subtrees of the root. At all other nodes, the resultant-computation cost is $C_2^{(\lambda)}$.

For simplicity, we assume that the recursion tree is a complete binary tree of height h, that is, $t + 1 = 2^h + 2$. We have $C_0^{(0)} = O(2^{2^h})$, $C_1^{(\lambda)} = O(2^{2^{h-\lambda-1}\times 3})$, and $C_2^{(\lambda)} = O(2^{2^{h-\lambda+1}})$. At level zero, we have the cost C_0, whereas at any other level λ we have exactly two cases of $C_1^{(\lambda)}$ and $2^\lambda - 2$ cases of $C_2^{(\lambda)}$. Moreover, $C_1^{(\lambda)} < C_2^{(\lambda)}$ for each fixed λ. Therefore, the total cost $C(t)$ of computing f_{t+1} is of the order of

$$C_0^{(0)} + \sum_{\lambda=1}^{h-1}\left(2C_1^{(\lambda)} + (2^\lambda - 2)C_2^{(\lambda)}\right) < C_0^{(0)} + \sum_{\lambda=1}^{h-1} 2^\lambda C_2^{(\lambda)}$$

$$= O\left(2^{2^h} + \sum_{\lambda=1}^{h-1} 2^{\lambda+2^{h-\lambda+1}}\right).$$

The inequality $\lambda + 2^{h-\lambda+1} > (\lambda+1) + 2^{h-(\lambda+1)+1}$ holds if and only if we have $2^{h-\lambda} > 1$. For all λ in the range $1 \leqslant \lambda \leqslant h - 1$, we have $2^{h-\lambda} > 1$. Therefore, $C(t)$ is of the order of

$$2^{2^h} + \sum_{\lambda=1}^{h-1}\left[2^{\lambda+2^{h-\lambda+1}}\right] = 2^{2^h} + \left[2^{1+2^h} + 2^{2+2^{h-1}} + \cdots + 2^{(h-1)+2^2}\right]$$

$$< 2^{2^h} + \sum_{i=0}^{1+2^h} 2^i < 2^{2^h} + 2^{2+2^h} = 2^{2^h} + 2^{2+2^h} = 5 \times 2^{2^h}.$$

Substituting 2^h by $t - 1$, we see that $C(t) = O(m)$, where $m = 2^t$.

The above analysis implies that the computation of the resultants at the top two levels determines the order of $C(t)$. For a general t of the form $2^{h-1} + 2 < t + 1 \leqslant 2^h + 2$, we let $\tau = \lceil \frac{t+1}{2} \rceil$, and conclude that $C(t)$ is of the order of

$$2^{\lceil \frac{t+1}{2} \rceil + \lfloor \frac{t+1}{2} \rfloor - 2} + 2 \times \left(2^{(\lceil \frac{\tau+1}{2} \rceil + \lfloor \frac{\tau+1}{2} \rfloor - 2)} \right)^2$$

$$= 2^{t-1} + 2^{2(\tau+1)-3} \leqslant 2^{t-1} + 2^t = \frac{3}{2} \times 2^t = O(m).$$

4.4 Security of SP

In this section, we prove the equivalence between the security of Algorithm SP and the security of the standard ECDSA* batch-verification algorithm. Suppose that the x-coordinates $r_1, r_2, \ldots, r_t$ in ECDSA signatures are available to an adversary and that the batch is accepted by Algorithm SP. By Eqn(10), there exist exactly two solutions $(y_1, y_2, \ldots, y_t)$ and $(-y_1, -y_2, \ldots, -y_t)$ for the y-coordinates satisfying $y_i^2 = r_i^3 + ar_i + b$ for $i = 1, 2, \ldots, t$ such that $(r_1, y_1) + (r_2, y_2) + \cdots + (r_t, y_t) = (\alpha, \beta)$, and $(r_1, -y_1) + (r_2, -y_2) + \cdots + (r_t, -y_t) = (\alpha, -\beta)$. These are the only cases in which $f_{t+1}(r_1, r_2, \ldots, r_t, \alpha) = 0$. Both these solutions are consistent with $\phi = 0$ (Step 9 of Algorithm SP). One of these solutions corresponds to the ECDSA* signatures based upon the disclosed values $r_1, r_2, \ldots, r_t$. For ECDSA*, the y-coordinates are known, and we have only one possibility $(r_1, y_1) + (r_2, y_2) + \cdots + (r_t, y_t) = (\alpha, \beta)$. Given r_i alone, the adversary can obtain the y-coordinates y_i up to sign by making t square-root computations which demand only moderate computing resources. The sign ambiguity can be removed by trying all of the 2^t sign combinations (as in Algorithm N). For small values of t (as we deal with), this too is a tolerable overhead to the adversary. To sum up, if the adversary can forge ECDSA signatures that pass Algorithm SP, (s)he can produce in feasible time ECDSA* signatures too that pass the standard ECDSA* batch-verification algorithm. The converse is obvious.

4.5 Necessity of the Sanity Check

The security proof in the last section assumes that all y_i reside in $\mathbb{F}_p$ itself, that is, the points (r_i, y_i) lie on the curve E defined over $\mathbb{F}_p$. The sanity check made in Step 1 of Algorithm 1 ensures this.

The sanity check may be unnecessary in many situations. Suppose that an adversary chooses an r_i for which $r_i^3 + ar_i + b$ is a quadratic non-residue modulo p. The square roots of all quadratic non-residues in $\mathbb{F}_p$ lie in $\mathbb{F}_{p^2}$, that is, we now get two y-coordinates in $\mathbb{F}_{p^2}$ (but outside $\mathbb{F}_p$). The corresponding points $(r_i, \pm y_i)$ lie in $E(\mathbb{F}_{p^2})$. The right sides of Eqns(3) and (5) always lie in the group $E(\mathbb{F}_p)$ generated by the base point P. The batch-verification condition demands the sum of $R_1, R_2, \ldots, R_t$ to lie in $E(\mathbb{F}_p)$ in order to pass the test $f_{t+1}(r_1, r_2, \ldots, r_t, \alpha) = 0$ (see Eqn(9)). If one or more of the points R_i are defined over $\mathbb{F}_{p^2}$ (but not over $\mathbb{F}_p$), then what is the probability of $\sum_{i=1}^{t} R_i \in E(\mathbb{F}_p)$?

A satisfactory answer to this question can be given if the group structure of $E(\mathbb{F}_{p^2})$ is known to us. $E(\mathbb{F}_p)$ is already a cyclic subgroup of $E(\mathbb{F}_{p^2})$ of large prime order n. If $E(\mathbb{F}_{p^2})$ is cyclic too, randomly chosen points $R_i \in E(\mathbb{F}_{p^2})$ have a probability of about $1/p$ to have their sum in $E(\mathbb{F}_p)$. Even when $E(\mathbb{F}_{p^2})$ is of rank two with no small-order subgroups (like $\mathbb{Z}_n \oplus \mathbb{Z}_n$), there may be little problem. The use of randomizers makes the probability of $\sum_{i=1}^{t} R_i \in E(\mathbb{F}_p)$ negligible even when the x-coordinates r_i are carefully crafted by the adversary. Only when $E(\mathbb{F}_{p^2})$ contains subgroups of small orders, the adversary may win with non-negligible probability. Randomizers do not seem to help much in this case. Section 8 deals with the cases of some of the NIST curves.

In Algorithm 1, the sanity check involves the computation of t Legendre symbols $\left(\frac{r_i^3 + a r_i + b}{p}\right)$. This is anyway not a huge overhead compared to the computation of f_{t+1} (unless t is very small). Consequently, there is little harm in conducting the sanity check even when the probability of $\sum_{i=1}^{t} R_i \in E(\mathbb{F}_p)$ for points R_i defined over $\mathbb{F}_{p^2}$ is overwhelmingly small.

A sanity check like this may be needed for the previously published algorithms S2 and S2$'$ too. This issue is only mentioned but not discussed in detail in [13].

4.6   Cases of Failure of SP

The symbolic-manipulation algorithms of [13] have a few cases of failure. Algorithm SP is robust against most of these failures. First, computations which treat y_i as symbols cannot distinguish between the cases of point addition and point doubling. On the contrary, summation polynomials work equally well for both of these operations. Second, Algorithms S1, S2, S1$'$ and S2$'$ fail when the point $R = (\alpha, \beta)$ computed from the right side of Eqn(3) or (5) is the point $\mathcal{O}$ at infinity. Algorithm SP continues to work. Eqn(10) is now rewritten as $(r_1', y_1') + (r_2', y_2') + \cdots + (r_t', y_t') = \mathcal{O}$. That is, instead of computing $f_{t+1}(r_1', r_2', \ldots, r_t', \alpha)$, we now compute $f_t(r_1', r_2', \ldots, r_t')$.

5   Adaptation of Algorithm SP to Koblitz Curves

Let E be a Koblitz curve defined over a binary field $\mathbb{F}_{2^d}$ by the equation

$$E : y^2 + xy = x^3 + ax^2 + 1, \text{ where } a \in \{0, 1\}. \tag{15}$$

Let n be the order of the group we work in, and $\hat{h} = |E(\mathbb{F}_{2^d})|/n$ the cofactor. For Koblitz curves, $\hat{h} = 2$ or 4. Because $\hat{h}$ is small, appending a few extra bit(s) to ECDSA signatures, we can uniquely retrieve the x-coordinates from the published value of r in a signature. We therefore assume that the x-coordinates are known to us. We denote these x-coordinates by r_i itself. We can apply our batch-verification Algorithm SP *mutatis mutandis* to Koblitz curves.

5.1 Summation Polynomials for Koblitz Curves

Here, we supply only the first three base cases of summation polynomials f_2, f_3, and f_4. The recurrence relation for Koblitz-curve summation polynomials f_t with $t \geqslant 5$ is identical to the case of prime curves.

$$f_2(x_1, x_2) = x_1 + x_2,$$
$$f_3(x_1, x_2, x_3) = (x_1 x_2 + x_1 x_3 + x_2 x_3)^2 + x_1 x_2 x_3 + 1,$$
$$f_4(x_1, x_2, x_3, x_4) = (x_1 + x_2 + x_3 + x_4)^4 + (x_1 x_2 x_3 + x_1 x_2 x_4 + x_1 x_3 x_4 + x_2 x_3 x_4)^4 +$$
$$x_1 x_2 x_3 x_4 (x_1 x_2 x_3 + x_1 x_2 x_4 + x_1 x_3 x_4 + x_2 x_3 x_4 + x_1 + x_2 + x_3 + x_4)^2 +$$
$$(x_1 x_2 x_3 x_4)^2 (x_1 + x_2 + x_3 + x_4)^2 + (x_1 x_2 x_3 + x_1 x_2 x_4 + x_1 x_3 x_4 + x_2 x_3 x_4)^2.$$

Eqn(9) holds for Koblitz curve too, that is, there exist $y_1, y_2, \ldots, y_t \in \mathbb{F}_{2^d}$ with each (x_i, y_i) satisfying Eqn (15) if and only if $f_t(x_1, x_2, \ldots, x_t) = 0$.

For prime curves, we always reduce the recursion to the computation of f_3, since the explicit formula for f_4 is rather clumsy. For Koblitz curves, we use both the cases f_3 and f_4 as those that terminate recursion. This helps us to reduce the height of the recursion tree for most of the batch sizes.

Notice that all batch-verification algorithms for Koblitz curves can be readily adapted to other ordinary (non-supersingular) curves over binary fields. We deal with the NIST family of Koblitz curves as an illustrative sample.

5.2 Adaptation of the Sanity Check

The sanity check (the equivalent of Step 1 in Algorithm 1) is quite easy in the context of NIST Koblitz curves. In order that the point $R_i = (r_i, y_i)$ is defined over $\mathbb{F}_{2^d}$, we now need the equation $y_i^2 + r_i y_i + (r_i^3 + a r_i^2 + 1) = 0$ to be solvable (for y_i) in $\mathbb{F}_{2^d}$. This is equivalent to the condition that the trace of $\frac{r_i^3 + a r_i^2 + 1}{r_i^2}$ over $\mathbb{F}_2$ is zero. Let the field $\mathbb{F}_{2^d} = \mathbb{F}_2[X]/\langle F(X) \rangle$ be defined by the irreducible polynomial $F(X) = X^d + a_{d-1} X^{d-1} + \cdots + a_1 X + a_0$, where $a_i \in \mathbb{F}_2$. Let $\theta \in \mathbb{F}_{2^d}$ be a root of $F(X)$. Any element $c \in \mathbb{F}_{2^d}$ can be represented as $c = \sum_{k=0}^{d-1} c_k \theta^k$. We can compute the trace of c as $\mathrm{Tr}(c) = c_0 + \sum_{k=1}^{d-1} k c_k a_{d-k}$ (see [8] for a discussion). For NIST Koblitz curves, the defining polynomial $F(X)$ has very few non-zero coefficients, so the computation of $\mathrm{Tr}(c)$ is essentially a constant-time effort given any $c \in \mathbb{F}_{2^d}$.

Even when the solutions for y_i lie in $\mathbb{F}_{2^d}$, there is no guarantee that the point $R_i = (r_i, y_i)$ belongs to the subgroup of $E(\mathbb{F}_{2^d})$ generated by the base point P, since Koblitz curves have cofactors $\hat{h} > 1$. At present, we do not know any efficient solution of this problem. If $E(\mathbb{F}_{2^d})$ is cyclic, then R_i is in the subgroup generated by P if and only if $n R_i = \mathcal{O}$. However, computing the scalar multiplication $n R_i$ for each i lets us forfeit the speedup obtained by batch verification.

Table 1. Times (in ms) for finding y_i from r_i

Square-root method in prime fields	P-256	0.28
	P-521	0.76
Factorization method in binary fields	K-283	8.31
	K-571	30.83

Table 2. Times (in ms) of scalar multiplication for prime curves

Scalar-multiplication algorithm	P-256		P-521		
	$l = 128$	$l = 256$	$l = 128$	$l = 256$	$l = 521$
Numeric scalar multiplication	2.04	3.92	2.69	5.48	10.60
Seminumeric scalar multiplication	2.04	4.12	2.81	5.92	11.44
Multiple scalar multiplication $\xi_1 R_1 + \xi_2 R_2$	2.93	5.67	4.37	7.89	16.30

l is the bit length of the randomizers

Table 3. Times (in ms) of scalar multiplication for Koblitz curves

Scalar-multiplication algorithm	K-283		K-571		
	$l = 128$	$l = 283$	$l = 128$	$l = 256$	$l = 571$
Numeric scalar multiplication	200.00	216.00	517.00	964.00	1076.00
Seminumeric scalar multiplication	267.10	288.93	718.88	1378.06	1532.89
Multiple scalar multiplication $\xi_1 R_1 + \xi_2 R_2$	443.46	973.75	1170.09	2344.40	5215.14

l is the bit length of the randomizers

6   Experimental Results

All experiments are carried out in a 2.33 GHz Xeon server running Ubuntu Linux Server Version 2012 LTS. The algorithms are implemented using the GP/PARI calculator [20] (version 2.5.0 compiled by the GNU C compiler 4.6.2). We have used the symbolic-computation facilities of the calculator in our programs. All other functions (like scalar multiplication and square-root computation) are written as subroutines in which function-call overheads are minimized as much as possible. We have used the best formulas supplied in [5,8]. We only used the built-in field arithmetic provided by the calculator. Since all algorithms are evaluated in terms of number of field operations, this gives a fare comparison of experimental data with the theoretical estimates. The GP/PARI library is much slower for binary fields than for prime fields. However, this speed difference matters only slightly in the experimental speedup figures which are ratios. As argued in Section 2.3, we consider only the case of the same signer.

The average times of finding the roots y_i from r_i are listed in Table 1. The average times of randomization achieved by the seminumeric algorithm [14] and numeric scalar multiplication are listed in Tables 2 and 3 for prime curves and Koblitz curves. Here, l denotes the length of the randomizers. We consider only two cryptographically meaningful values of l: 128 (giving 128-bit security irrespective of the difficulty of the ECDLP) and half-length (same security as offered by the square-root methods for the ECDLP). Tables 4 and 5 list the overheads associated with different ECDSA batch-verification algorithms for several batch sizes with all the signatures coming from the same signer. Finally, the speedup figures (over individual verification) are listed in Tables 6 and 7 for prime curves and Koblitz curves.

Table 4. Overheads (in ms) of different batch-verification algorithms for prime curves

Batch size	N		N′		S2′		SP	
(t)	P-256	P-521	P-256	P-521	P-256	P-521	P-256	P-521
2	0.091	0.126	0.022	0.031	–	–	0.038	0.080
3	0.289	0.401	0.034	0.050	0.081	0.158	0.121	0.153
4	0.788	1.097	0.048	0.067	0.183	0.315	0.144	0.267
5	1.813	2.585	0.063	0.086	0.391	0.596	0.211	0.377
6	4.316	6.229	0.075	0.106	0.701	1.062	0.446	0.789
7	10.104	14.667	0.080	0.112	1.493	2.213	0.663	1.167
8	23.191	33.265	0.098	0.130	3.574	5.398	1.464	2.698
9	–	–	–	–	–	–	2.385	4.240
10	–	–	–	–	–	–	8.234	15.598

Table 5. Overheads (in ms) of different batch-verification algorithms for Koblitz curves

Batch size	N		N′		S2′		SP	
(t)	K-283	K-571	K-283	K-571	K-283	K-571	K-283	K-571
2	19.75	53.16	4.96	13.86	3.96	10.57	1.640	4.545
3	73.60	200.21	9.42	25.87	12.00	32.71	4.378	12.710
4	212.18	581.49	13.80	37.65	33.84	91.12	48.927	179.337
5	556.25	1544.59	18.16	49.03	131.00	354.30	62.790	220.271
6	1372.07	3791.10	22.34	60.61	303.08	825.00	141.345	458.448
7	3356.48	9161.95	27.00	72.89	1000.61	2749.37	585.654	1784.127
8	–	–	–	–	–	–	734.916	2277.102
9	–	–	–	–	–	–	1409.530	4340.618
10	–	–	–	–	–	–	3258.385	9602.883

In Algorithm N′, there is a possibility of using multiple scalar multiplication. The times for computing the sum $\xi_1 R_1 + \xi_2 R_2$ using a single double-and-add loop are also listed in the Tables 2 and 3. For prime curves, the multiple scalar-multiplication times are significantly less than that of two separate scalar multiplications by the most efficient windowed NAF variant. However, for Koblitz curves, the sum of times to compute two numeric scalar multiplications by the τ-NAF method [22] is much smaller than the time of a double scalar multiplication. While calculating the speedup figures, we have considered the best available options. Algorithm N′ is suited to ECDSA#. We first obtain each y_i uniquely by a square-root computation. Randomization in this case uses numeric scalar multiplication (or double scalar multiplication whichever is better).

Table 6. Speedup obtained by batch-verification algorithms for prime curves

Batch-verification algorithm	Randomization algorithm	t	P-256		P-521		
			None*	$l = 128$	None*	$l = 128$	$l = 256$
N	Numeric	3	2.50	1.32	2.58	1.81	1.38
		4	2.99	1.44	3.19	2.09	1.54
		5	3.19	1.49	3.59	2.26	1.63
		6	2.92	1.42	3.61	2.26	1.63
		7	2.24	1.24	3.14	2.07	1.53
		8	1.46	0.96	2.34	1.69	1.31
N'	Numeric	3	2.60	1.48	2.63	1.90	1.53
		4	3.32	1.79	3.36	2.32	1.85
		5	3.98	1.89	4.04	2.58	1.97
		6	4.59	2.10	4.67	2.87	2.19
		7	5.15	2.14	5.25	3.04	2.24
		8	5.68	2.31	5.80	3.27	2.41
S2'	Seminumeric	3	2.96	1.36	2.97	1.96	1.43
		4	3.87	1.53	3.92	2.34	1.62
		5	4.68	1.64	4.82	2.63	1.75
		6	5.34	1.72	5.63	2.86	1.85
		7	5.54	1.74	6.16	2.99	1.90
		8	4.91	1.67	6.01	2.95	1.89
SP	Seminumeric	3	2.94	1.36	2.97	1.97	1.43
		4	3.90	1.54	3.94	2.34	1.62
		5	4.82	1.66	4.89	2.65	1.76
		6	5.56	1.74	5.72	2.88	1.86
		7	6.27	1.80	6.53	3.07	1.94
		8	6.36	1.81	6.86	3.14	1.97
		9	6.34	1.81	7.14	3.20	1.99
		10	4.08	1.56	5.11	2.72	1.79

*Without randomization

The experimental results clearly indicate that SP is the most efficient batch-verification algorithm for standard ECDSA signatures. Even for ECDSA# signatures, Algorithm SP often outperforms the naive method N'. The optimal batch size for Algorithm S2' is $t = 7$ (for prime curves) and $t = 5$ or 6 (for Koblitz curves). With Algorithm SP, the optimal batch sizes are $t = 9$ (for prime curves) and $t = 6$ (for Koblitz curves). For both these families, the maximum speedup is noticeably higher in Algorithm SP than what is achieved by Algorithm S2'.

The implications associated with the sanity check (Step 1 of Algorithm 1) are now discussed. For prime curves, the sanity check incurs negligible overhead. Without this check, the maximum achievable speedup figures for $t = 9$ are 6.55, 1.95, 7.25, 3.22 and 2.00. The corresponding row in Table 6 shows slightly smaller speedup values 6.34, 1.81, 7.14, 3.20 and 1.99 caused by the check. Similar observations hold for Algorithm S2' too. For Koblitz curves, the sanity check is very efficient and does not produce noticeable performance degradation.

Table 7. Speedup obtained by batch-verification algorithms for Koblitz curves

Batch-verification algorithm	Randomization algorithm	t	K-283 None*	K-283 $l=128$	K-571 None*	K-571 $l=128$	K-571 $l=256$
N	Numeric	2	1.84	0.99	1.90	1.30	1.03
		3	2.44	1.15	2.64	1.62	1.21
		4	2.55	1.17	3.01	1.75	1.28
		5	2.10	1.06	2.79	1.67	1.24
		6	1.40	0.85	2.11	1.40	1.08
		7	0.79	0.58	1.31	0.99	0.82
N'	Numeric	2	1.90	1.01	1.93	1.32	1.04
		3	2.78	1.22	2.84	1.69	1.25
		4	3.61	1.35	3.72	1.96	1.40
		5	4.39	1.45	4.57	2.18	1.50
		6	5.14	1.52	5.39	2.35	1.58
		7	5.85	1.58	6.17	2.49	1.64
S2'	Seminumeric	2	1.99	1.18	1.99	1.49	1.17
		3	2.94	1.46	2.97	1.98	1.45
		4	3.78	1.64	3.88	2.35	1.64
		5	4.08	1.69	4.48	2.55	1.74
		6	3.94	1.67	4.73	2.63	1.78
		7	2.56	1.36	3.69	2.27	1.61
SP	Seminumeric	2	1.99	1.18	2.00	1.49	1.17
		3	2.98	1.47	2.99	1.99	1.46
		4	3.69	1.62	3.78	2.31	1.62
		5	4.51	1.76	4.66	2.61	1.77
		6	4.82	1.81	5.22	2.78	1.84
		7	3.48	1.58	4.42	2.53	1.78
		8	3.52	1.59	4.59	2.59	1.76
		9	2.62	1.37	3.73	2.29	1.61
		10	1.51	0.99	2.42	1.72	1.31

*Without randomization

7 Summation Polynomial for Edwards Curves

Edwards curves are introduced by Edwards in [10]. Bernstein and Lange apply these curves to cryptographic usage [4]. Edwards curves offer faster addition and doubling formulas than elliptic curves. Moreover, the unified addition and doubling formulas make Edwards-curve cryptosystems resistant to simple side-channel attacks. An Edwards curve over a prime field is defined by the equation:

$$x^2 + y^2 = c^2(1 + dx^2y^2), \text{ where } cd(1 - dc^4) \neq 0.$$

The sum of two points $P_1 = (x_1, y_1)$ and $P_2 = (x_2, y_2)$ on this curve is given as

$$(x_3, y_3) = \left(\frac{x_1 y_2 + x_2 y_1}{c(1 + d x_1 x_2 y_1 y_2)}, \frac{y_1 y_2 - x_1 x_2}{c(1 - d x_1 x_2 y_1 y_2)} \right).$$

This formula holds even when $P_1 = \pm P_2$.

EdDSA is the Edwards-curve equivalent of ECDSA [3]. Like ECDSA, only the y-coordinate of an Edwards-curve point is sent in an EdDSA signature. An extra bit to identify the correct x-coordinate is included in the signature. As a result, all the batch-verification algorithms studied in connection with ECDSA apply equally well to EdDSA signatures. Here, we mention the adaptation necessary to make Algorithm SP work for EdDSA batch verification. The original proposal of EdDSA refers to a batch-verification method akin to Algorithm N′.

The two base cases f_2 and f_3 of Edwards-curve summation polynomials are given by

$$f_2(y_1, y_2) = y_1 - y_2,$$
$$f_3(y_1, y_2, y_3) = c^2 (B - d^2 A y_1^2 y_2^2) y_3^2 - 2 y_1 y_2 (B - dA) y_3 + (B y_1^2 y_2^2 - A),$$
$$\text{where } A = (c^2 - y_1^2)(c^2 - y_2^2) \text{ and } B = (1 - c^2 d y_1^2)(1 - c^2 d y_2^2).$$

The recurrence relation for Edwards-curve summation polynomials f_t for $t \geqslant 4$ is the same as for prime/Koblitz curves. The sanity check for Edwards curves follows the same procedure as for elliptic curves.

8   The Group Structures in Quadratic Extensions

Here, we investigate the groups $E(\mathbb{F}_{p^2})$ and $E(\mathbb{F}_{2^{2d}})$ for the NIST prime and Koblitz curves [19] for which we have reported our experimental results. Since the sizes of the groups over the base fields are known, it is easy to compute the orders of the groups over quadratic extensions using a well-known result by Weil [8]. These sizes give an initial (sometimes complete) understanding of the structures of the groups over the extension fields.

The curve P-256 is defined over $\mathbb{F}_p$ for a 256-bit prime p. The order of $E(\mathbb{F}_p)$ is a prime n, so $E(\mathbb{F}_p)$ is cyclic. The size of $E(\mathbb{F}_{p^2})$ is $|E(\mathbb{F}_{p^2})| = 3 \times 5 \times 13 \times 179 \times n \times n'$, where $n' \neq n$ is a 241-bit prime. Since $|E(\mathbb{F}_{p^2})|$ is square-free, the group $E(\mathbb{F}_{p^2})$ is cyclic. However, it contains subgroups of small orders.

The curve P-521 is defined over $\mathbb{F}_p$ for a 521-bit prime p. The order of $E(\mathbb{F}_p)$ is a prime n, so $E(\mathbb{F}_p)$ is cyclic. The size of $E(\mathbb{F}_{p^2})$ is $|E(\mathbb{F}_{p^2})| = 5 \times 7 \times 69697531 \times 635884237 \times n \times n'$, where $n' \neq n$ is a 461-bit prime. Again $E(\mathbb{F}_{p^2})$ is cyclic, since its order is square-free. This group too has subgroups of small orders.

The Koblitz curve K-283 is defined over $\mathbb{F}_{2^d}$, $d = 283$, and has an order $4n$ for a prime n. If the group $E(\mathbb{F}_{2^d})$ is not cyclic, we must have $E(\mathbb{F}_{2^d}) \cong \mathbb{Z}_{2n} \oplus \mathbb{Z}_2$. But then, by the structure theorem of elliptic-curve groups of rank two, we have $2|(2^d - 1)$, which is impossible. So $E(\mathbb{F}_{2^{283}})$ is cyclic. In the quadratic extension $\mathbb{F}_{2^{2d}}$, the group has order $|E(\mathbb{F}_{2^{2d}})| = 2^3 \times 5 \times 250057 \times 43611431 \times n \times n'$ for a 238-bit prime n' (different from n). As argued above, $E(\mathbb{F}_{2^{2d}})$ is easily seen to be cyclic. However, it contains subgroups of small orders.

The Koblitz curve K-571 is defined over $\mathbb{F}_{2^d}$, $d = 571$, and has order $4n$ for a prime n. We have the order $|E(\mathbb{F}_{2^{2d}})| = 2^3 \times 835205577201087993065806699 \times 596201686362718542354710701 \times n \times n'$ for a 395-bit prime $n' \neq n$. Both $E(\mathbb{F}_{2^d})$ and $E(\mathbb{F}_{2^{2d}})$ are cyclic. Again, $E(\mathbb{F}_{2^{2d}})$ contains subgroups of small orders.

Since each of these groups in the quadratic extension has small-order subgroups, the sanity check is apparently preferred for all these curves. However, if the points of small orders on a curve over the quadratic extension do not have x-coordinates in the base field, then we can eliminate the sanity check.

9   Conclusion

In this paper, we propose a new and efficient batch-verification algorithm for original ECDSA signatures. Our algorithm outperforms all previously known batch-verification algorithms for ECDSA. We theoretically and experimentally establish this superiority for the NIST prime and Koblitz families of elliptic curves. We also mention how the methods can be adapted to EdDSA signatures. Theoretical and experimental performance comparisons of different batch-verification algorithms for EdDSA signatures remains an open (albeit fairly straightforward) problem. The elliptic-curve group structures over quadratic extensions of the base fields need to be determined for all NIST curves, at the minimum to gauge the necessity of running the sanity check.

References

1. Bellare, M., Garay, J.A., Rabin, T.: Fast batch verification for modular exponentiation and digital signatures. In: Nyberg, K. (ed.) EUROCRYPT 1998. LNCS, vol. 1403, pp. 236–250. Springer, Heidelberg (1998)
2. Bernstein, D.J., Doumen, J., Lange, T., Oosterwijk, J.-J.: Faster batch forgery identification. In: Galbraith, S., Nandi, M. (eds.) INDOCRYPT 2012. LNCS, vol. 7668, pp. 454–473. Springer, Heidelberg (2012)
3. Ghosh, S., Roychowdhury, D., Das, A.: High speed cryptoprocessor for η_T pairing on 128-bit secure supersingular elliptic curves over characteristic two fields. In: Preneel, B., Takagi, T. (eds.) CHES 2011. LNCS, vol. 6917, pp. 442–458. Springer, Heidelberg (2011)
4. Bernstein, D.J., Lange, T.: Faster addition and doubling on elliptic curves. In: Kurosawa, K. (ed.) ASIACRYPT 2007. LNCS, vol. 4833, pp. 29–50. Springer, Heidelberg (2007)
5. Bernstein, D.J., Lange, T.: Explicit-formulas database (2007),
   http://www.hyperelliptic.org/EFD/
6. Brown, W.S.: The subresultant PRS algorithm. ACM Transactions on Mathematical Software 4(3), 237–249 (1978)
7. Cheon, J.H., Yi, J.H.: Fast batch verification of multiple signatures. In: Okamoto, T., Wang, X. (eds.) PKC 2007. LNCS, vol. 4450, pp. 442–457. Springer, Heidelberg (2007)

8. Cohen, H., Frey, G., Avanzi, R., Doche, C., Lange, T., Nguyen, K., Vercauteren, F.: Handbook of elliptic and hyperelliptic curve cryptography. CRC Press (2006)
9. Collins, G.E.: Subresultants and reduced polynomial remainder sequences. Journal of ACM 14(1), 128–142 (1967)
10. Edwards, H.M.: A normal form for elliptic curves. Bulletin of American Mathematical Society 44(3), 393–422 (2007)
11. Harn, L.: Batch verifying multiple RSA digital signatures. Electronics Letters 34(12), 1219–1220 (1998)
12. Johnson, D., Menezes, A.J., Vanstone, S.A.: The Elliptic Curve Digital Signature Algorithm (ECDSA). International Journal of Information Security 1(1), 36–63 (2001)
13. Karati, S., Das, A., Roychowdhury, D., Bellur, B., Bhattacharya, D., Iyer, A.: Batch verification of ECDSA signatures. In: Mitrokotsa, A., Vaudenay, S. (eds.) AFRICACRYPT 2012. LNCS, vol. 7374, pp. 1–18. Springer, Heidelberg (2012)
14. Karati, S., Das, A., Roychowdhury, D.: Using randomizers for batch verification of ECDSA signatures, IACR Cryptology ePrint Archive (2012), http://eprint.iacr.org/2012/582
15. Montgomery, P.L.: Speeding up Pollard and elliptic curve methods of factorization. Mathematics of Computation 48(177), 243–264 (1987)
16. Naccache, D., M'Raïhi, D., Vaudenay, S., Raphaeli, D.: Can D.S.A. Be improved? In: De Santis, A. (ed.) EUROCRYPT 1994. LNCS, vol. 950, pp. 77–85. Springer, Heidelberg (1995)
17. NIST: Digital Signature Standard (DSS), http://csrc.nist.gov/publications/drafts/fips_186-3/Draft-FIPS-186-3
18. NIST: Secure Hash Standard, SHS (2007), http://csrc.nist.gov/publications/drafts/fips_180-3/draft_fips-180-3_June-08-2007.pdf
19. NIST: Recommended elliptic curves for federal government use (1999), http://csrc.nist.gov/groups/ST/toolkit/documents/dss/NISTReCur.pdf
20. PARI Group: PARI/GP Home (2003-2013), http://pari.math.u-bordeaux.fr/
21. Semaev, I.: Summation polynomials and the discrete logarithm problem on elliptic curves (2004), http://eprint.iacr.org/2004/031
22. Solinas, J.A.: Improved algorithms for arithmetic on anomalous binary curves, Combinatorics and Optimization Research Report CORR 99-46, University of Waterloo (1999), http://www.cacr.math.uwaterloo.ca/techreports/1999/corr99-46.ps

On Updatable Redactable Signatures

Henrich C. Pöhls[1,2,*], Kai Samelin[**]

[1] Chair of IT-Security, University of Passau, Germany
[2] Institute of IT-Security and Security Law (ISL), University of Passau, Germany
{hp,ks}@sec.uni-passau.de

Abstract. Redactable signatures allow removing parts from signed documents. State-of-the-art security models do not capture the possibility that the signer can "update" signatures, i.e., add new elements. Neglecting this, third parties can generate forgeries. Moreover, there are constructions which permit creating a signature by merging two redacted messages, if they stem from the same original. Our adjusted definition captures both possibilities. We present a provably secure construction in the standard model, which makes use of a novel trapdoor-accumulator.

1 Introduction

Assume we sign a set $\mathcal{S} = \{v_1, v_2, \ldots, v_\ell\}$, generating a signature σ protecting $\mathcal{S}$.[1] The use of a redactable signature scheme ($\mathcal{RSS}$) now allows removing elements from $\mathcal{S}$: a verifying signature σ' for a subset $\mathcal{S}' \subseteq \mathcal{S}$ can be derived by anyone. This action is called a *redaction*. For this, no secret key is not required, i.e., redacting is a public operation. This possibility is contrary to standard digital signatures, which do not permit any alterations. Public redactions are especially useful, if the original signer is not reachable anymore, e.g., in case of death, or if it produces too much overhead to resign a message every time an alteration is necessary, e.g., if communication is too costly. Hence, $\mathcal{RSS}$s partially address the "digital document sanitization problem" [36]. Formally, $\mathcal{RSS}$s are a proper subset of ($\mathcal{P}$-)homomorphic signatures [1]. The obvious applications for $\mathcal{RSS}$s are privacy-preserving handling of medical records, the removal of the date-of-birth from certificates from job applications, and the removal of identifying information for age-restricted locations from XML-files or the cloud [7,27,30,40,41,42,43,45]. Real implementations are given in [40,44,46]. However, existing provably secure constructions offer the possibility of "dynamic updates". In a nutshell, dynamic updates allow the signer to add new elements to existing signatures. This captures the ideas given in [8,29]. Hence, a signer can add new elements without the need to re-sign everything, e.g., to add new

---

[*] The research leading to these results has received support from the European Union's Seventh Framework Programme (FP7/2007-2013) under grant agreement n° 609094.

[**] This work was partly supported by the German Federal Ministry of Education and Research (BMBF) within EC SPRIDE and by the Hessian LOEWE excellence initiative within CASED, while working at CASED.

[1] [14,19,43] show how to treat more complex data-structures with an $\mathcal{RSS}$ for sets.

I. Boureanu, P. Owesarski, and S. Vaudenay (Eds.): ACNS 2014, LNCS 8479, pp. 457–475, 2014.
© Springer International Publishing Switzerland 2014

credentials or new database entries. This is useful in many situations, e.g., if it is too costly to re-sign a database completely for each new entry added. In other words, updates may become less expensive than a complete re-sign. Unfortunately, this also allows forgeries according to the existing security models whenever the *adversary* is given access to an "update-oracle". Jumping ahead, this oracle essentially models the adversary's possibility to ask the signer to adaptively "update" signatures with elements of its own choice. Given the aforementioned application scenarios, this possibility must not be neglected. Related, and present in many $\mathcal{RSS}$s in the literature is the possibility of "merging": given two set/signature pairs derived from the same signature, one can combine them into a single *merged*, set/signature pair $(\mathcal{S}, \sigma)$.

Example. Consider bio data banks, which are collections of samples of human bodily substances (e.g., DNA) that are associated with personal data. While the personal data part might be quite small, the medical data is often very large. However, from the association with personal data follows the necessity to obey strict data protection requirements. Once this association is removed, the protection can be (partly) forgo and the handling of this data becomes simpler. Hence, one wants to store tables containing columns with personally identifying information separate from those that contain other data, which on its own is anonymous. Splitting the data allows to store it on servers with different security requirements, and possibly different costs. Also, the outsourcing party wants to allow the database service provider to repartition the database as it sees suitable for an optimal operation. The use of a private, updatable and mergeable $\mathcal{RSS}$ now allows protecting the integrity by signing each single field of each row in each table as an element. In $\mathcal{RSS}$s, privacy says that no information about redacted elements can be derived from signatures, *if one has no access to them*. In our example, this means that the low-security servers gain *no* information about the high-security columns. A formal definition is given in Sect. 2. To clarify, consider a simple database with one table and three columns (id, Name, DNA). When this database is signed, we get one signature over the complete database. Now, we can split the complete record into one table containing only (id, Name) pairs, and a second one holding (id, DNA) pairs. To do so, we generate two separate signatures by using the redact operation of the $\mathcal{RSS}$. Now, the $\mathcal{RSS}$ can further be used by each database server to generate and hand valid signature over to clients for any elements returned by their queries. If a query only returns one row, the database server redacts all other rows and sends the resulting signature to the client. The client is able to verify that the result set is from the original signer and the returned values have not been modified. In turn, mergeability now allows deriving a *single* valid signature from formerly split database records. Hence, the database service provider can undo the splitting by merging the result set, and the signatures, before returning it. A property we define in Sect. 2, named *merge transparency*, even hides the information that a signature has been created through a merge operation from the verifying client.

If the splitting was done for privacy, any client or third-party service which is allowed to query for private data, e.g., (id, Name), and (id, DNA) can merge the database server's answers and gain assurance that the merged result containing data with three columns (id, Name, DNA) comes from the trusted source and establish that the records have not been modified. On the other hand, dynamic updates have been motivated in previous work before and allow the signer, i.e., the database owner, to dynamically add new records to the database.

In our scenario, we require that: (1) an attacker cannot generate non-legitimate signatures, (2) redacted information remains hidden, and (3) that all algorithms create *linkable* versions of the same document. The third requirement makes $\mathcal{RSS}$s useable in practice: an attacker must not be able to generate "clones" of a signed set by gradually redacting different elements. As an example, assume that Name consists of several columns (FirstName, MiddleName, FamilyName). Then, we do not want that the DNA record of "Rose" "Fitzgerald" "Kennedy" can be duplicated without detection into several sets by redaction of some of the elements, e.g., pretending two signed DNA records exist: one for a member of the "Kennedy" family and another one for a woman with the first name of "Rose". Merging thus serves as a test when its questionable whether or not two records are derived from the same original: once two signed sets are available, their signatures only merge, if they are linkable.

State-of-the-Art. The concept of $\mathcal{RSS}$s has been introduced as "content extraction signatures" by *Steinfeld* et al. [45], and, in the same year, as "homomorphic signatures" [28] by *Johnson* et al. A security model for sets has been given by *Miyazaki* et al. [37]. Their ideas have been extended to work on trees [14,30,42], on lists [19,43], and also on arbitrary graphs [30]. There are also some schemes which offer *context-hiding*, a very strong privacy notion, and variations thereof, e.g., [1,3,4]. Context-hiding schemes allow to generate signatures on derived sets with no possibility to detect whether these correspond to an already signed set in a statistical sense. To some extend, the concept of sanitizable signature schemes ($\mathcal{SSS}$) is related [2,13,15,16,17,21,31]. In an $\mathcal{SSS}$, the sanitizer does not redact elements, but can change "admissible elements" to arbitrary strings, i.e., $v_i' \in \{0, 1\}^*$. $\mathcal{SSS}$s require sanitizers to know a secret and therefore do not allow public alterations. Even though they seem to be related, the aims and security models of $\mathcal{SSS}$s and $\mathcal{RSS}$s substantially differ on a detailed level [22]. Hence, $\mathcal{SSS}$s are not discussed in any more detail in this paper. Most recent advances generalize similar concepts. These are normally referred to as "($\mathcal{P}$-)homomorphic signatures", "functional signatures", and/or "delegateable signatures". Noteworthy work includes [1,3,4,5,10,12,20,23]. In this paper, we focus on $\mathcal{RSS}$s, while our results are applicable to the aforementioned primitives.

In the field of $\mathcal{RSS}$s, all existing provably *private* constructions only consider how to redact elements. The opposite — reinstating previously redacted elements, i.e., merging signatures — in a controlled way has neither been formalized nor have security models been properly discussed. Notions of mergeability are initially given by *Merkle* for hash-trees [35], but these are not private in the context of $\mathcal{RSS}$s. The closest existing works mentioning merging in our context are [28,33,38,39]. However, neither of the mentioned schemes is fully private in our model, while [28] is even forgeable — merging from any signed set is possible.

Contribution. As aforementioned, current security models do not correctly capture the possibility that some signatures can be updated, i.e., that the signer can freely add new elements. Additionally, they also do not discuss that signatures can, under certain circumstances, be merged. In this paper, we introduce an extended security model explicitly capturing both possibilities. Our contribution is therefore manifold: (1) We present some shortcomings in existing security models, which do not consider the case of updating signatures by the signer. We show how an adversary can construct forgeries, if this possibility is neglected. (2) We propose a countermeasure: we augment the state-of-the-art security model with explicit access to an "update-oracle", which an adversary can query adaptively. We also rigorously define the notions of "update privacy" and "update transparency". Jumping ahead, both properties describe which information can be derived from an updated signature. (3) We introduce a formal definition of "mergeability", i.e., under which circumstances signatures can be merged into a single one. With private and transparent mergeability, we give the first security model of the inverse operation of redaction, extending the work done in [33]. Again, both properties aim to formalize which information an adversary can obtain from a merged signature. We prove that merging signatures has no negative impact on existing security properties. (4) We show how the new and old notions are related to each other, extending the work by *Brzuska* et al. [14]. (5) We derive a provably secure construction, meeting our enhanced definitions. (6) For our construction, we deploy trapdoor-accumulators. This construction is of independent interest. Moreover, it turns out that we do not require any kind of standard signature scheme, which is a very surprising result on its own. Also, our construction proves that the statement given in [30] that accumulators are not sufficient for $\mathcal{RSS}$s is not true.

2   Preliminaries and Security Model

We heavily modify the security model introduced by *Brzuska* et al. [14], as we explicitly allow merging and updating signatures. We do so by introducing the algorithms Merge[2] and Update.

Definition 1 (Mergeable and Updatable $\mathcal{RSS}$). *A mergeable and updatable $\mathcal{RSS}$ consists of six efficient algorithms. Let $\mathcal{RSS} := (KeyGen, Sign, Verify, Redact, Update, Merge)$, such that:*

KeyGen. *The algorithm KeyGen outputs the public and private key of the signer, i.e., $(\mathrm{pk}, \mathrm{sk}) \leftarrow KeyGen(1^\lambda)$, where λ is the security parameter*
Sign. *The algorithm Sign gets as input the secret key sk and the set $\mathcal{S}$. It outputs $(\mathcal{S}, \sigma, \tau) \leftarrow Sign(1^\lambda, \mathrm{sk}, \mathcal{S})$. Here, τ is a tag*

---
[2] Merge was named "combine" in [33].

Verify. *The algorithm* Verify *outputs a bit* $d \in \{0, 1\}$ *indicating the correctness of the signature* σ, *w.r.t.* pk *and* τ, *protecting* S. *1 stands for a valid signature, while 0 indicates the opposite. In particular:* $d \leftarrow$ Verify$(1^\lambda, \mathrm{pk}, S, \sigma, \tau)$

Redact. *The algorithm* Redact *takes as input a set* S, *the public key* pk *of the signer, a tag* τ, *and a valid signature* σ *and a set* $\mathcal{R} \subset S$ *of elements to be redacted. The algorithm outputs* $(S', \sigma', \tau) \leftarrow$ Redact$(1^\lambda, \mathrm{pk}, S, \sigma, \mathcal{R}, \tau)$, *where* $S' = S \setminus \mathcal{R}$. $\mathcal{R}$ *is allowed to be* $\emptyset$. *On error, the algorithm outputs* $\bot$

Update. *The algorithm* Update *takes as input a verifying set/signature/tag tuple* (S, σ, τ), *the secret key* sk *and a second set* $\mathcal{U}$. *It outputs* $(S', \sigma', \tau) \leftarrow$ Update$(1^\lambda, \mathrm{sk}, S, \sigma, \mathcal{U}, \tau)$, *where* $S' = S \cup \mathcal{U}$, *and* σ' *is a verifying signature on* S'. *On error, the algorithm outputs* $\bot$

Merge. *The algorithm* Merge *takes as input the public key* pk *of the signer, two sets* S *and* $\mathcal{V}$, *a tag* τ, *and the corresponding signatures* σ_S *and* $\sigma_\mathcal{V}$. *We require that* σ_S *and* $\sigma_\mathcal{V}$ *are valid on* S *and* $\mathcal{V}$. *It outputs the merged set/signature/tag tuple* $(\mathcal{U}, \sigma_\mathcal{U}, \tau) \leftarrow$ Merge$(1^\lambda, \mathrm{pk}, S, \sigma_S, \mathcal{V}, \sigma_\mathcal{V}, \tau)$, *where* $\mathcal{U} = S \cup \mathcal{V}$ *and* $\sigma_\mathcal{U}$ *is valid on* $\mathcal{U}$. *On error, the algorithm outputs* $\bot$

We assume that one can efficiently, and uniquely, identify all the elements $v_i \in S$ from a given set S. All algorithms, except Sign and Update, are public operations, as common in $\mathcal{RSS}$s. In other words, all parties can redact and merge sets, which includes the signer, as well as any intermediate recipient. The correctness properties must also hold, i.e., every genuinely signed, redacted, merged, or updated set must verify. The same is true for updates and merging signatures. This must even hold transitively, i.e., the history of the signature must not matter. τ does not change on any operation. As we allow merging signatures, unlinkability cannot be achieved: τ makes signatures linkable.

On the Security Implications of Dynamic Updates. In our model, Update and Merge are explicitly defined, while in existing work they are present only *implicitly*. The schemes we want to review have in common that they allow dynamic updates and merging of signatures. In particular, there is a very subtle possibility, undermining existing schemes' unforgeability in current security models. Even without explicit algorithms, the following succeeds regardless of a scheme's implementation.

For the following, all signatures share the same tag τ. An adversary $\mathcal{A}$ can break the state-of-the-art unforgeability [14] of an $\mathcal{RSS}$ in the following way: $\mathcal{A}$ queries its signing oracle with a set $\{A\}$, receiving a signature σ_A. Afterward, $\mathcal{A}$ requests the signer to update $\{A\}$ to $\{A, B\}$, receiving a signature $\sigma_{A,B}$. Additionally, $\mathcal{A}$ requests a second update of $\{A\}$ to $\{A, C\}$, receiving $\sigma_{A,C}$. $\mathcal{A}$ can then "merge" $(\{A, B\}, \sigma_{A,B})$ and $(\{A, C\}, \sigma_{A,C})$ to a new verifying signature $(\{A, B, C\}, \sigma^*)$. This set/signature pair is considered a forgery in existing models, while this may be a wanted behavior, e.g., if in medical records new diseases are appended by two different medical doctors. Let us stress that we have introduced a new oracle, namely the update-oracle. However, even if the adversary cannot request updates of his own choosing, it can merge them into a forgery, according to existing models, once the signer performs two different updates on a signed set. Hence, either dynamic updates must be completely prohibited, or the existing security model must be altered. As our application scenario proves, dynamic updates have their merits and enable many practical applications. Therefore, we chose to take the second path. Note, that our example is tailored for sets, while some schemes address lists and trees. However, the aforementioned possibility is not limited to sets, but works on all the schemes aforementioned with minor adjustments. We stress that we explicitly took care that most current existing schemes, e.g., [14,37,42,43], can be considered secure in our enhanced security model. An exception are schemes which offer context-hiding (and their variants). This property discourages any discussions about dynamic updates, as an updated signature cannot be linked against an "old" one. This allows meeting the property of (statistical) unlinkability: derived signatures must be indistinguishable from fresh signatures. For this reason we explicitly split updating and signing signatures: updating a signature does *not* draw a new tag.

Security Model. Next, we introduce the extended security model and define the notions of transparency, privacy, unforgeability, merge privacy, merge transparency, update privacy, and update transparency. We then show how these properties are related to each other. As before, we use the definitions given in [14,37,42,43] as our starting point.

As common in $\mathcal{RSS}$s, all of the following definitions specifically address the additional knowledge a third party can gain from the signature σ alone: if in real documents the redactions or updates are obvious due to additional context information or from the message contents itself, e.g., missing parts of a well known document structure, it may be trivial for attackers to detect them. This observation is general and also applies to schemes which offer context-hiding and cannot be avoided.

Unforgeability. No one must be able to produce a valid signature on a set $\mathcal{S}^*$ verifying under pk with elements not endorsed by the holder of sk, i.e., the signer. That is, even if an attacker can adaptively request signatures on different documents, and also can *adaptively update* them, it remains impossible to forge a signature for a new set or new elements not queried. In Fig. 1 we use $\mathcal{S}_{\tau^*}$ to remember all elements signed by the oracle under tag τ^* and $\mathcal{T}$ to collect all tags. This unforgeability definition is analogous to the standard unforgeability requirement of standard digital signature schemes [26]. We say that an $\mathcal{RSS}$ is *unforgeable*, if for every probabilistic polynomial time (PPT) adversary $\mathcal{A}$ the probability that the game depicted in Fig. 1 returns 1, is negligible.

Privacy. The verifier should not be able to gain any knowledge about redacted elements without having access to them. In this definition, the adversary chooses two tuples $(\mathcal{S}_0, \mathcal{R}_0)$ and $(\mathcal{S}_1, \mathcal{R}_1)$, where $\mathcal{R}_i \subseteq \mathcal{S}_i$ describes what shall be removed from $\mathcal{S}_i$. A redaction of $\mathcal{R}_0$ from $\mathcal{S}_0$ is required to result in the same set as redacting $\mathcal{R}_1$ from $\mathcal{S}_1$. The two sets are input to a "Left-or-Right"-oracle which

Experiment Unforgeability$_{\mathcal{A}}^{\mathcal{RSS}}(\lambda)$
   $(pk, sk) \leftarrow$ KeyGen(1^λ)
   Set $T \leftarrow \emptyset$
   $(\mathcal{S}^*, \sigma^*, \tau^*) \leftarrow \mathcal{A}_{\mathsf{Update}(1^\lambda, sk, \cdot, \cdot, \cdot, \cdot)}^{\mathsf{Sign}(1^\lambda, sk, \cdot)}(1^\lambda, pk)$
    For each query to oracle Sign:
      let $(\mathcal{S}, \sigma, \tau)$ denote the answer from Sign
      Set $\mathcal{S}_\tau \leftarrow \mathcal{S}$
      Set $T \leftarrow T \cup \{\tau\}$
    For each call to oracle Update:
      let $(\mathcal{S}, \sigma, \tau)$ denote the answer from Update
      Set $\mathcal{S}_\tau \leftarrow \mathcal{S}_\tau \cup \mathcal{S}$
   return 1, if
    Verify$(1^\lambda, pk, \mathcal{S}^*, \sigma^*, \tau^*) = 1$ and
    $\tau^* \notin T$ or $\mathcal{S}^* \not\subseteq \mathcal{S}_{\tau^*}$

Fig. 1. Unforgeability

Experiment Privacy$_{\mathcal{A}}^{\mathcal{RSS}}(\lambda)$
   $(pk, sk) \leftarrow$ KeyGen(1^λ)
   $b \xleftarrow{\$} \{0, 1\}$
   $d \leftarrow \mathcal{A}_{\mathsf{Update}(1^\lambda, sk, \cdot, \cdot, \cdot, \cdot)}^{\mathsf{Sign}(1^\lambda, sk, \cdot), \mathsf{LoRRedact}(1^\lambda, \cdot, \cdot, \cdot, \cdot, \cdot, sk, b)}(1^\lambda, pk)$
    where oracle LoRRedact
     for input $\mathcal{S}_0, \mathcal{S}_1, \mathcal{R}_0, \mathcal{R}_1$:
     If $\mathcal{R}_0 \not\subseteq \mathcal{S}_0 \vee \mathcal{R}_1 \not\subseteq \mathcal{S}_1$, return $\perp$
     if $\mathcal{S}_0 \setminus \mathcal{R}_0 \neq \mathcal{S}_1 \setminus \mathcal{R}_1$, return $\perp$
     $(\mathcal{S}, \sigma, \tau) \leftarrow$ Sign$(1^\lambda, sk, \mathcal{S}_b, \tau)$
     return $(\mathcal{S}', \sigma', \tau) \leftarrow$ Redact$(1^\lambda, pk, \mathcal{S}, \sigma, \mathcal{R}_b, \tau)$.
   return 1, if $b = d$

Fig. 2. Privacy

Experiment Transparency$_{\mathcal{A}}^{\mathcal{RSS}}(\lambda)$
   $(pk, sk) \leftarrow$ KeyGen(1^λ)
   $b \xleftarrow{\$} \{0, 1\}$
   $d \leftarrow \mathcal{A}^{\mathsf{Sign}(1^\lambda, sk, \cdot), \mathsf{Sign/Redact}(1^\lambda, \cdot, \cdot, sk, b), \mathsf{Update}(1^\lambda, sk, \cdot, \cdot, \cdot, \cdot)}(1^\lambda, pk)$
    where oracle Sign/Redact for input $\mathcal{S}, \mathcal{R}$:
     if $\mathcal{R} \not\subseteq \mathcal{S}$, return $\perp$
     $(\mathcal{S}, \sigma, \tau) \leftarrow$ Sign$(1^\lambda, sk, \mathcal{S})$,
     $(\mathcal{S}', \sigma', \tau) \leftarrow$ Redact$(1^\lambda, pk, \mathcal{S}, \sigma, \mathcal{R}, \tau)$
     if $b = 1$:
      $(\mathcal{S}', \sigma', \tau) \leftarrow$ Sign$(1^\lambda, sk, \mathcal{S}')$
     return $(\mathcal{S}', \sigma', \tau)$
   return 1, if $b = d$

Fig. 3. Transparency

signs $\mathcal{S}_b$ and then redacts $\mathcal{R}_b$. The adversary wins, if it can decide which pair was used by the oracle as the input to create its corresponding output. This is similar to the standard indistinguishability notion for encryption schemes [25]. We say that an $\mathcal{RSS}$ is *private*, if for every PPT adversary $\mathcal{A}$ the probability that the game depicted in Fig. 2 returns 1, is negligibly close to $\frac{1}{2}$. Note, this definition does not capture unlinkability.

Transparency. The verifier should not be able to decide whether a signature has been created by the signer directly, or through the redaction algorithm Redact. The adversary can choose one tuple $(\mathcal{S}, \mathcal{R})$, where $\mathcal{R} \subseteq \mathcal{S}$ describes what shall be removed from $\mathcal{S}$. The pair is input for a "Sign/Redact" oracle that either signs and redacts elements (using Redact) or remove elements as a redaction would do $(\mathcal{S} \setminus \mathcal{R})$ before signing it. The adversary wins, if it can decide which way was taken. We say that an $\mathcal{RSS}$ is *transparent*, if for every PPT adversary $\mathcal{A}$, the probability that the game depicted in Fig. 3 returns 1, is negligibly close to $\frac{1}{2}$.

Experiment Merge Privacy$_{\mathcal{A}}^{\mathcal{RSS}}(\lambda)$

$(pk, sk) \leftarrow \mathsf{KeyGen}(1^\lambda)$

$b \xleftarrow{\$} \{0, 1\}$

$d \leftarrow \mathcal{A}^{\mathsf{Sign}(1^\lambda, sk, \cdot), \mathsf{LoRMerge}(1^\lambda, \cdot, \cdot, \cdot, sk, b)}_{\mathsf{Update}(1^\lambda, sk, \cdot, \cdot, \cdot)}(1^\lambda, pk)$

    where oracle LoRMerge

    for input $\mathcal{S}, \mathcal{R}_0, \mathcal{R}_1$:

      if $\mathcal{R}_0 \not\subseteq \mathcal{S} \vee \mathcal{R}_1 \not\subseteq \mathcal{S}$, return $\bot$

      $(\mathcal{S}, \sigma_\mathcal{S}, \tau) \leftarrow \mathsf{Sign}(1^\lambda, sk, \mathcal{S})$

      $(\mathcal{S}', \sigma'_\mathcal{S}, \tau) \leftarrow \mathsf{Redact}(1^\lambda, pk, \mathcal{S}, \sigma_\mathcal{S}, \mathcal{R}_b, \tau)$

      $(\mathcal{S}'', \sigma''_\mathcal{S}, \tau) \leftarrow \mathsf{Redact}(1^\lambda, pk, \mathcal{S}, \sigma_\mathcal{S}, \mathcal{S} \setminus \mathcal{R}_b, \tau)$

      return $\mathsf{Merge}(1^\lambda, pk, \mathcal{S}', \sigma'_\mathcal{S}, \mathcal{S}'', \sigma''_\mathcal{S}, \tau)$

  return 1, if $b = d$

Experiment Merge Transparency$_{\mathcal{A}}^{\mathcal{RSS}}(\lambda)$

$(pk, sk) \leftarrow \mathsf{KeyGen}(1^\lambda)$

$b \xleftarrow{\$} \{0, 1\}$

$d \leftarrow \mathcal{A}^{\mathsf{Sign}(1^\lambda, sk, \cdot), \mathsf{Sign/Merge}(1^\lambda, \cdot, \cdot, sk, b)}_{\mathsf{Update}(1^\lambda, sk, \cdot, \cdot, \cdot)}(1^\lambda, pk)$

    where oracle Sign/Merge for input $\mathcal{S}, \mathcal{R}$:

      if $\mathcal{R} \not\subseteq \mathcal{S}$, return $\bot$

      $(\mathcal{S}, \sigma, \tau) \leftarrow \mathsf{Sign}(1^\lambda, sk, \mathcal{S})$

      if $b = 0$:

        $(\mathcal{T}', \sigma'_\mathcal{T}, \tau) \leftarrow \mathsf{Redact}(1^\lambda, pk, \mathcal{S}, \sigma_\mathcal{S}, \mathcal{R}, \tau)$

        $(\mathcal{R}', \sigma'_\mathcal{R}, \tau) \leftarrow \mathsf{Redact}(1^\lambda, pk, \mathcal{S}, \sigma_\mathcal{S}, \mathcal{S} \setminus \mathcal{R}, \tau)$

        $(\mathcal{S}', \sigma', \tau) \leftarrow \mathsf{Merge}(1^\lambda, pk, \mathcal{T}', \sigma'_\mathcal{T}, \mathcal{R}', \sigma'_\mathcal{R}, \tau)$

      if $b = 1$: $(\mathcal{S}', \sigma', \tau) \leftarrow (\mathcal{S}, \sigma_\mathcal{S}, \tau)$

      return $(\mathcal{S}', \sigma', \tau)$

  return 1, if $b = d$

Fig. 4. Merge Privacy   **Fig. 5.** Merge Transparency

Merge Privacy. If a merged set is given to another third party, the party should not be able to derive any information besides what is contained in the merged set, i.e., a verifier should not be able to decide which elements have been merged from what set. In this definition, the adversary can choose three sets $\mathcal{S}, \mathcal{R}_0, \mathcal{R}_1$. The oracle LoRMerge signs $\mathcal{S}$ and then generates two signed redacted versions $\mathcal{S}' = \mathcal{S} \setminus \mathcal{R}_b$ and $\mathcal{S}'' = \mathcal{R}_b$. Then, it merges the signatures again. The adversary wins, if it can decide if $\mathcal{R}_0$ or $\mathcal{R}_1$ was first redacted from $\mathcal{S}$ and then merged back. We say that an $\mathcal{RSS}$ is *merge private*, if for every PPT adversary $\mathcal{A}$, the probability that the game depicted in Fig. 4 returns 1, is negligibly close to $\frac{1}{2}$.

Merge Transparency. If a set is given to a third party, the party should not be able to decide whether the set has been created only by Sign or through Sign and Merge. The adversary can choose one tuple $(\mathcal{S}, \mathcal{R})$ with $\mathcal{R} \subseteq \mathcal{S}$. This pair is input to a Sign/Merge oracle that signs the set $\mathcal{S}$ and either returns this set/signature pair directly ($b = 1$) or redacts the $\mathcal{S}$ into two signed "halves" $\mathcal{R}$ and $\mathcal{T}$ only to merge them together again and return the set/signature pair derived using Merge ($b = 0$). The adversary wins, if it can decide which way was taken. We say that an $\mathcal{RSS}$ is *merge transparent*, if for every PPT adversary $\mathcal{A}$, the probability that the game depicted in Fig. 5 returns 1, is negligibly close to $\frac{1}{2}$.

We emphasize that the notions of merge transparency and merge privacy are very similar to the notions of privacy and transparency, as they achieve comparable goals.

Update Privacy. If an updated set is given to another third party, the party should not be able to derive which elements have been added. In the game, the adversary wins, if it can decide which elements were added after signature generation. In this definition, the adversary can choose three sets $\mathcal{S}, \mathcal{R}_0, \mathcal{R}_1$. The oracle LoRUpdate signs $\mathcal{S} \cup \mathcal{R}_b$ and then adds $\mathcal{R}_{b-1}$ to the signature. The adversary wins, if it can decide which set was used for the update. A scheme $\mathcal{RSS}$ is *update private*, if for every PPT adversary $\mathcal{A}$, the probability that the game depicted in Fig. 6 returns 1, is negligibly close to $\frac{1}{2}$.

Experiment Update Privacy$_{\mathcal{A}}^{\mathcal{RSS}}(\lambda)$
$(pk, sk) \leftarrow \mathsf{KeyGen}(1^\lambda)$
$b \xleftarrow{\$} \{0, 1\}$
$d \leftarrow \mathcal{A}_{\mathsf{Update}(1^\lambda, sk, \cdot, \cdot, \cdot, \cdot)}^{\mathsf{Sign}(1^\lambda, sk, \cdot), \mathsf{LoRUpdate}(1^\lambda, \cdot, \cdot, \cdot, \cdot, sk, b)}(1^\lambda, pk)$
  where oracle $\mathsf{LoRUpdate}$ for input $\mathcal{S}, \mathcal{R}_0, \mathcal{R}_1$:
    $(\mathcal{S}', \sigma'_{\mathcal{S}}, \tau) \leftarrow \mathsf{Sign}(1^\lambda, sk, \mathcal{S} \cup \mathcal{R}_b)$
    return $\mathsf{Update}(1^\lambda, sk, \mathcal{S}', \sigma'_{\mathcal{S}}, \mathcal{R}_{1-b}, \tau)$
return 1, if $b = d$

Fig. 6. Update Privacy

Experiment Update Transparency$_{\mathcal{A}}^{\mathcal{RSS}}(\lambda)$
$(pk, sk) \leftarrow \mathsf{KeyGen}(1^\lambda)$
$b \xleftarrow{\$} \{0, 1\}$
$d \leftarrow \mathcal{A}_{\mathsf{Update}(1^\lambda, sk, \cdot, \cdot, \cdot, \cdot)}^{\mathsf{Sign}(1^\lambda, sk, \cdot), \mathsf{Sign}/\mathsf{Update}(1^\lambda, \cdot, \cdot, sk, b)}(1^\lambda, pk)$
  where oracle $\mathsf{Sign}/\mathsf{Update}$ for input $\mathcal{S}, \mathcal{R}$:
    if $b = 1$: $(\mathcal{S}', \sigma', \tau) \leftarrow \mathsf{Sign}(1^\lambda, sk, \mathcal{S} \cup \mathcal{R})$,
    if $b = 0$: $(\mathcal{T}', \sigma'_{\mathcal{T}}, \tau) \leftarrow \mathsf{Sign}(1^\lambda, sk, \mathcal{S})$
           $(\mathcal{S}', \sigma', \tau) \leftarrow \mathsf{Update}(1^\lambda, sk, \mathcal{T}', \sigma'_{\mathcal{T}}, \mathcal{R}, \tau)$
    return $(\mathcal{S}', \sigma', \tau)$
return 1, if $b = d$

Fig. 7. Update Transparency

Update Transparency. A verifying party should not be able to decide whether the received set has been created by Sign or through Update. The adversary can choose one pair $(\mathcal{S}, \mathcal{R})$. This pair is input to a $\mathsf{Sign}/\mathsf{Update}$ oracle that either signs the set $\mathcal{S} \cup \mathcal{R}$ ($b = 1$) or signs $\mathcal{S}$ and then adds $\mathcal{R}$ using Update ($b = 0$). The adversary wins, if it can decide which way was taken. We say that a scheme $\mathcal{RSS}$ is *update transparent*, if for every PPT adversary $\mathcal{A}$, the probability that the game depicted in Fig. 7 returns 1, is negligibly close to $\frac{1}{2}$.

As before, the notions of update transparency and update privacy are, on purpose, kept very similar to the notions of privacy and transparency due to their similar goals.

Definition 2 (Secure $\mathcal{RSS}$). *We call an $\mathcal{RSS}$ secure, if it is unforgeable, transparent, private, merge transparent, merge private, update private, and update transparent.*

We now give some relations between the security properties. This section can be kept brief, as we tailored the definitions to be similar (in terms of relation) to the ones given in [14]. This is intentional, to keep consistent with existing wording and to blend into the large body of existing work. We have to explicitly consider the update-oracle, as it may leak information about the secret key sk.

Theorem 1 (Merge Transparency $\implies$ Merge Privacy). *Every scheme which is merge transparent, is also merge private.*

Proof. Intuitively, the proof formalizes the following idea: if an adversary can decide which elements have been merged, then it can decide that the signature cannot be created by Sign, but by Merge.

Assume an (efficient) adversary $\mathcal{A}$ that wins our merge privacy with probability $\frac{1}{2} + \epsilon$. We can then construct an (efficient) adversary $\mathcal{B}$ which wins the merge transparency game with probability $\frac{1}{2} + \frac{\epsilon}{2}$. According to the merge transparency game, $\mathcal{B}$ receives a public key pk and oracle access to $\mathcal{O}^{\mathsf{Sign}}$, $\mathcal{O}^{\mathsf{Sign}/\mathsf{Merge}}$, and $\mathcal{O}^{\mathsf{Update}}$. Let $\mathcal{B}$ randomly pick a bit $b' \in \{0, 1\}$. $\mathcal{B}$ forwards pk to $\mathcal{A}$. Whenever $\mathcal{A}$ requests access to the signing oracle $\mathcal{O}^{\mathsf{Sign}}$, $\mathcal{B}$ honestly forwards the query to its oracle and returns the unmodified answer to $\mathcal{A}$. The same is true for $\mathcal{O}^{\mathsf{Update}}$. When $\mathcal{A}$ requests access to $\mathcal{O}^{\mathsf{LoRMerge}}$, i.e., when it sends a query $(\mathcal{S}, \mathcal{R}_0, \mathcal{R}_1)$, then $\mathcal{B}$ checks that $\mathcal{R}_0 \subset \mathcal{S} \wedge \mathcal{R}_1 \subset \mathcal{S}$ and forwards $(\mathcal{S}, \mathcal{R}_{b'})$ to $\mathcal{O}^{\mathsf{Sign/Merge}}$ and returns the answer to $\mathcal{A}$. Eventually, $\mathcal{A}$ outputs its guess d. Our adversary $\mathcal{B}$ outputs 0, if $d = b'$ and 1 otherwise. What is the probability that $\mathcal{B}$ is correct? We have to consider two cases:

1. If $b = 0$, then $\mathcal{O}^{\mathsf{Sign/Merge}}$ signs, redacts, and merges the set. This gives exactly the same answer as $\mathcal{O}^{\mathsf{LoRRedact}}$ would do, if using the bit b'. Hence, $\mathcal{A}$ can correctly guess the bit b' with probability at least $\frac{1}{2} + \epsilon$, if $b = 0$.
2. If $b = 1$, then $\mathcal{O}^{\mathsf{Sign/Merge}}$ always signs the set as is. Hence, the answer is independent of b'. $\Pr[\mathcal{B} = 1 \mid b = 1] = \frac{1}{2}$ follows.

Hence, due to the probability of $\frac{1}{2}$ that $b = 1$, it follows that $\Pr[\mathcal{B} = b] = \frac{1}{2} + \frac{\epsilon}{2}$. Hence, $\mathcal{B}$ has non-negligible advantage, if ϵ is non-negligible.

Theorem 2 (Merge Privacy $\not\Rightarrow$ Merge Transparency). *There is a scheme which is merge private, but not merge transparent.*

Proof. At sign, we append a bit $d = 0$. For all other algorithms d is cut off, and appended after the algorithm finished. However, we set $d = 1$ once signatures are merged. Obviously, we leave all other properties intact.

Theorem 3 (Update Transparency $\Longrightarrow$ Update Privacy). *Every scheme which is update transparent, is also update private.*

Proof. The proof is essentially the same as for Th. 1.

Theorem 4 (Update Privacy $\not\Rightarrow$ Update Transparency). *There is a scheme which is update private, but not update transparent.*

Proof. The proof is essentially the same as for Th. 2.

Theorem 5 (Merge Transparency is independent). *There is a scheme which fulfills all mentioned security goals but merge transparency.*

Proof. The proof is essentially the same as for Th. 2.

Theorem 6 (Update Transparency is independent). *There is a scheme which fulfills all mentioned security goals but update transparency.*

Proof. The proof is essentially the same as for Th. 2.

Theorem 7 (Unforgeability is independent). *There is a scheme which fulfills all mentioned security goals but unforgeability.*

Proof. We simply use a verify algorithm which always accepts all inputs.

Theorem 8 (Transparency $\Longrightarrow$ Privacy). *Every scheme which is transparent, is also private. Similar to [14].*

Theorem 9 (Privacy $\not\Rightarrow$ Transparency). *There is a scheme which is private, but not transparent. Similar to [14].*

Theorem 10 (Transparency is independent). *There is a scheme which fulfills all mentioned security goals but transparency. Similar to [14].*

Even though the transparency properties give stronger security guarantees, legislation requires that altered signatures must be distinguishable from new ones [16]. However, privacy is the absolute minimum to be useful [16]. We therefore need to split the definitions: depending on the use-case, one can then decide which properties are required.

3   Trapdoor-Accumulators and Constructions

Cryptographic accumulators have been introduced by *Benaloh* and *de Mare* [9]. They hash a potentially very large set S into a short single value a, called the accumulator. For each element accumulated, a witness is generated, which vouches for the accumulation. A trapdoor-accumulator allows generating proofs for new elements not contained by use of a trapdoor. Our construction is based upon such an accumulator. Using an accumulator allows us to achieve mergeability "for free", as we can add and remove witnesses and the corresponding elements freely. We do not require non-membership witnesses [32], or non-deniability [34] for our scheme to work. We do note that there exists the possibility of dynamically updating an accumulator [18]. However, they also allow removing accumulated elements, while they need to adjust every single witness. This is not necessary for our goals. However, accumulators are very versatile. We leave it as open work to discuss the impact of accumulators with different properties plugged into our construction.

Algorithmic Description and Security Model. We now introduce trapdoor accumulators. The definition is derived from [6].

Definition 3 (Trapdoor Cryptographic Accumulators). *A cryptographic trapdoor accumulator $\mathcal{ACC}$ consists of four efficient (PPT) algorithms. In particular, $\mathcal{ACC} := (\mathsf{Gen}, \mathsf{Dig}, \mathsf{Proof}, \mathsf{Verf})$ such that:*

Gen. *The algorithm* Gen *is the key generator. On input of the security parameter λ, it outputs the key pair $(\mathrm{sk}_{\mathcal{ACC}}, \mathrm{pk}_{\mathcal{ACC}}) \leftarrow \mathsf{Gen}(1^\lambda)$*

Dig. *The algorithm* Dig *takes as input the set S to accumulate, the public parameters $\mathrm{pk}_{\mathcal{ACC}}$. It outputs an accumulator value $a \leftarrow \mathsf{Dig}(1^\lambda, \mathrm{pk}_{\mathcal{ACC}}, S)$*

Proof. *The deterministic algorithm* Proof *takes as input the secret key $\mathrm{sk}_{\mathcal{ACC}}$, the accumulator a, and a value v and returns a witness p for v. Hence, it outputs $p \leftarrow \mathsf{Proof}(1^\lambda, \mathrm{sk}_{\mathcal{ACC}}, a, v)$*

Verf. *The verification algorithm* Verf *takes as input the public key $\mathrm{pk}_{\mathcal{ACC}}$, an accumulator a, a witness p, and a value v and outputs a bit $d \in \{0, 1\}$, indicating whether p is a valid witness for v w.r.t. a and $\mathrm{pk}_{\mathcal{ACC}}$. Hence, it outputs $d \leftarrow \mathsf{Verf}(1^\lambda, \mathrm{pk}_{\mathcal{ACC}}, a, v, p)$*

We require the usual correctness properties to hold. Refer to [6] for a formal definition of the correctness properties for accumulators.

Experiment Strong − Coll. − Res.$_{\mathcal{A}}^{\mathcal{ACC}}(\lambda)$
$(sk_{\mathcal{ACC}}, pk_{\mathcal{ACC}}) \leftarrow \mathsf{Gen}(1^\lambda)$
$(S^*, st) \leftarrow \mathcal{A}_1(1^\lambda, pk_{\mathcal{ACC}})$ //st denotes $\mathcal{A}$'s state
$a \leftarrow \mathsf{Dig}(1^\lambda, pk_{\mathcal{ACC}}, S^*)$
$(v^*, p^*) \leftarrow \mathcal{A}_2^{\mathsf{Proof}(1^\lambda, sk_{\mathcal{ACC}}, a, \cdot)}(st, a)$
return 1, if
$\quad \mathsf{Verf}(1^\lambda, pk_{\mathcal{ACC}}, a, v^*, p^*) = 1$,
$\quad$ and v^* has not been queried to Proof

Fig. 8. Strong Collision-Resistance

Strong Collision-Resistance. An adversary should not be able find a valid witness/element pair (p^*, v^*) for a given accumulator a, even if it is allowed to adaptively query for elements not contained in the original set accumulated and to choose the original set to be accumulated. We call a family of trapdoor accumulators *strongly collision-resistant*, if the probability that the experiment depicted in Fig. 8 returns 1, is negligible. We do note that this definition is very similar to the standard unforgeability of signature schemes. The naming is due to historical reasons [6].

Trapdoor-Accumulators. Next, we show how a trapdoor-accumulator can be build. We use the ideas given in [6], but make use of the trapdoor $\varphi(n)$.

Construction 1 (Trapdoor-Accumulator $\mathcal{ACC}$). *We require a division-intractable hash-function* $\mathcal{H} : \{0,1\}^* \to \{0,1\}^\lambda$ *mapping to odd numbers. A formal definition is given in [24]. Let* $\mathcal{ACC} := (\mathsf{Gen}, \mathsf{Dig}, \mathsf{Proof}, \mathsf{Verf})$ *such that:*

Gen. *Generate* $n = pq$, *where* p *and* q *are distinct safe primes of length* λ.[3] *Return* $(\varphi(n), (n, \mathcal{H}))$, *where* $\varphi(pq) := (p-1) \cdot (q-1)$.
Dig. *To improve efficiency, we use the build-in trapdoor. A new digest can therefore be drawn at random. Return* $a \in_R \mathbb{Z}_n^\times$.
Proof. *To generate a witness* p_i *for an element* v_i, *set* $v_i' \leftarrow \mathcal{H}(v_i)$. *Output* $p_i \leftarrow a^{v_i'^{-1} \pmod{\varphi(n)}} \mod n$
Verf. *To check the correctness of a proof* p *w.r.t. an accumulator* a, *the public key* $\mathrm{pk}_{\mathcal{ACC}}$, *and a value* v, *output 1, if* $a \stackrel{?}{=} p^{\mathcal{H}(v)} \pmod{n}$, *and 0 otherwise*

We do note that this construction is related to GHR-signatures [24]. Due to the build-in trapdoor, we do not require any auxiliary information as proposed in [6]. The use of safe primes allows us to almost always find a root for odd numbers. If we are not able to do so, we can trivially factor n. The proofs that our trapdoor-accumulator is strongly collision-resistant can be found in the appendix.

We want to explicitly stress that an adversary can simulate the Proof-oracle itself for the elements used for Dig. It calculates $a = x^{\prod_{v_i \in S} \mathcal{H}(v_i)} \mod n$ for a random $x \in_R \mathbb{Z}_n^\times$ and for each proof p_i, it lets $p_i = x^{\prod_{v_j \in S, i \neq j} \mathcal{H}(v_j)} \mod n$. For new elements, this technique does not work. Note, a is drawn at random

---

[3] A prime p is safe, if $p = 2p' + 1$, where p' is also prime.

for efficiency. We can also use the slower method aforementioned: a will be distributed exactly in the same way.

Updatable and Mergeable $\mathcal{RSS}$ — Construction. The basic ideas are: (1) Our trick is to fix the accumulator a for *all* signatures. Additionally, each element is tagged with a unique string τ to tackle mix-and-match attacks. Hence, all derived subset/signature pairs are linkable by the tag τ. τ is also accumulated to avoid trivial "empty-set"-attacks. (2) Redactions remove v_i and its corresponding witness p_i. The redactions are private, as without knowledge of the proof p_i nobody can verify if v_i is "in" the accumulator a. (3) Mergeability is achieved, as supplying an element/witness pair allows a third party to add it back into the signature. (4) Unforgeability comes from the strong collision-resistance of $\mathcal{ACC}$. (5) Dynamic updates are possible due to a trapdoor in $\mathcal{ACC}$, only known to the signer. (6) Privacy directly follows from definitions, i.e., the number of proofs is fixed, while the proofs itself are deterministically generated, without taking already generated proofs into account. We do note that we can also use aggregate-signatures to reduce the signature size [11]. However, we want to show that an accumulator is enough to build $\mathcal{RSS}$s. Having a suitable security model, we can now derive an efficient, stateless, yet simple construction. Our construction is inspired by [28]. However, their construction is forgeable and non-private in our model, as they allow for arbitrary merging, and do not hide redacted elements completely. One may argue that a very straight-forward construction exists: one signs each element $v_i \in \mathcal{S}$ and gives out the signatures. However, our approach has some advantages: we can exchange the accumulator to derive new properties, e.g., prohibiting updates using a trapdoor-free accumulator [34]. Moreover, we prove that using accumulators are sufficient, opposing the results of [30].

Construction 2 (Updatable and Mergeable $\mathcal{RSS}$). *We use $\|$ to denote a uniquely reversible concatenation of strings. Let $\mathsf{RSS} := (\mathsf{KeyGen}, \mathsf{Sign}, \mathsf{Verify}, \mathsf{Redact}, \mathsf{Update}, \mathsf{Merge})$ such that:*

KeyGen. *The algorithm KeyGen generates the key pair in the following way:*
 1. *Generate key pair required for $\mathcal{ACC}$, i.e., run $(\mathrm{sk}_{\mathcal{ACC}}, \mathrm{pk}_{\mathcal{ACC}}) \leftarrow \mathsf{Gen}(1^\lambda)$*
 2. *Call $a \leftarrow \mathsf{Dig}(\mathrm{pk}_{\mathcal{ACC}}, \emptyset)$*
 3. *Output $(\mathrm{sk}_{\mathcal{ACC}}, (\mathrm{pk}_{\mathcal{ACC}}, a))$*

Sign. *To sign a set $\mathcal{S}$, perform the following steps:*
 1. *Draw a tag $\tau \in_R \{0,1\}^\lambda$*
 2. *Let $p_\tau \leftarrow \mathsf{Proof}(\mathrm{sk}_{\mathcal{ACC}}, a, \tau)$*
 3. *Output $(\mathcal{S}, \sigma, \tau)$, where $\sigma = (p_\tau, \{(v_i, p_i) \mid v_i \in \mathcal{S} \wedge p_i \leftarrow \mathsf{Proof}(\mathrm{sk}_{\mathcal{ACC}}, a, v_i\|\tau)\})$*

Verify. *To verify signature $\sigma = (p_\tau, \{(v_1, p_1), \dots, (v_k, p_k)\})$ with tag τ, perform:*
 1. *For all $v_i \in \mathcal{S}$ check that $\mathsf{Verf}(\mathrm{pk}_{\mathcal{ACC}}, a, v_i\|\tau, p_i) = 1$*
 2. *Check that $\mathsf{Verf}(\mathrm{pk}_{\mathcal{ACC}}, a, \tau, p_\tau) = 1$*
 3. *If Verf succeeded for all elements, output 1, otherwise 0*

Redact. *To redact a subset $\mathcal{R}$ from a valid signed set $(\mathcal{S}, \sigma)$ with tag τ, with $\mathcal{R} \subseteq \mathcal{S}$, the algorithm performs the following steps:*

   1. *Check the validity of σ using* **Verify**. *If σ is not valid, return $\bot$*
   2. *Output (S', σ', τ), where $\sigma' = (p_\tau, \{(v_i, p_i) \mid v_i \in S \setminus R\})$*

Update. *To update a valid signed set (S, σ) with tag τ by adding U and knowing sk_{ACC}, the algorithm performs the following steps:*
   1. *Verify σ w.r.t. τ using* **Verify**. *If σ is not valid, return $\bot$*
   2. *Output $(S \cup U, \sigma', \tau)$, where $\sigma' = (p_\tau, \{(v_i, p_i) \mid v_i \in S\} \cup \{(v_k, p_k) \mid v_k \in U, p_k \leftarrow \mathsf{Proof}(\mathrm{sk}_{ACC}, a, v_k \| \tau)\})$*

Merge. *To merge two valid set/signature pairs (S, σ_S) and (T, σ_T) with an equal tag τ, the algorithm performs the following steps:*
   1. *Verify σ_S and σ_T w.r.t. τ using* **Verify**. *If they do not verify, return $\bot$*
   2. *Check, that both have the same tag τ*
   3. *Output $(S \cup T, \sigma_U, \tau)$, where $\sigma_U = (p_\tau, \{(v_i, p_i) \mid v_i \in S \cup T\})$, where p_i is taken from the corresponding signature*

Our construction is elegantly simple, yet fulfills all security goals (all but un-forgeability even perfectly), and is therefore useable in practice. The proofs of security are in the appendix. All reductions are tight, i.e., we have no reduction losses. We want to explicitly clarify that we do not see the transitive closure of the updates as forgeries. If we want to disallow the "transitive update merging", we can deploy accumulators which also update the witnesses, e.g., [18]. This requires a new security model, which renders existing constructions insecure, which we wanted to avoid. We leave this as future work.

4   Conclusion and Open Questions

We have revised existing notions of redactable signature schemes. We derived a security model, addressing the shortcomings of existing ones. We presented an attack on existing RSSs, if dynamic updates are not carefully considered. Moreover, we have formalized the notion of mergeability, the inverse of redactions. These properties allow using RSSs in more application scenarios, e.g., distributed databases and general cloud-storage. Finally, we have presented a provably secure construction in the standard model, based on a novel trapdoor-accumulator. It is unclear how we can prohibit dynamic updates and merging signatures, how accumulators and signatures are related to each other, and if efficient constructions for more complex data-structures exist.

References

1. Ahn, J.H., Boneh, D., Camenisch, J., Hohenberger, S., Shelat, A., Waters, B.: Computing on authenticated data. ePrint Report 2011/096 (2011)
2. Ateniese, G., Chou, D.H., de Medeiros, B., Tsudik, G.: Sanitizable signatures. In: de Capitani di Vimercati, S., Syverson, P.F., Gollmann, D. (eds.) ESORICS 2005. LNCS, vol. 3679, pp. 159–177. Springer, Heidelberg (2005)
3. Attrapadung, N., Libert, B., Peters, T.: Computing on authenticated data: New privacy definitions and constructions. In: Wang, X., Sako, K. (eds.) ASIACRYPT 2012. LNCS, vol. 7658, pp. 367–385. Springer, Heidelberg (2012)

4. Attrapadung, N., Libert, B., Peters, T.: Efficient completely context-hiding quotable and linearly homomorphic signatures. In: Kurosawa, K., Hanaoka, G. (eds.) PKC 2013. LNCS, vol. 7778, pp. 386–404. Springer, Heidelberg (2013)
5. Backes, M., Meiser, S., Schröder, D.: Delegatable functional signatures. IACR Cryptology ePrint Archive, 408 (2013)
6. Barić, N., Pfitzmann, B.: Collision-free accumulators and fail-stop signature schemes without trees. In: Fumy, W. (ed.) EUROCRYPT 1997. LNCS, vol. 1233, pp. 480–494. Springer, Heidelberg (1997)
7. Becker, A., Jensen, M.: Secure combination of xml signature application with message aggregation in multicast settings. In: ICWS, pp. 531–538 (2013)
8. Bellare, M., Goldreich, O., Goldwasser, S.: Incremental cryptography: The case of hashing and signing. In: Desmedt, Y.G. (ed.) CRYPTO 1994. LNCS, vol. 839, pp. 216–233. Springer, Heidelberg (1994)
9. Benaloh, J.C., de Mare, M.: One-way accumulators: A decentralized alternative to digital signatures. In: Helleseth, T. (ed.) EUROCRYPT 1993. LNCS, vol. 765, pp. 274–285. Springer, Heidelberg (1994)
10. Boneh, D., Freeman, D.M.: Homomorphic signatures for polynomial functions. In: Paterson, K.G. (ed.) EUROCRYPT 2011. LNCS, vol. 6632, pp. 149–168. Springer, Heidelberg (2011)
11. Boneh, D., Gentry, C., Lynn, B., Shacham, H.: Aggregate and Verifiably Encrypted Signatures from Bilinear Maps. In: Biham, E. (ed.) EUROCRYPT 2003. LNCS, vol. 2656, pp. 416–432. Springer, Heidelberg (2003)
12. Boyle, E., Goldwasser, S., Ivan, I.: Functional signatures and pseudorandom functions. IACR Cryptology ePrint Archive 401 (2013)
13. Brzuska, C., Fischlin, M., Freudenreich, T., Lehmann, A., Page, M., Schelbert, J., Schröder, D., Volk, F.: Security of Sanitizable Signatures Revisited. In: Jarecki, S., Tsudik, G. (eds.) PKC 2009. LNCS, vol. 5443, pp. 317–336. Springer, Heidelberg (2009)
14. Brzuska, C., et al.: Redactable Signatures for Tree-Structured Data: Definitions and Constructions. In: Zhou, J., Yung, M. (eds.) ACNS 2010. LNCS, vol. 6123, pp. 87–104. Springer, Heidelberg (2010)
15. Brzuska, C., Fischlin, M., Lehmann, A., Schröder, D.: Unlinkability of sanitizable signatures. In: Nguyen, P.Q., Pointcheval, D. (eds.) PKC 2010. LNCS, vol. 6056, pp. 444–461. Springer, Heidelberg (2010)
16. Brzuska, C., Pöhls, H.C., Samelin, K.: Non-Interactive Public Accountability for Sanitizable Signatures. In: De Capitani di Vimercati, S., Mitchell, C. (eds.) EuroPKI 2012. LNCS, vol. 7868, pp. 178–193. Springer, Heidelberg (2013)
17. Brzuska, C., Pöhls, H.C., Samelin, K.: Efficient and Perfectly Unlinkable Sanitizable Signatures without Group Signatures. In: Katsikas, S., Agudo, I. (eds.) EuroPKI 2013. LNCS, vol. 8341, pp. 12–30. Springer, Heidelberg (2014)
18. Camenisch, J.L., Lysyanskaya, A.: Dynamic accumulators and application to efficient revocation of anonymous credentials. In: Yung, M. (ed.) CRYPTO 2002. LNCS, vol. 2442, pp. 61–76. Springer, Heidelberg (2002)
19. Chang, E.-C., Lim, C.L., Xu, J.: Short Redactable Signatures Using Random Trees. In: Fischlin, M. (ed.) CT-RSA 2009. LNCS, vol. 5473, pp. 133–147. Springer, Heidelberg (2009)
20. Chase, M., Kohlweiss, M., Lysyanskaya, A., Meiklejohn, S.: Malleable signatures: Complex unary transformations and delegatable anonymous credentials. IACR Cryptology ePrint Archive 179 (2013)
21. de Meer, H., Pöhls, H.C., Posegga, J., Samelin, K.: Scope of security properties of sanitizable signatures revisited. In: ARES, pp. 188–197 (2013)

22. de Meer, H., Pöhls, H.C., Posegga, J., Samelin, K.: On the relation between redactable and sanitizable signature schemes. In: Jürjens, J., Piessens, F., Bielova, N. (eds.) ESSoS. LNCS, vol. 8364, pp. 113–130. Springer, Heidelberg (2014)

23. Deiseroth, B., Fehr, V., Fischlin, M., Maasz, M., Reimers, N.F., Stein, R.: Computing on authenticated data for adjustable predicates. In: Jacobson, M., Locasto, M., Mohassel, P., Safavi-Naini, R. (eds.) ACNS 2013. LNCS, vol. 7954, pp. 53–68. Springer, Heidelberg (2013)

24. Gennaro, R., Halevi, S., Rabin, T.: Secure hash-and-sign signatures without the random oracle. In: Stern, J. (ed.) EUROCRYPT 1999. LNCS, vol. 1592, pp. 123–139. Springer, Heidelberg (1999)

25. Goldwasser, S., Micali, S.: Probabilistic encryption. J. Comput. Syst. Sci. 28(2), 270–299 (1984)

26. Goldwasser, S., Micali, S., Rivest, R.L.: A Digital Signature Scheme Secure Against Adaptive Chosen-Message Attacks. SIAM JoC 17, 281–308 (1988)

27. Herkenhöner, R., Jensen, M., Pöhls, H.C., De Meer, H.: Towards automated processing of the right of access in inter-organizational web service compositions. In: IEEE WSBPS 2010. IEEE (July 2010)

28. Johnson, R., Molnar, D., Song, D., Wagner, D.: Homomorphic signature schemes. In: Preneel, B. (ed.) CT-RSA 2002. LNCS, vol. 2271, pp. 244–262. Springer, Heidelberg (2002)

29. Kiltz, E., Mityagin, A., Panjwani, S., Raghavan, B.: Append-only signatures. In: Caires, L., Italiano, G.F., Monteiro, L., Palamidessi, C., Yung, M. (eds.) ICALP 2005. LNCS, vol. 3580, pp. 434–445. Springer, Heidelberg (2005)

30. Kundu, A., Bertino, E.: Privacy-preserving authentication of trees and graphs. Int. J. Inf. Sec. 12(6), 467–494 (2013)

31. Lai, J., Ding, X., Wu, Y.: Accountable trapdoor sanitizable signatures. In: Deng, R.H., Feng, T. (eds.) ISPEC 2013. LNCS, vol. 7863, pp. 117–131. Springer, Heidelberg (2013)

32. Li, J., Li, N., Xue, R.: Universal accumulators with efficient nonmembership proofs. In: Katz, J., Yung, M. (eds.) ACNS 2007. LNCS, vol. 4521, pp. 253–269. Springer, Heidelberg (2007)

33. Lim, S., Lee, E., Park, C.-M.: A short redactable signature scheme using pairing. SCN 5(5), 523–534 (2012)

34. Lipmaa, H.: Secure accumulators from euclidean rings without trusted setup. In: Bao, F., Samarati, P., Zhou, J. (eds.) ACNS 2012. LNCS, vol. 7341, pp. 224–240. Springer, Heidelberg (2012)

35. Merkle, R.C.: A certified digital signature. In: Brassard, G. (ed.) CRYPTO 1989. LNCS, vol. 435, pp. 218–238. Springer, Heidelberg (1990)

36. Miyazaki, et al.: Digital documents sanitizing problem. Institute of Electronics, Information and Communication Engineers Technical Reports 103(195), 61–67 (2003)

37. Miyazaki, K., Hanaoka, G., Imai, H.: Digitally signed document sanitizing scheme based on bilinear maps. In: ASIACCS 2006, pp. 343–354. ACM (2006)

38. Pöhls, H.C.: Verifiable and revocable expression of consent to processing of aggregated personal data. In: Chen, L., Ryan, M.D., Wang, G. (eds.) ICICS 2008. LNCS, vol. 5308, pp. 279–293. Springer, Heidelberg (2008)

39. Pöhls, H.C., Bilzhause, A., Samelin, K., Posegga, J.: Sanitizable signed privacy preferences for social networks. In: DICCDI 2011. LNI. GI (2011)

40. Pöhls, H.C., Samelin, K., Posegga, J.: Sanitizable Signatures in XML Signature - Performance, Mixing Properties, and Revisiting the Property of Transparency. In: Lopez, J., Tsudik, G. (eds.) ACNS 2011. LNCS, vol. 6715, pp. 166–182. Springer, Heidelberg (2011)
41. Rass, S., Slamanig, D.: Cryptography for Security and Privacy in Cloud Computing. Artech House (2013)
42. Samelin, K., Pöhls, H.C., Bilzhause, A., Posegga, J., de Meer, H.: On Structural Signatures for Tree Data Structures. In: Bao, F., Samarati, P., Zhou, J. (eds.) ACNS 2012. LNCS, vol. 7341, pp. 171–187. Springer, Heidelberg (2012)
43. Samelin, K., Pöhls, H.C., Bilzhause, A., Posegga, J., de Meer, H.: Redactable signatures for independent removal of structure and content. In: Ryan, M.D., Smyth, B., Wang, G. (eds.) ISPEC 2012. LNCS, vol. 7232, pp. 17–33. Springer, Heidelberg (2012)
44. Slamanig, D., Rass, S.: Generalizations and extensions of redactable signatures with applications to electronic healthcare. In: De Decker, B., Schaumüller-Bichl, I. (eds.) CMS 2010. LNCS, vol. 6109, pp. 201–213. Springer, Heidelberg (2010)
45. Steinfeld, R., Bull, L., Zheng, Y.: Content extraction signatures. In: Kim, K.-c. (ed.) ICISC 2001. LNCS, vol. 2288, pp. 285–304. Springer, Heidelberg (2002)
46. Wu, Z.-Y., Hsueh, C.-W., Tsai, C.-Y., Lai, F., Lee, H.-C., Chung, Y.: Redactable Signatures for Signed CDA Documents. Journal of Medical Systems, 1–14 (December 2010)

A Security Proofs

Theorem 11 (Our Construction is Unforgeable). *Our construction is unforgeable, if the underlying accumulator is strongly collision-resistant.*

Proof. We do not consider tag collisions, as they only appear with negligible probability. $S^* \subseteq S_\tau$ for some signed τ is not a forgery, but a redaction. We denote the adversary winning the unforgeability game as $\mathcal{A}$. We can now derive that the forgery must fall into exactly one of the following categories:

> Case 1: $S^* \not\subseteq S_{\tau^*}$, and τ^* was used as a tag by Sign
> Case 2: S^* verifies, and τ^* was never used as a tag by Sign

Each case leads to a contradiction about the security of our accumulator.

Case 1. In this case, an element v^* not been returned by the Proof-oracle for the accumulator a, but is contained in S^*. We break the strong collision-resistance of the underlying accumulator by letting $\mathcal{B}$ use $\mathcal{A}$ as a black-box:

1. $\mathcal{B}$ receives pk_{ACC} from the challenger
2. $\mathcal{B}$ requests an accumulator a for $\emptyset$
3. $\mathcal{B}$ receives a from its own challenger
4. $\mathcal{B}$ forwards $pk = (pk_{ACC}, a)$ to $\mathcal{A}$
5. For each query to the signing oracle, $\mathcal{B}$ answers it honestly: it draws τ honestly and uses the Proof-oracle provided to get a witness for each $v_j \in S_i$ queried, with τ concatenated as the label. Also, $\mathcal{B}$ gets a proof for τ

6. For each call to the Update-oracle, $\mathcal{B}$ uses its Proof-oracle provided to get a witness for each $v_j \in \mathcal{S}_i$ queried, with τ concatenated as the label
7. Eventually, $\mathcal{A}$ outputs a pair (S^*, σ^*)
8. $\mathcal{B}$ looks for (v^*, p^*), v^* not queried to Proof, in (S^*, σ^*) and returns them

In other words, there exists an element $v^* \in \mathcal{S}^*$ with a corresponding witness p^*. If v^* has not been asked to the Proof-oracle, $\mathcal{B}$ breaks the collision-resistance of the underlying accumulator by outputting (v^*, p^*). This happens with the same probability as $\mathcal{A}$ breaks unforgeability in case 1. Hence, the reduction is tight.

Case 2. In case 2, the tag τ^* has not been accumulated. We break the strong collision-resistance of the underlying accumulator by letting $\mathcal{B}$ use $\mathcal{A}$:

1. $\mathcal{B}$ receives $pk_{\mathcal{ACC}}$ from the challenger
2. $\mathcal{B}$ requests an accumulator a for $\emptyset$
3. $\mathcal{B}$ forwards $pk = (pk_{\mathcal{ACC}}, a)$ to $\mathcal{A}$
4. For each query to the signing oracle, $\mathcal{B}$ answers it honestly: it draws τ honestly and uses the Proof-oracle provided to get a witness for each $v_j \in \mathcal{S}_i$ queried, with τ concatenated as the label. Also, $\mathcal{B}$ gets a proof for τ
5. For calls to the Update-oracle, $\mathcal{B}$ uses its Proof-oracle provided to get a witness for each $v_j \in \mathcal{S}_i$ queried, with τ concatenated as the label
6. Eventually, $\mathcal{A}$ outputs a pair (S^*, σ^*, τ^*)
7. $\mathcal{B}$ returns (p_τ^*, τ^*). Both is contained in σ^*

In other words, there exists an element $\tau^* \in \sigma^*$ with a corresponding witness p_τ^*, as otherwise σ^* would not verify. We know that τ^* was not queried to Proof, because otherwise we have case 1. This happens with the same probability as $\mathcal{A}$ breaks the unforgeability in case 2. Note, we can ignore additional elements here. Again, the simulation is perfect.

Theorem 12 (Our Construction is Merge Private and Transparent). *Our construction is merge private and merge transparent.*

Proof. The distributions of merged and freshly signed signatures are *equal*. In other words, the distributions are the same. This implies, that our construction is *perfectly* merge private and *perfectly* merge transparent.

Theorem 13 (Our Construction is Transparent and Private).

Proof. As the number of proofs only depends on n, which are also deterministically generated, without taking existing proofs into account, an adversary has zero advantage on deciding how many additional proofs have been generated. Moreover, redacting only removes elements and proofs from the signatures. Hence, fresh and redacted signatures are distributed *identically*. *Perfect* transparency, and therefore also *perfect* privacy, is implied.

Theorem 14 (Our Construction is Update Private and Transparent). *Our construction is update private and update transparent.*

Proof. The distributions of updated and freshly signed signatures are *equal*. In other words, the distributions are the same. This implies, that our construction is *perfectly* update private and *perfectly* update transparent.

Theorem 15 (The Accumulator is Strongly Collision-Resistant).

Proof. Let $\mathcal{A}$ be an adversary breaking the strong-collision-resistance of our accumulator. We can then turn $\mathcal{A}$ into an adversary $\mathcal{B}$ which breaks the unforgeability of the GHR-signature [24] in the following way:

1. $\mathcal{B}$ receives the modulus n, the hash-function $\mathcal{H}$, and the value s. All is provided by the GHR-challenger
2. $\mathcal{B}$ sends $pk = (n, \mathcal{H})$ to $\mathcal{A}$. Then, $\mathcal{B}$ waits for $\mathcal{S}$ from $\mathcal{A}$
3. $\mathcal{B}$ sends s to $\mathcal{A}$. Note, we have a *perfect* simulation here, even as we ignore $\mathcal{S}$, as the GHR-signature scheme draws s in the *exact* same way as we do for our accumulator
4. For each Proof-oracle query v_i, $\mathcal{B}$ asks its signing oracle provided, which returns a signature σ_i. Send σ_i as the witness p_i back to $\mathcal{A}$
5. Eventually, $\mathcal{A}$ comes up with an attempted forgery (v^*, p^*)
6. $\mathcal{B}$ returns (v^*, p^*) as its own forgery attempt

Now let $y = v^*$, and $p = \sigma^*$. As $s = p^{\mathcal{H}(y)} \pmod{n}$, and we have embedded our challenges accordingly, $\mathcal{B}$ breaks the GHR-signature with the same probability as $\mathcal{A}$ breaks the strong collision-resistance of our trapdoor-accumulator. [24] shows how to break the strong-RSA-assumption with the given forgery.

Practical Signatures from the Partial Fourier Recovery Problem

Jeff Hoffstein[1], Jill Pipher[1], John M. Schanck[2],
Joseph H. Silverman[1], and William Whyte[2]

[1] Brown University, Providence, RI, 02912
{jhoff,jpipher,jhs}@math.brown.edu
[2] Security Innovation, Wilmington, MA 01887
{jschanck,wwhyte}@securityinnovation.com

Abstract. We present PASS$_{RS}$, a variant of the prior PASS and PASS-2 proposals, as a candidate for a practical post-quantum signature scheme. Its hardness is based on the problem of recovering a ring element with small norm from an incomplete description of its Chinese remainder representation. For our particular instantiation, this corresponds to the recovery of a vector with small infinity norm from a limited set of its Fourier coefficients.

The key improvement over previous versions of PASS is the introduction of a rejection sampling technique from Lyubashevsky (2009) which assures that transcript distributions are completely decoupled from the keys that generate them.

Although the scheme is not supported by a formal security reduction, we present extensive arguments for its security and derive concrete parameters based on the performance of state of the art lattice reduction and enumeration techniques.

1 Introduction

In the late 1990s two authors of the present paper proposed authentication and signature schemes based on the problem of recovering a polynomial with tightly concentrated coefficients given a small number of evaluations of that polynomial. The heuristic justification for the security of the scheme was that the uncertainty principle severely restricts how concentrated a signal can be in two mutually incoherent bases.

An early incarnation of the scheme is found in [12], and a later version, called PASS-2 was published in [13]. A rough description goes as follows. Let N be a positive integer, and choose a prime $q = rN+1$, with $r \geq 1$. We will denote by R_q the ring $\mathbb{Z}_q[x]/(x^N - 1)$, though we will often treat elements of R_q as vectors in $\mathbb{Z}_q^N$ equipped with the $\star$-multiplication of R_q. To avoid confusion, we will denote component-wise multiplication of vectors by $\odot$. For any β, with $(\beta, q) = 1$, it follows from Fermat's little theorem that $\beta^{rN} \equiv 1 \pmod{q}$. Consequently, the mapping $\boldsymbol{f} \rightarrow \boldsymbol{f}(\beta^r)$ is well defined for any $\boldsymbol{f}$ in R_q. In addition to being well

I. Boureanu, P. Owesarski, and S. Vaudenay (Eds.): ACNS 2014, LNCS 8479, pp. 476–493, 2014.
© Springer International Publishing Switzerland 2014

defined, it is also a ring homomorphism, for the simple reason that for any $\boldsymbol{f}_1, \boldsymbol{f}_2 \in R_q$,

$$(\boldsymbol{f}_1 + \boldsymbol{f}_2)(\beta^r) = \boldsymbol{f}_1(\beta^r) + \boldsymbol{f}_2(\beta^r) \quad \text{and} \quad (\boldsymbol{f}_1 \star \boldsymbol{f}_2)(\beta^r) = \boldsymbol{f}_1(\beta^r)\boldsymbol{f}_2(\beta^r).$$

More generally, for any $\Omega = \{\beta_1^r, \beta_2^r, \ldots, \beta_t^r\}$, the mapping $\mathcal{F} : R_q \to \mathbb{Z}_q^t$ given by

$$\mathcal{F}_\Omega \boldsymbol{f} = (\boldsymbol{f}(\beta_1^r), \boldsymbol{f}(\beta_2^r), \ldots, \boldsymbol{f}(\beta_t^r))^T$$

is a ring homomorphism, with addition and $\odot$-multiplication modulo q done on the right hand side. This is an example of the more general phenomenon of the ring homomorphism mapping functions to their Fourier transforms.

In the above setting, the uncertainty principle implies that a ring element with a coefficient vector drawn from a small region of $\mathbb{Z}_q^N$ will have widely dispersed discrete Fourier coefficients. For instance a vector with small infinity norm, e.g. with coefficients in $\{-1, 0, 1\}$, will likely be supported on all powers of a primitive N^{th} root ω and will have Fourier coefficients which are essentially uniformly distributed in $\mathbb{Z}_q$.

The hard problem in PASS can be stated as the following underdetermined linear inversion problem, which we will refer to as the *partial Fourier recovery problem*. Let ω be a primitive N^{th} root of unity modulo q. We define the discrete Fourier transform over $\mathbb{Z}_q$ to be the linear transformation $\mathcal{F}\boldsymbol{f} = \widehat{\boldsymbol{f}} : \mathbb{Z}_q^N \to \mathbb{Z}_q^N$ given by

$$(\mathcal{F})_{i,j} = \omega^{ij}.$$

Furthermore, let $\mathcal{F}_\Omega$ be the restriction of $\mathcal{F}$ to the set of t rows specified by an index set Ω,

$$(\mathcal{F}_\Omega)_{i,j} = \omega^{\Omega_i j}.$$

The partial Fourier recovery problem is: given an evaluation $\widehat{\boldsymbol{f}}|_\Omega \in \mathbb{Z}_q^t$, find $\boldsymbol{x}$ with small norm such that $\widehat{\boldsymbol{x}}|_\Omega = \widehat{\boldsymbol{f}}|_\Omega \pmod{q}$.

The problem of recovering a signal from a restricted number of its Fourier coefficients is well studied and known to be quite difficult in general. The restricted image $\widehat{\boldsymbol{f}}|_\Omega$ is expected to contain very little information about the unobserved Fourier coefficients (the evaluations of $\boldsymbol{f}$ on ω^i for i not in Ω), and often the only way to recover $\boldsymbol{f}$ will be an expensive combinatorial optimization procedure. However, there are cases (some quite surprising) in which the problem is known to be easy.

Certainly, if $t \log q$ is small, brute force search over $\boldsymbol{f}'$ with appropriate norm may be a viable solution – each randomly chosen candidate having essentially a q^{-t} chance of evaluating to $\widehat{\boldsymbol{f}}|_\Omega$.

The problem is trivial in the large t regime, $t \geq N$, since any rank N submatrix of the chosen Vandermonde matrix will be invertible. As t decreases slightly below N, or we allow some portion of the coefficients to be corrupted, the problem essentially becomes that of decoding Reed-Solomon codes and we can expect to recover f by list-decoding or similar techniques. Efficient recovery of general signals when t is much less than N would have significant coding theoretic implications.

For t in an intermediate range, say $t \approx N/2$, the situation is more complicated. Were one to consider the complex Fourier transform rather than the number theoretic transform, one might be able to apply techniques from the field of compressed sensing. Recent work in this field has delineated cases in which a *sparse* signal can be recovered from a limited number of its (complex) Fourier coefficients by an L^1 optimization procedure. For this to be successful the signals must be very sparse, having a number of non-zero coefficients which is less than $|\Omega|/2$ [2]. It is not clear how these results translate into the finite field setting.

As far as we are aware, the best technique for solving the partial Fourier recovery problem is by solving an associated closest vector problem. Specifically, let $\Lambda^{\perp}(\mathcal{F}_{\Omega})$ be the lattice of vectors in the kernel of $\mathcal{F}_{\Omega}$. That is,

$$\Lambda^{\perp}(\mathcal{F}_{\Omega}) = \left\{ \boldsymbol{a} \in \mathbb{Z}_q^N \ : \ \mathcal{F}_{\Omega}\boldsymbol{a} = \boldsymbol{0} \pmod{q} \right\}.$$

If, given $\boldsymbol{y} \in \mathbb{Z}_q^N$, a point $\boldsymbol{x} \in \Lambda^{\perp}(\mathcal{F}_{\Omega})$ can be found such that $\|\boldsymbol{y} - \boldsymbol{x}\|_{\infty} \leq \beta$, then $\mathcal{F}_{\Omega}(\boldsymbol{y} - \boldsymbol{x}) = \widehat{\boldsymbol{y}}|_{\Omega}$ and $\|\boldsymbol{y} - \boldsymbol{x}\|_{\infty} \leq \beta$. Since one can easily find (large) $\boldsymbol{y}$ such that $\widehat{\boldsymbol{y}}|_{\Omega} = \widehat{\boldsymbol{f}}|_{\Omega}$ for any evaluation set $\widehat{\boldsymbol{f}}|_{\Omega}$, the ability to solve CVP in $\Lambda^{\perp}(\mathcal{F}_{\Omega})$ implies the ability to solve arbitrary partial Fourier recovery instances

While there is no known reduction from standard lattice problems to the partial Fourier recovery problem, there is at very least a superficial relationship between finding short preimages of $\mathcal{F}_{\Omega}$ and another well studied hard problem. A great deal of the research in lattice based cryptography throughout the last decade has focused on a type of underdetermined linear inverse problem referred to as the small integer solution (SIS) problem.

SIS is the problem of of finding a vector $\boldsymbol{y}$ in the kernel of a specified linear transformation $\boldsymbol{A} : \mathbb{Z}_q^n \rightarrow \mathbb{Z}_q^m$ such that $\boldsymbol{y}$ is small with respect to a given norm. That is, the goal is to solve

$$\boldsymbol{A}\boldsymbol{y} = \boldsymbol{0} \pmod{q} \quad \text{and} \quad \|\boldsymbol{y}\| \leq \beta.$$

Ajtai showed in [1] that, for certain parameters and uniform random $\boldsymbol{A}$, SIS enjoys a remarkable average-case correspondence with worst-case lattice problems. That is to say that the ability to solve random SIS instances with non-negligible probability implies an ability to find short vectors in any lattice. This correspondence between worst and average cases is attractive from a provable security point of view, offering strong assurance that easy to generate instances of the SIS problem will be hard to solve, but it does not yield particularly efficient cryptosystems without additional assumptions.

The most efficient and compact SIS schemes in the literature are based on the Ideal-SIS problem, wherein the matrix $\boldsymbol{A}$ is replaced by several uniform random elements, $\boldsymbol{a}_1, \boldsymbol{a}_2, \dots \boldsymbol{a}_k$ of a quotient ring $R_q^{\varphi} = \mathbb{Z}_q[x]/(\varphi)$. The polynomial φ is typically, but not necessarily, cyclotomic. A solution to Ideal-SIS is $\boldsymbol{y}_1, \boldsymbol{y}_2, \dots \boldsymbol{y}_k$ in the ring such that:

$$\sum_{i=1}^{k} a_i \star y_i = 0 \quad \text{and} \quad \sum_{i=1}^{k} \|y_i\|^2 \leq \beta^2.$$

These schemes derive their security from the presumed hardness of Ideal-SVP – the shortest vector problem in the restricted class of lattices generated by matrix representations of elements of R_q^φ. Reductions from worst-case Ideal-SVP to average-case Ideal-SIS were presented in [17] [20]. Unfortunately, even with the reduced storage requirements and fast multiplication algorithms available in some rings, provably secure Ideal-SIS based constructions are still too inefficient to be competitive with existing (non-quantum resistant) schemes.

The security of PASS can be said to rest on the assumed average-case hardness of Vandermonde-SIS. We are not aware of any technique for reducing a worst-case lattice problem to Vandermonde-SIS, nor will we postulate the existence of such a reduction. We do however raise the question of whether there might be a characterization of hard instances of SIS which does not rely on structural properties of the matrix A. Or more generally, when is a constrained linear inverse problem hard?

We believe an answer to this problem would likely simultaneously explain the hardness of Uniform-, Ideal- and Vandermonde-SIS, as well as delineate new classes.

2   Related Work

2.1   The Original PASS Protocols

Given a (padded) message μ, a secret key f with small norm, and a public key $\widehat{f}|_\Omega = \mathcal{F}_\Omega f$, the objective is to construct a signature that mixes f and μ and can be verified by means of $\widehat{f}|_\Omega$. A prototype of this was presented in [12].

To sign, Alice

- Computes and keeps secret a short polynomial $g \in R_q$ and reveals the commitment $\widehat{g}|_\Omega = \mathcal{F}_\Omega g$.
- Computes and reveals a short challenge polynomial $c \in R_q$ from $\mathsf{Hash}(\widehat{g}|_\Omega, \mu)$.
- Computes and reveals $h = g \star (f + c)$.

To verify, Bob

- Verifies that h has norm less than a specific upper bound.
- Verifies that $c = \mathsf{Hash}(\widehat{h}|_\Omega / (\widehat{f}|_\Omega + \widehat{c}|_\Omega), \mu)$

The first condition for verification is met because

$$\|g \star (f + c)\| \approx \|g\| \, \|f + c\| .$$

The fact that $\|\boldsymbol{f}\|, \|\boldsymbol{g}\|, \|\boldsymbol{c}\|$ are small thus implies that $\|\boldsymbol{h}\|$ is small[1]. The second condition is true because $\mathcal{F}_\Omega$ is a ring homomorphism.

To forge a signature, a third party would need to produce an $\boldsymbol{h}$ which is short, and which satisfies the required evaluations at points in Ω. It is conjectured that finding such an $\boldsymbol{h}$ is no easier than solving the associated CVP .

2.2   Transcript Weaknesses in Previous PASS Protocols

The difficulty with this PASS prototype is that a transcript of signatures produced by a single signer on any set of messages leaks information about that signer's secret key. One way to see this is via a ring homomorphism $\rho : R_q \to R_q$ given by

$$\rho(a_0 + a_1 x + a_2 x^2 + \cdots + a_{N-1} x^{N-1}) = a_0 + a_{N-1} x + a_{N-2} x^2 + \cdots + a_1 x^{N-1}.$$

The homomorphism ρ plays the same role that conjugation would play if x were replaced by a primitive N^{th} root of unity. If a polynomial $p \in R_q$ is drawn randomly from a distribution, let $\mathbb{E}[p]$ denote the expectation of p, that is, the average of p over many samples. A third party observing many examples of $\boldsymbol{g} \star (\boldsymbol{f} + \boldsymbol{c})$ could compute

$$\mathbb{E}[\boldsymbol{g} \star (\boldsymbol{f} + \boldsymbol{c}) \star \rho(\boldsymbol{g} \star (\boldsymbol{f} + \boldsymbol{c}))] = \mathbb{E}[\boldsymbol{g} \star \rho(\boldsymbol{g})]\, \mathbb{E}[(\boldsymbol{f} + \boldsymbol{c}) \star \rho(\boldsymbol{f} + \boldsymbol{c})]$$

For simplicity assume that $\mathbb{E}[\boldsymbol{c}] = 0$, then, since $\boldsymbol{f}$ is constant, the above becomes

$$\mathbb{E}[\boldsymbol{g} \star \rho(\boldsymbol{g})]\, (\mathbb{E}[\boldsymbol{c} \star \rho(\boldsymbol{c})] + \boldsymbol{f} \star \rho(\boldsymbol{f})) .$$

The distributions from which $\boldsymbol{c}$ and $\boldsymbol{g}$ are drawn are known, and thus a sufficiently long transcript will reveal $\boldsymbol{f} \star \rho(\boldsymbol{f})$ from which $\boldsymbol{f}$ may be computed by a technique from Gentry and Szydlo [8].

2.3   Recent Developments and Countermeasures

The problem with PASS was not that individual signatures leaked information about the secret key, but rather that an average over a collection of signatures would converge to a secret key dependent value. This is not a concern for signature schemes based on number theoretic trapdoor permutations, as such schemes enjoy relatively simple proofs that their signatures are uniformly distributed over the full range of possibilities. However, the requirement that PASS signatures have small norm, i.e. that they occupy a small region of the full domain, necessitates throwing out much of the algebraic structure that makes such uniformity

---

[1] The original PASS protocol used the centered L^2 norm - the L^2 norm about the mean of the vector. This norm can be seen to enjoy the above quasi-multiplicative property for independent random polynomials by considering the product in the complex Fourier domain, noting that the centering operation has the effect of zeroing the constant terms, and by applying Parseval's theorem.

guarantees possible. Full decoupling of secret keys from transcripts was a difficult barrier for the construction of secure lattice based signature schemes, and more so for the construction of efficient schemes.

The first successful decoupling, the signature scheme of Gentry, Peikert, and Vaikuntanathan [7], involved computing a candidate signature point x and then adding noise sampled from a discrete Gaussian distribution centered at $-x$. The resulting signatures have a distribution which is computationally indistinguishable from a spherical discrete Gaussian centered at the origin.

Lyubashevsky, in [14], constructed a lattice based identification scheme which avoids transcript analysis attacks with a technique he called "aborting." In this scheme, provers are capable of determining when their response to a challenge will leak information about their secret key. Whenever this occurs they abort the protocol rather than supply a response.

In [15], Lyubashevsky improved his aborting technique and constructed a signature scheme through the Fiat-Shamir transform with hardness based on the Ring-SIS problem. Improvements and variants of this scheme with different hardness assumptions were presented in [16].

The first truly practical lattice signature scheme to avoid transcript attacks was developed by Güneysu, Lyubashevsky, and Pöppelmann [9]. Their scheme is a highly optimized variant of [16] and relies on a stronger hardness assumption.

The current state of the art would appear to be the new scheme, called BLISS, by Ducas, Durmus, Lepoint, and Lyubashevsky [4]. This scheme makes use of an NTRU-like key generation procedure and a bimodal discrete Gaussian noise distribution to produce very compact signatures. The efficiency of the scheme is also very impressive, especially considering the complexity of sampling discrete Gaussians.

3   PASS$_{RS}$ – PASS with Rejection Sampling

We now present PASS$_{RS}$ a new variant of PASS which completely decouples the transcript distribution from the secret key. Table 1 lists the public parameters of the system and gives a brief description of each.

Table 1. Public parameters

N - Dimension
q - Prime $\equiv 1 \pmod{N}$
g - a primitive N^{th} root of unity in $\mathbb{Z}_q$
Ω - A subset of $\{g^j : 1 \leq j \leq N - 1\}$
t - $|\Omega|$
k - Infinity norm of noise polynomials
b - 1-norm of challenge polynomials

Some notes on notation: R_q is the ring $\mathbb{Z}_q[x]/(x^N - 1)$; elements $\boldsymbol{a} \in R_q$ are represented as polynomials $\boldsymbol{a} = a_0 + a_1\boldsymbol{x} + a_2\boldsymbol{x}^2 + \cdots + a_{N-1}\boldsymbol{x}^{N-1}$, with coefficients in $a_i \in \mathbb{Z}_q$. We freely transition between this polynomial representation and a coefficient vector representation, $\boldsymbol{a} = [a_0, a_1, a_2, \ldots, a_{N-1}]^T$, wherever convenient.

Norms, such as $\|\boldsymbol{a}\|_\infty$ and $\|\boldsymbol{a}\|_1$, are the standard L^p norms on coefficient vectors; for numerical calculations we consistently identify a_i with an integer such that $|a_i| \le q/2$.

We write $\mathcal{B}^1(b)$ to denote the elements of R_q with 1-norm $\le b$, and $\mathcal{B}^\infty(k)$ to denote the elements of R_q with ∞-norm $\le k$.

Lastly, The indicator function $\mathbf{1}_S(x)$ yields 1 if $x \in S$ and 0 otherwise.

3.1 Key Generation

A secret key is a polynomial with L^∞ norm equal to 1. We recommend the simple strategy of choosing each coefficient independently and uniformly from $\{-1, 0, 1\}$. Binary coefficients, though attractive for several reasons, would open the system up to a UniqueSVP gap amplification attack similar to that used by Nguyen in his cryptanalysis of GGH [19].

The public key corresponding to the secret key $\boldsymbol{f}$ is $\widehat{\boldsymbol{f}}|_\Omega = \mathcal{F}_\Omega \boldsymbol{f}$.

3.2 Signing

Signing is an iterated process consisting of the generation of a candidate signature followed by a rejection sampling step to prevent the publication of candidates that could leak secret key information.

A party with secret key $\boldsymbol{f}$, who wishes to sign a message μ, first selects a commitment polynomial $\boldsymbol{y}$ uniformly at random from $\mathcal{B}^\infty(k)$. The commitment $\boldsymbol{y}$ serves to mask the private key and must be treated with the same care as the private key itself. The signer then computes and stores $\widehat{\boldsymbol{y}}|_\Omega = \mathcal{F}_\Omega \boldsymbol{y}$, which will ultimately be made public if the candidate passes rejection sampling.[2]

Next, the signer computes a challenge, $\boldsymbol{c}$, which binds $\widehat{\boldsymbol{y}}|_\Omega$ to μ. To do so she makes use of the public algorithms:

$$\mathsf{Hash} : \mathbb{Z}_q^t \times \{0, 1\}^* \to \{0, 1\}^\ell, \text{ and}$$

$$\mathsf{FormatC} : \{0, 1\}^\ell \hookrightarrow \mathcal{B}^1(b).$$

Hash concatenates its inputs and passes the result through a cryptographic hash function such as SHA-512. FormatC maps the set of bitstrings output by Hash into a set of sparse polynomials. We avoid further description of the algorithms for now and simply say that

$$\boldsymbol{c} = \mathsf{FormatC}(\mathsf{Hash}(\widehat{\boldsymbol{y}}|_\Omega, \mu)).$$

---

[2] Note that the generation of $\boldsymbol{y}$ and the computation of $\widehat{\boldsymbol{y}}|_\Omega$ can both be done offline, oblivious to the message to be signed.

Finally, the signer computes a candidate signature point

$$z = f \star c + y \in R_q,$$

if any of the coefficients of z fall outside the interval $[-k + b, k - b]$, then y, c, and z are discarded and the signing process is repeated. Otherwise, the signer outputs the signature (c, z, μ).

In section 4 we will prove that signatures that pass the rejection sampling procedure have z values that are uniformly distributed over $\mathcal{B}^\infty(k - b)$.

3.3 Verification

The signature (c, z, μ) is valid if z is in $\mathcal{B}^\infty(k - b)$ and if

$$c = \mathsf{FormatC}(\mathsf{Hash}(\widehat{z}|_\Omega - \widehat{f}|_\Omega \odot \widehat{c}|_\Omega, \mu)).$$

Since $\mathcal{F}_\Omega$ is a ring homomorphism, it is the case that $\widehat{z}|_\Omega = \widehat{f}|_\Omega \odot \widehat{c}|_\Omega + \widehat{y}|_\Omega$. Therefore, on receipt of (c, z, μ), any verifier in possession of the appropriate public key $\widehat{f}|_\Omega$ can evaluate z and c and compute $\widehat{y}|_\Omega = \widehat{z}|_\Omega - \widehat{f}|_\Omega \odot \widehat{c}|_\Omega$. The correctness of the scheme is immediate.

Algorithm 1. Sign	Algorithm 2. Verify
Input: (μ, f)	**Input:** $(c, z, \mu, \widehat{f}|_\Omega)$
1. **repeat**	1. *result* $\leftarrow$ invalid
2. $y \xleftarrow{\$} \mathcal{B}^\infty(k)$	2. **if** $z \in \mathcal{B}^\infty(k - b)$ **then**
3. $h \leftarrow \mathsf{Hash}(\widehat{y}|_\Omega, \mu)$	3. $h' \leftarrow \mathsf{Hash}(\widehat{z}|_\Omega - \widehat{f}|_\Omega \odot \widehat{c}|_\Omega, \mu)$
4. $c \leftarrow \mathsf{FormatC}(h)$	4. $c' \leftarrow \mathsf{FormatC}(h')$
5. $z \leftarrow f \star c + y$	5. **if** $c = c'$ **then**
6. **until** $z \in \mathcal{B}^\infty(k - b)$	6. *result* $\leftarrow$ valid
Output: (c, z, μ)	7. **end if**
	8. **end if**
	Output: *result*

4 Rejection Sampling

Each iteration of the signature generation routine produces a candidate signature which is accepted or rejected based on its infinity norm alone. In this section we will argue that this rejection sampling procedure completely decouples the distribution of signature points from the private key.

We will make use of the following fact:

Fact 1. *Each candidate signature z is in $\mathcal{B}^\infty(k + b)$.*

Proof. By definition we have $\|z\|_\infty = \|f \star c + y\|_\infty$ and by the triangle inequality: $\|f \star c + y\|_\infty \leq \|f \star c\|_\infty + \|y\|_\infty$. Again by the triangle inequality, $\|f \star c\|_\infty \leq \|f\|_\infty \|c\|_1$, thus

$$\|z\|_\infty \leq \|f\|_\infty \|c\|_1 + \|y\|_\infty \leq b + k.$$

We will also make use of the following assumption on instantiations of Hash and FormatC.

Assumption 1. *Let the public parameters* (N, q, k, b, Ω) *be fixed and let* $c \in \mathcal{B}^1(b)$, $y \in \mathcal{B}^\infty(k)$, $\mu \in \{0,1\}^*$ *be random variables related by*

$$c = \mathsf{FormatC}(\mathsf{Hash}(\widehat{y}|_\Omega, \mu)).$$

We assume that Hash *is a collision resistant hash function, that* c *and* y *are independent, and that* c *is uniform over the range of* FormatC. *More explicitly, for any fixed* $c_0 \in \mathcal{B}^1(b)$ *and fixed* $y_0 \in \mathcal{B}^\infty(k)$,

$$\Pr\left[c = c_0 \mid y = y_0\right] = \frac{\Pr\left[c = c_0\right]\Pr\left[y = y_0\right]}{\Pr\left[y = y_0\right]} = |\mathcal{B}^1(b)|^{-1}.$$

Note that assumption 1 is no stronger than the standard random oracle assumption, so the reader may assume we are working in the random oracle model. We state the assumption in the above form to aid in the analysis of concrete instantiations. Clearly the assumption that the joint distribution of y and c factors is untenable - no deterministic instantiation of Hash can satisfy it while maintaining collision resistance. Yet by choosing an appropriate padding scheme for μ one should be able to approximately satisfy the assumption. We leave the exploration of padding schemes and analysis of the practical impact of assumption 1 to future work.

The following proposition describes the distribution of candidate signatures.

Proposition 1. *Fix vectors* $f_0 \in \mathcal{B}^\infty(1)$ *and* $z_0 \in \mathcal{B}^\infty(k + b)$. *Then as the pair* (c, y) *is chosen uniformly from the space* $\mathcal{B}^1(1) \times \mathcal{B}^\infty(k)$, *we have*

$$\Pr\left[f_0 \star c + y = z_0\right] = |\mathcal{B}^\infty(k)|^{-1} \sum_{c_0 \in \mathcal{B}^1(b)} \Pr\left[c = c_0\right] \mathbf{1}_{\mathcal{B}^\infty(k)}(z_0 - f_0 \star c_0).$$

Proof. For any fixed $c_0 \in \mathcal{B}^1(b)$ we have

$$\Pr\left[f_0 \star c_0 + y = z_0\right] = \Pr\left[y = z_0 - f_0 \star c_0\right]$$

$$= \begin{cases} |\mathcal{B}^\infty(k)|^{-1} & \text{if } (z_0 - f_0 \star c_0) \in \mathcal{B}^\infty(k) \\ 0 & \text{otherwise.} \end{cases}$$

By application of the law of total probability and the assumption that the c and y are independent:

$$\Pr\left[f_0 \star c + y = z_0\right] = \sum_{c_0 \in \mathcal{B}^1(b)} \Pr\left[c = c_0\right] \Pr\left[f_0 \star c + y = z_0 \mid c = c_0\right]$$

$$= \sum_{c_0 \in \mathcal{B}^1(b)} \Pr\left[c = c_0\right] \Pr\left[y = z_0 - f_0 \star c_0\right]$$

$$= |\mathcal{B}^\infty(k)|^{-1} \sum_{c_0 \in \mathcal{B}^1(b)} \Pr\left[c = c_0\right] \mathbf{1}_{\mathcal{B}^\infty(k)}(z_0 - f_0 \star c_0).$$

Recall from section 3.2 that a candidate signature is rejected unless its z component is contained in $\mathcal{B}^\infty(k-b)$. The following proposition shows that each point in $\mathcal{B}^\infty(k-b)$ is selected as a candidate signature with equal probability.

Proposition 2. *Fix vectors f_0 in $\mathcal{B}^\infty(1)$ and z_0 in $\mathcal{B}^\infty(k-b)$. Then as the pair (c, y) is chosen uniformly from the space $\mathcal{B}^1(b) \times \mathcal{B}^\infty(k)$, we have*

$$\Pr\left[f_0 \star c + y = z_0\right] = |\mathcal{B}^\infty(k)|^{-1}.$$

Proof. We first note that $\mathcal{B}^\infty(k-b)$ is contained within $\mathcal{B}^\infty(k+b)$, so proposition 1 applies. Additionally, it is the case that $\|z_0\|_\infty \leq k - b$ and consequently, for any fixed $c_0 \in \mathcal{B}^1(b)$, we have $\|z_0 - f_0 \star c_0\|_\infty \leq k$. Thus $z_0 - f_0 \star c_0$ is contained in $\mathcal{B}^\infty(k)$ and the indicator function in proposition 1 is unconditionally satisfied. Therefore,

$$\Pr\left[f_0 \star c + y = z_0\right] = |\mathcal{B}^\infty(k)|^{-1} \sum_{c_0 \in \mathcal{B}^1(b)} \Pr\left[c = c_0\right] = |\mathcal{B}^\infty(k)|^{-1}.$$

Proposition 2 informs us that each of the $|\mathcal{B}^\infty(k-b)|$ acceptable signature points is chosen with probability $|\mathcal{B}^\infty(k)|^{-1}$. We infer that each pass through the signature generation routine has probability

$$\Pr\left[accept\right] = \frac{|\mathcal{B}^\infty(k-b)|}{|\mathcal{B}^\infty(k)|} = \left(1 - \frac{2b}{2k+1}\right)^N \approx e^{-\frac{Nb}{k}}$$

of generating a valid signature point, where the approximation is valid provided that both N and k/b are large.

A *transcript* is a set of signatures published by an honest signer. For instance, a signer who uses private key f to sign messages $\mu_1, \mu_2, \ldots, \mu_k$ produces a transcript

$$T = \{(c_i, z_i) : (c_i, z_i, \mu_i) = \mathsf{Sign}(\mu_i, f)\}.$$

Proposition 3. *A transcript T generated by an honest signer with private key f is indistinguishable from a set of points drawn uniformly from $\mathcal{B}^1(b) \times \mathcal{B}^\infty(k-b)$. Furthermore, for any fixed $c_0 \in \mathcal{B}^1(b)$, $z_0 \in \mathcal{B}^\infty(k-b)$ and $f_0 \in \mathcal{B}^1(1)$, the events $(c_0, z_0) \in T$ and $f = f_0$ are independent.*

Proof. The c components of T are uniformly distributed over $\mathcal{B}^1(b)$ by assumption 1. Proposition 2 establishes not only that the z components of T are uniformly distributed over $\mathcal{B}^\infty(k-b)$, but also that the distribution of z depends *only* on the distribution of y. Again by assumption 1, c and y are independent and therefore c and z are independent. The distribution of transcript points is consequently the product distribution of c and z, i.e. uniform over $\mathcal{B}^1(b) \times \mathcal{B}^\infty(k-b)$.

Independence of transcript points from the secret key follows from the fact that proposition 2 holds for all choices of f_0 in $\mathcal{B}^\infty(1)$.

5   Security Analysis

Our security analysis will focus on two types of attacks, those that target the hash function (or the combination FormatC ∘ Hash), and those that target the partial Fourier transform $\mathcal{F}_\Omega$. Other attacks may be possible, and investigating them is an area for future work.

As our aim is to develop a practical quantum-resistant signature scheme, we will assume that the adversary has access to a quantum computer. Relatively little is known about the existence or non-existence of quantum algorithms for lattice problems, so our assumptions related to quantum computers will only address their ability to solve k-element black-box search problems in $\Theta(\sqrt{k})$ time.

5.1   Attacks on the Hash Function

The most obvious constraint on the security of the system comes from the entropy of c. An adversary who can find a Hash preimage of a particular c can produce forgeries on structured messages from any user's public key. To do so, the adversary:

1. Chooses arbitrary z and c from the appropriate domains.
2. Computes $\widehat{g}|_\Omega = \widehat{z}|_\Omega - \widehat{f}|_\Omega \odot \widehat{c}|_\Omega$, where $\widehat{f}|_\Omega$ is the victim's public key.
3. Finds a preimage of c in $\mathsf{Hash}(\widehat{g}|_\Omega, \cdot)$.

While attacks against specific hash functions can have arbitrarily low complexity, we will assume that a strong hash function is chosen, and only consider generic attacks. If the output of Hash is r bits, a quantum adversary can find preimages in time $\Theta(2^{r/2})$. For κ-bit security, the range of FormatC ∘ Hash should produce an essentially uniform distribution on a set of cardinality $2^{2\kappa}$.

5.2   Attacks on the Partial Fourier Transform

An adversary who can find $\mathcal{F}_\Omega$ preimages which are in $\mathcal{B}^\infty(k - b)$ can forge signatures on arbitrary messages from any user's public key.

1. Adversary chooses random point g_F in $\mathcal{B}^\infty(k)$
2. $c_F = \mathsf{FormatC}(\mathsf{Hash}(\mathcal{F}_\Omega g_F, \mu))$
3. $\widehat{z_F}|_\Omega = \widehat{g_F}|_\Omega + \widehat{f}|_\Omega \widehat{c_F}|_\Omega$
4. Adversary uses preimage attack on $\widehat{z_F}|_\Omega$ to find appropriate z_F.

Adversaries could also try to recover the secret key directly with their preimage algorithm, but in order for this to be effective they must be able to find exceptionally short preimages. The problem of secret key recovery seems, at least intuitively then, to be harder than forgery. Yet, surprisingly, given the particular parameters of the scheme, lattice attacks may be better suited for solving the secret key recovery problem than they are for forging messages. Some care must be taken when choosing parameters to balance the difficulty of the two problems.

Lattice Attacks on $\mathcal{F}_\Omega$. As mentioned briefly in the introduction, the partial Fourier recovery problem can easily be seen to be no harder than a specific class of closest vector problem CVP. Presented with the evaluation set, Ω, and a partial Fourier representation $\widehat{z}|_\Omega$, an adversary can construct a lattice in which solving the CVP associated to any arbitrary preimage of $\widehat{z}|_\Omega$ allows them to construct a short preimage of $\widehat{z}|_\Omega$.

That lattice, which we denote $\Lambda^\perp(\mathcal{F}_\Omega)$, is equivalent to the kernel of $\mathcal{F}_\Omega$,

$$\Lambda^\perp(\mathcal{F}_\Omega) = \left\{ a \in \mathbb{Z}_q^N \ : \ \mathcal{F}_\Omega a = 0 \pmod q \right\}.$$

In practice, CVP instances are almost always solved by transforming the problem into an SVP in dimension $N+1$. If z' is an arbitrary preimage of the target $\widehat{z}|_\Omega$, i.e. $\mathcal{F}_\Omega z' = \widehat{z}|_\Omega$ but $\|z'\|$ is large, and $\{b_1, b_2, \ldots, b_m\}$ form a Hermite Normal Form basis for $\Lambda^\perp(\mathcal{F}_\Omega)$, then solving SVP in the lattice generated by the columns of

$$\mathcal{L}_{z'}^{\mathsf{SVP}} = \begin{pmatrix} q & & 0 & b_{1,0} & \cdots & b_{m,0} & z'_0 \\ & \ddots & & \vdots & \ddots & \vdots & \vdots \\ 0 & & q & b_{1,t-1} & \cdots & b_{m,t-1} & z'_{t-1} \\ 0 & \cdots & 0 & \vdots & \ddots & \vdots & \vdots \\ \vdots & \ddots & \vdots & b_{1,N-1} & \cdots & b_{m,N-1} & z'_{N-1} \\ 0 & \cdots & 0 & 0 & \cdots & 0 & 1 \end{pmatrix}$$

is likely to yield a short z such that $\mathcal{F}_\Omega z = \widehat{z}|_\Omega$.

Experiments by Micciancio and Regev [18] have demonstrated that lattice reduction algorithms perform best against the kernel lattices, $\Lambda^\perp(A)$, of $t \times N$ matrices A when $N \approx \sqrt{t \log(q)/\log(\gamma)}$ for some $\gamma \approx 1.01$ determined experimentally for each reduction algorithm. In the PASS$_{\mathsf{RS}}$ setting this places restrictions on t and q that we have obeyed in all of our proposed parameter sets. As such there should be no benefit to attacking a sublattice of $\mathcal{L}^{\mathsf{SVP}}$, and we proceed under this assumption.

The performance of lattice reduction algorithms, particularly LLL and BKZ, on lattices such as $\mathcal{L}_{z'}^{\mathsf{SVP}}$ is difficult to analyze in practice. Perhaps the most surprising complicating factor is that the performance depends crucially on the coset of $\mathbb{Z}_q^N/\Lambda^\perp(\mathcal{F}_\Omega)$ to which z' belongs, and not strongly on z' itself. This dependence gives rise to two regimes that we will analyze separately. The extreme case, when z' is very close to the kernel lattice, produces instances of the UniqueSVP problem and determines the difficulty of the secret key recovery problem in PASS$_{\mathsf{RS}}$. The average case produces instances of ApproxSVP which will inform our discussion of the signature forgery problem.

UniqueSVP is the problem of finding a shortest vector in a lattice that is known to have a significant gap between the lengths of its first and second successive minima. Such is the case[3] in the lattices $\mathcal{L}_{f'}^{\mathsf{SVP}}$, as the the secret key, f, has an expected norm of $\sqrt{2N/3}$ and $[f, 1]^T \in \mathcal{L}_{f'}^{\mathsf{SVP}}$.

---

[3] Curiously, the fact that the kernel lattice always contains the exceptionally short vector $[1, 1, \ldots, 1]$ seems to have no impact here.

Lattice reduction algorithms can be ranked according to the so-called Hermite factor that they achieve. Algorithms that achieve Hermite factor γ can be expected to find the shortest vector in a lattice when the UniqueSVP-gap, $\lambda_2(\mathcal{L})/\lambda_1(\mathcal{L})$, is greater than a constant fraction of γ. This behavior was first examined by Gama and Nguyen, whose experiments determined that for a certain class of random lattices the constant is approximately 0.48 [5]. They exhibited classes of lattices for which the constant was smaller, but these appear to be somewhat exceptional. Ducas et al. [4] performed similar experiments on the lattices that occur in BLISS, and found the constant again to be 0.48, and we have found the same to be true of the lattices related to PASS$_{RS}$.

Table 2 contains estimates on the Hermite factor needed to recover PASS$_{RS}$ secret keys at several concrete parameter levels. We estimate $\lambda_2(\mathcal{L}_{f'}^{SVP})$ by the Gaussian heuristic in the L^2 norm. This predicts that N successive minima of a lattice will be tightly clustered around the radius of the smallest N-ball that has volume equal to the determinant of the lattice. The q-ary lattices, $\Lambda^{\perp}(\mathcal{F}_{\Omega})$, have determinant q^t, and the Gaussian heuristic therefore predicts

$$\lambda_2(\mathcal{L}_{f'}^{SVP}) = \lambda_1(\Lambda^{\perp}(\mathcal{F}_{\Omega})) \approx \det(\Lambda^{\perp}(\mathcal{F}_{\Omega}))^{1/N} \sqrt{\tfrac{N}{2\pi e}} = q^{t/N} \sqrt{\tfrac{N}{2\pi e}}.$$

As mentioned above, we estimate λ_1 as $\sqrt{2N/3}$, the length of the secret key. This gives us a UniqueSVP-gap, $\lambda_2/\lambda_1 \approx q^{t/N} \sqrt{3/(4\pi e)}$. Incorporating the constant 0.48 adjustment, we find that lattice reduction algorithms must achieve Hermite factor

$$\gamma = 0.62 \cdot q^{t/N} \tag{1}$$

in order to recover PASS$_{RS}$ secret keys.

The analysis for forgery attacks is very similar, only now the target $\widehat{z}|_{\Omega}$ will lie in an essentially random coset of $\mathbb{Z}_q^N/\Lambda^{\perp}(\mathcal{F}_{\Omega})$. The relevant problem is now ApproxSVP$_{\alpha}$ the problem of finding a short vector that is more than α factor of being optimal, in other words a vector that is no longer than $\alpha\lambda_1(\mathcal{L}_{z'}^{SVP})$. Lattice reduction algorithms that achieve Hermite factor γ can solve ApproxSVP with factor $\alpha = \gamma^2$ in the worst case. That said, $\alpha = \gamma$ seems achievable on average [5], so we use this estimate in our analysis.

PASS$_{RS}$ signatures are validated by the L^{∞} norm, but lattice reduction algorithms typically only guarantee the L^2 norm of their results. A vector of L^2 norm $\sqrt{N} \cdot (k-b)$ could potentially serve as a forgery, but this is highly unlikely. We estimate the approximation factor to be the ratio of the expected length of a forgery to the volume of the lattice, which is

$$\alpha = \sqrt{N} \cdot V/q^{t/N}, \tag{2}$$

where V is the variance of the discrete uniform distribution on $[-k+b, k-b]$.

Concrete Performance of Lattice Reduction Algorithms. Current folklore is that lattice reduction algorithms can achieve Hermite factor $\approx 1.01^N$ in reasonable time but that Hermite factor 1.005^N is completely out of reach.

These are useful heuristics, but they reflect more our ignorance about the concrete performance of lattice reduction and enumeration algorithms than they do our knowledge. Unfortunately, it seems that we know far too little about how these algorithms perform in high dimension to give precise "bit-security" estimates. We can, however, roughly determine which of the currently available lattice reduction algorithms might be useful for attacking PASS$_{RS}$.

Experiments by Schneider and Buchmann [21] indicate that the Hermite factor reachable by BKZ with blocksize β is approximately:

$$1.01655 - 0.000196185 \cdot \beta,$$

which for Hermite factors relevant to our parameter sets yields:

Blocksize (β)	15	30	40	55
Root Hermite factor	1.0136	1.0107	1.0087	1.0058

Table 2 lists several PASS$_{RS}$ parameter sets, the line labeled "Lattice security factor" represents our best guess as to the Hermite factor needed to launch either a key recovery or forgery attack (whichever is easier). We expect that our toy parameter set, $N = 433$, could be defeated by running BKZ-15 to completion. Although we do not have a good estimate on how long this would take, it should be possible with current technology.

Our other parameter sets should be significantly more difficult to attack. While Hermite factor 1.01^N is nominally within reach of today's technology, this has only been verified in relatively small dimensions. We know very little about how the algorithms will perform in dimension 577. Key recovery attacks on this parameter set should be possible with BKZ-30, but other approaches are likely needed to make the attack practical.

Chen and Nguyen have had impressive success with their BKZ-2.0 algorithm [3], which combines extreme pruning, developed in [6], with an early termination procedure, theoretically justified by [11]. BKZ-2.0 runs BKZ at phenomenally high blocksizes for a small number of rounds under the experimentally justified belief that most of the progress of BKZ is made in the early rounds. It is difficult to extrapolate security estimates from the results published thus far on BKZ-2.0's performance, but it would appear that our $577, 769$, and 1153 parameter sets could be within reach of terminated BKZ-75, 122, and 229 respectively.

For $N = 577$, our experiments with a BKZ-2.0 simulator similar to that presented in [3] indicate that 56 rounds of BKZ-75 would be sufficient to reach root hermite factor 1.0106; for $N = 769$, 47 rounds of BKZ-122 would suffice to reach 1.0084; and for $N = 1153$, 42 rounds of BKZ-229 would reach 1.0058.

Following the analysis of [3], we expecte enumeration to be the most expensive subroutine of BKZ-2.0. Each round consists of approximately N enumerations, and the cost of each enumeration depends on the the number of nodes visited in the enumeration tree. The estimated bit security is

$$\log_2(N \cdot rounds) + \log_2(nodes\ per\ enumeration) + \log_2(cost\ per\ node)$$

Using number-of-node and cost-per-node estimates from [3], we have that the estimated security of our $N = 769$ parameter is $\log_2(769 \cdot 47) + 53 + \log_2(200) \approx 76$ bits.

For $N = 1153$, a single enumeration in BKZ-229 is expected to take over 2^{130} time, which is greater than the expected time for a quantum attack on the hash function.

Table 2. Parameter sets and security indicators. UniqueSVP gap refers to λ_2/λ_1 without any correction for the performance of specific lattice reduction algorithms.

N	433	577	769	1153
q	775937	743177	1047379	968521
g	268673	296108	421722	56574
k	$2^{12} - 1$	$2^{14} - 1$	$2^{15} - 1$	$2^{15} - 1$
b	19	24	29	36
t	200	280	386	600
$\Pr[Accept]$	0.78	0.57	0.49	0.72
UniqueSVP gap	1.0117	1.0093	1.0075	1.0052
ApproxSVP factor	1.0105	1.0101	1.0081	1.0054
Lattice security factor	1.0134	1.0106	1.0084	1.0058
Entropy of c	124	160	200	260
Bit-security bound	$\ll 62$	$\ll 80$	< 100	≤ 130

6   Reference Implementation

We have created a reference implementation of PASS$_{RS}$ in C and made it available[4] under the GNU General Public License. Table 3 gives some idea of the performance of PASS$_{RS}$ relative to the recent proposal of Ducas et al. (BLISS [4]) and to RSA and ECDSA. BLISS was tested using the June 13, 2013 version[5]. The implementations of RSA and ECDSA are from OpenSSL 1.0.1e. All benchmarks were run on a single 2.8GHz core of an Intel Core i7-2640M with hyper threading and turbo boost disabled. We make no claims as to the accuracy of these benchmarks - the timing methods used internally by the three libraries tested are incommensurate and many variables have been left uncontrolled. However, we do feel that these preliminary performance estimates are worth reporting, as they indicate that the schemes are competitive with each other and that further comparisons would be interesting.

---

[4] https://github.com/NTRUOpenSourceProject/ntru-crypto
[5] http://bliss.di.ens.fr/

6.1   Performance Considerations

The two most computationally intensive parts of $PASS_{RS}$ are the number theo-retic transforms (NTT) used to compute $\mathcal{F}_\Omega$, and the sparse cyclic convolution used in computing $z = f \star c + y$. To compute $\mathcal{F}_\Omega$ we use Rader's algorithm to decompose the prime length NTT into cyclic convolution of length $N - 1$. We compute the resulting convolution as a pair of Fourier transforms over $\mathbb{C}$ using version 3.3.3 of FFTW. For all of the parameter sets presented above we have chosen chosen N to be a Pierpont prime (a prime of the form $2^u \cdot 3^v + 1$) as these yield very fast Fourier transform algorithms. Fermat primes $(2^u + 1)$ would yield a faster transforms, but there are no Fermat primes in our preferred parameter range.

We have made little effort to optimize the computation of sparse convolutions, and these often dominate the running time of the signing process.

6.2   Concrete Instantiations of Public Functions

Our reference implementation uses SHA-512 to instantiate Hash for all parameter sets. The input passed to SHA-512 is the concatenation of the low order byte of each coefficient of $\widehat{y}|_\Omega$ followed by the SHA-512 digest of μ.

$$\mathsf{Hash}(\widehat{y}, \mu) = \text{SHA-512}(lowbyte(\widehat{y}_0) \mid \ldots \mid lowbyte(\widehat{y}_{t-1}) \mid \text{SHA-512}(\mu))$$

We have not implemented any message padding.

Our instantiation of FormatC sets aside the first 64 bits of $h_0 = \mathsf{Hash}(\widehat{y}|_\Omega, \mu)$ to use as signs of the nonzero coefficients of c. The remaining bits of h_0 are used, 16 at a time, in a rejection sampling procedure to generate uniform random values in the interval $[0, N-1]$. Each such value becomes the index of a non-zero

Table 3. Benchmarks. Times are averages over many operations.

Algorithm	Parameter Set	Sign (μs)	Verify (μs)	Sig. (bytes)	Pub. key (bytes)
	577	62	31	1115	700
$PASS_{RS}$	769	73	40	1578	965
	1153	203	69	2360	1500
	0	321	25	413	413
	I	164	44	700	875
BLISS	II	642	43	625	875
	III	270	45	750	875
	IV	496	47	813	875
	1024	225	15	128	128
RSA	2048	1591	50	256	256
	4096	11532	185	512	512
	secp160r1	80	270	40	20
ECDSA	nistp256	146	348	64	32
	nistp384	268	1151	96	48

coefficient of c. If the pool of bits is ever exhausted, the process continues on $h_i = \text{SHA-}512(h_{i-1})$.

The random coefficients of y are generated by a rejection sampling procedure on the output of a stream cipher. Specifically we use the procedure from [10] of keying the Salsa20 stream cipher with a short seed from the Linux kernel random number generator.

Table 4. Sandy Bridge cycle counts for PASS_{RS}. 100k samples.

Parameter Set	Sign		Verify	
	Median	Average	Median	Average
577	121996	171753	86828	87031
769	174900	205456	120204	120374
1153	421904	584230	172428	172641

References

1. Ajtai, M.: Generating hard instances of lattice problems (extended abstract). In: Proceedings of the Twenty-eighth Annual ACM Symposium on Theory of Computing, STOC 1996, pp. 99–108. ACM (1996)

2. Candes, E., Romberg, J., Tao, T.: Robust uncertainty principles: exact signal reconstruction from highly incomplete frequency information. IEEE Transactions on Information Theory 52(2), 489–509 (2006)

3. Chen, Y., Nguyen, P.Q.: BKZ 2.0: Better lattice security estimates. In: Lee, D.H., Wang, X. (eds.) ASIACRYPT 2011. LNCS, vol. 7073, pp. 1–20. Springer, Heidelberg (2011)

4. Ducas, L., Durmus, A., Lepoint, T., Lyubashevsky, V.: Lattice signatures and bimodal gaussians. In: Canetti, R., Garay, J.A. (eds.) CRYPTO 2013, Part I. LNCS, vol. 8042, pp. 40–56. Springer, Heidelberg (2013)

5. Gama, N., Nguyen, P.Q.: Predicting lattice reduction. In: Smart, N.P. (ed.) EUROCRYPT 2008. LNCS, vol. 4965, pp. 31–51. Springer, Heidelberg (2008)

6. Gama, N., Nguyen, P.Q., Regev, O.: Lattice enumeration using extreme pruning. In: Gilbert, H. (ed.) EUROCRYPT 2010. LNCS, vol. 6110, pp. 257–278. Springer, Heidelberg (2010)

7. Gentry, C., Peikert, C., Vaikuntanathan, V.: Trapdoors for hard lattices and new cryptographic constructions. In: Proceedings of the 40th Annual ACM Symposium on Theory of Computing, pp. 197–206. ACM (2008)

8. Gentry, C., Szydlo, M.: Cryptanalysis of the revised NTRU signature scheme. In: Knudsen, L.R. (ed.) EUROCRYPT 2002. LNCS, vol. 2332, pp. 299–320. Springer, Heidelberg (2002)

9. Güneysu, T., Lyubashevsky, V., Pöppelmann, T.: Practical lattice-based cryptography: A signature scheme for embedded systems. In: Prouff, E., Schaumont, P. (eds.) CHES 2012. LNCS, vol. 7428, pp. 530–547. Springer, Heidelberg (2012)

10. Güneysu, T., Oder, T., Pöppelmann, T., Schwabe, P.: Software speed records for lattice-based signatures. In: Gaborit, P. (ed.) PQCrypto 2013. LNCS, vol. 7932, pp. 67–82. Springer, Heidelberg (2013)

11. Hanrot, G., Pujol, X., Stehlé, D.: Analyzing blockwise lattice algorithms using dynamical systems. In: Rogaway, P. (ed.) CRYPTO 2011. LNCS, vol. 6841, pp. 447–464. Springer, Heidelberg (2011)
12. Hoffstein, J., Kaliski, B.S.J., Lieman, D.B., Robshaw, M.J.B., Yin, Y.L.: Secure user identification based on constrained polynomials, U.S. Classification: 713/168; 380/28; 380/30; 713/170; 713/176 International Classification: H04L 932; H04L 928; H04L 930 (2000)
13. Hoffstein, J., Silverman, J.H.: Polynomial rings and efficient public key authentication II. In: Lam, K.-Y., Shparlinski, I., Wang, H., Xing, C. (eds.) Cryptography and Computational Number Theory, Progress in Computer Science and Applied Logic, vol. 20, pp. 269–286. Birkhäuser (2001)
14. Lyubashevsky, V.: Lattice-based identification schemes secure under active attacks. In: Cramer, R. (ed.) PKC 2008. LNCS, vol. 4939, pp. 162–179. Springer, Heidelberg (2008)
15. Lyubashevsky, V.: Fiat-shamir with aborts: Applications to lattice and factoring-based signatures. In: Matsui, M. (ed.) ASIACRYPT 2009. LNCS, vol. 5912, pp. 598–616. Springer, Heidelberg (2009)
16. Lyubashevsky, V.: Lattice signatures without trapdoors. In: Pointcheval, D., Johansson, T. (eds.) EUROCRYPT 2012. LNCS, vol. 7237, pp. 738–755. Springer, Heidelberg (2012)
17. Lyubashevsky, V., Micciancio, D.: Generalized compact knapsacks are collision resistant. In: Bugliesi, M., Preneel, B., Sassone, V., Wegener, I. (eds.) ICALP 2006. LNCS, vol. 4052, pp. 144–155. Springer, Heidelberg (2006)
18. Micciancio, D., Regev, O.: Lattice-based cryptography. In: Bernstein, D.J., Buchmann, J., Dahmen, E. (eds.) Post-Quantum Cryptography, pp. 147–191. Springer (2009)
19. Nguyên, P.Q.: Cryptanalysis of the Goldreich-Goldwasser-Halevi Cryptosystem from Crypto 1997. In: Wiener, M. (ed.) CRYPTO 1999. LNCS, vol. 1666, pp. 288–304. Springer, Heidelberg (1999)
20. Peikert, C., Rosen, A.: Efficient collision-resistant hashing from worst-case assumptions on cyclic lattices. In: Halevi, S., Rabin, T. (eds.) TCC 2006. LNCS, vol. 3876, pp. 145–166. Springer, Heidelberg (2006)
21. Schneider, M., Buchmann, J.: Extended lattice reduction experiments using the BKZ algorithm. In: Sicherheit, Gesellschaft für Informatik. LNI, vol. 170, pp. 241–252 (2010)

Activity Spoofing and Its Defense in Android Smartphones

Brett Cooley[1], Haining Wang[1], and Angelos Stavrou[2]

[1] The College of William and Mary, Williamsburg, VA, USA
[2] George Mason University, Fairfax, VA, USA
{brcooley,hnw}@cs.wm.edu, astavrou@gmu.edu

Abstract. Smartphones have become ubiquitous in today's digital world as a mobile platform allowing anytime access to email, social platforms, banking, and shopping. Many providers supply native applications as a method to access their services, allowing users to login directly through a downloadable app. In this paper, we first expose a security vulnerability in the Android framework that allows for third party apps to spoof native app activities, or screens. This can lead to a wide variety of security risks including the capture and silent exfiltration of login credentials and private data. We then compare current defense mechanisms, and introduce the concept of Trusted Activity Chains as a lightweight protection against common spoofing attacks. We develop a proof of concept implementation and evaluate its effectiveness and performance overhead.

1 Introduction

In the recent years, global smartphone sales have grown 73%, while Android phone sales have grown 379% [1]. Due to this massive growth, mobile platforms are being used for a wide variety of services. By accessing these services, end users have become accustomed to authenticating to multiple third parties. This experience can be similar to more traditional models if the services utilize a web-based application. However, more and more services are deploying native applications, which is a departure from the web interfaces more frequently found on a desktop or laptop computing model. Therefore, users are not familiar with the expected results of common tasks like launching an app or navigating between apps when unfamiliar windowing system is in use. These factors lower the barrier of entry for malicious code to fool a user into doing something unintended.

While malware is written to use any and all possible security holes, widespread threats will generally target the most lucrative opportunities with the largest possible user base. Due to the relative unfamiliarity users have for mobile devices and the lack of standardized interface paradigms, taking advantage of this has the potential to affect the vast majority of smartphone users. It also has the potential to be incredibly lucrative, as the possibilities for surreptitious logging of highly personal data like bank account credentials or credit card numbers are both numerous and take little effort. In a compounding effect, there are few to no technical challenges needed to deceive users.

I. Boureanu, P. Owesarski, and S. Vaudenay (Eds.): ACNS 2014, LNCS 8479, pp. 494–512, 2014.
© Springer International Publishing Switzerland 2014

Traditionally, phishing or web spoofing are targeted attacks designed to trick users into revealing sensitive information or credentials to a third party, often without the user's knowledge that something bad has happened. Most phishing attempts do not need to exploit security vulnerabilities in websites, but rely on social engineering, look-alike links, and persuasive or seemingly urgent emails to lure users to release their private information [2]. Many studies have focused on the prevention of phishing, both via automated detection of malicious websites [3–5] and training and informing users [2]. However, all of these studies and tools are focused on web-based phishing, and many of the methods involved are unsuitable for a mobile environment. They are either too specific to be useful in the context of native applications or rely on services which would be too resource intensive and non-trivial to port to mobile devices. All of these roadblocks are due to the difference in the interaction model used by native mobile apps. To fully understand phishing in the context of a native app, we must look at the framework from which native apps are built.

Android is designed with a strong inter-process communication framework, enabling third party apps to integrate both with Android services and other apps. One of the major design goals was to enable component reuse among apps. For example, Android devices with a camera ship with an associated app, allowing third parties to treat the camera as a service, from which they can make simple requests and get back a picture in a variety of forms. At the same time, the user is presented with a familiar camera interface, then returned to the app they were originally interacting with. The Android framework was designed to make this use-case simple to achieve for developers, and interactions with the myriad of hardware devices on a smartphone predictable and easy to manage for users. These goals are made possible by two major portions of the framework, Activities and Intents.

In this paper, we explore how the ability to reuse activities changes user expectations, thus allowing activities to be spoofed by almost any third party app. We show how this can lead to exfiltration of account credentials among other breaches of privacy. We further explore how such an attack can be embedded in a legitimate application, and a proof-of-concept attack is demonstrated. We then discuss different defenses, including simple solutions and more sophisticated approaches already developed. We propose a framework for Trusted Activity Chains, which provide a lightweight, transparent system with a variable level of protection and user interaction. We evaluate the effectiveness of our defense along with its performance overhead. In addition, we discuss how our adaptation can protect against a larger surface of attacks than just credential-focused phishing attacks, and possible areas for future work and analysis.

The remainder of the paper is structured as follows. Section 2 describes the background information on Android activity. Section 3 presents the vulnerability of activity spoofing. Section 4 details different defense mechanisms and our proposed approach. Section 5 evaluates the effectiveness of our solution and its performance overhead. Section 6 surveys related work. Finally, Section 7 concludes the paper with the discussion of future work.

2   Background

Activities can be considered an abstraction for all of the code required to both display and handle events on a single screen. Activities can also serve as the entry point to an app, when properly designated as such. This allows any activity to be reused by an app other than its own as long as the third party app knows the correct message, or intent, to send that activity. The associated framework that enables the aforementioned messages is a custom facility, which Android calls intents. Intents can be constructed in any activity, and are used to either explicitly bring another activity into view or to implicitly request a certain type of activity to handle the attached data. When an activity is requested for use by an intent, it is brought to the foreground and displayed to a user for interaction. Once the user is finished with an activity or the activity in turn sends an intent to yet another activity, the current activity finishes and is stopped. This returns the user to the previous foreground activity or the newly started one. This model is designed around a stack of activities [6], and allows for a fluid exchange of data between apps, and a seamless experience for the user.

Android does provide some methods for limiting the scope of an activity, but they alone do not provide adequate protection for developers or users. The two major methods of protection are permission preconditions and private scoping of activities. Optionally, activities can require apps which send them intents to possess certain permissions, such as the ability to access a user's location. This can be used to ensure correct functionality of an activity, or ensure that some data collected by an app with certain permissions is only passed to other apps with the same or similar permissions. This feature, while helpful, is widely unused [7], and users cannot rely upon apps to safeguard their information to any greater degree than the Android system requires. Even with the use of these permission checks, there are well-known permission escalation attacks [8]. Another privatization method for activities is requiring a custom "key", thereby ensuring that any invoking app knows the exact string required to launch that particular activity. More frequently, they can receive standard system messages, allowing any app which asks for a particular kind of service to possibly be routed to the activity in question. The final, and default option is for an activity to require explicit invocation by name. However, as we will discuss below, this is actually the least effective method of protecting an activity from third party access.

Android does not place any restrictions on what types of apps are allowed to request the execution of activities. By default, without flagging an activity for a certain type of action, activities can only be launched outside of their respective apps via invoking them by their full name including the package in which they reside. However, easy to use tools [9] exist which enable finding the package and full class names of all activities in any published app. This effectively makes securing components the job of the developer, which has been shown to be problematic [7,10,11]. Due to these limitations, a variety of patterns of misuse are available to app developers. We will focus on a particularly dangerous pattern, called *activity spoofing*.

Fig. 1. Facebook's login activity

3   Activity Spoofing

Due to the relative lack or inadequacy of protections for activities, one cannot be assured of which activities belong to which apps. When one app displays an activity which is visually similar or identical to an activity from another app, users will become confused as to which application they are interacting with. This is called activity spoofing. We give an overview of how activity spoofing works, then discuss the properties and magnitude of the attack surface, and finally look into a particular attack vector.

3.1   Overview of Threat Model

Activities consist of many different kinds of information and interactions. We are interested primarily in authentication screens, or other activities that require a user to enter some kind of credentials or private data. These kinds of screens are commonly found in many types of apps, including popular social network apps like Facebook (Figure 1) and Twitter (Figure 2). Activity spoofing normally occurs when a user launches an app, which attempts to display an activity (the *intended activity*), but another activity is immediately launched (the *spoofed activity*) afterwards, which mimics the intended activity in appearance but is not the activity the user is expecting. Activity spoofing which does not have a temporal context can also be executed by an app advertising some kind of interoperability, like the ability to tweet about something from within the app. When the user goes to exercise this functionality, the app is free to launch an activity which mirrors the official app's appearance and feel.

Fig. 2. Twitter's generic login activity, which could further encourage spoofing

When users are presented with the spoofed activity, they assume that it is in fact the intended activity; as it looks identical to the intended activity and is exactly what they expect by launching the intended app. This is primarily because Android operates with only one activity visible at a time. This deprives users of any possible knowledge that there are two activities which mirror each other in appearance. Another enabling factor is that Android does not force activities to actively display what app they belong to. Therefore, users have no way of knowing that the spoofed activity does not belong to the app it appears to originate from. When the user interacts with the spoofed activity, it has full control over what is done with any information the user provides.

If users do enter whatever credentials are required to authenticate to the service which the spoofed activity is masquerading as, such as a login ID or email address and a password or PIN, they are handing the spoofed activity full access to that service. The spoofed activity can capture these values, and is free to exfiltrate them as it pleases. Moreover, the likelihood of these credentials being correct is much higher than more traditional methods of credential collection. This is because users are trying to actively use the service being portrayed, ensuring they are making a good-faith effort to provide current login and password data. Since most apps send credentials to a server to be authenticated, active network I/O is very common after submitting credentials to a login activity. This creates a perfect opportunity to send the data collected by the spoofed activity to an external server associated with the spoofed activity's app. Combining legitimate network traffic with data exfiltration makes detection of the private data leakage more difficult.

To keep users unaware of the data leakage, the spoofed activity can act in a variety of ways after it has captured the entered credentials. It can display an error message to the users, and exit silently. This has the effect of redirecting the users to the intended activity, which allows them to re-enter their credentials without interference. Another option is to pass the data on to the intended activity and initiate the submission of the data, bypassing the intended activity and displaying the next activity in app. Note that either of the two approaches could raise some suspicions.

By displaying an error message to users, the spoofed activity is returning control to the intended activity's app as quickly as possible, thereby minimizing the chances for detection due to lag in the user-interface or other abnormalities. However, over time, the prevalence of these errors could arouse suspicion. Also, this requires the spoofed activity to closely mimic the intended activity's error dialog. This adds complexity to the spoofing code, which increases the code's footprint. To combat these issues, the app containing the spoofed activity could only launch the spoofed activity a fraction of the times the user attempts to interact with the intended activity. This allows for a more realistic error rate, which users will be more willing to tolerate. If the spoofed activity passes the data on, the expected workflow is uninterrupted. This decreases the likelihood of user suspicion, as the sequence of activities displayed to the user is unchanged by the spoofed activity. However, Android must update the display when the spoofed activity exits, and the ability to programmatically bypass an activity is dependent on the authentication model employed. This delay could potentially draw attention from a trained user. We next describe what common types of interactions are vulnerable to activity spoofing.

3.2 Properties of Vulnerable Apps

Despite Android's unhindered access model, not every activity can be easily spoofed. Activities which display real-time data, or frequently updated streams which aren't publicly available can present real challenges to spoofing. Also, activities which make API-specific request from services over the network typically employ the use of an API key, which would require a spoofed activity to also obtain an API key. While this is significantly more difficult than spoofing a basic activity, there are common weaknesses in this approach which could allow for bypassing the need for an API key [12]. Nevertheless, we will focus on those activities that do not make use of private API's. This covers the large majority of activities, most of which are vulnerable to spoofing, but are also relatively harmless. The harmful activities require user interaction, typically asking users to enter some sort of login credentials or private information. As discussed before, these kinds of activities are prime for spoofing. Depending on the exact methods used for mimicking an application, the spoofed activity could look anywhere from close to an exact replica of the intended activity. In some cases, apps provide very generic login activities which can lead to confusion as to what app is requesting the user's credentials, even without the introduction of spoofing attacks. While many kinds of activities fit these criteria, we now present social networking apps as a particular attack vector.

3.3 Spoofing Social Network Logins

Social networking has been exponentially increasing in the past few years, with the rise in popularity largely due to the sites like Myspace, Facebook, and Twitter. With a website like Facebook having well over 1.2 Billion active users [13], social network users account for one of the largest user-bases available. Combined with the fact that both Facebook and Twitter apps come preinstalled on many Android smartphones, the attack surface available to spoof a social networking application is very large. However, users do not hold access to their social networking accounts as important as access to more important accounts, like bank accounts and online shopping sites. This leads to weaker passwords, and password reuse [14] which furthers the expected value of intercepting this data. As an added benefit, some social networks use the user's email address as the account identifier. By capturing this data along with a valid password, a malicious app would have the ability to access some percentage of users email accounts, due to password reuse as mentioned previously. Many online services allow someone with access to the email address associated with an account to reset the password, thereby gaining access without knowing the chosen password *a priori*. All of these factors combine to make users' social network credentials highly desirable targets. To demonstrate the ease of these kinds of attacks, a proof-of-concept app was developed, and is discussed below.

3.4 Spoofed Activity Attack

In order to demonstrate the ease and effectiveness of spoofing popular applications, we have created a proof-of-concept attack on the Facebook app for Android. A true attacker would implement the activity spoofing code within another seemingly benign app; however, for our purposes, we have simply implemented a stand-alone app. Regardless of how the code is loaded, the app will generally follow a *monitor-capture-exfiltrate* cycle.

Monitoring. In order to spoof an activity, the attacking app must know when the intended activity is being launched. This is trivial if the user is already using the attacking app; but if they aren't, Android provides the ability for apps to launch background tasks called *services*. Our app uses a service which is detached from the app itself, allowing for it to continue to run in the background even after the app's activities are stopped. This service monitors Android's `ActivityManager`, which allows it to launch the spoofed activity as soon as any app requests for the intended activity to be launched.

Capture. Once the intended activity has been launched, our monitor launches the spoofed activity. This ensures it appears after, and therefore, above the intended activity. By utilizing Apktool [9], we have simply copied the relevant design assets and XML files which describe the look and feel of Facebook's app into our own, making the intended and spoofed activities appear identical (Fig. 1 is taken from our proof-of-concept). The users have no possible way of knowing that they are interacting with the spoofed activity, instead of the

Fig. 3. User's credentials captured by a spoofed activity

intended activity. Once the users attempt to authenticate, the spoofing app will intercept and capture their credentials, unbeknown to them.

Exfiltrate. While our proof of concept simply displays the captured values back to the user (Figure 3), a real application could exfiltrate this data, possibly over the network to a remote server. This presents the most challenging part of the spoofing attack, as tools like TaintDroid [15] exist to track this kind of information flow. However, none of the currently available flow analysis tools would flag this particular information leak, as the user is providing the information willingly, and from their memory or other medium outside the control of the phone. Therefore, any systems-based approach [16–18] wouldn't be able to differentiate this kind of data from valid data captured by the intended app itself. Significantly more intrusive and resource intensive methods would have to be employed for one of these systems to be able to differentiate between spoofed and valid authentication attempts at the activity level.

4   Defenses

While activity spoofing is hard to prevent and easy to implement, there exist a wide range of possible defenses. Any defensive measure must prevent activity spoofing from occurring while allowing benign apps to continue to reuse third party components. In addition, if the defense is to be practical, it must have a very low level of false positives (benevolent apps which are flagged as malicious) and have minimal impact on the user. False negatives (spoofed activities which are not caught) are acceptable as some protection is better than no protection; but false positives will lead to users bypassing any protections offered in order to simply achieve their desired functionality. Correctly identifying spoofing attempts is difficult because of the plethora of ways to emulate another activities functionality. Below we discuss two fundamental types of preventative measures, including analysis of a current solution [19]. We then offer a refinement on one of our proposed models, which offers a variable level of required user interaction, and protects against a wide range of attacks.

One strategy to defend against phishing is to deploy other apps which monitor or otherwise protect against phishing attempts. This approach has a low barrier to entry, and allows for widespread distribution even to older Android devices which may not receive official system updates. However, app-based solutions will have a limited ability to actively protect the user from other apps, and while monitoring and alerting users to potential threats is worthwhile, a better defense mechanism might be sought when valuable personal information is at risk.

4.1 Secure Phrases

On the Internet, websites have long dealt with phishing and spoofing attacks. One of the most popular methods of combating these attacks is the use of secure phrases and images [21–23]. These images or phrases are set up after successfully authenticating for the first time, and are displayed on the authentication page the subsequent times when users visit the site. This approach requires app developers to modify the apps' implementation. However, most major providers already have the infrastructure in place to offer this service via their web apps. All that would be required is a translation of the feature to work on an Android device. However, since this approach requires minimal work at the Android device, it is also the least effective. While rendering the simple implementation discussed previously ineffective, adding a secure phrase wouldn't prevent more complex spoofing attacks. For example, the spoofing activity could simply implement a transparent frame. If placed in the correct spot on screen, this transparency would give the appearance of displaying the secure phrase or image as if it was being displayed by the spoofing activity itself.[1] On the other hand, this approach introduces zero false positive, and does not restrict activity reuse in any way.

4.2 Spoof Killer

The main idea behind Spoof Killer [19] is to introduce a system interrupt into the login procedure, during which the system verifies that the current context, or the application from which the login request was generated, matches some sort of internal whitelist or certificate list. If the context is safe, the login proceeds, and is otherwise aborted. This system interrupt takes the form of requesting the user activate a pre-defined interrupt key, like the home key on Android phones. This requires users to correctly execute an additional step every time they login

---

[1] As of Android 4.0, there are built-in measures to guard against such attacks. But by 2014, the top five banking and social network apps have not yet implemented any sort of secondary security measures.

to any app. From a usability perspective this may not be advantageous, as it introduces another step during which a user could fail the login procedure. This may lead users to find the feature cumbersome, and disable it or find an alternate (and thereby more insecure) method of authentication. However, as was outlined in the cited page, when correctly used this feature builds a behavior into users that provides inertia against attacks that try and bypass this mechanism.

From a technical standpoint, requiring a global interrupt for any app authentication must be handled by the app developers, as there is no way for the system to detect every application's version of authentication unless they are using some standardized authentication feature. This could hamper usability as not all applications will implement the system interrupt feature, leading users to either distrust valid applications, or to not form the habit of initiating the interrupt, which weakens the protection provided. Also, by relying on a whitelist, Spoof Killer implicitly places the burden of ensuring an up-to-date whitelist on the end user's system, which may or may not be feasible for all platforms, specifically enterprise infrastructures which largely follow out-of-band update cycles. These concerns lead us to an alternate paradigm for less intrusive protection that requires no prior knowledge of trust.

5   Trusted Activity Chains

We now propose a system-level defense which provides a new framework feature to app developers, called Trusted Activity Chains. We will give an overview of the approach, discuss the components of our framework, potential issues which arise from this model, and the impacts it has on both the usability and security of an Android device.

5.1   Overview

Our framework introduces the concept of sequences of activities which should not be interrupted. App developers should be able to simply annotate a chain of activities with a request that they not be interrupted, and the system should handle the rest. In keeping with the design ideas of the Android framework, at any given time only one activity is displayed in the foreground. The app which owns this activity can therefore be considered the "foreground app". When an activity is brought into the foreground, it requests a lock, signaling that it should not be interrupted. Once this lock is granted by the operating system, the system will begin to monitor any attempts by other apps, background services, or other process to launch a new activity. Depending on the configuration, the system will handle these requests differently than it normally would (e.g. let the activity launch). Once the foreground activity is finished, the next activity in the uninterrupted chain will be launched, or the lock will be given up and the system will revert to standard behavior, allowing any activity to be launched.

5.2 Components

There are a number of interactions that Trusted Activity Chains give rise to. In order for the concept to work, we need to have processes to deal with how an activity acquires the interrupt lock, how it releases the same lock, how the OS manages the lock, and what happens when there is an attempted interruption while the lock is being held. Figure 4 gives a state diagram for the possible states of the lock, which will be referenced below.

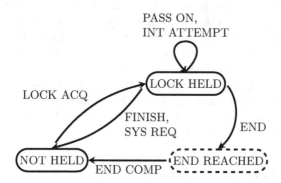

Fig. 4. State Diagram for Lock Life Cycle

Acquisition and Release. To acquire the interrupt lock, an activity simply needs to be marked as requesting the lock. When the `ActivityManager` launches such an activity, it will also check if the lock is free (`NOT HELD`). If so, it assigns the lock to the launching activity (`LOCK ACQ`), and allows it to launch without further interference. The activity now holds the lock (`LOCK HELD`), and may do any number of things with it. If the activity (such as a login screen) wants to assure that the next activity the user is shown upon successful authentication in the app's home screen, then the home screen can be tagged as the end point for the lock (`END`). This allows for the application to ensure that no other activities will be launched before its home screen is displayed (`END REACHED`, `END COMP`), which protects against post-authentication spoofing, such as a malicious activity launching a cloned version of the intended activity's error dialog for a failed authentication, and asking the user to try again. If the chain of activities which request the lock does not end at the app's home screen, the lock is simply transferred to the next activity (`PASS ON`), and the cycle continues.

Alternatively, the lock-holding activity may simply release the lock when it is paused or removed from the foreground (`FINISH`). This can be caused either by design when the activity is the last one the app wishes to display for the moment; or by the system if it needs to execute an action such as locking the screen or displaying information on an incoming call (`SYS REQ`). Since these activities can only be initiated by the system or the user via hardware buttons, they are safely allowed to override the lock.

Management. The Android framework already handles all activity lifetime services through a central class, the `ActivityManager` [20]. Using this class to simply keep track of which activity, if any, currently has the lock allows for all of the features discussed. The OS must simply pass control back through the `ActivityManager` any time it requests control from activities, so that the lock can correctly be released in these scenarios. This both encapsulates all modifications, and keeps the overhead imposed to a minimum.

Interrupt Handling. While the lock is held, if a third party app attempts to launch an activity, the `ActivityManager` intercepts this request, and can handle it depending upon the configuration of the system. Some options include alerting the user that a third party activity is trying to launch, and notify the user that the third party activity will be launched at the completion of the current app's sequence (`INT ATTEMPT`). While effective, this may be too heavy-handed, and so the OS could allow the third party activity to be launched, but require it identify itself as a third party. The Android framework already includes a mechanism for this by way of title bars. Title bars are an UI element that may optionally be turned off, depending on the theme selected by the app developer. This allows for a visual cue that the current activity is different from the activity that was just in focus.

5.3   Potential Issues

Trusted Activity Chains allow for a very robust defense against many kinds of spoofing and phishing attacks. However, there are some potential drawbacks which could limit the effectiveness of this mechanism. As with any system which employs a locking mechanism, we must handle the possibility of race conditions and deadlocks. Because Trusted Activity Chains require developers to adapt their apps to the framework, we also must address intentional and unintentional misuse by developers, along with issues of adoption.

Race Conditions and Deadlocks. Race conditions could occur when two or more activities are launched, each of which requests the interrupt lock. Due to the nature of Android, the order of activity launches is not precise, but is atomic. That is, one of the activities that is attempting to launch will be first, and will be launched before any of the other activities are picked by the system to begin the launch process. This ensures that one activity will always be able to fully acquire the lock before another activity is allowed to check the status of the lock. Therefore, while the activity receiving the lock may not always be the one expected to receive it, there is never a situation in which two activities simultaneously will have the lock.

Similarly, deadlocks are never an issue, as even in the case where an activity never manually releases the lock, any actionable item the system has to deal with automatically releases the lock. This includes the user pressing the hardware buttons, allowing the user control even in the event of a malfunction.

Developer Misuse. In order for Trusted Activity Chains to protect an activity, the developers of that activity must flag that it requests the lock. This kind of control can of course be misused by developers unfamiliar with the system, as well as opening up a possible attack vector. Fortunately, Trusted Activity Chains are resilient against all forms of misuse. If a developer were to tag an activity as requesting the lock unintentionally, the app will still function, but will simply prevent third party activities from launching. Even if the mistakenly tagged activity requires data from a third party activity to function, because the launch request for the third party activity originates from the activity with the lock, it will be allowed to launch and run as normal.

While inadvertent misuse is a honest scenario to consider when designing a framework, malicious misuse generally is more potentially damaging. However, because our framework is overridden when the system has tasks to handle, a malicious developer is not granted any more power than they already have within the larger Android framework.

Adoption. There are innumerable proposed extensions to Android for the purpose of enhanced security [15–19], all of which have varying levels of security, usability, and overhead. In addition to the vast number of users who are either indifferent or unaware of the security concerns with Android, this plethora of options makes adoption of any one strategy difficult. Furthermore, Trusted Activity Chains require developers to write apps with them in mind in order to be of use.

While these obstacles do exist, Trusted Activity Chains are still useful even without a widespread adoption. We allow for apps using our modifications to interact seamlessly with other apps and the system as a whole. This incremental approach allows for developers to slowly integrate Trusted Activity Chains into their apps at their own pace, which slowly builds momentum. It also relieves the pressure to patch all old apps immediately, as they too can be slowly phased in as time allows.

Trusted Activity Chains can be easily added to old and new applications with very few lines of code. Since the locking and unlocking mechanism does not impair application functionality even when misused, developers can integrate Trusted Activity Chains with confidence that they are not introducing bugs. We also note that by adding support, developers are taking an action which protects their users, which can generate positive press for the developer's apps. It can also call attention to other apps which fail to use this feature. This form of peer pressure can further drive adoption.

5.4   Implications

While providing a high level of protection, our framework could hurt usability. Therefore, we offer a less defensive, but more transparent method of functionality, wherein third party activities which launch during other app's activity chains are required to identify themselves to the user. This would alert the user to the presence of a activity which did not belong to the foreground app. While this

Fig. 5. The spoofed activity with Trusted Activity Chains enabled

does not guarantee that a user won't fall for a spoofed activity, it does allow easy identification of the intended activity in contrast with the spoofed activity. This defense has the added benefit of giving apps more control over how they interact with other portions of the Android system.

We note that this approach, like that of [19] requires developers to actively implement new features in the apps for the defense to function. However, apps which lack our approach do not function incorrectly in its absence, but are merely less secure. This allows for our approach to be implemented without prior widespread adoption as discussed above. Also, our approach is both flexible and extendable, and can be used for non-security related problems as well as protecting against many kinds of malicious behaviors.

6   Evaluation

To validate the efficacy of our proposed defense mechanism, we developed a prototype of Trusted Activity Chains. Then, we evaluated its effectiveness and usability via a case study, as well as performance impact on the Android smartphone. It is important that the proposed Trusted Activity Chains can be easily used by normal users, while its performance overhead is minor for using them. Our experiments were conducted using a Motorola device with a 550MHz ARM A8 processor and 256MB of RAM, running Android 2.2.3. For the purposes of evaluation, our defense mechanism was configured to simply block third-party app execution while a Trusted Activity Chain is underway. This allows for the most accurate performance measurements to be collected.

6.1   Effectiveness and Usability

Obviously, in the mode where third party launches are forbidden during a Trusted Activity Chain, a user will be simply unaware of the attempt assuming that the app developer has correctly annotated their app. So, we have only validated the effectiveness and usability when the mechanism is configured to allow third party apps to launch, but force them to show their title bars. We conducted a case study with a small group of users (<10) who do not use an Android device on a regular basis. We explained the purpose of the study, and told them to use the test device to log on to Facebook, take a photo, and share it. We did not give any information on how Trusted Activity Chains work, nor that there was any modification to the Android device. The Facebook app leverages the stock Android camera app to take photos, which means that it will allow third party code to run when the users attempt to take a picture. We have modified the Facebook app so that this action will occur during a Trusted Activity Chain to simulate developer misuse. We have also left our attack application running, which means the users will be confronted with the spoofed Facebook login activity before getting to the real activity. However, as per our configuration, the spoofed activity will be forced to display a title bar, which will display the app name to which the activity belongs.

During the initial launch, the users correctly identified that the spoofed activity was not the true Facebook login screen, but could not pinpoint the reason beyond that it looked different than what they were used to. This shows that

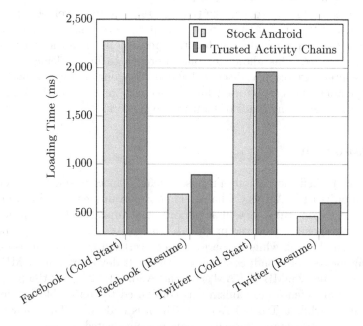

Fig. 6. Average load time for social networking app

even if a malicious application chose a name very similar to the one of the app it was attempting to spoof, users may still be able to discern the difference under our framework. After identifying the fraud, the users were unsure what to do to proceed, but were able to complete a valid login. However, when they attempted to take a picture, they again noticed that the camera app seemed different, and decided to cancel taking the picture. While this outcome is not a failure of our framework but rather due to developer misuse, our future work will consider how to resolve this type of false-positives.

6.2 Performance

In order to measure the performance overhead associated with Trusted Activity Chains, we took measurements of the total time elapsed to launch two social networking apps with and without the defense mechanism enabled. We tested both a cold start of the app along with resuming the app after five minutes of web browsing. We installed our attack application, which monitors for the launch of either app, and attempts to launch its own spoofed version of the login screens. These scenarios were repeated 10 times each, and we took the average time after dropping the highest and lowest times for each.

As we can see in Figure 6, the overhead during a cold start is barely recognizable. This is due to the initialization which must be undertaken for an app to be started for the first time taking much more time than our monitoring. However, on a resume we do see an extra delay. Note that the overall times it takes to resume the app are already rather high at 690ms and 460ms, respectively, under normal conditions. Thus, even though we introduce an extra delay of ~170ms, a user will likely not notice it because the normal transition delays are more than two to three times larger than this additional delay. Furthermore, users expect there to be some delay when moving between apps, as Android's UI shows transition effects when performing a context switch. From these observations, we can conclude that Trusted Activity Chains does not impair normal functionality of an Android device, and can be included without noticeable performance degradation.

7   Related Work

Previous work has identified flaws with both the Android IPC model [7] and the permission model [11]. This work identifies similar possible attack models, including Intent spoofing and activities external to the launcher's app returning information to the launcher. We take this a step further by silently monitoring for valid launches of activities and inject spoofed versions of these activities. A similar attack was presented in [24], however no publications have resulted.

Felt and Wagner [25] detailed numerous categories of phishing attacks levied at mobile devices, including spoofing an activities login screen. This work builds on their result to show an embedded approach, as well as revealing some of the technical features which enable this class of attacks. Further, we provide a robust defense mechanism which could protect against many of their listed attacks.

Russello *et al.* [17] built on TaintDroid [15] to provide information flow tracking as well as a fine-grained label system which allows users to allow or deny access to information on an per-app basis. Their work requires no action on the developer's behalf, but does require users to specify what data should be labeled. Users are generally less aware of application and data security concerns than developers, and this strategy might be too technical for many users.

Quire [18] offers call chain tracking to prevent confused deputy attacks [26] along with a signature scheme which allows intents to be signed and verified. This approach is limited to protecting well-meaning services from being duped by other less benevolent apps, but does not stop information leakage like what is possible via activity spoofing. More recently, ScreenPass [27] secures user passwords on touchscreen by providing a trusted password-entry user interface and defends against spoofing via optical character recognition.

Like Spoof Killer [19], we demonstrate a defense against spoofing attacks. However, our modification requires no whitelists, and protects users from a broad class of attacks as opposed to only protecting against login phishing attacks. Similar to the cited method, our approach does require developer involvement.

8   Conclusion

In this paper, we have presented a simple but dangerous exploit of the Android framework that allows arbitrary applications to spoof sensitive activities of other applications in order to collect private data without users' knowledge. This can be accomplished because of an inability to identify what app a given activity belongs to. We have developed a simple method for constructing spoof activities and integrating them into stand-alone or existing code. The danger of this exploit lies in the simplicity of engineering a spoofed activity for any service that provides a native app for Android, and the ease of collecting the harvested data from user devices. We have then described possible defenses to this class of attacks, considering some existing methods before introducing Trusted Activity Chains. We have demonstrated that Trusted Activity Chains are robust and provide an easy way to optimize for security and usability. We have also shown that they have minor impact on performance. We have further discussed the details of how Trusted Activity Chains support spoofing prevention without the pitfalls generally associated with locking mechanisms.

Our future work includes expanding the proposed defense mechanism, along with a large scale usability study to further demonstrate both the severity of the exploit and the effectiveness of our defense framework. The requirement of developer action to secure users' devices is less than ideal, and we would like to develop an automated method to detect which activities need to be protected and which do not. We also would like to implement a full version of our defense, and integrate it into the Android open source project.

References

[1] Canalys. Press Release 2011/081. Android takes almost 50% share of worldwide smartphone market (August 1, 2011),
http://www.canalys.com/newsroom/android-takes-almost-50-share-worldwide-smart-phone-market

[2] Sheng, S., Magnien, B., Kumaraguru, P., Acquisti, A., Cranor, L.F., Hong, J., Nunge, E.: Anti-Phishing Phil: The Design and Evaluation of a Game That Teaches People Not to Fall for Phish. In: Symposium On Usable Privacy and Security, pp. 88–99 (2007)

[3] Abu-Nimeh, S., Nappa, D., Wang, X., Nair, S.: A Comparison of Machine Learning Techniques for Phishing Detection. In: APWG eCrime Researchers Summit, Pittsburgh, PA, pp. 60–69 (2007)

[4] Bian, K., Park, J., Hsiao, M.S., Bélanger, F., Hiller, J.: Evaluation of Online Resources in Assisting Phishing Detection. In: 9th IEEE International Symposium on Applications and the Internet, Bellevue, WA, pp. 30–36 (2009)

[5] Xiang, G., Hong, J., Rose, C.P., Cranor, L.F.: CANTINA+: A Feature-rich Machine Learning Framework for Detecting Phishing Web Sites. ACM Trans. on Inf. and Syst. Security 14(21) (2011)

[6] Android Dev Guide. Tasks and Back Stack (August 28, 2011),
http://developer.android.com/guide/topics/fundamentals/tasks-and-back-stack.html

[7] Chin, E., Felt, A.P., Greenwood, K., Wagner, D.: Analyzing Inter-Application Communication in Android. In: ACM MobiSys, Washington, D.C., pp. 239–252 (2011)

[8] Davi, L., Dmitrienko, A., Sadeghi, A.-R., Winandy, M.: Privilege escalation attacks on android. In: Burmester, M., Tsudik, G., Magliveras, S., Ilić, I. (eds.) ISC 2010. LNCS, vol. 6531, pp. 346–360. Springer, Heidelberg (2011)

[9] Brut.alll. Apktool (May 15, 2011), http://code.google.com/p/android-apktool

[10] Enck, W., Octeau, D., McDaniel, P., Chaudhuri, S.: A Study of Android Application Security. In: USENIX Security, San Francisco, CA (2011)

[11] Felt, A.P., Chin, E., Hanna, S., Song, D., Wagner, D., et al.: Android Permissions Demystified. In: ACM Conference on Computer and Communication Security, Chicago, IL, pp. 627–638 (2011)

[12] Farrel, S.: API Keys to the Kingdom. IEEE Internet Computing 13(5), 91–96 (2009)

[13] Facebook. Facebook Fact Sheet (March 31, 2012),
http://newsroom.fb.com/content/default.aspx?NewsAreaId=22

[14] Ives, B., Walsh, K.R., Schneider, H.: The Domino Effect of Password Reuse. C. ACM 47(4), 75–78 (2004)

[15] Enck, W., Gilbert, P., Chun, B., Cox, L.P., Jung, J., McDaniel, P., Sheth, A.N.: TaintDroid: An Information-Flow Tracking System for Real-time Privacy Monitoring on Smartphones. In: USENIX Operation Systems Design and Implementation, Vancouver, B.C (2010)

[16] Beresford, A.R., Rice, A., Skehin, N., Sohan, R.: MockDroid: Trading privacy for application functionality on smartphones. In: 12th Workshop on Mobile Computing Systems and Applications, Phoenix, AZ, pp. 49–54 (2011)

[17] Russello, G., Crispo, B., Fernandes, E., Zhuniarovich, Y.: YAASE: Yet Another Android Security Extension. In: 3rd Conference on Privacy, Security, Risk, and Trust (PASSAT), Boston, MA, pp. 1033–1040 (2011)

[18] Dietz, M., Shekhar, S., Pisetsky, Y., Shu, A., Wallach, D.S.: Quire: Lightweight Provenance for Smartphone Operating Systems. In: USENIX Security, San Francisco, CA (2011)

[19] Jakobsson, M., Leddy, W.: Spoof Killer (May 21, 2011),
http://www.spoofkiller.com

[20] Android API Reference. ActivityManager (Mar 13, 2012),
http://developer.android.com/reference/android/
app/ActivityManager.html

[21] Dhamija, R., Tygar, J.: The battle against phishing: Dynamic security skins. In: Proceedings of the Symposium on Usable Privacy and Security (SOUPS), pp. 77–88. ACM (2005)

[22] Whalen, T., Inkpen, K.M.: Gathering evidence: use of visual security cues in web browsers. In: Proceedings of 2005 Graphics Interface (GI), pp. 137–144. Canadian Human-Computer Communications Society (2005)

[23] Schecter, S., Dhamija, R., Ozment, A., Fischer, I.: The emperor's new security indicators: An evaluation of website authentication and the effect of role playing on usability studies. In: Proceedings of IEEE Symposium on Security and Privacy (S&P), pp. 51–65 (2007)

[24] Hassell, R.: Hacking Androids for Profit (August 31, 2011),
http://conference.hitb.org/hitbsecconf2011kul/?page_id=1740

[25] Felt, A.P., Wagner, D.: Phishing on Mobile Devices. In: Web 2.0 Security and Privacy, Oakland, CA (2011)

[26] Hardy, N.: The Confused Deputy. ACM Operating Systems Review 22(4), 36–38 (1988)

[27] Liu, D., Cuervo, E., Pistol, V., Scudellari, R., Cox, L.: ScreenPass: Secure Password Entry on Touchscreen Devices. In: Proceedings of ACM MobiSys 2013, Taipei, Taiwan (June 2013)

Polymorphism as a Defense
for Automated Attack of Websites

Xinran Wang[1], Tadayoshi Kohno[2], and Bob Blakley[3]

[1] Shape Security
xinran@shapesecurity.com
[2] University of Washington
yoshi@cs.washington.edu
[3] Citigroup
bob.blakley@citi.com

Abstract. We propose PolyRef, a method for a polymorphic defense to defeat automated attacks on web applications. Many websites are vulnerable to automated attacks. Basic anti-automation countermeasures such as Turing tests provide minimal efficacy and negatively impact the usability and the accessibility of the protected application. Motivated by the observation that many automated attacks rely on interaction with the publicly visible code transmitted to the browser, PolyRef proposes to make critical elements of the underlying webpage code polymorphic, rendering machine automation impractical to implement. We categorize the threats that rely on automation and the available anti-automation approaches. We present two techniques for using polymorphism as an anti-automation defense.

1   Introduction

A web user interface (UI) is designed for manual use. The intent is that a human interacts with a web UI in a browser, and the web browser acts as a user agent to communicate with a web server. Unfortunately, by design the source code (HTML, JavaScript, and CSS) of every web page is publicly visible, and thus can be exploited by attackers in numerous ways including subjecting the website to automated attacks.

The past decade has seen a staggering diversity and volume of automated attacks on web applications. Man-in-the-Browser (MitB) attacks, such as the notorious Zeus, seize control of the end user's browser and can modify bank transactions without possessing authentication credentials or compromising any of the bank's technology infrastructure. For example, in 2007 the online banking services of KBC Bank were compromised with MitB techniques despite two-factor transactional authentication [1]. Credential stuffing attacks test a list of authentication credentials stolen from one website on a different website to discover where users have re-used their credentials. When originating from a botnet, these attacks can be indistinguishable from legitimate traffic [11]. Business logic denial-of-service (DoS) attacks interact with a website and exercise resource-intensive business logic: these attacks knock over sites without

I. Boureanu, P. Owesarski, and S. Vaudenay (Eds.): ACNS 2014, LNCS 8479, pp. 513–530, 2014.

requiring a significant volume of traffic. Furthermore, these attacks are unstoppable using traditional network DoS defenses [8].

Automation by attackers is not a new problem in web security. For lack of better options, Turing tests are widely used to block automation. As attackers have become more sophisticated about solving Turing tests, either with automation or human solvers, the tests have increased in difficulty to the point that the failure rate of humans approaches the failure rate of bots. Combinations of reputation and rate thresholds are currently promoted by application delivery controller (ADC) and web application firewall (WAF) vendors, [2] but are largely rendered obsolete by the widespread availability of botnets, which reside on the same machines as the legitimate website users.

We propose PolyRef, a novel technique using polymorphism for defense, which may offer a practical path to block certain classes of automation. Our approach is driven by the observation that today's automated interaction with a website often requires interacting with page content transmitted to the browser. By dynamically re-writing the page content, PolyRef impedes two types of attack: HTTP attacks, which rely on known POST or URL parameters to directly construct HTTP requests and DOM attacks, which manipulate DOM elements.

As shown in Fig. 1, PolyRef sits between a firewall and a web server. When a web page sent by the web server arrives, PolyRef finds the target forms and then applies reference and/or field polymorphism techniques. Note that the replacement happens for each page request. When the form is submitted, PolyRef restores the field names of the form back to their original values.

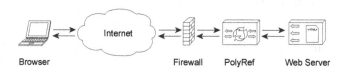

Fig. 1. PolyRef as a transparent proxy

We study several actual automated attack cases, and show how PolyRef uses reference and field polymorphism to impede unwanted automation. We also discuss potential counter attacks for PolyRef and the limitations of PolyRef.

The contributions of this Paper are summarized below.

- The paper systematically analyzes automated attacks against web applications defining a representative threat model, identifying relevant vulnerabilities, applications for automation, and implementation archetypes.
- We propose PolyRef, a new defense concept using polymorphism. We show how PolyRef deflects current generation automated attacks, and analyze impact of potential attacker evolution.
- We implement a prototype of PolyRef as a transparent proxy to protect web servers. We evaluate PolyRef in two experiments: a fake account creation attack and a Zeus MitB attack. The evaluation shows PolyRef is effective to deflect these attacks. We also evaluate PolyRef with a real world large e-commerce website and show latency is very low with caching turned on.

2   Background: Automated Attacks

We observed that many notable attacks on websites seemed to be rooted in automation, yet there are surprisingly few options for a viable defense. We set out to appreciate the extent to which automation is a current problem and look for options to mitigate the threat.

Definition 1. *Automated Attack/Automation. An interaction performed by a program on the user interface of a website where the user interface is intended exclusively for use by a human.*

2.1   Threat Model

To generalize the kinds of threats connected to automated attack of websites, we made a list of archetypical example threats. The list is derived from surveys of security practitioners for large scale websites in e-commerce, financial services, healthcare, national government, and social media, and is also informed by key threats listed in the OWASP Top 10.[1] We discarded threats and vectors not connected to automated attacks and the remainder are shown in the "Surveyed Threats" column of Table 1.

The "Attack Vectors" column of the table lists examples of the corresponding vulnerabilities that might be exploited by automation to realize a successful attack:

Credential Stuffing— The attacker tests a list of authentication credentials stolen from one website on other websites to discover where users have re-used these same credentials. Particularly useful when multiple websites can be correlated with the same credentials such as credit card and e-commerce sites.

Business Logic DoS— Denial-of-service attacks that interact with a website as if they were a human operated browser and exercise resource-intensive business logic. For example, loading a shopping cart on an e-commerce site often causes numerous writes to an underlying database.

Fake Account— Accounts used for the sole purpose of manipulation. Often created or exercised in a sufficiently large volume that they are impractical without automation.

Account Aggregation— Account aggregation services (for example, mint.com) collect and use login credentials to access their customer's bank accounts electronically and scrape information from the bank's website.

Carding— Small purchases used to verify the validity of stolen credit card data. Often operated on a large volume of low quality data and therefore reliant on automation. Particularly damaging to certain e-commerce sites as the chargeback fees can be much larger than the transactions.

Man-in-the-Browser (MitB)— A kind of man-in-the middle attack where the attacker controls the user's browser, and may observe or change information that is transmitted between the browser and the website.

---

[1] Open Web Application Security Project, www.owasp.org

Table 1. Relationship of threats to automated attack vectors

Surveyed Threats	Attack Vectors	Automation Application	Vulnerability Category
Account takeover Database scraping	Credential stuffing	Iteration	Inherent
Protection racketeering Hacktivism Masking of other attacks	Business logic DoS		
Comment SPAM Rating/review skewing Database scraping	Fake account		
Customer disintermediation Reduced security posture Database scraping	Account aggregation		
Chargeback fees	Carding		
Credential harvesting Account takeover Transaction manipulation	MitB	Manipulation	
Information leakage Loss of control	XSS CSRF		Inadvertent

XSS/CSRF— Non-persistent cross-site scripting and cross-site request forgery as defined by OWASP.

For the purpose of this threat model, we further narrowed the list of vulnerabilities and vectors to the cases where automation is required. For an attacker, automation is applied for at least two fundamentally different reasons which are noted in the "Automation Application" column of the table.

Iteration— A repeated interaction with a web user interface where a high number of iterations are required to realize value.

Manipulation— A one-time operation performed autonomously by a program over a specific web interface, because it is not practically accessible to a human attacker at the time of attack.

We distinguish between *Inadvertent* and *Inherent* vulnerabilities to highlight an observation[2] that the majority of concerns for large scale websites are for vulnerabilities not contemplated in the OWASP Top 10.

Inadvertent vulnerabilities Some attacks rely on vulnerabilities that are the product of implementation errors or design failures. In theory, this category of vulnerability never need exist and when discovered can be corrected without impacting user experience, business requirements, or application functionality. Many well known web application vulnerabilities such as CSRF, XSS, SQL injection, and the remainder of the OWASP Top 10 belong to this category.

Inherent vulnerabilities Many modern website attacks rely on vulnerabilities that are the byproducts of fundamental design requirements or conditions not

---

[2] Perhaps our survey suffered from a type of selection bias where our sample had sufficient budgets to remediate the better understood inadvertent vulnerabilities.

under the control of the solution architect. For example, a credential stuffing vulnerability stems from the requirement that sites must allow anonymous connections to attempt authentication, or they fail to meet the most fundamental business need: access from the Internet. To illustrate with a specific example, consider that an attacker could abuse the common security protocol of locking out an account after five consecutive login failures to create a denial-of-service attack. Depending on the design objectives of website, the solution to stop locking out accounts may not be an option. Unlike inadvertent vulnerability attacks, inherent vulnerabilities cannot be mitigated by "fixing" the application as the "fix" is at odds with a design requirement.

2.2   Methods of Automated Attacks

We classify the methods of automated attacks into three categories, each with fundamentally different approaches: *HTTP attack*, *DOM attack*, and *GUI attack*.

HTTP attack— This approach relies on manipulating the target of attack by transmitting GET or POST messages, but without any appreciation of how the target page would be rendered in a browser. A common example is a credential stuffing attack where a simple POST request is transmitted with the username and password key-value pairs. Another variation employed for manipulation instead of iteration is a CSRF attack where the HTTP GET is in the form of URL embedded in an HTML email message.

DOM attack— This attack operates inside a browser and uses JavaScript to feed input into DOM elements and perform submission. In DOM attacks, the target web page and all referenced content including JavaScript is loaded in a browser. The attack software now examines the DOM and feeds input into input elements of a target form. Because DOM attacks drive a real web browser, JavaScript, application state, cookies, nonces, sessions, properly set referrers, and other dependencies that arise in a complex web application are handled seamlessly. MitB attacks take this form (*e.g.*, Fig. 13). Most existing inherent vulnerability attacks, which exploit automation test tools such as Selenium and HtmlUnit, also take this form (*e.g.*, Fig. 11).

GUI attack— A more complicated option is when the attacker takes full control of a real browser to render the image of the target web page and interact with the web page by directing mouse movement/click and keystrokes. It can position the input focus by tab key press, x, y coordinates, or relative vectors, and then stream keystrokes into fields of focus. DOM manipulation is not necessary in this method. Note that GUI attacks need full control of a real browser and cannot be performed inside a web page by JavaScript. Although JavaScript in a web page can simulate a mouse event and cause browsers to fire the default action for the event (e.g., navigate to the link's href, or submit a form), browsers do not perform the default action for simulated keystroke events by JavaScript (e.g., browsers do not assign the value to an input field), and the actual mouse location cannot be changed by JavaScript. Many automated attacks presently implemented with the HTTP or DOM approaches could be adopted to the GUI approach by implementing them in open source automation test tools like PhantomJS.

Note that CSRF is limited to the HTTP approach, as it has no possibility to control the browser or to access the DOM of the target domain due to the same-origin policy limit. Non-persistent XSS is limited to the HTTP approach or the DOM approach, as it has no control of a browser. Other attacks may choose any of the three methods. The choice of methods depends on the attack requirements, and the methods are used differently due to the required attacker resources and the properties of the targeted web application.

2.3   Scope

In this paper, we focus on HTTP and DOM attacks. GUI attacks are out of scope. As PolyRef forces an adversary to perform GUI attacks with keyboard and mouse activity, the behavioral biometric method [13, 14] mentioned in Section 3, which can tell the difference between mouse and keystroke behaviors of a human and those of a bot, can be used to complement the PolyRef method.

2.4   Requirements for a Theoretical Ideal Mitigation Solution

Having defined automation as a fundamental and significant threat it seems clear a protection is needed. We were not able to identify any well accepted industry term of art for this class of solution and chose the term "botwall," a portmanteau of *botnet* and *firewall*.

Definition 2. *Botwall. A website security layer intended to mitigate programmatic or automated use of a website user interface that is intended exclusively for use by a human.*

We propose the following design objectives for an ideal botwall:
Preventive— Able to deflect automation.
Transparent— Does not impact the user experience.
Comprehensive— Broadly useful; not a point solution.
Facile— Easily applied to legacy websites.

3   Related Work

There is a wealth of research on web security, we survey the most relevant works here. Numerous protection techniques have been introduced during the last decade which create some friction for automation. However, all of them either have a low efficacy or a negative impact on usability.

Turing Test— CAPTCHAs [22] are widely used on web to mitigate some automated attacks. However, CAPTCHAs negatively impact the usability and the accessibility of the protected application [23]. In addition, CAPTCHAs do not work for MitB attacks.

Browser Detection— Examination of headers such as "user-agent" or exploration of expected browsers capabilities like running a JavaScript program that calculates the answer to a selected problem.

Reputation— Reputation methods are based on information about the historical activity of endpoints and their connection to activities of ill repute. These methods hinge on being able to establish the unique identity of the endpoint. Common approaches of creating a unique identity include IP address, cookies, and fingerprinting [10, 18]. IP address methods are not reliable because of dynamic IP addressing. Cookie methods are easily bypassed by removing tracking cookies [19]. The fingerprint algorithm collects information such as browser fonts, timezone, and installed plugin to uniquely identify a browser. Fingerprints may be used in combination with other techniques to facilitate a whitelist of known customer devices, or blacklists of problematic devices.

Honeypot— In the honeypot method, faked fields, links, and forms are inserted in the web page. They are invisible to users and only bots can perform the tasks in the honeypot. As honeypot forms are not real forms, honeypot methods cannot be used to prevent inherent vulnerability attacks such as MitB and credential stuffing. This method has been used to detect bots performing reconnaissance attacks [4]. This method can be used to complement PolyRef. PolyRef makes forms polymorphic and the "original" forms can be used as a honeypot.

Rate Threshold— Rate thresholds can be used to detect bots performing iteration attacks. Some application delivery controllers (load balancers) and web application firewalls (WAFs) detect bots by measuring volume and speed in the context of endpoint identity [2]. Often these implementations rely entirely on the IP address for endpoint identity but may also use cookies or browser fingerprinting. This solution is at best a modest barrier today given the widespread availability of botnets to distribute the traffic from rather broad selections of endpoints with a low request rate. This technique generally fails on the efficacy prong of our test as attackers may limit their request rate or generate requests from a botnet to bypass this form of detection. Furthermore, it also fails on the user impact test as well: IP rate-limiting may generate false positives in cases where multiple users are NATed through the same IP address.

Behavioral Biometrics— User keyboard and mouse activity can also be used to detect bots. The method injects a piece of JavaScript code in web pages which collects the user keyboard and mouse activity. The activity is sent back to web servers, and the web servers check if the results fit an expected human behavior distribution. This technique has been used to detect game bots [13], chat bots [14], and twitter and blog bots [6, 7].

Token—The secret validation token method [15, 17, 21] is a approach to defend against CSRF attacks. A secret validation token is attached to each HTTP request. If a request is missing a validation token or if the token does not match the expected value, the server rejects the request. Ollmann [20] proposed token-based methods to protect web applications against some malicious automated scanning tools. One disadvantage of this approach is that a website must maintain a large state table to validate the tokens.

Header Validation— Referer header checking is a common method to prevent CSRF. The header contains the URL of the site making the request, and thus can differentiate a same-site request from a cross-site request. A website can prevent CSRF by checking if a request was issued by the site itself. One problem of referer header checking is that it causes privacy leaking. Barth et al. [5] proposed a defense against CSRF by introducing an origin header with POST requests in the browser. It provides the security benefit of the referer header while responding to privacy concerns. Czeskis et al. [9] proposed a developer-friendly and complete coverage method called Allowed Referrer Lists (ARLs) to prevent CSRF. An ARL is a whitelist of referrer uniform resource locators (URLs) that allows browsers to withhold sending ambient authority credentials for websites wishing to be resilient against CSRF attacks.

Multi-Factor Authentication— It can be used to prevent password dictionary attacks and credential stuffing attacks. The approach requires the presentation of two or more of the three authentication factors: a knowledge factor ("something only the user knows"), a possession factor ("something only the user has"), and an inherent factor ("something only the user is"). However, this approach cannot stop MitB attacks [3].

Out-of-Band Verification— It is an effective method of combating MitB attacks. It overcomes MitB attacks by verifying the transaction details to the user over a channel other than the browser (for example, an automated telephone call or SMS). The downside of Out-of-Band Verification is a negative impact to the user experience from more and slower steps.

4   Proposal: PolyRef

The idea of PolyRef is motivated by the observation that all automated attacks are based on the fixed web page of a web user interface. PolyRef makes the web page of any web user interface polymorphic: the web page is different every time it is served. The variation introduced by PolyRef makes it hard for the attacker to predict how to automatically operate a future page. In this paper, we define Polymorphism as follows:

Definition 3. *Polymorphism. [As applied in this paper] Any technique which makes key elements of a web user interface (for example, HTML/JavaScript references) sufficiently varied for each request so that future constructions of the page are non-deterministic and render automated operation impractical.*

Unlike the use of polymorphism for the construction of malware, it is not our objective to protect intellectual property, obfuscate design, or even impede the manual reverse engineering of a given case, but to make the next case unpredictable or impede automatic program analysis.

We propose two types of polymorphism: reference and field polymorphism. Note that PolyRef is not limited to these two types. It can accommodate new types of polymorphism for any elements of HTML as attack evolves.

4.1   Reference Polymorphism

In reference polymorphism, HTML symbols such as form names, field names, and element identifiers are replaced with random character strings. Fig. 2 shows an example where the form name `Login`, the field name `lastname` and the element identifier `lastname_id` are randomized.

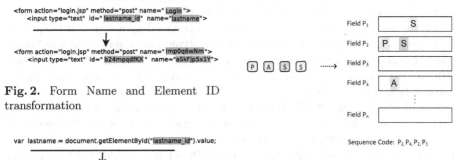

Fig. 2. Form Name and Element ID transformation

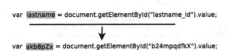

Fig. 3. Example JavaScript with transformed HTML reference

Fig. 5. Sequence code determines the order of field alternation

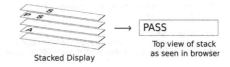

Stacked Display

PASS

Top view of stack as seen in browser

Fig. 4. Example JavaScript with a variable name randomized

Fig. 6. Stacked display preserves user experience

Form name and element identifier randomization will prevent attackers from directly locating a field. For example, using the JavaScript statement `document.-getElementByID(lastname_id)` to locate `lastname` field in Fig. 2 will not work anymore. As form name and element identifier may also be referenced in JavaScript/CSS, the randomization should be consistent. Fig. 3 shows an example of JavaScript changed with HTML symbol randomization.

Similarly, symbols in JavaScript should also be randomized. The JavaScript shown in Fig. 3 makes it clear to an attacker that the field `b24mpqdfKX` should contain a last name due to the JavaScript variable name `lastname`. A simple regular expression could allow an attacker to script the scraping of the field name from the page. Fig. 4 shows that we extend the concept of HTML polymorphism to JavaScript.

4.2   Field Polymorphism

Reference polymorphism is effective for HTTP attacks and existing DOM attacks. However, it is vulnerable to advanced DOM attacks. Advanced DOM attacks can indirectly find fields to defeat reference polymorphism. For example, instead of looking for the field `lastname`, an adversary could refer to it as the third field of the first form in DOM or even find fields based on the page structure after page rendering.

We propose field polymorphism to impede advanced DOM attacks. In field polymorphism, a field is broken into multiple fields. Keystrokes are distributed between the multiple fields in a pattern that is unique for each page served.

As shown in Fig. 5, focus is alternated between several input fields as each keystroke is typed. The alternation sequence is defined by a constant (sequence code), and a unique code is embedded into the dynamically generated JavaScript added to each page. From the website visitor's perspective, the user experience remains largely unchanged, as all fields are stacked in the display and appear like one field. (See Fig. 6.)

Examination of the POST shows the characters of a single field split between multiple name-value pairs. The constant required to reassemble the sequence was determined in advance, encrypted by a shared key only residing in the PolyRef server. It is embedded in the return POST as a hidden field. In Fig. 7, "KYTr29y7rhKJP6" is the hidden field containing the encrypted constant.

```
POST login.jsp HTTP/1.1
Host: example.com
Content-Type: application/x-www-form-urlencoded
Content-Length: 18

P1=S&P2=PS&P3&P4=A&
KYTr29y7rhKJP6=QmFzZTY0IGVuY29aW5nIHNjaGVtZXMgYXJlIGNvb
W1vbmx5IHVzZWQgd2hlbiB0aGVyZSBpcyBhIG5lZWQgdG8gZW5jb2Rl
```

```
POST /Locator/retrieveLocation.jsp  HTTP /1.1
Host:  bank.com
Content-Type: application/x-ww-form-urlencoded
Content-Length:127

latitude=37.3986039&longitude=-121.9643745&
atm=on&branch=on&specialServiceIndex=0&
service=null&region=US&distSelected=25
```

Fig. 7. Value distributed across multiple fields   **Fig. 8.** Business logic attack

5   Case Study

We study several real-world automated attack cases, and show how PolyRef defeats them with only reference polymorphism. Note that we only consider contemporary attacks (i.e., attacks that already exist today) in this Section. We will discuss future attacks in Section 8.

5.1   Cross-Site Request Forgery

Let's look at a cross-site request forgery (CSRF) attack on `bank.com`. It has a web page with a form that allows its customers to transfer money.

Assume Alice wants to transfer $50 to Bob. Although the POST method is used in the money transfer form, `bank.com` has accidentally allowed GET requests as well. Our malicious attacker, Mallet, exploits the vulnerability to automate a form submit with the URL `http://bank.com/transfer.jsp?to_account=Mall et&amount=1000` which will transfer $1000 from an unwitting victim to himself.

There are a couple of ways Mallet can trick Alice into submitting the URL. One way is to include the request as an HTML image element in an email to Alice.

Her browser will make the request automatically as if it were any other image content on a page <img src=http://bank.com/transfer?to_account=Mallet &amount=1000>. If Alice's bank keeps her authentication information in a cookie, and if the cookie has not expired, then the attempt by Alice's browser to load the image will submit the transfer request along with her cookie, thus authorizing a transaction without Alice's knowledge.

We can see that in this case, the CSRF attack must have fixed symbols for the forms parameters to work. Polymorphic references therefore stop these attacks.

5.2   Business Logic Denial-of-Service

Denial-of-service attacks have moved up the web stack from early Smurf attacks to syn floods to more modern socket exhaustion attacks. The next generation of DoS attacks focus on computationally intensive requests on back-end servers.

For web applications that must remain up-to-date or for content that cannot be cached for other reasons, distributing content on a worldwide content delivery network (CDN) is not an option. Thus requests must reach back to centralized back-end servers. One example of an attack that reaches back to a back-end server is a branch locator function.

An attacker could craft a POST like the one shown in Fig. 8 that asks a website for branch locations. This computationally intensive request could be made at arbitrary rates from a botnet until the server collapses under the computational load.

This attack is difficult to stop using current defenses. It bypasses CDN caching and does not rely on volume to overwhelm servers. It contains no malicious signature as it is, in fact, a perfectly valid request. However, if the site operator stops automation the attack is stopped.

It is clear to see that the attack shown in Fig. 8 will fail by applying reference polymorphism.

6   Design and Implementation

We constructed a prototype of PolyRef, implemented as a special case of a transparent HTTP proxy located adjacent to the web server. When a web page passes through this special proxy, PolyRef finds the target forms and then replaces selected content with a revised version applying reference polymorphism described in Section 4. Note that a different polymorphic variant is applied for each page request. When the form is later submitted, the same special proxy restores the key/value pairs of the form to the expected content so the protected web application continues to operate without modification. Since many websites terminate SSL at the load balancer, our special proxy would never see HTTPS and hence our implementation does not handle SSL directly.

Our implementation addresses the following scenario: A company — without modifying its own web servers — installs PolyRef as per Fig. 1. The implementation therefore needs to handle the complexity of modern web page design, including the use of CSS and JavaScript. There are two distinct phases for handling each web page. The first is a *pre-computation* phase, in which PolyRef learns the relevant symbols. This phase is performed automatically the first time a new page is processed and then cached, and hence can employ heavyweight techniques. Following the pre-computation phase is the *application* phase, in which the polymorphic techniques are applied. Our description below focuses on the pre-computation phase.

6.1   Web Page Transformation

If an HTTP response contains a web page, PolyRef will transform it to its polymorphic version with the polymorphic techniques described in Section 4. The transformation is trivial, if the page contains only plain HTML without CSS and JavaScript. However, today almost all web pages contain CSS and JavaScript. We must make symbols consistent among JavaScript, HTML, and CSS; otherwise, the functionality may be broken.

The process of the web page transformation is as follows. In the first step, we find target forms for transformation. The target forms are configured in a profile. We use a HTML parser to parse the web page into a DOM tree. The target forms are identified in the DOM tree. To keep consistency, once we find all relevant symbols, we need to accurately identify all references to them in CSS and JavaScript. A simple regular expression match may have problems. For example, the string `username` in line 12 of Fig. 9 is a reference to the field `username`, while the one in line 16 is not. To make symbols consistent among JavaScript, HTML, and CSS, in the second step, we parsed JavaScript and CSS into abstract syntax trees (ASTs). ASTs can tell us if a symbol is a property of a form. For example, as shown in Fig. 10 (2), `username` is the property of the form; while `username` in Fig. 10 (1) is not.

There are cases where relying on ASTs alone is not enough. For example, variable `pwd` in line 11 of Fig. 9 will be used to get the reference to field `password` and should be made consistent. To handle these cases, we do a static analysis in the analyzer step. We exploit several compiler optimization techniques such as constant folding and propagation in this step. By exploiting constant folding and propagation, the value of variable in line 11 of Fig. 9 will be made consistent. After all references are identified, symbols are randomized consistently across HTML, JavaScript, and CSS, and a new web page is generated in the serializer stage.

In this implementation, two cases are handled with human assistance. First, the fields of forms may be referenced in the `eval` function. Second, forms may be dynamically generated by JavaScript. Future work could potentially address these cases via more sophisticated automation or – changing the model slightly – combining the earlier approach with annotations or support at the web server.

6.2   HTTP Request Restoration

When the transformation is made, the mapping between symbols and randomized values is encrypted and added to the target form as a hidden field. When

```
1: <html>
2: <head>
3: <meta content="text/html; charset=utf-8" http-equiv=
4:    "Content-Type">
5: <style>
6:    input[name="username"] { background-color:red; }
7:    input[name="password"] { background-color:green; }
8: </style>
9: <script>
10:    function validate_input (form) {
11:       var pwd = "pass" + "word"
12:       var name = form.username.value;
13:       var pass = form[pwd].value;
14:       var tmp=" can not be empty";
15:       if (name == "") {
16:          alert("username" + tmp );
17:       }
18:       if (pass == "") {
19:          alert("password" + tmp);
20:       }
21:    }
22: </script>
23: </head>

24: <body>
25:    <h1>This is a test page.</h1>
26:    <form action="http://test.com/web/login00.asp" id="00"
27:       method="post" name="login00">
28:       Name:<input name="username" size="20" type="text">
29:       Password:<input name="password" size="20" type="text">
30:       <input name="button_00" type="button" value="login"
31:          onclick="validate_input(this.form) >
32:    </form>
33: </body>
34:</html>
```

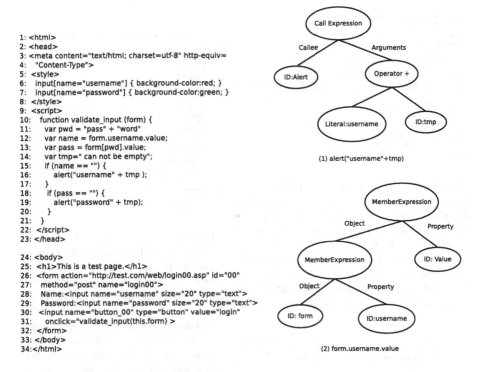

(1) alert("username"+tmp)

(2) form.username.value

Fig. 9. HTML consistency example   **Fig. 10.** AST examples

an HTTP POST request arrives, PolyRef decrypts the mapping and restores the names in the name-value pairs of the HTTP POST back to original values so the underlying web application requires no changes to work with the PolyRef. Note the encryption key is a only known by PolyRef and can be periodically rotated.

7   Evaluation

We designed three experiments to evaluate the prototype implementation of PolyRef. The first two experiments tested the effectiveness, and the third experiment tested the performance. We will discuss future attacks in Section 8.

7.1   Fake Account Creation Attack

In this Section, we first demonstrate a fake account creation attack, and then show the result after applying PolyRef. We examined the Top 10 Alexa websites, found four of them (Facebook, Yahoo, Twitter, and LinkedIn) did not require CAPTCHAs in the account creation page. We used Facebook as an example for our attack. To avoid directly attacking Facebook, we mirrored the front page (login and account creation page) of Facebook.com. We wrote a simple back-end which stored the created accounts in a database.

```
def create_fake_account(ssURL , ssFN , ssLN , ssMail , ssPass ,ssDomTag ,
    ssBm , ssBd , ssBy , ssSx ):

ssBrowserDriver = webdriver.Firefox();
ssBrowserDriver.get(ssURL);

ssLoginSignin = ssBrowserDriver.find_element_by_id("u_0_2");
ssFirstName = ssBrowserDriver.find_element_by_name("firstname");
ssLastName = ssBrowserDriver.find_element_by_name("lastname");
ssEmail = ssBrowserDriver.find_element_by_name("reg_email__");
ssEmailConfirm = ssBrowserDriver.find_element_by_name("reg_email_confirmation__");
ssPassword = ssBrowserDriver.find_element_by_name("reg_passwd__");

ssFirstName.send_keys(ssFN);
ssLastName.send_keys(ssLN);
ssEmail.send_keys(ssMail);
ssEmailConfirm.send_keys(ssMail);
ssPassword.clear();
ssPassword.send_keys(ssPass);
// Birth year, month and day are removed in the code due to space limit

ssLoginSignin.click();
```

Fig. 11. Fake account creation function. It begins by creating a Firefox driver and visiting the account creation page. It then uses the web driver API `find_element_by_id` and `find_element_by_name` to find all fields of the account creation form. It fills the fake account data into the fields by `send_keys` API and `pick_select_item` and `pick_radio_item` functions. Finally, it clicks the form submission.

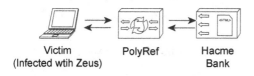

Victim   **PolyRef**   **Hacme**
(Infected wtih Zeus)   **Bank**

Fig. 12. Zeus MitB experiment setup

```
set_url "hacmebank"main.aspx?function=AccountTransfer" GP

data_before
value="Transfer" onclick="
data_end
data_inject
doTransfer();
data_end
data_after
data_end

data_before
    <body>
data_end
data_inject
<script>
    function doTransfer() {
        var destination_account = "5204320422040005";
        var tform = document.getElementById("WelComeForm");
        tform.ctl03$InternalOrExternalPayment[0].checked = false;
        tform.ctl03$InternalOrExternalPayment[1].checked = true;
        tform.ctl03_txtExternalPaymentAccount.value=destination_account;
    }
</script>
data_end
data_after
data_end
```

Fig. 13. Page injection Config for Hacmebank. The config tells Zeus to find the Hacme bank transfer account page to inject two pieces of code. The first one hijacks onclick function of "transfer" button. The second one performs the malicious transfer: replaces the transfer destination to the attacker's account 05. Parameter `set_url` sets the attack target; Parameter `data_before` describes the data to search for before the injection; Parameter `data_inject` is the actual script that will be injected.

The attack is written as a Python script using Selenium Webdriver API. Selenium is a software testing framework for web applications. The attack script exploits Selenium Webdriver API to drive a Firefox browser to launch the attack. Fig. 11 shows the source code of the fake account creation function. It only contains tens of lines of Python code. Note that the Python import header is ignored for brevity.

We used the attack script to attack our mirrored Facebook.com and we successfully created 1000 accounts. We deployed a PolyRef in front of the mirrored Facebook.com. We launched the attack again, and all 1000 attempts failed. We tested the account creation manually through the user interface and creation still works with PolyRef deployed.

7.2   Zeus MitB Attack

In this experiment, we show how Zeus performs a Man-in-the-Browser attack. Then, we demonstrate how our PolyRef blocks Zeus's attack.

Experiment Setup. Fig. 12 shows the setup of this experiment. We used McAfee's Hacme Bank, a security training bank application built on Microsoft

IIS/.Net framework. It is a database driven application. Hacme Bank provides a minimal representation of a financial institution such as authenticated accounts with balances and fund transfers between accounts.

Alex is a customer of Hacme Bank. Unfortunately, Alex's laptop is infected with Zeus malware. When Alex logs into Hacme Bank, the Zeus malware hijacks the session by page injection and secretly transfers money to attacker Mallet. One benefit of page injection is that Zeus is able to bypass two-factor authentication.

Victim Alex's machine is installed with Windows 7, Service pack 1, and IE 10 is installed and used as the browser. The victim machine was infected with our custom Zeus, created with a Zeus 2.0.8.9 builder. It is configured with a page injection file webinjects.txt, shown in Fig. 13.

Experiment. In the experiment, we show account transfers from a clean machine and a machine infected with Zeus. We created user Alex and two accounts 01 and 02. We also deposited $10000 and $100 into these two accounts, respectively. We started the victim machine without Zeus infection. We logged into Hacme Bank as Alex. We did an account transfer: $1000 from account 01 to 02. The account balance of account 01 and 02 became $9000 and $1100, respectively.

Then, we infected the victim machine with the Zeus sample created in our setup. We did another transfer after infection: $500 from account 01 to 02. The account balance shows $500 was deducted from account 01, but the balance of account 02 did not increase. The transaction details show the transfer destination is account 05 instead of account 02. This transaction was hijacked by Zeus.

We then deployed the PolyRef. We did a final transfer: $400 from account 01 to account 02. We checked the account balance and transaction details. There are no malicious transactions. The result shows PolyRef successfully deflected the Zeus MitB attack. The Zeus MitB attack failed to reference the account transfer form `WelComeForm` and the payment destination field `ctl03_txtExternalPaymen tAccount` in the `doTransfer` function (Fig. 13) because of the reference polymorphism.

7.3   Performance

In this experiment, we showed that the additional latency to deliver the login page for a popular e-commerce website is very low—if we cache the results of our first-time analysis. We ran PolyRef on a laptop with a quad-core Intel CPU and 16G memory. We used the laptop as a proxy to visit the login page of the tested website, stubhub.com[3]. The average additional latency to load the login page is shown in Table 2. We tested the latency with 1 to 32 concurrent threads in 6 tests, and each test was performed for 60 seconds. We used Apache JMeter to measure the result. Note that we started our test after page analysis cache was created during the first visit. Although the first-time analysis of the page (particularly the JavaScript) is time-consuming, it only needs to be done once.

---

[3] One of the largest online ticket marketplaces.

Table 2. The latency generated by PolyRef

Concurrent threads	1	4	8	16	24	32
Average latency (ms)	4	4	6	10	13	13

8 Discussion

We view PolyRef as the first step in polymorphic defense for websites. Adversaries, once they learn about PolyRef, may be able to tailor their attack techniques to target PolyRef's current defenses. In this section we discuss potential challenges and next steps, and we encourage future research on polymorphic defenses for web security.

8.1 Attacker Response

Field polymorphism raises the bar for advanced DOM attacks. An adversary may respond to field polymorphism by automatically extracting the sequence code from the dynamically generated JavaScript for each page served. It may be not hard for a skilled adversary to manually reverse the obfuscated JavaScript code of a page and extract the sequence code. However, DOM attacks have to perform automatic static analysis, as the sequence code is unique for each page served. Automatic static analysis of JavaScript is difficult, if not impossible, due to a number of dynamic features [16] and hard-to-understand semantic features [12] of JavaScript. In addition, the dynamically generated JavaScript can be highly obfuscated which makes the automatic analysis even harder. Obfuscation techniques including, but not limited to, variable and function name replacement, dead code insertion, encryption, string and number encoding, eval hiding, and opaque predicates, can be used to impede future attacks.

Eval hiding — hides the usage of eval function. Eval is commonly used to run code stored as a string in a variable which makes static analysis hard or even impossible. To hide uses of eval function, eval functions are assigned to various randomly named variables.

Opaque predicate — is defined as an expression for which the outcome is predetermined to be always true or false. The most simple example of this is expression *if (true)*. Opaque predicates can thwart static analysis by constructing expressions that are not so simple to determine without evaluating them inside the targeted environment.

8.2 Limitations

The limitation of PolyRef is that it does not prevent GUI attacks (where the attacker controls a real browser and interacts by directing mouse movement and keystrokes) as defined in Section 2. A GUI attack is equipped with a fully functional browser and sends OS mouse and keyboard events to the browser to simulate human interaction. It positions the input focus by x, y coordinates or relative vectors, and then streams keystrokes into the field of focus. As the attack relies on fixed x, y coordinates of web UI elements, a new type of polymorphism—view polymorphism, where view will be varied for each page served, may be used to impede such attacks. For example, locations of forms and fields can be changed slightly for each HTTP request, so that the x and y coordinates are unpredictable. In practice, moving a form slightly down in the browser may not affect the user experience. On the other hand, as mentioned in Section 2, the attack relies on simulating keyboard and mouse activity so the behavioral biometric method [13,14] mentioned in Section 3, which can tell the difference of mouse and keystroke behaviors between human and bot, could be used to complement PolyRef. Finally, the impact of GUI attacks is limited; that method does not enable CSRF or non-persistent XSS attacks.

9 Conclusion

We propose PolyRef, a method for a polymorphic defense to defeat automated attacks on web applications. PolyRef broadly deflects many types of automated attacks. As a preventive technique, it does not have false positive or false negatives. Further, the PolyRef concept is transparent to the web server, and most importantly, it has no deleterious user impact.

References

1. Belgisch gerecht ontdekt oplichting bij internetbankieren (2010)
   http://www.hbvl.be/nieuws/economie/aid956766/
   belgisch-gerecht-ontdekt-grootschalige-bankfraude.aspx
2. BIG-IP application security manager (2013),
   http://www.f5.com/pdf/products/
   big-ip-application-security-manager-ds.pdf
3. Multi-factor authentication (2013),
   http://en.wikipedia.org/wiki/Multi-factor_authentication
4. Mykonos web security (2013),
   http://www.mykonossoftware.com
5. Barth, A., Jackson, C., Mitchell, J.C.: Robust defenses for cross-site request forgery. In: Proceedings of the 15th ACM Conference on Computer and Communications Security, CCS 2008, pp. 75–88. ACM, New York (2008)
6. Chu, Z., Gianvecchio, S., Koehl, A., Wang, H., Jajodia, S.: Blog or block: Detecting blog bots through behavioral biometrics. Comput. Netw. 57(3), 634–646 (2013)
7. Chu, Z., Gianvecchio, S., Wang, H., Jajodia, S.: Who is tweeting on twitter: Human, bot, or cyborg? In: Proceedings of the 26th Annual Computer Security Applications Conference. ACM, New York (2010)
8. Crosby, S.A., Wallach, D.S.: Denial of service via algorithmic complexity attacks. In: Proceedings of the Usenix Security Symposium 2003, Berkeley, CA, USA, pp. 243–255. USENIX Association (2003)

9. Czeskis, A., Moshchuk, A., Kohno, T., Wang, H.J.: Lightweight server support for browser-based csrf protection. In: Proceedings of the 22nd International Conference on World Wide Web, WWW 2013 Companion, Republic and Canton of Geneva, Switzerland, pp. 273–284. International World Wide Web Conferences Steering Committee (2013)

10. Eckersley, P.: How unique is your web browser? In: Atallah, M.J., Hopper, N.J. (eds.) PETS 2010. LNCS, vol. 6205, pp. 1–18. Springer, Heidelberg (2010)

11. Fontana, J.: Password's rotten core not complexity but reuse (March 2013), http://www.zdnet.com/passwords-rotten-core-not-complexity-but-reuse-7000013019/

12. Gardner, P.A., Maffeis, S., Smith, G.D.: Towards a program logic for JavaScript. In: Proceedings of the 39th Annual ACM SIGPLAN-SIGACT Symposium on Principles of Programming Languages, POPL 2012, pp. 31–44. ACM, New York (2012)

13. Gianvecchio, S., Wu, Z., Xie, M., Wang, H.: Battle of botcraft: Fighting bots in online games with human observational proofs. In: Proceedings of the 16th ACM Conference on Computer and Communications Security, CCS 2009, pp. 256–268. ACM, New York (2009)

14. Gianvecchio, S., Xie, M., Wu, Z., Wang, H.: Measurement and classification of humans and bots in internet chat. In: Proceedings of the 17th Conference on Security Symposium, SS 2008, pp. 155–169. USENIX Association, Berkeley (2008)

15. Heiderich, M.: Csrfx (2007), http://php-ids.org/category/csrfx/

16. Jensen, S.H., Jonsson, P.A., Møller, A.: Remedying the eval that men do. In: Proceedings of the 2012 International Symposium on Software Testing and Analysis, pp. 34–44. ACM, New York (2012)

17. Jovanovic, N., Kirda, E., Kruegel, C.: Preventing cross site request forgery attacks. In: Second IEEE Communications Society/CreateNet International Conference on Security and Privacy in Communication Networks. IEEE (2006)

18. Kee, T.: Beyond cookies: digital fingerprints may track personal devices (December 2010), http://econsultancy.com

19. Miessler, D.: Bypassing WAF anti-automation using burp's cookie jar (September 2013), http://www.danielmiessler.com

20. Ollmann, G.: Stopping automated application attack tools. Technical report, Black Hat Europe 2006 (2006)

21. Sheridan, E.: OWASP CSRFGuard project (2008), http://www.owasp.org/index.php/CSRF_Guard

22. von Ahn, L., Blum, M., Hopper, N.J., Langford, J.: CAPTCHA: using hard ai problems for security. In: Biham, E. (ed.) EUROCRYPT 2003. LNCS, vol. 2656, pp. 294–311. Springer, Heidelberg (2003)

23. Yan, J., El Ahmad, A.S.: Usability of CAPTCHAs or usability issues in CAPTCHA design. In: Proceedings of the 4th Symposium on Usable Privacy and Security, SOUPS 2008, pp. 44–52. ACM, New York (2008)

Fragmentation Considered Leaking: Port Inference for DNS Poisoning

Haya Shulman and Michael Waidner

Fachbereich Informatik
Technische Universität Darmstadt
Darmstadt, Germany
{haya.shulman,michael.waidner}@cased.de

Abstract. Internet systems and networks have a long history of attacks by off-path adversaries. An off-path adversary cannot see the traffic exchanged by the legitimate end points, and in the course of an attack it attempts to impersonate some victim by injecting spoofed packets into the communication flow. Such attacks subvert the correctness and availability of Internet services and, among others, were applied for DNS cache poisoning, TCP injections, reflection DDoS attacks.

A significant research effort is aimed at hardening client systems against off-path attacks by designing challenge-response defences, whereby random challenges are sent with the request and the responses are validated to echo the corresponding values.

In this work we study the security of a standard and widely deployed challenge-response defence port randomisation, and show that off-path attackers can *efficiently* and *stealthily* learn the ports selected by end systems.

We show how to apply our techniques for DNS cache poisoning. We tested our attacks against standard and patched operating systems and popular DNS resolvers software. Our results motivate speeding up adoption of cryptographic defences for DNS.

Keywords: Challenge-response defences, DNS cache poisoning, fragmentation.

1 Introduction

Cryptography has known decades of research with numerous schemes, however, very few of those results are actually used in practice. Most Internet traffic is still not cryptographically protected, and basic systems and protocols, such as routing and naming, that constitute foundations of the Internet, are not protected. There is some (albeit limited) deployment of cryptography, mainly for protection of web traffic, e.g., based on the CAIDA dataset of 3 million packets [1] we found that only about 6% of the TCP traffic is cryptographically protected with SSL/TLS.

Currently, most systems deploy challenge-response defences, which provide security guarantees against off-path adversaries. Unlike a man-in-the-middle (MitM) adversary, an off-path adversary cannot observe nor modify legitimate

I. Boureanu, P. Owesarski, and S. Vaudenay (Eds.): ACNS 2014, LNCS 8479, pp. 531–548, 2014.

packets exchanged between other parties. Off-path adversaries typically launch attacks by transmiting packets that contain a *spoofed* (fake) source IP address - impersonating some legitimate party; see attacker model in Figure 1. Spoofed packets are used in many attacks, most notably, in cache poisoning and Denial of Service (DoS) attacks. Significant efforts are invested to enforce ingress filtering, [RFC3704], in order to prevent spoofing. However, IP spoofing is still possible via many ISPs and networks, [2].

Challenge-response authentication provides means to distinguish between packets sent from spoofed source IP addresses and packets exchanged between legitimate communication end-points. In order to authenticate a response from a server, a client sends a random *challenge* within the request, which the server echoes in the *response*. Since an off-path attacker cannot eavesdrop on the packets exchanged between the server and the client, it

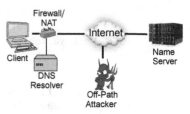

Fig. 1. Off-Path Attacker Model

appears that it would have to guess the challenge. Thus, a challenge, selected at random from a large distribution, should suffice to prevent an off-path attacker from crafting a response packet with valid challenge values.

The security of most Internet services, e.g., email, web surfing, DNS, peer-to-peer applications, relies on challenge-response mechanisms, mainly as part of the underlying *transport* and *application* layer protocols. A popular defence at the transport layer, supported by vast majority of the systems, is port randomisation, whereby the response is validated to have arrived on the same port from which the request was sent. Challenge-response defences in the application layer include widely-used web-security mechanisms based on cookies, such as in HTTP, or identifiers, such as in DNS. Trivially, challenge-response mechanisms are ineffective against MitM adversaries, since they can eavesdrop on the challenges and copy their values to responses. However, there is 'hope' that challenge-response defences should suffice to foil attacks by off-path adversaries.

In this work we focus on DNS security against off-path adversaries, especially in light of the recent standardisation efforts to further enhance DNS security with challenge-response mechanisms, [RFC6056, RFC4697, RFC5452]. These recommendations were standardised following Kaminsky's DNS cache poisoning attack in 2008, but most of them were known security measures also before.

In a DNS cache poisoning attack the attacker triggers a DNS request and then sends multiple spoofed responses, each containing different values, trying to guess the correct challenges. The first response with the correct values in challenge fields is accepted and cached by the DNS resolver; subsequent responses are ignored.

The attacker can use DNS cache poisoning to redirect clients to incorrect addresses, e.g., for spam, or malware distribution, credentials theft, or even to gain MitM capabilities for communication to the victim domain.

1.1   Challenge-Response Authentication

Following Kaminsky's cache poisoning attack, DNS resolvers were quickly patched to support challenge-response defences against cache poisoning. Most existing challenge-response mechanisms are 'patches', randomising and validating existing fields in the TCP/IP protocols. We next review standardised and most commonly used challenge-response authentication mechanisms.

DNS uses a random 16-bit *TXID (transaction identifier)* field that associates a DNS response with its corresponding request. DNS implementations additionally support a random selection of name servers each time they send a request. The main defence, that makes poisoning impractical is a (16-bit) *source port randomisation* recommended in [RFC5452], which together with a TXID result in a search space containing 2^{32} possible values; a source port identifies the client-side application in requests, and is echoed (as a destination port) in responses. Specific recommendations for port randomisation algorithms were recently provided in [RFC6056]. Due to the significance of port randomisation for preventing off-path attacks, e.g., cache poisoning and injections into TCP, multiple studies were conducted to measure support of port randomisation in the Internet, and it seems that many resolvers adopted port randomisation methods that were recommended in [RFC6056]; we also confirmed this using CAIDA's data traces [1], see Section 3. Furthermore, a number of DNS checker services, e.g., [3–5], were set up to enable clients to validate predictability of the ports supported by client systems, and algorithms recommended in [RFC6056] are reported secure.

Indeed, security of most DNS resolvers relies on these challenge-response mechanisms, and support of TXID together with source port randomisation, are believed to provide sufficient defence against attacks by off-path adversaries.

Notice however, that port randomisation, as well as other challenge-response mechanisms, do not prevent attacks by MitM adversaries. To protect DNS against a MitM, a cryptographic mechanism, DNSSEC [RFC4033-4035], was standardised already in 1997. DNSSEC is a standard for signing DNS records, allowing resolvers to validate DNS responses. However, so far, DNSSEC is not widely deployed, both at the zones as well as at the resolvers. For example, Google reports that less than 1% of the DNS records it retrieves are signed; and [6,7] tested queries to `org` and found that 0.8% of the resolvers were validating. Clearly, the deployment of DNSSEC is still very limited.

The goal of our work is twofold. (1) The vulnerabilities that we found and present in this work indicate the dangers of incorrect modelling of adversarial capabilities. In this work we present techniques allowing off-path attackers to efficiently reconstruct the (believed to be secure) ephemeral ports that are allocated in random kernel mode, thus allowing to derandomise standard port randomisation algorithms. Our techniques use fragmented DNS responses in order to elicit timing side channels. These side channels can be used to identify the ephemeral ports' sequence used by the victim system to a specific destination. We recommend fixes against our attacks in the short term. We notified the operating systems vendors and recent Linux kernel was patched to support our (immediate) short term recommendations [8]. (2) Our main message is to emphasise the significance of cryptographic defence, DNSSEC, which provides systematic protection even against other unforeseen vulnerabilities which may be discovered in the future, and prevents attacks not only by off-path but also by a stronger MitM adversary. We hope that the vulnerabilities that we found will encourage wider adoption of DNSSEC.

1.2 Related Work

Recently, a number of DNS cache poisoning attacks were published. We review them and put our contribution in context. The attacks can be grossly categorised into three distinct classes: (1) injection of spoofed records via fragmentation, (2) resolvers behind middleboxes and (3) source port inference.

Injection of Spoofed Records. When a DNS response is fragmented and the second fragment is sufficiently large to contain a DNS record, an attacker can replace the second fragment with a spoofed one, which contains malicious records, e.g., redirecting the client to incorrect hosts, [9]. Most DNS responses are not fragmented, however, [9], presented techniques allowing to cause fragmentation.

Resolvers-Behind-Middleboxes. Resolvers behind middleboxes, e.g., NAT devices or upstream forwarders, is a common setting in the Internet. However, attacks were shown allowing port inferences in both settings, [10–12]. The idea behind attacks is that the middlebox allows to attack the 2^{32} search space sequentially: the attacker first learns the port, and then, when it known the port, it sends 2^{16} packets to match the correct TXID.

Source Port Inference. Kernel processing of incoming packets introduces side channels which can be used to differentiate an open port from a closed one. Recently, [13] showed how to apply it for port inference. However, the techniques are effective on LANs and may be not suitable when the attacker is located on a different network due to the noise introduced by the routers and intermediate Internet devices.

In our work we improve over the results in [13], and present an effective and a much more efficient technique, requiring much less traffic and resilient to network noise.

Our Contributions

We show how off-path attackers can exploit fragmented DNS responses in order to infer ports allocated by common operating systems that support algorithms recommended in [RFC6056]. The ability to predict ports can be used for DNS cache poisoning, and we show how to extend our attacks to poison patched DNS resolvers software; we tested our attacks against Bind 9.8.1 and Unbound 1.4.19 DNS software.

Our techniques improve over the attacks presented in [10], which showed how to predict ports of the resolvers located behind NAT devices. The limitation of [10] is that the attacks apply only when resolvers are behind NAT devices, and require a user-priviledged malware on the LAN. We show that using our techniques much more efficient attacks are possible, which also do not require a malware, and apply to a general scenario, as well as to resolvers behind NAT devices.

We show how to extend our attacks for DNS responses interception. The limitation of applying our techniques for packet interception is that it requires a compromised host on the same LAN with the resolver, behind NAT or firewall device. DNS responses interception allows to circumvent more sophisticated defenses against cache poisoning, such as Eastlake cookies.

2 IP-Defragmentation Cache-Poisoning

In this section we present the basic technique *IP defragmentation cache poisoning* which we apply as a building block throughout the rest of this paper.

IP Fragmentation. TCP/IP networks impose a limit, maximal transmission unit (MTU), on the size of IP packets that they can support. If a packet exceeds the MTU of the link to which it is being forwarded, it is fragmented to smaller packets, i.e., fragments. Each fragment, of the original IP packet, is stamped with the same IP identifier (IP-ID) as the IP-ID value in the original IP packet, and is marked with an offset that corresponds to its location in the byte stream of the original IP packet.

Fragments are stored in an IP defragmentation cache at the destination. When all fragments comprising the original IP packet are received, they are reassembled. Operating systems typically impose a limit on the number of cached fragments per each (source, destination, protocol) triple. For example, in recent versions of the Linux kernel, the default value is 64, and older versions support up to several hundreds of fragments. This limit is imposed via the *ipfrag_max_dist* variable; see [14]. In order for fragments to be reassembled, they must match in four parameters: source and destination IP addresses, transport protocol and the IP-ID field. In IPv4, the IP-ID is a 16 bit field[1] selected by the source.

If some fragments are lost or missing, the cached fragments cannot be reassembled and are discarded after a timeout (default value is 30 seconds). The reassembled IP packet is then moved from the defragmentation cache, for transport layer processing.

We performed a study of typical DNS response sizes of Top Level Domains (TLDs) and top Alexa domains, [15], signed and non-signed; the results are plotted in Figure 2. As can be seen, DNS responses signed with DNSSEC result in much larger packets than traditional (unsigned) responses, and even the 'non-existing domain (NXD)' responses that are signed, often exceed the maximal transmission unit (MTU).

---

[1] In IPv6, the IP-ID is 32 bits; we focus on IPv4, since adoption of IPv6 is still limited.

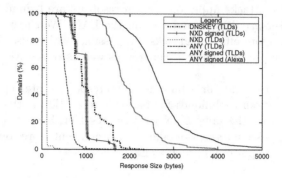

Fig. 2. Length of responses for signed and non-signed Alexa and TLDs, for `ANY`, `DNSKEY` and `A` resource records; `A` records were sent for random subdomains of tested domains, and resulted in NXD responses

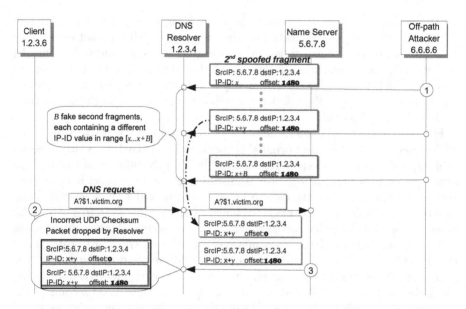

Fig. 3. Defragmentation-cache poisoning via a spoofed second fragment

Replacing IP Fragments. Defragmentation-cache poisoning is reassembly of spoofed IP fragments together with authentic fragments into a correct IP packet. To perform IP defragmentation cache poisoning, the attacker has to cache in the IP defragmentation cache of the victim, spoofed fragments, which contain the same IP addresses as the authentic fragments, sent by the victim, the same IP-ID and protocol fields. Using IP defragmentation cache poisoning, the attacker can replace any authentic fragment, first, middle or last, with a spoofed fragment.

In order for IP to merge a spoofed fragment with a legitimate fragment, the two fragments must match in four parameters: source and destination IP addresses, transport protocol and the *IP identifier (IP-ID)* field. In our setting, the attacker knows the IP addresses, and the transport protocol is UDP. Hence, the only parameter, which the attacker may not know, is the value of the IP-ID. A naive (brute-force) strategy is to try all possible IP-ID values, by sending multiple spoofed fragments, each containing a different IP-ID value. The efficiency of the attack can be significantly improved since most servers support predictable IP-ID values. We collected statistics for name servers of top-level domains (TLDs) and found the following common IP-ID allocation methods: *sequentially incrementing* (supported by more than 70% of the name servers) and *random* (supported by less than 1% of the name servers); see [9], for techniques to predict and hit the correct IP-ID for each allocation method.

Let B denote the number of spoofed fragments sent by the attacker. The defragmentation-cache poisoning attack for a special case[2] where attacker replaces a second authentic fragment with a spoofed one is illustrated in Figure 3. The attack begins when the attacker sends B spoofed second fragments (step 1), which are stored at the defragmentation cache of the destination (for 30 seconds by default), and triggers a DNS request via a puppet (step 2). If one of the B spoofed fragments, that the attacker sent, matches the reassembly parameters in the authentic first fragment, they are reassembled.

The only value that the attacker may need to guess is the IP-ID value in responses from the name server. The probability that the IP-ID of a legitimate (fragmented) response matches the IP-ID of one of the (up to B) spoofed second fragments, which the attacker sent, depends on the IP-ID assignment method; see analysis of the efficiency of defragmentation-cache poisoning for common IP-ID allocation methods: *incrementing* and *random* in [9], we briefly provide it here for completeness.

RANDOM IP-ID. In a random IP-ID allocation the name server selects the IP-ID values in each response uniformly. Let n be the number of DNS requests triggered by the attacker and B the number of spoofed second fragments sent by the attacker. The probability for a successful poisoning can be expressed as follows:

$$\Pr[success] \cong 1 - \left(1 - \frac{B}{2^{16}}\right)^n \qquad (1)$$

See graph representing defragmentation cache-poisoning success probability, based on Eq. (1), in Figure 4. As can be seen, for a default defragmentation buffer of $64 = 2^6$ and 256 parallel DNS requests, the chances are rather slim, i.e., below 0.4. However, random IP-ID is not common among servers, e.g., less than 1% of top-level domain name servers support it, and most deploy (variations of) incrementing IP-ID assignment. As we next show, incrementing IP-ID allows much more efficient prediction strategy.

---

[2] Extension to a general case is easy, and in this work, we focus on replacing second fragments.

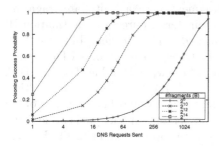 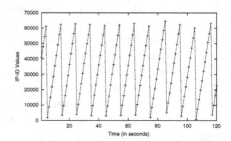

Fig. 4. Defragmentation-cache poisoning success probability per attempt, by analysis (Eq. (1)), for $B \in \{64, 1024, 4096, 16384\}$ (number of fake second fragments in cache)

Fig. 5. Progress of globally incrementing IP-ID values of `a0.org.affilias-nst.info` name server of `org` TLD.

INCREMENTING IP-ID. A significant fraction (more than 70%) of the name servers use incrementing IP-ID allocation methods. An attacker can query the name server directly and find out the current IP-ID value (since the same counter is used for sending packets to the attacker and to all other destinations, including the resolver). However, the IP-ID may considerably change between the query of the attacker and the query of the resolver, since the name server receives queries from other sources too. Therefore, in busy nameservers, that receive queries at a high rate, the IP-ID may grow very rapidly. Notice though that even if the DNS requests' rate to popular name servers is high, it is typically predictable. For example, in Figure 5, we show the measurements we ran on `a0.org.affilias-nst.info`, one of the name servers of `org`, that supports globally-incrementing IP-ID allocation; notice how rapidly the IP-ID 'grows' across the cyclic 16-bit counter field, yet it can be seen that the increments are predictable.

Indeed, the IP-ID value can be extrapolated, and the reason for this is that the query rate to name servers is stable, see [16].

To find the IP-ID value, the attacker measures the rate at which the name server receives requests, then measures the latency between itself and the victim resolver, and estimates the latency between the victim resolver and the name server. Then it samples the current IP-ID value, by seding a query to the name server. The attacker uses the response from the name server to extrapolate the value of the IP-ID that will be assigned by the name server to the response that it will generate for the resolver.

3   Port Derandomisation via IP Defrag-Cache Poisoning

In this section we describe port randomisation methods, standardised and deployed in popular systems, and show how to apply IP defragmentation cache poisoning, described in Section 2, for port derandomisation and discovery. IP defragmentation cache poisoning was applied in prior art, but mainly for attacks on performance, e.g., to ruin an IP packet, e.g., for denial of service attacks see [RFC6274] and [17], or name server pinning, [10] or for injection, [9]. In this work we present the first port derandomisation attacks using defragmentation cache poisoning. Our techniques apply to standard, and widely deployed, port assignment methods, supported by popular operating systems. This allows off-path attackers to predict client ports for a wide range of attacks, including DNS cache poisoning.

The Myth of Per-Destination Ports Security. A globally incrementing port allocation is not considered secure, since the attacker can sample the current port value, and then use it to extrapolate the next port value that will have been assigned by the client to its DNS requests. Indeed, most systems currently support a per-destination incrementing port allocation algorithms, recommended in [RFC6056]. A per-destination incrementing port is believed to be secure, since different ports' sequences are assigned by the resolver to different destinations; in particular learning the port value to one destination does not leak the port value assigned to some other destination. We checked, in [11], the *predictability rate* assigned by the popular DNS checker service provided by the OARC [4], to resolvers that send DNS requests with per-destination incrementing port. The tool reported (the highest) GREAT score, indicating that per-destination allocation methods are believed to be secure by the DNS experts. However, our results (within) show otherwise.

The idea behind per-destination incrementing ports is that a different sequence is selected to each destination as follows: the first port to some destination is selected at random, and subsequent packets to that destination are assigned sequentially incrementing ports. As a result, each destination knows only the port sequence that is used for communication to it, and cannot learn anything about communication to other destinations. Per-destination ports allocation underlies most of the algorithms proposed in [RFC6056]; more details in Section 3.2.

We collected statistics, [11], from two CAIDA datasets from 2012 [1] and found that many DNS requests support incrementing ports; the packets' traces are collected by CAIDA on (several) *backbone (OC192) links*. We used the traces to collect all the DNS requests (destination port 53) over UDP, and then filtered out IP addresses with a single DNS request, and collected only the sources that sent two or more requests. This allowed us to infer information about the source port allocation of the remaining DNS requests. We found that 54% of the requests were sent from incrementing ports.

In this section, we present attacks against standard and widely deployed port randomisation algorithms. We first show an attack against a popular per-destination algorithm, supported by Linux kernel OS, and then show extensions against other algorithms recommended in [RFC6056].

3.1   Predicting Linux OS Ports

In Linux OS kernel, the initial port to some destination is selected at random, and subsequent ports to that destination are incremented sequentially. This method is in fact a special case of Algorithm #3 [RFC6056] in Section 3.2, except that a distinct counter is maintained to each destination (instead of a global counter for all destinations). We show how to apply fragmentation to traverse the ports' range, in descending order, from the highest to lowest until correct port is found[3].

When traversing the ports' range, at each iteration i the attacker can sample more than a single port. For instance, if attacker samples p ports at each iteration, in the worst case, the attacker 'meets the resolver' after $\frac{2^{16}}{2^p}$ attempts.

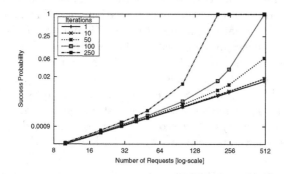

Fig. 6. Discovery of 'random' ephemeral ports' sequences against Linux Kernel, by applying defragmentation cache poisoning. The attacker uses the latency of DNS responses as a timing side channel to learn whether the correct port was hit.

The search distribution is composed of ports' pool and of the TXIDs range. We next show how to apply IP defragmentation-cache poisoning to *split* the distribution of TXIDs and ports values to two separate distributions of size (at most) 2^{16} each (assuming an ideal case where a maximal number of ports is used).

The steps of the attack are illustrated in Figure 7. We assume that the attacker already discovered the IP-ID value using techniques described in Section 2.

The idea is to use fragmentation to overwrite the transport layer header of the fragmented IP packet sent by the name server to the resolver. In each such attempt the attacker sends a spoofed fragment with a source IP of the name server and includes a guess for a port. If the guess is correct - the response is accepted and cached by the resolver. Otherwise, if the port in the spoofed fragment is incorrect - the resolver rejects the response, and retransmits the

---

[3] Often not all ports are used by the OS. DNS running on Windows server 2008 uses ports range $(49152-65535)$ and Windows 2000/XP/server 2003 use ports from range $(1025 - 5000)$. Older Bind versions use fixed ports. This results in ranges that are significantly smaller than 2^{16}, e.g., it is considered safe to use ports in the range $(1024 - 49152)$, [RFC5452].

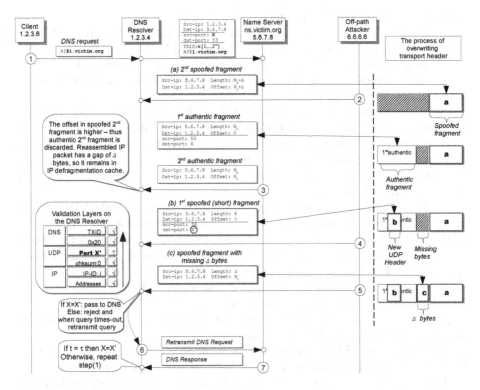

Fig. 7. DNS request port discovery: in step 1, the attacker plants a spoofed fragment in the resolver's defragmentation cache and then in step 2 the puppet triggers a DNS request to a resource within the victim's domain. The off-path attacker, in step 3, sends its guess for a port. If failure, timeout event occurs, and the resolver retransmits the DNS request. Otherwise, the attacker guessed the correct port.

request. The attacker uses the time till the response arrives, as a side channel, to distinguish between the correct and an incorrect ports.

In order to overwrite the (UDP) transport layer header, the attacker has to craft a spoofed first fragment, which is smaller than the original first fragment. The spoofed first fragment is 8 bytes long, and contains a guess for a new port; its purpose is to overwrite only the UDP header (also 8 bytes long) in the authentic first fragment. Notice that when two fragments contain identical offsets, then the last arriving fragment overwrites the first. Therefore, in order for the spoofed fragment to overwrite the transport header of the authentic fragment, it must arrive at the resolver *after* the first authentic fragment, and *before* the IP packet is reassembled, when the authentic second fragment arrives. Notice that this is not trivial, since once the two legitimate fragments arrive, they are immediately reassembled. Thus the attacker has to ensure that the first legitimate fragment remains in the defragmentation so that its header can be overwritten. To achieve that, the attacker has to plant a spoofed second fragment, similarly to attack in Section 2, which will be reassembled with the legitimate first fragment.

Attack. We next describe the steps of the attack.

Let $f = f_1 || f_2$ be the IP packet consisting of two fragments f_1 starts at offset 0 and is of length N_1 and f_2 starts at offset N_1 and is of length N_2.

(1) attacker triggers a DNS request (whose response is fragmented).

(2) the attacker sends a spoofed second fragment f_2', starting at offset $(N_1+\Delta)$, where Δ is some number of bytes.

(3) When the first authentic fragment f_1 arrives it is reassembled with the spoofed second fragment f_2' that is already waiting in the defragmentation cache; when the authentic second fragment f_2 arrives, it is discarded since a spoofed fragment starts and ends at a higher offset $(N_1 + \Delta)$. However, the reassembled IP packet does not leave the defragmentation cache since there is a gap of Δ bytes that are still missing.

(4) The attacker sends a short fragment that overwrites *only* the UDP header in the original first fragment. This fragment overlaps with the first 8 bytes (the UDP header) in the authentic first fragment; the spoofed fragment contains checksum 0, which indicates that checksum validation is disabled[4], more fragments is set to 1 (mf=1), and offset is 0. When initiating the attack, the attacker sets the UDP port in this spoofed first fragment to 2^{16}, and decrements its value during each subsequent iteration.

(5) Finally, the attacker sends a fragment that starts at an offset N_1 and is of size Δ. This fragment fills the missing gap.

Following reassembly, these fragments result in a complete IP packet, that leaves the IP defragmentation cache and is passed to upper UDP layer.

If the attacker guessed the port correctly, in step (4), the DNS resolver will cache and forward the response to the puppet. In contrast, if the port is incorrect, the resolver will discard the DNS response; as a result, a timeout event will occur, and the resolver will retransmit the request again. The attacker uses the differences in responses' latencies as a side channel to detect guessing the correct port.

Analysis. Let r be a DNS response size in bytes. Let R bytes/sec be the transmission rate of the attacker. Let t seconds be a limit on the timeout for a DNS request (i.e., including all retransmitted requests for that query) and let q be a number of times a pending query is retransmitted until it is terminated and SERVERFAIL is returned.

Resolvers implement retransmission policy based on round trip time estimates of the name servers, [RFC1536], and support timeout management with exponential backoff. When a timeout occurs resolver enters an exponential backoff phase, i.e., the timeout is doubled, and query is retransmitted. Resolvers implement variable timeout and retransmission values, typically up to 45 seconds (which is also a recommended ceiling for total timeout for a query [RFC1536]), and attempt up to 15 retransmissions. For instance, Unbound 1.4.19 sets t to a

---

[4] UDP checksum validation is optional, and it can be disabled by name servers by setting it to 0 (0000 in hexadecimal). When the checksum is disabled it is not validated by the resolvers.

maximal value of 40 seconds and Bind 9.8.1 sets $t \leq 30$ seconds and $q \leq 10$, i.e., supports up to 10 retransmissions before terminating a query.

In each retransmission the resolver advances the port (in case an incrementing allocation is supported). This allows the attacker to sample a number of ports in a single iteration (since with each retransmission there is a new pending request). Once the port is known the attacker launches a DNS cache poisoning attack, i.e., sends 2^{16} spoofed DNS responses, for some victim domain, such that each response contains a different TXID value.

The number of iterations required to hit the correct port in the worst case is: $\frac{2^{15}}{(q+1)}$ for a per-destination incrementing port assignment; during each iteration the attacker matches the original query and up to q query retransmissions. Since the attacker does not need to match the TXID, at each iteration only 3 fragments are sent; this significantly reduces the complexity of the naive cache poisoning attack, where the attacker attempts to hit both the correct port and the correct TXID.

The worst-case number of requests required to guess the port is $\frac{2^{15}}{(q+1)}$. During each iteration $3(q+1)$ fragments are sent, thus the worst case number of fragments is $3(q+1) \cdot \frac{2^{15}}{(q+1)} = 3 \cdot 2^{15}$.

Once the port sequence is known, the attacker launches the traditional DNS cache poisoning attack: (1) triggers a DNS request and (2) generates and transmits 2^{16} forged DNS responses (with a spoofed IP address of the victim name server) such that each DNS response contains a different value of the TXID, and the port number, which was guessed earlier. One of the responses, that contains the correct value of TXID, is accepted and cached by the resolver. The analysis of the attack is presented in Figure 6.

We next calculate the success probability, the required worst case number of attack iterations and the number of requests triggered by the puppet, and the number of fragments sent by an off-path attacker.

The probability of hitting the correct port in a single attempt, when triggering Q DNS queries, is: $\Pr[success] = \frac{Q}{2^{16}}$.
The success probability during i^{th} iteration of the attack is:
$\Pr[success] = \frac{Q}{2^{16} - i \cdot Q}$.

In the worst case the attack has to be repeated at most $i \leq \frac{2^{16}}{2 \cdot Q} = \frac{2^{15}}{Q}$ iterations (assuming that at each iteration the attacker sends Q queries). The number of DNS requests, sent by the client, in the worst case is: $Q \cdot \frac{2^{15}}{Q} = 2^{15}$. Total number of sets of fragments (i.e., three fragments each time, as described in Figure 7), sent by off-path attacker is: $N \cdot \frac{2^{15}}{Q}$.

Notice that the attacker can reduce the number of iterations by sampling more ports in each iteration, and it can also reduce the number of requests in each iteration by circumventing a 'birthday protection'.

3.2 Inferring Ports Supported by other Algorithms

In each following subsection, we give an abstract presentation of the port allocation method recommended in [RFC6056] and show how it can be circumvented
using IP defragmentation cache poisoning.

Notice that only Algorithms #1 and #2, [RFC6056], select random port for
each outgoing packet, and thus are not vulnerable to port prediction attacks via
fragmentation. However, they are vulnerable to port exhaustion attacks, [10],
whereby the attacker occupies all the available ports except one, which is then
assigned to the query of the resolver.

Simple Hash-Based Port Selection. Simple hash based port assignment
method is described in Algorithm #3, [RFC6056]. The port selection algorithm,
at the sender, maintains a *different offset* to each destination. The offset is a
result of a pseudorandom function computed over a tuple (*source IP address,
destination IP address, destination port, secret key*). The algorithm uses *a single
counter*, incremented globally, by one, for each port allocation, and added to the
offset of the relevant destination. As a result, connections to different destinations will have different sequences of port numbers, and one destination should
not be able to anticipate the ports allocated to the other. This algorithm was
supported by Linux OS kernel version 2.6, and was believed to be secure against
off-path attackers. Recent Linux versions also use a variation of per-destination
incrementing ports, see Section 3.1.

We show how to apply our IP defragmentation cache poisoning technique to
discover the ephemeral port used by a victim resolver to some destination name
server. The attacker learns the typical delay δ for a request to some name server.
The attacker then triggers DNS requests (via the puppet on the LAN), and
sends spoofed fragments for each candidate port that it samples, starting with
the highest port, and decrementing the port during each attempt. The attacker
learns when the correct port is hit, via the response latency. The ephemeral
port is found if during sampling of a candidate port z the response arrives after
$\tau > \delta$ seconds. Otherwise, the attacker repeats the attack with a new port $z-1$;
following a descending order of ports. When the correct port is hit, the resolver
accepts the DNS response. Otherwise, when an incorrect port is hit, the resolver
discards the response. This results in query retransmission by the resolver, and
adds more than a second to the response[5].

Once the port is discovered, the attacker can use its value for attacks at some
later time, without the need to discover the port again. This is due to the fact
that the same counter is used to all destinations, thus the attacker only needs to
trigger a DNS request to a server that it controls, to check the current counter
value, and adjust the port value accordingly.

Double-Hash Port Selection. Algorithm #4, [RFC6056], builds on Algorithm #3 (Section 3.2), but instead of keeping a globally incrementing counter

---

[5] Typical latency for a DNS request and response is in the order of 100 ms.

for all destinations, it groups the destinations to m sets and uses a separate counter to each set. The recommended value of m is 10, [18,19], however, as [19] notes, larger m values provide for better port obfuscation, since the same counter is not shared between too many clients. Notice that the special case of $m = 1$ is supported in Linux kernel (Section 3.1).

Port derandomisation attack proceeds as follows: first, the attacker attempts to find an IP address that *falls within the same set as the target name server* (the goal of the attacker is to eventually discover the port, used by the resolver, to that name server); the attacker may employ for its attack a number of compromised hosts, e.g., bot computers that it controls (located in different networks and not necessarily on the same LAN with the resolver). The idea is to trigger a request to some host i, and then launch IP defragmentation cache poisoning to check if the current port, allocated to the target server, was incremented; the port sampling attack steps are similar to those presented against *simple hash-based port selection*. If the port was incremented, then the host at IP address i falls within the same set as the target name server. This host i can be used to sample port increments.

Random-Increments Port Selection. Algorithm #5, [RFC6056], maintains a globally incrementing counter to all the destinations, which is incremented by (a randomly selected) N at each invocation of the ephemeral port allocation procedure. For $N = 1$ this is exactly the globally incrementing algorithm implemented in Windows and FreeBSD operating systems.

The attack against *simple hash-based port selection* applies with a slight modification: the attacker has to sample N ports, instead of one, in each attempt. Notice, that the actual value selected by the port allocation procedure can be less than N, but since the attacker does not know its value, it has to sample N ports each time in the worst case. Furthermore, when hitting the correct port, the attacker cannot tell which, out of the sampled N ports, it was, and it only learns that it was one the sampled ports. To reduce the success of port derandomisation attacks, N should be as large as possible. On the other hand, large N increases the chance for port collisions due to ports' reuse from previous connections, and smaller values of N are required to reduce collisions.

4   Resolvers behind NAT Devices

A natural question is what is the impact of port derandomisation attack against resolvers behind NAT devices. In fact, the same attack step, illustrated in Figure 7, apply, since the NAT itself reassembles IP fragments in order to be able to forward the packet to the correct internal host on the LAN based on the ports. This also improves over the attack in [10] which required a zombie order to leak the port number used by the NAT, in packets payload, to the external attacker, and used significantly more packets, rendering the attack impractical.

4.1 Are They Common?

To estimate what fraction of resolvers are located behind NAT devices, we ran statistics on two CAIDA datasets from 2012 [1], that were collected on equinix-chicago and equinix-sanjose monitors on high-speed Internet backbone links. Both traces contained packets sent from distinct 89750 source IP addresses, collected over two minutes interval. We ran the following test to check for DNS resolvers behind NAT devices: (1) we collected all DNS requests, i.e., packets sent to port 53; (2) we created a set of IP addresses that sent at least one DNS request per second (to ensure that we do not mistakenly interpret a host for a resolver behind a NAT; (3) we then parsed the traces to check if those IP addresses also sent packets to other ports, including port 80, and 443. We then concluded with high probability that those resolvers were behind NAT devices. We came up with a total of 3492, out of 89750, resolvers behind NAT devices.

4.2 Packet Interception

In a setting where a victim resolver is located behind a NAT device, and the off-path attacker controls a host on the same LAN, it can use the technique described in Section 3 to *intercept* DNS requests sent by the resolver. Notice that such a setting is common, e.g., the attacker may be a legitimate user on the same organisational network with the resolver, or on a public wireless access network, or it may control an infected host, i.e., user space malware would suffice (many computers are infected with malware), on the same network with a resolver. The same attack steps as in Section 3 apply, except that the target is the NAT device. The internal host first sends a packet (or a number of packets) to the name server, in order to create a mapping in the NAT table. The off-path attacker sends the spoofed fragments (as in Section 3), to overwrite the port of authentic response from the name server. The outcome of overwriting the port of inbound packets traversing the NAT, is that the DNS response is sent to a different internal host, i.e., the one that is identified by the new port which was used by the off-path attacker in its spoofed fragment, instead of the designated recipient (i.e., the resolver). Such attacks would enable circumvention of Eastlake cookies, and all other *non cryptographic defences.*

5 Defenses

The vulnerabilities described in this paper are severe and apply to many systems that support (variations of) per-destination ports assignment. We recommend a number of short term client-side defences. Most notably, proper port randomisation, which would prevent these attacks. Client side defences also include firewall-based mechanisms, such as [20]. In particular, in [20] we showed two techniques which make cache poisoning impractical: (1) we showed how to artificially increase the number of IP addresses allocated to a resolver, and (2) how to detect poisoning attacks by keeping track of responses which contain incorrect challenge-response values.

Another simple defence is to deploy IPv6. Its much larger IPv6 address space, makes the attack impractical.

In the long term we recommend to deploy systematic defences, most notably DNSSEC [RFC4033-RFC4035], which is the best defense against the poisoning attacks. DNSSEC provides security not only against off-path but also against MitM attackers. However, deployment faces multiple challenges and obstacles, see [7, 21, 22] for details. We hope that our results will help motivate speeding up adoption of DNSSEC and focusing efforts on investigation of the deployment challenges.

6   Conclusions

We presented port inference techniques using timing side channels which IP defragmentation cache poisoning makes available. Our techniques allow to predict source ports selected by client systems supporting port randomisation algorithms recommended in [RFC6056]. Our attacks effectively circumvent the 'source port randomisation (SPR)' defence making DNS cache poisoning, and other attacks which rely on ports' prediction, practical. We applied our techniques for DNS cache poisoning attacks agaist standard DNS resolvers, Bind 9.8.1 and Unbound 1.4.19, and popular operating system, Linux kernel OS. This attack is significant, since a large and growing number of networks support per-destination algorithms recommended in [RFC6056].

Acknowledgements. We are grateful for support for CAIDA's Internet Traces [1] that is provided by the National Science Foundation, the US Department of Homeland Security, and CAIDA Members.

References

1. Paulo, S.L.M., Barreto, S.D., Galbraith, C.O.: hEigeartaigh, and Michael Scott. Efficient pairing computation on supersingular abelian varieties. IACR Cryptology ePrint Archive, 375 (2004)
2. Beverly, R., Koga, R., Claffy, K.: Initial Longitudinal Analysis of IP Source Spoofing Capability on the Internet. Internet Society Article (July 2013)
3. Corporation, G.R.: DNS Nameserver Spoofability Test (2012),
   https://www.grc.com/dns/dns.htm
4. DNS-OARC: Domain Name System Operations Analysis and Research Center (2008), https://www.dns-oarc.net/oarc/services/porttest
5. Provos, N.: DNS Testing Image (July 2008),
   http://www.provos.org/index.php?/archives/43-DNS-Testing-Image.html
6. Gudmundsson, O., Crocker, S.D.: Observing DNSSEC Validation in the Wild. In: SATIN (March 2011)
7. Lian, W., Rescorla, E., Shacham, H., Savage, S.: Measuring the practical impact of dnssec deployment. In: Proceedings of USENIX Security (2013)
8. Neira, P.: Patchset of Netfilter Updates (2013),
   http://patchwork.ozlabs.org/patch/307041/

9. Herzberg, A., Shulman, H.: Fragmentation Considered Poisonous: or one-domain-to-rule-them-all.org. In: The Conference on Communications and Network Security, CNS 2013. IEEE (2013)

10. Herzberg, A., Shulman, H.: Security of Patched DNS. In: Foresti, S., Yung, M., Martinelli, F. (eds.) ESORICS 2012. LNCS, vol. 7459, pp. 271–288. Springer, Heidelberg (2012)

11. Herzberg, A., Shulman, H.: Vulnerable Delegation of DNS Resolution. In: Crampton, J., Jajodia, S., Mayes, K. (eds.) ESORICS 2013. LNCS, vol. 8134, pp. 219–236. Springer, Heidelberg (2013)

12. Gilad, Y., Herzberg, A., Shulman, H.: Off-Path Hacking: The Illusion of Challenge-Response Authentication. IEEE Security & Privacy (2014)

13. Herzberg, A., Shulman, H.: Socket Overloading for Fun and Cache Poisoning. In: ACM Annual Computer Security Applications Conference (ACM ACSAC) (December 2013)

14. Kernel.org: Linux Kernel Documentation (2011), http://www.kernel.org/doc/Documentation/networking/ip-sysctl.txt

15. Alexa: The web information company, http://www.alexa.com/

16. Wessels, D., Fomenkov, M.: Wow, thats a lot of packets. In: Proceedings of Passive and Active Measurement Workshop, PAM (2003)

17. Gont, F.: Security Implications of Predictable Fragment Identification Values. Internet-Draft of the IETF IPv6 maintenance Working Group (6man) (March 2012) (expires September 30, 2012)

18. Larsen, M., Gont, F.: Recommendations for Transport-Protocol Port Randomization. RFC 6056 (Best Current Practice) (January 2011)

19. Allman, M.: Comments on selecting ephemeral ports. ACM SIGCOMM Computer Communication Review 39(2), 13–19 (2009)

20. Herzberg, A., Shulman, H.: Unilateral antidotes to DNS poisoning. In: Rajarajan, M., Piper, F., Wang, H., Kesidis, G. (eds.) SecureComm 2011. LNICST, vol. 96, pp. 319–336. Springer, Heidelberg (2012)

21. Herzberg, A., Shulman, H.: Dnssec: Security and availability challenges. In: 2013 IEEE Conference on Communications and Network Security (CNS), pp. 365–366. IEEE (2013)

22. Herzberg, A., Shulman, H.: Retrofitting Security into Network Protocols: The Case of DNSSEC. IEEE Internet Computing 18(1), 66–71 (2014)

Delegating a Pairing Can Be Both Secure and Efficient

Sébastien Canard[1], Julien Devigne[1,2], and Olivier Sanders[1,3]

[1] Orange Labs, Applied Crypto Group, Caen, France
[2] UCBN, GREYC, Caen, France
[3] École normale supérieure, CNRS & INRIA, Paris, France

Abstract. Bilinear pairings have been widely used in cryptographic protocols since they provide very interesting functionalities in regard of identity based cryptography, short signatures or cryptographic tools with complex properties. Unfortunately their implementation on limited devices remains complex and even if a lot of work has been done on the subject, the current results in terms of computational complexity may still be prohibitive. This is clearly not for today to find the implementation of a bilinear pairing in every smart card. One possibility to avoid this problem of efficiency is to delegate the pairing computation to a third party. The result should clearly be both secure and efficient. Regarding security, the resulting computation of a pairing $e(A, B)$ by the third party should be verifiable by the smart card. Moreover, if the points A and/or B are secret at the beginning of the protocol, they should also be secret after its execution. Regarding efficiency, besides some specific cases, existing protocols for delegating a pairing are costlier than a true embedded computation inside the smart card. This is due to the fact that they require several exponentiations to check the validity of the result.

In this paper we first propose a formal security model for the delegation of pairings that fixes some weakness of the previous models. We also provide efficient ways to delegate the computation of a pairing $e(A, B)$, depending on the status of A and B. Our protocols enable the limited device to verify the value received from the third party with mostly one exponentiation and can be improved to also ensure secrecy of $e(A, B)$.

Keywords: pairings, secure delegation, elliptic curve.

1 Introduction

Pairings. Since the publication of the paper by Joux [23], elliptic-curve bilinear pairings have been frequently used in cryptography because they offer more functionalities than RSA groups while keeping a lower size. One of their most famous application was due to Boneh and Franklin [8] who used them to solve the open problem of constructing an efficient identity-based encryption scheme. Other known usefulness of pairings is their capacity to shorten signatures [9,10,6] and to obtain constructions in the standard model for cryptographic tools with complex properties (see *e.g.* [5]).

I. Boureanu, P. Owesarski, and S. Vaudenay (Eds.): ACNS 2014, LNCS 8479, pp. 549–565, 2014.

In the following, we more generally consider a bilinear environment, which corresponds to a set of two additive groups $\mathbb{G}_1$, $\mathbb{G}_2$ and one multiplicative group $\mathbb{G}_T$, all of known prime order l, along with an efficiently computable bilinear map $e : \mathbb{G}_1 \times \mathbb{G}_2 \to \mathbb{G}_T$. The way to describe such bilinear map has first been proposed by Miller in his unpublished paper. This work was next improved in many other ones, especially regarding the way to efficiently compute such mathematical function. Unfortunately, despite several improvements (one can find some of them in [2,3]), the computational cost of a pairing still remains high and may be prohibitive for restricted devices such as smart cards or RFID tags/sensor nodes. This may be a problem in some practical applications where the properties of a pairing are very useful.

Delegation. One way to solve this problem is to delegate the pairing computation to a more powerful entity such as a mobile phone (which is now possible in an efficient way [14,28]), a computer or a server. But this cannot be done at the detriment of the security. Indeed, if a smart card may today be considered as secure, this does not remain true for a mobile phone, a computer or a server that may be controlled by some dishonest entity (by the way of *e.g.* a malware).

In the setting of the delegation of a pairing, two security properties could be taken into account. The first one is *secrecy*, requiring that the more powerful entity should not learn anything about the inputs of the pairings (unless they are public). The second one is *verifiability* (also called correctness) and requires that the restricted device cannot accept a wrong value for the pairing which is delegated to the more powerful entity. We emphasize that a delegation protocol that does not ensure verifiability may cause severe security problems. As evidence, if the pairing occurs in the verification algorithm of some digital signature scheme, as the ones from [9,7], an incorrect value may lead for the restricted device to accept an invalid signature.

Related Work. The delegation of cryptographic operations is a technique which has been known since a long time (see *e.g.* [27,15,26]) and it now exists some constructions in the generic case [32,13]. The particular case of the pairing computation has first been studied, as far as we know, in a work by Girault and Lefranc [20]. But they have only considered the secrecy of the computation. Verifiable protocols for delegating a pairing $e(A, B)$ have first been provided by Chevallier-Mames *et al.* ([16,17]) and later by Kang *et al.* [25]. However their efficiency depends on the status of A and B. More specifically, their protocols remain rather efficient as long as one of the involved points is constant. Indeed, the *online* phase of the proposal for *variable* A and B in [16] (resp. [25]) necessitates 5 (resp. 3) exponentiations in $\mathbb{G}_T$, 3 tests of membership in $\mathbb{G}_T$ (resp. 3), plus additional scalar multiplications in $\mathbb{G}_1$ and $\mathbb{G}_2$, for the case of secret values. The proposal in [16] for a verifiable (but for public variable values) pairing delegation requires 3 exponentiations in $\mathbb{G}_T$ and 3 tests of membership in $\mathbb{G}_T$. Even if the computational costs of a pairing and of group operations depend on the choice of the parameters, the recent results of [28], implementing an optimal-Ate pairing over Barreto-Naehrig curves [4] (the most popular choice), seem to confirm that, regarding efficiency, it is better to directly embed the pairing computation inside the restricted device than using these solutions. Otherwise, the main contribution will be the save of area that is required to implement a pairing in a smart card, which is certainly a good point, but not enough in most contexts.

In [31], the authors have considered the more general case of delegating several pairings all at once. They pointed out the lack of formal security models in the previous works and therefore proposed a candidate for it. They have also described a protocol fulfilling this model but which can only handle one variable point (the other one has to be constant). Unfortunately, as illustrated by the results of the previous works, the trickiest case is the one where both A and B are variable which is commonly found in the verification of signature schemes [9,7] where verifiability is particularly relevant.

Our Methodology. For variable A and B, both papers [16,25] make use of the same methodology. They started by providing a protocol for secret points A and B, and they then convert it into a protocol where A and/or B are publicly known. We argue that it is far more interesting to convert a protocol for public A and B into a protocol for secret A and B. Indeed, if we assume the existence of a verifiable delegation protocol $\mathcal{P}$ to compute the pairing $e(A, B)$ for public A and B, then the case of the protocol $\mathcal{P}'$ for secret A and B can be treated, as in [20], by simply computing $A' \leftarrow [u]A$ and $B' \leftarrow [v]B$ for random u and v, and then running $\mathcal{P}$ with A' and B'. From $e(A', B')$, it is then easy to recover $e(A, B) \leftarrow e(A', B')^{(uv)^{-1}}$, and A' and B' need not to be secret. Then, the conversion from $\mathcal{P}$ into $\mathcal{P}'$ mostly requires one additional exponentiation in $\mathbb{G}_T$. Moreover, the result is obviously secure.

Curiously, the opposite is not true. If we consider a secure (verifiable and secret) pairing delegation protocol $\mathcal{P}'$ for secret values, the execution of this protocol for public values of A and B is not necessarily true, in particular depending on the kind of verifiability fulfilled by $\mathcal{P}'$. As evidence, we show in Section 3, using the protocol in [25], that this may permit the adversary to break the verifiability property from the knowledge of the secret points. We consequently describe a complete security model for pairing delegation. Our model is close to the one of [31] but with some necessary modifications, especially for the secrecy property.

In this paper, we will then focus on the design of an efficient scheme for public variable points since it leads to a scheme for secret ones. We will also study a specific case where we can ensure both secrecy and verifiability with better efficiency than the previous generic conversion.

Organization of the Paper. Section 2 gives some preliminaries for our study and Section 3 provides a security model for the delegation of a pairing. We describe in Section 4 verifiable protocols for public variable A and B, which necessitate the low-power entity to only compute one exponentiation (in the most important group). We explain in Section 5 how to achieve secrecy using the above idea but also provide an improved protocol for a specific case. Eventually, our last section compares our work with related ones and gives an example of the expected gain for a specific family of curve.

2   Preliminaries

In this section we recall some necessary definitions that will be used throughout the document.

Some Notations. In the following, $\overset{\$}{\leftarrow}$ corresponds to a random choice, while $\leftarrow$ is used to indicate an assignment of a variable.

Bilinear Groups. Bilinear groups are a set of three groups $\mathbb{G}_1, \mathbb{G}_2$ (with additive notations, as for elliptic curves) and $\mathbb{G}_T$ (with multiplicative notation), all of prime order l, along with a bilinear map $e : \mathbb{G}_1 \times \mathbb{G}_2 \to \mathbb{G}_T$ with the following properties:

1. for all $X_1 \in \mathbb{G}_1, X_2 \in \mathbb{G}_2$ and $a, b \in \mathbb{Z}_l$ we have $e([a]X_1, [b]X_2) = e(X_1, X_2)^{ab}$;
2. for $X_1 \neq 1_{\mathbb{G}_1}$ and $X_2 \neq 1_{\mathbb{G}_2}$, $e(X_1, X_2) \neq 1_{\mathbb{G}_T}$;
3. e is efficiently computable;

where $1_{\mathbb{G}_1}$ (resp. $1_{\mathbb{G}_2}$ and $1_{\mathbb{G}_T}$) is the neutral element of the group $\mathbb{G}_1$ (resp. $\mathbb{G}_2$ and $\mathbb{G}_T$).

Elliptic Curve Pairings. Our first protocol (see section 4.1) works for any bilinear groups while the second one (see section 4.2) works only for pairing computations on elliptic curves (which is currently the common case) and thus requires some additional definitions. We refer to [19,18] for a more extensive background on pairings.

Let p be a prime number. Let $E(\mathbb{F}_p)$ be an elliptic curve over the field $\mathbb{F}_p$. We usually define $\mathbb{G}_1$ as a subgroup of $E(\mathbb{F}_p)$, $\mathbb{G}_2$ as a subgroup of $E(\mathbb{F}_{p^k})$ and $\mathbb{G}_T$ as a subgroup of $(\mathbb{F}_{p^k})^*$, where k, called the embedding degree, is the smallest integer such that l divides $p^k - 1$.

Remark 1. In cryptography, the family of Tate's algorithms [19] is most of the time used to compute a pairing. These algorithms are divided in two parts: the Miller loop and the final exponentiation. This last step makes use of the exponent defined as $c = \frac{p^k - 1}{l}$. In the following, $\forall \alpha \in \mathbb{G}_T$, $\tilde{\alpha}$ will denote an element of $(\mathbb{F}_{p^k})^*$ such that $\tilde{\alpha}^c = \alpha$. Thus, considering that $\tilde{\alpha}$ is the output of the Miller's algorithm, α corresponds to the expected pairing value.

Testing Membership in $\mathbb{G}_T$. As said in the introduction, existing works [16,25,31] necessitate to test whether a value α belongs to $\mathbb{G}_T$ or not. The simplest way to test this membership is to check whether $\alpha^l = 1$ or not. However, this method requests one exponentiation in $\mathbb{F}_{p^k}$. As we will explain later (Remark 6), the only purpose of this check in our protocols (or the ones of [16,25,31]) is to ensure that the server does not return an element of $\mathbb{F}_{p^k}$ of small order. In [29], the author provides a very efficient way to avoid such a case. For example, for $k = 12$ (the usual choice for a 128-bit security), since pairing values are elements of the cyclotomic subgroup of order $\phi_{12}(p) = p^4 - p^2 + 1$, one may check membership of α to this subgroup by testing if $\alpha \cdot \alpha^{p^4} = \alpha^{p^2}$. Using the Frobenius action this can be done almost for free. However, this is useful as long as the cofactor $h := \frac{\phi_{12}(p)}{l}$ does not have small factors (for example, if h is prime and greater than l) which requires a special care when choosing the curve parameters. In the following, we will thus distinguish a test of membership from an exponentiation in $\mathbb{F}_{p^k}$.

3   Security Model

In this section, we give the security properties that we require for a secure pairing delegation. Let $A \in \mathbb{G}_1$ and $B \in \mathbb{G}_2$. We consider a restricted device, usually called a client, wanting to obtain the output of $e(A, B)$. For this purpose, the client interacts with a more powerful device, usually called the server, which is not necessarily trusted. We thus need to describe an interactive protocol between the client and the server where the output for the client is $e(A, B)$.

3.1   Syntax

A pairing delegation scheme consists of the three algorithms defined below, where *params* are some public parameters (see Remark 2 below).

- Init(*params*, A, B): this probabilistic algorithm takes as inputs two points A and B and outputs σ, sent to the server to compute with, and τ, kept secret by the client.
- Compute(*params*, σ): this deterministic algorithm is run by the server to compute α, which value is sent to the client.
- Extract(*params*, σ, τ, α): this algorithm is run by the client which uses the known secret (τ) and public values (σ) to check whether the computations (α) performed by the server are valid or not. The client finally outputs either a value μ (equals to $e(A, B)$ in the former case) or an error message $\perp$ (in the latter case).

Remark 2. We do not add a Setup algorithm since we assume that our delegation scheme will be used to compute pairings in cryptographic protocols where the public parameters *params* (containing, for example, a description of the bilinear groups) are already defined.

In practice, there are mainly two cases, considering the values A and B. In the first case, A or B is a *constant* value that never changes from one pairing computation to another, while the other is said *variable*. The other case is when both A and B are variables.

3.2   Security Notions

Regarding security, the authors of [16] and [25] have considered the three following informal security notions: (i) *completeness* (an honest client, interacting with an honest server, obtains $e(A, B)$ after completion of the protocol), (ii) *correctness* (a client interacting with a cheating server will output $\perp$ with overwhelming probability) and (iii) *secrecy* (even a dishonest server cannot learn any information about A and B).

As in [31], we rather define our security notions through experiments since they describe more precisely the power and knowledge of the adversary. Our correctness/verifiability (see the remark below) experiment is similar with the one from [31]. However, we propose a stronger definition of secrecy. Our security notions make use of the following oracle.

- $\mathcal{O}\mathtt{Sim}(params, A, B)$: is an oracle that executes the client's side of the protocol. In this case, the adversary plays the role of the corrupted server.

Remark 3. In this paper we will talk about *verifiability* rather than *correctness* since the latter is frequently used to denote *completeness* in cryptographic protocols.

Completeness. Informally, our definition of completeness is the same as the one provided by [16]. More formally, we define the completeness experiment $\mathbf{Exp}_{\mathcal{A}}^{comp}(params)$ as follows, where $\mathcal{A}^{\mathcal{O}\mathtt{Sim}}$ denotes an adversary $\mathcal{A}$ having an unconditional access to the $\mathcal{O}\mathtt{Sim}$ oracle, in an interactive way.

1. $(A, B) \leftarrow \mathcal{A}^{\mathcal{O}\mathtt{Sim}}(params)$.
2. $(\sigma, \tau) \leftarrow \mathtt{Init}(params, A, B)$.
3. $\alpha \leftarrow \mathtt{Compute}(params, \sigma)$.
4. $\mu \leftarrow \mathtt{Extract}(params, \sigma, \tau, \alpha)$.
5. If $\mu = e(A, B)$ then return 1.

A pairing protocol is *complete* if the probability $\Pr[\mathbf{Exp}_{\mathcal{A}}^{comp}(params) = 1]$ is overwhelming for all $\mathcal{A}$.

Verifiability. Regarding the literature on the subject, the definitions that one can find in [16,25] on the verifiability property are not very satisfying. In fact, they do not clearly specify the status (known or unknown) of A and B w.r.t. the server. Indeed, it seems that the status of A and B w.r.t. the adversary in the experiment related to the verifiability property depends, in their definition, of their status w.r.t. the server in the real protocol. Then, the probability of success of an adversary against the verifiability property may depend on the one against the secrecy, which is not very common in security where property definitions are usually independent one with each other.

A REMARK ON RELATED WORK SECURITY. In fact, this may even lead to some defaults related to security, and we can illustrate that using [25]. Let us consider a server being able to recover the secret points A and B with non-negligible probability λ for the protocol described in [25] (see Figure 1). It is then possible to show that such adversary is able to break the verifiability of this protocol with the same probability λ.

Indeed, if the server sends (instead of specified values), $\alpha_3 = e(R_1, R_2)^{1+z}$ and $\alpha_4 = e(T_1, T_2).e(A, B)^z$, for a randomly chosen z, then the client will output $e(A, B)^{1+z}$ instead of $e(A, B)$ since $\alpha_1, \alpha_2, \alpha_3$ and α_4 still satisfy the last equality test on α_4. The adversary will then succeed against the verifiability property with probability at least λ.

As a conclusion, we think that it is better to consider another definition for the verifiability property, which does not depend on the status (known or unknown) of A and B.

---

client $(A, B, G_1, G_2, G_T = e(G_1, G_2))$ server(G_1, G_2)

$g_1, g_2 \xleftarrow{\$} \mathbb{Z}_l$
$R_1 \leftarrow [g_1]A; \ R_2 \leftarrow [g_2]B$

$$\xrightarrow{\quad R_1, R_2 \quad}$$

$\qquad\qquad\qquad\qquad\qquad\qquad\qquad\qquad\qquad\qquad \alpha_1 \leftarrow (R_1, G_2); \ \alpha_2 \leftarrow (G_1, R_2);$
$\qquad\qquad\qquad\qquad\qquad\qquad\qquad\qquad\qquad\qquad \alpha_3 \leftarrow e(R_1, R_2)$

$$\xleftarrow{\quad \alpha_1, \alpha_2, \alpha_3 \quad}$$

For $i \in \{1, 2, 3\}$:
$\quad$ If $\alpha_i \notin \mathbb{G}_T$, return $\bot$
$r_1, r_2 \xleftarrow{\$} \mathbb{Z}_l$
$T_1 \leftarrow A + [r_1]G_1; \ T_2 \leftarrow B + [r_2]G_2$

$$\xrightarrow{\quad T_1, T_2 \quad}$$

$\qquad\qquad\qquad\qquad\qquad\qquad\qquad\qquad\qquad\qquad \alpha_4 \leftarrow e(T_1, T_2)$

$$\xleftarrow{\quad \alpha_4 \quad}$$

If $\alpha_4 = \alpha_3^{(g_1 g_2)^{-1}} \cdot \alpha_1^{g_1^{-1} r_2} \cdot \alpha_2^{g_2^{-1} r_1} \cdot G_T^{r_1 r_2}$
$\quad$ Return $\mu := \alpha_3^{(g_1 g_2)^{-1}}$
Else, return $\bot$

Fig. 1. The Kang *et al* protocol [25] for secret A and B

FORMAL DEFINITION OF VERIFIABILITY. Informally, verifiability requires that the client, even interacting with a dishonest server, will not output a wrong value for $e(A, B)$. We define the verifiability experiment $\mathbf{Exp}_{\mathcal{A}}^{verif}(params)$ as follows.

1. $(A, B, st) \leftarrow \mathcal{A}^{\mathcal{O}\text{Sim}}(params)$.
2. $(\sigma, \tau) \leftarrow \text{Init}(params, A, B)$.
3. $\alpha \leftarrow \mathcal{A}^{\mathcal{O}\text{Sim}}(params, \sigma, st)$.
4. $\mu \leftarrow \text{Extract}(params, \sigma, \tau, \alpha)$.
5. If $\mu = \bot$ or $\mu = e(A, B)$ then return 0.
6. Else return 1.

We define $\mathbf{Adv}_{\mathcal{A}}^{verif}(params) = \Pr[\mathbf{Exp}_{\mathcal{A}}^{verif}(params) = 1]$. A pairing delegation protocol is *verifiable* if, for any probabilistic polynomial time adversary, this advantage is negligible.

Secrecy. Informally, secrecy requires that the server cannot learn any information about A or B. We define the secrecy experiment $\mathbf{Exp}_{\mathcal{A}}^{sec}(params)$ as follows.

1. $(A_0, B_0, A_1, B_1, st) \leftarrow \mathcal{A}^{\mathcal{O}\mathtt{Sim}}(params)$.
2. $b \xleftarrow{\$} \{0,1\}$.
3. $(\sigma, \tau) \leftarrow \mathtt{Init}(params, A_b, B_b)$.
4. $b^* \leftarrow \mathcal{A}^{\mathcal{O}\mathtt{Sim}}(params, \sigma, st)$.
5. If $b^* = b$ then return 1. Else return 0.

We define $\mathbf{Adv}_{\mathcal{A}}^{sec}(params) = |\Pr[\mathbf{Exp}_{\mathcal{A}}^{sec}(params) = 1] - \frac{1}{2}|$. A pairing delegation protocol is *secret* if, for any probabilistic polynomial time adversary, this advantage is negligible.

In [31], the adversary against the secrecy property must distinguish a valid transcript from a simulated one without knowing the secret points. Our model is then stronger since it allows the adversary to choose the challenge points A and B. It is similar to the IND-CPA notion for public key encryption schemes.

4   Protocols with Public A and B

We provide in this section two efficient protocols to delegate the computation of public A and B, even if both of them are variable. For clarity's sake we first describe a protocol whose efficiency is equivalent to one exponentiation and one test of membership and then show how to modify it to suit the case where this last operation cannot be performed cheaply.

4.1   A Protocol with Test of Membership

We assume, as the authors of [16], [25] and [31], that the public parameters contain 3 elements: $G_1 \in \mathbb{G}_1$, $G_2 \in \mathbb{G}_2$ and $\rho = e(G_1, G_2)$.

Remark 4. Papers [16,25] do not explain how the client obtains the values G_1, G_2 and ρ. As mentioned in [31], there are two ways to treat this. For example, the client could generate G_1 and G_2 and compute ρ once for all. This computation can also be done by a trusted authority, which one could then embed the values in the client. In the latter case, there is no longer need for implementing the whole pairing computation algorithm in the client since our protocols only require group operations in the bilinear groups. This may justify, besides the efficiency, the use of our solutions since it saves some area needed to implement cryptographic operations. Indeed, there exist several different pairings, such as the Weil pairing, the Tate pairing or one of its variants [1,22]. Our protocols are then compatible with all of them as long as the values $e(G_1, G_2)$ (one for each type of pairing) are loaded in the client's memory.

The three algorithms defining our pairing delegation scheme are described in Figure 2 and enable the client to delegate the computation of $e(A, B)$ with public $A \neq 1_{\mathbb{G}_1}$ and $B \neq 1_{\mathbb{G}_2}$.

---

client (A, B, G_1, G_2, ρ) server(A, B)

Init$(params, A, B)$:

  $x_1, x_2 \xleftarrow{\$} \mathbb{Z}_l$

  $X_1 \leftarrow [x_1]G_1$; $X_2 \leftarrow [x_2]G_2$

  $\chi \leftarrow \rho^{x_1 \cdot x_2}$

  $T_1 \leftarrow [x_2^{-1}]A + X_1$; $T_2 \leftarrow [x_1^{-1}]B + X_2$

  Return $(\sigma, \tau) := ((T_1, T_2), (x_1, x_2))$

$$\xrightarrow{\quad \sigma \quad}$$

                                                             Compute$(params, \sigma)$:

                                                               $\alpha_1 \leftarrow e(T_1, T_2)[e(G_1, B)e(A, G_2)]^{-1}$

                                                               $\alpha_2 \leftarrow e(A, B)$

                                                               Return $\alpha := (\alpha_1, \alpha_2)$

$$\xleftarrow{\quad \alpha \quad}$$

Extract$(params, \sigma, \tau, \alpha)$:

  If $\alpha_1 = \chi \cdot \alpha_2^{(x_1 \cdot x_2)^{-1}}$ and $\alpha_2 \in \mathbb{G}_T$

    Return $\mu := \alpha_2$

  Else, return $\bot$

Fig. 2. Delegation protocol for public A and B

Computational Cost. Since X_1, X_2 and χ are easily pre-computable (they do not need the knowledge of A and B), the client only has to compute *online* a scalar multiplication in $\mathbb{G}_1$, another one in $\mathbb{G}_2$, an exponentiation in $\mathbb{G}_T$ and a test of membership in $\mathbb{G}_T$. The efficiency of our method strongly depends on the parameters of the bilinear groups, especially if they allow us to use the idea from [29] to avoid an exponentiation in $\mathbb{F}_{p^k}$ for the test of membership (see end of Section 2). To get an idea of the order of magnitude of the computational cost, one may look at the results from [12,11]. For every family of curves, their timings indicate that the cost of our protocol (assuming that the test of membership in $\mathbb{G}_T$ is cheap) is significantly smaller than the one of a pairing. One example (for an optimal ate pairing on a KSS-18 curve [24]) is given in Table 1 at the end of this paper.

Security. As A and B are public, we only need to verify that our protocol ensures the completeness and the verifiability properties.

Completeness. The protocol is complete since:

$$\alpha_1 = e([x_2^{-1}]A + X_1, [x_1^{-1}]B + X_2)[e(G_1, B)e(A, G_2)]^{-1}$$
$$= e(A, B)^{(x_1 \cdot x_2)^{-1}} e(X_1, X_2) = \chi \cdot \alpha_2^{(x_1 \cdot x_2)^{-1}}.$$

Verifiability. The main idea of our protocol is to request from the server the computations of α_1 and α_2, involved in a relation with the secret value τ. So, an adversary trying to cheat the client has to provide α_1' and α_2' satisfying the same relation. In the following, we argue that he is unable to do so, which ensures the verifiability of our protocol.

Remark 5. Our following proof is verified in the generic group model (extended to the bilinear setting). Even if we do not really provide a formal theorem that the underlying new assumption is valid, the methodology we adopt in the sequel is quite similar to a proof in the generic group model.

In the verifiability experiment, the server is controlled by the adversary who wants to convince the client to accept a wrong value for $e(A, B)$. This means that the adversary sends an element $\alpha_2' \neq \alpha_2 = e(A, B)$ belonging to $\mathbb{G}_T$ (since we test membership in this subgroup). So we have $\alpha_2' = \alpha_2.\delta$ for some $\delta \in \mathbb{G}_T$. It follows that the server has to send $\alpha_1' = \alpha_1 \cdot \gamma$ verifying:

$$\alpha_1' = \chi \cdot (\alpha_2')^{(x_1 \cdot x_2)^{-1}} \iff \alpha_1 \cdot \gamma = \chi \cdot (\alpha_2 \cdot \delta)^{(x_1 \cdot x_2)^{-1}} \iff \gamma = \delta^{(x_1 \cdot x_2)^{-1}}.$$

For the adversary, breaking the verifiability is then equivalent to find any two values $\gamma, \delta \in \mathbb{G}_T$ such that $\gamma = \delta^{(x_1 \cdot x_2)^{-1}}$. However, finding such a pair $(\delta, \delta^{(x_1 \cdot x_2)^{-1}}) \in \mathbb{G}_T^2$ does not match any standard computational assumption. So we cannot directly conclude. We then study the probability of recovering $(\delta, \delta^{(x_1 \cdot x_2)^{-1}})$ by using combinations of elements involved in the protocol. We consider the case of type 3 pairings (*i.e.* there is no efficiently computable isomorphism between $\mathbb{G}_1$ and $\mathbb{G}_2$) in order to reduce the number of possible combinations. However, our proof can also be done for other types of pairings.

Let $a, b, x_1, x_2 \in \mathbb{Z}_l$ be such that:

$$A = [a]G_1, \ B = [b]G_2, \ X_1 = [x_1]G_1 \text{ and } X_2 = [x_2]G_2.$$

Our security model defined in the previous section allows the adversary to choose A and B and we consequently assume that he knows a and b. Since we work with bilinear groups, we assume that the adversary is only able to compute pairings or algebraic combinations in $\mathbb{G}_1$ or $\mathbb{G}_2$, *i.e.* the adversary is only able to choose $a_1, a_2, a_3, a_4 \in \mathbb{Z}_l$ and computes:

$$e([a_1]G_1 + [a_2]T_1, [a_3]G_2 + [a_4]T_2) = e(G_1, G_2)^{s \cdot (x_1 \cdot x_2)^{-1} + t},$$

with $s = a_2 a_4 ab$ and $t = a_1 a_3 + a_1 a_4 b(x_1)^{-1} + a_1 a_4 x_2 + a_2 a_3 a(x_2)^{-1} + a_2 a_4 a + a_2 a_3 x_1 + a_2 a_4 b + a_2 a_4 x_1 x_2$. The only way (unless to guess $(x_1 \cdot x_2)^{-1}$ with probability $\frac{1}{l}$) for the server to find a suitable pair $(\delta, \delta^{(x_1 \cdot x_2)^{-1}})$ is then to recover:

$$(e(G_1, G_2)^s, e(G_1, G_2)^{s \cdot (x_1 \cdot x_2)^{-1}})$$

which means that it must find a_1, a_2, a_3, a_4 cancelling t but not s. The map

$$\psi : (\mathbb{Z}_l)^4 \to \mathbb{Z}_l$$
$$(a_1, ..., a_4) \mapsto t$$

is a quadratic form, its matrix M is:

$$2^{-1} \begin{pmatrix} 0 & 0 & 1 & b(x_1)^{-1} + x_2 \\ 0 & 0 & a(x_2)^{-1} + x_1 & a + b + x_1 x_2 \\ 1 & a(x_2)^{-1} + x_1 & 0 & 0 \\ b(x_1)^{-1} + x_2 & a + b + x_1 x_2 & 0 & 0 \end{pmatrix}$$

$$= \begin{pmatrix} 0 & N \\ N^T & 0 \end{pmatrix}$$

where N^T is the transpose of N. $\forall\, a, b \in \mathbb{Z}_l^*$ the rank of $N_{a,b}$ is 2, the number of zeroes of ψ is then:

$$|\{(a_1, \cdots, a_4) \in \mathbb{Z}_l^4 : \psi(a_1, \cdots, a_4) = 0\}| \leq l^3 + l^2 - l \leq 2l^3.$$

Since the server does not know x_1 or x_2, he must guess suitable values for $v = (a_1, a_2, a_3, a_4)$. However, the probability that v is an isotropic vector (*i.e.* $t = 0$) is negligible ($\frac{l^3 + l^2 - l}{l^4} \leq \frac{2}{l}$). Then, if $\alpha_2 \neq e(A, B)$, the client outputs $\perp$ with overwhelming probability, which concludes the fact that our protocol is verifiable.

Remark 6. In our protocol, as in previous works, the client has to test membership in $\mathbb{G}_T$ of some values returned by the server. However, the purpose of such test is to ensure that the server does not return elements of $(\mathbb{F}_{p^k})^*$ of small orders. Indeed, as shown in the above security study, the adversary has to find a pair $(\delta, \delta^{(x_1 \cdot x_2)^{-1}})$ to break the verifiability property. If the order of α_2 is not checked, then the adversary can choose an element of $(\mathbb{F}_{p^k})^*$ of order 2, and would then succeed with probability $\frac{1}{2}$, since it just has to guess the parity of $(x_1 \cdot x_2)^{-1}$.

4.2   Efficient Variant with One Exponentiation

As explained above, the efficiency of our protocol mainly depends on the computational cost of the test of membership. If the curve parameters do not allow the client to use the idea from [29], then the test of membership in $\mathbb{G}_T$ will require a costly exponentiation in $(\mathbb{F}_{p^k})^*$, making the speed-up of the delegation less obvious. Our aim in this section is to remove this test while ensuring verifiability.

In a nutshell, we will make use of Remark 1 given in Section 2 so that the fact that the order of α_2 is implicitly l, without the necessity to verify such fact. More precisely, the client will now compute $\widetilde{\chi}$ (instead of χ) such that $\chi = \rho^{x_1 x_2}$. As explained in Remark 1, $\widetilde{\chi}^c = \chi$, where $c = \frac{p^k - 1}{l}$. Then, the client and the server proceed as in the protocol of Figure 2, except that the server now returns $\widetilde{\alpha}_1$ (where $\widetilde{\alpha}_1^c = \alpha_1$) and α_2. Then, the client needs to check that

$$\alpha_2 = (\widetilde{\alpha}_1 \cdot \widetilde{\chi}^{-1})^{c \cdot x_1 \cdot x_2}.$$

Obviously, checking that α_2 is equal to an element of $(\mathbb{F}_{p^k})^*$, raised to the power c, necessarily ensures that it belongs to $\mathbb{G}_T$ (since this group contains all the elements of order l). As a conclusion, we no longer need to verify that α_2 belongs to $\mathbb{G}_T$. It follows that no adversary is able to cheat unless to provide a pair $(\delta, \delta^{(x_1 \cdot x_2)^{-1}})$ with δ of order l. The security of this variant is thus the same as the one of the original protocol.

Regarding efficiency, our protocol now requires 1 scalar multiplication in $\mathbb{G}_1$, 1 scalar multiplication in $\mathbb{G}_2$ and only one exponentiation in $(\mathbb{F}_{p^k})^*$. Since the exponent involved in this last operation is close to the one (namely c) involved in the last step of the Tate pairing, usually called the final exponentiation, we may use a similar methodology as the one in [30]. It thus remains to compare the computational cost of a Miller loop against 1 scalar multiplication in $\mathbb{G}_1$ and 1 scalar multiplication in $\mathbb{G}_2$. Using the timings from [28], we may conclude that our protocol is still more efficient than computing the pairing. Again, an estimated ratio is given in Table 1 for this variant.

4.3   Batch Delegation

In [31], the authors have considered the delegation of several pairings all at once but they have only proposed protocols with one constant point to each pairing. There are two reasons why batch delegation does not suit our protocol. First, with one constant point A, one may efficiently check the validity of the requested $e(A, B_1), ..., e(A, B_n)$ by using the bilinearity of the pairing since $e(A, B_1 + B_2 + ... + B_n) = e(A, B_1) \cdot ... \cdot e(A, B_n)$. However this is not possible with our protocol since we do not assume that one of the pairing's input is constant. More specifically, assuming that we want to delegate $e(A_1, B_1), ..., e(A_n, B_n)$, the computation of $e(A_1 + ... + A_n, B_1 + ... + B_n)$ is useless because it also involves several unknown values (the values $e(A_i, B_j)$ for $i \neq j$) that the client will have to cancel, which leads to additional computations. Second, the goal of batch delegation is to check validity of the n delegated pairings with less than n equality tests. However, when two pairings $\alpha_i = e(A_i, B_i)$ and $\alpha_j = e(A_j, B_j)$ are involved in the same equality test, they must be raised to different powers, else, an adversary could return $\alpha_i \cdot \delta$ and $\alpha_j \cdot \delta^{-1}$, for some $\delta \in \mathbb{G}_T$, and still satisfy the test. It then seems hard to construct a protocol for delegating n pairings with less than n exponentiations in $\mathbb{G}_T$ which is roughly the cost of n runs of our protocol (in the case of a cheap test of membership in $\mathbb{G}_T$).

5   Ensuring both Verifiability and Secrecy

We now consider the case where the points A and/or B are/is secret. We first explain how to modify our previous protocols to achieve secrecy and then propose an improved protocol which suits the case where B is a constant public point.

5.1   A Generic Conversion

There is an easy way to reach the secrecy property from the protocols described in the previous section, using the ideas given in [20]. If A and B are secret, one can simply compute $A' \leftarrow [u]A$ and $B' \leftarrow [v]B$ for randomly chosen u and v in $\mathbb{Z}_l$. Then, the client and the server play one of the protocols given in the previous section to get $e(A', B')$. Finally, $e(A, B)$ is obtained by simply computing $e(A', B')^{(uv)^{-1}}$. The completeness and verifiability of this protocol directly follow from the ones of the protocols given in the previous section. The secrecy is then obvious since A' and B' are seen as random elements in $\mathbb{G}_1$ and $\mathbb{G}_2$ respectively. This leads to a secure protocol requiring mainly two exponentiations in $\mathbb{G}_T$ and either one test of membership if we use the protocol described in Section 4.1, or one exponentiation in $\mathbb{G}_T$ and another one in $(\mathbb{F}_{p^k})^*$ if we use the protocol described in Section 4.2. Since all of these exponentiations require the knowledge of A and B, they have to be performed *online*.

5.2   A Protocol with Public Constant B

The case where A is a secret variable point and B is a constant public one can be found in some cryptographic protocols such as the one of Hess [21]. It was consider in [25] and [31]. But, on one hand, the solution provided in the former is not enough secure (see Section 3.2), since the verifiability depends on the secrecy. On the other hand, the solution of the latter requires two exponentiations in $\mathbb{G}_T$, one test of membership and additional computations in $\mathbb{G}_1$ and $\mathbb{G}_2$ during the *online* phase.

We here assume that the client already knows $\varrho \leftarrow e(G_1, B)$ (G_1 is a parameter and B is constant). We then provide a more efficient protocol, which is described in Figure 3.

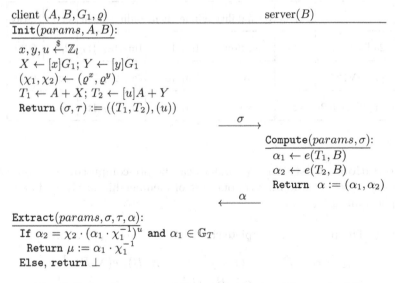

Fig. 3. Delegation protocol for secret A and public constant B

Table 1. Efficiency and security comparison, where m_1 (resp. m_2) stands for a scalar multiplication in $\mathbb{G}_1$ (resp. $\mathbb{G}_2$), e_T stands for an exponentiation in $\mathbb{G}_T$, e_F for an exponentiation in $(\mathbb{F}_{p^k})^*$, t_T for a test of membership in $\mathbb{G}_T$ and p_T stands for a pairing. We say that the verifiability is "conditional" when it depends on the secrecy (see section 3.2). Provided ratios assume that the test of membership can be performed cheaply [29]. The amount of storage required to store the pre-computed values is implicitly given in the column "offline client". Indeed, if an operation in a group is pre-computed, then the result, which is an element of this group, must be stored.

Protocols with variable A and B

	secrecy	verifiability	offline client	online client	server	Ratios
[20]	yes	no	-	$1m_1,1m_2,1e_T$	$1p_T$	0.46
[16,17] [Sect 4.1]	yes	yes	$2m_1,2m_2,2e_T$	$1m_1,1m_2,5e_T,3t_T$	$4p_T$	1.46
[16,17] [Sect 5.2]	no	yes	$1m_1,1m_2,1e_T$	$1m_1,1m_2,3e_T,3t_T$	$4p_T$	0.96
[25]	yes	conditional	$1m_1,1m_2,1e_T$	$1m_1,1m_2,3e_T,3t_T$	$4p_T$	0.96
Ours [Sect 4.1]	no	yes	$1m_1,1m_2,1e_T$	$1m_1,1m_2,1e_T,1t_T$	$4p_T$	0.46
Ours [Sect 4.2]	no	yes	$1m_1,1m_2,1e_T$	$1m_1,1m_2,1e_F$	$4p_T$	0.84
Ours + [20][Sect 5.1]	yes	yes	$1m_1,1m_2,1e_T$	$2m_1,2m_2,2e_T,1t_T$	$4p_T$	0.92

Protocols with variable secret A and constant public B

	secrecy	verifiability	offline client	online client	server	Ratios
[25][Sect 4.3]	yes	conditional	$1m_1,1e_T$	$1m_1,1e_T,1t_T$	$2p_T$	0.30
[31][SVPC]	yes	yes	$1m_1,1e_T$	$2m_1,2e_T,1t_T$	$2p_T$	0.60
Ours [Sect 5.2]	yes	yes	$2m_1,2e_T$	$1m_1,1e_T,1t_T$	$2p_T$	0.30

Computational Cost. Since χ_1 and χ_2 can be pre-computed, our protocol requires one exponentiation in $\mathbb{G}_T$, one test of membership in $\mathbb{G}_T$ and one scalar multiplication in $\mathbb{G}_1$.

Security. The protocol is complete since $e(A,B) = \alpha_1 \cdot \chi_1^{-1}$ and:

$$\chi_2 \cdot (\alpha_1 \cdot \chi_1^{-1})^u = e(Y,B) \cdot (e(A+X,B) \cdot e(X,B)^{-1})^u$$
$$= e(Y,B) \cdot e(A,B)^u$$
$$= \alpha_2.$$

T_1 and T_2 are random elements of $\mathbb{G}_1$ and thus do not reveal any information about A. As in the previous section, a pair (α'_1, α'_2) will satisfy the equality test if and only if $\alpha'_1 = \alpha_1 \cdot \delta$ and $\alpha'_2 = \alpha_2 \cdot \delta^u$. Since u is only involved in the computation of T_2, an adversary, even knowing A, will not be able to find a couple $(\delta, \delta^u) \in \mathbb{G}_T^2$ unless to guess Y. Our protocol ensures then both secrecy and verifiability with less computations than the one from [31], as we will see in the next section.

6 Conclusion and Efficiency Comparison

In this paper, we have provided several delegation processes for a bilinear pairing. We argue that our results are much more efficient than the state-of-the-art, for a comparable or improved security. As evidence, we provide in Table 1 a global comparison between our results and related works.

We use in this table the timings from [12,11] since this paper precisely describes the computational cost of operations in each group. Moreover, the authors have implemented their algorithms so that ratios between their different benchmark results do not depend on the platforms. They therefore remain relevant even considering an implementation on a smart card.

We emphasize that the efficiency of our protocols depends on the chosen pairing and curve. We do not claim that our protocols are more efficient than any implementation of pairing on any curve. However, there are some curves for which the efficiency gain is significant. As evidence, we give in the last column of Table 1 the estimated ratios between the online computational cost of our protocols and the one of a pairing for the KSS-18 [24] family of curves.

Acknowledgments. This work was supported in part by the French ANR-12-INSE-0014 SIMPATIC Project. We are also grateful to anonymous referees for their valuable comments.

References

1. Paulo, S.L.M., Barreto, S.D., Galbraith, C.O.: hEigeartaigh, and Michael Scott. Efficient pairing computation on supersingular abelian varieties. IACR Cryptology ePrint Archive, 375 (2004)
2. Barreto, P.S.L.M., Kim, H.Y., Lynn, B., Scott, M.: Efficient algorithms for pairing-based cryptosystems. In: Yung, M. (ed.) CRYPTO 2002. LNCS, vol. 2442, pp. 354–368. Springer, Heidelberg (2002)
3. Barreto, P.S.L.M., Lynn, B., Scott, M.: On the selection of pairing-friendly groups. In: Matsui, M., Zuccherato, R.J. (eds.) SAC 2003. LNCS, vol. 3006, pp. 17–25. Springer, Heidelberg (2004)
4. Barreto, P.S.L.M., Naehrig, M.: Pairing-friendly elliptic curves of prime order. In: Preneel, B., Tavares, S. (eds.) SAC 2005. LNCS, vol. 3897, pp. 319–331. Springer, Heidelberg (2006)

5. David Bernhard, Georg Fuchsbauer, Essam Ghadafi, Nigel P. Smart, and Bogdan Warinschi. Anonymous attestation with user-controlled linkability. IACR Cryptology ePrint Archive, 658 (2011)

6. Bichsel, P., Camenisch, J., Neven, G., Smart, N.P., Warinschi, B.: Get shorty via group signatures without encryption. In: Garay, J.A., De Prisco, R. (eds.) SCN 2010. LNCS, vol. 6280, pp. 381–398. Springer, Heidelberg (2010)

7. Boneh, D., Boyen, X.: Short signatures without random oracles and the sdh assumption in bilinear groups. J. Cryptology 21(2), 149–177 (2008)

8. Boneh, D., Franklin, M.: Identity-based encryption from the weil pairing. In: Kilian, J. (ed.) CRYPTO 2001. LNCS, vol. 2139, pp. 213–229. Springer, Heidelberg (2001)

9. Boneh, D., Lynn, B., Shacham, H.: Short signatures from the weil pairing. In: Boyd, C. (ed.) ASIACRYPT 2001. LNCS, vol. 2248, pp. 514–532. Springer, Heidelberg (2001)

10. Boneh, D., Shacham, H.: Group signatures with verifier-local revocation. In: ACM Conference on Computer and Communications Security 2004, pp. 168–177. ACM (2004)

11. Bos, J.W., Costello, C., Naehrig, M.: Exponentiating in pairing groups. In: Selected Areas in Cryptography (2013) (to appear)

12. Bos, J.W., Costello, C., Naehrig, M.: Exponentiating in pairing groups. IACR Cryptology ePrint Archive, 458 (2013)

13. Canard, S., Coisel, I., Devigne, J., Gallais, C., Peters, T., Sanders, O.: Toward Generic Method for Server-Aided Cryptography. In: Qing, S., Zhou, J., Liu, D. (eds.) ICICS 2013. LNCS, vol. 8233, pp. 373–392. Springer, Heidelberg (2013)

14. Canard, S., Desmoulins, N., Devigne, J., Traoré, J.: On the implementation of a pairing-based cryptographic protocol in a constrained device. In: Abdalla, M., Lange, T. (eds.) Pairing 2012. LNCS, vol. 7708, pp. 210–217. Springer, Heidelberg (2013)

15. Chaum, D., Pedersen, T.P.: Wallet databases with observers. In: Brickell, E.F. (ed.) CRYPTO 1992. LNCS, vol. 740, pp. 89–105. Springer, Heidelberg (1993)

16. Chevallier-Mames, B., Coron, J.-S., McCullagh, N., Naccache, D., Scott, M.: Secure delegation of elliptic-curve pairing. IACR Cryptology ePrint Archive, 150 (2005)

17. Chevallier-Mames, B., Coron, J.-S., McCullagh, N., Naccache, D., Scott, M.: Secure delegation of elliptic-curve pairing. In: Gollmann, D., Lanet, J.-L., Iguchi-Cartigny, J. (eds.) CARDIS 2010. LNCS, vol. 6035, pp. 24–35. Springer, Heidelberg (2010)

18. Freeman, D., Scott, M., Teske, E.: A taxonomy of pairing-friendly elliptic curves. J. Cryptology 23(2), 224–280 (2010)

19. Galbraith, S.D., Paterson, K.G., Smart, N.P.: Pairings for cryptographers. Discrete Applied Mathematics 156(16), 3113–3121 (2008)

20. Girault, M., Lefranc, D.: Server-aided verification: Theory and practice. In: Roy, B. (ed.) ASIACRYPT 2005. LNCS, vol. 3788, pp. 605–623. Springer, Heidelberg (2005)

21. Hess, F.: Efficient identity based signature schemes based on pairings. In: Nyberg, K., Heys, H.M. (eds.) SAC 2002. LNCS, vol. 2595, pp. 310–324. Springer, Heidelberg (2003)

22. Hess, F., Smart, N.P., Vercauteren, F.: The eta pairing revisited. IEEE Transactions on Information Theory 52(10), 4595–4602 (2006)

23. Joux, A.: A one round protocol for tripartite diffie-hellman. In: Bosma, W. (ed.) ANTS 2000. LNCS, vol. 1838, pp. 385–394. Springer, Heidelberg (2000)

24. Kachisa, E.J., Schaefer, E.F., Scott, M.: Constructing brezing-weng pairing-friendly elliptic curves using elements in the cyclotomic field. In: Galbraith, S.D., Paterson, K.G. (eds.) Pairing 2008. LNCS, vol. 5209, pp. 126–135. Springer, Heidelberg (2008)
25. Kang, B.G., Lee, M.S., Park, J.H.: Efficient delegation of pairing computation. IACR Cryptology ePrint Archive, 259 (2005)
26. Lim, C.H., Lee, P.J.: Server (Prover/Signer)-aided verification of identity proofs and signatures. In: Guillou, L.C., Quisquater, J.-J. (eds.) EUROCRYPT 1995. LNCS, vol. 921, pp. 64–78. Springer, Heidelberg (1995)
27. Matsumoto, T., Kato, K., Imai, H.: Speeding up secret computations with insecure auxiliary devices. In: Goldwasser, S. (ed.) CRYPTO 1988. LNCS, vol. 403, pp. 497–506. Springer, Heidelberg (1990)
28. Sánchez, A.H., Rodríguez-Henríquez, F.: NEON implementation of an attribute-based encryption scheme. In: Jacobson, M., Locasto, M., Mohassel, P., Safavi-Naini, R. (eds.) ACNS 2013. LNCS, vol. 7954, pp. 322–338. Springer, Heidelberg (2013)
29. Scott, M.: Unbalancing pairing-based key exchange protocols. Cryptology ePrint Archive, Report 2013/688 (2013), http://eprint.iacr.org/
30. Scott, M., Benger, N., Charlemagne, M., Dominguez Perez, L.J., Kachisa, E.J.: On the final exponentiation for calculating pairings on ordinary elliptic curves. In: Shacham, H., Waters, B. (eds.) Pairing 2009. LNCS, vol. 5671, pp. 78–88. Springer, Heidelberg (2009)
31. Tsang, P.P., Chow, S.S.M., Smith, S.W.: Batch pairing delegation. In: Miyaji, A., Kikuchi, H., Rannenberg, K. (eds.) IWSEC 2007. LNCS, vol. 4752, pp. 74–90. Springer, Heidelberg (2007)
32. Yao, A.C.-C.: Protocols for Secure Computations (extended abstract). In: FOCS, pp. 160–164. IEEE Computer Society (1982)

Automatic Protocol Selection
in Secure Two-Party Computations

Florian Kerschbaum[1], Thomas Schneider[2], and Axel Schröpfer[1]

[1] SAP, Karlsruhe, Germany
{florian.kerschbaum,axel.schroepfer}@sap.com
[2] Technische Universität Darmstadt, Germany
thomas.schneider@ec-spride.de

Abstract. Performance of secure computation is still often an obstacle to its practical adaption. There are different protocols for secure computation that compete for the best performance. In this paper we propose *automatic protocol selection* which selects a protocol for each operation resulting in a mix with the best performance so far. Based on an elaborate performance model, we propose an optimization algorithm and an efficient heuristic for this selection problem. We show that our mixed protocols achieve the best performance on a set of use cases. Furthermore, our results underpin that the selection problem is so complicated and large in size, that a programmer is unlikely to manually make the optimal selection. Our proposed algorithms nevertheless can be integrated into a compiler in order to yield the best (or near-optimal) performance.

Keywords: Secure Two-Party Computation, Performance, Optimization, Protocol Selection.

1 Introduction

Secure two-party computation allows two parties to compute a function f over their joint, private inputs x and y, respectively without revealing their private inputs or relying on a trusted third party. Afterwards, no party can infer anything about the other party's input except what can be inferred from her own input and the output $f(x, y)$. Secure computation has many applications, e.g., in the financial sector, and has been successfully deployed in commercial and industrial settings [6,25,5].

Performance is still often an obstacle to practical adoption of secure computation, even in the widely used semi-honest security model. A number of protocols compete for the best performance in this model. Recently, the garbled circuit implementation FastGC [20] has been used in several privacy-preserving applications, including [19,18], but still garbled circuits have some inherent limitations, e.g., due to the large circuit size of some functionalities such as multiplication. In this paper we propose a different approach. Instead of relying on a single protocol we mix protocols. Then, based on an extended performance model we *automatically* select the best protocol for a sub-operation. In all prior works this

I. Boureanu, P. Owesarski, and S. Vaudenay (Eds.): ACNS 2014, LNCS 8479, pp. 566–584, 2014.

selection was done manually, e.g., [17,21,3]. We present two algorithms for the protocol selection – an optimization based on integer programming and a heuristic. We apply these to three use cases from the literature: secure joint economic lot-size, biometric identification, and data mining. We use the evaluation of their implementation in the intermediate language of [43] to test three hypotheses:

- Our mixed protocols are faster than a pure garbled circuit implementation.
- The results of our heuristic and the optimum found by integer programming are close.
- The protocol selection problem is too complicated to be solved manually by the programmer.

Our heuristic can then be used in a compiler to automatically select the fastest sub-protocols in secure computations.

Our Contributions and Outline. In summary, this paper contributes

- an *extended performance model* for mixed protocol secure computation,
- two *selection algorithms* to automatically select mixed protocols with (near-) optimal performance based on this model,
- an *evaluation* based on three use cases from the literature.

Our paper is structured as follows: In §2 we review related work. In §3 we describe our mixed protocols for secure computation. §4 explains the corresponding cost model including conversion costs. We present our selection algorithms in §5 and our evaluation results in §6. Our conclusions are summarized in §7.

2   Related Work

Our results are based on the performance model framework of [43] for forecasting runtimes of secure two-party computations based on garbled circuits and homomorphic encryption. In §4.1 we provide a summary of this framework and extend it in §4.2 to cover conversion between the protocols. For completeness, we note that there are also other techniques for secure two-party computation beyond the ones we cover in this work, e.g., the GMW protocol [16] implemented in [8]. However, as this protocol also favors Boolean circuits, but differently from garbled circuits has a non-constant number of rounds, we chose garbled circuits in our work. Furthermore, this and other protocols can be integrated into our main approach by extending the performance model of [43] accordingly.

[24] describes automatic optimizations of secure computation protocols that automatically infer which operations can be performed locally by each party. This approach is orthogonal to ours that automatically selects the most efficient sub-protocol; combining both approaches yields even more efficient protocols.

There are several implementation frameworks for secure computation. Frameworks for secure two-party computation are either based on garbled circuits (e.g., Fairplay [33], FastGC [20], VMCrypt [32], and CBMC-GC [18]) or homomorphic encryption (e.g., VIFF [9]). The L1 framework [44] allows to describe secure computation protocols that employ both techniques, garbled circuits and homomorphic encryption. The TASTY framework [17] provides additional support for conversions between these two approaches. Both, L1 and TASTY require to specify which part of the protocol should be run with which technique. We provide the first method to automatically partition a functionality into sub-techniques.

The Sharemind framework [4] implements secure multi-party computation for three players using an additive secret sharing scheme over the ring $\mathbb{Z}_{2^{32}}$. The compiler of [31] implements secure two-party computations expressed using operations in the field $\mathbb{Z}_q$ of integers modulo a prime q and in the multiplicative subgroup of order q in $\mathbb{Z}_p^*$ for $q|p-1$ with generator g. Our protocols use additive secret sharing over $\mathbb{Z}_{2^l}$ among the two players for intermediate values (cf. §3.2).

Several protocols benefit from the combination of homomorphic encryption and garbled circuits, including [17,21,3]. In these protocols, the partitioning into sub-protocols was defined manually, whereas our methods allow to automatically find a good partition.

The authors of [35] describe a technique to compile functionalities described in Fairplay's Secure Function Definition Language (SFDL) [33] into Boolean circuits in a memory-efficient way. For this, they first compile the SFDL program into an intermediate language that represents operations as three-operand code. As we use a similar three-operand code language to describe the functionality that needs to be computed securely (cf. §4.1), the compiler of [35] could be easily extended to compile SFDL programs into our input language.

3   Secure Computation Protocols

We integrate two protocols for performing secure two-party computations – garbled circuits and homomorphic encryption. Both protocols are generic, i.e., they can securely implement any ideal functionality. Nevertheless they have different performance characteristics as shown by the performance evaluations in [17,43]. Throughout the paper we name the two parties Alice A and Bob B.

Next we explain the two basic protocols in §3.1 and §3.2, give the conversions that allow to combine and automatically select between both protocols in §3.3, and give background on the underlying semi-honest security model in §3.4.

3.1   Garbled Circuits

Garbled circuits, introduced by Yao [45], were the first generic protocol for secure two-party computation. An excellent introduction can be found in [33] which also presents the first implementation of this protocol. For the purposes of this paper a high-level overview without the technical details of encryption suffices.

Yao's garbled circuits protocol allows secure computation of an arbitrary ideal functionality that is represented as a Boolean circuit C. The basic idea is that C is evaluated on symmetric keys where one key corresponds to the plain value 0 and another to the plain value 1. Alice creates for each gate of C an encrypted table such that given the gate's input keys only the corresponding output key can be decrypted. Then, Alice sends to Bob the keys for the input wires of C in an oblivious manner: For each of Bob's inputs, both parties run a 1-out-of-2 oblivious transfer (OT) protocol. The OT protocol ensures that Bob obtains only the key corresponding to his input whereas Alice does not learn Bob's input. Now, Bob can use the encrypted tables to evaluate C under encryption. Finally, Bob sends the keys that correspond to Alice's outputs back to Alice. For his outputs, he is given a mapping that allows him to decrypt the output keys into plain output values.

For Yao's garbled circuits protocol we use the following optimizations and instantiations that are implemented in FastGC [20] (which is used in many recent works such as [19,18]) and VMCrypt [32]: For OT we use OT extensions of [22] with the OT protocol of [36] for the base OTs. For garbled circuits we use free XOR gates [28], garbled row reduction [37,41], and pipelining [20]. All these protocols and constructions are proven secure against semi-honest adversaries based on the random oracle and the computational Diffie-Hellman assumptions.

3.2 Homomorphic Encryption

Secure computation can also be implemented based on additively homomorphic encryption. On the one hand, opposed to fully homomorphic encryption [12], additively homomorphic encryption only implements addition (modulo a key-dependent constant) as the homomorphic operation. On the other hand, additively homomorphic encryption is almost as fast as standard public-key cryptography, whereas the practicality of fully homomorphic encryption schemes is still subject to research, e.g., [13].

Let $E_X(x)$ denote the encryption of plaintext x encrypted under X's (Alice's or Bob's) public key and $D_X(c)$ the corresponding decryption of ciphertext c. Then the additive homomorphism can be expressed as $D_X(E_X(x) \cdot E_X(y)) = x+y$. Multiplication with a constant c can easily be derived as $D_X(E_X(x)^c) = cx$.

Secure computation of an arbitrary functionality represented as arithmetic circuit can be built from homomorphic encryption as follows. Each variable is secretly shared between Alice and Bob. Let x be a variable of bit length l. Then Alice has share x_A and Bob has share x_B, such that $x = x_A + x_B \bmod 2^l$.

In order to securely implement the ideal functionality it suffices to securely implement addition and multiplication of shares. Addition of $x = x_A + x_B$ and $y = y_A + y_B$ (of the same bit-length l) can be implemented locally by addition of each party's shares. Multiplication $z = x \cdot y$ needs to be implemented as a protocol. Let σ be the statistical security parameter in the share conversion protocol of [10] and r be a uniformly random number of bit length $2l + \sigma + 1$. We use the following protocol for secure multiplication of shares:

$A \longrightarrow B$: $E_A(x_A), E_A(y_A)$
$B \longrightarrow A$: $E_A(c) = E_A(x_A)^{y_B} E_A(y_A)^{x_B} E_A(r) = E_A(x_a y_B + y_A x_B + r)$
$\quad A$: $\quad c = D_A(E_A(c))$, $z_A = x_A y_A + c \bmod 2^l$
$\quad B$: $\quad z_B = x_B y_B - r \bmod 2^l$.

It is easy to verify that $z_A + z_B = (x_A + x_B)(y_A + y_B) \bmod 2^l$. Also other operations can be implemented using homomorphic encryption (cf. §4.1).

In our implementation we use Paillier's cryptosystem [39] which is secure against chosen plaintext attacks (IND-CPA) under the decisional composite residuosity assumption.

3.3 Conversion

In the following, we describe how secure computations based on garbled circuits and homomorphic encryption can be combined by converting from one representation of intermediate values to the other. Our methods used for these conversions are similar to those of previous works [17,27], but more efficient as we directly compute on l-bit shares instead of computing on ciphertexts with longer masks: In previous approaches, one party held an l-bit value that is additively homomorphically encrypted under the public key of the other party. To convert such a value into an input of a garbled circuit required to add a $(\sigma + l)$-bit mask to the encrypted value, send this ciphertext back, and after decryption take off the $(\sigma + l)$-bit mask in the garbled circuit. Conversion in the opposite direction is similar. In these previous approaches the mask had to be σ bits longer than l in order to statistically hide the l-bit value. In our approach described below we directly combine the shares modulo 2^l and hence do not require expensive masking, decryption, and transfer of the ciphertext.

Homomorphic Encryption to Garbled Circuits. Assume that we want to compute a sub-functionality f using garbled circuits where one of the l-bit inputs x was computed using homomorphic encryption, i.e., x is represented as shares x_A, x_B with $x = x_A + x_B \bmod 2^l$. To use x as input for the garbled circuit, we extend the inputs of the garbled circuit computing f with an l-bit addition circuit to which A provides input x_A and B provides input x_B, i.e., the slightly larger garbled circuit computes $f(\ldots, x_A + x_B \bmod 2^l, \ldots)$. Note that reduction modulo 2^l is easily obtained by dropping the most significant carry bit.

Garbled Circuits to Homomorphic Encryption. Similarly, we can convert the output z of a sub-functionality that has been computed using garbled circuits into secret shares z_A, z_B that can later on be used for secure computations using homomorphic encryption. For this, we extend the output of the garbled circuit with an l-bit subtraction circuit whose subtrahend is a randomly chosen l-bit share z_A provided by A. We modify the garbled circuit protocol such that only B obtains the output $z_B = z - z_A \bmod 2^l$, i.e., he does not send the output keys back to A. Again, reduction modulo 2^l is easily obtained by dropping the most significant carry bit.

Optimization. Note that we only need to convert the inputs and outputs of operations that are securely computed with a different protocol type. Furthermore, each variable needs to be converted at most once and then can be used as input to all sub-functionalities.

3.4   Security

All protocols described in this section—garbled circuits, homomorphic encryption, and mixed protocols—are secure in the semi-honest model. In this model participants follow the protocol as prescribed, but keep a record of the messages received and try to infer as much information as possible about the other party's input [15]. Protocols secure in the semi-honest model ensure that an adversary cannot infer any information beyond what he can infer from its input and output of the protocol. This model covers many real-life threats such as attacks by honest but curious insiders.

For garbled circuits a proof of security can be found in [30]. Proofs for the protocols using homomorphic encryption can be found in [1,14,23]. For security of the mixed protocol we refer to Goldreich's composition theorem [15].

4   Cost Model

In order to choose which operation to implement using which protocol we need to compare their costs. By cost we mean the (wall clock) run-time of the protocol and its communication. Since the protocol can be composed from sub-protocols of both protocol types – garbled circuits and homomorphic encryption – we need to be able to assess their performance while taking care of additional conversion costs. We base our cost model on the model of [43] which can (reasonably) reliably forecast the protocol run-time and communication for both types of protocols. The accuracy of the forecast mainly determines the effectiveness of our approach. We summarize the layers of the cost model in §4.1 and give the costs for conversions in §4.2.

4.1   Layers

The cost model of [43] is divided into four layers. The top three layers are parameterized by the implemented algorithm and security parameters. The lowest layer is parameterized by the performance of the actual systems on which the protocols are deployed. This performance is measured for some basic operations once. Then, different protocols can be compiled. Alternatively, pre-configured costs for representative environments can be chosen by the programmer.

The first layer captures the number of input and output variables of every player, as well as the bit-length of these variables. The second layer captures the algorithm as a sequential list O of operations. An operation $o = \{l, \circ, r\} \in O$ consists of an assigned variable, a left-operand, an operator and a right-operand (3-operand code). All assignments are single static assignments. We adopt the intermediate language of [43] for our selection algorithms.

The intermediate language currently supports the following operations for which secure protocols are given in [1,14,23,27]. Some of these operations leverage the specific advantages of the respective protocol type, i.e., direct access to single bits and shift operations for garbled circuits or arithmetic operations for homomorphic encryption: addition $\oplus$, subtraction $\ominus$, dot product $\odot_e$, multiplication by a constant $\odot_c$, division by a constant $\oslash_c$, left shift by a constant $\ll_c$, right shift by a constant $\gg_c$, less-or-equal $\leq$. All operands are scalars with the exception of dot product which concurrently multiplies vectors of e elements.

The third layer captures the protocol type and their security parameters, i.e., the lengths of keys in garbled circuits, homomorphic encryption, and oblivious transfer. The fourth layer captures the performance of the systems and the network, i.e., the times for performing local operations (e.g., a homomorphic encryption or a hash-function), and network bandwidth and latency.

Given these parameters, a run-time forecast (cost) of the protocol is computed in the respective model. We implement the cost computation using the arithmetic formulas from [43]. Using an empirical evaluation, the authors of [43] show that these formulas estimate the run-time reasonably precisely: for n forecasts f_i and measurements e_i the average error is only $\left| 1 - \frac{1}{n} \sum_{i=1}^{n} \frac{f_i}{e_i} \right| = 3.6\%$.

4.2   Conversion Costs

The model of [43] actually distinguishes the two protocol types. We now need to additionally estimate the conversion costs between the two protocols.

Recall that all operations in the intermediate language are represented in 3-operand code (cf. §4.1). Let $a = b \cdot c$ be such a 3-operand operation. As each variable is assigned exactly once (single static assignment), we can use the assigned variable a as a short notation for the operation. There are two cases when we need to consider conversion costs according to the conversions described in §3.3: If a is implemented using homomorphic encryption, but b (or c) is implemented using garbled circuits, then we need to convert b (or c) from their garbled circuit representation into secret shares by adding an input for Bob's random share z_B and extending the garbled circuit with a subtraction circuit. If a is implemented using garbled circuits, but b (or c) is implemented using homomorphic encryption, then we need to convert b (or c) from their representation as secret shares into inputs for the garbled circuit by adding an addition circuit and inputs for the shares. Again, we emphasize that each operand needs to be converted at most once in the entire mixed protocol.

We can then compute the cost of the mixed protocol as the sum of its parts. For the costs of each part implemented as either protocol type we use the formulas of [43] for homomorphic encryption, the improved formula described in the full version [26] for garbled circuits, and the conversion costs described above.

5   Optimal Partitioning

Given the cost model described in §4 we can define the problem of an optimal partitioning of the operations into the protocol types. Consider a compiler that translates a programming language into the intermediate language described in §4.1. In order to construct a cost-optimal (i.e., the fastest) protocol it needs to assign each operation of the intermediate language a protocol type, also considering the conversion costs.

We setup the problem formulation as follows. Let the elements x_i correspond to the left hand-side variable assigned in an operation. We denote with $\mathbb{X}$ the set of these elements (variables). The operator mapping function op maps x_i to the right hand-side operators of that operation. The cost function $a(x_i)$ corresponds to the costs for computing x_i using garbled circuits and $b(x_i)$ to the costs using homomorphic encryption, respectively. The cost functions $c(x_i)$ and $d(x_i)$ correspond to the costs for converting x_i from homomorphic encryption to garbled circuits and vice-versa, respectively. The set $\mathbb{Y} \subseteq \mathbb{X}$ of instructions will be implemented using garbled circuits; the set $\mathbb{X} \setminus \mathbb{Y}$ using homomorphic encryption. We formally define the problem as follows:

Definition 1 (Problem Definition). Let $\mathbb{X}$ be a set of elements $x_1, \ldots, x_n$; $op(x_i)$ be a function mapping x_i to a set $\mathbb{F}_i \subseteq \mathbb{X}$; and $a(x_i)$, $b(x_i)$, $c(x_i)$, $d(x_i)$ be four cost functions. Find the subset $\mathbb{Y} \subseteq \mathbb{X}$ that optimizes the following cost function

$$\sum_{\{x|x\in\mathbb{Y}\}} a(x) + \sum_{\{x|x\in\mathbb{X}\setminus\mathbb{Y}\}} b(x)+$$
$$\sum_{\{x|x\in\mathbb{X}\setminus\mathbb{Y}, \exists y.y\in\mathbb{Y}, x\in op(y)\}} c(x)+$$
$$\sum_{\{x|x\in\mathbb{Y}, \exists y.y\in\mathbb{X}\setminus\mathbb{Y}, x\in op(y)\}} d(x).$$

There are some restrictions on the function op that are not captured in this problem definition. First, the set $\mathbb{F}_i$ is restricted to a size of at most 2 (three operand code). Second, the set $\mathbb{X}$ is ordered and $op(x_i)$ may only include elements $x_{i'}$ that have been computed already, i.e., $i' < i$. Nevertheless, if we solve the general problem we also solve the restricted problem.

A further complication is that the cost functions in the cost model of [43] do not only depend on the individual operation, but also on its neighbors. As such this already complex problem can only be seen as an approximation of the performance model. We address this in §5.1.

Partitioning problems, e.g., graph partitioning, are typically NP-hard, but unfortunately we cannot provide a hardness proof for our specific instance. First, our specific parameters for the maximum sizes of the partitions (almost the entire set) have not yet been proven NP-hard. Second, our restrictions on the function $op(x)$ complicates the reduction. Nevertheless, we conjecture that the problem is NP-hard.

5.1 Integer Programming (IP)

We search for the best solution to the partitioning problem defined above using an optimization algorithm. However, due to the size of the problem (our largest example considered in §6 has 383 operations) an exhaustive search is prohibitive, such that a more efficient approach for optimization is needed. $0, 1$-integer programming is a suitable candidate, but we have to consider some non-linear costs.

In $0, 1$ integer programming there are variables z for which an assignment is sought which minimizes a linear objective function $c(z)^T z$ subject to certain constraints. In its standard form it is represented as

$$\min c^T z$$
$$Az \le b$$
$$z \in \overrightarrow{\{0,1\}}.$$

For each element x_i in the set of variables $\mathbb{X}$ we add the following three variables to the integer program:

- $z_i' \in \{0,1\}$ indicates whether the operation assigning x_i will be executed using homomorphic encryption (0) or garbled circuits (1).
- $z_i'' \in \{0,1\}$ indicates whether the variable x_i needs to be converted from homomorphic encryption to garbled circuits (1) or not (0).
- $z_i''' \in \{0,1\}$ indicates whether the variable x_i needs to be converted from garbled circuits to homomorphic encryption (1) or not (0).

An element x_i is either implemented as garbled circuits or homomorphic encryption. So one variable suffices, but for conversion we need two variables. An element might not be converted at all, but is never converted in both directions. The objective function to be minimized follows directly from this construction:

$$\min \left(\sum_i a(x_i) z_i' - \sum_i b(x_i) z_i' + \sum_i c(x_i) z_i'' + \sum_i d(x_i) z_i''' \right).$$

One complication of this objective function is the non-linearity of garbled circuit execution time. As described in [43], side effects on OS and hardware level (like JIT compilation, CPU caching, etc.) lead to non-linear costs per gate if the number of gates is below a certain threshold. These effects have an influence on the cost objective of the integer program. Sums of costs for single garbled circuits of adjacent operations of the SSA algorithm are likely (due to their small size) to be higher than costs of a garbled circuit of combined operations (exceeding the threshold).

Our method to incorporate a correction in the objective function is to add different (decreasing) costs for a respective operation x_i, depending on whether the previous operations $i' < i$ have been computed using garbled circuits ($z_{i'} = 1$). In order to limit the number of additional variables in the integer program, we consider at most $k = 20$ previous operations. Let $a_j(x_i)$ ($a_0(x_i) > \cdots > a_k(x_i)$) be the cost of an operation x_i if it and the previous j ($0 \le j \le k$) consecutive operations are executed as garbled circuits. We then introduce new variables $z_{i,j}'$ and replace each term $a(x_i) z_i'$ of operation i in the objective function by

$$a_0(x_i) z_{i,0}' + a_1(x_i) z_{i,1}' + \cdots + a_k(x_i) z_{i,k}'.$$

We add a constraint to allow only one new variable $z_{i,j}'$ per operation to be set to 1 such that only its cost is added

$$z_{i,0}' + \cdots + z_{i,k}' - z_i' = 0.$$

We then add constraints for previous operations that are executed as garbled circuits in order to select the correct (minimal) j'th cost $a_j(x_i)$

$$z'_{i,j} - z'_{i-0} \leq 0$$
$$\cdots$$
$$z'_{i,j} - z'_{i-j} \leq 0.$$

The following constraints implement the conditions for the conversions based on the operator mapping function op. For each operation (element) $x_i \in \mathbb{X}$ and each of its operands $x_j \in op(x_i)$ we add the following constraint that determines whether x_j needs to be converted from garbled circuits to homomorphic encryption

$$z'_i - z'_j - z''_j \leq 0,$$

i.e., if z'_i is set (x_i is to be computed using garbled circuits), but z'_j is not set (x_j was computed using homomorphic encryption), then z''_j must be set (x_j must be converted).

Similarly, for each operation $x_i \in \mathbb{X}$ and each of its operands $x_j \in op(x_i)$ we add the following constraint that determines whether x_j needs to be converted from homomorphic encryption to garbled circuits

$$-z'_i + z'_j - z'''_j \leq 0,$$

i.e., if z'_i is not set (x_i is to be computed using homomorphic encryption) and z'_j is set (x_j was computed using garbled circuits), then z'''_j must be set (x_j must be converted).

Let $n = |\mathbb{X}|$ be the number of operations. Then, our integer program has $kn + 4n$ variables and at most $\frac{k(k-1)n}{2} + 5n$ constraints.

5.2 Heuristic

Integer programming is NP-complete and can become very slow for large instances. We therefore also implement a heuristic using a greedy algorithm. We start with all operations executed as garbled circuits. Then we consecutively scan each operation in a loop. If the overall cost decreases when converting this operation to homomorphic encryption we do so. We repeat until no more operations are converted.

The heuristic algorithm is shown in Algorithm 1. We use the same variables z'_i as above in §5.1 for each operation representing its assignment to either protocol type. We infer the variables z''_i and z'''_i using a helper routine and implement the remainder of the cost function in COST also as described above in §5.1. Initially we set all z'_i to 1 for garbled circuits (line 1). The algorithm has worst-case complexity $\mathcal{O}(n^2)$, since the inner loop (lines 6 - 17) is executed at most n times (at least one operation must be converted per iteration of the outer loop).

Algorithm 1. Cost-Driven Heuristic

Require: Cost function $\text{COST}(\cdot)$
Ensure: Partitioning z' of the operations into protocols
1: $z' \leftarrow 1$
2: $cost \leftarrow \text{COST}(z')$
3: $flag \leftarrow 1$
4: **while** $flag = 1$ **do**
5:     $flag \leftarrow 0$
6:     **for** $0 \leq i < n$ **do**
7:         **if** $z'_i = 1$ **then**
8:             $z'_i \leftarrow 0$
9:             $c \leftarrow \text{COST}(z')$
10:           **if** $c < cost$ **then**
11:               $flag \leftarrow 1$
12:               $cost \leftarrow c$
13:           **else**
14:               $z'_i \leftarrow 1$
15:           **end if**
16:         **end if**
17:     **end for**
18: **end while**

---

6 Use Cases

In order to validate the complexity of manual partitioning and the cost advantage of our algorithmic approach, we consider three use cases for secure computation from the literature: joint economic-lot-size (§6.1), biometric identification (§6.2), and data mining (§6.3). Afterwards, we evaluate their performance in §6.4.

6.1 Secure Joint Economic Lot-Size

The secure joint economic lot-size problem describes a two-party scenario between a vendor and a buyer of a product. Both try to align the process of production, shipping, and warehousing according to an overall buyer's demand. Specifically, they try to agree on a joint lot-size q for production and shipping. We call the demand known to both parties d, vendor's setup cost f_A, vendor's capacity c, supplier's ordering cost f_B, vendor's holding cost h_A, and supplier's holding cost h_B. Using the formula of [2] we can compute q as $q^2 = \frac{2 \cdot d \cdot f_A + 2 \cdot d \cdot f_B}{d \cdot \frac{h_A}{c} + h_B}$. The inputs to this calculation are sensitive (such as costs and capacities), since they disclose information about the cost calculation and influence future price negotiations if revealed. As described in [40] and can be seen above, the confidentiality-preserving computation of q can be reduced to secure division, see e.g. [1,7]. Secure division is also relevant for many other real world secure computations, e.g., k-means clustering [7]. As our use case we consider two division algorithms: the Newton-Raphson algorithm described in [1,43] and the long division algorithm described in [40]. That is, we compute for 32 bit inputs x and y held as shares x_A, y_A and

x_B, y_B by the respective parties (cf. §3.2) $f(x_A, y_A, x_B, y_B) = \left\lfloor \frac{x_A + x_B}{y_A + y_B} \right\rfloor$. The Newton-Raphson algorithm has 302 operations in the intermediate language and the long division algorithms has 383 operations.

6.2   Biometric Identification

Comparing and matching biometric data is a highly privacy-sensitive task in systems that are widely used in law enforcement, including fingerprint-, iris-, and face-recognition systems, e.g., [11,21,3]. The identification is based on comparing the submitted biometric information to values in a database, determining the closest match with respect to some metric (e.g., Euclidean distance). As use case we consider an algorithm for biometric identification, computing the distances using Euclidean distance as metric which is commonly used for fingerprints and faces. We compute $min\left(\sum_{i=1}^{M}(S_{1,i} - C_i)^2, \cdots, \sum_{i=1}^{M}(S_{N,i} - C_i)^2\right)$ for $N = 5$ vectors of $M = 4$ elements $S_{i,j}$ in the server database and a client vector C_i of M elements, for elements of 32 bit. The algorithm has 80 operations in the intermediate language.

6.3   Data Mining

Data mining aims to extract knowledge from databases, connecting the worlds of databases, artificial intelligence, and statistics. Various data mining algorithm for different purposes have been proposed in the literature. One particular purpose is that of structuring data sets in order to provide decision mechanisms that can be used for classification. A well known algorithm for decision tree learning is the ID3 algorithm described in [42]. A privacy-preserving classification variant of ID3, described in [29] as one of the first privacy-preserving data mining algorithms, enables new applications where multiple private databases can be used to act as training set (e.g., medical databases). The authors of [29] use entropy to compute the best attributes, with the privacy-preserving computation of the natural logarithm as the basis operation. As our use case we consider an algorithm to compute the natural logarithm. To the best of our knowledge, this is the first implementation of this privacy-preserving data mining algorithm. That is, we compute the natural logarithm of a 32 bit input $x = 2^n(1 + \epsilon)$ held as shares x_A and x_B by the respective parties where 2^n is the power of 2 which is closest to x and $-1/2 \leq \epsilon < 1/2$. The natural logarithm is approximated with a Taylor series with $k = 10$ iterations: $\ln(x) = \ln(2^n(1 + \epsilon)) = n \ln 2 + \epsilon - \frac{\epsilon^2}{2} + \cdots \frac{\epsilon^k}{k}$. The algorithm has 270 operations in the intermediate language.

6.4   Evaluation

In the following we evaluate our partitioning algorithms of §5 on the three use cases introduced in §6.1, §6.2, and §6.3. Using these results we compare the performance of mixed protocols to garbled circuit protocols, the optimization

Table 1. Runtime forecasts in [seconds] for long division (LD), Newton-Raphson (NR), Euclidean distance (ED), and natural logarithm (LOG) on 32 bit inputs

Security	Partitioning	LD		NR		ED		LOG	
		LAN	WAN	LAN	WAN	LAN	WAN	LAN	WAN
short-term	HE-only	81.6	104.7	93.6	119.5	14.8	18.4	72.6	95.7
	GC-only	2.0	5.6	12.3	82.2	6.1	16.6	1.6	4.0
	Heuristic	2.0	5.5	12.3	59.5	6.0	11.4	1.5	3.3
	IP	2.0	5.5	12.3	59.5	6.0	11.4	1.4	3.1
mid-term	HE-only	588.6	611.7	675.0	700.9	106.8	110.4	523.3	546.4
	GC-only	2.1	7.8	12.1	115.0	5.9	23.1	1.6	5.4
	Heuristic	2.0	7.7	12.1	115.0	5.8	22.8	1.4	4.6
	IP	2.0	7.6	12.1	115.0	5.8	22.7	1.4	4.4
long-term	HE-only	1,974.2	1,997.3	2,264.9	2,290.9	359.5	363.1	1,749.2	1,772.4
	GC-only	2.1	8.8	12.1	131.4	5.9	26.3	1.6	6.2
	Heuristic	2.0	8.8	12.1	131.4	5.8	25.9	1.4	5.2
	IP	2.0	8.6	12.1	131.4	5.8	25.9	1.4	4.9

of the heuristic to that of integer programming, and the automatic optimal partitioning to the manual partitioning approach.

As execution environment of the secure computation protocols we consider a LAN environment (bandwidth $b = 100$ Mbit/s, latency $t_{LAT} = 1$ μs) and a WAN environment (bandwidth $b = 1$ Mbit/s, latency $t_{LAT} = 100$ ms). The performance of local operations has been measured on servers with four AMD Opteron 885 dual-core 64-bit CPUs and 16 GB RAM using a single-threaded implementation (cf. the full version [26] for details). We use Java Version 6 and instantiate security parameters according to NIST recommendations [38] (cf. the full version [26] for details).

In a brief experimental study we confirmed the accuracy of the performance model described in §4. We executed all four use cases in the LAN/WAN setting with short-term security (80 bit) using the mixed partitioning. Our forecasts were always within the same error bound as reported in [43].

Tab. 1 summarizes the runtime forecasts. The table consists of the respective results in seconds for partitions that are computed entirely using homomorphic encryption (HE-only) or garbled circuits (GC-only), and for mixed partitions that were found by our heuristic and by integer programming (IP).

Mixed versus Non-mixed Protocols. The results in Tab. 1 show that for our use cases, mixed protocols can reduce runtimes below those of single protocols. For pure homomorphic encryption and garbled circuits we draw two conclusions.

First, in all use cases and settings the HE-based encryption protocols result in highest runtimes. In particular for growing key lengths of mid- and long-term security settings, HE is slower than GC by orders of magnitudes.

Second, GC-based protocols are sometimes competitive, but may be improved by mixed protocols. In 16 out of 24 experimental settings, garbled circuits have runtimes close to the best results (not more than 5% deviation). In four cases

Table 2. Communication forecasts in [kb] for long division (LD), Newton-Raphson (NR), Euclidean distance (ED), and natural logarithm (LOG) on 32 bit inputs

Security	Partitioning	LD	NR	ED	LOG
short-term	HE-only	776	852	96	892
	GC-only	5,057	76,668	15,147	3,384
	Heuristic	5,012	76,668	14,877	3,361
	IP	4,938	76,668	14,945	2,648
mid-term	HE-only	1,552	1,704	192	1,784
	GC-only	7,080	107,336	21,192	4,737
	Heuristic	7,017	107,336	20,814	4,706
	IP	6,914	107,336	20,908	3,692
long-term	HE-only	2,328	2,556	288	2,676
	GC-only	8,092	122,669	24,214	5,414
	Heuristic	8,020	122,669	23,782	5,378
	IP	7,901	122,669	23,890	4,214

the GC protocol results in the best performance. In all experimental settings, both partitioning mechanisms for computing optimal mixed protocols result in the best performance, including the previously mentioned four pure garbled circuit cases. In 8 of 24 settings, the mixed protocols result in an average of 20% less runtime. The largest improvement is 31% lower runtime compared to the protocol entirely implemented as garbled circuit (Euclidean distance, short-term security, WAN).

We infer that network conditions are essential in the context of performance measurements. For LAN settings, mixed protocols obtain on average an improvement over the garbled circuit protocol of 4%. For WAN settings, however, the improvement is significantly higher, namely 11%.

Tab. 2 depicts the communication complexities of the protocols in kilobytes. Clearly, non-mixed protocols yield either most (GC-only) or least (HE-only) communication traffic. From the perspective of communication and related costs (e.g., fees charged in mobile networks), HE-only as well as mixed protocols clearly have an advantage over GC-only protocols. The reason are the corresponding operators and sub-protocols of HE sub-protocols that, compared to GC-only protocols, have to transmit only a low amount of data. Additional communication savings can be obtained by packing these data. A good example is the use-case of calculating the Euclidean distance. Considering the amount of data to transmit, in Tab. 2 we see a difference of magnitudes between GC-only and HE-only and a reasonable difference to the mixed protocol. Regarding the example, a joint view on Tab. 1 and Tab. 2 shows how a mixed protocol (by both, Heuristic and IP) can significantly reduce runtime as well as network traffic.

Heuristic versus Integer Programming. Both optimization approaches result in mixed protocols that perform, in almost half of all experimental settings, noticeably better than pure protocols. As seen from the results in Tab. 1, the heuristic based partitioning results are close to those of integer programming

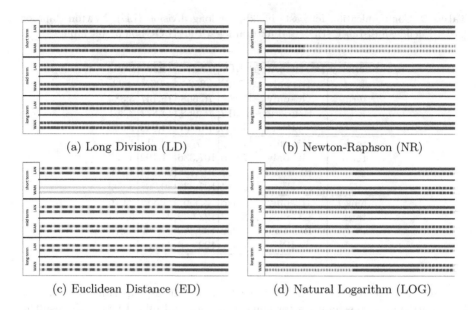

(a) Long Division (LD)   (b) Newton-Raphson (NR)

(c) Euclidean Distance (ED)   (d) Natural Logarithm (LOG)

Fig. 1. Partitioning of algorithms for 32 bit inputs. Operations computed using GC are depicted in dark-gray, those computed using HE in gray. The upper and lower bar depict the partitioning found by the heuristic and integer program, respectively.

(deviating not more than 2.7% on average, at maximum 7.6%). While the heuristic only requires seconds to compute the partitioning per use case and setting, the integer program requires several hours using the LP solver SoPlex[1] on the aforementioned server hardware. While the performance of the mixed protocols found by the two partitioning algorithms is similar, the resulting partitionings differ in several aspects (see the full version [26] for details). The heuristic, in comparison to the integer program, tends to reduce the number of blocks. A block is a sequence of consecutive operations with the same protocol type. For long division and natural logarithm, over all settings, the ratio between number of blocks and number of operations is less than 0.025, while it is more than 0.279 (i.e., larger by a factor of 10) for the integer program. On the contrary, results for Netwton-Raphson and Euclidean distance show that both partitioning algorithms may result in similarly high (0.5) or low (0.003) ratios.

Manual versus Automated Partitioning. Using an analysis of the partitions found by our algorithms – independent of heuristic or integer program – we argue that it is complicated to find the same partition manually. Fig. 1 shows how the optimization approaches partitioned the use cases in the various settings. Operations computed using garbled circuits are depicted in dark-gray, those computed using homomorphic encryption in gray.

---

[1] Version 1.6.0, available at http://soplex.zib.de/

Fig. 1 shows that the mixed protocols are heavily fragmented in order to achieve the optimal performance (cf. the full version [26] for details). We obtain a wide spectrum of fragmentations. For Euclidean distance we have 40 blocks (of at most two operations per block) within only 80 operations in total. Similarly, for Newton-Raphson we obtain 113 blocks (of 1 to 26 operations per block) within 302 operations. Regarding partitions with at least two blocks, we obtain the largest block for natural logarithm (of 221 operations) within 270 operations.

Although there seem to be patterns in some areas of the diagrams, it is difficult to infer a general conclusion that can be used to manually derive a partitioning with similar performance. Fig. 1 shows that for some sub-sequences partitions are constant (within the same network setting but for changing security levels, e.g., long division). Others change within the same network setting for changing security levels (e.g., Euclidean distance and Newton-Raphson). In only 3 out of 12 cases there is no change in the partitioning across different network settings. We provide more details in the full version [26].

7 Conclusions

In this paper we have presented algorithms to automatically select a protocol – garbled circuits or homomorphic encryption – in secure two-party computation. Based on a performance model our algorithms minimize the costs of a mixed protocol. We present an evaluation based on three use cases from the literature: secure joint economic lot-size, biometric identification, and data mining.

Our results support that mixed protocols perform better than pure garbled circuit implementations. In 8 out of 24 experiments we achieve a performance gain of 20% on average. We conclude that the option to mix protocols improves performance of secure two-party computation.

Our results also support that our heuristic is close to the optimization algorithm based on integer programming. In all experiments our heuristic achieved a performance within 2.7% of the optimum on average. Nevertheless, the heuristic runs within seconds whereas the integer program requires hours. We conclude that it is practically feasible to automatically do the (near-optimal) selection.

Furthermore, our detailed analysis of the experiments also revealed that there is no discernible pattern of the selection. A programmer cannot rely on simple hints in order to perform the selection manually. We therefore conclude that the protocol selection problem is too complicated to be solved manually by the programmer and needs to be solved automatically, e.g., by a compiler.

Acknowledgements. The research leading to these results has received funding from the European Union Seventh Framework Programme (FP7/2007-2013) under grant agreement n. 609611 (PRACTICE). Thomas Schneider was supported by the German Federal Ministry of Education and Research (BMBF) within EC SPRIDE and by the Hessian LOEWE excellence initiative within CASED.

References

1. Atallah, M., Bykova, M., Li, J., Frikken, K., Topkara, M.: Private Collaborative Forecasting and Benchmarking. In: ACM Privacy in the Electronic Society, WPES (2004)
2. Banerjee, A.: A Joint Economic-Lot-Size Model For Purchaser and Vendor. Decision Sciences 17(3) (1986)
3. Blanton, M., Gasti, P.: Secure and Efficient Protocols for Iris and Fingerprint Identification. In: Atluri, V., Diaz, C. (eds.) ESORICS 2011. LNCS, vol. 6879, pp. 190–209. Springer, Heidelberg (2011)
4. Bogdanov, D., Laur, S., Willemson, J.: Sharemind: A Framework for Fast Privacy-Preserving Computations. In: Jajodia, S., Lopez, J. (eds.) ESORICS 2008. LNCS, vol. 5283, pp. 192–206. Springer, Heidelberg (2008)
5. Bogdanov, D., Talviste, R., Willemson, J.: Deploying Secure Multi-Party Computation for Financial Data Analysis. In: Keromytis, A.D. (ed.) FC 2012. LNCS, vol. 7397, pp. 57–64. Springer, Heidelberg (2012)
6. Bogetoft, P., Christensen, D.L., Damgård, I., Geisler, M., Jakobsen, T., Krøigaard, M., Nielsen, J.D., Nielsen, J.B., Nielsen, K., Pagter, J., Schwartzbach, M., Toft, T.: Secure Multiparty Computation Goes Live. In: Dingledine, R., Golle, P. (eds.) FC 2009. LNCS, vol. 5628, pp. 325–343. Springer, Heidelberg (2009)
7. Bunn, P., Ostrovsky, R.: Secure Two-Party k-Means Clustering. ACM Computer and Communications Security, CCS (2007)
8. Choi, S.G., Hwang, K.-W., Katz, J., Malkin, T., Rubenstein, D.: Secure Multi-Party Computation of Boolean Circuits with Applications to Privacy in On-Line Marketplaces. In: Dunkelman, O. (ed.) CT-RSA 2012. LNCS, vol. 7178, pp. 416–432. Springer, Heidelberg (2012)
9. Damgård, I., Geisler, M., Krøigaard, M., Nielsen, J.B.: Asynchronous Multiparty Computation: Theory and Implementation. In: Jarecki, S., Tsudik, G. (eds.) PKC 2009. LNCS, vol. 5443, pp. 160–179. Springer, Heidelberg (2009)
10. Damgård, I., Thorbek, R.: Efficient Conversion of Secret-Shared Values Between Different Fields, http://eprint.iacr.org/2008/221
11. De Cristofaro, E., Jarecki, S., Kim, J., Tsudik, G.: Privacy-Preserving Policy-Based Information Transfer. In: Goldberg, I., Atallah, M.J. (eds.) PETS 2009. LNCS, vol. 5672, pp. 164–184. Springer, Heidelberg (2009)
12. Gentry, C.: Fully Homomorphic Encryption using Ideal Lattices. In: ACM Symposium on Theory of Computing, STOC (2009)
13. Gentry, C., Halevi, S.: Implementing Gentry's Fully-Homomorphic Encryption Scheme. In: Paterson, K.G. (ed.) EUROCRYPT 2011. LNCS, vol. 6632, pp. 129–148. Springer, Heidelberg (2011)
14. Goethals, B., Laur, S., Lipmaa, H., Mielikäinen, T.: On Private Scalar Product Computation for Privacy-Preserving Data Mining. In: Park, C.-S., Chee, S. (eds.) ICISC 2004. LNCS, vol. 3506, pp. 104–120. Springer, Heidelberg (2005)
15. Goldreich, O.: Foundations of Cryptography: Volume 2 – Basic Applications. Cambridge Univ. Press (2004)
16. Goldreich, O., Micali, S., Wigderson, A.: How to Play Any Mental Game. In: ACM Symposium on Theory of Computing, STOC (1987)
17. Henecka, W., Kögl, S., Sadeghi, A.-R., Schneider, T., Wehrenberg, I.: TASTY: Tool for Automating Secure Two-partY computations. In: ACM Computer and Communications Security, CCS (2010)

18. Holzer, A., Franz, M., Katzenbeisser, S., Veith, H.: Secure Two-Party Computation in ANSI C. In: ACM Computer and Communications Security, CCS (2012)
19. Huang, Y., Evans, D., Katz, J.: Private Set Intersection: Are Garbled Circuits Better than Custom Protocols? In: Network and Distributed System Security, NDSS (2012)
20. Huang, Y., Evans, D., Katz, J., Malka, L.: Faster Secure Two-Party Computation Using Garbled Circuits. In: USENIX Security Symposium (2011)
21. Huang, Y., Malka, L., Evans, D., Katz, J.: Efficient Privacy-Preserving Biometric Identification. In: Network and Distributed System Security, NDSS (2011)
22. Ishai, Y., Kilian, J., Nissim, K., Petrank, E.: Extending Oblivious Transfers Efficiently. In: Boneh, D. (ed.) CRYPTO 2003. LNCS, vol. 2729, pp. 145–161. Springer, Heidelberg (2003)
23. Kerschbaum, F.: Practical Privacy-Preserving Benchmarking. In: IFIP International Information Security Conference, SEC (2008)
24. Kerschbaum, F.: Automatically Optimizing Secure Computation. In: ACM Computer and Communications Security, CCS (2011)
25. Kerschbaum, F., Schröpfer, A., Zilli, A., Pibernik, R., Catrina, O., de Hoogh, S., Schoenmakers, B., Cimato, S., Damiani, E.: Secure Collaborative Supply Chain Management. IEEE Computer 44(9) (2011)
26. Kerschbaum, F., Schneider, T., Schröpfer, A.: Automatic Protocol Selection in Secure Two-Party Computations (Full Version), http://eprint.iacr.org/2014/200
27. Kolesnikov, V., Sadeghi, A.-R., Schneider, T.: Improved Garbled Circuit Building Blocks and Applications to Auctions and Computing Minima. In: Garay, J.A., Miyaji, A., Otsuka, A. (eds.) CANS 2009. LNCS, vol. 5888, pp. 1–20. Springer, Heidelberg (2009)
28. Kolesnikov, V., Schneider, T.: Improved Garbled Circuit: Free XOR Gates and Applications. In: Aceto, L., Damgård, I., Goldberg, L.A., Halldórsson, M.M., Ingólfsdóttir, A., Walukiewicz, I. (eds.) ICALP 2008, Part II. LNCS, vol. 5126, pp. 486–498. Springer, Heidelberg (2008)
29. Lindell, Y., Pinkas, B.: Privacy Preserving Data Mining. Journal of Cryptology 15(3) (2002)
30. Lindell, Y., Pinkas, B.: A Proof of Yao's Protocol for Secure Two-Party Computation. Journal of Cryptology 22(2) (2009)
31. MacKenzie, P.D., Oprea, A., Reiter, M.K.: Automatic Generation of Two-Party Computations. ACM Computer and Communications Security, CCS (2003)
32. Malka, L.: VMCrypt - Modular Software Architecture for Scalable Secure Computation. ACM Computer and Communications Security, CCS (2011)
33. Malkhi, D., Nisan, N., Pinkas, B., Sella, Y.: Fairplay - A Secure Two-party Computation System. In: USENIX Security Symposium (2004)
34. Mitchell, T.M.: Machine Learning. McGraw-Hill (1997)
35. Mood, B., Letaw, L., Butler, K.: Memory-Efficient Garbled Circuit Generation for Mobile Devices. In: Keromytis, A.D. (ed.) FC 2012. LNCS, vol. 7397, pp. 254–268. Springer, Heidelberg (2012)
36. Naor, M., Pinkas, B.: Efficient Oblivious Transfer Protocols. In: Symposium on Data Structures and Algorithms, SODA (2001)
37. Naor, M., Pinkas, B., Sumner, R.: Privacy Preserving Auctions and Mechanism Design. In: ACM Conference on Electronic Commerce (EC) (1999)
38. NIST. Recommendation for Key Management. Special Publication 800-57 Part 1 Rev. 3, 07/2012

39. Paillier, P.: Public-Key Cryptosystems Based on Composite Degree Residuosity Classes. In: Stern, J. (ed.) EUROCRYPT 1999. LNCS, vol. 1592, pp. 223–238. Springer, Heidelberg (1999)
40. Pibernik, R., Zhang, Y., Kerschbaum, F., Schröpfer, A.: Secure Collaborative Supply Chain Planning and Inverse Optimization - The JELS Model. European Journal of Operational Research (EJOR) 208(1) (2011)
41. Pinkas, B., Schneider, T., Smart, N.P., Williams, S.C.: Secure Two-Party Computation Is Practical. In: Matsui, M. (ed.) ASIACRYPT 2009. LNCS, vol. 5912, pp. 250–267. Springer, Heidelberg (2009)
42. Quinlan, J.R.: Induction of Decision Trees. Machine Learning 1(1) (1986)
43. Schröpfer, A., Kerschbaum, F.: Forecasting Run-Times of Secure Two-Party Computation. In: Int. Conference on Quantitative Evaluation of Systems, QEST (2011)
44. Schröpfer, A., Kerschbaum, F., Müller, G.: L1 - An Intermediate Language for Mixed-Protocol Secure Computation. In: IEEE Computer Software and Applications Conference, COMPSAC (2011)
45. Yao, A.C.: How to Generate and Exchange Secrets. In: IEEE Foundations of Computer Science, FOCS (1986)

Author Index